Religious Traditions of the World

Religious Traditions of the World

A Journey Through Africa, Mesoamerica, North America, Judaism, Christianity, Islam, Hinduism, Buddhism, China, and Japan

Edited by
H. Byron Earhart

HarperSanFrancisco
A Division of HarperCollins*Publishers*

Credits begin on page 1205.

Parts of this book were previously published as: *Religions of Africa: Traditions in Transformation.* Copyright © 1985 by E. Thomas Lawson. *Religions of Mesoamerica: Cosmovision and Ceremonial Center.* Copyright © 1990 by David Carrasco. *Native Religions of North America: The Power of Visions and Fertility.* Copyright © 1987 by Åke Hultkrantz. *Judaism: Revelation and Traditions.* Copyright © 1987 by Michael A. Fishbane. *Christianity: A Way of Salvation.* Copyright © 1985 by Sandra Sizer Frankiel. *Islam and the Muslim Community.* Copyright © 1987 by Frederick M. Denny. *Hinduism: Experiments in the Sacred.* Copyright © 1991 by David M. Knipe. *Buddhism: The Path to Nirvana.* Copyright © 1987 by Robert C. Lester. *Religions of China: The World as a Living System.* Copyright © 1986 by Daniel L. Overmyer. *Religions of Japan: Many Traditions Within One Sacred Way.* Copyright © 1984 by H. Byron Earhart. These works have been revised for this combined edition.

Design and production by TBH/Typecast, Cotati, California

FIRST EDITION

Library of Congress Cataloging-in-Publication Data

Religious traditions of the world : a journey through Africa,
  Mesoamerica, North America, Judaism, Christianity, Islam, Hinduism,
  Buddhism, China, and Japan / edited by H. Byron Earhart. — 1st ed.
      p.   cm.
    Includes bibliographical references and index.
    ISBN 0–06–062115–X
    1. Religions. I. Earhart, H. Byron.
  BL80.2.R448 1992
  291—dc20   91-55481
                                                           CIP

---

01   02   RRD(C)   10   9   8   7   6   5

This edition is printed on acid-free paper that meets the American National Standards Institute Z39.48 Standard.

Brief Contents

Contents

PART FOUR

Judaism: Revelation and Traditions   373

PART FIVE

Christianity: A Way of Salvation   485

PART NINE

Religions of China: The World as a Living System 973

Acknowledgments

OVER THE PAST DECADE a large number of people helped in various ways to turn this publishing project into a reality. All cannot be acknowledged but some cannot go unmentioned.

As editor, my thanks go first to the authors of the individual parts of the book. The authors worked hard and creatively in writing the original volumes that are the foundation for the present work; they also cooperated in revising and rewriting their volumes in the preparation for this edition.

Also indispensable was the support of the publisher, Harper & Row (now HarperSanFrancisco), and its staff. John Loudon first accepted the project, which later received the guidance of Clayton Carlson and Thomas Grady; this book was seen through the press by Kandace Hawkinson; Janet Reed improved the final version.

A number of colleagues and many students read and commented on the individual volumes, aiding in their early revision and the preparation of the present book. Two people who must be singled out are my son David, who edited most of the original volumes, and my former student John DeRoo, who edited each of the individual parts of the book.

H. Byron Earhart
Editor

Preface

ONE OF HUMAN HISTORY'S most fascinating aspects is the richness and variety of its religious traditions—from the earliest times to the present, in every area of the world. The ideal way to learn about all these religions would be to visit the homeland of each—to discuss the scriptures or myths with members of these traditions, explore their shrines and sacred places, view their customs and rituals. Few people have the luxury of leisure and money to take such trips, of course; nor are many prepared to make a systematic study of even those religions that are close at hand. This book is a substitute for an around-the-world trip to study many different religious traditions: It is an armchair pilgrimage through a number of traditions both distant and different from one another, as well as some situated close to one another in time, space, and religious commitment.

This book is based on the ten previously published individual volumes of the Religious Traditions of the World Series. These volumes have been well received and will continue to be published separately. However, for those who want to read or teach about a number of these traditions, reasons of convenience and economy argue for combining the ten volumes into a single text edition. Teachers who previously used individual volumes can treat the present parts in the same way as the original books, because each part stands alone as a self-contained unit, and the parts may be taken up in any order.

The basic content and framework of the individual volumes have been retained, but the parts of the present book include a number of improvements and additions. Each volume has been carefully reread and revised for classroom use. New features designed to maximize the unity of this ten-in-one edition and make for ease of use include: a general introduction and a general index, cross-references to the various parts, additional diagrams, and study questions.

The introductory chapter, "Journeying Through Religious Traditions," prepares readers for their trip by discussing the nature of religion and the study of religion, providing a general definition of religion and a basic model for studying religion with this book, and giving an overview of the traditions in the ten parts. Cross-references direct the reader from one part to another, locating historically related materials (such as the relationship between Judaism and Christianity), or comparable materials (such as objects of worship and rites of passage). Cross-references can also serve as the basis for brief papers, or the beginning point for term papers. For example, the page references—to such subjects as god, scriptures, rites of passage, birth, marriage, and death—give the location of basic information on these topics in various traditions, and form the foundation for comparison and contrast in framing a paper. All cross-references are enclosed in brackets. The comprehensive index for all parts at the end of the book enables readers to quickly find terms and subjects in one or more parts.

Teachers, students, and general readers may have their own preference for the order in which they take up the various religious traditions and how they choose to study them, in the process making use of chronologies, maps, glossaries, diagrams, and reading lists in each part. The common format for presenting all traditions is the triple approach of treating each religion through its history, system, and dynamics; this is explained in detail in the introductory chapter. In order to study successfully and understand a religion it is essential to be able to place it in time and space, identify and define its key terms, visualize it, grasp the core of its system, and gain access to more information about it.

A chronology at the beginning of each part lists major cultural and religious events and characteristics with corresponding dates to locate the tradition in time.* One or more maps place the tradition in its global space (or spaces). Photographs enable readers to see the religion about which they are reading. Diagrams make it possible to view at a glance the overall unity of a religious system.

At the end of each part appears study questions, glossary, and selected reading list. The glossary gives an alphabetical list of key terms and defines them; the reader is alerted to glossary terms in the text, which are printed in boldface on their first appearance. The selected reading list recommends general and specialized publications to assist the interested reader in pursuing the subject further.

Highly recommended as a "before" and "after" study technique for each part is the study questions section. Looking at the study questions before reading each chapter of a part will lead the reader to the key terms, facts, and patterns of each tradition. Study questions are "open-ended," asking the reader to focus on general objectives while reading a chapter, helping him or her to recognize the more important facts and ideas. After reading a chapter, reviewing the study questions is a good way to check comprehension. (Professors may ask students to write brief answers to each question, an efficient means of preparing both for classes and for later exams or essays.)

Keeping in mind the various features of the book, the reader is now ready to begin a pilgrimage through individual religious traditions.

---

* All references to dates in the text use C.E. for the common era and B.C.E. for before the common era.

Journeying Through Religious Traditions: Religion and the Study of Religion

The Starting Point

WHOEVER TRAVELS AROUND the world cannot fail to be impressed by the presence of religion in every country and culture. Whether it is the glory of the past (the pyramids of Egypt and the altars of Mesoamerica) or the grandeur of the present (the Vatican in Rome and the Taj Mahal in India) religion has made its mark on history and continues to shape and be shaped by contemporary life.

Indeed, there is no need to take a trip to be convinced of the significance of religion in all parts of the globe. Almost every day, television and newspapers provide accounts of important religious events. Unfortunately, all too often the media information about religion is focused on sensational aspects of religion—scandal within a certain religion or conflict between several religious groups. What we see and hear about religions other than our own usually is the exceptional—the "newsworthy" stories of huge numbers of pilgrims or inter-religious conflict.

The average person, whether deeply religious or not, is familiar with another side of religion, one often taken for granted—the day to day common events. Many people attend regular worship services; and even if a person is not strongly committed to one religion, he or she from time to time will attend a religious ceremony honoring the birth, marriage, or death of a friend or relative. So an individual may not be a follower or member of a particular religion, but may still know the major religious options in the larger community and the appropriate behavior for the people of these religious groups.

This illustrates what we "know" about religion simply as part of our store of common knowledge. For example, by the way in which each of us chooses to be religious (or nonreligious), we acknowledge the fact that every individual is either religious or at least has the potential (and choice) for being so. As human beings—as members of our own culture—we realize that our culture has its

1

religious dimension, whether or not we decide to take an active part in it. And, as we place ourselves within the larger family of the human race, we recognize that every culture has its religious dimension, too: Although other religious traditions may be quite different from the one or more traditions with which we are familiar, nevertheless, every culture has its own religious aspect and possibilities. Without becoming a world traveler, just by virtue of our own humanity, we have a sense that all individuals and cultures are or can be religious.

We do not have to be professional scholars of religion in order to recognize the presence of religion in our life and culture and the existence of religion in other people and cultures. In fact, two of the most obvious reasons we look into other religious traditions are natural curiosity and an innocent kind of "selfishness." We are curious about other peoples' religions, to see how they live their lives and to learn how their experience of the world is similar to and different from our own. This interest in the "other" always brings each of us back to an interest in "self"—an inevitable *self*ishness as the tendency for self-understanding, in wondering how our own religious heritage shares with or departs from other religions. We like to know how others are religious, for to be religious is a central part of what it means to be human, and everyone has a personal interest in how he or she fits into the larger picture of the human race as a whole.

Although it is easy for the average person to recognize the universal presence of religion in one's own and other cultures, by no means does this imply that religion is a rather simple matter. Nor is religion something uniform—the same in all cultures. Layperson and scholar alike face an amazing variety of beliefs and practices in the huge number of religious traditions that have appeared in human history. Something that fascinates us and persuades us to explore religion is the fact that its universality in all cultures is matched by an amazing diversity of particular forms.

The Academic Journey

In the study of religion, as in the study of many other human subjects, there is a tension between focus on the generic character of the subject and its particular historical forms. This is clear in the distinction between "art" and "arts." Study can concentrate on the nature of art as a generic aspect of human life and history (and like religion, art is found in every individual life as well as the life of all cultures). Or the study of art can focus on a specific art form, such as painting or ceramics, and a particular culture (and historical period)—such as early Chinese landscape painting. The same can be said for music and language: Each of these kinds of human expression is universally present in all cultures, and each has its generic quality. But neither music nor art exists "in general." The music we hear and the art we see are quite specific: They always appear in a given culture and time in very concrete and distinctive forms. Similar examples could be multiplied for other aspects of human life, such as society, and politics: We know they are found in all cultures and can make general statements about them, but in any culture they appear in actual, discrete shapes and forms.

This side trip into several human subjects shows us that just as there is an important distinction between art (as a generic subject) and arts (as specific art forms), so also there is a big difference between religion (as a generic human activity) and religions (meaning the religious traditions of particular cultures). In any field of study, concern for either the generic character of a subject or its specific forms goes beyond practical or existential involvement in the subject.

In the study of religion, it is essential to recognize the difference between experiencing one's personal faith or practice of religion and exploring one or more religious traditions other than one's own. Of course, some people may not consider themselves religious, in the sense of being active in an organized religion, but every person is more familiar with one or two traditions than with all the others. The important point here is that the religious tradition in which a person is active, or with which a person is most familiar, is not the best conceptual beginning for the study of other cultures. In other words, we cannot assume that the specific features of our own religious tradition are the same as the specific features of other cultures; the characteristics of one religious heritage do not define the generic character of all religion. To take a very simple example, in America many people regard religion as belief in God, belonging to a church, and going to church to worship God on Sunday. But this does not mean we can assume that all religions share these same specifics—so it would not be fruitful to ask about another tradition and its members such questions as: Do they believe in God? What church do they belong to? When do they go to church?

These questions are not necessarily wrong, in fact every one must begin from some concrete starting point. However, scholars of religion can help refine such questions so that they are more open to the distinctive features of any particular religious tradition. For example, we can ask instead: What do they worship? What religious institution are they a part of? Where, when, and how do they worship? These questions enable us to find out how American religion is practiced, but also they are flexible enough to obtain answers and information about almost any religious tradition. In the academic study of religion it is important to keep in mind the nature of religion in general while paying attention to the concrete details and specific features of a particular tradition.

The study of religion as an academic discipline and the practice of religion as a personal commitment are not necessarily contradictory, but they are different. Each is characterized by different intentions and questions. The practice of religion is a personal and existential quest for meaning, commitment, and action—involving one's own relationship to a religious reality. The personal quest leads to such questions as: Who am I? What religious reality defines me? How can (should) I lead my life? What religious practices may (should) I follow, and how do they lead me to a personal realization or fulfillment? These personal questions lead to existential decisions—choosing religious options and practicing them as one's own religious career.

By contrast, the academic study of religion is universal in scope—interested not just in one's own tradition and personal choices, but concerned with the entire range of religious beliefs and practices, for all people in all times and places. The study of religion includes comprehensive questions, such as: What is the meaning of religion in human history? How do we explain and interpret the similarities and differences between and among religious traditions? What and how do people in various traditions worship? What are the major religious practices, and how may they be compared and contrasted? These academic questions aim at the description and analysis of particular traditions, the understanding of religion in general, and interpretation of the human condition through the materials of religion.

If we contrast the personal or existential interest in religion with the academic study of religion, we find that not only do they originate from different intentions and lead to different questions, but also they arrive at answers which are quite divergent. In short, existential questions lead to existential answers, and academic questions lead to academic answers.

One thing that distinguishes a scholar of religion from the person on the street (or the scholar of other subjects) is a conscious decision to study religion thoroughly and systematically. Because no one can study comprehensively all religions, there must be a division of labor, and scholars must balance breadth of knowledge in as many traditions as possible with depth of knowledge in one tradition or several related traditions. Indeed, no single scholar can master all there is to learn about any one tradition, because every religion is quite complex. But a scholar of religion accepts the challenge to find out as much as possible about religion in general and one or more religious traditions in particular. Usually this requires learning at least one new language, in order to read the texts and/or speak with the members and specialists of a religion; it may mean travel to the area where the religion is practiced and observation of its rituals and festivals. Often lengthy study and distant travel entail hardships for the scholar and his or her family, but such difficulties are more than offset by the excitement and reward of seeing firsthand the customs and practices one has read about in books and articles.

Most people enjoy travel, and the individuals who take up the study of world religions are especially interested in other cultures and religions—so fascinated that they spend long years in graduate school in order to learn enough to teach and write about their chosen subject. One of the fringe benefits of such work is occasionally being able to spend an extended period traveling to and living within the culture and religion the scholar is studying; another benefit is the experience of sharing with others, through teaching and writing, what one has seen and learned. The study of world religions is like an academic pilgrimage through various traditions, and the authors of this book are comparable to professional tour guides, who take the reader to other times, places, cultures, and religious worlds.

Religion and the Study of Religion

Even an armchair journey through the religious traditions of the world, like any major trip, is best begun with a clear picture of the itinerary—what will be visited and how the tour will proceed. The object of this pilgrimage, what we will visit, is at once both obvious and elusive. "Religion" is self-evident to most of us, as is demonstrated by the fact that it has been the subject of our attention up to this point without being defined. Religion is something we have a feel for, in our own or other cultures, even when it is not precisely defined. However, both the person on the street and scholar of religion run into considerable difficulty as well as heated disagreement when it comes to actually defining religion. Like the notion of "time," religion is something we have a sense of, but can not easily pin down and define with precision. Nevertheless, if we do not go beyond a commonsense "feel" for religion, our pilgrimage will lack focus and we may lose sight of our tour objective.

It is hard enough to define one religion, but to arrive at a definition suitable for all religions is much more difficult. In fact, most definitions of religion, although attempting to include all traditions, tend to emphasize one or two major aspects of religiosity. For example, we have already seen the personal or existential *experience* of religion, with its concern for a personal answer, or in general the "answer" to the question of the meaning of life. It is possible to focus on the existential nature of religion in the *study* of religion and to follow this clue in interpreting all religions. Religion can be approached and defined as an existential process or goal—for example, salvation in Christianity or enlightenment in Buddhism. A psychological variation of this existential approach is to emphasize participation in religion as self-fulfillment or self-realization—especially the overcoming of a fragmented life through achieving wholeness and health.

Another way of defining religion is to focus on the object of worship; in Christian circles the reflection on the nature of God is called theology, and some have attempted to expand the term "theology" to include reflection on divinity or the object of worship in other religions. Some scholars of Buddhism refer to this kind of reflection on Buddhist teaching (or truth) as Buddhology. A similar way of reflecting on the nature or truth of religion, but not limiting this to divinity, is philosophy of religion. A philosophical approach to or definition of religion emphasizes the nature of human existence and the reality or truth of religious realization.

Religion may be seen as an ideal or aspiration, something to be aimed at even if not fully achieved. Existential, psychological, theological, and philosophical approaches tend to be more "idealistic." Social science approaches to religion are more concerned with the actual conditions of religion, focusing especially on the social circumstances that shape and influence religion (and how religion, in turn, shapes and influences the social setting). For example, sociologists want to know how social factors such as age, gender, income, and occupation influence religious commitment; or they examine how religious commitment influences people's social, ethical, and political involvement and activities. In other words, religion can be approached not just as a lofty ideal beyond the world, but as an actual function in the world here and now. Scholars of religion who utilize a social science position may not stop at describing the actual situation of religion, but also may criticize a particular connection between religion and society (such as the role of churches in apartheid in South Africa), and prescribe a preferred situation.

Other scholars of religion have tried to go around the ideal of religion and the function of religion to approach the phenomena of religion as such. "Phenomenology," when applied to the study of religion, has sought to separate religious facts (or phenomena) from their surroundings and to discover their intrinsic meaning. This phenomenological approach has defined religion as "power" or "the sacred," and has insisted on the unity of all religious life, from the earliest prehistoric times to the present (even though this "power" or "sacred" has its distinctive expression in every culture).

Another way of studying religion, the structural approach, is similar to phenomenology in that it sidesteps the ideal and function of religion to focus on the nature and meaning of religion. Scholars who see religion as structure explore the relationships among various beliefs and practices to discover the total system or world of meaning which they constitute. Structural approaches to religion favor constructing (or reconstructing) the worldview of a tradition through analysis of the relationships among its various parts.

There are so many ways to approach and define religion that the uninitiated reader may give up on mastering such a difficult set of methods and techniques. A complaint raised about scholars of every stripe—not just scholars of religion—is that they make study more difficult than it needs to be. This closes the door to a subject rather than welcoming the inquiring newcomer. Admittedly, specialists in any field can make matters unnecessarily complicated, but usually this is not intentional—there are always complex issues in any academic field. However, it is not necessary to become a professional scholar of religion in order to study and appreciate the religious life of humankind. Although any academic discipline is complex, it can also present materials as clearly, directly, and simply as possible. To borrow a term from the field of computers, this journey through religions of the world is planned as a "user-friendly" experience.

Religion as Tradition:
History, System, and Dynamics

If we enter the study of religions of the world with a sympathetic and inquiring mind, every religion has a story to tell us about how people in that heritage make sense out of the world and live their lives. In turn, knowledge and appreciation about other religious worlds can help us better understand our own religious lives. Taking these modest but worthwhile goals as our clue, we can fashion a working definition of religion and a model for the study of religion.

Religion as Tradition

For our purposes of exploring religions of the world, religion can be defined as a distinctive set of beliefs, symbols, rituals, doctrines, institutions, and practices that enables the members of the tradition to establish, maintain, and celebrate a meaningful world. As a distinctive pattern of human thought and action, religion is a tradition that is handed down, moving through time and manifesting a continuous identity along with a tendency to change and be transformed.

In order to study a particular religious tradition we need to have at least three kinds of information about it: its history, system, and dynamics. This triad of material can be phrased in a number of ways, for example: origin(s), structure, and practices. But however we label these three divisions (and they are bound to overlap), they will include most of the approaches and ways of looking at religion. We need to treat briefly each of these modes of studying religion.

History and Religion

History in the study of religion, as in other subjects, asks the question: "*When?*" One of the simplest questions about religion is when did it arise. Especially with founded religious traditions such as Buddhism, Christianity, and Islam, there are important queries about who the founder was, how the founder happened to establish the religion, and thereafter how the religion developed from the first followers to the later institutions and continued to the present time. One reason why these questions at least appear to be simpler than other questions is that it is much easier to arrange facts in chronological sequence, and most of us are familiar with handling religion in terms of a sequence of persons and events.

Historical study of religion, of course, does not stop at origins, and is not satisfied with mere sequencing of facts. History is concerned with questions of how a tradition develops, changes, and is transformed. This involves both continuity and discontinuity, as well as unity and diversity. In other words, how do we account for the amazing variety of sub-traditions within each tradition? And when we look at the historical career of a religion, we must take into account all the other social and cultural factors with which religion is intertwined. There is always a process of mutual influence between (and among) religion and other cultural forms.

System and Religion

System in the study of religion asks the question: "What is the *structure,* or the overall unity of a religious tradition?" A religion has its scriptures, myths, beliefs, symbols, doctrines, institutions, priests, and so on, and yet the structure is not necessarily one visible part. Rather, structure is the foundation or framework that holds the tradition together. Just as the skeleton of an animal holds it together or the steel framework of a building supports it, so structure in a religious tradition is what is behind and within it and expresses its unity.

A religion is a tradition moving through time, but a tradition is not a static entity. A religion is always in process, balancing continuity (preservation of the old) with discontinuity (the acceptance of the new). System or structure is the unity of the entity as it moves along and constitutes its continuity. The notion of structure is more difficult to grasp than the idea of history, because most of us are more familiar with the study of history and chronological sequencing. But knowledge of the structure of religion is crucial for two reasons: First, it helps us distinguish between the less important or peripheral and the more important or central components of a religion; second, it enables us to see the relationship of the parts as a unified whole (and to keep track of it as we follow it through history).

Dynamics and Religion

Dynamics in the study of religion asks the question: "What are the actual *practices* of a religion?" Most people within any religion know very little about its history, and usually are unable to provide an interpretation of it as a system. There is good reason for this, because most individuals do not experience religion as a historical process or a unified system, at least not in the way that they directly participate in the activities, ceremonies, rituals, and practices of a religion. An oversimplified way of phrasing the importance of dynamics is: Religion is what religion does. Religion has a heritage, that is, a history or past; religion has a system or structure, a worldview or codified order; by the same token, religion has its own pattern of action in dynamics.

The dynamics of religion are never separate from history and structure, for practices are rooted in history and are the practical expression of structure. Every religion has its own ways of practicing religion, be it in collective worship and festivals, or in individual prayer and meditation. However, three broad categories of religious action are found in almost all traditions: the annual cycle, the life cycle, and personal experience. The annual cycle is the circle of rituals and celebrations marked by a calendar year and usually repeated every year. The life cycle is the round of rituals linked to the stages of a person's life, from birth to death, although they may begin even before birth and continue long after death. Life-cycle rituals (or "rites of passage") may vary between males and females and are not uniform for every individual, but generally they are repeated in the career of most individuals. Just as the annual cycle and the life cycle form two of the most important patterns of religious practice, so does individual experience constitute a universal and valuable resource for getting an "inside" view of religious life. Personal experience of a religion can be recorded through listening to one person's life story (a "life history"), can be portrayed through a sketch of a typical life, or can be presented through biographies.

By paying attention to the history, structure, and dynamics of a religion we learn the story that tradition has to tell.

Each of the ten parts of this book describes and interprets a major tradition, including treatment of its history, structure, and dynamics. The author of every part is a scholar of religion who has completed extensive study in that tradition. There is a general format for every part, but each is a self-contained unit; therefore, the parts can be read in any order the reader desires. A preview of the ten parts may help the reader plan the journey through these traditions.

Religious Traditions of the World: An Overview

Africa, Mesoamerica, and North America

Parts 1, 2, and 3—Religions of Africa, Religions of Mesoamerica, and Native Religions of North America—deal with what have sometimes been called "primitive religions," but the authors of these parts argue convincingly against this category. These three traditions often are set apart from "world religions" because world religions usually are founded traditions in large-scale civilizations that have spread over vast areas of the globe. However, even if there are some differences between these traditions and the usual group of "world religions," these differences are not sufficient to isolate them from other traditions in the study of religion. The religions of Africa, Mesoamerica, and North America should be considered together with all other religions.

AFRICA Part 1, Religions of Africa, takes up religion in the land where the first human beings emerged. There is no one "African religion," in fact, hundreds of traditions are found within this vast continent. Therefore, Lawson has selected for case study two different traditions, the Zulu and the Yoruba. Zulu religion is centered around the village, especially its circle of huts and the cattle enclosure; the Zulu religious system is shown to be a pattern of interaction between powers and roles. The dynamics of Zulu religion are illustrated through description of the rites and observances at the death of a headman and following the life cycle of the new headman from birth through marriage. Yoruba religion is a tradition of ancient cities and a complex pantheon of many deities (called *orisha*) and features lengthy divination rites; the system of Yoruba religion is presented as a pattern of mediation (through ritual mediators) between worshipers and powers such as the *orisha*. The practice of Yoruba religion is followed through the process of divination and also the life cycle of a typical person from birth to death. The transformation of Zulu and Yoruba religion is demonstrated through the analysis of Christian new religious movements.

MESOAMERICA Part 2, Religions of Mesoamerica, takes us to a land of mystery and misunderstanding, as intriguing for us today as for the Spanish explorers who first "discovered" it about five centuries ago. The peoples of Mesoamerica developed large-scale city-states whose monuments still dazzle our imagination. Although these lost civilizations are no longer active, Carrasco has analyzed a variety of materials, especially archaeological finds, to reconstruct the "Mesoamerican cosmovision" with its emphasis on worldmaking, worldcentering, and worldrenewing. Singled out for special attention are the Aztec and the Maya. Aztec religion is interpreted through the tales of great deities, the record in stone of the great Aztec temple, and the drama of human sacrifice. Maya religion is portrayed through the symbolism of the cosmic tree and sacred kingship, as well as the regeneration of time in a remarkable calendar. The dynamics of Mesoamerican religion today are found in such examples as the distinctive tradition of the Virgin of Guadalupe (a blending of the Christian cult of the Virgin Mary with an Aztec mother goddess) and the peyote hunt of the Huichol Indians (a pilgrimage led by a shaman to find and eat peyote).

NORTH AMERICA   Part 3, Native Religions of North America, takes us to the traditions of people popularly known as "American Indians," focusing on the areas of the American continent north of Mesoamerica. Like Africa, the North American continent includes hundreds of religious traditions; Hultkrantz has selected two different examples, the Shoshoni and the Zuni. The Shoshoni, who lived on the western plains and Great Basin area, followed a nomadic hunting life. They had a rich mythology that in many ways contrasted with their ritual life, centered around the Sun Dance. The dynamics of Shoshoni religion come to life in a lengthy description of the annual Sun Dance, in which the participants build a lodge as a replica of the cosmos and dance while enduring severe physical hardships in order to seek a vision. The Zuni of the Southwest are famous for their agricultural lifestyle and pueblos, as well as for having one of the most elaborate and complex ritual patterns of all native Americans. The practice of Zuni religion is highlighted in the description of their ritual organizations (which meet in underground chambers called *kivas*), and the ritual year, which culminates in the *shalako* rite of renewal, "possibly the greatest ceremony in aboriginal North America." New religious movements among the Shoshoni and Zuni peoples show the interaction of native traditions with Christianity.

Judaism, Christianity, and Islam

Parts 4, 5, and 6 include Judaism, Christianity, and Islam—three traditions that are in close historical relationship to each other, which display some important similarities but at the same time are distinctively different in their respective messages and rituals. Historically, Judaism was the first to appear, followed by Christianity and then Islam, but the latter two include theological claims that precede their "founders" and go back to Creation itself. These three religions are sometimes thought of collectively as "religions of the West," because they originated in and have dominated the West—the area around the Mediterranean,

Europe, and North America. And yet their influence goes far beyond these regions. They are often considered as monotheistic traditions because of their emphasis on the sovereignty of God; they have also been called "religions of the Book" because of the importance they place on one revealed scripture. Nevertheless, the diversity within each of these three traditions defies any simple labels.

JUDAISM Part 4, Judaism, takes us to what are known as biblical lands at the eastern end of the Mediterranean Sea, but also to a people who, along with their religion, are scattered throughout much of the world. Judaism has no single founding figure, although it does have an abundance of religious leaders, of whom the greatest are Abraham and Moses. Judaism is founded on covenants between God and humans, the record of which is found in God's revelation known as Torah. Fishbane relates the history of this covenant along with the extensive commentary on it—in writings such as the Talmud and Mishnah—that is so important to the life of Judaism. The practice of Judaism is made clear in the calendrical cycle of holiness (including daily and weekly prayers and patterns as well as yearly festivals and sacred days) and the life cycle of holiness (from birth and circumcision to death and crisis rituals). Contemporary diversity in Judaism is exemplified in two tales: "a tale of two cities," showing the differences between great representatives of Orthodox Judaism in Vilna, Lithuania, and of Reform Judaism in Frankfurt am Main; and "a tale of two centers," contrasting the practice of Judaism in Israel, the major spiritual and spatial focus for Jewry today, and in the United States, where liberal and orthodox Jews have tended to cooperate in common causes.

CHRISTIANITY Part 5, Christianity, takes us first to the biblical lands shared with Judaism, and then through Europe and other areas where this religion is dominant. Christianity is closely related to Judaism in its origins, and shares much with Judaism, especially its emphasis on one God and one revealed scripture. But of course Christianity was "founded" by Jesus, and the divinity of Jesus is one of the dividing points between Judaism and Christianity. Frankiel traces the origins of Christianity and tells the story of its universal message of salvation based on the life, death, and resurrection of Christ. The development of the church (and churches) is treated, and the structures of the Christian life are presented through discussion of creeds, the drama of rituals such as baptism and Eucharist, and Jesus as a model for personal life. The dynamics of Christian practice are illustrated through two major examples: through description of a medieval Spanish Catholic pilgrimage, a lengthy and dangerous trip visiting many sacred sites and participating in many church services, all in order to enable pilgrims to purge themselves of sin; and through reflection on two figures of a famous American Protestant family, Lyman Beecher and his daughter Harriet Beecher Stowe (author of *Uncle Tom's Cabin*), whose lives represent very different responses to the Calvinist creed and its emphasis on "conviction of sin."

ISLAM Part 6, Islam, takes us first to the land of Arabia, where this religion originated, and then to the lands where it spread, across Africa and Europe and much of Asia. From a historical viewpoint, Islam was preceded in time by Judaism and Christianity and shares much of the heritage of both Abraham and Jesus. Like Judaism and Christianity, Islam insists on the worship of one God and on one revealed book (which for Islam is the Qur'ān); on the other hand, these similarities should not keep us from seeing Islam's own message. From a modern viewpoint Muḥammad may be considered the founder of Islam, but within Islam, Muḥammad is revered as a prophet rather than worshiped as a divinity. Although Islam is a religion, it also defines an inclusive community, follows its own law, and in fact constitutes a total way of life. Central to this community is a highly formal worship service, performed five times daily. Worship is one of the five pillars of Islam, all of which are described. Denny presents the dynamics of Muslim institutions through such practices as recitation of the Qur'ān, veneration of saints, and the Muslim life cycle. Islam's interaction with the West is discussed in terms of Muslim rejection of the West, the growing presence of Muslims in Western countries (including the life of a mosque in Toledo, Ohio), and a discussion of the meaning of "Islamic fundamentalism."

Hinduism, Buddhism, China, and Japan

Parts 7, 8, 9, and 10 treat Hinduism, Buddhism, Religions of China, and Religions of Japan. Usually these four traditions are grouped together as "Asian religions," or "religions of the East," in contrast to the "religions of the West." In recent times, however, these religions have developed branches in the West and all parts of the world, both through Asian immigrants outside Asia, and through conversion of non-Asians in other regions. Hinduism and Buddhism are very closely related through their common origin in ancient India, but also exhibit remarkable differences: Hinduism has been mainly a religion of the Indian people, whereas the founded religion of Buddhism spread a universal teaching of enlightenment. In the religions of China and the religions of Japan we see both cultures as well as religions. Buddhism, a strong missionary religion, was welcomed in these two countries, but also competed (and interacted) with pre-existing traditions. China and Japan each had their native traditions: China developed Daoism (Taoism) and Confucianism (both of which had influence beyond China), and Japan gave birth to Shinto (which remained a national tradition). The story of these "Asian religions," partly because they present strong contrasts with the monotheistic traditions of the West, have fascinated the Westerners who have become familiar with them.

HINDUISM Part 7, Hinduism, takes us to India, repository of one of the most ancient religious heritages in the world. Actually, the origins of Hinduism lie outside India, among the pastoralists who entered northern India about five thousand years ago and mixed with the people living there to form the rich tradition eventually known in the West as Hinduism. Knipe relates the myths, epics, and history of this religion, which itself is somewhat skeptical of formal or written history. Sacred scriptures such as the *Vedas* abound, but until recent times they were memorized and recited rather than written down and read. An almost bewildering array of divinities, and devotions at home and temple, are central to Hinduism. From prehistoric times elaborate rituals were performed by a priestly class; some of these rituals are still performed today, while others have been interiorized through processes of thought and meditation. Hinduism has never been neatly codified and uniformly institutionalized, but it does have its own worldview, which can be seen in five dimensions: listening to, mythologizing, classifying, recycling, and swallowing the universe. The dynamics of Hinduism are presented in "the journey of a lifebody" (the life cycle), the record of a woman's daily devotions and the details of her pilgrimage to a regional shrine, and the forty-year religious career of a man told through his life history.

BUDDHISM Part 8, Buddhism, takes us first to India, which Buddhism shares with Hinduism (and other religions) as its place of origin, and then follows Buddhism's spread throughout Asia. Buddhism emerged out of Hinduism, and while sharing many concepts and much mythology with this religion, developed its own universal message. It was founded by the Buddha and centers around his experience of enlightenment, which became a model for all people to follow. Summed up in the Buddha's teaching of the Four Noble Truths and the Eightfold Path, this universal message spread beyond India to most parts of Asia. Buddhism developed an elaborate set of scriptures and commentaries recording and interpreting the teachings of the Buddha; it also established many monastic centers to continue the Buddha's practice of meditation. Monks have been considered a kind of "pool of merit" that devout lay persons can draw from. Lester has presented the historical development of Buddhism, in its various forms, as well as its basic teachings. The dynamics of Buddhist practice are illustrated in the rituals and festivals of the Buddhist life and described at greater length in two case studies: the Theravada Buddhism of an agricultural village in Thailand (where the emphasis is on merit sharing or other-power) and the Mahayana Buddhism of a Zen monastery in Japan (which stresses self-discipline or self-power).

CHINA Part 9, Religions of China, takes us to the eastern extremity of the Asian continent, to what has become one of the largest and most populous countries in the world. Overmyer tells us this is also the oldest continuous culture, because its form of writing dating from about four thousand years ago is still in use today. From ancient times Chinese culture developed a distinctive worldview, which can be expressed as "the world as a living system." Notions such as *yin/yang* are part of this cosmic system. In early China there developed a number of philosophical and religious traditions, the most important of which are the ethical teachings of Confucius and the mystical and religious activities of Daoism. Buddhism entered China and interacted with both of these native traditions, as a result of which all three shared mutual influence. There is no one "Chinese religion"; rather, a number of religions coexist within a unified worldview. The components of this worldview—such as sacred space, sacred time, symbols of superhuman power, and rituals relating people to superhuman power—are analyzed and interpreted. The dynamics of the Chinese worldview are presented through description of: a spring festival honoring a family's dead in a mountain graveyard, the Buddhist enlightenment of a young monk, exorcism of a ghost from a lake after the drowning of a child, and spirit-writing as the religious vocation of a housewife.

JAPAN   Part 10, Religions of Japan, takes us to the Japanese islands east of the Asian mainland. Japan is the recipient of culture and religious influence from distant India as well as China (partly through Korea), and yet Japanese culture also developed its own particular style. Buddhism, Confucianism, and Daoism entered Japan, which contributed its own religious tradition of Shinto to form a distinctively Japanese religious heritage. Earhart portrays this Japanese worldview as "many traditions within one sacred way." The history of the appearance and interrelationship of these formal traditions, and also folk religion and new religious movements, is sketched. This provides background for discussion of the Japanese worldview by analyzing and interpreting what is worshiped, who worships, when worship takes place, where worship is held, and how it affects human life. The dynamics of Japanese religion are presented in two lengthy case studies: a rural agricultural spring festival in which village representatives climb a sacred mountain to celebrate annual renewal and fertility of the rice field and the life history of an urban member of a new religious movement, who defines religion as the power that enables people to live.

The preceding overview of each of the ten parts may help guide readers in entering the lands and religions to be visited in this journey through religious traditions of the world. On returning from this trip, readers should bring home memories that will reflect their appreciation of other cultures and also help them see the religion of their own culture in a new light.

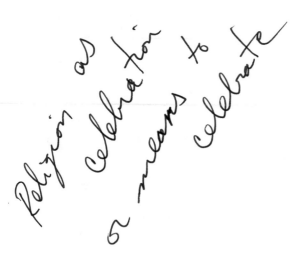

PART ONE

Religions
of
Africa

*Traditions
in Transformation*

E. Thomas Lawson

Chronology of African History and Religion

With Particular Reference to Zulu and Yoruba Societies

Chronology	Historical Features
	BEGINNINGS
Late Miocene	
5 million years ago	African apes and hominids diverge and hominids begin to diversify
Pliocene	
3.7 million years ago	Laetoli footprints in Tanzania (proof of bipedalism)
3 million years ago	"Lucy," Australopithecus Afarensis
2 million years ago	Homo habilis
Early Pleistocene	
1.75 million years ago	Homo erectus, stone tools begin to be used
700,000 years ago	The discovery of fire for human purposes
700,000 to 40,000 years ago	Archaic Homo sapiens becomes established
40,000 years ago	Modern Homo sapiens spreads throughout Africa
10,000 years ago	Indigenous African peoples are already forming their societies according to specific cultural patterns
2,900 years ago	The Nok culture of northern Nigeria uses iron and terra cotta in creative cultural ways
2,900 to 1,000 years ago	Migrations of large groups of people from central Africa in both an easterly and a southerly direction
	EARLY AFRICAN HISTORY
1,400 years ago	The birth of Islam (622 C.E.); Muslim conquest of Egypt, Palestine, Syria, Iraq, and Iran occurs very rapidly
1,300 years ago	Islam has conquered all of North Africa (by 700 C.E.) and has begun to establish connections with both West and East Africa

Chronology	*Historical Features*
	EARLY AFRICAN HISTORY (continued)
1,200 to 1,000 years ago	Islam is carried across the Sahara by traders along trade routes to both West and East Africa
1,000 years ago	Yoruba are already building large cities with walled compounds; slow migration of Bantu-speaking peoples from central to southeastern Africa moving as far south as the Transvaal
500 years ago	The ancestors of the Zulu begin to settle in Natal
	RECENT AFRICAN HISTORY
1471	Portuguese settle in West Africa
1652	The Dutch settle at the Cape and come into contact with the Khoisan people to the eventual detriment of the latter
1652 to 1795	The establishment of Afrikaanerdom and Calvinist culture and religion in South Africa
1750 to 1800	Exportation of 100,000 slaves a year to the Americas from the western coast of Africa; most of the European nations participate in the slave trade
1795 and 1806	British invasions of Cape Colony, which unsettles the Afrikaaners
1814	British take over Cape Colony
1816 to 1828	Reign of Shaka, the great Zulu king
1828 to 1840	Dingane, successor to Shaka
1836	The "Great Trek": The Afrikaaners leave the Cape Colony and begin to move north where they eventually come into hostile contact with the Zulu
1840 to 1872	Mpande, successor to Dingane
1842	Christianity introduced into Nigeria
1872 to 1884	Cetshwayo, successor to Mpande
1879	British invade Zulu kingdom and exile Cetshwayo, the last independent Zulu king
1884 to 1913	Dinizulu, successor to Cetshwayo
1894	Natal Native Code permits the confiscation of two-thirds of Zululand
1897	Zululand ceded to British colony of Natal

Chronology	*Historical Features*
	RECENT AFRICAN HISTORY (continued)
1900 to present	The proliferation of new religious movements, such as Isaiah Shembe's amaNazaretha Church in southern Africa and Aladura in Nigeria
1910	The Union of South Africa is formed as part of the British Commonwealth; the Union continues until 1961
1948	The launching of the doctrine of "apartheid" with the election of the Nationalists and a victory of Afrikaanerdom; vigorous attempts to separate the races and undo many of the gains made by the black people of South Africa
1960	Nigeria gains its independence from Great Britain; Zulu Chief Albert Luthuli awarded Nobel Peace Prize.
1961 to present	The Republic of South Africa is established and ties with the British Commonwealth are cut; this increases the unrest among the oppressed black people of South Africa and leads to the imprisonment of a large number of resisters against apartheid. Finally by the end of the 1980s, apartheid started to crumble and significant constitutional change began to be planned.

Prologue

THIS PART IS ENTITLED Religions of Africa, not *The* Religions of Africa, because it lays no claim to being comprehensive; a comprehensive treatment of the religions of Africa would be impossible in this short a space. Depending upon how one defines religious traditions, there are either hundreds or thousands of religions in Africa. The aims of this work are more modest. It is my intention to introduce the student to some of the religions of Africa by describing the worldview they embody and the acts that illustrate it. I also intend to show that these are living and lively traditions in process of transformation, possessing profound internal resources to respond to new situations and modes of thought with creativity and depth.

1

Introduction

Perceptions of Africa

THE AFRICA KNOWN BY TOURISTS is a vast continent punctuated with modern, skyscrapered cities that are encroaching on game reserves populated by freely roaming wild animals, little villages with thatched roofs on circular huts, grass plains merging into dense and often impenetrable jungles, and black people clothed in colorful garments or nothing at all. For those not given to travel but to reading novels, watching television, going to the movies, and reading the local newspaper, it is both the land of three-million-year-old Lucy, whose fossilized bones testify to the origins of the ancestors of Homo sapiens, and the land of Tarzan and the apes. And for those drawn to the esoteric it is the dark continent of bizarre ritual practices and farfetched stories about the origins of the world and the beings who inhabit it.

This essay is about some of the religious traditions of Africa. In it we shall consider these seemingly bizarre practices and ideas. Our purpose is to place them in a context in which they may be more readily understood. In this attempt at understanding the modes of thought and practice of people who, at least on the surface, lead lives quite different from ours in the West, we follow the paths of an illustrious band of inquirers who have preceded us. Inquiry into the traditions of Africa has been going on for a long time; over the last few decades there has been an increasing interest, both scholarly and popular, in the worlds of Africa.

But despite a developing interest in Africa spurred by the establishment of the Peace Corps in the sixties, the recent paleontological discoveries, and various revolutions and coups, Africa still carries the image of the dark continent, a vast geographical area that is little known, essentially backward, and rather mysterious. This is surprising, because Africa has been explored and studied for a long time. The Phoenicians had already circumnavigated the continent in the sixth century B.C.E. Vasco da Gama and Bartholomew Dias explored it as a route to India four hundred years ago, and the Dutch had begun to settle its southern regions by the mid–seventeenth century. [See Religions of Mesoamerica pp. 119–26 and Native Religions of North America pp. 261–64 for discussion of Western stereotypes.]

Serious scientific study of this land is more recent but is at least a hundred years old; it is not as if Africa is a newly discovered Atlantis emerging from mysterious waters, waiting to be explored. Yet Africa *does* need to be rediscovered, because, despite its image of mystery, strangeness, and radical otherness, its story is our own. *We are all Africans.*

That assertion, that we are all Africans, might ring strange to our ears but it points to scientific truth about human origins on this planet. A few million years ago some very important evolutionary events were taking place in the eastern part of Africa, specifically in the area now known as the Great Rift valley.

Briefly, the first hominids, our earliest human ancestors, appeared about four million years ago in what is now known as Tanzania and Ethiopia. Within two million years a number of hominid species were roaming the eastern plains of Africa. Homo erectus, who appeared over a million years ago, is particularly interesting. Homo erectus made and used tools and discovered fire, some of the very first marks of "culture." Homo sapiens emerged about 40,000 years ago and rapidly established itself as the dominant species. Homo sapiens created even more sophisticated tools than Homo erectus, developed hunting skills, used fire systematically, and engaged in both ritual and artistic activities.

So it is in Africa, too, that the first cultural discoveries were made, discoveries we now take for granted: the first tool was invented, the first fire lighted by a human hand, the first crop planted, the first village established, the first language spoken. These activities are some of the marks of human civilization. The original humans then began their slow journey to other continents, where they began to establish a wide range of lifestyles. This story of our African origins has been painstakingly assembled during the last century; it is now a basic assumption of Western scientific thought. To this day, of course, many African peoples continue to retell their own stories of beginnings. The content of their stories is different from the story we have been writing recently, but the interest in origins is identical to our own and testifies to the same seriousness of intellectual purpose.

The Reality of Africa

What is the context for the religious traditions we shall be examining? How can the dark continent become illumined for us? We shall start by learning something about the realities of Africa.

Africa is the second largest of the continents on our planet. Its population today is estimated to be about four hundred million. The land consists of thick forests, high plateaus covered with tall grasses and acacia trees, and severe deserts. An astonishing variety of human societies occupy its land areas, and a wide range of languages reverberate on its streets and pathways. In the

Niger-Congo language family alone there are nine hundred languages, each having numerous dialects; the **Bantu*** languages, each consisting of many forms, are only one subgroup of this vast array of languages in the Niger-Congo family.

The sheer massiveness of Africa is sufficient to overwhelm anyone who wishes to study some aspect of its contours, whether the interest is in languages, human origins, social organization, political change, or animal life. Decisions have to be made, therefore, as to what one will study. Some general divisions have been accepted by most scholars; for example, the continent is usually divided into two parts for investigation. One area of study starts at the Mediterranean and reaches to the lower edge of the Sahara Desert. This is usually known as Islamic Africa. The other area of study consists of the rest of the continent and is known as sub-Saharan Africa, or black Africa. This term is quite misleading, for the people of Africa below the Sahara come in many shades, sizes, and traditions. And despite the fact that the upper part of Africa is known as Islamic Africa, it is not true that Islam has had no influence below the Sahara. In fact, over the centuries Islam has vigorously pursued a policy of conversion and has been quite successful in many sub-Saharan countries. It has made great strides in Nigeria in the last few centuries, and the **Yoruba** people, which we will be studying, have been partially converted to it.

We shall focus upon the religious life of people in the sub-Saharan part of Africa. Many books have been written about these Africans. There are also many books about "primitive religions" in which these peoples and their religious traditions are lumped together with small-scale societies from Polynesia, South America, North America, and even the Arctic. The assumption in these books is that such widely disparate societies have something important in common. But there is little agreement as to precisely what that is; often it means little more than that such people have not used writing as a form of cultural expression and that they are "small-scale." We shall not use the term *primitive* in this book; nor shall we operate according to any of its questionable assumptions. We shall avoid lumping together all the people of sub-Saharan Africa, and we shall not argue that they are all alike. Nothing could be further from the truth. [See Native Religions of North America p. 263 for a discussion of "primitive religions"; see Religions of Mesoamerica pp. 122–25 for a treatment of "the noble savage/wild man."]

One of the realities of Africa is its diversity. This can be seen in the fact that its societies exhibit a wide range of social organization. Some are vast kingdoms with millions of subjects, thus belying the term *small-scale*. Nigeria is a good example of such a society. Others are small groups of families wandering in the hot sands of the Kalahari Desert. Some Africans from the earliest times developed town life, for example, the Yoruba of West Africa. Other Africans, such as the **Zulu** of South Africa, have lived for centuries in small villages. [See

---

*Terms defined in the glossary, pp. 101–4, are printed in boldface type where they first appear in the text.

Religions of Mesoamerica pp. 117–19, Native Religions of North America pp. 263–64, Judaism pp. 389, 426, 456–75, Christianity pp. 492–94, Islam pp. 607–8, Hinduism pp. 719–21, Buddhism pp. 853–55, Religions of China pp. 990–1015, and Religions of Japan pp. 1090–92 for discussion of the diversity of religious traditions.]

Political arrangements also vary considerably from society to society. Some political systems are centrally controlled under the absolute rule of a king. Others are almost completely decentralized, with power in the hands of a village council or a village headman. Still others have a tribal organization, with authority residing in a chief. And some consist of small wandering bands dependent for a living on hunting and gathering and governed by consensus.

Of course, the coming of the Europeans and the Muslims changed some of these social and political arrangements. New boundaries were carved out of the old territories, resulting in the division of cultural wholes. New styles of politics were introduced. In Nigeria, the British used the principle of indirect rule to control the population and gave to the chiefs powers they had never had before. Some of the problems encountered in Africa today are the direct result of the artificial boundaries and political structures imposed by the colonial powers.

The coming of the Muslims and Europeans also introduced new religious ideas and practices. Islam and Christianity in their various forms were carried to most of the African societies. What is clear is that neither Islam nor Christianity was successful in eradicating the traditional religious thought and practices of the societies into which they were introduced. Though Muslim and Christian symbols are everywhere in evidence in Africa, they are often merely an additional element in the religious life of the people. We shall have occasion later to pay some attention to the relationship between the indigenous religions and the introduced religions. In this introduction we need only say that over the last century, especially, there have been religiously based movements that have arisen in response to these external religious traditions. These new religious movements, identical with neither Christianity nor Islam nor, for that matter, the indigenous religions, have been powerful forces, expressing not only political and nationalistic power but a new kind of religious creativity. [See Religions of Mesoamerica pp. 112–14, 215–21, Native Religions of North America pp. 320–21, 325, Hinduism pp. 766–67, 770, and Religions of China p. 988–89 for discussion of invasion and colonization.]

Some scholars have gone so far as to argue that an understanding and explanation of the causes and functions of these new religions will provide important clues to the nature of religion wherever it is found. Some of these new religious movements have appropriated symbols from traditional African religions but given them a new twist. Other movements have employed Christian imagery and given it a novel interpretation. Some have developed followings with thousands of members; others, after a brief moment of glory, have withered away as their leaders have died.

Not only have these new religious movements been examples of religious creativity, they have also been vehicles for the expression of the demand for independence, equality, freedom, and nationhood. Those governments interested in "keeping the natives in their place" have shown considerable interest in these movements and expressed fear of them because of their involvement in the forces for social change.

For those scholars who wish to make a clear distinction between religious and political action, these movements have proved to be particularly difficult to analyze. This should not be at all surprising when one considers that a people with a long tradition of their own have developed an elaborate worldview. If change does occur, it will be within the terms of that worldview. Whatever is novel in any society is at least partly traceable to one or more elements in the worldview that has developed over time. Two countries, Nigeria and South Africa, have proven to be especially fertile areas for the development of new religions.

Many scholars have remarked upon the proliferation of new religious movements in the Republic of South Africa, a nation with four million whites who effectively control the lives of twenty-five million Africans. Though many of these religious movements employ Christian imagery, such imagery is often combined with strong anti-white sentiment. Some scholars, therefore, tend to downplay the religious dimensions of these movements and interpret them as political movements in religious garb. But the situation is far more complicated. In the case of the Zulu we see a complex symbol system in place that is quite capable of being transformed to deal with new situations in a new setting. Similar systems exist among the Yoruba of Nigeria. They have a complex and differentiated symbol system that not only has consistently undergone internal transformation but, when confronted with other radically alien systems, has been able to adapt and adjust certain elements into new forms.

Whether we examine the traditional religious systems or the innovations brought about by new religious movements, we still need to develop an approach that will increase our understanding of the structure and dynamics of African religions. In deciding upon an approach we will first describe the paths we will not take.

It would be easy and tempting to develop a collection of overarching generalizations about the religious life of Africans. With some imagination, it might be possible to identify certain themes in African beliefs and practices. Some books do just that, and they make interesting reading. Or we might attempt a personal odyssey. Starting in the south and journeying slowly to the Congo, we might describe briefly our encounters with the beliefs and practices of the people we meet. Or we might start out with a specific notion, such as the idea of "belief." Having defined what a belief is, we could then systematize the various beliefs of various African societies into a kind of catalogue, and we might show that in some way everything that Africans believe we also believe in some way or another. Or we might decide to stay put and examine only one African society, delineating its thoughts and practices in a careful and systematic manner; some of the most helpful books on Africa are those that do exactly that. Or we might simply attempt to be comprehensive on the basis of what is available.

We will do none of these. We have already called attention to the vastness of Africa, its cultural and linguistic variety. Rather than spreading ourselves too thin, we shall narrow our focus down to two African peoples, the Zulu and the Yoruba. It is our hope that through such focusing we shall be able to give a better and more comprehensible picture of what two particular African religious worlds look like.

In our discussion of these two religious traditions we shall try to show what their religious worlds are like and how the Zulu and Yoruba live and act within these frameworks. In describing their religious worlds we shall show that each consists, first, of special places that provide a ritual environment and dramatic setting for the performing of religious acts. Second, such worlds consist of special roles that define the purpose of the actors in the religious drama. Third, they consist of special powers, presences, or beings with which the actors form prescribed relationships within the dramatic setting. Once we have achieved familiarity with the religious places, roles, and powers, we shall be prepared for a description and analysis of religious activities. In other words, we will know something about how the Zulu and Yoruba live and act in a religious world.

In order to make these religious activities as informative as possible, we shall describe the many religious symbols that are present in, and inform, the actions that characterize the stages on life's way. We shall see how, at important periods of Zulu and Yoruba life, the religious world is a significant presence. The focus here will be on what Zulu and Yoruba traditions are and how such ancient traditions are still reflected in present forms of life and thought—even under conditions of change.

No religious world remains the same over long periods of time for reasons having to do with both the internal experience of the people and with their relationships between other religions, other people, and other social and cultural forms. Among both the Zulu and the Yoruba other systems of thought and action have been introduced. As a creative response, old forms have been redefined and new forms have been developed. Old places, roles, and powers have attained new meanings, and new places, roles, and powers have been recognized. In other words, transformation of the two traditions has taken place. We shall attempt to describe the interesting and complex relationships that these new forms have to the traditional ones and show how flexible a tradition can be.

The Zulu and the Yoruba, then, will provide the focus of our attention, and the notions of "religious system" and "religious action" will provide the lenses through which we can view their religions. We shall certainly discover that ideas such as "primitive" and "simple" do little to advance our understanding of other peoples and their religious thought and action.

The Zulu live in the southern part of the African continent. The Yoruba live in the western part of central Africa. These two peoples are widely separated and have different histories, different social and political organizations, and different cultures and languages. They are distinct enough in style and tradition to provide us with the basis for individual analysis, as well as comparison. And yet they are not completely unrelated. First, they do occupy the same continent. Second, many of the people now occupying the southeastern part of the continent migrated from central Africa over the last two thousand years, and so at least some continuity, however tenuous, can be assumed. The Zulu and the Yoruba have been the subject of both scholarly and popular interest. In the case of the Zulu the popular imagination associates them with the picture of the warrior courageously fighting the British and the **Boers** (the white settlers of Dutch extraction who colonized southern Africa in the seventeenth century).

In the case of the Yoruba we have a complex image of **witchcraft, divination,** and art. In fact a recent novel on the practice of witchcraft in New York City traces it back to the Yoruba. Although widely separated from each other on the African continent and radically different from each other in social and religious institutions, the Zulu and the Yoruba belong to the same language family, the Niger-Congo. Although consisting of hundreds of languages and dialects, this language family can be divided into six groups: Among these six groups, Yoruba belongs to the Kwa group and Zulu to the Benue-Congo group. More than seven million people speak Yoruba, and about four million speak Zulu.

Zulu belongs to a subgroup within the Benue-Congo called the Bantu set of languages. These languages are called Bantu because the word for "people" is *bantu* in this assortment of languages. So, for example, when the Zulu give their account of the origins of **Unkulunkulu,** the first human being, they use the word *bantu* to describe him and the people who issue forth from him.

The Zulu and the Yoruba are happy choices to focus on for a number of reasons. They both have been the subject of sufficient scholarly study so that a good basis for analysis exists. They both have the kind of systems that appear in similar forms in some other African societies, so that a knowledge of their religions opens a door to knowledge of other African religions. Understanding the religion of the Zulu, for example, opens the door to understanding the religion of the Swazi, Xhosa, and other Nguni people. Both Zulu and Yoruba have also been subject to the forces of colonialism and Christianization, and new religious movements have appeared in both contexts. They also have systems sufficiently different so that comparing and contrasting them becomes interesting and fruitful.

Today the Zulu are still under the domination of the white South African government, although its recent moves (for example, legalizing the African National Congress) provides some hope for significant change. The Yoruba are free and are an important part of the complex, modern state of Nigeria. But bound or free, their religious systems continue to exist and to provide the basis for continuing traditional practices and inventing new ones. These flexible religious traditions are our subject.

Our focus on these religions of Africa will consist of showing how in each case their religious places, roles, powers, and actions are expressions of a coherent system of thought that informs the conduct of the lives of the people who participate in them. We shall not ignore the obvious diversity of practice and belief in each religion. Instead we shall lay the groundwork for showing that, even granting religious diversity, there is an underlying unity of thought that provides a set of profound answers to fundamental questions about what is real, important, personal, dangerous, and desirable.

Specifically, chapter 2 will provide the setting for understanding Zulu religion, chapter 3 for understanding Yoruba religion. Chapter 4 will be an analysis of how individual participants in these religious traditions, the roles they occupy, and the actions they perform lead us to the conclusion that each religion is an example of a system of thought about the world and the place of human life in it. Each religion also contributes to our common human heritage.

2

The Zulu and Their Religious Tradition

The Origins of the Zulu People

THE ORIGINS OF THE ZULU PEOPLE are shrouded in the mists of oral tradition. But by using a variety of specialized methods, scholars have been able to penetrate the mists and discover some of the Zulu past. They have concluded that within the last two thousand years there have been a series of migrations of large numbers of people from central Africa into the southern part of the continent. These migrants from the north had a linguistic identity, and they are referred to as Bantu-speaking peoples. This means that although these people spoke many different languages the languages were similar enough in form and structure to deserve a common name, Bantu. Scholars chose the name Bantu because this word, meaning "people," occurs in a large array of languages spoken by the migrants. These people slowly settled the southeastern area of Africa all the way down to what is now known as the province of Natal in the Republic of South Africa. As they settled the land they began to form special groups. One large group is now known as the Nguni people. The Nguni group consisted of many tribes and clans: the Xhosa, the Fingo, the Tembu, the Pondo, the Swazi, and the Zulu. This process of migration and solidification into special groups, each with a distinct language, was complete by the seventeenth century.

The Zulu at this stage of development were one group of people among many. According to their own traditions, an ancestor named Malandela had two sons named Qwabe and Zulu. These two sons became the chiefs of two clans. Chief Zulu extended his quest for territory until he came to the Mfolosi Valley, an area north of the Thukela River in the present-day province of Natal. There Chief Zulu settled. His clan remained stable and unremarkable until the renowned Zulu chief **Shaka** (1787–1828) emerged as a dynamic leader and warrior at the beginning of the nineteenth century. Shaka in a very short time welded many different clans together into one powerful kingdom. He was successful in this endeavor because he developed completely new methods of military conquest, establishing highly disciplined regiments of young men and inventing new ways of deploying them in battle. It is Shaka's prowess as a general that has captivated the imagination of Western novelists and filmmakers. Movies about the Zulu warrior continue to be made to this day.

Zululand in its African context.

Today there are about four million Zulu in South Africa. They continue to live primarily on a small portion of their original land in the northeast section of Natal. However, many Zulu can also be found throughout South Africa working in the mines, as domestic servants, and in those positions in the world of industry and business not reserved for whites (although this picture is now in the process of change). Even under such very difficult conditions some Zulu have been able to attain a high level of education and thus will be found either at the segregated universities provided by the South African government or, in special cases, at one of the English-speaking universities, such as the University of Cape Town or Rhodes University. (Recently the picture has changed and predominantly white universities, including Afrikaans-speaking universities, have a more open admissions policy.)

When the government of South Africa declared a portion of the province of Natal as the Zulu "homeland," they named it Kwazulu. Supposedly, within this area the Zulu would finally have some political rights. Whether or not this occurs, this greatly diminished area has not proved to be self-sufficient. The Zulu therefore have been forced to continue their dependence on white South Africa, with its system of **apartheid.** Apartheid is a governmental policy intended to keep the various groups of people living in South Africa separate from each other. Its practical effect has been to keep all black people in a position of servitude, without political rights of any kind. The "homeland" is certainly far less in area than the traditional Zulu kingdom. At this moment the Zulu are strongly insisting through two different organizations, the African National Congress and the Inkatha party, on their autonomy and freedom. Zulu leaders have often been some of the most eloquent spokesmen for the rights of all black people in South Africa. In fact, the Zulu chief **Albert Luthuli** was granted the Nobel Peace Prize in 1960 (the first African to be so honored) for his articulate and peaceful presentation of the case for all the oppressed people of South Africa.

While the Zulu people continue in such an oppressed situation it remains impossible to speak of an independent kingdom or nation, despite their possession of the small territory, Kwazulu. Long before this possession, the buffeting that these people had received from both British and Boer had already destroyed their autonomy.

In 1879 the British invaded the Zulu kingdom established by Shaka and maintained by the succeeding chiefs. Cetshwayo was the last of the Zulu kings or great chiefs. After the British invasion of Zululand he was exiled; the invasion and his exile signaled the end of Zulu territorial and political independence. In 1897 Zululand was ceded to the British colony of Natal. Shortly after this cession, the British and the **Afrikaaners** engaged in a war disastrous for both. This war created a deep enmity between the two white groups. In 1910 the Union of South Africa was formed as a state within the British Commonwealth. In 1913 the South African government promulgated the Native Land Act, naming a portion of traditional Zululand as a "native reserve." In fact, by 1906 much of the territory that the Zulu regarded as their own kingdom had already been overrun and was possessed by white Natal settlers of both British and Boer stock. It is the remnants of this native reserve that has now been designated as Kwazulu, the "homeland" of the Zulu people.

Despite this tragic ending to an illustrious history, Zulu social and religious traditions have survived. The Zulu have not forgotten their past, and even those Zulu who have become Westernized are very careful to insist upon the worth and significance of their own traditions. Of course, this does not mean that the Zulu are static. There have been changes, often subtle ones, in the Zulu worldview. But there is clearly a continuity of thought and practice between present and past forms of Zulu life. In the town of Ulundi to this day on special occasions the chief, dressed in traditional garb and carrying the traditional spear (***assegai***) and shield, assembles the men of the community into their regiments, and they sing the praises of their great ancestors, especially Shaka, who made of them one people.

The Religious System of the Zulu People

Though I have briefly called attention to the history of the Zulu, I do not intend to discuss the historical development of Zulu religion. There are many good reasons for not engaging in a historical analysis, the most important being lack

Villages on the hills of Zululand. (Photograph by the author.)

of information. To study the historical development of a religious tradition means tracing its progress from its inception through its various changes to its present situation. Unfortunately, as with most African religions, such historical documentation is simply not available. We are dealing with an oral culture in which traditions are handed down by word of mouth, for example, by praise songs. Documentation is not, of course, entirely lacking. We do have the diaries of Westerners who lived with the Zulu for a period. Some missionaries did make a very serious attempt to record the thought and practice of the Zulu. But such records are too sparse and too unsystematic to give us the kind of information that would permit significant historical analysis.

Rather than getting lost in unclear historical detail, I prefer to look directly at the known patterns of Zulu thought and practice. This way of studying a religion provides a key for opening the doors to at least some of the complex religious world of the Zulu. This approach starts out by viewing Zulu thought and practice as parts of a whole. It assumes unity in Zulu life; through the changes brought about in history there is a continuity. Though such an approach acknowledges change, it insists that the Zulu religious system is flexible enough to deal with new situations in terms of its own ideas and practices.

A responsible description of the Zulu religious world must, however, choose some time frame, because, although history is not the focus, it cannot be ignored. It would be whistling in the dark to assert—without evidence—that the Zulu religious world of today is identical with that of 500 years ago. In the first place, strictly speaking, Zulu identity can only be traced back as far as Chief Zulu, and some argue that it can only be traced back as far as Shaka. I have chosen to describe a system that has been in place for the last 150 years. Whatever documents we do have are from this period, and they are of sufficiently high quality to give us the kind of information we need. These documents are diaries, reports written by missionaries on the basis of interviews with Zulu, accounts by colonial administrators, and descriptions by various anthropologists and other social scientists. Obviously such documents reflect the biases of those who wrote them, and the information generated depends upon the kinds of questions asked. But they are sufficiently informative to furnish us with the materials we need to provide a description of Zulu thought and practice.

Such thought and practice can be understood more clearly when we begin to identify their context. The Zulu people live and act in a religious world. This means that, whether one is talking about the birth of a child, a boy coming of age, the marriage of a young couple, or the death of a person in the family, there will be distinctive places, people, and powers that give these events special significance.

One way of getting a clearer view of the Zulu religious world is to pay attention to the places where religious acts take place, the roles assumed by the Zulu in the performance of these acts, the focus of the acts, and the style of action. In what follows, therefore, we shall organize our description of the Zulu religious system according to religious places, religious roles, religious powers, and religious acts.

As one wanders the dusty, red roads of present-day Zululand, one is struck by the simple beauty of the gently contoured green hills stretching to the horizon. These hills have great religious significance for the Zulu, for many of them provide the sites for the **umuzi** or Zulu village, also known as **kraals.** (The word *kraal*—from the Portuguese *curral*—is often used to refer either to the Zulu village or to its cattle enclosure; for the sake of clarity, we will use "village" or "cattle enclosure.") Some of these hills will not have villages built on them, and it is such unpopulated hills that provide sites for special rituals the Zulu occasionally perform. But the Zulu village is the primary locus for ritual action. It is in this sacred space that crucial religious performances occur periodically.

The traditional village consists of a circular arrangement of thatched huts, each shaped something like a beehive. This circle of huts surrounds a cattle enclosure at the very center of the village. This inner circle is called an **isibaya.** In effect, you have a circle within a circle, a cattle enclosure within a human enclosure. The village is built on the side of the hill and slopes downward, with the entryways to both the outer circle of huts and the inner circle for the cattle facing toward the bottom of the hill. These entryways invariably face east.

The location of the huts in the circular arrangement is significant, for it indicates both social and ritual relationships of the occupants. The chief hut, on the west side of the circular arrangement, is the hut of the headman, who is also the priest of the village. This chief hut is balanced on each side by the huts of the headman's wives, one of whom will be known as the "great wife." Lower down are the huts for the children of the family, for appropriate relatives, and for guests or visitors. Such relatives, guests, or visitors will always have a particular association with this village, usually a relationship of kinship.

The inner circle is the cattle enclosure. As with all Bantu-speaking peoples, cattle are of extreme practical and religious importance. It is in the cattle enclosure that most of the important Zulu religious rituals are performed. In fact

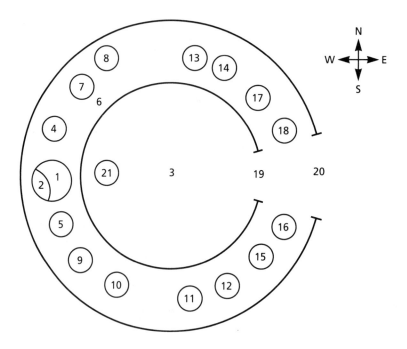

1. Chief Hut (Headman/Priest)
2. *Umsamo*
3. Cattle Enclosure
4, 5. Huts of Great Wife
6. Fence Around Cattle Enclosure
7, 8. Huts of Chief Wife of the Left Section
9, 10. Huts of Chief Wife of the Right Section

11, 12. Huts of the Sons
13, 14. Huts of the Daughters
15, 16, 17, 18. Huts for Guests and Visitors
19. Entrance to Cattle Enclosure
20. Entrance to Village
21. Site for Ritual Ceremonies for Ancestors

Figure 1-1. Traditional Zulu Village.

some scholars call the cattle enclosure the "temple" of the Zulu people. Although the particular inhabitants of a village might very well own other types of animals, such as sheep and goats, in the traditional Zulu village such other animals will be kept in separate enclosures outside the village proper. Only in cases of extreme poverty—a family that owns no cattle at all—will one find sheep or goats in the inner circle. Such a situation is much more likely today than it was in the heyday of the Zulu kingdom.

In each hut in the village will be found the **umsamo.** This is a special place set aside for various objects with ritual significance. In the hut of the head-man/priest there will be found a very special *umsamo.* Its particular purpose is to provide a ritual ground for communing with the ever present family ances-tors. Likewise, on the west side of the inner cattle enclosure there is a ritual ground for the performance of religious ceremonies directed to the ancestors.

Besides the unoccupied but specially marked hills, then, the village turns out to be not only a place to live but also a place to serve the ancestral powers in the manner that they require. Both places serve as sacred ground for the religious acts that the Zulu regularly perform.

These sacred grounds provide the stage for the many roles assumed by the actors in the Zulu religious drama. What is particularly interesting about these roles is that they identify who the leaders and specialists in the Zulu community are. An examination of them will show how political, social, and religious functions in Zulu society overlap and interact with each other. For example, the headman/priest of the village leads the rituals for the ancestors, makes decisions that affect the everyday lives of its inhabitants, and maintains the correct relationships between every person in the village.

Of the many Zulu roles, eight—headman/priest, **diviner, herbalist,** patient, **heaven-herd**, supplicant, sorcerer, and witch—hold particularly important places in the religious practice.

The headman of each Zulu village is the hereditary chief official of the village and also that person most directly responsible for the performance of the ritual acts expected of all Zulu, especially those that address the ancestors. His role is, therefore, political, social, and religious in nature. He is called *umnumzane.* Religiously, he represents the people of the village to the ancestors and the ancestors of the headman's lineage to the people. This position is of great ritual significance in the religious world of the Zulu because the ancestors are a focal point of their religion. The ancestors have great power, and they act for the good or ill of the villagers. These ancestors require reverence and devotion, and the *umnumzane* ensures that both in attitude and in act the members of the community for which he is responsible perform their religious duty. Whether it be birth, marriage, or death, the headman will be involved in some manner, and it is in the village that such acts will be performed. [See Religions of Mesoamerica pp. 198–201, Native Religions of North America pp. 347–48, Judaism pp. 391–92, Christianity pp. 503–505, Islam pp. 632–33, Hinduism p. 748, Buddhism pp. 875–77, 952–53, Religions of China pp. 991–93, and Religions of Japan pp. 1095–96, 1105–6 for the relationship of religion to political leaders.]

Divination, the ritual acts performed by ritual specialists to diagnose the reason for a misfortune or the means to the solution of some human problem, is widespread throughout Africa. As we shall see, it has achieved a highly systematic and intricate character among the Yoruba. Divination is also an important activity among the Zulu, and the role of the diviner is widespread in Zulu society.

Though both men and women can become diviners, this is a vocation in Zulu society that is most often assumed by women. One needs a special calling from the ancestral spirits in order to become a diviner. Such a calling takes a specific form, often that of a vision or a dream. The visitation is frequently accompanied by aches, pains, or other bodily disorders. Those who have been called receive special training under an experienced diviner; divining is not regarded as a casual affair, for identifying the cause of a problem takes great skill.

Once a diviner finds the cause of a problem, an herbalist prescribes the cure. Although most Zulu know something about herbs and other kinds of **medicines,** and many Zulu are experts in the knowledge of and prescription of particular medicines, there are Zulu who are specialists in medicine, who have a wide range of medical knowledge. Such a Zulu specialist is known as an *izinyanga zemithi,* a specialist in medicine, or *izinyanga zokwelapha,* a specialist in healing.

Whereas most diviners are women, most herbalists are men. Knowledge of medicine is usually handed down from father to son. But as I have already indicated, there is widespread knowledge of medicine, and particular people in the community will have knowledge of special medicines for special purposes.

One of the most interesting features of Zulu medicine is that it is not a completely traditional system. By this I mean that the specialist is in constant search for new and more effective medicines, and records show that medicines introduced by Westerners have been enthusiastically received and have become part of the Zulu medical repertoire. Thus, though it has a strong traditional base, Zulu medicine is a flexible system that has proven to be quite open to new knowledge. [See Native Religions of North America pp. 268, 273, 279–80, 298–300, 316–20, 344–46 for discussion of medicine, medicine man, and related subjects.]

Whereas the roles of headman/priest, diviner, and herbalist are formal and public roles, that of patient—the user of medicine—is an informal and private one. Because of the flexibility of Zulu medicine both with regard to the practitioner and to the materials used, many of the people can diagnose and cure their own illnesses. Thus the patient may either consult an herbalist or engage in self-prescription; in either case there is a direct relationship between the patient and the power of medicine. Strictly speaking, mediation on the part of the herbalist is not necessary to tap that power.

The *izinyanga zezulu,* the specialists in matters having to do with the sky —for example, thunderstorms and lightning—have a very important ritual role to play in the Zulu religious drama. These individuals are responsible for "herding" the thunderstorms that frequent Zululand, and they are known, therefore, as "heaven-herds." It should be remembered that cattle are of fundamental importance to the Zulu, and therefore the imagery of cattle and the activities associated with cattle occur quite frequently. (The role of the heaven-herd is always occupied by a Zulu male because of the close symbolic association between men and cattle.)

Heaven-herding is a vocation; it is a role to which a man is called in a special way by the **God of the Sky:** For example, the individual might receive a special sign, perhaps an especially close encounter with a bolt of lightning, that will convince him that the God of the Sky has chosen him for this work. The candidate for the role will then go through a period of apprenticeship with an experienced heaven-herd. Part of his initiation will be having special cuts made on his face by an experienced heaven-herd. This is a special, permanent marking of the face called scarification.

What is special about the role of the heaven-herd is that he will have a ritual relationship with the God of the Sky instead of the ancestors. The weather is under the control of the God of the Sky; it is he who sends the lightning and the wind and the rain. So the job of the heaven-herd is to repel or divert the approaching storm and to mitigate its effects. Just like the **umfaan,** the young lad who herds the cattle to their special grazing spots, the heaven-herd guides the weather for human benefit.

Most of Zulu religious life centers upon reverence for the ancestors and the ritual obligations associated with these revered predecessors. But occasions do arise when it is thought necessary for special acts to be performed over which the ancestors have no control or into which the ancestors have given no indication that they care to intrude. The Zulu supplicant, that is, anyone who communes directly with the God of the Sky, will know that in such a situation of dire need, help is possible from the God of the Sky. The God of the Sky is communicated with only in such special situations, when neither the headman/priest nor the diviner nor the herbalist have demonstrated an ability to help. Only then are special acts of supplication to the God of the Sky in order. Such communication with the God of the Sky will take place on those hills known by the Zulu supplicant to be arenas for an encounter with him. It should be noted, then, that what the heaven-herd and the supplicant have in common is a special ritual location—the hills of God—on which to worship him.

Any Zulu can be a sorcerer. The role of the sorcerer is general; no one person or set of persons is always and consistently a sorcerer. The reason is that **sorcery** depends upon the situation; a special grievance has to arise for one Zulu to feel that the occasion is ripe for the expression of the grievance. This angered individual will consult with either a diviner or an herbalist. A diviner is the likely consultant if the cause of the problem needs clarification. Of course, if the diviner traffics in medicine then two jobs can be done at the same time. If the aggrieved person is convinced of the cause but requires the means of sorcery, he or she will consult an herbalist with knowledge of those medicines that can have the desired effect.

To engage in sorcery is to have access to medicinal and spiritual power and to use such powers for destructive ends. The sorcerer's intent is to harm through the straightforward means made available by the herbalist's and/or the diviner's knowledge. The motive is often revenge. Anyone with a knowledge of medicine can perform sorcery. One simply devises the techniques to use its power (**amandla**) for evil ends. Sorcery is an activity similar to but not as destructive as witchcraft.

There is nothing straightforward about the role of the **abathakati** (witch) in the Zulu religious world. First of all, no one really knows who the witches are. The role of witch is completely private. It is also completely secret. It is important to note this secrecy, because the headman/priest, the heaven-herd, the diviner, and the herbalist are open, traditionally prescribed, and public roles. But the maker of witchcraft is that unknown individual, almost always considered to be a woman, who misuses valid and good power for invalid and evil ends. Witchcraft is a threat to public order, an unbearable strain on traditional social organization, a challenge to revered tradition. Witches derive their power from, and base their operations in, a shadowy world that is neither that of the ancestors nor that of the God of the Sky. And their purpose is the destruction of what is good, especially those processes that create and enhance life. The witch is the specialist in evil, the one who twists the system with its centers of power for destructive purposes. [See Native Religions of North America pp. 339, 342–43 for other examples of witchcraft.]

Failure to show due reverence for the ancestors may result in sickness and suffering; the consequences of witchcraft are destruction and death. Such destruction and death does not come from the God of the Sky, the ancestors, or medicine. Nor does it come even from sorcery, which is the straightforward expression of anger due to justifiable grievances. It comes from the twisted use of power for evil ends.

Any woman can become a witch; she becomes one through the experience of possession by evil power. It is possible, however, for a Zulu to be a witch without even knowing it. This cannot be said of any other role in Zulu society. Witches are regarded as having superhuman properties; they can fly at night, can become invisible, and can act on others at a distance. Witches also have a relationship to special kinds of snakes, and the presence of a snake of a certain kind is a clue to the operation of witchcraft.

Understanding the nature and function of these eight roles advances our knowledge of the worldview of the Zulu and leads us to questions about the centers of power around which they revolve.

We now have two locations for the Zulu religious drama, the village and specially designated unoccupied hills. We have the roles played by those enacting the drama: the headman/priest, the diviner, the herbalist, the heaven-herd, the supplicant, the patient, the sorcerer, and the witch. What is the drama about? It is about the use and misuse of power. But what is power for the Zulu, and how is such power expressed?

Power, *amandla,* is that which is capable of bringing about a change in a situation, an alteration of a status, a variation in a condition. For the Zulu there are three legitimate elements that are capable of exerting power in this sense. These sources of power are the ancestors, the God of the Sky, and medicine. As we have already seen in our discussion of witchcraft, there is also evil power. Evil power is the misuse of power for destructive ends. Legitimate power sustains life in an orderly, customary fashion. When judgment on human actions is necessary it follows from the acknowledged structure of the Zulu religious world. Illegitimate power destroys life. It introduces disorder, disrupts human relationships, unleashes vengeance, and destroys the equilibrium that characterizes the intricate balances of everyday Zulu life.

The role of ritual is to maintain and enhance the relationships the Zulu have to the powers of life. The following sections describe the Zulu conceptions of each of these powers in more detail.

The ancestral spirits variously known as the **amalozi, amakhosi,** or **amathonga** are of fundamental significance for the Zulu. They are the departed souls of the deceased. Although they are regarded as having gone to abide in the earth, they continue to have a relationship with those still living in the village. They are regarded as positive, constructive, and creative presences. They are also capable of meting out punishment when they have been wronged or ignored. Veneration is their due. Failure to show proper respect to them invites misfortune; proper veneration ensures benefit. The ancestors, therefore, are powers for either good or ill. When such power is judgmental it is not regarded as destructive, for its purpose is to maintain traditional relationships. For an ancestor to bring misfortune on a living member of the village is viewed as a legitimate expression of wrath attributable to the failure of one or more living members of the village to do their duty.

The Zulu make a distinction among ancestors. Zulu society is patrilineal, that is, authority and inheritance proceed through the male line from father to son. The important ancestors for a village are male ancestors, particularly the former headman/priest. Of course the great chiefs of the Zulu nation are also very important ancestors, and there will be occasions when they are addressed by praise songs and appealed to for help.

The ancestors are regarded as living in or under the earth. They are also identified with the earth. But they have a particular association with two places in the village, the *umsamo* and the cattle enclosure, especially that place where the important religious rituals are performed. They are constantly watching over the activities of their descendants (see fig. 1-1, nos. 1 and 21).

The Zulu word for the sky is **izulu.** It is clear, therefore, that the Zulu have a religious relationship to the sky as well as to the earth, the abode of the ancestors. In fact, the Zulu trace their ancestry to an act of creation by the God of the Sky. The God of the Sky, **Inkosi Yezulu** (literally, "chief of the sky"), also has a special name, **Umvelinqangi,** which means "that which appeared first." It also implies "the first of twins." Presumably, the other twin is the earth. The God of the Sky is male, father; the earth is female, mother. Upon death the ancestors return to mother. Only in special circumstances do people go to be with Umvelinqangi.

The God of the Sky and the earth are regarded as having brought forth **abantu** ("the people"). But the view of the origin of the *abantu* is a complicated one. First, the Zulu do believe that the *amazulu* (the Zulu people) come from the God of the Sky, who sent a male still attached to an umbilical cord through a hole in the dome of the sky. A reed was used to cut the umbilical cord. Second, the Zulu also say that humankind came from the breaking off of reeds. These two accounts might reflect two traditions, now merged, or they might reflect a distinction between the origins of the Zulu and the origins of all people, or it might indicate that the creation of the first man by the God of the Sky is a later story. Some scholars argue that it is a later story developed under the influence of the Christian missionaries.

What is interesting is that both the God of the Sky and the ancestors are referred to as *inkosi* by the Zulu. But the ancestors are usually referred to as a group, the *amakhosi,* whereas the singular, *inkosi,* refers to the God of the Sky. Yet the ancestors are clearly referred to as people of the earth. It is probable that the God of the Sky is not a later addition but has been present for a long time in the religious system of the Zulu. But the role of the **High God,** the supreme but remote deity who dwells in the heavens, has been misunderstood and misinterpreted. Clearly, in the earliest accounts recorded by travelers and missionaries, he appears but is confused with Unkulunkulu, the first man, who also had a creator-like role in establishing the first people. [See Native Religions of North America pp. 289–91, 330–31 for discussion of Supreme Being, God, and gods, and Religions of Mesoamerica p. 166 for mention of High God.]

The God of the Sky has praise names associated with him.[1] Praise names (**izibongo**) and the highly stylized poetry associated with praise names are of fundamental importance in Zulu life. All important personages in the history of the Zulu people have praise names associated with them, and praise poems are sung at important occasions. The fact of Umvelinqangi having praise names is important proof of his traditional and continuing importance in the Zulu religious world.

Praise is important in Zulu social relations, and the ceremonial use of praise names is one very important method the Zulu use to recapitulate their history. In fact there are transcriptions of the *izibongo* of all the Zulu kings back to King Zulu himself. These praise poems are an important source of historical information and clearly reflect the Zulu attitudes toward their past leaders. They also express reverence and respect for all sources of power, whether these be ancestors or the High God.

As we have already indicated, it is unusual for a Zulu to approach the God of the Sky; it is the ancestors who are most frequently addressed. But there do arise conditions of dire need, both for individuals and for groups—for example, a severe drought—and on such occasions, when neither medicine nor the ancestors have been effective in alleviating a bad situation, the Zulu will address the God of the Sky as supplicants. Then the Zulu will take to the hills, there to commune with Umvelinqangi in isolation from the world of the village and the ancestors occupying it.

The God of the Sky has a special relationship with thunder and lightning. Storms are his direct acts. Should a person be killed by lightning, he or she is regarded as having been taken by Umvelinqangi. Such people do not become ancestors. They do not reside under the earth, are not present in any of their usual locations; in fact, they are to be buried as close as possible to where they were taken, and they are not ever to be talked about. They are said to be "with the God of the Sky." Because of this, no mourning for them is encouraged or permitted. Whereas the ancestors have gone down into the earth, the people killed by lightning have gone up to the sky. [See Religions of Mesoamerica pp. 157–58, 186–89, Native Religions of North America pp. 274–76, 288–305, 330–332, Judaism pp. 414–15, Christianity pp. 537–38, Islam pp. 635–37, Hinduism pp. 739–41, 759–61, 780–84, Buddhism pp. 900–903, Religions of China pp. 1024–26, and Religions of Japan pp. 1112–27 for discussion of God, gods, and objects of worship.]

The third type of power acknowledged by the Zulu is the power of medicine. The power of medicine is neither the power of the ancestors nor the power of the God of the Sky; it has its own power. One might almost say that medicine represents a system of its own. The God of the Sky, the ancestors, and medicine can each act for the good or ill of people. All are capable of bringing about change in a situation, alteration of a status, variation of a condition.

All three powers are capable of treating illness, but it is the particular nature of medicine to maintain or restore health, although it can be misused in acts of sorcery. The point to remember is that medicine does not depend upon either the power of Umvelinqangi or the ancestors for its efficacy. It stands on its own, and its *amandla* can be added to by new knowledge.

Evil power is negative and destructive. It is not an independent, autonomous power as are the God of the Sky, the ancestors, and medicine; it derives its influence from these three positive elements in the Zulu religious world. The three positive elements maintain and enhance and ensure normal, traditional relationships. *Abathakatha* is the misuse of positive power for destructive ends. As such it is a serious and constant threat to the social fabric. Those who manipulate this evil power tamper with established objects, actions, and roles. When the three other sources of power are expressed, legitimate action occurs even if its consequences entail pain, suffering, and death, for in such instances there has been failure to perform an appropriate obligation. To use witchcraft is to participate in the shadowy world of evil and to go outside the bounds of all that is good and right and prescribed. Whereas the practitioners of medicine are known and public, the practitioners of evil are hidden from view. Whereas the sorcerer will misuse the *amandla* of medicine for bad ends, the witch will twist the entire fabric of the system for destructive purposes and introduce death into the world.

We now know who the practitioners of the various religious roles are, and we know the various expressions of power in the Zulu religious world. The question is, How does the system work? How do those who assume the roles that they do in the Zulu religious world relate themselves to the sources of power?

First I will summarize with a diagram of what we have seen thus far (see fig. 1-2).

This diagram uses a set of interlocking triangles to represent the relationships that hold in Zulu religion between the ritual roles and sources of power. The base of each triangle symbolizes the observable, ritual aspect of Zulu religion. The apex of each triangle indicates the power each role is designed to tap.

There are four triangles, which represent the four powers (the God of the Sky, the ancestors, medicine, and evil) and the four sets of roles that can be discerned in Zulu religion. The four triangles are interlocked to emphasize the interconnectedness of the various roles with each other and with the sources of power.

In the case of the God of the Sky, it is the heaven-herd and the supplicant who perform the ritual actions necessary to provide the power available from that source. In the case of the ancestors, it is the headman/priest and the diviner who are responsible for the rites that establish and maintain the right relationship with these sources of power. In the case of medicine, it is the herbalist and the patient who have the knowledge and perform the deeds necessary to derive the healing and the protection available from this source. In the case of evil, it is the sorcerer and the witch who have the knowledge and intent to distort and twist the power generally available from the other sources for destructive ends.

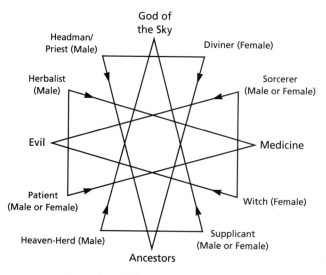

Figure 1-2. The Zulu Religious System.

Such a diagram graphically describes roles and relationships that the Zulu believe to be important, real, and effective; it permits us to organize the information available from the observers of Zulu life as well as from the Zulu themselves and to ask further questions.

I now propose to show how particular events in Zulu life can be seen as expressing the Zulu religious system in action. We shall see how the various roles in the religious system function in the everyday life of the Zulu, especially in those important events understood as stages on life's way. [See Religions of Mesoamerica pp. 201–6, Native Religions of North America pp. 278–79, 295–98, 306–8, Judaism pp. 445–50, Christianity pp. 542–43, 555–57, Islam pp. 677–78, 680–86, Hinduism pp. 747, 807–14, Buddhism pp. 915–17, 921, 931–37, Religions of China pp. 1019–21, and Religions of Japan pp. 1146–50 for description and discussion of rites of passage.]

Rites at the Death of a Headman/Priest

Consider the following situation: The headman/priest of a particular Zulu village has died in the prime of life of an unexpected illness. How will the religious system come into play? Who will do what?

If the members of the Zulu village still follow the traditional Zulu ways, there are a number of rituals that will be performed. First, the body of the deceased headman/priest will be prepared. This will involve the ritual washing of his face, the shaving of his head (the hair will be retained and buried with him), and the manipulation of his body into a sitting position with his knees drawn up to his chin. Then his body will be bound in ox hide or, if this is not available, in a blanket and placed against one of the poles supporting the main hut, where it will then be shielded from view by a covering of some sort. These actions will be performed under the supervision of the new headman/priest, the first son of the deceased leader.[2]

After these initial acts a grave will be dug near the main hut of the village by the first son. The burial will occur at night. In recent times this aspect of the ritual has not always been adhered to except in the case of especially distinguished figures. The less frequent adherence is due to the influence of Christianity, which usually performs burial services during the day. When the body is placed in the grave near the main hut, it is positioned so that the head of the body faces the hut. During these activities there will have been the sounds of wailing and lamenting; the actual funeral procession takes place in complete silence.

For a month after the burial, the behavior required of everyone in the village is quite specific. There can be no work. There is quiet and inactivity. No sexual activity is permitted during this month-long period of mourning.

The event of death in a Zulu village is regarded as a time of great danger for everyone. This means that everyone must be protected from the powers that have caused the death. In the situation we are discussing, the death is untimely. Such deaths will either be regarded by the members of the village as punishment from the ancestors for failure to perform some obligation to them or for having offended them in some way, or may be regarded as having been caused by an act of either sorcery or witchcraft. The point is that, although there may have already developed some suspicion among the mourners about the possible cause, no one knows yet exactly why the death has occurred. It is important, therefore, for the people to find out why. It is also important for the survivors to avoid further problems. Two of the roles we have described will therefore come into play: that of the diviner and that of the herbalist or specialist in medicine. It will be the diviner's obligation to identify the cause of the untimely death and the herbalist's to provide the medicines that will protect the villagers. The diviner's activities will stretch over a considerable period; those of the herbalist are more immediate.

Directly after the headman has been buried, the people of the village will begin taking medicines as a protective device. As we have already found, medicine has its own power and is not reducible to the other powers in the Zulu religious world. Either the herbalist will prescribe the appropriate medicines to take or, because knowledge of medicine is quite widespread in the Zulu community, there will be self-prescription. This act of taking medicine is so important that no one from the affected village is permitted to leave it or to communicate with people in other villages until the medical treatment has occurred. Some of the medicine will be placed on the *umsamo* in the main hut and some of it will also be used to treat the cattle.

Having taken the medicines that will provide the strength and protection necessary in such a dangerous situation, the people will then perform other important ritual acts. There will be a ritual washing in the closest stream; the ritual slaughter of an animal, such as a goat; and the purification of the hut of the deceased headman/priest. The slaughter of the goat is not regarded as a sacrifice to the ancestors but as yet another form of medicine to protect the survivors from danger. The goat, in fact, is called **imbuzi yamakhubalo,** "the goat of medicine."

The general period of mourning lasts for a month, but this period does not apply to the widow of the deceased headman, for whom the period of mourning is a year.

The month-long period of mourning for all but the closest relatives comes to an end with the **ihlambo** ceremony. *Ihlambo* means "the washing of the spears" of all the men associated with the village. In actual practice the ritual is more complicated than the washing of the spears, for both the men and the women of the village are expected to perform those acts that signal the end of the period of mourning. In practice, the men ritually wash their spears and the women ritually wash their hoes. They are "washed," however, not with water but with action. The men wash their spears by going on a hunt and the women by hoeing in the fields. After these religious acts have been performed, the implements are regarded as having been cleaned, and the people are free to return to their normal patterns of living. But one more ritual has to be accomplished during the *ihlambo;* the praises of the departed headman must be sung, an animal must be sacrificed, and there must be a final taking of medicine. [See Religions of Mesoamerica pp. 142–43, 227 and Native Religions of North America pp. 260, 268, 272–73, 277, 309–12, 332–33 for the religious significance of animals and hunting.]

Now the great wife of the headman continues in mourning for the rest of the year. To symbolize her mourning, she will wear an *intambo* (a grass headband), refrain from sexual relations, and live a life of great circumspection. At the end of the year-long period of mourning, she will be ritually purified with the appropriate medicines and then be ready either for marriage to one of the brothers of the deceased or for the journey back to her parents' village.

And now the village is ready for the final ritual, the **ukubuyisa idlozi,** "the bringing home of the ancestor." All this time the deceased headman has been in an "in-between" state, neither here nor there. He is now ready to be joined with the other ancestors by being brought home, for the ancestors though living in an "underworld" also live right in the village. The deceased headman must, therefore, be brought back to his rightful place among the living, there to continue to exert his influence collectively with the *amakhosi,* the group of ancestors. His presence in the *umsamo,* in the doorways, in the cattle enclosure, and in the hearts and minds of the people needs to be ensured. Failure to perform the *ukubuyisa idlozi* would create danger for all members of the village. It clearly would be treated by the ancestors as an insult.

The *ukubuyisa* is a festive occasion involving joy, feasting, and fellowship. A special ox is sacrificed, and other animals are also killed. Special portions of the ox are placed on the *umsamo,* other portions are ritually burned, and the rest remains in the hut of the deceased headman. The following day all of the ox is eaten; none of it can be left over or removed from the village. The other meat and food prepared can be removed or given as gifts to members of other villages. The ancestor may be guided to the *umsamo* from the grave site by the new headman/priest, the chief son of the former headman/priest, who makes marks with twigs. At the *umsamo* the **idlozi** (ancestor) may be called upon to return to his rightful place. This will be the first time that the ancestor is addressed and praised along with the other ancestors. For it is now right and good to show him reverence and respect and to treat him as a source of power for good or ill. And now the chief son is ready to assume completely the role of headman/priest. [See Religions of Mesoamerica pp. 144, 229–33, Native Religions of North America pp. 300–301, 307–8, 335–37, Judaism pp. 448–50, Christianity p. 557, Islam pp. 684–85, Hinduism pp. 813–14, Buddhism pp. 935–37, Religions of China pp. 1021, 1041–44, and Religions of Japan pp. 1149–50 for description and discussion of death and funeral rites.]

It should be clear from the description of the death of the headman/priest and the actions performed by the members of the village that key elements of the religious system are at work. Special places have provided the ritual ground for religious actions, special roles have come into play, and special powers have been acknowledged. The village provides the scene for the burial rites and the burial plot. And within the village the *umsamo* assumes particular importance as one place where the ancestors are communicated with. There are also specific roles at work—those of the headman/priest, the diviner, and the herbalist. And special powers are acknowledged, the power of evil that has caused the death because of the activities of witchcraft, the power of medicine that prevents the danger from spreading, the power of the ancestors who maintain the people and situation in balance and who receive the deceased into their world. This description has given us the occasion to examine some of the details of a **rite of passage,** in this case from the everyday world to the world of the ancestors. It also provides the opportunity to discuss other rites of passage practiced by the Zulu, under the rubric of the stages on life's way. A rite of passage is a special religious ceremony that makes or brings about a transition from one role in a religious system to another, for example, from son of headman/priest to headman/priest.

Rites for a New Headman/Priest

Let us now consider the new headman/priest to whom the mantle of leadership has passed. How did he achieve this prominent position? What has been his career? What stages did he have to pass through in order to arrive at his present position? We shall give him a name, Bhudaza, and trace the orderly progression of his life starting from the time of his birth.[3] [See Native Religions of North

America p. 307, Judaism pp. 445–46, Christianity p. 556, Islam p. 682, Hinduism pp. 810–11, Buddhism p. 932, Religions of China pp. 1019–20, and Religions of Japan pp. 1146–47 for description and discussion of birth rites.]

From the moment his mother recognized that she was pregnant, Bhudaza was part of a religious world. When she felt his first stirrings, his mother immediately regarded herself as being in a dangerous situation. The powers spelled potential danger for the developing child, and precautions had to be taken to protect the mother and her coming child from the wrath of the ancestors and the acts of sorcerers and witches. She called upon the knowledge of the herbalist to prescribe the right protective medicines and began eating only those foods ritually permitted.

When the time came for Bhudaza's delivery, his mother was attended by the old women of the village in their capacity as midwives. She knew that her first son's birth would be auspicious, because before his birth she saw an ancestor in the form of a snake.

As soon as Bhudaza was born he was taken to the *umsamo;* a special hole was dug in this sacred place, and he was bathed in the hole. The water used in the bathing was treated with medicine, and his umbilical cord was buried in the hole in the *umsamo.* Cattle, and the milk of cattle, are of great religious significance, and so, before he was permitted to drink his mother's milk, he was fed cows' milk or *amasi,* the specially treated curds of milk. The religious significance lay in the fact that Zulu identity is intimately connected with the imagery of cattle.

Because medicine has a power of its own, the first few days after his birth he was treated again with medicines, and because of the danger of the wrath of his ancestors and the powers of sorcery and witchcraft, he and his mother were isolated. The period of isolation was brought to an end by the ritual purification of the mother. This involved taking medicine prescribed by the herbalist.

Only then was the father permitted to see the child. The father's first ritual act was to sacrifice an ox to the ancestors. This was an act of both thanksgiving and precaution. This sacrifice ensured the protection of the ancestors and identified him with his lineage. The baby was then ready to be named. His name involved a great deal of careful thought and consultation. When it was decided upon, this name was either based upon some significant event, or it referred to some ancestor. In this case the name Bhudaza was chosen because it figures prominently in a praise song to Macingwane, son of Lubhoko of the Chunu clan, and Bhudaza was a new member of that clan.

Sometime before puberty Bhudaza had his ears pierced. A special ceremony marked this occasion, which occurred either at the appearance of the new moon or when the moon was full.

Isolation or seclusion is always used to mark transition, and so the night before the ear-piercing (**qhumbaza**) Bhudaza was isolated. On the day of the ritual, which is performed either by an herbalist or an experienced ear-piercer in the village, a sacrifice of a male animal was performed. His father, the headman/priest, went to the *umsamo* with special cuts of the sacrificial animal, and there he thanked the ancestors for having given him a first son and for keeping him safe to that day. It is then that the operation on his ears was performed at the entrance to the cattle enclosure, the abode of the ancestors.

The next important event in Bhudaza's life was the **thomba** ceremony, which marks the onset of puberty. Every Zulu boy is taught to watch for the sign that will mark the next significant event in his life, namely, his first nocturnal emission.

The morning after this sexual event, long before the sun had risen, Bhudaza took the cattle from his village's cattle enclosure, and perhaps even the cattle from neighboring villages, and hid them in a place difficult to find. Once the cattle were hidden he ritually bathed in the closest stream and then waited for his agemates to come and find him.

The disappearance of the cattle alerted everyone in his village to the significance of the event, and the search for the missing cattle and boy commenced. While the search was in progress Bhudaza's father began to make preparations for the ritual events to follow. The most important of these was the preparation of medicines. When the boy and the cattle were discovered, they were driven back into the cattle enclosure. After the father welcomed him and treated him with medicine, he was taken to one of the huts and told to sit right in the *umsamo.* He would have been in such close proximity to this sacred place at only one other time, at the ritual bathing attending his birth. The *umsamo* at all other times is strictly off limits; it is sacred space not to be violated. As Bhudaza sat in the *umsamo* area of the hut he was covered with a screen to shield him from view. Only his agemates were permitted to visit with him during this in-between period. If he left the hut at all, it would have been with great circumspection; under no conditions was he permitted to see or come into contact with women.

While Bhudaza had been driven—like a cow—back to the cattle enclosure, his father had made preparations for the special day of the puberty feast. When that day arrived, the boy Bhudaza was led from his place of seclusion to the cattle enclosure. There an ox was sacrificed, *izibongo* (praise poems) were sung to the ancestors, and he was treated with medicines. Then offerings were made to the ancestors by the headman/priest in the *umsamo,* and the boy was led back to the hut. After a further addressing of the ancestors, and before the feast began, he was taken by his agemates to the river and ritually bathed; his old garments were removed and destroyed, and he was given new clothes. He was also given a new name. He now had two names: his birth name, Bhudaza, and the name Mdingi, given to him by his agemates.

Not only were his old clothes destroyed but also the screen that had shielded him from view. In his new finery Bhudaza and his agemates then started to dance. At first the boy followed the others, but gradually he assumed the role of the leader of the dance. The spirit of the dance took over, and soon the entire assembly was dancing and feasting.

On the evening of the next day Bhudaza went again to the *umsamo* where, as he communicated with his ancestors, he ate meat from the sacrificial ox that had been specially treated with medicine. He was now ready for the next stage of his life.

Before its sovereignty was destroyed by the combined forces of British colonialism and the developing white South African state, the Zulu kingdom was armed with numerous regiments. The great Zulu chief Shaka had devised a plan for forming efficient, well-disciplined regiments to be the military arm of the new Zulu kingdom. An important stage in the career of the young Zulu male was induction into one of these regiments, which occurred within a year or two after the *thomba* ritual. Even though this ritual induction into the regiment is fast disappearing today, the concept still survives. If Bhudaza were living in the time of the full flower of the Zulu nation he would be so inducted.

The first part of the **ukubuthwa,** or "grouping-up," ritual consisted of an ordeal, undergoing harsh treatment at the hands of experienced members of the regiment, hard work, ritual combat, and serious competition among those grouping up together.

The second part consisted of instruction. During this stage of the initiation ceremony, Bhudaza learned the rules of regimental life—especially obedience and respect for authority, abstinence from sexual relations with women during the induction period, and the eating of special foods meant to strengthen the inductees.

During the third part of the induction ceremony the regiment to which Bhudaza was giving his allegiance received its name. This naming was the prerogative of the king only. After the king announced the name, a ritual chanting of important *izibongo,* or praise names, took place accompanied by dancing.

The fourth part of the ritual was the presentation of the weapons of war. These *assegais,* or spears, after being given to each member of the regiment, were then presented to the headman of the district in which each young man lived, to remain there until needed for battle.

After Bhudaza had completed his induction or "grouping up" into his regiment he returned to his village where he was greeted joyously by his father. A special ox was sacrificed, the ancestors were praised, and there was general feasting and merrymaking. In the heyday of the Zulu kingdom such an induction could last as long as six months depending upon the king's decision. It could also be little more than a week or two.

Bhudaza was now ready for marriage. His life had changed. Up until this point he was an *umfaan,* a boy whose main responsibility was the herding of the cattle of the village. Now he was released from such duties and could begin the joyful time of courting. As with every other stage of his life, this period of courtship and marriage involved religious activity for the appropriation of power. One important source of power is, of course, medicine, and so Bhudaza used medicine to aid him in his search for a wife. Love potions would give him the kind of power to attract the right maiden.

Besides taking love potions, Bhudaza also wore the **kehla,** or headring, as a special religious symbol of the imminence of his marriage. And when he had found a wife, marriage plans were put into effect. Such plans involved a number of actions. The first of these is known as *lobola,* the practice of transferring cattle from his village to that of his future wife. Rather than being a bride price, this was regarded as a contract on the part of both families. The second activity for Bhudaza was receiving the consent of his future wife's older sisters and her parents. Complex negotiations between the two villages then ensued. Finally, after many intricate maneuvers, his bride arrived at his village for the wedding activities.

The most important of the wedding rituals was the exchange of gifts between the two villages involved in the wedding. Bhudaza's bride, upon her arrival with her family, began to sing a special song to her ancestors. Shortly thereafter, his mother and the other wives of his father began to sing a song also. Slowly two groups formed on each side of the cattle enclosure. The bridal party

Young Zulu woman.
(Photograph by the author.)

occupied the ground on the right side of the cattle enclosure and the bride-groom's party was on the left side. The two sides sang to each other. They also shouted and played the drums. This activity continued through the night.

The next day the bridal party left the village, the bride was secluded, and the bridal party dressed for the occasion. After a while they returned to the vil-lage and there was more dancing. Then the **umbeka** beast—usually an ox—which represents the ancestors of the bride in her new home, was guided to a position between the two wedding parties. The father of the bride addressed the ancestors, requesting them to accept the bride in her new status. Bhudaza's uncle addressed the ancestors of his village, apologized for the loss of cattle to the bride's village, but informed them of the exchange of these cattle for a bride and the *umbeka* beast. Then the cattle belonging to Bhudaza's father were paraded before the assembled people.

After this there was a general celebration and feast. The bride, after a brief seclusion, returned to the village of the groom. The **umqholiso** ox, the wedding ox to be sacrificed to the ancestors, was killed, and the gall of the ox was poured over the bride. The ancestors have a particular liking for gall, and this act associ-ated the bride with the ancestors of Bhudaza. The sacrificed ox was eaten by both families, and the bride then entered Bhudaza's hut. That night the bride and groom consummated their marriage.

On the following day the ceremony of the beads took place. Bhudaza had to choose a bead from the left hand of his wife. His wife concealed the beads from him by rolling them around in her hand. The beads were black, red, and white

Dancing and drumming at a Zulu wedding. (Photograph by Brian Jones.)

in color. The groom hoped for a white bead as this would signal a good marriage. (If it were red she would not be a virgin, and if black it would indicate that she had been promiscuous.) Then the bride handed out articles that she herself had made for her new relatives. The bride was then anointed with fat by her mother-in-law, and she donned the standard dress of a married woman.

On the fourth morning of the wedding, the bride ritually cleaned the village of the bridegroom's family, helped by her friends who then left for their own villages. Only one ritual act remained: The bride had to cut a piece of cow dung with a knife before she could begin to eat the regular food of her new village.

The bride had now left the home of her ancestors and taken up a new dwelling with the ancestors of her husband. While Bhudaza had simply changed from an unmarried to a married man, his wife had also moved from one ancestral abode to another, a much more radical change, quite capable of introducing dangerous powers into both situations. Great care and circumspection were, therefore, required on her part. This meant living strictly according to the obligations of a new wife in a new situation. Especially significant was the requirement that she cover her face as she moved about the village. Failure to cover her face would have indicated a lack of reverence for the ancestors present there and could have brought upon her and everyone in the village the ancestors' anger. After a few months she was permitted to remove this sign of respect. Now Bhudaza and his new wife would look forward to the birth of their first child. If this child were a son, he would automatically become the heir, and the cycle with which we began this account of the stages on life's way would begin again. At Bhudaza's death the same rituals that were performed for his father would be performed for him, and the life cycle would be complete. [See Judaism pp. 447–48, Christianity p. 556, Islam pp. 683–84, Hinduism pp. 809–810, Buddhism p. 935, Religions of China p. 1020, and Religions of Japan p. 1148 for description and discussion of marriage rites.]

Organizing Life Religiously

In our own society we are usually quite aware of when our behavior is religious and when it is not. We know the difference between praising the cook for her excellent apple pie and praising God for Her mercies, the difference between raising the flag and raising the host during the celebration of mass. Such distinctions are usually easy to make, because we have been taught to make them from an early age. But when we study another society we discover that they are not obvious at all. It is much more difficult to make such a distinction when talking about the Zulu. Almost every act that a Zulu performs is religious. Perhaps a simpler way to put it is that the way the Zulu live their lives is organized religiously. This means that the stages on life's way are invested with significance; there are appropriate and inappropriate forms of action. The new bride appropriately covers her head in the presence of her husband's ancestors; not to do so is to show disrespect. But this religious system also changes. In earlier times, the bridegroom chose the hidden bead from the bride's hand. But if he did not get the white one, it was rather traumatic. Today the groom often hits the beads out of her hand and grabs the white one, thus ensuring the right outcome. The point is that the Zulu religious system has changed over the last 150 years. One of the reasons for the change has been the encounter with the cultures of the West, which include such notions as the difference between religious and nonreligious action. But what is most impressive is the ability of the Zulu religious system to deal with new situations and ideas in a flexible and creative manner. The belief in the power of the ancestors has not changed, but under the influence of Western religions such as Christianity, Islam, and even Indian religions (for there are many Indians living in the province of Natal), elements of the Zulu religious system have been given increased significance.

The belief in the God of the Sky is a very old Zulu belief. But until the encounter with other religions, there never had been much ritual action associated with this source of power. With the incursion of Christianity, and especially with the introduction of the **Zionist** church and other new religions into Zulu life, a much greater emphasis has been placed by some Zulu on communication with the God of the Sky. So the special hilltops associated with his worship are scenes of increasing activity as the influence of the Zionist and other independent churches grows. The God of the Sky, though an important presence and source of power in the Zulu religious world, has never been in the forefront of religious attention. But the very acknowledgment of such a power has made it possible for the Zulu to respond to both internal and external challenges to their religious system. Such is its flexibility.

Another example of flexibility is the power of medicine. Traditional medicine is still practiced in Zululand to this day, but Western medicines are slowly being added to—not replacing—such traditional medicines. Clearly, whatever medicine is used is treated as a source of more than physical and chemical changes, for medicine is an independent source of healing power, where healing involves more than purely physical well-being.

Yet another example of the flexibility of the religious system can be seen in the ritual actions of women. Zulu society is patrilineal in organization. In practical terms this means males are dominant in the social and religious order. Women nevertheless have significant areas for religious action. Some of these have already been noted. For example, though the headman/priest is the main conduit to and the main representative of the ancestors, the woman diviner also has access to them through the ritual activity of divination. Zulu certainly have a healthy respect for witchcraft and sorcery, and the role of women in these activities is thought to be prominent. But there are also specific important rituals that are the exclusive province of women.

In the diagram of the Zulu religious world in figure 1-2 there is one element missing, namely, the Princess of the Sky, **Inkosazana.** Although the ancestors and the God of the Sky receive the most attention, the religious system is flexible enough to provide room for a ritual role for women. Nowhere is this role clearer than in the relationship between women and the Princess of the Sky. The princess has a number of significant features that contribute to the overall complexity of the religious system. She is associated with both virginity and fertility of all creatures. But most significantly, she is capable of instituting rules of behavior and ritual action that are distinct from those of both the God of the Sky and the ancestors. For example, the herding of cattle is an activity confined to young men. But under the instructions of the Princess of the Sky, young women, clothed like men, do engage in this activity at special times. This is a clear example of role reversal in which the power normally associated with one religious role is transferred, ritually, to another.

The Princess of the Sky is also capable of acting as a mediator between the people and the God of the Sky. Under one transformation of the religious system, it is the princess rather than the heaven-herd who persuades the God of the Sky to send rain.

The location for the appearances and revelations of the princess is never the village but always specific hills or mountains. When communication takes place between her and young women, these women herd some cattle into the hills and there perform a ritual to the princess.

What is interesting about all of this is that it shows that the religious system of the Zulu has resources within itself to handle the inevitable tensions that arise in a system that so emphasizes the role of the male. In fact, the princess can be quite dangerous to Zulu men, and she is neither to be approached nor seen by them. She also provides avenues of information to women that otherwise would be closed to them.

What is also clear is that the presence of this creative and responsive capacity in the religious system of the Zulu makes the system capable of dealing with new situations as they arise. We now turn to this responsive and creative capacity.

Transformations of the Religious System

Religious systems are dynamic. They change in various ways. In fact religious systems are very flexible, capable of expressing themselves in novel ways in new settings. The reader will remember that the Zulu village was the primary locus of religious action, but the unoccupied hills also played an important role in Zulu religious life. The village has a direct relationship to the ancestors; the hills have a direct relationship with the God of the Sky. And though the headman/priest is the ritual practitioner responsible for maintaining relationships with the ancestors, the heaven-herd is responsible for communication with the God of the Sky.

But this duality in the religious system points to a very strong tension within it. Under usual conditions the roles of the two ritual practitioners are clearly defined. The headman/priest pays due reverence to the ancestors; the heaven-herd controls the storm by the power of the High God. Only when dire situations arise will the members of the Zulu village appeal to the God of the Sky.

But the Zulu people have maintained and developed their identity in the context of a very complex history. The colonial powers made their presence and power increasingly felt in the nineteenth century; Christians began to establish missions among the Zulu; the concepts of Western culture began to exert their influence. Perhaps most importantly, gold was discovered near **Johannesburg** in 1885, and many young Zulu men were recruited to work in the mines. One of the consequences of the work in the mines was disruption of traditional Zulu life.

In this setting of change the development of new religious movements among the Zulu accelerated. Many scholars writing about the development of these new religious movements have interpreted them as a Zulu reaction to Christian symbols. Such an interpretation is far too simple; it does not give due credit to the religious creativity involved and ignores the inherent power of the Zulu symbols themselves to achieve new forms in new situations. Given that there is a built-in tension in the Zulu system, it should not surprise us that these separate elements may undergo a transformation and find new expression under new conditions. We shall see in our discussion of a founder of a new religious movement one form that such a transformation can take. [See Religions of Mesoamerica p. 240, Native Religions of North America pp. 287, 320–22, 357–58, Judaism pp. 427–31, 456–75, Christianity pp. 529–33, Islam pp. 698–700, Hinduism pp. 770–74, 823–31, Buddhism pp. 952–56, Religions of China pp. 998–1002, 1055–59, and Religions of Japan pp. 1132–33, 1163–72 for discussion of new religious movements.]

Isaiah Shembe was a Zulu prophet (d. 1935) and a creative religious leader who established a large following in Zululand with his church, the ama-Nazaretha. Shembe combined Zulu and Christian symbols into a new form of religious life; some scholars interpret it as a Zulu form of Christianity. So, for example, Shembe's claim that he received a revelation from Jehovah attracts a great deal of attention, as does his exorcism of demons by the power of the Holy Spirit. But the Zulu religious context is clear and cannot be ignored. Shembe received revelations on separate occasions when he had narrowly escaped from being struck by lightning. In the first experience, he had a vision commanding him to stop being immoral. In the second experience, he had a vision of his own death. In the third, he was told to abandon his four wives. In his fourth encounter, his best ox was killed by lightning, and he suffered severe burns. Shembe interpreted this fourth experience as a divine ultimatum to convey his new message to the people.

In the religious system of the Zulu the heaven-herd receives the call to his ritual role with the God of the Sky through a close encounter with lightning; the hills provide the locus for his religious acts. What is interesting is that when Shembe built his first church it was on top of a hill and was called "The High

Place." And one of the first pilgrimages that Shembe led was to Nhlangakazi Mountain in Natal, a mountain that has since become the setting for the New Year festival of the amaNazaretha church.

Both the form and content of Shembe's experience illustrate that transformation has been at work. There is both a traditional and a new element in this emerging religious system. The traditional element is the entire set of symbols connected with the God of the Sky: the heaven-herd, the hills, lightning, and the experience of possession or visions or dreams. The new element is the association of these symbols with the imagery provided by Christianity, such as Jehovah, Holy Spirit, and spiritual healing. Shembe also retained, unchanged, many of the other aspects of the Zulu system, such as the practice of sorcery and witchcraft.

In effect, what Shembe accomplished was the transformation of the role of the heaven-herd from that of controller of severe weather by the power available from the God of the Sky to that of the prophet of the God of the Sky with a message of healing for the Zulu in their time of suffering. This message from above did not deny the reality and importance of the ancestors or of the power of medicine or of the destructive power of sorcery and witchcraft. If he had adopted such an approach he would have been ignored. But the silent God of the Sky became capable of speaking, capable of using the heaven-herd as the conduit of his message when his people needed it. And Zulu practice had always acknowledged the power of the God of the Sky. Only an extreme situation, however, that went beyond the needs of individuals to that of the society as a whole could transform traditional roles. Zulu society, by the end of the nineteenth century,

Isaiah Shembe, Zulu prophet, a creative religious leader who established the amaNazaretha Church. (Photograph by Lynn Acutt; used with permission of Oxford University Press for the International African Institute.)

was in desperate straits. Its land had been taken away, its king exiled, its religion called into question by Christian missionaries. Its young men had been torn out of the fabric of village life and sent to the mines many hundreds of miles away. All these factors conspired to create a religious crisis in Zulu life and thought. Shembe's message showed a way out of this crisis for some. And so his message took hold. It pointed the way to a kind of healing available to those who felt the suffering most severely. The message had a new form, but it was familiar enough to be heard and understood.

But the relationship between Christianity and traditional Zulu religion worked in the opposite direction as well. Because the Zulu acknowledged the reality of the God of the Sky, their religious system provided a meeting point with Christianity. Christians could appeal to this meeting point as the bridge over which elements, at least, of their religious world could journey and gain entrance to the system of the Zulu people. But the character of the God of the Sky became in the process transformed from a remote creator and sustainer of the world who was appealed to only in time of dire need, or when the forces of nature threatened destruction, into a God closer at hand. Isaiah Shembe was one bridge for this encounter between two religious worlds. In one mind and in one movement we can see the Zulu religious world making both an accommodation and a creative response to a new situation while at the same time maintaining its own coherence and integrity. The Christian world tended to make exclusive claims, but the Zulu system as transformed in the mind and movement of Shembe tended to be inclusive; that is, it contained both Christian and Zulu elements. [See Christianity p. 529 for the relationship between the ancient African heritage and black American Christianity.]

Shembe's movement was not alone in its confrontation with the world of the whites. The oppression and suffering experienced by the Zulu was fertile ground for the emergence of other movements. One of these was the development of Christian groups known as **Ethiopian churches.** These churches did not encourage the role of the prophetic and even revolutionary leader represented in Shembe's person and movement. Instead they emphasized the importance of organization and adaptability to the new situation in which the Zulu found themselves. Whereas Shembe's movement was radically anti-white in sentiment, the Ethiopian churches were ambivalent about the oppressors. They imitated white modes of organization in their churches, and the ministers of the churches were expected to be pastors, leaders of the flock.

Once again we need to be reminded that in the religious world of the Zulu the headman/priest is that official who assumes responsibility for the entire life of the village. We must add to this the importance given to rank throughout Zulu society. Now in a new setting that calls forth creative responses to new situations, it is this role of the headman/priest that becomes transformed into that of the church leader, who emphasizes diplomacy and rank. What is old is the emphasis upon the centrality of headman/priest; what is new is the Christian imagery that is added to the traditional system. Whereas Shembe's movement transformed the role of the heaven-herd, the Ethiopian churches transformed the role of the headman/priest. In both cases the traditional system has roles that are flexible enough to be interpreted in new ways when warranted. In both cases traditional values are maintained even as they become filled with partially new content. [See Religions of Mesoamerica pp. 152, 163–68, Native Religions of North America pp. 266–67, Christianity pp. 495–97, 531–32, 534–35, Islam pp. 622–28, 698–99, Hinduism pp. 769, 770–72, Buddhism pp. 860, 861–68, 892–99, Religions of China pp. 993–95, and Religions of Japan pp. 1090, 1100, 1122–23 for discussion of religious founders.]

In South Africa there have been two standard responses by the Zulu to white oppression—that of accommodation and that of resistance. These responses have assumed not only a political form but also a religious one. And very often these responses to oppression have been combined in one movement. Among the Zulu it is very difficult to finally separate the religious and the political. Though no Zulu chief accepts white oppression, the Zulu chief has tended to be more accommodating than leaders of the various movements for liberation that have developed in South Africa. This standard form of accommodation had failed; new forms of action were required. The Ethiopian church created a new form of expression of the traditional role. There is still accommodation, but of an ambivalent kind. Their church "is as good as the church of the whites," because it has the same forms of organization and the same type of leadership. But their church is their own; it is a black church, a Zulu church with its own access to power. One might have to live under the numbing shadow of the whites, but one could still live according to the resources of one's own traditions.

What is most interesting is that many Zulu have insisted upon maintaining the traditional system without resorting to such new interpretations. For them the religious system they have inherited makes sense no matter what the world is like. These Zulu continue to regard the village and the hills as the locus of religious activity; the God of the Sky, the ancestors, medicine, and evil are the powers to be reckoned with. And the traditional roles designed to bring these powers to bear on their lives are still valued, for that is what it means to live one's life as a Zulu. From their point of view, their thought and practice has never been understood by the whites in any case. When the Christian missionaries, in all their sincerity, translated the Bible into Zulu, they called their Christian God Unkulunkulu, thinking that that was the name of the Zulu God. But for the Zulu, Unkulunkulu was the first man, not the God of the Sky. This first man was a creator, however. After having come from the sky he was the creative source of all other human beings. The Christians showed their inability to understand by confusing these two different roles.

Nevertheless, even Zulu "traditionalists" have demonstrated a remarkable capacity for recognizing what is of value in the thoughts and actions of the people who came from across the sea. The values of a formal educational system, the discoveries of science, the political and social theories that describe and explain human behavior have all made an impression. And many Zulu have set as their goal the acquisition of new knowledge in whatever context it is available. Some of the white universities have been accessible, and some have not, although this is now changing because of recent political events. When they are not accessible, the Zulu have devised their own means for educating themselves.

The Zulu have demonstrated that they are willing to face the challenges of a new world and have the resources to meet the challenge no matter what the whites have decided about the meaning and end of Zulu life.

What emerges is that the religious system of the Zulu continues in various creative ways to provide a foundation for the Zulu to live in a new world with dignity and grace. This world is a world in transformation and a world of transformations. We have been looking at a dynamic, not a static, tradition. As a tradition in the process of transformation, its world provides a context and a means of living in and thinking about the natural and social worlds. We have caught glimpses of what that world is like by becoming acquainted with its places, roles, powers, and actions, and we have learned something about such a world in action. We have also observed its ability to express itself in new ways; it has provided a bridge to other worlds, including that of Western medicine, and traffic over the bridge moves in both directions.

It is also a world of transformations. Transformation here does not refer to a process of change and accommodation but to the complex relationships that exist within the religious system. This means that within one system there are alternative modes of thought and action, but one alternative receives its significance only in relationship to the other alternatives. For example, the position of men and women differ in the Zulu world. And yet these positions have a relationship to each other. Though the headman/priest provides the link between the present and the past, between the living and the dead, between the world of everyday life and the world of ancestral power, nevertheless women have an alternative access to the sources of power through divination, witchcraft, and special rites that are their exclusive province.

It is a world of transformation also because new religious forms are not simply alien, imported forms but responses to what is new and strange and attractive on the basis of a coherent system of thought and action. In chapter 4 we shall see just how such a system provides answers to important questions about what is real, important, personal, dangerous, and desirable. We shall also discover that the Zulu system, though it has some elements in common with Yoruba religion, also has a distinctiveness and integrity of its own.

3

The Yoruba and Their Religious Tradition

The Origins of the Yoruba People

THE MODERN STATE OF NIGERIA is a large and complex country consisting of diverse ethnic groups with different languages, traditions, and religious systems. One of these groups of people is known as the Yoruba, who live mainly in the western part of Nigeria and continue to practice their own traditions. Our purpose in this chapter is to describe this religion.

As with any culture in which the traditions of origins are preserved orally, the details of the beginnings of Yoruba culture are difficult to specify with any degree of accuracy. What is clear for the Yoruba is that there is a continuity to their culture that stretches into the very distant past. Many contemporary Yoruba have spent a great deal of time dealing with the question of their origins. Some have gone so far as to postulate a relationship with Middle Eastern countries. Linguistics and archaeology have been important tools in these investigations. We do know that a city such as **Ife** was founded nearly a thousand years ago and has continuously been a center of Yoruba religion ever since. Whether the establishment of the Yoruba people as a distinct tradition is traceable to migrations of people from the Middle East, or whether they are the result of a culture born of contact between indigenous African forest people and people from the dry regions beyond the Niger River is immaterial for our purpose, because we shall be examining the religious thought and practice of a people who by now possess a very ancient heritage. [See Religions of Mesoamerica pp. 114–15, Hinduism pp. 732–33, and Religions of China p. 986 for discussion of early cities.]

Who are these Yoruba people, then? Estimates of their number vary according to the references one consults. There seem to be anywhere from five million to ten million Yoruba. The largest number live in the western part of Nigeria, but others can be found in Ghana, Togo, and Dahomey. During the period of slavery in the seventeenth and eighteenth centuries many of them were taken by force to the New World. Some people of African descent still practice at least some aspects of Yoruba tradition in Cuba, Brazil, and even the United States. There are residents of New York City, some of whom are Yoruba descendants, who still perform rituals in honor of the Yoruba divinity Sango.

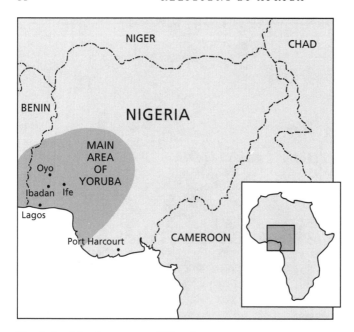

Yorubaland in the context of Nigeria.

Though all Yoruba speak a common language and subscribe to the same worldview, they actually consist of a number of social and political groups. Each of these groups, with its own tradition, has had a specific urban center. Each of these centers has an **oba** (chief) as the symbol of supreme authority, authority both political and religious in nature.

Each of these cities provides the focus for one of the various social groups in **Yorubaland;** nevertheless, the city of Ife was and still is regarded by the Yoruba as the center of their culture and religion. Each of the urban centers traces its own origin to Ife. New chiefs receive confirmation of their status from the paramount chief of Ife. Though other cities, such as **Oyo,** have, on occasion, had greater military and political strength, none has been able to supplant the cultural and religious preeminence of Ife.

The dominant occupation of the Yoruba is farming. Although people live in the cities, these cities are surrounded by farms where they work. Secondary dwellings are often built on these farms, especially if the farm is a long distance from the city, but these second houses are never as important as the primary dwellings in the city.

The Yoruba have had a much lighter contact with the forces of colonialism than the Zulu. Whereas the Zulu suffered colonization by the British and the expansion of the Afrikaaners into their territory and, further, became subservient to an imposed white state in which they and other indigenous Africans could play no political role, the Yoruba were subjected only to indirect rule. This meant that the traditional Yoruba structure remained largely intact. Also, the

British did not permit immigration of white colonists into the country. Hence the Yoruba never had to contend with a large alien population.

But external influences have had their effect on Yoruba culture. Both Islam and Christianity have developed roots within Yoruba society. Actually, the influence of Islam preceded Christian missionary activity by a number of centuries. Some scholars date the introduction of Islam in the seventeenth century. Christianity was introduced in 1842 but was at first most successful with the newly freed slaves, released from slave ships bound for America by the British navy, who in turn attempted to spread it among the indigenous Yoruba. This meant the establishment of mission churches and, after some time, the development of independent African Christian churches.

In 1960 Nigeria, of which Yorubaland is an important part, was granted its independence and became a member of the British Commonwealth. Contemporary Nigeria is a complex mix of old and new. Skyscrapers, universities, and banks can be found in many of the cities. But along with these new symbols of contemporary life, the traditions of the Yoruba survive. It is to these traditions that we now turn our attention.

The Religious System of the Yoruba People

As with the Zulu people, the historical origins and development of Yoruba religion are too complex and too indefinite for a quick summary. Therefore, rather than discussing such problematic matters, we shall focus our attention upon the coherent worldview of the Yoruba people. We shall proceed on the basis that there is both underlying unity and great diversity in the religious thought and practice of these people.

The diversity of Yoruba thought and practice is so great that some scholars —tongue in cheek—recommend studying its art instead. But there is little reason to be intimidated by the complexity, because Yoruba scholars have themselves already demonstrated elements of the unity in the religious worldview that underlie the thought and practice of the Yoruba. We shall use the results of such scholarship in our own description of Yoruba religion.[4]

Whereas the religious world of the Zulu is centered upon practices in the sacred places of the village and nearby hills, the Yoruba system has a dual focus on one major center and many local sites. On the one hand, it has its foundation in the city of Ife as the center of all religious power. On the other hand, it is represented in every compound, city, shrine, grove, temple, rock, tree, hill, crossroads, diviner, priest, chief, and family head in the land. Ife is the center because it was there that the god **Orisa-nla** commenced with the very first acts of creation. But all the other places and roles are sources of power also, because they derive their status from Ife.

In any religion there will not only be ritual action but people who are responsible for ensuring that such action occurs. These ritual practitioners

A Yoruba healing specialist performing a healing ritual. (Photograph by Raymond Prince.)

either perform these actions themselves or direct those who do. In this section we shall briefly identify the roles assumed by Yoruba ritual practitioners.

In each Yoruba household, if the vitality of the religious symbols is still treasured, there will be found a family shrine. It is at this shrine that the head of the family, known as the **olori ebi,** assumes ritual powers for communicating with the objects of devotion. Of particular importance is his ritual relationship with the ancestors, who are regarded as being important sources of power. No important event in the household can occur without the *olori ebi's* involvement. For example, the birth of a child, the departure of a daughter to be married, and the funeral of a family member will all require his guidance and his ritual action. Any infraction of the rules of Yoruba life on the part of a family member will be brought to his attention; it is his obligation to mete out the appropriate punishment and to perform the correct rites to the ancestors who have been offended by such infractions.

Whereas among the Zulu nearly all the ritual activity is concentrated in and around the village, among the Yoruba one finds different levels of ritual action. One level is the home, and it is the family head who provides the center of action. The second level is the town or city, and it is the town *oba* who assumes ritual responsibility. The *oba* is the ruler or king or paramount chief of the town. In the Yoruba view all such rulers originally came from Ife, for it was there that the gods established the earthly kingdom. In traditional Yoruba thought each *oba* is invested with religious power. In fact, their very position means that they are below only the gods in both power and status and, therefore, worthy of great respect. Without the presence of the *oba* certain rituals would not be performed. The *oba,* then, controls a level of religious power above that of the family head. There are annual festivals at which his presence is required.

At yet another ritual level the *oba* and the priests of Ife provide the focus of religious action. And intersecting all these levels are the priests associated with the many shrines in Yorubaland, who mediate between the human and the divine worlds. It should be clear, then, that we are dealing with a very complex system of ritual relationships and roles. One way of increasing our understanding of these roles, relationships, and objects of devotion is to identify the role of the priests in the religious system.

Among the Yoruba there are many gods, and each of these divine beings is attended by a priesthood. One kind of priest, or ***aworo,*** is the ***babalawo,*** or diviner. It is he who communicates with **Orunmila** (the god most closely associated with the practice of ***ifa***) through divination and who is most frequently consulted by the Yoruba for advice about all matters of importance. Becoming a *babalawo* involves a long training period. But all the other priests also have an important function to perform in the religious system. They are in charge of the many shrines and are associated with one of the many divinities worshiped in the various areas of Yorubaland. Particular urban centers have particular divinities associated with them, and particular Yoruba will develop a ritual relationship to one or more of the shrines in the area. These priests are responsible for the sacrifices performed by the devotees of a particular divinity and communicate the commands and wishes of the gods to the people. They are also responsible for arranging the many festivals that are characteristic of Yorubaland.

In addition to the priestly role there is that of the ***elegun,*** the medium who is spiritually possessed. Among the Zulu, divine possession (either by trance, dream, or sign) is a condition for being called to perform the role of the diviner, but among the Yoruba anyone can become a medium for divine powers without becoming a diviner. In fact, in the context of a religious festival such experiences of possession frequently occur. In such ecstatic states the divine powers communicate through the *elegun* to the other worshipers. But such an experience does not lead to the assumption of a formal ritual role like that of the Yoruba diviner, which takes many years of training and most probably involves having inherited the calling.

The role of the specialist in medicine is very similar to that in the Zulu system. Though all Yoruba have knowledge of medicine, the ***oloogun,*** the specialist in identifying the causes and prescribing the cures for the various illnesses that beset the Yoruba, plays a key role. He is the repository of medicinal knowledge. What is particularly interesting is that he usually works in cooperation with the *babalawo,* for it is the diviner who is supposed to be particularly adept at uncovering the reasons for an illness. But medicine is not an autonomous system. Its power comes from the gods. In that sense the *oloogun* is a conduit for healing power.

The ***egungun*** are masked dancers who perform at festivals and other important ritual occasions. They wear opaque nets over their faces to prevent their identification, wear long and colorful robes, and are regarded as the representatives of the ancestors. The masks they wear are handed down from generation to generation and are seen by the Yoruba as possessing great power. Special rites must be performed by the men who wear them, and they are believed to be particularly dangerous to women. But there is one woman who is permitted contact with them; she is known as the **iya agan,** and it is her function to supervise the dressing of the *egungun*.

Each of these roles provides an access to one or more aspects of the world of power. The most inclusive symbol for that world is the Yoruba concept of **Orun** (heaven or "the above"). In our discussion of religious powers in the following section we shall describe the many ways in which Orun is the locus for such power.

The Yoruba divide the cosmos into two parts, Orun and **Aiye** (earth), which are connected by ritual space. Orun is heaven, or the sky, and is the abode of the Yoruba High God, known by two names, **Olorun** and Olodumare. (For the purpose of this discussion, the High God will be referred to as Olorun.) It is also the abode of the other deities (known as **orisa**) and the ancestors. It is populated with other sources of religious power as well. Aiye is the earth, the world of human habitation. In this second world live people and animals and "the children of the world," known as **omoraiye.** This latter group is responsible for sorcery and witchcraft. It is clear, then, that both heaven and earth contain many sources of power. What is important is how they are connected ritually.

A Yoruba egungun *masked dancer. (Photograph by William Bascom; used with permission of Lowie Museum of Anthropology, University of California, Berkeley.)*

Although Yoruba cosmology is complex and not centered in one deity or principle, it is possible to understand it by seeing it as organized according to three main elements located at three levels. Olorun is the chief source of power. He is also the most remote, and in the world of worship, he is hardly ever approached directly except in prayer. The *orisa* represent a level of power that is approachable directly through ritual action and so provide one very important focus for Yoruba religion. The ancestors exist at yet another level of power. In family worship, they assume an important place in religious activity.

All these sources of power have an intricate relationship to each other. We shall first describe some of their features and then attempt to clarify some of the relationships.

The Yoruba word *Olorun* literally means "owner of the sky" and refers to the High God who lives in the heavens. But there is a considerable range of opinion among the Yoruba themselves about his nature and origin. Some see it as a relatively recent concept added to the indigenous religion under the influence of Christianity and Islam. Other Yoruba think that it is a long-standing concept in the indigenous religion and integral to the Yoruba worldview. From the latter point of view, the Yoruba were quite capable of conceiving of a High God apart from external religious influences.

Such diversity of opinion reflects a more general problem in Western scholarship about the nature and origin of the High God in the development of religion. Some Western scholars think that the High God occurs early in the emergence of religion. Others, using an evolutionary metaphor, argue for the late development of the concept and give particular credit to the Jewish, Christian, and Muslim religions for its discovery. [See Native Religions of North America pp. 289–91, 330–31 for discussion of Supreme Being, God, and gods; see Religions of Mesoamerica p. 166 for mention of High God.]

Whatever version of these views one adopts, however, is irrelevant for our purposes, because it is generally agreed that Olorun has played a significant role in Yoruba religious thought for some time and that he does represent the most basic level of religious power.

Olorun is the originating power in the cosmos. All other powers, such as the *orisa,* the ancestors, and, in fact, all forms of life, owe their form and being to him. But he has delegated many of his powers to the other divinities. An elaborate system of mediators is interposed between him and the world of human life.

Thus Olorun is often regarded as austere, remote, and difficult to approach. Although he is prayed to, no shrines are erected in his honor, no rituals are directed toward him, and no sacrifices are made to placate him. Such ritual activities are to be directed to the gods at a lower level of power. They are the ones who act as mediators between this world and the other world. And they were brought into being in order to serve the purposes of Olorun.

Some scholars refer to the *orisa* of Yoruba religion as lesser divinities or lesser deities. The fact is that these gods are regarded by the ritual practitioners as superhuman agents who are sources of religious power that can act for their good or ill, and they are an important focus for religious action. The point in the religious system of the Yoruba is that there are many such foci, and their power is based finally on the power of the High God.

Who are these *orisa?* There are many of them. And their large number corresponds to the variety of forms that Yoruba religion takes. A particular *orisa* may only be worshiped by one descent group in one town. And there he or she will have a shrine for that purpose. Another *orisa* may be regional in influence and may, therefore, be worshiped at a number of shrines. Some *orisa* are worshiped throughout Yorubaland. All this is an indication of the diversity of religious expression in Yoruba religion.

The *orisa* provide a key focus for religious worship among the Yoruba. Some Yoruba claim that there are over four hundred of them. We shall pay attention to only a representative few; the ones we have chosen are widely known throughout Yorubaland.

Orisa-nla, also known as Obatala, is one of the *orisa* worshiped throughout Yorubaland. He has many religious functions, one of the most important being his role in the creation of the earth and the bringing to earth of the first sixteen persons already created by Olorun. Orisa-nla is, in fact, credited with the sculpting or shaping of the first humans and, interestingly, is also responsible for the existence of albinos, hunchbacks, cripples, dwarfs, and mutes. These unfortunate people are not regarded as having been punished but as being sacred; they are meant to remind the more fortunate of their obligation to worship Orisa-nla.

Two important taboos are associated with him: There should be no drinking of palm wine and no contact with dogs. He has a particular association with the color white; he is said to live in a white palace and to wear white raiment, and his followers often wear white clothes. He is the chief of the "white gods," of whom there seem to be about fifty. But there is a problem here, because these may simply be different names for the same god. He has a priesthood associated with him, and shrines in his honor are to be found throughout Yorubaland where sacrifices to him are regularly made.

As has been mentioned, there is more than one version of the creation story among the Yoruba. In the tradition held at the city of Ife it is **Oduduwa** who preempts the role of creation normally associated with Orisa-nla. This story says that Orisa-nla became drunk with palm wine and failed to follow Olorun's instructions correctly, and Oduduwa therefore had to rectify Orisa-nla's errors. Whereas Orisa-nla is clearly a male deity, the status of Oduduwa is not nearly as clear. In some versions "he" is the wife of Orisa-nla. Scholars argue that the various stories reflect layers of tradition, with Oduduwa replacing Orisa-nla in ritual importance. What is perhaps most interesting about Oduduwa is that he is also regarded as having at one time been human; at his death he was transformed into an ancestor with the status of an *orisa.*

Orisa-nla is worshiped throughout Yorubaland; Oduduwa has shrines and a priesthood mainly in the city of Ife. But because of his association with this sacred city, he is, nevertheless, recognized as an important deity throughout the land.

Orunmila is the god associated with practice of *ifa,* a method for acquiring knowledge through divination. In fact, some investigators also refer to him as

Ifa, a deity, but Yoruba scholars regard this as a confusion between the practice of divination and the object of divination. In any case Orunmila is a god with great knowledge and wisdom who was present at the creation of the human race and has knowledge of human destiny. It is particularly appropriate, therefore, that he be the source of information about the future of humankind. [See Religions of Mesoamerica pp. 129–35, 154–55, 163–68, Native Religions of North America pp. 288–95, 327–29, 333–42, Judaism pp. 380–84, Christianity pp. 534–35, Hinduism pp. 739–41, 743–46, Buddhism p. 890, and Religions of Japan pp. 1094–96 for discussion of myth and mythology.]

An important element in the Yoruba religious system is that the destiny or fate of humankind was decided by Olorun from the very beginning, that humans have forgotten their fate, and that such knowledge can be recovered through the process of divination (*ifa*).

Esu is one of the most complex of the Yoruba deities. Christian missionaries, in their early encounters with Yoruba religion, tended to equate him with the concept of the Devil, but this is most unfortunate and distorts his nature, because, though he has certain evil properties, he is by no means the incarnation of evil. In Yoruba religion Esu is regarded as having taught Orunmila the secrets of divination. He is also an important extension of Olorun's power. In fact, it is one of his major roles to provide tests for the people in order to determine their character. He is also conceived of as a mediating power between heaven and earth; any sacrifice to the *orisa* must include a portion for him to ensure his cooperation in mediating between the two worlds. Failure to perform the appropriate obligations to the *orisa* brings about Esu's wrath and consequent punishment. Proper respect for the divine powers brings about his suitable rewards.

The complexity of Esu's nature is revealed by his tendency to incite the Yoruba ritual practitioner to give offense to the other *orisa* by failing to sacrifice to them. But this aspect of his character can also be misinterpreted, for his intention is to ensure that, as a consequence of such offense, the ritual practitioner will then perform the sacrifices required as a result of the offense. This preserves the continuing worship of the gods. [See Religions of Mesoamerica pp. 166–67, 177, 186, 237–38, Judaism pp. 399–400, Christianity pp. 543–44, 550, Islam p. 646, and Hinduism pp. 743–45, 747–48 for description and discussion of sacrifice.]

Although Esu is an important deity and is constantly on the minds of the worshipers, he has no special set of worshipers and no special shrine. Instead, all places of worship and all acts of worship contain a place for him. As a result he is an object of indirect attention even when other *orisa* are the focus of a ritual act.

It is precisely because Esu contains within himself forces of both good and evil, both reverence and irreverence, and because he encourages both worshiping and giving offense that he is able to mediate between heaven and earth. It is his contrary qualities that make it possible for him to assume the key role of mediator between the many levels of power conceived of in Yoruba thought, particularly between the worlds of divine and human power.

Esu, then, is the ambiguous god. **Trickster**, mischief maker, punisher, rewarder, source of wisdom and knowledge, confuser of situations, mediator—all of these things can be said of him. A failure to understand Esu's role in the Yoruba religious system is a failure to understand the lineaments of that world. [See Native Religions of North America pp. 268–69, 288–89 for a discussion of trickster.]

Esu may be one of the most complex of the Yoruba gods, but **Ogun** is one of the most puzzling. He is variously regarded as one of the original gods and as a human ancestor who became a god. The puzzlement might be removed by looking closely at his characteristics.

According to the religious traditions of the city of Ife, Ogun was its first king. It should be remembered that, according to Yoruba tradition, all kings originally were descendants of the first king of Ife, where the world was established by the gods and where the gods first expressed their power. Having been established at Ife as its first ruler, Ogun ruled the city and its territories as a chief is supposed to. His people were obliged to be obedient and respectful toward him. But some of his people failed to show proper respect. As a result of this insult, Ogun lost control of himself and started to kill his own subjects. When he realized the gravity of his acts, he killed himself with his own sword and disappeared into the bosom of the earth. His last words were a promise to respond to those who called upon him in dire need.

Now, according to Yoruba tradition, Ogun is the god of metals and war. There are also traditions that emphasize it was Ogun who, with his metal ax, cleared the path for the other divinities when they came to the earth. Thus Ogun has a special relation to all acts of tool making and all functions and roles associated with these acts. The Yoruba know that the discovery of metals and the making of tools was later than the act of creation and yet is a fundamental and creative step forward in human progress. Also, such implements are capable of destructive and constructive use. As such they have a divine and a human element, and thus both the divine and the human worlds are credited with this great discovery. Ogun's status reflects this duality. Ogun is associated both with the heavens and the earth; his abode is in the heavens as well as on (or within) the earth. He is both a living god and a dead ancestor. If one were to place the gods on a line extending from Olorun to the ancestors, Ogun would be on the borderline between the gods and the ancestors. It is this special place that makes it possible for Ogun to stand for justice, the justice of the gods and the justice required in human action. In courts of law, Yoruba who still live by their traditional customs swear to tell the truth by kissing a piece of iron in the name of Ogun. And because of his association with metals, drivers of motor vehicles of all sorts often carry a representation of Ogun as a charm to prevent accidents and ensure their own safety.

We have already seen how important the ancestors were in Zulu religion; they are equally important in Yoruba religion. We have also seen that among the Zulu there is clear distinction between the God of the Sky (and the heavenly princess) and the sacred ancestors. In Yoruba religion, not only is the world of the divine divided into the realms of the High God and the *orisa,* the world of the ancestors is similarly divided.

In the Yoruba religion the ancestors are agents with religious powers capable of acting for the good or ill of their descendants. Therefore the ancestors are treated with great respect and devotion. In fact, special shrines and rituals exist as contexts for maintaining proper relationships with them.

There are two classes of ancestors, family ancestors and "deified" ancestors. We shall discuss these two classes separately. As with the Zulu, not all people who die become ancestors, or at least ancestors to whom any ritual attention is paid. They must have special qualities to attain such ritual attention. The most important quality in a family ancestor is that he or she lived a good life, and as a consequence, achieved the state of **orun rere,** which literally means being in the "good heaven," the world of Olorun and the *orisa*. The next important quality is the attainment of a ripe old age, for this is a good indication that the ancestor has fulfilled his or her destiny. Yet another quality is the possession of dutiful descendants who remember the ancestor with appreciation and are willing to continue to perform the ceremonies in his or her honor.

Such family ancestors will be venerated or worshiped by their descendants and will be represented by the *egungun;* the Yoruba believe that the ancestors are ritually present in these masked dancers. Such ritual practitioners become conduits for messages from and to the ancestors and, in fact, assume the role of mediators between the family and the departed loved ones. On special occasions, for example at a festival, all the ancestors may be brought back and represented by many *egungun.* In many regions of Yorubaland such festivals are eagerly awaited and provide a focus for community celebrations; they may even be linked to the planting of the new crops for the year.

The "deified ancestors" are tied not to particular families but to the history of the cities or to important factors in the development of Yoruba culture. These ancestors have shrines not simply in the home but in towns, often throughout the country. Some scholars, in fact, refer to them as *orisa*. Whatever the term used, such ancestors are considerable sources of power and ritual practices are associated with them. Sango, Orisa-oko, and Ayelala are examples of ancestors who have attained a very special status in Yoruba religion, although in some cases their influence does not spread throughout Yorubaland. Sango has a specific association with lightning, Orisa-oko with farming, and Ayelala with punishment for wrongdoing. What is interesting is that their human origins are preserved in Yoruba stories; yet there is no doubt about their status as superhuman agents with the ability to exert power for good or ill and the necessity of worshiping them.

We now have a picture of the many places of religious action in Yoruba religion, the different roles assumed by the religious practitioners, and the levels of religious power addressed in the wide variety of rituals. But one additional concept is needed to help us understand how places, roles, and religious powers are related to each other, namely, the concept of mediation.

In the Yoruba religious system mediation plays a particularly important part. Mediation occurs in many contexts, involves many agents, and implicates many sources of power. The first of these contexts is that of the family. As we have already learned, the family head is the key ritual figure, and one of his most important functions is to maintain ritual relationships with the ancestors. He is the channel for communication with the ancestors, and as such a channel, he acts as a mediating agent between heaven and earth—but with a specific focus upon the family ancestors. He represents the people to the ancestors by sacrificing to them on behalf of the people, and he represents the ancestors to the people by informing the family members of their obligations to the ancestors.

On special occasions, however, the ancestors are represented by the *egungun* rather than by the family head. One such occasion is the death of an important family member. The *egungun* will emerge from the house of the deceased, imitate this newly departed person, and convey messages of consolation from the dead to the living members of the family.

The second context for mediation is that of the shrine. Here the priest of the particular form of Yoruba religion practiced in the area assumes the mediating role between the member of the cult and the particular *orisa*. For example, if the *orisa* is Orunmila, the god of divination, then a *babalawo* (one of the many kinds of priests) will be the mediating link between the devotee and Orunmila, the keeper of his or her destiny.

The third context for mediation is that of the city. Here the mediator is the chief, who, by virtue of his direct descent from the original kings of the sacred city of Ife, is capable of representing the entire population of a city and its environs to the *orisa*. His mediating role is expressed in many ways. For example, on festival occasions he will be the leader of the procession, and his important role will signal the presence of the *orisa*. In fact, some festivals cannot proceed without his mediating presence.

The fourth context for mediation is every act of worship in which one *orisa* is required to mediate between the ritual practitioner and another *orisa*. The clearest example of this is the role of the *orisa* Esu, who, though possessing no shrines of his own, is always acknowledged whenever the worshiper sacrifices to another *orisa*. Failure to acknowledge the mediating role of Esu will disrupt communication between the worshiper and the world of sacred power.

These various contexts for mediation between the Yoruba and the world of sacred powers point to the complex structure of Yoruba life and reflect the many forms of ritual action that their religious system makes necessary and possible. Whether the worshiper seeks knowledge of his or her destiny, pays respect to the deceased, offers a sacrifice, or marches in a procession, there will be a mediator operating to establish a line of communication between worshiper and object of devotion.

The diagram in figure 1-3 provides one way of organizing and representing the ritual roles and religious powers that play such an important part in the Yoruba religious system. It shows that there are two levels of power, within which there are multiple foci. Within the first level, known as Orun (heaven), there is Olorun, the High God, and the *orisa*, the deities who are subordinate to Olorun but who also provide the focus of ritual attention for the worshiper.

There are also the family and deified ancestors. What distinguishes these two kinds of ancestors from each other is that the family ancestors are venerated

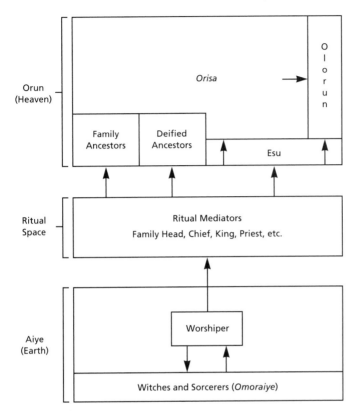

Figure 1-3. The Yoruba Religious System.

exclusively within the context of the descent group whereas the deified ancestors are the objects of worship of a specific cult tied not to a family but to a locality. Such a cult does not exist in competition with the family ancestors or the *orisa* but provides an additional context for the performance of sacrifices. Thus an individual Yoruba may be found to be sacrificing to a family ancestor in the context of the home, to a deified ancestor at a local shrine, and to an *orisa* at a regional or national shrine. And all such sacrifices will require some mediator or process of mediation to be effective.

The second level of power is that of Aiye (or Aye), which means earth. The worshiper is the focus of power here, as are the *omoraiye*—the witches and sorcerers who are known as "children of the earth." These are not *orisa* and are able to accomplish their destructive aims by manipulating and twisting the human personality.

Having described the roles and powers, the process of mediation, and the various contexts in which the powers are addressed, we shall now illustrate how all these factors operate in specific situations. There is no better place to start such an analysis than with that most characteristic of all Yoruba religious practices: divination, or *ifa.*

Divination Ritual and Destiny

The Yoruba people practice many forms of divination. The most widespread and highly regarded of these is the consultation of the divine oracle. In observing a divination ritual one will notice that there are three elements in the ritual: the diviner, known as a *babalawo;* the ritual apparatus that the diviner uses in the consultation; and the person who is consulting with the diviner. In order to understand what is occurring, we need to know something about the Yoruba concept of the person, something about the diviner and the consulter, and something about the procedures and objects used in divination.

In Yoruba religion each person is regarded as both a physical and a spiritual being. The physical aspect of the person is known as **ara.** This is the word for the body of the person. The spiritual aspect is described in two ways, first as **emi,** or "breath," and second as **ori,** or "head." Without *emi,* the power that gives life to the body, there would be no person at all. Without *ori* the human body would be incapable of thought and be unable to communicate with the world of religious power. One of the most important aspects of *ori* is its relationship to the course of the life of the individual. Each person has chosen his or her identity before birth, and that identity includes a life plan that is the person's fate. Because this identity has a heavenly origin, it is also the guardian of that individual and is identified with an ancestor.

Each person, therefore, can also be considered as the reincarnation of an ancestor. Each person, because of his or her *ori,* is of spiritual origin, having come from the domain of the ancestors, the world of Orun. Birth into this world

A babalawo *performing* ifa *divination. (Photograph by William R. Bascom; used with permission of the Lowie Museum of Anthropology, University of California, Berkeley.)*

is accompanied by a failure of memory. Such a memory of destiny needs to be recovered or rediscovered. Consulting the divining oracle fulfills that function. Therefore, when consulting the oracle through the mediation of the diviner, a Yoruba is attempting to come to terms with his or her destiny. Although such destiny has the ring of inevitability about it, nevertheless, it needs to be "protected" by ritual action and discovered using the knowledge available through the diviner. It also is capable of being "modified" under certain conditions.

And so the Yoruba consults the diviner, the *babalawo.* Who is this ritual practitioner? The *babalawo* is one of many kinds of priests to be found in Yoruba religion, because each god has his or her own priesthood. The *babalawo* is the priest who has a special ritual relationship to the god Orunmila. *Babalawo* literally means "father of secret things." The *babalawo* is the priest who through the process of divination mediates between human and divine and reveals the human patterns of destiny.

The procedures and objects used in the divining process are as follows: When the Yoruba who desires to consult an oracle comes to the diviner, the diviner arranges the ritual elements and prepares for the act of divination. The elements are sixteen kola nuts (or a divining chain), a divining board, and divining powder. If the diviner uses the kola nut method (and this is regarded as more reliable than the chain) he will place the sixteen nuts in his left hand and then attempt to take as many of them with his right hand as possible. If only one nut remains, then he will make a double mark in the divining powder on the divining board. If two nuts remain, he will make a single mark. If no nuts or more than two remain, he will make no marks. The purpose is to end with two columns with four sets of marks in each column. A particular result might look as follows:

There are 256 possible combinations of such marks. Each of these sets of marks has a set of traditional stories associated with it. The *babalawo* will know at least four such parables, or **odu,** for each of these 256 sets. Experienced *babalawo* will have memorized many more. In fact the diviner's expertise is measured by the amount of wisdom in the form of such parables that he knows. When a particular set has been arrived at by the diviner and the appropriate story has been chosen, he will inform the consulter what action the story recommends be performed. A sacrifice of some kind will almost always be part of the requirement, because a sacrificial offering is the basic form of communication with the religious powers.

In this act of divination, then, one has a number of elements: a worldview in which a forgotten destiny needs to be discovered, an action that must be performed to keep this destiny on course, a method for determining the action, a priest who is expert at determining the problem to be solved and the means for solving it, and a consulter with a problem. To understand the operation of these key elements is to understand something about the Yoruba view of how one's destiny can be both discovered and ensured.

Destiny is not, however, only an individual matter; it also involves the future course of community life and experience.

In a world in which farming is still the predominant activity, one of the most important annual events involving matters of destiny is the harvesting of crops. Nowhere is the delicate system of equilibrium that binds gods and people together more obvious and more immediate. A good crop means plenty, and a poor crop means famine.

One of the most important crops of the Yoruba is yams. They are a staple in the Yoruba diet, and much depends upon their bounty. Because *orisa,* ancestors, and humans are mutually interrelated, all are involved in the success or failure of the crops. The harvest festival provides a context for the establishment and maintenance of these relationships; the roles of the people and the sacred powers are particularly important for the destiny of the crops.

One such festival is the New Yam festival, known in some parts of Yorubaland as **Eje.**[5] In this annual festival the god of the sea, **Malokun,** plays an important role, but many other types and levels of religious power play a part as well. In fact, the entire range of religious power from the ancestors to the gods becomes involved in this celebration.

The festival lasts for two days and consists of a number of activities: purification rites, presentation rites, divining rites, and thanksgiving rites. On the first day it is important to ritually purify the areas in which the rites will take place. Two such places are the sacred grove and the sacred shrine. After these areas have been purified, the rest of the festival may proceed. The yams have already been taken to the *oba's* farm, where they have been placed in heaps. These yams must be presented in a ritual manner to the appropriate religious powers. Some of them are placed at the shrine of the *orisa* Malokun. Upon their arrival, which is announced in a loud voice, the people congregate together to joyously welcome the new harvest. A new year is about to be born, and the priest of the shrine prays it will be a good and successful one.

On the night of the first day of Eje, after the yams have been installed in the shrine, the people remain outside, where they give continual thanks to the religious powers generally and address the ancestors specifically, making offerings of palm wine and kola nuts to them.

But although the yams are already in the shrine, they have not yet been formally offered in sacrifice and have not played a role in divination. The ritual of presentation to the *orisa* involves a number of elements. First is the requirement that both *oba* and priests purify themselves by fasting throughout the day. On the morning of the second day the *oba*, dressed in a white garment, makes an offering of a white kola nut and a white pigeon and prays with the priests to Malokun. This is followed by a procession to the shrine, where the yams are now presented to the religious powers, namely, Malokun and the ancestors.

One of the high points of the festival is the divination rite that will determine the destiny of the life of the community, especially the success or failure of the crops in the following year. In this rite one of the recently harvested yams is taken and divided into two parts. They are cast, and if one falls face up and the other face down everybody is pleased, for this is a positive sign. If both fall either face downward or face upward there is concern, for it indicates problems ahead. [See Religions of Mesoamerica pp. 229–38, Native Religions of North America pp. 308–16, 351–57, Judaism pp. 439–45, Christianity pp. 551–55, Islam pp. 674, 677–79, Hinduism p. 829, Buddhism pp. 937–41, Religions of China pp. 1021–24, and Religions of Japan pp. 1140–46, 1153–62 for description and discussion of festivals and annual celebrations.]

Another ceremony, also involving divination, then takes place in the other sacred area, the grove. The people all move in a procession to the grove, where, once again, a yam is divided and its two parts cast in an act of divination. And once again there is rejoicing if the signs are positive and concern if they are negative. The people and the priests then proceed to the palace, where they are met by the *oba*, who then joins the procession and leads them in a dance through the town. An important part of this dancing procession is the stops it makes at each of the shrines of the many divinities worshiped in the town. Sacrifices are made to the *orisa* venerated at each shrine. The fast of *oba* and the priests is then broken, and a general celebration begins. The town has been purified, the yams have been presented; the future has been divined; the *orisa* and the ancestors have been served; and the new year has begun when new crops can be planted with confidence that the act of divination has ensured their destiny.

Stages on Life's Way

One way of understanding a religious system better is to see how it defines the important events in the life of an individual. We shall follow the career of an individual from birth to death and show how key elements of the religious system make their presence felt in the stages on life's way. The information we shall use is a summary of extended discussions the author has held with Yoruba informants. The individual whose career we shall be tracing will be called Ogunbode Akinsaya. Ogunbode is his religious name, and Akinsaya is his family name.

One of the first actions that Ogunbode's mother performed, when she discovered that she was pregnant, was to pay a call on the diviner (*babalawo*) who was resident in her city. There were two purposes for her visit: first to have him divine the destiny of the unborn child and second to have him both prescribe the right medicines to take to ensure a good birth and tell her which taboos to observe. The medicines would be decided by a consultation between the diviner and a specialist in medicines (*oloogun*).

Having performed these important tasks, she returned home and began her preparations for the birth of the child. Very soon after the child was born, he was taken to the *babalawo,* who again performed the divining ritual to determine the child's destiny. After knowledge of his destiny was acquired, the parents made an offering at the shrine of the *orisa* named Ogun, because it was to him that Ogunbode's family felt the deepest attachment; a great deal of their religious life was centered around Ogun. The offering that the parents made was a sacrifice and was regarded by them as being crucial for maintaining a correct relationship with Ogun in a time of danger. They were also very careful to include a portion of the sacrifice for Esu to avoid any mischief from this powerful and puzzling *orisa.*

Because Ogunbode was a boy he was given his name on the ninth day after his birth. Had his mother given birth to a girl the naming ceremony would have taken place on the seventh day. If twins had been born they would have been named on the eighth day. His name, Ogunbode, was chosen by his parents because of their religious relationship to Ogun and was one of a set of possible names that exist to honor this *orisa.* The other names in the set are Ogunlake, Ogundolam, Ogunyale, Ogunsanya, and Ogundele. A name, then, gives to its bearer an obvious and immediate connection to the divine world.

From the time of Ogunbode's birth certain foods were automatically forbidden to him. His parents knew which foods to withhold because of what the diviner had said. Such a set of taboos was not permanent, however, for in the process of growing up Ogunbode could decide to eat what was forbidden when he observed someone else doing so.

Ogunbode's place of residence was not with his mother and father but with his grandfather, who, because of his status as family head (*olori ebi*), was the most direct link with the family ancestors. Ogunbode was from the very beginning of his life taught both the ritual and the family responsibilities that go with being a Yoruba who still believes in the importance of the ancestral traditions. As well as learning the religious traditions, Ogunbode also learned from his grandfather the intricacies of farm work, for the compound in the city had its own farm in the countryside.

Before he reached his second birthday Ogunbode was circumcised. No special ceremonies of a religious nature (that is, having any reference to either the ancestors or the *orisa*) were performed at this time. This act was simply to ensure that he would have an important qualification for marriage, because no Yoruba male can be married without having undergone circumcision. [See Judaism pp. 385–86, 445–46, Christianity p. 496, and Islam pp. 677–78, 680, 682 for discussion of circumcision.]

From his earliest days Ogunbode was regarded as being part of an age group. This meant that boys of roughly the same age formed a community of their own. The same was true for the girls. All through his life his friends and acquaintances would have a special attachment to him because of his relationship to such an age group.

Many Yoruba believe that there are only three important events in the career of a person: birth, marriage, and death. While Ogunbode underwent circumcision and participated in the life and experiences of all those belonging to his age group, nothing of religious significance characterized his development until he was ready for marriage.

When he was ready for marriage, Ogunbode faced two alternatives. Either he could have an arranged marriage (perhaps his parents had long ago made a commitment to some other family) or he could have informed his parents that a particular young woman had caught his eye and he wished them to start inquiries and negotiations about her availability. In Ogunbode's own case, he fell in love with an attractive young woman in his own city and so wished his parents to make it possible for them to be married.

It was at this point that mediation between the two families became important. Not only is mediation a fundamental process in Yoruba religion; it is generally fundamental in Yoruba life. In a ritual context it involves the establishment of relationships by an official between the human and the divine worlds. In matters such as marriage it involves the establishment of connections between family groups by the intervention of a middle person.

Such a middle person, or mediator, is known as the **alarena,** and it is her role to ensure that the proper procedures are followed in the intricate negotiations that take place. The particular functions of the *alarena* in this case were to know or to learn about the family of Ogunbode's prospective bride. Such negotiations always take a great deal of time, and the attitude of the bride-to-be's parents is crucial for a successful completion to the maneuvers. But finally the future bride's parents were sufficiently convinced of the good character of Ogunbode, and the parents of Ogunbode about the qualities of the future bride, to proceed with the arrangements. At this stage the future bride's parents arranged a consultation with the diviner, in the presence of the *alarena,* in order to determine the prospects for the marriage, which both families knew had already been determined by the *orisa.*

In this particular case the diviner predicted a good and fruitful marriage for the young couple. Secure in this information, but also to ensure that this destiny came to pass, Ogunbode then went to Ogun's shrine and offered a sacrifice to him and Esu.

All the right actions having been performed, Ogunbode was now ready to talk, for the first time, to his future bride. And his parents, secure in their knowledge that the marriage was destined to be a good one, arranged the bride price, once again through the intermediary. The wedding date was then set. This date could either be seven, fourteen, or twenty-one days after the completion of the final arrangements.

On the day of the wedding separate ceremonies, independent of each other, took place in each of the two family compounds. At the bride's house, aside from the expected festivities of eating and dancing, the women in the compound performed a ritual in which they circled the compound both weeping and chanting *okun iyawa,* which are special sayings such as "I am leaving for my husband's house; pray for me that I will have children."

At the compound of the bridegroom there was general revelry and much eating, drinking, and dancing along with an air of expectancy and excitement as they awaited the appearance of the bride. In both compounds sacrifices were performed by the family head to ensure the blessings of the ancestors on the marriage.

As the time came for the bride to leave she made a special visit to the family head in her own compound. All her attendants accompanied her on this visit, and when they arrived in his presence they respectfully seated themselves around him and silently listened to him pray to the ancestors in her behalf.

In the meantime the women from the bridegroom's compound had come to the bride's compound but had not entered through its gates. Instead they waited outside and could be heard continually chanting, "We are ready to take our wife." Upon hearing this persistent chanting, the bride knew that the time had come to leave. She covered her head and was led out by her own attendants. They introduced her to her new escorts, who then proceeded with her to her new home.

At the entrance of her new home a calabash had been placed in a conspicuous position. She was expected to shatter the calabash with a strong blow. The number of pieces into which the calabash broke was an indication of the number of children she would bear.

Then she entered the compound. There near the entrance her legs were washed, and she was taken to the oldest woman living in the compound. This old woman then led her to the family head of the compound, and she was introduced to him as the most junior wife of the compound. After the introduction to the family head, she was then introduced to the other family members living in the compound. Conspicuous by his absence during these introductions was Ogunbode himself, who was not permitted to be in the compound during these ceremonies. It was more important that his bride become part of the family and recognize where the family and ritual authority lay. In fact Ogunbode was not permitted to have any contact with his new bride on this first day. Only on the following day, perhaps even the third day, was he finally permitted to see her and then, on the evening of that day, to consummate their marriage.

Ogunbode lived to a ripe old age. When his father died, he became the new family head in his compound, and when Ogunbode died all the many members of his family were notified of the event. Unlike the death of a child or a young person (which is a sign of evil afoot), there was no particular urgency to bury him. Thus there was time for all the relatives to gather together from far and near.

Ogunbode had done a great deal of hunting in his lifetime and, therefore, much firing of guns into the air took place. Some of the male members of the family even went on a brief hunting expedition into the forest to try to kill an elephant in his memory.

Very soon after his death his body was thoroughly washed and then laid out in his hut. He was dressed in the finest clothes, and a bed was made out of the best wood available. His grave was dug in the compound. If he had been a Christian he would have had the option of being buried in the local cemetery. But even Yoruba Christians do not particularly care for such a practice. According to Yoruba tradition, burial in the compound, the home of the ancestors as well as the living, is the most desirable. Because Ogunbode was a follower of Ogun, the Christian alternative would not even have been considered.

The grave was dug with the help of the other followers of Ogun. But because Ogunbode died in old age, the *babalawo* was not consulted about the cause of his death. Only when someone dies young would the bereaved members of the family seek to identify the causes of such an untimely event. The priests from Ogun's shrine were in attendance, and after his body was placed on the specially made bed that had already been placed in the grave, they prayed that he would be accepted into the good heaven (*orun rere*) and be judged worthy of taking his place with the ancestors. The priests also made a sacrifice to Ogun. Then the *egungun* emerged from Ogunbode's hut and danced throughout the compound. There was further feasting and dancing, and all the visiting relatives slowly took their leave.

At the burial spot a new shrine was erected, for here a new ancestor would now be called upon and praises would be sung to his name. Ogunbode the ancestor would continue to be in this compound and to make his presence felt in many ways. [See Native Religions of North America pp. 318–20, Judaism pp. 457–69, Christianity pp. 573–86, Hinduism pp. 820–26, Religions of China pp. 1040–54, and Religions of Japan pp. 1163–72 for description and discussion of life histories and personal accounts.]

Transformations of the Religious System

No religious system remains static over time; new conditions and new discoveries change it in significant ways. Perhaps one of the most serious challenges to any system is contact with new religious systems. All religions experience it, and Yoruba religion, like Zulu religion, is no exception. Long before the coming of Islam and Christianity, Yoruba religion was in a constant process of transformation. In fact the term *Yoruba* itself seems to be a rather recent (nineteenth century) innovation in describing a large group of people with important connections to each other.

Islam and Christianity represented two distinctive religious systems, to which the Yoruba responded in a number of ways. Some individuals accepted either Christianity or Islam; others attempted to maintain their traditions; still others developed new religious forms that transformed the recently introduced religious ideas into the terms of the traditional system. These complex responses brought even greater diversity to the religious life of the Yoruba. We shall attempt to deal with one kind of response by discussing the **Aladura** religious movement, which will help us understand how new religious movements are not merely reactions to alien symbolic systems but creative responses to them. Such creativity transforms an old idea into a new one while maintaining much of the previous religious structure.

Although Christianity was reasonably successful in establishing itself in Yorubaland via the mission churches, clearly neither the external control of religious development nor the form of religious worship satisfied all those people who developed an association with Christianity. The Aladura movement in particular shows evidence of such dissatisfaction. Originally this movement was not intended to be an alternative to Christianity but a supplement to the Christian rituals and organization among the Yoruba.[6]

There are two kinds of Aladura churches in the movement, the apostolic and the visionary. The apostolic churches in their organization and activities reflect many of the values and attitudes of the mission churches. The visionary churches are much freer in form. There has been considerable argument among scholars about whether these new religious movements are Christian or not. Certainly the mission churches regarded them with some hostility, seeing them as heretical offshoots. Whether these churches are to be regarded as Christian, however, is beside the point for our purposes: The practices of these churches are interesting in their own right for the information they provide about the creativity and flexibility of the traditional Yoruba religious system. Whether or not Christianity can claim them, they have a clear Yoruba quality. [See Christianity p. 529 for the relationship between the ancient African heritage and black American Christianity.]

We shall focus our attention on one of the Aladura religious movements, that of the Seraphim. In 1925 a young woman, fifteen years of age and named **Abiodun Akinsowon,** had a religious experience while watching the Corpus Christi procession in Lagos. This Christian procession takes place in honor of the presence of Christ in the Eucharist. According to her own account, one of the angels under the canopy that carried the Christian sacrament followed her home. There she became possessed and had visions of the heavens, received revelations, and successfully passed tests given to her in the state of possession. A man named Moses Orimolade was sent to pray for her. Akinsowon then came out of the state of possession and shortly thereafter founded a society with the help of Orimolade. The society's name, **Egbe Serafu** (the Seraphim Society), was given in a vision, and all subsequent additions to the society's thought and practice were given by visions. The society began to flourish and attracted many people by its focus upon the importance of prayer and healing. The society also attacked the traditional Yoruba use of medicine and specific Yoruba gods. There were injunctions against possession of clay representations of the gods and all the many ritual uses of medicine to be found throughout Yorubaland. The movement achieved high visibility by organizing large processions each year to celebrate the original revelation. Though Akinsowon was the receiver of the revelation, Orimolade became the leader of the movement and Akinsowon his assistant. Her official title was Captain Abiodun.

At a certain point a split developed in the movement between Orimolade and Akinsowon. This first split was by no means the last one, and various forms of Seraphim became established in various cities. The movement continues to be strong to the present day, despite its fracture into a number of movements.

From its beginning the movement has emphasized the importance of prayer. The name *Aladura* means "the ones who pray," and members of the movement believe that God always answers the prayers of his followers. The movement has also stressed the importance of dreams and visions, which are viewed as the sources of information and direction. They illuminate the causes of problems and identify courses of action to be taken. As such, they become the means by which the members of the movement can focus their prayers, and a special time is set aside for the recording and reporting of these dreams and visions. We have already made it clear that the Seraphim Society was not intended to replace the Christian churches but to supplement them by stressing the importance of prayer in daily life. Much of its imagery is Christian, but with novel twists. For example, the following hymn is sung:

> Witches cannot control us
> Under the war-staff of Jesus;
> Before the Seraphim,
> All witches jump out of the way;
> Holy Michael (the archangel)
> Is the Captain of our society.

Many of the themes of the Seraphim Society are apparent in these verses, and it would be easy to interpret the movement as a form of Christianity. But such an interpretation would not account for the success of the movement among the Yoruba. Whatever success the movement has had depends on the traditional forms available for transformation in the light of special conditions and upon the characteristics of the people who become involved in the movement. In fact, many Aladura members had been involved in other Christian churches before they were attracted to Aladura practices.

One of the attractions of the movement lies in its reordering of traditional symbols. For example, the existence and power of witches is not denied, but the Archangel Michael can make them jump out of the way. The efficacy of traditional medicines is not denied, but it is superseded by the power of Christ. One of the many reasons that Yoruba Christians were attracted by Aladura was the emphasis upon the healing power of Christ and the opportunities this provided for a new form of "medicine." Though traditional medicine was attacked, the traditional emphasis upon the availability of healing power in a ritual context was not forgotten. Aladura transformed the form of healing, but not its importance, and made the means available for healing.

The Aladura do not practice divination in the traditional manner, but their emphasis upon the importance of dreams and visions reflects a continuing interest in the issues of destiny present in the traditional system. Thus the participant in Aladura is every bit as interested as the tradition-oriented Yoruba in knowing the future and knowing which acts should be performed to assure progress in the right direction. God still decides human fate. Just as there is flexibility in the traditional Yoruba view—though one's fate has been decided, nevertheless adjustments are possible through sacrifice—so this same flexibility is revealed through the means of prayer and visions. God answers all prayers, and prayer changes things.

Processions are frequent in Yoruba life—in the Eje festival, for example, a key element was the procession led by the *oba*—so it should not surprise us that a procession provided the context for the revelation that Abiodun received. Processions are also an important element in many annual festivals. Pilgrimages to sacred groves and sacred hills are widespread annual events; the Aladura churches have transformed these in their own way to express their new religious forms. Nor should we be surprised that it was an angel who provided the medium for Abiodun's revelation; the angel was a physical representation of a source of power, and such representations are fundamental forms of Yoruba religious expression. The angel represents the element of mediation. The prominence of the Archangel Michael can be seen as a transformation of one of the Yoruba mediators. Michael and the other archangels have a religious connection with earth, air, fire, and water and are regarded as guarding the gates of heaven. They assume the same mediating function as some of the *orisa* do in the traditional Yoruba system. All of this demonstrates the flexibility of the religious system of the Yoruba and its internal power to make new forms out of old forms in the presence of new conditions.

Therein lies the power of a religious system in concept and practice—in established and novel ways—to provide an intricate and interesting context for the living of a good life.

4

Individuals, Roles, and Systems

ANY RELIGIOUS TRADITION, seriously considered, presents a puzzle to the student. One of the most intriguing elements in this puzzle is the sheer variety of practices and beliefs one discovers as one begins to pay close attention to the religious tradition under investigation. This diversity is as characteristic of the religions of America as it is of the religions of other times and other places. Readers only have to examine the yellow pages of the telephone directory in their own community to recognize the diversity of names religions have. Of course, from the point of view of the participants of a specific religion, such diversity is relatively minor and trivial. What counts is the underlying unity. But the student of religion cannot afford to ignore such diversity. It must be dealt with.

One way of doing so is to imagine what religion in America looks like to a serious student from another culture. If, for example, a visitor from Yorubaland were to come to America to study Christianity, he or she would experience both familiarity and strangeness. Familiarity would stem from encounters with, and knowledge of, Christianity in Nigeria; we have already learned that Christianity has taken root in Nigeria and that it has assumed not only "standard" but also new forms. The strangeness the visitor would experience would come from the bewildering variety of forms that Christianity takes in America, forms that are not duplicated in Nigeria. This variety would be expressed in many ways: Imposing cathedrals, suburban ranch-roofed churches, and storefronts with exotic-sounding names all compete for attention. Were the student to commence study of any one of these Christian churches, he or she would discover an even more interesting fact. Even within the limits of one church, great variations in practice and belief among the members of the congregation would be found. It would not be at all surprising to hear the Yoruba student exclaim at a certain point: With all this diversity, what is American Christianity really like?

In the same way, an American student studying Yoruba religion in its own context would be struck by the variety of forms that it takes, both within one area and between various areas. Traveling from Lagos to Oyo to Ife would disclose a wide range of practices, beliefs, and institutions. Further complicating the picture are many hybrid forms in which Christianity and Islam seem to have become united with the traditional forms of Yoruba religion. The wider the net is cast, the more complex the picture becomes. At a certain point such a student might very well exclaim: Not only do I not know what Yoruba religion is, but I cannot even identify Christianity in this context!

Given such a complex picture, we could easily conclude that the religious tradition is chaos. Were we to do so, then understanding that religious tradition would be impossible: We can experience chaos, but we cannot understand it. Chaos means that there are no significant connections among the variations that we have discovered.[7]

But neither the Western religions with which you are probably most familiar nor the African religions to which you have been introduced are nearly as chaotic as they appear. The constantly changing, kaleidoscopic image that appears through the viewfinder of our investigations can be analyzed to reveal the principles underlying the variations.

How we analyze this set of variations depends upon what we focus our attention on. There are three useful ways to bring order out of the apparent chaos. Each of them will permit us to make the problem of assembling the puzzle into a reasonably clear picture more manageable. The first way is to analyze the thought and practice of the individual participants in the religious tradition. We have already done some of this by examining the life stages of Bhudaza and Ogunbode. This is the most concrete level of analysis and permits us to get a view of religion as it appears to participants in it. It is also the level at which extreme variations will be discovered.

The second way is to analyze the religious roles available to, and occupied by, the individuals within a religious tradition. The emphasis here will be upon roles, not individuals. It became clear in our chapters on the Zulu and the Yoruba that, even when we do analyze the religious career of an individual, some reference to the roles characteristic of the religion is inevitable. For example, we can talk about the roles of the headman/priest, the diviner, and the herbalist in Zulu religion without any reference to the individuals that occupy those roles.

The third way is to attempt to discover the system of thought that underlies both the practices and the beliefs of individuals and the religious roles and their relationships to each other. Each of these topics—individuals, roles, and systems —will be discussed separately in the following sections.

Individuals

The diversity of a religious tradition becomes most apparent when one talks to its various participants. It seems that no two individuals do exactly the same things, think the same thoughts, or interpret the meaning and significance of what they do and think in the same way. This produces a context fraught with fascination and frustration. Obviously, the variety of beliefs and practices is interesting and can lead to all kinds of questions about the wide range of human behavior. Equally obviously, it is frustrating to attempt to identify in some relatively simple way what is being studied.

Scholars have employed a number of methods to handle these variations. One approach is to search for representative informants, with the hope that some individuals might be found who have given serious thought to the unity underlying the diversity. In fact some scholars appear to have become quite adept at identifying particular people in a religious tradition who have developed a remarkable perceptiveness about the unity underlying the diversity in their tradition. Some of the most interesting work on African religions has been done by scholars who have lived with the Yoruba and the Zulu long enough to be able to identify these individuals and record their interpretations and accounts of their religious traditions.

But there are also problems with such an approach. How do we decide who is representative and who is not? For example, scholars studying the Yoruba have spent a great deal of time speaking to the diviners, and the diviners have not been at all hesitant to tell what Yoruba religion really is. But there are different diviners, not all of whom agree with each other. How do we know who is right? Further, even if the problem of representativeness could be solved, we are still left with the interpretations proposed by these apparent representatives; are the interpretations solutions to the problem of diversity or do they just add to it? Clearly the student of religion cannot ignore what the informant says, for what he or she says is itself an instance of religious reflection that must be accounted for. Such interpretations suggested by the informants must be analyzed; they are part of the puzzle. What is most significant about these interpretations is that they disclose that people within a religious tradition, even when they disagree with each other, do think that there is an underlying unity—even when they cannot articulate it.

Another approach to diversity has been statistical. Given a range of responses to a set of questions we can attempt to identify the frequency with which similar types of answers appear. Some scholars have used the questionnaire method to identify the common practices and beliefs of a wide range of people. This approach is something like taking the pulse of a large group of people at the same time in order to come up with averages. One of the advantages of such an approach is that if it is done over a sufficiently long period of time it will provide a picture not only of continuity but also of change over time.

But this statistical approach also brings problems. What questions are to appear on the questionnaire? To ask a question means that we will be making one or more assumptions. For example, if the question is about the relationship between political and religious institutions, the question might assume a radical discontinuity between these forms of human behavior.

But whether the student of African religions relies on representative informants or statistical methods or some other approach in order to deal with the diversity within a religious tradition, he or she will discover one very important fact, namely, that different individuals participate in a religion to different degrees and in different ways. In other words, there will be levels of participation in a religion and there will be different kinds of participation in that religious tradition. Some people will, according to their own lights, faithfully practice all or nearly all of the rites and duties made available to them in their own context. Others will practice only some of these rites and duties. And there will be a wide range between these extremes. It will be important to identify some of the reasons for varying degrees of participation.

Not all of the reasons will have to do with interest or commitment. For example, a Zulu working in the Johannesburg gold mines will not perform all of the rituals that he would if he were still living in the village in Zululand. And we already know why from our study of the locus of religious action: In Zulu religion the primary places for ritual activity are in the village and on the sacred hills. The village is the abode of the ancestors, and it is there that they must be approached; they cannot be approached hundreds of miles away in a mining compound in Johannesburg. On the other hand, this Zulu mine worker might very well be found practicing rituals of sorcery and witchcraft. In fact, being removed from the environment of the ancestors automatically exposes him to the power of sorcerers and witches, and the best way to fight sorcery under such conditions of dislocation is with sorcery. So an examination of the context of the religious life of this particular Zulu will disclose that his actions differ both in range and in kind. In fact, the amaNazaretha church in Johannesburg might provide him with a context for his religious life that both assures him of some continuity between his past and his present and (because of its differences with traditional Zulu religion) makes sense in such a strange situation.

In the case of the Yoruba a similar distinction between kind and degree of participation can be made. For example, a bank clerk working in the Nigerian city of Lagos, who was born and brought up in the city of Oyo, may occasionally make offerings at one or more of the many Yoruba shrines in Lagos. She may occasionally also consult a diviner. But her primary religious identification may still be with the particular traditions of Oyo. In spite of this sense of identifications she might also spend some of her religious energies in a Baptist church in Lagos. Yet whenever she returns to Oyo she might not only make offerings to her ancestors in the family compound but, if the season is right, participate in one of the annual festivals for Ogun. Thus to the student of African religions she might identify herself as a Christian of Baptist persuasion and yet be married in the traditional Yoruba manner characteristic of Oyo and expect to be buried not in the Christian cemetery but in the family compound according to Yoruba custom. Her degree of participation in Yoruba religion will differ from the family head who has remained in Oyo, and the kind of participation will differ also, because she is attempting to live in a religious world that is both Christian and Yoruba simultaneously.

But individuals come and go, and Zulu and Yoruba religion remain. It is at this juncture that we need to recognize that there is more to a religion than the practices and beliefs of individuals. What this more is becomes clearer as we begin to examine the roles characteristically present in a religion.

Roles

Whereas a religious individual participates in a religious tradition according to circumstance, custom, and interest, the various roles characteristic of the religious system in which he or she participates are not nearly as flexible. There are usually "standard" roles in the religion that are defined by the tradition and not by the individuals who have a relationship to it. And there should be nothing surprising about this. The fact that there is a headman/priest, a diviner, a heaven-herd, and an herbalist in Zulu religion is not decided by a particular Zulu. These roles were there before they were born, and unless the religion completely disintegrates in their lifetime, the roles will be there after they have died. Of course, if the particular Zulu happens to be Isaiah Shembe and has a revelation and a call to establish a new form of worship, then what he or she does might very well have an impact on the total religious system. Under the impact of an Isaiah Shembe, the total system might change in some way or it might assume a number of different forms that continue on together. It is clear that some of the variation in a religious tradition can be accounted for by new experiences and new revelations that permit the establishment of new or transformed systems of thought and action. What all of this shows, then, is that, apart from the participation of individuals, and because of new revelations and new interpretations, a religious system has a history, which is to say that it can and does change. Both Zulu and Yoruba religion have been a long time in the making, and the many roles they contain are the result of a complex transmission of practices from generation to generation.

As we have indicated, it is possible for such a system, despite its long history, to collapse, and it will do so if it does not make sense to a sufficient number of individuals. No system can continue if the roles defined by the religious system are not occupied by individuals. But given a living religion with a history, we can examine the roles themselves and learn something about that religion without having to inspect what goes on in the mental life of the participants (although we can never afford to ignore this level of analysis in the long run).

When we begin to examine the roles in Zulu and Yoruba religion one of the first discoveries we make is that no role in either religion makes sense in isolation. For example, to attempt to understand the role of the heaven-herd in the religious system of the Zulu without reference to the other seven roles leaves us with a picture of a disturbed individual standing in splendid isolation on a mountaintop speaking to bad weather. But when we examine the eight roles in their relationship to each other, we know that, in the context of the religious system of the Zulu, the heaven-herd and the headman/priest have opposite roles. The heaven-herd has a ritual relationship with the God of the Sky, whereas the headman/priest is the ritual mediator between the ancestors and the people of the village. But we also know that neither of these ritual functions is exclusively identified with the heaven-herd or the headman/priest. The supplicant also has

access to the God of the Sky, and the diviner can communicate with the ancestors on behalf of the people. In fact, once we know what the sources of power
in Zulu religion are we can show that for each source of power there is a dual
set of roles available in the system to make a connection between the human
and the other world.

The more we learn about the relationships among the roles the more we
can discover about the complex system of thought that is expressed not only in
what the Zulu and the Yoruba say but in what they do and what they take as
important. In fact, examining the roles in their complex relationships leads us
to the recognition that there is a structure to a religious tradition and that such
a structure has a history. However we analyze this structure, we will discover
that questions about one element will lead to questions about other elements.
For example, questions about the role of the Zulu herbalist will lead to questions
about the ritual relationships between the specialists in medicine and the
patients. They will also lead to questions about the status of medicine as a power
and to questions about the destructive use of medicine in sorcery and witchcraft. And questions about sorcery and witchcraft will lead to questions about
the nature and power of evil; the relationship between the power of the God of
the Sky, medicine, and evil; and the relationship of all these to the power of the
ancestors. They will also make possible questions about Zulu views of the
causes of evil and the role that diviners play in disclosing good and evil.

In the structure of Yoruba religion a similar chain of questioning, based
upon our identification of Yoruba ritual roles, can be undertaken. Because the
roles vary from situation to situation, and because not all roles identified in
chapter 3 are found in every variant, we can analyze the roles according to one
or more of their functions. For example, mediation is a characteristic of Yoruba
religion. Many of the roles provide the context and conduit for specific relationships that individual Yoruba are attempting to establish between themselves and
the sources of power. Examining the mediating function of a particular role will
give us information not only about the experience of the individual Yoruba worshiper but also about the way that the role of the worshiper becomes connected
via the mediation of the *babalawo* to the role of Olorun, Esu, and a particular
sorcerer.

Let us examine, for example, the case of a worshiper who is faced with a
major decision about her occupation. She has decided to move from the city of
Oyo to Lagos to teach in a school. This worshiper has focused her religious energies on the god Ogun. She has regularly sacrificed to him (and to Esu); she has
regularly participated in his festivals. How does the role of such a worshiper
make a connection with the world of the gods? By paying a visit to the diviner
or *babalawo*. The diviner represents the mediating role between the worshiper
and her destiny. We already know that her destiny has been determined in the
other world. So the diviner, on the basis of manipulating the kola nuts, will provide her with the knowledge of how to decide about the move. But the diviner
will also recommend that she make an offering to Ogun and Esu, for only Ogun
gives the power to act. But even this power to act can be interfered with by Esu,

so an offering must be made to him as well. This offering will be made at a local shrine to Ogun, and at that shrine there will be a priest who is a mediator between the worshiper and Ogun. Thus the role of the diviner becomes linked with the role of the priest. But we also know that it is Orunmila, not Ogun, who is responsible for human destiny and divination that provides access to it. And so in the other world Ogun mediates between Orunmila and the priest who is mediating between the worshiper and Ogun. But what is most interesting of all is that, from a Yoruba point of view, the role of Ogun and Orunmila depends upon the role of the worshiper. The *orisa* depend upon the offerings for their power. They would be diminished without the sacrifices.

Another example of how the roles work and what they tell us about the structure of Yoruba religion, and the system of thought that such a structure represents, is that of a man beset by a serious illness. Upon consultation with the *babalawo,* the worshiper might discover that sorcery is involved. Now, in Yoruba religion sorcerers are human, not divine, powers; they are "children of the world." They are able to accomplish what they do by virtue of the destructive resources within the human personality and not by a relationship to the *orisa.* They do not have to harness special evil powers or forces; they simply have to be adept at mischief and destruction. Worshipers in such a situation have a number of options available to them: They might attempt to counter sorcery with sorcery. Or they might try to deal with the threat by taking medicine from the *oloogun,* the specialist in medicine. Or they might attempt to call upon the power of the *orisa.* They might even call upon the power of the Aladura church, which is known for its power over sorcerers and witches. But whatever they do, they will consult the *babalawo,* for it is this kind of priest who has access to knowledge about the causes of the illness.

What we discover, then, is that there is a variety of roles relevant to this situation, that these roles have a connection with each other, and that the sources of power made available by the ritual roles can be in either heaven or earth. Not only is understanding the roles in all these examples impossible without seeing how they all fit together, but analyzing the practice of one role in one situation inevitably leads to the practice of another. So in either Zululand or Yorubaland, if you come across a diviner performing rituals, you will sooner or later discover that other roles have come into play as well.

But even a thorough knowledge of all the roles in all their contexts will not be adequate for understanding these two religions. We shall still have only partial knowledge of what these religions are. The reason has already become apparent: We could not discuss the roles in either Zulu or Yoruba religion apart from their reference to the sources of power that make them important to the individuals who occupy them. Individuals and roles are elements in a system that gives them their coherence and unity—the roles, and the experiences of individuals in all their variety, are expressions of a coherent system of thought. To discover what this system of thought is like is crucial, therefore, for understanding how the roles obtain their definition and the individuals their experience.

Systems

How, then, do we understand and describe such a system? Many analogies have been available, but one of the most useful is that of a language.[8] A language has variants, a structure, and a dynamics. The variants of a language are known as dialects; these can be regional, occupational, or a matter of status or social level. In fact, one way of defining a language is as the sum of its variants. The structure of a language can be described in a number of ways. At its most basic level of analysis, a language consists of a set of sounds combined to form words. These words are combined to form sentences, and the sentences are combined to form either oral or written discourse. The dynamics of a language can be described by paying attention to the many uses to which it is put by its speakers. Most generally the dynamics disclose that language is a vehicle for both thought and action.

Like a language, a religious system has variants, as we have already seen in our discussion of the beliefs and practices of individuals. Such variants can be regional or a matter of religious roles or degree and level of participation. A religion, like a language, can also be defined as the sum of its variants. Where and when we analyze it makes a difference in what we discover. But just because there are variants does not mean that these variants are unrelated to each other. Just as the various English dialects are still English, so the variants of Yoruba religion and Zulu religion are still Yoruba and Zulu, respectively. In fact, one way of looking at these many variants of each tradition is to understand them as transformations of each other, as different arrangements of the elements that they have in common. One way of describing these elements is as a worldview; this worldview can be expressed in many different ways, in many variants. Different expressions bring into focus different arrangements of the elements. For example, in the Yoruba worldview, there are Olorun, the *orisa,* the ancestors, and humans and all other forms of life. Each of these is a source of power, and ideally, each exists in a relationship of equilibrium with the others. But in a particular place, at a particular time, for particular reasons, only one of the *orisa* or one of the ancestors may be the focus of ritual action. And it is quite possible that, at least for a time, an entire tradition might develop around one source of power almost to the exclusion of all the others. Nevertheless, there will still be subtle ways in which the other sources of power are recognized and acknowledged.

We must, however, look beyond these variants in order to discover other interesting properties of the religions of Africa. We must also examine their structure and dynamics.

A structural analysis of a religious system, such as that of the Yoruba, will disclose that a religion, like a language, consists of a set of elements. These elements are the individual acts that occur in the course of religious behavior in general and ritual behavior in particular. A ritual consists of a set of acts. When we observe a sequence of these acts, we are, in fact, observing a ritual in progress. For example, if one is studying the marriage rites, one can show how individual acts form a sequence of acts and how a number of sequences form a very complex ceremony. We can concentrate on an analysis of the individual acts and talk about their meaning and importance, or we can concentrate upon a particular sequence of acts and show how they accomplish a specific objective—for example, how they change a man and a woman from the status of being unmarried to the status of being married, or how being married is part of an even larger picture that describes an entire style of life.

Paying attention to the dynamics of a religious system will clarify more of its characteristics, especially when we keep the language analogy in mind. Consider the many uses to which the sentences in a language can be put. We can ask questions and give answers. We can prohibit actions, command attention, tell the truth, conceal our motives, invent elaborate metaphors, speak in riddles, describe events, and imagine possible and impossible worlds. We can communicate or deliberately misinform, express our emotions, explain our theories, and state our beliefs. We can even play with words. In fact, the power of a language lies in its flexibility.

A religious system is equally flexible. Just as it is a mistake to think of a language as having only one purpose, so it is a mistake to think of religion as having but a single purpose. Its infinitely large set of purposes is discovered according to the categories that one brings to the analysis. And it can be analyzed in its own terms or in terms originating outside of it. Consider, for example, Zulu religion in the context of a system of oppression. Such a religion in one of its variants can be analyzed in its own terms. So that when the Zulu speaks about power (*amandla*) as being necessary to overthrow the oppressors, such an appeal can be interpreted in Zulu terms as being a call to the ancestors, or the God of the Sky, or the power of medicine, or all of these together, to get rid of the evils of apartheid. But it is also possible to analyze this call to overthrow the oppressors in political and economic terms that are "outside" the Zulu system of thought. Whichever way we proceed in such a case we must be careful not to conclude that the Zulu religion is nothing but a political system, for it means more than that to the Zulu people, and, in fact, it is more than that in any adequate theory of the role that religion plays in a human society.

Analyzing a particular religious system by taking into account the complex and intricate relationships among the roles occupied by individuals and the kinds and levels of religious power the people believe to be real leads to the discovery of its importance for shaping human life for good or ill. And one can understand how its flexible forms can be used for composing compelling narratives, providing solace and comfort in time of need, enhancing the human capacity for reflection and meditation, encouraging the emergence of structures for overthrowing the oppressors, and even causing families and societies to be torn asunder. Religion can become a vehicle for the expression of lofty and abstract thoughts, or an occasion for the cruel, the mean, and the petty.

Perhaps the most compelling analogy between a language and a religion is that a religion, like a language, provides a vehicle or a context for thought. In

the case of a religion, it is not only what people say within the context of a particular ritual or series of rituals, or what they say about a particular ritual or
series of rituals, that shows that we are dealing with a system of thought. The
religion of the particular people we are studying is itself the direct vehicle for
the expression of their thoughts. In other words, the way the rituals fit together
and the way the various roles mesh tell us something about how the people
understand themselves and their place in the world. Ritual actions, roles, and
relationships are, in fact, like statements, a special language expressing a special
form of knowledge. To understand how the religious system fits together is to
know something about the view of the world that the system represents.

Learning about what the Yoruba and the Zulu take to be knowledge comes
not only by talking to their representatives but by seeing what they do, how they
organize their lives, how they divide their time, what places they venerate, what
kind of relationships they value, what they welcome and what they avoid. Chapters 2 and 3 have provided us with some of the information needed to engage
in this task of analysis.

In what follows we shall attempt to reveal that on the basis of the information we possess we can show how these two religious systems can be understood
as systems of thought that provide answers to some quite specific questions.
These are: (1) What is real? (2) What is important? (3) What is a person? (4) What
is dangerous? (5) What is the form for maintaining right relationships with all
sources of power?

Let us start with the Yoruba. If we grant that there is something called the
Yoruba religious system and that it is contained not only in Yoruba words but
also in Yoruba rituals, roles, and relationships, then there are five answers to the
five key questions listed above. The first question is, What is real? The Yoruba
answer is both simple and complex. On the simple level it is that whatever has
power is real. This answer is revealed not only in what the Yoruba say but in
what they do. Their deeds as well as their words show what they regard as having power, namely Olorun, the *orisa,* the leaders of the society, and every individual person.

On the most fundamental level Olorun, the High God, is real by virtue of
his power. Such power has been expressed in the creation of the world and the
founding of the city of Ife. The Yoruba, no matter what the change in political
structure, no matter where the center of earthly authority lies, treat the city of
Ife as the place where the High God has revealed his power and intentions. Now,
by virtue of the fact that Olorun is real because of his power, other forms derive
their reality and power from him and become sources of power also. So because
the *orisa* are real and exert power, the ancestors, kings, chiefs, diviners, family
heads, and ultimately every individual human being has power. In addition
other forms of life have power as well. Even inanimate objects, under certain
ritual conditions, are sources of power. Medicine is particularly powerful for
both good and ill. Even witches and sorcerers are sources of power. But there
is an important difference between the power of witches and sorcerers and all
the other kinds. All the other kinds of power are part of a closely interrelated

network. The major characteristic of this network is that unless it is disrupted it exists in a state of balance or equilibrium. Sorcerers and witches are perverted human beings; something has gone wrong with them or inside them. As a consequence, they can upset the balance of powers with disastrous results for individual and community.

The second question to which the system provides an answer is, What is important? The Yoruba answer is that it is important for human beings to discover their destiny and live according to it. Once again, this answer is not simply a verbal one elicited from Yoruba still trying to be faithful to their tradition. Rather, it emerges from analyzing what the Yoruba do at key moments of life such as birth, marriage, and death, and from understanding the value they place on the roles and relationships among the roles in their society. The diviner aids in the discovery of personal destiny and its relationship to social destiny. The diviner, by manipulating the kola nuts and connecting their numbers to the memorized texts handed down by the tradition, connects heaven and earth. On the personal level destiny is nothing but the course of the individual's life starting and ending with the world of the gods. On the social level destiny is the group fulfilling its obligations to all sources of power in heaven and on earth. That means respecting elders; deferring to authority; valuing traditional places, times, roles, and arrangements; and maintaining the cohesion and solidarity of the group.

The third question is, What is a person? A person is a living being with a destiny determined in heaven. A person can either be balanced or unbalanced. A balanced person is one who "feeds his head," who makes the appropriate offerings to *orisa* and ancestors at their shrines and recognizes their presence within his or her own being. These sources of power are both far away and as close as one's breath. They are both inside and outside. To the extent that they are inside, the person is a source of power with the ability to make a difference in and to the world.

A balanced person honors the ancestors. That means ensuring that they are buried in the right place and in the appropriate way. It also means continuing to revere them by making offerings to them, by consulting them about important decisions, by keeping them in memory, and by not offending them in any way.

A balanced person performs the rituals to the *orisa* and does not forget Esu. Which *orisa* one worships is a matter of history, of geography, and of personal choice. In fact, the diversity in Yoruba religion can be traced partly to this principle, namely, that one's location in space determines the range of ritual choices and ritual objects to which one can become related.

Finally, a balanced person is one who uses his or her own power to maintain the *orisa* by participating in the rites and festivals, making offerings to the *orisa* and the ancestors, and preserving the traditions of the society. Without such human use of power, the gods begin to lose their power and disappear from the scene.

An unbalanced person is an *omoraiye,* a "child of the earth." This means a number of things. It means, first of all, the perversion of human power for destructive ends—humans turning on humans to harm and destroy them. It means one who has been cut off from heaven and lives only off the turmoil created by being out of balance. It means acting in the terms of witchcraft and sorcery.

The discussion of an unbalanced person leads naturally, then, to the fourth question to which the religious system of the Yoruba provides an answer: What is dangerous? Anything that upsets the intricate balances among the many sources of power in heaven and earth is dangerous. Literally this means giving offense to any source of power, whether this be another human, an ancestor, or an *orisa*. And how does one give offense? By failing to recognize what is real, do what is important (and not do what is forbidden), and live the way a person in balance should live. A strong sense of tradition will show the way, and divination will provide the details.

The fifth question is, What is the form for maintaining right relationships with all sources of power? The Yoruba answer is mediation. Mediating persons, roles, and objects provide the forms for maintaining such relationships, whether it is the *alarena* mediating a wedding contract, the priest mediating a ritual offering, a *babalawo* mediating a decision concerning destiny, or a set of kola nuts mediating an offense. In each case there is an appropriate form available for the Yoruba person who wishes to remain in balance with that vast and intricate network that establishes the structure of the world in which he or she lives.

It can be shown that the same questions are answered by the Zulu system of religion. As we proceed, we shall also be able to note certain similarities between the Zulu and the Yoruba forms of thought, as well as important differences. What we cannot fail to notice is that, if the analysis presented here is correct, then there is no basis for regarding these two societies as being primitive or irrational or bizarre.

To the first question, What is real? the Zulu answer at the lowest level is remarkably similar to the Yoruba. Whatever has power (*amandla*) is real. But when we move up a level and analyze what is meant by the term *power*, that is, what the term applies to, then we note both important similarities and important differences between the two systems of thought. What has power in the Zulu system is the God of the Sky, the ancestors, and medicine. Sorcerers and witches have a derived power, but, whereas in Yoruba religion such beings are perverted human beings, in Zulu religion they are perversions of the total system of powers. Furthermore, whereas in the Yoruba system the *orisa* play an important and separate role from both the High God and the ancestors, in the Zulu system no such separate source of power is available. This is not to say that there is no complexity in the God of the Sky. As we have already indicated in the chapter on the Zulu religious system, the Princess of the Sky adds a dimension to the character of the source of power that the God of the Sky represents. But when we examine the actual rituals the Zulu perform, we see that only a certain set of women has ritual access to such a source of power.

The Zulu system also provides an answer to the second question, What is important? Whereas the Yoruba system implies that it is important for a human being to discover his or her destiny and live according to it, the Zulu system implies that it is important for a human being to uncover the seeds of destruction that if permitted to grow will distort the orderly arrangements of social life. The method for the discovery of destructive elements and the maintenance of order can be either divination or the ordeal. Which of these it is depends upon the status, position, and nature of the people involved. For example, in the Zulu grouping-up ceremony the ordeal overcomes destructive elements and establishes order; whereas in the funeral ceremony divination uncovers the causes of illness and death (and medicine restores order). The notion of personal destiny, so crucial to Yoruba belief and practice, does not enter into the Zulu religious system. As a consequence of this emphasis upon order, individualism is less possible in Zulu society than in Yoruba. Among the Yoruba there is always that element of choice, tied, of course, to the fact that each person does have a destiny decided in heaven.

The third question is, What is a person? To the Zulu system, a person is a social being with intricate relationships and obligations to the members of the village and to the ancestors who dwell there. A person is also one who acknowledges that all the villages are intricately related to each other by custom, ceremony, marriage, and tradition. There are some ancestors who not only have a primary identification with a particular village but an identification with all the Zulu people. These ancestors are acknowledged in the praise songs that all Zulu know. Although it is the obligation of a particular clan to remember, chant, and preserve these songs about the great cultural heroes, they are the heroes of all.

Thus, though the concept of balance and equilibrium is present, the possibility of that balance being disrupted is always real; the emphasis is not on balance but on praising the ancestors in song and maintaining right relationships with them.

The fourth question is, What is dangerous? For the Zulu, it is whatever gives offense to the ancestors. To give offense to the ancestors by not "bringing them home," by not acknowledging them in the appropriate rites in the *umsamo,* by arranging marriages without taking into account the ruptures caused by new alliances are all examples of giving offense. This is doubly dangerous because, not only can the ancestors punish the offender, but by giving offense the offender rends the fabric of social life and opens the world to perversion of the sources of power exemplified in the activity of sorcerers and witches. In such a situation even the ancestors may be rendered ineffective.

The fifth question is, What is the form for maintaining right relationships with all sources of power? The answer to this question depends upon the two contexts for Zulu ritual acts. As we have seen in chapter 2, these are the hills and the village. The hills are a natural, and the village a social, environment for religious action. Both provide places for communion with sacred power. In the natural environment the heaven-herd and the supplicant approach the God of the Sky directly and without mediation. So when the God of the Sky is the source of power with which right relationships must be established, the form is one of solitariness and isolation, away from the human, social world in the hills of God.

But when the ancestors are the source of power, the form is one of group activity mediated in every case by the precisely defined roles of the religious system. There is little question that this second context is in the foreground of Zulu religion. This is why the Zulu, although they acknowledge the importance of the God of the Sky in the creation of the natural world and the making of the first human, do not spend much time emphasizing this. Instead, the social world and the solidarity required of it are at the center of the stage. There are historical reasons for this view that lie deep in Zulu experience. These reasons go all the way back to Shaka's emphasis upon uniting many clans into one Zulu kingdom. Throughout their history there were persistent attempts from within the Zulu kingdom to destroy such solidarity. And their encounter with the territorial designs of the colonial powers demonstrated its importance again.

To this day, the Zulu continue to emphasize such solidarity and to express it in their relationships both with the white people of South Africa and with the neighboring African groups possessing traditions of their own.

Tradition and Transformation

The answers to these questions provided by the two systems of thought show that any claim that all African religions are alike is a very superficial one. On the contrary, they show different understandings of what the world is like and the place and power that humans have in it. There are obviously similarities—for example, both include the ancestors as an important source of power, and both take sorcery and witchcraft very seriously—but the systems differ greatly in the way they fit together. We are obviously dealing with two different religions with different elements and different views about how life is to be lived and reflected upon.

In the contemporary situation both Zulu and Yoruba face a complex future. Not only do both peoples have continuing and complex relationships with the other indigenous people around them, but they also have continuing and complex relationships with the worlds of Christianity and Islam. In addition, secular modes of thought and action that propose new concepts of power and new relationships to place and role continue to make their presence felt. It seems clear that Zulu and Yoruba systems of thought and action are flexible enough to respond to these different systems in a creative and responsible manner. Our discussion of traditions in transformation and transformations in tradition have attempted to provide a form for analyzing this process and set of relationships.

There is a reemphasis upon the importance of their traditions among the many peoples of Nigeria today. In this context the Yoruba people are no exception. At the same time, in Nigeria generally and among the Yoruba in particular there is an emphasis upon new styles of decision making, new ways of advancing knowledge, new ways of developing relationships with the peoples of Africa and the rest of the world. It is as if there is a double movement. As a relief from the strictures of colonialism there is a reemphasis upon Yoruba identity and the traditions that have defined it. The Yoruba have demonstrated a new pride in their cultural and religious heritage. At the same time new forms of thought, action, and organization continue to be taken seriously. We can expect this double movement of reappropriation and new appropriation to continue. Worldviews are always in the making. But whatever the form and content of this new worldview, we can reasonably expect that the Yoruba religious system will play a formative role in that process of transformation.

Among the Zulu there is also an acknowledgment of the importance of tradition. But whereas the Yoruba have experienced liberation from colonialism, none of the black people of South Africa, including the Zulu, have had this experience; they continue to live under the system of apartheid, although by 1990 this system finally began to crumble. In a situation of large-scale white oppression symbolized by the system of apartheid there is an increasing tendency among some Zulu leaders to modify the emphasis upon Zulu identity with an increasing emphasis upon the unity of all the oppressed peoples of South Africa. Nevertheless, even those who emphasize unity continue to draw on a set of symbols and images to apply to a revolutionary situation. One of these symbols has already achieved prominence in the resistance movement, as this was represented in the African National Congress. The Zulu word *amandla* (power) has become a symbol that signals not only that the Zulu have resources for resistance but that all the oppressed people of South Africa have similar resources. Accommodation is giving way to resistance, both passive and active. And other African peoples on the rest of the continent are beginning to support such resistance with action, not mere words. Whatever new worlds of thought and action emerge in both the Yoruba and the Zulu societies, they will have a continuity with the great traditions that characterize these two religions of Africa and illustrate the process of traditions in transformation and transformations in tradition.

Study Questions

Before you begin to read this part, take a mental inventory of what you know and think about Africa. What images do you have of Africa and African people? Make a list of African "things" that you know—music, dance, drums, masks, clothing, houses, and so on. What would you imagine religion in Africa to be like? Keep these images and things in mind as you read this section and develop new notions about Africa.

CHAPTER 1

Introduction

1. How is Africa usually perceived? What are the realities of Africa?
2. What is the meaning of the term *primitive religions* and why does the author prefer not to use this term?
3. Why are we all Africans?
4. What are the "marks of human civilization"?
5. What does the author mean by "religious system" and "religious action"?

CHAPTER 2

The Zulu and Their Religious Tradition

1. In what sense do the Zulu live and act in a religious world?
2. How does the Zulu village symbolize important aspects of the Zulu religious system?
3. Analyze the Zulu religious significance of the Zulu village as diagrammed in figure 1-1.
4. What are the major Zulu religious roles?
5. What are the major Zulu religious powers?
6. How do the religious acts relate roles and powers?
7. Is an ancestor a god?
8. Analyze the Zulu religious system as diagrammed in figure 1-2.
9. What does the term *transformation* mean, and how does this concept enable us to understand important aspects of Zulu religion?
10. In what sense was Isaiah Shembe a Christian?
11. How are religion and politics related in the Zulu religious system?
12. Why do the Zulu not mention someone killed by lightning?

CHAPTER 3

The Yoruba and Their Religious Tradition

1. In what sense are there different levels of religious action among the Yoruba?
2. What are the major religious roles among the Yoruba?
3. What are the major religious powers among the Yoruba?
4. How do the religious acts relate roles and powers?
5. How do Yoruba witchcraft and sorcery differ from Zulu witchcraft and sorcery?
6. How does the Yoruba High God compare with the Zulu God of the Sky?
7. What is Esu like? Would he make sense in a Zulu context?
8. What similarities and differences are there between Zulu and Yoruba medicine?
9. Why are witches women in both Yoruba and Zulu religion?
10. What is divination?
11. What is mediation? What role does it play in Yoruba religion? How would Yoruba religion look without it?
12. Analyze the Yoruba religious system as diagrammed in figure 1-3.
13. What similarities and differences are there between Yoruba and Zulu ancestors? What would both religions look like without them?
14. How does transformation take place in the Yoruba religious system as seen in the Aladura religious movements?

CHAPTER 4

Individuals, Roles, and Systems

1. What is a religious system?
2. Why is a religious system like a language?
3. What is the difference between an individual and a role in a religious system?
4. What is real, important, personal, dangerous, and desirable for Zulu and Yoruba?
5. What does the concept of primitive mean? Does the term apply to the two religions you have studied?
6. If you were able to change these two religions in any way how would you change them?

Recall the mental inventory of African images and things that you made before reading this work. What is there in African religion that is most like your own religious tradition? What in African religion is most different from your own tradition? What is most interesting? How has your understanding of Africa changed as a result of reading this section? Can you now imagine yourself participating in African religion?

Notes

My indebtedness runs deep. For the Zulu material, three works provided the informative bedrock on which my superstructure was built. These are Eileen Jensen Krige's classic *The Social System of the Zulus,* Axel-Ivar Berglund's illuminating *Zulu Thought-Patterns and Symbolism,* and Bengt G. M. Sundkler's *Bantu Prophets in South Africa.* Each of these three volumes is a treasure house of information and detailed description of ritual practices and beliefs. I recommend them to all students who wish to move beyond this introductory text.

After reading through many books on the Yoruba, I decided that three of them provided particularly significant information about the Yoruba religious system. These are J. Omosade Awolalu's *Yoruba Beliefs and Sacrificial Rites,* E. Bolaji Idowu's *Olodumare: God in Yoruba Belief,* and J. D. Y. Peel's *Aladura: A Religious Movement Among the Yoruba.* Each is an outstanding work and provides the kind of precise detail necessary for general summaries. But all the books listed in the selected reading list were helpful in the formative stages of this work.

I am also indebted to the Yoruba people who so willingly acted as informants to me. I am particularly grateful to Emmanuel Oladepo Alaye, who, over a three-month period, spent many hours a week giving me firsthand information about his traditions. He was at all times patient and gracious.

1. See Axel-Ivar Berglund, *Zulu Thought-Patterns and Symbolism* (London: C. Hurst, 1976), 35 for a discussion of the use of praise names for Umvelinqangi.
2. For a detailed analysis of funeral practices see Eileen Jensen Krige, *The Social System of the Zulus,* 2d ed. (Pietermaritzburg: Shuter & Shooter, 1950), 159–75.
3. The best complete description of the rites of passage can be found in Krige, *Social System,* 81–119.
4. See especially J. S. Eades, *The Yoruba Today* (Cambridge: Cambridge University Press, 1980) and J. Omosade Awolalu, *Yoruba Beliefs and Sacrificial Rites* (London: Longman, 1979).
5. For a firsthand description of the Eje festival see Awolalu, *Yoruba Beliefs,* 144–47.
6. The most thorough and systematic treatment of this movement remains J. D. Y. Peel, *Aladura: A Religious Movement Among the Yoruba* (Oxford: Oxford University Press, 1968).
7. For an interesting theory of how traditional knowledge is acquired, see Pascal Boyer, *Tradition as Truth and Communication* (Cambridge: Cambridge University Press, 1990).
8. For a recent development of this idea, see E. Thomas Lawson and Robert N. McCauley, *Rethinking Religion: Connecting Cognition and Culture* (Cambridge: Cambridge University Press, 1990).

Glossary

A note on Zulu terms. Zulu nouns consist of a root with a prefix that indicates whether the word is singular or plural. So the root *-ntu* is singular when *umu-* is added to it to form *umuntu*. When *aba-* is added it comes the plural *abantu*. Similarly, *isi-* is singular, *izi-* is plural. So *isibongo* and *izibongo* are the singular and plural forms of the word meaning "praise songs." (One convention is to capitalize *the stem,* as in "aBantu.")

abantu The Zulu word for "the people." This name occurs in all of the Bantu languages and has the same meaning in all of them.
abathakati The Zulu name for a witch, that special person who manipulates powers for evil and destructive ends.
Afrikaaner One of the two groups of white South Africans who trace their ancestry to the Dutch settlers who arrived at the Cape in 1652. The other group is known as "English-speaking South Africans," whose ancestors arrived in 1820 and became known as the 1820 settlers.
Aiye (Aye) The earth, the abode of all creatures.
Akinsowon, Abiodun The young Yoruba woman who had a revelation that became the foundation for the Aladura Movement.
Aladura A new religious movement among the Yoruba that has connections with both traditional and Christian religious forms. Literally it means: "those who pray."
alarena A mediator between Yoruba families arranging a marriage.
amalozi, amakhosi, amathonga Zulu words referring to the ancestors, shades, or spirits.
amandla The Zulu word meaning "power." The word is used both literally and figuratively. Power appears in four forms: the God of the Sky, the ancestors, medicine, and evil. Recently it has also been used as a political slogan as in "power to the people."
apartheid The policy and doctrine of the South African white minority government ensuring that people of different ethnic origin, but especially white and black, be kept separate from each other socially, geographically, and culturally.
ara In Yoruba thought this term refers to the physical aspect of a person.
assegai The Zulu term for the traditional Zulu spear.
aworo A Yoruba word for priest, the person qualified to perform ritual actions on behalf of others.
babalawo The Yoruba word for diviner, the one who performs special rites such as *ifa*. Literally it means: "father of secret things."
bantu The same word as *abantu* but in anglicized form.
Boer The white settlers of Dutch extraction who colonized southern Africa in the seventeenth century; another name for Afrikaaner, but emphasizing the fact that the Afrikaaners were originally and predominantly farmers. The Boer War was a conflict between the British and the Afrikaaners, or Boers.

divination A technique used by a religious specialist for identifying both the cause of a personal or social problem and the means for solving it or predicting its outcome, often using special methods such as throwing bones or manipulating cowrie shells or kola nuts.

diviner One who is qualified to engage in the art of divination, the activity of deriving information from reading signs.

Egbe Serafu The Seraphim Society among the Yoruba based upon the revelation to Abiodun Akinsowon about the way of prayer.

egungun A Yoruba masked dancer (masquerader).

Eje The Yoruba New Yam festival.

elegun A Yoruba person who is a medium for spirits and who becomes possessed by them.

emi Power that gives life to the body. Literally it means: "breath."

Esu A Yoruba deity with both good and evil qualities, also known as a trickster. The Yoruba believed it essential to sacrifice to him.

Ethiopian church A form of Christianity with special African roots, especially in Ethiopia, that has spread to other parts of Africa including South Africa.

God of the Sky The supreme deity of the Zulu people. He is called Umvelinqangi and also frequently is simply referred to as *inkosi*, which means "Chief" or "King."

heaven-herd (*izinyanga zezulu*) The religious specialist in Zulu religion who is responsible for controlling the weather.

herbalist (*izinyanga zemithi*) A medical specialist with knowledge of what will cure and what will harm people.

High God Another name used by religion scholars for the Zulu supreme deity, God of the Sky. He is characterized by his seeming remoteness and majesty and his non-involvement in the day to day affairs of the people.

idlozi **(plural: *amalozi*)** One of the Zulu terms for referring to the ancestors. It is also used to refer to an old person.

ifa A special form of Yoruba divination using kola nuts and a distinctive system of marks. The marks are used to choose the *odu* or special parables that are meant to state the meaning of the results of the divination. The term Ifa is sometimes used to refer to the Yoruba deity Orunmila.

Ife The most sacred city of Yorubaland, the place where the world began.

ihlambo The washing of spears, a Zulu rite performed on very special occasions.

imbuzi yamakhubalo "The goat of medicine" in Zulu religion.

Inkosazana Princess of the Sky, of special significance for Zulu women.

Inkosi Yezulu Another Zulu name for the God of the Sky.

isibaya The cattle enclosure within the Zulu villiage.

isibongo **(plural: *izibongo*)** A Zulu praise name, praise song, or praise poem that celebrates ancestors and cultural heroes.

iya agan The woman whose function it is to supervise the dressing of the *egungun,* or masked dancers.

izinyanga zemithi A Zulu herbalist, a specialist in the use of the wide range of medicines available.

izinyanga zezulu The heaven-herd, the Zulu specialist in charge of the weather.

izinyanga zokwelapha A Zulu specialist in healing.

izulu The Zulu word meaning "the sky." (*uzulu:* the Zulu people; *isizulu:* the Zulu language).

Johannesburg The largest city in South Africa and the center of the gold-mining industry in which many Zulu work.

kehla The headring worn by a young Zulu male as a signal that he is shortly to be married.

kraal A word (similar to the English "corral") derived from the Portuguese *curral*; it refers to the Zulu village. The Zulu word is *umuzi*.

Luthuli, Albert A famous Zulu chief who received the Nobel Peace Prize in 1960 for his efforts at bringing about social change without violence for all black South Africans.

Malokun The Yoruba god of the sea.

medicine A special power, often viewed as a superhuman agent in the Zulu religious system. It is capable of good or ill. The use of medicine is ritually mediated.

oba The Yoruba term meaning "chief."

odu Parables used in Yoruba divination.

Oduduwa A Yoruba deity associated with the creation of the world and having a special connection to the city of Ife.

Ogun The Yoruba god of iron; he is a deified ancestor and the first king of Ife.

oloogun A specialist in identifying the causes and prescribing the cures for the various illnesses that beset the Yoruba.

olori ebe The Yoruba term meaning "head of the family."

Olorun The Yoruba High God. Literally it means: "owner of the sky."

omoraiye (omoraye) Earthly powers of destruction in Yoruba religion who engage in witchcraft and sorcery.

ori Literally "head"; makes Yoruba capable of thought and communication with the world of religious power.

orisa Yoruba deities who provide the major focus of ritual action.

Orisa-nla One of the Yoruba deities worshiped throughout Yorubaland. He is regarded as having an essential role in the creation of the world, particularly the sculpting of human beings.

Orun Heaven, the sky, the abode of Olorun.

orun rere The state of being in the "good heaven" characteristic of a Yoruba ancestor who has lived a good life.

Orunmila The Yoruba deity most closely associated with the practice of *ifa* and sometimes even identified as the personification of that practice.

Oyo An important city in Yorubaland and the center of political power in important periods of Yoruba history.

qhumbaza Zulu term for the ritual piercing of the ears.

rite of passage A special ceremony marking or bringing about a change of social status or condition; a transitional rite from one role in a religious system to another.

Shaka (Chaka) The Zulu chief who welded many Nguni clans into one powerful Zulu nation, and who developed many new forms of warfare.

Shembe, Isaiah A Zulu prophet who established the amaNazaretha Church in South Africa.

sorcery The use of power for destructive ends.

thomba A puberty rite among the Zulu.

trickster A superhuman agent or deity with a capacity for good or ill with a mischievous nature and a tendency to trick people to their discomfort, detriment, and, occasionally, salvation.

ukubuthwa The Zulu grouping-up ritual.

ukubuyisa idlozi The ritual performed by the Zulu to "bring home the ancestor." Often abbreviated to *ukubuyisa*.

umbeka An ox that represents the ancestors of the Zulu bride in her new home.

umfaan A young Zulu male who is responsible for herding the cattle.

umnumzane The head of the Zulu village.

umqholiso The wedding ox sacrificed at a Zulu wedding.

umsamo A place set aside for various objects with special ritual significance. The special *umsamo* in the *umnumzane's* hut in the Zulu village is where the ancestors are ritually approached.

umuzi The Zulu word for village.

Umvelinqangi The Zulu High God.

Unkulunkulu The first created being, also used to refer to God.

witchcraft The use of special powers and techniques by a witch to destroy accepted social structures and to cause serious injury or death to individuals.

Yoruba An individual member of a group of people with a long historical and cultural tradition traceable at least to the founding of the city of Ife.

Yorubaland That area of contemporary Nigeria where the majority of the Yoruba people live. This is a cultural rather than a political entity as its areas do not coincide with the borders established during the colonial period.

Zionist A member of the church of Zion in South Africa, a unique blend of indigenous and imported religion.

Zulu A member of the former Zulu kingdom with a historical and cultural tradition traceable to Chief Zulu. It is at present a "tribal group" in South Africa.

Selected Reading List

Awolalu, J. Omosade. *Yoruba Beliefs and Sacrificial Rites.* London: Longman, 1979.

Berglund, Axel-Ivar. *Zulu Thought-Patterns and Symbolism.* London: C. Hurst, 1976.

Biobaku, S. O., ed. *Sources of Yoruba History.* Oxford: Clarendon Press, 1973.

Bryant, A. T. *The Zulu People As They Were Before the White Man Came.* Pietermaritzburg: Shuter & Shooter, 1949.

Callan, Edward. *Albert John Luthuli and the South African Race Conflict.* Kalamazoo: Western Michigan University, 1962.

Calloway, Rev. Canon. *Nursery Tales, Traditions and Histories.* Westport: Negro Universities Press, 1970.

———. *The Religious System of the Amazulu.* London: Turner, 1870.

Cope, Trevor, ed. *Izibongo: Zulu Praise-Poems.* Collected by James Stuart, translated by Daniel Malcolm. Oxford: Clarendon Press, 1968.

Cowley, Cecil. *Kwa Zulu: Queen Mkabi's Story.* Cape Town: C. Struik, 1966.

Dennett, R. E. *Nigerian Studies or The Religious and Political System of the Yoruba.* London: Frank Cass, 1968.

Eades, J. S. *The Yoruba Today.* Cambridge: Cambridge University Press, 1980.

Gleason, Judith. *Orisha: The Gods of Yorubaland.* New York: Atheneum, 1973.

Gonzalez-Wippler, Migene. *Santeria: African Magic in Latin America.* New York: The Julian Press, 1973.

Guy, Jeff. *The Destruction of the Zulu Kingdom.* London: Longman, 1979.

Hastings, Adrian. *A History of African Christianity, 1950–1975.* Cambridge: Cambridge University Press, 1979.

Idowu, E. Bolaji. *Olodumare: God in Yoruba Belief.* New York: Frederick A. Praeger, 1963.

Krapf-Askari, Eva. *Yoruba Towns and Cities.* Oxford: Clarendon Press, 1969.

Krige, Eileen Jensen. *The Social System of the Zulus.* 2d ed. Pietermaritzburg: Shuter & Shooter, 1950.

Lucas, J. Olumide. *The Religion of the Yorubas.* Lagos: C. M. S. Bookshop, 1948.

Niven, C. R. *A Short History of the Yoruba Peoples.* London: Longmans, Green, 1958.

Oduyaye, Modupe. *The Vocabulary of Yoruba Religious Discourse.* Ibadan: Daystar Press, 1971.

Peel, J. D. Y. *Aladura: A Religious Movement Among the Yoruba.* Oxford: Oxford University Press, 1968.

Soyinka, Wole. *Ake: The Years of Childhood.* New York: Vintage Books, 1981.

Sundkler, Bengt G. M. *Bantu Prophets in South Africa.* 2d ed. Oxford: Oxford University Press, 1961.

PART TWO

Religions of Mesoamerica

Cosmovision and Ceremonial Centers

Davíd Carrasco

Chronology of Mesoamerican Religions

Dates	Major Events
50,000 to 6500 B.C.E.	Groups of peoples from northeast Asia enter the Americas through Bering Strait land bridge bringing hunting cultures, shamanism, and animal ceremonialism
6500 to 1500 B.C.E.	Incipient agricultural development focusing on maize, beans, squashes, cotton, and chili peppers leads to village formation and the importance of religious cults associated with rain and fertility; settlement in villages with ceremonial centers, burial mounds, and sacred rulers
1500 to 900 B.C.E.	Rise of Olmec civilization centered on eastern coast of Mesoamerica in humid lowlands of Veracruz and Tabasco and spreading into western and southern Mesoamerica; the appearance of monumental architecture characterized by a superb sculptural tradition in gigantic basalt monuments and miniature jade work: Examples include the "Colossal Heads" of San Lorenzo and the hybrid art style of animal (jaguar, bird, reptile) and human forms demonstrating the importance of shamanic specialists; the rise of intense social stratification
900 to 300 B.C.E.	Florescence of Olmec cosmovision and ceremonial style throughout parts of Mesoamerica; formation of the monumental ceremonial center of La Venta, where rich burials reveal intense social stratification; proliferation of religious cults dedicated to gods of rain, fire, maize, Plumed Serpent, the Earth, and the Underworld
600 to 300 B.C.E.	Formation of monumental ceremonial center at Monte Albán in Oaxaca, with evidence of astronomical alignments of ceremonial buildings, elaborate public ceremonies, and royal tombs; rise of Iztapan civilization in Chiapas, where eighty pyramidal mounds, upright stelae, long count calendar dates, and writing appear, indicating that the Mesoamerican cosmovision is generalized

Dates	Major Events
300 B.C.E. *to 100 C.E.*	Early formation of the Maya civilization in Petén area of south-central Mesoamerica; sites at Uaxactun, Yaxchilán, El Mirador, and Tikal take shape
100 to *700 C.E.*	Teotihuacan becomes the imperial capital of an empire: This four-quartered city with towering pyramids, palaces, stairways, marketplaces, and monumental sculpture demonstrates that the cosmovision has become imprinted on the entire urban form; cults of rain, war, jaguars, Feathered Serpent, stars develop; the great ceremonial city of Cholula, organized by the largest pyramid on earth, develops during this period; other important sites include Xochicalco and El Tajín
200 to *900 C.E.*	The Classic Period; Mesoamerican culture is integrated in a number of major areas: Teotihuacan in the central plateau, Maya cultures of the lowlands, and Monte Albán in Oaxaca
300 to *900 C.E.*	The extravagant cosmovision of the Classic Maya develops in the lowlands; this cosmovision includes the long count calendar, intense presentation of royal families, complex writing system, and rich but scattered ceremonial centers at Tikal, Yaxchilán, Palenque, Uxmal, Copán, Quiriguá, and elsewhere are flourishing; the cosmovision of the cosmic tree, dynastic records, the journey through Xibalba, autosacrifice, and human sacrifice appear in iconography
830 to *900 C.E.*	Collapse of segments of Maya civilization
900 to *1100 C.E.*	The Toltec empire centered at Tollan (Tula), famous for the Quetzalcoatl tradition; iconography reveals presence of warrior cults, long-distance trading, and the prestige of having originated and perfected the arts, astronomy, and a cosmovision that influenced subsequent cultures; Chichén Itzá in Yucatan flourishes and integrates Toltec traditions.
900 to *1500 C.E.*	Post-Classic Mesoamerica; the rise and fall of the Toltec empire and the development of the Aztec world; ceremonial centers at Mitla in Oaxaca and Chichén Itzá are flourishing
1200 to *1350 C.E.*	Migrating farmers and warriors move into the Lake Cultures of the central plateau, which had been developing at the same time as Teotihuacan and the Toltec empire; Chichimecas (the Aztecs) partially assimilate with existing social patterns of farming, warfare, market exchange, and religious cults

Dates	Major Events
1325 C.E.	Chichimecas (the Aztecs) settle the swampy island of Tenochtitlan led by their deity, Huitzilopochtli, in the form of an eagle; the settlement is eventually divided into four great quarters surrounding the temple Coatepec (Serpent Mountain), and over seventy-five ceremonial buildings; the cults of Tlaloc, god of agriculture and water, and Huitzilopochtli, god of war and tribute, are combined at the Great Temple
1350 C.E.	Another Chichimec group settles the nearby island of Tlatelolco, which becomes the market center for the Lake Cultures and the site of a great ceremonial center
1425 to 1428 C.E.	The Mexicas, under the leadership of warriors, lead the rebellion against the city-state of Azcapotzalco and form the Triple Alliance of Tenochtitlan, Tlacopan, and Texcoco, which rules central Mesoamerica
1440 to 1468 C.E.	The Aztec Tlatoani Moctezuma Ilhuicamina rules and expands Coatepec (the Great Temple), the monumental ceremonial center in the capital, the tribute network, and warfare efforts; eventually the city is populated by over 200,000 people
1473 C.E.	The Aztecs of Tenochtitlan impose their rule on Tlatelolco and take control of the great market system, solidifying the core of their empire
1502 C.E.	Moctezuma Xocoyotzin comes to the throne
1510 C.E.	Spaniards begin reconnaissance along east coast in Mexico
1521 C.E.	Tenochtitlan falls when Cuauhtemoc surrenders to Cortés at Tlatelolco.
1531 C.E.	Juan Diego experiences the apparition of the Virgin of Guadalupe at Tepeyac
1737 C.E.	Virgin of Guadalupe made patroness of Mexico
1754 C.E.	Pope Benedict XIV officially recognizes Our Lady of Guadalupe
1790 C.E.	Aztec calendar stone, also known as sun stone, discovered beneath the street in Mexico City

Prologue

Raise your spirit. . . . Hear about the new discovery!
Peter Martyr, September 13, 1493

ONE OF THE MOMENTOUS TRANSFORMATIONS in the history of the Western world took place on the shores and in the villages and cities of Mesoamerica between 1492 and 1521. This transformation was initiated with the voyages of Cristóbal Colón (we know him as Christopher Columbus) and reached a culmination, of sorts, with the fall of the Aztec capital, **Tenochtitlan,*** in 1521. Within three quick decades the European image of the world was radically changed and a previously unimaginable universe—Nueva España, America, and above all, the New World—was discovered, invaded, and invented. As Tzvetan Todorov notes, the discovery and conquest of Mesoamerica was the "most astonishing encounter of our history," which "heralds our present identity" as citizens of the world and interpreters of culture.[1] [See Religions of Africa pp. 24, 31, 60–61, Native Religions of North America pp. 320–21, 325, Hinduism pp. 766–67, 770, and Religions of China pp. 988–89 for discussion of invasion and colonization.]

We have the vantage point of a grand eyewitness account of a pivotal episode in this transformation provided by Bernal Díaz del Castillo, a sergeant in Cortés's invading army, who describes the Spanish *entrada* into the Aztec capital in 1519 this way:

> During the morning we arrived at a broad causeway and continued our march towards Iztapalapa and when we saw so many cities and villages built in the water and other great towns on dry land and that straight and level causeway going towards Mexico, we were amazed and said that it was like the enchantments they tell of in the legend of Amadis, on account of the great towers and buildings rising from the water, and all built of masonry. And some of the soldiers even asked whether the things that we saw were not a dream.

Once the Spaniards entered the city the palaces appeared even more amazing to their eyes.

---

*Terms defined in the glossary, pp. 248–51, are printed in boldface type where they first appear in the text.

How spacious and well built they were, of beautiful stone work and cedar wood, and the wood of other sweet scented trees, with great rooms and courts, wonderful to behold, covered with awnings of cotton cloth.

And the natural world of the city was also wonderful.

When we had looked well at all of this, we went to the orchard and garden, which was such a wonderful thing to see and walk in, that I was never tired of looking at the diversity of the trees, and noting the scent which each one had, and the paths full of roses and flowers, and the many fruit trees and native roses, and the pond of fresh water. There was another thing to observe, the great canoes were able to pass into the garden from the lake through an opening that had been made so that there was no need for their occupants to land. And all was cemented and very splendid with many kinds of stone (monuments) with pictures on them. . . . I say again that I stood looking at it and thought that never in the world would there be discovered other lands such as these, for at that time there was no Peru, nor any thought of it. Of all these wonders that I then beheld today all is overthrown and lost, nothing left standing.[2]

This and other eyewitness accounts show that the Spaniards were astonished by the architectural wonders, agricultural abundance, royal luxuries, ritual violence, social stratification, and spatial organization of the capital. To their great surprise Mesoamerica was an urban civilization organized by powerful, pervasive religious beliefs and practices.

Within eighteen months, however, distrust, intrigue, torture, murder, and conquest dominated the interaction between Spaniard and Aztec. The last Aztec ruler, **Cuauhtemoc** (Diving Eagle), surrendered to Cortés and his army of Spaniards and Indian allies on November 15, 1521, at the ceremonial center of **Tlatelolco** in the capital. The Aztec view of the events leading up to this terrible change appear in this native lament:

Broken spears lie in the road;
we have torn our hair in our grief.
The houses are roofless now, and their walls
are red with blood.

We have pounded our hands in despair
against the adobe walls,
for our inheritance, our city, is lost and dead.
The shields of our warriors were its defense,
but they could not save it. . . .

They set a price on all of us
on the young men, the priests, the boys and the girls
the price of a poor man was only two handfuls of corn
or ten cakes made from mosses or twenty cakes
of salty couch-grass.

Gold, jade, rich cloths, quetzal feathers—
everything that once was precious was now considered
worthless.[3]

In spite of the human devastation and cultural transformation brought on
by the conquest and European colonialism, significant versions of the native
images of space, time, the cosmos, social and economic relations, and the
underworld are available to us. The archaeological, ethnohistorical, and literary
evidence provides us with the eloquent statement that the story of Mesoamerican religions is the story of cities and symbols of cities. In fact Mesoamerica was
a world organized by hundreds of carefully planned **ceremonial centers** and
scores of monumental, even majestic cities and city-states. It is usually overlooked that Mesoamerica was one of the seven places on the globe—with China,
Mesopotamia, Egypt, the Indus Valley, Nigeria, and Peru—where human culture
managed the great transformation from preurban society to urban society.
These urban societies, while different from one another in many ways, all developed traditions of art, symbolism, politics, and social organization that became
the heart and nexus of human culture. It is also remarkable that in each of these
seven cases of **primary urban generation** the societies at large were *regulated
and organized by monumental ceremonial centers that contained such architectural
structures as temples, platform mounds, pyramids, palaces, terraces, staircases,
courts, stelae, and spacious ritual precincts.*[4] The little footprints crossing the
ancient Mesoamerican maps and the portrayal of ritual life in the art of various
cities show that ancient peoples visited such places as **Teotihuacan,** Abode

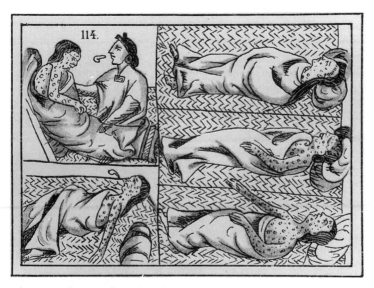

These panels come from the Florentine Codex *and they depict the suffering and
medical care of smallpox victims. The Spanish brought to Mexico with them a
number of foreign diseases that devastated the indigenous population in a very short
time. (*Paso y Troncoso *edition.)*

of the Gods; Xochicalco, Place of the House of Flowers; Chichén Itzá, Mouth of the Well of the Itza; Colhuacan, Place of the Ancestors; **Tollan,** Place of Reeds; and Teocolhuacan, Place of the Divine Ancestors. In this way ancient Mesoamerican history is the story of people and their symbols moving to and from cities and their ceremonial centers. [See Religions of Africa p. 59, Hinduism pp. 732-33, and Religions of China p. 986 for discussion of early cities.]

This urban image of place and action provides the plan for this book. The controlling idea for the entire study is that the ceremonial precincts of Mesoamerica were the centers and theaters for the acting out of religious and social life. These ceremonial centers served as powerful magnets attracting people, goods, authority, and sacred forces into their precincts, ceremonies, and marketplaces. Once within the power, drama, and order of the ceremonial center people and their goods underwent experiences that changed them and their sense of orientation and value. But these ceremonial centers, operating under the control of royal and priestly elites, also had a *centrifugal* force, which redistributed goods, values, and people outward into the society at large.

Another important term in the subtitle is **cosmovision,** which means the ways in which Mesoamericans *combined their cosmological notions relating to time and space into a structured and systematic worldview.* This worldview included a strong sense of parallelism between the celestial, supernatural forces of the cosmos (macrocosmos) and the biological, human patterns of life on earth (microcosmos). As we shall see, the spatial organization, architecture, and calendrical rituals of many ceremonial centers in Mesoamerican history expressed intimate parallels between the time and space of the deities and the time and space of humans and terrestrial beings. One of the most important points to understand at the outset is that in Mesoamerican religions *time* and *space* were inseparable realities.

Chapter 5 surveys the challenge of studying Mesoamerican religions and the rich ensemble of resources available for the study of Mesoamerican religions. It discusses three characteristics of religious history in Mesoamerica: worldmaking (cosmovision and sacred space), worldcentering (cosmovision and the human body), and worldrenewing (the ceremonial rejuvenation of time, human life, agriculture, and the gods). Chapter 6 develops a historic overview of the diversity and richness of major ceremonial centers and ritual traditions in Mesoamerican culture. It begins with the artistic and trading achievements of the Olmecs (1500–300 B.C.E.); outlines the superb creativity of **Classic Maya** ceremonial life (200–900 C.E.); discusses the grand imperial capital of Teotihuacan (200–750 C.E.); outlines the utopian image of **Quetzalcoatl's** kingdom in Tollan (900–1100 C.E.); and ends with the religious world of the Aztec empire (1325–1521 C.E.). Chapter 7 focuses on the religion of the warrior: the power of ritual violence in Aztec religion expressed in the cult of the warrior, warrior kings, and the sacrificial ceremonies at the Great Aztec Temple of Tenochtitlan. This chapter also includes a discussion of the art of Aztec speech. Chapter 8 explores the "blood of kings," that is, the royal religion of Maya ceremonial settlements that were organized around the symbolism of the flowering sacred tree and the careers of royal families and their ancestors.[5] In this discussion of the

Maya achievement we will examine one of the most pervasive meanings of all Mesoamerican religions: the sacred powers of agricultural life. Chapter 9 summarizes several continuities and innovations in Mesoamerican religions during the colonial period and in contemporary communities. We will discuss the New World as a world of social and spiritual crisis for indigenous and *mestizo* (mixed Spanish/Indian parentage) peoples. We will look at an array of religious expressions of worldmaking (Huichol peyote hunt), worldcentering (Day of the Dead ceremonies), and worldrenewing (cults of Guadalupe and Santiago). In this array we will see clear examples of both religious pilgrimages and religious **syncretism.**

5

Introduction: Approaching Mesoamerican Religions

Inventions and Fantasies of Mesoamerica

AROUND 1510 A SPANISH RECONNAISSANCE EXPEDITION from the island of Cuba made contact with a small group of Maya Indians on a beach bordering territory that the people called the Land of the Turkey and the Deer. Attempting to figure out their location the Spaniards shouted, "What is this place called?" The natives replied, *"Uic athan,"* meaning, "We do not understand your words." In an ironic turn of meaning characteristic of many changes that were to follow, the Spaniards decided to call this area Yucatan, a place name that is now the permanent designation for this eastern part of Mesoamerica.[6]

Mesoamerica is a term given by scholars to designate a geographical and cultural area covering the southern two-thirds of mainland Mexico, Guatemala, Belize, El Salvador, and parts of Honduras, Nicaragua, and Costa Rica. In this area the powerful processes of urban generation began with sophisticated agricultural production in the second millennium B.C.E. and ended with the Spanish conquest in the sixteenth century C.E. Extensive research shows that Mesoamerica was inhabited by a wide spectrum of social groups with various levels of social integration; but the permanent, extensive ceremonial centers at the heart of social worlds resembling small-scale city-states became the most powerful social unit in a few different regions beginning around 1500 B.C.E. It is also clear that the earliest and most influential institutions contributing to the organization of peoples into urban centers were sacred ceremonial precincts. Therefore it is useful to approach the study of Mesoamerican religions through the continuous patterns and presence of cosmovision and ritual action created and celebrated within these ceremonial centers and their city-states.

As the naming of Yucatan suggests, however, knowledge of these places and peoples was subject to inventions and fantasies that have had long-term influences. Unless we acknowledge their presence, they can silently distort our understanding of religion in Mesoamerican cultures. In fact Mesoamerica

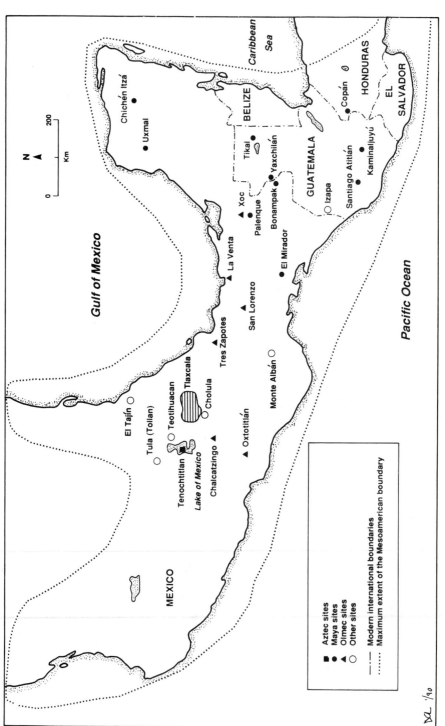

Mesoamerica.

was a powerful European fantasy long before it was mapped or lived in. It was believed to be at once the Garden of Eden and the land of wild men, monstrosities, and devil worship. As the quote that opens the prologue to this part indicates, there was excitement and even euphoria in Europe at the news of Columbus's landfall. This excitement extended beyond the Italian humanist Peter Martyr, as indicated by the fact that Columbus's first letter to the crown was published nine times in 1493 and twenty times by 1500. However, it was not easy or comfortable for Europeans to fit the incredible news of entirely unknown lands, peoples, empires, souls, and gold, into their intellectual horizon. America became, for centuries, a "strange new world" with different languages, customs, symbols, cuisines, philosophies, manners, and landscapes. Juxtaposed to Peter Martyr's happy announcement is the cleric Cornelius De Pauw's claim, three hundred years later, that the "discovery of the New World was the most calamitous event in human history."[7]

Europeans struggled in diverse ways to observe, perceive, and understand the New World of America. In the process they produced many inventions and fantasies. The many inventions and fantasies concerning Mesoamerica can be divided into two groups: fantasies about Mesoamerican geography and inventions about the nature of human beings. It is important to review these fantasies and inventions before we study the religions of the Aztecs, Mayas, and their neighbors and contemporary religious expressions. This will help us see how Mesoamerican peoples and places were both attractive and threatening to European consciousness. It is important to be aware of this powerful ambivalence concerning religions and peoples in the New World so we can lessen its influence in our approach to Mesoamerican cultures, religious practices, and creativity. It is also important to recognize the religious themes that were woven into the European inventions about Mesoamerica. [See Religions of Africa pp. 23–24, Native Religions of North America pp. 263–64, Judaism pp. 389, 426, 456–75, Christianity pp. 492–94, Islam pp. 607–8, Hinduism pp. 719–21, Buddhism pp. 853–55, Religions of China pp. 990–1015, and Religions of Japan pp. 1090–92 for discussion of the diversity and variety of religious traditions.]

Mesoamerica as an Earthly Paradise

From their first sightings of the "Indies" to the end of the sixteenth century, Europeans hoped they had discovered an earthly paradise filled with the Garden of Eden, the Seven Enchanted Cities of Gold, and the Fountain of Youth. These wonderful images had been deposited in European traditions for centuries, and it made sense to compare the exotic reports of the explorers with these fabulous places. It is significant that two major English literary works, Shakespeare's *The Tempest* and Thomas More's *Utopia,* reflect the fantasy that Europe was going to be renewed and transformed for the good by the settlement of the New World. We see the energy of this fantasy in Miranda's lines to Prospero in the last scene of *The Tempest.* In describing her "vision of the island" (at once Naples and America) she states,

MIRANDA: O Wonder!
How many goodly creatures are there here!
How beauteous mankind is.
O, brave new world, that has such people in't.

PROSPERO: Tis new to thee.

> (act 5, scene 1)

While classical and European society had long dreamed and written about
ideal social societies where human possibility could be fulfilled, Thomas More's

This stylized map of the Aztec world depicts Tenochtitlan, where an eagle is perched on a prickly pear cactus in the center of the four quadrants. Warriors with shields and flint-studded clubs are shown next to two conquered communities, represented by smoking temples and tilted and thatched roofs. From the Codex Mendoza, *a post-conquest manuscript prepared by the first viceroy of New Spain.*

image of Utopia (meaning "good place" and "no place") reflects the renewed sense that the dream was about to be realized in America. In fact the narrator of *Utopia*, Ralph Hythloday, was portrayed as the companion of Amerigo Vespucci, the Italian explorer who was credited with concluding in 1507 that the landmass of South America was not part of Asia, but was in fact a new continent. For this insight America was named after him.

The voyages of discovery stimulated both great interest and defensiveness on the part of Europeans, whose maps of geography and of humankind were being quickly and radically challenged. On the one hand there seemed to be "newness" coming in many forms. New lands, peoples, languages, colors, animals, vegetation, and religions were appearing on the European frontier. On the other hand these novelties appeared so "other," different, and—in Europeans' views—undeveloped that the Europeans felt the peoples of the New World of America had not evolved or progressed as they believed their own culture had.

All this evoked some important questions: What is a human being? What is the difference between a civilized and a barbaric language? Is Europe the center of the world? We can see this new ambivalence in a passage from the 1512 edition of Pomponius Mela's *Cosmographia*. The humanist Cochlaeus wrote in the introduction,

> In our lifetime, Amerigo Vespucci is said to have discovered that New World with ships belonging to the kings of Spain and Portugal; he sailed not only beyond the torrid zone but far beyond the Tropic of Capricorn. He says Africa stretches as far: and that his New World is quite distinct from it and bigger than our Europe. Whether this is true or a lie, it has nothing . . . to do with Cosmography and the knowledge of History. For the peoples and places of that continent are unknown and unnamed to us and sailings are only made there with the greatest dangers. Therefore it is of no interest to geographers at all.[8]

In other words the discovery of a new continent was not about to alter the European map of the world as presented in school textbooks! [See Religions of Africa pp. 21–22 and Native Religions of North America pp. 261–64 for discussion of Western stereotypes.]

The landscape of the islands near Mexico and the beauty of the South American mainland stimulated stories that the earthly paradise written of in the Bible and medieval books had finally been discovered. Reports passed through European capitals that the land was indeed inhabited by humans who had not changed since the time of Adam and Eve. A quarter of a century later, in central Mexico, these hopes took the form of a belief that a **millennial kingdom** ruled by priests who would convert the masses of natives into Christians was about to be established. Franciscan missionaries believed they faced the opportunity to create an earthly Christian community that would fulfill New Testament prophecies and herald the return of Jesus Christ on earth. The belief that the place of the Aztec capital was central to this biblical event was symbolized by the arrival, in a grand ceremony in the spring of 1524, of twelve Franciscan priests (referred to as the "apostles") into Mexico City. It was thought they were reenacting the presence of the twelve disciples on earth and heralding the dawn of a heavenly kingdom. In subsequent decades some members of this order organized their Indian followers (whom they considered "like angels" or "soft wax" waiting for the impression of Christ on their hearts) into utopian communities to prepare the way for the end of time and the Second Coming of Jesus. A related belief, sometimes preached from pulpits in Mexico, was that the Apostle Thomas, the wandering disciple of Christ, had preached in Mexico fifteen centuries before, introducing Christian teachings that had subsequently been distorted with time. Both the hope in a millennial kingdom and the belief that Saint Thomas had preached in the New World centuries before reflected the primary attitude of the Catholic church toward the native peoples. They were "souls to be saved" in a global process of conversion. [See Christianity pp. 527–33 for discussion of Christianity in the "New Worlds."]

The Mesoamerican landscape was also considered an abundant resource of gold. The desire for wealth resulted in extraordinary fantasies and tragedies in the settling of New Spain. Stories of El Dorado (cities of silver and gold) and rumors of **Moctezuma's** buried treasure motivated otherwise rational human beings to face immense challenges and dangers in search of mineral resources for a luxurious and powerful life. Consider this eyewitness account made by Aztec survivors of the conquest:

> And when they were given these presents (of gold, quetzal feathers, and golden necklaces), the Spaniards burst into smiles; their eyes shone with pleasure; they were delighted by them. They picked up the gold and fingered it like monkeys; they seemed to be transported by joy, as if their hearts were illumined and made new.
>
> The truth is that they longed and lusted for gold. Their bodies swelled with greed, and their hunger was ravenous. They hungered like pigs for the gold. . . . They were like one who speaks a barbarous tongue: everything they said was in a barbarous tongue.[9]

This belief in Moctezuma's treasure of gold resurfaced again in Mexico City in 1982, when rumors spread that the archaeologists excavating the Great Aztec Temple had found the gold and were keeping it secret.

The Noble Savage/Wild Man

The most influential and degrading fantasy was the belief in the natural inferiority of the Indians. Some Europeans believed that the indigenous peoples were halfway between beasts and humans. American Indians were portrayed, in the first decades after the discovery of the New World, as cannibals, sexually promiscuous, lawless, and misdirected by pagan gods. They were, in short, humans, but wild humans whose evolution and development had taken a very different direction than did the civilizations that led to European cultures.

Other Europeans, however, argued that while these beings were indeed savages, they had not yet suffered the debilitating effects of civilization associated with greed, cruelty, and bad manners. Rather than being a wild human race they felt that the Indians were noble and pure in their hearts but still savages. Research has taught us that both these images, the wild man and the noble savage, were already deeply embedded in the European mind before Mesoamerica was discovered.

A third response to the natives of Mesoamerica became apparent as the sixteenth century unfolded and more contact between the Old World and the New World took place. A number of Spaniards realized that a complex mystery, a radically different world, was being revealed, which demanded careful and sustained analysis. This group became determined to discover where the Indians fit into the scheme of creation, society, and religion. For all three groups of European interpreters, Mesoamerica became the big screen upon which Europeans could either project these fantasies and at the same time believe these projections were realities, or carry out their comparative experiments in thinking and classification.

Treatment of native peoples became so brutal and dehumanizing, justified in part by these racial stereotypes, that in 1550 Charles V of Spain suspended all expeditions to America and summoned into session a *junta* of foremost theologians. This Council of the Fourteen, in Valladolid, Spain, was called to consider a debate on the question of whether it is "lawful for the King to wage war on the Indians before preaching the faith to them in order to subject them to his rule, so that afterwards, they may more easily be instructed in the faith."[10] The debate focused on two major questions: (1) What is the true nature of the Indian? and (2) Could Europeans justifiably use coercion, violence, and war to eliminate Indian religions and force the people to become Christians and obey the Spaniards?

This "Great Debate," as Lewis Hanke calls it in *Aristotle and the American Indians,* set in motion the written expression of ideas and racial prejudices that some people still use today in naming and interpreting Native American life and culture. At the heart of this conflict was a religious bias that Aztec and Maya religions were "ancient idolatries and false religion with which the devil was worshiped until the Holy Gospel was brought to this land."[11]

On one side of the debate was the Spanish philosopher **Juan Ginés de Sepulveda,** admirer of Cortés, friend of Erasmus, and translator of Aristotle's *Poetics* into Latin. He argued in a five-hundred-page treatise that the Indians were "as inferior to Spaniards . . . as children to adults, as women to men . . . as great a difference between them . . . as monkeys to men."[12] Therefore the natural condition of the Indians was social slavery and obedience to the more rational Europeans. In other words Indians, by *nature,* not as a result of military weakness, deserved an eternally inferior social position in the New World. Further, any Indian refusal to obedience and the acceptance of a life of servitude was seen as the reasonable basis for using force, violence, and warfare against them. Lodged within this argument of Aristotelian logic is a destructive, grandiose conception of European superiority, perfection, and virtue. Conquerors never had it so good!

The Indian side was taken by the Dominican priest **Bartolomé de las Casas** (no native Mesoamericans were present), who had served as the Bishop of

Chiapas while ministering in Maya communities. His extensive defense of the Indians contains aggressive discussions of such categories as "barbarian," "city," "Christian," "language," and "natural slavery" as a means to argue that preconquest Indian societies met all the Aristotelian criteria for a civil society. He argued that the people he saw every day were rational beings and should be brought to Christianity through persuasion, not violence. "Every man can become a Christian," he argued, because they already displayed a "wild" Christianity. Therefore there was no basis for a just war against the natives. Las Casas advanced the idea—which astonished many Spaniards during his day—that the American Indians compared favorably with peoples in ancient Old World civilizations, were eminently rational beings, and in fact fulfilled every one of Aristotle's requirements for the good life. He even argued that the Greeks and Romans were inferior to the Indians in child rearing, education of children, marriage arrangements, law, and architecture, and that the Indians were in some ways superior to the Spaniards. [See Religions of Africa p. 23 and Native Religions of North America p. 263 for discussion of "primitive religions."]

Two points must be made about the way this kind of debate influences our attempts to understand the aesthetics, ritual, and cosmovision of Mesoamerican religions. First, a terrible alienation has already been set in motion whenever a society debates whether others "are human and do we have the right to kill them?" Subsequent generations are faced with the task of either elaborating these positions, or eliminating them so genuine methods of understanding and caring for the "others" can be developed. These debates in Spain, and in New Spain during the sixteenth century, took place long before the settlements of the New England colonies. The categories, prejudices, and clichés about Mesoamerican peoples were often the basis for the attitudes and policies of discrimination later developed toward American Indians in North America. Second, even though we may all wish to side with las Casas, it must be noted that both he and Sepulveda argued that the Indians must be changed into Christians in order to take a fully human place in society. Las Casas argued that the most impressive feature of the Indians was their similarity to Christians! Neither the priest nor the philosopher displayed a fundamental ability to appreciate these peoples for their own cultural style and content. Yet it is important to repeat that there were a number of people like las Casas and especially José de Acosta, author of a remarkable work, *Historia Natural y Moral de las Indies,* who did believe in the essential sameness of all human minds and made admirable efforts to figure out how the Indian world worked and how it could be reasonably related to the European worldview and lifestyle.

Clearly all European involvements with Mesoamerican cultures were not negative. While there were widespread attempts to degrade Indian art, clothes, cuisine, length of hair, and so on, there were also expressions of curiosity and admiration among a number of theologians, artists, and priests. Subsequent centuries have shown a remarkable interest in Mesoamerican art, politics, social structure, and religious practices. As Benjamin Keen has shown in *The Aztec Image in Western Thought,* Mesoamerica has been much on the minds of playwrights, poets, novelists, and painters as well as scholars. Among the significant cultural figures who have been drawn to Mesoamerican cultures for political, cultural, and intellectual materials are the German naturalist, traveler, and statesman Alexander von Humboldt; philosopher and writer Johann Gottfried von Herder; anthropologist E. B. Tylor; poet and critic Heinrich Heine; poets William Carlos Williams and John Dryden; Napoleon Bonaparte; writer Hart Crane, and others.

Two Controversies

Two major controversies have been advanced in recent years, allowing for more fruitful understanding of the Mayas, the Aztecs, and their precursors. The first was whether or not Mesoamerican peoples attained a level of social and symbolic complexity associated with urban civilizations. The second was why human sacrifice and cannibalism took place on such a large scale.

Each of these issues, one concerning the social organization of Mesoamerica, the other concerning the ritual traditions of the Aztecs and Mayas, has involved heated and sometimes fantastic formulations. For instance in his article "Montezuma's Dinner," written in 1876, one of the founders of cultural anthropology, Lewis H. Morgan, claimed that the Aztecs were "still a breech cloth people wearing the rag of barbarism as the unmistakable evidence of their condition." The intellectual milieu of Morgan's generation was inspired by the evolutionary framework of Charles Darwin and his followers, some of whom attempted to extend the new picture of biological development to the development of societies. Morgan had developed a scheme of human society's progress through three stages—savage, barbarism, and civilized—and argued that the Aztecs and their neighbors had only developed to the stage of barbarism. He argued that the Aztec palaces described by Hernán Cortés and Bernal Díaz del Castillo were, according to Morgan (who could see it all more clearly 350 years later), "joint tenement houses" that "reflected the weakness of the Indian family and inability to face alone the struggle of life." That the barbarian chief Moctezuma might have eaten on a tablecloth scandalized Morgan, who wrote, "There was neither a political society nor a state, nor any civilization in America, when it was discovered and excluding the Eskimo, but one race of Indians, the Red Race."[13]

Although Morgan's thesis was very influential well into the twentieth century, subsequent research by archaeologists and ethnohistorians has shown that it is not a question of whether Native Americans developed cities or not, but of what kinds of cities they did develop. In fact scholars have discovered a number of striking similarities between Mesoamerican cities and the urban civilizations of China, Egypt, Mesopotamia, India, Nigeria, and Peru.

More recently, in 1979, a furious controversy broke out in academic journals and books concerning what Marvin Harris called the "Cannibal Kingdom" of the Aztecs. Again, as in Morgan's day, the general intellectual atmosphere influenced the interpretation of the specifics of Mesoamerican culture in a distorted fashion. Anthropological literature in the 1970s was awash with the theory of cultural materialism, an approach that tended to reduce cultural developments to the material conditions and forces in society. At the center of this debate were the extraordinary ritual practices of bloodletting, human sacrifice, and ritual cannibalism practiced by Mesoamerican peoples. The debate divided into two camps: (1) the ecological explanation, which stated that "they ate humans for protein and profit"; and (2) the cultural explanation, which stated that "they were ritually exchanging gifts in the forms of thighs, hearts, skulls, and blood." But neither of these approaches was solidly based on Aztec or Maya conceptions of matter, the human body, or human/deity relations. As we shall see Mesoamerican religions were animated, in part, by ritual bloodletting and the sacrifice of human beings, who were ritually transformed into deities. But neither of these explanations was based on a secure understanding of what these peoples actually did and what they meant when they did it. We will study these unusual practices in chapters 7 and 8.

Sources for Understanding: The Ensemble Approach to Evidence

In 1982 a Mexican journalist visiting France was given permission to study the Aztec ritual manuscript the *Tonalamatl Aubin* in the confines of the rare books room at the National Library in Paris. With a certain stealth and unusual luck he stole the manuscript from the museum and fled to Yucatan, Mexico, where he was eventually tracked down by Interpol. He announced in the newspapers that the precious manuscript had been illegally taken from Mexico in 1840 and that he had returned an indigenous treasure to its homeland. While the two governments disputed the rightful ownership of the *Aubin* the journalist became something of a national hero. Today the manuscript is in the Biblioteca Nacional in Mexico City.

The cultural pride associated with the recovery of the *Tonalamatl Aubin* symbolizes some of the problems and possibilities facing the study of Mesoamerican religions. On the one hand we are faced with the scattered remnants of the pictorial, archaeological, and literary evidence. Hernán Cortés's march from Villa Rica de la Vera Cruz to Tenochtitlan was punctuated with the defacing, whitewashing, and removing of religious monuments and images. In case after case the Spaniards destroyed the images of deities and ceremonial life, replacing them with Christian crosses on the spot. Later, in 1535, the apostolic inquisitor of Mexico, Juan de Zumarraga, ordered the collection and destruction of the pictorial records belonging to the Nahuatl cultural capital of Texcoco. Tradition tells us that the beautifully painted historical, ritual, and genealogical screenfolds were gathered into a huge pile in the local marketplace, set afire, and turned to ashes. It is a bitter fact that of the hundreds of pictorial manu-scripts extant in Mesoamerica in 1517 only eleven remain today.

On the other hand extensive archaeological discoveries, excellent reproduc-tions of the existing pictorials, recent translations of Maya script and Nahuatl documents, and an abundance of ethnohistorical writings composed in the six-teenth and seventeenth centuries provide us with revealing accounts of reli-gious patterns and practices from a variety of local city-states in different parts of Mesoamerica. In addition there are millions of Nahuatl- and Maya-speaking people alive today who know elements of the ancient cosmovision and practice religious rituals in ceremonial centers that have dimensions of pre-Hispanic symbolism.

Given this abundant evidence the most useful approach to the study of Mesoamerican religions is an ensemble approach: the integration of a variety of types of evidence including such pictorial manuscripts as the *Codex Borgia* and *Codex Mendoza;* ritual objects such as the masks and statues of the Great Aztec Temple; the Aztec Calendar Stone; such myths as the *Leyenda de los Soles* or the *teocuitl* (divine song) of the birth of the Aztec war god **Huitzilopochtli;** carvings as the reliefs from the Maya cities of Yaxchilán and **Palenque;** archaeological material such as the excavations at Copán, Tlatelolco, Teotihuacan, Cacaxtla, or Rio Azul; ethnohistorical descriptions such as those found in Diego de Landa's *Relacíon de las Cosas de Yucatan,* Diego Durán's *Book of the Gods and the Rites and the Ancient Calendar,* or extensive mythologies found, for instance, in the Maya book **Popul Vuh.** Rather than approaching religion from the privileged position of the star performance of one text, say a pictorial manuscript or a Spanish eyewitness account, we will combine four kinds of evidence: archaeological records, literary testimony, pictorial manuscripts, and contemporary fieldwork reports.

Archaeological Records

Archaeological discoveries have uncovered major ritual artifacts and large portions of ceremonial centers from numerous Mesoamerican cultures during the last three hundred years. In 1790, for instance, the Great Aztec Calendar Stone was uncovered below a street in Mexico City revealing the Aztec cos-mogony, or story of the ages of the universe. Later, in 1841, John L. Stephens and Frank Catherwood, after exploring and drawing a number of Maya ceremonial centers long abandoned and covered by the jungle, published *Incidents of Travel in Central America, Chiapas, and Yucatan, Mexico.* They startled the English-speaking world with their reports of pyramids, tombs, ball courts, and huge stat-ues of lavishly dressed lords and gods. Stephens actually purchased the ruins of the ancient city of Copán for thirty-five dollars! In 1810 Alexander von Hum-boldt published valuable paintings and reports of his visits to numerous Mexi-can ruins and awakened in German universities and other parts of Europe a real interest in visiting and studying Mesoamerican society. Between 1900 and 1915

Mexican archaeologists uncovered the great pyramids of Teotihuacan, showing the truly monumental nature of an ancient capital. In the following decades Mexican archaeologists discovered tombs, temples, pyramids, ball courts, and palaces in such cities as Monte Albán, Xochicalco, Quirigua, Palenque, Tikal, Tula, Copán, Yaxchilán, and El Mirador. During the last twenty years a veritable revolution in our view of the ancient Maya has been accomplished, in part through archaeological and iconographic analysis of sculptured images and written inscriptions. Information about the daily life, political alliances, astronomical influences, crafts, dynastic privilege, and cosmovision of the Classic Maya is increasing every month. Another major development has been the excellent reproductions of the Mixtec pictorials by publishing houses in Europe. Each of these discoveries has yielded extensive information on the cities, architecture, and ritual actions in Mesoamerica.

Among the most significant archaeological discoveries in this century, reflecting the interplay between the religious imagination and urban centers, was the 1978 to 1983 excavation of the Great Aztec Temple of Tenochtitlan in Mexico City. This temple, called **Coatepec** or Mountain of the Serpent, was located in the center of the ancient capital. But it was not only the political and symbolic center of the Aztec empire, it was also one of the end products of a thousand years of temple architecture, religious symbolism, and ritual construction. For five years truly fabulous discoveries startled public and scholars alike as some seven thousand ritual objects were excavated within the eleven enlargements of the temple situated in the heart of Mexico City. Most of these treasures were obtained from offertory caches including effigies of deities, ritual masks, sacrificial knives, jade beads, marine animals and seashells, human sacrifices, and major and minor sculptures, which were deposited together with an enormous number of animal species. Significantly, a large percentage of these objects came from distant regions of the empire as well as the Pacific Ocean and the Gulf of Mexico. The study of this temple will serve as one of the focusing lenses for our vision and understanding of the ways communities, cities, and even empires were organized by a religious cosmovision. And in the Maya areas a series of remarkable excavations at Rio Azul and Tikal are changing the way we understand the purpose and meaning of the pyramids and tombs, which organize much of the Maya ceremonial world.

Another exciting development is the recent decipherment of Maya writing and iconography. The so-called Mysterious Maya of the third to ninth centuries C.E. achieved an elaborate writing system combining phonetic and ideographic script in inscriptions that covered temples, stairways, reliefs, pictorial manuscripts, stelae (upright stones in ceremonial centers), and vases. Scholars have discovered that the Maya carved vivid narratives showing the powerful interaction of their gods, mythical time, agricultural cycles, dynasties, ancestors, and ritual life in numerous ceremonial centers. These elaborate narratives, not unlike episodes in a play, show fantastic scenes of bloodletting, descent into the underworld, and the enthronement of royal figures at the cosmic tree. This material shows how the sanctified character of kingship and social stratification played a major role in Mesoamerican religions.

Literary Testimony

In addition to the remains of ceremonial centers and the iconography of the writing systems that survived the conquest, the student is fortunate to have a series of valued translations of selected written documents from the colonial period, including such rich accounts as the *Popul Vuh* or *Book of Council* of the Quiché Maya, Landa's *Relación de las Cosas de Yucatan,* and *The Book of Chilam Balam of Tizimin* of the Yucatan Maya, and the *Anales de Cuauhtitlan,* the *Leyenda de los Soles,* the *Codex Cantares Mexicanos,* and the **Florentine Codex** from the Aztec region. Each of these documents, originally written in Quiché Maya or Nahuatl and Spanish (after the conquest) contain abundant information about the religious symbols and rites, and views of warfare, kingship, and human destiny on earth and in the afterlife as perceived in Aztec and Maya religion. For instance, this passage about the Dual God, **Ometeotl,** expresses one of the major elements of central Mesoamerican cosmovision:

> And the Toltecs knew
> that many are the heavens.
> They said there are twelve superimposed divisions.
> There dwells the true god and his consort.
> The celestial god is called the Lord of Duality.
> And his consort is called the Lady of Duality, the celestial Lady
> which means
> he is king, he is Lord, above the twelve heavens.
> In the place of sovereignty, in the place of sovereignty, we rule;
> my supreme Lord so commands.
> Mirror which illumines things.
> Now they will join us, now they are prepared.
> Drink, drink!
> The God of Duality is at work,
> Creator of men,
> mirror which illumines things.[14]

Here we see two major notions: (1) the organization of the cosmos into thirteen levels (the Dual God occupies the thirteenth); and (2) the division of the cosmos into a dual supernatural reality, male and female, which gives light and understanding (illumines things) to the world.

Of extraordinary value for the study of Maya religion is the *Popul Vuh,* an 8,500-line document containing creation myths, sacred histories, and descriptions of ritual performance, representing a long tradition of Maya religious thought. We see that in Maya mythology the cosmos was created as an extensive ritual performance. "It takes a long performance and account to complete the emergence of all the sky-earth" within a four-quartered world, which was animated through the continual process of "sowing and dawning," that is, planting and harvesting, burial and rebirth, sunset and sunrise. This pattern of planting and rebirth, so vital to the Maya mentality, was also expressed in the periodic rebirth of the cosmos, which passed through four (or six) ages. In the *Popul Vuh* these cycles of repeated cosmic creations and destructions are the setting in which a number of heroes and characters face ordeals and fabulous transformations in journeys through, among other places, **Xibalba,** the Maya underworld. We meet such characters as Heart of Heaven, Crunching Jaguar, Maker of the Blue Green Plate, Blood Woman, Raw Thunderbolt, Plumed Serpent, and the Jaguar Twins, who perpetuated the sowing and dawning of the Maya world through their actions and misdeeds. Study of the postconquest *Popul Vuh* as well as the *Books of Chilam Balam* (books of the Spokesman of the Jaguar), and recent research in contemporary Maya and Mixtec communities herald an awareness that the religious worldviews of the Maya and the Mixtec were not destroyed at the conquest. As we shall see in chapter 9 a number of ritual practices similar to those of the ancient Maya are still carried out today.

The major role played by war and the warrior in the religious worldview of Mesoamerica is richly portrayed in monumental architecture and small sculptured objects as well as pictorial and literary documents. In most parts of Mesoamerica, war and the aesthetic, ritual character of the warrior was overtly religious. Great care was given to regulate, through art and aesthetic expression, the profound transformation a human being underwent in training, costuming, combat, victory, defeat, sacrifice, and the afterlife. These actions were guided by a cosmovision saturated with military motifs. For instance the patron deity of the Aztecs, Huitzilopochtli, was the model warrior who, after being magically dressed in his power costume, slew hundreds of enemy deities at the sacred mountain at the center of the world. It was "said that he set men's hearts on fire and gave them courage for war."[15] The religious significance of war in Aztec thought is shown when the birth of this god is immediately followed by his transformation into a ferocious warrior.

Perhaps the richest resource for the study of central Mesoamerican religions is the *Florentine Codex,* a twelve-volume encyclopedic study carried out by the Franciscan priest **Bernardino de Sahagun** within decades after the fall of the Aztec capital. Gods, ceremonies, creation myths, costumes, royalty, animals, medical practices, and the cosmic meaning of the human body are presented in rich and vivid detail. For instance we have many descriptions of how *teotl* (gods, in Nahuatl) and **teotl ixiptla** (human images of gods) were dressed for their ceremonial events. Here is a description of how the *ixiptla* of Xilonen, goddess of the tender maize, was dressed:

> On the tenth day, then the woman (who was the likeness of) Xilonen died. Her face was painted in two colors; she was yellow about her lips, she was chili-red on her forehead. Her paper cap had ears at the four corners; it had quetzal feathers in the form of maize tassels; (she wore) a plaited neck band. Her neck piece consisted of many strings of green stone; a golden disc went over it. (She had) her shift with the water lily (flower and leaf design), and she had her skirt with the water lily (flower and leaf design. She had) her obsidian sandals, her carmine-colored sandals. Her shield and her rattle stick were chili-red. In four directions she entered . . .[16]

In this description we see that the image of the goddess is a living symbol of fertility and powerful objects (obsidian) that, like corn, come out of the earth.

Another important resource combining literary and pictorial information are the Relaciones Geographica, which described political, social, and geographical realities of pre-Hispanic and colonial society. Often, these documents included maps painted in native and colonial styles.

Pictorial Manuscripts

The most beautiful resources for the study of Mesoamerican religions are the eleven surviving preconquest pictorials drawn and painted on bark or deerskin. These colorful documents show that Mesoamerican peoples conceived of *time* and *space* as thoroughly intertwined. It was the function of ritual life acted out in the ceremonial centers to regulate and restore the detailed interaction of spatial directions, colors, and towns with time periods, anniversaries, births, deaths, journeys, ancestors, and war.

These documents and the sculptural tradition clearly indicate that there were different degrees of writing in Mesoamerican culture, including a spectrum moving from pictorial signs to phonetic scripts. In central Mexico screenfolds and codices show that the cosmological, genealogical, ritual, and historical information was communicated to the community by a combination of pictorial sign and oral interpreter who used images as the basis for verbal presentation. In this way they were storybooks—pictorial books used for the oral description and interpretation of genealogies, town histories, astronomical events, and ritual prescriptions. The pictorial signs and phonetic syllabary depicting the gods, nature, places, kings, warriors, bodily parts, and ritual objects were combined with oral traditions to direct ritual life in all its aspects. This communication of cosmovision and ceremonial life was controlled by the ruling classes.

These documents, plus the remarkable postconquest pictorials (with commentaries in Spanish and sometimes Italian) such as the *Codex Mendoza,* display a powerful obsession with the cycles of agriculture and stars (macrocosmos and microcosmos) and the forces and meaning of sacred time and sacred place. Time was closely observed and each day was considered loaded with celestial and divine influences that determined the inner character and destiny of a person and actions carried out at specific times. This pattern of timekeeping is displayed in the puzzling manuscript called the *Dresden Codex,* a ritual almanac depicting the detailed intimacy of humans, deities, and celestial bodies.

Contemporary Fieldwork Reports

A fourth resource for the study of Mesoamerican religions is contemporary fieldwork carried out in many indigenous communities. New studies into the calendars, processions, mythology, dream life, healing practices, clothes, market systems, and syncretistic cults reveal both continuities with and changes from the pre-Columbian world.

Given this remarkable ensemble of resources for approaching Mesoamerican religions, what was the religious character of the ancient world of ceremonial centers?

Religion as Worldmaking, Worldcentering, Worldrenewing

As we look at the map of Mesoamerican traditions we see the many locations of different cultures and ceremonial centers (see p. 118). In fact Mesoamerican history was characterized by an eccentric periodicity of creativity, stability, and settlement. The urban tradition was not controlled by one or even several capitals during its distinguished history. Ecological variation and instability as well as intense competition between city-states resulted in periodic collapses of regional capitals, followed by periods of reorganization in which particular ceremonial capitals dominated specific regions. This pattern of order/collapse/recentering/order/collapse and so on was stabilized by certain distinguished periods of creative order. These periods and places of creative order include the Olmecs (1500–300 B.C.E.), Iztapan Culture (300 B.C.E.–100 C.E.), Classic Maya (200–900 C.E.), Kaminaljuyú (500 B.C.E.–800 C.E.), Monte Albán (350–1200 C.E.), Mixtec (1200–1521 C.E.), Toltec (900–1250 C.E.), and Aztec (1300–1521 C.E.).

What was the social and religious character of these major periods of cultural integration? In all the cultures listed above three essential processes animated the world of the ceremonial center: worldmaking, worldcentering, and worldrenewing. These processes often interacted to form the religious traditions of Mesoamerican capitals.

Worldmaking

In every case society was organized by and around ceremonial centers modeled on a vision of the structure of the universe. The model of the structure of the universe was contained in the treasured mythology of each community, which told how the world was made and how supernatural forces organized the cosmos.

These ceremonial centers controlled what one scholar has called an **ecological complex** consisting of agricultural production and technological potentials, including art, trading networks, and movements in human population. Each such community, called (in the Aztec world) a *tlatocayotl* (domain of the *tlatoani* or chief speaker), had a ceremonial precinct, often with monumental architecture that served as the ritual theater for acting out the ways in which the world was made and would be remade. Each of the ceremonial centers was a pivot of the universe, acting as a magnet drawing all manner of goods, peoples, and powers into its space.

An example of this magnetic power is described in the sixteenth-century Spanish eyewitness account of Díaz del Castillo:

To go back to the facts, it seems to me that the circuit of the great pyramid was equal to that of six large town lots, such as they measure in this country, and from below up to where a small tower stood, where they kept their Idols, it narrowed. . . . There was a report that at the time they began to build that great pyramid, all the inhabitants of that mighty city had placed as offerings in the foundation, gold and silver and pearls and precious stones, and had bathed them with blood of the many Indian prisoners of war who were sacrificed, and had placed there every sort and kind of seed that the land produces, so that their Idols should insure victories and riches, and large crops.[17]

By giving precious offerings to the ***axis mundi,*** the center of the world of the community, their world got made and remade in terms of agriculture and war.

Perhaps the best example of worldmaking I can use to clarify the term comes from the Aztec myth of the creation of the Fifth Age, the age in which they lived. We are told that before the present world was made, "When no sun had shown and no dawn had broken," the gods gathered in the great ceremonial city of Teotihuacan (Abode of the Gods) to create a new sun. For four days they did penances in the cosmic darkness around a divine fire, which was burning for the duration. Two deities, Nanauatzin (the Pimply One) and Tecuciztecatl (Lord of the Snails) hurled themselves into the fire. The gods sat looking in all directions to see the sun rise. One god, Quetzalcoatl, faced toward the east and there the sun rose. The world was now made. A ceremonial center (Teotihuacan) and a celestial event (sunrise) are linked and aligned uniting heaven and earth. But it was still not centered. The sun was not on its course through the sky, because "when the sun burst forth, he appeared to be red; he kept swaying from side to side." The world has been made with the appearance of the sun, but it had no stability, no process, no center. It has been made through sacrifice, but as we shall see, the world still needed to be centered.

Worldcentering

The cultural world was made and ordered at the ceremonial centers through the creative work of human beings. Human beings acted as the "centering" agents of cultural and religious life in two decisive ways. First, the human body was considered the nexus and unifying structure of the universe. In cosmology, ritual, social structure, and art it is a religious conception of the human body that gives Mesoamerican religions a powerful focus. Second, the world was centered through the work of sacred specialists and royal lineages. Each of these communities operated under the religious authority of an elite corps of priests, rulers, and warriors, who controlled the ritual actions and social groups of farmers, warriors, artists, astronomers, builders, traders, and commoners. This elite community took charge of the goods, peoples, and powers who were drawn into the villages, cities, and capitals and redistributed them according to their own needs. While these leadership groups also insured the well-being of the masses by dispensing food and technology, and organizing rituals and warfare, they made decisive moves to increase their own luxuries and powers in a highly disproportionate way. This led to an extraordinary focus on elite human beings.

Let's return to the myth of the creation of the Fifth Age. How did the cosmos become "centered"? That is, how did it find a pattern, orbit, process? Faced with the threatening condition in which the sun "could only remain still and motionless," the remaining gods committed themselves to a course of action that had a profound influence on the human communities that were created later. One elite god, Ecatl, was chosen to sacrifice *all* the remaining gods to set the sun in motion. Afterward he "arose and exerted himself fiercely and violently as he blew. At once he could move him, who thereupon went on his way" (that is, the sun moved along its orbit). It is through further sacrifice of extraordinary beings that the world becomes centered and regular as the sun moves along its path, dividing time into night and day.

Worldrenewing

The entire style of life of these hierarchical societies was organized by a worldview emphasizing the daily, monthly, and yearly rejuvenation of society and the cosmos. This rejuvenation depended on a complicated range of ritual performances that replayed the myths and images of the origins and transformations of the cosmos and its many parts. These rituals and mythic traditions were not mere repetitions of ancient ways. New rituals and mythic stories were produced to respond to ecological, social, and economic changes and crises. The priests, operating within the sacred confines of their ceremonial centers, used complex calendar systems, divination, and stargazing to direct these extraordinary public rituals to communicate the structure and dynamics of the universe.

An artist's reconstruction of the Maya ceremonial center, called the Acropolis, at Copán during the Late Classic Period. (From An Album of Maya Architecture *by Tatiana Proskouriakoff. New edition copyright © 1963 by the University of Oklahoma Press.)*

As we shall see in several upcoming chapters, astronomy played a major role in the calendrical, ritual, and military traditions of Mesoamerica. As with the celestial cycles, so the world of the humans, animals, and plants was renewed constantly within a tight system of ritual displays, pilgrimages, dances, songs, combats, sacrifices, and coronations.

And just as the cosmos was made (sunrise) and centered (sunpath) through sacrifice, so it is renewed through daily, weekly, monthly, and yearly sacrifices of different kinds. These sacrifices take many forms, including bleeding, heart sacrificing, drinking, abstaining from sexual behaviors, and expending money on food for the Day of the Dead.

These three major elements of the ceremonial center and celestial event (worldmaking), human creativity and sacrifice in the hands of an elite (world-centering), and the commitment to rejuvenation (worldrenewing) will guide the discussion in each of the subsequent chapters. Let us now turn to the history of Mesoamerican religions in order to view its chronology and creative periods.

6

History and Cosmovision in Mesoamerican Religions

And so then they put into words
  the Creation,
  the shaping
  of our first mother and father.
Only yellow corn
and white corn were their bodies.
Only food were the legs
and arms of man.
    Popul Vuh[18]

In many ways Mesoamerica is the most different of the world's early civili-
zations. It arose in a land where communication was exceptionally difficult
and natural disaster was frequent; its occupants had a wealth of domestic
plants but few domestic animals. This meant that not only economics but
also the metaphors of daily life, or of religion and politics, were different
from those of other civilizations: there could neither be "a bull of heaven"
nor a "lamb of God" in ancient Mexico. For all these reasons, Mesoamerica
is a critical case for developing and evaluating general ideas about world
view as a context for understanding the developing cultural complexity
and for the importance of what we term "religion" in the rise of the first
hierarchical polities.
    Henry T. Wright[19]

WHERE DID THE PEOPLES AND CULTURES of Mesoamerica originate? This question has challenged scholar and layperson alike from the earliest contacts with
indigenous American peoples to the twentieth century. Theologians in the sixteenth century, shocked by the sudden appearance of masses of peoples never
before imagined, asked, "Are they descendants of Adam and Eve?" Some Europeans, troubled by how to treat the Indians, wondered, "When Christ died for the

sins of humankind, did he also die for the natives of America?" In anthropological terms Europeans asked, "How do we take people who are scarcely human, or only half human, and teach them to become fully human, as we are?" Central to these questions was the search for the original geographical and cultural homeland of the Aztecs, Mayas, and their ancestors.

Within academic studies it was once thought that native Mesoamericans migrated from Egypt, bringing artistic, political, and religious ideas and symbols with them. The fact that both civilizations produced what appear to be pyramids and hieroglyphics was used to argue that Mesoamerican culture originated in the Old World and traveled to the Americas by various means. Other scholars have argued that they came from Asia, either sailing in *Kon-Tiki*-like boats across the Pacific or gradually migrating down the western coast of America, bringing elements of civilization that served as the basis for the ceremonial centers, calendars, and rituals of the Mayas and Aztecs. Recently some scholars have argued that Asian cultures strongly influenced the Costa Rican area of Mesoamerica, bringing Buddhist artistic and theological traditions to the New World more than two thousand years ago. This type of approach, called the diffusionist approach, argues that the great civilizations of the Americas were developed by migrating peoples who left original centers of cultures and transplanted the roots of civilization (monumental architecture, writing, calendrics) in American soil. This approach is largely based on a series of similarities (pyramids, art motifs, toys, cotton) found in Cambodia, India, China, and the Americas.

One extreme example of diffusionist thought very popular in the nineteenth century claimed that the lost continent of Atlantis, or Mu, was the original home of ancient American civilizations. Using Plato's description of the sinking of the legendary continent of Atlantis, proponents of the submerged continent theory argued that the aboriginal Americans saved themselves in the nick of time and brought to America their great civilization. An English nobleman, Lord Kingsborough, spent much of his family fortune trying to demonstrate that the native inhabitants of Mesoamerica were the descendants of the thirteen lost tribes of Israel. Perhaps the most fantastic formulation, popular in the twentieth century, is Erik von Daniken's claim that ancient astronauts brought the genius of extraterrestrial civilizations to ancient Mesoamerica. The theory of cultural diffusion raises many intriguing questions for the researcher interested in tracing the history of ancient transportation and communication patterns. But similarities in cultures do not demonstrate close or significant contact. This is especially the case when we realize that not a single object from Asian cultures has been discovered in the Americas. And many objects vital in Old World culture, such as the wheel, the cart, the plough, iron, and stringed instruments, are missing in the pre-Columbian New World.

In the case of the Americas such ridiculous formulations as von Daniken's, Kingsborough's, and some others may conceal a powerful ethnocentric bias. The implication of some diffusionist interpretations is that Native Americans were not capable of achieving extraordinary levels of cultural creativity on their own but needed the stimulus and remnants of superior foreigners to become civilized.

Scholars have clearly shown that Mesoamerican civilizations, in fact all New World civilizations and cultures, *developed as a result of cultural creativity indigenous to the Americas.* This is not to deny that impressive similarities between Old and New World cultures exist. Monumental architectural structures, which we refer to as pyramids, existed in Egypt, Indonesia, Mexico, Guatemala, and other parts of Mesoamerica. But the so-called pyramids of Mesoamerica were actually huge platforms constructed to support temples, which together served as theatrical stages upon which were acted out the pomp, cosmovision, and political spectacles of the city. It is true that some Mesoamerican pyramid/temples served (as in the case of Egypt) as royal tombs and monuments to ancestors, but it is more likely that they were primarily places of public performance of religious ceremonies linking the living and the dead in a day-to-day fashion. Also, in Mesoamerica, specific pyramid/temples could be utilized by *successive rulers* for exterior displays of cosmovision and politics as well as for interior burials of individuals and treasure.

Another major difference between the monumental cities of the Old and New Worlds was the intricate and widespread 260-day ritual calendar so influential among many Mesoamerican peoples. Although it appears that limited contact between Asian cultures and the peoples of Mesoamerica took place, the Olmecs, Huastecs, Mayas, Tlaxcalans, Toltecs, Mixtecs, Otomis, Aztecs, and all other indigenous cultures developed their own cultural processes independent of significant contributions from outside civilizations. These cultural processes were concentrated and crystallized in the numerous ceremonial centers, city-states, and cosmovisions that organized Mesoamerican society.

In this chapter we will present an overview of the history of Mesoamerican religions from two points of view. We will describe the patterns of worldmaking, worldcentering, and worldrenewing in chronological order beginning with the rise of agriculture, proceeding through the three major stages of historical development called the Formative Period (1800 B.C.E.–200 C.E.), the Classic Period (200–900 C.E.), and the Post-Classic Period (900–1500 C.E.). And we will also emphasize the creative moments of and major contributions to the formation of Mesoamerican religions.

Plants and the Sacred Dead

Mesoamerica was a geographical and cultural area covering the southern two-thirds of Mexico and significant portions of Central America. In this extensive region human populations developed intensive agricultures, which served as the partial basis for the rise of urban civilizations. It is evident that human populations from northeast Asia (groups of Mongoloid peoples) entered the New World as early as 50,000 B.C.E. and as late as the time of Christ over and along the Bering Strait land bridge that connected Siberia and Alaska. These hunting and gathering peoples migrated southward and eventually reached the Basin of Mexico by 20,000 B.C.E. They carried a circumpolar and circumboreal hunting culture into the Americas, which included shamanism and ceremonial ties to animals and their spirits. Various human physical types speaking many languages migrated into North America and Mesoamerica; over 250 languages for the area covering Mexico and Guatemala have been identified. [See Native Religions of North America pp. 264–66 for a discussion of the origins of Native Americans.]

As these peoples moved into Mesoamerica, they encountered a geography of contrasts and wonders, highlands and lowlands, with an astonishing variety of ecosystems. High mountain ranges, periodically volcanic, form high valley systems and plateaus where major cultural centers developed at different periods in history. These high, mountainous areas sweep down on the eastern and western sides into lowland areas that give way to the Gulf of Mexico, the Caribbean Sea, and the Pacific Ocean. One writer has compared sections of Mesoamerica to the shape of a pyramid with temples and open spaces on top. The plateaus and high valleys as well as the fertile areas of the lowlands served as important centers of pre-Hispanic cultures.

The most creative cultural event in the preurban history of Mesoamerica was the control of food energy contained in plants. As the quotation that begins this chapter indicates, the natives compared the creation of human life with the creation of corn: The substance of the human body consisted of yellow and white corn! The domestication of agriculture, fundamental to the eventual rise of permanent villages, ceremonial centers, and social differentiation developed slowly between 6500 B.C.E. and 2000 B.C.E. as peoples learned to plant and harvest corn, beans, squash, avocados, cotton, and chilies. All of these plants were perceived as imbued with sacred powers and came to play important roles in the mythology, calendar, ritual, costumes, ancestor worship, and performances of Mesoamerican religions. Centuries later, in the Aztec capital of Tenochtitlan, corn was one of the rewards for the good citizen who acted diligently. In the ceremony Teotleco (The Gods Arrive) the ritual began when a priest provided

> a small basket of dried grains of maize, or else four ears of maize: in some places, three ears of maize; if [the householders] were very poor, it was two ears of maize that he gave them. . . . And no one just idly ate the maize toasted on the embers; only those who were diligent, acceptable, careful, wakeful, who trusted not too much their own diligence.[20]

Archaeologists have discerned that during the last part of these agricultural periods people developed some of the ritual relationships to the human body that eventually became central to the religions of numerous Mesoamerican peoples. These included shamanism, special offerings to the dead, the dismemberment of human beings, sacrifice, and cremation. Cultures practiced rituals dedicated to the hunting and restoration of animals and their spirits as well as to the planting, fertilization, and harvesting of plants. It appears that some powerful beliefs in the longevity of the human spirit and an afterlife were present. Some humans were buried with companions whose involuntary death provided assistance to the leader or master in the world of supernatural entities. Around 2500 B.C.E. multiple forms of ritual and domestic pottery, including cooking utensils, clay figurines of women, animals, and deities, were developed in central Mexico; and by 1800 B.C.E. the stage was set for what Eric Wolf called "villages and holy towns," in which some of the basic cultural religious patterns for the next three thousand years were established.

The subsequent period of cultural history has been designated by historians as the Formative Period (see chronology, p. 109). Between 1800 B.C.E. and 200 C.E. cultures began to form permanent ceremonial centers containing impressive monumental, ceremonial architecture including pyramids, palaces, tombs, and spacious outdoor ritual precincts. It was within these sacred precincts, examples of what we have called worldmaking, that ritual performances were acted out and directed by priestly elites who managed the integration of economic, political, artistic, astronomical, and spiritual forces. One pervasive performance was ritual dancing in community ceremonial centers. Archaeologists working in Oaxaca, Mexico, have uncovered figurines depicting dance societies as well as conch-shell trumpets and turtle-shell drums dating from 1200 B.C.E. to 600 B.C.E. The dancers are dressed as fantastic animals and as jaguars, birds, and pumas reflecting the sacralization of human-animal relationship. Dance societies dressed in these animal motifs were active when the Spaniards arrived and are still performing in indigenous communities and for tourists today.

It is also apparent that important private and public ceremonies of ritual bloodletting were carried out. We know that in the Classic (200–900 C.E.) and Post-Classic (900–1500 C.E.) periods priests drew blood from tongues, earlobes, thighs, and sexual organs using fish spines, maguey thorns, obsidian blades, or, in the case of Mayan lords, knotted strings of thorns. Some of these bloodletting instruments have been found in ruins of private households of public ceremonial precincts in Oaxaca that date from between 1200 B.C.E. and 600 B.C.E. These discoveries indicate that ceremonial centers were within domestic dwellings as well as in the larger community spaces.[21]

It is also important that a number of public ceremonial buildings in the Oaxaca region share astronomical orientations (that is, they are aligned toward horizon points where sun, moon, Venus, or other celestial bodies appear) with ceremonial structures hundreds of miles away. This indicates a shared cosmovision that influenced ceremonial architecture and ritual very early in Mesoamerican history. This combination of ceremonial center (microcosmos) and astronomical event (macrocosmos) is what helps create order in the world.

The art and architecture of the earliest Mesoamerican civilization, called the Olmecs by archaeologists, shows that religious ideas and symbols were not only mental activities, but rather tied up with daily work, trade, social order, and warfare.

The Olmec World:
Jaguars and Giants in Stone

One of the real challenges for students of religion in general and Mesoamerica in particular is to understand cultures that did not produce what we consider writing. Many Mesoamerican cultures were primarily oral in their modes of expression. Others, such as the Mixtec, the Maya, and the Aztec, produced pictorial systems with varying degrees of symbolic expressions including pictograms, ideograms, and phonetic script. The range of expression in Mesoamerica is so complex and varied that it has challenged scholars to rethink the category of "writing" and to reevaluate the status of cultural superiority that has too long accompanied it.

In addition to the important task of interpreting oral traditions, we are often faced with the need to work with "mute texts"—stones, sacred stones, ceremonial architecture, pottery, and even human and animal bones. The most vivid example of this situation is the Olmec culture (*Olmec* means "people from the land of the rubber trees"), whose scattered ceremonial centers took shape around 1800 B.C.E. and collapsed by 300 B.C.E. The name Olmec was used by an indigenous group living in this area at the time of the conquest. It is not known what the ancient community called itself.

The social history of permanent Mesoamerican ceremonial centers begins around 1800 B.C.E. with the rise of the **Olmec Style** of art and architecture found in a variety of sacred precincts and caves, originating in the lowland regions of southern Vera Cruz and western Tabasco near the coast of the Gulf of Mexico. This region is one of the richest archaeological zones in the world, probably having the highest density of sites per square mile in all of Mesoamerica. Called the "Mother Culture" of later Mesoamerican civilizations by the Mexican artist and scholar Miguel Covarrubias, the Olmecs set in motion certain religious patterns that were elaborated and developed by later peoples. Evidence of these patterns is found in a glorious tradition of stone carvings, rock paintings, and religious imagery for us to admire and interpret.

The most impressive pattern of Olmec culture was the manner in which the earth was reshaped as a means of religious expression. The Olmec media for art and symbolic expression were jade, basalt, clay, and the earth itself in the forms of caves, hills, and artificial volcanoes such as was used at **La Venta** to represent an earth pyramid. Each of these media was transformed to represent the realities of social hierarchy and religious imagination. Caves became the setting for cave paintings and rituals of mythic events while cliffs became the place of carvings of human-animal-spirit relations. The ceremonial centers were assemblages of sacred spaces made of redesigned earthly materials arranged on and *within* the earth. This tie to the earth is reflected in Olmec mythology expressing themes of emergence from caves, human-jaguar transformation, and the relations of animals to rulers. We can see the fabric of nature-human relations in the bas relief from Chalcatzingo where an Olmec ruler or man-god is seated in a cave holding a box surrounded by clouds, water, jade (circular motifs), vegetation, and the stone representing the earth itself. And in at least one case, archaeologists have found large mosaics laid out to form a jaguar mask buried in multiple layers beneath the surface of the earth.

The Olmec heartland of the coastal region has been compared to the "fertile crescent" of Mesopotamia because of its extraordinary potential for corn farming and its rich supply of fish, aquatic birds, frogs, and toads. In this region of abundant natural resources the Olmecs built permanent ceremonial centers accompanied by an alluring art style appearing in jade miniatures, pottery, stelae (upright standing stones with carved imagery), and large sculpture. The culture managed to spread its religious, political, and artistic conceptions up into the central Mexican highlands, into the western lowlands, and as far south as El Salvador through the control of long-distance trade routes and exploration.

Although we cannot tell if the Olmecs achieved territorial control over large parts of Mesoamerica, it is clear that their artistic and conceptual style was spread far and wide. This style included the ritual calendar and ritual burials and a profound relationship with animals whose visages permeate their art. In fact Olmec ceremonial centers were ornamented with a number of fantastic religious motifs depicting animal-human relations. Such combinations as human-jaguar, jaguar-bird, bird-jaguar-caiman (alligator), jaguar-caiman-fish, and caiman-human appear in different sites. Rattlesnakes, fer-de-lances (venomous pit vipers), harpy eagles, and monkeys were also considered manifestations of the sacred sky, earth, and underworld. It is possible that these carefully carved, sometimes precious stone images reflect the belief in spirit helpers who took the form of powerful, aggressive, even dangerous animals serving in the practice of shamans. We know from later Maya and Aztec periods that real and fantastic animals or entities became intimately associated with all individuals. They could function as the spiritual guides of sacred specialists, warriors, priests, and the ruling class. [See Religions of Africa p. 44 and Native Religions of North America pp. 260, 268, 272–73, 277, 309–12, 332–33 for the religious significance of animals and hunting.]

This stone carving depicts a person seated in a stylized cave, symbolizing the earth-monster. The emerging scroll represents wind or the sound of thunder, while precious raindrops, representing fertility, fall from the clouds. Monument 1 El-Rey, Chalcatzingo, Morelos, Mexico c. 600 B.C.E. (Courtesy of Michael Coe.)

One site that depicts early conceptions of Mesoamerican deities was San Lorenzo, which was fully formed by 1200 B.C.E. It was suddenly destroyed around 900 B.C.E., when many of its religious and historical images were mutilated and buried. In addition to the over two hundred ceremonial mounds identified at this site, the most astonishing discovery was the six colossal stone heads carved with powerful simplicity depicting individual human faces with mongoloid features, each wearing a helmetlike headgear. Up to nine feet in height, weighing forty tons, these heads, along with a number of other huge stone monuments, are carved from rocks in the Tuxtla mountains over forty-five miles from the site. Their transportation to San Lorenzo over land and water, as well as their artistic sophistication, reflects both a complex level of social organization and a deep concern for religious symbolism. It is difficult to understand the meaning of these giant stone heads, which were in some cases lined up at the edge of a ceremonial area. It has been suggested that they represent the heads of dead warriors or portraits of rulers, whose images guarded the sacred

One of many colossal basalt heads carved by the Olmecs at ceremonial centers on Mexico's gulf coast. This monolith is nearly three meters in height and was transported over fifty miles from its quarry site. Monument 1 from San Lorenzo, c. 1200 B.C.E. (Photograph courtesy of Michael Coe.)

precincts from invaders. It is likely that they represent the Olmec concern with royal genealogy by memorializing rulers who appear as gigantic beings influencing daily life.

Another impressive site is the ceremonial center of La Venta, where jaguar motifs and giant heads sculpted in stone embroider a small, swampy, stoneless island. In the heart of this carefully planned site stands Mesoamerica's first great pyramid. It is a fluted, cone-shaped natural structure 420 feet in diameter and 100 feet high, with its outward surface consisting of alternating rises and depressions that give it the appearance of a volcano. Nearby, archaeologists found the buried remains of two juveniles heavily covered with thick cinnabar pigment accompanied by offerings of jade beads and stingray spines. This ceremonious concern for the dead buried near the heart of the sacred precinct shows a special relation between certain human groups and the *axis mundi*. This combination of human and temple at the heart of a settlement indicates the early pattern of what we have called worldcentering. In a number of later cultures the royal dead were buried in tombs within the sacred precincts, suggesting a special relation between sacred space, ceremonial structures, the earth, the dead, and the underworld. A number of other spectacular caches, perhaps offerings to the gods, containing jade, jaguar mosaics, and pierced concave mirrors made of iron ore, were excavated at La Venta.

One of the greatest religious achievements of Mesoamerica was the invention of a ritual calendar of extraordinary accuracy. At a third major site, Tres Zapotes, all of the Olmec artistic and religious characteristics, plus one, were combined in the sacred center. The most famous monument of Tres Zapotes is called stela C. It contains a jaguar monster mask on one side and a column of bars and dot numerals on the other. However, it has been determined that this is a post-Olmec monument containing bars and dots that have been deciphered as the date 31 B.C.E. The suggestion is that the Olmec and not the Maya, as previously thought, invented, toward the end of their history, the great calendar system called the **long count,** which was instrumental in organizing ritual and social life in parts of Mesoamerica. [See Native Religions of North America pp. 280–82, 351–54, Judaism pp. 431–33, Christianity pp. 551–53, Islam pp. 674, 707, Hinduism pp. 727, 793–94, Buddhism pp. 890–91, Religions of China pp. 1021–24, and Religions of Japan pp. 1141–46 for discussion of religious calendar and time.]

Astronomy and the Sacred Ball Game

One of the most intriguing types of ceremonial centers was the sacred ball court (*tlachco* in Nahuatl, *Pok-ta-pok* in Maya) where the ball game was played. Spread throughout Mesoamerica, this ritual tradition has one of its most impressive expressions at the site of El Tajín in modern-day Vera Cruz, where it was developed as a major cosmic symbol between 200 C.E. and 500 C.E. Typically the game was played on a ball court laid out like a capital letter I with a central narrow gallery or playing court leading at both ends to short perpendicular spaces. This was a stylized representation of the four-quartered universe joined by the central or fifth region. The court and the game constituted a cosmogram (image of the cosmos) and religious drama. Detailed carvings of the ball game ritual from El Tajín show the dress, action, and religious meaning of this game. It appeared that on certain occasions the losing warriors, or at least a representative, were publicly and ritually sacrificed and beheaded in the shrine.

Later, in Aztec times, it appears that the playing court represented the narrow passageway of the underworld through which the sun traveled at night. The game represented a cosmic struggle between competing factions to see which group could bring the sun out of the underworld by hitting the ball through one of the two perforated rings on the sides of the court. The ball court, then, is a kind of temple in which the solar drama is acted out in human time and space. The sacrifice of the losing player may represent the offering of energy in the form of blood and human life in order to give birth to the new sun.

Fortunately the Dominican priest Diego Durán, who lived in New Spain between 1545 and 1588, asked his native parishioners about the native ball game. He wrote,

So that we can understand its form and begin to appreciate the skill and dexterity with which this game was played, it must be noted that ball courts existed in all the illustrious, civilized, and powerful cities and towns, in those ruled by either the community or the lords, the latter stressing [the game] inordinately. A regular competition existed between the two [types of communities]. [The ball courts] were enclosed with ornate and handsomely

A ceremonial ball court at the Late Classic Maya site of Copán, in Honduras. (Courtesy of Linda Schele, photographer.)

carved walls. The interior floor was of stucco, finely polished and decorated with figures of the god and demons to whom the game was dedicated and whom the players held to be their patrons in that sport. These ball courts were larger in some places than in others.

Durán describes the walls, sculptures, and crowds this way:

> The height of the wall was anywhere between eight and eleven feet high, running all around [the court]. Because of heathen custom, around [the wall] were planted wild palms or trees which give red seeds, whose wood is soft and light. Crucifixes and carved images are made of it today. The surrounding walls were adorned with merlons or stone statues, all spaced out. [These places] became filled to bursting when there was a game of all the lords, when warlike activities ceased, owing to truces or other causes, thus permitting [the games].[22]

Two other important religious innovations, astronomical alignments and pictorial narratives, took place by the time the ceremonial centers of Monte Albán (600–300 B.C.E.) and Izapa (200 B.C.E.–100 C.E.) were formed. At the heart of over two hundred permanent sites near the present-day city of Oaxaca in southern Mexico stood the elaborately built Zapotec hilltop center of Monte Albán. It consisted of temples, courtyards, ball courts, and tombs for elites scattered throughout the site. Among its many characteristics are the alignment of buildings with particular astronomical events plus the appearance of writing and the elaboration of the long count calendar system. Several buildings were built so as to face a particular horizon appearance of a celestial body or a constellation. This relationship of the orientation of ceremonial buildings to astronomical events such as the solstices, equinoxes, and Venus cycles is of major importance in our understanding of cosmovision. It shows that early in the architectural record Mesoamericans were expressing the conviction that human and cultural spaces (such as homes, pyramids, temples, ball courts) had to be in tune or aligned with celestial bodies and their patterns. This integration of sky and earth and human society in Mesoamerica has been intensely studied by archaeoastronomers such as Anthony Aveni, who has shown that in some cases ceremonial buildings were constructed to mark the passage of Venus from its first to its last appearance in the Venus cycle, above the horizon. We will see more of this relationship of stargazing and temple alignment in later cultures.

Recently archaeologists have realized that Iztapa, in Guatemala, which contained over seventy-five pyramid mounds and a large number of stone stelae, was a major transition point between the Olmec style and the Maya achievement. Of particular importance are the pictorial narratives, stories carved in stone depicting human and celestial forces. We see humans and deities involved in battles, sacrifices (including decapitation), and rituals, all associated with a stylized sacred world tree. Many of these religious ideas and actions were to find their most brilliant expression among the Classic Maya, who now entered the stage.

The Classic Maya:
Kings and Cosmic Trees

The astonishing achievements of the Classic Maya civilization have inspired awe and admiration in all who come to study them. A number of religious innovations appear to crystallize in Maya society between 200 C.E. and 900 C.E., a period designated as the Classic Maya. Among the major elements of the Maya achievement were the mathematically ingenious calendar; lavishly decorated ceremonial centers; a heightened conception of the royal person; writing; and a complex mythology of the underworld and cosmic regeneration. It is also amazing that these city-states and achievements developed in the forests and jungle environments, where civilizations have usually had a difficult time taking hold. Called the "Mysterious Maya" for generations, they were once believed to have been a peace-loving civilization of stargazing priests whose theological vision should be imitated by modern people. Recent studies have revealed a more typical civilization motivated by warfare, the desire to dominate, hierarchies, elaborate ceremonies associated with lineage and ancestors, and complex esoteric religious ideas. One of the greatest mysteries about the Classic Mayas is the **Maya collapse:** the rapid and near total collapse of many of their ceremonial centers during the short period of 790 C.E. to 900 C.E. It appears that a pervasive series of crises shattered the Maya world, stimulated by interlocking collapses in the agricultural, ceremonial, and political systems that held the society together.

The character of the Classic Maya world is well represented in a small jade plaque discovered in 1864 by workers digging a canal in eastern Guatemala. Called the Leiden Plate because eventually it was taken to Leiden, Holland, this 8.5-inch object contains two typical images of Maya life. On one side we find a long count calendar date corresponding to 320 C.E., while on the other side we see an extravagantly dressed Maya lord stepping on a midget-sized captive cowering underneath him. This combination of sacred time, warfare, and social hierarchy carved in fine jade illustrates the integration of vital elements of the Maya achievement.

One of the most creative religious achievements attributed to the Classic Maya was the long count calendar. Although this calendric system had earlier origins based on intense astronomical observations, it was the Maya who elaborated the cosmological conviction that human life would be most favorable if it mirrored the mathematically expressible cycles of the heavens. As a means of recording important human events and attuning human order to the celestial order, the Maya developed a calendar system with many different counts including the Tzolkin (260-day count related to human gestation), the Haab (365-day count related to solar cycle), the long count (related to ancestor worship and lineages), the **calendar round** (a 52-year cycle), the Lords of the Night (9-day interval), and the lunar cycle. The largest count in this system was the long count, which measured each day from the beginning date of the present cosmic era in 3114 B.C.E. and prophesied its end on December 23, 2012. Each day was measured by a system of five subunits and enabled the priest to compute dates in colossal cycles going back to at least nine million years B.C.E. as marked on inscriptions in several ceremonial centers.[23] Mathematicians have pointed out that an understanding of the concept zero is necessary for such computations. The Maya marked these days so they could be in conscious contact with the sacred forces appearing in the terrestrial world at carefully determined intervals. Unfortunately this calendar system largely faded from use, except in scattered parts of Yucatan, after the Classic Maya society collapsed.

The social style of this universe appears in the murals of **Bonampak** ("city of painted walls"), which were discovered by accident in 1946. A photographer following a jungle deer saw it go into a small temple barely visible in the overgrowth. Once within he was surprised to find murals covering the walls and ceilings of three rooms depicting the formal aspects of Maya court life and a series of scenes of bloodletting, warfare, human sacrifice, ceremonial processions, and dances on pyramids, all surrounded by astronomical and calendrical signs. In one alluring scene a procession of deity impersonators dressed as animals (crocodiles, crabs, jaguars) accompany a musical ensemble preparing to process.

During this long period of cultural creativity the Maya elaborated a profound religious cosmovision based on the "symbolism of the center." The Maya

This painted wall depicts the arraignment of prisoners by a victorious procession of elites and warriors. The prisoners are being tortured by having their fingernails plucked before their final sacrifice. Structure 1, Room 2, Bonampak, Chiapas, Mexico, eighth century C.E. (Photograph courtesy of the Peabody Museum, Harvard University; photograph by F. P. Orchard.)

believed the world was centered by a combination of the sacred flowering cosmic tree and the royal person (**Mah K'ina,** Great Sun Lord), both linked to the world of ancestors. This cosmovision is made clearest at the beautiful site of Palenque, where pictorial programs, carved on a series of ceremonial temples and buildings, show how the royal families ruled, communicated with gods, died, and passed power from the dead to the living and rejuvenated the agricultural world. As we shall see in chapter 8, the Maya lords had a grandiose conception of their role in sacred history. Let us now move over four hundred miles to the north where the imperial capital of Teotihuacan was constructed.

Teotihuacan: The Imperial Capital

The most frequently visited archaeological site in the Americas is Teotihuacan, known to most people as the "pyramids." Located in the central highlands thirty miles northeast of present-day Mexico City, Teotihuacan (as known to the Aztecs five hundred years after the city collapsed) means "the place where one becomes deified." Not only did it contain monumental architecture, but it was also designed as a gigantic image of the cosmos. At its peak, around 500 C.E., Teotihuacan was populated by over two hundred thousand people who shared in the prestige of a capital that influenced many cities and towns within and beyond the central plateau of Mexico.

Surprisingly, Teotihuacan had its beginnings in a cave. This greatest of Classic cities, with its immense towering pyramids of the sun and moon, elaborate ceremonial courtyards, and residential palaces (the city contains over seventy-five temples), originated underground at the mouth of a well. Recent excavations show that directly under the Pyramid of the Sun lie the remains of an ancient tunnel and shrine area, which was an early, if not the original, sacred center for ritual and perhaps the goal of pilgrimages. Throughout Mesoamerican history caves are valued as the places of origin of ancestral peoples and the openings to the powers and gods of the underworld. Like the city that was to spread out above it, this cave was artificially reshaped and decorated into the form of a four-petaled flower. In some of the later paintings and pictorial narratives the Mesoamerican cosmos is symbolized by a four-petaled flower representing the division of space into four cardinal regions around a center. It is possible that the cave was Teotihuacan's earliest *imago mundi,* or sacred image of the cosmos.

The entire city of Teotihuacan was laid out by its planners and architects as a four-part imitation of the cosmos. In this way it was not only a container of religious symbolism, it was itself a religious symbol. The city's hundreds of residential, ritual, and craft buildings followed a grid pattern that was organized by two main avenues: the Street of the Dead (over two thousand meters long) and the East West Avenue, which crossed at right angles in the center of the city dividing it into four huge quadrants. It is important to note that a number of natural features such as creeks and hills were altered to conform to this scheme.

This layout had clear linkages to astronomical events. The great stairway of the Pyramid of the Sun, for example, faces a westerly point on the horizon where the **Pleiades,** called Tianquitzli, meaning "marketplace" (or Miec meaning "heap") by later Nahuatl peoples, sat directly in front of it. What exact religious moment in the city's calendar this day signified may never be clear; but it is obvious that there was a noble attempt to achieve a harmony and to express that harmony publicly between the great pyramid and celestial patterns. This is also demonstrated by the fact that the Pleiades made its first yearly appearance above the horizon before sunrise on the day the Sun passed through the zenith. It is likely that these two stellar events, key to the cosmovision of so many Mesoamerican cultures, signaled the moment when the elites organized the masses of people to ritually prepare for the new agricultural season.

The art of Teotihuacan also reveals an abundance of cults dedicated to the activities of warfare, titular deities, fertility, ball games, dynastic rulers, and burials. The earlier evidence of these religious themes that we have studied now takes center stage in the evidence at Teotihuacan. And although we have no written material and very limited oral tradition directly related to Teotihuacan, it appears that deities, which in later cultures are identified as Quetzalcoatl (the Feathered Serpent), **Tlaloc** (the Rain God), Xipe Totec (the God of Vegetation), and Xochiquetzal (the Goddess of Sexuality), were highly revered in the great capital.

It is clear that later cultures, especially the Aztecs, looked to Teotihuacan as the Place of Origins. They claimed in their sacred history that the Fifth Sun, the Aztec Era, was born out of sacrificial fire in the great city at the beginning of

The Pyramid of the Sun at Teotihuacan. This monumental structure dominated the ceremonial center and imperial capital of the Valley of Mexico from 200 until 750 C.E. In the foreground are platforms along the Street of the Dead that supported other smaller temples and dwellings. At the height of its urban expansion (300–600 C.E.), Teotihuacan rivaled the most populated of Old World cities. (Photograph courtesy of Lawrence G. Desmond.)

time. The story of the creation of the Fifth Age of the cosmos, the age of the Aztecs, begins:

> It is told that when yet [all] was in darkness, when yet no sun had shown and no dawn had broken—it is said—the gods gathered themselves there at Teotihuacan. They spoke . . . "Who will take it upon himself to be the sun, to bring the dawn?"[24]

Teotihuacan's monumental magnificence, precise spatial order, exuberant craft and market systems, and sacred prestige helped make this city the center of an expanding, pulsating empire. Although its position of absolute dominance over many other cities appears to have lasted for less than two hundred years, its status as the center for this region of the Mesoamerican world cannot be limited to the time when its art styles were imitated. For Teotihuacan was the first true capital, the first great place in central Mexico, where a fully integrated, rich, and well-fed society operated under the authority of supernatural forces and cosmo-magical formulas.

Tollan: City of the Plumed Serpent

> Quetzalcoatl was looked upon as a god. He was worshiped and prayed to in former times in Tollan, and there his temple stood: very high, very tall. Extremely tall, extremely high.[25]

This passage, recited by an Aztec elder to the Spanish priest-researcher Bernardino de Sahagun, refers to one of the most creative periods of the history of Mesoamerican religions, namely the Toltec empire. In Aztec times (1325–1521 C.E.) young people were educated about the cultural brilliance and religious genius of the ancient kingdom of Tollan (Place of Reeds) ruled by the priest-king **Topiltzin Quetzalcoatl** (Our Young Prince the Feathered Serpent), who was a devotee of the great god Quetzalcoatl. Following the rapid eighth-century collapse of Teotihuacan as the center of the Mesoamerican world, the "Great Tollan" was formed, consisting of over twenty sizable settlements surrounding the capital of Tollan, also called Tula. According to the sacred history taught in Aztec *calmecacs,* or schools, Tollan existed in a golden age where agricultural abundance, technological excellence, artistic perfection, and spiritual genius were united under the patronage of the great divine being, Quetzalcoatl, the Plumed Serpent. Tollan was inhabited by the legendary Toltecs, whose very name signified artistic excellence. They were remembered as

> very wise. Their works were all good, all perfect, all wonderful, all miraculous, their houses beautiful, tiled in mosaics, smooth stuccoed, very marvelous.[26]

In this setting of cultural genius and economic stability, the Toltecs invented the calendar, originated the year count, they established the way in which the night, the day would work . . . they discerned the orbits of the stars. . . .[27]

and invented rituals of divination. Of course we have already seen that many of these cultural forms were invented and developed a millennium before the Toltecs. But with the rapid collapse of earlier cultures these traditions were periodically reinvented and developed. Also, in Aztec times, all societies seeking prestige claimed their descent from the Toltec lineage.

All this abundance and creativity was organized by a ceremonial center consisting of a great pyramid surrounded by four temples, beautifully decorated, facing the four cardinal points of the universe. At the center of this world lived the priest-king Quetzalcoatl, who had fabulous powers endowed upon him by his god. It was recited in the Aztec schools, "Truly with him it began, truly from him it flowed out, from Quetzalcoatl—all art and knowledge."

Scholars have worked diligently through the pictorial, architectural, and ethnohistorical evidence to discover that there were at least two Quetzalcoatls. One, a powerful creator god, was one of the four children of the divine duality, Ometeotl, who dwelled in the innermost part of heaven, above the twelfth level. In different accounts Quetzalcoatl creates the cosmos, recovers the ancestral bones from the underworld (**Mictlan**), and acquires corn from the **Mountain of Sustenance** for humans. The other was his human representative or *hombre-dios* (man-god) who ruled Tollan and brought it to its apex of greatness. The human Quetzalcoatl was also known by his calendrical name as Ce Acatl Topiltzin Quetzalcoatl (One Reed, Our Young Prince the Feathered Serpent). He was remembered in song, poetry, and art as having a miraculous birth, a rigorous training for the priesthood that included mountain asceticism, a fierce career as a warrior, and a brief period as a triumphant king. During his kingship he apparently attempted a religious revolution. According to one source Topiltzin Quetzalcoatl changed the ritual tradition of sacrificing human beings and substituted quail, butterflies, and rabbits. This radical departure provoked the magical attacks of his archrival Tezcatlipoca, Lord of the Smoking Mirror, whose sacrificial cults drove Topiltzin Quetzalcoatl into exile. In one surviving tradition it was believed that the fleeing prince might return in a future calendar round in the year *ce acatl* or One Reed. One Reed also corresponded to the year 1519, when the Spaniards arrived in Mexico; and Cortés was believed, for a time, to be the return of Quetzalcoatl's power. Around the eleventh century, Tollan, like the Maya and the culture of Teotihuacan, fell into rapid ruin, perhaps as a result of Quetzalcoatl's defeat. But the Toltec tradition lived on and was to become one of the keys to the rise of the warrior religion of the Aztecs.

Aztec War, Cosmic Conflict

A fragment of Aztec poetry reads like a combination of cosmic security and military boast.

Proud of Itself
Is the city of Mexico-Tenochtitlan
Here no one fears to die in war
This is our glory
This is your Command
Oh Giver of Life
Have this in mind, oh princes
Who could conquer Tenochtitlan?
Who could shake the foundation of heaven?[28]

Four elements in this verse guide our historical overview of Aztec religion: warfare; the concentration of order within the capital of Tenochtitlan; a fear of cosmic instability; and a connection to the intentions of the gods. In fact the formation of Aztec religion was accomplished in the capital city of Tenochtitlan, located in the central Valley of Mexico between the fourteenth and sixteenth centuries C.E. The Aztec religious tradition combined and transformed a number of ritual, mythic, and cosmological elements from the heterogeneous cultural groups, including the Toltecs, who inhabited the central plateau of Mesoamerica.

When the Aztec precursors, the **Chichimecas** (from *chichi,* meaning "dog" and *mecatl,* meaning " rope," or "lineage"), migrated into the lake region (there were five interconnected lakes covering the valley floor) in the thirteenth century, the valley was organized by warring city-states constantly competing for land and tribute payments of food, luxuries, and military prisoners. This fragmented world was partly the result of the twelfth-century collapse of the Toltec empire. The Toltec collapse brought waves of Chichimecas and Toltec remnants into the Valley of Mexico, where they interacted with different city-states and religious traditions in periodic and intense conflict. One Chichimec group, who called itself the Mexica, settled on a swampy island in the middle of the lakes and within a hundred years organized a ferocious military and political unit with the capacity of dominating by force and persuasion an increasing number of city-states in central Mexico. They achieved dominance during the revolution of 1424–1426 against the ruling capital of the Tepanec empire, Azcapotzalco. Along with two other rebelling city-states, Tlacopan and Texcoco, they formed the feared Triple Alliance; but it was the Aztecs of Tenochtitlan who assumed supreme power in central Mesoamerica. They did this through the control of trade routes, an aggressive cosmovision, and large-scale military campaigns that were celebrated in the lavish rituals held in the various ceremonial centers of the capital.

Seldom has a capital city fit the category of "center of the world" more completely than Tenochtitlan. While the high plateau of Mexico was roughly the center of Mesoamerica, the Valley of Mexico was the heart of the plateau; interconnected lakes formed the center of the valley and Tenochtitlan was constructed near the center of the lakes. From the beginning of the Common Era, when the great imperial capital of Teotihuacan was organized into four great quarters around a massive ceremonial center thirty miles to the north of the Valley of Mexico, the central highlands had been the dominant cultural region of central Mesoamerica. Even though Mesoamerican civilization was periodically fragmented, its reintegration was controlled, at least in the cultural regions north of the Maya regions, by cities located at the top of the geographical pyramid. Between 1300 and 1521 all roads of central Mesoamerica led into the lake region of the valley from which the magnificent capital of the Aztecs arose. Like Teotihuacan before it, it was a four-quartered city inspired by a cosmovision with several distinctive qualities.

Many cosmologies, or statements of world order, stress the achievement of stability, security, and control over the forces of chaos. The Aztec cosmology, however, had several distinctive qualities, including the fact that the cosmic setting was a dynamic, unstable, destructive one distinguished by sharp alternations between order and disorder, cosmic life, and cosmic death. This cosmic order was marked on both the celestial and terrestrial levels by combats, sacrifice, and rebellion as well as by harmony, cooperation, and stability. But the former actions always seemed to overcome the latter. The formal expression of this is the **Myth of the Suns,** which was carved in splendid symbolism on the face of the Calendar Stone, or Sun Stone, which stands today in the Museo Nacional de Antropología (National Museum of Anthropology) in Mexico City. The stone, along with a number of other pre-Columbian and postconquest accounts, depicts the Four Ages, or Four Suns, through which the universe passed prior to the present age, the Fifth Age.

The First Age, called Sun 4-Tiger, was brought into order out of primordial chaos. Then a struggle between the gods ensued, resulting in a collapse of the cosmos and, according to one tradition, its reorganization by the winning deity, Tezcatlipoca. The beings who lived in this era were eaten by ocelots. This process of order and collapse was repeated four times. The Second Age was called Sun 4-Wind, and the beings who lived there were carried away by wind. The Third Age was Sun 4-Rain, and fire rained on people and they became turkeys. The Fourth Age was Sun 4-Water, and water swallowed the people and they became fish. Then, the present age, Sun 4-Movement, was created out of the

The Great Aztec Calendar Stone, carved sometime after 1502 C.E. during the reign of Moctezuma II. In the center is the sun god of the current age surrounded by four mythical dates that symbolize previous epochs of creation and destruction. The twenty-day signs circle the central core of the stone. Two sky serpents facing each other at the bottom represent time and space. (Photograph courtesy of Museo Nacional de Mexico.)

sacrifice of a large number of deities in Teotihuacan, or elsewhere, depending on the tradition. It was believed that this age would end in earthquakes and famine. What is clear is that cosmic order is achieved in the Aztec universe out of conflict, sacrifice, and the death of humans and gods.

This cosmic understanding, that cosmic order comes from conflict and sacrifice, was at the basis of the extraordinary practices of bloodletting and human sacrifice throughout Mesoamerica. Each of the 18 twenty-day months involved the public sacrifices of captured warriors, or in rare cases children or young women. But in each case the purpose was to acquire the divine forces embedded in the physiology of human beings in order to nourish the sun, earth, and rain so that the stability of the Fifth Age would be maintained. These ceremonies were elaborate musical, artistic, public displays of Aztec cosmology and political will.

Aztec ceremonies, guided by detailed ritual calendars, varied from settlement to settlement. Typically, however, they involved three stages: days of ritual preparation, ceremonial sacrifice, and acts of nourishing the gods and the community. The days of ritual preparation included fasting, lengthy processions (sometimes to many mountain and lake shrines), and offerings of food, flowers, and paper. There were extensive purification techniques, embowering, songs, and processions of deity impersonators (*teotl ixiptlas*) to different temples in ceremonial precincts. Following these elaborate preparations blood sacrifices were carried out on pyramidal and temple platforms by priestly groups trained to dispense the victims swiftly. This involved different types of **autosacrifice** (bleeding of self) and the heart sacrifice of enemy warriors and purchased slaves. Though a variety of methods were used, including decapitation, burning, hurling from great heights, strangulation, and arrow sacrifice, the typical ritual involved the dramatic heart sacrifice and the placing of the heart in a ceremonial vessel (sometimes the *cuauhxicalli*-eagle vessel) in order to nourish the gods. We will look more deeply into the religious meaning of these amazing actions in the next chapter.

Aztec warfare was intimately tied to this cosmovision and ritual tradition. War, as we shall see, was a religious and aesthetic affair designed not only to dominate one's enemies but also to rejuvenate the deities by "debt-payment" (***nextlaoaliztli***), returning to the "Giver of Life" some of the sacred energy he had provided and sacrificed in the beginning and which needs rejuvenation each month. Reflecting themes we have seen as far back as Olmec times, war was the place "where the jaguars roar," where "feathered war bonnets heave about like foam in the waves." And death on the battlefield was called *xochimiquiztli*, the flowery death.

The entire situation of stability/instability, war, and empire is reflected in the **Xochiyaoyotl** or Wars of the Flowers, which were practiced between 1450 and 1519. These Flowery Wars consisted of a series of scheduled battlefield confrontations primarily between warriors from the Triple Alliance and warriors from the Tlaxcalan-Pueblan Valley Kingdoms to the east. The purpose of these wars, which pitted the most powerful eagle and jaguar knights of the Aztecs against their enemies, was to acquire sacrificial victims for the ritual festivals in the ceremonial centers, to keep warriors in training, and to reaffirm and raise the status of warriors. However, it is often overlooked that these Flowery Wars also had a vital political significance, namely to reestablish or disrupt the borders and balance of power between competing city-states.

All this activity was directed by *tlatoanis* or chief speakers, the name for lords or kings. The line of Aztec kings, which included the two Moctezumas (Ilhuicamina [1440–1454] and Xocoyotzin [1503–1519], the king Westerners know as Montezuma), were warriors, priests, and artists all in one. But one of their primary responsibilities was to lead successful wars of conquest resulting in rich tributary payments of foods, luxuries, feathers, servants, and captured warriors in order to keep the capital rich and publicly triumphant, "the foundation of heaven."

But all was not conflict and aggression in Aztec religion. As we shall see in chapter 7 the Aztecs were skilled poets and philosophers who developed artistic techniques in order to realize human spiritual potential. These techniques included skillful linguistic formulations that were believed to enable the human personality to achieve elevated spiritual experiences and raise the human heart to unforeseen levels of insight and power. The practitioners of this ritual art, called the **tlamatinime** or "knowers of things," also developed, according to some scholars, a critique against the spiritual crisis caused by the dominant cosmovision of conflict and warfare. Rather than attempt to achieve knowledge of the divine through blood sacrifice, they argued that the Place of Duality, or Omeyocan, referred to as the "innermost part of heaven," could be known through the creation of true words or supreme poems or aesthetic works. In this way the innermost self, the heart (*yollotl*), became inspired by a divine force— that is, was deified, and united with the gods in a spiritual sense rather than through heart sacrifice. One of the geniuses who developed this approach was the Tlatoani of Texcoco, **Nezahualcoyotl,** the Fasting Coyote. He was not only a poet, warrior, and spiritual leader of this ceremonial city, but he also organized public festivals where Aztec arts and philosophy were presented and refined.

A number of other remarkable cultures and city-states shaped the course of Mesoamerican religions. Among important cultures we have not discussed were the Totonacs, Tarascans, Otomis, and Mixtecs. The latter culture in particular made a remarkable contribution through a series of beautifully painted pictorial histories depicting the Mixtec pantheon, ritual system of cosmogony, and cosmology. It is clear that the Mixtecs utilized a powerful calendric system to communicate sacred genealogies and the histories of royal families and towns. Several examples of this pictorial art appear in this book.

This historical overview has concentrated on a general chronology and creative moments in Mesoamerican ceremonial centers. Now we will take a look at the general cosmovision that has emerged. Although there were important variations in the different regions and periods of Mesoamerican history (and we have not covered many significant groups), it is fair to say that certain general patterns of worldmaking, worldcentering, and worldrenewing were shared by nearly all Mesoamerican cultures.

The Mesoamerican Cosmovision

As stated earlier, the term *cosmovision* points to the ways in which cultures combine their cosmological notions relating to time and space into a structural and systematic whole. The following discussion of the Mesoamerican cosmovision will be divided into the structure of the cosmos, the cosmic significance of the human being, and the patterns of time.

The Structure of the Cosmos

The Mesoamerican universe, in its various formulations, had a geometry consisting of three general levels: an overworld or celestial space, the middle-world or earthly level, and the underworld (Mictlan, Place of the Dead). One of the most sophisticated images of this universe appears on the sarcophagus lid of the ruler **Pacal** at Palenque, the majestic ceremonial center of the Classic Maya. We see all three levels of the cosmos expressed in the roots, trunk, branches, and top of the World Tree, which is embroidered with serpents, jewels, plants, mirrors, and other valuable items. There were, at least among the ancient Nahuas, thirteen celestial levels (in some sources there are nine celestial levels) and nine underworld levels, each inhabited by diverse gods and supernatural beings, often depicted as conjugal pairs. The top level was inhabited by Ometeotl, the God of Duality.

Each of these realms, which in the Nahua imagination were divided into smaller, powerful units, were permeated with supernatural powers circulating up and down the cosmic levels through spiral-shaped passages called *malinallis.* Some levels, especially the lower terrestrial and aquatic levels, including the mountains, were filled with abundant, valuable forces such as seeds, water, and precious stones upon which farmers, families, and craftsmen depended. One Mexican scholar notes that the ancient Nahuas

> believed this earthly and aquatic world to be contaminated by death and jealously guarded by the dangerous "lords" of springs and woods. Even today, the places from which wealth derives—fountains, forests and mines—are thought to be points of communication between the worlds of men and that of death, guarded by the Ohuican Chaneque, "lords of the dangerous places."[29]

In some versions of the universe these supernatural entities and forces flowed into the human level through giant ceiba trees, which held up the sky at the four quarters of the world and stood at the center of the universe. As we can see when we look at the ideal image of the universe as pictured in the *Codex Fejérváry-Mayer,* the four-quartered universe is structured by four flowering trees, each with a supernatural bird on its crown (see page 170). In some cultures a flowering tree or a sacred mountain stood at the center of the universe linking up, like a vertical shaft, the upper, middle, and lower worlds.

In Maya cosmology the souls of the dead and supernatural forces often traveled from level to level via the extravagant flowering trees at the axis of the universe. For instance the great Maya king Ah Pacal (Lord Shield) is pictured on his sarcophagus lid as falling down the shaft of this tree, along with the setting sun, into the gaping jaws of the earth monster after his death. But once in the underworld it was believed that he was transformed into a supernatural entity who continued to influence life on earth, especially at intersections between cosmic levels, such as the temples he built during his reign.

These supernatural forces, from below and above, could also enter the world through caves, fire, sunlight, animals, stones—any place where there was a spiral or opening connecting humans with the spaces or temporal cycles of the gods. In the Aztec cosmovision some of the pyramids or great temples in the ceremonial centers served as replicas of the cosmic mountain, or *axis mundi,* which in ritual performances connected the sun, stars, and celestial influences to earth. These monumental architectural structures were also seen as openings to the underworld and sometimes had caves or special rooms built at the base where subterranean forces could enter and exit the earthly level. The ceremonial centers of Teotihuacan, Palenque, Chichén Itzá, Tollan, and Tenochtitlan were organized as replicas of this cosmic geometry so that elites, warriors, captives, traders, farmers, poets, and commoners could experience this cosmovision and participate in its nurturance.

Cosmovision and the Human Being

Another type of "center" in Mesoamerican religions was the human being, especially the human body and the "career" of the human being. The three levels of the cosmos corresponded to the human body. *Ilhuicatl,* or heavenly water, was linked to the head, while one of the lower heavens was associated with the heart. The liver was linked to the spiritual forces of the underworld. As Alfredo Lopez Austin has abundantly shown in *The Human Body and Ideology,* Mesoamerican peoples saw the human body as the nucleus and unifying body of the cosmos, which was permeated—in fact, "loaded"—with specific supernatural powers and entities. The human body was progressively filled—at conception, birth, the first exposure to fire and sunlight, and at points of special achievements in life—with powers originating in the celestial spaces above and in sacred events that took place in mythical time. Although all parts of the human body were loaded with these special powers, they were concentrated in three parts of the human physiology. The head (especially in the hair and in the fontanel area, the soft spot on an infant's skull) was filled with **tonalli,** an animating force or soul that provided vigor and the energy for growth and development. The heart received deposits of **teyolia** (what gives life to people), which provided emotion, memory, and knowledge to the human. This was the soul that could live and have influence after the body was dead. The liver received *ihiyotl,* which provided humans with bravery, desire, hatred, love, and happiness. It was thought of as a luminous gas that could attract and charm other people. These forces or "animating entities" directed the physiological process of a human body, gave the person character, and were highly valued by the family and sought after in warfare and ritual sacrifice. It was believed that some of these powers could be taken from a human body and either offered to the gods as a form of "debt payment" or acquired by the ritual person who touched the physical entity in which they resided.

Every human being was seen as the living center of these forces; but certain individuals—such as warriors, deity impersonators (*teotl ixiptla*, literally "images of the deity"), lords, or artists at the moment of creativity—contained extraordinary supernatural powers. One special type of human being, known to us through the reports of the Spanish chroniclers, was the *hombre-dios* or man-god who functioned as a religious virtuoso, an extraordinary model of religious conduct, power, and authority. These individuals were able to communicate directly, through the perception of their hearts, with the will and power of the deity, the symbols of whom they sometimes carried in sacred bundles. An outstanding example of this type of divine person was Topiltzin Quetzalcoatl, Our Lord the Feathered Serpent, the priest-king of Tollan. Tollan was the fabled and historical kingdom of the tenth-century Toltecs, who were renowned as having discovered the structure of the universe and having invented the most important world-renewing rituals.

The Cosmovision of Time

One of the most fascinating aspects of Mesoamerican religions was the fact that time was believed to exist in three different planes, each intersecting with one another. The meeting of human time with the time of the gods and the time before the gods filled human life with incredible power, changes, and significance.

Human beings dwelled in a time or cycle of time created on the surface of the earth by the gods. It was marked by a yearly calendar. Time and space were seen as an intertwined sacred entity. The passage of time was created by supernatural forces that emanated from the sky and underworld and converged on the earthly level. In this manner human time and space was filled with sacred forces. There was another temporal cycle prior to human time in which the gods had undergone struggles, abductions, broken honor, death, and dismemberment. This cycle of time, the time of myths, had two special features influencing human experience within the first cycle of time. First, it resulted in the creation of supernatural beings who became intimately connected to daily life in human space on earth. Second, this cycle of time continues on into the present.

Beyond these two temporal realms, which touched each other constantly, was the third temporal realm, the transcendent time of the gods. The High Gods existed prior to the other two cycles but provided the original energy and structure of the universe. This primordial time of the gods, when order first appeared out of chaos, continues on in a celestial realm. We can conceive of these cycles as a wheel within a larger wheel within a larger wheel. Each hour and day in the early time is in touch with the particular forces of the time of the gods and the time of myth. In this way human life (time and space) is loaded up with a specific set of powers and entities each day. And each day these powers and entities are different. Lopez Austin summarizes this multiple view of time in the following manner.

> The second time, the time of myth, did not end after it had given birth to the time of man. The time of myth continued ruling, far from man's dwelling place. . . . When a moment of human time coincided with one of the ever-present moments of mythical time, man's time received an imprint from the world of the gods. The sequence of correspondences between one and another time resulted in cycles of different dimensions, making each moment happening in human time a meeting place for a plurality of divine forces, all combining to constitute its particular nature. . . . Thus, an hour of the day was characterized by being a moment of night or day; by the influence of a sign (one among the twenty day names) and a number (one among thirteen) in a cycle of 260 days; by the group of thirteen to which it belonged; by its month (among eighteen) and its position within the month (among twenty) by the year (among fifty-two) which in its turn was marked by the destiny of a sign (among four) and a number (among thirteen); and so on, successively, through the sequence of other cycles. . . . This made each moment on earth a complex combination of the different influences coming down from the heavens or arising from the underworld.[30]

The Mesoamerican calendars (found in sculpture or in *tonalamatls*, books of day counts) marked and regulated the passage of influences into human life. One of the great measuring devices for these calendars was astronomical observations, which guided a number of major ceremonies related to Venus, the Pleiades, and changes in the solar cycle. In some cases entire ceremonial centers or parts of ceremonial centers were laid out so that dramatic observations of these astronomical events could be celebrated and communicated through public rituals. One such ceremony was the **New Fire Ceremony,** or Binding of the Years, which marked the passage of the Pleiades through the meridian at midnight once every fifty-two years or 18,980 nights. In fact the Pleiades passed through the zenith every night, but it only passed through the zenith at midnight once a year. The complexity of Aztec observation appears when we realize that they regarded only one of every fifty-two passages as supremely important because it marked the exhaustion of possible interactions between two different calendar systems. This ceremony included the ritual sacrifice of an enemy warrior to mark the rejuvenation of all cycles of time.

Within these complicated formulas of time was a profound commitment and concern for ensuring the renewal of cosmic forces alive in plants, animals, humans, and dynasties. In Maya religion, for instance, bloodletting ceremonies by members of the royal household were enacted to bring the ancestors and deities and the time of myth into the realm of humans to nurture agriculture, empower a lord at the time of his enthronement, or prepare a community for war.

One dramatic ceremony, linking up the time of the gods with human time, involved the bloodletting ritual by **Lady Xoc** of Palenque. We see in the sculptures of Yaxchilán a giant, twisting, decorated serpent emerging from her blood. Out of the "jeweled serpent's" mouth comes what appears to be the body of a divine warrior returning to earth to empower the dynasty. It is through this ritual sacrifice that two realms of time, the time of the gods and the time of humans, are linked together and renewed.

Now that we have reconstructed parts of the history and structure of the ceremonial world and cosmovisions of Mesoamerica, it is time to examine the arresting case of Aztec religion, which was animated by the militancy of the warrior and the art of refined speech.

7

The Religion of the Aztecs: Ways of the Warrior, Words of the Sage

He was imitated by the incense keepers and the priests. The life of Quetzalcoatl became a pattern for the life of every priest: so it was established, the regimen of Tollan—so it was adopted here in Mexico.
Florentine Codex[31]

WHEN HERNÁN CORTÉS LED THE SPANISH ARMY of five hundred soldiers, accompanied by several thousand allied Indian warriors, into the Aztec capital of Tenochtitlan in 1519, Moctezuma Xocoyotzin believed, according to one account, "that this was Topiltzin Quetzalcoatl who had arrived." Topiltzin Quetzalcoatl was the model priest-king who had ruled the great eleventh-century Toltec kingdom of Tollan before he was forced into exile, promising to return one day. Moctezuma sent a number of rich gifts, including the ritual costume of the great deity Quetzalcoatl, to welcome the strangers on the coast.

Although it is unclear to what extent the native peoples identified Cortés as the return of Quetzalcoatl or one of his descendants, it is clear that important elements of the Aztec cosmovision were based on the ancestral tradition of the Toltecs. As we saw in the previous chapter this tradition included an emphasis on the intimate relationship between the great god Quetzalcoatl and the *hombre-dios* Topiltzin Quetzalcoatl (Our Young Prince the Feathered Serpent). The Aztecs, as well as many other cultures, followed, in part, "the pattern" of Toltec religion when developing their cosmology, priesthood, and sacred architecture. The Aztec shape of time and ceremonial renewal, which provided the framework for ritual sacrifice including human sacrifice, was influenced by the Toltec tradition. The identification of Cortés with the great priest-king of Tollan becomes more plausible when we realize that, in Aztec belief, Topiltzin was born in the year *ce acatl* (One Reed), departed his kingdom fifty-two years later in *ce acatl*,

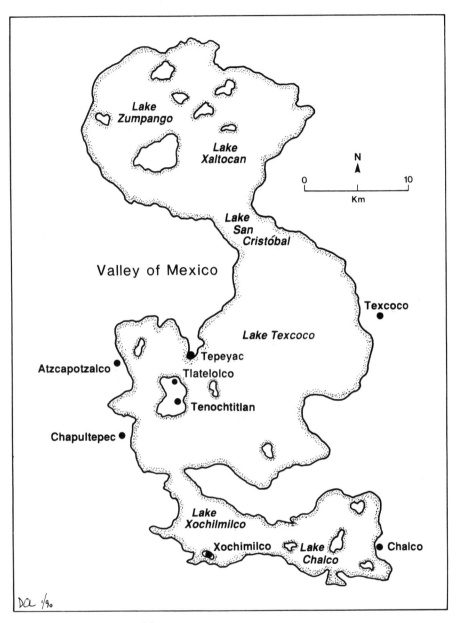

Core area of the Aztec world.

in *ce acatl,* and was expected to return in the year *ce acatl.* It is one of the amazing coincidences of history that the Aztec year *ce acatl* fell in the Christian year 1519, the year that Cortés appeared in Mexico.[32]

The significant role that Topiltzin Quetzalcoatl played in Mesoamerican religions after the twelfth century points to a major pattern in worldcentering. Each community was organized by expressions of authority rooted in sacred traditions and events. Sacred authority was often expressed in and through the career of certain exemplary human lives or types of religious virtuosos. Many religions, especially religions organized by urban centers, develop elaborate conceptions of social and symbolic authority associated with high-status positions and the paraphernalia associated with those positions. Religious authority can take many forms or be embedded in many kinds of objects, such as the Crown of Charlemagne, the Chair of the Pope, or the Chrysanthemum Throne of the Japanese Emperor, or in a sacred teaching like the Torah in Judaism. One of the most widespread and influential forms of authority (that is, authority as central value system and major symbols derived from tradition) is in certain types of human beings, such as prophets, founders, magicians, seers, or saints. The lives and personal experiences of these leaders embody the most sacred values and teachings of a tradition, providing it with a central image or exemplary pattern for proper conduct and religious devotion.

The Sacred Career of Topiltzin Quetzalcoatl

One of the most important ways in which a community expresses these values and symbols of authority is through the telling of stories, hymns, legends, or gospels that grow up around the life and death of a revered individual. In Mesoamerican capital cities from the twelfth century on a rich tradition of stories, songs, paintings, and sculpture depicted to young and old alike the inspired career of Topiltzin Quetzalcoatl and his relationship with his powerful divinity. [See Religions of Africa pp. 36–37, 64–67, Native Religions of North America pp. 288–95, 327–29, 333–42, Judaism pp. 380–84, Christianity pp. 534–35, Hinduism pp. 739–41, 743–46, Buddhism p. 890, and Religions of Japan pp. 1094–96 for discussion of myth and mythology.]

This tradition told how divine forces, originating on other levels of the cosmos, entered the world through Topiltzin's life and religious experiences. This career can be compared to a seven-act play depicting his (1) miraculous birth, (2) ritual training and ecstatic experiences, (3) ascension to the throne, (4) creation of his splendid capital, (5) downfall at the hands of his rival, Tezcatlipoca, (6) exile, and (7) death and transformation into Venus as the Morning Star, a divinity. All these "acts" had influence in later history, but we will focus on his birth and ritual training for the priesthood; his career as a warrior/sacrificer; his splendid capital; and the manner of his death and transformation into the Morning Star. In this way we will come to see how parts of Aztec religion were patterned on the dramatic career of Topiltzin Quetzalcoatl.

Birth and Ritual Training

According to one tradition Topiltzin Quetzalcoatl was conceived after his mother Chimalma (Earth Shield) swallowed an emerald. He was raised by his grandparents and underwent seven years of rigorous ritual training, living for a time as a mountain ascetic. He practiced autosacrifice, the bleeding of oneself through insertion of spines or other ritual implements into parts of one's body. These techniques were at once offerings to the gods and "openings" in the human body designed to enhance direct communication with deities. He also built ritual temples in order to meditate, pray, chant, and carry out sacrifices. His influence on Aztec ceremonial life was discovered by the sixteenth-century Spanish friar Diego Durán, who interviewed Aztec survivors of the wars with the Spanish. Durán wrote,

> all the ceremonies and rites, building temples and altars and placing idols in them, fasting, going nude and sleeping . . . on the floor, climbing mountains to preach the law there, kissing the earth, eating it with one's fingers and blowing trumpets and conch shells and flutes on the great feast days—all these things imitated the ways of the holy man, Topiltzin Quetzalcoatl.[33]

One of the most valued achievements in this holy man's career was his direct experience of Ometeotl, the Creative Heavenly Pair who dwelt in the innermost part of heaven at the top of the celestial levels. One text tells that in the year Two Reed, Ce Acatl Quetzalcoatl (another name for the hero) built a special temple facing the cardinal directions and fasted, did penance, and bathed in icy cold waters. He also set thorns into his flesh on the summit of four sacred mountains near Tollan. Following these ritual ordeals, he

> sent up his prayers, his supplications into the heart of the sky and called out to Skirt of Stars, Light of Day, Lady of Sustenance, Wrapped in Coal, Wrapped

Quetzalcoatl Ehecatl as lord of the wind is seated upon a jaguar throne next to a giant feathered serpent. This image comes from the Codex Laud, *a preconquest deerskin screenfold manuscript. (Courtesy of Akademische Druck und Verlagsanstalt, Graz, Austria, 1966 facsimile ed.)*

in Black, She who endows the earth with solidity, He who covers the earth with cotton.

This quest to communicate with the High God is successful, for

they knew that he was crying out to the place of Duality, which lies above the ninefold heaven. And thus they knew, they who dwell there, that he called upon them and petitioned them most humbly and contritely.[34]

These techniques of humble prayers, autosacrifice, bathing in cold water, and speaking in metaphors of duality became the priestly style for opening paths of communication with celestial forces in the Toltec world and in subsequent city-states, including the Aztec capital.

Model Warrior/Sacrificer

A controversial part of Topiltzin Quetzalcoatl's career was his experience as a warrior. During his lifetime he apparently changed his attitude toward war and ritual sacrifice, which were intimately linked throughout Mesoamerican history.

Topiltzin Quetzalcoatl was born into a world of war. According to many primary sources the gods were periodically at war with one another during the mythic eras prior to human existence. In the vivid creation story of the *Historia de los Mexicanos por Sus Pinturas,* the gods created the Chichimec people in order to gain sacrificial blood through human warfare and the ritual sacrifice of captive warriors. Within this cosmic order Topiltzin Quetzalcoatl spent seven years of ritual training to become a warrior, utilizing sacred forces to enhance his battlefield experience. He fights gallantly alongside his father, who is killed and buried in the sand by enemies. Topiltzin recovers his father's body and buries him at a shrine on Cloud Serpent Mountain. Enemy warriors led by Apanetcatl attack him, and Topiltzin

rose up, striking him full in the face, sent him tumbling down, and he fell to the base of the mountain. Next he seized Zolton and Cuilton and . . . he put them to death, he spread them with chili and slashed their flesh and he set out to make conquests.[35]

This action of attacking enemies and performing human sacrifices at mountain shrines became a model for Aztec warfare and sacrificial ceremonies, as we shall see in the upcoming section on the Great Aztec Temple.

However, according to several traditions, Topiltzin Quetzalcoatl initiated a reformation in sacrificial practices later in his career: He forbade human sacrifice. One text reads,

And it is told and related that many times during the life of Quetzalcoatl certain sorcerers attempted to shame him into making human offerings, into sacrificing humans. But he would not consent. He would not comply, because he loved his subjects who were Toltecs. The offerings he made were only of snakes, birds, and butterflies.[36]

This reformation provoked the trickery of a rival cult led by the priest of Tezcatlipoca, Lord of the Smoking Mirror. Topiltzin, now the wise king of Tollan, was tricked into a drunken episode during which he violated his priestly vows and was forced to abdicate and flee into exile.

One text describes his lament at his downfall:

Thereupon Quetzalcoatl said, "Unfortunate me!" Then he raised his lament he'd composed for his going away. And he sang:

> "No more.
> The days will be counted no more in my house and it
>   shall be empty."

Then his pages weeping sing,

> "No more we delight in him,
> Him our noble one,
> Him Quetzalcoatl
> No more thy precious crown!"[37]

This tension between sacrificing human beings or using other means to open ways of communicating with the deities continued on into Aztec history, as we shall see in the upcoming section on sacred words. For now let us look briefly at what the Aztecs claimed Topiltzin Quetzalcoatl lost as a result of this great defeat. [See Religions of Africa pp. 67, 88–89, Judaism pp. 399–400, Christianity pp. 543–44, 550, Islam p. 646, and Hinduism pp. 743–45, 747–48 for description and discussion of sacrifice.]

The Splendid City

When the Aztec elders spoke to Bernardino de Sahagun after the conquest about the cultural sources of their achievements, they stated that it was the Toltecs "who came to cause the cities to be founded." The Toltecs were considered the ancient geniuses who set culture on a new level of excellence. "The Tolteca were wise. Their works were all good, all perfect, all wonderful, all miraculous; their houses beautiful, tiled in mosaics, smoothed, stuccoed, very marvelous."[38] In fact the elders were describing the splendid city of Tollan, which emerged during the reign of Topiltzin Quetzalcoatl. It was remembered as having been the greatest urban achievement in human history. This grand prestige was due to the environmental and artistic plenitude of Quetzalcoatl's kingdom.

The wealth of Toltec fields was like an ancient Findhorn: All the "squashes were very large, and some quite round. And the ears of maize were as large as hand grinding stones, and long. They could hardly be embraced in one's arms." And the amaranth plants, so important in Aztec agriculture and ritual offerings, were as tall as trees, "verily they climbed up them; they could be climbed." Also the cotton farming produced fields of amazing colors, "burnt red, yellow, rose colored, violet, green, azure, verdigris colored, whitish, brown, shadowy, rose red and coyote colored . . . so they grew; they did not dye them."[39]

This part of the ecological complex was matched in excellence by the technological and artistic achievements of the Toltecs. The people of Quetzalcoatl were remembered as the finest feather workers, physicians, jewelers, astronomers, architects. Their ritual buildings were constructed to face the cardinal directions: The eastern building was the house of gold, the western building was the house of fine turquoise, the southern building was the house of shells and silver, and the northern house was inlaid with red precious stones. The achievements of these people are summed up in this passage: "In truth they invented all the wonderful, precious, marvelous things which they made. . . ."

But this splendid urban achievement of cosmovision, agricultural abundance, and technological excellence began to crumble when the priest-king went into exile.

Death and Deification of the Human Body

The exile of Topiltzin Quetzalcoatl was a well-known story in the Aztec capital. The places he stopped to rest, eat, and search for ritual objects are mentioned in the narratives about the fall of his kingdom. In one place it is known, from indentations on rocks, that he put his buttocks there. The religious meaning of his life becomes clear when he arrives at the seacoast (referred to as the celestial shore of divine water), weeps, and discards his ornaments, green mask, and feathers. Realizing that his earthly career has run its course, he sacrifices himself by cremation, and

> from his ashes, rose all the precious birds, the cotinga, the spoonbill, the parrots. . . . Then the heart of Quetzalcoatl rose into heaven and, according to the elders, was transformed into the Morning Star . . . and Quetzalcoatl was called Lord of the Dawn.[40]

This episode points to one of the most pervasive notions in Aztec religion: the sacrality of the human body and its potential to return its energy to the celestial forces that created it. It was widely believed that at death energies within the human body, especially the *teyolia* contained in the human heart, could become deified or grafted onto the celestial substance of a divinity. In this case Topiltzin Quetzalcoatl's *teyolia* becomes the planet Venus in its appearances as the morning star.

As we now turn to discussions of Aztec cosmology, temples, speech arts, and sacrifice, we will see why the Aztecs chanted, "From him it began, from Quetzalcoatl it flowed out, all art and knowledge." [See Religions of Africa pp. 29, 55–57, Native Religions of North America pp. 266–67, Christianity pp. 495–97, 531–32, 534–35, Islam pp. 622–28, 698–99, Hinduism pp. 769, 770–72, Buddhism pp. 860, 861–68, 892–99, Religions of China pp. 993–95, and Religions of Japan pp. 1090, 1100, 1122–23, for discussion of religious founders.]

Cosmovision and the Human Body

A prayer to Tezcatlipoca, spoken in the Aztec capital, and recorded by Sahagun:

> O master, O our lord, O lord of the near, of the nigh, O night, O wind: thou seest, thou knowest things within the trees, the rocks. And behold now, it is true that thou knowest of things within us: thou hearest us from within. Thou hearest, thou knowest that which is within us: what we say, what we think; our minds, our hearts.[41]

The history of religions teaches us that, at one time or another, almost everything has been considered sacred. Archaeological, textual, and ritual evidence shows that during the long and diverse experiences of the human species gestures, toys, games, books, buildings, animals, stars, sex, hunting, food, even athletics have been considered religious in nature. More specifically we see that there are holy books (Torah, *Vedas, Sutras,* Gospels, *I Ching,* Qur'ān); sacred buildings (St. Peter's, the Ka'ba, the Basilica of Guadalupe); sacred cities (Ife, Kyoto, Jerusalem, Rome); sacred mountains (Mt. Fuji, Mt. Sinai, Mt. Tlaloc); sacred people (Jesus, the Buddha, Joseph Smith, Confucius, Topiltzin Quetzalcoatl); and sacred offices (papacy, ayatollah, *ashiwanni*—Zuni rain priests). We also have persuasive evidence that in a number of cultures the human body is understood as a sacred container of cosmic powers.

The central ritual in Christianity, for example, is the ingestion of the "body and blood" of Jesus. His body, filled with divine love, is symbolically or actually (according to the particular tradition) taken into other human bodies, which become spiritually renewed. In the Buddhist tradition the bodily remains of Sakyamuni Buddha were believed to have been deposited in *stupas,* or stone monuments, after the Buddha's death. As time passed these *stupas* became objects of pilgrimage. Eventually new *stupas* were built to house the bodily remains and relics associated with outstanding Buddhist sages. In some cases pious Buddhists built their homes nearby so as to live close to these bodily remains. In a number of American Indian traditions vision quests included the offering of parts of bodies including skin, muscle, and fingers.

One of the most amazing examples of the sacred nature of the human body is the cult of mummies developed in Egypt and South America. In Egypt a chemical method was used to preserve the anointed and bandaged dead body so that the soul, which left at death, could return to take the food offerings left behind. Among the Inca of the fifteenth and sixteenth centuries in Peru, the bodies of rulers were mummified and consulted on major matters of state by living rulers, who believed that the deified, royal personality resided in the corpse. These mummies were housed in special temples and cared for by a group of specialists.

These diverse examples point to the importance of the human body in religious traditions. One of the most elaborate ritual expressions of the human body as a container of sacred forces was developed in Mesoamerica. In this section we will survey how Aztec peoples saw the human organism as the container par excellence of sacred powers and rhythms. On certain ritual occasions the human physique was treated as an extremely potent living image of cosmic forces. This study will prepare us for our discussion of the most difficult topics facing students of Mesoamerica: bloodletting and human sacrifice.

The Body at the Center of the World

We have seen that Mesoamerican religions were most vividly expressed in ceremonial centers. The most pervasive type of sacred space where elaborate ceremonies were carried out was the human body. The human body was considered a potent receptacle of cosmological forces, a living, moving center of the world.

Consider, for instance, the elaborate image of the cosmos from the *Codex Fejérváry-Mayer*. It reflects the typical Mesoamerican worldview divided into five sections. We see the four quarters, each containing a sacred tree with a celestial bird on top, surrounding the central region where **Xiuhtecuhtli,** the Fire God, is dressed in warrior regalia. According to scholars the body of Tezcatlipoca has been cut into pieces and divided over the four directions of the world, with his blood flowing into the center. The divine blood is flowing into the axis of the universe, which redistributes the divine energy to animals, body parts, vegetation, and the calendar, which is divided by the four quarters of the cosmos.

Page 1 of the **Codex Fejérváry-Mayer** *is a schematic representation of the cosmos, depicting the center and the four cardinal directions. It is also a divinatory calendar used to predict the fortune of future events. The Mesoamerican concepts of time and space were intimately linked to geographical and cosmological relationships. (Courtesy of Akademische Druck und Verlagsanstalt, Graz, Austria, 1971 facsimile ed.)*

Each quadrant shows two of the Nine Lords of the Night in ritual postures next to the cosmic tree. The dots surrounding the edges of the design represent the 260-day ritual calendar divided by the spatial structure of the universe.

In order to understand the religious power of the human body and to build a foundation for our discussion of human sacrifice, let us focus on the importance of two body parts in Aztec religions, the heart and the head.

The Mesoamerican cosmos was conceived as a series of thirteen celestial and nine underworld layers, each layer inhabited by gods, supernatural beings, and forces. These powers and beings entered the earthly level through a series of openings or avenues of communication including the four cosmic trees at the edges of the world, mountains, caves, the rays of the sun, the motion of the wind, and so forth. These lines of communication were pictured as two pairs of heliacal bands, called *malinalli,* which moved in constant motion, allowing the forces of the underworld to ascend and the forces of the overworld to descend. In this way the Turquoise World (sky) and the Obsidian World (underworld) were dynamically connected to the terrestrial world of nature, human beings, and society. These supernatural forces emerged each day from the sacred trees and spread across the landscape. They could be introduced into the human body by either ritual means or through the action of nature.

Tonalli

One of the most powerful divine forces was called *tonalli* (from *tona,* meaning "to irradiate or make warm with sun"), which was collected in the human head. The original source of *tonalli* was Ometeotl, the supreme Dual God residing at the top of the thirteen celestial layers. But the divine *tonalli* reached the human through the action of celestial beings inhabiting other levels of the sky. It was believed that at the moment of the conception of a human being Ometeotl intervened on one of the celestial levels and sent vital energy into the uterus of the female. This energy was deposited into the head of the embryo, resulting in the original shape of one's temperament and destiny. After the child was born containing this initial amount of *tonalli,* the child was ritually placed near a fire and eventually exposed to the sun in order to increase his or her *tonalli.* Although the sun was believed to be the most powerful visible source of *tonalli,* people could acquire *tonalli* from beings close to them after birth.

The term *tonalli* has a rich range of meanings referring to its vigor, warmth, solar heat, summertime, and soul. It infiltrated animals, gods, plants, humans, and objects used in rituals. The hair that covered the head, especially the fontanel area, was a major receptacle of *tonalli.* The hair prevented the *tonalli* from leaving the body and was therefore a major prize in warfare. It was believed that the fortitude and valor of a warrior resided, in part, in the hair, and we have many pictorial scenes showing Aztec warriors grabbing the hair of enemies. The hair of warriors captured in battle was kept by the captors in order to increase their *tonalli.* The decapitated heads of enemy warriors were a supreme prize for the city, which gained more *tonalli* through the ceremony.

Teyolia

Another divine force animating the human body was *teyolia,* which resided in the human heart. *Teyolia* was likened to "divine fire," and it animated the human being and gave shape to a person's sensibilities and thinking patterns. Every human heart contained this divine fire, but an extraordinary amount resided in the hearts of priests, *hombre-dioses,* artists, and the men and women who impersonated deities during festivals. Each of these human types was considered a living channel of *teyolia* into the social world. Extraordinary ritual achievements resulted in the increase of one's *teyolia.*

When a person died his or her *teyolia* traveled to the world of the dead, known as the "sky of the sun," where it was transformed into birds. This is the pattern of spiritual transformation we saw in the cremation of Topiltzin Quetzalcoatl. It was his *teyolia* that rose to heaven and changed into a divinity. This is the power to give energy to the sun, which was sought in the heart sacrifice of warriors. As one text says clearly, "Therefore, the ancients said that when they died, men did not perish, but began to live again almost as if awakened from a dream and that they became spirits or gods."[42]

Teyolia resided in mountains, lakes, towns, and temples. All important landscapes and living entities had *teyolia* or "heart." Each community had an *altepeyollotl* or heart of the town, a living divine force sometimes represented in a sculpture or decorated image. During the recent excavation of the Great Aztec Temple a number of statues were discovered representing the *teyolia* or heart of the sacred mountain. Our discussion now turns to a description and interpretation of this most powerful of Aztec places.

Serpent Mountain: The Great Aztec Temple

The Mesoamerican cosmos was centered in the physical characteristics of the human body. In this way each human being was a center of vital forces and changes. But each community had a public ceremonial precinct, which oriented all human activity and influenced social life. The most powerful sacred place in the Aztec empire was Coatepec or Serpent Mountain, the ritual name of the Great Temple of Tenochtitlan.

This identification of the great shrine with a sacred mountain points to one of the major religious patterns in Mesoamerican traditions, namely the identification of mountains as prodigious resources for abundance, danger, sacrality, and power. The Aztec temple/symbolic mountain stood in the center of the ceremonial precinct of the capital, which was the political center of an empire of more than four hundred towns and fifteen million people. The **Templo Mayor** of Tenochtitlan was significant not only because it supported the shrines of the great gods Tlaloc (god of rain and agriculture) and Huitzilopochtli (god of tribute and war), but also because, as the recent excavation of the structure revealed, it contained more than a hundred rich caches of ritual offerings buried in its floors.

Our discussion of the Great Temple will cover three important dimensions of Aztec religion: the theme of sacred mountains, the Aztec foundation myth, and the birth of the War God, Huitzilopochtli.

Cosmovision and the Sacred Mountain

One of the last impressions the Spaniards had of the Great Temple before the siege and conquest of the capital of Tenochtitlan involved a desperate sacrifice of a number of their fellow soldiers by the Aztecs. The Spanish soldier Bernal Díaz del Castillo describes the Spanish retreat from a ferocious battle near the Great Temple. Looking back toward the center of the city they saw the following:

> there was sounded the dismal drum of Huichilobos and many other shells and horns and things like trumpets and the sound of them all was terrifying, and we all looked toward the lofty Pyramid where they were being sounded, and saw that our comrades whom they had captured when they defeated Cortés were being carried by force up the steps, and they were taking them to be sacrificed. When they got them up to a small square in front of the oratory, where their accursed idols are kept, we saw them place plumes on the heads of many of them and with things like fans in their hands they forced them to dance before Huichilobos and after they had danced they immediately placed them on their backs on some rather narrow stones which had been prepared as places for sacrifice, and with some knives they sawed open their chests and drew out their palpitating hearts and offered them to the idols that were there, and they kicked the bodies down the steps, and the Indian butchers who were waiting below cut off the arms and feet and flayed the skin off their faces, and prepared it afterwards like glove leather with the beards on, and kept those for the festivals when they celebrated drunken orgies and the flesh they ate in chilimole.[43]

This amazing, shocking scene can only begin to make sense to us if we attempt to understand a few of the major assumptions associated with Aztec cosmovision.

The Aztecs called their world **cemanahuac,** or "land surrounded by water." This land was conceived as having five parts with four quadrants called *nauchampa,* literally the four directions of the wind, extending outward from the central section. Each of these quadrants were associated with specific names, colors, and influences. Though the pattern varied from culture to culture a typical Mesoamerican version was: East—Tlacopan, Place of Dawn, yellow, fertile, and good; North—Mictlampa, Region of the Underworld, red, barren, and bad; West—Cihuatlampa, Region of Women, blue, green, unfavorable, humid; South—Huitzlampa, Region of Thorns, white; Center—Tlalxico, Navel, black. The waters surrounding the inhabited land were called *ilhuica-atl,* the celestial water, which extended upward in a vertical direction merging with the sky and supporting the lower levels of heaven.

A reconstructed model of the Aztec ceremonial center in Tenochtitlan. The twin pyramid complex in the background was dedicated to two principal deities in Aztec cosmology, Tlaloc, representing water and fertility, and Huitzilopochtli, representing war and tribute. The circular temple in the foreground was dedicated to Quetzalcoatl Ehecatl, as lord of the wind. (Photograph courtesy of Lawrence G. Desmond.)

Through the navel flowed the vertical cosmos, which consisted of thirteen layers above and nine layers below the earth. As we saw in our historical overview of the Aztec city, it was believed to be the quintessential connecting point of the Above and the Below.

In Aztec cosmovision there were many connecting points between the supernatural spheres and the human sphere. The most outstanding examples were mountains, considered to be the sources of life-giving waters, deities, and diseases associated with rain, the *tlalocs* (rain gods), and other supernatural powers. The crucial role played by mountains in Aztec religion is reflected in the Nahuatl term for village, city, or community, **altepetl,** meaning "mountain filled with water." The human community with its various ceremonial centers was defined in terms of the landscape, the Mountain of Sustenance, which provided the resources for life. The many mountains surrounding the Valley of Mexico were conceived as huge hollow vessels or "houses" filled with water that came from subterranean streams that filled the space beneath the earth. This underworld realm was called Tlalocan, considered the paradise of the great water deity Tlaloc. In this way each mountain was also an *axis mundi* linking the watery underworld with the terrestrial level of the city to the celestial realms.

With this symbolism in mind we can turn back to the Great Aztec Temple with fresh understanding. The Great Temple consisted of a huge pyramidal base that supported two major shrines. Two stairways led up to the shrines of Tlaloc and Huitzilopochtli. The south side of the pyramid represented the legendary Coatepec, the mountain birthplace of the war god Huitzilopochtli. The north side of the temple represents the Mountain of Sustenance associated with Tlaloc's paradise, which provided the precious rains and moisture that regenerated the agricultural world of the capital. Imagine the visual power this pyramid/temple had on the populace, who saw it standing in the center of the city as a living image of these two great mythic mountains.

A Myth of Foundation

This "symbolism of the center" is expressed in two important myths or sacred stories about Tenochtitlan. Both stories focus on the worldcentering character of the Templo Mayor and the surrounding sacred precinct.

How Tenochtitlan became the center of the world is told in the Aztec foundation myth, a version of which is embroidered on the flag of modern Mexico. Fortunately we have an excellent depiction of this act of worldcentering from the frontispiece of the *Codex Mendoza*, a valuable pictorial manuscript painted by native artists a decade after the conquest. The first image of the codex pictures a huge eagle, *nopal*, and stone above a giant Aztec shield with seven eagle-down feathers and seven arrows attached to it. The eagle represents the god Huitzilopochtli landing on the spot where the Aztecs were to build their major temple, around which the entire community developed. According to Aztec lore Huitzilopochtli had earlier appeared to the tribe's *hombre-dios*, ordering him to lead the people south until they saw the image of the god sitting on the cactus. The shield with feathers and arrows is the ideogram for "place of authority" and the painted image can be read, "The Aztecs have arrived in Tenochtitlan, the

The Coyolxauhqui Stone, a large sculptured disc, eleven feet in diameter, depicting the dismembered Aztec goddess Coyolxauhqui, who according to myth was dismembered by Huitzilopochtli, the patron deity of warfare and tribute among the Aztecs. (Photograph, David Hiser.)

place of authority." The long-range truth of this image—capital equals center of world equals place of authority—is demonstrated by the fact that when Cortés wrote his second letter to the King of Spain in 1520 he reported that "all the Lords of the land who are vassals of the said Montezuma have houses in the city and reside therein for a certain time of year." In other words all the leaders in the empire were lodged in the capital, lending it extra prestige as the place of authority.

As this discussion shows, the central force in the foundation of the city, in the making of this social and architectural world, was the Aztec god Huit-zilopochtli. He inspired the ancestors of the Aztecs to take the risky journey to find their distant home. He was also renowned for setting "men's hearts on fire and preparing them for war." In fact Aztec mythology is permeated with warrior themes and symbolism. Nowhere is this military aspect of their culture more evident than in the *teocuitatl* or divine song, a kind of epic poem about Huit-zilopochtli's birth at Coatepec, the Serpent Mountain.

The Birth of the War God, Huitzilopochtli

The divine song of Huitzilopochtli's birth goes like this. On Coatepec (Serpent Mountain) the mother of the gods, Coatlicue (Lady of the Serpent Skirt) was sweeping out the temple. A ball of plumage "descended upon her" and she placed it in her bosom. Later she discovered it had disappeared and immediately realized she was pregnant. When the *centzon huitznahua* (the four hundred southerners, her children) heard of this pregnancy started at the sacred shrine, they were outraged. The text tells of this outrage:

> they were very angry, they were very agitated, as if the heart had gone out of them. Coyolxauhqui incited them, she inflamed the anger of her brothers, so that they should kill their mother.[44]

Led by the warrior sister **Coyolxauhqui,** the four hundred southerners

> felt very strong, adorned, decorated for war, they distributed among themselves their vestments of paper, their destiny, their nettles . . . their arrows had sharp points . . . they went in order, in an orderly squadron, Coyolxauhqui guided them.

Coatlicue was frightened for her life, but a voice spoke to her from her womb: "Have no fear, already I know what I must do." The army in full fury rushed the mountaintop. Just at the moment of attack the god Huitzilopochtli sprang from his mother's womb full grown, dressed as a warrior, and engaged his brothers and sisters in combat. He grabbed a serpent of fire, charged his sister in a rage, and decapitated her in one swipe. The text reads, "her body went falling below and it went crashing to pieces in various places, her arms, her legs, her body kept falling."

As is the case with all mythology there are several layers of meaning to this influential story. At one level Huitzilopochtli's birth and victorious battle against the four hundred siblings represents the solar dimension of Aztec religion. It

represents the daily sunrise above the sacred mountain (earth) and the elimination of the moon (Coyolxauhqui) and the stars (*centzon huitzhanua*). Second, this
daily experience of nature is viewed in terms of a celestial conflict, war, and
sacrifice. The natural order is a violent order. The world is renewed through
ritual combat at the sacred mountain.

A third level of significance in the myth is historical. Records tell of a crucial
battle at a mountain called Coatepec in which a leader named Huitzilopochtli
killed an enemy woman warrior named Coyolxauhqui and decapitated her.

It is important to focus on the meaning of Coatepec in the drama. The Templo Mayor, called Coatepec by the Aztecs, consisted of a huge pyramid base supporting two temples, one to Huitzilopochtli and one to Tlaloc. Two grand
stairways led up to the shrines. The Coyolxauhqui stone was found in 1978, during the excavation of the remains of the Great Temple, directly at the base of the
stairways leading up to Huitzilopochtli's temple. On both sides of the stone and
the two stairways were two large, grinning serpent heads. The Templo Mayor is
the image of Coatepec or Serpent Mountain. Just as Huitzilopochtli triumphed
at the top of the mountain, while his sister was dismembered and fell to pieces
below, so Huitzilopochtli's temple and icon sat triumphantly at the top of Templo Mayor while the carving of the dismembered goddess was placed at the base
of the stairway far below.

Most interpretations of the myth end with the dismemberment of Coyolxauhqui and the realization that the Templo Mayor and the architectural arrangement of Huitzilopochtli's temple and the Coyolxauhqui stone represent the
drama of the myth. However, if we read on, we discover the mythic source for
large-scale human sacrifice.

Following the dismemberment of Coyolxauhqui, Huitzilopochtli turns and
attacks the rest of his siblings, "the four hundred gods of the south, he drove
them away, he humbled them."

This increment of sacrifice is made emphatic in the text. After driving the
four hundred off the mountain of the snake, Huitzilopochtli

> pursued them, he chased them like rabbits, all around the mountain . . . with
> nothing could they defend themselves. Huitzilopochtli chased them, he
> drove them away, he humbled them, he destroyed them, he annihilated
> them.

This mythic action of sacrifice on the sacred mountain, an elaboration of
the sacrificial pattern in the early part of Topiltzin Quetzalcoatl's career, became
a model in Aztec times for the sacrifice of large numbers of enemy warriors at
the Great Temple of Tenochtitlan. Now we can see the meaning of that sacrifice
of Spanish soldiers, which opened this section of our study. Much more than just
a butchering of Spaniards was taking place. For when they ascended the Great
Temple, dressed in plumes, and danced before Huitzilopochtli's image, they
were being forced to reenact the myth of the attack of the four hundred
southerners at Serpent Mountain. And as in the myth they were sacrificed, dismembered, and thrown down the sacred steps in order to give power to the
Aztec age of the Fifth Sun.

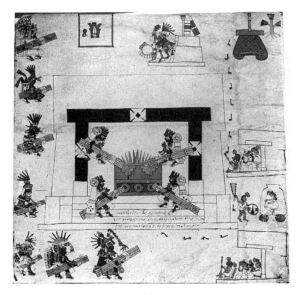

The New Fire Ceremony was performed at midnight every fifty-two years at the beginning/end of each calendar round. Seven deity impersonators with a fire-making implement are about to produce the fire of the new age that will be relayed to extinguished hearths throughout the empire. From the Aztec manuscript Codex Borbonicus, *page 34. (Courtesy of Akademische Druck und Verlagsanstalt, Graz, Austria, 1974 facsimile ed.)*

Sacred Words

> Among the Mexicans, . . . the wise, superior, and effective rhetoricians were held in high regard. And they elected these to be high priests, lords, leaders, and captains, no matter how humble their estate. These ruled the states, led the armies, and presided in the temples.[45]

It is erroneous to think of Aztec society and religion as primarily concerned with violence and aggression. As the pictorial images and ethnographic texts show, Nahuatl-speaking peoples worked cooperatively in farming communities, developed exquisite crafts and art forms, sponsored poetry festivals, cared deeply for children, worried about the power of gossip, loved telling stories, and warmed to the excitement, color, and tensions of the marketplace. All of these activities, the human life cycle, cultural expressions, farming, and trading were regulated and renewed by ceremonial performances.

Like all traditional urban societies the Aztec world was permeated by a formal sense of order and beauty. Feather work, dance, pottery, sculpture, mural painting, and philosophical discourse were vivid elements of the social landscape. One of the most refined and influential art forms was human speech. The Aztecs and their neighbors put great effort into developing both eloquent speech forms and profound metaphorical content in their spoken interactions. It is not easy for contemporary students, raised in a culture where "free speech" is a leading guide to language usage, to appreciate the power and meaning of those languages based on traditionally formal speech patterns and expressions. But Nahuatl was a highly formalized language that has often led outsiders to misunderstand its intentions and meanings. When Moctezuma Xocoyotzin greeted Hernán Cortés, for instance, he used conventional Nahuatl polite speech, which elevated the Spanish leader to a level of high honor. A number of scholars unfamiliar with Aztec language arts wrongly concluded that the welcoming speech showed the ruler to be a weak and docile leader. In fact he was greeting a state visitor in the proper respectful style of a welcoming Tlatoani.

When the Franciscan priest Bernardino de Sahagun did his extraordinary study of Aztec life and language in the 1540s, he discovered how florid, elegant, and meaningful Indian languages were. The most beautiful single volume of the twelve-volume encyclopedic *Florentine Codex* is Book VI, *Rhetoric and Moral Philosophy,* which presents the formal speeches and moral philosophy of the Aztecs. It contains forty extensive prayers, some over five pages long, plus exhortations and orations spoken by parents, rulers, midwives, and citizens. This remarkable volume concludes with a collection of proverbs, riddles, and metaphors portraying wit, insight, and vivid imagery.

These verbal arts, filled with beauty and complexity of thought, are comparable to the great literatures of the world. We will discuss three dimensions: the *tlamatinime,* or wise people trained in verbal arts; the **huehuetlatolli,** or the Ancient Word; and riddles. In each case we will see how the cosmovision of Mesoamerica turned speech into a ceremony between humans. [See Native Religions of North America p. 285, Judaism pp. 390–94, Christianity pp. 497, 499, Islam pp. 635–37, 648–53, 665–72, Hinduism pp. 728–29, 738–43, 750–53, Buddhism p. 861, Religions of China pp. 995–96, 999–1000, 1031, and Religions of Japan pp. 1100, 1101 for discussion of Bible, scriptures, and religious texts.]

The Tlamatinime

Although rhetorical polish was appreciated in many social situations, there was a group of trained specialists, *tlamatinime* (knowers of things), who used the art of language to raise philosophical questions about human nature and its relations to ultimate truth. This group explored an alternate religious worldview to the mystico-military religion of the Aztec warrior class. They used language, instead of blood, to communicate with and make offerings to the gods.

Compared to "a stout torch that does not smoke," the *tlamatinime* were trained in *calmecacs,* or schools of higher learning, to be ideal guides in human affairs. They preserved honored traditions, produced and read the painted manuscripts, and developed refined metaphors and poems to probe the true foundations of human existence. The clearest examples of its expression come from a series of texts showing the talents and insights of such rulers as Nezahualcoyotl (Fasting Coyote), King of Texcoco; Tecayehuatzin, Prince of Huexotzinco; and a dozen other *tlamatinime.* In other words this type of verbal art was largely practiced by the elites.

These poet-philosophers saw human existence as essentially fragile and ephemeral, as this poem attributed to Nezahualcoyotl indicates.

> I comprehend the secret, the hidden:
> O my lords!
> Thus we are,
> we are mortal,
> men through and through,
> we all will have to go away,
> we all will have to die on earth . . .
> Like a painting,
> we will be erased.
> Like a flower,
> we will dry up
> here on earth . . .
> Think on this my lords,
> eagles and ocelots,
> though you be of jade,
> though you be of gold
> you also will go there
> to the place of the fleshless.[46]

The precious aspects of life (jade, gold, flowers, paintings) are transitory and vulnerable rather than solid and with a firm foundation. Faced with this cosmic condition of instability and illusion, the *tlamatinime* developed a rhetorical strategy aimed at discovering and experiencing the nature of truth, a solid foundation to existence. They believed that there was such a reality beyond human existence, "in the region of the gods above and in the region of the dead below." In order to penetrate these regions and discover a stable reality, they had to devise techniques to open the depths of the human personality to the elusive world of truth. The main technique was the creation of *in xochitl, in cuicatl,* or flowers and songs, artistic expressions in the forms of words, songs, and paintings that connected the human personality, referred to as "face and heart," with the divine.

The Fasting Coyote also wrote of this connection,

> My flowers will not come to an end,
> my songs will not come to an end,
> I, the singer, raise them up:
> they are scattered, they are bestowed.[47]

Speaking of the power of poetry to express a lasting truth, he wrote,

> Even though flowers on earth
> may wither and yellow,
> they will be carried there,
> to the interior of the house
> of the bird with the golden feathers.[48]

This approach of linking the "face and heart" (personality) to the divine through the medium of "flower and song" was based on a religious conception of duality. In Nahuatl culture the cosmos was originally created and structured by a supreme Dual God, Ometeotl. This duality was manifested in the dualities, which combined to make forms of reality such as male/female, hot/cold, left/right, underworld/celestial world, above/below, darkness/light, rain/drought, death/life. At the level of human language this duality could be expressed in metaphors that generally consisted of two words or phrases joined to form a single idea, like "flower and song," meaning poetry or truth. At the level of the gods the High God or Ometeotl (Giver of Life) was the combined forces of Ometecuhtli and Omecihuatl. The language form used to inculcate this divine duality into words, called a *difrasismo*, includes two phrases joined to mean one thing. For example:

in xochitl, in cuicatl = flower and song = poetry or truth

in atl, in tepetl = water and hill = a town

in topan, in mictlan = what is above us, the region of the dead = the world beyond humans

topco, petlacalco = in the bag and in the box = a secret

in cueitl, in huipilli = the skirt, the blouse = the sexual nature of women.

In the rhetorical and aesthetic program worked out by the *tlamatinime*, a correspondence was revealed linking the human personality, poetic structures, and the divine foundation of the universe together, through the use of this language art. In the moment when the speaker or artist truly expressed his or her heart in flower and song, the inner self was deified or filled with divine energy. This achievement meant that poetry and the human personality became linked to the divine duality above. The most profound truth—the reliable foundation of the cosmos—was the Lord and Lady of Duality, who were beyond "all time, beyond the heavens in Omeyocan." As with our discussion of the cosmos and human body, so with the Lord of Duality and the language of duality—the power and truth of celestial forces could be encapsulated in the spoken word.

The Huehuetlatolli

One of the most influential instruments for organizing human behavior was the *huehuetlatolli*, or the Ancient Word. These rhetorical orations were florid, elegant, metaphorical speeches, which were memorized and presented at ceremonial occasions such as the coronation of a ruler, the entry of a youth into the *calmecac*, the work of a midwife, or a marriage ceremony. *Huehuetlatolli* were also utilized when nobles gathered every eighty days in a special setting to receive admonitions and instructions of how to conduct themselves in war and peace. In this way these ancient words instructed Aztec peoples on friendship, learning, aspects of beauty, and proper worship of gods.

Consider the beauty and tenderness expressed in this *huehuetlatolli* spoken by a midwife to a newborn baby. Note how this formal speech required in midwife training reflects the patterns of cosmos and human body as well as divine duality and human language:

And when the baby had arrived on earth, then the midwife shouted: she gave war cries, which meant that the little woman had fought a good battle, had become a brave warrior, had taken a captive, had captured a baby.

Then the midwife spoke to it. If it was a male, she said to it: "Thou has arrived on earth, my youngest one, my beloved boy, my beloved youth."

If it was a female, she said to it: "My beloved maiden, my youngest one, noblewoman, thou hast suffered exhaustion, thou hast become fatigued. Thy beloved father, the master the lord of the near, of the nigh, the creator of men, the maker of men, hath sent thee: . . . My youngest one! Perhaps thou wilt live for a little while! Art thou our reward? Art thou our merit? Perhaps thou wilt know thy grandfather, thy grandmothers, thy kinsmen, thy lineage.

In what way have thy mother, thy father Ome tecutli, Ome ciuatl, arrayed thee? In what manner have they endowed thee?"[49]

Some of the same elements of cosmovision appear in this opening passage of the *huehuetlatolli* spoken by a nobleman to his son exhorting him to sexual chastity.

Thou who art my son, thou who art my youth, hear the words; place, inscribe in the chambers of thy heart the word or two which our forefathers departed leaving: the old men, the old women, the regarded ones, the admired ones, and the advised one on earth. Here is that which they gave us, entrusted to us as they left the words of the old men, that which is bound, the well-guarded words. They left saying that the pure life is considered as a well-smoked, precious turquoise: as a round, reedlike, well-formed, precious green stone. There is no blotch, no blemish. Those perfect in their hearts, in their manner of life, those of pure life—like these are the precious green stone, the precious turquoise, which are glistening, shining before the Lord of the Near, of the Close. . . . For the Lord of the Near and Close has said, you are ordained one woman for one man. However, you are not to ruin yourself impetuously; you are not to devour, to gulp down the carnal life as if you were a dog.[50]

The force of these metaphors of affection, sexuality, and the gods combines to focus the listener on the main message: The gods befriend those who abstain from sex before and outside of marriage.

One of the Franciscan priests remarked around the middle of the sixteenth century that "no people loved their children more" than did the Aztecs. This love was also expressed in artistic speech. Rulers spoke to their daughters when they reached the age of discretion:

Here you are, my little girl, my necklace of precious stones, my plumage, my human creation, born of me. You are my blood, my color, my image. . . .

Listen. Much do I want you to understand that you are noble. See that you are very precious, even while you are still only a little lady. You are a precious stone, you are a turquoise.[51]

Riddles

While Nahuatl language arts were florid, noble, and highly formal, they also contained a capacity for word pictures and wit. *Huehuetlatolli* included riddles, which were part of daily speech acts. Knowing the correct answer to riddles indicated that a person was from a good family. Note the ways that humankind and nature, cosmovision and human action, are related in these riddles:

> What is a little blue-green jar filled with popcorn? Someone is sure to guess our riddle; it is the sky.
>
> What is a warrior's hair-dress that knows the way to the region of the dead? Someone is sure to guess our riddle: it is a jug for drawing water from the well.
>
> What is a mountainside that has a spring of water in it? Our nose.
>
> What is it that goes along with foothills of the mountain patting out tortillas with its hands? A butterfly.
>
> What is it that bends over us all over the world? The maize tassel.[52]

Finally let us review a series of proverbs used in social discourse, which reflect many of the religious dimensions discussed in this chapter.

Moxoxolotitlani = A page is sent. This is said about someone who is sent with a message and fails to return with an answer, or else does not go where he was sent. It is said for this reason. They say that when Quetzalcoatl was King of Tollan, two women were bathing in his pool. When he saw them he sent some messengers to see who they were. And the messengers just stayed there watching the women bathing and did not take him the information. Then Quetzalcoatl sent another of his pages to see who the bathers were and the same thing happened: he did not return with an answer either. . . . From that time on they began, they started saying: A page is sent.

Niquauhtlamelaoa, tiquauhtlamelaoa = I am a fruitless tree, you are a fruitless tree. This is said when I study something but cannot learn it. It is exactly as if I were a fruit tree that bears no fruit.

Ipal nonixpatlaoa = Because of him my face becomes wide. This is said when someone's child—a boy or girl—or else someone's pupil, was well-taught, well-brought up.

And finally from the section on metaphors.

Tzopelic, auiyac = Sweet and fragrant. This was said about a city where there was prosperity and joy, or about a king who brought joy to the people.

In otitochtiac, in otimazatiac = You have turned into a rabbit, you have turned into a deer. This was said about someone who no longer lived at home. He no longer paid any attention to his father and mother but ran away when they wanted to correct him.

Yollotl, eztli = Heart and blood. These words were said of chocolate because in the past it was precious and rare. The common people and the poor did not drink it. They also said it was deranging and it was thought to be like the mushroom, for it intoxicated people.[53]

With this sense of language and the sacred that we have gained, let us now turn to a different understanding of "heart and blood" equally as precious as chocolate but not nearly so rare.

Rites of Renewal and Human Sacrifice

We have explored four pervasive themes in Aztec religion as a means of understanding how their world was made, centered, and renewed: the tradition of Quetzalcoatl and Tollan, the cosmology of the human body, the Great Temple as *axis mundi,* and the art of language. All of these dimensions influenced the dynamics or splendid ceremonial cycles of Aztec religion, which involved different forms of sacrifice, including human sacrifice, and wove together economic, political, military, and aesthetic institutions. The high priests who officiated and spoke at the major festivals involving human sacrifice at the Templo Mayor, for example, were called *quequetzalcoa* after the priest-king of Tollan. Now it is time to turn to two of these remarkable human celebrations: the New Fire Ceremony held only once every fifty-two years; and the festival of **Toxcatl** in honor of the awesome deity Tezcatlipoca, Lord of the Smoking Mirror. Each ceremony will be described in some detail and then interpreted within the context of Aztec religion as a whole.

The New Fire Ceremony

On a morning in the middle of November 1507 a procession of fire priests with a captive warrior "arranged in order and wearing the garb of the gods" processed out of the city of Tenochtitlan toward the ceremonial center on the Hill of the Star. During the days prior to this auspicious night the populace of the Aztec world participated together in the ritual extinction of fires, the casting of statues and hearthstones into the water, and the clean sweeping of houses, patios, and walkways. In anticipation of this fearful night women were closed up in granaries to avoid their transformation into fierce beasts who would eat men, pregnant women would put on masks of maguey leaves, and children were punched and nudged awake to avoid being turned into mice while asleep. For on this one night in the calendar round of 18,980 nights the Aztec fire priests celebrated "when the night was divided in half": the New Fire Ceremony that ensured the rebirth of the sun and the movement of the cosmos for another fifty-two years. This rebirth was achieved symbolically through the heart sacrifice of a brave, captured warrior specifically chosen by the king. We are told that when the procession arrived "in the deep night" at the Hill of the Star the populace climbed onto their roofs. With unwavering attention and necks craned toward the hill they became filled with dread that the sun would be destroyed forever.

It was thought that if the fire could not be drawn, the demons of darkness would descend to eat human beings. As the ceremony proceeded the priest watched the sky carefully for the movement of a star group known as Tian-quitzli or Marketplace, the cluster we call the Pleiades. As it passed through the meridian signaling that the movement of the heavens had not ceased, a small fire was started on the outstretched chest of a warrior. The text reads, "When a little fire fell, then speedily the priests slashed open the breast with a flint knife, seized the heart, and thrust it into the fire. In the open chest a new fire was drawn and people could see it from everywhere."[54] The populace cut their ears—even the ears of children in cradles, the text tells us—and "spattered their blood in the ritual flicking of fingers in the direction of fire on the mountain." Then the new fire was taken down the mountain and carried to the pyramid temple of Huitzilopochtli in the center of the city of Tenochtitlan, where it was placed in the fire holder of the statue of the god. Then messengers, runners, and fire priests who had come from everywhere took the fire back to the cities where the common folk, after blistering themselves with the fire, placed it in their homes, and "all were quieted in their hearts."

This dramatic performance is extraordinarily thick and complex with meanings related to astronomy, calendars, ritual theaters, human sacrifice, and even child rearing. It is a clear example of what we have called worldcenter-ing and worldrenewing. What is especially instructive is that the New Fire Ceremony integrates two major ceremonial centers and two cycles of time in one ceremony. Worldcentering and worldrenewing are doubly expressed.

The New Fire Ceremony, also called the Toxiuhmolpilia, Binding of the Years, actually tied together two important but very different ceremonial cen-ters: the Great Temple of Tenochtitlan and the Hill of the Star. This rare cere-mony, seen only once in a human lifetime, begins in the capital when the ruler Moctezuma orders a captive warrior be found whose name contains the word *xiuitl,* meaning turquoise, grass, or comet, a symbolic name connoting precious time. The procession of priests and deity impersonators moves along a pre-scribed passageway, presumably seen and heard by masses of people before arriving at the Hill of the Star. (In another report of this ceremony we are told that Moctezuma had a special devotion and reverence for this hill and shrine.) Then, having walked the twenty kilometers and climbed the ceremonial hill, the group of priests and lords, sharing a heightened sense of expectation and fear, seeks another procession: the procession of the stars through the meridian. Once the procession of stars is recognized, the heart sacrifice is carried out, and new fire is lit amid universal rejoicing and bleeding. Then, in the primary action that links the two "centers," the fire is taken back to the Templo Mayor. Next, in what I see as the most meaningful social and symbolic gesture, messengers, priests, and runners who have "come from all directions" to the Templo Mayor take the fire back to the towns and cities on the periphery, where it ignites the new fire or time periods locally. In this way all the lesser units of the society, with their local shrines, are illuminated by the new fire, which links them to both the capital and the sacred hill. The fiery display ignites the imperial landscape by linking up all the sacred spaces in the Az-tec world.

Aztec time is also renewed in this ceremony. Mesoamerican life was organized by two major calendar rounds, a 365-day solar cycle and a 260-day ritual cycle. Both calendars were divided into months, which were marked by carefully choreographed ritual performances and processions involving different cults, priestly groups, and communities. Mesoamerican priesthoods interlocked these cycles together, noting that all the possible interactive combinations became exhausted after 18,980 days or every fifty-two years. The end of this great cycle marked a point of cosmological crisis and transition. The New Fire Ceremony, focused on the heart sacrifice of a captive warrior, functioned to renew the beginning of these cycles for another fifty-two years. The power of this renewal came from two forces: the heart (*teyolia*) of humans and a new fire, which was ignited in the "hearth" created by the heart's extraction. When we remember divine forces were believed to reside in the human heart—and that the *teyolia* was believed to rise into the Sky of the Sun upon the death of a warrior—we can understand *what they believed they were accomplishing in this otherwise strange ceremony*. The Sun and celestial dynamics, or time, was being renewed from the gift of the *teyolia* that was being returned to the divine beings above.

Toxcatl: The Festival for Tezcatlipoca

Human sacrifice was not a random or occasional ritual practice: It took place in the Aztec world every month. Given what we have already studied about cosmology and the human body, and the New Fire Ceremony, we should now be able to understand—regardless of our sense of discomfort—the meaning and purpose of these rituals, described so shockingly by Díaz del Castillo earlier in this chapter. In order to further understand the meaning of human sacrifice in Aztec terms, let us look at one of the yearly festivals, Toxcatl.

Toxcatl was celebrated in honor of the "god of gods," Tezcatlipoca (Lord of the Smoking Mirror), one of the four creator gods who ordered the cosmos. The central act was the sacrifice of a captive warrior chosen for his perfect physical features. This youth was ritually changed into a *teotl ixiptla*, or image of the god, who paraded for one year throughout the Aztec city. At the end of the year the impersonator of Tezcatlipoca was sacrificed on top of a pyramid/temple, when his heart was extracted and offered to the sun. The impersonator was beheaded and his skull displayed on the skull rack in the ceremonial courtyard.

Let us consider the following stages of this ritual as described directly in the text.

The Aztec priests chose the most attractive physical male from a group of enemy warriors. There was a ritual prescription for the body type, as this excerpt shows.

> Indeed he who was thus chosen was . . . of good understanding, quick, of clean body, slender . . . long and thin, . . . like a stone column all over. . . .
>
> Indeed it became his defect if someone were exceedingly tall. The woman said to him, "Tall fellow; tree-shaker; star gatherer."

A litany of detailed physical characteristics outlines the type of human body needed for the ceremony:

> He who was chosen as impersonator was without defects. He was like something smoothed, like a tomato, like a pebble, as if sculptured in wood, he was not curly haired, curly headed. . . . He was not rough of forehead; he had not pimples on his forehead. He did not have a forehead like a tomato: he did not have a baglike forehead . . . he was not swollen cheeked; he was not of injured eyes; he was not of downcast face; he was not flat-nosed, not crooked nosed, but his nose was averagely placed. . . . He was not thick lipped, he was not big lipped, he was not bowl lipped; he was not a stutterer, he did not speak a barbarous language. He was not buck-toothed, he was not yellow toothed, he was not ugly toothed, he was not rotten toothed, his teeth were like sea shells; they lay well, they lay in order . . . he was not fat, he was not big bellied, he was not of protruding navel, he was not of hatchet shaped navel, he was not of wrinkled stomach, he was not of hatchet shaped buttocks, he was not of flabby buttocks.[55]

We see here the prime importance of the human body in the ritual of Toxcatl. The perfect container of divine energy is being chosen in recognition of Tezcatlipoca's status as a High God. After this individual is chosen he goes through a formal training period in the art of flower carrying, flute playing, speech arts, and whistle blowing in order to appear as the perfect image of Tezcatlipoca on earth. The impersonator and a specially trained guard/entourage of servants roam freely throughout the city for one year, showing the populace

A postconquest depiction of human sacrifice from the Codex Magliabechiano. *The victim is held over the sacrificial stone while a priest cuts his heart out with a flint knife. Once the heart is removed, the victim is thrown down the steps of the temple. The divine power in the heart ascends into the sky. (Courtesy of University of California Press, Berkeley.)*

the living image of Lord of the Smoking Mirror. At the appointed time he is taken before the king Moctezuma and adorned with lavish cloaks, gifts, and luxuries, transforming the appearance of the impersonator into that of the living god. Following more public display the impersonator is given four wives, who are impersonating goddesses of agriculture, with whom he apparently has orgiastic sexual relations for twenty days prior to this sacrifice. Then he sheds his luscious ornaments in various places and his hair is cut into the style of a seasoned warrior.

With his deified wives he visits, dances, and sings at four ceremonial precincts, distributing food and gifts to the commoners before departing from the women and processing to the temple of Tlacochcalco. The text reads,

> He ascended by himself, he went up of his own free will, to where he was to die. As he was taken up a step, as he passed one step, there he broke, he shattered his flute, his whistle.
>
> And when he had mounted all the steps, when he had risen to the summit, then the offering priests seized him. They threw him upon his back on the sacrificial stone; then one of them cut open his breast; he took his heart from him, he also raised it in dedication to the sun. . . . But his body they did not roll down; rather, they lowered it. And his severed head they strung on the skull rack.[56]

In the extraordinary treatment given to Tezcatlipoca's living image on earth, we see the integration of a number of major elements of Aztec religion. The sacrificial victim is a captured warrior, as in the case of the mythical sacrifice at Coatepec. In this ceremony more than just the divine forces in the heart are released into the cosmos. Because the impersonator is Tezcatlipoca, the *tonalli* embedded in the skull of the perfect warrior is also offered as a gift to the god. Second, we see the importance of artistic display in the music, costume, rhetoric, and poise of Tezcatlipoca. He is a living example of "flower and song," the divine truth on earth. The ceremony ends with the following statement of "truth on earth."

> And this betokened our life on earth. For he who rejoiced, who possessed riches, who sought, who esteemed our lord's sweetness, his fragrance—richness, prosperity—thus ended in great misery. Indeed it was said: "No one on earth went exhausting happiness, riches, wealth."[57]

In this remarkable ceremony we are seeing the Aztec conception of the perfect life and ideal death of the warrior displayed for all to see as he parades, sings, plays music, and is sacrificed in public.

It is often asked whether sacrificial victims voluntarily surrendered themselves in the manner described here. Sources reveal that in some cases the warriors attempted to escape during the ceremonies. We also know that victims fainted from fear as they approached the top of the temple. In other cases it appears that some deity impersonators, especially women, did not know that they were soon to be ritually killed. But it is also evident that, as in the festival of Toxcatl, some impersonators surrendered willingly, even with courageous displays of devotion to the sacrificial destiny. They believed that their hearts and minds would, like Quetzalcoatl, be transformed into eternal forces living in the heavens. This is perhaps the meaning of the claim that Tenochtitlan "is the foundation of heaven . . . where no one fears to die in war." [See Religions of Africa pp. 39–42, 64–69, Native Religions of North America pp. 274–76, 288–305, 330–32, Judaism pp. 414–15, Christianity pp. 537–38, Islam pp. 635–37, Hinduism pp. 739–41, 759–61, 780–84, Buddhism pp. 900–903, Religions of China pp. 1024–26, and Religions of Japan pp. 1112–27 for discussion of God, gods, and objects of worship.]

8

Maya Religion:
Cosmic Trees, Sacred Kings,
and the Underworld

"The dawn has approached, preparations have been made, and morning has come for the provider, nurturer, born in the light, begotten in the light. Morning has come for humankind, for the people of the face of the earth," they said. It all came together as they went on thinking in the darkness, in the night, as they searched and they sifted, they thought and they wondered.

Popul Vuh[58]

IN 1949 ALBERTO RUZ, the chief excavator of the Temple of the Inscriptions at the Maya city of Palenque (fourth–ninth centuries C.E.), deduced that the floor of the rear hall concealed something below. He lifted several huge polished floor stones and discovered a steep staircase leading downward and packed with tons of stone rubble. Three years later in 1952, after arduous and careful work, Ruz opened for the first time in more than one thousand years the fabulous tomb of the Maya king Pacal (Lord Shield), who had ruled for sixty-eight years until his death in 683.

In the center of the tomb stood the sarcophagus of Pacal, whose remains were found within, covered with remnants of a jade mask, necklaces, ear spools, rings, and a collection of jade and mother of pearl ornaments. On the walls and floors around the sarcophagus were reliefs of stucco, pottery vessels, stuccoed portrait heads, and the corpses of six sacrificial victims probably sacrificed on the occasion of Pacal's funeral. After the crypt was sealed a hollow miniature stairway made of thin slabs of stone leading upward from the crypt to the upper Temple floor provided for communication between Pacal and the upper world. But the most revealing part of the tomb was the intricately carved sarcophagus lid, measuring more than twelve by seven feet, which depicted the image of the Maya cosmos and Pacal's movement through it. It consisted in part of

- a fantastic tree, decorated with jewels, mirrors, bloodletting bowls, dragons, bones, and a celestial bird on top
- the image of Pacal, with a small bone attached to his nose at the moment of death, falling

1. Bloodletting Bowl
4. Double-Headed Serpent Bar Represents the Middle World
2. Bowls with Dragons
3. Jaws of the Underworld Formed by Two Skeletal Dragons

Carved from a single slab of limestone, this lid covered the tomb of Lord Pacal, who ruled Palenque for sixty-eight years. It depicts the cosmos at the moment of his death, as he descends down the World Tree into the underworld. Sarcophagus Lid, Temple of the Inscriptions, Palenque, Chiapas, Mexico, 684. (Courtesy of Editions Albert Guillot, 4 rue de Seze, Lyon, France.)

- into the gaping jaws of the underworld, pictured as two huge skeletal dragons joined at the chin to form a U-shaped opening representing the passage to Xibalba. Other underworld symbols decorate the lid.

Around the sides of the sarcophagus were vertically carved images of Pacal's ancestors emerging from trees, and on the floor were five or six human sacrificial victims who had been killed when the tomb was sealed. This interrelated imagery of tree, king, ancestor sacrifice, and the underworld tells us that

> for the Maya, the world was a complex and awesome place, alive with sacred power. This power was part of the landscape, of the fabric of space and time, of things both living and inanimate and of the forces of nature—storms, wind, smoke, mist, rain, earth, sky and water. Sacred beings moved between the three levels of the cosmos, the Overworld which is the heavens, the Middleworld where humans live and the Underworld of Xibalba, the source of disease and death. The king acted as a transformer through whom in ritual acts, the unspeakable power of the supernatural passed into the lives of mortal men and their works. The person of the king was also sacred. His clothing reflected more than wealth and prestige: it was a symbolic array identifying rank, ritual context and the sacred person he manifested.[59]

This chapter will explore the awesome, sacred world of the Maya, which was centered on the flowering cosmic tree and the lives of royal families and their intimate ties to ancestors. We will also see, following our general concern for "world renewal," how various means of sacrifice and mythical and spiritual journeys through the underworld revitalized the Maya cosmos. We will see that just as the bone attached to Pacal's nose symbolizes a large seed or his regeneration, so the Maya believed that it was possible, through cosmo-magical struggles, to overcome death and experience a spiritual future including return visits to the earthly level. In this way we can, like King Pacal, descend into the rich world of meaning that filled the Maya cosmos.

The Lost Civilization of the Maya

There has always been a mystique surrounding the jungle civilization of the Classic Maya, who flourished between 200 and 900 C.E. Whether referred to in a number of books as the "Lost Civilization," or superficially depicted in movies as treasure houses for *Raiders of the Lost Ark* or *Star Wars* rebel bases, the lost Maya have been like screens upon which modern cultures have projected their own ideas about noble savages. In the works of novelists, scholars, and travel agencies of the early twentieth century they have been portrayed as the great exception to the patterns of settlement and human character found in other ancient civilizations. This process of making the Maya so exceptional began, in part, with the discovery of the ruins of Copán in the Honduran jungle by the traveling diplomat John L. Stephens and the artist Frederick Catherwood. Stephens wrote after struggling through the jungle-covered site,

> We sat down on the very edge of the wall and strove in vain to penetrate the mystery by which we were surrounded. Who were the people that built this city? In the ruined cities of Egypt, even in the long lost Petra, the stranger knows the story of the people whose vestiges are around him. America, say historians, was peopled by savages: but savages never reared these structures, savages never carved these stones. . . . There were no associations connected with the place; none of those stirring recollections which hallow Rome, Athens, and "the world's great mistress" on the Egyptian plain; but architecture, sculpture, and painting, all the arts which embellished life, had flourished in this overgrown forest; orators, warriors and statesmen, beauty, ambition and glory had lived and passed away, and none knew that such things had been, or could tell of their past existence.[60]

These attempts to relate in one way or another the Maya cities with the great civilizations of the so-called Old World continued on in the nineteenth century and received a fantastic series of twists by the French photographer and explorer Augustus Le Plongeon, who did archaeological and photographic work in Yucatan between 1873 and 1884. Le Plongeon made a splendid photographic record of Maya ritual buildings, iconography, and sculpture, which demands universal respect today. But at the same time he developed fantastic theories about the original homeland of the Maya and of their cultural achievements. He argued in a series of publications that the Maya were descendants of the lost civilization of Atlantis and the founders of Egyptian and Babylonian civilizations. Later scholars argued the reverse, that the Maya had migrated from Egypt. It appears unlikely that there were any such migrations of cultural significance. Le Plongeon also believed that the Maya's hieroglyphics indicated that they had prophesied that one day the telegraph would be used!

A more modern vision of the Maya, developed during the first half of the twentieth century, persisted until thirty years ago. In this vision the Maya were presented in popular and academic books as being a peaceful civilization directed by priests who were intense stargazers and mathematical geniuses. It was also believed that they lived in settlements that were neither village nor city but some vague utopian form of human habitation. This image was often put forth with glee in the face of the Aztec portrait of thundering warriors with bloodthirsty intentions celebrated on pyramids of carnage and cruelty. The more general claim was that the Maya were an ideal civilization unique in world history.

This view of the lost Maya ideal was shattered in the 1946 discovery of the murals at the ceremonial center of Bonampak in southern Mexico. Three rooms containing elaborate paintings presented a narrative of Maya life as a society dedicated to warfare and public human sacrifice under the direction of a royal family involved in the investiture of a prince into the line of succession to the sacred royal throne. Further research revealed that the Maya lived in socially stratified societies spatially organized around monumental ceremonial centers directed by sacred priesthoods who shared immense power with royal families in whom the ultimate authority, on earth, resided. It has become clear that Maya life was animated by an obsession with lineage. In a number of cases these ceremonial cities contained three distinctive zones of habitation: a central zone, adjacent to the ceremonial core where the elite class lived; a closely surrounding residential zone with mixed elites and commoner homes; and a peripheral residential area, where commoners and agricultural workers resided. This spatial layering was accompanied with distinctive degrees of access to status, goods, and power. A very serious collaborative effort by scholars from various disciplines has developed this more realistic and yet fascinating view of Maya religion and society.

The Maya region has been divided by scholars into three subregions: the southern subregion of the Guatemala highlands and the Pacific coast, the central subregion of northern Guatemala and its adjacent lowlands and the Petén region of Guatemala, and the northern region of the Yucatan Peninsula north of the Petén.

The greatest Maya achievements took place in the central and northern subregions in a number of major and minor ceremonial centers during what archaeologists have designated the Classic Period. For practical purposes scholars have divided Maya history in particular (Mesoamerican history in general) into three major phases. The Formative Period (1800 B.C.E.–100 C.E.) was characterized by the gradual rise of complex ceremonial centers and the appearance of monumental architecture. During this period hieroglyphic writing and calendrics, the induction of social stratification, short and long-distance trade routes, and the first outlines of political statehood developed in several areas. A few large-scale city-states organized by dominant cities such as El Mirador and Kaminaljuyú appear to have emerged toward the end of this period. New evidence indicates that the long count calendar, which eventually flourished in the Classic Period, was developing in the southern regions during this Formative Period. The Classic Period (200 C.E.–900 C.E.), which we are focusing on in this chapter, resulted in the maturation of these processes, including the proliferation of ritual and solar calendrical systems, sizable agricultural bureaucracies, and the emergence in several areas of intense, even brutal, competition between powerful ceremonial centers. In the Maya area, however, the pattern of state organization was generally restricted to a series of competing city-states, a few of which extended strong religious and political influence to other regional sites.

The Post-Classic Period covers the development of the Maya world down to the conquest. It is quite astonishing that the greatest Maya achievements took place in the forests and jungles of Guatemala and Mexico. The extraordinary range of religious forms can only be illustrated here through reference to a handful of major sites.

Many of the Maya ceremonial centers were architectural wonders containing steep pyramid temples, large and small standing stelae or stone columns with writing and images, ball courts, palaces, and stairways. Throughout these ceremonial centers was spread a writing system that has puzzled and frustrated scholars for four hundred years. A major breakthrough in reading the Maya texts occurred in 1960, when Tatiana Proskouriakoff revealed that Maya inscriptions could be read and that they were primarily historical accounts of lives, families, and deaths of Maya royalty though not without astronomical references. Due to an unusual cooperative effort among Maya specialists we are gaining an in-depth understanding of the dynastic histories and sacred cosmologies of such beautifully built cities as Palenque, Caracol, Copán, Tikal, Dos Pilas, Yaxchilán, and many others. It has been discovered that the Maya told their histories and cosmologies in "pictorial programs" carved and painted on buildings throughout their ceremonial centers. One cosmic symbol that organizes and renews the Maya world is the sacred, flowering tree.

The Cosmic Tree

In order to get a good focus on the Maya cosmic tree we must first discuss the general idea of the cosmic tree. Then we will return to the ceremonial center of Palenque, where the cosmic tree is depicted in various, fantastic forms in a number of ceremonial buildings.

The Maya world was covered with vegetation. The people survived and prospered, in large part, through agricultural cultivation and production. We can tell from the rich images and clusters of images in Maya art that the people shared an agricultural mentality, that is, they were deeply committed to the con-tinual regeneration of the plant world. This mentality springs from the insight that agriculture is not just a profane skill, but that it deals with powers and life forces that dwell in the seeds, furrows, rain, and sunshine. Human society and the agricultural process are viewed as set within and dependent upon the dra-matic and tense cosmic cycles that insure the vital process of plant fertilization, ripening, harvest, decay, death, and rebirth. The forces in the plants, land, and rains are viewed as sacred forces, which reveal themselves in dramatic and criti-cal moments that are never to be taken for granted. In fact the Maya not only considered the plants and seeds as in need of regeneration, but the entire cosmos depended on various processes of rebirth.

We can see the pervasive power of an agricultural mentality in the names and attributes of certain Maya gods. For instance, Itzamna was one of the most powerful Classic Maya gods associated with both the earth and sky, represented with reptilian features combining crocodile, lizard, and snake. He was the source of life-nurturing rains that produced the abundance of the Maya fields and forest. Another fertility force was Ah K'in, the sun who represented not only the forces of warmth that insured the reappearance of plant life, but also the threatening droughts. In the latter case Ah K'in was appeased to avoid agricul-tural disaster. All the Maya, but especially the peasants, worshiped the Chacs, who were associated with the four world directions from which flowed the rain that nurtured the fields and the trees. Equally important were the maize gods, who lived in the ever-present *milpas* or cornfields that surrounded the Maya ceremonial centers.

In the great myth of creation, recorded in the Quiché Maya book *Popul Vuh* or *Book of Council,* the cosmos is created in an agricultural style. At the beginning of time the gods created an abundant world of vegetation after they asked about the sky-earth (world):

> How should it be sown, how should it dawn? . . . Let it be this way, think about it: this water should be removed, emptied out for the formation of the earth's own plate and platform, then comes the sowing, the dawning of the sky-earth . . .
>
> And then the earth arose because of them, it was simply their word that brought it forth. For the forming of the earth they said "Earth." It arose suddenly just like a cloud, like a mist, now forming, unfolding. Then the mountains were separated from the water, all at once the great mountains came forth. By their genius alone, by their cutting edge alone they carried out the conception of the mountain-plain, whose face grew instant groves of cypress and pine.[61]

This cosmic sowing and dawning provides the model for all subsequent creations, innovations, and changes. In Maya mythology seeds are sown in the earth to dawn as plants; celestial bodies are sown beneath the earth to dawn in their rising; humans are sown in mothers' wombs to dawn into life; and the dead are sown in the underworld to dawn as sparks of light in the darkness. The world's first dawn, brought forth through the sun's rays, emerges with the appearance of the planet Venus:

> And here is the dawning and sowing of the Sun, Moon, and Stars, and Jaguar Quitze, Jaguar Night, Mahucutah, and True Jaguar were overjoyed when they saw the daybringer. It came up first. It looked brilliant when it came up since it was ahead of the sun.[62]

In the Maya theory of creation, reflected in this pattern of the first and therefore subsequent sunrises, the world is in a continual process of sowing, and dawning (sprouting). The Maya conceived of this process as "a long performance," which hopefully would never end.

It is important to remark that this pattern of birth, death, and rebirth reflects a worldwide pattern of religious symbolism in which the cosmos is likened to a cosmic tree or some form of vegetation. The cosmic tree symbol, which is found in China, Egypt, Mesopotamia, Africa, and other Native American cultures, represents in Mircea Eliade's words the "world as a living totality, periodically regenerating itself and, because of this regeneration, continually fruitful, rich and inexhaustible."[63] [See Native Religions of North America pp. 269, 275 for discussion of the World Tree; see Hinduism pp. 740–41, 747–49 for treatment of the cult of the divine plant *soma.*] The Maya version of this worldwide symbolism is still a vital symbolic force among some Maya, including the **Tzutujil** Mayas of present-day Guatemala. One of the most powerful images of daily and ritual life is expressed in the words *kotsej juyu ruchiliev* or "flowering mountain earth." The entire terrestrial level inhabited by animals, plants, and humans is viewed as a tree or maize plant that repeatedly sprouts, blossoms, wilts, dies, and is reborn. According to Tzutujil mythology there existed a god in the form of a tree before the creation began. This tree stood in the center of chaos. This god-tree became pregnant with potential life as the creation of the universe approached. It began to flower and grew, in the form of fruit, one of everything that was to exist in the created world. Robert Carlsen and Martin Prechtel, who have learned the religious patterns of the contemporary Maya, summarize this process:

> Not only were there gross physical objects like rocks, maize and deer hanging from the branches of this tree, there were also such elements as lightning and even individual segments of time. Eventually this abundance became too much for the tree to support, and the fruit fell. Smashing open, the fruit spread their seeds, and soon there were numerous seedlings growing at the foot of the old tree. The great tree provided shelter to the young "plants," nurturing them, until finally the old tree was itself crowded out by the new. Since then, this tree has existed as a stump at the center of the world. This stump is what remains of the original "Father/Mother" (Te Tie Te Tixel), the source and purpose of life. Moreover, this tree stump constitutes that force which allows the world to flower anew. In this way the world was created.[64]

A number of fascinating details about the Maya cosmic tree of the Classic Period reflect this view. Let us return to the image on Pacal's sarcophagus and concentrate on the Classic Maya image (see the illustration on p. 191).

The Maya tree typically, as in this case, is rooted in the underworld, has its trunk in the middleworld, and its high branches or top ascending into heaven or the upperworld. In this way it unites, through a vertical column, the cosmos and its diverse powers, forces, deities, and dangers. It was believed that the souls of the dead—in this case the soul of Pacal—descend and ascend along the axis provided by the tree. Characteristically the Maya tree has a supernatural bird perched on the top symbolizing the celestial realm of the universe.

In the case of Pacal's tomb, the tree emerges out of the underworld shown as two gaping skeletal jaws of the earth. Pacal is seated on the head of the Four-Sided Sun Monster, which is shown at the moment of sunset. Like Pacal the sun is descending into the night of Xibalba, the underworld. The meaning is also that Pacal, like the sun, will emerge from the underworld in a new form. The trunk of the tree is marked with mirror symbols, indicating that it has brilliance and power—or in Maya religion, sacred energy. At the top of the trunk (1) is a bloodletting bowl outlined with beads of blood. At the edges of the branches (2) are two more bloodletting bowls with square-nosed dragons with jade cylinders and beads lining their mouths, signifying that they are very sacred and represent the heavens. These symbols have cosmic meaning. The skeletal dragons below (3) represent the world of death into which Pacal is descending.

The earthly level is represented by the double-headed serpent bar (4) wrapped around the branches of the world tree, from which fleshed dragon heads with open mouths emerge. These fleshed beings represent the earthly level where the human community organized around the ruler (symbolized by the double-headed serpent bar) is situated.

But this entire scene is in motion. Pacal is pictured at the moment of his fall into the underworld, the sun is sinking below the horizon, and the tree is alive with its miraculous energies and beings. This dynamic motion is also present in the ancestral portraits carved on the side of the sarcophagus. Pacal's ancestors are depicted as emerging with a fruit tree from a crack in the earth, signifying the complementary action of dying and rising, descent and ascent.

One of the most impressive aspects of the art and architecture of Palenque is the series of cosmic trees that adorn the Temple of the Foliated Cross and the Temple of the Cross. Each has a significant variation on the themes discussed above. The central image of the Temple of the Foliated Cross, for example, depicts the cosmic tree rising from a symbol of the ancestral abode. The central tree is actually a composite of the four sacred trees associated with the four directions of the universe. The tie between agriculture and humans is signified when the tree is transformed into a flowering corn plant. However, instead of producing ears of corn, the plant creates the heads of young males, which rest on the leaves. For in Maya thought, the beauty of young males may symbolize the ripe maize, which may in turn represent the young male ruler ascending (or sprouting) to the throne.

This pattern of corn and rebirth reflects another major theme in Maya thought, that is, the meaning of the sun as a divine regenerative force. This pattern has recently been illuminated in Gary Gossen's *Chamulas in the World of the Sun*, a study of a Tzotzil-speaking Maya community in southern Mexico. The oral tradition of this contemporary Maya community reveals that the sun deity is the major symbol connecting ideas of order, verticality, heat, light, maleness, age, and renewal. All Chamula rituals include references to the great drama of the sun's ascent into the cosmos. It is possible that these contemporary patterns reflect ideas that animated the Classic Maya ceremonial world.

The symbol of the *axis mundi* is associated with many of the major elements of the religious world: agriculture, warfare, heaven, ancestors, the underworld, and kingship. The most powerful earthly being associated with the cosmic tree was the king, who was considered the human *axis mundi* of the Maya world.

Sacred Kingship

We have seen throughout our study of Mesoamerican religion that human beings were "centers" of religious power and prestige. The human body, warriors, priests, and especially individuals such as Topiltzin Quetzalcoatl, Nezahualcoyotl, and Pacal oriented human consciousness and provided immediate contact with the sacred. The highest expression of human sacrality in the Maya world was in the royal families and especially the supreme rulers who descended from sacred lineages. Not only did their bodies contain divine fire and energy, but their clothes, bloodlines, paraphernalia, and especially their ritual actions brought the divine into the terrestrial level of existence. To understand this extraordinarily powerful type of individual in Maya religion we will look at the general nature of sacred kingship and then turn to two dimensions of Maya kings: the royal clothes and rites of bloodletting expressive of royal authority.

One way to appreciate the awesome influence of Maya kings is to ask, "What were they the center *of?*" The answer is both simple and complex. Kings or rulers were the center of everything in heaven and earth. They were the living *axis mundi,* the embodiment of tradition and the symbol of totality. In broader terms rulers, especially in urban societies, stood at the center of an "ecological complex" consisting of five dimensions of society: cultivation of the natural environment, movements of the human population, developments of technology, conflict and warfare, and developments of social status and structure. The king was the supreme authority who, with the advice of his ruling family and council, directed the work of intensive agriculture and trading; the ceremonial cycles that attracted peoples to the city; the use and innovations in arts, crafts, tool making, and weaponry; initiated the outbreak of conflicts with other communities; and regulated the rewards for the maintenance of social status. All this was managed from the supremely sacred location of the temple communities at the heart of society. The sources of the authority to carry out the immense power of kingship were the cosmic beings and especially ancestors, in the Maya case, who became incarnate in the body, blood, actions, and costume of the ruler.

This pattern of rulership was present, in a particular form, in Maya society. It was based on four basic assumptions lodged in the Maya worldview. First, it was believed that a powerful cosmic order permeated every level and dimension of the world from the heavens, through the clouds, through the things on the earth and into the realms of the underworld. Second, it was believed that human society would be stable as long as it operated as a microcosm or approximate imitation of the cosmic order constructed by the gods. Third, it was the role of the sacred kings to align the social world of the humans with the supernatural world of the gods. Fourth, the king had to demonstrate through ritual his line of descent from the first ancestor, who was the source of sacrality. The main technique for Maya kings to bring the social and supernatural world into alignment was ritual action. [See Religions of Africa pp. 24, 35, 60, Native Religions of North America pp. 347–48, Judaism pp. 391–92, Christianity pp. 503, 505, Islam pp. 632–33, Hinduism p. 748, Buddhism pp. 875–77, 952–53, Religions of China pp. 991–93, and Religions of Japan pp. 1095–96, 1105–6 for the relationship of religion to political leaders.]

Maya Kings Dressed to Kill

Maya rulers were called Mah K'ina (Great Sun Lords), or Ahau (Lord). Unlike the social pattern in Aztec culture, where competing city-states gave way to imperial centers such as Teotihuacan and Tenochtitlan, Maya culture tended to maintain regional centers of power such as Palenque, Yaxchilán, Copán, and Quiriguá. The result was a series of powerful local or regional rulers in periodic competition with other city-states. We know of such rulers as Smoke Jaguar, Yax Pac (First Dawn), Kakukpacal (Fire Is His Shield), Shield Jaguar, and Two-Legged Sky. What we know about these rulers and their ritual techniques comes primarily from the fabulous art, writing, and architectural traditions imprinted in the surviving ceremonial centers, pottery, and sculpture. Let us turn to a consideration of the royal costume to see how the supernatural and the king became so closely identified.

The Great Sun Lords were sacred, in part, because of the clothes they wore. They were carefully and richly adorned with arrays of brilliant and colorful objects made of wood, cloth, feathers (quetzal, macaw, parrot), shells, and stones (jade, pyrite, obsidian), which were transformed into belts, pectorals, knee guards, bracelets, and large undulating headdresses often in zoomorphic styles. They also carried sacred bundles filled with objects representing the presence of the divinities. Once arrayed with these prestigious and potent objects, they hardly appeared human at all. They represented a sacred presence organized by cosmic symbols of very high status. Embedded in their costumes were images of myths, gods, and spatial domains. These royal persons were living cosmograms designed to inspire awe, respect, and obedience.

Let us focus on one typical, extravagant image of a ruler dressed, literally, to kill (see the illustration on p. 201). The image of the ruler of Dos Pilas appears in frontal position with his head turned to the left. Our general impression is that we are looking at a human being who has been transformed into a fantastic series of circles, lines, waves, and images associated not only with high rank but also supernatural power. For instance the ruler has a fabulous, opulent headdress consisting of feathers, wood, jade, and beads organized by an animal image. The zoomorphic head (a) is mounted directly above the face and lacks a lower jaw, so that the ruler's head emerges from the mouth of the animal. In some cases rulers had several animal heads constituting their headdress associated with war or bloodletting, fertility, or kingship, according to the ritual occasion. These headdresses symbolized the intimate relations between the powers of these animals and the royal person who obtained and wielded these awesome forces. The ruler contains the powers of the god, as in the case of **Chac-Xib-Chac,** the god of war, sacrifice, and dancing.[65]

Let us focus our eyes on two other aspects of this image to see how ritual action involved kings in the practice of worldcentering and worldrenewing. When we move our eyes below the head (b) we see an intricately designed large, round pectoral with triple loops extending horizontally to cover the king's chest. These three loops indicated that the king was dressed as one of a group of immensely powerful gods who inspired and supported his actions. The idea is also that the powers of supernatural entities reside in the chest as well as the head of the king.

Below this (c) the ruler wears a knee-length apron with the image of a god, known only as God C, with a square-nosed serpent design framing both sides of his legs. This apron is a royal symbol of the cosmic tree and signifies that the king, like the symbolic tree we have just interpreted, was the center of the Maya cosmos. The king, like the flowering tree, is the central human image whose actions renew the world in ritual. The main ritual action that gave new life to the gods and agriculture was bloodletting. In the case of this king's costume imagery a number of elements are associated with the onset of warfare and the offering of captured warriors for sacrifice. This ruler is dressed to kill and offer blood.

Bleeding for a Vision of Regeneration

In order to understand the unusual practice of bloodletting we must place our discussion within the context of two important Maya cultural patterns: reciprocity and rites of passage. Reciprocity was established by the Maya gods during their struggle to create human beings. The Maya perform rites of passage in order to periodically renew their relationship with the forces that created them. [See Religions of Africa pp. 42–51, 76–79, Native Religions of North America pp. 278–79, 295–98, 306–8, Judaism pp. 445–50, Christianity pp. 542–43, 555–57, Islam pp. 677–78, 680–86, Hinduism pp. 747, 807–14, Buddhism pp. 915–17, 921, 931–37, Religions of China pp. 1019–21, and Religions of Japan pp. 1146–50 for description and discussion of rites of passage.]

RECIPROCITY In the Maya world, as in many religious traditions, humans and gods have a relationship based on some form of mutual care and nurturance. The gods create humans, who are therefore in their debt. The ongoing existence of human life depends on the generous gifts of life, which the gods continue to

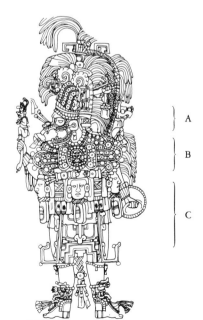

A

B

C

This drawing of Stela 1 from Dos Pilas shows a Maya ruler at the time of his accession to the throne. His elaborate costume is complemented with the heads of sacrificial captives, plumes, and precious jewels. (Drawing courtesy of Linda Schele.)

dispense through children, germination, rain, sunshine, the supply of animals, and objects of power. But the gods are also dependent beings, at least in the Maya world. They depend on humans to care, nurture, acknowledge, and renew their powers. [See Religions of China pp. 1026–29, 1060 for a discussion of reciprocity.]

The Quiché Maya story of creation reveals the character of this reciprocal relationship. The following excerpts come from the *Popul Vuh,* discovered and translated in Guatemala around 1702. Even though it was produced after the conquest it contains many myths and ritual traditions that relate to the time of Pacal and his precursors. Let's consider some opening passages that reveal the creative acts of the gods and the manner in which earthly existence depends on their power and generosity. These creative acts are the first step in the formation of reciprocity. We can also see some interesting parallels with Aztec creation stories.

> This is the beginning of the Ancient Word, here in this place called Quiché. Here we shall inscribe, we shall implant the Ancient Word, the potential and source for everything done in the citadel of Quiché in the nation of Quiché people.
>
>> And here we shall take up the demonstration,
>> revelation, and account of how things were put in
>> shadow and brought to light
>> by the Maker, Modeler, named Bearer, Begetter,
>> Hunahpu Possum Hunahpu Coyote,
>> Great White Peccary, Tapir,
>> Sovereign Plumed Serpent,
>> Heart of the Lake, Heart of the Sea,
>> Maker of the Blue-Green Plate,
>> Maker of the Blue-Green Bowl,
>
> as they are called, also named, also described as
>
>> the midwife, matchmaker
>> named Xpiyacoc, Xmucane,
>> defender, protector.
>> twice a midwife, twice a matchmaker,
>
> as is said in the words of Quiché. They accounted for everything—and did it, too—as enlightened beings, in enlightened words.[66]

In this opening section we see that the creation is likened to planting and sprouting or sowing and dawning, in the words of the text "things were put in shadow and brought to light." What was brought to light was a divine society made up of immensely powerful "enlightened beings" who made "everything."

The world was created as a great ritual action. In the words of the text, "It takes a long performance and account to complete the emergence of all the sky-earth." The world, in other words, is created both by a telling (account) and a doing (performance). This cosmos has order and structure for beings to dwell in. The sky-earth had

> the fourfold siding, fourfold cornering,
> measuring, fourfold staking,
> halving the cord, stretching the cord
> in the sky, on the earth,
> the four sides, the four corners.[67]

The beauty of this story continues when we are told of the "first eloquence," which describes the world before the gods decide to gather and create animals and humans.

> There is not yet one person, one animal, bird, fish, crab, tree, rock, hollow, canyon, meadow, forest. Only the sky alone is there; the face of the earth is not clear. Only the sea alone is there; the face of the earth is not clear. Only the sea alone is pooled under all the sky; there is nothing whatever gathered together. It is at rest; not a single thing stirs. It is held back, kept at rest under the sky.
>
> Whatever there is that might be is simply not there; only the pooled water, only the calm sea, only it alone is pooled.[68]

In this primordial stillness the gods in the sky and the "Bearers, Begetters are in the water, a glittering light" speak and plan for the "dawn of life. . . . How should it be sown, how should it dawn."

They decided to make trees, bushes, animals, and humans and set about to organize the terrestrial level. They were successful in all matters but one, the creation of humankind. Each of three attempts to create humans failed. And in the narrative of their attempts we see how *reciprocity* is intended in their creation of humans.

> Again there comes an experiment with the human work, the human design, by the maker, Modeler, Bearer, Begetter:
>
> "It must simply be tried again. The time for the planting and dawning is nearing. For this we must make a provider and nurturer. How else can we be invoked and remembered on the face of the earth? We have already made our first try at our work and design, but it turned out that they didn't keep our days, nor did they glorify us.
>
> "So now let's try to make a giver of praise, giver of respect, provider, nurturer," they said.[69]

Herein we see the reason for the creation of human life: so that the gods will have beings who can praise, respect, provide for, and nurture the gods. A short formula of this relationship can be stated, "We create your life so that you can praise, nurture, and call us into your community." The form of praising, respecting, and calling the gods into the Maya social world was, in part, bloodletting. This technique is part of a larger religious tradition humans use to fulfill their part of the bargain. It is referred to, in general terms, as "rites of passage."

RITES OF PASSAGE   Rites of passage are a category of rituals that mark the passage of a person through the life cycle, from one stage to another over time, from one role or social position to another, integrating the human and cultural experiences with biological destiny: birth, reproduction, and death. These rituals enable the individual to make a significant passage through a direct *experience* of the sacred and through *learning* about the human/divine relationship as defined by a particular culture. In Maya society there were rites of passage for all members of the society at birth, puberty, and marriage; at significant moments in the agricultural year; on becoming a warrior or priest; and at death. But in Maya religion, rites of passage extended beyond the death of the individual to include moments of reintegration into the terrestrial world. The most powerful rite of passage was the accession to the throne of royal persons. What is special about the rite of accession to the office of ruler in Maya religion is that another type of "passage" was sought and achieved through bloodletting, namely, the passage of ancestors and supernatural beings into the world of the human. The *opening* or passageway for this passage was the wound in the human body and blood. This opening was especially crucial for lords seeking to become rulers. For it was through bloodletting that a real reciprocity was achieved. On the one hand the royal person was passing to a higher social and sacred status, that of the supreme ruler. On the other hand the gods were passing into the world of humans to be reborn. The Maya gave blood in order to receive a vision in which the gods and ancestors appeared in the world of the ceremonial center and in order to perceive the spiritual presence of their ancestors.

Though it may seem strange to modern readers, bloodletting was not strange or unusual in Maya culture. It was described in the mythology of various communities, part of the public rituals of everyday life, and central to the ritual actions of the upper classes. Bloodletting was done at the dedication of buildings and monuments, the births of children, marriage ceremonies, all political events, moments of transition in the calendar, and at life-cycle rituals. It has been called the "mortar of Maya life" because it not only signaled major transitions, it also integrated the levels of the cosmos and the social groups into a sense of wholeness. In order to gain more detail and understanding about bloodletting we will focus on two religious meanings of this ritual practice. The first is the religious meaning of female blood. The second is the religious meaning of subincision or penis perforation.

We are fortunate to have a series of carved lintels from the ceremonial center of Yaxchilán that depict progressive scenes of a royal Maya woman, Lady Xoc, and the ruler Shield Jaguar participating in a bloodletting ritual. In lintel 24 we see the king, Shield Jaguar, holding a huge torch above his ritual partner, Lady Xoc. Both are dressed in exquisite costumes decorated with cosmic designs. Notable are the shrunken head of a past sacrificial victim on Shield Jaguar's headdress, the beaded necklace with its Sun God pectoral hanging from his neck, highback sandals made of jaguar pelts, and a cape with designs of the four world directions. Jade ornaments encircle his knees and wrists, and his loincloth carries the ancestral lineage emblem. The shrunken head signifies his role in nurturing the gods through sacrifice. Lady Xoc wears a fabulous *huipil* (blouse) woven in a diamond pattern with star designs and a skyband border symbolizing heaven and particular astronomical events. Her headdress is decorated with tassels and a head of the rain god Tlaloc, out of which feathers spring. Most important she is pulling a thorn-lined rope through her tongue. The rope falls into a woven basket, which contains paper with spots of blood on it. Her cheeks have scroll designs signifying the blood she is giving to the gods.

This remarkable scene, which probably took place at night, is associated with another depicted on Lintel 25 from Yaxchilán. Looking at the image we can see Lady Xoc crouching down but looking up at the gaping mouth of a Vision Serpent, from which emerges a fully armed Tlaloc warrior. This fantastic serpent emerges from the bloodied paper and rope in the ritual plate on the floor. The Tlaloc image on the headdress is associated with bloodletting, war, and sacrifice in Maya mythology.

In these scenes of ritual bleeding and the appearance of a vision we may be able to gain insight into the meaning of female blood in Maya religion. More work still needs to be done on the symbolism and political importance of these scenes. But we can postulate that they may indicate that female blood, shed in this sacrificial manner, opens the membrane between heaven and earth through which flow astronomical influences, the spirit of ancestors, and legitimate power for a ruler ascending the throne. It is not clear to scholars whether Lintel 25 depicts an ancestor emerging out of the mouth of the Vision Serpent or whether it is the birth of Shield Jaguar *as* a king.

This sculptured relief is an extraordinary depiction of a Late Classic Maya bloodletting rite. A king, Shield Jaguar, stands next to his ritual partner, Lady Xoc, who is engaged in pulling a thorned rope through her mutilated tongue. Dressed in cosmic symbols, she sheds the precious blood to sustain the gods and celebrates the king's accession to the throne. Lintel 24, Yaxchilán, Chiapas, Mexico, 725. (Photo © Justin Kerr, 1985. Courtesy of British Museum.)

Gods and Kings Bleeding for a Vision

As we might suspect, given our discussion of the Maya conception of reciprocity and rites of passage, gods also sacrificed their own blood and in some cases bled their genitals to stimulate visions. Maya art includes scenes in which gods create the ritual tradition of bleeding their penises. In one scene, on an elaborately carved pot, the Sun God who has performed a bloodletting rite is shown having a vision in the form of a Vision Serpent who spits out the Sun while another serpent in the same vision spits out the water of the underworld. In this vision the two halves of the cosmos, the sky and the earth, are visualized by the sacrificing deity. Within these cosmic spaces appear birds, plants, death, sacrifice, day, and night. "The god's bloodletting vision is thus the whole cosmos."[70]

Maya art shows us that one of the body parts bled in order to stimulate visions was the royal penis. There are many images depicting rulers and their male relatives piercing their genitals in public and private settings. What can be the meaning of males giving blood in this manner? Fortunately we have inscriptions associated with some of these scenes suggesting that the Maya lords sought to experience a *totality*, even a divine totality, by imitating the capacity of women to menstruate (bleed from their genitals) and to give birth. In several cases the Maya kings are referred to as "mother of the gods," who give birth—that is, bring the gods into being on a terrestrial level—through bloodletting. It is through the blood of the king that he becomes both male ruler and female nurturer of the Maya gods. This kind of giving, pain, and generosity was one of the ultimate means to participate in a truly reciprocal relationship with divine forces.

The Calendar and the Regeneration of Time

At the beginning of this chapter we viewed the imagery of Pacal's descent into the underworld. The symbolism of the seed on his nose represented his potential for regeneration following an ordeal of traveling through Xibalba. The journey through Xibalba was one of the great themes of Maya religion that influenced commoner, warrior, farmer, weaver, and ruler.

Before we travel along with the Maya through the underworld landscape and its ordeals, we need to describe and interpret one other major ritual pattern of Maya culture, the sacred calendar. The Maya calendar reveals two passions in Maya thought: the passion for pattern and the passion for regeneration of time and life. As we have implied throughout this study ancestors and ancestral powers are considered the source for agriculture and even the regeneration of time. It is in the calendars of Maya culture that we see these passions, which take the forms of mathematics and ritual joined in one unit, inscribed.

Unlike most other indigenous peoples of the Americas, the Maya developed an elaborate writing system capable of recording the range and meanings of their spoken language. Fortunately we have abundant evidence of this writing system on the ball courts, temples, stelae, stairways, codices, and pottery of the Classic Maya. The typical presentation of this writing system combines written texts, carved into the stone, with pictorial programs depicting ritual and political action. In this manner the viewer or reader had two sources of information about the scenes portrayed. In some cases the written texts told of events leading up to the pictorial scene in front of the viewer. Some Maya scholars have called these scenes with their inscriptions Maya "cartoons," because they contain frozen framed images with accompanying narrations.

Permeating almost all Maya writing and pictorial scenes are calendrical notations indicating to us that the Maya were deeply concerned to locate all events, especially period-ending dates, within a cosmological framework designed to ensure the regeneration of life. The Maya generally believed that the universe had passed through at least three previous ages, with the present age beginning on a date corresponding to 3114 B.C.E. Time was moving systematically toward the end of the present cycle on December 23, 2012 C.E. In other words time past and time future were fixed into a discernible pattern that could be read *and* predicted. In addition to this over five-thousand-year cycle were a series of other cycles, which the Maya marked, celebrated, and sometimes feared in detail.

First the Maya observed a temporal cycle we call the calendar round, which covered a fifty-two-year period. It consisted of two different calendars interlocked and rotating. The first, called Tzolkin or sacred round, consisted of 260 days built up by giving 1 of 20 day names to each day in succession and giving 1 of 13 numbers to each day in succession, resulting in a number and a day name for each day: for example, 4 Ahau. Each of the 260 days had a unique number and day combination. This was the basic ritual calendar utilized throughout Mesoamerica. This cycle interacted with the Haab (Cycle of Rains) or Vague Year, which divided the observed solar year of 360 days built up into eighteen months of twenty days plus one month of five days. Thus 2 Pop would be the second day of the first month of the Seasonal Year, which was named Pop. The five-day month at the end was called Uayeb and considered hazardous. The Maya named their days according to the intermeshing of each calendar so that, for instance, the day 4 Ahau 2 Pop marked a day on both the longer and shorter calendars. These two interlocking calendars exhausted all possible combinations after 18,980 days or 52 Haabs when 4 Ahau 2 Pop would recur. This marked the end of a significant time period and the regeneration of a new temporal order.

This system was common throughout much of Mesoamerica and was the guiding calendrical pattern when the Spaniards invaded Mesoamerica in the early sixteenth century. However, the religious sensibility for pattern and renewal within the flow of time was also expressed in another, much more elaborate long count calendar, which according to some scholars measured time along a spectrum of over nine million years. Maya monuments throughout the ceremonial centers of Palenque, Yaxchilán, Copán, Tikal, Quiriguá, Uaxactún, and many others are incised with long count notations marking the dates of births, marriages, bloodletting ceremonies, warfare, anniversaries, enthronements, deaths, and the emergence of royal persons from the underworld.

The long count system is based in a vigesimal count; that is, it has a base of twenty rather than the base of ten used by European civilization. Instead of taking the Vague Year as the basis for the long count, the Maya and other peoples employed the *tun,* a period of 360 days composed of eighteen divisions of 20 days each. Consider the spacious sense of time in the long count cycles, which include

1 *kin* = 1 day

20 *kins* = 1 *uinal* or 20 days

18 *uinals* = 1 *tun* or 360 days

20 *tuns* = 1 *katun* or 7,200 days

20 *katuns* = 1 *baktun* or 144,000 days

Long count dates inscribed by the Maya on their monuments consist of the above cycles listed from top to bottom in descending order of magnitude, each with its numerical coefficient, and all to be added up so as to express the number of days elapsed since the end of the last great cycle, a period of thirteen *baktuns,* whose ending fell on the date 4 Ahau 8 Cumku. Thus a long count date conventionally written as 9. 10. 19. 5. 11. would be calculated as follows:

9 *baktuns* = 1,296,000 days

10 *katuns* = 72,000 days

19 *tuns* = 6,840 days

15 *uinals* = 100 days

11 *kins* = 11 days

In sum, this is 1,374,951 days since the close of the last great cycle, reaching the calendar round position 10 Chuen 4 Cumku.[71] It is important to reiterate that the Maya had come to understand the concept of zero, which was necessary to perform calculations in this positional count.

At important divisions in this long count system the entire Maya world took time and gave significant effort to celebrate transitions and new beginnings. The Maya lords offered blood in public settings at the end of each *katun* or 7,200 days as well as at each five-year interval within this twenty-year period. In this and in every way the Maya marked time with sacred rituals in order to both locate themselves with the great cycle of the cosmos and regenerate their smaller cycles of agricultural, social, and cosmic changes. It now is clear that the reason the Maya added the long count to the calendar round system was because they took dynastic succession to be the foundation of their society. Great lengths of time became important when remembering long chains of ancestors.

Archaeoastronomy and the Maya

Intimately related to the Maya calendar was the careful alignment of particular buildings and ceremonies with the dramatic cycles and appearances of celestial bodies, including the moon, sun, Venus, and so on. Recently a new academic discipline called archaeoastronomy has made major strides in understanding the relationships among ancient Mesoamerican astronomy, the natural landscape, ceremonial buildings, and human life. Defined as "the interdisciplinary study of the practice of astronomy by ancient peoples using both the written and unwritten record," archaeoastronomy has shown how major temples, entire ceremonial centers, and the calendars that guided ritual and social life were dependent, in part, on astronomical events and patterns. Although there are many interesting examples of the interrelationship of ceremonial centers and astronomy in Mesoamerica, I will briefly summarize just one as reported in the work of Anthony Aveni.[72]

A principal idea in the archaeoastronomy of Maya religion is the idea of "axiality," or the major orientation of a ceremonial center or building with reference to the local culture's notion of cardinal directionality. The Maya city of Chichén Itzá, for instance, is laid out so that the oldest part of the city is aligned eleven to fourteen degrees east of north. This orientation/layout appears to have some particular astronomical pattern as its key.

More specifically, archaeoastronomers have been able to determine that **special assemblages** or groups of buildings misaligned in relationship to other buildings often have some precise architectural connection to astronomy. In the Maya area there is a group of buildings known as "E-VII/sub" in a number of architectural sites. At Uaxactún this group consists of four buildings, including a large platform on the west side of a plaza, which faces three other buildings to the east. When ritual specialists stood on the western platform looking east they would have observed summer and winter solstice sunrises appearing over the north and south buildings, respectively, and the equinox sunrise occurring over the middle building. In this way the entire complex becomes a solar observatory that tells the elites when to prepare the community at large for planting, harvesting, warfare, and other crucial events regulated by the solar year.

This pattern of Maya ceremonial architecture is an excellent example of how cosmovision, the parallelism between celestial and earthly cycles, became inscribed on the material world of the ceremonial center.

The Ordeals of Xibalba

Death is a fact of the life cycle. Religions the world over teach us that human beings have developed meaningful ways of overcoming death. The basic human stance, whether expressed in statements such as "Death Be Not Proud," or funerary rituals, or visions of paradise, has been a stance of defeating death through rituals of transformation. These rituals include rites of separation such as human burial or cremation. But they also include songs, imagery, and stories that express the hope and belief that some core dimension of the human continues to live on past death and is reborn into a spiritual or divinized community. This pattern of death and rebirth was particularly powerful in the Maya world where war, sacrifice, and a short life span were accepted patterns of destiny.

One of the elaborate ways in which the Maya expressed their hope and belief in a life after death and after the struggles of earthly existence was through the pattern of the heroic journey through the Underworld of Xibalba. (Xibalba was simultaneously the Place of Death and the Place of Regenerative Powers symbolized by the ancestral seeds and skulls, the symbols of fertility.) As in many other classic statements about the underworld, such as Dante's *Inferno,* the Maya heroes faced extraordinary ordeals that had to be overcome before emerging once more to see the heavens with their orderly rhythm.

The belief in another world, or underworld, is widespread in the history of religions. Often the underworld is a place of punishment, pain, and frightening beings, who test and overcome the spirits of the deceased. A common theme is the descent of a hero into a cave, earth monster, belly of a whale, or some other creature of the Abyss. The hero undergoes terrible ordeals, including being dismembered, becoming paralyzed by fear, encountering the lords of the dead face-to-face, and experiencing other kinds of contests during which one's ultimate destiny is at stake. One of the goals of these ordeals is new knowledge about the mysteries of existence, the afterlife, and powers of rebirth. Ideally the hero, usually with the help of some friendly spirit, overcomes the lords of the underworld, reemerges from the earth, and achieves immortality. In Mesoamerica, as we saw in the case of Quetzalcoatl, the hero who is reborn often takes the form of an ancestral spirit or becomes part of a celestial body (or maize plant or World Tree) now fully integrated into the patterns of the heavens.

Fortunately we have full and partial written accounts of the Maya version of this pattern, which we saw so vividly in the image of Palenque's ruler Pacal entering the underworld with the setting sun. The implication was that he would be regenerated with the rising sun. In works such as the *Chilam Balam of Tizimin, Chilam Balam of Chumayel,* and the *Popul Vuh* or *Book of Council,* we find valuable information about the Maya view of the cosmos and the powers that inhabit it. In the amazing narrative of the *Popul Vuh* we see the Maya underworld as a dangerous landscape where gods and human spirits struggle to deceive, trick, sacrifice, and overcome one another. In some ways the Maya underworld is a sarcastic replica of life on earth. In other ways Xibalba is a landscape of awesome, dangerous beings who usually have their way.

One of the most revealing episodes in the underworld described by the *Popul Vuh* is the contest, in the form of a sacred ball game, between the Hero Twins **Hunahpu and Xbalanque** and the Lords of Xibalba. In the narrative the Hero Twins are playing ball at the ball court where their father and uncle had played a generation before. These ancestors had been invited down into Xibalba (that is, they had died), where they had been defeated and destroyed by the Lords of the underworld. Now, a generation later, the boys are playing a game and disturb the Lords of Death by stomping around and bouncing the ball loudly. One Death and Seven Death and the other Lords summon them into the underworld to play a game and undergo great ordeals. The message reaches them: "In seven days they are to come here. We'll play ball. Their gaming equipment must come along; rubber ball yokes, arm guards, kilts. This will make for some excitement here . . . " The boys

> went down to Xibalba, quickly going down the face of a cliff, and they crossed over the bottom of a canyon with rapids. They passed right through the birds—the ones called thorn birds—and then they crossed Pus River and Blood River, intended as traps by Xibalba. They did not step in, but simply crossed over on their blowguns and they went on over to the Cross roads. But they knew about the roads of Xibalba: Black Road, White Road, Red Road, Green Road.[73]

With the help of a mosquito the Twins learn the names of the Lords: One Death, Seven Death, House Corner, Blood Gatherer, Pus Master, Jaundice Master, Bone Scepter, Skull Scepter, Wing, Packstrap, Bloody Teeth, Bloody Claws. These Lords put the Twins through a series of ordeals. First, they are placed in the Dark House and given an impossible challenge. They are given a torch and two cigars and told that they must return them unconsumed in the morning. The Twins take the tails of macaw birds, which look like torches to the sentries, and put fireflies on the tips of the cigars, giving the false appearance of having them lit all night.

Undefeated by this trial, the Twins are then placed in a series of houses on different nights, each one representing an ordeal. They are first tested in the Razor House and survive by persuading "each and every knife (to) put down its point." Then the Xibalbans put them in the Cold House, where "countless drafts, thick falling hail" threaten to freeze them to death. Through cunning they survive and "were alive when it dawned." Then they were placed in the Jaguar House, the "jaguar-packed home of jaguars," who threaten to eat them. They scatter bones before the jaguars, who wrestle over the bones, ignoring the Twins. Then they are placed in the Fire House, where they are only simmered instead of burned. The "Xibalbans . . . lost heart over this." Finally they are forced into the Bat House, where "monstrous beasts, their snouts like knives, the instruments of death" threaten to "finish them off at once." The Twins slept in their blowguns and avoided this horrible death.

One of the twins, Hunahpu, meets his death; but the other Twin figures out a way to resurrect him. In other words they learn the secret of overcoming death. Hunahpu peeks out of his blowgun, attempting to see the dawn, and is decapitated. The Xibalbans are delighted to see Hunahpu's head rolling on to the ball court. Xbalanque replaces it with a carved squash and the Twins, now one with a squash for a head, play ball with the Xibalbans. Through trickery Xbalanque retrieves the original head and rejoins it to Hunahpu's body, regenerating his human form.

The text reads, "They did whatever they were instructed to do, going through all the dangers, the troubles that were made for them, but they did not die from the tests of Xibalba, nor were they defeated by all the voracious animals that inhabit Xibalba."[74] Yet they realize that their death is inevitable in the underworld and instruct two helpful shamans to tell the Lords of Death to kill them in a certain fashion that will, unknown to the Xibalbans, lead to their rebirth and defeat of Death. The Lords burn the Hero Twins in an oven and grind their bones into powder, which is thrown into the water. "On the fifth day they reappeared . . . having germinated in the waters." The Twins reappear in the disguise of vagabonds "with rags before and rags behind" dancing the Dance of the Poorwill, the Dance of the Weasel, and the Dance of the Armadillo. Like tricksters they travel about performing miracles and dancing before the Xibalbans. The most impressive miracles include sacrificing a dog that revives, and burning a house that is not consumed.

> Then the lord said to them: "Sacrifice my dog, then bring him back to life again," they were told.

> > "Yes," they said.
> > When they sacrificed the dog
> > he then came back to life.
> > And that dog was really happy
> > when he came back to life.

Then the Lords of Death insist that they carry out a human sacrifice and regenerate the victim.

> > And they took hold of a human sacrifice.
> > And they held up a human heart on high.
> > And they showed its roundness to the lords.

> And now One and Seven Death admired it, and now that person was brought right back to life. His heart was overjoyed when he came back to life, and the lords were amazed.[75]

So amazed were the Lords that they commanded the distinguished Twins to sacrifice and regenerate themselves. So Hunahpu was sacrificed by Xbalanque. "His heart, dug out, was smothered in a leaf, and all the Xibalbans went crazy at the sight." Then Hunahpu is revived. " 'Get up!' he said, and Hunahpu came back to life."

Overwhelmed by these magical powers, the Lords of Death ask the inevitable. "Do it to us! Sacrifice us!" said One and Seven Death. Realizing they have gained the crucial upper hand the Twins sacrifice the Lords but *do not* bring them back to life.

Through trickery the Twins have triumphed in the midst of an extraordinary ordeal through achieving self-knowledge and the powers of self-transformation: "Such was the defeat of the rulers of Xibalba. The boys accomplished it only through wonders, only through self-transformation."

The Twins order the remaining Xibalbans to cease their destructive ways or face the same ultimate death as their lords. Then, in a scene reminiscent of the final passage of Dante's *Inferno*, "the two boys ascended this way, here into the middle of the light and they ascended straight on into the sky, and the sun belongs to one and the moon to the other."[76]

In this way the Twins suffered the tortures of the underworld but gained the knowledge of self-transformation to overcome the threatened final static condition of death. Instead they learned the secrets of self-sacrifice and regeneration and ascended into the celestial levels to become a permanent pattern of renewal, a mythic model for Maya religion.

This engaging story helps us understand more clearly the meaning of the cosmic scene of Pacal's tomb. His descent is vitally important to record because it marked the beginning of another career, the career of struggling to overcome the Lords of Xibalba with the same cunning, courage, and self-transformation of the Twins. And like them Pacal rose to become, as all Maya kings did, the Sun, rising above the horizon in a regular pattern, passing regularly across the heavens, giving the Maya an experience of regeneration.

The Maya Collapse

In spite of these remarkable strategies to ensure the regeneration of their world, the Classic Maya civilization collapsed rapidly between 800 and 850 C.E. We know that in 790 C.E. at least nineteen different ceremonial centers erected monuments with the long count calendar inscribed on them. But by 889 C.E. only one ceremonial center in the entire Maya region was using this calendar system. Research at Palenque shows a 90 percent population decline over a two-hundred-year period. Other archaeological evidence makes it clear that the most sophisticated urban culture in Mesoamerican history fell into ruins and the population was decimated or fled the area in a rapid fashion.

Although the causes for this collapse are still mostly unknown, large areas of Maya civilization seem to have undergone a series of internal and external stresses, which combined to bring the ceremonial cities into ruin. It appears that intense trading, ceremonial and military expansion, *and* competition between centers led to a weakening of the interlocking fabric that constituted the Maya world. Population explosions likely put undue stress on the agricultural productivity leading to subsistence emergencies, which the population was unable to stop. Food shortages and weather changes may have led to malnutrition and epidemic diseases, which put increased pressures on ceremonial centers to utilize their religious powers to solve. This led to more intense needs for ceremonial displays and rituals that emphasized the role and power of the elites, who grew further and further away from the confidence of the masses. In order to maintain their own levels of luxury and superiority the elites may have intensified their warfare practices in order to obtain necessary goods and sacrificial victims. This may have led to internal rebellions or at least a loss of faith in the royal families.

One or two of these stresses might be manageable by an elite core of priest-kings, but taken as an interlocking series the stresses may have been too severe and total for the society to survive. In this way the Maya of Palenque, Tikal,

Copán, and other magnificent ceremonial centers withered from prominence. It is a pattern we in the modern world must learn about because, like the Maya, our remarkable material achievements may also fade back into the natural landscape.

At any rate the central role of the ceremonial city persisted into the Post-Classic Period and into the memory of the Maya of colonial Guatemala. One passage in the *Popul Vuh* reads,

> "Let us go ourselves and search,
> and we shall see for ourselves
> whether there is something to guard our sign.
> We will find what we should say before them,
> and thus we shall live.
> There are no guardians for us,"
> then said Jaguar Quiche,
> Jaguar Night,
> Nought, and Wind Jaguar.
> They heard news of a city
> and went there.[77]

9

Mesoamerica as a New World: Colonialism and Religious Creativity

Although they did not use the term "Latin America," Spaniards and Portuguese thought of America in a unitary way, as a "New World" so different and unknown that it had to be invented, a place where legends about earthly paradises, Amazon women, Prester John, cities of gold and millennial kingdoms might come true. The legends and fantasies of Latin America have continued to be reinvented in the form of romantic stories of island castaways like Robinson Crusoe, and in glossy travel brochures inviting the foreign visitor to unspoiled island paradises and golden lands.

    William B. Taylor[78]

. . . in Mexico City there is never tragedy but only outrage . . . city of the violated outrage, city witness to all we forget, city of fixed sun, city ancient in light, old city cradled among birds of omen, city tempested by domes, city woven by amnesias, bitch city, hungry city, city in the true image of gigantic heaven. Incandescent prickly pear.

    Carlos Fuentes[79]

WE HAVE COME TO the final chapter in our exploration of Mesoamerican religions and the interrelations between cosmovision and ceremonial centers. Throughout this study we have emphasized that religion is both a matter of the imagination and a matter of the social and material world within which humans dwell. Now we have the task of exploring some of the *continuities and changes* of Mesoamerican religions in the social and symbolic settings that became known as a New World.

In the first chapter we outlined some of the powerful and dehumanizing "inventions" of Mesoamerica and its native peoples. Europeans unleashed both powerful fantasies and colonial expeditions into Mesoamerica, attempting to transform the lands and peoples into extensions of themselves. On the surface Anahuac became Nueva España, the Mexica became Indians, and their religions were considered the devil's work. But beneath the surface indigenous and European traditions mixed together into a remarkable series of new cultural combinations. The food, language, medical practices, even the biological and cultural character of people were transformed into new social and symbolic forms. As Elizabeth Weismann writes in her invaluable *Mexico in Sculpture: 1521–1821,* "Two different kinds of life absorbed each other and produced things new and different from anything else in the world."[80] These new and different things had to be put into new relationships with one another. Most crucial of all, perhaps, were the efforts to locate where the natives and the *mestizos* (people of mixed blood) were to fit in the new social, legal, and religious schemes. The result has been a complex, varied, and sometimes mysterious social and symbolic landscape mixing Aztec, Maya, Otomi, Huichol, Tzutujil, and many other traditions with Catholic, Spanish, Portuguese, French, and other Old World cultural and religious patterns. The student of colonial and modern Mesoamerica is faced with, as the Mexican novelist Carlos Fuentes indicates, a world of outrage, Christian churches, denial of the damage of colonialism, ancient images still visible in daily life, and the persistence of a cosmovision embedded in the largest urban center of the world, Mexico City, "city in the true image of gigantic heaven." Mesoamerica's pre-Columbian traditions have continued to play a vital role in the colonial and postcolonial communities of Mexico, Guatemala, El Salvador, Honduras, Nicaragua, Costa Rica, and Belize. Meaningful traces of these traditions can even be found in the Chicano communities in the United States. And as the Latin American historian William B. Taylor notes above, fantasies about the paradises of Mesoamerica continue to attract people from all over the world.

In this chapter we will look at a series of creative religious responses to the crisis of colonialism that show some of the continuities and changes that have taken place in Mesoamerican religions. We will focus on the human trauma caused by the conquest and early colonial events and on a series of religious practices and responses in contemporary Mesoamerica. These include the peyote hunt of the Huichol Indians, the cult of the **Virgin of Guadalupe,** the **Dia de los Muertos** (Day of the Dead) ceremonies, and the Fiesta de Santiago in Santiago Atitlan, Guatemala. Each of these will be discussed in relation to two major dimensions of religious life in Mesoamerica: pilgrimage and syncretism. In each of these instances people take special journeys to or through a sacred landscape in order to have a direct experience and gain new knowledge of the sacred. These journeys involve, to varying degrees, the three processes we have emphasized in this book: worldmaking, worldcentering, and worldrenewing. The Fiesta of Santiago includes all three dimensions, but emphasizes worldrenewing by symbolically traveling from the *axis mundi* of the community to the four quarters of the universe and back to the center. The Huichol peyote hunt emphasizes worldcentering by traveling to the ancestral lands to gather and consume peyote in order to discover the relationship between humans and ancestral gods and thereby to find the meaning of what it is to be Huichol. And the Dia de los Muertos, practiced in almost every home in Tlaxcala, Mexico, focuses on the family altar, full of foods, gifts, and photographs of the dead, which is an example of worldmaking. But in each case a pilgrimage of humans or spirits is central to the religious action.

A second important dimension of these activities is what scholars call syncretism. Though syncretism can work in a complex fashion involving languages, religions, and other cultural elements, it can be defined simply as "the combination of different forms of beliefs and practices into new patterns of meaning."[81] In religious terms this usually involves the mixing of symbols, ritual elements, or images from different traditions, such as Catholic and Aztec fertility rites, Maya and Catholic devotion to deities, or observances of the dead.

Throughout Mesoamerica today groups carry out ceremonies combining a wide range of native and Catholic symbols and beliefs into new patterns of meanings. And it is primarily within the experience of ritual action that syncretism becomes an authentic dimension of life. For the rituals create the legitimate setting and charged atmosphere for the placing of incongruent objects, symbols, sounds, and ideas together in an acceptable way. This results in new versions of older patterns. The images of Christ and the saints have received a rich series of innovations in Mexico. A good example are the many colonial churchyard crosses that still stand in Mexico. Many appear, on first glance, to be symbols of a European Christian presence. But on closer view it is clear that many echo preconquest designs, emotions, conceptions of spatial arrangement, and style. Further reflection leads to the realization that these crosses are neither European nor Indian, but Mexican—a fluid syncretic image of new power, decoration, and combined meanings. Often it is the *mestizo* or Indian community that takes the initiative in forming these meaningful combinations as a means of gaining some measure of power within a cultural situation that has diminished their status or degraded their power. Throughout this chapter we shall see examples of syncretistic combinations and ritual processes in Mesoamerican religions.

The Social and Symbolic Crisis of the Colonial New World

It is also important to recall that this part began with a report of the European invasion and so-called conquest of Mesoamerica. The violent, transformative process of colonialism, which began in the 1520s in Mexico, Guatemala, and other regions of Mesoamerica, radically altered (to varying degrees) the social and symbolic worlds of the Moctezumas, Quetzalcoatls, Hero Twins, *altepetls,* ceremonial centers, and communities at large. This process has been consistently referred to as having created a "New World" with its smaller "New Spain," and then eventually "New Mexico" and along the north Atlantic coast "New York," "New England," "New Jersey," "Nova Scotia," and so forth. However, the natives of Mesoamerica who underwent the process of colonialism experienced this newness more as forms of dependency, oppression, starvation, disease, death, and dehumanization than as opportunities for salvation and revitalization. It was a "newness" they could just as well have done without. The formation of new religious movements and cults and mixtures of pre-Hispanic and Catholic religious meanings emerged as strategies to survive and maintain human integrity in relation to their lands and selves.

Although we cannot go into an extensive description of the social and biological disasters of the Spanish conquest of Mesoamerica, it is important to state directly how the human population suffered. And it is vital to remember that the colonial process in Mesoamerica began almost one hundred years before the English explored the North American coast and established their settlements at Plymouth and Massachusetts Bay. By the early 1600s, when parts of northern Europe were abuzz with rumors, stories, and prejudices about the people and lands in the New World (these stories and prejudices had largely filtered up from Spain and Portugal), most of the great ceremonial centers and local shrines in the Aztec, Tlaxcalan, Tarascan, and other kingdoms had been dismantled and replaced by Christian churches well under construction. American history does not begin in New England, as is still taught in public schools in the United States. It started in Yucatan, Tlaxcala, Cholula, Tenochtitlan, and it was characterized by misunderstanding, greed, warfare, theft, disease, debate, economic exchange, and a ferocious clash of two types of cosmovisions.

The conquest and colonial process in Mesoamerica had a devastating impact on the human population. The tie between the colonizer and the colonized was often violent and authoritarian. But what really devastated the indigenous population was disease. Although it is not easy to determine the quantitative loss of life, historians have been able to estimate with reliable plausibility that in 1500 around eighty million inhabitants occupied the New World. By 1550 only ten million natives were alive. In Mexico there were close to twenty-five million people in 1500. By 1600 only one million native Mesoamericans were still alive. This incredible loss of life was caused by either direct murder in warfare; cruelty in the mines, fields, and towns; or "microbe shock," that is, disease. The majority of the indigenous population who died during the sixteenth century were the victims of diseases transmitted by the "lethal handshake"—the physical contact with Europeans including baptism by Catholic priests. These diseases turned into epidemics fueled by malnutrition, fatigue, and the destruction of the indigenous social relations and medical practices. People in Mesoamerica had had their own diseases and epidemics, which periodically caused crisis prior to the European colonies. But the immune systems developed in the pre-Columbian periods were not prepared to face the diseases transmitted by Europeans and the result was catastrophic.

When surveying the destructive consequences of European presence in Mesoamerica, it is important to also state that many Europeans cared deeply for the native people and made serious and sustained efforts to understand the native culture and to work out ways of fitting it into the new society. It is also very important to realize that the natives responded in varying degrees to the problems and challenges of the new society. Some fell into complete despair, whereas others strove with varying degrees of success to find places in society that combined indigenous and foreign elements into their lives. During the sixteenth and seventeenth centuries a new society and culture, unique in the history of humankind, took form and expression in Mesoamerica.

We can see both the pressures to change indigenous society and the attempt by natives to find a place in the strange, new world created by the conquest in this passage from the *Book of Chilam Balam of Tizimin.*[82]

> Your older brothers are arriving
> To change your pants,
> To change your clothes,
> To whiten your dress,
> To whiten your pants—
> The foreign judges,
> The bearded men
> Of heaven born Merida,
> The seat of the lands.
> And they
> Are the sun priests
> Of the living God,
> The true God.
> He shall be worshiped
> In one communion
> On earth
> Below:
> An additional rule.
> And for the fatherless,
> And for the motherless—
> Jaguar was the head
> And urged his people
> To be sprinkled
> In the changed city.

The passage tells how the Maya were told that the Spaniards were coming to change society, customs, and religion. The Maya will be forced to change their clothes, new judges will issue laws from Merida, the capital, and the religion of what the missionaries said was the true God was being introduced. Finally, the Maya leader, the "Jaguar" in the text, urges the people to become converted to Catholicism, "to be sprinkled in the changed city," that is, the colonial city of Merida.

But in the early part of the colonial process the Indian population was in grave crisis. The gravity of the colonial situation is reflected in the writings of the Franciscan priest Motolinia, who compared the devastation of the indigenous populations with the ten plagues sent by God to chastise the Egyptians in the Old Testament. The first plague was smallpox: "They died in heaps, like bedbugs." The second plague was the death by Spanish weapons. The third was the famine that accompanied the Spanish destruction of Indian harvests. The fourth plague was the vicious overseers who tortured the natives. The fifth plague was the taxes in the forms of lands and goods levied on the natives. The Indians were under such pressure that when they had no goods they were forced to sell their children to the Spaniards, and eventually to sell themselves. The sixth plague was the mines in which Indians were forced to work long hours in dangerous conditions and sometimes carry loads as heavy as 250 pounds up steep underground ascents. The seventh plague was the building of the city of Mexico, during which scores of Indians died in falls, were crushed by beams, or were crushed by buildings being torn down. The eighth plague was the slavery of the mines. Slaves were branded by the letters of all those who bought and sold them. In some cases a slave was tattooed with brands on many parts of his or her body. The ninth plague was the open graveyards around the mines. One eyewitness wrote,

> For half a league around these mines and along a great part of the road one could scarcely avoid walking over dead bodies or bones, and the flocks of birds and crows that came to feed upon the corpses were so numerous that they darkened the sun . . . [83]

The tenth plague was the in-fighting, factions, and scapegoating among the Spaniards. Their internal social problems often led to frustrated excuses for executing large numbers of Indians without legal or rational justification. Consider, for instance, this unbelievable report by the priest Bartolomé de las Casas. One day, after a picnic, a group of Spaniards decided to test whether their swords were sharp.

> A Spaniard, in whom the devil is thought to have clothed himself, suddenly drew his sword. Then the whole hundred drew theirs and began to rip open the bellies, to cut and kill those lambs—men, women, children, and old folk all of whom were seated, off guard and frightened, watching the mares and the Spaniards. And within two credos, not a man of all of them remains alive. The Spaniards enter the large house nearby, for this was happening at its door, and in the same way, with cuts and stabs, begin to kill as many as they found there, so that a stream of blood was running, as if a great number of cows had perished. [84]

It is important to reiterate that there was another community of Spaniards, usually led by priests and nuns, who not only strove to understand the nature of Indian societies but also struggled, sometimes at serious personal risk, to stop the abuse, killing, and exploitation of native peoples.

The near extermination of the indigenous population began to be reversed in the eighteenth century. By 1800, as astonishing as it may seem, there were six million Indians living, struggling, and in isolated cases thinking rebellion, which occasionally broke out, in different parts of Mesoamerica. There were also a growing number of castas or mestizos or people of mixed blood who had more rights and privileges than the native communities.

The point is that Mesoamerica, in fact all of Latin America, became an incredibly complex world. This complexity has been outlined by William Taylor in his writing on Latin American social history. Taylor notes that on the one hand there are a number of common features in the colonial history of the New World, such as

> degradation of the labor force, rural estates, village communities (many of which were "peasant" communities in the anthropologists' specialized meaning), Independence Wars, urbanizations, and large-scale collective actions . . . a conflict society . . . the Spanish Conquest, the Comunero Rebellions, the Tupac Amaru Rebellion, slave revolts, the Independence Wars, wars of reform, United States interventions, millenarian movements, and social and socialist revolutions.[85]

But scholars have also become impressed with the local variations of social developments and religious responses to the order of the world in the New World. As Taylor notes,

> Recent scholarship describes a notable fluidity of communities—much leaving and returning, some movement across lines of rank, ethnicity, and class, and vague and permeable boundaries—and significant regional variation in structural changes and institutions. . . .[86]

One way of talking about these significant fluidities in terms of religious response is through the category of syncretism, or the process of mixing together elements from different religious traditions. Syncretism is a sign of important religious change taking place in a culture, and the primary instrument of that change appears to be ritual and ceremonial life. Throughout Mesoamerica today indigenous and *mestizo* groups carry out ceremonies combining native and Catholic symbols and beliefs all the time. One of the most powerful Christian images that has been joined to indigenous religious ideas is the image of Jesus Christ as suffering savior. The bleeding, pained image of Jesus on the Cross has had special attraction to all social groups and classes in Latin America including native communities, who see a version of their own sacred traditions in stories of Christ's passion. A special example of syncretism that joins the image of the crucified Christ to native religion appears in the following tale from Zinacantan, a highland Maya community in Chiapas, Mexico. In it we see an example of religious change at the level of story and myth.

When Christ Was Crucified

> When the world was made long ago, the Holy father walked. He made the rocks and sea, corn and trees, everything there is on earth.
>
> When he was chased by the devils he ran. But the devils were right behind him. They saw that there were trees already, peach trees, white sapotes, everything.

"Hurry up, you bastards, he's here now, he's near now.
He's planted everything already."
Our Lord ran around the world. Ooh, he was tired out.
He hid under some banana trees to rest.
"He's near now" said the devils.
The Magpie-jay was there. He was a human then.
"Is it Our Lord you're looking for?" asked the jay.
"He's here now. Seize him!"
They captured Our Lord. They made him carry a cross.
Our Lord bent low to the ground.
They hung him on the cross. He cried. He bled.
"Let's eat! He's dead now," said the devils.
Our Lord was left hanging.
A rooster landed on the arm of the cross.
"Tell me if they are coming," said Our Lord.
"I'll climb back up the cross right away.
"I have more work to do. You call out!"
"All right," said the rooster. "Cock-a doodle-doo!"
Quickly Our Lord climbed up the cross.
"Where are the devils?" he asked.
"Nowhere, they aren't coming," said the rooster.
"What are you good for?" said the Lord.
"This is what you're good for!"
He wrung the rooster's neck until it was dead.
A sparrow appeared.
"You sing out," said our Lord.
"I'm going to work a little while."
The Lord came down from the cross. He looked for a blue pebble.
He threw it into the air. The sky was made.
The sparrow called out. Our Lord climbed up the cross.
All the devils arrived.
"He's still hanging here," they said.
"We killed him. Let's bury him."
He died. He was buried.
"We'll come back three days from now," said the devils.
"They thought I died," said the Lord.
"But I'll revive in three days."
Living he rose to heaven. He left a substitute here on earth.
"The rooster is no good. He can be sacrificed.
"The sparrow mustn't be harmed," said Our Lord.
So, living, he rose to heaven.
He arrived at the right hand of the judge.[87]

This story cannot be fully interpreted here, but syncretism is richly illustrated in this combination of both an indigenous myth about the creation
of the cosmos and the story of Jesus' career, crucifixion, and resurrection. In

Zinacantec mythology, predating the imposition of Catholicism, the world was made in three stages. In the beginning the rocks and ground were made, then the ocean, trees, and animals appeared. Finally the sky was created. Part of the indigenous creation story appears here with Christ coming down from the cross and throwing a blue pebble into the air to complete the third stage of the creation of the cosmos. "He threw it into the air. The sky was made." Catholic influences mixed with local cosmology appear when the tale tells of Christ rising into heaven to sit at the right hand of the judge. The judge is the Christian saint San Salvador, who occupies the center of the sky. According to the storyteller, Romin Teratol, San Salvador is the older brother of the sun or Christ who was sent to travel around the world to record and report back on the sins of humans.

It is clear that the Zinacantecs know and have incorporated bits of the gospel stories into their creation stories. We see Christ's temptation by the devil, the betrayal by Judas (here in the form of the magpie), his crucifixion, and conversations with the other two crucified victims on Golgotha, and his resurrection included in their version. The story also provides the indigenous ritual prescription that roosters can be used as sacrificial birds in curing ceremonies, house dedications, and agricultural rites. In ceremonies focusing on the treatment of illnesses these birds become the "substitute" of a patient. On the other hand the story is telling that the rufous-collared sparrow cannot be killed by the community because "Our Lord," who is at once Christ and a pre-Columbian deity, blessed the bird.

Syncretism is a rich and varied process of combining religious elements from different traditions; but it is important to emphasize the creativity involved in forming new religious and social combinations, especially in colonial settings like Mesoamerica between 1520 and 1900. One of the most vivid, moving, and beautiful examples of creative syncretism is the pervasive cult of the Virgin of Guadalupe in Mexico, which began within two decades after the conquest and continues to thrive to this day.

The Virgin of Guadalupe

The Virgin of Guadalupe is part of a much larger cult of the Virgin Mary of Immaculate Conception, which permeates religious art, meaning, and practice throughout Latin America. Images of the different sacred Virgins are found on statues, clothes, and jewelry in every conceivable place in Latin countries, including churches, bars, discotheques, restaurants, ballfields, hotels, museums, chapels, ice cream shops, parks, and automobiles.

From 1540 to today the cult of Mary has dominated churches and even entire villages, which turn to her as the go-between to God the Father and believe that the destiny of the whole community depends on her powers. Powerful cults dedicated to Mary include the cult of the Virgin of los Remedios, the Virgin of Candelaria at San Juan de los Lagos, and the Virgin of Zapopan. It is obvious that the Virgin Mary is a European importation into Mesoamerica. Each Iberian colonial incursion into Mesoamerica was accompanied, if not led, by the standard of one of the Virgins, who protected, inspired, and comforted the invaders as they claimed new territories and peoples for the Spanish empire. But in each case new meanings were given to the Spanish cult of the Virgin by *mestizos,* Indians, and creoles (Spaniards born in the New World). This remarkable creativity shows in clearer outline what we saw suggested in the Zinacantec story of Jesus, namely, that the native peoples and *mestizos* did, in varying degrees, embrace elements of Christianity, come to regard themselves as Christians, and develop new forms of Christian stories, art, and ritual expression. But this process of becoming and transforming Christian meanings and practices was wonderfully complex and difficult to describe adequately.

The cult of the Virgin of Guadalupe contains many of the rich patterns of religious life we have studied in this book, including pilgrimage, *axis mundi,* world renewal, ecstasy, and syncretism. According to the official tradition in Mexico a dark-skinned Virgin of Guadalupe appeared to a lowly Indian who was passing by the hill of Tepeyac in 1531, just ten years after the capital of Tenochtitlan fell to Cortés's forces. When the Indian, Juan Diego, reported the apparition to church authorities, they immediately scoffed at the idea that the Mother of Jesus would reveal herself to an Indian. When Juan Diego returned to the site to ask for the apparition's assistance she told him in Nahuatl to take roses from a nearby bush that was blooming out of season and roll them up in his cloak.

This anonymous painting depicts Juan Diego presenting a bouquet of roses and the image of Guadalupe to Bishop Zumárraga, not shown, that according to legend he received from an apparition of the Virgin. Guadalupe spoke to him in Nahuatl from the hilltop previously dedicated to the Aztec goddess Tonantzin. The cult surrounding Our Lady of Guadalupe played a powerful role in integrating colonial society, and the image became a precious symbol of Mexican nationalism. Today, the original image of Guadalupe can be viewed in her basilica in Mexico City. (Photograph courtesy of the National Catholic News Service.)

He did as he was told, and when he unrolled the cloak a magnificent color image of the Virgin of Guadalupe, surrounded by a blazing solar corona, was imprinted on it. When Juan Diego took the cloak to the Archbishop of Mexico, according to popular legend, the astonishing miracle was accepted and the site of the revelation was chosen for the future cathedral. Today Mexico's greatest basilica stands at the bottom of the hill and is visited every day by thousands of the faithful, who gaze upward at the glass-encased cloak with the miraculously painted image of the Virgin. Some come in pilgrimages from hundreds of miles away and walk the last part on their knees, praying along the way.

Even in the middle of the sixteenth century, priests complained that there were "idols behind altars" (pre-Columbian pagan statues, or memories of statues, behind the Catholic altars) at places like Tepeyac. On the one hand, however, the apparition of Guadalupe was familiar and even affirmed by the Spaniards who brought a tradition of apparitions and shrines to the New World. Mexico was a training ground for priests who expected apparitions to be part of their ministry. On the other hand the Franciscans and Dominican priests, who spoke Nahuatl and observed the indigenous peoples adjusting painfully to the colonial order, realized that the Indians were not merely adopting Spanish Catholic practices. Rather they were mixing native and European beliefs together and sometimes disguising their continued worship of their spirits, deities, and ancestors in their devotion to Mary and other saints. It was known that the site of Juan Diego's experience was the sacred hill dedicated to the Aztec mother goddess, Tonantzin, who was worshiped throughout the history of the Aztec empire. Recently archaeoastronomers and historians of religions have shown how Tepeyac was associated with important pre-Columbian ceremonial routes traveled to stimulate the rain-giving mountains to release their vital waters. It appears that Aztec ceremonial life involved ceremonial pilgrimages and processions to many of the sacred mountains around the Valley of Mexico and that Tepeyac and its nearby hills were shrines of high importance to the rain god cults of Tenochtitlan. The point is that the cult of Guadalupe, while strongly Catholic in meaning, also expresses an Indian sense of sacred space and worship of a goddess and her cults.

One of the most difficult realizations for students of religion to reach is the multiple, sometimes contradictory meanings of symbols or religious images. In a religious cosmovision, whether in Mesoamerica or Europe or China, a single symbol will have multiple meanings. An obvious example of this multivalence is the Christian cross. On the one hand it represents the betrayal, suffering, sacrifice, and death of Jesus Christ. But on the other hand it represents resurrection, life, victory over death, and faith in God. This multiplicity of meanings is also stimulated by the local variations a symbol or deity may take according to local history, geography, politics, and ecology. There are many local meanings and stories associated with the different holy Virgins in Mexico. At the same time Guadalupe is special because she integrates the tensions of Indians and Spaniard, *mestizo* and Indian, Spaniard and *mestizo* into *one* community of faith and devotion.

We can see very different images and meanings associated with Guadalupe during her career in Mexico. First, she is considered the nurturing Mother who embraces, protects, and loves the people and nation of Mexico. She is kind, loving, forgiving, and accessible in all the shrines and images dedicated to her. Second, she is the wonderful intercessor, the go-between to whom humans turn in order to reach the miraculous power of God the Father. Third, she can also become the female warrior of the revolution. At different, violent upheavals in Mexican history, priests and rebels have turned to her power and authority to inspire them to overthrow the oppressive government. She becomes the natural ally of the common people, often Indians and *mestizos,* in their spirit of rebellion. She is approached for aid in the resistance against hated taxes. For example, in the Indian uprising in Tulancingo in 1769, rebel leaders called for the death of Spanish officials and the creation of an Indian priesthood.

> They dreamed of the day when bishops and the alcaldes mayores would kneel and kiss the rings of the native priests. Their new theocratic utopia was led by an Indian who called himself the New Savior and by a consort who was reputed to be the Virgin of Guadalupe.[88]

In Guadalupe we see a curious and even furious syncretistic mixture. She is Indian and Spaniard. She is an Earth Mother and a Holy Mother. She is a comforter and a revolutionary. She is the magnet for pilgrimages and she is a pilgrim herself, traveling in front of the rebel soldiers and entering every heart who needs her protection and comfort, as did the poor Indian Juan Diego in 1531. [See Christianity pp. 518, 528 for discussion of the cult of Mary and Our Lady of Guadalupe; see Native Religions of North America p. 358 for description of the (Zuni) Church of Our Lady of Guadalupe.]

The Peyote Hunt of the Huichol Indians

Not all religious practices in contemporary Mesoamerica have a mixture of indigenous and imported symbols and beliefs. In some cases Nahuatl and Maya-speaking peoples practice pre-Columbian rituals that have very little Catholic or Protestant influence. One outstanding example, witnessed by cultural anthropologist Barbara Myerhoff, is the yearly Huichol pilgrimage to **Wirikuta,** the land of the ancestors where *hikuri,* or peyote, grows.

The Huichol peoples live in the mountainous regions of the Mexican states of Durango, Jalisco, Nayarit, and Zacatecas. The Huichols are famous for their brilliantly colored yarn paintings, which depict myths, images, and fantastic beings from their worldview and environment. Their social and symbolic life is complex and varied, but they are best known for their yearly journey to the ancestral territory of Wirikuta, two hundred miles from the city of Guadalajara, in search of peyote and peyote visions. These pilgrimages are always led by a shaman-priest or **mara'akame** such as Ramon Medina Silva, who was the chief inform-ant in Barbara Myerhoff's study *Peyote Hunt: The Sacred Journey of the Huichol Indians.*

Ramon's role and original decision to become a *mara'akame* reflects our earlier discussion about the human career as a way of worldcentering. When he was between six and nine years old Ramon began to have a series of amazing dreams in which the Huichol deity Tayaupa (Our Father Sun) spoke to him, revealing that he was being chosen to become a spiritual leader of the Huichols.

> Tayaupa spoke to me. He said, "Look, son, do not worry. You must grow a little more so you can go out and become wise, so that you can support your-self. . . . You will make fine things, things of color. You will understand this and that. It is for this that you were born." At first, I was frightened. I did not know. I began to reflect.[89]

During this period of reflection Ramon was bitten by a snake and nearly died. His grandfather, a *mara'akame,* healed him and it was slowly revealed to the community that Ramon had been chosen by the Huichol gods to become a shaman-priest. This combination of religious dreams and injury/healing is typi-cal of individuals who become set apart from the community into a status of sacred leader.

Years later Barbara Myerhoff was introduced to the adult artist shaman Ramon Medina and became a trusted friend of his family. After two summers of visits, conversations, and taped question-and-answer sessions Myerhoff was invited to participate, under Ramon's guidance, in the sacred journey to Wirikuta.

The peyote hunt, which is described in some detail by Myerhoff, and which appears in Peter Furst's 1969 film *To Find Our Life,* has many stages and powerful transitions in it. According to Myerhoff the journey to Wirikuta, two hundred miles to the north, is the Huichol version of a universal human quest, namely the search for Paradise, or the original center of the world where god, human, animal, and plant were at one with each other during a primordial era. This search for a total unity or *communitas* with all of life is reflected in two major themes of the peyote hunt. First, the pilgrims are changed, through a ritual, into living images of the first peyote pilgrims, who were gods. The pilgrims are gods in human form. Second, the peyote plant is also identified with the deer (animal ancestor). In the Huichol past the deer was a source of food and beauty, a magi-cal animal who is remembered as having given the first peyote to the first peyote hunters. On each subsequent hunt it is believed that the peyote is left by the ancestral deer who comes from the sky. Only the *mara'akame* can see him, while the other pilgrims can see his footprints in the forms of peyote plants in the des-ert floor. This unity of animal and plant is further enriched by the symbolism of the maize in Huichol thought. Maize is the source of life today, abundant and all around. In the Huichol cosmovision the peyote hunt is a time and action of unity bringing together animal and plant, past and present, ancestor, spirit, and the human. Therefore the peyote hunt must be carried out with the utmost care.

This experience of unity is achieved through a series of stages that make up the drama of the hunt. The Huichols sing, dance, play music, and chant during the peyote hunt, which can be said to have the following stages: Stage one is preparation and rehearsal, stage two is taking the names of deities, and stage three is preparing the fire and confessions. These first three stages take place at a private home before stage four, departure for Wirikuta, which is about a twenty-day walk from Huichol communities. Today they drive in cars and trucks. Arrival at Tatei Matinieri (Where Our Mother Dwells), a place of natural springs in the desert, is stage five. There the pilgrims witness the sunrise and "help Tayaupa come up."

At each stage there are meaningful and emotional moments of sadness, joy, exuberance, and solemnity, according to the occasion. In stage six reversals are established in which the people, now considered living images of the first peyote pilgrims, are designated as the opposite of what they in fact are. For instance,

> Merriment and excitement filled the car and animated chatter and laughter. By way of explaining the laughter, Ramón reached over and taking some of my hair in his hand said that now it was cactus fiber. Pointing to himself, he said that he was the Pope, that Lupe was an "ugly boy," Victoria a gringa, and Francisco a nunutsi (little child).[90]

The meaning of these reversals is that the *peyoteros* are participating in *another mode of being,* a religious way of being human, and as such change or reverse who they are. This is partly due to the fact that each peyote hunt repeats the first peyote hunt, when the ancestral gods journeyed to Wirikuta.

The seventh stage is the arrival at Wirikuta, which is signified by the "knotting-in," an act of unification of the pilgrims when they tie knots in a string that links them together at the entrance to the sacred land. Stage eight includes the actual "hunt" of peyote, which is considered in Huichol symbolism to be a deer. Myerhoff's description helps us understand this identification of plant and animal.

> The hikuritamete (peyote companions) set out across the desert, moving briskly toward the mountains but fanning out instead of following the single file usually observed for ritual processions. Everyone was completely quiet and grave, looking closely at the ground for tracks. As they approached the mountains, the peyoteros' pace slackened for peyote was more likely to be found here and the tension mounted. Their behavior was precisely that of stalking an animal. There were no sudden movements, no talking. The pilgrims bent over close to the ground, moved in the brush on tiptoe, gingerly raising a branch or poking under a cactus in hopes of catching sight of the small gray-green peyote plant which is so inconspicuous, growing nearly parallel to the earth's surface and exactly the same color as surrounding vegetation in this region. . . . Finally Ramon beckoned everyone to his side—he had found peyote, seen the deer. Quickly we all gathered behind him as he drew his arrow and readied the bow. We peered down at the barely noticeable round flat-topped plant, two inches in diameter, segregated into eight sections. Everyone prayed quietly as Ramon began to stalk it, moving ever closer until when he was only a few feet away he aimed and shot one arrow into the

base of the plant toward the east and crossed it quickly with another arrow pointing north so that the peyote was impaled in the center. The peyote-deer was thus secured and unable to escape.[91]

Following a series of prescribed ritual actions the *peyoteros* collect, sort, clean, and pack a large number of peyote buttons. During several following nights peyote is eaten by the group gathered around the fire in order to induce visions. The pilgrims laugh and discuss the beautiful colors and little animals in their visions, finally falling quiet as they stare into the fire. During this entire episode the *mara'akame* gazes quietly into the fire seeing visions of the ancestral pilgrims, the spirits of the Huichol cosmos. He sees and talks with the main deities, receiving new knowledge about life and the sacred.

Stage nine is the departure from Wirikuta. This involves the giving of peyote names, the eating of salt, and the untying of the cord that united the group before entering the sacred land.

In this remarkable sacred journey, the Huichol regenerate their sense of identity. In their words, they "find our life," meaning they commune with the beauty and powers of Wirikuta and come to experience what it feels like and what one "sees" when one is a Huichol. All this is a reiteration of how the world of the peyote hunt was first made. [See Native Religions of North America pp. 287, 322 for description of "peyotism" as a "new religion" in North America.]

Having looked at a pilgrimage in which people travel to a sacred space to find their life, let us now turn to the yearly celebrations called Day of the Dead, in which the spirits of deceased friends and relatives make the pilgrimage back into the world of the living. [See Judaism pp. 469–70, Christianity pp. 562–73, Islam pp. 645–47, Hinduism pp. 815–20, Buddhism p. 874, Religions of China pp. 1041–44 and Religions of Japan pp. 1154–60 for description and discussion of pilgrimage.]

Dia de los Muertos (Day of the Dead)

One of the most meaningful yearly celebrations in Mexico, in fact throughout Latin America, is the Dia de los Muertos (Day of the Dead) celebrated for nearly a week at the end of October and beginning of November. This elaborate celebration, dedicated to the cult of the dead (also referred to as Todos Santos, All Saints Day), combines pre-Hispanic rituals and beliefs with Catholic practices and symbols. The central idea is that during this period of public and private (family) rituals the living and dead family members and friends are joined together in an atmosphere of communion and spiritual regeneration.

It is important to note that the rituals, symbols, and elaborate decorations of home altars and cemeteries are somewhat different according to region. Some communities will emphasize elaborate cemetery altars and decorations, while others will emphasize the processions between home and cemetery. Still others make unusual efforts to decorate their home altars to dead ancestors in baroque, lavish ways. Some communities have open-air competitions of altars and offerings to the dead, ranging from small altars to some that are ten feet high and fifty feet long. But all Day of the Dead celebrations focus on a spiritual covenant between the human community and supernatural entities of deceased family members, friends, or saints. The following description is taken largely from Day of the Dead celebrations in the Mexican state of Tlaxcala, east of Mexico City, as reported by Hugo Nutini.

The Day of the Dead rituals are complex and difficult to categorize, but we can emphasize three outstanding dimensions: the preparations for the ceremonies (worldmaking), the symbolism of the family altars to the dead (worldcentering), and the ceremonial feast of the dead and spiritual union with the dead at the home and cemetery (worldrenewing).

Scholars have determined that important elements of the Day of the Dead festivities were practiced in pre-Hispanic times and have become integrated into the Catholic traditions of Latin America. Bernardino de Sahagun discovered the following ritual practices associated with the month of Tepeilhuitl in the Aztec capital. In this description we see the importance of the cult of the dead associated with a ceremonial place:

> They also used to place the image of the dead on those grass wreaths. Then at dawn they put these images in their shrines, on top of beds of reed mace, sedge, or rush. Once the images were placed there, they offered them food, tamales, and gruel, or a stew made of chicken (turkey) or dog's meat. Then they offered the images incense from an incense burner, which was a big cup full of coals, and this ceremony they called calonoac.
>
> And the rich sang and drank pulcre (fermented agave juice) in honor of these gods and their dead, while the poor offered them only food, as has been mentioned.[92]

This same pattern of offering food to the spirits of dead ancestors in ceremonial shrines is carried out today after elaborate and sometimes economically stressful preparations.

In each household, which is the center of the cult of the dead, it is believed that the souls of the dead have taken a journey to the world beyond. The souls of good people travel a straight and narrow path to another world, while the souls of bad people travel a wide and labyrinthine way. All souls arrive at a deep and broad river that can only be crossed with the help of a dog, which lifts the souls on his shoulders and carries them over to the other side. In Tlaxcala, at least, it is believed that the bad souls would be refused transportation across this river, while good souls could persuade the dog to carry them more easily if they had the coins that were placed in the mouth or hand of the dead at their funerals. In many communities it is believed that dogs must be treated well in this life because they are spirit helpers in the next.

What is outstanding in all cases is the belief that one's life on this earth is dependent, in part, on treating the dead well. People believe that if the dead are not worshiped, nurtured, and remembered in the proper manner their own economic security, family stability, and health will be in jeopardy. Therefore careful and generous preparations are carried out. [See Religions of Africa pp. 42–45, 78–79, Native Religions of North America pp. 300–301, 307–308, 335–37, Judaism pp. 448–50, Christianity p. 557, Islam pp. 684–85, Hinduism pp. 813–14, Buddhism pp. 935–37, Religions of China p. 1021, and Religions of Japan pp. 1149–50 for description and discussion of death and funeral rites.]

Preparations (Worldmaking)

Prominent in the decorations of family altars and cemetery altars are the marigold flowers or **zempoalxochitl** (a Nahuatl word meaning "twenty-flower"). Most households grow their own *zempoalxochitl* in their own gardens and plant the seeds in the middle of August so that the flowers bloom by the last part of October. This sense of preparation for Dia de los Muertos intensifies at the start of October, when people set out the necessary cash and other goods to be used in the generous decorations of altars, tombs, and at the ceremonial meals for the dead and the living. Also, careful arrangements are made to be free from jobs so that the proper ritual responsibilities can be carried out. In Latin America, where poverty is so widespread, this responsibility entails a sense of sacrifice on behalf of the family. Journeys are made to local and regional markets, sometimes covering several hundred miles, so that the correct foods and decorations can be purchased in time for the sacred week.

Most important are preparations of special foods for the dead. These include baked breads, candied fruit, skulls made of sugar, and human figurines made of pumpkin seeds, as well as apple, pear, and quince preserves. Papier-mâché images of various kinds are purchased or made, to be used in the decorations of the altars and the cemetery graves. The last and most crucial item to be picked or purchased are the *zempoalxochitl* flowers. Since these flowers will last for only four days, they are placed on altars and tombs and as pathways between the cemeteries and the homes on the day before Dia de los Muertos begins.

The Family Altar (Worldcentering)

Day of the Dead altars can appear in public plazas, in schools, and even in competitions, but the most important altar appears in the individual household. Within the family home it serves as the *axis mundi* of the ritual and ceremonial life of the family. Most homes in the Tlaxcala region will have an altar in place all year round, but it becomes elaborately and colorfully decorated during this ritual period. This altar becomes a sacred precinct or a ceremonial center within the home made up of at least ten kinds of objects—breads, sweets, cooked dishes, delicacies, fruits and vegetables, liquors and liquids, flowers and plants, clothing, adornments, and (perhaps most important) pictures, images, and statues. These pictures and statues are usually placed in a *retablo* (a structure forming the back of an altar), where images of the Virgin, Christ, the cross, and saints watch over the *ofrenda,* or offering to the dead. This offering takes the shape of a wonderful feast for the spirits of the dead who will return and be nourished on specific nights during Dia de los Muertos. A typical *ofrenda* in Tlaxcala is shaped like a four-sided pyramid decorated along the edges by *zempoalxochitl* flowers. At each of the four corners are placed mounds of mandarins and oranges on top of sugar cane cuttings. Cooked dishes, liquids, finger foods, *pan de muerto* loaves, candied fruits, tamales, bananas, and oranges constitute the bulk of the offering. The most impressive objects of the *ofrenda* are crystallized sugar skulls of different sizes and with various kinds of decorations. These skulls represent the dead infants, children, and adults being honored that year.

Many rich symbolic and social meanings are expressed in this crowded, organic ceremonial center. This cornucopia of goods represents the quest for fertility and the renewal of relations with dead friends and family members. But the overall image is that of a sacred Mountain of Sustenance that orients and nourishes the family community. As we have seen in our chapter on the Aztec ceremonial pyramids the Mountain of Sustenance is a pre-Catholic symbol of rain, fertility, and the container of the most valued supernatural powers. In part the Dia de los Muertos altars and *ofrendas* symbolize the body of the life-giving earth with its forces of regeneration.

Communion with the Dead (Worldrenewing)

The actual moments of reunion with the dead and the regeneration of family ties are carefully orchestrated. In fact, according to the detailed practices of the Tlaxcala region, there are five categories of the dead souls—those who die in accidents, those who die violently, those who die as infants, as children, and as adults—who return on five consecutive days. On November 2, which is the climax of Todos Santos, all the dead are remembered.

According to Hugo Nutini's research in Tlaxcala, the people believe that the souls of the dead begin to return and hover around their family households beginning at 3 P.M. on October 31. In order for the souls of the dead to return to the house where they lived, a trail of *zempoalxochitl* flowers must be laid out for them to find their way. Early in the morning the women in the family prepare a basket of fragrant flower petals, which are sprinkled with holy water from the church. Then the male adults and children lay the petals in a line marking a trail from the street through the yard or courtyard to the foot of the family altar. This trail is intended to show the spirits of the dead the path home from the cemetery. It is important that the flowers be fragrant because it is believed that while the souls of the dead are blind, they have acute senses of smell and can find their way home on the path of aroma created by the petals.

By 9 P.M. on November 1 it is believed that all the souls of the dead have traveled along the fragrant path of flowers to their old homes. In some homes the room containing the altar/*ofrenda* is closed between 10 P.M. and 6 A.M. so that the returning souls can enjoy the food and treats and reminisce together about their past lives in the human world. Then it is believed that the souls of the dead return to the cemetery to join the living in a vigil of communion.

This vigil is called Xochatl in Nahuatl or La Llorada in Spanish (the Weeping), and it is the time when the living and dead join together as a living spiritual community. The souls of the dead reassure the living of their continued protection, and the living reassure the dead that they will remember and nurture them in their daily lives.

In the local cemetery a community band with *teponaxtle y chirimia* (native drum and flute) ensemble play both melancholy and vibrant tunes for eight hours while candles are lit on the graves and rosaries are said as church bells toll out pleasing music for the souls of the dead who are about to return to their graves. The living ask the dead souls to protect their families, crops, businesses, health, and property for another year. Part of the ritual speech goes, "Oh, blessed souls who have kindly returned to us . . . to participate with us in this day of remembrance, find it in the goodness of your hearts to protect us and shelter us."[93]

Here we see a moving example of modern-day Mesoamericans, heirs of centuries of both a pre-Hispanic cosmovision and Catholic patterns of rosaries and altars, regenerating their own sense of family and community by participating in the cult of the dead.

The Fiesta of Santiago Among the Tzutujil Maya

Earlier we studied the symbolism of the cosmic tree and the rituals of bleeding for a vision of regeneration among the Classic Maya (third to tenth centuries C.E.). We also traveled through the underworld with the Maya Hero Twins of the seventeenth-century document *Popul Vuh*. Now we will turn to the festival of Santiago, held the third week in July in the Guatemalan Maya community of Santiago Atitlan. In spite of the harsh history the Maya have undergone since the first half of the sixteenth century, the contemporary Maya of Santiago Atitlan (known regionally as Atitecos) have devised effective strategies to maintain many of their traditional ways of worldrenewing by mixing them with Catholic practices and holidays. Agricultural fertility and renewal was an essential dimension of all Maya communities. Consider the contemporary ritual methods for ensuring worldrenewal during the Feast of Santiago or, as the Maya call it, **nim q'ij Santiag** or Big Sun Santiago.

This ceremony takes place when the first corn is being harvested in the highland Maya region, around July 23, which is also the saint's day of Santiago (Saint James) in the Catholic calendar. Throughout contemporary Mesoamerica, Santiago has a rich range of meanings in the many local societies where he is represented in rite, iconography, and theology. To the Atitecos, Santiago is identified as a Catholic saint and also as a *bokunab*, a category of deity characterized by the power to multiply elements of the world they come in contact with. Although this characteristic is most notable for its relationship to agricultural abundance, with Santiago it is portrayed symbolically by his sword. When Santiago whacks people with a sword it doesn't kill, but instead divides his target into two. If he touches corn it increases in number. In other words *bokunabs* not only regenerate the world, they make it more abundant. This idea is combined in Maya religion with the belief that humans have a responsibility for assisting in this process of enrichment by carrying out certain rituals in a correct manner. This is a way of taking care of the divine forces so they will continue to regenerate the cosmos. [See Christianity pp. 569–73 for description and interpretation of the pilgrimage to Saint James (Santiago) of Compostela in Spain.]

The following description of the ritual celebration of Santiago comes from interviews with Robert Carlsen, a cultural anthropologist who has lived among the Tzutujil Maya for parts of ten years during which he witnessed and participated in the *nim q'ij*. His experience has been significantly enriched by a personal, working relationship with Martin Prechtel, a shaman healer (*a'kun*) who was initiated by Nicolas Chiveleyo, a renowned Maya leader, into Maya ritual traditions. Speaking of the almost twelve-hour ritual procession, which symbolically travels to the four quarters of the Atiteco universe, Carlsen stated,

> The celebration begins early in the morning when members of the town's ten different *cofradias* (traditional religious organizations) gather at the cathedral in their colorful, woven costumes. Several of the *cofradias* bring the statue of a saint, each lavishly dressed and mounted on a platform which is carried on the shoulders of members of the *cofradia*. These saints have been in the church for several days, waiting for the long, slow walk around the block, which is also the Tzutujil cosmos in miniature. In the minds of the Atitecos, these statues are living images of the deities, which combine Christian and Maya attributes, and these living images are pleased to gather together once a year in the church and celebration. To the Atitecos the center of the church is the **r'kux ruchiliev** or umbilicus of the world, the center of

The procession associated with the festival of Santiago begins and ends at the centuries-old church in Santiago Atitlan. Depicted here are members of the town's ten public cofradias, attired in their best ceremonial clothes, waiting for the procession to begin. At the foreground is the image of Santiago, the patron saint of the town. (Photo courtesy of Paul Harbaugh.)

the world which was the birthplace of all that exists. In fact there is a carefully marked hole in the center of the church that marks the spot of the center.

At a time when the mood is right the appropriate *cofradía* members bring the saints out of the church onto the front steps. In a way the celebration begins on this ancient and beautiful semicircular stairway. Around 7 AM, amidst the sounds of singing, personal greetings, and conversation, with incense floating through the morning air, *cofradía* members with their wives, family, and friends, now numbering about five hundred people, lift the platforms of saints and descend the stairs in their colorful, striking headdresses and clothes. Crowded together they slowly move across the church courtyard as *bombas* (sticks of dynamite) are lofted high into the air and explode. The percussion is so great that you must open your mouth to keep your ears from splitting in pain.

The procession is slow. It is difficult to imagine how slow the Maya move and with natural ease. They go down the stairs, slow, really slow. They proceed through the church courtyard following an imaginary line that divides the ritual space in half. This line also represents the middle of the ritual year, or ritual time. As Martin Prechtel and I have explained in our writings, the primary symbolic function of the Atiteco *cofradía* system is to help carry the sun across the sky. Beginning at a point at the symbolic center of the year, this and other similar *cofradía* processions are understood as walking the path of the sun. To walk this path, what in Tzutujil is called "Foot of the Dawn, Foot of the Sun," is necessary for the sun's progression across the sky.

The procession, always led by a drummer and flute player, plus the litters of Santiago and two other saints, covers about 200 yards in the first half hour. Inevitably tourists are busy taking pictures and videos from different angles, while the Maya do their best to ignore them or nudge them out of the way when necessary. Once the procession leaves the churchyard it turns left, amid singing, drinking, friendly conversation, and proceeds to the first corner, where a shrine covered with pine needles houses the precious image of a saint. The procession puts all the litters down, kneels, and—following the *cabecera* or *cofradía* leader—offers prayers and the sacred beverage of *aguardiente* to the saint. This is understood as an offering that nurtures the saint, that actually feeds the little shrine and the corner of the world it represents. The *cabecera* prays hard in Tzutujil, calling out the names of deities and sacred places. Then the singers sing special prayers for roughly forty-five minutes. The group—now without the tourists, who have become bored and drifted away—has swelled in numbers of native participants. For these people believe that they are doing rituals that need to take place in this corner of the world to make the process of regeneration work.

Then, amid another series of *bomba* explosions, the procession sets off, ever so slowly, with people becoming progressively drunk to the second corner of the world. They cover about 100 yards in forty-five minutes and arrive at a second shrine. The same putting down of litters, prayers, songs, and drinking takes place for an hour or so at this shrine. Communal drinking cups are passed through the crowd, full of one of two types of alcoholic beverage. There is the *de la ley* or legal drink known as *aguardiente*. It is potent and tunes you up after a few drinks. Then there is the *contra ley* or illegal *ptzihuan ya* or "canyon water." This is very hard to drink but it cannot be refused. By now the procession consists of an intoxicated unit, a kind of Dionysian band, drunk, happy, talking serious shit loudly in each other's ears, making pledges for life, helping each other through the ritual.

At the time when the mood is right, the group, amidst the *bombas*, singing, and marimba music playing the background, sets off for the third corner of the world. But halfway to the third station, just at the point of intersection of the middle line I mentioned as we were leaving the courtyard, everyone stops and puts down the saints. This is the point of transferal of the "cargo" or religious material/responsibility from this past year's *cofradia* of Santiago to next year's group. It is immensely sad for the retiring group. Members cry, pledge lifelong faithfulness to Santiago, and speak of the power and blessing they felt during their year of having his sacred life in their care and home. *Bombas* go off as the responsibility of Santiago is transferred to his new keepers and last year's group gets up and walks away from the procession. Explicit in this ceremony is the knowledge that this transferal of care and responsibility insures the continuation of the sacred force of the saint within the human community.

Then the colorful, swaying, singing, growing throng, which by now has grown to over a thousand people, picks up the litters of saints and slowly, ever so slowly, walks to the third corner. This corner has a big house on it and the front porch serves as the shrine for the saints to be set up and worshiped. More *bombas*, drinking, prayers, feelings of commitment and unity are generated. Then it's on to the fourth corner.

Here the ritual symbolism gets complex and rich. On this corner, where the shrine would normally be, stands the Centro Americana church, the largest and oldest Protestant denomination in Guatemala. The front door of this Church stands right where the Santiago chapel should be. In fact, when the huge procession arrives, members of the church are sitting on the front steps staring smugly and disapprovingly at this "pagan" throng. So the procession goes across the street and celebrates there. And there is a *cantina* on this corner. By now the group has passed over into the rhythm of an inebriated mass, singing, swaying, praying, pledging loudly in each other's ears. Long prayers are offered, *bombas* explode, the world seems awash in color, smoke, noise, and yet a feeling of the sacred and sacrifice hovers around the group.

The ritual has gone on for over nine hours and the procession, having symbolically walked around the cosmos, returns to the area in front of the entrance to the church courtyard. Directly facing the church is the building of the municipal government and, depending on the religious and political attitudes of the mayor, the procession is either let into the courtyard of the *municipio* or made to celebrate on the steps outside. Again, prayers, toasts, the display of the saints, songs all come together with the music of a marimba band, which has been playing sacred music for hours. The group is now in the thousands. One feels surrounded, embraced, encapsulated within the atmosphere of a separate reality, intensely communal, joyful, yet on the edge of vomiting, which has taken place many times by now. It is like a time of myth when all kinds of different beings and forces came together to make the cosmos.

Then, at the right mood, the community slowly reenters the courtyard, exhausted, spent, and nearly delirious. Up until now, we have gone so slow, so slow, for ten hours going slowly. Then the devices to shoot the *bombas* into the air are collected together in an area of the courtyard. All of a sudden all the *bombas* go off in a colossal series of explosions, boom, boom, boom, boom, boom, and the entire mass rushes as fast as it can up the stairs, jostling, bumping, lifting, surging forward into the church with the litters in the lead. It is as though the rhythm of the world has been reversed from slow to rapid. This is such a powerful experience as the outside world is left behind. The saints are taken up to the main altar. More prayers, hymns, with the saints and people back at the umbilicus of the world, having traveled to and remade the cosmos. There are Indians from all over the country in the church, which is lit, in the dusk of day, with thousands of white candles.

After some time the group thins out. Members of the *cofradia* stay in the church as lines of Indians come and pray to the saints, give thanks, ask for blessings, miracles, help to end suffering, good fortune. These *cofradia* members are also guarding the saints' clothes and canopies, some of which were made in the seventeenth and eighteenth centuries of hammered silver. But they are guarding these precious items from the church officials, who they believe may try and confiscate them.

I am left with the image of Maya women, dressed with their colorful *x'kap's* or cloth halos, praying, lighting candles, singing, and eventually moving out of the ceremonial space to return home.

Amazingly, the members of the new *cofradia* of Santiago return to their ceremonial home and celebrate for three more days!

Then, five days later, the entire community repeats this walking trip around the four quarters of their universe again![94]

What can we understand, in religious terms, from this extraordinary firsthand account of the contemporary Maya pilgrimage around the cosmos? In the terms of this book at least three patterns are outstanding. First, a clear statement of cosmovision is revealed in the relationship of the people to the saints. In the Maya worldview, life is a sacred gift from the deities for which humans are responsible to nurture. As Martin Prechtel has noted, "The world is a gift, but it isn't a free gift. You must put back, if you don't do these *costumbres* (ceremonies), if you don't put things back, then the world will stop." The Maya literally believe that if they don't do these things the world will die. Something must be put back, in terms of responsible ritual actions, in order to effectively take the powers of saints and deities into one's life.

Second, this ritual helps us understand one of the major patterns in Mesoamerican religions, namely sacrifice. For the Maya to carry out this ritual, extraordinary sacrifices are made. The Maya say this ritual involves *sacrificio* in terms of the serious expense incurred by the *cofradia* members who care for, nurture, and pay some of the expenses of this and other rituals. Also, the drinking to full drunkenness is difficult, painful, and has a stunning effect for weeks afterward. This drunkenness is a *passage* into the sacred time of Santiago, a time marked by the theme of division of realities. Just as Santiago has the capacity to divide things in two so that they become more abundant, the ritual drunkenness makes one's sense of self, community, time, and health more abundant, multivalent, larger. This is also a sacrifice because of the pain, vomiting, in fact "ritual illness," which is incurred in order to take someone to another level of reality. In this ritual the Maya, as Carlsen makes so clear, exhaust their financial and emotional resources in order to become reduced to a basic economic, social, and emotional community that is in the process of starting over, fresh and full of new potency.

Third, the action of responsible ritual care and sacrifice is done in order to renew the cosmos. This worldrenewing is done by symbolically retracing the cosmic image of the center and the four quarters. It is significant that the cosmology of great cities such as Teotihuacan, Tollan, and Tenochtitlan, with their ceremonial centers and four cardinal directions, is replicated in the microcosm of the block surrounding the main church in Santiago Atitlan. [See Religions of Africa pp. 74–75, Native Religions of North America pp. 308–16, 351–57, Judaism pp. 439–45, Christianity pp. 551–55, Islam pp. 674, 677–79, Hinduism p. 829, Buddhism pp. 937–41, Religions of China pp. 1021–24, and Religions of Japan pp. 1140–46, 1153–62 for description and discussion of festivals and annual celebrations.]

Conclusions

WE HAVE, LIKE THE PILGRIMS in Santiago Atitlan, come full circle. In our introductory chapter we noticed that the study of Mesoamerican religions is the
study of ceremonial centers where peoples acted out the dramas of their cosmovisions, which outlined the relations of celestial and human beings. In each
historical period, Olmec, Maya, Teotihuacan, Toltec, and Aztec peoples built
monumental ceremonial cities inscribed with images and symbols of their intimate relations with supernatural forces. We have seen how the human body,
mountains, stars, kings, warriors, ancestors, language, buildings, plants, and
the underworld were experienced and viewed as living containers of spiritual
power originating above and below the human level of existence. And we have
witnessed the various ritual means used by humans to make, center, and renew
their cosmos in a multiplicity of ceremonial centers. In the postconquest setting, characterized by surprising continuities and ingenious changes, we have
seen how new combinations of native and European religious elements were
joined to create new types of ceremonial centers in homes, in deserts, at pre-
Columbian sites and surrounding Christian churches. Like the Atiteco Maya
we have circumambulated a part of the history of religions in Mesoamerica.
At every stop we find a ceremonial center orienting religious experience and
expression.

It is important to remember that one of the most distinctive aspects of the
history of Mesoamerican religions is its relationship to the urban world and primary urban generation. The religious patterns that helped give birth to the
Mesoamerican urban tradition are one of the keys to understanding the role of
religion in what scholars have called the "birth of civilization" in human experience. In studying the religions of Mesoamerica we are observing and interpreting one of the greatest transformations and developments in the imagination
and social organization of the human species. In social terms we are studying
the role of religion in the emergence and development of hierarchical societies
organized on a political and territorial basis around monumental ceremonial
centers that served as the quintessential sacred meeting points between supernatural forces and human life. In a way, by studying Mesoamerican religions as
we have in this part, we are studying the formation and history of that great
artifact, the city, which, though it has undergone many significant transformations, is the setting we live in today.

But what is the future of Mesoamerica and its religious imagination? The pattern of the future can be seen in the patterns of its past. Both Mesoamerican cosmology and history were characterized by "eccentric periodicities," meaning periods of stability forcefully interrupted by collapses, rebellions, violent transformations, and new beginnings. Some people consider the reign of the Virgin of Guadalupe as the Sixth Age or Sun of central Mesoamerica. And with the prodigious complexities of change taking place in parts of Latin America today, we will likely see more rather than fewer manifestations of syncretism appearing in new reports, anthropological research, and creative literature. Mesoamerican religions today constitute one of the great fields for the study of social and religious change, innovation, and persistence. As the cults of Guadalupe, Santiago, and the peyote hunt demonstrate, even when a new urban tradition (European) was imposed on Mesoamerica, ancient ritual patterns competed with the more powerful (politically speaking) theological ideas for a significant place in the novel combinations that emerged. With new technologies and weapons spreading across Mesoamerica it is very difficult to know what the future holds, what kind of city will stand, what forms the cults of Guadalupe, Santiago, and the peyote hunt will take. It follows from the approach of this section that as long as they have their ceremonial centers for worship, orientation, and vision they will continue to mix native and imposed religious patterns.

There is also an ironic dimension to the conquest of the indigenous urban tradition by the Europeans. Every year in Mesoamerican cities and in rural areas where ancient cities once stood, new discoveries of ruins awaken the modern sensibility to the haunting presence of the pre-Columbian ceremonial world. When the subway was installed in Mexico City in the 1960s through 1980s impressive finds of temples, burials, and statues continually made the news. In a sense the more modern Mesoamerica becomes, the more it will recover its pre-Hispanic roots. As Carlos Fuentes stated about modern Mexico City, it is a "city ancient in light . . . city witness to all we forget."

One of the most interesting responses to the changes of the modern West comes from the Chicano movement in the United States. This response includes the utilization and celebration of the pre-Hispanic past in the aesthetic and political expressions for Chicano liberation in the United States. Chicanos are Americans of Mexican descent who have formed a movement to liberate themselves from Anglo stereotypes, political oppression, poverty, unequal opportunity, and spiritual doubt. This movement, also called the Chicano Renaissance, was most vocally represented in the Farmworkers' Union led by Cesar Chavez, in the Centro de la Raza led by Corky Gonzalez in Denver, and by the movement to recover ancestral lands in New Mexico. It receives its most vivid expression in the music, mural art work, and community services programs found in every Chicano community from El Paso, Texas, to Washington, D.C. Over the course of this movement there has been a remarkable interest in and representation of Aztec, Maya, Olmec, and Teotihuacan symbolism. [See Religions of Africa pp. 25, 54–57, 79–82, Native Religions of North America pp. 287, 320–22, 357–58, Judaism pp. 427–31, 456–75, Christianity pp. 529–33, Islam pp. 698–700, Hinduism pp. 770–74, 828–31, Buddhism pp. 952–56, Religions of China pp. 998–1002,

1055–59, and Religions of Japan pp. 1132–33, 1163–72 for discussion of new religious movements.]

In Chicago's Pilsen Community, for instance, where Chicanos have gained important political power, stands Casa Aztlan, an all-purpose community center housing colorful murals depicting Mexican history from the time of the Toltecs to the present. Casa Aztlan (the Home of Aztlan) is named after the mythical homeland, north of the Aztec capital, from which the Mexica ancestors left in order to build their great center, Tenochtitlan. Chicanos in Chicago claim that that original homeland is their *barrio,* where struggle and celebration are joined in a movement to ease the pain of urban living. They know in their minds that, geographically speaking, Aztlan is much further south. But in the religious imagination a sacred place can be anywhere there is a revelation of the spiritual resources and destiny of a people. Casa Aztlan is a modern-day ceremonial center for Chicanos to recall the pre-Columbian past and use that recall to strengthen themselves. In every Chicano community in the United States there are educational projects (some named after Quetzalcoatl), political movements (some named after Cuauhtemoc), and cultural centers (named after the Toltecs or the Mayas) that reflect a reaching back for power and inspiration from distant ancestors who, like the family spirits in the Dia de los Muertos, are given a path to reenter the world of the living. It is a special gift of the religious imagination that allows a people, after five hundred years of colonialism, dependency, oppression, and resistance, to turn to the ancient Mesoamerican past for symbols of a cosmovision that help make a world meaningful, give it a standing center, and provide for social and spiritual renewal. [See Christianity p. 531 for mention of Mexican-American Catholic churches.]

And this Chicano example of utilizing the creative past for regeneration in the present is part of a wider significance to be found in studying Mesoamerica. To study its ceremonial cities and religious imagination leads us to consider comparisons with other ancient urban traditions. And to consider Mesoamerica's unique colonial history leads us to realize just how novel the New World was and is. As Díaz del Castillo wrote long ago, when reminiscing about his youthful attacks on the Aztec capital,

> And some of our soldiers even asked whether the things that we saw were not a dream. It is not to be wondered at that I here write it down in this manner, for there is so much to think over that I do not know how to describe it, seeing things as we did that had never been heard of or seen before, not even dreamed about.[95]

Of course the native Mesoamericans had never dreamed of the European world, either, and when the two came together they created a wonderfully complex world that we must continue to strive to understand and appreciate. It is the purpose of this essay to help us understand and appreciate Mesoamerican religions, not only because they are Mesoamerican but also because they reveal to us dimensions of the human imagination and its expression in the work of the human body.

Study Questions

Before you begin to read this part, take a mental inventory of what you know and think about Mesoamerica and the people of Mesoamerica. Make a list of Mesoamerican "things" that you know—Mexico, Mexican music and foods, the Maya and Aztecs, human sacrifice, and so on. What would you imagine religion in Mesoamerica to be like? Keep these images and things in mind as you read this section and develop new notions about Mesoamerica.

PROLOGUE

1. How does the author characterize the meeting of European culture and peoples with the culture and people of Mesoamerica?
2. How did Europeans view their "discovery" of Mesoamerica?

CHAPTER 5

Introduction: Approaching Mesoamerican Religions

1. Identify the geographical location of Mesoamerica and its major cultural features.
2. How were European views of Mesoamerica influenced by European preconceptions?
3. What materials will the author use to describe the religions of Mesoamerica and what concepts will he use to interpret them?

CHAPTER 6

History and Cosmovision in Mesoamerican Religions

1. When, where, and how did Mesoamerican civilizations develop?
2. What were the major features of the "cosmovision" in Mesoamerica—its mythology and cultural achievements?
3. Characterize ancient Mesoamerican cities.
4. Sum up in your own words the Mesoamerican cosmovision—its view of the cosmos, human beings, and time.

CHAPTER 7

The Religion of the Aztecs: Ways of the Warrior, Words of the Sage

1. How is Aztec religion closely related to "ways of the warrior"?
2. Summarize the sacred career of Topiltzin Quetzalcoatl.

3. What is the significance of the human body in Aztec religion?
4. What are the major features of the Aztec temple?
5. How is Aztec religion related to the "words of the sage"?
6. What were the major ways language was used to communicate and make offerings to the gods?
7. Identify and interpret the major aspects of the New Fire Ceremony and human sacrifice.

CHAPTER 8

Maya Religion: Cosmic Trees, Sacred Kings, and the Underworld

1. From the first few pages of this chapter frame a picture of "the image of the Maya cosmos."
2. Identify the major aspects of the cosmic tree and sacred kingship.
3. Describe the Maya calendar and the regeneration of time.
4. Summarize the pattern of the heroic journey through the underworld of Xibalba.

CHAPTER 9

Mesoamerica as a New World: Colonialism and Religious Creativity

1. How does Carrasco interpret Mesoamerica as a "new world"? How was colonialism a crisis for Mesoamerican culture?
2. Describe and interpret the Virgin of Guadalupe as an example of the interaction of Christianity with indigenous religious life.
3. Describe and interpret the peyote hunt of the Huichol Indians as an example of the continuation of pre-Columbian rituals.
4. Interpret the Day of the Dead as an expression of worldmaking, worldcentering, and worldrenewing.
5. Trace the events of the Fiesta of Santiago as a way of preserving traditional customs within Catholic practices.

Recall the mental inventory of Mesoamerican images and things that you made before reading this part. What is there in Mesoamerican religion that is most like your own religious tradition? What in Mesoamerican religion is most different from your own tradition? What is most interesting? How has your understanding of Mesoamerican religion changed as a result of reading this section? Can you now imagine yourself participating in Mesoamerican religion?

Notes

Throughout this book I use the spelling *Moctezuma* to refer to the Aztec rulers usually called, in English, *Montezuma*. There were two Moctezumas, Moctezuma Ilhuicamina 1440–1454 and Moctezuma Xocoyotzin 1502–1520. The Nahuatl spelling in the *Florentine Codex* is *Motecuzoma*, though some scholars use *Moteuczomah* while others use *Moteuczoma*. I am following the translation of Dibble and Anderson, who consistently use *Moctezuma*.

This work is dedicated to my parents David and Marji Carrasco. I want to thank the colleagues and friends who helped me during the writing of this work. They include Lois Middleton and Linda Cohen, who organized many important details of research; Peter van der Loo, Robert Carlsen, Carolyn Tate, and Anthony Aveni, who gave advice on certain chapters; Scott Sessions, who helped with the codices; and Richard Griswold del Castillo and Jose (Dr. Loco) Cuellar, who helped me direct the narrative for use in Chicano studies programs. William B. Taylor urged me to take a long second look at the presentation of colonialism and syncretism. Michio Araki, from the University of Tsukuba, Tsukuba, Japan, opened the resources of the Institute of Philosophy to me during the early drafts of this work. I thank him and the students who assisted me in library research while in the land of the rising sun.

This work has been enriched as well by a number of scholars, who participated in summer seminars at the Mesoamerican Archive. They include Elizabeth Boone, Robert Bye, Charles Long, Jane Day, Johanna Broda, Edward Calnek, Doris Heyden, Cecelia Klein, Eduardo Matos Moctezuma, Alfredo Lopez Austin, Edelmira Linares, H. B. Nicholson, Richard Townsend, Jorge Klor de Alva, Lawrence Desmond, and Lawrence Sullivan. Paul Wheatley's work has nurtured this project from the beginning. Finally, my gratitude extends to Raphael and Fletcher Lee Moses for their timely and generous support.

1. Tzvetan Todorov, *The Conquest of America: The Question of the Other* (New York: Harper & Row, 1982), 4.
2. Bernal Díaz del Castillo, *The Discovery and Conquest of Mexico* (New York: Farrar, Straus & Giroux, 1956), 191.
3. Miguel Leon-Portilla, *The Broken Spears* (Boston: Beacon Press, 1962), 138.
4. Paul Wheatley, *The Pivot of the Four Quarters: A Preliminary Enquiry into the Origins and Nature of the Ancient Chinese City* (Chicago: Aldine, 1971), especially chapter 3.
5. The "blood of kings" is the title of an outstanding book on Maya religion: Linda Schele and Mary Ellen Miller, *The Blood of Kings: Dynasty and Ritual in Maya Art* (Fort Worth, TX: Kimbell Art Museum, 1986).
6. Inga Clendinnen, *Ambivalent Conquests: Maya and Spaniard in Yucatan, 1517–1570* (Cambridge, MA: Cambridge University Press, 1988), iii.
7. J. H. Elliott, *The Old World and the New: 1492–1650* (Cambridge, MA: Cambridge University Press, 1970), 1.

8. *First Images of America: The Impact of the New World on the Old* (Berkeley: University of California Press, 1976), vol. 1, 14.

9. Leon-Portilla, *Broken Spears,* 51–52.

10. Lewis B. Hanke, *Aristotle and the American Indians: A Study in Race Prejudice in the Modern World* (Bloomington: University of Indiana Press, 1959), 38.

11. Diego Durán, *Book of the Gods and the Rites and the Ancient Calendar,* trans. and ed. Doris Heyden and Fernando Horcasitas (Norman: University of Oklahoma Press, 1970), 51.

12. Hanke, *Aristotle,* 47.

13. Quoted in Davíd Carrasco, "City as Symbol in Aztec Religion: Clues from the Codex Mendoza," *History of Religions Journal, 20,* No. 3 (February/1981): 200.

14. Miguel Leon-Portilla, *Native Mesoamerican Spirituality* (New York: Paulist Press, 1980), 201.

15. Durán, *Book of the Gods,* 70.

16. Bernardino de Sahagun, *The Florentine Codex: The General History of the Things of New Spain,* ed. Arthur J. O. Anderson and Charles Dibble, 12 vols (Sante Fe, NM: School of American Research and University of Utah, 1950–1969), vol. II, 103.

17. Díaz del Castillo, *Discovery and Conquest of Mexico,* 222.

18. Munro S. Edmonson, *The Book of Counsel: The Popol Vuh of the Quiché Maya of Guatemala* (New Orleans: Middle American Research Institute, Tulane University, 1971), 148.

19. Henry T. Wright, "Mesopotamia to Mesoamerica," *Archaeology* (January/February 1989).

20. Sahagun, *Florentine Codex,* Book II, 127.

21. Kent V. Flannery, "Contextual Analysis of Ritual Paraphernalia from Formative Oaxaca," in *The Early Mesoamerican Village,* ed. Kent V. Flannery (New York: Academic Press 1982), 333–45.

22. Durán, *Book of the Gods,* 314.

23. Schele and Miller, *The Blood of Kings,* 318.

24. Sahagun, *Florentine Codex,* Book VII, 4.

25. Ibid., Book III, 39.

26. Ibid., Book X, 166.

27. Ibid., 168.

28. Miguel Leon-Portilla, *Precolumbian Literatures of Mexico* (Norman: University of Oklahoma Press, 1969), 87.

29. Alfredo Lopez Austin, *The Human Body and Ideology: Concepts Among the Ancient Nahuas,* trans. Bernardo Ortiz de Montellano (Salt Lake City: University of Utah Press, 1988), 57.

30. Ibid., 65.

31. Sahagun, *Florentine Codex,* Book III, 15.

32. See Davíd Carrasco, *Quetzalcoatl and the Irony of Empire: Myths and Prophecies in the Aztec Tradition* (Chicago: University of Chicago Press, 1982). The authoritative work on the Toltec tradition is H. B. Nicholson, "Topiltzin Quetzalcoatl of Tollan: A Problem in Mesoamerican Ethnohistory," Ph.D. diss., Harvard University, 1957.

33. Durán, *The Book of the Gods,* 59.

34. *Anales de Cuauhtitlan,* quoted in Leon-Portilla, *Mesoamerican Spirituality,* 169.

35. Leyenda de los Soles, *Four Masterworks of American Indian Literature,* trans. John Bierhorst (New York: Farrar, Straus & Giroux, 1974), 21.

36. *Anales de Cuauhtitlan,* in ibid., 29.

37. Ibid.

38. Sahagun, *Florentine Codex,* Book X, 166.

39. Ibid.

40. *Anales de Cuauhtitlan,* quoted in Bierhorst, *Four Masterworks,* 62.

41. Sahagun, *Florentine Codex*, Book VI, 25.
42. Lopez Austin, *Human Body and Ideology*, 328.
43. Bernal Díaz del Castillo, *Discovery and Conquest of Mexico*, 436. See also the many works by Johanna Broda on sacred mountains.
44. All the quotes in this section about the birth of Huitzilopochtli come from Book III of Sahagun's *Florentine Codex*. I am using Leon-Portilla's more literary translation as found in *Mesoamerican Spirituality*, 220–25.
45. Sahagun, *Florentine Codex: Introduction and Indices*, 65.
46. Leon-Portilla, *Mesoamerican Spirituality*, 241–42.
47. Ibid., 243.
48. Ibid.
49. Sahagun, *Florentine Codex*, Book VI, 167.
50. Ibid., 113–18.
51. Leon-Portilla, *Mesoamerican Spirituality*, 63–64.
52. All the riddles in this section are from Book VI of Sahagun, *Florentine Codex*, 237–40.
53. Ibid., 219–35.
54. Ibid., Book VII, 26.
55. Ibid., Book II, 67.
56. Ibid., 71.
57. Ibid.
58. Dennis Tedlock, *Popul Vuh* (New York: Simon & Schuster, 1985), 163.
59. Schele and Miller, *The Blood of Kings*, 300.
60. John L. Stephens, *Incidents of Travel in Central America, Chiapas and Yucatan* (London: 1844), 82–83.
61. Dennis Tedlock, *Popul Vuh*, 73.
62. Ibid., 181.
63. Mircea Eliade, *Patterns in Comparative Religions* (New York: Meridian Books, 1963), 345.
64. Robert S. Carlsen and Martin Prechtel, "The Flowering of the Dead: Mayan Notions of Sacred Change," unpublished manuscript, 5.
65. In this section I have utilized the remarkable achievements in interpreting the Maya by Schele and Miller in *The Blood of Kings*.
66. Tedlock, *Popul Vuh*, 71.
67. Ibid., 72.
68. Ibid.
69. Ibid., 79.
70. Schele and Miller, *The Blood of Kings*, 181.
71. Michael Coe, *The Maya* (New York: Praeger, 1973), 58.
72. See a series of works by Anthony F. Aveni, especially *Skywatchers of Ancient Mexico* (Austin: University of Texas Press, 1980).
73. Tedlock, *Popul Vuh*, 134.
74. Ibid., 147.
75. Ibid., 152.
76. Ibid., 160.
77. Leon-Portilla, *Mesoamerican Spirituality*, 134.
78. William B. Taylor, "Between Global Process and Local Knowledge: An Inquiry into Early Latin American Social History, 1500–1900" in *Reliving the Past: The Worlds of Social History*, ed. Oliver Zunz (Chapel Hill: University of North Carolina Press, 1985), 116.
79. Carlos Fuentes, *Where the Air Is Clear* (New York: Farrar, Straus & Giroux, 1971), 5.
80. Elizabeth Wilder Weismann, *Mexico in Sculpture: 1521–1821* (Cambridge, MA: Harvard University Press, 1950), 5.
81. For a general discussion of religious syncretism see the article on Syncretism in the *Encyclopedia of Religion*, gen. ed. Mircea Eliade (New York: Macmillan, 1987), 218–26.

82. *The Ancient Future of the Itza: Book of Chilam Balam of Tizimin* (Austin: University of Texas Press, 1982), 45.
83. Quoted in Todorov, *The Conquest of America,* 138.
84. Ibid., 141.
85. Taylor, "Global Process," 117.
86. Ibid., 123.
87. Carol Karasik, ed., Robert M. Laughlin, collector and trans., *The People of the Bat: Mayan Tales and Dreams from Zinacantan* (Washington, D.C.: Smithsonian Institution Press, 1988), 137–38.
88. William B. Taylor, "The Virgin of Guadalupe in New Spain: An Inquiry Into the Social History of Marian Devotion," *American Ethnologist,* 14, No. 1 (February, 1987): 9–33.
89. Barbara Myerhoff, *Peyote Hunt: The Sacred Journey of the Huichol Indians* (Ithaca, NY: Cornell University Press, 1974), 33.
90. Ibid., 147.
91. Ibid., 153.
92. Quoted in Hugo Nutini, *Todos Santos in Rural Tlaxcala: A Syncretic, Expressive, and Symbolic Analysis of the Cult of the Dead* (Princeton, NJ: Princeton University Press, 1988), 56.
93. Ibid., 152.
94. Robert Carlsen, a Ph.D. student at the University of Colorado, personal interview.
95. Díaz del Castillo, *Discovery and Conquest of Mexico,* 192.

Glossary

altepetl A mountain filled with water; the Aztec term meaning a community or city.

autosacrifice The bleeding of one's own body (tongue, earlobes, thighs, genitals, and so on) as an offering to the gods, or as a means to induce a vision of a supernatural being or ancestor. Autosacrifice was often associated with legitimation of royalty.

axis mundi The center of the world of the community.

Bonampak Classic Maya ceremonial center discovered in 1946. It contained a number of monumental buildings, including one palace whose interior walls were covered with murals depicting courtly life, warfare, ceremonial processions, and ritual sacrifice associated with continuity of the royal lineage.

calendar round A fifty-two year period determined by the intermeshing of the 260-day ritual calendar and the 365-day solar calendar. All possible combinations of the two calendars are exhausted after 18,980 days, equaling fifty-two years.

cemanahuac Land surrounded by water; the Aztec term for the terrestrial level of the cosmos.

ceremonial center The ritual and spatial center of Mesoamerican homes, cities, and communities, where the cosmovision was expressed in decoration, sculpture, painting, and ritual performance. In urban societies the major ceremonial centers consisted of monumental buildings including pyramids, temples, stairways, stelae, ball courts, and palaces.

Chac-Xib-Chac The Maya god of war, sacrifice, and dancing.

Chichimecas From *chichi,* meaning "dog" and *mecatl,* meaning "rope" or "lineage"; a general term for the migrating tribes who settled in the Valley of Mexico (including Tenochtitlan and Tlatelolco) in the twelfth and thirteenth centuries.

Classic Maya The Maya culture of 200–900 C.E., which achieved extraordinarily complex mathematical, calendrical, astronomical, and architectural traditions organized in ceremonial cities in southern Mexico, Guatemala, Honduras, and other locations.

Coatepec Serpent Mountain; the mythical mountain where Coatlicue, Lady of the Serpent Skirt, gave birth to the Aztec patron god, Huitzilopochtli, Hummingbird on the Left. The Aztecs gave this name to their greatest shrine, the Templo Mayor of Tenochtitlan.

cosmovision A worldview that integrates the structure of space and the rhythms of time into a unified whole. See photographs of the Sun Stone (see p. 154) and the *Codex Fejérváry-Mayer* for examples.

Coyolxauhqui The female warrior who led the attack against Coatlicue in the Aztec mythic episode of Huitzilopochtli's birth.

Cuauhtemoc Diving Eagle; the last Aztec ruler who resisted the Spanish attack on Tlatelolco. A nephew of Moctezuma Xocoyotzin.

Dia de los Muertos Day of the Dead; yearly celebrations during the end of October and beginning of November that celebrate the reunion of the souls of the dead with living family members and friends.

ecological complex The context of urban centers consisting of the human population, agriculture, geography, technology, and social stratification.

Florentine Codex The twelve-volume encyclopedia of Aztec life describing the supernatural, human, and natural world of pre-Columbian central Mesoamerica. Compiled by Bernardino de Sahagun with the help of native informants.

hombre-dios Man-god; a Spanish term referring to the native idea of human beings imbued with special capacities to communicate with and contain the will of deities within their hearts.

huehuetlatolli The Ancient Word or Sayings of the Elders; elegant, florid, rhetorical orations representing the traditional teachings about ethics, aesthetics, symbolism, politics, and authority in the Aztec world.

Huitzilopochtli Patron deity of the Aztec capital. His royal shrine was at the Templo Mayor.

Hunahpu and Xbalanque The Hero Twins of the *Popul Vuh*. They successfully undergo the ordeals of Xibalba, the Maya underworld.

in xochitl, in cuicatl Flower and song; an Aztec term meaning poetry, the Truth on earth.

Lady Xoc Maya royal person (ritual partner of Yaxchilán's Shield Jaguar), who is depicted in sculpture carrying out autosacrifice and having a vision of an ancestral warrior.

las Casas, Bartolomé de The Bishop of Chiapas, who defended the natives of Mesoamerica in the debates of Valladolid, Spain, in 1550–1555.

La Venta An early (1500–800 B.C.E.) Olmec ceremonial center containing one of the earliest pyramids in Mesoamerica.

long count The Maya calendar system, which utilized the concept of zero to calculate the passage of time by marking five units of measurement, constructed in part to relate contemporary rulers to an ancient chain of ancestors.

Mah K'ina Great Sun Lord; the title of Maya rulers in the Classic Period.

mara'akame Huichol shaman who guides the pilgrims on the peyote hunt, knows the sacred traditions of the community, and heals.

Maya collapse Classic Maya civilization disintegrated rapidly between 790–900 C.E. Its causes are still only partially understood.

Mictlan Region of the Dead; the ninth level of the Aztec underworld, where the souls of people who died ordinary deaths resided.

millennial kingdom The Franciscan idea (derived from the Book of Revelation) that the thorough conversion of the Indians would result in the realization of heaven on earth.

Moctezuma The modern name given to the two Aztec rulers, Moteuczoma Ilhuicamina (1440–1454) and Moteuczoma Xocoyotzin (1503–1519).

Mountain of Sustenance A mythic mountain that was the source of abundance, rain, seeds, corn, food. This mountain was symbolized in the Tlaloc section of the Great Temple of Tenochtitlan.

Myth of the Suns The story of the Four Ages of the cosmos leading up to the Fifth Age of the Aztecs.

New Fire Ceremony The ceremony held once every fifty-two years to mark the passage of one major cycle into another. All fires were extinguished and a new fire representing a new time period was lit at a precise astronomical moment.

nextlaoaliztli The Aztec term for debt-payment, which often took the form of elaborate ceremonies lasting twenty days and culminating in human sacrifices.

Nezahualcoyotl Fasting Coyote; the Aztec Tlatoani or Chief Speaker of the cultural capital of Texcoco.

nim q'ij Santiag Big Sun Santiago; the Atiteco Maya name for the Feast of Santiago, in which the participants circumambulate the town block around the cathedral to renew the cosmos.

Olmec style The extraordinary artistic and political style of Olmec culture (1500 B.C.E.–300 B.C.E.) characterized by the reshaping of earth materials into a religious cosmovision. The Olmec emphasized jade and stone work depicting animal and animal/human combinations. The Olmec influence spread throughout many parts of Mesoamerica during the Formative Period.

Ometeotl Aztec God of Duality, who resided in the highest level of heaven from which he or she created the cosmos and continually creates life.

Pacal Seventh-century Maya ruler of Palenque, whose tomb depicts the descent of the ruler into the underworld.

Palenque A beautiful Maya ceremonial center (fourth–ninth centuries C.E.). It contains a series of temples known as the Group of the Cross, which depict the Maya cosmology in detail. The site of Pacal's tomb.

Pleiades A star cluster that the Aztecs called Tianquitzli (Marketplace). Its movements had influence on the spatial layout of cities and the ritual calendars of Mesoamerica.

Popul Vuh Book of Council of the Quiché Maya, discovered in Chichicastenango, Guatemala, in 1701. It contains a rich account of cosmovision and ritual actions of preconquest and postconquest Maya peoples.

primary urban generation The complex process of original urban formation in Mesoamerica, China, Mesopotamia, Egypt, Indus Valley, Nigeria, Peru.

Quetzalcoatl The Plumed Serpent or Precious Twin was a Toltec and Aztec god; one of the four sons of Ometeotl, who created the cosmos and ruled over periods of its history.

r'kux ruchiliev Umbilicus of the world located in the center of the Atiteco Maya cosmos.

Sahagun, Bernardino de The Franciscan priest whose research and writing (in Nahuatl and Spanish) on Nahuatl/Aztec culture resulted in *The Florentine Codex: The General History of the Things of New Spain.*

Sepulveda, Juan Ginés de Spanish philosopher who utilized Aristotle's vision of social relations to argue that the natives of Mesoamerica were slaves by nature.

special assemblages Groups of buildings misaligned in relation to other buildings but aligned to enable viewers to see important astronomical events along the horizon.

syncretism The complex process by which rituals, beliefs, and symbols from different religions are combined to create new meanings. Syncretism is most clearly represented in ritual performances that enable people to locate themselves within the new world of meaning.

Templo Mayor Great Temple; a number of Aztec communities had a Templo Mayor, but this term usually refers to the Great Aztec Temple of Tenochtitlan.

Tenochtitlan Place of the Prickly Pear Cactus; the capital city of the Aztec empire, founded around 1325 and conquered by the Spanish in 1521. Site of Mexico City.

Teotihuacan Place Where the Gods Were Born; the imperial capital of second to seventh century C.E. central Mesoamerica. Known today as the pyramids, it was populated by over 200,000 people. The Aztec considered it the place where the Fifth Sun was created.

teotl ixiptla Aztec term meaning "image of a god." These images were sometimes humans, usually destined for sacrifice in one of the major festivals of the Aztec calendar.

teyolia Aztec term for a spiritual force that resided in the human heart and provided the person with intelligence, fondness, and inclinations.

tlachco The Aztec ball court where the sacred ball game was played.

Tlaloc The rain god who brought moisture, fertility, and regeneration, and whose powers resided in mountains, caves, and the fertile earth. Tlaloc's major shrine was at the Templo Mayor of Tenochtitlan.

tlamatinime Knowers of things; these Aztec wisemen used language arts to seek and teach profound truths.

Tlatelolco The sister city of Tenochtitlan; it became the site of the imperial marketplace and a major ceremonial center.

Tollan Place of Reeds; this was the fabulous Toltec City (ninth–eleventh centuries C.E.).

tonalli Spiritual force sent by the Aztec god Ometeotl, the sun, and fire into the human body, giving it character, intelligence, and will. *Tonalli* was concentrated in the head of humans.

Topiltzin Quetzalcoatl Our Young Prince the Feathered Serpent; the priest-ruler of Tollan, whose career became a model for Aztec rulers, priests, and artists.

Toxcatl Dry Season; the Aztec festival dedicated to Tezcatlipoca, Lord of the Smoking Mirror, in which the *teotl ixiptla,* image of the god, paraded through the capital for one year prior to his sacrifice.

Tzutujil The Maya community residing in and around Santiago Atitlan in Guatemala.

Virgin of Guadalupe The patron saint of Mexico appeared to the Indian Juan Diego near the Aztec shrine of Tepeyac in 1531. She is the loving guardian, intermediary to God, and courageous warrior of the faithful.

Wirikuta The ancestral land of peyote for the Huichol peoples of Mexico. Each year pilgrimages under the guidance of *mara'akame* go to Wirikuta to renew, through peyote visions, their community.

Xibalba The Maya underworld; a place of ordeals and transformations where the Hero Twins overcame the Lords of the Dead. Xibalba is the place through which all people must travel in order to be regenerated.

Xiuhtecuhtli The Aztec Fire God who dwelled at the center of homes, ceremonial centers, communities, and the cosmos.

Xochiyaoyotl Wars of the Flowers; a series of scheduled battlefield confrontations between the Aztecs and enemy city-states. Their purpose was to reestablish political balance, train warriors, and supply sacrificial victims.

zempoalxochitl Marigolds cultivated for Day of the Dead celebrations in Mexico. They decorate altars and are laid out to mark a path, which the dead souls can smell and thus follow during their return to the human community.

Selected Reading List

Adams, Robert McC. *The Evolution of Urban Society.* Chicago: Aldine Press, 1967.

Aveni, Anthony F. *Skywatchers of Ancient Mexico.* Austin: University of Texas Press, 1980.

Bernal, Ignacio. *The Olmec World.* Berkeley: University of California Press, 1969.

Boone, Elizabeth Hill. *The Codex Magliabechiano.* 2 vols. Berkeley: University of California Press, 1983.

Broda, Johanna, Davíd Carrasco, and Eduardo Matos Moctezuma. *The Great Temple of Tenochtitlan.* Berkeley: University of California Press, 1987.

Brundage, Burr. *The Fifth Sun.* Austin: University of Texas Press, 1979.

Calnek, Edward. "The Internal Structure of Tenochtitlan." In *The Valley of Mexico,* edited by Eric Wolf. Albuquerque: University of New Mexico Press, 1976.

Carrasco, Davíd. *Quetzalcoatl and the Irony of Empire: Myths and Prophecies in the Aztec Tradition.* Chicago: University of Chicago Press, 1982.

————. *To Change Place: Aztec Ceremonial Landscapes.* Niwot: Univ. Press of Colorado, 1991.

Coe, Michael. *The Maya.* 3d. ed. New York: Thames and Hudson, 1984.

Culbert, T. Patrick, ed. *The Classic Maya Collapse.* Albuquerque: University of New Mexico Press, 1973.

Díaz del Castillo, Bernal. *The Discovery and Conquest of Mexico.* New York: Farrar, Straus & Giroux, 1956.

Durán, Diego. *Book of the Gods and the Rites and the Ancient Calendar.* Translated and edited by Fernando Horcasitas and Doris Heyden. Norman: University of Oklahoma Press, 1970.

Edmonson, Munro S. *The Ancient Future of the Itza.* Austin: University of Texas Press, 1982.

Elliott, J. H. *The Old World and the New: 1492–1650.* Cambridge, MA: Cambridge University Press, 1970.

Gossen, Gary H. *Chamulas in the World of the Sun.* Cambridge, MA: Harvard University Press, 1974.

Hanke, Lewis. *Aristotle and the American Indians: A Study in Race Prejudice in the Modern World.* Bloomington: Indiana University Press, 1959.

Heyden, Doris. "An Interpretation of the Cave Underneath the Pyramid of the Sun in Teotihuacan, Mexico." *American Antiquity* 40(2) (1975): 131–47.

Katz, Friedrich. *Ancient American Civilizations.* New York: Praeger, 1972.

Keen, Benjamin. *The Aztec Image in Western Thought.* New Brunswick, NJ: Rutgers University Press, 1971.

Klein, Cecelia. "Who was Tlaloc?" *Journal of Latin American Lore* 6(2) (1980): 155–204.

Landa, Diego de. *Relacion de las Cosas de Yucatan.* Edited by Alfred Tozzer. Cambridge, MA: Harvard University Press, 1941.

Leon-Portilla, Miguel. *Aztec Thought and Culture.* Norman: University of Oklahoma Press, 1963.

————. *Native Mesoamerican Spirituality.* New York: Paulist Press, 1980.

Lopez Austin, Alfredo. *Hombre-Dios: Religion y Politica en el Mundo Nahuatl.* Mexico: Universidad Nacional Autonoma de Mexico, 1973.

————. *The Human Body and Ideology.* Translated by Bernardo Ortiz de Montellano. Salt Lake City: University of Utah Press, 1988.

Matos Moctezuma, Eduardo. *El Templo Mayor: Excavaciones y Estudios.* Mexico: Instituto Nacional de Antropología y Historia, 1982.

Millon, Rene. *Urbanization at Teotihuacan, Mexico: The Teotihuacan Map.* Austin: University of Texas Press, 1973.

Nicholson, H. B. "Religion in Pre-Hispanic Central Mexico." In *Handbook of Middle American Indians* 10:395–445. Austin: University of Texas Press, 1964–1976.

Pasztory, Esther. *Aztec Art.* New York: Henry N. Abrams, 1983.

Paz, Octavio. *The Other Mexico.* New York: Grove Press, 1972.

Sahagun, Fray Bernardino de. *The Florentine Codex: The General History of the Things of New Spain.* Edited by Arthur J. O. Anderson and Charles Dibble. 12 vols. Sante Fe, NM: School of American Research and University of Utah, 1950–1969.

Schele, Linda and Mary Ellen Miller. *The Blood of Kings: Dynasty and Ritual in Maya Art.* Fort Worth, TX: Kimbell Art Museum, 1986.

Stuart, George E. and Gene S. Stuart. *The Mysterious Maya.* Washington, D.C.: National Geographic Society, 1977.

Tedlock, Dennis. *Popul Vuh.* New York: Simon & Schuster, 1985.

Townsend, Richard. *State and Cosmos in the Art of Tenochtitlan.* Studies in Pre-Columbian Art and Archaeology 20. Washington, D.C.: Dumbarton Oaks, Trustees for Harvard University, 1979.

van der Loo, Peter. *Codices, Costumbres, Continuidad.* Leiden: Archeoligish Centrum R. V. Leiden, 1987.

Weismann, Elizabeth Wilder. *Mexico in Sculpture: 1521–1821.* Cambridge, MA: Harvard University Press, 1950.

Wheatley, Paul. *The Pivot of the Four Quarters: A Preliminary Enquiry into the Origins and Nature of the Ancient Chinese City.* Chicago: Aldine, 1971.

PART THREE

Native Religions of North America

The Power of Visions and Fertility

Åke Hultkrantz

Chronology of Native American Culture and Religions

With Particular References to Shoshoni and Zuni History

Chronology	Major Cultural and Religious Features
	FIRST INHABITANTS
60,000 to 30,000 years ago	Arrival of groups of peoples from northeast Asia, carriers of a circumpolar and circumboreal hunting culture; religion: animal ceremonialism, masters of the animals, shamanism
4000 B.C.E. to birth of Christ	Last immigrants of prehistoric times: the Athapascan Indians; religion: hunting religion, girls' puberty rites
	PREHISTORIC DEVELOPMENTS
8000 to 5000 B.C.E.	Immigrants reach Tierra del Fuego; in North America increase in population density and differentiation into two great cultural traditions: the Archaic hunting tradition east of the Rockies and the "Desert" (or "Desert Archaic" or "Western Archaic") culture in the greater Southwest (including California, the Plateau, and northwestern Mexico); the latter was adapted to the harvesting of acorns, piñon nuts, grass seeds, roots, and berries; religion: rituals around the gathering of plant foods, an attenuated shamanism (this is partly the basis of Shoshoni religion)
5000 B.C.E.	Introduction of agriculture in Central America, followed by settlement in villages, the construction of ritual centers and burial mounds, and social and ceremonial differentiation; religion: plant spirits, ceremonial calendar, incipient cult of the dead, sacred rulers
1500 B.C.E. to 1000 C.E.	Formative period of Mexican civilizations; growth of city culture, with temples and plazas, sacred kings and powerful gods; these cultures have had an impact on those of North America

Chronology	Major Cultural and Religious Features
1000 B.C.E.	Eastern Woodlands cultures, influenced from Mexico, with houses on mounds formed like birds, and burials in mounds; presence of Mother Earth statuettes
300 B.C.E. to 700 C.E.	Hopewell culture in the Ohio area and its surroundings, characterized by burial mounds, ceremonial centers, and cosmological symbolism, but very little agriculture
1 to 500 C.E.	Beginning of maize farming settlements in the Southwest and ceremonial constructions inspired from Mexico; original habitations in the eastern part of the area were pit houses, which later became the Pueblo ceremonial chambers
700 to 800	Possible origin of the Zuni pueblo in the Southwestern Basketmaker period; Mississippian culture period, stimulated from Mexico, with maize agriculture, platform mounds and sacred kings, and rich ceremonial symbolism; fertility religion and elaborate ceremonies (called the "Southern cult," or "Southeastern Ceremonial complex") radiated out over the Eastern Woodlands cultures
1000 to 1200	Building of Zuni pueblo houses
1000 to 1400	Mississippian culture invades the eastern plains, or prairies, introducing horticulture and cosmological symbolism and ceremonialism; part of this complex later sifted into the tribes of the western high plains, which were not semi-sedentary, however, but nomadic
1100 to 1200	Founding of the Hopi pueblo of Oraibi
	HISTORICAL TIMES
1540 to 1541	Arrival in Zuni ("Cibola") of Spanish expedition under Francisco Vasquez Coronado, who then continued to the southern Plains
1598	Beginning of Franciscan missionary activities in Zuni
1629	First mission established in Zuni
1680 to 1692	The Pueblo rebellion against the Spaniards; thereafter concentration of the Zuni population to one pueblo and the desertion of five others; rearrangement of Zuni ritual organization
1699	The main church in Zuni is erected

Chronology	*Major Cultural and Religious Features*
1700 to 1800	Invasion of northern and eastern tribes into the Plains area as a consequence of white population pressure; the Sun Dance complex is diffused to most Plains tribes from intruding groups
1775 to 1825	Restructuring of Shoshoni religion in Wyoming: general vision quest, Sun Dance, High God concept activated
1868	Creation of the Wind River Reservation for Plains Shoshoni and Sheepeaters
1877	Creation of Zuni Reservation
1883	Episcopal mission opened at Wind River
1890	Introduction of Christian symbolism into the Sun Dance at Wind River; Ghost Dance
1919	Introduction of the peyote religion on the Wind River Reservation

Prologue

NORTH AMERICAN ABORIGINAL RELIGIONS represent a vast subject, and no introductory work can do justice to their immense richness and variety. This work should be considered a brief introduction to the study of these religions. It attempts to provide an orientation to the American Indian religious world and at the same time an insight into the structure and functioning of living tribal religions.

To this end the treatment has been divided into two main parts. The first part, designed to cover the most essential features and the basic scope of Native American religions, presents a general overview of the most important phenomena and historical developments (where these may be traced). The second part sketches two separate religions that illustrate the two main branches of religious expression among the Native peoples: the religions of the hunters and the religions of the agriculturists. Like most other religions outside the range of more complex Eurasiatic religions, North American indigenous religions are, in their organizational structure and choice of religious imagery, dependent on the nature around them and on their ecological use of this nature. This is why the division into "hunting religion" and "agricultural religion" is so important.

There are of course many variations in these two main types of religions in North America, and the two I have selected certainly do not exhaust the possibilities in matters of religious expression and religious organization. Still, they are representative of the tendencies in the two structural religious patterns. The agricultural Zuni of New Mexico were selected because of their tendency toward organization, a tendency that has made their religion the most complex in aboriginal North America. The Wind River Shoshoni, hunting Indians on the western high plains, are the Indians among whom I conducted fieldwork during a number of years (particularly 1948–1958). Their religion is presented in some detail here for the first time. Both religions manifest the historical depth of their traditions, and the faithfulness of the people, particularly the Zuni, to these traditions is evident in these pages. At the same time there is a continuous innovative process going on, particularly among the Shoshoni, that re-creates religion in new patterns. During recent decades **Pan-Indianism** and secularization have changed many old religious forms.

It is my hope that this work will illuminate both the traditional religions and the major changes they have undergone. I also trust that it will open the richness and beauty of American Indian religion to a larger public.

10

Introduction to Native American Religions

The Diversity and Richness of American Indian Religions

THE RELIGIOUS LIFE of Native Americans is a rich panorama featuring many diverse beliefs, ceremonies, and ways of life, but little of this rich tradition is reflected in the popular notions about these peoples. Probably the most familiar image of the "American Indian" is the Plains Indian, whose life centered around the hunt; in this popular image we see Plains Indians of recent centuries riding horses to hunt buffalo (bison). However, this presents an incomplete picture of American Indians—it overlooks the farming heritage of Native Americans and does not even scratch the surface of their ancient hunting culture and related religious beliefs and practices. [See Religions of Mesoamerica pp. 119–26 and Religions of Africa pp. 21–22 for discussion of Western stereotypes.]

These Native Americans of the Plains shared not only a hunting culture but also a common religious heritage, especially a midsummer **Sun Dance*** that emphasized the bravery, courage, and individual initiative so highly prized by these hunting people. Although the horse is a rather recent newcomer to the Americas (having been introduced by the Spaniards in the sixteenth century), a hunting life and the religious rituals associated with hunting were important for all Native American cultures, even the sophisticated Maya, Aztecs, and Incas in Central and South America.

These hunting rituals can tell us something about the religious life not only of Native Americans, but also of the so-called world religions. In fact, many of the spiritual ideas and ritual expressions of contemporary religions—even Christianity—have their origins in hunting religions of the same type as those found in North and South America. One reason those of us who are not Native Americans study their religious beliefs and customs is to recover a religious heritage that we all, as descendants of hunters in ages past, share.

---

*Terms defined in the glossary, pp. 369–71, are printed in boldface type where they first appear in the text.

Native American Tribes of North America.

Another more important reason for studying American Indian religions is their intrinsic interest. Just as Native American cultures exhibit a colorful series of tribal or "national" lifestyles (not limited to the pattern of horse-riding hunters on the Plains), so too the religions of these cultures provide a rich and varied tapestry of approaches to the supernatural. Indigenous American religions are as dramatic and exciting as the art forms through which they are expressed. These traditions possess a treasure trove of myths and tales of all varieties, some humorous and even obscene, others beautiful and highly spiritual. These traditions also contain beliefs and ideas about the world that achieve high levels of sophistication, as in the notions about the beginning of the world, the concepts of a lofty Supreme Being, and the elaboration of cosmic harmony. In ritual, too, the Native American traditions present a rich and varied heritage of dramatic beauty and spiritual force, primarily expressed in dancing and repetitive movements, prayers, and songs.

Some people, and even some scholars, have viewed Native American religions as examples of what has been called "primitive religion." If by "primitive" is meant crude cultural manifestations devoid of deeper feelings and subtle thoughts, American Indian religions are far from primitive. Some scholars of religion who specialize in the study of world religions but are not familiar with the rich symbolism and profound speculative thought in Native American religions have neglected them in their consideration of comparative religion. This is an unfortunate mistake, based on a lack of concrete knowledge of American Indians and a misconception about their "primitive" character. It is unfortunate because it overlooks a treasury of myths and tales, speculative thought, and ritual activity. Indeed, questions about the creation of the world, the origin of human life, the nature of the divine or supernatural, and the afterlife—all topics discussed in the "advanced" world religions—have also been posed by the indigenous religions of North and South America. Such questions are found among all peoples and occur in all cultures, even though the "answers" to these questions are distinctively different in each tradition. By studying the Native American answers we not only will learn about their traditions but also will become more sensitive to the answers of our own traditions. [See Religions of Africa p. 23 for discussion of "primitive religions"; see Religions of Mesoamerica pp. 122–25 for a treatment of "the noble savage/wild man."]

It is difficult to generalize about Native American cultures and religions because in the Americas there is a multitude of tribes and other social units. The diversity of these traditions cannot be reduced to a single tradition, for there is no simple entity such as *the* Native American religion." A number of tribes may be grouped together because they participate in a similar cultural life, such as the buffalo hunting tribes on the Plains or the fishing and manioc cultivating tribes in the Amazonian lowlands. These tribes that share a similar cultural life also tend to share a similar religious life. Nevertheless, each tribe has its own practices and customs, and we must remember that there are as many Native American religions as there are tribes.

No single work can present a satisfactory survey of all these religions. The purpose of this brief work is to first provide some general information on all Native American religions and then focus more closely on two examples of Native American religions in North America. This chapter takes up the thorny question of the origin and development of Native American religions—considering the manner in which these traditions were formed and how this helps us understand the rather flexible character of these traditions. Chapter 11 discusses some general features of all Native American religions. Chapters 12 and 13 provide case studies of two contrasting examples of Native American traditions:

the Wind River Shoshoni of the Utah and Wyoming area and the Zuni of the American Southwest. Each tradition will be presented and discussed through its historical development, its structure as a religious tradition, and examples of its religious dynamics. [See Religions of Africa pp. 23–24, Religions of Mesoamerica pp. 117–19, 263–64, Judaism pp. 389, 426, Christianity pp. 492–94, Islam pp. 607–8, Hinduism pp. 719–21, Buddhism pp. 853–55, Religions of China pp. 990–1015, and Religions of Japan pp. 1090–92 for discussion of the diversity and variety of religious traditions.]

Ethnic and Religious Origins

Native Americans did not keep written records of their history, and the written records by Europeans cover only the time since the arrival of Columbus in 1492. Of course Native Americans preserve an oral tradition of their beliefs and customs, but this does not include a close sequence of historical events. And the history recorded by whites has been distorted and fragmentary. For all these reasons it is not possible to reconstruct the history of Zuni or Shoshoni culture over a long span of time such as can be done, for example, with ancient Greece and Rome. The earliest documents on the Zuni date from 1540, and the Zuni themselves have been hesitant about providing information to outsiders. For the Shoshoni, detailed information was lacking until the beginning of the nineteenth century.

A similar lack of historical information holds for the rest of native North America. In spite of the collection and publication of much ethnographic information during the past century, we still do not know the full story of the historical development of American Indian religions. However, the general knowledge we have of the historical and cultural background of North American Indian religions can be summarized briefly as a means of throwing light on the contrast between Shoshoni and Zuni.

The origins of Native Americans are found in the migration of groups of northeast Asiatic peoples into Alaska and Canada from about sixty thousand to thirty thousand years ago. In that period of extended glaciation the sea level was much lower than at present, and east Siberia and Alaska formed a continuous landmass. The new arrivals could follow ice-free valleys, such as the Mackenzie Valley, down into regions with a milder climate and high plains where big game was plentiful. The immigrants penetrated deeper and deeper into the American continent, and at least by about 8000 B.C.E. they had moved from the northern extreme of North America to the southernmost tip of South America, the stormy sounds of Tierra del Fuego.

Who were these early invaders, the ancestors of the American Indian tribes? In all likelihood they were an offshoot of a proto-Mongoloid population in the northeastern part of Asia. Their exact ties with later linguistic stocks and archaeological remains in Asia have not been discovered so far, but their cultural heritage in North America seems to indicate that they were part of the rather uniform **circumpolar** and **circumboreal** culture that stretched from Scandinavia across northern Russia to Siberia. It is not surprising that the religious features of the historically related peoples in this broad culture are almost identical. Thus, hunting **taboos, animal ceremonialism,** beliefs in spirits, and **shamanism** have been common to such geographically distant peoples as the Saamis (Lapps) of northern Europe and the Samoyeds of northern Asia as well as the Algonkian Indians of eastern Canada. Even myths and mythical motifs have their counterparts in Old World and New World circumpolar religions. Seen in an evolutionary context, the circumpolar stratum clearly contains the beginnings of religion in aboriginal North America.[1]

The immigration of these groups to America took place over several thousand years. The last to arrive from northeast Asia were probably the Athapascan Indians who now occupy western Canada and Alaska, but who also may have filtered down into the Southwest where their late descendants are the Apache and Navajo. The Athapascans are probably related to the Sino-Tibetan linguistic stock and may have carried with them religious ideas and rituals predating Chinese sacred kingship and Tibetan lamaism. Their original ideology was a religion of the hunters, modified by matrilinear customs such as girls' puberty rites.

The general picture of the northern Asian origins of Native Americans is clouded by the lack of precise knowledge of exactly when and how particular groups moved to certain areas and how they came to share certain cultural features while developing other distinctive ones. For example, one feature that appears to have remained relatively consistent throughout much of the Americas is the original hunting religion brought with the first immigrants to North America. However, there remain many intriguing and unanswered questions about the origins of various cultures and their relationships to other cultures. One interesting case is the speculation concerning the origins of the **totem poles** of the Northwest Coast Indians, which have been compared to ceremonial poles found in the cultures of the South Pacific as well as among the Maori of New Zealand. Some scholars have argued that the similarity among these cultural objects points to a common Pacific origin, but most American anthropologists reject these arguments. It is just as likely that totem poles (or myths showing similarity to Polynesian mythology) developed in North America independent of an origin or influence from the Pacific area.

The discussion of a trans-Pacific source of some religious traits becomes more relevant when we consider the origins of agricultural religious ideology, because of the more obvious parallels between the agricultural rituals of the Old World and those of the New World. In contrast to the preservation of the hunting life in the northern and southern extremities of the two Americas (doubtless for climatic reasons), from about 5000 B.C.E. the temperate and tropical areas of the Americas developed maize and manioc horticulture. Anthropologists are in general agreement about the indigenous origins and development of agriculture in America, but the picture is complicated by the fact that the American religious ideas and rituals related to agriculture are very similar to those in the Old World. Indeed, the same tales about agricultural spirits appear in both hemispheres. One example is the American story of the **Corn Maiden,** whose departure from the human world causes the disappearance of vegetable food but whose return to this world after a long absence results in abundant crops. This is a remarkable parallel to the myth of the flight and return of the fertility goddess in Europe and the Middle East. However, it is possible to argue that this tale simply depicts the passing of the seasons of the agricultural year and could have originated independently in both hemispheres. But whatever the ultimate origin or origins of Native American agriculture, a religious pattern associated with horticulture spread over northern South America and southern North America. [See Religions of Mesoamerica pp. 136–38 for a discussion of the migration of peoples into North America and Central America.]

The end result of the long history of migration of peoples and development of cultures in both of the American continents is the existence of two contrasting religious orientations: the old hunting religions and the new horticultural religions. In general these two patterns can be characterized by two sets of features:

HUNTING PATTERN	HORTICULTURAL PATTERN
Animal ceremonialism	Rain and fertility ceremonies
Quest for spiritual power	Priestly ritual
Male Supreme Being	Goddesses and gods
Annual ceremony of cosmic rejuvenation	Yearly round of fertility rites
Few stationary cult places	Permanent shrines and temples
Shamanism	**Medicine society** ritualism
Life after death beyond the horizon or in the sky	Life after death in the underworld or among the clouds

Of course each of these two patterns is only an ideal model. Every Native American tribe has its own emphasis on one pattern or the other or in many cases a distinctive blending of the two patterns. Our sketch of Shoshoni religion and Zuni religion will illustrate two "typical" cases of these two kinds of religious orientations.

The Formation of Religious Traditions

Native American religious traditions took shape in a manner somewhat different from world religions such as Christianity and Islam. Of course, all religious traditions are based in part on the previous religious heritage. For example, the formation of Christianity is not comprehensible without knowledge of Judaism, the Old Testament, Gnosticism, and Hellenism; similarly, Islam is not comprehensible without knowledge of pre-Islamic customs, Judaism, Syrian Christianity, and Manichaeism. Even though religions such as Christianity and Islam are established by founders—Jesus and Muḥammad—as distinctively "new" religions, they still preserve elements of the preexisting religious situation. All religions tend to be conservative, because their sacred authority lies in the sanctity of the past: a myth records the sacred origin of a ritual, a legend explains the acquisition of a sacred object, a tradition preserves the account of a god's message to humans. At the same time, most religions remain open to the personal experiences of the spiritual world. The balance between faithfulness to tradition and openness to new experience is what constitutes the religious life. [See Religions of Africa pp. 29, 55–57, Religions of Mesoamerica pp. 152, 163–68, Christianity pp. 495–97, 531–32, 534–35, Islam pp. 622–28, 698–99, Hinduism pp. 769, 770–72, Buddhism pp. 860, 861–68, 892–99, Religions of China pp. 993–95, and Religions of Japan pp. 1090, 1100, 1122–23 for discussion of religious founders.]

A major difference between the formation of world religions such as Christianity and Islam, on the one hand, and Native American traditions, on the other, is that these world religions were established by particular founders and preserved as literary traditions, whereas Native American religions were handed down by tribes as oral traditions. [See Judaism pp. 386–87, Christianity pp. 538–42, and Islam pp. 612–13, 639–40 for discussion of creed; see Religions of China pp. 1017–1018 for comparison with Native American religions.]

In general, the weight of the past—the emphasis on preserving the "letter" of the written record, such as Christianity's conformity to the Bible and Islam's conformity to the Qur'ān (Koran)—is much heavier within written traditions than within oral traditions. Of course, oral traditions can and indeed have been passed down through many generations for long periods of time, among Native Americans as well as many other peoples. In native North America, oral traditions were the only means of transmitting beliefs and practices until the beginning of the nineteenth century, when the Cherokee tribe developed an alphabet and wrote down some of their heritage. Toward the end of the last century Indians increasingly entered missionary schools and came to read and write English, but still they tended to maintain their sacred traditions through oral transmission. [See Religions of Mesoamerica p. 179, Judaism pp. 390–94, Christianity pp. 497, 499, Islam pp. 635–37, 648–53, 652–72, Hinduism pp. 728–29, 733–43, 750–53, Buddhism p. 861, Religions of China pp. 995–96, 999–1000, 1031, and Religions of Japan pp. 1100–1101 for discussion of Bible, scriptures, and religious texts.]

This major dependence on oral traditions has meant that native Indian religions have not been so dogmatically bound by what was handed down from the past. Over the whole continent, with the exception of parts of the Southwest, it was common for a person to enter into direct contact with the supernatural powers and receive their directions and personal protection. New cults and new ritual songs were introduced by the supernatural beings in visions and dreams. Native religion was thus quite charismatic and innovative, modifying and even replacing older traditions with new revelations. Probably no other cultures have given visions such importance in daily religious life as those of native North America.

Native American religions are formed through the interaction of preserving the prior tradition and at the same time accepting new visions. Old traditions, such as the Sun Dance of the Plains Indians, have been changed through visions, and visions have given rise to new traditions, as seen in the origin legends of the **medicine bundles** in eastern North America. While it is true that the New World preserves many old mythical accounts that connect it with Eurasia, such as the myths of the Flood and the **Mythic Twins** (described below), the visionary reformulations of some of these myths have often made them very different from their Old World counterparts. The origin of some rituals and practices is found in mythical accounts; other rituals and practices are authoritative because they were revealed in the visionary experiences of heroes in ages past—often experiences during situations of social and economic difficulty.

This explains the manifold and complex character of many American Indian traditions. On the Plains and in the Midwest not only tribes and clans but also families have their special oral traditions. For instance, among the Winnebago each clan has its own myth of the origin of the world, and each of these myths deviates from the others. In the same fashion, among Southwest Indians different clans of the same **pueblo** may perform the same ritual, but with significant variations. It seems that the authority for a myth or ritual does not rest in a fixed tradition as such but in the revelation of supernatural beings who are the ultimate source of all religious traditions.

Although there is considerable variation to mythical accounts and ritual practices, some have persisted as important patterns in Native American religious history. Among customs preserved from remote hunting times we find the **bear ceremonialism,** a continuous tradition of beliefs, myths, and rituals centered on the bear and practiced by a whole range of cultures from the Saamis (Lapps) of northern Europe to the Lenape (Delawares) along the Atlantic coast of North America. Bear ceremonialism involves the ritual appeasement and ceremonial disposal of a slain bear so that other bears will feel honored to be caught and killed. The ritual may be performed for other game animals as well (and was probably originally meant for all game animals killed). This animal ceremonialism is perhaps the most characteristic complex of hunting religion practiced in both America and the Old World. It is part of circumpolar culture and seems to go back to Paleolithic times in the Old World. In North America the best example of this complex is found among the Algonkian Indians of eastern Canada and the United States, who are known as the greatest preservers of old circumboreal religion. However, there are traces of animal ceremonialism throughout the religions of North America, including those in California and the Southwest. Remains of the old bear ceremonialism may be found even in the Pueblo Southwest.[2]

Another pattern of myths and beliefs at least partially deriving from Old World accounts is the Mythic Twins, or Dual Creators. This theme appears in two forms: the incipient dualism (or tension) between the Supreme Being and the **culture hero** or **trickster** and the dualism between two world-ordering culture heroes.

The former theme of dualism is discernible in most parts of North America and implies a rivalry in mythical times between a divine figure (usually identified with the Supreme Being who is prominent in prayer and ritual) and the culture hero who only appears in mythology (and does not play a role in ritual). In essence the two represent similar functions, and in some places, for instance California, the culture hero (usually **Coyote**) is at the same time conceived as a Supreme Being. In the majority of tribes, however, there is a clear distinction between the two personages associated with their abilities as creators: The main creator stands for the beneficial and complete creations and the culture hero takes care of lesser tasks (such as the founding of cultural and religious institutions) or makes less beneficial or ambiguous contributions to creation (such as the introduction of death). The culture hero's failures turn him into a comic figure, a trickster. Egotistical and obscene, this character has given rise to the largest and most important part of American Indian mythology, the trickster cycle.[3] The culture hero and trickster came to be seen as having an evil disposition when the opposition between the two divine figures was overlaid with the more pronounced dualism between the Dual Creators, an Asiatic theme that was spread through North America (along with the Earthdiver Myth). However, the evilness belongs only to the mythological figure and has not turned American religions into dualistic ethic traditions. [See Religions of Africa p. 68 for discussion of the trickster.]

In its second form the Mythic Twins theme is connected with the twin culture heroes, one a positive transformer of the landscape and founder of institutions, the other one a destructive and unfriendly being. We find this cycle of tales primarily represented in certain horticultural milieus such as among the Pueblos of the Southwest and the Iroquois of the Northeast. Secondarily this theme has also spread to such neighboring nonfarming peoples as the Navajo. A separate widespread myth, the Star Husband Tale, makes the divine twins the children of a heavenly god and the goddess of vegetation.

Another prominent pattern of Native American religion, found among horticultural peoples in the South, is the mythical account in which the cosmic beginning was not focused on the creation of the world but on the emergence of the first human beings from the interior of the earth. There is mention of four or five worlds, one on top of the other, through which the first humans climbed, with the aid of a vine or a tree (probably the **World Tree**). Each of the worlds had its own color but was generally dark. The last world into which the first humans arrived is the present world, and the hole through which they emerged is the navel of the world. As we shall see later, it is symbolized in the sacred *sipapu* hollow of the Pueblo cult chamber. This is the **Emergence Myth**, diffused over the southern and horticultural Indian areas of the United States. It is easy to see that the appearance of humans on earth is here paralleled with the rise of the plants from the earth's interior. [See Religions of Mesoamerica pp. 195–98 for discussion of the cosmic tree; see Hinduism pp. 740–41, 747–48 for treatment of the cult of the divine plant *soma.*]

These three widespread patterns—animal ceremonialism, the Mythic Twins (or Dual Creators), and the Emergence Myth—help illustrate the nature of religion among Native Americans. These patterns are directly related to religious patterns of northern Europe and Asia and came to be disseminated over most of the American continent. However, unlike the founded traditions of Christianity and Islam, Native American religions were not linked directly to particular founders and restricted by bodies of doctrine until the rise of Indian religious movements inspired by Christianity, especially in the nineteenth century. Native American religions developed very freely, bound only by the limits of the natural setting, social structure, and general cultural patterns.

11

Native American Religions: An Overview

THERE ARE SO MANY NATIVE AMERICAN RELIGIONS and their expressions are so varied that it is difficult to generalize upon all Native American religions. As we shall see in chapters 12 and 13, the religious life of the Shoshoni and that of the Zuni Indians show amazing diversity between two North American tribal groups and even a large amount of variation within each group. Nevertheless, if we keep in mind the distinctive religious differences of individual tribes, some general features are found among most groups. For example, we have already seen that there are two basic patterns—a hunting culture and a farming culture—throughout the Americas, with each tribe emphasizing one or the other pattern or a blending of the two patterns. Some other general features can be isolated in the religions of North American Indians, with greater or lesser emphasis depending on the particular group.

Four prominent features in North American Indian religions are a similar worldview, a shared notion of cosmic harmony, emphasis on directly experiencing powers and visions, and a common view of the cycle of life and death. These features will be treated separately, but it is useful to provide an initial identification of each. Worldview is the total understanding of life and the universe held by a particular people or culture. North American Indians have worldviews that in many respects are remarkably similar, particularly in the way they perceive the interrelationship of humans and animals. Many North American Indians also share a notion of cosmic harmony, in which humans, animals, plants, all of nature, and even supernatural figures cooperate to bring about a balanced and harmonious universe. North American Indian traditions emphasize a direct experience of spiritual power through dreams and visions; as we have already seen, the sacredness and prestige of these striking revelations often result in the modification or replacement of previous traditional elements. Native Americans have a common view of time as a recurring cycle; they are interested mainly in how this cycle affects people in this life and have only a vague notion of another existence after death.

Worldview

If we want to grasp the essential character of North American Indian religions it is natural to start with their worldview. Worldview is a concept that may be interpreted in different ways. The American anthropologist Robert Redfield defines worldview as "the way a people characteristically look outward upon the universe,"[4] and it may be convenient to apply that definition here. In our context worldview then stands for a people's concept of existence and their view of the universe and its powers.

Most North American Indians consider that human existence was designed by the creator divinities at the time of the "first beginning." Mythological tales report that in those days all beings on earth were more or less human, but a change took place that turned many primeval beings into animals and birds. Only those who today are human beings retained their forms. Because of this genesis there is still today a close affinity between people and animals: They are brothers, and it is people's task to respect and be in harmony with the animals. It is interesting that domesticated animals such as dogs have not been included in this brotherhood, whereas domesticated horses have. Indeed, on the Plains there is even a cult of the horse. It is difficult to tell whether the fact that the horse is of foreign, European origin has contributed to its lofty position. In the main, however, it is the wild, independent animals to which Native Americans' religious attention has been paid. All over the Americas they have been thought to manifest the mysterious qualities of existence.

One consequence of the close kinship between humans and animals has been the tendency for Native Americans to imitate the animals in dress, actions, and projective thought. The feather-lined shirts, the feather ornaments for dancing, and the feather plumes in the hair of the American Indians are all measures to instill the capacities of birds (spirit birds) in the human being. Some feather arrangements in the hair seem to have obtained a secondary meaning—marking the number of enemies killed, success in scalping an enemy, or other deeds. The Mandan and their neighbors near the Upper Missouri developed the large war bonnets with a row of feathers in a headband, trailing down the back; these were more a symbol of dignity and intrepidity than of spiritual assistance—although the latter possibility cannot be excluded. These war bonnets were later adopted by other Indians. The feather decorations of American Indians remind us of those of the Siberian **shaman,** which is a further testimony of the spiritual background of the "feather complex." Apparently feathers manifest spiritual essence, particularly of beings on high.

The bond between animals and humans is also expressed in ritual activities. Plains Indian dances in which the men imitate the movements of buffaloes or wear their horns and skins are supposed to bring forth this valuable game. They are not, as earlier research took for granted, magic rituals to multiply the animals. They are rather acts of supplication in which Indians, by imitating the wild, express their desires and expectations. Such a ritual tells us of the Indian's veneration for the active powers of the universe: It is a prayer.

The final consequence of Native Americans' close affinity to the animals is **animalism,** that is, the concept of spirits as animals. This is a characteristic feature in North American Indian religions. Of course, wherever hunting cultures are to be found, supernatural beings come dressed in animal attire. In North America, however, the vision complex, of which more will be said shortly, has strengthened and perpetuated the belief in animal spirits.

Here we may well ask whether we should speak about "animal spirits" or "spirit animals." The former term may indicate either the notion of spirits in animal form or the concept of the spirits—or souls—of animals. The latter term suggests that some animals may not be real animals, but spirits. In North American traditions both designations seem to apply, because the boundary between animals and spirits here is very vague. Therefore, both terms will be used in the following.

Indians think that animals are by nature mysterious, as their behavior is both similar to and different from that of humans. Such a tension between known and understood, and unknown and not understood, usually creates a sentiment of something uncanny, something not quite belonging to normal reality. The Ojibway of the Great Lakes think that, although most stones are not alive, some are. They can be seen rolling of their own accord, and a **medicine man** or a **medicine woman** can talk to them and receive their answers. Apparently, stones are divided according to their possession of or lack of mysterious qualities. A similar rule holds for animals. All bears are mysterious in their various ways, but some bears are more mysterious than others, being able to talk or change forms (as experienced in dreams and visions). The former bears are, in spite of everything, ordinary bears; the latter are spirits. However, sometimes it is difficult to find out which category of bears Indian informants are referring to.

We are here reminded of the fact that to Native American religious thinking there is a dividing line between what belongs to the ordinary or natural world around us and what belongs to the supernatural or spiritual world. In some scholarly quarters it has been denied that any such categorization exists among the Indians, or it has been said that it only occurs among those Indians who have been touched by Christianity. However, a consideration of all the evidence makes it quite clear that in their spontaneous experience of religious miracles and in some cases in their thinking about such experiences and existence as such, Indians distinguish between an ordinary and a spiritual world. It is difficult for us to pinpoint which things belong to either category. As mentioned above, a bear may be an ordinary animal, or it may represent the shape of a supernatural being. To some tribes certain mountains are supernatural, to others they are not.

Indeed, some natural phenomena and cultural objects are so saturated with supernaturalness that they are set aside from all other things. They are sacred and therefore dangerous, taboo. For instance, the Indians surrounding Yellowstone National Park feared its spouting geysers. Their eruptions were thought to spring from the operations of capricious spirits. Archaeological evidence seems to suggest that the Indians may have offered axes and other implements to the underground spirits. Otherwise, however, they avoided the dangerous spots.

There are many other examples of the distinction between natural and supernatural. Plains Indians received in visions spirit instructions to leave alone certain tools or abstain from certain actions. The sacred Arapaho flatpipe cannot be touched except under proper ritual conditions. It is preserved in a special lodge and carefully wrapped in blankets. One Shoshoni medicine man refused to dine with me at a restaurant because his spirit had forbidden him to eat with cutlery. Whoever transgresses such taboo rules runs the risk of becoming sick or paralyzed, or even of dying. That person will bring misery and misfortune not only to self, family, and kin, but to the whole community.

Some Indian pronouncements sound as if the whole universe, particularly the natural environment, is sacred. This is not so; if it were, Indians would not point out certain stones, mountains, and lakes as sacred. Conservationists have mistakenly assumed that Indians are ecologists because they supposedly care for all of nature. In fact, there are many examples of the devastation of nature by Indians.[5] However, Indians have paid more attention to nature than perhaps any other peoples, and Indian hunters have tended to protect nature, or parts of nature, as a manifestation of the supernatural. They care about the trees, because trees give evidence of the supernatural; they care about the animals, because animals may represent spirits; they care about the vast lands, because the lands may reveal God. Nature is potentially sacred, or rather, it turns into sacred matter when humans experience the supernatural in vision, meditation, or ritual.

There has been no remarkable speculation on the relations between the natural world and the spiritual world in the Indian worldview. Perhaps one could say that for the Indians the spiritual reveals the true nature of the ordinary world around us, but this inference should not be emphasized. The Western religious dichotomy between a world of spiritual plenitude and a world of material imperfection, a dualism pertaining to Christian and Gnostic doctrines, has no counterpart in American Indian thinking. Indians highly value life on earth, and their religion supports their existence in this world. The whole spirit of their religion is one of harmony, vitality, and appreciation of the world around them.

Perhaps the Western concept of "nature" is too narrow to use in this connection. Nature, the world, and the universe are concepts that flow into one another in Indian consciousness. What some scholars describe as "nature rituals," Indians view as affecting the whole of the universe. The Sun Dance is not just a ritual that promotes the vegetation and animal life during the new year that it introduces, it is a recapitulation of the creation; in fact, it is creation, and its effects concern the whole evolution and sustenance of the universe.

The universe is usually divided into three levels—heaven, earth, and underworld—a division that is a heritage from ancient times and is also known in northern Eurasia. However, there are some variations in this world picture. The Bella Coola of British Columbia believe that there are five worlds on top of one another, of which ours is the middle one. Many Pueblo peoples of the Southwest believe in the existence of four underworlds and four upper worlds, and the Navajo have taken over their idea of the four subterranean realms, one over the other.

The various worlds are often united through the World Tree, which has its roots in the underworld, stretches through the world of humans and animals, and has its crown in the sky world. The World Tree is represented by such ritual structures as the Sun Dance post (which is an uprooted tree) or the Omaha sacred pole. The three levels of the universe are marked on the Sun Dance post: The eagle at its top manifests the sky world, the buffalo skull on its trunk or at its base is the world of animals and humans, and the offerings of tobacco and water on the earth close to the base, destined for Mother Earth, symbolize the relations to the underworld. The myths of the tree or vine on which the ancestors climbed up from the underworld(s), according to Southwestern Indians, also remind us of the idea of the World Tree.

In myths and rituals the sacred areas of the supernatural powers are drawing close to people. They may become identical with the areas people occupy today. Thus, the mythic world of the Navajo supernatural beings is situated between the four sacred mountains that enclose the central country of the Navajo people: Big Sheep Peak in the north, Pelado Mountain in the east, Mount Taylor in the south, and the San Francisco Peaks in the west. To take another example, the Shoshonean myths portray a landscape in the Great Basin that still is the home of many Shoshoni groups today.

The supernatural powers that govern the universe are multifarious. There is usually a heavenly god who rules over the sky, a host of spirits who control the atmospheric powers, an innumerable crowd of spirits who influence human life on earth, and also some beings, including Mother Earth, who roam the netherworld. Very often these spirits, or a large number of them, are conceived as a unity. This unity may consist of a collectivity of spirits or of a Supreme Being (usually identified with the sky god) supervising or taking in the functions of various spiritual powers. On the Plains, both these concepts may exist side by side. Thus **Wakan Tanka** of the Lakota Sioux is a term comprehending a set of spirits from different levels, functions, and areas—sixteen all together. (The number is the speculation of holy men.) However, it is also the name of a personal god, the quintessence of all powers. To one Lakota division, the Oglala Lakota, the concept of Wakan Tanka swings between the two poles of unity and collectivity. [See Religions of Africa pp. 39–42, 64–69, Religions of Mesoamerica pp. 157–58, 186–89, Judaism pp. 414–15, Christianity pp. 537–38, Islam pp. 635–37, Hinduism pp. 739–41, 759–61, 780–84, Buddhism pp. 900–903, Religions of China pp. 1024–26, and Religions of Japan pp. 1112–27 for discussion of God, gods, and objects of worship.]

Psychologically seen, the two cognitive elaborations represent two ways of looking at the supernatural. When people perceive the universe as a unit, whole and indivisible, the figure of the single godhead stands in focus. When human attention is drawn to the particular acts of the divine, such as thunder, food giving, and healing, particular powers appear that express the activities referred to. The Supreme Being fades into the background, unless he is especially bound up with one of these activities. There is thus a tension between universalism and particularism in the concepts of the supernatural and the universe.

The worldview of North American Indians reveals a concept of existence contrasting sharply with that of the Western world and the Judeo-Christian tradition. There is no sharp differentiation between divinity and humans, nor is there a clear distinction between humans and animals. Not only is there a different relationship between these beings, but also the beings themselves are viewed in a distinctive fashion calling for their own terms. The Western world focuses on one divinity as "God," but Native Americans, although they have the notion of a Supreme Being, emphasize an abundance of "powers" and "spirits." These powers are not far removed from humans but interact freely with humans, especially in dreams and visions (as will be seen later in this chapter). Some animals are spirits, as some spirits are animals. In general, the Native American view of "nature" is much more alive and filled with spiritual activity than the Western view of nature. The Native American worldview can in some instances be characterized as emphasizing cosmic harmony.

Cosmic Harmony

Today's Indians often emphasize the unitary, balanced system of the universe as made up of humans, animals, trees and plants, nature as a whole, and the supernaturals. For instance, Jackson Beardy, a modern Cree Indian artist, sees the world as a unit dominated by the sacred number four. He told me that the world has four basic elements: air, water, fire, and stone. The creation took place in four processes: the creation of the earth, the plants, the animals, and the human beings. There are four basic colors in the universe; and so on. Now, this is scarcely the original worldview of the artist's people, the Woodland Cree of Manitoba, because Canadian Woodland Indians are not known to have such concepts. It is rather a worldview that has striking resemblances with the cosmic speculations of Plains and Pueblo Indians. As a matter of fact, when questioned, Jackson Beardy admitted that he had absorbed ideas from the Plains Indians, the Northwest Coast Indians, and other Indians. He is convinced that there are no real differences between Indian religions, only different names.

The same position is taken today by most young Indians who believe in Pan-Indianism; that is, they consider that all Native American tribes basically share the same culture and the same religion and they want to revert to this culture and religion. They present a "North American religion" as an integrated system of beliefs and rituals with fixed symbolism, the same for all tribes. This is, however, a late idea, formed under the pressure of white domination. Still, its foundation, the concept of cosmic harmony, a harmony in which living beings also take part, is much older. It is an outgrowth of the speculations among priests in predominantly agrarian societies where religious ideas, natural phenomena, humans, and other beings have been drawn together as parallels, analogues, and symbols in a connected religio-philosophical pattern. Certainly, the very germs of this speculation may be retraced to the ancient hunting milieu. However, it is particularly in the horticultural milieu with its developed and intricate ritualism, its grandiose mythology and speculating priest-thinkers that the idea of cosmic harmony is really at home.

To show the uniqueness of this ideology we may here contrast the thought systems of a hunting tribe like the Naskapi of Labrador and a horticultural group like the Tewa of New Mexico. The Naskapi, says an expert on their religion, Frank G. Speck, do not classify their religious ideas. "For a system is scarcely to be expected to appear on the surface as covering the aggregation of metaphysical ideas so rudimentary as those exhibited in Montagnais-Naskapi thought. . . . That any conception of categories is alien to the thought of the people must be apparent to anyone who has viewed their undisciplined life."[6] On the other hand, there is an unconscious thought system that sometimes has a ring of Platonism, because earthly forms are seen as having their supernatural ideal forms. Each animal species has its master (lord, boss); this **master of the animals** is usually conceived as a mysterious animal spirit larger than ordinary animals of the same kind. Thus, the giant beaver who governs the beavers decides their allotment as game food to the hunters and their return to the world after death. The fish also have a master, but he is identified with the moose-fly, strangely enough. The principle remains, however: Living beings have their supernatural guardians. In the case of humans, it is the Supreme Being who plays the superior role.

This simple system of the hunters contrasts with the rich symbolism of the agricultural Tewa, a Pueblo tribe in New Mexico described in detail in an excellent work by a Tewa (San Juan) Indian scholar, Alfonso Ortiz. The Tewa are organized in two **ceremonial moieties** or halves that are responsible in particular for the rituals of the calendar. These rituals regulate the seasons and serve the supernatural cosmic system. Whereas in the inchoate religion of the Naskapi the supernatural beings stand out as the powers who decide the course of events, in the Tewa worldview they are part of the ritual machinery, impersonated in the rituals by members of the moiety divisions. It is the cooperation between the two moieties that brings together the wholeness of Tewa existence. A symbol of this wholeness is the sacred center, the navel of the Earth Mother, a keyhole-shaped arrangement of stones on the southern plaza. Late in the winter seeds are placed in this navel to symbolize the reawakening of nature. From this navel the world is oriented. The world has four quarters, and so has its ritual manifestation on earth, the pueblo.

The complementary powers of the universe are contained in the two moieties, which represent summer and winter and are protected by the Blue Corn Mother and the White Corn Mother, respectively. The summer moiety is particularly associated with the furthering of vegetation, the winter moiety with the furthering of hunting. Moreover, the moieties are combined with symbolic colors, the summer moiety with black (for clouds), green (for crops), and yellow (for sunshine), the winter moiety with white (for winter moisture) and red (for warfare and hunting). As a consequence of this division, the summer moiety stands for femaleness and the winter moiety for maleness. The summer moiety impersonates in its rituals the gods from the warm south, the winter moiety, the gods from the cold north. In this way everything that exists is divided between the ceremonial moieties.[7]

There are also secret societies belonging to the moieties or balancing between them. In the annual cycle of rituals (called "works") these societies perform retreats and prayer sessions associated with the progression of the year and its economic activities. "The intent of each work is to harmonize man's relations with the spirits, and to insure that the desired cyclical changes will continue to come about in nature."[8]

Why is there this difference in outlook between the Naskapi and the Tewa? One reason is certainly the wide differences in their conditions of existence. In their hard struggle in an Arctic environment the Naskapi, strewn over the country in small hunting camps, had few possibilities and few incentives to create bodies of speculative thought and little ritualism that made such speculation necessary. The agricultural, closely connected Tewa Indians, inhabiting a circumscribed pueblo and living in a more pleasant climate, had enough surplus time to consider their affinity with the universe. The picture of this universe was taken from their own cultural structure. Their dualistic cosmology may, as Ortiz suggests, have been stimulated by a dual subsistence system (hunting and horticulture). In a wider perspective their thought system is part of a Pueblo Indian philosophy that may go back to tendencies in archaic American Indian thinking.

Powers and Visions

The Jesuit missionaries of the 1630s who had arrived in the area of the Great Lakes to convert the Indians there were astonished to find religions so different in structure and expression from their own Catholic faith. "Their superstitions are infinite," wrote Father de Brébeuf on the Huron, an Iroquoian people, and Father François du Perron made the following statement: "All their actions are dictated to them directly by the devil, who speaks to them now in the form of a crow or some similar bird, now in the form of a flame or a ghost, and all this in dreams, to which they show great deference. They consider the dream as the master of their lives; it is the God of the country. It is this which dictates to them their feasts, their hunting, their fishing, their war, their trade with the French, their remedies, their dances, their games, their songs."[9]

Behind these theological comments we have here the earliest Western descriptions of the role that dreams and visions have played in Native American religion. All over North America, with exception of the Southwest, spiritual power has come to people in their dreams or in visions they have received in isolated places in the wilderness. Indeed, it is possible to say that the **vision quest** is the most characteristic feature of North American religions outside the Pueblo area. For the lone hunter safety and success depended on the guardian spirit acquired through the vision quest. The guardian spirit was closer at hand than the High God or other spirits. The connection between a person and a protective spirit could become so intense that the person took part in the spirit's qualities and even in its life. In northern Mexico, this close bond is called **nagualism,** after the Indian term *nagual* (the guardian animal that is the individual's second ego). When the spirit died (and spirits could die), the person also succumbed.

The relationship to a guardian spirit through vision is evidence of the importance of spiritual contact in American Indian religion. Indians "believe" when they see or feel the supernatural being. A historical document from the seventeenth-century Southwest illustrates this point. The Spanish missionary Fray Alonso de Benavides tells us how he was visited by a Jicarilla Apache chieftain who much admired his altar and was informed that God was on that altar. However, the Apache was not satisfied, for God was not visible on the altar. When he left he was very disappointed, for he wished to have seen God. In Indian religion, the vision quest provided an opportunity for direct contact with the supernatural.

The basic vision quest in North America is connected with puberty or the years immediately preceding puberty. The young boy (girls do not usually participate in the vision quest) is required to seek the assistance of a guardian spirit to withstand the trials of existence and have luck in hunting, warfare, love, and so on. The parents or elders send him out, usually together with other boys, into the forest or mountains to fast and suffer from the cold and the attacks of dangerous wild animals. In his weakened state he may have a vision of the spirit that henceforth becomes his guardian spirit. (There are many cases told of supplicants who were not blessed by spirits.) This quest, which we may call the **puberty quest,** was transformed into a quest for full-grown men on the Plains and in parts of adjacent territories. On the Plains the warriors repeatedly withdrew into the wilderness to seek spirits. A Plains Indian may therefore have a variety of guardian spirits, each of which is good for a different purpose.

Consequently, the boundary line between common visionaries and medicine men has been very slight among Plains Indians (medicine women will be discussed later). One can say that in comparison with ordinary Indians medicine men have more spirits, and their spirits are specialized to help cure the diseases of their clients. The medicine man receives his mission to cure from the spirits that come to him, and in his visions he receives instructions in the ways of doctoring.

The most common therapeutic method is to remove the agent of the disease, whether it be an object or a spirit. Sucking, blowing, and drawing it out (with a feather fan) are the most common techniques. In some areas, and particularly along the Northwest Coast, the medicine man falls into a trance or ecstasy to enable his soul to transcend the boundaries to the other world. In his trance he gathers information from the spirits of the dead, or even steals away the soul of a patient that has gone to the realm of the dead during the feverish coma of its owner. The medicine man then brings the soul back to the sick person, usually by pressing his hands against the latter's crown. Such a medicine man who falls recurringly into a deep trance to save a person's life is called a shaman.

Shamans, however, are not only doctors. They are able to divine the whereabouts of game, the location of a missing person, and the course of future events. Among the Athapascans of the Southwest (Apache and Navajo) the shaman goes into a trance to find out the nature of the disease before other medicine men start their doctoring.

Common visionaries, medicine men, and shamans all have their authority from spiritual revelations in visions. As said before, this direct contact with the supernatural world through visions means more to American Indians outside the Pueblo area than the knowledge of supernatural powers through traditional lore. Sometimes spiritual revelation comes not through the sought vision, but in a spontaneous dream, particularly among the Iroquois in New York State and the Mohave in western Arizona and southern California. The Iroquois decide their actions from interpretations of dreams, and the Mohave even dream their myths, that is, construct their myths on the basis of dream contents. Medicine men and shamans west of the Rocky Mountains receive their powers not through the vision quest, but through spontaneous dreams and visions.

Since time immemorial Indian shamans have facilitated their contacts with the supernatural through potent psychotropic drugs, drugs that affect consciousness and behavior. Tobacco is a well-known and important ingredient in American Indian rituals. In the Eastern Woodlands and on the Plains, the smoking of a pipe introduces most ceremonies and most peace talks. There is reasonable evidence to suggest that in bygone times the pipe without the bowl functioned as a suction instrument through which the shaman could both remove a disease object from a patient and intoxicate himself with tobacco fumes.

Many psychotropic plants have been used for the attainment of trance states. Datura was used in California, the Southwest, and the Southeast. In recent times peyote, the small spineless cactus, plays a similar role. A whole religion has grown up around peyote, particularly on the Plains. (This subject will be further discussed in chapter 12.)

The Cycle of Life and Death

In contrast to Western cultures, Native Americans conceive of time not in a linear, but in a cyclical form. Western time concepts include a beginning and an end; American Indians understand time as an eternally recurring cycle of events and years. Some Indian languages lack terms for the past and the future; everything is resting in the present. This explains to us how mythical events apparently thought to have happened long ago may repeat themselves in present ritual occurrences. The Lakota define the year as a circle around the border of the world. The circle is a symbol of both the earth (with its encircling horizons) and time. The changes of sunup and sundown around the horizon during the course of the year delineate the contours of time, time as a part of space.[10] An illustration of this way of counting time is indicated in stone arrangements on mountaintops and plateaus in the Rocky Mountains: The stones are laid in a wide circle around a central hub, and the place of the summer solstice is marked. The **medicine wheels,** as these stone structures are called, served as some sort of calendars, among other things. [See Religions of Mesoamerica pp. 159–60, 206–9, Judaism pp. 431–33, Christianity pp. 551–53, Islam pp. 674, 707, Hinduism pp. 727, 793–94, Buddhism pp. 890–91, Religions of China pp. 1021–24, and Religions of Japan pp. 1141–46 for discussion of religious calendar and time.]

The cyclical time concept applies not only to the macrocosmos, the world and the year's rhythm, but also to the microcosmos, the human being. Each person makes a cycle of time from birth to death. Rituals mark the important changes of life: birth ceremonies, puberty rituals, initiation rites into tribal societies, and death rituals. The cyclical concept demands that death is not an end, but a beginning of new life, either on this earth (**reincarnation** as another human or **transmigration** into some animal, most often an owl) or in a transcendent hereafter. Very often one individual might hold several ideas about the dead at the same time: the dead as residing in the other world, the dead as reincarnated in other persons, and the dead as haunting ghosts. This may appear to be a logical inconsistency in Indian thinking, but it should not be so considered. Different situations call for different interpretations of the fate of humans after death. (And in fact Western people themselves do not reconcile their apparent inconsistencies on the fate of individuals following death.)

Native Americans usually avoided the issue of death, thinking that nothing could be known with certainty about the state of the dead. The question of a person's survival after his or her demise has never been a prominent theme for American Indian speculation (although the Jesuit fathers thought so). As said before, religion in aboriginal America has always been in the service of life, not death. Beliefs about the dead are abstruse, vague, and of little consequence. The best descriptions there are emanate from shamans who have gone beyond life to liberate sick people's souls entrapped by the dead. These descriptions tell us much about the difficult roads to the other world and the obstacles to be met. With Paul Radin we may say that these tales are folkloristically reworked, rich in detail, but scarcely meaningful to the ordinary person who primarily trusts his or her own religious experiences.[11] Conditions in the next life are not so well documented, although there are occasionally illuminating reports. These are usually modeled on the setting and conditions in this life and consequently vary with cultural background.

In popular contexts we often talk about the "happy hunting grounds." It has been said by some authorities that Indians never believed in them, but this is wrong. Hunting tribes usually think that there is a happy land after death, at least for those who have conformed to the norms of society. There is plenty of game in that land. Horticulturists tend to believe in a subterranean realm of the dead, the place of Mother Earth who produces the new life of vegetation. For obvious reasons this realm portrays a gloomier picture of afterlife. However, often the horticulturists retain the old idea of a happy paradise, whatever its location, filled with the bounty of the earth. The question of whether there were different realms of the dead based on good and bad deeds in pre-Columbian

Indian belief is difficult to answer. However, we know definitely that such ideas developed under the impact of Christianity, for cyclical thinking does not provide for a resuscitation of the dead in this life. As an Indian told me, those who are gone are gone forever. Only in religious movements that have been inspired by Christian ideas, such as the **Ghost Dance** around 1890, is the return of the dead possible.

The overview of Native American religions in this chapter provides us with a general understanding of the worldview, cosmic harmony, powers and visions, and the cycle of life and death so important to this religious heritage. But because this overview has attempted to characterize Native American religion as a whole, especially in North America, it has necessarily been quite general. The next two chapters offer more concrete description of the richness of two specific Native American traditions.

12

The Religion of the Wind River Shoshoni: Hunting, Power, and Visions

THE RICHNESS AND VARIETY of Native American religions seen in the two previous chapters make it difficult to provide a general overview of so many complex and fascinating traditions. Limiting our focus to just two tribal groups, the Wind River Shoshoni and the Zuni, at first glance may seem to simplify the interpretation of a Native American religious tradition. However, the full richness and diversity of Native American religions can be appreciated only when they are seen in the context of a particular tribal group.

The nature of every Native American religion is in sharp contrast to such traditions as the founded religions of Christianity, Islam, and Buddhism. These religions are organized around the experience of the founding figure: The scriptures record the life of the founder and the religious texts comment on this experience; the community of religious practice is drawn together as a following of the founder. Especially because these traditions became codified in writing by a professional religious leadership, it is rather easy to identify the formal teaching or message of these religions: for example, the Nicene Creed in Christianity, the Four Noble Truths of Buddhism, and the confession of faith in Allah and Muḥammad (the Shahada) in Islam. Of course, the beliefs and practices of individual members of these religions are much more diverse than what is seen in these very formal statements, but this individual variation can be measured against the codified formal statement.

In a Native American religious tradition there is no single founder, no scriptural authority, no specific church or religious organization, no professional religious leadership. Rather, religion has been handed down as an oral tradition from one generation to another. The tribal group itself is the total religious community that receives, modifies, and transmits the religious tradition to the next generation. Because they are oral traditions, they are not bound so closely to the fixed character of the written word and past precedent as seen in founded religions, and because Native American religions emphasize direct contact with

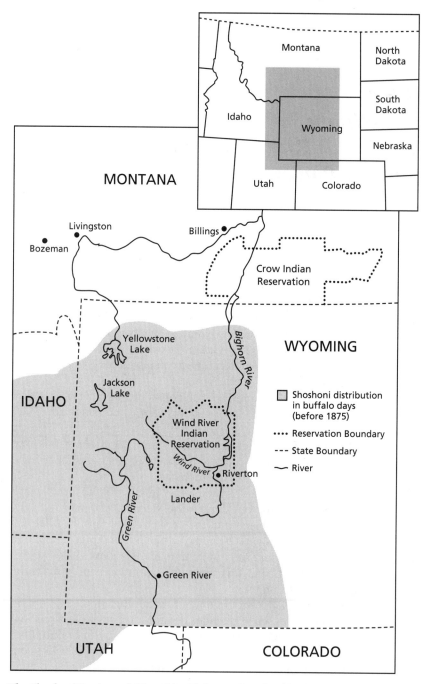

The Shoshoni Regions of Wyoming, Idaho, and Utah.

supernatural beings in visions and dreams, these traditions have more readily been transformed by the powerful experiences of remarkable individuals. In short, the oral traditions of Native American religions are more fluid and vary more greatly among individual members of a tradition than is the case with most world religions.

Because there is no written creed or codified doctrine for Native American religions, we must observe the rituals practiced and listen to the myths and beliefs told by the members of a particular tribe to discover the tribe's worldview. By paying close attention to their beliefs and practices we will come to see their view of human life and the cosmos as a total world of meaning. As we saw in chapter 10, there are basically two kinds of religious orientation in Native American traditions, a hunting pattern and a horticultural pattern. In this chapter the religion of the Wind River Shoshoni is described and interpreted as an example of the hunting pattern; in the next chapter the religion of the Zuni will be treated as an example of the horticultural pattern. For each religion, we will look first at the historical conditions of its development, then explore more closely the religious beliefs and practices, and finally provide more detailed description of some concrete examples of religious life.

The Development of Shoshoni Culture and Religion

The Wind River Shoshoni are named after their reservation in the central western part of the state of Wyoming. Their land is a sagebrush plain intersected by the upper course of the Wind River and bordered by the Rocky Mountains on the west and the open short grass plains on the east. The Indians on the reservation, Shoshoni and Arapaho, have access both to the warm valleys of the river and the rich hunting grounds up in the mountains. This country was chosen as a reservation in 1868 by the famous Chief Washakie, leader of the Shoshoni for almost sixty years. Their former enemies, the Arapaho, an Algonkian Plains tribe, were transferred to the reservation ten years later. The two tribes kept apart from each other.

Before they were collected on the reservation, the ancestors of the present Wind River Shoshoni belonged to different Shoshonean groups. In a larger perspective they formed part of the widely spread Shoshonean population (known linguistically as Numic) that for many centuries had been at home in the semi-deserts of the Great Basin and southern California. The Basin Numic Indians, divided into many groups such as the Ute, Paiute, Chemehuevi, Gosiute, and so on, were seed and nut gatherers and hunters of small game. They had one of the simplest cultures in North America: They lived in wickiups (brushwood huts or brush shelters), had little social organization above the family level, spent much time traveling from one source of food to another, and held very elementary thanksgiving feasts with round dances. Their eastern offshoots are the Shoshoni of Wyoming and the Comanche of the southern Plains. Because of ecological and historical influences, the culture of these Indians changed considerably from their Basin heritage.

Because the Wind River Shoshoni religion is closely related to this complex cultural background, a description of their prereservation history is necessary. The majority of them were Plains Shoshoni, mounted warriors whose Basin culture had been partially overlayered by Plains culture from the eighteenth century. They hunted buffalo, lived in portable tents of buffalo skin (**tipis**), and had a strict military organization under a powerful paramount chief but at the same time kept a flexible band organization under lesser chiefs. They had societies for men, at least from the nineteenth century, and celebrated the Sun Dance as their great annual ceremony. However, in many respects they departed from the Plains cultural pattern as we know it among the Crow, Lakota, Kiowa, and Cheyenne, which was characterized by a more intricate social and ceremonial organization, more reliance on the buffalo for food, the sole use of tipis for shelter, and a geometric art. For example, the Shoshoni groups, in addition to their use of the tipi, which was typical of the Plains, also built mat houses. They shared some crafts in common with Plains groups, such as a particular bead technique and rawhide work, but unlike the Plains Indians they also made baskets. When the buffalo hunting was over for the season the various bands and family groups spread among the foothill areas and along mountain rivers where they hunted deer, mountain sheep, and small game, as well as fished and gathered bulbs, berries, and wild plants—remnants of the old Basin way of living.

This style of mountain life was more typical for another group of Wyoming Shoshoni, the Sheepeaters. They were part of a small but widely spread out population in the mountain districts of Wyoming, Idaho, and Montana that had adapted itself to mountain conditions. Indeed, they owed their name to the fact that, more than other Shoshoni, they hunted the bighorn sheep. Their pattern of life was ancient Shoshonean, combined with such Plateau Indian features from the north as salmon and trout fishing in the mountain rivers. Until the 1860s they lacked horses and therefore were called "walkers." They lived in brush lodges and did not associate with other groups.

There were other Shoshoni groups in southwestern Wyoming, in the Bear River country. Originally representing a very simple Basin culture, they mixed with white trappers in the beginning of the nineteenth century and became traders on the active Fort Laramie–Fort Bridger–Salt Lake City trade route. They developed a culture of their own, part white, part Indian.

After the Indian wars of the nineteenth century, all these Shoshoni Indians (and half-breeds) were collected on reservations in Idaho (Lemni, Fort Hall) and Wyoming (Wind River). Because there has always been lively interaction among the various groups and much intermarriage, it is natural that some Wyoming Indians settled in Idaho, and some Idaho Indians in Wyoming. Another factor in the shifting of Shoshoni Indians was the moving of all the Yellowstone

National Park Sheepeaters to reservations in Idaho. However, the present Wind River Shoshoni are mainly descendants of former Wyoming Shoshoni.

This complex cultural and historical background is reflected in the makeup of Wind River Shoshoni religion as we know it during the present century. There is, first of all, the religious complex related to the culture of the hunters and gatherers manifested in hunting ideas, shamanism, and mythology. Second, there is the overlay of Plains ideas and ritualism represented by the vision quest, the Sun Dance, an active High God concept, and belief in a happy hunting ground after death. This restructuring of religion may have taken place between 1775 and 1825, possibly earlier, and was accompanied by a strong emphasis on war ceremonialism. Since the Plains Shoshoni were the dominant group in Wyoming's Shoshonean population, they also put a strong stamp on the religion of the Wind River Shoshoni in modern reservation times.

Nevertheless, about the time of the first settlement on the reservation and particularly in connection with the defeat of the militant Ghost Dance religion about 1890–1891, another reorientation of religion took place, this time in a more peaceful direction: Beliefs and practices associated with war were discarded and there was a greater concern with health and happiness. This was the time when the traditional form of the vision quest was gradually abandoned and was even declared harmful to its participants; at the same time the Sun Dance was reinterpreted as a ritual for healing of diseases and for tribal coherence, and Christian symbolism and values penetrated traditional religion. The introduction of **Peyotism,** the peyote religion, dates from this period. (Peyote is a cactus that grows in Mexico and southern Texas; it is eaten by some Native Americans to, among other things, experience a vision.) Developments during the nineteenth century have been characterized by the Christianization of some religious activities, the spread of Peyotism, and the adoption of new "cults"—but also the reinvigoration of religious tribalism.

The contribution of Sheepeater religion to Shoshoni religion represents a separate issue and the extent of its influence is difficult to judge. There is some evidence that the concepts of mountain spirits and rock ogres were particularly characteristic of this religion.[12] On the other hand, the interaction among the various groups of the Wind River Shoshoni so thoroughly blended the several kinds of religious influence that today it is not possible to separate the different strands.

The following presentation of Shoshoni religion is an interpretation of the forms practiced by medicine men and medicine women and traditionalists until very recent times. Today, practically all the old-style medicine men and women are gone, and those who now claim to be a medicine man or woman operate without the benefit of the complete traditional setting, combining glimpses of Shoshoni practice with a Pan-Indian outlook. If we want to study the earlier style of Wind River Shoshoni religion as once practiced during their days as a hunting people, we have to rely on the testimony given by traditional Shoshoni believers, who preserve many of the beliefs and practices of an age long past.

The Structure of Shoshoni Religion: Spirits, Powers and Supernatural Power, and Visions

Supreme Being: Mythology of Wolf and "Our Father" in Everyday Religion

The complex historical background of Shoshoni culture and religion is reflected in the composite character of Wind River Shoshoni religion as known in recent times. This is conspicuous especially in the remarkable gap between everyday religious practice and mythology. The mythology expresses the ancient world of the hunters and gatherers of the Great Basin, depicting the landscape, the lifestyle, and the animal figures of the Great Basin Shoshoni. The stories themselves are common to the Numic tribes of that area and the Wind River Shoshoni east of the Rocky Mountains. On the other hand, the religion practiced in everyday life presents a sharp contrast, referring to a world and lifestyle predominantly Plains Indian in character. Most of the active spirits in everyday religion, too, are animal figures, but these are animals found on the Plains. For example, the buffalo spirit has no importance in the mythic tales, but it turns up again and again in vision narratives and historical legends, and it plays an important role in rituals. Also the rituals of everyday religion are very similar to those of Plains Indians—the Sun Dance is a good example.

The gap between mythology and everyday religion creates a tension in Shoshoni religion, a tension that sometimes leads to openly conflicting views on the same subject. Take for instance the belief in a Supreme Being. Some scholars have thought that this belief is fairly recent, an outcome of Christian missionary teaching, and that in earlier Shoshoni religion there was only belief in many spirits all on the same level. However, there is plenty of evidence that not only the Wyoming Shoshoni but also the Shoshoneans of the Great Basin have believed in a Supreme Being since ancient times. This divinity is almost everywhere called "father." He is sometimes thought of as anthropomorphic, that is, humanlike, and sometimes as zoomorphic, or animal-like; in the latter case he is portrayed as **Wolf,** a wolf that speaks with a human tongue and thinks human thoughts.

Among the Wind River Shoshoni he is Wolf in mythology, but not in everyday religion. The mythology tells us that he supervises the world, an Indian chief in the disguise of a wolf, aided by "little wolf," or Coyote, a trickster who pulls many pranks. His surrounding host of figures are all represented as animals, although (as in the Greek fables) their thinking and actions are predominantly human. At the end of the ancient mythological times all these zoomorphic beings turned into real animals and became the ancestors of now-living animal species. In the mythological world Wolf is not so much the creator as the arranger of an already existing world. Coyote is partly his assistant in this work, partly his adversary, blamed for having introduced death into the world. Mostly, however,

Coyote is just a trickster with bad habits. [See Religions of Africa pp. 36–37, 64–67, Religions of Mesoamerica pp. 129–35, 154–55, 163–68, Judaism pp. 380–84, Christianity pp. 534–35, Hinduism pp. 739–41, 743–46, Buddhism p. 890, and Religions of Japan pp. 1094–96 for discussion of myth and mythology.]

In everyday religion the scene is different. In the first place, the mythological dualism is gone. Coyote plays no role at all, and no cult is directed to him. The primordial animal characters of mythology—Porcupine, Skunk, Weasel, Cottontail, and so on—have given way to other animal spirits that appear in visions. Most important, Wolf has disappeared, and in his place a vaguely anthropomorphic Supreme Being, "Our Father" (**Tam Apo**), has made his entrance. He is, at least in later tradition, supposed to be the creator of the world and of humans and may be manifested in the sun. In the old days, people told me, there was not much worship of Our Father. Only in exceptional cases—for instance when a person was all alone out on the plains suffering from thirst, hunger, or cold—did he or she turn in prayer to the Supreme Being as a last resort. Usually they prayed to auxiliary spirits. However, from about 1800 when the Sun Dance was introduced, people could more easily approach their High God in the annual ceremonies. In this way the godhead became more active. At least in one medicine man's theology a kind of hierarchical structure developed, with "Our Father" being enthroned above the mass of spirits whom he controls and directs.

One of my informants, now dead, gave me the following description of Tam Apo and of the cult associated with him:

> We think about him as the whole sky; he covers the whole world. He is a human being above the sky. His power extends over the whole earth. In ancient times we did not pray to him, but we prayed to different spirits. Still, we believed in God. Only in the Sun Dance did we pray directly to God.

However, this is not the general situation of Shoshoni beliefs. For most traditional Shoshoni, the spirits work largely independent of the Supreme Being. When people need individual help they turn to their guardian spirits or to medicine men and women whose possession of such spirits enables them to help people out. When aid is sought for the whole tribe or for individuals coming together, they call on Our Father, especially in the Sun Dance. The nature of the Supreme Being in recent times can be seen in the following prayer to Tam Apo at the sunrise ceremony by a leader of the Sun Dance in 1948:

> Tam Apo, here we are, standing up and facing towards the sunrise. I am offering a prayer again, asking your blessing. The sun you made has come up, it is shining towards us, all over; and it is the light from you and we like to have this every day of our life, and we want to live a long time. Because we are suffering for our homes, families, friends, and all kinds of nations, I want you to bless us. And I ask you to bless the service boys [in the U.S. Armed Forces] so that they will be safe and nothing will happen to them. . . . I ask you to see to it that there will be no war, make it that way through your willpower. And

when we get to the end of these three days, when we get out, give us our water and our food. The powerful water will give us good strength, and so will the food—what we eat will give us good strength. For we want to live as long as we possibly can.

How can we account for this discrepancy of beliefs in a Supreme Being—on the one hand mythological tales focusing on Wolf and on the other hand ritual practices directed to "Our Father" (Tam Apo)? Because of the divergence in beliefs in a Supreme Being, it may appear that the whole tribe suffers from a split personality, but this is not the case. Rather, this discrepancy is the direct influence of two distinct religious traditions having their roots in different cultural milieus upon the Shoshoni religious heritage. Of course, for some Shoshoni Indians the old stories of Wolf and Coyote are just "fictional" tales not to be taken seriously (something like Grimm's fairy tales for modern Europeans and Americans). These tales are usually told during the dark seasons of the year (as with most American Indian storytelling) as entertainment for both grownups and children, but mostly for children. Some stories about the Cannibal Owl and other monsters that are supposed to catch and devour children are more than anything else pedagogical tales told to make children behave properly.

However, in the Great Basin area this mythology has been a matter of belief, and among the Wind River Shoshoni such mythological tales are considered to be true stories. For example, stories such as the myth of how Coyote brought death into the world are not fictional tales but a subject of belief—at least, that was the case during my field research some thirty years ago. Therefore, the discrepancy of beliefs in a Supreme Being in mythology and everyday religion cannot be dismissed as the difference between religion and fictional accounts (or fairy tales). The best way to understand the relationship between the two kinds of belief is to observe how the individual deals personally with the tension and to see how different social settings call into play different orientations of religious beliefs. Viewing Shoshoni religion in this fashion enables us to understand how it is possible for an individual to isolate particular sets of belief for particular situations. For example, when Shoshoni Indians spend a winter evening listening to mythological stories they may accept the mythological figures and believe in their world and activities; the reactions of the listeners around the storyteller may vary from credulity to amusement to skepticism. By contrast, in another setting, the summer Sun Dance celebration, all religious belief is concentrated on the anthropomorphic Supreme Being and the spirits surrounding him. And as we shall see later, in a third situation, when an individual dreams of guardian spirits, the Supreme Being does not appear at all. This demonstrates that in the hunting religion of the Shoshoni, beliefs are not codified in a neat system such as a formal theology (as found in Christianity and Islam). Rather, the individual experiences the supernatural world in what could be called alternating configurations or compartments. Different religious complexes appear in different cultural and social situations. There are even watertight compartments separating these religious complexes, so that the mythteller can speak about a Supreme Being in animal form, while the Sun Dance dancer refers to a Supreme

Being in human form. The tensions among various aspects of Shoshoni religion show us the flexible nature of Native American religion and also throw light on the composite character of all religious traditions.[13] [See Religions of Africa pp. 39–40, 64–68 and Religions of Mesoamerica p. 166 for mention of the High God.]

Spirits and Powers

Everyday religious life, sometimes called "practical religion," is quite different from the beliefs and tales of mythology. In everyday religion the Supreme Being is always thought to reside in the sky and may express his splendor through the sun, but the stars do not play any role in religious ritual. (Conversely, the stars and constellations figure frequently in the mythological tales, where they are transformations of the mythological beings.) However, next to the Supreme Being there is a class of spirits of the atmosphere that are powerful, although they are not greater than the Supreme Being. There are many of these spirits or powers in the atmosphere and throughout nature, some more important than others, but they are not arranged in a clear hierarchy or theology.

One particular atmospheric power is inherent in the first thunder to be heard in the spring. Prayers to the thunder spirits at this time promote health and well-being. Lightning spirits and thunder spirits are sometimes identified with each other, sometimes conceived of as independent of each other. An old Shoshoni woman informed me that small brown birds that jump up and down close to the creeks—apparently blackbirds—control the thunder. The lightning, on the other hand, she ascribed to the activities of a bird with a red spot that she had seen at Trout Creek. She was here obviously referring to the hummingbird.

An aged medicine man had somewhat different ideas, although he shared the old woman's opinion that the thunderbird has a diminutive form. To him, **tongwoyaget** ("crying clouds") is like a hummingbird, but even smaller. He seems like "a sharp-nosed bird, little as a thumb, looks like the hummingbird, but is faster." This is how the thunderbird looked in his visionary dreams. The same informant was convinced that the thunderbird collects the water in the clouds and makes them thunder. "This gives us rain and snow," he said. Lightning he had seen as a fire or as a blue streak of light, but never as a being. However, it can talk to people in his dreams. In practice, though, this medicine man could not distinguish clearly between thunder and lightning spirits.

The idea that the thunder spirit looks like a hummingbird is apparently an old one among Indians of the Uto-Aztecan linguistic stock to whom the Shoshoni belong, for the ancient protective god of the Aztecs, Huitzilopochtli, was connected with hummingbirds. Actually, his name means "hummingbird to the left," and two hummingbirds decorated his statue in the great temple of Tenochtitlan, present-day Mexico City.

There is also, however, the notion among the Shoshoni that the thunderbird looks like an eagle. This is a general Plains idea the Shoshoni have possibly taken over from other Plains tribes. The eagle itself is respected by the Shoshoni as the bird of peace, connected with the sky and the Supreme Being. As a messenger from God a stuffed eagle is placed in its nest on the top of the Sun Dance pole.

Other atmospheric spirits are the winds. While some winds are controlled by the thunderbirds, others are subordinated to **nyipij,** the "wind master." Nobody has seen this spirit, whose appearance is unknown, but Indians sense its presence; its residence is high in the mountains. Whirlwinds are apparitions of dead people and may be dangerous, as illustrated in the following account. Not long ago a company of women were out walking. They encountered a whirlwind. One of the women got angry and cursed the whirlwind. It turned against her, destroyed her tent, and broke one of her legs.

Atmospheric spirits are numerous; there are also many other spirits closer to the human landscape, spirits associated with animals, plants, mountains, and lakes. The spirits assume various forms, as can be expected in a religion dominated by visions, and they exercise different powers—some benevolent, some malevolent. These spirits are so numerous we can only touch on a few here.

One of the most respected of all spirits is **Tam Sogobia,** "Our Mother Earth." The Supreme Being and the powers associated with him, especially Mother Earth, completely dominate the Sun Dance. Mother Earth receives offerings in the Sun Dance (tobacco is poured on the surface of the earth) and appears in ever so many prayers. Whenever there is a feast and the bowl of water is brought in, a little water is first poured on the ground for Mother Earth. She is identical with the earth itself and nourishes the plants and animals on which human beings live.

The spirits that dwell close to humans may be met in the surrounding natural environment and in visionary and dream experiences. We do not find, however, that spirits occupy houses or ranches. The idea of house spirits does not belong to a hunting people who not long ago lived in tipis transported from place to place. The spirits are found in nature. The locations of spirits are places avoided by humans, because they are sacred and dangerous places. The boundary line between these two categories is vague, but the common element is that they are risky for people to visit.

Sacred and dangerous places do occur all over the land that the Wind River Shoshoni once roamed, from Salt Lake City to the Medicine Bow Mountains and Yellowstone National Park. Our comments will be restricted to the lands that the Shoshoni have occupied during the past hundred years, the Wind River Valley and Wind River Mountains, and to the areas they frequent in the Grand Teton and Yellowstone parks. Because the Shoshoni have inhabited this area since ancient times (and were not moved to a reservation distant from their ancient homelands, as were some tribes), the sacred places within this general area are very old.

The sagebrush plains have few sacred places, except among rivers and creeks and in the high scraggy hills. The verdure of the Wind River and its confluences has been the hiding place of the feared dwarf spirits called **nynymbi,** which are usually unseen but sometimes may be dressed in old-fashioned buckskin suits and armed with bows and arrows. These dwarf spirits are evil. They shoot arrows into the lone traveler so that the latter falls from his or her horse with a hemorrhage in the lungs. This is a supernatural explanation for the many cases of tuberculosis among the Shoshoni. The *nynymbi* may also be found in the mountains, and there are many legends of these spirits being attacked by eagles. If a Shoshoni shoots an eagle, the dwarf spirit shows thankfulness by helping the person find a dead game animal. (This story is a version of the widespread Indian tale of the battle between the heavenly eagles and the dark powers of the earth and the underworld.)

In the waters there are water sprites of various kinds, such as water babies, the water woman (usually just one), and water buffalo. Formerly, water babies could be heard crying in the Wind River. They sound like babies and look like small human beings. They are one and a half feet tall but so heavy that a person cannot move them. One of them may devour a woman's baby and put itself in the baby's place. The water woman, or fish woman, with pretty, long hair is a full-sized water spirit. She is counted as a kind of water baby and is supposed to be evil, dragging people down through a hole in the ice. Some skeptical Shoshoni suggest that white trappers introduced this belief. This is possible, for in several tales she has a long fish tail like a European sea maiden. Nevertheless, she has been seen by Shoshoni Indians in the Big Wind River, Bull Lake, and the Dinwoody Lakes.

Bull Lake is a favorite haunt of water sprites. In particular it houses the remarkable water buffalo. (In Shoshoni Bull Lake is called "water buffalo lake.") Water sprites look like buffalo but are supernatural. They can be heard in the spring when the ice cracks. There is a story of how two Shoshoni scouts found a water buffalo on the shore and killed it. One of the men ate pieces of the buffalo. His comrade watched him gradually turn into a buffalo, go down into the water, and disappear. Bull Lake is a dangerous place; many Shoshoni stayed away from it in the old days. They were respectful when passing the lake and abstained from making fun of it. If a person happened to see a water buffalo there, it was a bad sign.

The buttes and foothills are full of spirits. On the north side of Crowheart Butte, a legendary place in Shoshoni war records, there are said to be lots of spirits that may be good guardian spirits if you receive their help. However, it is dangerous to climb the butte, for the person who does so may disappear. Other buttes are sites of rock drawings, and the spirits are in their neighborhood. Thus, there are several reports of people receiving a guardian spirit in a vision at Medicine Butte and Cedar Buttes and in the foothills at the headwaters of Sage Creek, Willow Creek, and Owl Creek. The rock drawings are supposed to represent spirits and have been made in the winter by these spirits themselves. Each spirit draws its picture. Indians have told me that in the spring and summer they have discovered new drawings on the rockface, apparently pecked by spirits since their last visit. Some Shoshoni who approach the rock drawing places in wintertime may hear the spirits working at them. As they come closer, the sound ceases. When they withdraw from the place they can again hear the knocking.

The spirits are not as common today as they were in the old days. The power lines and poles especially have scared them away. They have retreated for good to the mountains. Even rock drawing sites have been abandoned. When a white built a cabin close to the rock drawings at Sage Creek, Indian vision seekers did not go there anymore—it was useless.

At South Fork Canyon (of Little Wind River) there is a deep cave where until about 1910 the Shoshoni buried their dead. The corpses were carried on horses up the steep slopes and laid side by side. The place is avoided.

The high mountains were formerly haunted by dangerous spirits, the **dzoavits** or **pandzoavits.** They were humanlike monsters made of stone with stone packs on their backs; but their faces and hands were of soft material. They ate people and could come to the camps to do so. It was risky to talk about them. Most Shoshoni I asked said that this kind of spirit is extinct nowadays. However, they may exist underground and underwater.

The majestic Teton peaks are powerful beings. They do not allow people to climb them, and those who try succumb. Nor do they accept being called by their right name, which in Shoshoni is "black standing up." If a person traveling through the Teton Pass makes use of the true name of these mountains, it will cause a flood or, in wintertime, a terrible snowstorm. It is also forbidden to point at the peaks with a finger. Like other northwestern Plains Indians, the Shoshoni once feared the geyser basins of Yellowstone National Park, ascribing their activities to dangerous spirits. However, in this respect the Sheepeaters were less fearful, having made the park their home.[14]

There is a medicine wheel close to Pinedale, west of the Wind River Mountains. Some Shoshoni Indians say it is a plan of the sacred Sun Dance, its spokes corresponding to the "rays" left by the dancers on the sandy ground of the Sun Dance hall. In modern times at least one Shoshoni has gone up there to sleep between the spokes to receive a power dream. Not far away from this place is a rock in the mountains around which Indians have to pass to be safe when traveling. However, people dare not walk there unless they bring a gift; to go without making an offering is to invite bad luck.

The examples of sacred places given here could be complemented with others farther away from the Wind River Reservation, but still situated in ancient Shoshoni country. They all give evidence that there are sacred places scattered around the territory used by the Shoshoni, so that a wanderer or mounted traveler always has to be prepared for ritual precautions. Indeed, one never

Spiritual power radiates like electricity from one of the pandzoavits *(depicted here in a rock drawing)—dangerous, mysterious ogres and visionary spirits of the Shoshoni.*

knows for sure when one might be confronted by a supernatural being, for these spirits can reveal themselves anywhere and at any time. This is the case in particular with all those spirits that may provide an individual with **puha,** supernatural power; these are the guardian spirits, and they are also called *puha.*

Puha: *Supernatural Power, Visions, and Guardian Spirits*

With the mention of guardian spirit beliefs we enter the central tenets of old Shoshoni religion. All the previously mentioned spirits of the atmosphere and nature, including "Our Father" and Mother Earth, possess a kind of power. However, Shoshoni distinguish the power of spirits in general from *puha,* which can mean either supernatural power acquired by humans, or guardian spirits who grant such supernatural power. *Puha* is central to Shoshoni religion because the heart of this tradition is receiving supernatural power from guardian spirits, especially through visions and dreams.

The persons who have power from the spirits are not so numerous today as in former times, when all males were supposed to withdraw into the solitude of the wilderness to obtain the favors of the spirits. Still, there are some Shoshoni today who have such powers, although they do not like to talk about them. Nowadays *puha* is received in spontaneous dreams or in dreams during unconscious states due to exhaustion in Sun Dance dancing. Earlier, persons interested in supernatural power submitted themselves to the hardships of a vision quest to get it.

In Shoshoni tradition, dreams and the vision quest have long been acceptable means of receiving power, but the acquisition of supernatural power in spontaneous dreams is probably the older way, with roots in Great Basin culture. The vision quest most likely came later, institutionalized through the influence from the Plains Indians. Thereafter, the two ways existed side by side until, after the Indian wars and the establishment of the reservation system, it was found to be rather superfluous to seek visions for warfare, prowess, and hunting in a time that no longer had use of such pursuits. During World War I, a medicine man received a vision; according to this vision, all deliberately sought visions were imparted by *pandzoavits* and were therefore dangerous to the visionary. This message was in a way a rationalization of the gradual disappearance of the vision quest. It also signaled the return of the importance of spontaneous dreams.

In view of the modern revival of vision quests among such Plains peoples as the Cheyenne and the Lakota, it is possible that the vision quest has regained some of its old status among some Shoshoni who still cling to traditional beliefs. However, during my first visit to the Shoshoni in 1948 there were only a few persons, among them the famous medicine man Tudy Roberts, who were supposed to have power from sought visions. (The career of Tudy Roberts will be presented later.) Another medicine man offered to go through a vision quest with me, an offer that was not realized because of the onset of cold weather (summer, the appropriate time for vision quests, was over).

Stories of people who have experienced the vision quest circulate among Shoshoni, but they all refer to persons who are now dead. Although the Shoshoni have been more open and direct about their religious beliefs and experiences than most Plains Indians, they do not volunteer to disclose the details of their visionary experiences except to close kin and friends. However, the main elements of their experiences are known and even told to non-Indians.

The general rules of the Shoshoni vision quest have been the following. The supplicant, usually male, rides a horse up to the foothills where the rock drawings are—the foremost places of spirit revelation. At a distance of some two hundred yards from the rock with pictographs he tethers his horse. Then he takes a bath to cleanse himself in the nearest creek or lake. Without moccasins he walks up to the rock ledge just beneath the drawings and makes his camp there. Naked except for a blanket around him, he lies down there under the open sky, waiting for the spirits to appear. Sometimes, I was told, the supplicant directs a prayer to a particular spirit depicted on the rock panel, anxious to receive that very spirit's power. As we shall see, each spirit that blesses its client does so with a special gift related to the spirit's own abilities.

The vision is induced by fasting, enduring the cold and lack of sleep, and smoking the pipe. Sometimes the vision comes rather quickly, in other cases after a longer time, and in still other cases not at all. There are reports that the vision appears after three or four nights and days, but this information may be doubtful, constructed perhaps to make the nights of suffering conform with the sacred numbers three or four.

It is difficult to tell whether the Indian is awake or dreaming when he finally is blessed with a vision. The Shoshoni word **navushieip** covers both dreaming and visions. One medicine man told me that he had spontaneously received waking visions, and they appeared like dreams. He also made a distinction between common dreams and "power dreams," that is, dreams or visions in which spirits appear. These dreams are, he said, clearer than other dreams and hold your attention so you cannot awaken until they are over. There is also a peculiar feeling that you are going away somewhere.[15]

What appears in the vision itself may be quite changeable. The same medicine man said that he had had a vision of a lightning spirit that changed its shape: It was first like a body of water, then like a human being, then like an animal, and finally it faded away. We shall soon see more examples of this spiritual ability. It is obvious that the spirit of the dream or vision takes part of the latter's inconstancy and changing panorama. Some instances of sought visions among Shoshoni may give further illustrations of the drama and visual contents involved.

Taivotsi ("Little White Man") had a dream in which he was informed in a mysterious way that he should go to the rock drawings of Willow Creek if he wanted to get **medicine**. He did as he was told. He cleansed himself from impurity by bathing there, and early in the evening he lay down. He did not quite know if he was asleep or not, but thought he was awake when an owl suddenly flew down upon him and started pecking him. The owl tried to scare him away but did not succeed and finally left him. A little later there appeared a bear. It grabbed hold of Taivotsi and threw him around. Taivotsi, however, did not care, so the bear gave up and trotted off. Next, a deer came forth and jumped straight at Taivotsi. It repeated this movement several times, but Taivotsi remained calm. A coyote then stole upon him and bit him, but Taivotsi did not mind. Finally, a big rattlesnake came writhing against him, rattling its tail. Taivotsi had always been afraid of snakes, so he jumped up and ran away. That was his misfortune. If he had stayed on the spot, the snake would have entrusted him with supernatural medicine, for this snake was the spirit. Instead, his legs became lame shortly afterward, and he was forced to walk with crutches.

This story demonstrates what deprivations the supplicant has to experience, and what psychic strength he must possess. Four visitations strike him that he has to endure. Finally, there comes the spirit itself. When the client flees from it he has not only forfeited his luck, he has also committed a crime against the spirit, a crime punished by paralysis. Many a vision seeker does not even come that far. If there are no trials from dangerous animals, this is a sign that the spirit does not accept him as its ward. It may be that the spirit does not consider him humble and good-natured or that he has not made the right ritual preparations. Of course, a supplicant who cannot face the four fearsome animals (four being the sacred number) has no chance to meet the spirit.

The appearance of the spirit is the great moment in the vision quest. Sometimes the seeker is not aware that he stands before the spirit itself, as in Taivotsi's case. Usually, however, there is no doubt. "The *puha* approaches you like a strong light," said one Shoshoni medicine man. The mysterious way of spirits is well accounted for in Morgan Moon's memories of his visionary experiences. Once, when he was lying in trance, a spirit looking like an Indian slowly approached him. It stopped at his feet, granted him its supernatural medicine, and sang for him its sacred song. Then, as it were, the spirit dissolved, gradually fading away. In vain Morgan tried to find it. On another occasion Morgan saw the spirit emerge from the willow thicket and slowly approach him. It handed over to him its powers and the instructions connected with the power. Then it turned around and went back into the willow brush. In an instant it was gone.

Appearing mysteriously, transferring power, imparting instructions with the power (such as rules for dress and the wearing of feathers, rules for making a medicine bundle, or rules for avoiding things, persons, or actions), and singing a sacred song—these are the guardian spirit's activities in a successful vision quest. It is then the client's task to take on the responsibility for the right administration of the marvelous gifts. Careless manipulation of the power, disobedience of the rules laid down, and neglect of ritual observances leads implacably to loss of power, paralysis, or other disease, injury, or even death.

However, in some cases where the "medicine" has been lost, the spirit may again take pity on its former ward. Let us return to Taivotsi. In one vision quest he met a falcon spirit that endowed him with the ability to win in the so-called handgame, one of the most popular pastimes among the Plains Indians. There were certain conditions for the reception of this gift, and Taivotsi unfortunately happened to transgress them. As a consequence he became almost blind. Sometime afterward he was walking over the plains when suddenly the same spirit again showed itself to him. "You trespassed against my instructions," the spirit said. "Now you are a poor fellow. However, I feel pity on you. I will help you once again. Tomorrow you shall go to Willow Creek. You will find a huge deer there. This deer you shall have." Next morning Taivotsi rode to the place that the spirit had pointed out to him. His sight was bad, and he did not indulge in great expectations. But lo, there was a big deer! He killed it and returned home with it. Thereafter his sight changed and became as sharp as it had been in the good old days. And the spirit often appeared to him and told him where to hunt with success.

These vision narratives tell us that the guardian spirit may show itself as a person or as an animal. From the material at my disposal it seems that the animal form is more common. At least one medicine man who had many guardian spirits referred to animal shapes in 95 percent of the cases. As stated before, this is natural in a hunting religion. As we have noticed, the change from animal to human being and vice versa is the usual pattern in these visions. The animal form possibly says something about the nature of the power that the visionary receives. The beaver makes the person a good swimmer, the deer or antelope a swift runner, the magpie a good scout, and so on; each of these special abilities relates to the abilities of the animal form of the protective spirit. There are certain conditions for the use of this power. For instance, the deer spirit whose gift is quick running may direct its client to have a deer tail fixed to his shirt or hanging on a ribbon around his neck. The client may also be told to pray to the spirit about power before, say, a running competition.

Possessors of Power: Visionaries and Medicine Men

Shoshoni visionaries could acquire several guardian spirits, one after another, sometimes in such a way that one spirit paved the way for the other. One medicine man even constructed a hierarchy of spirits, with the lightning spirit on top and with other spirits of lesser dignity subordinated in a descending scale. This was, however, not a typical case. The guardian spirit world is rather chaotic to most Shoshoni because the spirits operate as they please.

The medicine man, or inspired healer, has the largest number of spirits and is an expert on spirit lore. Otherwise he is little distinguished from other visionaries, except that he is usually blessed by spirits that have given him the ability to cure sick people. Such spirits are often stronger than other spirits. This was the case particularly in the past when medicine men could travel in their spirits to the land of the dead to receive information or liberate some lost soul that had been taken there by the dead. However, a spirit that gives curing *puha* may also give other abilities that have nothing at all to do with curing.

The medicine men have always been few in Shoshoni society. It is indeed difficult to know their numbers even in comparatively recent times, for two reasons. First, there is no proper term for a "medicine man"—both common visionaries and medicine men are called **puhagan,** or "possessors of power." This linguistic usage reflects the only slight difference between a medicine man and an ordinary Shoshoni, at least in older times when most men were supposed to seek out guardian spirits. Second, there have been many individuals with super-natural power who have been able to handle minor diseases without being con-sidered medicine men. A real medicine man cures many difficult diseases, although some specialize in certain diseases, and is socially accepted as a doctor. During my stay among the Shoshoni only five persons passed as medicine men, but several other persons were supposed to have power to heal a few minor, nar-rowly defined diseases. This should be compared with the estimation of some Shoshoni that in the old days about 10 percent of the population were *puhagan*. Perhaps a tenth of these *puhagan* were proper medicine men.

Some women may become medicine women. However, this happens late in life. As long as they are young and menstruate, they are considered impure and cannot approach the spirits. Only after menopause can they establish a connec-tion with the spirits. This means that there are no particular spirits for women, as there are in other hunting cultures; not even Mother Earth is accessible to young women. It also means that they cannot, like young men, participate in vision quests. However, older women after menopause are free to pursue vision quests, unless they receive their power in dreams. Some medicine women have been very powerful. One such woman, the mother of one of my informants, a medicine man, was reputed to have healed a sick person just by touching him once with her hand. During my time among the Shoshoni I met two medicine women, both very capable.

Some medicine men are specialized in curing rattlesnake bites, or pneumo-nia, or other specific diseases. A clever medicine man is also expected to show his spiritual abilities in ways other than curing. He may be able to disclose the whereabouts of the game animals, to find lost items, or to foretell the future. Such competent medicine men who have recourse to some sort of trance are known to us as shamans.

One particular kind of medicine man that used to exist among the Shoshoni and Paiute of the Great Basin were the antelope medicine men. They had super-natural power to attract the antelope (pronghorns). Together with his tribesmen such a medicine man would go out to the antelope flats carrying a gourd deco-rated with antelope hooves. Standing on a hilltop, he shook the gourd and sang the "antelope song." This song called the animals and ended with a sound imitat-ing them. The antelope drew near and were surrounded by the hunters, who easily caught or killed them. There are no antelope medicine men left today.

Strictly speaking, these antelope medicine men are not doctors, and there-fore not medicine men in our sense of the word. However, the Shoshoni con-sider them medicine men because of their great powers and perhaps also because they serve the whole community. As we have seen, "medicine man" is a white concept. To the Shoshoni, "a *puhagan* with great *puha*" is a more ade-quate expression, implying that the great *puha* may be used for the help of oth-ers, whether for curing or for a collective antelope hunt. One medicine man went so far as designating himself and his colleagues "sacred" because of their possession of *puha*. However, there has been no particular veneration of medi-cine men, but rather great fear of them if they were known for turning their powers against people. Such medicine men appeared in the past and were shunned because they practiced witchcraft. All medicine men who use their powers for the good of the tribe are respected in proportion to their ability.

Medicine men are usually forceful personalities who, because of their knowledge of the supernatural, are valuable as ceremonial leaders, for instance in the Sun Dance. All Shoshoni ceremonies are based on some revelatory experiences with which medicine men are quite familiar. It is therefore natural that they sponsor a Sun Dance, or lead such a dance, or perform curing rites in the ceremonial hall of the dance. We shall later see how the medicine men proceed when they cure their patients. [See Religions of Africa pp. 35–36, 38, 40–41, 52, 63 for discussion of medicine.]

Death and the Land of the Dead

When the medicine man's art fails, as it finally does, his patient leaves for the world of the dead. For the Shoshoni, there are many ways of conceiving of the dead. Either they go to a particular realm in the other world, or they remain on earth as ghosts, or they are born again as people, or they transmigrate into insects, birds, or even such inanimate objects as wood and rocks. There is also the belief, possibly post-Christian, that the dead person goes to Our Father. The beliefs in reincarnation and transmigration seem to have been very weak and to have disappeared at least fifty years ago. All these afterlife alternatives illustrate what we have said above about so-called alternating configurations of belief: They are adapted to particular situations and are called into focus when such situations appear.

The beliefs in a land of the dead are not really vital today but deserve mention. Medicine men who have gone there in trance, and sick people who have been there in coma, tell about this land. One Shoshoni woman, the granddaughter of Chief Washakie, "died"—which in their language also means lost consciousness—and found herself in a foreign place looking down from a high hill. She saw the land of the dead, a pretty country with many tipis and people. Other "travelers" report the same thing, adding a detail or two here and there: You arrive in that land through a tunnel; the dead sleep in the day, but are up in the night; they spend the time there singing, dancing, and gambling; they hunt buffalo on horseback in beautiful surroundings. In short, this is the blessed land of the dead of the Plains Indians. We have reason to suspect that in the pre-horse, pre-Plains days the Shoshoni land of the dead had a slightly different tone, being more in line with the concept of the afterlife held by the Great Basin tribes. However, even in earlier times this land was described as delightful and happy with plenty of food.

To come to this paradise the dead person follows the Milky Way, "the backbone of the world." This indicates a realm of the dead in heaven, an old belief also found among the Basin Shoshoni. This belief is somewhat at variance with another belief in which the land of the dead is situated beyond the mountains.

There is a very strong belief in ghosts that haunt the living. Some say these ghosts are the dead who have followed the wrong branch of the Milky Way and turned back. The idea seems to be that good tribal people go to the land beyond, while those who have behaved badly (for instance, killed or robbed a member of the tribe) come back to wander eternally "as a man, as a voice, as an echo" (as one Shoshoni expressed it). Ghosts might disguise themselves as whirlwinds. Some ghosts appear as walking skeletons; they are visible in the moonlight and frighten people with their rattling. Favors done for these ghosts may result in their granting supernatural powers to their benefactors—however, this is rare. Usually ghosts afflict people in some way, and even medicine men may be hurt by contact with them.

Personal experiences and legends elaborate the ideas of the afterlife. However, most Shoshoni express only a slight interest in the next life and often declare that they know nothing about it—the dead do not come back to tell us. Only those who have gone to the other world in trance or coma are more explicit about what it is like. Here, as elsewhere among the Shoshoni, the rule holds that only visions and dreams open the gates of the other world. [See Religions of Africa pp. 42–45, 78–79, Religions of Mesoamerica pp. 144, 229–33, Judaism pp. 448–50, Christianity p. 557, Islam pp. 684–85, Hinduism pp. 813–14, Buddhism pp. 935–37, Religions of China pp. 1021, 1041–44, and Religions of Japan pp. 1149–50 for description and discussion of funeral rites.]

Summary of the Structure of Shoshoni Religion: Honoring Spirits and Acquiring Power

Shoshoni religion is as complex as the total Shoshoni cultural heritage, with roots in the Great Basin traditions and more recent contributions from Plains traditions. As was seen with basic beliefs about the Supreme Being, the Shoshoni have both mythological notions of Wolf and ritual practices directed to Our Father. Shoshoni religion may be seen as a composite of various strands within different Shoshoni groups and influence from the major Plains traditions; but, as we saw in chapter 10, every religious tradition, even a world religion, is the sum total of its previous history and therefore is a kind of composite religion. Shoshoni religion, like every religious tradition, incorporates various historical influences while forming a distinctive worldview. The several religious complexes present within the Shoshoni tradition are experienced by the individual as a whole worldview.

The hunting culture and religious tradition of Shoshoni are more loosely organized than life among horticulturists, for example, the Zuni (to be discussed in the next chapter). There is no codified theology, and yet the Shoshoni worldview presents a clear and consistent picture of religious reality. Central to this worldview is the reality of spirits, some of which are important in the mythological tales forming a distinctive religious complex of beliefs and stories; other spirits are related to the separate religious complex of everyday ritual life. Paramount among these spirits is Our Father, who is located in the sky, associated with the sun, and worshiped in the all-important Sun Dance. In addition to Our Father, there are many atmospheric spirits such as thunder, lightning, and wind (and associated birds). These atmospheric forces have power, which is dangerous, and may even be used to harm humans, as in the case of whirlwinds.

Other forces of what in English is called "nature" are also spirits. Not all of nature is sacred for the Shoshoni, but certain natural phenomena such as mountains and lakes are viewed as having special association with certain spirits. Mother Earth is one of the most important of these spirits, to whom offerings are made in the Sun Dance and on many other religious occasions. As we will see in the next section, the erection of the lodge during the Sun Dance ceremony is a ritual reconstruction of the world, a microcosm.

Places where spirits are found are sacred, and some locations are so powerful or so filled with evil spirits that it is dangerous for people to visit them: Sacred and dangerous places are approached with caution or avoided. Some specific places are especially sacred or dangerous, but generally the nomadic heritage of the Shoshoni has meant that these places are scattered throughout the territory they roamed; there is no special sacredness to the home or a permanent dwelling place such as a village. Supernatural beings may reveal themselves at any place or time, and the individual must always be ready to recognize and revere them. Generally a Shoshoni should live life in harmony with these spirits, respecting them and praying to them, honoring sacred places and avoiding dangerous places. There are special rules such as not saying the true name of the Teton peaks or pointing a finger at them. Honoring the spirits and sacred places enhances one's life; neglecting the spirits and overstepping the bounds of dangerous places invites misfortune.

These spirits and sacred places are important, but the heart of Shoshoni religion is the *puha* or supernatural power of guardian spirits, which individuals can receive through a sought vision or a dream. As has been mentioned throughout, the flexibility of Shoshoni religion is mainly due to the emphasis on adapting beliefs and rituals to newly received visions or dreams of supernatural power. In earlier times every young man was expected to seek a vision and receive a guardian spirit, undergoing lengthy and arduous ritual procedures; in recent times the dream has become more important as a means of obtaining supernatural power. The important Shoshoni religious leaders are the "possessors of power," the medicine men, visionaries, and shamans who have received supernatural power, usually only after the difficult ordeal of the vision quest or the Sun Dance. These are the religious figures with the power to heal, to take the lead in important ceremonies such as the Sun Dance, and to initiate the hunt. The gist of Shoshoni religion is to maintain purity and honor spirits and sacred places, while seeking the supernatural power of visions and dreams. It should be noted that although much of this questing for supernatural power is individual, it usually benefits the community as a whole, as seen in the collective blessing in the Sun Dance or in the antelope medicine man's aid in the collective hunt.

As was mentioned previously, Native American religions present a sharp contrast with world religions, because native religions are not based on the messages of particular founders and are not organized according to literary traditions and theological teachings. Rather, Native American religions have emphasized oral traditions and openness to new visions and revelations. Shoshoni religion is a good example of this tendency to be more fluid and flexible in religious life. However, the fact that Shoshoni religion does not have a particular founder or a written body of doctrine or creed should not lead us to the conclusion that Shoshoni religion is incoherent or inconsistent. Shoshoni religion, like other Native American traditions, has an unconscious thought system that is implicit within its distinctive pattern of beliefs and practices.

The Shoshoni religious way can be outlined as shown in the following diagram. This diagram can be read from top to bottom and from the center both to the left and to the right. At the top are the cosmic powers, headed by Tam Apo. Beneath Tam Apo are various spirits and particular powers and also power itself (*puha*); below these are humans and human life. At the very center of this world is a concentration of power; to the left is the diminishing of power, to the right is the enhancing of power. Left of center, starting at the top, we find Coyote (especially in mythology), and malevolent spirits, as well as conditions such as ritual impurity that lead to lack or loss of power and being an unsuccessful hunter or experiencing undesirable conditions such as sickness or punishment. Right of center, we find benevolent spirits and guardian spirits, as well as the rites, such as the Sun Dance, and the means, such as dreams and visions, for acquiring communal and individual power (and becoming a successful hunter or medicine man and benefiting from healing or blessing). In general, then, the diagram is based on the two major emphases of the Shoshoni world: to maximize enhancing of power and to minimize diminishing of power. This diagram will become clearer as it is illustrated by concrete examples of Shoshoni religious life in the next section; the structure of Shoshoni religion can also be interpreted as a total way of life.

The Shoshoni way of life is based on the notion that people live in this world and are expected to use it carefully while fulfilling their roles as husband and wife and as social members of their community. Their relative success is dependent on their relationship to the Supreme Being (Tam Apo, "Our Father"), their blessing by the spirits, and their abstention from ritual impurity. The highest figure in the Shoshoni worldview is the Supreme Being, Tam Apo, who controls the world and makes it new every year. Central to this worldview is *puha* or power. Many spirits of the atmosphere and nature express this power but are not more powerful than the Supreme Being. Some of these spirits, such as the water sprites, tend to be malevolent while others can be benevolent. Guardian deities are beneficial because they are able to grant supernatural power directly.

The character of human life is dependent on the way humans are related to the various powers of the world. When humans are related positively to the Supreme Being and other powers of the universe, their welfare is enhanced; rituals such as the Sun Dance and general ritual purity enable individuals, the community, and the world to come into contact with these powers and to be renewed. Individuals may be blessed with power involuntarily through dreams, or they may seek power through vision quests. Such experiences may result in the acquisition of power (*puha*). Persons who gain special power are called medicine men or women (*puhagan*). They become successful hunters and doctors.

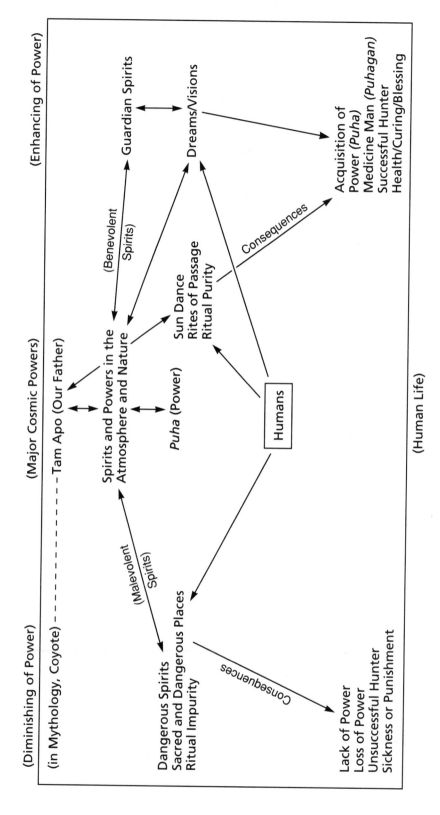

The Shoshoni Religious Way.

On the other hand, humans may have a negative relationship with the various spirits and powers of the world, by failing to act in accordance with tribal rules. In a very simple sense, not to participate in the rituals of the Sun Dance and other ceremonies means that a person loses opportunities for enhancing health, prosperity, and personal power. If a person approaches spirits and powers when impure (especially in association with menstruation and death) one can be punished. Some spirits such as water spirits are often malevolent and are to be avoided, because they may harm people. When spirits of the atmosphere and nature are not respected, they may attack the offending party. Some places are especially sacred or dangerous, and are to be avoided or respected if approached, because of the threat to human fortune and life. All these examples of negative behavior, whether expressed in failure to participate in rituals, or in participating directly in negative practices, result in lack of power or loss of power for a person. In Shoshoni life this especially means being a poor hunter or being sick or otherwise afflicted.

The Dynamics of Shoshoni Religion: Rituals of Human Change, the Sun Dance, and Curing

The many ideas and notions of the supernatural are not just philosophical concepts—thought tools to explain the world around them—to the Shoshoni, although of course they do also fulfill this intellectual ambition. They are lived through, experienced, "danced out," as the great European scholar R. R. Marett expressed it at the beginning of this century. Notions of the supernatural are inextricably associated with daily life, with rites, and with observances.

Here we must nevertheless be careful not to draw hasty conclusions: The *beliefs* are transformed into active ritual behavior, but the *myths* are not. We saw how mythology operates at variance with religious beliefs, sometimes even contradicting them. Mythology represents an older worldview and thus does not reflect everyday religious reality, with a few exceptions. For example, a ritual like the Sun Dance has a foundation legend—that is, a story of the meeting between supernaturals and mortals in what is described as historical times. However, there is no foundation myth or tale of divine decisions in distant mythic times. The Sun Dance is a creation of Plains religions and has nothing to do with the mythology developed while the Shoshoni were part of the Great Basin cultural area.

In this connection we should observe that the Shoshoni rituals are relatively few in comparison to those of, for instance, the Zuni. As a hunting people they concentrated on the rituals of human change, of curing, and of thanksgiving. Of these, the original thanksgiving rite has given way to the Plains Indian Sun Dance, which is indeed a ceremony with the same aims, but one that is much more intricate.

We may well wonder what has become of animal ceremonialism, so typical for hunting peoples in the northern area of the continent. The answer is that it does exist among the Shoshoni, but rather rudimentarily. In mythology there are numerous references to the resuscitation of game animals from their preserved bones; sometimes the requirement is that the bones be thrown into water. There is also the story of a medicine man with buffalo power who arranged a circle of buffalo skulls on the ground, sang a song to them, and asked them to get up. The buffalo then arose, but there were now ten times as many buffalo as before.

This legend actually illuminates what has happened to the old animal ceremonialism: It has been reinterpreted to suit the dominant religious pattern, the vision complex. The visionary, the medicine man, the *puhagan,* has taken over the role once played by the master of the species and also the mysterious mechanism we sometimes call magic. The vision complex has grown so strong that it has practically ousted animal ceremonialism and beliefs in supernatural masters of animal species.[16] Even the bear cult has apparently fallen into oblivion. What is left are tales of the bear's mysterious abilities; its strong *puha,* which may turn a man with bear power into a bear; and its granting medical powers.

The rituals that have remained in Shoshoni religion are fairly simple, with the exception of the Sun Dance, which is of course not at all of Shoshoni origin (although some Shoshoni declare the opposite). It exhibits the lavish Plains ceremonialism, although modified to suit the Shoshoni taste.

Rituals of Human Change: Puberty, Childbirth, and Death

Rituals of human change, rituals that mark an individual's main life crises, have been called rites of passage by Arnold van Gennep. According to van Gennep, the main phases of each rite of passage are first separation, then transition, then incorporation, and they indicate the individual's passage from one state of existence (or rank or prestige) to another.[17] Thus, puberty, childbirth, and death are accompanied by rites of passage among the Wind River Shoshoni. Also rituals of disease could be mentioned in this context, but they deserve mention primarily in connection with the medicine men, so their discussion will be deferred. [See Religions of Africa pp. 42–51, 76–79, Religions of Mesoamerica pp. 201–6, Judaism pp. 445–50, Christianity pp. 542–43, 555–57, Islam pp. 677–78, 680–86, Hinduism pp. 747, 807–14, Buddhism pp. 915–17, 921, 931–37, Religions of China pp. 1019–21, and Religions of Japan pp. 1146–50 for description and discussion of rites of passage.]

At puberty there are—or were—different rituals for boys and girls, but both types are designed to secure their transition to adult life with its trials and responsibilities. The boys do not undergo vision quests (as had been the case in Indian cultures in the north and east of the North American continent) but participate in the Sun Dance, usually on their own initiative. However, today their motives are mainly social: to show other youths their strength and endurance and of course to impress the girls. In a way their present participation in the Sun Dance takes the place of the vision quest as a mark of the attainment of adulthood.

For the girls, puberty officially begins with the start of menstruation,[18] which is considered a state of uncleanliness and very dangerous to men. The menstruating girl withdraws to a brush lodge or (more recently) a wooden shed at a stone's throw distance from the main settlement. She abstains from eating meat but may eat roots and drink water. After a few days or maybe a week, the girl appears again, shrouded in new clothes and painted. One Indian complained to me that this custom is no longer rigorously observed, with the consequence that men no longer receive clear visions and dreams and therefore do not acquire spiritual powers.

The same ritual observances were until recently required of the woman about to give birth. She was supposed to abstain from fattening foods and had to drink hot water. When her time came she moved to the menstrual hut, where she stayed until a month after the birth. She was not confined there but could walk around, although she was not allowed to visit the family quarters. Food was brought to her daily, and she was assisted at the birth by a midwife who had had a dream of serving that profession. The pregnant woman was forbidden to scratch her head with her fingers but could use scratching sticks. She was also instructed not to eat meat. In fact, she mostly subsisted on soups. If the woman ate too much it was assumed her baby would become fat and lazy.

All these precautions give evidence that a menstruating or pregnant woman is in a dangerous, tabooed state. Spirits avoid her, animals flee from her if she touches them, and men fear her. If a man enters her lodge during menstruation or childbirth, it is believed that he will start bleeding in the nose or the mouth and bleed to death. The woman is on these occasions loaded with electric impurity, as it were, and is dangerous even to herself. Balance or purity is restored to the pregnant woman thirty days after giving birth. She then returns with her baby to her home, and she, her husband, and the baby take a bath in the creek and put red paint on themselves. The paint is considered a blessing. [See Religions of Africa pp. 45–46, 76, Judaism pp. 385–86, 445–46, Christianity p. 556, Islam p. 682, Hinduism pp. 810–11, Buddhism p. 932, Religions of China pp. 1019–20, and Religions of Japan pp. 1146–47 for description and discussion of birth rites.]

During the critical times of menstruation and childbirth the husband manifests specific behaviors as a sign of his sharing in the states of his wife and child. While his wife is menstruating, a period that usually spans four days, he is fasting, restricting his food to bread and water. He also runs several miles a day. The idea seems to be that in this way he contributes to his wife's overcoming the pains and hastens her recovery. This kind of behavior by the husband at childbirth is known in many cultures and is called **couvade.** He consumes light food—but no meat—and drinks much water, evidently to facilitate his wife's labor. As the newborn baby is bathed in warm water, the father dips himself in the cold creek, thus symbolically taking on himself the role of his child. He rises early and moves around, the idea being, said my informants, that as he behaves, so will the child behave in times to come. This parallels the mother's behavior as well: A few hours after the delivery she gets up and starts some easy work, "because she wants her child to become in that way."[19]

The last rites of passage given to an individual are those at death. For two or three days the bereaved cry at the dead person's grave. Women slash their legs and arms with knives so the blood runs; they cut their hair short to the ears and keep it loose. The men cut their hair to the shoulder and untie their braids. The corpse is immediately removed from the tipi in which the person lived to a shade, formerly of buckskin, close by. The dead person is painted with the colors and patterns used on festive occasions during his or her lifetime, usually red and white streaks. The painting process is accompanied by a prayer in which the survivors express the hope that the dead person leaves them and does not come back to scare them. The dead person is dressed in his or her best clothes, with some clothing items donated by relatives and friends. A woman is wrapped in her tent cover; a headdress is placed on the head of a dead man. If there are many such headdresses they are placed on trees or sticks in the close vicinity of the grave. All the dead person's goods, in particular the horses, are distributed among relatives and friends, but some goods are spared for the grave.

On the third or fourth day after death the corpse is transported to the burial place. Silver dollars are placed on the eyes and mouth if these have not been shut. The family tent is buried with the deceased person (and the family moves to another place). For a male the best horse is killed on the spot so that it can serve as its master's mount to the land of the dead; on this horse he hunts buffalo in the beyond. Some of the dead person's belongings are brought to the grave to remain with him or her. A medicine man has his medicine pouch around his neck or packed in a blanket next to him when he is buried; it goes with him to the next world. A woman is equipped in the grave with her kitchen utensils. Finally the corpse is covered with a pile of rocks to protect it from wild animals.

In some cases the crying of the mourners could continue for up to ten days after the burial. Weeping, the women pray that the dead person follows the straight way to the realm of death and does not get lost. Mourning does not cease until after a dance has been arranged one to six months later. On this occasion a specially selected individual paints the bereaved with red and admonishes them to be happy again and join the dance. The mourners abandon the ragged clothes that they have worn until now and don new ones.

These rites of passage go back to very ancient times and express the anxieties experienced by individuals in their fight and concern for fitness and survival as well as in their fear of death—not of dying, but of the state of death. Such rituals and observances originated long ago in the small hunting societies and were continued by the Shoshoni Indians when they had been transformed into mounted, well-disciplined warriors along the lines of Plains Indians.

The Sun Dance: Thanksgiving Ceremony, Microcosm, Visions, and Curing

The main ritual of the Shoshoni is the Sun Dance. It is basically a thanksgiving ceremony in which the Supreme Being is thanked for the year that has passed and is petitioned to guarantee a happy and healthy year to come, a year of plenty. We find such annual thanksgiving ceremonies among many North American tribes. The Great Basin Indians had a simplified version of such a thanksgiving ceremony, and it was preserved among the Wind River Shoshoni until it was replaced by the Sun Dance. (As we shall see, it continued as a Ghost Dance ritual on into this century.) The "Father Dance," as it was called, was a round dance in which men and women formed a circle around a cedar tree, clasping hands and shuffling sideways. Singing, they thanked Our Father for his bounty and implored him to send rain and plenty of food and make the people survive. It is probable, although it is difficult to prove, that the cedar tree represented the World Tree in the middle of the world, the symbol of Our Father's presence.

This ancient ceremony faded into the background when the Plains Indian Sun Dance was introduced about 1820 by the great Shoshoni chief and medicine man Yellow Hand.[20] Of course, the Shoshoni claim they invented the Sun Dance long, long ago, and other Plains tribes were merely late recipients of this rite. As some elderly Shoshoni remember, it is indeed the other way around. Yellow Hand, who was originally a Comanche Indian well initiated into Plains Indian ceremonialism, transmitted the Kiowa-Comanche type of Sun Dance to his Shoshoni. Since then, the Sun Dance has undergone a series of changes. The Sun Dance that is danced today, usually in July (and often succeeded by one or two additional Sun Dances in July and August), has been reinterpreted to suit reservation conditions and the impact of Christian ideology. For one thing, prayers for good health and the curing of diseases have emerged as a major concern.

According to Shoshoni beliefs the Sun Dance was initiated by two men, one of them sometimes identified with Yellow Hand, who had sacred visions. These men lived at different times and their visions may be termed the first vision and the second vision. In the legend of the first vision it is said that "many, many years ago" a Shoshoni, some say a chief, was guarding the horses of the camp. He brought them to a butte and sat down there to scout for smoke from enemy camps. As he watched the horizon at sunrise he saw something rushing toward him from the east. Soon he found out it was a buffalo. The man thought it had been scared by hunting Indians. However, the buffalo surprised him by coming close to him. It spoke to him. It told him not to be frightened but to listen to good news. The buffalo said that it had been sent by Our Father[21] to inform the Shoshoni about a way to cure the sick by faith and prayer.[22] The buffalo looked down upon the camp at the foot of the butte and instructed the man on how to plan and arrange what is today the first phase of the Sun Dance. Among the many instructions was an order to send out warriors to kill the biggest bull they saw in a buffalo herd. The head had to be severed behind the ears but left joined to a strip of skin along the back including the tail. Nobody was to molest the rest of the body, which was left to the coyotes; in this way the skeleton was preserved.[23] The buffalo head should then be put on a structure during the four initial praying nights of the Sun Dance. The buffalo spirit of the vision said furthermore that Our Father had sent it because the buffalo was the foremost of all animals and superior to them all.

Many generations had passed when there occurred a second vision. This time it was a young man who one night had a dream of seeing an eagle flying toward him eastward from the sunset and entering his tipi. The eagle had been sent by Our Father to instruct the people through the young man to put up a cottonwood pole, fix the buffalo head to this pole, and make a nest for the eagle at the top of the pole. A lodge would then be built around it, and the dancing would take place inside this lodge. This is the second and essential phase of the Sun Dance. The eagle had been chosen as God's messenger because it is superior to all birds, soaring high above them in the sky, a symbol of purity.

The Sun Dance was thus, according to legend, started through visions of supernatural beings, and visions have continued to be part of the ceremony. Many Shoshoni, fatigued by fasting, thirst, and dancing for days, have fallen unconscious or into deep sleep and in this state received power visions. Said one knowledgeable Shoshoni, "Everything we know we have learned through visions in the Sun Dance." It is characteristic that a person who sponsors a Sun Dance should first have a dream of doing so. One may have a dream at night of an old Indian arranging two sticks to form a cross, or a spirit may tell one in a dream, "You are going to put up a Sun Dance." Or a voice comes from the Sun Dance hall area admonishing the listener to initiate a Sun Dance. (It may however also happen that a person puts up a Sun Dance after having vowed solemnly to do so, in gratitude for the safe return of a soldier son or as a votive offering for the safe homecoming of a dear person.)

In accordance with the first vision, the so-called buffalo vision, the Sun Dance is begun with a preliminary dance before a skin or brush shelter suspended between four poles set in a row not far from the future dancing lodge. It is July and the grass is in places still very green. One to four men dance here for four consecutive nights, praying to Our Father for protection, health, and happiness. The dancers usually include the sponsor, who is also the main ceremonial leader of the dance, the second ceremonial leader who is a man the sponsor trusts, and one or two other experienced dancers. A fire burns in front of the dancers, who take steps back and forth between the wind screen and the buffalo head. These dance evenings usually end with a cleansing bath.

Thereafter follows the main Sun Dance as outlined in the eagle vision. A company of young men are sent out to bring back a tree to serve as a center pole in the Sun Dance lodge. It has to be a cottonwood tree growing by a stream. The young men find the tree and count coup on it, just as in the old days a warrior counted coup, or points of merit, on the first enemy he could touch with his rod. Special ceremonies are observed when cutting down the tree, which is then carried to the Sun Dance field. Formerly the returning young men were met by a crowd of other young men on horseback, and a sham battle took place between the two groups. However, since there are no more warriors left from the Indian wars, no one has the right to take part in sham battles, so these have been dropped.

When the tree has been brought home, a hole for it is dug in the center of the planned lodge. The buffalo head—now a stuffed head, but formerly a skeleton of a head covered with buffalo skin with sweetgrass in the eyes and nostrils—is fastened halfway up the trunk facing west. The raising of the pole illustrates the emphasis that is placed on ritualism in the Sun Dance: Four prayer songs are sung, and four times the pole is raised to the height of the breast, then laid down again. This is done with hand clapping, songs, and war whoops. Thereafter, eight persons lift the pole again and place it in its hole.

The lodge will now be erected. At a distance of some fifty feet from the center pole and encircling it, twelve sturdy poles are placed. They are connected with crossbeams at the top and joined to the center pole with rafters. One of these rafters has a stuffed eagle at the point where it connects with the center pole. The space between the twelve standing poles is interlaced with cottonwood brush. When finished, the lodge presents an airy building, partly shaded from the sun. This is important for the comfort of the dancers. Their special area is the sacred half-circle at the rear of the lodge. During the course of the ceremony the dancers arrange individual booths along the brush wall where they can rest and redecorate themselves (see the illustration on page 313).

Originally the Sun Dance of the Plains Indians was a ceremony that safeguarded the progress of the coming year by recapitulating and dramatically representing the creation. As far as we know this has never been the Shoshoni interpretation, although during this century the High God's role as creator (for Our Father) has been accepted by some Shoshoni. On the other hand, the idea of the Sun Dance lodge as a replica of the cosmos has been basic to Shoshoni thinking, as will emerge from the following.[24]

Thus it was said explicitly by the Indians that the lodge is sacred because it is a symbol of the world. People coming in to get healed are requested to take off their moccasins and boots. When the Sun Dance is over, the lodge is left to decay—no human agency may destroy it, in any case not the center pole. Here and there on the flats around Fort Washakie old center poles are still standing, monuments of past Sun Dances. The center pole is the most sacred part of the lodge, as we can see from the rites performed around it. It is seen as a communication channel between the people and God, a vehicle for people's prayers, and a source of divine power. It even represents Our Father. At the same time it stands for the Milky Way, the road to the beyond. The forked top of the pole symbolizes the two branches of the Milky Way. Obviously, the center pole is a cultic replica of the World Tree. It has the same function in other Plains Sun Dances.

This interpretation is strengthened by the presence of the buffalo head and the eagle (and eagle's nest) on the pole. The buffalo head, which reminds the Shoshoni of the first founding vision, represents the game animals and is itself a representative of the foremost game species—the chief of all animals, as one knowledgeable informant assured me. The eagle placed on a rafter at the fork of the center pole is not only the bringer of the second message, it is the leader of all birds and stands in an intimate relationship to the Supreme Being himself. Sometimes the eagle body is replaced with eagle feathers. The bunch of willows that is attached to the fork of the pole is now the eagle's nest, but was probably originally the grass on which the buffalo feeds. In earlier days it was apparently placed under the buffalo head. At any rate, the buffalo head and the eagle stand for two tiers of the universe, earth and sky. The World Tree penetrates both of them.

Buffalo head attached to the center pole of the Shoshoni Sun Dance lodge. The buffalo spirit stands for food and nourishment and is the chief of all animals. Over the buffalo head an eagle's nest is placed where the rafters come together.

In modern times there has been a Christian reinterpretation of this symbolism, so that the center pole symbolizes Christ, the peripheral twelve poles his apostles, the buffalo head the Old Testament and the eagle the New Testament. This is an interpretation that may have appealed to missionaries and Indian agents, but it is void of deeper meaning. It hides the rich traditional cosmological symbolism in which the Sun Dance lodge with all its details is a microcosmic representation of the world. Prayers and dramatic behavior during the Sun Dance also give evidence that in recent times this old ideological context has been forgotten. The Sun Dance has turned into a ceremonial complex where the main concern is the restoration of health.

When the Sun Dance lodge stands ready on the day after the last preliminary dance, the families taking part in the ceremony pitch their tents and adjoining arbors in a wide circle around the open place that has the dance lodge as its center. The dancers, all men of varying ages, make themselves ready. They decorate themselves partly with spots of clay, partly with paint. The first day the paint is usually red; black dots are painted on the face and arms. The second day the paint is yellow. The hair is braided, and in some cases false braids are used with headband and pendants. Occasionally a few feathers may be stuck in the hair of a mature dancer, a sign that he has a guardian spirit. Around the neck each dancer wears an eaglebone whistle with eagle down and a tribal necklace or hanging beads. Eagle down is also attached to the little finger of each hand. The upper body and the feet are naked, while the lower body is covered with a richly decorated apron.

We shall now follow the progress of the Sun Dance from day to day.

FIRST DAY When the evening star rises over the horizon, the dancers march into the dance lodge in a long row. Their numbers vary, but there may be as many as forty or fifty. They arrange themselves in the back of the lodge. The drummers and the choir of women take their seats in the foreground to the left, as is shown in figure 3-1. Standing at the center post, the main ceremonial leader prays to Our Father, a prayer in which his blessing is called down. Then the dancing and singing begin. Each song is repeated four times and finished by

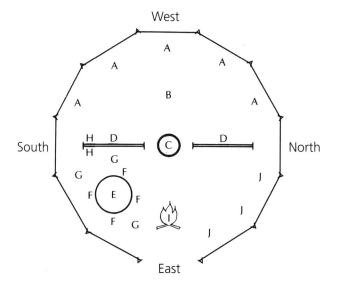

A   Booths for Dancers, Separated by Saplings of Cottonwood or Pine

B   Sacred Area

C   Center Pole

D   Log on the Ground Separating the Sacred Area from the Rest of the Lodge

E   Drum

F   Drummers and Male Singers

G   Female Singers

H   Old Men

I   Fire

J   Spectators

Figure 3-1. Plan of the Sun Dance Lodge.

whistles from the dancers' eaglebones. The dancing is a monotonous rocking up and down, now and then interrupted with shuffling steps toward the center pole and back again. The dancers turn their faces toward the east. This first evening the dancing is a concerted action by all participants and is quite vigorous.

The Shoshoni name of the Sun Dance is "dry-standing-dance." It designates the two most characteristic features of this ceremony, the protracted dancing and the abstention from water. With pauses for rest and sleep, particularly during the night hours, the dancing goes on for the next three days. All this time the dancers are forced to fast and abstain from drinks. Their feet get sore on the sandy and twiggy ground; the thirst, the heat of the day, and the cold of the night are trying. According to old Plains Indian standards this suffering is meaningful: It should make the supernatural powers take pity on the dancers and help them and their people. It is the same technique to win the powers that has been used in the vision quest. Psychologically expressed, it is a technique that stimulates a trance or state of altered consciousness and thus invites visions. Ever so many Shoshoni have acquired their supernatural powers in the twilight states of the Sun Dance.

Opening of the Shoshoni Sun Dance ritual. The leader prays in front of the dancers.

Dancing in the Shoshoni Sun Dance ritual.

Blessing of people in the Shoshoni Sun Dance.

SECOND DAY   At dawn there is sporadic dancing by single dancers or pairs of dancers. Most dancers are sitting shivering in their blankets before a big fire in front of the center pole. At sunrise the dancers form five lines behind the center pole. As the sun appears over the eastern horizon there is intense drumming and whistling, and the dancers stretch their hands toward the red globe. Thereafter they sit down to listen to the leader's morning prayer. This morning ceremony, which is repeated each of the following days, is followed by rest, morning toilet, and repainting.

This day the curing rites begin. About ten o'clock the dancing is resumed on a large scale, and after an hour's dancing, drumming, and singing the persons to be cured appear on the scene. They remove their moccasins and shoes and proceed to the center pole where they are treated by a medicine man, usually one of the ceremony leaders. With the aid of an eagle wing, the medicine man brushes the patients' sore spots, now and then filling his wing with power by touching it to the center pole. Later in the day groups of dancers are blessed by the medicine man in the same way. There is no observable difference between the curing and blessing procedures. They have the same aim: to strengthen the human being with supernatural power.

THIRD DAY   This day is said to be the hardest but also the most powerful day. Those who have medicine bags bring them forth, and sacred pipes circulate among drummers and dancers. Most curing rites are performed before midday, that is, while the sun is rising in the sky. The dancing is stronger than ever, and war whoops are heard over the drumming, singing, and whistling. The intense dancing has by now created circular tracks on the ground.

This is the day when sacred visions may appear to dancers. Some dancers are exhausted and lie prostrate on the ground, now and then tended to by the medicine men who massage them. Staggering dancers gaze at the sun or look steadfastly at the buffalo head. Dancers have told me how they have seen the head shaking and steam coming out of the nostrils.

FOURTH DAY   The curing and blessing rites continue. All the dancers appear in turns at the center pole to be blessed by the medicine men, alone or in groups. After noon all curing and blessing activities cease. Instead, again and again announcements are made that money has been donated by cured persons. More and more money is thrown upon a blanket spread out on the ground. Clothes and blankets are also heaped there by relatives of the dancers.

Late in the afternoon a couple of buckets of water are brought in and placed close to the center post. One of the medicine men steps forward to the buckets, faces east, prays over the water, and pours some water on the ground. This is an offering to Mother Earth. The buckets are then passed among the dancers who now rest behind screens in their booths. This is their first sip of water since the dance's commencement. This marks the end of the Sun Dance.

The donated gifts are distributed among the women of the camp. Some blankets are put down at the base of the sacred pole and remain there as offerings to the Supreme Being, an act of gratefulness for his help and blessings.

In the evening there is feasting, round dancing, and war dancing (the Wolf Dance), all dances of social entertainment. However, this concluding celebration, which is attended by all participating families, is very often moved to the evening of the following day. [See Religions of Africa pp. 74–75, Religions of Mesoamerica pp. 229–38, Judaism pp. 439–45, Christianity pp. 551–55, Islam pp. 674, 677–79, Hinduism p. 829, Buddhism pp. 937–41, Religions of China pp. 1021–24, and Religions of Japan pp. 1140–46, 1153–62 for description and discussion of festivals and annual celebrations.]

In retrospect, there is nothing in the Shoshoni Sun Dance expounding the new creation motif, which is so explicit in the Arapaho and Cheyenne sun dances.[25] Maybe the new creation motif was never clear to the Shoshoni or maybe the strong emphasis on curing and reception of supernatural powers after 1890 concealed it (which I find less probable, however). There is a cosmological interpretation implied in the structure of the dancing lodge, as we have seen, but it refers to Our Father as lord of the world, and not to creation.

Curing: Soul Loss and Spirit Intrusion

The concern about curing in the Sun Dance is directly related to the general Shoshoni curing complex. What the medicine men perform in their Sun Dance cures does not deviate from their ordinary methods of coming to grips with diseases; as mentioned previously, their curing activities have been inspired by their guardian spirits.

Among tribal peoples there is a close correspondence between disease etiology—the ideas of the causes of the disease—and the practical treatments of a disease. Whatever the ultimate causes of the disease, whether taboo infringement, sorcery, the wrath of the spirits, or something else, the immediate causes may be defined as **spirit** (or **object**) **intrusion** and **soul loss.** If we take a wider comparative view of these diagnoses as they occur among hunting peoples in Eurasia and America, they correspond to two different types of curing practices. Soul loss is usually cured by the medicine man's catching the lost soul and bringing it back to its owner. Object or spirit intrusion, on the other hand, is healed by the medicine man's removal of the foreign body from the patient. However, sometimes in a certain culture one diagnosis becomes dominant or one sort of treatment becomes dominant. In such cases the causal relationship between theory and practice breaks down. The Shoshoni curing complex is a case in point.

In earlier practice the Shoshoni medicine man cured soul loss by falling into a trance. In this state his own soul traveled toward the land of the dead where the lost souls of sick people usually made their way. Such trance expeditions still occurred at the beginning of this century. There are reports of how the medicine man, or shaman, could see his own body lying there on the ground, motionless, while in spirit form he floated away to the other world. Some medicine men could easily visit the land of the dead and return again, provided they did not eat any food there. Others dared not go "over that hill" separating the land of the dead from this world. A lost soul that had passed the boundary line could be lost forever.

Soul loss usually refers to a weakening or change of consciousness, such as during high fever or coma. The disappearance during this century of shamanic soul excursions, which my informants described as demanding tremendous power resources not possessed by present-day medicine men, resulted in the application of techniques of intrusion curing to diseases of mind and consciousness. Regarding this, I was told the following story.

An apparently dead child was brought to the medicine man Morgan Moon. Everybody thought the child was gone for good, but the medicine man said, "No, her soul has just temporarily left the body, but I shall bring it back." Then he touched the top of the child's head, passing his hand over and around it. Suddenly the child opened her eyes and looked at him. The next day she could play again and was completely recovered. Here, as it is in most Native American cultures, the crown of the head is considered the passage by which the soul leaves the body. According to Morgan's surviving sister (whom I interviewed), the presupposition was that the child's spirit had remained in the neighborhood of the body. However, the treatment applied (rubbing the head) is adapted from the technique of intrusion curing.

Today, the very diagnosis of soul loss is gone. All diseases are ascribed to intrusion by harmful objects or spirits. Originally, however, intrusion diseases were deadly diseases, wounds, infections, aches, interior diseases, and so on.

In former days the medicine men had to be invited to come and help in a formal ritual way. In the cases I had the privilege of watching there were no formalities, but much attention was paid to the economic satisfaction demanded by the medicine man.

As is the case in modern professional medicine, the doctor starts by finding out the causes and nature of the disease. (I only know of one medicine man who was supposed to have a precognition of the disease, Tudy Roberts, soon to be discussed.) One medicine man diagnosed the disease by looking through a black scarf, another by seeing with closed eyes. The idea is that the medicine man sees through the patient's body with his interior eye, a sort of X-ray process.

Shoshoni medicine man
Tudy Roberts.

When the diagnosis is made, that is, the supernatural cause has been revealed, the medicine man prays to his guardian spirit to come and help him. An experienced medicine man turns to the particular guardian spirit known to cure the disease that has just been diagnosed. Depending on the type of disease and on the blessings received from the guardian spirit, the medicine man has recourse to different methods to remove the disease agent.

We saw how in the Sun Dance the medicine man brushes the dancers and sick people with his eagle wing. The same method may be used when a patient seeks his help privately. I was told that the feathers draw out the disease object, which the medicine man then brushes away onto something nearby, such as the antlers of a deer that is running away. In the Sun Dance he puts the disease object on the center pole. Then, when the pole is touched again with the feather wing, the feather wing receives new power, which is then transferred to the patient. Another use of eagle feathers was demonstrated by the medicine man Tom Wesaw. He cured people who had been afflicted with tuberculosis by arrows shot from the *nynymbi's* bows. For this purpose he had recourse to eagle feathers, since the eagle, as we have seen, is the *nynymbi's* enemy. Tom touched the center of the patient's stomach with his feathers, then struck the feathers and, he asserted, felt the little arrow, which he put in his pocket. Then he went out in the dark and blew the arrow away.

The same operation can be achieved with a stick or other object (a buffalo horn, some say). The blowing away of the disease can be a curing method in itself: The medicine man blows on the sick spot through his rolled up fingers. In the past diseases were sometimes blown away to the whites—perhaps to return them to those who had introduced diseases that became devastating epidemics among the Indians.

Another familiar therapy is sucking out the disease. Like the curing by the use of feathers, sucking may also be tried in the Sun Dance. Different medicine men have different ways of sucking. One medicine man put his mouth to the sick spot, sucked, and spat out the evil thing into a vessel. Next, he threw it into the fire. An older colleague of his placed his elbow on the sick spot and sucked at the birthmark he had on the elbow, the idea being that the disease went up into the medicine man's arm and could be sucked out from there. It is difficult for people other than medicine men to see the disease object or disease spirit, but it has sometimes been described as a little being with arms and legs of a finger's length.

The world of the medicine men is best approached by focusing on one particular medicine man. Tudy Roberts (1883–1957), one of the most respected medicine men, was the head of a family known for its strict adherence to traditional religion and was a Ghost Dance leader in the conservative Sage Creek district. Still, like most Shoshoni, he had listened to what missionaries had to tell, so that some aspects of Christian ideas slipped into his conceptual world.

Tudy was reputed to have received his foremost power, lightning, at the rock drawings, but in direct conversation he denied this. He himself thought that dream visions did not grant sufficient powers—waking visions did. Tudy had experienced several waking visions, but apparently not at rock drawing places. He described and explained these experiences as follows:

> Our Father above empowered the spirits, those powers which are around us in the country. I have seen them many times: they have their hair braided, tied with strips of skin, and they all appear like Indians, not as animals. Once in a while such a [spirit] Indian appears to me when I am awake, although in a twilight state, not sleeping however. The Indian may also arrive in the dream, but then seems to come in a different way.

Tudy had many spirits of different kinds. He told me that the spirits liked him and that is why they came to him. Other people, he pointed out, were not liked so well by spirits. Only a few persons were as privileged as he was. The following report by Tudy on his acquisition of invulnerability medicine may serve as an example of a traditional dream vision.

> I dreamt that I looked toward the east at sunup and saw three bears sitting under some pine trees. I shot at them. One of them approached me and said, "Look now, you see all these bullets twisting the fur here?" "Yeah, I see them," said I. "This is the way I am," said the bear. "The bullets can't kill me." They looked like mud twisted in the fur. The bear said, "I want you to cut off one of my ears, and hang it in a thong at your side. This is the way you should be in the Sun Dance." The dream ended there. Later I found a dead bear, cut off the ear, and wear it now in the Sun Dance. No bullet can kill me. This is true. I never tell lies. That's the way I like to be.

Some dream visions authorized Tudy to initiate and lead a Sun Dance. Sometimes he received supernatural messages affecting other persons. Once in a vision he saw a woodpecker with a pinkish belly seated on the top of the Sun Dance pole singing a new song. The spirit told Tudy to keep this song secret, for one of the younger men would discover it soon and use it. Sometime afterward when the Sun Dance ceremony was held, this young man dreamed about Tudy giving him that song. The young man sang it in his sleep, and upon awakening he went down to the Sun Dance camp, joined the drummers, and introduced the new melody as a song to the American flag. (A flagpole is nowadays raised close to the entrance of the Sun Dance lodge.)

Tudy had secret powers. He knew, in a way that he could not explain, what the weather was going to be. No wonder, then, that he was counted as a great medicine man by most Shoshoni (although not by the Peyotists, followers of the peyote religion, to which he did not belong). Many spirits had blessed him with medicine power, the most important of which were the lightning spirits. Once, Tudy told me, he had just finished the Sun Dance and was sleeping on the ground in the foothills of Fort Washakie. In his dream he saw three spirits looking like men and dressed up like the Indians are today, except they wore very clean clothes and had feathers in their hats. They were singing. They were the lightning spirits. They told him to call upon them, "black clouds and lightning," when somebody had been struck by lightning. They would help him doctor the patient. Since that time Tudy had used for his doctoring an eagle tail and an eagle wing with a zigzag mark, made according to the instruction of the spirits. The feathers were hanging on the wall in his timber house. These feathers could also be used for other purposes. For instance, when Tudy did not feel well, he fanned himself with the eagle wing, for the spirits had told him to do so.

Although Tudy had the power to cure diseases like colds, measles, and paralysis, he never cured anybody unless he had received directions to do so in a dream. For instance, if somebody was very badly ill and Tudy was called upon to help out that person, he did not do so until he had prayed for assistance during the night and as a consequence a spirit had appeared and given him the right instructions. The methods used varied according to these instructions. A person with a sore throat was cured by Tudy sticking his finger down the person's throat. In most other cases he used his eagle wing, touching the sick spot with it, drawing the disease out with the wing, and destroying it or blowing it away. For instance, one of my informants, an old woman, had paralyzed legs. Tudy brushed away the "impurity" with his eagle wing, and little by little the woman recovered. In all cures Tudy started by praying to the spirit helping him and by singing a prayer song.

Tudy told me that only he himself could see the disease object. He described it as a round, red thing. If he was unable to extract it in the right way, it would return to the patient. There were diseases that Tudy knew how to cure but didn't do so because he had not received the authorization of the spirits. Wounds resulting from shots by the *nynymbi* belonged to this category. Whatever doctoring Tudy took on himself, he was humble and straightforward in his attitude and never overcharged his patients. He refused to accept money but gratefully received a blanket or a horse, because the spirits had told him to do so.

As mentioned, Tudy was a prominent member of the conservative Indians of the Sage Creek group. He arranged Ghost Dances, feeble echoes of the great Ghost Dance at the end of the last century. He told me that in the dance he was accompanied by the dead and sang with them. In dreams he had seen the dead, who, he said, look just like us. Since then, old Tudy has gone to live with the dead, forever. [See Religions of Africa pp. 45–51, 75–79, Judaism pp. 457–69, Christianity pp. 573–86, Hinduism pp. 820–26, Religions of China pp. 1040–54, and Religions of Japan pp. 1163–72 for description and discussion of life histories and personal accounts.]

New Religious Approaches

Religion, although conservative, is always changing. Shoshoni religion has changed considerably during the span of time we can view it, that is, since the beginning of the nineteenth century. Influences from Plains tribes were responsible for the adoption of the Sun Dance at that time. Influences from Christianity made themselves known at least from the 1840s, possibly earlier, since there was close contact between white trappers and Shoshoni Indians from the 1820s onward.[26] Christian influence was strengthened during the course of the century, both directly and indirectly. [See Religions of Africa pp. 24, 31, 60–61, Religions of Mesoamerica pp. 112–14, 215–21, Hinduism pp. 766–67, 770, and Religions of China pp. 988–89 for discussion of invasion and colonization.]

In a direct way, Christian ideas entered the Shoshoni scene partly through the French Catholic and Iroquois trappers who had joined the tribe and partly through Catholic missionaries. In July 1840 the well-known Catholic Father Pierre-Jean de Smet held the first holy mass for Shoshoni Indians close to the town of Daniel, on the upper Green River (the famous *la prairie de la messe,* "the prairie where Mass was held"). For some time the Mormons exerted a considerable influence, and to this day there are Indians who have been "washed" (baptized), as they say, by Mormons. The introduction of first Episcopalian and then Catholic missions on the reservation in the 1880s contributed to a general spread of Christian ideas, but also to a relativization of the Christian message through the divergent doctrines and rituals of the two churches. In this century also other Christian denominations have appeared on the reservation.

The impact of Christianity is difficult to measure. Certainly practically all Wind River Shoshoni are in some way affiliated with Christian schools or churches. However, at the same time many Indians retain ideas and celebrate rituals belonging to traditional Shoshoni religion. And, as we shall see, a good deal of them cling to new Indian religious faiths. Christian control through the missions has declined in recent times. However, as assimilation to white civilization intensifies, conventional Christianity becomes more accessible as a natural spiritual path.

Indirectly, Christianity has played a role by inspiring new religious movements, on one hand, and by stimulating a partial reorientation of old traditional religious rituals, on the other. The Ghost Dance was one of these new religious movements. It had crystallized out of old traditional and new Christian ideas and received its definitive form in the divine message of a Paiute Indian from Nevada named Wovoka. In visions Wovoka had been informed that the spirits of the dead would return and that the old Indian world would be regained if people danced the round dance and prayed. This was an attractive message to dispirited tribes that had lost the wars for their land and independence and were now threatened by political, social, cultural, and religious dissolution. Representatives of many tribes, among them Wind River Shoshoni, visited the Paiute prophet and were taught his doctrines. The Ghost Dance spread like a prairie fire among the Basin and Plains tribes in 1890. However, its appearance among the Sioux led to severe clashes between them and the U.S. military. This spelled the doom of the Ghost Dance. It was repressed and survived only on a small scale on some reservations. We have seen how the Shoshoni Tudy Roberts conducted Ghost Dances even in the 1950s. These dances were the last of a great religious movement—and also the last traces of the Shoshoni Father Dance.[27] [See Religions of Africa pp. 25, 54–57, 79–82, Religions of Mesoamerica p. 240, Judaism pp. 427–31, 456–75, Christianity pp. 529–33, Islam pp. 698–700, Hinduism pp. 770–74, 828–31, Buddhism pp. 952–56, Religions of China pp. 998–1002,

1055–59, and Religions of Japan pp. 1132–33, 1163–72 for discussion of new religious movements.]

Another new religion, peyotism, has been more tenacious. This is a Pan-Indian religion that has grown out of an old pre-Columbian ritual in northern Mexico and southern Texas centered around the small spineless peyote cactus (*Lophophora williamsii*). The believers in peyote's power gather at night meetings where they consume the cactus. Peyote is a hallucinogenic (vision-producing) herb and creates feelings of sincere fellowship and solidarity. A peculiar ritual has developed around the eating of peyote. This new religion, which absorbed Catholic concepts and rituals, slowly spread among the southern Plains Indians in the last century and was introduced to the Shoshoni about 1919. It now is used by about 75 percent of the Shoshoni population. On Saturdays the quick drumming from a lit-up tipi or wooden house marks the presence of a peyote meeting. The drumming, singing, praying, and consuming of peyote goes on the whole night. Peyotism has accomplished what Christianity apparently failed to do—unite the Indians in a church of their own, the Native American Church, and offer them a faith that satisfies their "Indianness," while providing relief and meaning in a discordant new age. [See Religions of Mesoamerica pp. 226–29 for description of the peyote hunt of the Huichol Indians.]

At the same time the old traditional religion has continued to live on, at least in fragments. Its central feature today, the Sun Dance, is still practiced, although its form has changed as times have changed. About 1890 its old associations with war were discarded, and it took on the character of a curing ceremony, the details of which we have seen. At the same time its symbolism began to be reinterpreted in a Christian spirit so that, for instance, the twelve roof rafters that had been thought to represent the tailfeathers of the eagle were transformed into a representation of the twelve apostles of Jesus. Thus Christian ideas were absorbed into the Sun Dance, changes that certainly pleased the white authorities, but the basic religious structure was not changed. Finally, the Sun Dance absorbed older independent rites, such as the vision quest. Visionaries today receive their supernatural power through the Sun Dance; practically all the old beliefs and rituals are now to be found concentrated in it. We may even talk about a "Sun Dance religion." Moreover, the Sun Dance is today the main manifestation of Shoshoni tribal cohesion.

Christianity, Peyotism, Sun Dance religion—they are all available to Shoshoni, whose traditional application of religious compartmentalization has taught them to accept the variability of religious forms.

13

The Religion of the Zuni: Farming, Masked Dancers, and the Power of Fertility

The Development of Zuni Religion and Culture

ZUNI IS THE NAME of both an Indian pueblo, or town, and the people of this pueblo.[28] The pueblo of Zuni is situated in westernmost New Mexico, close to the Arizona state line. Its environment could be characterized as a broad valley of high altitude between wooded mountains in the east and arid plains in the west, partly covered by greasewood, yucca, and cactus. The pueblo itself is located on the north bank of the main drainage, the Upper Zuni River. It gives the impression of being situated on a height, for it is built on the mounds of former houses.

Indian neighbors are the once roving Navajo in the north and Apache groups in the south. The closest Pueblo Indians are the Acoma and Laguna in the east. In the northwest, within the boundaries of Arizona, the westernmost Pueblo Indians, the Hopi and their "guests" since the 1680s, the Tewa, have their homes in a series of pueblos. Zuni's rather isolated position in relation to the other pueblos has probably been one of the factors that contributed to its characteristic tendency to combine religious and social organization. Indeed, the Zuni are famous for having constructed the most complex ritual organization of aboriginal North America.

The prehistory of the Zuni is veiled in darkness, but so far as we know, they have always resided in the area where they live today. The Zuni have no linguistic kin. They may have come from the west, as their own traditions tell us, but there is no substantial evidence to support these claims. Proof that the Hopi pueblo of Oraibi has been occupied since 1100 C.E. marks it as the oldest continuously inhabited town in North America, but there are reasons to presume that the Zuni may have occupied their present location even earlier. At any

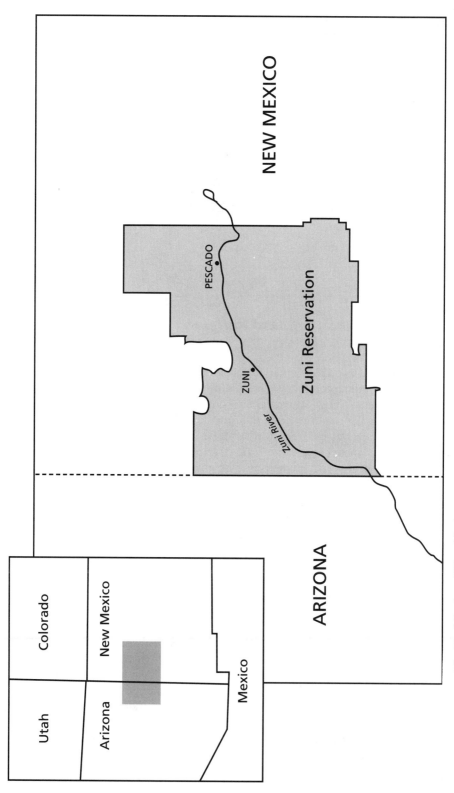

The Zuni Region of New Mexico.

rate, archaeologists have been able to follow an unbroken line of development in this area from the early Basketmaker III times about 700 or 800 C.E. to the later Pueblo eras. These Basketmaker Indians (probably Zuni) cultivated corn and lived in settlements of four or five oval pit houses. About 1000 C.E. these pit houses functioned as ritual meeting places, or *kivas,* while big masonry buildings had taken their place as living quarters. Typical to both house constructions was the entrance through an opening at the top joined to the bottom floor by a ladder. When the Spaniards arrived in 1540 the Zuni people occupied six masonry structures, or pueblos, each one with hundreds of rooms. It is obvious that the period 1000–1200 C.E. when these houses were built marked the transition of Zuni society and religion to greater complexity. The many rectangular *kivas* in close proximity to the houses or even attached to them at this time testify to the growth of ceremonialism.

The history of the Zuni while under Spanish rule is characterized by increasing Spanish influence on administration and religion. The Zuni establishment of a secular administration under a governor and his assistants—all of them appointed by the high religious hierarchy in Zuni—dates from this period. The Catholic mission efforts made little progress, although churches were established and saints' fiestas and other festival occasions exerted Catholic influences.

From 1680 to 1692 a general Pueblo uprising against the Spanish meant a major drawback for the Spanish rule and mission, but also a decline for the Zuni. They deserted their towns in fear of Spanish revenge. When they finally returned, they had decreased in numbers and from that time occupied only one of their old pueblos, which they still inhabit today as Zuni pueblo. In addition, many Zuni currently live in outlying villages close to the farmlands, originally the tribe's summer villages.

When Zuni territory became part of the United States in 1846, a new period of active interaction with the whites began. In 1877 the United States government established the Zuni Reservation. In spite of pressure first from Catholics and then Presbyterians, the Zuni tended to close the doors to missionary efforts, although they formally accepted Catholic ritualism. There were considerable difficulties with accusations of witchcraft during the last decades of the nineteenth century and the first decades of the present century. When tribal warfare became obsolete, the powerful Bow Priesthood, which was formerly composed of warriors who had taken enemy scalps and had the particular duty of protecting the town from enemies, turned its attention to the persecution of witches accused of upsetting the general welfare of the tribe.

Zuni culture is part of the well-known Pueblo culture of the Southwest, one of the most interesting aboriginal cultures of North America. It is particularly famous for its exquisite art in pottery and silver and turquoise jewelry, its architectural accomplishments, its conservatism that has managed to retain both traditional and spiritual culture, and its beautiful ceremonialism. Basic to this cultural flowering have been the achievements of horticulture and, since Spanish days, sheepherding. Nowhere else in native North America has the tilling of the soil been as intense as among the Pueblo Indians. Not only has this distinctive agricultural practice formed the basis of their economy and sedentary lifestyle, but it has also been an integral part of their religious beliefs and aesthetic expressions. Their success in keeping out white intruders has enabled them to preserve their ancient traditions intact. Many rituals are still being performed in secrecy and remain unknown to us, although the Zuni and the Hopi are more open in this respect than the eastern Pueblo Indians; for the latter anthropologists have had to resort to more or less clandestine methods of recording beliefs and practices.

There is a cultural boundary between the western and the eastern Pueblos, especially in social and ceremonial respects. For example, the eastern Pueblo Indians lack clans but are divided into two ceremonial halves or moieties and follow a patrilineal kinship system, instead of the matrilineal kinship system of the western Pueblo Indians. However, the general cultural picture is very much the same over the entire Pueblo area. The characteristic ethnographic traits are heavy dependence on maize, squash, and beans, with men as cultivators of the soil; the use of cultivated cotton as textile material, with men weaving cloth on standing looms; habitation in multistoried and clustered houses of masonry and adobe; and the manufacture of pottery with polychrome or glazed decoration (red and black among the Zuni) on a whitish ground. Other craftwork includes the production of **kachina** dolls (among the Hopi), silverwork, and the manufacture of turquoise and shell beads (in Santo Domingo and Zuni about 90 percent of Zuni men and women work on silver and turquoise ornaments). Add to this an elaborate ceremonialism with priests, dancers, altars, sand paintings, and masked performances centering around concern for rain and fertility, and we have before us one of the most dramatic and expressive traditions in native North America.

Within this cultural configuration the Zuni hold a prominent position. They are the most populous of the Pueblo nations—they number more than seven thousand—and they are, as said before, the pueblo with the most complex ceremonial organization. To outsiders it is also the best known of the pueblos, having been documented in the 1880s by such writers as Frank Hamilton Cushing and Matilda Coxe Stevenson and since then intensely analyzed by many anthropologists and scholars of religion.

The sight of Zuni pueblo is currently not as imposing as, for instance, the multistoried pueblo Taos or the pueblo Acoma on its high mesa. There was once a mighty town called Halona with terraced houses up to five stories on the site where Zuni now stands. Today the houses are single story, built around a plaza. As in some other pueblos the Catholic main church has a dominant position close to the plaza. It was erected about 1699, just after the end of the rebellion, and marks the height of Catholic reconquest, but since that time it has fallen into disuse. Characteristic of Zuni are the small gardens surrounded by stone walls.

In spite of modernization of living conditions and the introduction of commercialism and higher education, the Zuni hold tenaciously to their old religion. We know very little about the development of Zuni religion besides what has been mentioned above. One researcher, Alfred Kroeber, suggests that the concentration of all Zuni to one pueblo in the 1690s meant the rise of the intricate priestly and ritual organization at this time. Earlier, he maintains, the organizational pattern had been less systematized, as in the more easterly pueblos.[29] This is possible. At the same time, there are traces of an even more complex organization in the past. Thus there probably once existed, as among the eastern Pueblos, a sacred moiety organization between a south or summer people, with a Sun Priest, and a north or winter people, with a Rain Priest. There seems also to have been a grouping of clans into major units, so-called phratries, corresponding to the six sacred directions: the four cardinal points, zenith, and nadir.[30] It is thus reasonable to suppose that the complicated ritual system is rather ancient, but that a thorough reorganization and elaboration took place in the years after 1700.

As we shall discover, the outcome of this process is an organization in which different socioreligious groups criss-cross one another: extended family household groups (which are the foundation of Zuni social and ceremonial organization), clans, *kiva* dance groups, rain societies, medicine societies, and priesthoods. All these groups are marvelously integrated into a coherent ceremonial system that makes up the backbone of Zuni religion.

However, no religion is understandable unless it is related to basic principles of faith. Even a religion as expressly ceremonial as Zuni religion has its premises in people's personal religiosity. Dreams and visions sometimes support religious beliefs, although not to the same extent as among the Plains Indians. Because of the highly integrated character of Zuni religion, the ideological premises are given in the myths. Myth and religion form a unit in Zuni religion, the rituals furnishing the practice and the myths the code of religion.

The Structure of Zuni Religion: Emergence from the Earth and the Reemergence of the Spirits

The Myth of Origins

Zuni religious thought takes its departure from the myth of origins. There are two different forms of this origin myth. According to the form known as an **Emanation Myth,** the world emanated from two primeval beings; according to the form known as an Emergence Myth, humankind emerged from the interior of the earth. In fact, the latter account may be considered a continuation of the former. However, during the present century only the Emergence Myth seems to have been known (as reported by recording anthropologists).

The Emanation Myth tells how the Sky Father (or Sun Father) appeared out of the mists of the primeval world. He cohabited with Mother Earth, and life was conceived in the deepest, fourth womb of the earth. This is what has been called the "world-parents myth," known among some Pueblo peoples and tribes in southern California, with analogues in Polynesia and East Asia.[31] It links the origin of the world to sexual procreation and probably is associated with agrarian fertility beliefs.

The Emergence Myth, diffused over large parts of horticultural Indian North America, is definitely part of such agrarian beliefs. The Zuni know it in several versions, but the religiously significant points are roughly the same in all versions. The following is a summary of the Emergence Myth as presented by Elsie Clews Parsons, Kroeber, and Cushing.

In the beginning the world was empty. Only the Sun Father and Moon Mother were up in the sky, while the people were down in the fourth dark underworld. The Sun asked his two sons, the twin war gods *ahayuta,* to descend there and bring the people up in his light. The two gods, who are described as stars, did so. They instructed the people, who made themselves ready. They took with them all their sacred bundles for making rain, making snow, and making seeds grow, and climbed up along a reed (in some versions, using a pine tree as a ladder). They passed through four underworlds: the soot world, the sulfur-smell world, the fog world, and the feather-wing world, where they perceived faint light. Finally, they emerged into the bright world of the Sun Father.

There was an old man who was fetched by the two war gods to become **pekwin** (the Sun Priest, the spiritual leader). Spider inspired him to tell the people the identity of the various sacred bundles. Two witches were discovered who said that they had come up from the underworld to kill some people so that the world would not become crowded. They also brought corn of different colors and were therefore accepted. The witches were given a Rain Chief's little daughter to try their powers on. She died and went back to the place of origin. She told two people who came to see her that she would stay there forever and that whoever died would come there.

After this incident the people moved about in an easterly direction, now and then stopping at a certain place for four years before continuing again. At the first stop the people, who had webbed feet and tails, cut their tails off and cut their fingers and toes apart and thus became human. At another stop the son and daughter of a Rain Chief had incestuous relations with each other and were transformed into clowns, "mudheads." Then they formed two mountains with a river between. When crossing the river many women could not hold on to their small children and lost them. Shortly afterward the people heard singing and dancing from the bottom of a lake: It was their drowned children. The dead children said they would stay there forever, instead of being stationed at the first place of the dead, which was too far away from the living. However, the people continued migrating, and at one place they accepted clan names.

The people then arrived at a place where other beings tried to prevent their passage. Fierce fighting ensued. In their desperation the people turned to the two *ahayuta,* the divine twins of war. The younger twin managed to shoot down the giantess that was leading the enemies, and the war came to an end. And so the tale proceeds until the navel of the world, Zuni, was found.[32]

There are several important observations one can make in connection with this myth. It belongs to the class of Emergence Myths common among southern maize-cultivating Indians. Like many other myths, its focus is limited in that it deals primarily with the Zuni (and the Hopi, Havasupai, and Navajo secondarily). What is more important, the incidents of this myth are recited to confirm supernatural validation for rituals and ceremonies, clan organizations, societies, patron animals, and so on.[33] Indeed, depending on the narrator and the situation, particular rituals and sacred objects are emphasized in different myth versions. The most detailed instructions are put in the mouths of the mythical beings. Conversely, deities and spirits that have little or no connection with rituals are scarcely mentioned. The myth is a charter of Zuni rituals.

Zuni myth outlines the major aspects of the Zuni understanding of the nature of the cosmos. In turn, rituals are firmly rooted in Zuni cosmogony and cosmology. This cosmology is closely connected with the surrounding landscape.[34] It was said in the foregoing that the Zuni pueblo is represented as the navel of the earth, the middle around which all cosmic orientation takes place. In ceremonies people observe six sacred points of orientation in the order of north, west, south, east, zenith, and nadir. The six ceremonial rooms, or *kivas,* are correlated with these points, and the fourteen clans are subsumed under them. North is associated with the color yellow and air, west with blue and water, south with red and fire, east with white and earth—associations that have apparently been inspired by heavenly colors and experiences of climate and geography. The zenith is multicolored (the changing sky) and nadir is black (the underworld). As there are four underworlds, there are also four upper worlds, the lowest one for crows, the highest one for eagles.

The Zuni Cosmos

The cosmos, then, consists of four underworlds, a middle world that is the home of the human beings, and four sky worlds. Attention is naturally drawn to the lower worlds, which, in this horticultural society, represent the origins of the human beings. In all horizontal directions the land is surrounded by the ocean, or rather the four oceans, connected with the four cardinal directions. The Sun Father has one house in the eastern and another in the western ocean. The sky is formed like a bowl and is solid. The stars are lights fixed to the sky vault. Apparently there is no observation of the movements of the stars.

In this cosmography the sacred number six appears again and again: There are six directions, and the supernatural beings are connected with them. Thus, there are six places for the rain gods, the lightning and thunder gods, the **beast gods,** the hoofed animal spirits, and so on. Sometimes seven sacred locations are mentioned, the "middle" being added to the other six. However, many supernatural beings are located in the four cardinal directions, and in rituals the most important number seems to be four. This horizontal symbolism means more to the Zuni and other Pueblo tribes than the vertical symbolism among the North American hunting tribes, which focuses on the World Tree.

The sacred geography is oriented around Zuni, or rather, the Zuni center (*itiwana,* "the middle place"). Inside a room in one of the houses there is "the heart of the world," symbolized by an altar containing two columns of rock, one of crystal and one of turquoise. Only the high priest of the foremost Rain Priesthood has access to this center of the world.

The pueblo is spiritually divided into seven parts. The clans are grouped in clusters within these parts, so that "north," for instance, includes all clans with totemic names referring to this direction: the Crane, Grouse, and Evergreen Oak clans. Several houses contain the sacred medicine bundles the Zuni once brought up from the underworld, according to the myth. These bundles are wrapped around jars with water and seeds, stone images (**fetishes**) of beast and prey gods, and masks belonging to the society of masked dancers (*kachinas*). In the storerooms are kept the "corn mothers," the harvested corn ears with the colors of the six directions: yellow, blue, red, white, speckled, and black corn. Zuni as the center of the world thus holds some of the most sacred objects of the universe. Just northwest of the town the Scalp House preserves enemy scalps, which are supposed to promote fertility. These scalps are "water and seed beings" and bestow water, seeds, wealth, longevity, power, and strong spirit.

Spirits and Gods

Many spirits and gods have their residences on mountaintops, in cairns, and in the lakes not far from Zuni. Thus, the *kachina* spirits have their central realm at the bottom of a lake west of Zuni, as the origin myth tells us. People who go there risk their lives, as Stevenson informs us. The twin gods, the *ahayuta,* are celebrated with shrines situated in the close vicinity of Zuni. East of Zuni in the surroundings of the Sandia Mountains lives the lord of the medicine societies, the culture hero **Poshayanki,** who is also head of the beast gods. Unlike most other culture heroes in North America he is the object of worship in a cult.

Springs all over the country are the living quarters of the rain gods. Indeed the supernatural powers are everywhere in nature, a part of the world surrounding humankind. Still, they are different from humans in that they belong to another order of being. The Zuni indicate this by distinguishing the "raw people," the spirits (and gods), from the "cooked people," or "daylight people," the ordinary human beings.[35] The spirits are raw because they eat food that is raw or receive offerings of food that may be raw. Thus, the Zuni throw pieces of food into the fire or on the floor while they say a short prayer. The spirits are supposed to nourish themselves on the spiritual essence of the food. There is however a certain ambiguity in the concept of raw beings. One pioneering investigator, Cushing, thought that the concept stood for game animals, water animals and water sprites, and prey animals and prey gods, but not for other beings. This seems to indicate that the raw beings primarily should be the animal spirits, and that any animal is potentially an animal spirit—you never know whether an animal you meet is a spirit or not. Any extension of the concept to cover other spiritual categories is secondary. The plain fact is that there is no generic term for supernatural beings.

Nor is there a set of terms corresponding to our distinction between spirits and gods. In North American research it has been common usage to talk about the supernaturals as spirits and reserve the term *god* for the Supreme Being. Students of Zuni religion, however, have called the more important spirits "gods." That rule will be followed here: Supernatural beings that have strong ritual functions will be referred to as gods, although the Zuni linguistic usage does not provide for this distinction.

There are, on the other hand, classes of supernatural beings that in Zuni can be comprehended under a single term. One such term is **awonawilona.** The first ethnologists to explore it thought that it stood for the Sun Father or for a bisexual creator. Apparently, *awonawilona,* "holder of the paths of life," is an epithet for two high beings, the Sun Father and the Moon Mother. In the plural it includes a large range of supernaturals. The misinterpretation of a bisexual divinity derives from the fact that both male and female spirits are contained in the collective concept; if the concept is misunderstood as indicating one being, the result is the mistaken notion of one divinity with a bisexual character. The alternate use of a supreme metaphysical concept for a specific divine being and a collective reference to supernaturals in general is well known in other American Indian tribes. (Compare, for example, the term Wakan Tanka among Lakota Sioux Indians.)

Father Sun is the paramount figure in the Zuni pantheon, as he is among many Pueblo groups, although among the Zuni's eastern Pueblo neighbors the Corn Mother is the dominating divinity—a not infrequent phenomenon in a matrilinear agricultural community. In Zuni the Sun is the life-giving god, connected with the Dawn People (Spirits of the Dawn). According to one source it was due to his will that human beings came out of the underground. When nobody would give him prayer sticks—short rods with feathers "planted" in the ground to embody a prayer—he sent for human beings who then ascended from their underworld. Another myth has it that the culture hero Poshayanki prayed to the Sun to deliver humankind from the dark world in the interior of the earth. Although the Moon is called our mother she is certainly not a sexual partner of the Sun. She shares however in the cult dedicated to the Sun. She is reborn each month, grows into maturity, and then wanes. [See Religions of Africa pp. 64–66, and Religions of Mesoamerica p. 166 for mention of the High God.]

The Sun begets offspring with other female beings. The diminutive war gods, *ahayuta,* were born when the rays of the Sun had penetrated the mist surrounding a waterfall. In mythic times they were people's helpers at the emergence from the underworld; in our own days they are the source of wind and snow. They live on the mountaintops where people have erected their shrines. The myths describe them as playful little boys ready for mischief of all sorts, obscene and ridiculous, but they save humans from monsters—they are simultaneously culture heroes and tricksters in the same form.

Other beings also figure as culture heroes. One of them is Poshayanki, "the wisest of men," who once instituted the medicine fraternities. He is thought to have implored Sun to save humankind from the underworld, in some versions of the Emergence Myth. Another culture hero is **Payatamu,** who taught the people to cultivate corn and then disappeared. He is connected with the myth of the flight of the Corn Maidens (see below). His flute is the male sexual symbol.

In the sea and underground waters dwells the water serpent, conceived of as a plumed or horned snake. This monster can bring rain and may impregnate bathing women. He controls floods, landslides, and earthquakes. Powers of rain and dew belong to the **uwanammi,** who live along the ocean shores and in springs all over the country. They travel as clouds and patches of fog. Some of them are responsible for lightning and thunder. As gods of the rain they do not stand alone, for most Zuni supernaturals are rainmakers. Also the *kachina* spirits bring rain when they leave their abodes in the lake "whispering spring" west of Zuni and appear as clouds. The *kachinas,* or **koko,** are the spirits of the dead who, like the dead in other horticultural religions, further fertility through the life-giving rains. Also the spirits of the dead enemies, through the preserved scalps, bring rain. There are indications that some of the *uwanammi* are ancestors, like the *kachinas,* but the two categories are obviously otherwise not identical. Indeed, the ancestors seem to form a vague collectivity of spirits that are identical with several spirit categories, but more generally with *kachinas.*

Hunting and Animal Spirits

Some of the supernaturals, and also some of the *kachinas,* supervise hunting and game animals. Considering the emphasis placed on agricultural pursuits, it may seem surprising that hunting is at all tied to Zuni religion. But we must remember that the hunting substructure of American Indian cultures is conspicuous within the life of all tribes and that the hunt is a subsidiary economic pursuit in Pueblo culture. Therefore, it is to be expected that clear traces of the old hunting ideology are found among the Zuni. They are careful to see that the bones of slain animals are not molested, they honor the dead animal with blankets and jewelry, and their designs of animals on pottery and symbolic shields belonging to the priesthoods display a line drawn between mouth and heart—the "lifeline" of the animals.[36]

The ancient heritage of hunting and its continued importance explains the belief in animal spirits among the Zuni. One category of animal spirits is the beast or prey gods, which are the masters or patrons of animal species. Foremost among them is the Mountain Lion, guardian of the north (for he is yellow, the color of the north). Next in rank come the Bear, guardian of the west, the Badger, guardian of the south, the Wolf, guardian of the east, the Eagle, guardian of the upper regions, and the Mole, guardian of the lower regions—all of them colored or speckled in a way that associates them with the respective regions. However, in line with Zuni religious organization, these prey gods are subordinated to Poshayanki, the chief of the twelve medicine societies, and are his personal guardians. In other words, the representatives of hunting culture and untamed "nature" have been organized into the socioreligious system of the urban, agricultural Zuni. Animal spirits have assumed healing functions in addition to their old functions of providing good luck in hunting. The latter functions have been eclipsed by the former. Animal spirits have also become gods of magic and witchcraft.

Another category of animal spirits are the masters of the "hoofed game animals." They are also arranged according to the sacred directions, although their numbers have been expanded with other game lords to make up the necessary six varieties: the Mule Deer in the north, the Mountain Sheep in the west, the Antelope in the south, the Whitetail Deer in the east, the Jackrabbit in the zenith, and the Cottontail in the nadir. There is also mention of a mother of all game animals who furthers their propagation and who lives at a place south of Zuni. This tradition is obviously in conflict with another one, according to which dead game animals go to the great Kachina Village at the bottom of the sacred lake west of Zuni and are restored there. Not unexpectedly, therefore, this mother of the game is represented as an enemy of the lake *kachinas.*

Farming and the Corn Maidens

While the animal spirits or gods are important as mediators between the medicine societies and the culture hero Poshayanki, the spirits of earth and vegetation are directly related to horticulture. Thus we turn again to Mother Earth, who in the Emanation Myth is described as a sexual partner of Father Sun. In general beliefs she is always recognized as a vague personification of the earth and its growth. As we have noted, the four underworlds are her wombs. The Zuni pray to her in wintertime "that our earth mother may wrap herself in a fourfold robe of white meal, that she may be covered with frost flowers." Then comes spring "when our earth mother is replete with living waters," and the Zuni pray for summer, or

> That our earth mother
> May wear a fourfold green robe,
> Full of moss,
> Full of flowers,
> Full of pollen.[37]

The flowering season is a work of many forces in addition to Mother Earth—the rain and thunder gods, the *kachinas,* the water monsters, and of course the life-giving Father Sun. The most important aspect of vegetation, maize, is of many different colors, all personified in the Corn Maidens. Also in this case the spiritual beings are vaguely identical to their plant forms, the corn. The corn plants have been described as personified beings whose tassels are their heads and who hold the maturing corn ears in their arms. This treatment of earth and corn as live forces is a good illustration of the way the Zuni combine the spiritual and material.

These identifications between spirit and matter may make us wonder whether the general division between this world and a world of another order is applicable here. The answer to this question is that we must not expect strict conformity to abstract logic by American Indians. In principle the Zuni maintain a distinction between the two worlds; in practice the boundary between the two worlds is often disregarded as a result of the human tendency to give concrete form to religious concepts: in this way they become more realistic. Earth and corn are more palpable substances than sky and ethereal ghosts; therefore they give a more "realistic" impression. This is further complicated by the fact that Zuni religion tends to combine the spiritual and the material in ritual performances and mask ceremonialism.

The Corn Maidens are a good example of Zuni myth and ritual: They are the main persons in a dramatic myth describing (like some ancient Near Eastern myths) the flight of the fertility and vegetation goddesses from the lands and their return. There are many versions of this myth in Zuni, but they are similar in their general structure and course of events.[38] The myth recounts how the Corn Maidens are insulted by the people in their storerooms—they are not cared for or are even assaulted by a man who is described as a Bow Priest or as one of the divine twins. (This really means the same thing, for the *ahayuta* are the supernatural counterparts of the Bow Priests.) As a result, the Corn Maidens flee the land, or at least hide themselves under the wings of ducks (in the ocean), causing a famine. The people send out messengers to find the vegetation goddesses. In one version the seeker is the culture hero Payatamu, the initiator of the corn cultivation. This handsome flute player, patron of the Flute Cult associated with one of the medicine societies, recovers the Corn Maidens and lures them back to the people. They consent to "give their flesh" to the people, and the famine is over.

Like other Zuni myths, this corn myth is dramatized in ritual: in the Thlahewe ceremony (a corn ceremony every four years), in the harvest rituals each fall, and in the **Shalako** ceremony in wintertime. On these occasions the Corn Maidens are impersonated, or their corn ear representatives are treated like persons. It is interesting to note that the Zuni are reluctant to sell corn from their homes, because they fear that all their corn may follow what is sold, exactly as the stored corn in mythical times followed the fleeing Corn Maidens.

There are other female spirits as well that play a role in the life of the Zuni Indians. For instance, the maker of Zuni prayer sticks—short rods with feathers that are "planted" in the ground to embody a prayer—calls on the three "mothers": Clay Woman, Black Paint Woman, and Cotton Woman. These spirits help him in turn to tie the cotton around the stick and to "clothe the plume wands with their flesh."[39]

The remarkable thing about all these divinities and spirits we have just reviewed is that they are integrated into some ritual: All these divinities and spirits have their main function in these rituals rather than appearing as beings who reveal themselves out in nature or in people's dreams. With only slight overstatement we could say that the spirits are primarily important in relation to the ritual aims they fulfill and to the ritual organizations they preside over and protect.

An example of this integration is the connection between sacred time, rituals, and spirits—what is usually called the calendar round. As in other Native American cultures, the Zuni have a time concept according to which year follows after year, season after season, in what some scholars have called an "undulating" or cyclical pattern. It is true that in modern times a more linear concept of time has been recorded, manifested in ideas that at the end of the world all things made by humankind will rise against them and hot rain will fall. However, such ideas obviously have originated in Western (and Christian) notions of a final catastrophe. The typical agricultural time pattern is the cyclical pattern, and this seems to be an ancient form with the Zuni.

This pattern takes its beginning each year with the rituals for a successful corn cultivation and therewith a healthy and happy life for all Zuni. The year ends when the powers of fertility have been exhausted and have to be renewed. Thus a sacred year begins, with a calendar of festivals and rituals closely correlated with the growth, maturing, and harvesting of the grain. We have here clear parallels to the agricultural calendars in Europe and Asia. Like other Pueblo tribes, the Zuni divide their year into two halves, one period between midwinter and midsummer, and another period from midsummer to the following midwinter. The first period is marked by cleansing rituals and ritual dances to ensure growth and flowering. The second period is dedicated to rain-promoting ceremonies, so that the harvest will be assured. We may conclude that the two seasons of the calendar year are ecologically adjusted to the welfare of the maize and, accordingly, to the lives of human beings. (A more detailed account of the progress of the ritual year will be given in the next section.)

Kachinas

The main spirits figuring in this calendar are the *kachinas,* Zuni *koko. Kachina* is actually a Hopi word and is the general term by which all spirits of this kind among Pueblo peoples have come to be known to the outside world, so it will be used here to refer to Zuni spirits. *Kachinas* are, in Zuni thought, all "masked" beings, that is, all those spirits that can be impersonated in ritual dances with masks. The *kachinas* serve many purposes. They are, among other things, cloud and rainmakers who approach the pueblo in the form of ducks. They come from the mountains or from the "Kachina Village" at the bottom of the sacred lake southwest of Zuni, which is the home for most of them.

This area is also the home of the dead, or rather, those dead that have been initiated into the *kachina* society—and, as we shall see, the majority of all men belong to this society. At death, the corpse is buried in the churchyard with its head to the east. For four days the spirit of the dead person lingers. During this time his surviving spouse fasts and purifies herself by scattering cornmeal. At the end of the fourth day the dead person turns into a *kachina* and departs for the sacred lake, while the bereaved burn his personal property.

Scholars have discussed whether the *kachinas* were originally the dead or the rain spirits. We know from other horticultural peoples that there is a tendency to identify ancestors with fertility spirits. Scholars have pointed out that in Pueblo culture the idea of fertilization dominates practically every area of thought and that therefore the spirits of the deceased were interpreted in conformity with this pattern.[40] As we have noted, among the Zuni most groups of spirits, including the *uwanammi,* the water monsters, the *kachinas,* and even the enemy scalps, may send rain. The *kachina* complex also may have outside influence. There is evidence that this particular form of *kachina* worship was introduced from Mexico, perhaps not so very long ago.

There are among the *kachinas* three categories of deceased persons. First, there are those who have recently died. They may or may not produce rain. Second, there are the ancestors who have been dead for some time. The Zuni pray to them for health and survival, rain, and a good corn harvest. Third, there are the original *koko,* the children who died by drowning after the Emergence and apparently also those who died and went back to the underworld. Sometimes all three categories are termed *koko;* sometimes people make a distinction between ancestors and *kachinas.* Apparently only those who in life were members of the *kachina* society, especially those who have been officers in the society and bring their own masks, go to the Kachina Village where they are welcomed. Members of the rain priesthoods join the *uwanammi,* and distinguished members of other priesthoods and societies join their respective spiritual protectors in the other world. What happens to women and children is not always clear. On the whole, the picture of the destination of people after death is quite varied and confusing. This is not surprising, because most beliefs about the afterlife among American Indians are ambiguous and even contradictory. Besides, the Zuni are known to observe ritual details more rigorously than matters of belief and to pay less attention to concepts about an afterlife.

The conditions after death, as far as they are known, are described in rather positive terms. Husbands and wives (to the extent that they get along) live together in the Kachina Village, but there is some doubt whether their young deceased children can join them; it is sometimes said that these children turn into water animals. As *kachinas* the dead spend a happy time in their underwater realm. They are beautifully dressed and adorned with beads and feathers —just like their masked human representatives on earth. They dance and sing and feast. If they wish, they may visit their living kin. They do that now and then, arriving in clouds. It is said that at the beginning of time they often came to dance in the plaza of the pueblo. However, because on their return to the Kachina Village they happened to take somebody back with them to the other world (that is, the person died), they decided "no longer to come in person." Instead, people were told to imitate their costumes and dances, and they would be with them in spirit. They have done so ever since. The *kachinas* come flying to Zuni in the shape of ducks, and the members of the *kachina* society impersonate them by dressing up in their costumes, particularly their masks. The impersonators have to make food offerings before they can put on the masks. It is said that when the dancer dons the mask he is assisted by the invisible *kachina* spirit who stands behind or in front of him. After the performances, the spirits return to their village, again in the guise of ducks.

We have here another testimony of the close integration between religious concepts and rituals in Zuni: In this case it is the dead ancestors who play a part in rituals. In fact, the Zuni *kachina* cult is the most conspicuous example of ancestor worship in North America. The Hopi are also famous for their *kachina* cult, but the associations between the dead and the *kachinas* are not as concrete there as they are among the Zuni.

In view of this ancestor worship it seems strange that the name of a person who has died is taboo. The explanation could be that the dead person, tabooed because of his or her dangerousness, loses individual identity and goes up in the great collectivity of *kachina* spirits. When the Zuni turn to the *kachinas* in prayers and throw sacrificial food to them in the Wide River west of the town (the food is thought to be carried by the river to the sacred lake where the *kachinas* have their home), it is to the ancestors as a whole that the Zuni direct themselves, not to individual ancestors.

As is often the case in Native American beliefs about life after death, the Zuni believe the dead will die again. There are different views of what then happens to them. Some people apparently hold that for each death a dead person descends deeper into the underworlds, finally reaching the fourth underworld from which the first ancestors once emerged. Thereafter the person transmigrates into an animal, the nature of which is decided by the individual's activities in this life. Thus, a witch may become a coyote, lizard, bullsnake, or owl, all detested animals, whereas a prominent member of the *kachina* society turns into a deer.

The Zuni Version of the Orpheus Tradition

The Zuni, like many peoples of North America, tell versions of the touching story of how a man tries to follow his dead wife on her way to the realm of the dead to bring her back to life again. (This story, reminiscent of the Greek tale of Orpheus traveling to the underworld to find his dead wife, is sometimes called the North American Orpheus tradition.) In the American tradition the story often gives the impression of being linked to experiences in trance or deep sleep, but whatever the background, this tale supplies us with some interesting details of Zuni notions of the afterlife. It relates how a witch girl, overcome by jealousy in her love for a young hunter, kills the man's young wife. The wife is buried, and her husband sits mourning at her grave. After dark he sees a light at the grave. His wife talks to him: "My husband, do not sit facing the west. You are not dead yet. Face to the east. I am still here in this country. On the fourth day I shall go to Kachina Village." The hunter tells her that he wants to go with her. She agrees he can go with her but instructs him to dress in his best clothes, as if for a funeral, and to bring along extra moccasins, four pairs, and a downy eagle feather to tie in her hair. He does as she says, and early in the morning of the fourth day he has everything ready. He ties the eagle feather to the crown of her head, and she tells him to follow the feather. They start their way westward, crossing large fields of cactus. She moves swiftly (she is a spirit), but he gets tired and wears out his moccasins, one pair after another. After some time they arrive at an open country without cactus and come to a chasm. He sees the feather way down below but cannot follow it anymore. As he stands there crying, a squirrel turns up and offers to help him. He climbs onto the squirrel's back and is carried down the canyon and up the other side. As he turns around and looks back, he cannot see any chasm. He then continues walking. Soon he sees the feather far ahead at the bottom of a big cliff. He cries, and again a squirrel comes to his rescue and carries him down the cliff. As he looks back he does not see more than a plain. He continues on his path, but in the long run loses track of the feather. He cries, for he loves his wife. Nevertheless, he goes on and finally catches sight of the feather. At the end of the day he discovers Kachina Village. His wife tells him to wait outside of the village for four days, because he is not dead yet. She goes into the lake, while her husband sits there weeping. "And that is why, when a husband or wife dies, we tell the one who is left not to weep or he will die soon."[41]

This Orpheus tale does not correspond exactly to the general pattern of the North American Orpheus tradition, because the question of the return of the dead woman is not answered. However, the tale does illustrate some basic Zuni concepts about the dead. Thus, the dead do not depart for the underworld until four days after the time of death. They go west, traveling on this earth, but are invisible; only the feather on their heads belonging to this world can be seen. The dead can traverse obstacles the living cannot, and they are not hurt by the cactus on the way. From the quarters of the other world, canyons and mountains do not look like obstacles on the path. Only a really dead person can penetrate the lake of the *kachinas*.

These ideas about the dead are confirmed in the myth of the Emergence, in which it is maintained that the dead have no bodies, they are like the wind, and they take form from within of their own wills. At the same time they have a part in the common life within the world. Wind is identical with breath, which is the symbol of life. At the end of a prayer or a chant, people inhale as an act of ritual blessing. We have noticed that the feather is a visual manifestation of breath. This idea is common in Native American culture and religion.

Summary of the Structure of Zuni Religion: Mythical Emergence and Ritual Reemergence

Zuni religion, like Shoshoni religion, is not codified as a written theology, but in comparing the two traditions, the Zuni heritage is more concisely formulated in the myth of origins and more uniformly carried out in the collective rituals. One reason the Zuni have a more clear and compact religious system is that they have lived in the same general area for many centuries and have been able to retain a rather unbroken line of beliefs and practices. The farming culture of the Zuni has been the material foundation of a rich religious life permanently settled at and around the present town of Zuni.

The myth of origins sets the tone for most Zuni religious concepts with the notion of the emanation of the world from the primeval parents Sky Father (or Sun Father) and Mother Earth: As a result of their cohabitation, life was conceived within the deepest womb of the earth. Another version of the myth of origins depicts the emergence of people from within the womb of the earth. This myth, or pair of myths, reveals an interesting aspect of the Zuni spiritual world. Of the many spirits or "gods," Sun Father is the most important figure in the pantheon, but more attention is paid to the earth and female forces of fertility. Indeed, the most important spirits are the *kachinas*, and the *kachina* dances in the Shalako ceremony are the main annual religious performances because they depict the annual reemergence from the earth. In other words, Sky Father (or Sun Father) was important in the origin of the cosmos, but power is concentrated mainly in Mother Earth and fertility. This power is seen in the maize and in the Corn Maidens: We can talk of the Corn Maidens being embodied in the maize, or the corn plants as personified Corn Maidens. In fact, there is a separate myth to account for the gift of corn to the Zuni by the Corn Maidens, who then are offended and leave the land, later to be persuaded to return to Zuni with their blessings of corn.

Such myths can be seen as the foundation of ritual, but because of the dominant role of collective rituals in Zuni religion, it is also possible to see ritual as the justification for retaining the myth. What is important in the structure of Zuni religion is the close integration of myth and ritual, with all ritual grounded in mythical tales. Indeed, the masked dancers of the Shalako represent an annual reemergence of power from the world and a renewal of time and the world for the Zuni. As we shall see later, time, or the annual ritual year, is divided into two halves by the winter and summer solstices; the Shalako at the winter solstice marks not only the seasonal turning back of the sun but also the ushering in of the new year by masked gods. The myth of origins lays down the precedent for sacred time and also establishes the site of Zuni as the center of the world, or sacred space. The Zuni pueblo (or town) is seen as the navel or middle of the earth, and all cosmic orientation takes place around this center. For the Zuni this means not just the four cardinal directions, but the sky (zenith) and especially the underground (nadir). The *kiva* is the ceremonial room of the Zuni imitating this cosmic model, including the *sipapu* or hole of emergence. Just as the Sun Dance lodge represents a microcosm for the Shoshoni, the *kiva* is a miniature cosmos for the Zuni.

The heart of Zuni religion is the elaborate ritual life of interrelated ceremonial societies and groups, each with its own set of rules for membership and procedures. The careful conformity to ritual precedents may make Zuni religion appear to be mere mechanical performance, but we should not lose sight of the thrust of all these activities, which is to bring the individual and the group into conformity with the spirit of the universe. Zuni see their participation in the rituals as part of a larger drama in which they come into harmony with the universe. Some of the obvious intentions of these rituals are to assure the fertility, growth, and harvest of maize in its various stages, as well as thanksgiving. But for the Zuni the growing of maize is not simply a means of making money, it is a way of life, a way of taking part in the drama of the emergence and reemergence of plant and animal life. We have seen that for the Shoshoni the ideal of religious life is the intense personal vision; the vision is the goal of much religious activity, especially the Sun Dance, and visions are the authority and sources of new ritual. Among the Zuni the ideal religious life is more a submersion of the individual in the group ritual activity, such that all work together in unison with the rhythms of the cosmos. Indeed, a person who acts too much on his or her own is thought to be using religious power for evil intentions and may be accused of witchcraft. (Witches and witchcraft will be discussed in the next section.) Zuni emphasis on collective ritual even spills over from this life to the next, for all Zuni men belong to the *kachina* society, thus assuring their permanent abode in the Kachina Village at the bottom of the sacred lake near Zuni.

The Zuni religious way can be outlined as shown in the following diagram, which shows how myth, ritual, and religious organizations mutually reinforce

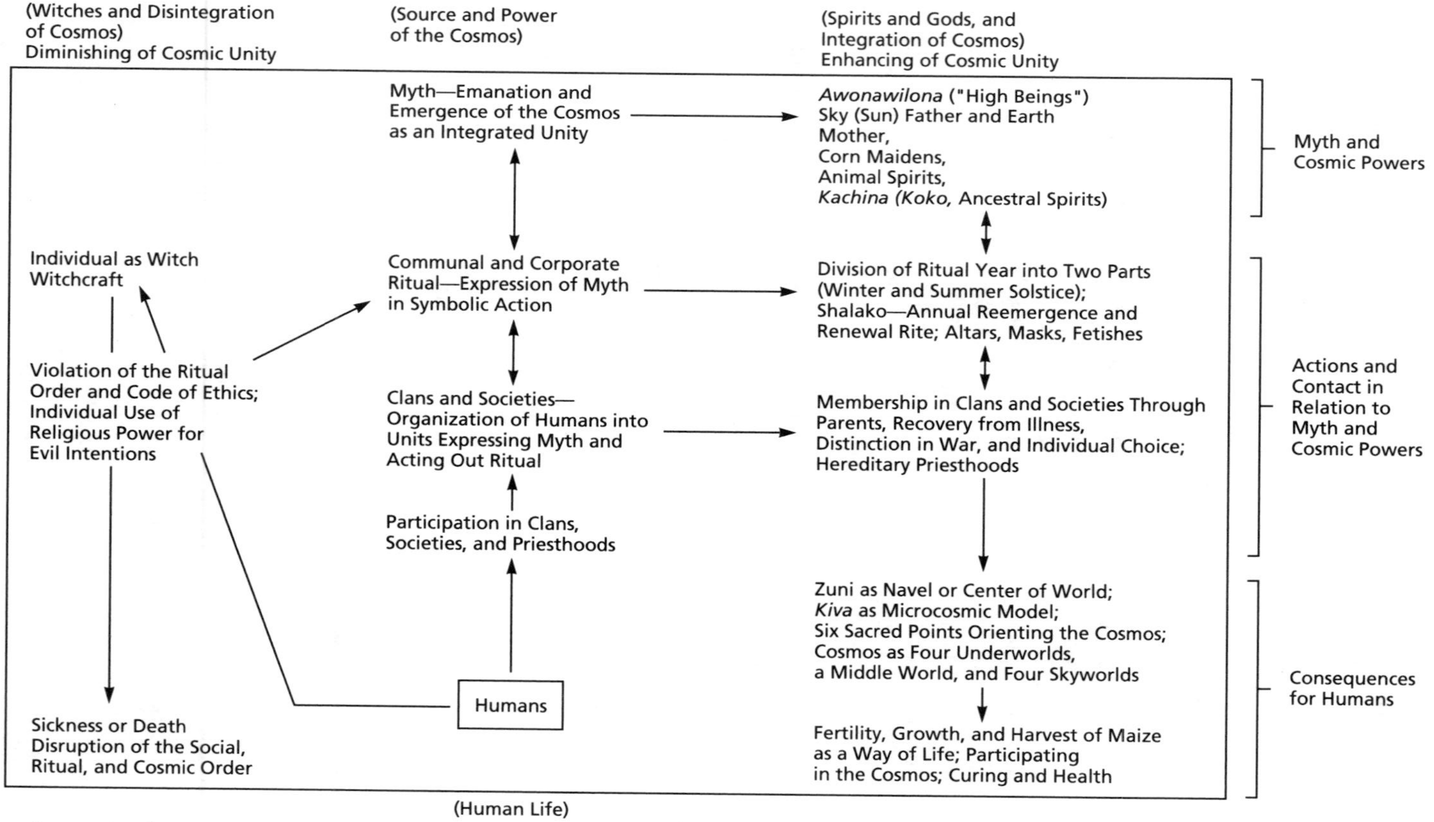
(Witches and Disintegration of Cosmos) Diminishing of Cosmic Unity
(Source and Power of the Cosmos)
(Spirits and Gods, and Integration of Cosmos) Enhancing of Cosmic Unity
Myth—Emanation and Emergence of the Cosmos as an Integrated Unity
Awonawilona ("High Beings") Sky (Sun) Father and Earth Mother, Corn Maidens, Animal Spirits, *Kachina (Koko,* Ancestral Spirits)
Myth and Cosmic Powers
Individual as Witch Witchcraft
Communal and Corporate Ritual—Expression of Myth in Symbolic Action
Division of Ritual Year into Two Parts (Winter and Summer Solstice); Shalako—Annual Reemergence and Renewal Rite; Altars, Masks, Fetishes
Violation of the Ritual Order and Code of Ethics; Individual Use of Religious Power for Evil Intentions
Clans and Societies—Organization of Humans into Units Expressing Myth and Acting Out Ritual
Membership in Clans and Societies Through Parents, Recovery from Illness, Distinction in War, and Individual Choice; Hereditary Priesthoods
Actions and Contact in Relation to Myth and Cosmic Powers
Participation in Clans, Societies, and Priesthoods
Zuni as Navel or Center of World; *Kiva* as Microcosmic Model; Six Sacred Points Orienting the Cosmos; Cosmos as Four Underworlds, a Middle World, and Four Skyworlds
Humans
Consequences for Humans
Sickness or Death Disruption of the Social, Ritual, and Cosmic Order
Fertility, Growth, and Harvest of Maize as a Way of Life; Participating in the Cosmos; Curing and Health
(Human Life)

The Zuni Religious Way.

the notion of an integrated cosmos. This diagram can be read from top to bottom and from the center both to the left and to the right. At the top are the myths that express the source and power of the cosmos, out of which come both religious action in ritual and also the spirits and gods. In the center are the highly developed clans and societies for acting out myth in ritual; below these are the humans who participate in the clans, societies, and priestly roles, and also human life in general. At the very center is the concentration of religious societies and ritual action necessary for celebrating and maintaining the cosmos; to the left is the diminishing or disintegration of cosmic unity. Left of center we find witchcraft, violation of the ritual order, and individual use of religious power for evil intentions—all of which are conditions leading to sickness or death and disruption of the social, ritual, and cosmic order. Right of center, we find the various gods and spirits (*awonawilona*, Sky or Sun Father, Moon Mother, Corn Maidens, animal spirits, and *kachinas*), and the ritual calendar and altars, which are the means for acting out and enhancing cosmic unity; this is seen concretely in the imagery of Zuni as the navel of the world and the *kiva* as a microcosmic model and is realized through the fertility of maize and participation in the life of the cosmos (in curing and health). In general, then, the diagram is based on the two major emphases of the Zuni world: to maximize the enhancing of cosmic unity and to minimize the diminishing of cosmic unity. This diagram will become clearer as it is illustrated by concrete examples of Zuni religious life in the next section on the dynamics of Zuni religion; the structure of Zuni religion can also be interpreted as a total way of life.

Myth relates how the world appeared as a result of divine emanation and how people emerged out of the underworld to serve Father Sun. This Emergence Myth is the charter of Zuni rituals and the basis for organization of clans, societies, and priesthoods. In general, a fruitful and prosperous life is dependent on the right cosmic balance between man, nature, and the powers—as related in myth, acted out in ritual, and conducted by religious organizations.

Awonawilona, the "high beings," were responsible for the beginning of the cosmos, but later Sun Father and Moon Mother were more important for the ongoing life of the world. In particular, Moon Mother and Corn Maidens are responsible for the growth of vegetation, especially corn. Animal spirits also are worshiped, but the *kachinas* (or *koko*, ancestral spirits) are crucial in the all-important Shalako ceremony. Rituals are the direct expression of myths, and the Zuni ritual drama establishes the harmony of the universe. The ritual year is divided into two parts by the summer and winter solstice, and the *kachina* dancers in the Shalako ceremony represent the annual reemergence from the underworld.

Humans enter this cosmic drama by being active members in their clan, joining other societies and participating in the collective ritual life that is closely related to the horticultural cycle. Participation in religious organizations and their rituals enhances the cosmic unity symbolized in the pueblo as the navel of the world, the *kiva* as the microcosm, the six directions orienting the cosmos, and the larger picture of the cosmos (the combination of four underworlds, a middle world, and four sky worlds). The positive result of enhancing the cosmos is not merely the growth and harvesting of maize, but the fulfillment of life as maintaining the cosmic balance. This is seen personally in curing and health.

There is also a negative side to the Zuni religious way, which is generally the direct opposite of the collective ritual life previously outlined. Any person who violates the ritual order or goes against the code of ethics of social and ritual life sets him- or herself outside the pattern of cosmic integration and risks the accusation of witchcraft, especially the individual who uses religious power for evil intentions. These witches may cause sickness or death and generally diminish cosmic unity by disruption of the social, ritual, and cosmic order.

The Dynamics of Zuni Religion: Harmony with the Cosmos Through Collective Ritual

Religious Societies and Collective Ritual

Ruth Bunzel, a leading scholar and writer on Zuni culture and religion, writes about the Zuni male: "The only sphere in which he acts as an individual rather than as a member of a group is that of sex."[42] Indeed, a Zuni man is normally a member of several ritual organizations and disappears, as it were, behind the collectivistic ritual machinery. This is the background of Ruth Benedict's famous characterization of the Zuni as Apollonian, in Nietzsche's sense, with a sober faithfulness to tradition and a playing down of the individual and personal experiences. Benedict's portrait of the modest, unassuming Zuni personality has been challenged and is certainly exaggerated, as we shall soon see, but it contains some elements of truth.

There is no doubt that conformity to traditional customs and usage and adherence to established ritual practice are esteemed virtues in Zuni society: These virtues constitute the "ideal personality type." A person with these qualities keeps the life-sustaining and cosmically important rituals going, thereby preserving Zuni life both in its worldly and in its metaphysical dimensions. Every person has a place in the rich and complex ritual apparatus, and everyone is expected to do his or her share.

Those who openly violate this order or code of ethics or are even accused of going against it jeopardize their social reputation and even their lives. They may be accused of witchcraft. This happens, for instance, if a person is suspected by the relatives of a deceased Zuni to have caused the latter's death. According to general belief, all diseases that are not the result of an accident are due to the evil operations of witches. It is the task of the Bow Priests to find out whether the accusation is justified. Not so long ago they did this by relying on torture to extort a confession from supposed culprits. The arms of the suspects were crossed behind their backs, and they were suspended by their thumbs or wrists from a beam of the church wall. They might hang there for several days without food or drink, now and then knocked and kicked by the priests. Witch trials could end in expulsion from Zuni or even in execution. In later times flogging has also been a form of punishment. [See Religions of Africa pp. 37–38 for another example of witchcraft.]

For the well-behaved male Zuni, the best proof of his unassuming and loyal character is to join a good number of the societies and cult associations that are at his disposal. Membership in these organizations may come about through recovery from an illness, distinction in war, and individual choice. In some cases they are restricted by clan affiliation. Indeed, what we have here is an intricate system of social and ceremonial connections, in which different principles of order interlock with one another in a bewildering complexity.

We have first of all the kinship ties. The Zuni reckon kinship on the mother's side and belong from birth to the mother's clan and household. To some extent these matrilineal connections determine the positions of office that an individual might hold in the religious system. However, this structure is complicated by a man's being at the same time a "child of the father's clan," for he also has responsibilities to his father's clan, although these are less important positions.

In the past there were a great number of clans. Today, however, there are fourteen clans, all matrilineal, all exogamous. Indeed, Zuni even avoid marrying a spouse taken from the father's clan. Each clan is totemic, that is, it has a clan emblem that is usually an animal or a plant. For instance, we find Eagle, Turkey, Bear, and Deer totems and Dogwood, Corn, Tobacco, and Mustard totems. There is, however, no real cult of these totems and no concept of spirits behind them. The clans have the right to place their members into the rain priesthoods. These are important offices and represent the highest positions a Zuni can attain as a member of a clan.

Next, we have what could be called the free associations. Memberships in *kiva* groups and medicine societies are based on a variety of reasons, such as individual choice, paternal choice, or recovery from a specific illness. However, such a membership may be limited by clan affiliations, as noted above.

A third category is war achievements. Male Zuni who have taken scalps are introduced into the Bow Priesthood. We may of course wonder how this priesthood could still exist today, when there is no tribal warfare. It seems that veterans from the two World Wars, the Korean War, and the Vietnam War could take on the roles of Bow Priests but rarely have done so. These modern wars lack the ritual values of the old tribal wars.

We have so far talked only about the men. In many respects they are dominant in the ritual life, although women certainly have access to medicine societies and some priesthoods. The emphasis on males ties in with their economic dominance: The man is the cultivator of the soil, the builder, and the weaver. This is a pattern that was also practiced in pre-Columbian Mexico and is no doubt related to the incipient urban civilization there. Where the man's ancient role as hunter has fallen away, as was the case in classical Mexico, his activities are transferred to the main economic activity, horticulture. Here we face another hint of the strong impact of ancient Mexico on Pueblo Indian culture.

On the other hand, women play important roles in other connections. The housewife, with her mother, brothers, and sisters, owns the family rooms, and she and the other women of the family are rulers there. The husband is a guest in her home and may be dismissed when she so wishes. To her belong also the sacred fetishes, a most precious part of Zuni sacred paraphernalia.

Having discussed the rules of joining the ritual societies, including the woman's part in the social and ceremonial system (which, it must be stressed, in many respects constitutes a unit) we shall now turn to a presentation of the most common and most important religious and ceremonial organizations.

Ceremonial Organizations

THE *KACHINA* SOCIETY   All young males, but very rarely girls, are introduced into one of the six "*kiva* groups" that exist in Zuni. Usually the parents decide which *kiva* group a child should join. Later in life the initiated may change to a *kiva* group of his own choice. The initiation is spread over two periods. Sometime between the ages of five and nine the child undergoes a preliminary initiation in the *kiva*. He is whipped by masked *kachinas*, probably for purifying reasons or, as it is expressed, "to take away the bad luck." (Whipping is never used as a means of punishment.) The whole ritual signifies that the young child is put in the charge of the *kachinas*. The second, final initiation takes place between the ages of ten and twelve years. The children are then whipped a second time and taught the secrets of the *kachina* ritualism.

The *kiva* groups represent the *kachina* society. This all-embracing society is headed by a chief who always belongs to the Antelope clan. His deputy or "speaker" is a member of the Badger clan. Two Bow Priests also belong to the "board." The rituals of the society are, as always in Zuni, characterized by prayers, chants, and dramatic performances. Symbolic actions and objects, such as the offering of cornmeal and prayer sticks, are frequently involved.

Each *kiva* group is bound to a particular *kiva*. As said before, the six *kivas* are modeled on the four cardinal directions and the zenith and nadir. The *kivas* are usually rectangular rooms in the house units and are situated above ground, not subterranean as among the eastern Pueblo peoples. There is a ceremonial order to the *kivas*, so that each season the dances begin with the *kiva* on the main plaza and then continue in a counterclockwise direction among the other *kivas*. The performances in the *kivas* are secret. We know that rehearsals take place there and also purifications when some sacred matter has been defiled. The splendid *kachina* dances and shows that take place on the plaza and are open to the public will be discussed later.

MEDICINE AND HUNTING SOCIETIES   These are twelve societies into which men and women who have fallen ill and have been treated by members of a medicine society are recruited. Indeed, anyone who has received such treatment is required to join the society; otherwise his or her life is in danger. The medicine society is a secret society that a person may enter only after expensive gift feasts. The initiation ceremony takes place under the supervision of a "ceremonial father"—the person who cured the individual. In a few of these societies it is customary or even demanded that the leading members of the society belong to certain clans. Women who have been recruited may not appear in more advanced curing functions.

The medicine societies have as their patrons the beast gods for whose cults they are responsible. These gods are the givers of medicine and long life, but also of witchcraft. The most powerful of the gods is Bear, the god of the west. In the Bear Dance the dancers have bear paws attached to their arms, growl like bears, and dash about wildly as if possessed by bears. In other words, they impersonate the bear. This is interesting, for over large parts of North America the bear is the particular guardian spirit of healing medicine men. The Zuni have apparently taken over the ancient function of the individual bear medicine man and collectivized it into a group of bear medicine men.

Characteristically, members of the medicine societies remove the disease object by sucking, as is the case among native medicine men in most of North America. Furthermore, the different medicine societies are experts about particular kinds of diseases and hold rituals featuring altars, fetishes, and other sacred things. Each society has its peculiar fetish, kept by the main household of the associated clan. In addition, each member of the society has his or her own personal fetish, a feathered ear of corn, placed on the altar. All this reminds us of

Members of the newekwe *or "Clown People," a Zuni medicine society. (Photo by M. C. Stevenson 1909, National Anthropological Archives, Smithsonian Institution, Neg. No. 2372–C–19.)*

the functions of individual medicine men in other areas and of their ritual paraphernalia. In other words, the medicine society is a corporation of medicine men and women, but these have not gone through the guardian vision quest and they do not perform curing while in a state of trance. This is a typical case of Pueblo collectivization: We see in these medical practices the attitudes of a hunting people expressed in the collective form of horticulturists.

Another interesting item is the connection between these societies and hunting. For instance, the members of the Coyote society formerly took part in the communal rabbit hunts. They are said to be good deer hunters and cure all illnesses thought to be caused by the deer. The emphasis on male pursuits in this society explains why no women are allowed membership. In most other medicine societies women are welcome, although they are not allowed to hold office.

The combination of medicine for curing and medicine for hunting echoes the characteristic capabilities of American Indian medicine men in hunting societies, for instance, on the Plains. However, the extreme individualism of these doctors has no counterpart in Pueblo culture. It is noteworthy that practically all medical practice in Zuni is in the hands of the medicine societies.

These medicine societies are very active in cultic and ceremonial practices. The time for their regular performances is fall and winter. At the winter solstice the initiated have their retreats in their sacred houses (not *kivas*) to make prayer sticks for the ancestors and to pray for rain and fertility. Thereafter, they call on the beast gods and demonstrate to the public their powers of curing. They also appear publicly now and then when there are occasions of curing or initiation. Members of other societies are often invited to be present at the ceremonies.

THE RAIN PRIESTS (*ASHIWANNI*) In contrast to the societies, the priesthoods are hereditary offices limited to a few persons. There are sixteen rain priesthoods, each one constituted by two to six members who have inherited their positions within matrilineal household groups. The power of the priests resides in the sacred fetish, one for each priesthood; these are the most sacred fetishes among the Zuni. The households keeping these fetishes are considered the most important families in the town. In the houses where the fetishes (representing the *uwanammi*) are kept their priests hold secret ceremonies for the supernatural rainmakers, the *uwanammi*.

The main period to pray for rain and for ritual activities of the **ashiwanni** is the rainy season, the months of July through September. Prayer sticks are planted at sacred springs, and thereafter the priests spend their time night and day for four days in their rooms, praying to the *uwanammi* and singing and fasting. One priesthood after another repeats the procedure. It is characteristic that the Rain Priests never engage in public ceremonies. Their main concern is the rain, and they promote its coming by quiet meditation. They are also doctors and diviners. The Rain Priests are expected to be peaceful and kind and have no quarrels with anybody. They are considered holy men and women. Formerly, they were not allowed to have any work to do other than that belonging to their sacerdotal duties. This is as close to a professional priesthood that one will see among Native Americans.

THE BOW PRIESTS (*APILA ASHIWANNI*)   The priesthood of the Bow Priests is associated with war and the *ahayuta*, the twin gods, the warlike sons of the Sun we have seen mentioned in the Emergence Myth. The *apila ashiwanni,* recruited from warriors who have killed and scalped an enemy, were formerly war chiefs whose job it also was to protect the pueblo from witches. In earlier times a killer had to protect himself from the revenge of the ghost of his victim. He did that by becoming initiated into the Bow Priesthood at the same time that a scalp dance was conducted to propitiate the dangerous ghost.

Today there are only two Bow Priests left, for obvious reasons: There are no more tribal wars, no scalping, and (officially at least) no witches. It was different in the old days, as recorded by Matilda Coxe Stevenson, when there was a chief priest and a battle chief and different functionaries for special tasks. Like other sacred organizations, the Bow Priests have a ceremonial chamber in a house in town where they keep their paraphernalia. Some of the fetishes they use are kept by officers outside their own ranks. The idols of the war twins, which figure in their ceremonies, have been carved by men of the Deer and Bear clans. These images play a role in the winter solstice ceremonies, the great annual occasion of the appearance of the Bow Priests. At that time new images are made of the twin gods, forming the center of a night of ceremonial singing. At dawn the following morning the idols are brought to two of the mountain shrines of the *ahayuta*. In the old days the Bow Priests held a great public dance after the harvest of the corn in the fall. As often has been the case in agricultural ceremonies around the world, the celebrations were accompanied by sexual license.

THE PRIEST OF THE SUN (*PEKWIN*)   Besides these religious organizations, there have been other, smaller societies, which at the present time are mostly phenomena of the past. There is, however, one ceremonial figure who rises in power and sanctity above all others and that is the *pekwin,* the priest of the Sun. The Sun, the father of all, is venerated at the midwinter and summer solstices on days decided upon by his priest. It seems that observation of the rising and setting of the sun at certain landmarks helps the *pekwin* determine the dates of these sacred periods. Another public ceremony, the Corn Dance each fourth summer, is also controlled by the *pekwin*. However, this ceremony is not primarily directed to the Sun, but to the departure and return of the Corn Maidens. Also other rituals are supervised by the priest of the Sun who is, in effect, the keeper of the calendar. He is also the chief of the other priests, officiating whenever the other priests come together. He installs the new priests and sanctions the impersonators of the *kachina* spirits. In addition he presides over the council of priests, six priests in all who have been the real political authority of the Zuni tribe. [See Religions of Africa pp. 24, 35, 60, Religions of Mesoamerica pp. 198–201, Judaism pp. 391–92, Christianity pp. 503, 505, Islam pp. 632–33, Hinduism p. 748, Buddhism pp. 875–77, 952–53, Religions of China pp. 991–93, and Religions of Japan pp. 1095–96, 1105–6 for the relationship of religion to political leaders.]

However, the functions of the high priest are not carried out at present, because his position has been vacant since the 1940s. The ritual machinery

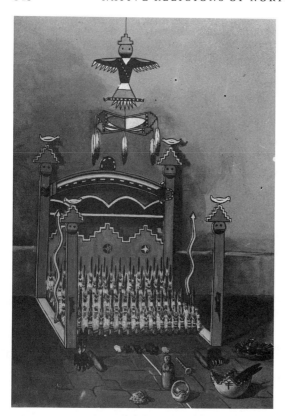

The altar of the Eagle Down Fraternity is one of the most attractive altars in the Zuni religious tradition. A variety of stone fetishes are placed around this altar, including figures of a bison, a bear, and a woman. (National Anthropological Archives, Smithsonian Institution, Neg. No. 2359–C–1.)

moves on, but its main controller, the man who is responsible for the spiritual and material welfare of the Zuni, is gone. Perhaps this is convincing proof of the inherent strength in the ceremonial organization: It can run without its foremost director.

Altars, Masks, and Fetishes

The ceremonial system of the Zuni would be inexplicable without reference to the sacred objects handled by the organizations: the altars, masks, and fetishes. The altar is the focus of attention in ceremonies. It is placed in the room of ceremonies on the side away from the door and consists of fetishes and other sacred objects set on the floor in front of painted wooden slabs. This is the description of a Rain Society altar: Eight corn-ear fetishes rest on a cloud terrace design, from which lead eight discs of cornmeal terminating in two forked lines tipped with arrowheads. Along the discs there is a line of stone fetishes, and over the cloud terrace there are a number of arrowheads. Turtle shells surround the corn-ear fetishes. Four lines of cornmeal form two crosses that are placed in a circle; as always in North America, such crosses placed within a circle are symbols of the world and the cardinal points.

As mentioned above, dancers and impersonators of gods turn into these beings by donning masks. In fact, it is said that the *kachina* spirits, who are the chief "masked beings," at a certain time declined to visit human settlements in person, because on their return to the other world they "drew" the people along to their sacred lake. Instead, they told the Zuni to put on masks representing them and to perform the ceremonies they otherwise would have performed themselves. A mask is therefore naturally sacred and takes on the attributes of the god.

The representation of supernatural beings by masks is common in secret societies that have developed in horticultural settings. The mysterious experience of spirits received in visions has here been supplanted by the collective demonstration of spirits in dramatic performances, in which the presence of the spirit is expressed through the mask and skin of the spirit animal. There are certainly cases of visionary experiences among the Zuni, for example, as requirements for initiation into curing societies. (The shamanic background of the curing societies was pointed out above.) Moreover, the Rain Priests ingest a psychotropic drug, *Datura stramonium,* to become entranced and thus able to cure or perform divination. However, it is thought that the regular experience of the supernatural takes place in the ceremonies, not in visionary states. The masks are manifestations of the supernatural.

Masks are of many types. Half-masks, or strips of leather worn over the face from the hairline to the mouth and from ear to ear, are often worn by female deities. Complete face masks have a molded nose and lips and eye holes but are not realistically formed; rather the faces are exaggerated into caricatures. Helmet masks encircle the head like a rounded bag over the top of the head. These masks, which completely cover the dancer's head, are made of deer or buffalo skin or simply cowhide. The mask is usually crowned by bunches of feathers; the more feathers, the more important is the *kachina*. Downy feathers represent "the breath of the rain." Realistic symbols like attached deer horns or stylized geometric symbols indicate possible supernatural associations. In addition, masks are painted with the same designs as those we find on ceremonial pottery, altar boards, and sand paintings, a testimony of strong religious integration. The masks generally display a fine degree of craftsmanship.

There are more than a hundred types of masks, each one having a particular name and portraying a particular god or spirit. All may be classified into two general divisions. One division is composed of very ancient masks that remain tribal property. They represent high-ranking *kachina* gods and are considered most dangerous. They are kept in sealed jars in houses, and their hereditary guardians are the owners of these houses. Such masks demand food sacrifices in the river to the ancestors before anyone can wear them, and the planting of prayer sticks and four days of sexual continence after wearing. The other main category is masks that are individual property. Such a mask serves as a person's personal fetish. Some have several such masks. After an individual's death the mask is buried at the Kachina Village to maintain that person's status among the *kachinas* just joined. Only the departed who have such masks may return in spirit to visit the Zuni in *kachina* dances.

We come finally to all the talismans, stones, feathers, ears of corn, and other objects scholars include under the general term *fetish,* which was originally a term that the Portuguese applied to the sacred objects of West Africa. However, it has been commonly used about Zuni sacred objects since Cushing wrote his classic (but confused) study, *Zuñi Fetiches,* in 1883. These fetishes—which also include masks—do not stand isolated from other American Indian cultic phenomena. Just as the Zuni masked beings in ritual processions are substitutes for the visionary spirits in the rest of North America, so the different sorts of Zuni fetishes supplant the medicine bags found elsewhere. Their functions are the same: Both the fetish and the medicine bag are visible signs of the bonds between the supernatural order and humans. The fetish is itself powerful: If neglected or desecrated it may strike its keeper with misfortune.

No Pueblo Indians make such extensive use of ceremonialism as the Zuni, and no Pueblo Indians have paid such great attention to fetishes as the Zuni. Everyone may have a personal fetish, such as a little stone found in the mountains, which, owing to its peculiar form or color, is thought to have supernatural properties. Such smaller fetishes are usually the individual's hunting charms and are kept in buckskin bags hanging around the owner's neck when hunting. They are the most common fetishes and help people catch and slay wild game. A relic of the old animal ceremonialism is the idea that by proper use of the fetish the spirit of the slain animal attains life after death.

The more powerful fetishes are not individual property but associated with the ceremonial societies, particularly with the priests. The fetishes of the Rain Priests, the **ettowe,** are the most sacrosanct objects in Zuni and the source of power of the priests. They are of two kinds, water fetishes and corn fetishes. They are said to be petrified supernatural beings. According to tradition they were carried by the first ancestors from the fourth underworld and are now preserved in sealed pottery jars in the same houses where they have been since Emergence days. The medicine societies have in their custody large animal-like fetishes, such as stone images of the beast gods. They decorate the painted slab altars of these societies. Each image is fed regularly at mealtime every day by some woman living in the house where it is kept. There is a hole one to four inches in diameter in one side of the jar, and through this hole the fetish is fed.

The fetishes that often vaguely resemble animals are used in a most concrete way in curative rites. For instance, the Ant society cures skin diseases by placing its fetish, an effigy of a red ant tied to a horn medicine pouch, on the patient's pillow near the face. The red ant takes the disease away through the sick person's mouth. The procedure is accompanied by chanting each morning for twelve days by the society members.

Offerings

The feeding of fetishes is of course not the only form of offerings in Zuni religion. Other supernaturals who receive food offerings are the ancestors. Before a meal everyone participating in it selects a bit of each food dish, breathes on it, and says, "Receive! (Oh, souls of) my ancestry, and eat; resuscitate by means of your wondrous knowledge, your hearts; return unto us of yours the water we need, of yours the seeds of earth, of yours the means of attaining great age." When this grace has been said the selected food is cast into the fire. Cushing, who in the nineteenth century reported this prayer, added that he had never seen a Zuni, young or old, taste food without first giving this invocation, although sometimes in abbreviated form.[43] There is one great offering day to the ancestors, Grandmothers' Day (the same as All Souls' Day in Christianity), when great quantities of food are sacrificed in the river or in the fire. Catholic and indigenous religious practices have merged in this rite.

Offerings of food are made regularly to ancestors, *kachinas,* and fetishes. Another type of offering consists of a prayer meal, that is, cornmeal mixed with ground white shells and turquoise. This meal is offered to the Sun each morning and sprinkled as a sanctifying element on sacred objects and *kachina* dancers. It is also used to delineate sacred paths, and it is rubbed on the newborn and the dead.

Prayer sticks are also a kind of offering. They usually consist of red willow staffs to which feathers are attached; they are painted with symbolic colors (for instance, blue and yellow for fecundity). They are planted in corn fields, springs, and mountain shrines, and followed by restrictions on sexual intercourse and food for the one who plants them. Prayer sticks communicate a prayer and are accompanied by oral prayers. As Bunzel has noted, prayers constitute the heart of each ceremony, and are—like fetishes—sacred and powerful in themselves. Prayers are directed to the supernaturals, who are the controllers of the universe.

The offerings can be understood partly as gifts to the supernaturals, in particular the food offerings, but most of all they express the sentiment of communion with the supernatural powers. However, prayer meal and prayer sticks are primarily expressions of a feeling of the balance within life: the balance between humans and the supernatural as well as the balance within all ingredients in an ordered universe. It is people's task to contribute to this cosmic balance through personal behavior and through participation in the necessary rituals. Prayer meal and prayer sticks are parts of these rituals and a personal means of promoting the individual and collective welfare that is an integral part of the all-pervasive cosmic balance.

The Ritual Year

There has been much talk here of ritual performances and little demonstration of them. The reasons are obvious. The rituals are so many, so diversified, and so rich that it would be an impossible task to present them in this short survey. After all, each society—and as we have seen there are many societies—has its own set of rituals in the annual round. We will have to be satisfied here with a general account of the ceremonial round—in which the main ritual procedures and the major appearances of the ritual organizations will be mentioned—and a closer view of one of these organizations, the most renowned and popular of them all, the *kachina* dancers.

A preliminary presentation of the calendar year in its basic outline and meaning has already been given. As is so common in American Indian ceremonialism, the ritual year has a double reference: It relates to cosmic events, the harmony between spirits and humans, and also to the changes of the seasons that have meaning for human subsistence. In an agricultural setting it is the vegetative year that is important. Changes in plant life are marked with ritual measures and the appearances of ceremonial organizations. Among the Zuni these interrelationships are extremely complicated and not known in every detail; or the details vary according to the accounts of field investigators.[44]

As pointed out, the ritual year is divided into two halves separated by the winter and summer solstices. The winter and spring ceremonies are concerned with medicine, war, and fertility; the summer and fall ceremonies with rain and crops. The exact time of the winter solstice (the month of "Turning Back," that is, of the sun) is determined by the priest of the Sun, the *pekwin*, who, from a cornfield east of the town, observes the time when the sun rises over a certain point of Corn Mountain. The celebrations are introduced by a period of ceremonial constraint indicating the critical juncture between the old year and the new: No fire must be seen, animal food must be avoided, trading is forbidden, and sexual continence has to be observed. However, in one of the *kivas* a sacred fire is kept burning. If these regulations should be disregarded, the safe transition of the world from one period to another might be endangered.

This is therefore a period of intense ritual activity. Thus, the medicine societies have their nightly retreats, followed by the planting of prayer sticks to the beast gods and the *kachinas*. The priests, in their retreats, pray for rain and fertility and then deposit prayer sticks at springs. Each family sets out ears of corn, rain fetishes, and personal fetishes at night, praying for good crops, flocks of sheep, and the fecundity of women.

On the twentieth day of these celebrations the new year is brought from the east by two masked gods. They arrive at the chief *kiva* and dance together with the priests assembled there all through the night. The old year is "sent out," and a new fire is kindled in the morning. All over the town of Zuni, people enjoy the occasion and come to fetch live coals from this fire, returning with the coals to light their home fires. Many people go to the main *kiva* to be blessed by the masked gods, and all rejoice and dance until sundown.

There is now a cleaning of the previous year's refuse from the houses, a ritual procedure that is coupled to the fate of the corn. The man of each household takes out the accumulated refuse and stacks it on the ground as if it were corn: The refuse represents the corn. Similarly, the woman carries out the ashes and sprinkles them as she would sprinkle cornmeal at the harvest. Everybody, indeed, sprinkles cornmeal and prays to the Sun. Omens of a good or bad harvest are studied. Houses are symbolically cleansed from witchcraft. At the same time, the men who have been chosen to impersonate the *kachina* gods, to appear at the end of the year in the Shalako ceremony, are summoned by the Bow Priests to start their ritual training. This training will continue throughout the year, always in the evenings.

Corn Mountain as seen from the Pueblo of Zuni. (Photo from Laboratory of Anthropology, Ben Wittick Collection; Courtesy Museum of New Mexico, Neg. No. 4996.)

After the midwinter rites have ended the *kachina* dancers begin their season of public dances, which lasts from February to September. This is also the season of the growth of the corn, which is stimulated by these dances. The ears of corn exposed at the midwinter celebrations are planted in March. The planting must always be carried out ceremonially in holes representing the six directions. The planter sprinkles a cross of meal and places a prayer stick at its intersection, all the time chanting sacred songs. Then he fasts for four days.

The midsummer is spent planting prayer sticks, making offerings, and saying prayers to the rainmakers. Impersonators of the *kachina* clowns, the **koyemshi,** visit all houses and are doused with water by the women—a symbolic reference to the need to water the corn plants. A few days later the summer rain dances start, to promote the coming of the rains. At this time every fourth year there is a pilgrimage to Kachina Village, the lake about eighty miles west of Zuni. A deputation of *kachina* dancers offers prayer sticks at the shrines there.

As the first ears ripen in August they are brought home and put together with a perfect ear, the "corn father," and a double ear, the "corn mother," both taken from the granary. This green corn ritual refers to the return of the Corn Maidens, according to the myth.

November is general harvest time. The woman of the house sets aside the finest ears of new corn, greets them in a ceremonial way and sprinkles them with flowers, pollen, and water. She preserves them in a pouch, bringing them out again at midwinter and at spring planting next year. This feast is accompanied by sexual license, which in all fertility religions is part of the ritual reproduction process.

The year ends with the coming of the *shalako* at the end of November, possibly the greatest ceremony in aboriginal North America. The *shalako* are the messengers of the rain gods (the dead) and probably, as Parsons thought, spirits of the deer; the six gigantic masked figures that represent them symbolize the six directions and the deer. They make an enormous impression. The dancers impersonating them carry a ten-foot-long pole in their hands that holds up the costume and has the facial mask on the top. The dancer has to look out through a hole in the blanket covering the "upper body."

These supernatural beings come from the desert bringing blessings of fertility and long life. Their arrival is a great occasion. In the words of a well-initiated Zuni to that famous pioneer ethnographer Frank Cushing: "Little brother, make your heart glad—a great festival is now everyone's thought. Eighteen days more, and from the west will come the *Sha-la-k'o;* it welcomes the return of the *Ka-ka* [*kachinas*] and speeds the departure of the Sun."[45] What has been called "the coming of the gods" is a public festival of fourteen days duration in the late part of November or early part of December.[46] Preceded by the *koyemshi* clowns and accompanied by singers, the giant figures approach the town and halt on the south bank of the Zuni River. Bunzel has ably described her impression of the coming of the gods: "As soon as it is quite dark the six Ca'lako [*shalako*] cross the river quietly and then suddenly rise out of the river bed, each surrounded by a group of singers from his *kiva,* all singing antiphonal songs. This is the most impressive moment in the Ca'lako [*shalako*] ceremonies. The songs are magnificent, and the sudden appearance of the six giant figures in the moonlight is superb." Thereafter the masked beings go to their respective houses where they spend the night dancing. The peculiar figure "fills the room, from floor to ceiling, and its crest of eagle feathers brushes the beams. Dancing in the house they [the impersonators] resemble nothing so much as animated gargoyles with their huge heads and tiny legs and their clattering beaks. They bend over and clap their beaks in the face of anyone who dozes in the house."[47]

During these festivals, which are open to the public, even white visitors, there are prayers for fertility, corn growth, and health. As one informant told Bunzel, "When Ca'lako [*shalako*] comes he brings in all different kinds of seeds, wild things, and peaches and pumpkins and beans and corn. Then when spring comes, the man who has had Ca'lako [*shalako*] house plants these seeds in his fields."[48] When the *shalako* leave for the west again the dances continue for some time, and everybody is happy. That ends the year.

Kachina *Dancers*

Next we turn to the ritual organization to which the *shalako* dancers may be counted, the *kachina* dancers. As mentioned in the foregoing, the *kachinas*, or *koko,* are spirits of the first ancestors, the dead, the clouds and rains who live in the sacred lake or the clouds who live up on the mountains. They are the masked gods, that is, they are primarily known through the performances of the masked Zuni dancers who represent them. The *kachina* cult is, as Bunzel says, the dominant Zuni cult, both because of its spectacular ceremonies and because of its support by all males; no man refrains from playing an active role in the organization if he wants to be certain of living on after death. The ritual contribution that a man can make in the *kachina* ceremonies and that lasts at least until he is in later middle age is necessary work to align the Zuni with the cosmic forces that keep everything, including their very existence, alive. The *kachina* organization membership is more than a social duty, it is a religious necessity. We are indeed far from the individualism of Shoshoni religion!

One could certainly account for the attraction of the *kachina* cult also in other terms, for example, its beauty and gaiety. This and the friendliness and easy ways of the *kachina* spirits are qualities that have no doubt endeared them and their pageants to the Zuni people. And yet, it is a fact that the *kachina* spirits severely punish any impersonator who does not represent them correctly: The mask might choke him. Persons appearing in *kachina* apparel, in turn, demand respect from the onlookers, for they are the gods as soon as they have put on the masks. Besides the masks, which as fetishes have been described in the foregoing, *kachina* dancers wear costumes, in particular white cotton kilts, sashes, and high buckskin moccasins. They carry gourd rattles or bow and arrows or feather staves, depending on their roles.

Some *kachina* figures are very sacred and have individual names. These are the **kachina priests,** the priestly hierarchy that rules the Kachina Village in the beyond. There is, for instance, the chief of these *kachinas,* **Pautiwa.** He is impersonated by a member of one particular clan who is venerably treated in connection with his appearance at the New Year ceremonies. Another important figure is **Long Horn,** who sends the deer—apparently an old supernatural master of the animals. Impersonators of the *shalako* form a cult group for the time they serve, as do the impersonators of the *koyemshi* ("mudheads"), clown *kachinas.* At the New Year celebrations the priests appoint a leader of the clowns, Father Koyemshi, who in his turn appoints nine other clowns. They all serve for four years, entertaining between rain dances with comic and obscene performances. The Shalako festival, for instance, is introduced by obscene appearances of the sacred clowns.

The sacred clowns, whose buffooneries amuse small children as well as adults, represent on a ritual level the trickster personage in mythology. (Stories about the trickster Coyote are found also among the Zuni.) The clowns disrupt the ceremonial stress, release tensions, and make ceremonies endurable. Generally in North American ceremonialism, mirth and sacred gravity exist side by side, and this is the case with the Zuni. However, the *koyemshi* are dangerous— whoever touches them becomes crazy. The Zuni never forget the supernatural, irrational character of the beings they impersonate.

The *kachina* dancers appear in two series of performances, the winter dances after the midwinter solstice held in the *kivas* and the summer dances (rain dances) held on the open plaza in the town. They also participate as assistant dancers when other societies and priesthoods have their ritual performances

These Zuni Shalako kachinas are ten-to-twelve feet high. The dancer, carrying a tall pole supporting a head and surrounded by hanging robes, peeps out through a hole in the midriff. (National Anthropological Archives, Smithsonian Institution, Neg. No. 2374.)

They are indeed the backbone of Zuni ceremonialism, supposed to bring health, rain, and fertility in their masked appearances. This is an extract of the prayer a Shalako *kachina* recites when he enters a Zuni house in early December:

> I have come from the sacred lake and I have come by all the springs. . . . I have come to see my people. For many years I have heard of my people living here at Itiwana [the middle of the world] and for long I have wanted to come. I want them to be happy, and I have been praying for them; and especially I want the women to be fortunate with their babies. I bring my people all kinds of seeds, all the different kinds of corn and all different kinds of fruit and wild green things. I have been praying for my people to have long life; and whoever has an evil heart should stand up in the daylight. I have been praying that my people may have all different kinds of seeds and that their rooms may be full of corn of all colors and beans of all colors and pumpkins and water gourds, and that they may have plenty of fresh water, so that they may look well and be healthy because of the pumpkins and the beans and the corn. I want to see them healthy.[49]

This is the kind of prayer found among all North American Indians, although in this case it is the *shalako* or divine protectors, once living members of the Zuni tribe, who offer the prayer. Life, security, food, and drink—these are the gifts for people if they comply with the ritual and metaphysical order.

Indeed, the concept of harmony with the supernatural order brings to the fore parallels in other religions—for instance, Vedic *rita* and Chinese *Dao* (*Tao*). The wealth and beauty of Zuni rituals to adapt humans and their society to the cosmic harmony is well known and surpasses everything we know in North American ceremonialism. [See Hinduism p. 740 for mention of *rita;* see Religions of China pp. 995–97 for discussion of *Dao* (*Tao*).]

Zuni Religion Today

No religion that is so intimately connected with culture and society as Zuni religion can in the long run withstand the change of time, especially when the presuppositions of this culture become altered. This is what is happening in our day. The new type of tribal government today is reducing the importance of sacral leaders. The pressure from a new social style and way of life makes itself felt. There is also a transition from horticulture to new ways of living such as working for money (employment among the whites), trade, and commercialism (for instance, in the distribution of Zuni art objects). As could be expected, religion, although conservative, slowly follows suit and also changes.

Old myths have disappeared, and many old ideas and rituals have become forgotten. On the other hand, some spectacular rituals have become more elaborate. Thus, the *kachina* cult has become more important in this century than it ever was before. Its elaboration is certainly associated with the decline of priesthoods and secret societies. The latter do not seem to respond to the demands of a changing lifestyle. The war priests, for example, also called Bow Priests, cannot function meaningfully now after the end of tribal wars. Some Zuni have been involved in the global wars of the last fifty years, but they are reluctant to equate modern warfare with ancient Zuni war practice. The result has been that there is no longer natural recruitment to the Bow Priesthood. The same applies to the other organizations: It is difficult to find people who are interested in practicing old-fashioned medicine or invoking the rain.

Just as among the Plains Indians the old religion has become concentrated in the Sun Dance ceremony, so with the Zuni Indians religion is increasingly receiving its main support from *kachina* ceremonies. It is difficult to know if in the long run this development will overthrow the structure of the Zuni religious system, but it will certainly modify the picture that we have presented here. Until now this system has been sufficiently closed to exclude many new Indian religious currents, such as the peyote religion, which is so important for contemporary Shoshoni. The individualistic character of Peyotism and its socially disruptive emphasis on personal experiences are not at all in line with the spirit of Zuni religion. The same is true for other Pueblo groups, except for the Plains-influenced Taos among whom use of peyote has been allowed, although not fully accepted.

The role of the Catholic church is an interesting chapter in Zuni religious development. There are church buildings both in Zuni itself and in the surrounding area, and the Catholic fathers certainly have Zuni in attendance at their services. However, the Zuni circumstances are not favorable to Catholicism on a more genuine level. Cushing has called attention to the nature of aboriginal reactions to the Catholic mission. When in the 1770s the Church of Our Lady of Guadalupe was built, Zuni artists painted the walls with traditional symbols of the gods of wind, rain, lightning, sunlight, tempest, and war and with emblems of the Corn Maidens amidst Christian decorations. The Catholic fathers did not realize the nature of this symbolism but were happy to see the zeal of the native painters in working, as they thought, for Catholicism. From then on, the Indians were eager to attend mass, to be baptized, and have their names written in the baptismal registers—"names totemic of the sacred assemblies"—which were thus legitimized by the church representatives who did not understand their meanings. As Cushing says, the Indians did not even think of renouncing their allegiance to Zuni gods. Rather, the Zuni wanted to gain the force of purification and the name-potency of the God and spirits (angels, saints) of another people and at the same time to assure the recognition of their own gods and priests by the foreign gods and priests. Indeed, tribal medicine feathers and fetishes were hidden under the altar of the church.[50] [See Christianity pp. 518, 528 and Religions of Mesoamerica pp. 223–26 for discussion of the cult of Mary and Guadalupe.]

Such incidents have set the pattern for today's devotion to Catholicism. Catholic sacred beings and symbols are incorporated into Zuni religion insofar as they comply with the traditional pattern, and Catholic attendance is largely seen in the perspective of traditional religion. For instance, among the Zuni fetishes there is a Catholic **santo** (saint) that people took care of when an old mission was abandoned in the beginning of the last century. The image, twelve inches tall, portrays the Christ Child of Our Lady of Atocha. It is kept in a shrine under the Shalako ceiling altar. The shrine is crowned by a cross. The image, whose garments are adorned by votive offerings, is fed daily like other fetishes. According to the Zuni, the Christ Child was borne by a daughter of the Sun. There is a dance each fall for the *santo* who is supposed to bring fertility for humans, animals, and fields.[51]

It has been argued by some researchers that the *kachina* cult has been inspired by the Catholic veneration of saints. This argument could be accepted if we keep in mind that the *kachina* cult as such originated in pre-Christian times and later received a veneer of Catholicism. A closer investigation of Zuni religious and ceremonial forms might reveal many influences of this kind.

The mixture of Zuni traditional practices with Catholicism is no sign of deterioration of the Pueblo religious pattern, but rather of change and, in some respects, of enrichment. However, in a larger perspective, the change in the conditions of living and the impact of Western value standards may threaten the future of Zuni traditional religion.

14

Conclusion:
Unity and Diversity
in Native American Religions

THE PRECEDING SKETCHES of two North American Indian religions offer us examples of two ways in which humans have tried to solve the eternal question of the nature of reality and how people relate to that reality. "Religion" is the name usually given to the cultural constructions founded on this basic and yet quite complex human concern.[52] Of course ecology, society, and historical traditions contribute to the final shape of such religious forms. However, what is most important is the identification of a religious reality that goes beyond all natural, social, and historical conditions.

The earliest tribes who long ago took possession of North America were the bearers of a hunting culture and a hunter's outlook on the supernatural world. We have seen how elements of this hunting ideology are preserved in the traditions of all later Indian groups, even among such an agricultural tribe as the Zuni. However, as cultures became differentiated, and particularly with the rise of agriculture, new religious forms arose that corresponded more closely to the conditions of the new cultural patterns. There is no doubt that at present, facing integration with white material (and also social) culture, Indian religions are again on the verge of dramatic changes; older Native American forms that are no longer relevant will be threatened and may disappear, but Native American religions will not give way completely to Western religious (and areligious) values.

Wind River Shoshoni and Zuni religions demonstrate the great diversity of Native American traditions within very different ecological, social, and historical conditions. As was mentioned in chapter 10, there is no single "American Indian religion" that is uniform throughout North America (or North and South America). In general, there are two basic religious orientations found in North America, a hunting pattern (as seen among the Shoshoni) and a horticultural pattern (as among the Zuni). Each of these particular traditions has retained its distinctive religious heritage, while changing so that it is in tune with the historical and social context.

The Wind River Shoshoni have remained strong individualists long after the end of their hunting days on the open Plains and in the Rocky Mountain forests. The infusion of Plains culture from the east modified their cultural and social individualism: They became devoted to the more collective activities of the Sun Dance and military drill in warfare but in other aspects continued to be "wild and disorganized like birds," as one observer has put it. Their guardian spirit complex expresses the Shoshoni individual quest for supernatural help and protection in hunting, warfare, and other pursuits. On the other hand, the Sun Dance ceremony is a collective ritual of thanksgiving and petition for the success and well-being of the whole tribe from one summer to the next. In extraordinary situations, such as sickness, when the individual's religious and secular resources are of no avail, medicine men come to the rescue of the individual.

As is typical of hunting religions, Shoshoni religion features a rather loose integration of religion, society, and culture. The individual is emphasized at the expense of society and culture. This relative lack of integration is demonstrated in the tension between mythology and cult, with mutually exclusive ideological patterns. The tales of mythology have very little to do with everyday ritual, and rituals such as the Sun Dance have very little connection with mythology. Another example of the loose integration of Shoshoni religion is the high degree of diversity of religious concepts from individual to individual; within the boundaries of the religious pattern, ideas are flexible and shift considerably.

Because religious ideas are so flexible and the organization of the worldview is so loose, a number of belief complexes are formed that pull together and unify otherwise separate beliefs and practices. For example, individual beliefs form links, like links of a chain, and these connect an association of beliefs into a larger complex. This is seen in the interconnection of guardian spirits with the medicine man's spiritualism as well as with the diagnosis and cure of disease and ideas about the spirits of the dead. Each link can be seen as an individual belief when viewed separately, but in the actual practice of Shoshoni religion, these links become forged together into a unified "complex" of related beliefs and ritual action. Such links, as individual elements, may be at variance or even in apparent conflict with one another, but they become coordinated and unified within the religious complex. Shoshoni religion, which features both a loose social organization and a flexible set of ideas or "philosophy," tends to encourage the unification of individual elements as complexes. The general organization and philosophy within Shoshoni religion varies considerably from individual to individual, and is guided by personal religious experience such as dreams and visions.

The Zuni show a reverse picture, suppressing rather than emphasizing the individual and experiential side of religion. Some scholars such as Ruth Benedict may have exaggerated the Zuni preference for the collective tradition, but it does contrast sharply with the Shoshoni. And when viewed in terms of Native American religions in general, the Zuni represent the horticultural pattern of religious orientation and emphasize the collectivism and cooperation essential in an agricultural society with greater population density.

The Zuni form one of the clearest cases of the horticultural pattern: Their socioreligious organization is unsurpassed in complexity throughout North America. One probable historical reason for this complexity is that the organizations and functions in the ancient "seven cities of Cibola," as the Spaniards called the Zuni pueblos, came to be concentrated in one settlement after the Pueblo revolt in the 1680s. The ceremonial system was contracted and therefore became more complex with, as Parsons describes it, "reduplication or elaboration of ceremonials." In earlier times there was exclusive association of the Shalako ceremony with the ancient pueblo of Hawikuh. In modern days, there is overlapping of the functions of *pekwin* with those of the town chief. The concentration of Zuni religion resulted in an enormous machinery, an intertwined web of religious activities, social roles, and cultural objectives. Bunzel has remarked that, although religion pervades all activities and the Zuni are one of the most religious peoples of the world, "in all the enormous mass of rituals there is no single bit of religious feeling equal in intensity and exaltation to the usual vision quest of the North American Indian." Bunzel considers that among the Zuni, religion has been externalized in rituals instead of internalized in religious feelings.[53] Perhaps this is true in a generalized sense, but we can scarcely rule out the occurrence of individual piety.

Behind the elaborateness of Zuni ritual there is a unitary religious conviction that the world order is founded on a balance of interrelationships among humankind, the universe, and the supernatural powers. The ritual organization and processes are directed to conform to this conception of world harmony. The rituals operate together with, and thereby strengthen, the well-being of the pueblo. To call this system magic is to depreciate the nature of the convictions involved.

Bunzel has claimed that there is a lack of profounder cosmological thought and metaphysics in Zuni mythology. If so, there is a change from the days when Cushing recorded the origin tales. The inference of the Zuni ritual symbolism is clear: The cosmos is a harmonious whole or spiritual order that also includes humankind. There is no explicit statement in so many words of this thought— no prophets, no authoritative philosophers—but it illuminates the structure of Zuni religion.

The Shoshoni and Zuni represent the unity as well as the diversity of Native American religions. The Shoshoni and Zuni, like other American Indians, share many features such as a notion of affinity to plants, animals, and all of nature. The Shoshoni emphasize their relationship to animals; the Zuni retain some of the old animal ceremonialism but focus primarily on their relationship to maize. Shoshoni view the universe in the four sacred (cardinal) directions, while Zuni expand the four sacred directions to six—to include zenith and nadir.

All Native Americans look to "natural spirits" or the spirits of nature for revelation and power, and this is true of Shoshoni and Zuni. However, Shoshoni look more to animals and the sky, whereas Zuni look to plants and the underground. Religious architecture mirrors both their understanding of the universe and the two diverse forms of expression. For the Shoshoni the cosmos is reconstructed in the Sun Dance lodge, open to the sun and the elements, built on any site. For the Zuni, the cosmos and its "emergence" is reflected in the permanent *kiva,* with its *sipapu* or ceremonial hole of emergence; for rituals the Zuni "descend" into the *kiva.*

The Shoshoni recognize Mother Earth, but they focus mainly on the power in the sky; the Zuni recognize the preeminence of the Sun, but their main concern is with the sacredness of the wombs of the world and the underground. The supernatural reveals its power to American Indians: To Shoshoni, the power comes mainly to individuals in dreams and visions; to Zuni, the power is conveyed especially to groups in the myth of origin and in collective annual rituals.

Shoshoni and Zuni religions express two distinctive approaches to the mystery and sacredness of life, both stamped by their Indian heritage, but communicating the Indian conviction of religious reality to the rest of the world.

Study Questions

Before you begin to read this part, take a mental inventory of what you know and think about Native America and Native Americans—popularly known as "Indians." Make a list of facts that you know about Indians and Indian culture—the interaction of Europeans such as Pilgrims with Indians, Indian foods such as corn and turkey, Indian forms of dress and housing (for example, the tipi), Indian art, hunting, and warfare. What do you know about (or imagine about) Native American religion? Keep these images and things in mind as you read this section and develop new notions about Native Americans and their religious traditions.

CHAPTER 10

Introduction to Native American Religions

1. How does the author introduce the popular image of the "American Indian," and how does he propose to approach the Native Americans and their religious traditions?
2. Why does the author reject the notion of "primitive religion," and the concept of "*the* Native American religion"?
3. What do we know about the origins of Native American people and culture?
4. Characterize the "hunting pattern" and "horticultural pattern" of Native Americans.
5. How would you compare and contrast Native American religious traditions with world religions?

CHAPTER 11

Native American Religions: An Overview

1. What are the major features of North American Indian religions?
2. Characterize the worldview of North American Indians, indicating the role of humans, animals, spirits, and supernatural powers within this worldview.
3. How does the worldview of North American Indians compare with the worldview of the Western world and the Judaeo-Christian tradition?
4. What are some of the most important religious activities among Native North Americans?

CHAPTER 12

The Religion of the Wind River Shoshoni: Hunting, Power, and Visions

1. What is the basic difference between the Shoshoni and the Zuni?
2. Identify the basic components of Wind River Shoshoni religion.
3. Contrast mythology and everyday religion among the Shoshoni.
4. What is the relationship between the Supreme Being and spirits in Shoshoni religion?
5. Define *puha* and treat its importance in Shoshoni religion.
6. What is the role of dreams and the vision quest in the Shoshoni tradition?
7. Contrast the role of beliefs and myths in Shoshoni religion.
8. What is the significance of the Shoshoni Sun Dance?
9. Trace the accounts of the origin of the Sun Dance, and identify major features of the Sun Dance lodge.
10. Using figure 3-1, "Plan of the Sun Dance Lodge" on p. 313, analyze this lodge as a replica of the cosmos.
11. Describe the major activities in the Sun Dance.
12. Interpret the Shoshoni view of sickness and show how the medicine man acts to cure sickness.
13. In recent times how did Shoshoni religion interact with "new religious approaches"?

CHAPTER 13

The Religion of the Zuni: Farming, Masked Dancers,
and the Power of Fertility

1. Identify the basic features of Zuni life and religion.
2. Tell in your own words the Zuni origin myth.
3. Characterize the Zuni worldview by describing the significance of the pueblo and analyzing the levels in the Zuni cosmos.
4. What are the major figures in the Zuni pantheon?
5. Interpret the religious significance of the pattern of Mother Earth, vegetation, maize, and Corn Maidens.
6. Tell in your own words the Zuni version of the "Orpheus" Tradition.
7. Compare the role of myths in the Zuni and Shoshoni traditions.
8. What is the significance of "collective ritual" in Zuni religion?
9. Compare the role of *kiva* groups, medicine societies, and priesthoods, especially noting who is included in each category.
10. Describe the major features of Zuni ceremonies.
11. What characterizes the Zuni ritual year?
12. Define *kachina* and interpret the significance of the *kachina* cult in Zuni religion.
13. What is the relationship between the Catholic church and Zuni religion?

CHAPTER 14

Conclusion: Unity and Diversity in Native American Religions
1. In general how can Shoshoni religion be characterized?
2. In general how can Zuni religion be characterized?
3. How can we best compare Shoshoni religion and Zuni religion?

Recall the mental inventory of Native American images and things that you made before reading this part. What is there in Native American religion that is most like your own religious tradition? What in Native American religion is most different from your own tradition? What is most interesting? How has your understanding of Native American religion changed as a result of reading this section? Can you now imagine yourself participating in Native American religion?

Notes

For linguistic help and preparation of maps I am indebted to my dear wife, Geraldine. As a small token of my gratitude I dedicate the work to her. And my thoughts go to my Shoshoni friends, many now deceased, who with such dedication of spirit initiated me into Shoshoni religion.

1. Further discussion of this circumpolar heritage can be found in my article "North American Indian Religions in a Circumpolar Perspective," *North American Indian Studies: European Contributions,* ed. Pieter Hovens (Göttingen: Edition Herodot, 1981), 11–28.
2. A. Irving Hallowell, "Bear Ceremonialism in the Northern Hemisphere," *American Anthropologist* 28, no. 1 (1926): 1–175.
3. The trickster has been discussed from a humanistic perspective in Paul Radin, *The Trickster: A Study in American Indian Mythology* (New York: Philosophical Library, 1956); and from the perspective of comparative religion in my book, *The Religions of the American Indians* (Berkeley and Los Angeles: University of California Press, 1979), 29–43.
4. Robert Redfield, *The Primitive World and Its Transformations* (Ithaca, NY: Cornell University Press, 1953), 85.
5. Åke Hultkrantz, *Belief and Worship in Native North America,* ed. Christopher Vecsey (Syracuse, NY: Syracuse University Press, 1981), 117–34.
6. Frank G. Speck, *Nasukapi: The Savage Hunters of the Labrador Peninsula* (Norman, OK: University of Oklahoma Press, 1935), 33–34.
7. Alfonso Ortiz, *The Tewa World: Space, Time, Being and Becoming in a Pueblo Society* (Chicago: University of Chicago Press, 1969).
8. Ibid., 98.
9. Edna Kenton, ed., *The Jesuit Relations and Allied Documents* (New York: Vanguard Press, 1954), 113, 141–42.
10. James R. Walker, "The Sun Dance and Other Ceremonies of the Oglala Division of the Teton Dakota," *Anthropological Papers of the American Museum of Natural History* 16, no. 2 (New York, 1917): 157, 160. See also the interpretation in Werner Müller, *Amerika: Die Neue oder die Alte Welt?* (Berlin: Dietrich Reimer, 1982), 36–51.
11. Paul Radin, *Primitive Religion* (New York: Dover Publications, 1957), 3–4.
12. See my article, "Accommodation and Persistence: Ecological Analysis of the Religion of the Sheepeater Indians in Wyoming, U.S.A.," *Temenos* 17 (1981): 35–44.
13. See my *Belief and Worship,* 28–47, and my article, "An Ideological Dichotomy: Myths and Folk Beliefs Among the Shoshoni," in *Sacred Narrative: Readings in the Theory of Myth,* ed. Alan Dundes (Berkeley and Los Angeles: University of California Press, 1984), 152–65.
14. See my *Belief and Worship,* 157–84.
15. See my article, "The Concept of the Soul Held by the Wind River Shoshone," *Ethnos* 16, nos. 1–2 (Stockholm 1951): 18–44.

16. Although not being the supernatural owner of the animals the *puha* animal is supposed to control the animals. For an analysis of these problems among the Shoshoni, see my article, "The Master of the Animals among the Wind River Shoshoni," *Ethnos* 26, no. 4 (1961): 198–218.

17. Arnold van Gennep, *The Rites of Passage* (Chicago: University of Chicago Press, 1960).

18. There is no similar exact time for the boys' ceremonies. For customs at menstruation and childbirth, see also Demitri B. Shimkin, "Childhood and Development among the Wind River Shoshone," *Anthropological Records* 5, no. 5 (Berkeley and Los Angeles: University of California Press, 1947).

19. This holistic interpretation of couvade is preferable to the efforts made by some social anthropologists to regard it as a way of asserting the father's paternity or as a means to save the wife from evil spirits and transfer the latter on her husband.

20. Demitri B. Shimkin, "The Wind River Shoshone Sun Dance," *Bureau of American Ethnology,* Bulletin 151 (Washington: Smithsonian Institution, 1953): 409–17; Åke Hultkrantz, "Yellow Hand, Chief and Medicine-man among the Eastern Shoshoni," *Proceedings of the 38th Congress of Americanists,* vol. 2 (Stuttgart and München: Klaus Renner, 1968): 293–304.

21. This is one of the few visions where there is reference to Our Father. One of my informants even thought that it was Our Father himself who appeared in this vision.

22. The emphasis on curing is most certainly a reflection of the changed aims of the ceremony introduced about 1890.

23. This is of course an instance of animal ceremonialism.

24. A more exhaustive presentation will be found in my *Belief and Worship,* 235–63.

25. See also Hultkrantz, *Iconography of Religions: Prairie and Plains Indians* (Leiden: Brill, 1973), 9–18.

26. See my *Belief and Worship,* 212–34.

27. Ibid., 264–81.

28. Zuni—sometimes spelled Zuñi, but nowadays not pronounced that way—is a Keresan name of the pueblo. The Zuni themselves call their town Ashiwi. The Spaniards of the sixteenth century called the pueblos "los siete ciudades de Cibola," the seven towns of Cibola.

29. Alfred L. Kroeber, "Zuñi," *Encyclopaedia of Religion and Ethics,* ed. James Hastings (New York: Scribner, 1928), 12:868–73.

30. Fred Eggan, *Social Organization of the Western Pueblos* (Chicago: University of Chicago Press, 1950), 210–22.

31. Frank Cushing, "Outlines of Zuñi Creation Myths," *13th Annual Report of the Bureau of Ethnology* (Washington: Smithsonian Institution, 1896): 379–81. On the world-parents myth, see Anna Birgitta Rooth, "The Creation Myths of the North American Indians," in *Sacred Narrative: Readings in the Theory of Myth,* ed. Alan Dundes (Berkeley and Los Angeles: University of California Press, 1984), 171–73.

32. Elsie Clews Parsons, "The Origin Myth of Zuñi," *Journal of American Folk-Lore,* vol. 36 (1923): 135–62. Kroeber, "Zuñi," 869. Cushing, "Outlines of Zuñi Creation Myths": 379–447.

33. See Ruth Benedict, *Zuni Mythology* (New York: Columbia University Press, 1935), 1:256.

34. The universe is thus basically restricted to this landscape. A Hopi friend of mine told me of the shock he experienced when for the first time he saw the Pacific Ocean from the California coast.

35. Those who have studied the recent works of Claude Lévi-Strauss should know that in his book series *Mythologiques* he treats lengthily the distinction between "raw" and "cooked." His argument does not, however, concern us here.

36. See for instance plates X and XI in Frank H. Cushing, "Zuñi Fetiches," *2nd Annual Report of the Bureau of Ethnology* (Washington: Smithsonian Institution, 1883). The same "lifelines" are found on Zuni pottery.

37. Ruth L. Bunzel, "Introduction to Zuñi Ceremonialism," *47th Annual Report of the Bureau of American Ethnology* (Washington: Smithsonian Institution, 1932): 483–84.

38. Benedict, *Zuni Mythology,* vol. 1, 20–43, 269–72.

39. Ruth L. Bunzel, "Zuñi Ritual Poetry," *47th Annual Report of the Bureau of American Ethnology* (Washington: Smithsonian Institution, 1932): 804.

40. See Herman Karl Haeberlin, "The Idea of Fertilization in the Culture of the Pueblo Indians," *Memoirs of the American Anthropological Association* 3, no. 1 (Lancaster: American Anthropological Association, 1916). See also Hultkrantz, *Belief and Worship,* 107–11.

41. Quoted after Benedict, *Zuni Mythology,* vol. 2, 128–34. In a version given by Cushing, the wife is recovered from the Kachina Village by owls who instruct the man to observe continence on the way back to Zuni. However, he breaks the taboo, and his wife becomes an owl. From this event dates the mourning for the dead: Frank H. Cushing, *Zuni Folk Tales* (New York: Knopf, 1931), 18–32.

42. Bunzel, "Introduction to Zuñi Ceremonialism," 476.

43. Frank H. Cushing, *Zuñi: Selected Writings,* ed. by Jesse Green (Lincoln: University of Nebraska Press, 1979), 306–7.

44. See Elsie Clews Parsons, *Pueblo Indian Religion* (Chicago: University of Chicago Press, 1939), vol. 1, 514–31, vol. 2, 791–93; Parsons, "Notes on Zuñi, Part I," *Memoirs of the American Anthropological Association* IV, no. 3 (Lancaster, PA: American Anthropological Association, 1917); and Bunzel, "Introduction to Zuñi Ceremonialism," 534–40.

45. Cushing, *Zuñi: Selected Writings,* 75–76.

46. For the festivals, see Ruth L. Bunzel, "Zuñi Katcinas," *47th Annual Report of the Bureau of American Ethnology* (Washington: Smithsonian Institution, 1932): 941–75.

47. Bunzel, "Zuñi Katcinas," 973.

48. Ibid., 975.

49. Ibid., 974.

50. Cushing, *Zuñi: Selected Writings,* 176–78.

51. Ruth F. Kirk, "Introduction to Zuni Fetishism," *Papers of the School of American Research* (Sante Fe, NM: Archaeological Institute of America, 1943): 16–17.

52. See my article, "The Concept of the Supernatural in Primal Religion," *History of Religions* 22, no. 3 (1983): 231–53.

53. Bunzel, "Introduction to Zuñi Ceremonialism," 480.

Glossary

ahayuta The diminutive twin war gods of the Zuni.

animal ceremonialism The rituals around the slain game, in particular the disposal of the carcass whereby the bones are laid in their anatomical order and the head is sometimes elevated on a tree or a pole. The ceremonialism is intended to propitiate the animal or its spiritual master who is supposed to have been offended by the killing. The order of the bones is an objectification of the wish that the slain animal may rise again, in this world or the next one.

animalism The mysterious relation in hunting cultures between humans and animals manifested, for example, in the idea of spirits in animal form.

annual ceremony of cosmic rejuvenation The ceremony held at the beginning of each new vegetation year to bring humans in harmony with the rejuvenation not only of vegetation and animal life, but also of the world and the cosmos; it is a reiteration of the cosmic drama through which the world was once formed.

apila ashiwanni Zuni Bow Priests, once war chiefs, associated with the mythical *ahayuta*.

ashiwanni Zuni Rain Priests.

awonawilona A class of supernatural beings among the Zuni, in particular the Sun Father and Moon Mother.

bear ceremonialism The animal ceremonialism centered on the bear; bear ceremonialism is the most developed form of animal ceremonialism.

beast gods Zuni supernatural masters of animal species.

ceremonial moieties In some tribes the population is divided into two halves for the purpose of alternating at ritual performances; for instance, one moiety is supposed to bury the dead of the other moiety.

circumboreal religion The religions of the northern woodland areas in North America and Eurasia. They include animal ceremonialism, beliefs in masters of the game, worship of sky gods and atmospheric spirits, and shamanism.

circumpolar religion The religions of northernmost Arctic and sub-Arctic North America and Eurasia which, due to historical and ecological factors, show a certain likeness to one another.

Corn Maidens The protective spirits of the corn among the Pueblo Indians.

couvade The custom of the husband undergoing certain taboos and ritual injunctions during the latter part of his wife's pregnancy.

Coyote The prairie wolf, a mythic culture hero and trickster among the Shoshoni.

culture hero A supernatural being from the beginning of time who introduced cultural and religious institutions among humankind.

dzoavits Among the Shoshoni, monsters who eat people.

Emanation Myth A myth about the origin of the world in which the world is said to emanate from the sexual union of two divine beings.

Emergence Myth A myth about the emergence of the primeval mankind from the underworld.

ettowe The mighty fetishes of Zuni Rain Priests.

fetish Object radiating supernatural power. *Fetish,* a word adopted from the Portuguese *feitiço* (bewitched, enchanted thing), has been used by ethnographers to refer to Zuni sacred objects.

Ghost Dance A revivalistic movement originating among the Paiute of Nevada and California (1870–1890) and spreading to the Plains Indians where it caused clashes between Sioux Indians and the U.S. military. The movement is named for its round dancing, which was supposed to contribute to the return of the dead and the good times of yore.

intrusion See spirit or object intrusion.

itiwana "The middle place," the Zuni center.

kachina Among the Pueblo Indians a masked dancer and the spirit portrayed by this dancer—usually an ancestor and rain spirit.

kachina **priests** The supernatural rulers of the mysterious Kachina Village among the Zuni.

kiva The Hopi word for a partially subterranean cult chamber among the Pueblo Indians.

koko The Zuni term for *kachina.*

koyemshi The Zuni term for *kachina* clowns.

Long Horn The supernatural master of the deer among the Zuni.

master of the animals The idea that every animal species of importance has its own supernatural ruler or master who protects the animals of that species and either offers them to or withholds them from the hunters.

medicine A term usually applied to supernatural power, in particular the power received by an Indian from his or her personal protective spirit.

medicine bag, medicine bundle A bag or sack of animal skin in which an Indian, a clan, or a society keeps its sacred "medicines," that is, pieces of animal bones, claws, hooves, pollen meal, or feathers that constitute centers of sacred power. The bag or bundle is composed according to instructions given by guardian spirits in dreams or visions. Some clan or tribal bundles are inherited from one generation to the next and so on. The contents of Zuni bundles are often described as fetishes.

medicine man, medicine woman A person who has received special supernatural power of importance, in particular medical power.

medicine society A society composed of people blessed by the same supernatural power, in particular curative power.

medicine wheel Arrangements of stones in circles around a central hub by which certain calendar dates, such as the summer solstice, have been decided.

Mythic Twins The creative brothers or culture heroes; one of them is often identical with the Supreme Being, the other with the trickster. See also *ahayuta.*

nagualism A Mexican Indian term denoting such an intimate connection between an individual and the individual's guardian spirit that they share the same qualities and even the same life.

navushieip The Shoshoni word for dream or vision and the soul that has such experiences (the "dream soul").

nyipij "Wind master," the Shoshoni spirit controlling the winds.

nynymbi Dangerous dwarf spirits among the Shoshoni.

pandzoavits See *dzoavits.*

Pan-Indianism The (American Indian) interpretation that Indian religious symbols basically cover the same concepts in all tribes, since all Indians are really ethnically and culturally identical; the movement to realize this idea is also referred to as Pan-Indianism.

Pautiwa The chief of the *kachina* priests in Zuni religion.

Payatamu Zuni culture hero who introduced corn agriculture.

pekwin The Sun Priest and spiritual leader of the Zuni.

Peyotism A revivalistic religion based on the use of peyote, a small spineless psychotropic cactus from the Rio Grande area, that has spread from the southern Plains over the United States and southern Canada.

Poshayanki Zuni culture hero, head of the beast gods and patron of the medicine societies.

puberty quest A vision quest at puberty.

pueblo The Spanish word meaning "town"; it also means the people of the town. The concentrated Indian adobe settlements of New Mexico and Arizona are called pueblos, and the Indians living there are called Pueblo Indians.

puha The Shoshoni word for both supernatural power and the guardian spirit that grants such power.

puhagan In Shoshoni "possessor of supernatural power," the term for a medicine man or woman and any other person with such power.

reincarnation Rebirth as a human.

santo Spanish word meaning "saint" (used by the Zuni).

Shalako The great Zuni ritual at the end of the year; the *shalako* are powerful *kachinas*.

shaman A religio-magical practitioner who, on behalf of society and with the aid of guardian spirit(s), enters into a trance (ecstasy) to establish contact with the powers in the other world.

shamanism A complex of rituals, tales, and beliefs concentrated around the shaman.

sipapu In Pueblo religion the place of emergence from the underworld of the first people, symbolized by a sacred hollow in a cult chamber.

soul loss The idea that a disease is due to the loss of the patient's soul (or one of his or her souls).

spirit intrusion or **object intrusion** The idea that a disease is due to the intrusion into the body of a spirit or an object.

Sun Dance The annual cosmic rejuvenation ceremony of the Plains Indians.

taboo Scientific term taken from the South Sea islanders to denote what is forbidden, dangerous, and sacred; a prohibition with a religious or social sanction.

Tam Apo "Our Father," the Shoshoni name of the Supreme Being.

Tam Sogobia "Our Mother Earth," the Shoshoni goddess of the earth.

tipi The buffalo skin tent of Plains Indians.

tongwoyaget "Crying clouds," the Shoshoni thunderbird.

totem poles Heraldic poles among the Indians of the Northwest Coast raised to celebrate an important person's acquisition of a new name (or title), to commemorate a feast or a ceremonial occasion, or to preserve the remains of a dead person. The poles usually portray guardian spirits and the owner or the owner's ancestors.

transmigration Rebirth as an animal, tree, or inanimate thing.

trickster A character in the mythologies of many Native American peoples, often identical with the culture hero in his comic aspects.

uwanammi Zuni spirits of rain and dew.

vision quest The ritual quest for a guardian spirit performed by males in early youth or (on the Plains) repeatedly on later occasions and by some females. The Indian seeks the spirit in lone places where it may appear to him or her in a vision.

Wakan Tanka The collective term for supernatural beings of the Lakota (Dakota) Indians; it is often used to denote the Supreme Being—the interpretations of the Indians vacillate between spirit collectivity and a High God.

Wolf The chief of the Shoshoni myth world; among the Wind River Shoshoni, Wolf corresponds to the Supreme Being of everyday religion.

World Tree The cosmic tree that stretches through three worlds—sky, earth, and underworld; it is a symbol of the cosmic center or the Supreme Being, and serves as a communications channel between the sky powers and humans.

Selected Reading List

Benedict, Ruth. *Patterns of Culture.* London: Routledge, 1946.

———. *Zuni Mythology.* 2 vols. Columbia University Contributions to Anthropology 21. New York: Columbia University Press, 1935.

Bunzel, Ruth L. "Introduction to Zuñi Ceremonialism," "Zuñi Origin Myths," "Zuñi Ritual Poetry," "Zuñi Katcinas." *47th Annual Report of the Bureau of American Ethnology.* Washington: Smithsonian Institution, 1932.

Cazeneuve, Jean. *Les dieux dansent à Cibola.* Paris: Gallimard, 1957.

Cushing, Frank H. "Outlines of Zuni Creation Myths." *13th Annual Report of the Bureau of Ethnology.* Washington: Smithsonian Institution 1896.

———. *Zuñi: Selected Writings.* Edited by Jesse Green. Lincoln: University of Nebraska Press, 1979.

———. "Zuñi Fetiches." *2nd Annual Report of the Bureau of Ethnology.* Washington: Smithsonian Institution, 1883.

Handbook of North American Indians, vol. 9, Southwest. Edited by William C. Sturtevant and Alfonso Ortiz. Articles on the Zuni by, among others, Fred Eggan, Edmund J. Ladd, and Dennis Tedlock. Washington: Smithsonian Institution, 1979.

Hultkrantz, Åke. *Belief and Worship in Native North America.* Edited by Christopher Vecsey. Syracuse, NY: Syracuse University Press, 1981.

Kirk, Ruth F. "Introduction to Zuni Fetishism." *Papers of the School of American Research.* Santa Fe, NM: Archaeological Institute of America, 1943.

Lowie, Robert H. "The Northern Shoshone." *Anthropological Papers of the American Museum of Natural History,* vol. 2, part 2. New York: American Museum of Natural History, 1909.

Parsons, Elsie Clews. "Hopi and Zuñi Ceremonialism." *Memoirs of the American Anthropological Association* 39. Menasha, WI: American Anthropological Association, 1933.

———. "Notes on Zuñi." *Memoirs of the American Anthropological Association* 4, nos. 3–4. Lancaster, PA: American Anthropological Association, 1917.

———. *Pueblo Indian Religion.* 2 vols. Chicago: University of Chicago Press, 1939.

Quam, Alvina, ed. *The Zunis: Self-Portrayals.* Albuquerque: University of New Mexico Press, 1972.

Roediger, Virginia More. *Ceremonial Customs of the Pueblo Indians.* Berkeley and Los Angeles: University of California Press, 1961.

Shimkin, Demitri B. "The Wind River Shoshone Sun Dance." *Bureau of American Ethnology,* Bulletin 151. Washington: Smithsonian Institution, 1953.

Stevenson, Matilda Coxe. "The Zuñi Indians: Their Mythology, Esoteric Fraternities, and Ceremonies." *23rd Annual Report of the Bureau of American Ethnology.* Washington: Smithsonian Institution, 1904.

Voget, Fred W. *The Shoshoni-Crow Sun Dance.* Norman: University of Oklahoma Press, 1984.

PART FOUR

Judaism

*Revelation
and Traditions*

Michael Fishbane

Chronology of Jewish Religious History

Dates	Major Cultural and Religious Events
2000 to 1250 B.C.E.	Ancestors of the Jews migrate from Mesopotamia to the land of Canaan; formation of nomadic and early settlement; traditions of the patriarchs; development of tribal lineages
1250 to 1050 B.C.E.	Exodus from Egyptian bondage; formation of covenantal community; conquest and initial settlement of Canaan; development of tribal structures and forms of national leadership
1050 to 587/6 B.C.E.	Rise and establishment of monarchy under David (c. 1013 to 973 B.C.E.); First Temple built by Solomon, son of David; development of ancient Israelite institutions and literature; religious creativity; emergence of classical prophecy with Amos (mid–eighth century); Assyrians conquer Samaria; exile of ten northern tribes (722/1 B.C.E.); Jerusalem Temple and Judea destroyed by Babylonians; exile of Judeans to Babylon (587/6 B.C.E.)
539 B.C.E. to 70 C.E.	Beginning of return to Zion; restoration of ancient institutions and leadership; Temple rebuilt (515 B.C.E.) and prophecy revived; emergence of classical Judaism, centered around the law (revelation) and its interpretation (traditions); rise of Greek power and hegemony in Palestine (331 B.C.E.); Judaism prohibited by Antiochus IV; Maccabees revolt (168 B.C.E.); Temple restored and purified (165 B.C.E.); development of different religious groups in Palestine, including the community around the Dead Sea; the development of Jewish life in Alexandria; Philo combines Jewish culture with Hellenistic thought; emergence of Pharisees as dominant religious movement, and its consolidation of the ideals of scholarship and piety; rise of Roman rule; conquest of Palestine (63 B.C.E.)

Dates	*Major Cultural and Religious Events*
70 to 700 C.E.	Rabbinic Judaism in formation; development of class of sages and rabbinical schools of study and interpretation; fall of Second Temple to Romans (70 C.E.); Rabbi Yochanan ben Zakkai founds center for legal study and administrative rule in Yavneh (Jamnia); conference on canonization of biblical literature at Yavneh (90 C.E.); Rabbi Judah the Prince compiles the Mishnah, the written digest of the oral traditions and rules of the Tannaim; establishment of Babylonian rabbinical academies and the development of vast commentaries on the Mishnah, called Talmud, by Amoraim; consolidations of these comments and other traditions produce Palestinian and Babylonian Talmuds (mid–fifth to sixth centuries); midrashic (nonlegal) creativity in Palestine and Babylonia
700 to 1750 C.E.	Consolidation of legal traditions and liturgy; Massoretes establish traditional text of the Bible (Rabbinic Bible); Jewish life spreads from Israel to Spain, Morocco, Iraq, and beyond; development of Jewish institutions and literary creativity; Jewish life influenced by Christianity and Islamic civilizations; repeated persecutions and massacres of Jews, as in the Rhineland (1040), York, England (1190), Navarre (1328), Spain (1391), Poland (1648); ritual burning of Talmud in Paris (1244) and Italy (1553); repeated exile of Jews, as from England (1291), France (1309), Spain (1492), and Portugal (1496); ghetto introduced in Venice (1516); major thinkers (most notably Rashi, born in 1040) emerge to comment upon or consolidate the biblical and rabbinical traditions; development of systematic philosophical expressions of Jewish theology (most notably by Maimonides, born in 1135); emergence of new trends in Jewish mysticism in Spain and Germany (*Zohar* is written in Spain in the late thirteenth century); revival of Jewish mysticism in Safed, Palestine (sixteenth century), led by Joseph Karo and Isaac Luria; major compilation of Jewish law by Karo (Shulkhan Arukh); important period of Talmudic study in Poland (sixteenth to eighteenth centuries); Jewish community founded in New Amsterdam, New York, in 1654
1750 C.E. to present	Emergence of new patterns of Jewish life, due to social and ideological revolutions in Europe and challenges to old rabbinical structures in Eastern Europe; development of secular Jewish enlightenment and religious reform movements in Western Europe; pietistic revival, known as Hasidism, under spiritual leadership of Rabbi Israel Baal

Dates	**Major Cultural and Religious Events**
1750 C.E. *to present* (continued)	Shem, in Eastern Europe; resistance of traditional Orthodoxy in Eastern Europe; accommodations to European culture develop in the West; spread of new religious developments to America in the nineteenth century; foundation of Union of American Hebrew Congregations (Reform, 1873) and of the Jewish Theological Seminary of America (Conservative, 1886); revival of Jewish nationalism, called Zionism (from 1881); Herzl writes Zionist manifesto (*The Jewish State,* 1896), and the Zionist movement is founded (1897); resettlement of land of Israel and revival of Hebrew language; Tel Aviv founded (1909); Nazi war against the Jews of Europe (1933 to 1945); six million Jewish noncombatants murdered during World War II; development of Jewish resistance in Europe (Warsaw Ghetto uprising, 1943); resistance spreads to Jews in Palestine; Jews return en masse to land of Israel and develop social, cultural, and political institutions; state of Israel founded (1948); partition of Palestine between Jews and Arabs; frequent conflicts; Six Day War (1967) and Jewish reunification of Jerusalem; ancient Temple wall recovered and ancient holy sites declared accessible to all; revival of Jewish cultural and religious institutions in America; cultural ties deepened between Jews of Israel and Diaspora

Prologue

THIS SMALL WORK IS AN ATTEMPT to provide, in a concise and direct way, an introduction to the remarkable religious force and range of Judaism. An effort has therefore been made to present something of the historical diversity and complex variations of Judaism, as well as of its central and dynamic features. Over the course of the centuries, Judaism has never had a fixed or frozen form. Rather, it has expressed itself as a living historical phenomenon in ever new though identifiable variations. Basic beliefs and ideas as well as fundamental texts and rituals have all been subject to interpretation and reinterpretation. The animating forces of creativity, which have shaped the development of Judaism in and through its traditional texts and expressions of observance, are still alive in our own day.

15
Introduction

LET US IMAGINE the following historical event, one quite typical of Jewish life as it has been practiced worldwide for over two thousand years. On a **Sabbath*** day sometime in the mid-sixteenth century, the Jews of Cochin, a city on the Malabar coast of southwest India, gather in the **synagogue** for worship. On that day the readings from the Bible** include chapters from the Book of Exodus and a portion of chapter 46 from the prophecies of Jeremiah. The first of these readings recalls the slavery of the ancient Israelites in the land of Egypt (thirteenth century B.C.E.); the second announces a divine promise to a different generation (seventh century B.C.E.) that the nation would one day be restored to its ancestral homeland—the land of **Israel**—from all the far-flung lands of its dispersion. Reflecting on these matters, the **rabbi** or learned elder tells those assembled that the history and the hope just read from the Bible are not just words from the past. They are, he says, living words for them: The slavery in Egypt is their own national memory, and the promise of national renewal is their own collective hope. Hearing this, the congregation nods assent—just as they are doing in a synagogue in Alexandria (Egypt) on that same Sabbath, when Rabbi David **ben** Solomon ibn Abi Zimra gives his learned address, and just as they are doing in a synagogue in Safed (Palestine), after the discourse of the mystic and lawyer Rabbi Joseph Karo.

Thus, though separated east and west and ruled by all the kingdoms of the earth, the Jews the world over were and are one people sharing deep bonds despite external differences of custom and costume. They share similar national memories and hopes rooted in the same biblical texts, which they read throughout the year and in the same sequence. And they also share a book of common prayers for everyday worship and a fixed pattern of observances for every moment of the calendar year. In this way the teachings and **commandments** of the Bible, as explained or reformulated by scholars throughout the centuries, have been faithfully preserved and lovingly performed by Jews from Cochin to Krakow and from Bombay to Brooklyn—all to the glory and honor of God.

---

*Terms defined in the glossary, pp. 479–82, are printed in boldface where they first appear in the text.

**In this part the term Bible refers to the Hebrew Bible.

Judaism is thus the religious expression of the Jewish people from antiquity to the present day as it has tried to form and live a life of holiness before God. It is, on the one hand, an expression of recognizable uniformity, practiced commonly and communally by Jews across the centuries in different lands. But, on the other, it is also a religious expression with great historical variations. Never static, Judaism has changed and challenged its adherents for over two millennia, even as it has been changed and challenged by them in different circumstances and times. This relationship of continuity and change stands at the center of Jewish practice and belief. Since Judaism characteristically understands itself by commenting on its own earlier traditions, let us follow this lead and turn, by way of introduction, to two most instructive texts.

The first of these is a remarkable legend preserved in the Babylonian **Talmud,** the foremost collection of classical Jewish law and lore (edited in the fifth century C.E., but containing traditions from up to 750 years earlier). In just a few sentences, the narrative discloses the authoritative core of Jewish creative vigor and the very pulse of its unity within diversity. It shows Judaism to be at once a religion rooted in the Bible—in terms of its beliefs and behaviors, history and hopes—yet radically transformed by the ongoing teachings of the sages. All this is conveyed in a series of dramatic folk images (not abstract arguments) that extend literary hints found in the Bible itself.

The text has its point of departure in the biblical account of the revelation of the divine Law at Mount Sinai as recorded in the Book of Exodus. In the Bible, this is the central moment of ancient Israelite history and religion, for it is the moment, according to tradition, when the ancient Hebrews became a religious nation bound to God. Understandably, then, the divine revelation at Sinai has remained the central religious event for Jews and Judaism ever since. But when we look closely at the biblical text, which apparently only states that the Israelites received the Ten Commandments and a rather limited collection of ordinances at Sinai, we might well wonder how this event could also be the source of the voluminous laws and practices of historical Judaism.

The biblical passage (in Exodus 19) simply states that, while the nation waited below, "**Moses** ascended" the mountain to receive God's laws and instructions for them. However, according to Rab, the teacher (third century C.E.) in whose name the legend was transmitted in the Talmud[1], this textual reference is merely an allusion to a more profound spiritual moment for Moses and the future Jewish people. It is but the merest clue of what "really" took place on that occasion—namely, Moses' spiritual ascension to heaven. There, the legend tells us, the future lawgiver Moses found God adding little scribal flourishes to the letters of the Law, the **Torah.** Astonished and perplexed, Moses asked for an explanation. God then told him that a man would arise after many generations, **Akiba** ben Joseph by name, who would be able to derive "heaps of laws" from each jot and tittle of the Torah. Moses was thus given to understand that the written Law, which he was to receive from God and transmit to the nation, would be adapted to ever new historical situations through creative interpretations of even the smallest of its letters and calligraphic ornaments.

The legend relates that Moses wished to see this man and was granted his request. Turning around, Moses found himself in an academy of study where Akiba and his disciples were expounding the Torah (over a thousand years later). Thereupon, Moses sat himself in the rear of the hall among the novices and tried to follow the proceedings, but he was thoroughly dumbfounded. At long last, a student asked Akiba the basis for his argument and was told, "It is a law given to Moses at Sinai." Thus the new ruling was assured through having its basis and authority in the ancient written Torah of God. Hearing this, Moses was comforted. But then a deeper perplexity forced him to ask God, "Master of the Universe, you have such a man (as Akiba, who can elaborate the Torah to such an extent) and you give the Torah by me?!" "Be silent," answered God, "for this is how I have determined it."

Formulated in the first centuries of Judaism, this legend is very much a Jewish "myth of origins," for in the manner of myth the account provides a charter of authority for the basic ways and worldview of the culture. In this case, it serves to anchor the numerous and apparently nonbiblical legal expositions of the rabbis—the authoritative teachers of Judaism—in the most formative and primary document of Judaism: the Bible. It recounts for a later Jewish audience, subject to the Torah and its binding interpretations, how God prepared the basis for the oral teachings of the sages when the written Torah was divinely inscribed and given to Moses at Mount Sinai. Indeed, the audience is drawn behind the biblical narrative and into a mythic realm where the vast historical and spiritual unfoldings of Judaism are formally anticipated and justified. In the words of another formulation of this ideology: "Everything which a disciple of the wise (a rabbinic sage) might ever innovate was already given to Moses at Sinai." From

A Torah scribe. The task of copying a Torah scroll is one of great piety and rigor. All details have been fixed by tradition. (Photo by Bill Aron.)

the revealed Torah of God at Sinai, say the rabbis, flows a continuous revelation of teachings through their authoritative expositions. [See Religions of Africa pp. 36–37, 64–67, Religions of Mesoamerica pp. 129–35, 154–55, 163–68, Native Religions of North America pp. 288–95, 327–29, 333–42, Christianity pp. 380–84, Hinduism pp. 739–41, 743–46, Buddhism p. 890, and Religions of Japan pp. 1094–96 for discussion of myth and mythology.]

Another dimension of this "myth of origins" pertains to the actions or rituals that accompany the words and give them dramatic expression. A correlation between "sacred words" (Gk., *mythoi*) and "sacred actions" (Gk., *dramata*) is a common feature of so-called primitive and ancient religions. But it is also a feature of the great world religions and recurs in Judaism in various forms. In the present case, the text depicts a relationship between sacred words (the Torah) and ritual (Torah study) that is historically actualized whenever the written Torah is renewed through study and interpretation. From this perspective, every student of the Law renews through interpretation the first giving of the Torah at Sinai and extends that revelation into new historical circumstances. This, of course, is the mysterious relationship between Torah and interpretation that God communicates to Moses in the legend; for Moses, the lawgiver, needs sages such as Akiba for the sake of the ongoing life of the Torah, just as each sage (as Akiba) regards Moses as the first teacher of Judaism, whose Torah is the basis of all authoritative teaching. Without the studious deliberation of an Akiba, Moses' ancient text would become a dead letter. But without the Torah of Moses, the expositions of the sages would lack religious authority. It must therefore come as no surprise that, in time, Moses was called *rabbeynu*, "our rabbi." And so it has remained.

The revelation of divine instructions (the Torah) at Sinai is thus a central historical moment for Judaism and its history: It is the time when God and the ancestors of the Jews entered into a religious relationship, or **covenant,** based on these very teachings. In a strictly historical sense, therefore, the revelation at Sinai was a "one and only" time for Jewish religious destiny. But as we have seen, this event has also been something more than a one-time occurrence for Jews and Judaism: It has been something of a mythic moment, recurring "always and again" whenever the Torah is studied and its teachings interpreted. Thus the divine voice heard at Sinai does not cease, according to the traditional Jewish self-understanding, but is authoritatively developed through the human words of the sages. It is they who faithfully renew the event of Sinai and who generate "heaps of laws" that extend the covenant into new areas of life. In fact, for Judaism, no area of life was or is in principle excluded from this process: Every action and behavior, no matter how seemingly mundane, could be transformed into an expression of religious piety. For this reason, Judaism has often been called a positive religion, a religion that prescribes and regulates all the actions of its adherents. Through devoted obedience to the prescriptions of the Torah and its rabbinic elaborations, Judaism has taught that one might lead a life of divinely guided sanctity and ascend along just this path to religious perfection and communion with God.

For Judaism, then, the Torah and its vast tradition of interpretation is an elaborate but sure guide to holy living and nearness to God. But, as we have already suggested, Judaism is also a highly varied religion. It is not only a stable complex of beliefs and behaviors developed over millennia; it is also a religion capable of sustaining ideals and attitudes of the most diverse—and seemingly contradictory—sort. For example, in contrast to the above-mentioned focus on interpretation and formal observance of the commandments, there is a strand in Judaism that allows for a more spontaneous, simple meeting between a person and God. This feature of simple, unmediated encounters with the divine is exemplified in a legend found in the *Book of the Pious* from thirteenth-century Germany—nearly a thousand years after our rabbinic "myth" of Akiba and Moses.[2]

This legend tells of a herdsman who did not know how to pray, though it was his custom every day to say: "Lord of the world! Surely you know that if you had cattle and gave them to me to tend, though I would take wages from all others, from you I would take nothing—because I love you!" And so time passed. But a learned man who was going on his way came upon the herdsman praying thus, and said to him, "Fool, do not pray in this way." And when the herdsman asked him how to pray, the learned man taught him the traditional order of the prayers and all their set words. Thus it was that the herdsman ceased praying in his customary way. In time, however, the herdsman forgot what he had been taught and stopped praying altogether. He was even afraid to pray in his old style, for the learned man had told him not to. And so it was. But then one night the learned man had a dream and in it a voice said, "If you do not tell him to pray as he did before you came to him, know that evil will befall you, for you have robbed me of one who belongs to the world to come." And this the learned man did. "Behold," concludes the legend, "here there is neither Torah [study] nor works [obedience to the Law], but only this, that there was one who had it in his heart to do good, and he was rewarded for it, as if this were a great thing. For [tradition teaches that] 'the Merciful One desires the heart.' Therefore let people think good thoughts, and let these thoughts be turned to the Holy One, Blessed be He."

It is evident that this legend undercuts the Torah "myth" presented earlier, for here neither learning nor legal piety constitutes a life of holiness with God, only simplicity and purity of heart. Likewise, in this text God is not far off and mediated through the cultural traditions of the religious community, but near to anyone whose soul seeks the divine Presence without guile or self-consciousness. The holy herdsman is thus the opposite of the sage. He is both unsophisticated and natural, equally unaware of the Torah and its vast tradition of learning and practice. For him, religious devotion is not structured by a community of believers who share communal symbols and language; nor can he even effectively receive this communal heritage or make good use of it. Though taught the normative religious practices of Judaism by the sage, the herdsman soon forgets his instructions and becomes nonobservant. Indeed, it is the sage who is reproved by God in this legend, as his wise counsel has deprived heaven of an act of pure service.

For a classical tradition that had repeatedly affirmed the ancient rabbinic dictum that "a simple person cannot be pious," since such a one does not know the Law, the divinely given guide to piety, the legend of the herdsman is a powerful critique of essential values. Indeed, what is portrayed here is a piety that can be neither learned nor transmitted; nor is it divinely taught. The core of authentic religion, the legend counsels, is the authentic heart of the worshiper—his or her selfless humility. And it is just this service that God wants.

Taking both legends in hand, we go a long way toward understanding the powerful tensions and balances that have structured Judaism over the ages. Such tensions and balances have provided mechanisms whereby Judaism could revise or critique itself for the sake of its ongoing integrity. In the first case, we noted the dynamic relationship Judaism posits between the ancient Torah of Sinai and the ongoing interpretation of the sages. In the latter instance, the apparent tension between a "piety of strict obedience" and a "piety of simple spontaneity" has also proved salutary and regenerative for Judaism. Where the one or the other pole has predominated in Jewish history, it was counterbalanced by its opposite. In this way the observance of the divine Law, which could not be abrogated, was dynamically infused with the spirit of spontaneity, and the power of spontaneous worship of God was always structured by the norms of the community. Indeed, a balance was always struck—in each community and by each person—between what was called "the yoke of the commandments" and "the yoke of the kingdom of heaven." Their indissoluble combination is one of the unique and characteristic features of the religion, for it posits that there is no simple love of God that is not concretized through some customary form of behavior and no strict observance of these behaviors that is not also to be regarded as an expression of the love of God. According to one classic statement, the combination of these two values explains why the liturgical affirmation of divine unity and lordship, the **Shema**—"Hear, O Israel, the Lord is our God, the Lord is One"—is immediately followed by the exhortation: "You shall love the Lord, your God, with all your heart, with all your soul, and with all your might; and let these words which I [God] command you this day be upon your heart. . . ." Not content with observing that this prayer derives from a sequence of biblical citations (Deut. 6:4ff.), the ancient rabbis explained the first as an acknowledgment of divine sovereignty and the second as an injunction to practice the Law (the commandments) of God. First one accepts "the kingdom of heaven" (God's majesty), they said, then one assumes "the yoke of the commandments" (the Torah and its interpretation).

On the basis of the two legends discussed above, Judaism may be defined as the religious expression of the Jewish people based upon a Torah believed given them by God and on the teachings of this Torah as elaborated by trained sages for the sake of sanctifying human behavior and guiding nearness to God. To be sure, precisely because Judaism is a historical religion, every element of this definition—God, the Jewish people, Torah, and its interpretation—has undergone significant development or change. To speak, therefore, of Judaism as some timeless essence would be as misleading as asserting that, because of its historical variations, Judaism is a disconnected miscellany of beliefs and behaviors. The fact is that a fairly stable pattern of behaviors and beliefs has marked the expressions of traditional Judaism from classical times (the first centuries of our era) to the present day. Accordingly, if the very *history* of Judaism precludes our speaking of an abstract "essence of Judaism," one can nevertheless speak of its "essential features." This is constituted by the several elements of the definition. To better appreciate this unity (of stable elements) within diversity (of historical expressions), let us now retrieve some of the issues introduced in the preceding pages and say a bit more about them.

The Jews

Judaism is rooted in the people who have constituted it, beginning with the ancient Israelites of biblical times and continuing through all those who have assumed its traditions. These people are the Jews, whose name derives from a Hebrew word referring to the citizens of ancient Judea, part of the biblical land of Israel in Greco-Roman times (second century B.C.E.–fifth century C.E.). According to the biblical record, the ancestors of the Jews originated in families and tribal units who wandered from ancient Mesopotamia to the land of Canaan (some time in the mid–second millennium B.C.E.). The Bible presents this movement and settlement as based upon a divine call and promise to an ancestor named Abraham. With this call, a religious bond, or covenant, was established between Abraham and his descendants and his God. From the first, this covenantal bond and its ritual expression (**circumcision** of males) gave the people a self-conscious religious destiny. They were henceforth not solely part of the natural seed of Adam, the mythic progenitor of humankind, but part of the divinely constituted seed of Abraham, the bearers of special promises about settlement in the land of Canaan. Few ritual obligations are described at this early point in the Bible. It is only with the expansion of this covenant to all the multitudinous descendants of Abraham who came out of Egyptian bondage (in the mid–thirteenth century B.C.E.) that a true religious peoplehood was constituted. This came about through the divine covenant with the nation of Israel at Sinai. With it and its obligations, Israel and all of its descendants assumed their special spiritual destiny as "a priestly kingdom and a holy nation" (Exod. 19:6). [See Religions of Africa p. 76, Christianity p. 496, and Islam pp. 677–78, 680, 682 for discussion of circumcision.]

The people thus believed themselves doubly chosen: once in the time of Abraham and again in the time of Moses. And yet all persons could join this nation on the condition that they keep the covenant and fulfill its obligations. Thus ancient Israel combined two patterns of affiliation known to religions of antiquity. On the one hand, the nation of Israel was a "natural" people constituted by a special religious life, so that all those born into the nation were Israelites and practitioners of the Mosaic covenant law. This is a type of religious ethnicity well represented by the ancient Greeks and Chinese. In it one is born into a tribal unit or confederation and goes on to practice its customs and ceremonies. But beginning in the Hellenistic world, around the time of the earliest formations of Judaism (from the third century B.C.E.), there also developed the phenomenon sometimes referred to as "religions of salvation." These religions were not at all based on such primary affiliations as birth or descent, but rather on secondary associations assumed through special initiation ceremonies or rites of conversion. The so-called mystery cults of the Greeks and Romans as well as the early and later Christian church represent this type of spiritual affiliation. To be sure, the society of ancient Israel in early biblical times had already developed procedures for the incorporation of non-Israelites into its covenant community with full ethnic and ritual rights (through marriage for women; through circumcision for males). But when Judaism in Hellenistic times also developed an ideology and practice of conversion, propagandizing its theology and truth claims to non-Jews, this was an altogether new development. It opened Judaism to more spiritual forms of affiliation. [See Christianity p. 496 for discussion of conversion.]

In sum, Judaism combined (and still combines) two modes of religious association. The first derives from ancient Israel and pertains to the ancient ethnic core of the Jewish people. The second mode of affiliation also derives from antiquity, but it took on new forms in the classical period of the religion. Through it Judaism extended its divine covenant to anyone who would believe that the Torah is a divinely revealed way of holiness and salvation and who would practice that "way." Once converted by established procedures, such persons are Jews in all respects and their descendants are fully Jews "by nature" as it were. In the sense that Judaism is both grounded in a closed religious-ethnic community and open to all who would accept its teachings, the religion of Judaism includes both particularistic and universalistic elements. Other aspects of this combination of opposites, such as the fact that Jews have believed themselves divinely chosen via Abraham from among all the descendants of Adam for a particular covenantal destiny that includes a universal mission of witness to their God's teachings and reality, will be mentioned further on.

God

As indicated, the self-understanding of the Jewish people was and is that of a distinct people, a people whose uniqueness is constituted by its spiritual link with God and expressed through the ritual and ethical requirements of the covenant (the Torah and its traditional elaborations). God is therefore central to Judaism, but not in any abstract or impersonal sense. Rather, God is always the One *who* establishes a covenant, *who* reveals the Torah, *who* requires obedience and sanctity, *who* guides the people's destiny, and so on. This is particularly true of Judaism's central monotheistic proclamation (the Shema) that God is One and Unique. Such a creed was always taken to mean that the God who made a covenant with Moses, delivered the people of Israel from slavery in Egypt, revealed the Torah, and made a covenant with the entire nation at Sinai is the one and only God in the universe. To be sure, abstract formulations of the sovereignty or perfection of this God can be found in Jewish philosophical literature, and daring speculation on the hidden life or nature of divinity also recurs in the long history of Jewish mysticism. But even in these two cases of rational arguments and theological insights about God, the centerpoint for the religion remained the historical moment of divine revelation—the event of personal contact between God and the people of Israel at Sinai—and its ongoing covenantal implications. As a result, the active religious life of the Jew is not one of theory and deduction, but one entirely filled with ritual and moral obligations constantly making the reality of God present in the most personal and concrete terms. [See Christianity pp. 538–42, Islam pp. 612–13, 639–40, and Native Religions of North America pp. 267–68 for discussion of creeds.]

This feature of personal divine immediacy marks all the ritual sanctifications of life in Judaism, quite apart from whatever abstract theological system may justify it at more theoretical levels. For example, this immediacy is found in the traditional expressions of thanksgiving for blessings received from God, *who provides* all forms of life and sustenance (as in the standard liturgical formulation: "Blessed are you, O Lord our God, king of the universe, *who brings forth food from the ground*" or "*who clothes the naked*," and so on). And it is found in diverse expressions of hope for blessings to be received from God, *who may provide* them in the present or future (as in the liturgical phrases: "*May you heal us,* O Lord, that we may be healed" or "*May you restore us* to you" or "*May you hear our prayer*").

Reflecting on these two aspects of the religion, we may state that in its more developed forms Judaism is a two-tiered system that balances or integrates abstract concepts of God with notions and experiences of God as a personal covenantal Presence. But, this granted, it is vital to remember that the daily *life* of the religion is predicated on the latter, for Judaism is not just a "monotheism" in any abstract sense, but a "covenantal monotheism" in the specific sense in which it expresses a belief in one God who has chosen Israel from among the nations and revealed to it the Torah—for its obedience, holiness, and redemption. It is just this "covenantal monotheism" that has structured and conditioned the religious imagery and experience of God in Judaism over the ages.

Torah and Interpretation

Jewish covenantal monotheism can furthermore be seen to have a rule-governed, legal character. Everything is strictly regulated by the teachings and commandments of the Torah: eating, personal relations, work, and much more. Indeed, what is not explicitly set forth in the Torah of God is derived from or related to it by the interpretations of the sages over the centuries. There are thus three major intersecting structures of authority in Judaism: God, the Torah, and the interpretation of Torah by qualified sages. In theory, each of these structures is independent, though in actuality they converge and interrelate dynamically.

Thus, though it is believed that God expresses his will in the Torah for all time, it is the sages who explicate and apply this will for all historical situations. This, of course, is the essential point of the Talmudic legend about Moses discussed earlier. In another striking expression of this ideology, an appeal to divine intervention in order to resolve legal discussions is forcefully denounced. The reason provided is that "it [the Torah] is not in heaven." That is to say, the Torah and its ongoing application is given to the people of Israel; divine miracles may not override the logic of human interpretation. A final legendary coda reinforces the point: When the whole episode came before God, he laughed, we are told, and said, "My sons have defeated Me!"[3] [See Islam p. 609 for discussion of Torah.]

Tradition

The cumulative result of the converging authority structures of God, Torah, and interpretation is *tradition*—itself an authority structure and religious reality of major significance in Judaism. On the one hand, tradition embodies the cumulative legal and theological teachings of the sages in writings that have themselves assumed an aura of sanctity. But tradition also includes the sum of customary beliefs and practices of Jews at all times, though with specific reference to those features that are culturally alive for Jewish communities at any given period. And as with the rabbinic literary collections, these customs are also dignified by a religious, sacred aura, for they are believed to be generated out of Jewish living rooted in Torah piety. Such customs include what ancient Jewish authors referred to as "the traditions of the ancestors," many of which were eventually justified by linking them to scriptural passages (through interpretation), and all the variety of folkways and regional embellishments of legal practices that have thickened the atmosphere of Jewish life, affecting its styles and gestures, its cuisine and clothing, its language and imagery. Thus if the divine law together with the authoritative teachings of the sages came collectively to be known as "Torah," a medieval maxim even went so far as to add that "the customs of Israel are [also!] Torah." Though few Jews over the centuries would have denied this essential cultural equation because they did indeed experience the totality of Jewish life as "Torah," many objected to so sharp a formulation. In any event, for a Jew born into the lived reality of Jewish practice, tradition is the crown of all crowns, the total life-breath of Judaism.

The massive scope of the Jewish tradition and its fluid extension into every aspect of life constitute for the traditionalist nothing short of the immediate covenantal Presence of God at all times. The ancient theological dictum "there is no place devoid of him (God)" might thus with valid reason be applied to tradition as well, both as regards its pervasive scope and, as suggested above, as regards its functional character as a token of divine reality in the life of the Jew. In the ongoing history of Judaism, in which the prescriptions of the sacred

Torah have been safeguarded and extended by many levels of tradition (interpretation and custom), this tradition has itself become sacred. The result is that it, too, has been extended by many new levels of interpretation and authoritative custom. For Jews over the centuries, this complex pattern of life woven around the written Torah has been the sure way to God because it was the traditional way. Some even went so far as to believe that the entirety of traditional belief and practice was an expression of the will of God—an absolute value in its own right—though other Jews felt that something like the critique of the "holy herdsman" was necessary to caution the faithful that the garment of tradition was a means to holiness—not an end in itself.

In the preceding pages, we have taken some initial steps toward an understanding of Judaism. Through an introduction to its essential matrix of elements, Judaism was presented as a covenantal monotheism structured by such core features as God, Israel (the people), Torah, and interpretation. As suggested, these features have functioned organically and dynamically throughout the history of this religion, stabilizing its vast life system and generating new and renewing expressions. Thus, while these essential features have their own distinct histories over the long life of Judaism, their meanings have been further shaped through various recombinations. This has resulted in new hierarchies or orderings of meaning among the features and new modes of interaction among them. The way that God is understood and related to Torah, for example, or how Torah is conceived and related to interpretation and the people of Israel are thus matters of great diversity in the history of Judaism.

Such modifications and resynthesis of essential teachings have served to regenerate the phenomenon of Judaism for over twenty-five hundred years. Indeed, amid a highly inflexible sense of destiny and direction, this remarkable capacity for variation and reemphasis has helped the religion to adapt to new historical features and to transform them into authentic expressions of Jewish life and belief. It is to the historical unfolding of such expressions that we now turn. [See Religions of Africa pp. 23–24, Religions of Mesoamerica pp. 117–19, Native Religions of North America pp. 261–64, Christianity pp. 492–94, Islam pp. 607–8, Hinduism pp. 719–21, Buddhism pp. 853–55, Religions of China pp. 990–1015, and Religions of Japan pp. 1090–92 for discussion of the diversity and variety of religious traditions.]

16
Judaism as an Ideological System

WHEN WE THINK ABOUT A RELIGION, many things come to mind: first, a vast array of ideas, values, and beliefs; and second, alongside these, a host of verbal and nonverbal features connected with authoritative persons, symbols, and rituals. Altogether, these many elements combine to express a worldview. Sometimes, in response to a specific question or set of circumstances, only one or another aspect of the worldview is involved or given direct expression. More commonly, however, the various beliefs and symbols of a worldview mix with related rituals and values to constitute a thick cultural web. Indeed, when a religion truly does its cultural work, its worldview is always being enacted at personal and interpersonal levels. This is as much the case for laypeople, who are often incapable of articulating values and beliefs, as it is for the official teachers of a given religion.

In line with these considerations, we shall in this chapter treat Judaism as an ideological system, that is, both as a system of ideas about God, the world, and persons, and as a system of values directing action and feeling within society. These ideas and values have not remained fixed throughout Jewish religious history, so it will be important to pay attention to their *historical* growth and development. Moreover, the ideas and values of historical Judaism have not always coalesced in just one cultural configuration, so it will also be important to pay attention to the *varieties of Judaism* that have come to historical expression. Sometimes one or another of the features of the matrix dominates; and all the while different understandings of the role and meaning of Torah, interpretation, Israel, and tradition come to expression. Finally, having surveyed Judaism from an ideological and historical perspective, we shall turn our attention to the ritual expression of Jewish belief and values in chapter 17.

Rabbinic Patterns of This-Worldly Holiness and Salvation

The Biblical Heritage

The history of Judaism begins with the Bible and its religious-literary heritage, for the twenty-four books of the Hebrew Bible not only constitute the literary anthology of the religion and culture of ancient Israel, but for Jews and

Judaism they comprise *the foundation document* of the religion—*the* text Jews believe to contain the revealed teachings of God given to the house of Israel in antiquity and faithfully studied ever since. The Bible is not, therefore, an "Old Testament" whose historical recollections and religious teachings have subsequently lost their value or authority (wholly or in part). It rather remains *the* book of authoritative teachings and memories for Judaism, *the* work whose proper interpretation constitutes the vitality and authority of ongoing Jewish life. [See Religions of Africa p. 32, Religions of Mesoamerica p. 179, Native Religions of North America p. 285, Christianity pp. 497, 499, Islam pp. 635–37, 648–53, 665–72, Hinduism pp. 728–29, 738–43, 750–53, Buddhism p. 861, Religions of China pp. 995–96, 999–1000, 1031, and Religions of Japan pp. 1100, 1101 for discussion of Bible, scriptures, and religious texts.]

When we refer to the Bible as the foundation document of Judaism, therefore, at least two important issues must be considered. The first issue is a historical one and is rooted in the fact that Judaism has always perceived its origins to be found in the Bible. This perception has several interrelated aspects. First, Jews have viewed the persons in biblical antiquity as their own forebears and the events of that age as their own prehistory. Second, Jews have always considered the covenant between God and the ancient Israelites to be the basis of their own religious obligations. And finally, it has been believed since antiquity that no break whatever separates the religion of the ancient Hebrews and the religion of Judaism, and that the earliest "institutions" of classical Judaism were actually established by Ezra, a priest and scribe whose work is recorded in late biblical books.

The second issue bearing on the Bible as a foundation document is an ideological one and is rooted in the fact that this text has always been regarded as the prime source of Judaism. This consideration also has several interrelated aspects. First, Jews have regarded the beliefs and commandments recorded in the Bible as continuous with and continued by Judaism, albeit in highly reinterpreted ways. Second, Jews have always considered the prescriptions and institutions of this text as the model for their own behaviors, again often in radically transformed ways. And finally, it has been a tenet of rabbinic Judaism since antiquity that all the features of Judaism, no matter how innovative, have their ultimate source in the Bible. Indeed, it has been one of the principal tasks of traditional Jewish interpretation to establish just this point and to give it authority.

Now, since Judaism is so profoundly rooted in the Bible, it behooves us to ask what Judaism inherited from ancient Israel by way of the Bible. In purely literary terms, it inherited a vast anthology of texts spanning nearly a millennium or more, from the nomadic traditions of the patriarchs (c. 1500–1350 B.C.E.) to the historical traditions of the Jewish resistance to Hellenism recorded in the Book of Daniel (mid–second century B.C.E.). These texts include epic traditions of the Exodus from Egyptian bondage and the conquest and settlement of ancient Canaan, records of the royal courts and sacred shrines, moral teachings and admonitions of the prophets, liturgies and prayers of the kings and commoners, practical advice and speculative wisdom, religious rituals and civil rules, and much more. While certain perspectives dominate, there is no one religious or ideological viewpoint in this large literature. In fact, many view-points (prophetic, priestly, monarchic) and many concerns (theological, histori-cal, ethical) are to be found. One thinks, for example, of the diverse religious expressions of the northern (Ephraimite) and southern (Judahite) tribes; of the different prescriptions for various observances of the Priestly and Deutero-nomic writers (the books of Leviticus and Deuteronomy, respectively); and of the different views of God and the people held by early and late prophets, or even by contemporaries like Jeremiah and Ezekiel. There were thus many "Israels" within the house of ancient Israel in its homeland, just as many Juda-isms also constituted the house of Israel in all the lands of its dispersion.

Turning to the content of the Hebrew Bible, one might well wonder what kind of impact a document spanning one thousand years and many perspec-tives could have on Judaism. But the fact is that several ideological constants can be isolated from the material. These are somewhat evident in the thematic emphases that recur throughout the diverse periods and genres of the Bible. And they had a decisive impact upon the very formation of Judaism, guiding its ongoing appreciation of biblical personalities and events and helping to produce its religious ideology and hierarchy of values as well.

The Bible begins at the beginning, with an account of the creation of a habitable world by an almighty and sovereign God. Constrained by neither other gods nor nature, this God forms a good and bounteous world and gives over its stewardship to human care. Thus from the outset, being the product of a good and caring God, the world is presented as compatible with human creativity and salvation. One need not reject the natural world to experience divine grace, for, indeed, such grace is found in the creation itself—in the physical environment (called "good") and in persons (called "very good"). It is only through human dis-obedience to the directives of this God that pain, death, and want enter the world. Thus humans, created in the divine image, are free to obey or disobey this Lord—but they and their descendants will bear the consequences of their actions. God is therefore portrayed as a moral judge who is attentive to human action and who responds to it.

These several elements assume new forms as the biblical focus shifts from humans in general to a group chosen from among all peoples and tongues—the Hebrews, the ancestors of the Jews. The process begins with the responsiveness of the great ancestors of this people (Abraham, Isaac, and Jacob) to the demands of this God and their faithfulness to his promises of national blessing in a special homeland—the land of Canaan, later called the land of Israel. This divine prom-ise of national blessing within history is the ancestral covenant, renewed and expanded centuries later for the entire nation. At Sinai, after their divine redemption from Egyptian bondage, the people willingly responded to the obligations and promises revealed by God: They acknowledged his ongoing care and averred faithfulness to him alone. [See Religions of Africa pp. 24, 35, 60, Religions of Mesoamerica pp. 198–201, Native Religions of North America pp. 347–48, Christianity pp. 503, 505, Islam pp. 632–33, Hinduism p. 748, Bud-dhism pp. 875–77, 952–53, Religions of China pp. 991–93, and Religions of Japan pp. 1095–96, 1105–6 for the relationship of religion to political leaders.]

The stipulations of the covenant, preserved in the Torah, thus constitute the legal-religious bond between the people and their God. Through obedience to the commandments, the nation would find peace and rest in its homeland under a just king. But disobedience to the commandments, the fruit of sin, would result in natural peril and blight, national exile and the whirlwind of flight. Thus, again, it was believed that God was personally attentive to all the details of Israel's life and would judge them accordingly. As the divine covenant was deemed comprehensive, providing a collection of instructions embracing all the details of life (moral, civil, and religious), so was it also believed to be comprehensible, providing a framework of meaning that allowed the people to know and perform God's will. From the perspective of the covenant, moreover, no matter was believed too insignificant for God's concern. Accordingly, history was no meaningless barrage of events, and nature was no blind force. Rather, both were subject to the rule and judgment of God. From the perspective of biblical religious ideology, in fact, the rise and fall of nations and the weal and woe of nature were considered to be God's responses to Israel's covenantal behavior. Not even the arguments of Job would ultimately unsettle this view of the world and human destiny.

In the Bible, then, the context of human action is this world, and it is just here that salvation might be experienced—peace and bounty for the nation, and food and family for the individual. The commandments therefore serve both to regulate social and religious behavior and to regulate history and nature, all under God's ultimate rule. As a result, no political or natural state was final. The human world was always renewable through repentant and obedient behavior; but it was also subject to doom and despair through selfishness and sin. Knowing what was to be done and the consequences gives ancient Israelite religion its public, or exoteric, aspect. There were no divine secrets of any human significance that were withheld from the human world, just as there was no secret knowledge to be gained through mysterious means for the sake of salvation. What was needed for piety and salvation was given by God to all: "the hidden things are God's, but the revealed things are ours and our children's forever," reports Moses in the Torah (Deut. 29:28). The instructions are "not in heaven," he adds, but "in your mouth and heart" on earth (Deut. 30:14).

The people of ancient Israel are therefore bidden to serve God with faithfulness and love—in the heart and the home, in the community and the Temple, in the homeland and in exile. This service is, moreover, both a task of holiness for the individual in community and a work of witness for the world at large, for if, in the times of sin and disobedience, the nation of Israel would be punished by God through nature and the nations of the world, in the times of repentance and obedience Israel would, correspondingly, be the center of grace and hope toward which all nations would turn. The hope of history was thus the eventual restoration and unification of all the nations of the earth through their acceptance of the teachings of a just and righteous God. This would be the time of universal reconciliation when, in the words of the prophets, the harvest would overlap the time of planting, when swords would be turned into plowshares, and when all nations would go up to the Temple of the Lord for instruction and for

celebration. However painful the longing, this biblical hope was faithfully transmitted from one generation to the next and awaited in this world.

Taken altogether, the Hebrew Bible is thus a national book of memories and
hopes, of explanations and instructions, of commandments and covenants, of
faithfulness and rebellion, and of benefits and dooms. As events of history, the
great acts of divine deliverance recorded therein (like the Exodus) were one-
time events. But as events of memory these decisive moments also served as
images of hope in times of crisis (like the Babylonian exile). And so the first Exodus was taken over by the prophets as the token of future restorations from servitude, just as the first land settlement typified future returns of members of
the nation to their ancestral homeland. In similar ways, the old instructions to
Moses were not only revelations of the past, but also rules constantly revised
for new times and situations. Collectively, these biblical traditions served the
people from generation to generation, providing them with self-definition and
historical consciousness as well as with rules governing divine-human and
interpersonal relations. As these multiple traditions accumulated, they spun a
web around the nation and its imagination. No action or hope, no rule or celebration was conceivable apart from them. The inevitable result, taken in subsequent centuries, was the authoritative formulation of these traditions in one
fixed corpus: the Bible. Thereafter, in the words of a medieval adage, "Israel and
the Torah [were] one."

The Emergence of Classical Judaism
(From the End of the Babylonian Exile, 539/8 B.C.E.,
to the Fall of the Second Temple, 70 C.E.)

The traditions and institutions of ancient Israel took on new shapes after
the events of 587/6 B.C.E., when Jerusalem and Judea were destroyed by Nebu-
chadnezzar, king of Babylon. At that time, the majority of the Israelites were
exiled—with the result that three major geographical centers came to dominate
Jewish life and creativity: the province of Judea, in the land of Israel; the region
around Alexandria, in the Egyptian delta; and the areas around Babylon, in what
is now Iraq. It was, in part, the mixture of these three communities in the land
of Israel *after* the return from exile—each with its Torah traditions and practices
—that contributed to the controversies of the restoration period. This return to
the homeland began in 538 B.C.E. after a decree by Cyrus, the great king of
Persia who had just conquered Babylon. Nevertheless, many former Judeans
remained in their new homes with their new traditions. In fact, it was the ongoing vitality of these three cultural regions that affected the shapes of Jewish
religious expression over the next thousand years.

During the first centuries of national restoration, especially from the time
of Alexander the Great (born 333 B.C.E.) to the early second century C.E., the
land of Israel and Alexandria were the dominant religious and cultural centers.
Subsequently, the community in Israel remained a recognized center; but,
suffering from Roman hegemony, the Jewish institutions of learning and administration in this region were gradually eclipsed by those that had developed

in Babylonia. This shift eastward is of considerable historical significance not only because of the emergence of a new geographic sphere of importance (for it was, in many ways, the revival of the old exilic community), but because it also marks a series of decisive shifts in Jewish religious expression, as we shall see.

When the Jews returned to Jerusalem from the Babylonian exile (after 538 B.C.E.), they prepared to rebuild the ancient Temple destroyed a half-century earlier. Soon their ritual practices were restored, and Ezra, the leader of the period, set about to develop a full religious life based on the ancestral Torah of Moses. During this time, the Jews benefited from the benign foreign policy of the Persians. As regional overlords, the Persians actually sought to encourage the revival of native traditions among their vassal populations. Nevertheless, it was inevitable that Persian influences penetrated Jewish life from this early period. A number of religious ideas from ancient Zoroastrianism gradually made an impact and challenged existing beliefs. The Zoroastrian dualistic theology of two supreme gods—one good, the other evil—was naturally rejected by Jews; but more modified forms of this and other beliefs were gradually absorbed into the stream of developing Judaism. For example, many scholars view the new emphasis on eschatology (theories of the final days) and angelology (role of angels) in Judaism at this time as due to such Persian influence. The literature of the sectarian communities that lived at or near Qumran from the second century B.C.E. to the first century C.E. (commonly known as the Dead Sea Scrolls) clearly shows such Eastern influence. In these texts very strong emphasis is given to a separation and rivalry between the cosmic principles of good/light and evil/darkness (though under the rule of one supreme God); to a final cosmic-historical battle in which good/light and purity would be victorious; and to angelology, astrology, notions of personal fate, and so on. Nevertheless, these various ideas and beliefs were skillfully integrated into a viable religious pattern that actually claimed to be the most authentic Jewish expression of the time, one that would be vindicated by God in the end of days.

Unfortunately, very little is really known about this formative period in the history of Judaism—overall. But when Jewish literary sources do fully emerge in the late second century B.C.E., they clearly indicate the vitality of the times. For one thing, the Jews in Egypt, Israel, and Syria were under diverse Greek administrations (the Ptolomies in the south, the Seleucids in the north). This had a great impact on early economic patterns and also on the legal-social forms that entered classical Judaism. In addition, Jews and Judaism fell under the powerful cultural influence of Hellenism. This latter had an inestimable impact, shaping notions of wisdom and Torah study and affecting the language and ideology of Judaism for ages to come. For many Jews in the parochial highlands of Judea, the broad sweep of Hellenism presented unexpected cultural options and ideas. New challenges were in the air, eliciting diverse responses to the competing realities of Greek *paideia* (education and culture) and Torah piety. Three broad types of response can be isolated. Intriguingly, they also foreshadow the dominant patterns of Jewish cultural response to foreign cultures and religions over the centuries. They are *assimilating* into Judaism the foreign ideas and elements, *rejecting* them outright, or *renewing* the religion from within in response to them.

The cosmopolitan and metaphysical scope of Greek speculative thinking and the sophisticated Greek views of intellectual and ethical development made many Jews feel that their native Torah instructions were comparably naive, parochial, and unedifying. As a result, many sought actively to assimilate to the Greek culture, so that they might more fully participate in its alluring intellectual life. Others, just as impressed by the Greek world, nevertheless defended native Jewish traditions and promoted a cultural symbiosis of one sort or another.

Among those who sought a positive response to Hellenism through intellectual creativity, Philo of Alexandria (20 B.C.E.–50 C.E.) must be considered the most significant. As a Jew he was fully devoted to the ancient Torah, an observer of its commandments, and a student of its rabbinical reformulations; while as a Hellene, he was just as fully committed to contemporary Greek thought and ideals. Refusing to give up the first for the second, he regarded the instructions of the Torah as of preeminent value and truth. On the other hand, he just as adamantly refused to reject the path of philosophy as of merely subordinate significance or of no worth. His solution was to adjust the received philosophical tradition (Plato, Aristotle, and the Stoics) to the received Torah tradition (the teachings of Moses and the rabbis) through a sophisticated allegorical procedure. By this means, the divine truths of the Torah were presented not solely as equivalent with philosophical wisdom, but as containing them. Thus no Jew had to reject Torah in order to accept philosophy, for all the truths of philosophy were in the Torah in a most superior manner—if one only knew how to disclose them. Through Philo's guidance, the patriarchal narratives and legislative prescriptions were allegorically revealed to be teachings instructing the philosophical adept in the acquisition and development of spiritual, moral, and intellectual virtues. For example, biblical laws that instructed someone who committed accidental manslaughter to flee to a city of refuge were now shown to be also (in their "deep sense," or Gk. *hyponoia*) concerned with the flight of the human soul from material encumbrances to God. Similarly, Abraham and Sarah represented not only historical personalities but (again, more deeply) intellectual-moral virtues. In all this, Philo emerges as the first religious philosopher of the West, the first major thinker to integrate philosophical wisdom with divine revelation. In the alien and alluring environment of Alexandria (and elsewhere), Jews could be proud of the philosophical profundity of their ancient heritage (the Torah) and remain observant in practice.

The sophisticated intellectual syncretism of Philo is balanced by the comparably crass religious-intellectual syncretism promoted by some members of the priestly class and aristocracy in Jerusalem. These Jews, through bribery and intrigue, sought to introduce changes in the civil and religious life of Judaism and conspired with the Seleucid overlords to issue decrees, the intent of which was to compromise traditional life and observance. In the most significant instance, the Seleucid ruler Antiochus Epiphanes IV was induced to desecrate the high altar in the Temple in Jerusalem and require Jews to defile themselves through prohibited acts. What these priests and their followers wanted was nothing short of a Hellenization of Judaism. This would have turned the ancestral religion into just one more quasi-philosophical cult in the Hellenistic world. To be sure, their motivations were not entirely narrow-minded or only self-serving. But a majority of Jews soon perceived in these developments a serious challenge to the fundamentals of their national and religious integrity—and they responded accordingly.

Focus on the integrity of the ancestral religion and a violent rejection of foreign influence was thus a second typical response to Hellenism. Of enduring fame in Jewish historical and folk memory are the attacks launched against the Seleucids by a priestly family. Led by one Mattathias and his son, Judah Maccabee, and soon supported by the populace at large, this group won a decisive victory. Reclaiming their heritage from the assimilationists, they were able to repurify and rededicate the sacred Temple in Jerusalem on the 25th of Kislev (November–December), 165 B.C.E.—the day memorialized in the Jewish calendar as Hanukkah and celebrated as the (eight-day) Feast of Dedication. In their deeds and motivations, the Maccabees and their followers reflect the spirit of religious purism and fanatical devotion to native religious tradition that burned deeply in Judaism from the days of the ancient prophets.

The third major type of Jewish expression in this period was one that attempted to effect a dynamic renewal of the religion from within *in response* to outside influences. Rather than accommodating native traditions to new forms or merely rejecting them outright, the Pharisaic way (so-called after the Pharisees, an important rabbinic and lay religious group at this time) was to accommodate the nonnative features to the traditions of Torah, to naturalize them, as it were.

Of distinctive significance in early Pharisaism is the emergence of a Torah-centered piety rooted in tradition and interpretation and characterized by a democratic openness to the people as a whole. In fact, the earliest legends and historical fragments about Pharisaic teachers show the emergence of a new type of religious leader: a "disciple of the wise," who was neither priest nor holy man but, characteristically, a self-sustaining layperson who achieved prominence through mastery of the written Torah and the ancient oral traditions. Accordingly, study of the Torah and simplicity of manner remained high ideals of these "disciples," who constituted a fellowship of learning open to all who would study its traditions and practice them. Initially, the ancient oral traditions were not solely authorized by being linked to scriptural passages but constituted authoritative ancestral lore in and of themselves. By degrees, however, this linkage to Torah was achieved, so that by the end of the first century C.E. Pharisaism was distinguished by its belief that its oral tradition of interpretation was the true elucidation of written Scripture and that it had its origin (in principle, at least) within it.

Torah thus emerged as the absolute center of Pharisaism. All was believed to be contained in it—both the written Torah of Moses and the oral traditions of the "wise"—and the unfolding of the new applications of Torah was considered to be the ongoing historical unfolding of God's infinite word. Accordingly, in Pharisaic Judaism (and this is the pattern of Judaism that has survived to this day) study is a mode of piety. This ideal is noticeable from the earliest records of its founding teachers, such as **Hillel,** and has served as the means of cultural-religious renewal ever since. This is not to say that the Greco-Roman environment made no impact on early Pharisaism—it did. But these influences, such as they were, were thoroughly transformed and drawn into the very life-blood of Judaism. Thus anyone unaware of Stoic ideals of wisdom and sage-like behavior would hardly recognize the impact of these Greek traits upon the popular Pharisaic treatise *The Sayings of the Fathers,* just as anyone unaware of Greco-Roman rhetoric and terminology would not perceive their impact upon the methods and terms of classical rabbinic Bible interpretation, so thoroughly naturalized are they. By the same token, Greco-Roman legal patterns and terms were also incorporated into the earliest legal activity of the Pharisaic sages. A celebrated example comes from Hillel. Faced with the refusal of some people to lend money close to the time of the Sabbatical Year (every seventh year, during which creditors were required to release debtors from their loans [Deut. 15:1–2]), this sage ingeniously worked out a solution so that the Temple would function as a kind of intermediary between borrowers and lenders. In this way the biblical rule was retained and economic stability restored. Hillel's decree (based on Scripture but going beyond it) was called a *prozbul* in rabbinic law. The term itself is derived from the Greek expression *pros boule,* "before the assembly," and the very method Hillel used to establish his point was also Greek in origin.[4]

Thus Pharisaism did not attempt to align its teachings either to an alien wisdom or to an alien cultural system but rather sought to integrate the latter into Judaism. In all their work, the Pharisees evince an unswerving conviction in their cultural autonomy and its values, and throughout they project a profound confidence in the truth of the laws and teachings of Scripture. In this, as in other respects, they emerge as the true shapers of historical Judaism.

Rabbinic Judaism in Formation (From the Fall of the Temple, 70 C.E.) to the Redaction of the Two Talmuds, (Fifth–Sixth Centuries C.E.)

Reflecting on his Jewish heritage and its importance, an early Jewish sage named Simon the Righteous said: "The world depends upon three things: upon Torah, upon Worship (*avodah*), and upon Acts of Loving-kindness."[5] By this he was certainly referring, first, to the centrality in Judaism of Torah and the faithful performance of its commandments; second, to the maintenance of the Temple service (*avodah*) and the proper performance of its rituals; and, third, to a concern for human welfare and the extralegal concern for righteous behavior. Surely all three things derive from biblical antiquity: the traditions of the Torah, the celebrations of the Temple, and deeds of social kindness. And surely, too, each of these three things was basic in the beneficial maintenance of the divine-human relationship, for the fulfillment of the covenant depended upon obedience to the instructions of the Torah, on the performance of purifications by the priests, and on the expressions of grace and goodwill by all. But when Simon epitomizes these things in just this way he is also giving special power to each for maintaining the flow of divine blessing (natural and historical) to earth. Jews, so to speak, maintain the civilized and beneficent order of life through their actions, for without the teachings of Torah, without the divine-human reconciliations and influences of the Temple, and without gratuitous humanity there would be no "world" whatever—no moral-social order. The institutions of Judaism thus functioned, to speak the language of the sociology of religion, as a system of cultural-cosmic maintenance.

REPLACING THE TEMPLE The destruction of the Temple in Jerusalem in 70 C.E. and the subsequent desacralization of the Temple Mount by the Romans were thus a major watershed in the history of Judaism. Like all other religions of antiquity, Judaism also gave enormous centrality to its sacral institutions: to the Temple and its priesthood; to the ancient sacrifices of atonement, purification, and thanksgiving; and to the symbolic role of the Temple as the abode of God to which penitents and pilgrims came during seasonal celebrations and times of need. In a word, the Temple established a concrete domain of access to the holy and to divinity; and the priesthood, which controlled the rituals of the Temple, also established or administered the rules of holiness as they pertained to many other spheres of life (like rules of contagion and purification, or rules of required or votary donations). To envisage the loss of the Temple, therefore, would be to envisage religious life without its sacral forms of divine-human intercession, without the possibility of priestly purification for sins and disease, and without the ancient process for divine-human reconciliation.

But ancient Judaism had survived the Babylonian exile without its priestly institutions, and the loss of the Temple in 70 C.E. continued the processes begun centuries before and introduced new transformations. Thus earlier, without their rites and sacrifices, the Babylonian exiles of 587/6 B.C.E. developed new modes of piety (like communal prayer) and generated new treatments of the ancient Torah traditions (particularly their collation, study, and interpretation). During the successive centuries, traces of the increased development of such institutions as synagogues for prayer and houses of study for the learning and reinterpretation of the Torah can be observed—alongside, of course, the renewed and still dominant priestly institutions. Accordingly, when the Temple was destroyed, a multifaceted mechanism was already in place for the survival of a Judaism without sacrifices and the hierarchical authority of the priesthood. [See Religions of Africa pp. 67, 88–89, Religions of Mesoamerica pp. 166–67, 177, 186, 237–38, Christianity pp. 543–44, 550, Islam p. 646, and Hinduism pp. 744–45, 747–48 for description and discussion of sacrifice.]

And so two "Houses," the House of Prayer (*beit tefillah*) and the House of Study (*beit midrash*) replaced the Temple—the House (*bayit*) par excellence. Each contributed a new understanding of *avodah,* or divine service.

THE HOUSE OF PRAYER In the House of Prayer the language of supplication and praise came into its own as a distinct form. Prayer was in fact called a "service (*avodah*) of the heart," whose very order was modeled on the times of the old Temple sacrifices. We shall consider something of the forms and content of Jewish prayer in the next chapter. Here it is simply necessary to observe, first, that the rabbinic prayer service was performed thrice daily, morning, afternoon, and evening, in order to correspond to the perpetual offerings in Temple times (b. Berakhot 26b). In addition, this prayer service was also saturated with recollections of the ancient glory of the Temple and hopes for its speedy restoration, with Priestly recitations like the benediction derived from Numbers 6:24–26, and with continued respect for clerical pedigree when honoring individuals to bless the Torah when it is recited in the communal service. Gradually, recommended and fixed features of the prayer service emerged, and these were offered to God with all the hopes that such "offerings of the lips" would "find favor" with God, like the sacrifices of old. "May my prayer be established as fragrant incense before You," says the Psalmist (Ps. 141:2). Or in the words of the ancient rabbis, who only had words to offer: "Be favorable, O Lord our God, towards Your people Israel and their prayer. Restore the Service (*avodah*) to the Shrine of Your House (*bayit*), and lovingly accept the prayer of Israel. May the service (*avodah*) of Your people be always favorable before You."[6]

THE HOUSE OF STUDY This God of Israel, believed to be transcendent above the heavens, was also believed to be present to the needs of the people. Indeed, as a majestic and distant Lord, he was called Heaven and King and Power; as a near and caring Father he was also called Place and Presence and Blessed Holy One. He was referred to as a "seeing eye" and "hearing ear"—an attentive and responsive *personal* God. He was addressed as a God of justice and mercy who, in one striking image, wore phylacteries (prayer boxes, called **tefillin,** with Torah passages inside) just like his earthly servants. In another famous image, this God was portrayed as studying Torah and reviewing the daily interpretations given to it by his people. Thus dignified, the human study of the Torah was also regarded as a major form of religious *avodah*. In fact, the study of the rules of sacrifices found in the Torah was frequently considered to be the post-Temple equivalent of the sacrifices themselves; through the study of the rules for sacrifices it was "as if" they had actually been offered. With the emergence of the House of Study to independent status, Torah replaced Temple; study substituted for sacrifices.

With the removal of sacrifices and priests from the stage of Jewish history, the "disciples of the wise" and their texts moved in to fill the breach. It is therefore hardly fortuitous that, shortly after 70 C.E., the sacred Torah literature was effectively fixed and closed (i.e., canonized). A new stage was thus set for the rabbinic transformation of Scripture. One of the great sages of this period was Rabbi Yochanan ben Zakkai. A figure of history whose deeds were quickly shrouded in legend, Rabbi Yochanan used his political influence with the Roman leadership to have an accredited Pharisaic academy established in Yavneh (also known as Jamnia), a town on the coast of the Mediterranean Sea. Here, in the "vineyard of Yavneh," disciples gathered to revive Judaism from its spiritual and national catastrophe. Much in the manner that contemporary

Greeks gathered around their philosophical mentors, Jewish students gathered around their masters and attended to their every deed and word, for all life was the potential sphere of Torah. Thus how the rabbinic master inferred or deduced a legal ruling in this or that circumstance (real or theoretical) or how he comported himself on this or that occasion was of great practical religious importance. A celebrated ideal for a master of this class was "to raise up many disciples," as a contemporary exhortation put it; and for the student the corresponding ideal was "to serve the master gratuitously." As the potential sphere of Torah had "no measure," said the sages, so its spiritual rewards were correspondingly without measure. Torah thus became the consuming ideal of these sages and their students. And with this ideal they helped set Judaism on its new historical course: The academy was the new Temple; the sages were the new priesthood; and the great ritual was the study of Torah.

The vast project of the rabbis, of commenting on the Torah and adapting its teachings to all areas of life, was predicated upon their belief that God's Torah is a "foundation of the world" and that it alone provides a way of truth and holiness on earth. To study the Torah is thus inseparable from its practice, for one can only do God's will if one knows it. Indeed, no other matters than these—knowing the divine will ("study," *talmud torah*) and its performance ("action," *ma'aseh*)—were of greater importance to Judaism. It therefore makes sense to pause here and briefly spell out this project and its major contents.

After 70 C.E., the Torah teachings and rulings of the rabbinical schools (called "houses") of Hillel and Shammai were gathered together, along with other testimonies and interpretations still in oral form. As noted, new academies were set up, first in Yavneh and later in such places in Israel as Usha and Tiberias. In these settings, new rulings were derived from the old Torah, other rules were framed to fill in gaps left by biblical legislation, and a host of theological and homiletical comments were generated from biblical texts to clarify or reinforce Jewish values and perspectives. The gradual result of this "oral Torah"—legal and nonlegal—was the production of a postbiblical rabbinic literature, which was itself then later subject to reinterpretation and elaboration.

The process of textual interpretation is called **midrash,** and the interpretations of Torah for the sake of generating new rules (**halakha**) or justifying (by Scripture) customary ones is known as *midrash halakha.* Such interpretation is part of the native Jewish tradition; its earliest forms are in the Bible itself. It has continued to be the characteristic form of Jewish legal expression over the centuries. This point must be emphasized, for while *midrash halakha* has strong traces in the earliest strata of Jewish literature, the dominant legal work of this time, called the **Mishnah,** is without this explicit exegetical dimension. For this reason, a good deal of the *midrash halakha* that followed it was principally geared to provide (or make explicit) the scriptural basis for the abstractly formulated religious rules recorded in the Mishnah.

THE MISHNAH AND SUPPLEMENTS The Mishnah is the classical collection of laws and normative rules of behavior of ancient Judaism. In its content, this document reflects the growth and consolidation of halakhic traditions from the preceding centuries and builds upon the earlier (but no longer extant) collections of Rabbi Meier and Rabbi Akiba. The final form of the work is the great religious-intellectual achievement of Rabbi Judah the Prince (the Patriarch of the land of Israel, a political-legal title confirmed by the Romans) sometime in the late second or early third century C.E. It is therefore commonly referred to as "Rabbi's Mishnah."

As the written digest of the hitherto exclusively oral traditions of the Tannaim (the Pharisaic sages c. 200 B.C.E.–200 C.E.), the Mishnah reflects their legal-religious interests and the majority and minority opinions of their law schools. The abstract formulations and topical structure of the Mishnah resembles contemporary Roman codes, and in its content projects the code of behavior Rabbi Judah and the sages sought to impose on the people at large. In the course of time, the Mishnah did achieve this grand goal and became and still is *the* foundation document of rabbinic legalism. Subsequent to the Bible, the Mishnah, written by the sages, is thus *the* document of Pharisaism emergent and triumphant: the law code of a pattern of Judaism developed by rabbis for themselves and their followers. It soon attained the status of a sacred text.

In terms of its format, the Mishnah is divided into six major orders or divisions. These are called Seeds, Feasts, Women, Damages, Holy Matters, and Purities. In turn, each of these orders is subdivided into tractates (totaling sixty-three), and these are then subdivided into smaller teachings called *mishnahs*. The content of the six orders is thus quite complex—more, in fact, than appears at first sight. For example, the order called Seeds holds rulings on various agricultural issues (like tithing or crop mixtures) but also deals with rules for prayer and gleanings to be left for the poor. The order called Feasts covers rulings dealing with the major holy days (such as the Sabbath and **Passover**), but also includes discussions of monetary donations and aspects of the writing of sacred scrolls. The order called Women deals primarily with family laws (e.g., marriage and divorce), but it also includes rules about vows of various sorts. The fourth order, called Damages, covers civil and criminal laws and punishments in all their variety but also deals with matters concerning oaths and idolatry as well as a collection of moral maxims (*The Sayings of the Fathers*). The next order, called Holy Matters, includes sundry ritual rules (such as sacrificial offerings, types of sacrilege, and Temple measurements). And the sixth and final order, called Purities, considers impurities attached to such physical states as death, leprosy, or menstruation as well as with their methods of religious purification (through sacrifices or immersion in water).

The above listing does not encompass the entirety of Tannaitic legal material. To it must be added a large "Supplement" to the Mishnah with many significant variations (called *Tosephta*), a great many Tannaitic teachings (called *beraitot*) preserved in the Talmud (see presently), and a variety of ad hoc decrees and rulings (called *taqqanot* and *gezerot*) issued for the public good. Altogether, this literature (particularly the Mishnah) constitutes *the agenda* of rabbinic legal study (both theoretical and practical) over the centuries.

THE TALMUDS As noted earlier, the Mishnah is the starting point for the discussion of the next generation of sages (called Amoraim) in the land of Israel and Babylonia, from the second century C.E. on. The literary product of these discussions is the Talmud of the land of Israel (called the Jerusalem Talmud) redacted in the mid–fourth century, and the Talmud of Babylonia (called the Babylonian Talmud) redacted with final annotations in the fifth century. These two great collections from the two preeminent centers of Jewish life and scholarship form the next foundation document of developing Judaism. They both gradually achieved the status of authoritative and sacred texts, though only the Babylonian Talmud ever really dominated the academic and legal curriculum of Jewish study over the ages.

Both Talmuds develop the abstract and practical implications of the Tannaitic Mishnah (and its supplements), draw inferences about its logic and suppositions, harmonize contradictions among various legal positions (for theoretical and practical purposes), determine the relationship of the Mishnah to the Torah legislation, and include an enormous range of legendary, homiletical, and theological matters. The texts preserve the discussions of the sages (as remembered and as reconstructed) in highly compressed and elliptical forms. Accordingly, the Talmuds are enormously difficult to read, and traditional education is geared not only to the contents of the arguments but to the crucial matter of phrasing and sentence division. But because of the supreme importance of these documents for Jewish life and practice, the Talmud (the Amoraic content of which is called *gemara*, "study," though this term is often used generically for the entire Talmudic corpus) has remained the core document of traditional Jewish study. The two Talmuds overlap in almost all the topics dealt with in the second, third, and fourth orders of the Mishnah; though the Babylonian Talmud has no discussion on the first division (Seeds), and the Jerusalem Talmud has no discussion on the fifth (Holy Matters). Very little of the Amoraic treatment of the sixth division of the Mishnah (Purities) is preserved.

RABBINIC LITERATURE AND THE TORAH Faced with such a prodigious intellectual output, one may naturally wonder why such a proliferation was necessary in the first place. The place to begin is with the Bible itself. Despite its divine authority, the rabbis, who wanted to establish a comprehensive biblically based religion, had to deal with the fact that the Torah is not a comprehensive document. Numerous topics necessary for religious-legal life are missing. For example, little or nothing is said in the Torah about the laws of marriage and burial, adoption and contracts, and much more. In addition, where topics are specified in the Torah, they are frequently found to be either ambiguous or in need of supplementation. Thus, for the Torah to be the basis of *all* religious life it was necessary for the sages to make the general rules specific and draw out the implicit meanings of other laws. Because of its overall importance in Jewish life, and as a representative case, let us briefly consider the rules pertaining to Sabbath observance.

The Decalogue, or Ten Commandments, commands the Jew not to work on the Sabbath ("six days shall you labor and do all manner of work; but the seventh day is for the Lord, your God; *you shall not do on it any manner of work*" [Exod. 20:9–10; Deut. 5:13–14]). But aside from one or two further regulations elsewhere in the Bible (as the prohibition against lighting a fire), the nature of "work" is not specified, so the precise manner of obeying the divine law was left open. It was therefore necessary from early times for teachers to determine a whole host of issues such as: *when* the Sabbath day begins (for though new days are reckoned from eventide in Judaism, the strict prohibitions of Sabbath labor required special precision; hence the onset was variously "pushed back" to predusk or earlier); *what* constitutes a forbidden labor (as a formal guide, the thirty-nine Mishnaic rules of prohibited labors in the ancient Temple, like carrying objects and lighting or extinguishing fires, served as precedents); *where* certain of the prohibited Sabbath labors (like carrying objects) applied and where not (complex rules of "boundaries" establishing private vs. public domains were worked out; carrying being permitted in the former); *whether* one could walk beyond certain fixed limits and *in what circumstances* one could break the Sabbath rules for health reasons; and *how* one should comport oneself in demeanor, dress, and thought on the Sabbath day to make it holy and special.

The halakhic discussions of the rabbis on these matters in the Talmud especially are intense and legalistic and filled with great intellectual and theological passion. Gradually a whole complex of rules designed to make the Sabbath "sacred" were formulated or justified through biblical proof-texts. There is thus an overwhelming disproportion between the amount of divine legislation found in the Bible and the amount of human legislation preserved in rabbinic literature. But what is particularly significant about this is that the rabbinic rules are not only designed to help implement the biblical law but *to protect it*. An important legal category thus developed, known as "building a fence around the Torah"; that is, the rabbis typically added many rigorous circumscriptions ("fences") to the biblical law *so that the divine law it protects would not be broken*. The rabbis themselves recognized the ironies involved. According to one early remark found already in the Mishnah, the sages stated that the numerous halakhic prescriptions concerned with the proper observance of the Sabbath were like "mountains hanging by a thread." Yet this thread was strong enough to help weave the complex pattern of Jewish holiness and to spin the mysterious web of Jewish continuity. One may therefore concur with the pithy formulation of a later observer: Less than the Jews preserved the Sabbath, the Sabbath preserved the Jews.

Now all this may seem an inordinately complex form of religious concern. But it is just this complexity and legal piety that has informed Judaism over the ages. In their concern to establish and obey the positive ("thou shalt") and negative ("thou shalt not") commandments of the Bible with every nuance, and to make certain that rules pertaining to such daily practices as personal hygiene and eating were properly followed, the rabbis and Jews (of these and later times) believed that *in just this way* they were truly faithful to the covenant and God's will on earth. Scrupulous piety, it was hoped, would result in divine blessings in the here and now (what was called *olam hazeh,* "this world"), though the obscurities of fate often led the people to defer this hope to a future time (what was called *olam haba,* "the world to come"). Thus the commandments, or **mitzvot,** were a means of holiness and hope in this world.

The deferral of hope because of historical injustice or the mysteries of divine justice never compromised this mode of holy service. Indeed, for many the "world to come" was no radically transformed existence, but the full earthly realization of the hopes of the Bible: peace on earth, harmony in the family, natural bounty, political dignity (under a native, anointed king, or "**Messiah**"), and restoration of sacrifices (in a rebuilt or heavenly sent Temple). The frustrations of history, especially the abortive national uprising under Bar Kochba (132–135 C.E.), turned many Jews inward, away from issues of political power and toward the spiritual "history" of "the four cubits of the *halakha*," as the concerns of legal piety were sometimes dubbed. The Mishnah itself may reflect this very ideology. By contrast, other Jews longed for a radically transformed *olam haba* on earth; or they awaited the manifestation of divine justice in an altogether divine world. Either way, whether rewarded now or later, the unassailable belief and assumption was that the *mitzvot* are the mysterious means of personal and national salvation, and that these "works" were given by God for just that very purpose. [See Christianity pp. 491–92, 495–97 for discussion of the Messiah.]

EXTRALEGAL LITERATURE   The halakhic spirit may thus be summarized as legalistic in its nature, authoritative in its forms, and communal in its sphere of application and performance. A more personal spirit is reflected in the numerous theological interpretations of the Bible known as *midrash aggada.* Coming from the same Tannaitic and Amoraic academies as the legal teachings, the aggadic spirit reflects the theological quest and concerns of the rabbis as reflective interchanges among themselves and as highly stylized sermons delivered to the people on Sabbaths and holidays.

The *aggada* achieves its theological aims through the reapplication of biblical images and themes (e.g., creation or the Exodus), through passionate appeals for repentance and purity of service (i.e., against rote performance of the commandments and self-deception), and through the unrelenting advocation of moral action and personal perfection before God (by reflections on the great biblical models of moral action and religious decision). All this nonlegal material is found in special collections of interpretations of biblical books. Significantly, these aggadic anthologies typically include legal discourses and expositions as well. Similarly, aggadic materials are also woven around the halakhic discussions preserved in the Talmud. This frequent integration of the two types of content is of notable significance. For *halakha* and *aggada* are two sides of Judaism, not just two literary genres, constantly intertwining and mutually challenging. *Halakha* gives the *aggada* its social and public expression; *aggada* gives the *halakha* its spontaneity and extralegal spirit.

In addition to the great ideal of Torah study as a special substitute for the ancient sacrifices, there is another "service of the heart," whereby Judaism replaced and transformed the ancient powers of the Temple. It is the service of the repentant and gracious spirit. One expression of this is a justly celebrated teaching of Rabbi Yochanan ben Zakkai. While many fellow Jews were intensely mourning the loss of the Temple, this sage consoled his students by spiritualizing the meaning of the sacrifices through an adroit reinterpretation of a biblical passage. Picking up a remark of the prophet Hosea, Rabbi Yochanan said that acts of "loving-kindness" replaced and were greater than "sacrifices," and that acts of "repentance" replaced and were greater than "sacrifices of atonement."[7] Loss of the Temple need not, therefore, mean the loss of spiritual renewal and reconciliation with God. This could be achieved, he taught, through pious penitence toward God and personal devotion to one's neighbor. Other sages taught that the commandments themselves might serve as functional substitutes for the ancient sacrifices, insofar as their pious performance was an act of self-sacrifice of personal desire and will. Thus while one might perform the commandments solely as an act of legal piety and thus be considered a *tzaddik,* or just and honorable person, loving devotion to others beyond the strict letter of the law would be the acts of a *hasid,* or righteous person. Such a one goes beyond the needs of the self and sacrifices personal interests for the sake of a higher path of divine service. Such a standard was called the *mishnah* of the righteous, *mishnat hasidim.* It was not the way of the many, but of those who saw it as their concern to enact the reconciliations of the Temple through acts of neighborly devotion. This path had its faithful followers throughout the Middle Ages.

Prayer gathering at the "Wailing Wall," the only remaining portion of the ancient Temple in Jerusalem. It has served as a symbol of exile and hope for millennia. Since antiquity this site has been the locus of pilgrimages. (Photo by Bill Aron.)

Among the ideals of self-sacrifice of the early sages (preserved and transformed into a national ideal in medieval and modern times by historical necessity), none was greater than martyrdom. In this one act, as Jewish texts repeat, one no longer transfers one's offering to another creature but becomes that very sacrifice. For the rabbis, the patriarch Isaac and the events recorded in Genesis 22 came to constitute the biblical model for this "perfect and unblemished offering"—as midrashic texts speak of his trial on the altar. The story of Isaac was recited daily in the morning liturgy, elaborated upon with much pathos in the *aggada,* and rendered poetically in pious martyrologies throughout the Middle Ages. The great rabbinic scholar Akiba was another model of self-sacrifice for the Jews of classical antiquity and beyond, for during the Roman persecutions of 132–135 C.E., Akiba's flesh was stripped off and he was hung in the market stalls because he disobeyed the prohibition of Torah study and observance. According to tradition, his was an awesome display of devotion and piety; he died for the sanctification of God by reciting the proclamation of the unity of God (the Shema) at the climax of his suffering. [See Christianity p. 502 and Islam pp. 673, 678–79 for discussion of martyrs.]

One version of the foregoing event of Akiba's martyrdom is preserved in the Talmudic legend of Moses with which we opened this work. After the event in the study hall, when Moses queried God why he and not Akiba should have the merit of receiving the Torah and was abruptly silenced by God ("Be silent, for this is how I have determined it"), Moses asked to see Akiba's fate. Anticipating the reward due the righteous, Moses sees instead the martyrdom of the saint and the shame done to his body. Outraged, Moses exclaims, "This is Torah, and this its reward?!" Is this the result of a life devoted to Torah study and piety? Just as abruptly as before, God silences Moses and says, "Be silent, for this is how I have determined it." No further answer is given. The two scenes of the Talmudic account—of devoted study and ultimate faithfulness to God and his law—conjointly express the deepest ideals and ideology of Jews in this classical period: that Jewish renewal is achieved through devoted interpretation of Moses' Torah and that Jewish destiny is fatefully bound up with its ongoing life of Torah. Or, to reexpress the matter in the folk adage quoted earlier, "Israel and the Torah are one."

The Amoraic period ended in the land of Israel about 425 C.E. with the abolition of the Patriarchate by the Roman emperor Theodosius II. It was brought to a close in Babylonia about a century later, after persecutions of the Jews by the Sassanians. By that time the seat of the Jewish religious authority had long since shifted to the Babylonian Exilarch (as the leader of the Jewish community there was called) and to the great Babylonian academies established in the cities of Sura, Pumbedita, and Nehardea (in modern-day Iraq). It was here that such rabbinic authorities as Rab and Samuel left their mark on Jewish legal theory and literature for all time, as did the later pair of sages Abbaye and Rava. Through the efforts of these scholars, the rabbis of the Pharisaic tradition succeeded in establishing their legal and moral authority over most of the house of Israel.

Developments in Judaism from the Seventh
Through the Seventeenth Centuries

We have paused at some length to discuss the ideological system of Judaism during its formative phase (from 70 C.E. to the redaction of the two Talmuds) for three reasons. First, while Judaism changed in its emphases over succeeding centuries, the Tannaitic-Amoraic period of the religion is its classical expression and brings to focus the essential features of Judaism that dominated Jewish life for the next thousand years. That is, *the core features of the classical phase remained the matrix of traditional Jewish life:* Torah study and interpretation, legal piety through fulfillment of the commandments, human responsibility before God and God's responsiveness to human action and need, and the chosenness of Israel among the nations along with the hope in the eventual unification of all peoples in a just and righteous order.

The second reason for this emphasis on the formative phase of Judaism is that its core features were repeated daily by all Jews in the formulations of the liturgy. That is, *the ideological features of the classical phase were continuously reactivated in Jewish consciousness through the liturgy and its behaviors.* And finally, the theological and legal texts of classical Judaism became the agenda for subsequent Jewish speculation and interpretation. That is, *the halakhic and aggadic expressions of the formative phase were the basis for ongoing Jewish creativity and expression.*

With all this in mind, we shall now see at somewhat greater length how the classical rabbinic inheritance was variously complicated, consolidated, elaborated, and explained in the postclassical period.

ISRAEL   Already after the first exile (587/6 B.C.E.), the Jews were a dispersed nation subject to diverse national and religious influences. This remained so in the classical phase, when the two dominant centers were the land of Israel and Babylonia (with their Greco-Roman and Irano-Sassanian influences, respectively), and continued to characterize Jewish life in the Middle Ages. Gradually these two centers fell under the influence of Christianity and Islam and their temporal religious heads in Rome and Baghdad. As Jewish life fanned out from Israel to Spain and Morocco in the west, and to Iraq and Persia in the east, the Jewish cultural styles of these environments (known as **Ashkenazi** in Franco-Germany and Italy, and as **Sephardi** in Spain and the Near East) were continuously affected by their Christian and Islamic overlords. Inevitably, for all classes, these influences included participation in the regional dialect and folk repertoire and the more subtle factors of aesthetic taste and demeanor. Among the mercantile and scholarly classes, the influences extended to shared legal and economic conventions and common intellectual and literary interests.

Nevertheless, within this wider framework, the Jews carved out (at the discretion of the popes and princes of the church, and the sultans and *imāms* of the mosque, to be sure) their own autonomous (if largely second-class) culture. Here, in the Jewish domain, Ashkenazi and Sephardi communities developed their own linguistic jargon (like Yiddish, a mixture of Hebrew, German, and

Slavic elements; or Ladino, a mixture of Hebrew, old Spanish, and Provencal elements); their own folk heritage and art forms; and their own distinctive mores and styles of family life. And here, too, in the autonomous Jewish domains, the rabbinic lawyers (and their courts and halakhic rules) held sway. Issues of religious concern (such as prayer and food slaughter) were subject to Jewish authority, while issues of public status (as taxation and state service) and public behavior (as expressed support of the state and its leaders) were subject to external, non-Jewish authority. In the context of an often precarious balance between rights obtained and negotiated, Jews lived in separate enclaves where they established synagogues for prayer, academies for study, and whole networks for communal services (care for the sick and poor, or burial and aid societies) in all the lands of their settlement. Naturally, the communal patterns changed according to region and time; and they also varied in degrees of political or economic efficiency. But all told, Jewish self-government and accompanying bureaucracies were a reality throughout the Middle Ages and a reality the Jews depended upon for their support and safety.

Thus if the Jews found themselves dispersed abroad, they were nevertheless centralized within their local communities, often called "the holy community" of this city or that. And if, further, the Jews in Muslim lands were categorized as *dhimmis* (Arab.; i.e., non-Muslims formally protected by a "pact" with Muslim overlords), who were at best tolerated when not completely harassed, and the Jews of Christian Europe were totally outside the law and thoroughly dependent upon benign papal bulls and the goodwill of local electors (the Jews were called *servi camerae,* a Latin phrase meaning "servants of the royal chamber"), they still maintained their belief to be God's chosen people. The principle of *ahavat Yisrael,* the love and care for fellow Jews, was a central value for this oppressed minority, as was the principle that stated that "all Jews are responsible for one another." In normal times, where communal and intercommunal self-help was required, these principles were often the motivations for social kindness. During times of danger and oppression, these principles also motivated Jews to rescue merchants frequently kidnapped for high ransom, to defend their compatriots against frequent Christian blood libels (which outrageously imputed that Jews murdered Christian children to use their blood in their Passover holiday bread or that they "tormented" the blood and body of Jesus through desecrations of the Eucharist host and wine), and to provide a safe haven and care for Jews exiled from one city and country to another. [See Christianity pp. 514, 520 and Islam p. 626 for persecution of the Jews.]

Overall, Jewish literature and historical memory in the Middle Ages is a traumatized memory of "tears and martyrdom," as one historian put it, of national-cultural destructions that turned whole communities into rivers of blood or torrents of homeless exiles. Years like 1096, when the Jews of the Rhineland were plundered and killed by Christian pilgrims on their circuitous crusade to liberate Jerusalem, and 1648–1649, when hundreds of thousands of Jews were butchered by the Cossack chieftain Chmielnitzki and his hordes during Ukrainian uprisings, are deeply etched in the collective memory of the Jews. Equally cataclysmic are such dates as 1290, 1306, 1391, 1395, 1492, and

1497, times when Jews were expelled from England, France, Spain, and Portugal. Many more dates could be added. No wonder that the Jews of medieval Europe rarely regarded themselves as part of the history of the Gentile nations. Theirs, they believed, was a sacred history politically disrupted in 70 C.E. but to be revived again in the ever-near messianic future.

The focus of the people of Israel was thus neither politics nor power, but the maintenance of their halakhic patterns and the time-transcending demands of a comprehensive religious tradition. In this regard, Gentiles were treated with outward civil respect but inner suspicion and reserve, for the inescapable fact is that Jewish history in Christian Europe and the Muslim lands was a nightmare for medieval Jews, the ever-present confirmation of their life in **galut,** or exile. On the other hand, the messianic longing for redemption, outbreaks of which recurred repeatedly from the seventh century in Yemen to the seventeenth century in Europe and the Near East, reflects the deep Jewish passions for a restoration of their national dignity and the right to perform their religion freely.

These powerful messianic passions were fanned daily by the texts of the liturgy as well as by the pervasive Jewish belief—against all outward logic—that Jewish history was providentially guided by God and was thus ultimately subject to no temporal power. And so, while the outward course of history appeared under the bleak image of the "eternal Jew" wandering from one burning city to another, Jews as a whole held fast to a more inward course of history, a history believed to be a meaningful and God-directed affair within which the Jews played a pivotal role. No understanding of Judaism or Jewish historical resilience in the Middle Ages can begin or end without taking this belief into account.

HALAKHA Halakhic piety served to provide Jews with a special and autonomous life pattern and a buffer against political harassment and theological attack. It also provided *the consensus* for Jewish life the world over. Jews wandering from one land to another could easily adapt to the new environments because of the common calendar, common rituals, common sacred objects, and, especially, common legal norms. The latter grew out of the Talmudic traditions and expanded during the Middle Ages, first by the Geonim, the "Excellencies" or heads of the Babylonian academies from the seventh to the eleventh centuries (until the fall of the Baghdad Caliphate), and later by the Rishonim, the "Earlier Authorities," from the twelfth through the sixteenth centuries. The scattered and diverse halakhic norms were variously compiled by such scholars as Yehudai Gaon, in his eighth-century collection *Halakhot Pesukot;* by Simeon Kayyara, in his ninth-century collection *Halakhot Gedolot;* by Rabbi Isaac Alfasi (known by the acronym Rif), in his eleventh-century collection *Sefer ha-Halakhot;* by the extremely influential works of Rabbi Moses **Maimonides** (known by the acronym Rambam), in his thirteenth-century work *Mishneh Torah;* by Rabbi Jacob ben Asher, in his fourteenth-century codification *Turim* (known as "The Tur"); and by Rabbi Joseph Karo, in his sixteenth-century work *Shulkhan Arukh.* All these works are justly famous in Jewish life; they gave a systematic structure to Jewish legal piety over the ages. Some medieval scholars complained that the works of Maimonides and Karo, especially, formulated as they were without citing precedents of legal reasoning, tended to give Jews the impression of a fixed and apodictic legal system. This was not an altogether unjust complaint—especially as far as Jews with minimal rabbinic training were concerned. But the elaborate "Question and Answer" literature (called *Responsa*) from early Geonic times, in which new halakhic queries and their solutions were constantly being discussed, belie this impression of halakhic rigidity. This literature (and the process of discussion and reasoning involved) remains a window to the passions and perplexities of halakhic life to this day.

The halakhic consensus of traditional Jewish life also established the centrality of the rabbis as local lawyers and judges and as communal leaders and teachers of God's law. Faced with the fact that their legal reasoning was interpretative in nature, the rabbis sought to establish the legitimacy of their methods and conclusions by recording chains of authorities—something like spiritual-religious genealogies (comparable to the Islamic *isnads* or Buddhist lists of teachers). This concern was also motivated by the Karaite challenge from the seventh century on. This group, founded by one Anan ben David, rejected "Rabbinite" authority and halakhic reasoning and sought to develop its own "biblical" religion (the word "Karaite" derives from the nouns *mikra* or *kera,* as Scripture was called). They exhorted their followers to "search the Scriptures well," and to use natural reason and logic—not rabbinic exegesis—in developing new legal norms and rules from the Bible. The basis for this lay in the Karaite contention that the interpretative procedures of Talmudic antiquity distorted the meaning and application of the divine Law. [See Islam p. 654 for the "chain of transmitters."]

Despite the power and pervasiveness of the Rabbinite establishment, the Karaite challenge was strong and serious and frequently split the Jewish community into bitter factions for centuries. The great Gaons (or "Excellencies"), like Saadia of Sura, frequently debated the contentions of the Karaites, while many other rabbis used every opportunity to criticize the Karaites' calendrical calculations and their often literalist legal interpretations. Ostensibly, the issue was a concern for a halakhic consensus among all Jews and the "proper" interpretation of the divine law, but the desire for power and control over the Jewish populace cannot be excluded as a motivation. By the high Middle Ages (thirteenth–fifteenth centuries), the vituperative debates slackened somewhat, and the Karaites settled into enclaves with their own hegemony in such areas as Constantinople (modern Istanbul) and northwestern and southern Russia. The remnants of this Jewish community were sought out and many were killed, along with other Jews, during World War II.

The halakhic work of the rabbis reinforced and further extended the dimensions of Jewish legal piety. Every sphere of personal and communal life was regulated by it. But this was hardly abstract law, for as we have seen, the *mitzvot*—the visible expressions of *halakha*—were the commandments of God (as rabbinically formulated) that established the religious (not just legal) basis for life. Through performance of the *mitzvot* the Jew was constantly in relation to God, constantly sanctifying life by holy actions, and constantly accruing "merits" for future (earthly or otherworldly) blessedness. Thus, through the *mitzvot* life remained centered on earthly actions even as these commandments were simultaneously directed toward God, their source. It is characteristic of Jewish legal piety that the very codes that established halakhic order are also pervaded by great religious devotion. The Sephardic sage Moses Maimonides (author of the *Mishneh Torah*) and his Ashkenazi contemporary Rabbi Elazar of Worms (author of the *Rokeach*) both begin their important works with spiritually passionate sections dealing with the ideals of Torah study and its deep connection to the love of God and moral-religious perfection (through the *mitzvot*). "Arise like a lion, run like a deer, to fulfill the commandment of the Creator," charges Joseph Karo at the beginning of his own great legal code (the *Shulkhan Arukh*).

BIBLE STUDY As is understandable, a great deal of halakhic study was practical in nature (*halakha le-maʿaseh,* as it was called), for Jewish piety had to be defined, applied, and judged. At the same time, already in many Talmudic discussions and increasingly among the Franco-German "glossators" (called Tosaphists) and others, the concern for halakhic theory was prevalent—the natural process of law being the establishment of theoretical structures and the discussion of theoretical cases. But it should be noted that from the last stages of the Talmud on, in addition to trends toward more theoretical analysis, halakhic issues moved increasingly away from the Bible and focused on Tannaitic-Amoraic discourses (harmonizing them or reframing their concerns) as well as the subsequent formulations of the Geonim. The dependence of the rabbis upon rabbinic literature was certainly part of the Karaite critique, which, it will be recalled, urged a return to biblical foundations. While the rabbis did not restructure their halakhic reasoning on this account, they did return to Bible study in a new way.

The first new activity that must be mentioned is the work of the Massoretes. It is they who studied and annotated the biblical text. They were concerned that its letters and vowels along with its reading signs and oddities were preserved intact—for the sake of an exact tradition (the very name Massoretes, which means something like "traditioners," reflects this concern). The Massoretes collated Bible manuscripts, collated textual variants, and also noted linguistic idiosyncrasies or parallels in the texts. Their work seems to have begun around the seventh or eighth century and hit a high-water mark in the ninth and tenth centuries, though it continued for hundreds of years thereafter. The Massoretes established the traditional text of the Bible through their great compilations, and many of their remarks can be found in the margins or in sections following particular books in the so-called Rabbinic Bibles, *Mikraʾot Gedolot*, printed beginning in the sixteenth century and continuing up to today.

One of the hallmarks of the Rabbinic Bible is the inclusion in it of some of the popular or preeminent Jewish medieval commentators. Indeed, one of the special features of the work of these rabbis is their concern for the "plain sense" of the biblical text. In its earliest forms, this plain sense (called *peshat*) was not so easily distinguished from rabbinic modes of interpretation (called *derash*). In fact, the great early commentator of eleventh-century France, Rabbi Solomon ben Isaac (known by the acronym **Rashi**), who first set forth the program of a *peshat* commentary on the Bible, often slips into the mode of *derash* to support a narrative or legal point. Nevertheless, the very attempt to establish a working cultural distinction between something that would resemble the explicative and historical sense of the biblical text (the *peshat*), on the one hand, and the midrashic sense of the text (legal and theological *derash*), on the other, was of considerable importance for Jewish and Christian Bible studies. Other commentators soon elaborated upon this exegetical dichotomy. Among these was Rashi's own grandson, Rabbi Samuel ben Meier (known by the acronym Rashbam) of the eleventh–twelfth centuries. Indeed, he maintained a vigorous concern for the linguistic-historical sense of the Bible. In pursuing the sense of *peshat,* in fact, Rashbam even interpreted the Bible against the sense of the halakhic tradition (the *derash*). Presumably for Rashbam, and not for him alone, the Bible was believed to contain both senses in a noncontradictory way, though of course the midrashic sense was authoritative for halakhic behavior. It appears that pressures from outside Judaism (specifically, new Christian concerns and contentions) lie at the root of this new rabbinic interest in the *peshat* of Scripture.

The concern to penetrate the *peshat* of Scripture gradually became a Jewish scholarly concern in its own right. For the rabbinic scholars in Spain, this textual interest was further accelerated by growing developments in philology in the contemporary Islamic world. Among the notable new voices was that of Rabbi Abraham ibn Ezra in the twelfth century. In the introduction to his Bible commentary, he aggressively separated the different styles and interests of contemporary Bible commentators and opted for the plain, grammatical-historical sense of the text. Ibn Ezra's work is marked by a high literary style and a pithy acuity that set generations of students to work to discern the exact sense of his comments (such annotations are known as supercommentaries). Many other French scholars of this period, such as Rabbis Joseph and David Kimhi of Narbonne, and Rabbi Eliezar of Beaugency, labored to establish the method of *peshat* interpretation.

The important Bible commentary of the twelfth–thirteenth century Sephardic scholar Rabbi Moses ben Nachman (also called Nachmanides and known by the acronym Ramban) is more complex and synthetic than the preceding works. For one thing, he takes up and debates the earlier comments of the classical sages, of Rashi and ibn Ezra, though almost invariably providing a distinctive approach to the plain sense of a scriptural passage. However, Ramban was also a devoted traditionalist and important halakhist, and he turns his comments in that direction where matters of law or practice are concerned. Thus, though Ramban clearly saw it as the task of the Bible commentator to serve theoretical and scholarly interests, he also felt it to be his responsibility to write a work that would serve the religious community in its faith and practice. This helps explain another particular element in his Bible commentary: his mystical allusions. While he indicates his strong mystical concerns in his introduction (and his belief that the *peshat* hardly exhausts the meaning or truth of the Torah), Ramban was exceedingly careful not to be too explicit about these matters in a public commentary (as per rabbinic doctrine). He therefore often closes a cryptic mystical observation with the caveat "but the discerning one will understand" or "we have no (mystical) tradition on this."

By contrast with these various philological and mystical interests, the values of Renaissance humanism also penetrated into Jewish Bible commentaries. The voluminous work of the courtier Don Isaac Abarbanel (Spain and Italy; sixteenth century) typifies this trend, for here we have at once a highly systematic synthesis of the preceding centuries of Spanish exegesis as well as original literary and historical observations. At several points Abarbanel even includes elements characteristic of late Renaissance statecraft and political theory.

In all, this and the preceding works of scriptural interpretation provided many new insights into the text. Most significantly, much of this labor served to restore to Jews the study of the Bible as a document in its own right—neither as a source of *halakha* nor a repository of mystical symbols, but as a work whose very language, rhetoric, and logic was of cultural value. Perhaps one may perceive in this threefold interest an echo of the older medieval scholarly curriculum (the Latin *trivium*) within the study halls of the Jews.

THEOLOGY   The native theology of traditional Judaism is a biblical theology, a theology rooted in biblical images and ideas, in biblical language and hopes, and in biblical values and concerns, however much these images, hopes, and values were transformed through reinterpretation and reformulation. Being so biblically based, much of the ancient and early medieval theology is preserved in the books of *midrash aggada* spoken about earlier (i.e., in commentaries on biblical books and homilies on Torah readings and holiday themes). For this reason, too, the themes and topics of this early theology are not systematized under any abstract heading but follow the sequence of biblical texts and the lead of their topics: God, the creation, the patriarchs, Moses, the covenant, the homeland, kingship, and so on. Invariably, a particular verse sequence and its imagery elicit many other scriptural texts with similar or contrasting language or ideas. These are then coordinated with the biblical passage that initiates the aggadic reflection. The result is a vast web of ideas from the entirety of Scripture. Aggadic theology is therefore a total biblical theology; and because it is such, its images of God are anthropomorphic (i.e., God sees and speaks, loves and judges, and so on), not abstract; and its views on any given topic are as varied and contradictory as is the entire biblical inheritance. This bothered no one and actually gave Jewish theological life a nondogmatic flexibility—within the broad constraints of Judaism's "essential features," to be sure, and the more narrow limits of halakhic conformity.

Those medieval theologies like Judah Halevi's *Kuzari: Defense of a Despised Faith* (twelfth century, Spain), which retained the pathos of the living and guiding God of Abraham and Moses and did not neutralize this pathos through abstract philosophical analysis, thus remained true to the native theology of Judaism and captured the hearts of the Jewish populace. Little wonder, then, that Halevi was the great "sweet singer of Israel" in the Middle Ages, whose religious (and biblically rooted) poetry entered the prayer book of the Jews.

Lord, where shall I find You?
High and hidden is Your place.
And where shall I not find You?
The world is filled with Your Glory.

I have sought Your nearness,
With all my heart I have called You;
And going out to meet You,
I found You coming toward me.[8]

With these words Halevi speaks for all traditional Jews, of a God utterly exalted and hidden, but of a Presence also near and immediate. He speaks of the passions of religious yearning and the mystery of God's kingship, but also of the joy expressing the certainty that God responds to his creatures in love. This, too, is the biblical and rabbinic God of light and power, who also "clothes the naked" and "raises the downtrodden." Such a God is deemed a living Father and King, the revealer of covenant demands and promises; and he is also the One who is trusted to redeem his people and restore them to their ancestral homeland, to **Zion.** Of this longing for national redemption Halevi says: "My heart is in the east/and I am at the edge of the west." And with the melancholy of his entire nation, the poet cries to Zion: "I am like a jackal when I weep for your affliction; but when I dream of/the return of your exiles, I am a lute for your songs."[9] Similar hopes and longings were recited daily in the prayer service, as was the acknowledgment of God the Creator, who has chosen his people in love and revealed to them his teachings for their holiness and ultimate salvation. [See Religions of Africa pp. 39–42, 64–69, Religions of Mesoamerica pp. 157–58, 186–89, Native Religions of North America pp. 274–76, 288–305, 330–32, Christianity pp. 537–38, Islam pp. 635–37, Hinduism pp. 739–41, 759–61, 780–84, Buddhism pp. 900–903, Religions of China pp. 1024–26, and Religions of Japan pp. 1112–27 for discussion of God, gods, and objects of worship.]

More systematic, philosophical expressions of Jewish theology were introduced into Judaism during the course of its encounters with Islamic and Greek philosophy in the Middle Ages. The range of topics did not change from that found in the *aggada* or liturgy (God, Israel, covenant, Torah, and messianic hope), but much of the native pathos was neutralized by the rational and abstract tone of the philosophers. Typical of such efforts and of monumental significance for the history of Jewish thought is the philosophical work of Moses Maimonides, who was mentioned above as the author of one of Jewry's most influential legal codes. In his great work, *The Guide of the Perplexed*, Maimonides gave paramount importance to his philosophical reading of the ancient biblical tradition, though he conceded the value—even necessity—of a more naive and literalist understanding of Scripture for most Jews. In this way, he argued, those persons not capable of abstract philosophical analysis might nevertheless be guided on the way of truth through a reliance upon the concrete and anthropomorphic imagery of the Bible. Naturally, for him the philosophical approach was the higher and more individualistic way to truth. But the important point was that the seemingly naive biblical tradition was not therefore to be rejected: It was a necessary, though not final, level of meaning, the public expression, in fact, of God's revelation of Mount Sinai. Thus ordinary people had immediate access to divine truth through the revelation and subsequent rabbinic explanations of it, whereas the philosopher added the more arduous path of intellect and logical argument. Despite this high privilege accorded to philosophical reason, Maimonides nevertheless conceded that, without the biblical view of God as Creator in time (that is, not an Abstract Idea out of time), the whole foundation of Judaism—based on God's revelation and teachings, on divine guidance and redemption—would crumble.

A complex balance between reason and revealed truth was therefore a philosophical necessity. It is thus notable that when Maimonides formulated his "Thirteen Principles of Faith," he combined the abstract language and arrangement of the philosopher with the content of a living, biblical theology. This creedal statement, preserved in the daily prayer book, states: "I believe, in perfect faith, that the Creator, may His Name be blessed" is (1) the sole Creator, (2) uniquely One, (3) beyond all conception and form, (4) the First and the Last, and (5) the true God of prayer; that, further, (6) the words of the prophets are True, that (7) Moses is the True and First prophet, and that (8) the whole Torah was given to Moses; moreover, that (9) there is no new covenant; that (10) the Creator is Omniscient and (11) rewards and punishes for observance of the commandments; and further, that (12) in his own time God will yet bring the Messiah, and (13) resurrect the dead. A discerning review of this formulation will perceive both the abiding theological matrix of traditional Judaism *and* the outright rejection of the principles of Muslim and Christian belief (note numbers 2, 3, 5–9, and 12).

ETHICS The sphere of halakhic action has two main foci: ritual actions performed between the individual and God (*bein adam la-Makom*) and moral actions performed between one individual and another (*bein adam le-havero*). The first sphere includes prayer, physical purity, proper dietary regulations, and celebrations of the festivals; the second includes legal actions, business transactions, respect for parents, and the obligation to arrange the marriages of children and bury the dead. Both spheres are governed by the *halakha,* in the sense that strict norms of performance and behavior are imposed upon the Jew; the actions in both spheres are *mitzvot,* in the sense that they are ultimately derived from the Bible and performed in the service of God. In Judaism, then, ethical action is part of halakhic action and done with God in mind. It is just this double character of regulated interpersonal actions done for the glory of God that is the touchstone of traditional Jewish ethics.

Native Jewish ethics derive from the Bible and the whole library of aggadic literature. As with theology, the reflections on actions and duties, or motivations and ideal behavior, arise in the course of reflecting upon biblical actions. How the patriarchs acted, the dangers of pride and the value of penitence, and the duties to the "stranger, orphan, and widow" are among the biblical topics taken up in the *midrash aggada*. To be sure, the classical rabbinic literature does show some trends toward a more systematic collection of ethical actions. The Tannaitic treatise, *The Sayings of the Fathers*, for example, gathers together some ethical dicta of the early sages, and a hierarchical list of spiritual perfections has been preserved in the Talmud in the name of Phineas ben Yair.

Despite these trends toward systematization in the classical sources, traditional ethical behaviors and motivations were only gradually gathered and ordered in the post-Talmudic period. Soon a voluminous literature developed. The ethical work of Bahya ibn Pakuda (Spain, eleventh century) is a crucial turning point in this regard. His influential *Duties of the Heart* deliberately shifts focus from the outer, halakhic level of behavior (the "duties of the limbs") to the inner sphere of motivation and self-scrutiny (the "duties of the heart"). In an elegant and enticing way, this work guides the reader along an ideal path of perfection from proper belief in God, to the virtues of trust, sincerity, penitence, semi-asceticism, and fear and love of God, all in the context of discussing the traditional halakhic actions and their proper motivation. Bahya's *Duties* was of immense importance in medieval Europe and was devotedly studied by pietist circles from the Rhineland (the German Hasidim, twelfth–thirteenth centuries) to the Ukraine (the so-called new Hasidim, from the eighteenth century).

Other influential works, such as Rabbi Jonah Gerondi's *Gates of Repentance* (thirteenth century, Spain), or Rabbi Elijah de Vidas's *Beginning of Wisdom* (land of Israel, sixteenth century), or Rabbi Moses Luzzatto's *Path of the Upright* (Italy, eighteenth century) further directed the Jew toward holiness, self-purification, and unselfish actions. Most literate homes had some *musar* (ethical) books or pamphlets in their libraries. In their content and ideal value, then, these holy handbooks are to be considered central to appreciating the ever-renewed quest of Jewish spiritual life for devoting all actions to God alone. It was, in addition, a literature of the traditional community at large and did not require highly developed rabbinic skills for its comprehension.

By contrast, the philosophical ethical literature, which also derives from a biblical foundation, was written with elites in mind and was greatly influenced by ancient Greek ethical systems. Many of these works, like Solomon ibn Gabirol's *Perfection of the Qualities of the Soul* (eleventh century, Spain), linked Greek psychological theories to theories of ethical development. The several structures of the human soul (the so-called corporeal, divine, and supernal elements) were systematically related to the structures of ethical and spiritual development. Thus, one's actions might move from lesser to increasingly more refined instincts, and from there to higher intentions—like uniting one's highest soul element to God. The even "purer" philosophical ethics of Maimonides were also based upon biblical passages and Talmudic sayings as well as ancient and medieval psychological theories. But it is also very much distinguished by the influence of Aristotle's *Nichomachian Ethics*. The result is Greek ethics in a Jewish guise. It is chiefly when he is providing moral-spiritual explanations to the practical laws (as in the *Book of Knowledge* of the *Mishneh Torah*) or ordering the normative way of giving charity or doing repentance from rabbinic sources that Maimonides' ethics are distinctly characterized by biblical-rabbinic language and values. It is, further, in just this area of his work that the ancient Jewish passion for *religious perfection in and through society* is most clear.

Rabbinic Patterns of Hidden Meanings and Otherworldly Concerns

The patterns of rabbinic life and thought that were considered in the preceding section under the rubric of "this-worldly holiness and salvation" may be referred to as the exoteric or public level of Judaism. This level is rooted in the public nature of the biblical revelation and the social context of the commandments. Referring to the accessibility of the Torah, Moses reminds the people that this teaching "is not in heaven," for "the hidden things are God's, but the revealed things are for us and our children forever: to do all the teachings of the Torah (Deut. 29:28). Thus through the *mitzvot* and the *halakha*, the public, earthly nature of divine service is never lost in Judaism. The *mitzvot* are works done in this world and for the sake of this world. Moreover, through these earthly works people can relate to God, who is the source of the *mitzvot*. This world is thus the enduring context of holiness and of religious experience and expression, according to standard Jewish teaching.

Nevertheless, a distinct esoteric or hidden level of meaning is evident in Judaism over the ages, not particularly in the sense that special knowledge or secrets are withheld from the people-at-large (though this was sometimes the case), but in the sense that the texts and works of Judaism were believed to contain deeper and more hidden levels of meaning. And, indeed, precisely these deeper levels of meaning should be the true focus of the adept. The esotericists would thus interpret the foregoing Deuteronomic passage to mean that God's Torah contains *both* hidden and public meanings and that the former may be discerned by the adepts either through rational deduction (the way of philosophy) or spiritual disclosure (the way of mysticism). The esoteric trend is thus an elitist phenomenon that focuses on the individual and the special wisdom to be found in the Torah. It builds upon, but does not reject, the populist trend, which focuses on the halakhic consensus founded upon the Torah.

In what follows we shall not review each of the main periods of Jewish life from the detailed perspective of Jewish esotericism and its otherworldly meanings and concerns. Rather, a more selected focus shall be offered of the major historical types found in the philosophical and mystical approaches to Judaism. The ancient dictum that the world is founded upon "Torah, worship, and acts of loving-kindness" will have its echoes in the present review as well.

The Philosophical Path

The dominant image for this path may be "apples of gold set in silver traceries." It is an image made famous by Maimonides in the introduction to his monumental philosophical work, *The Guide of the Perplexed*. Commenting on the biblical adage that "a word fitly spoken is like apples of gold in settings of silver" (Prov. 25:11), Maimonides speaks of discerning the truth of Torah. For one who simply looks at Scripture at a distance, without close examination, the inner truth of the text is misperceived for its outer expressions, just like one looking "with imperfect attention" at golden apples around which silver filigree has been traced might imagine that these apples were solely silver. Only "with full attention" will the interior become clear to the viewer, and he or she will know the apples to be of pure gold.[10] Thus one must penetrate beyond the surface sense of Scripture, for while its external expressions are "useful for beliefs concerned with truth," they cover "truth as it is." The uncovering of the deeper sense of Scripture, of Torah, is through allegory.

Faced with the abstract and sophisticated philosophical view of God taught in the Hellenist schools, Philo of Alexandria (20 B.C.E.–50 C.E.), as remarked earlier, was concerned to show that the Torah, revealed Truth, was, despite its external imagery and anthropomorphic portrait of God, in accord with philosophical truth and reason. Through a complex retranslation of biblical imagery into Greek categories and a reinterpretation of the great personalities of the Bible in terms of Platonic and Stoic virtues, Philo claimed to penetrate to the "deep sense" of Scripture—its philosophical truth. Thus while he emphasized that this deeper level of the Bible—which the rabbis were to call *remez*—did not displace the *peshat* (plain sense) of Scripture or the halakhic actions based on rabbinic *derash,* his intellectual energy was nevertheless focused on philosophical concerns and the "intellectual love" of God. For him, Torah was no mere book of narratives portraying human virtues or vices and its view of God was not mere anthropomorphic presentation of a loving or wrathful deity. Rather, when rightly read, the Bible was nothing less than a divinely given handbook of philosophical truths.

Philo taught that the Bible as a revealed work of wisdom is replete with instructions concerned with guiding one to moral-intellectual perfection. Such instructions occur in the narratives, the laws, and the exhortations. For example, the constant human struggle between the rational and irrational parts of the psyche is for Philo symbolized in the Bible by the raising and lowering of Moses' arms in the battle against Amalek (Exod. 17). Or further, the ancient Greek theme of the soul's exile from its true divine homeland and its struggle to remove itself from the material world through a life of moral-intellectual perfection is particularly symbolized by the lives of the patriarchs. Accordingly, when Scripture reports that "the Lord said to Abraham: 'Go forth from your homeland, your kin and your father's house,' " the hidden instruction to us is the necessity to disengage from the body, sense perception, and speech (i.e., the illusions and attractions of language) in order to draw close to God, the truly "existent One," through contemplation. So guided by Scripture, Jews may live philosophically within their tradition. Far from turning them from philosophy, Philo taught, the proper study of the Bible is a philosophical exercise, for philosophical truths are contained *within* it.

Maimonides continued this ancient allegorical-intellectual tradition and provided its classical medieval expression. Concerned with demonstrating the

true philosophical sense of the Bible and purifying the text from its anthropomorphic images of God, Maimonides began his *Guide* with a virtual philosophical dictionary. Hereby, one anthropomorphic image after another is explained
—and in effect explained away. Thus, though the language of the text may
appear to indicate that God sees and talks and so on or that he has eyes and
hands, these images are reinterpreted in more abstract categories. What the text
"really means" is that God is omniscient, omnipotent, providential, and so on.
In this way the cruder features of the Bible are refined, as it were.

Now all this does not mean that the outer form of the Bible is false and an
offense against reason. Recalling the opening image of golden apples, what this
rather means is that this exterior level is *also* part of the sense and truth of the
biblical text—deliberately produced by God, says Maimonides, to enable common people to appreciate (via the metaphors and concrete language) the power
and beneficence of God. So impressed, they will undertake the performance of
the commandments and thus be guided to moral-social perfection. Were the biblical text merely philosophical in rigor and rhetoric, were it merely abstract and
logical, Maimonides contended, God's teachings would have been restricted to
the intellectual elite. In their present form, by contrast, the entire nation is
guided to perfection and true belief, each according to his or her intellectual
abilities and needs.

For Maimonides, then, Scripture is constituted by truth at its exterior and
deeper levels. The latter contains what are often called the *sitre torah,* or esoteric
"mysteries of the Torah" (such matters as the true nature of God, metaphysics,
and the divine realm as well as the true meaning of the biblical narratives and
the purposes of the positive and negative commandments). Hence the Bible is
a teaching for both the ordinary believer and the philosopher, who will be more
perplexed by the surface formulations of Scripture and more in need of expert
guidance—lest skepticism and rejection of religion result. "A person ignorant of
the secret meaning of Scripture and the deeper significance of the law" might
thus tend to misperceive the special wisdom of Judaism and be subject to doubts
or loss of faith. For this reason, Maimonides believed, it is necessary to enhance
this deeper knowledge—for the ordinary folk and the intellectual elite—in
different ways. And this he did through the moral-spiritual explanations of the
laws found in the *Mishneh Torah* and through the more penetrating interpretations of action and belief found in the *Guide.* Special effort is therefore made to
teach the deeper philosophical sense of God and the Torah through philosophical emphases and allegorical reinterpretation. And a special effort is also made
to inculcate the deeper sense of the *mitzvot* through an explication of the higher
moral and religious ends they serve.

Thus, teaches Maimonides, God, being utterly beyond human description,
can only be thought of negatively, by considering what he is not; and being
utterly perfect and One, God can hardly be thought of through the compound
features of language. By taking care in this regard, one will therefore refine one's
religious sensibility and be guided to a purer and more devoted divine service.
The language one uses about God is thus directly related, for Maimonides, to the
way one conceives of the meaning or motivation of human action. Crass views

of God, he judged, would lead to crass and self-centered expectations of personal benefit when performing the *mitzvot,* whereas a more philosophically purified perception of God would lead to a more spiritual and God-directed form of observance. Remarking on the commandments, he further observed: "Know that all the practices of worship, such as reading the Torah, prayer and the performance of the commandments have only the end of training you to occupy yourself with His commandments."[11] But, he continues, if your attention is weak and "you pray merely by moving your lips," or "read the Torah with your tongue while your heart is set" on personal matters, or "you perform a commandment merely with your limbs," such worship is a perfunctory and self-centered act.[12] By such rote behavior true love of God is not achieved, and the perfections of Torah are abused. One of the concerns of philosophical wisdom was, therefore, to challenge and readdress religious routinization through the proper comprehension of the nature of God and the goal of the commandments.

Still, it must be stressed, the path of philosophy was precarious and not for all comers. The weak-minded could easily be befuddled. For example, if God in the philosophical understanding is pure Intellect or Thought, one might naturally wonder how he is also the concerned revealer of Torah and the caring protector of Israel. Or further, if God is conceived of as a pure Unity and utterly Impassable, one could naturally imagine that such a God was not one to whom prayer and supplications might be addressed. In this light, some interpreters have argued that Maimonides was himself caught on the horns of this apparent series of contradictions and was really a philosopher who advocated religion for the welfare and perfection of humankind. Others have contended that Maimonides skillfully integrated the two modes of philosophy and religion and that for him the paths were thoroughly complementary—though on different levels.

Such speculations transcend the merely academic and have had serious practical consequences. For example, shortly after the publication of Maimonides' *Guide* the rabbis in France and Germany provoked a bitter controversy over its contents. It was their conviction that only a belief in the biblical-rabbinic God was faithful to Judaism and would ensure Jewish practice. Philosophical reinterpretations of Judaism, they believed, obscured the pathos and demands of the God of the covenant, and rather than being a means toward the purification of belief and practice were rather the alien alloy that would destroy it. There were, in fact, some grounds for this contention. Indeed, over a century earlier Judah Halevi had already remarked about a view that some philosophically minded Jews also held in Maimonides' day. In his *Kuzari,* a spokesman for this position is made to say: "Human actions are but instruments which lead up to philosophical heights. Having reached these I care not for religious ceremonies."[13]

But Maimonides' whole approach belied this facile trend. Knowing that the philosopher and the simple person of faith have different motivations and goals, Maimonides' great intellectual effort was to show that the two were not contradictory. For him, in fact, philosophy and (biblical) revelation were complementary paths to God and perfection. To be sure, the former was the rational way of the individual and the latter the faithful way of the community. But since the Jewish philosopher was also enjoined to obey the commandments of the revelation and participate in the halakhic consensus of the community, the role of philosophy could only enhance the participation of the philosopher in Jewish practice. For a long time such arguments fell on deaf ears; and the actual practice of many who pretended to philosophical interests seemed to confirm the tirades of the more literal traditionalists. It was a century and more before the steam of controversy evaporated somewhat, and it became clear that Maimonides' whole concern was to exalt Torah and the service of God.

The study of Maimonides' *Guide* went into some eclipse until the nineteenth century, when a new wave of rationalism burst on the Jewish scene. Even then, as earlier, this work was not popular among most Jews. For them, the more literalist style of Jewish belief fostered in France and Germany held sway, as did a whole range of mystical interpretations of Scripture and the commandments. In fact, a significant Jewish mystical revival developed in and around thirteenth-century Spain and spread to all the lands of Jewish settlement. Not the least of the motivations for this revival was a rejection of philosophical rationalism and allegory. Slowly, a new symbolic language emerged that dominated the nature and imagery of Judaism for centuries.

The Mystical Path

The dominant image for the mystical path may be "the maiden in the palace." It is an image made famous by the monumental mystical work of Judaism, the *Zohar*, or *The Book of Splendor* (thirteenth century, Spain). Referring to different levels of interpreting Torah and thus approaching God, the text likens the Torah to "a beautiful damsel who is hidden in a secluded room of her palace." She "has a secret lover" who "for love of her . . . keeps passing the gate of her house." And "what does she do? She opens the door of her hidden room ever so slightly and for a moment reveals her face to her lover." This she does gradually, out of love for him; and only he who loves her sees this and is drawn nigh. "So it is with the word of the Torah," says the text, "which reveals herself only to those who love her." The mystic (called the "wise of heart") is thus drawn to God through the Torah and its hints to him. Gradually, out of mutual faithfulness, the "hidden secrets" of God's Scripture are revealed to the lover, who, joined in understanding and love to the maiden, is called a "bridegroom of the Torah." Mystical longing is thus consummated with the bliss of understanding.[14]

Faced with the starkness and transcendence of the divine will, many Jews from antiquity on yearned for contact with the living God and for the hidden knowledge derived thereby. Already in early Tannaitic-Amoraic sources a type of Throne Mysticism is indicated, whereby mystical adepts ascended the cosmic spheres to behold in bliss the cosmic Chariot and Throne of God. Here, moreover, in this otherworldly focus one might also be vouchsafed the knowledge of the end of the world. Such a yearning was common in early rabbinic circles and expresses the somewhat world-weary hopes of those subjugated to the dominion of Greece and Rome and downtrodden by the fall of the Temple and the suppression of national hopes. To be sure, this did not lead to any lesser interest in the divine commandments. In fact, some of the great early mystical seekers—like Rabbi Akiba himself—were among the great halakhic specialists. Moreover, these otherworldly speculations did not proceed from outside the Torah, but rather from the reinterpretation of the prophetic and other scriptural passages.

Particular mention should be made in this regard concerning the mystical speculations of the anthropomorphic grandeur and form of God that developed at this time. Such speculations, which derived in part from reinterpretations of passages from the biblical Song of Songs, led in the Middle Ages to a whole anthropomorphic literature about the enormous humanlike features of God—the so-called *Shi'ur Komah* literature. While such speculations were a natural outgrowth of the biblical statement that humans are in the "image of God," they were nevertheless the subject of harsh critiques by the philosophers. These latter felt that such an anthropomorphic focus was a misreading and distortion of scriptural language. Certainly the strong anti-anthropomorphic concerns of Saadia (the Gaon of Sura) and Maimonides were motivated as much by a prophet-like rejection of such "images" of God as by purely philosophical principles. In any case, the ancient Jewish mystics studied and interpreted Scripture with an eye to its deeper spiritual or mystical sense, later called *sod.* This level of meaning was understood to supplement *but not replace* the other levels: of *peshat,* of *derash,* and of *remez.* The *sod* included hidden secrets of God's majestic realm, his form and glory, and the times of the end of history.

The *Zohar* provides one classical expression of the mystical trends current in Judaism in the Middle Ages. As with Maimonides, Moses de Leon also speaks of *sitre torah* ("secrets of Torah"), but these are now given a distinctly mystical (even mythical) meaning. While continuing earlier trends, the *Zohar* reflects a strong reaction to the abstractions and spiritualizations of the philosophers of

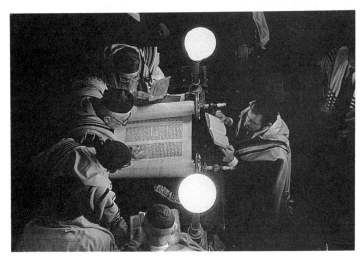

Yom Kippur Torah reading, recent Leningrad. Public reading and study of Torah is a sacred duty in Judaism. For Jews it is a renewal of the covenant and testimony to the ever-new teachings of ancient Scripture. (Photo by Bill Aron.)

the day and reconstructs Judaism—through new scriptural interpretations—on a strikingly new foundation. God was no longer perceived as separate from the world, as in the Bible, or utterly abstract and beyond attribution, as in the philosophical literature. God was rather understood as both the transcendent source of all being and the immanent presence of divinity in all things. Thus all creation and creativity was portrayed as flowing out of the infinity of God. Indeed, in the mystical apprehension, God's "image"—his complex structure of attributes (like mercy, power, generativity, and receptivity) and their interrelationships—is to be found in all life and in humans most fully. Thus, as the *Zohar* never ceases to emphasize, what "is below" is mirrored "on high" and vice versa. This being so, God is believed to be inseparable from the life of the world, being its ultimate influence. But, correspondingly, God is also believed to be subject to human influences, through actions and prayer, precisely because humans are so fully "in the image of God."

All these mysteries and more are contained in the Torah when correctly understood through the symbolism of *sod,* for the Torah is not merely a book of narratives and laws. "In the mystery of truth," as the *Zohar* says, the biblical narratives of individual and national history and the laws expressing patterns of proper action are most deeply concerned with the mysterious dynamics in the divine realm, for example, the mysterious relations between mercy and justice or the flow of perfection generated through the unification of such opposites as male and female. The mystical adept is privileged to learn of this deeper truth of the biblical text and, correspondingly, of the way his or her own inner life mirrors such divine dynamics. This knowledge of "higher things" is therefore no mere abstract privilege; its concrete effects are everywhere visible. In the degree to which individual and social life is unified and in harmony, the divine realm (of which human and social life is a part) is correspondingly strengthened; and the degree to which disintegration and discord run rampant in the human realm produces a corresponding fate in the totality of life and being.

For the Jewish mystic, then, the service of God through observance of the commandments is nothing less than a double act of personal and cosmic integration. Indeed, through a life of halakhic performances and prayer the mystic understands and enacts the deepest *sod* (mystery) of being, for he or she is in the privileged position of establishing hidden cosmic harmonies *even as* his or her actions establish social order and psychological integration. Thus the this-worldly focus of classical rabbinic Judaism, which saw in Torah study and obedience to the *mitzvot* a means to *tikkun olam* (the rectification of social life), is not bypassed by the mystic. In the performance of the *halakha,* the mystic combines this feature of religious action with the philosopher's and moralist's concern for *tikkun ha-middot* (the rectification of psychological qualities through proper study and observance) in pursuit of the ultimate goal: cosmic *tikkun* (or the rectification and unification of the divine spheres). Indeed, for the mystical path, this otherworldly realm is the true focus of human intention in the faithful observance of the commandments. [See Christianity pp. 500, 507, 519, Islam pp. 659–62, Hinduism pp. 752–53, Buddhism pp. 946–48, Religions of China pp. 1032–34, and Religions of Japan pp. 1102, 1121–27, 1151 for discussion of meditation and mysticism.]

Earlier, in connection with Akiba's martyrdom, the medieval adage referring to the unity of Israel and Torah was mentioned. In fact, this adage derives from the ideology of the Zoharic tradition just reviewed. In another formulation of it, the maxim states that "God, Israel, and Torah are one." Now a complete explication of this statement would involve discussing the mystical identities between the three terms in the supernal realms. Nevertheless, some sense of the adage has already been indicated, for since the Torah is an earthly expression of mysterious truths of God and since the commandments of the Torah given to Israel are the true means of establishing divine unity, the three terms comprise one interdependent whole.

Thus, both as an expression of historical reality (the fateful bond between God, Torah, and Israel in the world) and as an expression of theological truth (the mysterious unity between God, Torah, and Israel in the sustenance of this world and all cosmic realms), the foregoing adage captures many layers of Judaism in the Middle Ages. Not the least do we sense here the combination of two of its most salient features: the pathos of Jewish historical destiny and the self-proclaimed privileges of those who believed that their religious life served worldly and otherworldly ends. The gradual penetration of these attitudes into all strata of the Jewish people gave much of medieval Jewish life its distinct character. The belief in the cosmic power of the commandments was also the lever for some powerful eruptions of messianic activity in the sixteenth and seventeenth centuries. Such eruptions and beliefs appear, in retrospect, as among the final expressions of a worldwide Jewish consensus.

Convergences of Paths and Periods

Before turning from medieval to modern Judaism, something should be said of the convergence within historical Jewish life of many of the features just discussed, for it would appear, at first view, that each of the periods just described was utterly separate and that each of the paths and expressions quite distinct. Naturally, classical Judaism is not medieval Judaism, and the philosophical and mystical paths are not one and the same. Still, to not appreciate the organic relations of all these would do considerable disservice to Judaism as it has been lived and continues to be lived.

First, we should simply emphasize the fact that the texts of the classical phase of Judaism continued to be studied in all successive phases, so that the ideologies and halakhic regulations of the early rabbis continued to be discussed and practiced in successive generations. Rabbinical scholars, in fact, constantly related and correlated their various sources and tried to resolve differences between scholarly opinions sometimes spanning more than a thousand years. Their legal and aggadic literature reflects this constant interchange, and the anthological character of so much Jewish medieval literature bears this out as well. There were moral and mystical compendia and aggadic and legal ones.

Here many opinions sit alongside one another, all part of one stream of tradition. In many cases, just this anthological character denotes the open-endedness of all discussions. Indeed, already in the Talmud, sages over many centuries are found in close anthological proximity. Further, in the prayer book, the Jew could read thrice daily through a literature replete with many levels of tradition: from the biblical psalms to Tannaitic rulings and prayers to medieval hymns and poems. In this form, the full sweep of the tradition is constantly intoned in the community. And finally, the very format of the Rabbinic Bibles (the *Mikra'ot Gedolot*) from the sixteenth century on demonstrates the simultaneity of diverse interpretations in the lifetime of the Jew; every folio page is covered with dozens of commentaries from the first to the nineteenth centuries, with the biblical text in large boldface in the center. The ongoing and often polyvalent voice of tradition was thus an ever-present reality for the Jew (scholar and layperson alike) in both the synagogue and the study house.

It bears further comment in this connection that the creativity of the elite scholars was not compartmentalized, and simultaneous involvement in many levels of writing and thinking was not a rare phenomenon. Thus Akiba was both a halakhic lawyer and a mystic, as was Nachmanides a thousand years later, and Joseph Karo several centuries after him. Similarly, Akiba commented on the Bible and rabbinic literature, as did Rashi and Rashbam and Nachmanides. On the other hand, Saadia was a Bible commentator and a philosopher, as was Rabbi Levi ben Gerson centuries later. Maimonides, as we have seen, not only wrote a vast legal code but composed a rational philosophical treatise as well. Rabbi Joseph Karo, by contrast, not only wrote a legal code and folios of rational legal argument but also commented on the Mishnah through the mediation of a heavenly guide, which revealed legal instructions to him after he repeatedly recited portions of this legal text in mantralike fashion (also a practice of other mystics in his circle). Moses de Leon, the reputed author of the *Zohar,* was both a philosopher and mystic (consecutively), and his contemporary Abraham Abulafia combined the language and worldview of philosophy (notably of Maimonides' works) with a highly arcane linguistic technique for achieving mystical ecstasy. Quite clearly, some of the most diverse intellectual patterns and interest could be sustained by rabbinic scholars within a fixed, but broadly interpreted, halakhic framework. And as it was for the scholar, so it was for the layperson, though naturally at more modest levels. Indeed, a full grasp of the entire intellectual-religious tradition was an ideal for all. And all were encouraged to roam the rooms of this superstructure, built on the firm base of halakhic conformity.

Perhaps the very anchor of this remarkable diversity was the ancient belief—constantly echoed—that God produces new meanings of Torah every day and that *all* are "the words of the living God." The Torah has at least seventy facets, says a Talmudic tradition; and one medieval mystic even said that it had six hundred thousand—one for every Jew who heard the revelation of Sinai. Thus Torah was always believed to be a religious kaleidoscope of meanings, the rich product of God. To be sure, some meanings had to be fixed for ritual and halakhic life, but many others, of a more aggadic and speculative character, remained more fluid. In all, the diverse meanings of the four traditional methods of interpreting Scripture—*peshat, derash, remez,* and *sod*—were believed to constitute the simultaneous truths of one Torah.

By the Middle Ages, these four levels were coordinated more conceptually and known by the acronym *pardes. Pardes* itself means "garden," and this term soon became symbolic of the vast sphere of divine knowledge. As *pardes* was one, so no layer of Scripture canceled any other. Naturally, the halakhist gave chief emphasis to legal *derash,* while the philosopher and mystic emphasized the levels of *remez* and *sod.* Indeed, the philosopher and mystic commonly believed that these latter levels were of highest significance, and their evaluation of the *peshat* and the purposes of halakhic action were affected by this scale of values. We have indicated some aspects of this in our review of the paths of philosophy and mysticism in medieval Judaism.

The Modern Period (From the Eighteenth Century to the Present)

If we survey the scene of Jews and Judaism from the eighteenth century on from the perspective of our essential matrix of elements, one is struck by both the patterns of continuity and discontinuity. On the one hand, traditional Jewish life continued along quite established channels. As the period opened, the religious authority of the rabbis remained in force, and rabbinic procedure and courts controlled most areas of public and personal law. The halakhic consensus guided the daily and ceremonial life of the Jew in a full manner, and very little was not regulated by it. The Torah and its interpretations dominated the religious imagination and creativity, and this literature was pretty much the only literature traditional Jews read and studied. And the people of Israel remained in the physical and theological state of *galut,* and so felt themselves in exile from their homeland and aliens in the lands of their settlement.

To be sure, all was not static. Corruption in rabbinic leadership in eastern Europe, the lingering crisis of failed messianic expectations, and the effects of violent persecutions were among the factors that led to the emergence of new Jewish communal patterns and religious structures in southern Poland and the Ukraine in the eighteenth and nineteenth centuries. Particularly significant was the emergence of the pietist movement called Hasidism. In it greater emphasis was placed on personal relations with God and the community than on Torah study and halakhic discourse, and more value was given to the redemptive powers of joy and psychological integration than to ascetic acts of penitence and attempts to influence cosmic harmonies (features of older mystical practice). The new leaders were charismatic teachers and healers called Tzaddikim, rather than rabbinic scholars and halakhic experts. In one fell swoop, the pious acts and paradoxical teachings of these holy masters produced a groundswell that renovated the Jewish tradition from within.

Antitraditionalist in some respects (particularly in attitudes toward study, fixed prayer hours, and types of decorum), the new Hasidic movement provoked all the vituperative reactions of a "counterreformation" among the more rational traditionalists, who continued the more intellectual patterns of study and authority. The merest denigration of study was opposed, and the emotional emphases of Hasidic life, together with its belief in the power of the Tzaddikim to serve as religious mediators between the people and God, provoked ridicule and censure among those for whom the hallmark of Judaism was emotional propriety and the capacity of each person to stand before God. Yet the threat of a common enemy—outright secularism and radical religious reform—eventually pulled the Hasidim and their opponents (called Mitnaggedim) together. On occasion, the reaction to change was so severe as to provoke attempts to freeze the tradition. Maxims like "change is forbidden from the Torah" from such celebrated halakhists as Rabbi Akiba Eiger (c. 1720–1758) reflect the fears of traditionalists. Further symptomatic of these fears were the severe constraints imposed in matters of dress, language, and manner, let alone halakhic innovation. It is therefore not uncommon to see extreme traditionalists to this day dress in the "high style" of nineteenth-century Poland and convinced that "orthodoxy" means inflexibility to change.

Other traditionalists sought to renew the powers of their religious life in other ways: through attempts to renovate the more abstruse patterns of Talmud study that had developed and alienated all but halakhic virtuosi; through attempts to return to more demanding lives of esoteric study and penitential rigor; and through attempts to regenerate religious practice through emphasis on such traditional values as humility, self-scrutiny, and secret service to the poor (the so-called *musar,* or moralist, movement). The renovation of Talmud study led to the founding of great new rabbinical academies, as the celebrated *yeshiva* (rabbinic academy) founded in Volozhin, Lithuania. The return to esoteric piety led to the renewal of Cabalistic study in such celebrated mystical groups as the *"kloiz"* of Brody, Lithuania. And the concern to regenerate flagging or routinized piety through *musar* was the life work of Rabbi Israel Salanter.

But for all the power of these movements and many others that developed from them along more liberal lines the tide of nontradition was rising and threatened to flood Judaism everywhere. It is the discontinuities with tradition that began to emerge in European Jewish life in the eighteenth and nineteenth centuries that set apart this new period from all those that preceded it. In effect, the continuity of tradition was now just one feature among a great many expressions of Judaism on the historical stage. A clear consensus was a matter to be sought; it could not simply be pointed to.

By the mid–eighteenth century, western and central Europe were undergoing a social and ideological revolution. The class hierarchies of the medieval world were breaking down, notions of the "rights of man" began to develop and spread, ideas of equality among all peoples were advocated and fought for, and a shift in patterns of authority and privilege was in the air. The result was that marginal or suppressed social classes like the Jews were given unprecedented access to education and culture. For virtually the first time Jews mixed with

Gentiles on a common basis and had access to new professions. Common political ideals were formed, and Jews became increasingly devoted to the civil laws and educational curricula of the nations in which they lived. All this pulled them farther and farther away from an exclusive reliance on Jewish tradition and put greater demands on this tradition to conform to the new realities.

The social transformations of Jewish life were accompanied by profound shifts of ideology and value. The new "open" cultural climate of Europe—itself a revolutionary rejection of medieval patterns—advocated the ideals of reason and intellectual daring (one motto of this period, the Enlightenment, was *aude sapere,* a Latin phrase meaning "dare to know"). No longer was there a traditional, pregiven, and predetermined social-religious reality that people incorporated in themselves with mother's milk, as it were. Now the extent and nature of one's Jewish practice and identity would have to be chosen over against other religious and cultural options available in the society-at-large. This now meant that, for all practical purposes, one's Jewish identity was a matter of personal choice, not just fate. Naturally many Jews experienced intense conflict as they tried to balance new thoughts with traditional ones. One famous example of a search for an intellectual-religious synthesis based on these new realities was that of Moses Mendelssohn (1729–1786). In his celebrated volume *Jerusalem,* Mendelssohn formulated a Jewish ideology for the Age of Reason, a Judaism that conforms to natural reason in all its social-moral teachings and that is distinct only in its revealed ceremonial laws. The acceptance of this philosopher into Berlin intellectual society became a celebrated example for liberal Jews and non-Jews alike. It suggested that, with the appropriate adjustment of traditional education and habits, the Jew could "make it" in Gentile society. It was not a message that all Jews wanted to hear. Still, new attempts to integrate Judaism with general culture followed; and these paved the way for religious reforms on an unprecedented scale (see chapter 18). [See Religions of Africa pp. 25, 54–57, 79–82, Religions of Mesoamerica p. 240, Native Religions of North America pp. 287, 320–22, 357–58, Christianity pp. 529–33, Islam pp. 698–700, Hinduism pp. 770–74, 828–31, Buddhism pp. 952–56, Religions of China pp. 998–1002, 1055–59, and Religions of Japan pp. 1132–33, 1163–72 for discussion of new religious movements.]

All told, these changes were momentous and had a profound effect on the status of Torah and tradition. Earlier, when new values and concerns emerged from within the community or from without, they were set against tradition for evaluation. Now the situation was paradoxically reversed; now it was tradition that was set against the nontraditional values for evaluation. The result was that the ancient texts and rituals of Judaism were reevaluated. The Torah was now viewed as a changing and historically conditioned document (in accordance with new historical ideas), and the moral and legal content was judged accordingly. Judaism as a system of thought and practice was now seen in historically relative terms—not as some absolute and timeless essence. In response, some Jews rejected Judaism entirely as a pre-Enlightenment stage of religious culture. Others were spurred to rethink and reform the old faith, for if Judaism was no timeless essence but the ongoing historical product of Jewish creativity, the fate of the religion was something humans could and should take responsibility for. And this many did. A deep alliance therefore developed between those who studied Jewish sources "scientifically" (the movement was called "The Scientific Study of Judaism") and those who wished to present Judaism as an evolving religious-cultural civilization. If (to allude to our opening Talmudic legend) the pressures of modernity forced traditionalists increasingly to emphasize the "Torah of Moses revealed by God," the spirit of modernity also encouraged many others to stress the ever-changing human "interpretations of Akiba and the rabbis." The new ideal was to take historical responsibility for Judaism and Jewish culture and thus through moderate or radical reform to bring traditional Jewish values and practices "into the modern world."

Perhaps the most unexpected cultural reform, and equally the most revolutionary, was the attempt beginning in the late nineteenth century to revive the Jewish nation in its ancestral homeland. This reformist-nationalist movement is known as **Zionism.** Faced with a growing resurgence of anti-Semitism throughout Europe and Russia, many Jews came to fear that civic acceptance by non-Jews was not to be trusted and that they alone had to provide the means for their physical and cultural preservation. Old canards of the Gentiles that the Jews were a "state within the state" and subject to "dual loyalties" provoked old Jewish reactions and convinced them that despite apparent social advances they were still "a nation that dwells apart." Under the leadership of Theodor Herzl and others a concern to reform Jewish national life by establishing a new national settlement in Palestine was generated. A major plank in this platform was thus to ensure the physical safety and enfranchisement of Jews, when they could not rely upon their host country. The rescue of Jews from the bloodbath of Nazism after 1945 and of oriental Jews from Arab persecutions after the national State of Israel was founded in 1948 proved to all the essential importance of political Zionism. The role of Israel in providing a safe haven for oppressed Russian, Iranian, and Ethiopian Jews from the 1970s through the present has reinforced this attitude.

Thus, after almost two thousand years of exile, the Jews began to restore their ancestral nation and homeland, to revive the ancient Hebrew language, and to rebuild their political and cultural institutions. Indeed, after nearly two millennia of being powerless resident aliens, outside history and national states, many Jews sought to return to history and the task of building a society on a new Jewish basis. This spiritual-cultural aspect of Zionism is its second plank and was considered central to Zionist ideology by some of its earliest leaders, like Ahad Ha-Am. Rejecting many of the attitudes and patterns of traditional Judaism, the new cultural Zionists sought to establish a vigorous nontraditional Jewish culture *on the foundations* of its ancient heritage. This powerful reaction to tradition, together with its strong tone of self-reliance, alienated many traditional Jews from Zionism in the early years, for these traditionalists would not relinquish the ancient image of Zion as a religious symbol of Jewish historical fulfillment and the "return of Zion" as a messianic event to be inaugurated by God alone. Other, more temperate attitudes developed within traditional circles, and forms of religious Zionism gradually emerged in central Europe and

America. Today, religious Zionism is a vital component in the reshaping of Jewish life in Israel providing a strong share of new immigrants and challenging secular or non-Jewish laws and values with the teachings of tradition. Attempts to form a viable synthesis between traditional *halakha* and custom, and Western liberal humanism and its values are a major feature of the legal-cultural agenda of the modern State of Israel—though not without intense vigilance and lobbying on both sides to ensure that their "interests" are safeguarded and enhanced.

The development and revival of Jewish culture in Israel has had an incalculable effect on the nature of Jewish life elsewhere, particularly in twentieth-century America. It has generated new national pride, stimulated study of Hebrew and Jewish literature, and restored Israel to a land of pilgrimage for all. As the first cultural Zionists hoped, Israel has proved to be a center and catalyst for Jewish creativity everywhere. In addition, as a result of Zionism, new bonds have been formed between Jews the world over, so that the ancient value that "all Jews are responsible for each other" has received new meaning in the second half of the twentieth century. Massive financial and emotional support has been tendered the fledgling state by North American Jews especially, and Russian and other recent immigrants to Israel have been sustained by world Jewish charities. All this is done with the ancient virtue of self-help and with a new nonapologetic pride in Jewish destiny. For these reasons, Jews growing up after 1948 hardly conceive of a time when the Jewish people were harassed and utterly powerless. This has led to a revision of historical memory in some cases. Nevertheless, the constant concern to memorialize the murder of six million Jews during World War II keeps the pain of the Jewish historical past alive and has motivated a vigilant attitude that "never again" will Jews be powerless and unprepared in the face of persecution. Such collective attitudes have served to reinforce the sense among modern Jews that they remain one people, however scattered they may be across the globe and however diverse they may be with respect to their religious practices. In fact, this powerful concern for the preservation of the Jewish people serves virtually as the new consensus of Jewish life, binding traditional and nontraditional Jews to a common purpose.

Another virtual consensus of modern Judaism, despite all the variations and reinterpretations to which it has been subject, including the secular revision of its ancient symbols and terms, is the ancient calendar cycle. Whether they are traditionalists, nontraditionalists, or post-traditionalists and whether they are fundamentalists, liberals, or secularists, all modern Jews who are in any way conscious of their religious-national heritage acknowledge the Jewish New Year and the ancient national festivals in some way, for to live utterly and deliberately outside the traditional Jewish units of time—no matter how much these may be, for some, secondary to the civil calendar—is to live utterly and deliberately outside any expression of Jewish life. Thus today as much as in earlier times the calendar cycle carries the forms of Jewish life and sensibility. It is to the traditional pattern of this cycle that we now turn. Indeed, in one form or another these patterns still mark the physiognomy of modern Judaism.

17

Judaism as a Ritual System

IN TRADITIONAL JUDAISM, all aspects of life are ritualized through halakhic regulations—from the first thoughts and prayers in the morning through the final prayers upon one's bed at night, from permitted and unpermitted foods to permitted and unpermitted business practices, from the obligations of daily prayer to the requirements of festival celebration and personal mourning. Accordingly, all aspects of life take on the legal character of *mutar* and *asur,* or "permitted" and "forbidden," acts. Such other categories as *hayyav* and *patur,* or "obliged" and "free" (not obliged) and *qodesh* and *hol,* or "holy" and "profane" also dominate the daily religious consciousness and experience of the traditional Jew. Accordingly, the observant Jew will be typically scrupulous in performing his or her halakhic obligations, that is, highly attentive to the proper times and manner of performing the commandments. And further, since this pattern of performance is not merely individual, but often depends upon a quorum of others, halakhic observance also brings the Jew into conformity with other members of the community who feel equally "bound" by the legal-religious strictures of the *halakha.*

Invariably, then, the personal and interpersonal pattern of halakhic life dramatizes the ideology of Judaism in concrete forms. And it is just these forms that give the beliefs and attitudes of Judaism their daily texture, their lived quality. It has therefore been observed that the calendar is the true Jewish theology or ideology, for it is the calendar and its content that carries Judaism from one moment to the next. Indeed, the beliefs of Judaism become present each day through the prayers, study, and life actions of the Jew, for each act (ideally) brings to mind the historical memories, ritual affirmations, and moral values upon which Judaism is based. There is thus no abstract affirmation of faith in Judaism. Rather, one performs the *halakha* and, through it, affirms Jewish values and ideals. Characteristically, a traditional Jew is not called a "believer" but a *shomer mitzvot,* an "observer of the commandments," and a traditional Jew is not considered pious in the abstract but only through being quit of the halakhic obligation required on a given occasion. Halakhic piety is thus an ongoing expression—daily and seasonal—of Jewish religious life.

Before turning to the rituals themselves, a brief word about the all-important calendar is in order. First, the present calendar of traditional Judaism is lunisolar; that is, the months are reckoned according to the phases of the moon and the years according to the circuit of the sun. Now since a solar year exceeds a lunar one (twelve months) by about eleven days and since, too, the festivals are fixed both by the moon and by agricultural seasons, which are dependent upon a tropical solar year, the cycle of lunar months must be adjusted. If this were not done, the festivals would "wander" backwards, and the spring festival of Passover would eventually come in the winter and then in the summer. At the present time, the adjustment means the addition of an extra month (Adar II) seven times in nineteen years. For daily ritual purposes, time reckoning is deemed to begin at the end of twilight (i.e., after sunset, with the rising of the moon). Special rituals occur in connection with the new moon each month, and the beginning of a new lunisolar cycle is celebrated by holy convocations, as we shall see. [See Religions of Mesoamerica pp. 159–60, 206–9, Native Religions of North America pp. 280–82, 351–54, Christianity pp. 551–53, Islam pp. 674, 707, Hinduism pp. 727, 793–94, Buddhism pp. 890–91, Religions of China pp. 1021–24, and Religions of Japan pp. 1141–46 for discussion of religious calendar and time.]

It may be noted that, from biblical antiquity through the Middle Ages, the proper determination of the calendar was a major preoccupation and a source of bitter controversy. Many factors entered into these disputes, including (among the Qumran sectarians and others) belief in a purely solar reckoning. Of particular significance was the concern for a ritual or halakhic consensus among all Jews—based, naturally, on what each group believed to be the true interpretation of the biblical cycle of holy seasons. Dramatic breaks within ancient and medieval Judaism and of course between early Judaism and Christianity thus found concrete expression in calendrical terms. For example, when the early Christian church determined that the Sabbath was to be reckoned on Sunday and not on Saturday (as was the custom from ancient biblical times) or that Easter could not fall on the Passover festival, it became effectively impossible for early Christians (committed to Jesus as Messiah) to also remain Jews in practice. Similarly, the reckoning of time relative to the life of Jesus (e.g., A.D.) and the adjustment of the months to the pagan Roman civil calendar further distinguished the two communities. For Jews time was reckoned, through biblical chronologies, back to the creation, and the beginning of the year coincided with a late Babylonian calendar (discussed below). Thus the Jewish New Year beginning in autumn 1986 (October 4 or 5 of that year, but varying slightly in other years) was celebrated by Jews worldwide as the year 5477 since the creation of the world. Some Jews have also dated their times from the fall of the Temple in 70 C.E., but this was never common practice. Thus, even by such broad computational matters, the calendar conveys the significant religious and historical orientations of those who live by its structures. [See Christianity pp. 497–98, 535 for discussion of Passover and Easter.]

The Calendrical Cycle of Holiness

Daily Prayers and Patterns

The cycle of holiness begins for the traditional Jew upon awakening. The *halakha* regulates these initial acts, as it does all others. At this time it is customary (for the male after putting on a skullcap, called *kipa* or *yarmulke*) to wash and recite prayers that reflect the dependence of the human creature on the Creator and the need to be respectful of this attitude at all times. One of these morning prayers, and often the first young children are taught, states: "I give thanks to You, living and enduring King, who has restored me to my soul, with the great grace of Your trust-worthiness. The beginning of wisdom is the fear of the Lord . . . [whose] praise is everlasting." A series of prayers that emphasize the divine gift of knowledge, of daily sustenance and care, and of the consciousness of Jewish identity and its obligations begins the order of the service. These may be recited alone or with the community at morning worship. Traditionally, this prayer service and all other obligations whose "time is fixed" (a halakhic category) are incumbent upon the male but not obligatory for women with household responsibilities. Some of women's fixed obligations will be mentioned later.

All males thirteen years and over are required to pray three times daily and to wear phylacteries during the morning service. These phylacteries, called *tefillin,* are ritual prayer boxes containing biblical quotations that are secured to the forehead and customarily to the left arm by leather straps. This ancient practice is based on the biblical passages that say that one should bind the teachings of God as a "sign upon your hand and frontlets between your eyes," that is, as a constant reminder of divine duties. The *tefillin* on the head now symbolizes the obligation to serve God with one's mind and the one on the arm, near the heart, symbolizes divine service with one's emotions. In early rabbinic times and through the Middle Ages especially, saintly persons wore *tefillin* at all times. Women are also permitted to wear them but have been customarily discouraged from this practice until very recent times and only among certain more liberal though traditionally minded Jews. Similarly, a male wears a prayer shawl, called **tallit,** with special knots and fringes, during daily morning prayers, though the prayer leader also wears it at afternoon and evening services. It is common for Jews to raise the shawl over their heads in prayer as a means of facilitating private devotion and concentration. Very traditional males also wear such fringes attached to a type of undergarment, thus further fulfilling an ancient biblical injunction. Such prayer garments are not customary for women, though the outer shawl has begun to be worn in recent years. The purpose of the fringes is to aid one "to remember all [the] commandments."

The opening section of the morning prayers are composed of biblical psalms and of rabbinic prayers especially emphasizing the themes of creation, revelation, and redemption. Thus a variety of historical and theological issues are brought to mind, particularly one's dependence upon God in nature and history and the obligations one owes God for his guidance and teachings. The affirmation of divine unity (the Shema prayer, cited earlier) is a major event in this part of the service (and again when recited in the evening service). For Jews it is a moment of personal and collective testimony to the principles of mono-theism—the unity of God and all life under God. So central is this affirmation that it is customarily recited before sleep and as part of the death confession. It was also recited by Jews who died a martyr's death on account of these very principles.

A major prayer—called, in fact, "The Prayer" (*ha-Tefilla*)—climaxes the morning and virtually every Jewish service. The morning version has tradition-ally eighteen separate prayers (fewer on the Sabbath). These prayers proceed from praise to petition (for wisdom and health, for justice and peace, and for the restoration of the kingship of David and the ancient Temple service). "The Prayer" is silently recited while standing—hence it is also called "The Standing Prayer" or Amida—and immediately repeated aloud by the prayer leader along with a series of sanctifications recited communally. On Mondays and Thursdays (ancient market days), the weekly Torah portion is read publicly in an abbre-viated form, so that all Jews might "fulfill the commandment" of Torah study in public. Final prayers concerned with personal needs and collective redemption conclude the service.

The afternoon (*minhah*) and evening (*ma'ariv*) service are more abbreviated versions of the morning (*shaharit*) worship, with occasional variations on it. Most significantly, the Shema is recited twice daily, and "The Prayer" and an Adoration are recited in all three daily services. The Adoration is recited with great reverence (and in ancient and medieval times and still today on special occasions with an act of genuflection). It opens with the words: "It is incumbent upon us to praise the Master of All . . . who has not dealt with us as with other peoples." Acknowledging their special historical destiny, Jews go on to recite the messianic hope. "We therefore hope in You . . . to speedily see the splendor of Your might"—the end of idolatry, the national restoration of Jews to their home-land, and the reunification of all the peoples of the earth. The concluding line of the Adoration is commonly sung by all as the great climax of worship: "And as it has been said [in Scripture]: the Lord will be king over all the earth; on that day the Lord will be One, and His Name One."

Only after morning prayers does the traditional Jew eat breakfast. All meals are preceded by a ritual handwashing (with prayer) and a benediction over the food: "Blessed are You, Lord our God, king of the universe, who brings forth bread from the earth." Other blessings for other foods can be substituted, and these are carefully fixed by rabbinic *halakha*. After the meal, a cycle of prayers in thanks to God "who sustains all life" is recited. And all through the day, special events in nature (like seeing marvels or the simple wonder of a sunset) or between per-sons (like reunions and partings or beholding human grandeur or despair) can be the occasion for special prayers. In all this there is to be found a religious atten-tiveness to all life as a divine gift. An old rabbinic dictum states that one who receives the benefits of the earth without thanking God is "like a thief."

We may recall here the statement of Maimonides cited earlier, that the goal of the commandments is to teach the Jew proper service of God in all things. We may add, given that Maimonides was the author of a legal code, that this service extended from the prayer house to the community and business world. From the traditional perspective, the performance of all one's behaviors within the moral framework established by halakhic regulations (recall the categories of the Mishnah) was also a form of acknowledgment of divine lordship. There is thus daily verbal prayer (petition and praise) and daily nonverbal action (halakhic duty). Each in its own way expresses subservience to divine rule. Not restricting themselves to fixed halakhic regulations, the pietists called Hasidim further devoted themselves to serve God in all ways at all times. They spoke of *avoda be-gashmi'ut,* "service through physical nature," by which they meant the concern to sanctify God's creation in every way, even through the most mundane physical acts. By this they only expressed in a more passionate way the basic religious assumption of halakhic Judaism: that service to God is to be performed in and through the concrete details of daily life.

The traditional Jew is thus fully conscious at every moment of every day that he or she is responsible to the Torah and the commandments. Years of training, study, and practice make one highly sensitive to whether actions are halakhically permitted or not—and this sensitivity is, in fact, at a high level of daily awareness. But this does not mean that the traditional Jew normally feels constrained by this orientation or burdened by it, for the immediate goal is to become competent in the traditional practices in order to serve God through the commandments. The greater the skill and competence, the more completely will the practices be internalized and performed with an unconstrained sense of personal inflection. Accordingly, for the traditional Jew the *halakha* is experienced as a divine gift that guides one through the maze of possible actions. Indeed, via the *halakha* a Jew commonly feels the "rightness" and "order" of earthly actions, their "world-building" and "covenant-confirming" character.

Nor do traditional Jews normally feel burdened by the commandments, for their whole goal is obedience to God, and the commandments are the concrete means toward that end. There is thus very great emphasis in Jewish practice on resisting routinized performance and practicing the commandments with attention and joy. In fact, one of the most important value categories related to traditional observance is called *simhah shel mitzvah,* "the joy of the commandment." It may take various forms at various times. One form is mostly affective in nature and leads one to enact the details of the law with visible joy. The Psalmist's dictum to "serve the Lord with gladness" is thus internalized in this mode and given external expression through passionate involvement in the *mitzvot.* The second form of "joy," quite related to the preceding one, is focused on what is called *hiddur mitzvah,* "enhancing the commandment" through additional acts. It is thus the biblical dictum "this is my Lord and I shall exalt Him" that is internalized in this mode and expressed through the constant desire to dramatize one's loving performance of the *mitzvot* by adding more and more features to them. The frequent comment that one has the *mitzvah* or special merit and opportunity to perform a given *mitzvah* thus conveys the conviction of the Jew that in and through the joyful performance of the commandments one can continuously express the willing acceptance of God's covenant.

Weekly Prayers and Patterns

Perhaps no occasion in the life of the Jew is more dominated by the obligations of unstinting joy or more focused on the halakhic details of "permitted/forbidden" and "sacred/profane" acts than the Sabbath. Coming each week at Friday dusk and celebrated until Saturday eve (though routinely one "delays concluding the Sabbath and hastens to begin it"—this being *hiddur mitzvah*), the Sabbath is both the climax and focus of the week. Special foods are customarily prepared or set aside for the Sabbath, special guests or unexpected travelers are invited, and the labors and distractions of the work week are consciously disregarded. From classical times to the present day the Sabbath has been the day when every male Jew was king and his wife a queen, when the Jewish nation royally accepted "Queen Sabbath" into its midst, and when the joys of paradise and redemption were anticipated. Already in ancient sources the Sabbath is referred to as a "mystery" of God's, as a special expression of divine grace for the people of Israel. In one old midrashic source it is stated: "If one keeps one Sabbath as it should be kept, the Messiah will come. The Sabbath is equal to all the other precepts of the Torah." In the mystical tradition, the "mystery" of the Sabbath is profounder yet, symbolic of ultimate divine harmonies and cosmic restoration. A passage from the *Zohar* called *raza de-Shabbos,* "the mystery of the Sabbath," is still sung on Friday evening in many synagogues as part of the First Sabbath service.

In a traditional home, the approach of sundown on Friday marks the final stage of Sabbath preparations. Because the Sabbath day traditionally recalls the completion of the creation and God's rest from this labor, no work is permitted on this day. All cooking is completed before the onset of the Sabbath, and perhaps the stove is also lit for reheating the previously cooked food. Electric lights will also be switched on in advance of the Sabbath, since the strictly observant consider even the use of noncombustive types of burning produced by electricity an extension of the biblical prohibition against igniting a fire on this day. For this reason, nowadays electrical appliances are also avoided (except the refrigerator, since the surge of current is considered incidental and not the result of intent). In addition, business instruments and money are set aside for the duration of the Sabbath.

When these matters are completed, the more spiritual preparations are undertaken. In certain circles it remains customary to precede the Sabbath with a ritual ablution, to prepare special clothes for use (often white ones, an old symbol for purity and grace), and to get oneself into the proper frame of mind though mental reflection or study of a pious text. It remains customary to recite the Song of Songs, whose contents from ancient rabbinic times have been interpreted allegorically as God's love for Israel. More mystical understandings regard this relationship as symbolic of profound unifications in the divine realms. In many communities, the recitation is done in the synagogue immediately before the inaugural service on Friday (before sunset), when the "Queen Sabbath" is welcomed.

Shortly before sunset two Sabbath candles are lit and blessed by the mother of the home; this is one of her traditional obligations, along with the baking of Sabbath loaves (called *halah*) which are braided in a customary way. The candles and two loaves of bread (for the evening and next day) along with the wine for sanctifying the Sabbath day dominate the table. These accoutrements symbolize the fullness of blessing and resemble the setting of the candelabra and shewbread in the ancient Temple. In fact, an old rabbinic dictum states that "[one's] table is like an altar," and this interpretation gives a heightened ritual aura to the setting.

The traditional Sabbath service begins late Friday afternoon with psalms about the divine Majesty and Kingship, along with a medieval hymn welcoming Queen Sabbath. The regular evening service then continues with some special additions marking the Sabbath day. After these prayers, and throughout the Sabbath, the customary salutation is a blessing for Sabbath peace—in Hebrew *Shabbat Shalom* and in the colloquial Yiddish *gut Shabbos*. After the Sabbath evening service (recited in the synagogue or at home), the family then gathers at table where a special hymn to the "angels of peace" is recited and the children are individually blessed by their parents. Before the adult male recites the benediction over the wine and the sanctification over the day (the Kiddush prayer), he customarily sings a biblical hymn of praise to his wife (Prov. 31:10–31). In mystical understandings, this hymn is directed to the mysteries of cosmic union, symbolized by masculine and feminine imagery. After a ritual handwashing (as at every meal) and a benediction over the bread, a festive meal with traditional songs is enjoyed. If guests are present, they will be invited to lead a song or teach the gathering some "word of Torah." The guest is also often honored with leading the grace after meals.

The special holiness of the Sabbath day is thus marked by a festive mood called *oneg Shabbat,* "Sabbath joy." Indeed, one is enjoined to make the day joyous and different from other days in both deportment and attitude. Certainly the strict restriction ensuring "rest" gives the day a tone and rhythm affected by natural light and natural human relations—not artificial lights or goal-oriented behaviors. Many Jews are also concerned that the topics of conversation befit the spiritual character of the day and that thoughts be restricted to themes of Torah, God, and loving-kindness. Since ancient rabbinic times, in fact, a quasi-legal category called *shevut* has been recommended. This category emphasizes a concern for mental and emotional rest, for a general "letting go" of everyday concerns on the Sabbath.

The full rhythm of the day dramatizes the themes and ideology of Judaism. The Kiddush on Friday eve, along with the synagogue hymns, stresses the imagery of creation and new beginnings. The morning service on Saturday, which generally expands upon the regular daily service, climaxes with a communal reading of a lesson from the Torah (and also the Prophets), and so celebrates the divine revelation to the nation. And the late afternoon service on Saturday and the concluding prayers "separating" the Sabbath from the week (called the Havadalah, or "Separation" service) give special emphasis to the theme of messianic renewal and redemption. The celebrated medieval author Rabbi Isaac Arama, in his *Akedat Yitzhaq,* stressed that these major phases of the day symbolize the three central themes of Judaism: creation, revelation, and redemption. Moreover, already in ancient times the three phases of the day coincided with three Sabbath meals. In medieval mystical circles, special cosmic significance was attributed to the celebration of each one. More recently, among the Hasidim, the third meal (called *se'udah shelishit,* or colloquially *shale-shudes*) was deemed a most "favorable time" to commune with God, and the rabbi then delivered a special Torah teaching. Rhythmic chants, holy tales, and shared food add to the "messianic" atmosphere of the occasion. An additional fourth meal has been added by some, to prolong the holiness of the day and accompany the Sabbath Queen as she departs from the community. This festive time is called the *melave malke.*

As these final meals are dominated by Torah study, so is the whole Sabbath day affected by it—especially the central ceremony on Saturday morning when the weekly Torah portion is read out loud. It is a momentous occasion, preceded by taking the Torah scrolls from the ark (the Torah is still written on special skins in the ancient script) and parading them around the congregation. All congregants face the processional of the long scrolls, which are robed in fine cloth and adorned with high silver crowns. Many reach out to touch or kiss the holy objects with great veneration. Laid upon a high reading desk, the Torah of Moses is then unfurled and a selection chanted in the ancient melody. This is done each week of the year (with special readings on or near festivals). In ancient times, in the land of Israel, the entire Pentateuch (the Five Books of Moses) was recited over a three-year period, but the Babylonian custom to conclude the reading in one year now prevails. In more recent times, attempts to abridge the weekly lection have been innovated, but the idea of a continuous and unbroken reading of the Torah remains among traditional Jews. Symbolic of this is the custom of reading a brief excerpt from the following week's portion during the Sabbath afternoon service.

In all these ways the centrality of the Torah in the life of the people is dramatized. Significantly, too, only the Torah lection is read out in the service—even though members of the congregation will follow along with texts that include rabbinic comments, and even though all know that it is just these comments and interpretations that give the Torah its distinctly "Jewish" character. The reason for this is to emphasize the divine word alone and to distinguish that from the history of its interpretation. For the community, this high ceremony of reading the Torah is experienced as a renewal of the ancient revelation. It is therefore an occasion of deep mythic significance for Jews.

Yearly Festivals and Sacred Days

Although some of the festivals are agricultural in origin and others are not, there is calendrical continuity in the fact that the lunar phases that help to reckon the ancient seasons still determine the monthly countings. Thus many festivals occur on the fifteenth day, or full moon, of a month. And there is also a basic symmetry to the calendrical year. For example, preparation for the spring holiday of Passover (Pesah, often in April) begins on the tenth day of the first month (Nisan), and the festival itself commences on the fifteenth and lasts a week. Actually, according to Pharisaic tradition, the first day is celebrated for two days, as is the seventh, hence for a total of eight days, exceeding the biblical requirement. The reason has to do with the ancient problem of notifying communities in the Diaspora, those dispersed throughout other lands, when a new moon preceding a festival was sighted. Owing to communication delays, these communities did not always know if a certain month had thirty days rather than twenty-nine, and so they celebrated the ensuing festival with an extra day at the onset and at the conclusion for precautionary reasons. (This practice has become customary to this day outside the land of Israel, except for Reform Jews). Beginning with the second day of Passover (according to Pharisaic tradition) a period of forty-nine days is counted off, culminating with the festival of Pentecost, or Shavu'ot (celebrated for two days).

Balancing these spring holidays in the first month are a series of autumnal celebrations a half year later. The first of these is the New Year festival, called Rosh Hashanah (observed for two days) at the beginning of the seventh month (Tishri). It is followed ten days later by the Day of Atonement, known as Yom Kippur (a one-day fast). On the fifteenth of the month, the festival of Tabernacles, or Sukkot, is celebrated for a week plus a final eighth day of Solemn Assembly. Because of the custom of adding an extra day, the total holiday period is nine days in all—though since the Middle Ages this last day has been celebrated as a separate holiday called Simhat Torah, the day of the "Rejoicing of the Law." On this day, the annual Torah reading is both concluded and immediately inaugurated once again. Other annual festivals include the ancient Arbor Day celebration (called Tu Be-Shevat) on the fifteenth of the eleventh month (Shevat), once called the "New Year for Trees," and Purim, celebrating the Jews' ancient deliverance from a threatened persecution in the days of the ancient "Persians and Medes," on the fourteenth of the twelfth (Adar) month (but on the fifteenth day in ancient walled cities, like Jerusalem). The anomaly that the months are counted from the spring but the New Year occurs in the seventh month is due to the adoption during the Babylonian exile of a late Babylonian calendar (and its names).

As mentioned, many of the festivals originally had an agricultural origin (Passover celebrates the ripening of the barley grain, Pentecost is the time of the harvest of first fruits of the soil, and Tabernacles celebrates the ingathering of crops) and served in biblical and rabbinic times as pilgrimage seasons and times of ritual donations to the shrine and Temple. However, from early biblical times, many of these seasonal festivals were given historical significance. Thus the festival of Passover was reinterpreted in biblical antiquity as a commemoration of the Exodus from Egypt; and Pentecost, in later rabbinic times, came to commemorate the revelation of the Torah at Mount Sinai. Similarly, the rabbinically ordained festival of Hanukkah, commencing on the twenty-fifth of the ninth month (Kislev), may originally have been related to solar rites at the winter solstice (the holiday had the ancient name of "Festival of Lights") but came to commemorate the rededication of the Temple and the rekindling in it of the holy flame from pure oil preserved despite the desecration of sacred objects by the Greeks. According to a tradition, this cruze of oil miraculously burned for eight days, so the holiday is celebrated for this many nights with burning candles or wicks.

Other days, like the fast Tisha B'Av on the ninth of the fifth month (Av), may also have had agricultural roots (like the ancient festivals on the fifteenth of that month) but came to commemorate the destructions of the First and Second Temples, as well as the exile from Spain (in 1492). In recent years, this fast day is also a time when the horror of the Holocaust is recalled, though this latter event now also has its own memorial day (on the twenty-seventh of Nisan), immediately prior to the day recalling acts of Jewish heroism and resistance during World War II (on the anniversary of the Warsaw Ghetto uprising). Like these more recent occasions, the ancient and medieval calendar was full of days of fasting and commemoration, though not all are still observed. Thus there are minor fast days (like that commemorating the assassination of the governor Gedalia in biblical times; or the twentieth of the third month [Sivan], which was a major day throughout the Middle Ages for recalling martyrologies), as well as festivals of national liberation (like the day of Nicanor in antiquity; the many Second Purims of the Middle Ages celebrating local victories or release from tyranny; or the Day of Independence in recent times, on the fifth of the second month [Iyyar], celebrating the establishment of the State of Israel in 1948). Like the older festivals and now the newer ones, lore, customs, rituals, special foods, and symbolic interpretations provide the concrete expressions and thoughts of living Judaism.

Quite apart from the historical reinterpretation of the nature festivals of antiquity, another layer—of spiritual interpretation—is commonly added to the symbols and rites of the holidays. This transforms them into days of holiness and contrition, in accordance with the Jewish spirit. Thus, for example, the command to eat unleavened bread (called *matzah*) throughout the Passover period has come to indicate the need for penitential abandonment of the sin of pride and self-aggrandizement (the act of "swelling" with pride or "puffing" oneself up), as symbolized by the forbidden leavened bread. Similarly, the halakhic injunction to search one's home diligently to remove all leavened goods before the holiday has often been interpreted as the need simultaneously to cleanse one's inner being before the festival. In this way the celebration of the historical release from bondage is correlated with an act of personal transformation as well.

But all these and other spiritual reinterpretations of ancient holidays pale in emphasis and depth before the most holy and spiritual of days in the Jewish year: the days that occur before, during, and after the New Year (at the beginning of the seventh month Tishri). This period, known as the Days of Awe, traditionally begins in the preceding month of Elul and extends through the seventh day of Tabernacles (called Hoshana Rabba). It is a time of somber self-scrutiny and acts of repentance. Throughout this time blasts of the ram's horns (*shofar*) are blown, symbolizing the need to awaken from spiritual slumber and return to God. This concern for spiritual and moral renewal (called *teshuvah*) is especially marked during the period from Rosh Hashanah to Yom Kippur, which is known as the "Ten Days of Repentance." On Rosh Hashanah itself all Jews gather for communal prayers and high celebration of Beginnings. The extended synagogue liturgy emphasizes the themes of world and individual renewal; of God as Creator, King, and Judge; of the need for divine mercy; and the humbleness of mortal existence. The services are marked by special liturgical poetry that repeats in many modulations the religious themes of this holy period. Special liturgical melodies, which express the majesty of the divine kingship and the humble neediness of human life, also give the services a special and memorable timbre for the worshipers. The Torah readings chosen for this time and the complementary selections from the Prophets reinforce the liturgical themes as they stress the frailty of ongoing life and the eternal hopes of the human community.

In this connection, it is important to add that links between family and friends are especially marked during this period. Festive meals for relations and others are very much part of the socially integrating customs of the New Year. It is furthermore customary for Jews to visit the graves of ancestors during the period of penitence. In this way earlier generations have beseeched their "righteous dead" to intercede for them and their sins before the Mercy Seat of God and have integrated memories of loss with personal and communal hopes. Jews commonly greet one another during this period with the blessing "May you be written and sealed [in the divine Book of Life] for a good year" and with hopes for "a good and sweet year." On Rosh Hashanah it is traditional to dip apples in honey and to pray for a year of sweet renewal. It is also an old custom among Jews to buy new clothes for the New Year. In this way the prevalent themes of newness are dramatically expressed, for clothes typically symbolize spiritual status and hope. Similarly, many adult males wear white outer garments at this time to symbolize the desire for purity and spiritual rebirth. Often a male will receive and first wear a white robe (colloquially called a *kittel,* after the Greek *kiton*) on his marriage day; he then wears it yearly at the Passover meal, on Yom Kippur, called the "Sabbath of Sabbaths," and finally as a shroud.

Yom Kippur is the climax of the extended period of penitence and renewal beginning in the month of Elul and is observed through strict fasting and self-scrutiny. The liturgy for this most holy day begins a little before sunset (of the tenth of Tishri) and, after a night pause, continues from early the next morning through sunset of that day. This great Day of Awe emphasizes self-examination, repentance, and need for God-centeredness. The liturgy is filled with the hope and confidence of divine mercy, but humbly so; and it is replete with extensive confessions and meditations (read silently and aloud with the community). Significantly, an old ruling in the Mishnah emphasizes that the prayers and ritual of Yom Kippur only atone for sins between the individual and God, not for sins between one person and another. For this reason it is customary to seek personal forgiveness or reconciliation from members of one's family and community before the beginning of the prayers. The Jew thus moves first to strengthen links of interpersonal solidarity and then to the matter of the personal relationship with God. It should be emphasized that the transition to privacy before God is neither abrupt nor final. Throughout the liturgy the individual repeatedly recites confession in a collective voice ("we," "us") and bows down or sings with the community. Nevertheless, Yom Kippur is a time of great interiority and private reflections.

This most holy day ends with a final burst of theological confession and joy at the possibility of new beginnings and the sense of divine forgiveness. The Shema is proclaimed, as is the eternal Kingship of God, and the community joins with songs of hope in a speedy redemption. It is at this time that a long, final blast of the *shofar* is sounded (one hundred blasts are blown on Rosh Hashanah). This final blast is thus no longer a piercing or wailing call for self-awakening and contrition but a triumphant blast that follows the communal proclamation that it is one fellowship under One God. The Jew, robed in the solemn garments of death (the *kittel*) and behaving in many ways as a mourner, goes through an inner process of death and rebirth—as did the prophet Jonah, whose story of rebellion, repentance, and renewal (with the symbolism of death and rebirth through the episode of the great fish) is recited on this day. Significantly, at the close of the service family and friends gather for a festive meal that symbolizes the social solidarity of the community as each individual is drawn out of solitariness for the shared tasks of the new year.

As a further gesture of the return from the liminal, liturgical zone of Yom Kippur to the world of the community, it is customary on that very night to begin building an arbor booth, or *sukkah*. It is within this temporary structure that meals are taken during the festival of Tabernacles (Sukkot), which follows five days later. The fragility of the booth and its openness to the high heavens and raw nature symbolize for the Jew the fragility of all earthly constructions and the dependence of all creatures on their Creator. The building of the booth and the celebration of an ancient harvest rite with a bouquet of plants and fruits is thus the first act of world-building after the sustained period of penitential withdrawal beginning in Elul. Its repetition each year is part of the deep myth and ritual of Judaism.

While periods like the Days of Awe involve a balance between personal solitariness and communal solidarity, other holidays, like the festival of Passover (Pesah), give more complete expression to communal celebration. This national holiday emphasizes the collective nature of redemption from bondage in Egypt. It is traditionally celebrated as a family meal and recitation (thus preserving the ancient biblical rite), together with special synagogue observances. The Passover meal, or **seder,** is modeled on an old Roman banquet format (complete with the kinds of hors d'oeuvres Romans ate) but is linked to a recitation, called the *Haggadah,* of the wondrous events of the Exodus. The structure of the recitation involves questions and answers, discussions and rabbinic commentaries, and biblical narratives and hymns. Medieval rounds are sung with great gusto at the finale.

The recollection of redemption and divine power are the recurrent themes of the day, and personal and collective identification with Jewish history are the great imperatives. It is incumbent upon each Jew to identify with the story of the Exodus by elaborating on the original event or by discussions that seek to make the ancient event of liberation relevant in each generation. The Passover meal is also the time of somber historical recollection: The *matzah,* or unleavened bread (eaten during the entire festival), as well as the herbs and condiments eaten symbolize the suffering of the ancient Israelites and the mortar for the bricks during their forced labor. But the central meal, which interrupts the *Haggadah* recitation, is also a time of family joy and ingathering. Central to the family ritual on this night is the youngest child, the bearer of the future, who is raised to preeminence as the initiator of the questions that precede the *Haggadah* recitation. The other young children have other, more gamelike, roles to play in the *seder,* which turn the event into one of great mirth.

A more solemn time in the family service occurs after the meal, when the door of the house is opened to invite the prophet Elijah (the traditional harbinger of the Messiah) to partake of the celebration. This invitation with songs of future redemption has been supplemented since the Middle Ages with a curse against those who have killed the Jews over the centuries. And indeed, in Jewish memory Passover has not only been a time of hope but, falling as it does near Easter, a time of fear, for this was the time of frequent church-sponsored persecutions or vilifying blood libels (Jews being falsely accused, in the Middle Ages and up to recent years, of killing Christian children to use their blood for baking *matzah*). Heinrich Heine's famous story of *The Rabbi of Bachrach* strikes familiar dread in the hearts of Jewish readers. In this tale, at the moment when the door was opened for Elijah, it was not this messianic precursor who entered but rampaging Christian mobs. This and other accounts of destruction and bloodshed were told over and over again in Jewish historical chronicles.

But we should also add that the symbolism of liberation of Passover has also inspired great acts of spiritual resistance. Stories of the celebrations of the Passover in the Warsaw Ghetto and the concentration camps during World War II are as awesome for the human daring involved as they are powerful expressions of the Jewish use of myth and ritual for acts of antihistory, for a rejection of the history of brutality and power in favor of a history of spiritual dedication.

In all these forms, Jewish life has dramatized its deepest convictions and memories. Memory and ideology are thus not abstract matters but concretely represented throughout the course of the calendar year. Quite evidently, then, this calendar cycle determines the rhythm of thoughts and feelings of the Jew the year round, pacing and balancing religious moods and awareness and providing the occasions for living the religion. It is for this reason that *halakha* has often been popularly defined as a "way" of life and that the goal is not abstract belief but "being Jewish" through action and performance. The basic fact that ideology and belief are carried by the *halakha* and its rituals and are not of much independent value is paradoxically expressed in an ancient rabbinic comment. It is there stated by God that he would rather that the people of Israel rejected him but continued to obey his Torah. Jewishness is therefore expressed not in theological abstractions, but in the ongoing acts of life, acts that suffuse the order of the day and establish the tempo and content of

Judaism itself. Each act and gesture is thus part of a vast organic web of meaning and significance. The totality of all this is tradition. [See Religions of Africa pp. 74–75, Religions of Mesoamerica pp. 229–38, Native Religions of North America pp. 308–16, 351–57, Christianity pp. 551–55, Islam pp. 674, 677–79, Hinduism p. 829, Buddhism pp. 937–41, Religions of China pp. 1021–24, and Religions of Japan pp. 1140–46, 1153–62 for description and discussion of festivals and annual celebrations.]

The Life Cycle of Holiness

Rites of Passage

In addition to the recurrent daily and seasonal patterns of Judaism, the nonrecurrent moments of personal life are also given ritual distinction. These moments celebrate or mark times of new beginning and transition from one life stage to another. They dramatize the transience of individual existence, while highlighting those social symbols that give the community its identity and integrate the person into a larger sphere of meaning. Moments of passage are thus crucial in a double sense. First, while stressing the transience of life, they also provide the means of transcending this terror through the enduring symbols of religious meaning. Thus if the individual life is mortal, the ongoing community is a symbol of collective immortality and the permanence of values. Second, while stressing the transience of life, rites of passage also provide the means of transition from one life stage and one sphere of responsibility to another. They thus confirm the hierarchies of value of the community. And they also project an ideal sequence of personal development the individual can look forward to, so that, upon reaching each stage, a person can evaluate his or her maturation against a collective standard. [See Religions of Africa pp. 42–51, 76–79, Religions of Mesoamerica pp. 201–6, Native Religions of North America pp. 278–79, 295–98, 306–8, Christianity pp. 542–43, 555–57, Islam pp. 677–78, 680–86, Hinduism pp. 747, 807–14, Buddhism pp. 915–17, 921, 931–37, Religions of China pp. 1019–21, and Religions of Japan pp. 1146–50 for description and discussion of rites of passage.]

BIRTH Birth is naturally the first major moment in a person's individual and communal life. When a boy is born, a circumcision rite called a *brit* ("covenant," short for *brit milah*, "covenant of circumcision") can be expected eight days later. This ceremony, of great antiquity, confirms the transition of the infant from being a child of Adam, as it were, to a member of the Jewish people. Thus the boy enters the "covenant of Abraham." The minor operation is delegated by the father to a ritually trained surgeon, called *mohel*. The *mohel* receives the child after he has been passed among the relatives, beginning with the mother (in a separate room; she is customarily secluded at this time). Just before the boy is given to the godfather (called *sandek*) to hold while the operation is performed according to the ancient procedure, the *mohel* temporarily places the child on a "chair of Elijah"—symbolic of the hopes of redemption. After the actual circumcision, the child is handed to the father (or an honored guest) while the *mohel* recites blessings in praise of God and for the welfare of the child. It is then that the boy's name is announced. The name (e.g., David son of Abraham) will be how the boy will be "called up" when he is honored to bless the Torah in later years, and this name will be marked upon his tombstone at death. From antiquity some Jews have had double names, a Hebrew name and a related vernacular name (e.g., in Hellenistic times one might be Jonathan or Matthew and Theodore, names all meaning "gift of God") or names that could function in both the ritual and secular communities. Among Ashkenazi Jews, it is customary to name the boy after a deceased relative; Sephardis, however, do not adhere to this practice. A joyous moment in the circumcision ceremony is when the entire assembly exclaims: "Just as he has entered the covenant, so may he enter [the study of] Torah, the wedding canopy, and good deeds." Thus a life cycle is outlined, which all the adults confirm through their own lives. [See Religions of Africa p. 76, Christianity p. 496, and Islam pp. 677–78, 680, 682 for discussion of circumcision.]

The naming ceremony for a girl traditionally takes place in the synagogue during a subsequent Sabbath service, when her father is "called up" to the Torah. In recent times in more liberal contexts, the mother is involved in this occasion, and new rituals for the birth of a girl have been developed. One of the more popular designations for these ceremonies is *simhat bat,* "joy [for the birth] of a daughter." [See Religions of Africa pp. 45–46, 76, Native Religions of North America p. 307, Christianity p. 556, Islam p. 682, Hinduism pp. 810–11, Buddhism p. 932, Religions of China pp. 1019–20, and Religions of Japan pp. 1146–47 for description and discussion of birth rites.]

RELIGIOUS MAJORITY The *study of Torah* traditionally begins quite early, for boys perhaps when they are three or four years old; and, according to custom, this event is inaugurated by having the child find and trace the letters of his name which are covered with honey. This act symbolizes the hopes for the sweetness of life devoted to Torah and the commandments. From youth, a boy will be instructed in Hebrew and the traditional classics of Judaism, but he will not be a formal member of the halakhic community until he is thirteen years old. At that time he will become a **bar mitzvah,** literally a "son of the commandment(s)." He can then perform all the *mitzvot* and is required to do so with full responsibility for his religious behavior. When the boy is first "called up" to the Torah, symbolic of his attainment of majority, the father utters a blessing commemorating this transition to adulthood.

A girl traditionally achieves majority at twelve years and a day, a time symbolic of the onset of menstruation, and is by then fully instructed in the intricacies of maintaining a ritually correct home, in the traditional rules of menstrual purity, and in some of the sacred texts. In recent times, girls are given fuller academic instruction in the traditional literature (though this varies by group) and in liberal contexts a *bat mitzvah* ceremony ("daughter of the commandment[s]") has been developed to mark the rite of passage. The degree to which this ceremony is part of the traditional service depends upon the strictness of the group. Some communities give a girl the same Torah ceremony as a boy; others only give her some ritual part in the Friday evening service; and still others limit this involvement to some celebratory action outside the framework of the *halakha*. There is naturally a high correlation between how a girl celebrates her majority status as a doer of *mitzvot* and the role of women in a given ritual community. Strict traditionalists, concerned with the separation of the sexes and the more minor ritual status of the female, will thus regard the moment as a female affair. Those groups that variously reject traditional rules about women (particularly matters of segregation in prayer, formal exclusion from the prayer quorum, and fewer required positive commandments) will correspondingly regard the moment of a girl's majority as a more ritual event along the lines enjoyed by males. Nowadays, such matters are subject to local rabbinic-communal regulation, though the communities themselves feel subject to the authority of different rabbinical institutions and their rulings on these halakhic matters.

MARRIAGE   For traditionalists and nontraditionalists alike, the wedding canopy is a major moment of personal and social transition. The male and female take their place as productive communal citizens and fulfill the first *mitzvah* of the Torah: to "be fruitful and multiply." The wedding is thus the transition to the basic Jewish institution of the home and to responsibility for the welfare of the community. In earlier times and still in some ultratraditional circles, marriages are arranged among peer groups. In such traditional groups, a bridegroom will not see his bride until near or on the wedding day; though nowadays when marriages are generally affected by more romantic inclinations, and contact between groups is also more flexible, a period of acquaintance for the future couple is more common. Most modern traditionalists enjoy more flexible dating patterns, as do liberal Jews.

In Talmudic times, a stage of "betrothal" (*kiddushin* or *erusin*) preceded the "nuptials" (*nisu'in*) by some time period. The two stages were combined in the post-Talmudic period and are celebrated together in the present Jewish wedding marriage ceremony. This latter formally begins in the afternoon (the bridegroom and bride having separately returned from ritual ablutions, a traditional practice), when the ancient contract formulas are reviewed by the "Arranger of *kiddushin*" and the document (*ketubbah*) is signed by witnesses. This *ketubbah* is read at the ceremony itself, along with seven blessings extolling the beauty of creation and the joys of companionship. The male will customarily wear his white *kittel* and recite the traditional marriage formula ("You are betrothed to me, with this ring, in accordance with the laws of Moses and Israel"). In Ashkenazi ceremonies, the couple shares wine and the groom breaks a glass. One explanation of this old custom is that it is a popular defense against evil spirits. Another interpretation gives a more moral explanation, saying that it recalls the sadness of the Temple's destruction in moments of joy. Among some Sephardis, the cup is smashed with wine in it as a sign of plenty. Related to such gestures of good omen, or *mazel tov,* it is customary to perform weddings at nightfall in view of the stars (which symbolize the divine promise to Abraham that his descendants would be as numerous as the stars), and on Tuesday (because of the double repetition in the biblical creation account of the phrase "and God saw that it was *good*" on that day). In certain periods associated with death or unfulfillment, marriages may not be performed.

It is considered a special *mitzvah* to praise the bride and entertain the groom. A whole repertoire of how one should dance before the bride and of the mirthful or mocking songs are part of the rich tradition linked to the event. In strictly traditional groups the dancing is performed by males and females in separate groups, and the bridegroom and bride are each hoisted up on chairs as the guests whirl roundabout. It is also customary to extend these festivities over a long period of time after the wedding day. Thus friends in different locales may invite the couple to a joyous reception where the seven blessings of the marriage ceremony are recited by honored guests. Torah teachings are given, and the *mitzvah* "to make the bridegroom rejoice in his bride" is fulfilled. Since the covenant at Sinai was imagined by the ancient rabbis as a wedding between God and Israel, with the Torah as the *ketubbah* and Moses the "go-between," a deeper theological background is conveyed by the marriage occasion. The mystical understanding of the unity of male and female as symbolic of deeper divine and cosmic harmonies adds to the aura of the event. [See Religions of Africa pp. 48–51, 77–78, Christianity p. 556, Islam pp. 683–84, Hinduism pp. 809–10, Buddhism p. 935, Religions of China p. 1020, and Religions of Japan p. 1148 for description and discussion of marriage rites.]

DEATH The consummate symbol of new social life, marriage, is indirectly linked to the final life stage, death. First, the white *kittel* the groom first wears on his wedding day will be his shroud, just as the prayer shawl (*tallit*) he receives at marriage is often used to form the bridal canopy and will be wrapped around him at death. Second, the children who are the manifestation of new family life will provide for social continuity after a parent's death and will be obliged to mourn for the dead parent and care for the other. And finally, just as a special meal is provided after the circumcision and wedding ceremonies, so is it customary for a "meal of consolation" to be provided the mourners by relatives and friends upon the return from the gravesite. In this way the transition to death is linked to symbols of social celebration and continuity.

Since death is the liminal moment par excellence, dramatizing the ultimate changes of status for the deceased and relatives, and because the occasion of death is one of great anxiety and disrupts established social patterns, all the procedures connected with the event are carefully regulated by the *halakha* or fixed custom. There are thus several postmortem periods that require different actions by the living. These periods have traditionally been correlated with the stages of departure of the deceased's soul and are recognized by different terms.

The period between death and burial (usually within three days) is the first stage. Upon hearing of the death of near kin, the mourner (now called *onen*) rips his or her garments and acknowledges God as "the true Judge." Great restrictions are imposed upon the *onen*. Shaving, the wearing of leather, and certain types of washing are forbidden. He or she recites psalms, is exempt from most positive commandments, and makes sure that the body of the deceased is ritually purified and dressed in a shroud (earth from the land of Israel is customarily placed in the simple wood coffin for those dying "in exile"). "Watchers" stay awake with the corpse and recite psalms. After the burial ceremony and the first recitation of the **kaddish** prayer (a glorification of God's power and redemptive help), the second mourning stage begins. It is called *shiva* ("seven," in Hebrew), for this mourning period lasts seven days. From this time on the mourner is known as an *avel*. Near relatives stay together at the home of one for the week and customarily sit on low seats. During daily prayers performed in the house of the mourner certain prayers are deleted and psalms added. Consolation is bestowed by the community by visiting the bereaved after morning prayers, or before or after evening ones. This is considered an important *mitzvah*. Customarily a visitor will not initiate conversation with an *avel*, respecting the mourner's private mood; if a conversation is started, it is considered proper to restrict the topic to the merits of the deceased. Upon departing from an *avel*, one says (in Hebrew): "May the Almighty comfort you, together with all the mourners of Zion and Jerusalem."

After *shiva* the mourner returns to normal activities, though refraining from celebrations (also haircutting and newly pressed clothes) for thirty days. During this period (the third stage), too, and for eleven months thereafter (the fourth stage), the *kaddish* is recited in communal services. Throughout this period, the mourner will not sit in his or her customary seat in the synagogue— another sign of this liminal period. This stage closes with the unveiling of the tombstone. On the anniversary of death according to the Jewish calendar (called in Yiddish *Yahrzeit*) and during subsequent holy days when special memorial recitations occur, the former mourner again rises to recite the *kaddish*. During the *Yahrzeit* for a relative, the male will often be honored with leading communal prayer. In some circles, it is also customary to hire someone to recite the *kaddish* for the deceased if this would not otherwise be done. Such prayers for the "souls of the departed," that they "find rest in the Presence of the Almighty," are thus of important emotional and ritual significance.

Through such periodic memorials the dead are not "cut off" from the community. Moreover, as noted earlier, ancestors are remembered by having their names given to newborns and by visitation to gravesites before Rosh Hashanah (also on the *Yahrzeit*). In addition, martyrs of the past are remembered on Sabbaths and holy days, and graves of saints or sages of the past have often been sites of pilgrimage—pilgrims pray there for divine blessing through the intercession of this "righteous holy one" in Heaven. The graves of Rachel and the patriarchs in the land of Israel have been places of prayer and pilgrimage for certain Ashkenazis, especially Hasidim; and *hilula* ceremonies at the tombs of sages and relatives are still common among Sephardi Jews. In recent years, the death-camps where Jews were murdered in Europe during World War II have been the locale of memorial pilgrimages, as also the Yad Va-Shem shrine in Israel. The power of the memory of ancestors and persecution are thus very dominant in Jewish life and pervade the consciousness of Jews at different levels the year round. [See Religions of Africa pp. 42–45, 78–79, Religions of Mesoamerica pp. 144, 229–33, Native Religions of North America pp. 300–301, 307–8, 335–37, Christianity p. 557, Islam pp. 684–85, Hinduism pp. 813–14, Buddhism pp. 935–37, Religions of China pp. 1021, 1041–44, and Religions of Japan pp. 1149–50 for description and discussion of death and funeral rites.]

Crisis Rituals

If the ordinary cycle of Jewish life is something on the order of "one continuous worship service with minor interruptions," personal and communal crises engage another level of ritual behavior. In highly traditional circles, from antiquity to recent times, a whole range of popular and often officially sanctioned (though not always halakhic) behaviors have been practiced. Thus ancient Talmudic spells and medieval and later magical recipes (such as those found in the tract *The Angel Raziel*) have been used to ward off evil spirits at childbirth or special occasions, to promote fertility and counteract disease, and to dispel the effects of a bad dream. Among other crisis rituals still practiced in some traditional circles, one may particularly mention the practice of fasting in the wake of a bad dream. Such self-imposed fasts are regulated by halakhic norms. Another still common act is the custom of changing the name of a gravely ill or dying person in the hope that the new name will inaugurate a new lease on life (and also "trick" the Angel of Death into believing that the moribund person has died). Even persons who have otherwise little link to such procedures may nevertheless perform them as a gesture of desperation or hope. In a similar way, the custom of placing notes with petitions at the gravesite of a holy ancestor or especially of placing them in the cracks of the so-called Wailing Wall of the ancient Temple in Jerusalem is still common among Jews of all persuasions. For some, this act is of great supernatural benefit; for others, it remains a folk custom or charm—but one not to be disregarded for all that.

The performers of crisis rituals vary with the halakhic status of the acts. Thus, in medieval times individuals might divine their own daily fate through forms of bibliomancy (randomly opening the Bible—especially using Psalms—and taking this passage as a key to personal fortune); or, in particularly dire circumstances, they might have recourse to the special prayers and charms of a midwife or rabbi. On the other hand, rituals against drought, plague, or persecution affecting the entire community were integrated into the halakhic format of daily life and given official sanction, just as the crisis of martyrdom (called *kiddush ha-Shem*, "Sanctification of the Divine Name") was also a halakhically regulated procedure for both group and individual. In premodern times it was also quite common, in the face of natural or historical disasters, for persons to undertake great acts of penitence involving self-mortification but also almsgiving "to avert the severe decree." It must therefore be noted that in the history of Judaism crisis rituals were not only of a personal and self-centered nature, but they also involved special acts for the welfare of the community. Even more, in late medieval mystical groups especially, the supernatural dimension of the natural or historical crisis was the main focus of attention. And so rituals designed "to repair" a cosmic crisis or imbalance affecting human life below were performed with great passion and conviction. In all these ways and at all these levels, crisis rituals demonstrate the powerful function of ritual actions to order and sustain one's personal or social world.

The Social Circles of Holiness

The rituals of Jewish life typically occur in several expanding spheres, though the boundaries are not always firmly fixed between them and most activities can occur in all spheres. Thus, to move from the home to the synagogue does not mean that personal prayer is restricted to the home and group prayer to the synagogue or that table fellowship and study are greatly different in either place. Similarly, to move beyond these two spheres to the wider communal realm does not mean that the legal aspects of life or acts of charity are restricted to this latter domain. Nevertheless, each sphere (home, synagogue, and community) is a special locus involving distinct types of social interaction and frames of mind. They therefore require separate consideration.

Family and Home

Traditionally, the home is the nuclear holy space and the family the nuclear ritual unit of Judaism. To the doorpost at the right of entry a Jew affixes a **mezuzah,** a case with a Hebrew parchment on which the biblical Shema passage is inscribed. The *mezuzah* is thus an external sign that the house is "Jewish" and a symbol of the Jewish values and behavior espoused inside. Today most Jews continue this custom even if the home life is largely nonhalakhic. The *mezuzah* thus functions partially as a good-luck charm and loose badge of social identity. In more traditional homes, the *mezuzah* functions as a holy object separating the outside "profane" from the inside "sacred" space. Crossing the threshold (and venerating the *mezuzah* by touching it and kissing one's hand) is thus a ritual act: a movement inward, from the world to the distinctly Jewish domain.

Here, in the home, the dominant value is *shalom bayit* ("the peace of the home"), regulated by strong codes of parental respect and hierarchy. Honoring one's parents is a child's duty of great importance, a *mitzvah* advocated even in the most trying circumstances. Correspondingly, care for one's children, including educational and financial support, is considered a primary parental duty. Such patterns of respect and hierarchy are customarily expressed in many ways, but particularly at the table. Children do not sit in their parents' chairs, eat before parents say the blessing over food, or leave the table until parents conclude grace after meals. This hierarchy is somewhat disrupted during the Passover, when children inaugurate the *seder* rite with questions and songs, but it is also more fluidly interrupted at all family moments of ritual sharing, when the children are given acts of honor and involvement.

The table, compared earlier to an altar, dominates the home for festive and daily occasions. The food eaten is traditionally *kasher* (colloquially, **kosher;** i.e., halakhically "proper") in terms of the dietary regulations involved. Crustaceans and pork (among other "fish" and land animals) are prohibited by biblical law, and mixtures of dairy and flesh products (so-called milk and meat; colloquially, *milchig* and *fleishig*) are prohibited by rabbinic law. Moreover, permitted land animals (like cows, also fowl) must be ritually slaughtered by special procedures that include soaking and salting the meat so as to drain off the blood. [See Islam pp. 646, 681, 694 for discussion of kosher.]

Accordingly, all table fellowship is at the same time ritual fellowship. The related consideration is that, because of strict adherence to these regulations, strictly traditional Jews will not eat in Gentile homes or allow "nonkosher" food into their own. Thus, ritual fellowship determines table fellowship. In this way, food becomes a symbol of social difference and group maintenance. In modern times, minor gradations of observance of the ancient dietary rules are common, so that some traditional Jews will eat dairy or vegetable food outside the home under certain circumstances. The use of public (nonkosher) restaurants for such purposes is thus, further, a statement about one's halakhic position on these matters. Symbolically, where and how one eats extends the domain of the home and structures the types of personal contact one will have. For this reason, some lenient moderns may observe forms of dietary propriety (*kashrut*) at home but be more flexible outside, thereby indicating that their Jewishness is a "private matter" only. Observance of traditional food rules is thus a key indicator of a Jew's overall halakhic observance and general attitude toward assimilation to non-Jewish patterns.

The Synagogue

In traditional Jewish life, the synagogue has functioned as a house of prayer, a house of study, and a place of communal assembly. All these functions are interrelated (since gathering together for prayer includes the hearing or recitation of sacred texts; and the study of sacred texts commonly occurs in gatherings in prayer rooms). Because of this close relationship between prayer and study, the synagogue is colloquially (in the Ashkenazi sphere) referred to as Shul (*Shul* is a Yiddish word for synagogue and school). Moreover, "to go to Shul," in the common parlance, may mean to gather in the synagogue for prayer, for study, or for fellowship.

The synagogue is thus the center of the traditional Jewish community, the shared building and symbolic home for all. In its formal seating structures (the traditional segregation of male and female or the less traditional integration of male and female), in its informal seating patterns, and in its political structures and system of ritual honors, the Shul dramatizes the public values and social hierarchies of the particular community. Moreover, because traditional Jews are halakhically prohibited from driving on the Sabbath and festivals, they tend to live in close proximity to one another and to the Shul. This factor further heightens their social interdependence. Indeed, the fairly restricted nature

Great Leningrad Synagogue. Jews may gather for a prayer quorum in homes, in special buildings, or in nature. Synagogue architecture has varied with place and time. The Torah Ark is at the eastern side. (Photo by Bill Aron.)

of this reference group for esteem and fellowship has tended to encourage halakhic conformity and social propriety among the members. Formally, rabbinic scholars and the halakhically pious dominate the hierarchy of the traditional community; but the wealthy "householder" and the bestowers of synagogue honors have always exerted great informal social control. In less traditional circles, where driving is permitted (at the least to attend Sabbath or festival services), the synagogue is not within the near radius of all homes, and so it is also not the only place where members may interact communally. In these circumstances, the range of values and patterns of social evaluation are more varied and tend to conform to the social and value hierarchies of the wider society.

Nevertheless, to be a "Shul-goer" (or synagogue- or temple-goer) is somewhat synonymous with being a practicing Jew in accordance with the halakhic norms of one's immediate community. Synagogue membership is thus an assumed pattern of association where one can fulfill communal halakhic obligations, become more knowledgeable about Jewish life and culture, and generally mingle with other Jews who share similar lifestyles and values. Nowadays, in areas of great Jewish population density, there is an obvious correlation between how close one lives to a synagogue and the degree to which Jewish behaviors and attitudes are central. In the less populous Jewish areas of modern America, membership in a synagogue will be maintained even at great distances, since it not only provides for occasional ritual needs but expresses needs of ethnic-social identity as well.

The Community

As we have seen, a number of Jewish values are expressed in and through halakhic behaviors. Thus one is obliged to feed guests and give them shelter, to give charity to the poor and maintain Jewish charitable institutions, to help needy Jews worldwide through financial and political intercession, and to return lost objects and visit the sick. All these are fixed halakhic obligations, or *mitzvot*. But they may also tend to have a superhalakhic dimension too, for to say that it is a *mitzvah* to do the above behaviors does not simply imply them to be commandments, but the "right thing"—something that transcends individual convenience or personal satisfaction. Thus when a Jew says that "it is a *mitzvah*" to help the poor or to be just, he or she means that such acts are dominating values that take precedence over all else whenever the occasion arises. Moreover, to say that some behavior "is a *mitzvah*" is to give that act the ultimate authority and motivation. It is to say that it derives from the official code of Jewish behavior and that it is an essential feature of it. Today, when nontraditional Jews explain their involvement in social causes, philanthropic associations, or politically related Jewish activities, they may refer to such work as "a *mitzvah*." By this they regard their actions as "Jewish" in some sense and as expressive of their "Jewishness." Further, they tend to see their actions as expressions of Jewish moral teachings and their devotion to this work as "religious" in some sense. For this reason, many such moderns feel with strong conviction that in performing acts of Jewish communal service, they are "good Jews," though in traditional circles and in more formal terms this attribution is not a moral evaluation but a halakhic one, bestowed upon one who conforms to the halakhic consensus.

The obligation to work for the community is thus a traditional Jewish value with broad modern nuances. In fact, for Jews, there is no social value higher than "love of the people Israel" (*ahavat Yisrael*)—concern for the welfare of all Jews. Social factors of isolation, memories of persecution, and the historical need for communal self-reliance have certainly contributed to this. Nevertheless, the holy texts of Judaism, from the Bible on, together with the traditional daily liturgy all express the firm belief that the God of Israel is the Creator of all and that all creatures descend from Adam. Accordingly, the wider moral category of "love of fellow creatures" (*ahavat ha-beriyot*) as well as the ideals of universal peace and reconciliation remain essential and repeated traditional values in Judaism. The liberal wing of modern Judaism has promoted universal concerns to a preeminent status in its religious ideology. In this, such liberal Jews have kept the conscience of Judaism attuned to its ancient ideals.

The preceding treatment of Judaism as an ideological and ritual system can be expressed in abbreviated form in the following diagram. In brief, it shows the basis for covenantal monotheism in God's creation of humans to serve him in love. For guidance they were granted a covenant with obligations extending to every area of life. This teaching is mediated through Moses and the prophets in biblical times, and by the rabbinic sages thereafter. The Jewish community attempts to live a life of holiness and to follow Jewish principles and ideals. The covenantal monotheism of Judaism establishes patterns for the spiritual life, which are enacted by rituals, prayer, and study. The welfare of the needy is basic to its spiritual life.

God created humans to live a life of holiness before God, but giving humans freedom to obey or disobey God; due to disobedience, pain, death, and misfortune entered the world.

The divine call that made covenantal monotheism possible

THE SPIRITUAL LIFE OF COVENANTAL MONOTHEISM

to heed the call of God
to live as the chosen "people"
to serve God with faithfulness and love

Patterns for the spiritual life:
BIBLICAL PROPHETS (MOSES)   GREAT RABBIS/SAGES

Rituals and practices:

WORSHIP	RITES OF PASSAGE	STUDY	PRAYER	MYSTICAL PATH	DIETARY AND CULTURAL LAWS
sacrifices (in ancient and early Rabbinic times) Shema daily prayers weekly prayers (Sabbath) yearly festivals	birth/ circumcision *bar mitzvah* marriage death	Torah Mishnah *Midrash* Talmud			

Contact with holy things:
TORAH   SYNAGOGUE   PHYLACTERIES   ISRAEL (WAILING WALL, ETC.)

The great ancestors such as Abraham, Isaac, and Jacob responded to this message of God; Moses received God's laws and instructions for the Jewish people to live a life of holiness. The content of biblical revelation and prophetic and priestly tradition constitute Jewish covenantal monotheism. The content of the Bible and the transmission of prophetic messages and priestly practices constitute the religious expression (revelation and traditions) of the Jewish community.

THE JEWISH COMMUNITY

attempts to live a life of holiness
in obedience to and worship of God;

maintains a spiritual life of covenantal monotheism
(thisworldly holiness and salvation,
as well as otherworldly concerns);

and attempts to establish Jewish principles
in all areas of life and civilization (culture).

The ongoing acts that lead people away from a life of disobedience to a life of obedience and holiness in expression of covenantal monotheism and a meaningful human/cultural life

The monotheistic message that Jews affirm is the source of true religion (holiness) and meaningful human existence

Convenantal Monotheism in Judaism.

18
Jews and Judaism in Modern Times

AT THE CONCLUSION of our historical discussion in chapter 16, various changes affecting Jews and Judaism in modern times were considered. Central among these were transformations of a social and psychological nature, the increased decentralization of Torah, and the revival of Jewish nationalism. While these developments may be seen as separate phenomena, they are also deeply interrelated. The splintering of medieval Jewish communal and religious structures increasingly exposed Jews to the varieties of general culture around them and to such liberal concerns as natural reason and natural rights. For those subject to these influences, virtually nothing was left unexamined and virtually everything was subject to choice or decision. Should one remain a Jew and in what way? Is Judaism compatible with "general culture," or should it be changed? Are Scripture and rabbinic literature the only authoritative texts, or might one be instructed by literary creations from other cultures? And finally, should Judaism be one's only or primary loyalty or might there be other groups with compelling claims upon one's moral or religious sensibilities?

These and many more questions circulated among Jews from the mid-eighteenth century on. As noted earlier, some pockets of Jewry resisted change, but nowhere was the decision to change or to resist taken without thought or care. Each person had to make a choice of some kind. Accordingly, the modern world for Jews is characterized by the pressure of just this option: either to resist the power of tradition and commit oneself to a new and larger world or to resist the new ideas of modernity as threats to traditional truths and forms. Of course, only at the radical edges of the spectrum was the choice posed in such a polar way. Most Jews were more compromising, although these solutions were also asserted in manifesto-like forms in the early period.

The processes and possibilities set in motion in the eighteenth century are still very much part of Judaism today. Indeed, two hundred years is a comparatively short span of time within which responses to the modern assault on two thousand years of tradition might be worked out. In this sense, Judaism is still deeply involved in the dynamic of its "reformation," and the emergent shapes are still very much in flux in both traditional and nontraditional circles. To gain some sense of this variety, we shall first focus on several expressions found in two European cities and then on several others in two different countries, Israel and the United States. The examples are typical of the times and their temper.

A Tale of Two Cities: Vilna and Frankfurt am Main

Vilna

Soon after receiving the rights of settlement in the sixteenth century, the Jews of Vilna (now Vilnius), Lithuania, quickly established that city as the pre-eminent center of traditional Talmudic piety in northern Europe. Its stature reached unparalleled heights in modern Jewish life through the example of Rabbi Elijah ben Solomon. Also known as "The Gaon (Eminence, Genius) of Vilna," Rabbi Elijah Gaon was born in or near Vilna in 1720 and died in that city in 1797. He has been called the "last great theologian of classical rabbinism," and in the context of the new ritual and ideological developments of his day, Rabbi Elijah took his stand as a staunch, authoritarian supporter of Jewish medieval tradition. Rigidly and censoriously he resisted any deviance from the old Jewish norms. As one of the last towering figures of Talmudic rabbinism, the Gaon of Vilna became a symbol of resistance to "unauthorized change" in Judaism (that is, change not authorized by certain ultratraditionalists) as well as a model of devotion to tradition and its comprehensive truth claims.

Born to a distinguished family of scholars, Elijah ben Solomon was quickly recognized as a child prodigy when he had mastered the Bible and traversed "the sea of the Talmud" by the age of six. As a youth, he mastered the *Zohar,* practiced various mystical-magical behaviors, and expanded his interests to include mathematics, astronomy, and botany. He mastered all these disciplines on his own (for Jews were not part of any public educational system) in an attempt to comprehend his Jewish sources. For him, "everything that was, is, and will be is included in the Torah—and not only principles, but even the details of each species, the minutest details of each creature, plant, and mineral." According to Rabbi Baruch of Shklov in the introduction to his translation of Euclid done at the request of the Gaon (1780), Rabbi Elijah said that "to the degree that a man is lacking in knowledge of secular sciences he will lack one-hundred-fold in the wisdom of the Torah." Here then is a unique ideology for the use of Western science *in the service of the truth of Torah.*

The productive output of the Gaon's learning is astonishing. Over seventy scholarly books and pamphlets have been attributed to him. Some he penned himself, while others were culled from the marginalia he inscribed on his copies of classical texts or from the lecture notes of his faithful disciples. He was a profound annotator of virtually every book in the rich traditional library of Judaism: the Bible, the Mishnah, the Babylonian and Jerusalem Talmuds, the volumes of legal and homiletical *midrash,* assorted mystical texts (like the mystical-cosmological *Sepher Yetzirah* or obscure sections of the *Zohar*), and the legal codes (like the *Shulkhan Arukh*). He even wrote on Hebrew grammar in the medieval style. His all-absorbing and fanatical dedication to the truth of Jewish texts led Rabbi Elijah to become a scholarly and religious ascetic, who lived in his home with the shutters boarded up, studying by candlelight so as not to know if it was day or night. According to the testimony of his son, the Gaon never slept more than two hours a day and even then never more than a half hour at a time. Such was the stuff of legend, to be sure; but similar examples of scholarly devotion to the divine word are known from earlier ages and in the practices of sages of more recent times.

It may be because Rabbi Elijah had become an independent scholar at such an early age that he was remarkably free of the style of complex Talmudic dialectics (called *pilpul*) then still in vogue in Poland and Lithuania and was able to develop his own critical style of rabbinic study. Indeed, for all his traditionalism, the Gaon in a way paradoxically anticipates features of the modern critical study of the Talmud. For him, the primary condition for textual criticism was a disciplined reason, with no reliance upon the opinions of earlier authorities. In the course of his study, the Gaon became aware of what would later be called "lower textual criticism," for he came to realize that many older laws or formulations were based upon passages that had become corrupted in the course of their scribal transmission. He thus sought to restore original textual readings by conjectural emendations that are feats of intuitive genius. By this means he

Talmud study is a sacred obligation, performed alone or in study groups and often in the local synagogue. Talmud study is at the core of the traditional rabbinical curriculum. The Talmud is learned through an oral, singing recitation. (Photo by Bill Aron.)

hoped that the *halakha* would be firmly established upon the basis of the "original" readings of the sources, not upon the accumulated errors of their copyists. The Gaon was also involved in what would later be called "higher textual criticism," for he was also aware of discrepancies between parallel formulations of halakhic rules in the Mishnah and *midrash* or between the Babylonian and Jerusalem Talmuds, and he tried to resolve them and deal with such issues as their relative historical priority. Since the goal of all this study was to plumb the depths of divine Truth, Rabbi Elijah's rigor was ruthless and his independent spirit a subject of awe.

In all his ways the Gaon of Vilna was a distinct personality. And, as remarked, he represented the old path of traditional rabbinism in the face of the many new currents then swirling about in the Jewish world. A brief glance at the world to the west and east of Vilna in his day will bring out this point.

Glancing westward toward Berlin, we see Moses Mendelssohn (1729-1786) living among the rational philosophers and advocating the study of nontraditional subjects for spiritual and cultural development. Like his fellow Maskilim ("Enlightened Ones"), he felt that the old curriculum of learning was not sufficient for the proper cultivation of the human "spirit" or for furthering the integration of the Jews into the larger cultural mainstream of Europe. Clearly for Mendelssohn, unlike the Gaon, "everything" was not "included in the Torah." Moreover, he did not consider the Torah to be the *revealed* source of eternal truths. As a philosopher of the times, Mendelssohn distinguished between a religion of reason and empirical teachings. The truths of reason are eternal and open to all persons and they are not dependent upon a special revelation. Empirical teachings, on the other hand, are temporal truths of fact and subject to ongoing experience. So viewed, the Torah of Judaism is not unique for its eternal truths (which are accessible through reason to all), but rather because it contains revealed laws that guide and formally constitute the Jewish polity. As Mendelssohn argued in his book *Jerusalem* (1783), this polity exists no longer, so that the modern Jew is thoroughly a citizen of the secular state and *its* legislative constraints. For Mendelssohn and for his circle, religion was thus a private and inward matter; they argued that as long as people conformed to the outward public good there must be tolerance for divergent religions and their practices. Variations on this theme have resounded in modern Western religious life, both Jewish and non-Jewish.

The Gaon of Vilna never publicly turned against the Maskilim, perhaps because those of his day still remained observant Jews. But he could not have disagreed more strongly with their more diminished notion of Torah and their advocacy of secular study. Nor would he have appreciated the irony that his style of textual criticism would be developed in succeeding generations among Jews who advocated the "Scientific Study of Judaism" for the sake of pure historical reconstruction and also as a means of demonstrating the cultural richness of Judaism to Christians. Much closer to home, it was rather the ways of the Hasidim that evoked Rabbi Elijah's ire. Now since the Hasidim were observant Jews who also believed in the mystic and absolute truth of Torah, the Gaon's hostility to them must be traced to the threat this new movement posed to traditional structures of rabbinic authority.

As noted earlier, Hasidism developed patterns of charismatic authority and often demoted Torah study before such values as group and individual mystical experience. To the strict Talmudic traditionalists, these features reawakened memories of the failed messianic movement (led by the apostate Sabbatai Tzvi) that had rocked Jewry a century earlier. They were thus vigilant against any new expressions of nonconformist behavior in Judaism. In addition, there was also anger at some new variations introduced by the Hasidim into the liturgy and ritual slaughter. The combination of these factors, experienced at intense emotional levels, induced the Jews of Vilna to draw the Gaon into the thickening fray and issue edicts of excommunication against their fellow Jews. Given the animosity of the edicts and counteredicts over a long time, it is not the least of historical ironies that the new changes brought on by modernity eventually produced an unofficial alliance between the Hasidim and their erstwhile "opponents" (called Mitnaggedim) against the "godless secularists" or reformers. A further irony is that, in more recent times, the Hasidim have themselves emerged as the last bastion of conservative orthodoxy and regularly issue edicts against both the "godless" and other (even ultra-) traditionalists who deviate from their norms.

Let us return to Vilna. One of the Gaon's celebrated students, Rabbi Hayyim ben Isaac, sought to reinvigorate traditional life and piety with a new *yeshiva* (rabbinic academy) established near Vilna, in Volozhin. Founded in 1803, it became one of the most celebrated academies of Talmudic rationalism in the nineteenth century and contributed generations of rabbis to Jewish life until it was closed by the Russian government in 1892. A brief glimpse of the daily schedule in the *yeshiva* may give some indication of the structural pattern of a traditional Talmudic study regime and its passionate dedication and rigor.

The official day began with the morning *shaharit* prayers at 8 A.M., after which the students (which Rabbi Hayyim refered to as "the men of the *yeshiva*") had breakfast. Following this, the weekly portion of the Torah was studied and explained along with traditional commentaries by the principal. Study of the Talmud (and later commentaries and codes) then proceeded in groups (which Rabbi Hayyim preferred to self-study) from 10 A.M. to 1 P.M. After this, a major lecture was given. In the 1880s the lecture during the first part of the week was given by Rabbi Hayyim Soloveitchik and in the second half of the week by Rabbi Naftali Tzvi Berlin, both renowned for their incisive Talmudic analyses. Following the lecture, the midday meal was taken and the students were free until 4 P.M., when the afternoon *minhah* prayers were recited. Students then studied until 10 P.M., when the evening *ma'ariv* prayers were conducted and supper followed. Most students would then return to the *yeshiva* to study until midnight. They would then sleep until 3 A.M., when they would return to their benches to study until morning prayers. The method of study cultivated in the *yeshiva* was intense scrutiny of the Talmudic text and independent "straight thinking" (not excessive logical pyrotechnics). The ideal was *torah li-shemah,* study for the sake of pure understanding. According to Rabbi Hayyim, Torah study was a form of direct communion with God. Among the "men of the *yeshiva*," such study was combined with a strong emphasis on the objective performance of the commandments and a corresponding derogation of their subjective, experiential component (the Hasidic way). Students would remain for years in this intense atmosphere, and they were examined by the principal once each term.

The atmosphere of scholarly diligence and piety at the Eitz Hayyim *yeshiva* in Volozhin became legendary. Among the famous glorifications of such Talmudic asceticism and devotion was a poem written by one of its former students, the modern Jewish poet laureate Hayyim Nahman Bialik (1873–1934). In "The Eternal Student" and "On the Threshold of the House of Study," Bialik sings nostalgically of the faithful dedication of such divine service, a service that required the student to sublimate all feelings for nature and beauty for the sake of a single-minded devotion to the spiritual ideal. He recognized that this devotion had "formed the heart of the nation." But, like others of his generation who began to read widely in Western culture, the exclusivity of Talmud study and the fixed patterns of traditional Jewish life seemed narrow and repressive. Nostalgia was thus coupled with anger and rejection. The ancient theme of the Temple service (which we have repeatedly touched upon in these pages) is symptomatic of these changes. Bialik likens the house of study to the Temple of old and the decay of the ideals of traditional learning and self-sacrifice to the destruction of the ancient Shrine. Faced with this new loss and in despair over the crisis of faith, Bialik exhorts an entire generation to return to Zion and rebuild their ancient homeland. In a speech delivered at the opening of the Hebrew University in Jerusalem (1925), the poet likened the new builders of the land to the priests of the Temple. The new "service" was thus devotion to the renewal of national culture on a spiritual foundation. In this regard, Bialik worked tirelessly to revive the Hebrew language, reedit national religious classics in new forms for the modern imagination, and help establish educational institutions that would implement the ancient ideals of Judaism in new ways.

Bialik emigrated from Russia to the land of Israel and settled in the new city of Tel Aviv in solidarity with the new centers of creativity and work the pioneers had established throughout the land. Jerusalem was the ancient holy city, representing the traditional Zionist longings of millennia; Tel Aviv, the "Mound of Spring," was to be the symbol of the new Zionism, of the self-created life in the homeland with its ideals of a return to nature and physical labor. Thus, if the ancient Temple ideals of *avodah* (shrinal "service" and work) had been transformed over the centuries to include divine "service" through study and observance of the commandments, this term was utterly transformed in early Zionism to refer to physical "work" on the land. *Avodah* now became "service" to the nation and the national-spiritual renewal through productive and self-reliant "work." Indeed, this was the new form of "worship" for all those Jewish pioneers for whom the ancient faith no longer made a truth claim upon them, but who nevertheless remained Jews in both spirit and sensibility. Some of the new "returnees to Zion" were, in fact, aggressive secularists concerned with restoring a lost national connectedness to the cycles of nature (from ancient Canaanite and Israelite times). Others sought to transmute the spiritual teachings of the past into new forms—a sort of cultural alchemy. But all were dedicated to transforming the old *"galut* Jew" into a new breed, into a self-reliant actor in history, into a person devoted to physical and moral renewal in the homeland. In waves, the idealists and the oppressed of the ancient nation "went up" to the land "to build and be rebuilt in it" (as an early "work song" had it), just as generations before "went up" to the Temple and Torah service. The old word *aliyah* (the act of "going up") thus took on a thoroughly new meaning.

Through the reinterpretation of old religious symbols like *avodah,* through a renewal of the ancient ideal of a return to the ancestral homeland, and through the reapplication of traditional texts, Zionism is in many respects a continuation and new expression of the Jewish religious spirit. Even a staunch traditionalist like Rabbi Abraham Isaac ha-Cohen Kook (1865–1935), the Ashkenazi chief rabbi of the land of Israel from 1921 to his death, recognized this and regularly intervened with the ultratraditionalists on behalf of the secularists. Also a product of the Volozhin *yeshiva* and an almost exact contemporary of Bialik, Rabbi Kook understood the national awakening in traditional messianic terms and saw the socialist pioneers as the spiritual vanguard of the nation. In a famous defense of the secularists, Kook stressed that when the ancient Temple was being built even ordinary "workers" could stand where, later, only the high priest could "serve." Traditionalists, he argued, should see through the external expressions of the "builders" to the deep "love of Israel" that motivated them. A profound reinterpreter of the mystical tradition, Kook worked for unity at all levels of human life. He sought to fan the "sparks of holiness" wherever they glimmered and to build through them a "new light in Zion." In his great theological work *Lights of Holiness* (three volumes), Rabbi Kook retaught the ideals of devoted service to God and the need to enhance the divine creative force in all things. This is a redemptive task he felt would unify the Jewish people. His goal was thus a reinvigoration of rigid traditionalism and a transformation of traditionless secularism through the energy of a common national *avodah* in the holy land. The unification of Jews in Zion actively devoted to peace and divine creativity would, he believed, be "the beginning of the (ultimate) redemption" that he, as a traditional Jew, awaited in faith. Rabbi Kook inspired a generation of religious and nonreligious Zionists alike.

Frankfurt am Main

A different range of modern Jewish expression is exemplified by various personalities of the western European city of Frankfurt am Main. Jews had frequented the annual fall fairs of this city from 1074 on and had developed there a distinctive set of ritual procedures. Prayer books still mention the "rites of Frankfurt" along with the standard Ashkenazi and Sephardi rites. Frankfurt Jewry developed during the Middle Ages and, by the mid–nineteenth century, boasted major Orthodox and Reform rabbis. In subsequent decades, Frankfurt was also the scene of major moments in modern Jewish life and thought.

Among the distinguished citizens of Frankfurt am Main was Abraham Geiger (1810–1874), who was a leading proponent of Liberal-Reform Judaism and served as a communal rabbi there between 1863 and 1870. He was one of the great founders and contributors to the "Scientific Study of Judaism" movement as well, and through his historical researches in the biblical text and the liturgy he gave support to the liberal view that Judaism was an evolving religious civilization. He opposed orthodoxy, which he judged to have become ossified and unaesthetic, and was among the proponents of a Jewish "mission" to spread rational faith in One God and his moral teachings. Geiger strived, like other reformers of the time, to turn Judaism solely into a religious community and eliminate all features that would separate Jews from the Gentile nations. He thus advocated praying in the vernacular (and not Hebrew), removing references to a "return to Zion" from the prayer book, and changing prayer formulations that no longer reflected current beliefs (thus the ancient prayer that God was "reviver of the dead" was changed to refer to him as the "source of eternal life"). Also, like other reformers before and since, he permitted instrumental music in the synagogue service and was lenient regarding some forms of Sabbath work. However, he opposed changing the Sabbath from Saturday to Sunday and rejected proposals to abolish the rite of circumcision.

Geiger met his future Orthodox adversary Rabbi Samson Raphael Hirsch (1808–1888) at the university in Bonn (1829) while both were students there in ancient languages and history. Though Hirsch was a product of a traditional Talmudic education, he was also influenced by the more enlightened wing of Orthodoxy that countenanced the study of Western culture. Indeed, one of the famous bywords associated with Hirsch and that influenced generations of Orthodox Jews was "Torah with *derekh eretz*," "the (traditional) study of Torah *with* secular studies." In addition, as a communal rabbi (he served in Frankfurt from 1851 to 1888), Hirsch introduced some liturgical adjustments (like adding a choir and preaching occasionally in the vernacular).

Nevertheless, Rabbi Hirsch was an opponent of Reform Judaism. In his theological work *Nineteen Letters* (1836), he not only stated that Judaism is an expression of God's will through the Torah but, by emphasizing that the Torah is a feature of divine truth and *not* dependent upon society, he diminished the significance of historical process as a factor affecting the development of Judaism. Such an attitude was rejected by Geiger and this led to a split between the former friends. Moreover, Hirsch's notion that Judaism is not solely a religious community but a "national religious consciousness" whose mission it is to teach the nations "that God is the source of blessing" further divided him from Geiger and reformist ideology. Indeed, for him the cultivation of *Menschentum* (Ger., "humanity") is but a preparatory stage in the development of *Israeltum* (Ger., "Jewishness"), whereby one is truly led to perfection. These ideas had (and still have) a great impact on Orthodox Jewish life. Hirsch propagated them from the pulpit, through such popular forums as the *Jeschurun* journal, which he edited, and in his Bible translation and exegesis. The latter was based on traditional notions of revelation and, because of Hirsch's denial that Jewish values and ideals had a historical development, rejected the critical approach to biblical interpretation then making headway in the universities of Europe.

In some respects, the difference between Hirsch's Orthodoxy and Geiger's Liberalism is the difference between those (the Orthodox) who would argue for the a priori nature of Jewish belief and practice, regarding such as the "objective given" to which subjective attitudes must conform, and those (the Liberals) who would argue for the a priori nature of historical subjectivity, regarding Jewish belief and practice as a product of human experience. A more mediating position is represented by Franz Rosenzweig, who was born in Cassel, Germany, in 1886 and died in Frankfurt in 1929. He typifies the estranged modern Jew, the product of Western culture, who could nevertheless return to a vital and unapologetic Jewish *life beyond Liberalism and Orthodoxy.* For many contemporaries, the model of his intellectual transformation and the model of his piety and integrity during years of a degenerative illness have transfigured the life of Rosenzweig into the story of a modern saint and sage.

Franz Rosenzweig did not start his religious journey from within a firm Jewish center. A highly assimilated home that only minimally conformed to the outer trappings of Judaism, Rosenzweig's family was more attuned to the values and concerns of the *Frankfurter Zeitung,* an influential upper-class newspaper of the time, than to Jewish tradition. As for many others, this attitude was not especially marked by a hostile rejection of Jewish ideology. It was simply based on the fact that Judaism no longer appeared as a vital spiritual force and so simply faded into the background before other interests.

Rosenzweig himself studied history, medicine, and philosophy and eventually produced the significant *Hegel and the State.* But already as a youth, shortly before World War I, he keenly felt the need for a vital religious life. And so, along with several other friends, Rosenzweig considered conversion to Christianity. After long probing, he determined to enter the church in the way advocated by the earliest Christian missionaries to the Jews—as a Jew, not as a pagan. In the course of his preparations, he visited a small Orthodox synagogue in Berlin during the high holy days of 1913. Rosenzweig emerged from the Yom Kippur service with the decision to remain a Jew. As he expressed it in a powerful exchange of letters with Eugen Rosenstock, Judaism was not an antiquated or parochial religion without vibrancy in the modern age. Moreover, he, a born Jew, had no need to come to God the Father through the Son, as did the pagans, for he was *already* with the Father. Redemption and nearness to God are always immediately available to the Jew, he maintained; no mediation is necessary. But he added, this does not mean that Judaism is superior to Christianity and will replace it in some ultimate future; neither does Christianity, for its part, fulfill or negate Judaism. Both ways are true; both Judaism and Christianity are valid expressions of religious truth and will remain so until the final redemption. Until that time, Jews must maintain their eternal, community-centered life of religious observance, inwardly regenerating like the fire of the sun, while Christians will continue to be the sun's rays, outwardly extending in time and space to convert the unbeliever to God. In his idea of a "double covenant," according theological validity to Christianity and challenging this religion to a reciprocal acknowledgment of Judaism, Rosenzweig parted company with almost all Jewish thinkers before him. His position opened the way to the possibility of genuine interreligious dialogue—without the triumphalist pride of either group and without hidden agendas of conversion.

Rosenzweig came to reject German idealist philosophy, which regarded concrete experience as secondary to pure thought. For Rosenzweig, true thinking is not abstracted from life but is deeply a part of it, beginning with the awareness of personal death and the uniqueness of each human life. This is the core of his celebrated "New Thinking," a type of commonsense theology that explored the concreteness of life lived with the awareness of death. Stationed on the Balkan front during World War I, Rosenzweig wrote out his religious thoughts on postcards that were sent home and subsequently published in 1921 under the title *The Star of Redemption.* In this theological masterwork, he fully developed his religious existentialism or, better, coexistentialism, for he believed that the individual person was never alone, but always working out his or her destiny with God.

For Rosenzweig, the truth of Judaism lies precisely in the capacity of its categories and behaviors to aid one to live dynamically with God, open to the ever-renewed givenness of the world experienced as creation, responsive to the ever-new demands of life experienced as revelation, and devoted to the work of love in the world for the sake of redemption. The Bible is thus the ongoing record of the concrete life of Israel in relationship with God and illustrates the profound truths of religious revelation as it makes claims upon persons and the community. Thus, Rosenzweig argued, the ancient Israelite, like the Jew of yesteryear or today, when faced with the immediacy of God's presence, did not experience the demands presented at the moment as external laws imposed from without. They were rather experienced as immediate commandments, as tasks that must be done for the sake of integrity and truth. This, he claimed, is the living religious source of the commandments in the Bible and in Judaism, for they are dynamic translations into human terms of the experience of God's loving presence. For this reason, tradition, which is the community's record of its attempts to "institutionalize" these moments of divine-human meeting and extend their reality into human life, is a valuable vessel of the sacred. Naturally, through overuse or abuse, the forms of tradition may lose their immediate impact and religious vitality. And so it may become necessary from time to time for religious individuals and alienated Jews alike to reexperience them afresh as powerful vehicles of an engaged religious life.

For a modern Jew, this appropriation of the ancient tradition as the bearer of authentic religious expressions may be extremely difficult. Indeed, Rosenzweig's close friend, Martin Buber, could not make the move toward a God who gave laws. Rosenzweig felt that Buber misunderstood or chose not to understand the issue. As for himself, Rosenzweig was willing to risk seeing the laws of tradition as potential commandments, but he realized that this willingness, or readiness, was only the beginning. The reappropriation of Judaism by the modern

Jew could not be done at once, he said, or without honest struggle, for the modern Jew is neither simply a believer who accepts the *halakha* nor simply an unbeliever who rejects it; he or she accepts and rejects at once, responding to the demands of tradition with the sensibilities of his or her own life and thought. In this attitude, Rosenzweig reflects his unique stance in modern Jewish thought. Like the perspective of Orthodoxy, he accepted the objective givenness and authority of the tradition; but he did not accept it as an absolute or necessary truth for himself until he lived it part by part. And like the attitude of religious liberalism, Rosenzweig accepted the importance of subjective choice in the ritual expression of one's religious life; but he also did not accept the arbitrary assumption that certain traditions are either antiquated or sterile *until they are experienced and lived.* Thus, he argued, one must start with life, with a positive decision to *live Jewishly.* For the assimilated or alienated Jew of his time, Rosenzweig's words and personal example were a provocation all the more challenging for the honesty they assumed and demanded. Nothing modern had to be rejected; no sense of individual freedom, no secular knowledge, and no life experience had to be foregone. On the contrary, all this and more was to be brought to the service of one's Jewish life. Only in this way, he felt, would Judaism be revived as a vital religious expression.

In the years that followed the war, Rosenzweig made some decisive personal decisions and actualized his visions in institutional form. He realized that an important carrier of the Jewish traditions and the bridge to its inner life and self-renewal was study. He established a model "school," the Freies Juedisches Lehrhaus in Frankfurt. The name was not fortuitous. As a "House of Jewish Study," Rosenzweig hoped to signal his distance from the dispassionate academic study of Judaism or, indeed, from any uninvolved intellectual accumulation of details. And he further hoped to recapture in a modern form the older style of "learning" of sacred texts in which what was studied was transformed into life. No texts were in principle excluded from the curriculum, and not all of the instructors in the Lehrhaus were "experts." The ideal was that teachers were also expected to learn and the students were also expected to teach; each was to give and receive reciprocally out of personal knowledge and experience. All that was required was the willingness to study the texts and bring them alive—in whatever way—in one's own life as vital forces. In this way a return to the sources would be a modern return to the roots of Jewish expression, where one could always learn and be instructed—provided that there was "readiness."

The Lehrhaus assembled among its teachers some of the more remarkable intellectual personalities of the time (including Martin Buber, Erich Fromm, Nahum Glatzer, Gershom Scholem, and Ernst Simon) and quickly became an adult education enterprise of enormous cultural significance. This went on for a number of years, at first under the direct supervision of Rosenzweig himself. After 1921, when he began to notice the effect of progressive paralysis, the immediate supervision of the Lehrhaus was taken over by colleagues and a new, more intimate Lehrhaus was formed in the privacy of Rosenzweig's apartment. Here, remarkably, with virtually no physical powers save eye movements, Rosenzweig carried on a voluminous correspondence, studied Jewish sources, especially the Talmud, translated and commented upon the religious poetry of Judah Halvei, and from 1923 on worked with Martin Buber on a new German translation of the Bible—one that cannot be read passively but must be engaged with the eye and ear "in life." (Ten volumes were jointly completed; the remainder were done by Buber alone over the next three decades.) As was traditional, this more private Lehrhaus, the "house of study," was also a "house of prayer," and Rosenzweig's friends conducted religious services for him over the years of his illness. Near the end (and not disclosed until after Rosenzweig's death), Leo Baeck, a liberal rabbi and theologian of great distinction (who refused to leave his people during the horrors of World War II and preserved for them the image of human dignity in the concentration camp of Theresianstadt), conferred upon Franz Rosenzweig the ancient rabbinical title of *moreynu*, "Our Teacher." For such he had become and would remain for many, his life and thought a new link in an ancient tradition and a testimony that Judaism could be revived as a vital reality for the complex but honest modern Jew.

Martin Buber (1878–1965), the close friend of Franz Rosenzweig and his collaborator in their joint Bible translation, walked a different path to Jewish commitment. Buber's early years were marked by an intimate awareness of authentic eastern European piety and of Maskil-like scholarship and also by a deep involvement in the aesthetics and attitudes of late nineteenth-century Europe. As a boy, he spent considerable time in Galicia on the estate of his grandfather, Salomon Buber, who in his spare time devoted himself to producing critical editions of midrashic works scattered throughout the world's libraries. This early contact with the nonhalakhic sources of the Jewish spiritual imagination impressed young Buber, as did his trips to local Hasidic prayer houses. But Martin Buber was pulled in other directions. He became involved with the thinking of Nietzsche at an early age and studied Western philosophy and art history at various European universities. Though a nonpracticing Jew, Buber was nevertheless profoundly committed to the Jewish cultural renaissance of Zionism. His was an early and important voice for a nontraditional renewal of the spiritual resources of Jewish culture.

Buber's commitment to cultural Zionism took many forms. He was a serious advocate of the new agricultural settlements then being founded in the land of Israel (the *kibbutzim*), seeing in them important moral experiments in the renewing power of human community. In the 1930s Buber showed his true greatness in reviving the Lehrhaus and traveling throughout Germany in a heroic effort to teach the sources of Judaism to his beleaguered people and thus give them the cultural resources for a spiritual resistance to Fascism. After the war, Buber recognized that the task of rescuing the Jewish survivors of the death camps gave Herzl's program of political Zionism a special moral urgency. He nevertheless continued to speak out forcefully on behalf of cultural renewal in the State of Israel and tried to instill in the new refugees—many of whom had no previous Zionist training—his ideals of the creation of a new Jew, spiritually alert and proud, in touch with both a life of culture and a life on the earth.

Buber's concern for a broad cultural renewal led in many literary directions. He translated selections of Chinese folk tales, worked on the Finnish *Kalevala* epic, and wrote studies on Christian mysticism. At the same time, Buber began an intense study of Jewish religious sources, specifically those of Hasidism. Buber began a lifelong project of presenting these sources to the world-at-large, beginning with books of the tales of the Ba'al Shem Tov and Rabbi Nahman of Bratzlav and especially through his celebrated *Tales of the Hasidim*. In these and other writings, he presented Hasidism as the direct inheritor of the authentic teachings of Judaism and rooted in the Bible. These teachings included alertness to the demands of the living God; a consecration of daily life through "sacramental living," where every deed was given the highest moral and religious significance; concern for the unity of life and the tyranny of idolatry; and the restorative power of a human community unified around these ideals. His goal in these works was not detached historical reconstruction but engaged living for the sake of cultural renewal. Herein lay Buber's practical goals of creating a new Jewish person, of forming a new post-traditional but spiritually enriched Jewish existence, and of saving culture from encrustation by reviving the heart and soul of persons.

Beyond these involvements, Buber was particularly influential through his great theological meditation *I and Thou* (1923). In this work, Buber avowedly turned away from the mystical self-absorptions of his youth and toward dialogical living, a living wherein all life is "meeting" and "relationship" with nature, persons, and God. Buber saw life as turning around two poles of relationship: the "I-It" pole, where relations are detached, manipulative, and move between a subject (the self) and an object (things or other persons), and the "I-Thou" pole, where relations are spontaneous, reciprocal, and involve one's total being. Naturally, all "I-It" relations are not bad, and some are even necessary for living. But if the "I-It" pole predominates in life, as Buber feared it had come to do in modern technological society, it tends to block out the possibility of intense sharing. In the "I-Thou" relation, one subject is deeply responsive to the presence and need of another subject, who, while experienced as an "other," is not experienced as an "object" and is not swallowed up in one's subjectivity. Rather, the other person remains a wholly present reality who can only be known through shared living. God, in truth, is the "Eternal Thou," says Buber, the Thou that can never be objectified and Who shines forth in true meetings between persons or between them and other aspects of reality. God, then, is the eternal, living Presence that can be responded to through individuals and nature or reduced to idolatrous and manipulated forms. To respond to the living reality as it appears before the self is to respond to God's Presence, his eternal revelation. To ignore this living reality because of private needs or contrivances is to sin, for it is to objectify reality or God out of fear or for the sake of power and self-interest. The human task, says Buber, is to make the world "God-real," to make the Presence of the Eternal Thou more and more active and present in the human community.

For Buber, the great Jewish texts of the Bible and Hasidism preserve these insights and, if one is open to them, may direct the alienated, self-absorbed, and fearful human soul of the modern era to their life-giving power. Here was a reinterpretation of classical sources that was not a renewal of traditional Judaism per se, but a confidence in the truthfulness of parts of the Jewish tradition to renew Jewish life in unexpected and nonparochial ways. As observed earlier, Buber did not share Rosenzweig's belief that the commandments of Judaism were potential carriers of such religious renewal. He rather saw them as external constraints against responsiveness to the spiritual demands of the moment. It is for this reason, among others, that many modern Jewish traditionalists have found it difficult to appreciate aspects of Buber's teaching. But to dismiss Martin Buber as an inauthentic Jewish teacher because he was not traditionally observant is to err profoundly, for Buber's voice speaks out of the depths of Jewish religious sources—though for him the challenge of "Sinai" is everywhere and with no fixed form. Buber challenged the modern individual, and the Jew in particular, to live an authentic existence, one that demanded spiritual focus and integrity in every action and at every moment. In this Buber was one in his thought and life. Like the world of Simeon the Righteous of old, the world of Martin Buber also stood on three things: Torah study, committed service to the world, and good deeds. His model of choice and decision remains significant for contemporary Jews, in all their various forms of commitment to the Jewish religious tradition. [See Religions of Africa pp. 45–51, 75–79, Native Religions of North America pp. 318–20, Christianity pp. 573–86, Hinduism pp. 820–26, Religions of China pp. 1040–54, and Religions of Japan pp. 1163–72 for description and discussion of life histories and personal accounts.]

A Tale of Two Centers: Israel and the United States

Israel

The modern State of Israel is a major spiritual and spatial focus for contemporary Jewry. As the center of a renewed national life, its cultural and political achievements since 1948 are a source of pride for Jews the world over. Many make secular "pilgrimages" to the civil shrines of the new state—the communal farms (*kibbutzim*), the parliament (Knesset), the development towns in the desert, and the Holocaust memorials (as Yad Va-Shem)—and spend time studying at its universities or just touring the land. [See Religions of Mesoamerica pp. 226–33, Christianity pp. 562–73, Islam pp. 645–47, Hinduism pp. 815–20, Buddhism p. 874, Religions of China p. 1043, and Religions of Japan pp. 1154–60 for description and discussion of pilgrimage.]

Many others come to Israel with specifically religious goals in mind, though the two motivations are not mutually exclusive. Among the religious purposes for travel to Israel is the trend for American youngsters to celebrate a *bar mitzvah* at the old Temple wall (the Wailing Wall) in Jerusalem, for Orthodox high-school students to spend a year in a *yeshiva*, and for all Jews to participate in its diverse and intense synagogue life. The existence in Israel of thousands of prayer rooms and synagogues, where the customs of Jews from Poland to

Bukhara are actively practiced, imbues the visitor with wonder at the range of traditional Jewish culture and its many modes of modern expression. Being a virtual microcosm of Jewish diversity and commonality over the ages, the religious life in Israel thus often inspires new commitments to Jewish identity. And being itself a virtual microcosm of Jewish cultural creativity over the ages, the very land of Israel, with its archaeological ruins and Byzantine ramparts, inspires reflections on Jewish history and the imperatives of continuity. No matter how traditional or secular the individual, all these activities are interpreted by modern Jews in religious terms, and the feelings evoked by them are understood as religious experiences. However paradoxical to the outsider, this is a basic fact of contemporary Jewish life—a modern expression of Judaism as a national-religious culture.

Within Israel itself, the diversity of religious life must be seen as a more complex affair, for while there is a polar split between the traditionalists and the secularists, the traditionalist group covers a volatile range from the modern to the ultra-Orthodox. Thus, due to the politicization of religious interest groups and the increasing institutionalization of the chief rabbinate, certain areas of law have been given over to the Orthodox coalitions (e.g., control over such personal law as marriage and divorce and in some cities control over public issues as the prohibition of public transportation and the closing of movie theaters on the Sabbath). Such restrictions have often seemed to secularists to compromise their civil liberties, and tensions occasionally erupt when one group or the other lobbies to increase or consolidate its position (within or outside of the law). Because of the general inflexibility of the rabbinate to compromise on issues it believes to be divine law, the concern that even most secularists have that traditional *halakha* play a role in the development of a common law in the state is increasingly tested. The lack of separation between "religion" and "state" has thus turned religious versus secular values into political interests—a result that has left little room for a middle ground. There are thus very few expressions of liberal religion in Israel. And the few attempts in this direction have often been harassed by the strict traditionalists, from whom the liberals must receive political approval (and religious certifications); or they have been rejected by the secularists, who have become antagonistic to all religious groups and can hardly conceive of a nondogmatic form of traditionalism. Paradoxically, coalitions between traditionalists and secularists do occur when political or security interests are involved (though the often messianic motivation of the former will not be shared by the latter).

Among the traditionalists, there are great differences as well. In their common struggle against secularism, the various traditionalists are vitally concerned to determine the Jewish character of the state. The spectrum of traditionalism ranges from the modern Orthodox, whose lives are determined by *halakha* but who also promote the civic democratic concerns of a Western state, to the ultra-Orthodox, who either reject the state outright or wish to influence it by working politically for the totalization of halakhic norms in the public realm. Since these positions involve strongly diverse feelings about the Jewish character of the state, about Western democracy and respect for the law, and (increasingly) about the messianic character of the times (i.e., whether the "return to Zion" is part of the divine fulfillment of ancient prophecies), strongly diverse behaviors are generated. At one time, the players in this drama and their attitudes were easily identified by how Western their clothes were, the nature and size of their headcovering, and whether the "Holy Tongue" of Hebrew was spoken in daily life or only in prayer. Today, many of these distinctions are harder to make, and extreme traditionalists include new immigrants from the West or young Israelis imbued with the passion "to increase Torah and to strengthen it."

Quite certainly, each group in the State of Israel feels a responsibility to mold the Jewish character of the country in its own image. The political compromise to separate education into traditional and secularist branches simply ensures the fact that each group is only exposed to its own values. Thus where traditionalists will lobby so that halakhic values will determine medical ethics (including such matters as abortion, autopsy, and genetic testing), secularists will often reject these positions on political grounds and not necessarily on the basis of the values involved. Similarly, secularist concerns for civil liberties and democratic values are often spurned by traditionalists because they are sponsored by nonbelievers and nonhalakhists. The struggles go on every day, so that the future character of Jewish life in the State of Israel can only be guessed at. The higher birthrate of the ultratraditionalists and their development of committed voting blocs are viewed by them as positive indicators of eventual political predominance. Such developments evoke serious concern among the more liberal traditionalists and certainly among the completely secular Israeli Jews. The latter hope that the ancient ideal of the unity of the Jewish people will stimulate all to work for a conciliatory consensus.

The United States

If there is a concern among Jews in the State of Israel to find a unifying consensus to overcome their various political-religious polarizations, a concern for the cultural and physical survival of the Jewish people is the unifying consensus of Jews who enjoy a multifaceted political-religious pluralism in the United States. Founded on the principle of the separation of church and state, religious life in America has encouraged its diverse religious and ethnic constituencies to strengthen their respective communal positions. In the Jewish case, this has meant the development of regional and national federations that include religious *and* nonreligious interest groups. Since these federations are responsible for the whole (regional or national) Jewish community, a spirit of pluralism and conciliation has generally prevailed, even where the religious divisions have been quite marked. Moreover, since Jews have been an ethnic-religious minority, it has been important for them to remain unified to promote their interests at local and state levels, particularly in earlier decades when Jews were generally restricted from the use of certain medical or communal institutions and limited by (unofficial) quotas from enrollment in universities and acceptance in established Gentile law or business firms. For these and other reasons,

Jews in America have supported causes favoring participatory democracy and the role of small interest groups. Naturally, this has further affected its religious life. The acrimony once common in Europe between liberal and orthodox Jews has never been a common feature of Jewish life in America.

In the main, the immigrants to America from Europe and Russia in the nineteenth century determined its religious and communal patterns. Early waves of German Jews brought with them the Reform ideology developed by Geiger and others and thus promoted changes in the liturgy (e.g., abbreviated prayers, vernacular and responsive hymn singing, and mixed seating). A liberal attitude toward halakhic regulations was fostered: Dietary and Sabbath rules were relaxed or abandoned and traditional headcoverings were rejected or made optional. Devotion to America led in the early years to the rejection of the Jews as a nation (and so of Zionism) and the promotion of universal brotherhood. The fact that the first Reform rabbinical seminary was established in Ohio symbolizes the general early American orientation toward the Midwest heartlands. In many respects, Reform Judaism introduced features of the Protestant style of religion into Judaism and often turned the rabbi from a scholar into a preacher, who sat on a raised dais in clerical garb facing the congregation. Moreover, a result of alienation from the tradition was that many congregants would simply live out their religious affiliation through the rabbi and see religion as a sometime Saturday (or Friday night) affair with little relation to one's values and habits the work week long. In recent years, Reform Judaism has become more traditionally minded, a vanguard for liturgical creativity within traditional categories, and a supporter of the State of Israel. In its concern for universal and social causes and outrage at civil abuses in the United States and abroad, Reform Judaism has helped keep the moral conscience of American Jewry.

Those Jews who later came to America from eastern Europe and Russia near and after the turn of the twentieth century brought with them the older traditional patterns and their modern compromises. Conservative Judaism, for example, is derivative of the more moderate reform groups in Europe—those who maintained strong links to traditional study and piety, though recognizing the historical character of Judaism. In America, the Conservatives have permitted some changes in the liturgy and *halakha*, but this has been done with great caution. Thus, while some Conservatives introduced occasional responsive reading in English into the service and permitted mixed seating, a strong respect for the dietary and Sabbath regulations remained, and the liturgy has remained traditional in both content and language. As has always been customary in traditional circles, the local Conservative rabbi (though now also in consultation with his "ritual committee" and under the moral guidance of a rabbinical committee of "law and standards" at the Conservative seminary) is in control of the religious practices of his congregation. The result is a broad spectrum of behaviors and beliefs among those Jews who are affiliated with Conservative congregations. This pluralistic temper remains the case even around such controversial issues as permitting congregants to drive to Sabbath or festival services (only), allowing women to be called up to bless the Torah in their own right, and permitting women to be hired or to officiate as rabbis. This last is a very new matter for Conservative Jews, since only in recent years have women been accepted to its rabbinic school (the practice has been common in Reform seminaries for a decade and more).

Jews from eastern Europe also solidified the Orthodox community of America, which continued along traditional lines in matters of authority, practice, and education. Nevertheless, use of the public schools or secular studies was assumed. In the emergent "modern Orthodox" style, as it has been called, firm roots in tradition are maintained and business involvements and social contacts in the wider Gentile environment are accepted. Naturally, tensions arise over such compromises. But the "modern Orthodox" claim that their struggle for such integration is in the true spirit of tradition, which has always been open to the wider educational and economic world—though cautiously integrating these (or, at times, living in "two spheres"). The more traditional Orthodox in the United States, many of whom came as immigrants after World War II, generally resist contact with the secular world and live in isolated and self-imposed ghettos, where they claim they can authentically preserve the values and life patterns of a "Torah-true" Judaism. Jews in these spheres are largely restricted to traditional Jewish cultural patterns, and they have developed an intense and self-absorbed communal structure. For them, modernity is an outright blasphemy and threat to all that they hold sacred. These feelings are also related to their ideological concern for the soul of secular Jews and their attempts to convert these nonobservant coreligionists back to the true, traditional path.

Among the notable recent developments in modern Jewish life in America is the growth of day-school education, among the modern Orthodox and Conservative Jews especially. Such education integrates the serious study of classical Jewish sources along with the equally serious study of secular subjects, all within a framework where traditional values are lived. The day-school phenomenon reflects a new enhancement of traditional education among America's Jews and institutionalizes a new style of integrating Jewish and Western culture. According to their differing halakhic temperaments, the two religious movements promote the values and benefits of each. The further supplementation of day-school and afternoon (Hebrew school) education with intense Jewish summer camp experiences has also deepened the commitments of young Jews to Judaism and helped them to conceptualize and live models of Jewish identity that are thoroughly at home in the traditional culture and the secular ambience.

Patterns of adult education or study groups sponsored by synagogues try to foster greater Jewish knowledge among the older generations. Talmud study groups for men have always been customary in Orthodox settings, and some modern Orthodox have established Talmud classes for women as well. In Conservative and Reform circles, many of these study groups are also intense family fellowships (called *havurot*), which may meet for smaller prayer gatherings within the framework of the larger congregations. The "Havurah" movement has also promoted the organization of such small prayer-study communities in their own right. The style of prayer and adherence to tradition in these groups is determined by the members, and their nonhierarchical structure encourages egalitarian participation for men and women along with various types of liturgical innovations. In some ways, this movement transcends the ideologies of earlier American generations and, in its serious commitment to tradition in a style that is at once nondogmatic and concerned with reflecting the values of its participants (typically liberal, self-expressive, and participatory), a new synthesis of tradition and modernity is being formed—something uniquely American.

It may be added that the full participation of women in these groups, in Reform congregations and increasingly in Conservative synagogues, is a structural change in traditional Jewish practice of the greatest moment. The full implications of this change cannot yet be gauged. One can only surmise that the full involvement of women within Jewish piety and study will have serious implications for a yet-to-emerge liberal-traditional sensibility. Certainly one of the upshots of the Havurah pattern and new feminine involvements in Judaism, whose impact can already be felt, is the growing sense that Jews must take active and creative responsibility for their own religious lives. Not for nothing have Franz Rosenzweig and Martin Buber been the spiritual godfathers for many of the intellectuals involved in these developments. Together with this, a new emphasis on the aggadic imagination—an imagination that cultivates religious wonder and the delight in traditional literary images—has given the old halakhic patterns a new vibrancy for such "heterodox" Jews. From a historical point of view, the emergence of new motivations for practicing the commandments has always signaled vitality and renewal in Judaism.

The shapes and expressions of Jewish life in Israel and the United States at the close of the twentieth century could hardly have been anticipated a century

Celebration with Torah at the Western Wall, Jerusalem. Joy with the holy scroll is a communal act, for its words are the religious teachings of the people. According to an ancient prayer, "they are our life, and the length of our days." (Photo by Bill Aron.)

ago, and one may expect new syntheses and patterns in the future. The modern Jewish scholar and thinker, Simon Rawidowicz, once referred to Jews as the "ever-dying people," so precariously perched has Jewish civilization been on the twigs of alien trees. But Jews and Judaism are also being ever renewed and reborn—more so now than ever as Jews the world over have developed political power and a new will to determine their historical destiny. This new will and power has led to some fragmenting results, splitting Jewish groups among themselves. But it has also promoted new expressions of traditional practice and an unapologetic sense of national-religious vitality. Whether a new consensus can arise from this diversity will largely depend on the spirit of the Jews themselves. Certainly the basis for this new consensus is present in the calendrical cycle, which all Jews share in some way, as well as in the values of Torah, *halakha,* and peoplehood—no matter how diversely interpreted and implemented. Moreover, though the Jewish tradition has fostered dogmatic as well as nondogmatic trends and both flexible and inflexible constructions of its laws, what often determined which trend or construction was emphasized was a series of meta-halakhic values. Chief among these values are equity, loving-kindness, and *ahavat Yisrael,* "love of the people of Israel." Many Jews today believe that the role of these values will greatly determine the fate of the old-new religion of Judaism in the years to come.

Study Questions

Before you begin to read this part, take a mental inventory of what you know and think about Judaism and Jewish people. Make a list of Jewish images and "things" that you know—biblical materials, Israel, and Jewish foods and music. What religious acts and events do you associate with Judaism? Keep these images and things in mind as you read this section and develop new notions about Judaism.

CHAPTER 15

Introduction

1. How does the author use the story about sixteenth-century Jews in India to approach the unity of Judaism in the midst of historical variations?
2. How does the author use the stories of Moses in the Bible and in the Talmud to illustrate a Jewish "myth of origins"?
3. How are the notions of covenant, Torah, and God important for Judaism?
4. How is Judaism defined in this chapter?

CHAPTER 16

Judaism as an Ideological System

1. How does the author approach Judaism "as an ideological system"?
2. What is meant by "rabbinic patterns of this-worldly holiness and salvation"?
3. In what way does the biblical heritage form the foundation of Judaism?
4. Characterize the interaction of Judaism with other cultures and religions.
5. Explain how the destruction of the Temple in Jerusalem in 70 C.E. was a major watershed in the history of Judaism.
6. In addition to the Torah, what are the major writings in Judaism and what role do they play?
7. What is *halakha* and why is halakhic piety so important in the life of Judaism?
8. What is meant by "rabbinic patterns of hidden meanings and otherworldly concerns"?
9. Characterize the "philosophical path" and the "mystical path" in medieval Judaism.
10. What are the major developments in Judaism during the modern period (from the eighteenth century to the present)?

CHAPTER 17

Judaism as a Ritual System

1. How would you characterize Judaism as a ritual system?
2. What are the major features of the "calendrical cycle of holiness"?
3. Specifically, what are the daily, weekly, and yearly practices of traditional Judaism?
4. What are the major features of "the life cycle of holiness"?
5. Specifically, what are the practices related to birth, religious majority, marriage, and death?
6. What is the significance of the home and family in traditional Judaism?

CHAPTER 18

Jews and Judaism in Modern Times

1. Compare and contrast Judaism in "A Tale of Two Cities: Vilna and Frankfurt am Main."
2. Characterize Rabbi Elijah Gaon of Vilna and Moses Mendelssohn of Berlin, and Abraham Geiger and Samson Raphael Hirsch of Frankfurt am Main.
3. How do Franz Rosenzweig and Martin Buber present new possibilities for modern Judaism?
4. Compare and contrast Judaism in "A Tale of Two Centers: Israel and the United States."

Recall the initial inventory of Jewish images and things that you made before reading this part. What is there in Judaism that is most like your own religious tradition? What in Judaism is most different from your own tradition? What is most interesting? How has your understanding of Judaism changed as a result of reading this section? Can you now imagine yourself participating in Judaism?

Notes

In presenting this work to students and lay readers, it is my pleasure to thank various people. H. Byron Earhart, the series editor, was kind enough to invite me to participate in this educational project on Religious Traditions of the World. I am grateful for his courtesy and promptness in responding to my evolving ideas concerning the arrangement and content of the material. Various working drafts were tried out in the framework of courses on Judaism taught at Stanford University and at Brandeis University. Among my students, I am particularly grateful to Sebastiano C. Paiewonsky of Brandeis for his close reading of a working manuscript. His reactions to matters of style and content have been helpful.

As with all my writing, I have had the joy to share this with my wife, Mona. Many thoughts were talked through with her long before they reached the written page, and once my words became a written text, her sharp editorial eye and concrete judgment improved the work in many ways. My gratitude is lifelong.

In completing this work, I have had the special pleasure of the interest and involvement of my oldest son, Eitan. He did research on and provided the initial drafts for the glossary. My youngest son, Elisha, provided expert help with pagination. I want to thank him very much as well.

All of the photographs found herein are courtesy of Bill Aron, who has allowed me to use materials from his collection *From the Four Corners of the Earth* as well as from unpublished material. I am also grateful to the American Jewish Historical Society, located at Brandeis University, for archival assistance.

1. Babylonian Talmud, *Menahot* 29b.
2. The text occurs in J. Wistinetzki, *Sefer Hasidim (Das Buch der Frommen)* (Berlin: Itzkowski, 1891), 6.
3. Babylonian Talmud, *Baba Metzia* 59b.
4. *Mishnah Shevi'ith* X. 3-4.
5. *Mishnah Nezikin* I. 2 (*Ethics of the Fathers*). See R. T. Herford, ed. and trans., *The Ethics of the Talmud: Sayings of the Fathers* (New York: Schocken, 1966), 22.
6. See J. Hertz, ed., *The Authorized Daily Prayer Book* (New York: Bloch Publishing Company, 1955), 149.
7. S. Schechter, ed., *Avot de-Rabbi Nathan* (New York: Feldheim, 1967), version A, chap. 4, p. 21; see also J. Goldin, trans., *The Fathers According to Rabbi Nathan*, Yale Judaica Series X (New Haven, CT: Yale University Press, 1955), 34.
8. From "Lord, Where Shall I Find You?" in *The Penguin Book of Hebrew Verse*, ed. and trans. T. Carmi (New York: Penguin, 1981), 338–39.
9. See "Ode to Zion" in *The Penguin Book of Hebrew Verse*, 347.
10. S. Pines, trans., *The Guide of the Perplexed* (Chicago: University of Chicago Press, 1963), 11–12.
11. Ibid., 622.
12. Ibid.
13. *Kuzari* III. 65.
14. *Zohar* II. 99 a-b. See translation of D. Matt (New York: Paulist Press, 1983), 121–23.

Glossary

Akiba Distinguished rabbi in ancient Palestine (c. 50–135 C.E.). A major legal scholar, who established an academy in Bne Brak, Akiba ben Joseph was also a legendary mystic and martyr. He was tortured and killed by the Romans in 135 C.E.

Ashkenazi Originally the designation Ashkenaz referred to a people and country bordering on Armenia and the upper Euphrates; in medieval times, it referred to the Jewish area of settlement in northwest Europe. The whole cultural complex deriving from this region is known as Ashkenazi; hence it now refers to Jews of European and Russian background and their distinctive liturgical practices or religious and social customs. The term is in contradistinction to Sephardi.

bar (bat) mitzvah Literally, "son (daughter) of the commandment(s)." The phrase originally referred to a person responsible for performing the divine commandments of Judaism; it now refers to the occasion when a boy or girl reaches the age of religious majority and responsibility (thirteen years for a boy; twelve years and a day for a girl).

ben "Son," "son of" in Hebrew; Rabbi Akiba ben Joseph means Akiba son of Joseph.

circumcision The minor surgical removal of the foreskin when a Jewish boy is eight days old. The ceremony is called *brit milah,* which indicates that the ritual establishes a covenant between God and the individual.

commandments According to rabbinic tradition, there are 613 religious commandments referred to in the Torah (and elaborated upon by the rabbinic sages). Of these, 248 are positive commandments and 365 are negative. The numbers respectively symbolize the fact that divine service must be expressed through all one's bodily parts during all the days of the year. In Hebrew, the commandments are called *mitzvot* (sing., *mitzvah*). More generically, a *mitzvah* refers to any act of religious duty or obligation; more colloquially, a *mitzvah* refers to a "good deed."

covenant In the Bible, it refers to the religious bond between God and Israel contracted at Sinai with the giving of the Torah. For Judaism, it refers to the eternal bond between God and the people of Israel grounded in the nation's obedience to the divine commandments. It is a major theological concept, expressive of divine grace and concern for the Jews and their reciprocal obligations to God.

galut Literally, "exile." The term refers to the various expulsions of Jews from the ancestral homeland. Over time, it came to express the broader notion of Jewish homelessness and state of being aliens. Thus, colloquially, "to be in *galut*" means to live in the Diaspora and also to be in a state of physical and even spiritual alienation.

halakha Any normative Jewish law, custom, or practice—or the entire complex. *Halakha* is law established or custom ratified by authoritative rabbinic jurists and teachers. Colloquially, if something is deemed halakhic, it is considered proper and normative behavior.

Hillel Often called by the title "the Elder." Probably a Babylonian, Hillel was an important sage of the classical period. He lived c. 50 B.C.E.–first century C.E. His teachings convey the Pharisaic ideal, through many epigrams on humility and peace (found in *Ethics of the Fathers,* chaps. 1–2), and were fundamental in shaping the Pharisaic traditions and modes of interpretation. His style of legal reasoning is continued by his disciples, known as Beit Hillel ("House/School of Hillel"). It is typically contrasted with that of Shammai (a contemporary) and his school.

Israel In biblical times, this refers to the northern Israelite tribes, but also to the entire nation. Historically, Jews have continued to regard themselves as the true continuation of the ancient Israelite national-religious community. The term thus has a strong cultural sense. In modern times, it also refers to the political State of Israel.

kaddish Prayer recited by mourners for the dead. The prayer extols God's majesty and kingdom. There is also a version of the prayer recited by the prayer leader between major units of the public liturgy and a long version (called Rabbinic Kaddish) that follows an act of study. Most of the *kaddish* is in Aramaic.

kosher Literally, "proper," or "ritually permitted" food. Traditional Jewish dietary laws are based on biblical legislation. Only land animals that chew the cud and have cloven hoofs are permitted for use as food and must be slaughtered in a special way. Further, meat products may not be eaten with milk products or immediately thereafter. Only sea creatures (fish) having fins and scales are permitted. Fowl is considered a meat food and also has to be slaughtered in a special manner.

Maimonides Major medieval rabbi, physician, scientist, and philosopher (1135–1204), known by the acronym Rambam. Born in Spain, Maimonides fled from persecution to Morocco and finally settled in Egypt. His major works include a legal commentary on the Mishnah, a law code called *Mishneh Torah,* and the preeminent work of medieval Jewish rational philosophy, *The Guide of the Perplexed.*

Messiah Literally, "anointed one." Based on an old biblical belief that a descendant of King David (a royal "anointed one") would establish an era of peace and justice for the nation of Israel and the world, expectations of a universal or cosmic redeemer developed in classical Judaism and were further refined and developed over the centuries. The messianic age was believed by some Jews to be a time of perfection of human institutions; others believed it to be a time of radical new beginnings, a new heaven and earth, after divine judgment and destruction. The period known as "days of Messiah" may thus refer to this period of renewal, and not necessarily to an individual who inaugurates or rules the time.

mezuzah Literally, "doorpost"; the scroll and container affixed by Jews to the exterior doorposts (at the right side of the entrance) of their home. By custom, interior doorways are also often marked by a *mezuzah.* The practice of affixing a *mezuzah* is based on a biblical passage (Deut. 6:1–4).

midrash Literally, "exposition" or "inquiry" into the language, ideas, and narratives of the Torah. It constitutes a major literary achievement of classical and later Judaism. Its two major divisions are legal *midrash* (or *midrash halakha*) and nonlegal *midrash* (or *midrash aggada;* this includes grammatical explications, theology, ethics, and legends).

Mishnah Ancient code of Jewish law collated, edited, and revised by Rabbi Judah the Prince at the beginning of the third century C.E. The code is divided into six major units and sixty-three minor ones. The work is the authoritative legal tradition of the early sages and is the basis of the legal discussions of the Talmud.

mitzvot See commandments.

Moses The great biblical personality (c. thirteenth century B.C.E.) who led the nation out of Egyptian bondage and taught them the divine laws at Sinai. He is also presented as the first of the prophets. Throughout Jewish history he is the exalted man of faith and leadership without peer.

Passover Spring holiday celebrating the Exodus of the ancient Israelites from Egypt. The festival lasts eight days, during which Jews refrain from eating all leavened foods and products. A special ritual meal (called *seder*) is prepared, and a traditional narrative (called the *Haggadah*), supplemented by hymns and songs, marks the event.

rabbi Hebrew, "My Master"; an authorized teacher of the Jewish tradition. The role of the rabbi has changed considerably throughout the centuries. Traditionally, rabbis serve as the legal and spiritual guides of their congregations and communities. The title is conferred after considerable study of traditional Jewish sources. This conferral—and its responsibilities—is central to the chain of tradition in Judaism.

Rashi Acronym for Rabbi Solomon ben Isaac (1040–1105), a great medieval sage of Troyes, France. He is the author of fundamental commentaries on the Talmud, and one of the most beloved and influential commentators on the Bible. Characterized by great lucidity and pedagogy, his comments emphasized the plain, straightforward sense of a text.

Sabbath The seventh day of the week (Heb., *shabbat*), recalling the completion of the creation and the Exodus from Egypt. It is a day symbolic of new beginnings and one dedicated to God, a most holy day of rest. The commandment of rest is found in the Bible and has been elaborated by the rabbis. It is a special duty to study Torah on the Sabbath and to be joyful. Sabbaths near major festivals are known by special names.

seder The traditional service for the holiday of Passover, which includes special food symbols and narratives. The order of the service is highly regulated (*seder* means "order"), and the traditional narrative is known as the *Haggadah*.

Sephardi The designation Sepharad in biblical times refers to a colony of exiles from Jerusalem, possibly in or near Sardis; in the medieval period, Sephardi Jews were descendants of Jews living in Spain and Portugal before the expulsion of 1492. Later, as a cultural designation, the term came to refer to the cultural complex associated with Jews of this region and its related Diaspora in the Balkans and Middle East. The term is used in contradistinction to Ashkenazi, but it does not refer, thereby, to all Jews of non-Ashkenazi origin.

Shema Title of the fundamental, monotheistic statement of Judaism, found in Deut. 6:4 ("Hear, O Israel, the Lord is our God, the Lord is One"). This statement avers the unity of God and is recited daily in the liturgy (along with Deut. 6:5–9, and other passages) and customarily before sleep at night. This proclamation also climaxes special liturgies (like Yom Kippur) and is central to the confessional before death and the ritual of martyrdom. The Shema is inscribed on the *mezuzah* and the *tefillin*. In public services, it is recited in unison.

synagogue The central institution of Jewish communal worship and study since antiquity. The structure of the building has changed, though in all cases the ark containing the Torah scrolls faces the ancient Temple site in Jerusalem.

tallit A large shawl with fringes and special knots at the extremities, worn during morning prayers. The fringes, according to the Bible, remind the worshiper of God's commandments. It is traditional for the male to be buried in his *tallit*, but without its fringes.

Talmud Literally, "learning" or "study"; primarily used to refer to the classical rabbinic discussions of the Mishnah. These discussions are also known as *gemara*, which has become a colloquial, generic term for the Talmud and its study. There is a Babylonian Talmud and a Jerusalem Talmud. The first was completed in the fifth century C.E.; the second, also known as the Palestinian Talmud, was edited in the early fourth century C.E.

tefillin The two black boxes containing scriptural citation worn by men and boys (of majority age) during morning services, though not on Sabbath and festivals. The *tefillin*, also called phylacteries, have leather thongs attached. One box (with four sections) is placed on the head, the other (with one section) is placed (customarily) on the left arm, near the heart. The biblical passages emphasize the unity of God and the duty to love God and be mindful of him with "all one's heart and mind."

Torah The first five books of the Bible, also known as the Five Books of Moses, or the Pentateuch. The word *Torah*, literally "instruction," is commonly used to refer to the entire range of Jewish teachings and practices.

Zion, Zionism Zion is the ancient name for Jerusalem, but as early as biblical times it served to indicate the national homeland. In this latter sense it served as a focus for Jewish national-religious hopes of renewal over the centuries. Ancient hopes and attachments to Zion gave rise to Zionist longings and movements since antiquity, culminating in the modern national liberation movement of that name. The Zionist cause helped the Jews return to Palestine in this century and found the State of Israel in 1948. The goal of Zionism is the political and spiritual renewal of the Jewish people in their ancestral homeland.

Selected Reading List

CLASSICAL SOURCES IN TRANSLATION

Birnbaum, P., ed. *High Holiday Prayer Book.* New York: Hebrew Publishing Company, 1951.

Buber, M. *Tales of the Hasidim.* 2 vols. New York: Schocken, 1947–1948.

Carmi, T., ed. *The Penguin Book of Hebrew Verse.* New York: Penguin Books, 1981.

Danby, H., ed. *The Mishnah.* Oxford: Oxford University Press, 1933.

Epstein, I., ed. *The Babylonian Talmud.* 6 vols. London: Soncino, 1935–1952.

Freedman, H., ed. *The Midrash.* 10 vols. London: Soncino, 1939.

Ginzberg, L. *Legends of the Jews.* 7 vols. Philadelphia: Jewish Publication Society, 1909–1938.

Glatzer, N., ed. *In Time and Eternity: A Jewish Reader.* New York: Schocken, 1961.

———. *Language of Faith.* New York: Schocken, 1947.

Hertz, J., ed. *The Authorized Daily Prayer Book.* New York: Bloch Publishing Company, 1955.

———. *The Pentateuch and Haftorahs.* London: Soncino, 1965.

Matt, D., trans. *Zohar: The Book of Enlightenment.* New York: Paulist Press, 1983.

Montefiore, C. G., and H. J. Loewe, eds. *A Rabbinic Anthology.* London: MacMillan, 1938.

Sperling, H., and M. Simon, trans. *The Zohar.* 5 vols. London: Soncino, 1931–1934.

SURVEYS AND TOPICS IN JEWISH HISTORY AND THOUGHT WITH FULL BIBLIOGRAPHIES

Baron, S. *A Social and Religious History of the Jews.* 16 vols. New York: Columbia University Press, 1952–1973.

Cohen, A., and P. Mendes-Flohr, eds. *Contemporary Jewish Religious Thought.* New York: Scribner, 1987.

Encyclopedia Judaica. 16 vols. and suppl. Jerusalem: Keter Publishing House, 1971.

Finkelstein, L., ed. *The Jews: Their History, Culture and Religion.* 2 vols. New York: Harper & Brothers, 1949.

Green, A., ed. *Jewish Spirituality from the Bible Through the Middle Ages.* Vol. 1. New York: Crossroad, 1986.

Guttman, J. *Philosophies of Judaism.* New York: Holt, Rinehart & Winston, 1964.

Moore, G. F. *Judaism in the First Centuries of the Christian Era.* 2 vols. Cambridge, MA: Harvard University Press, 1927.

Scholem, G. *Major Trends in Jewish Mysticism.* New York: Schocken, 1956.

———. *The Messianic Idea in Judaism.* New York: Schocken, 1971.

Urbach, E. E. *The Sages.* Cambridge, MA: Harvard University Press, 1987.

PART FIVE

Christianity

A Way
of Salvation

Sandra Sizer Frankiel

Chronology of Christian History

Dates *(C.E.)*	Events
	THE EARLY CHURCH
26 to 29 C.E.	Ministry of Jesus of Nazareth in Judea, Samaria, and the Galil
29	Crucifixion of Jesus; beginnings of "churches"
c. 40 to 60	Paul's ministry and letters
54 to 68	Rule of Nero; first systematic persecution of Christians
c. 65 to c. 100	Writing and circulation of Gospels and other early Christian literature that became part of "New Testament"
66 to 70	War between the Jews and Rome in Palestine
70	Destruction of the Second Temple in Jerusalem
c. 100 to c. 165	Life of Justin Martyr
110	Martyrdom of Ignatius of Antioch
c. 185 to c. 254	Life of Origen
216 to 276?	Life of Mani in Persis; Manichean religion begins
249 to 251	Persecution of Christians by Emperor Decius
c. 250 to 356	Life of Anthony of Egypt, "father of monasticism"
263 to 339	Life of Eusebius of Caesarea, first church historian
284 to 305	Persecution of Christians by Emperor Diocletian
290 to 347	Life of Pachomius of Egypt, founder of first monastic community
296 to 359	Life of Simeon Stylites ("pillar-sitter"), saint of Syrian monasticism
305 to 311	Persecution of Christians by Emperor Galerius in the eastern empire

Dates (C.E.)	Events
	CHRISTIANITY IN THE ROMAN EMPIRE AND IN EUROPE
312	Constantine, patron of Christianity, becomes emperor
325	Council of Nicea to deal with Arian controversy; official establishment of four patriarchates at Jerusalem, Antioch, Alexandria, and Rome
354 to 430	Life of Augustine of Hippo
c. 400 to 700	Arian and Monophysite controversies in Eastern church
413	Augustine's *City of God*
c. 450 to 600	Barbarian attacks on Rome
451	Council of Chalcedon; Constantinople is made a patriarchate
476	Death of Romulus Augustus, last Western emperor, in Rome
496	Conversion of Clovis, king of the Franks
622	Beginning of Islam
638 to 640	Muslim conquest of Egypt and Syria, formerly major Christian centers
c. 675 to 754	Life of Boniface of England, missionary to Europe
726 to 843	Iconoclastic controversy in Eastern church
732	Charles Martel defeats Muslims at Poitiers
740 to 747	Reform of the Frankish church under Boniface
742 to 814	Life of Charlemagne
800	Charlemagne crowned Emperor of the Romans
800 to 1000	Conversion of Bulgars, other Balkan peoples, Slavs, and Russians to Eastern Orthodoxy; Barbarian wars in the West
932	Establishment of patriarchate at Preslav
1020	Peace of God in Western church; knights are bound to respect rules of war set by church
1054	Western and Eastern churches mutually excommunicate one another
1085	Conquest of Toledo (Spain) by Christian armies; beginnings of new scholarship using Muslim texts and translations
1095 to 1099	First Crusade
1000 to 1300	Development of *hesychasm,* mysticism, and theology of deification in Eastern church
1090 to 1153	Life of Bernard of Clairvaux, mystic and founder of abbey of Clairvaux

Dates (C.E.)	Events
1122	Concordat of Worms to settle church/state disputes in West
1170 to 1221	Life of Dominic
1182 to 1226	Life of Francis
1187	Muslims reconquer Jerusalem
1198 to 1216	Innocent III is pope; high point of papal power
1204	Fourth Crusade
1215	Fourth Lateran Council
1224/25 to 1274	Life of Thomas Aquinas
1290	Jews expelled from England
1305	Jews expelled from France
1309 to 1377	Papacy is at Avignon, France
1337 to 1443	Hundred Years' War
1348	Black Death epidemic begins
1377 to 1414	Western Schism in the papacy
1414 to 1417	Council of Constance to reunite papacy
1431 to 1449	Council of Basel, to deal with Wycliffe/Huss controversy and with the question of papal supremacy

THE AGE OF REFORM

1452 to 1498	Life of Savonarola, Dominican preacher and reformer in Florence, Italy
1453	Turks conquer Constantinople
1466 to 1536	Life of Desiderius Erasmus, humanist, Renaissance scholar
1476	Selling of plenary indulgences by Pope Sixtus IV
1483 to 1546	Life of Martin Luther, leader of German Reformation and "founder" of Protestantism
1484 to 1531	Life of Ulrich Zwingli, Swiss Protestant reformer
1491 to 1547	Life of Henry VIII, reforming English monarch
1491 to 1556	Life of Ignatius of Loyola, founder of Society of Jesus in the Roman Catholic church
1492	Jews expelled from Spain; Columbus reaches West Indian islands

Dates (C.E.)	Events
1497	Jews expelled from Portugal
1509 to 1564	Life of John Calvin, Protestant reformer in Geneva, Switzerland
1517	Luther nails "95 Theses" to the door of Wittenberg Chapel, marking the "official" beginning of the Protestant Reformation
1533 to 1603	Life of Elizabeth I, English Reforming monarch
1545 to 1563	Council of Trent, establishing principles of the Roman Catholic Reformation
1607, 1620 to 1630	Puritan colonies established in America
1649 to 1660	Puritan Revolution in England

MODERN DEVELOPMENTS

c. 1740 to c. 1760	First Great Awakening in America
1775 to 1863	Life of Lyman Beecher
1776 to 1789	American Revolution
1789 to 1794	French Revolution
1790 to 1835	Second Great Awakening in America
1792 to 1875	Life of Charles Grandison Finney
1803 to 1882	Life of Ralph Waldo Emerson, "father of Transcendentalism"
1811 to 1896	Life of Harriet Beecher Stowe
1830	Founding of Church of Jesus Christ of Latter-day Saints (Mormons)
1863	Founding of Seventh-day Adventist church
1879	Founding of Church of Christ, Scientist
c. 1880 to 1914	Holiness movement
c. 1900 to 1914	Pentecostal movement begins; Social Gospel developed in American churches
1962 to 1965	Second Vatican Council of the Roman Catholic church under Pope John XXIII

19
Introduction

BEGINNING THE STUDY OF CHRISTIANITY means opening a door to a world of fascinating figures, paradoxical beliefs, mysterious rites, and unending questions. For Western students especially it is an important enterprise, for Christianity is at once a familiar part of the environment and a hidden influence on our lives. Mention of Christianity often brings powerful questions to the fore: What is the significance, the deep meaning, of Christianity as a religion? How has it been so powerful in people's lives—how did it come to influence millions over two thousand years of history? What importance does it have in my life, in my society and culture? These questions might be asked of any religion, but they carry added weight in a society where virtually every day one meets Christian believers and confronts Christian influence in politics, education, and culture. The study of Christianity should provide students with at least some of the resources to answer such questions: basic information about Christianity; a grasp of some of the issues that have been important to Christians; and a sense of the depths of the religion, which have made it a motivating force in people's lives.

First, however, we need to establish a preliminary agreement on what we mean by the term *Christianity.* Most simply, Christianity is the religion of those people who believe in Jesus Christ as the savior of the world. But that immediately raises more questions: Who is Jesus Christ? What is a savior? What is meant by "believe in"?

In fact, we know very little about the man called Jesus Christ—more properly, Jesus the Christ, for "Christ" is derived from the Greek term for **Messiah,*** the "anointed" one of God. All we know comes from the New Testament writings about him, none earlier than about ten years after his death (Paul's letters, and Paul never knew Jesus alive) and most written down at least thirty years after his death (the Gospels). He seems to have been a wandering teacher in Palestine, mostly in Galilee and Samaria, for about three years. He preached the impending end of the world and the coming **kingdom of God.** He was a powerful

---

*Terms defined in the glossary, pp. 598–600, are printed in boldface type where they first appear in the text.

teacher and healer, and he probably instituted some customs among his disciples that later became rituals of the church. He was crucified by the Romans about 29 C.E.[1] More than that we cannot say for certain; we cannot even declare unequivocally which sayings attributed to him are actually his. Most of what we know as Christian teachings derives from the early church and the claims it made about Jesus; we cannot know how much actually came from him.

It is significant, however, that it was a "church," a defined community, that preached and wrote about Jesus. The people who believed in him formed a tightly organized community living a disciplined way of life. Part of Christianity since then has always been the community. The early Christian creeds, statements of right belief, referred to the church as the "Holy Church," meaning that their community was in some important ways separate from the rest of the world. They believed that they were continuing the mission of Jesus, preaching the coming kingdom until he returned.

For they believed he was the savior who would return. As a Jewish sect, they adopted one currently popular belief that God would send a Messiah at the end of time to rule as king over a new, perfect world. Jesus was that Messiah. But they also held that Jesus' life, death, and **resurrection** had changed their lives in the present and ensured their **salvation.** When the end came, some souls would be condemned to punishment and some saved; those who belonged to the church would be among the saved. In the present, they already felt some of the effects of that salvation; they had a foretaste, in the intense spiritual life that they lived, of what was to come. How Jesus accomplished this was a great mystery, embodied in the rites and doctrines of the church. It is this mystery of salvation that has stood at the heart of Christianity for almost all its history.

To "believe in" Jesus meant to accept what the church taught about him as true and to act accordingly: to be baptized, to participate in the rites and ongoing life of the church, to live a moral life according to the church's standards. Belief was the beginning of Christian life and a central pillar of it, but it led to much more.

Then, what do we mean by the "religion" of those who held these beliefs? We mean the set of practices, beliefs, and institutions that they established to maintain, express, and transmit their tradition. The religion includes the church and its hierarchy, the lay members and the **clergy,** the worldview that they held, the rites they performed, the ethics they taught, the doctrinal systems they developed, and the art, literature, and music that they used to express their religious feelings and ideas.

Immediately our scope widens enormously. For Christianity includes all the religious activities undertaken in the name of Christian belief. We soon discover we must speak not of "the church" but of churches, not of Christianity but of "Christianities." From the beginning there were disagreements among Christian churches: Paul disagreed with the church leaders at Jerusalem; the direction of the church at Corinth was different from that of the church at Rome. Dissent and "heresy" (as the church that won called the beliefs of the dissenting group) ran through the early centuries of Christianity—and never stopped. Even while Christians agreed that Jesus was their savior, they disagreed over whether he actually suffered and died on the cross, or only appeared to do so. Even as they agreed that they should celebrate the **Eucharist,** they disagreed over whether **icons**—portraits of Jesus, Mary, angels, and saints—should be used in the worship services. The Christianity of the warrior society of the eighth-century Franks differed sharply from that of the Byzantine Empire at the same period, and both differed from the Christianity of Martin Luther.

A simple view of Christianity dissolves, and the religion of those who believe in Jesus the Christ becomes a large family of religious groups. Its history looks more like an evolutionary tree with large and small branches, some stopping abruptly and others remaining small for a while, then suddenly blossoming into many twigs, some of which become substantial branches. The various churches share some features in common some of the time, but one can never be sure that two groups calling themselves Christian will hold the same views of Jesus, of salvation, of belief, or of what is essential to their religion. [See Religions of Africa pp. 23–24, Religions of Mesoamerica pp. 117–19, Native Religions of North America p. 263–64, Judaism pp. 389, 426, 456–75, Islam pp. 607–8, Hinduism pp. 719–21, Buddhism pp. 853–55, Religions of China pp. 990–1015, and Religions of Japan pp. 1090–92 for discussion of the diversity and variety of religious traditions.]

Christianity has a deceptively simple core but is an extremely diverse religion. We can best approach that diversity by a historical study that traces the contours of development, identifies some of the major different religious styles, worldviews, and directions within the religion. This is what we will attempt in chapter 20, beginning not with Jesus but with the earliest Christian communities as they spread from Asia Minor around the Mediterranean. We will see how the churches developed from a small Jewish sect into the official religion of the Roman Empire, and then split again into two great branches, the Eastern and Western, the Orthodox and the Roman Catholic churches. We will trace the history of each branch into the Middle Ages, and after the time of the Crusades, we will follow the development of the Western church through the Reformation, the translation of Christianity to many peoples of the world, and the emergence of modern Christianity. In each case we will be attempting to capture the religious spirit of the age, the style and worldview as much as the events and people that are the highlights of the period.

Because it accentuates diversity, however, history is only one dimension of any study of religion. There are also features that endure over time, which seem characteristic of one particular religion over against others. These we treat in chapter 21. These basic structures of Christianity also have their historical dimension, of course; practices change, people develop new interpretations of old features; some aspects decline in importance as others rise to prominence. Yet most of the elements that we would call basic structures appear in the early development of the religion and remain, even if only in fragmentary form, throughout most of the life of the religion.

Many of these enduring structures, moreover, are those that have counterparts in other religions. To mention just a few examples: Rituals of immersion in water and of sacred communal meals are common to many traditions; the idea of a holy community or holy people appears in some; the tension between the present world and an ideal state beyond, expressed in the Christian idea of salvation, is familiar to believers in different religions. It would be a mistake, however, to begin comparing these in isolation. The point is not that Christianity is like or unlike Buddhist, Judaic, or the African Ashanti tradition on any given point. Rather, the enduring structures of Christianity point to a ground that various religions share, where one can locate the deeper impulses of any religion. In other words, these enduring structures suggest the depth of Christianity's power as a religion, operating below the surface changes of history. Christianity, of course, expresses and shapes these common impulses in its own distinctive way: Salvation is not the same as enlightenment in Buddhism; the Eucharist is not equivalent to ancient practices of sacrifice. The deeply embedded common structures interact with the historical particularities to produce a distinctive religion. So we must learn to stretch our minds here to encompass both the universal and the particular religious impulses expressed in Christian religious structures.

We will take yet a third approach to understanding in chapter 22, filling out our outline of history and structure by looking at two specific examples of Christian belief and practice in a time of significant change. One example will be a twelfth-century pilgrimage to the Roman Catholic shrine of Saint James of Compostela in Spain. The second takes place within a family famous in nineteenth-century American religion, in which a daughter, Harriet Beecher Stowe, struggles with her spiritual inheritance from her father, Lyman Beecher. Both examples will give us brief but valuable glimpses into the rich and intricate dynamics of Christian life, showing us the interweaving of traditional beliefs and practices with new thoughts, desires, and goals. Chapter 23 will offer some general observations about Christianity and set forth a few of the problems faced by modern Christians.

This multidimensional approach aims to provide a rich picture of Christianity by utilizing a variety of perspectives, bringing some material into view more than once to reinforce learning and provoke questions. The student should be forewarned, however, that no work on so large a subject can be exhaustive. It is to be hoped that readers will supplement this information with some readings in primary text material, to encounter at first hand the words of Christians speaking for themselves about their beliefs, arguing with one another, praying, or singing. Such readings will enliven the discussion in the text and provide points of entry for deeper study and for questioning the interpretations put forward here.

For this essay is also meant to be argued with. History is being rewritten every day; our understanding of religion itself is undergoing dramatic change in this generation. As something to argue with, this work will serve a much greater purpose than it can by simply being read from an interested distance.

20

The Historical Development of Christianity

THE RELIGION WE KNOW as Christianity originated as a small sect within the religion of Judaism in the fourth decade of the first century. In the years 30–100 C.E. small groups of interested Jews and Gentiles (non-Jews) were beginning to gather themselves as a distinct body within Judaism, both in the land of Israel (Palestine) and in the larger Roman Empire. At the outset these groups kept many of the Jewish practices of their times: They observed some of the dietary laws and the Sabbath (Saturday), celebrated the major festivals, and honored the Holy Temple in Jerusalem, although they probably paid little attention to the priestly rituals of purity. Yet they had certain peculiarities: The members also gathered on Sunday, the first day of the week, for a common meal culminating in a ritual of bread and wine, and all members would have undergone a special ritual immersion, or **baptism,** before being admitted to their first ritual meal.

These new additions to Jewish ritual life were connected to a distinctive set of beliefs that formed the religious rationale of the new community. We can best grasp the nature of early Christianity by seeing how these beliefs and practices emerged. For example, we must understand that the ritual immersion was a baptism of repentance: Those who had repented of all their **sins and turned to a** new life would be cleansed in the natural waters of a river or lake. Just as many Jews, then and now, practiced immersion before Yom Kippur (the Day of Atonement, when they believe all people are judged for their sins), so these sectarian Jews immersed themselves in preparation for the final Day of Judgment, the great Yom Kippur that would mark the end of the present world.

Christian **eschatology** held that the world as we know it was about to end. A new world would soon be ushered in with the return of God's Messiah (Gk. *Christos,* source of the English word "Christ"), that is, God's chosen king. These new believers came to be called Christians, that is, believers in the Messiah. They had in common a faith that the Christ had in fact appeared on earth already in the form of a man named Jesus, who had been killed by the Romans, crucified as a suspected political rebel. His followers believed he had been resurrected after three days—a development of the belief held by many Jews that the messianic age would include a general resurrection of the dead. Jesus had then

495

returned to be with God in heaven. His suffering or "Passion," death, and resurrection signified a complete victory over sin and evil in the world, ensuring the salvation of all believers; soon he would return to earth, judge the world, and inaugurate God's kingdom. Christians celebrated a ritual meal of bread and wine based on the memory of what Jesus had instituted among his first followers, to eat the bread as his body and the wine as his blood, reminding themselves of him and his death until he returned. Sunday was the "Lord's day," the day on which they commemorated the resurrection from the tomb.

Such a sect was not a startling new development. Like other religions of the time, Judaism had become preoccupied with the question of salvation: How were people to redeem themselves from the evil of this world? Different groups offered different answers. A number of sects awaited the coming of a Messiah who would restore independence to the land of Israel, either by force or by a spiritual hand. The Zealots, for example, looked toward political revolution as a means of ushering in the messianic era. Later, around 130–135 C.E., many Jews, including important rabbis, pinned their hopes on a man named Bar Kochba ("Son of a Star") as the Messiah who would lead the final revolt against Rome. From at least the first century B.C.E. a quiet, ascetic Jewish community called the Essenes, living near the Dead Sea, anticipated a final war between the Sons of Light and the Sons of Darkness, with leadership by one or more messianic figures. A prophetic man known as John the Baptist preached repentance and the coming kingdom of God during Jesus' lifetime; indeed, Christian tradition holds that Jesus was baptized by John, in effect continuing John's mission. Some baptist groups, perhaps including John's, believed in a supernatural being who occasionally came to earth as a divine incarnation to reveal God's will. Besides this, groups of Jews and non-Jews often gathered for table-fellowship, sharing a common meal in a ritual way. The new Jewish group that believed in a crucified Messiah was therefore unique in some ways, but not so much as to stand out in a society of such diverse religious preferences as first-century Judaism. [See Judaism p. 405 for mention of the Messiah and Bar Kochba.]

☛ What soon began to make the Christians more noticeable was their intense **evangelizing** activity. Judaism had long made it a practice to accept converts, and in the Hellenistic period (the period of Greek cultural dominance, roughly 300 B.C.E.–300 C.E.) some Jews actively sought out Gentiles who would come to learn Jewish wisdom in the synagogues. Synagogue membership usually included a number of converts plus a number of "God-fearers," as they were called, who supported the synagogue and learned there without completing the conversion process (which included **circumcision** and ritual immersion). Jews and non-Jews, therefore, frequently intermingled. [See Judaism p. 386 for discussion of conversion; see Judaism pp. 385–86, 445–46, Islam pp. 677–678, 680, 682, and Religions of Africa p. 76 for discussion of circumcision.]

Christians, however, took on an active missionary effort far beyond what Jews had ever done. The original followers of Jesus, including the **apostles** and other early adherents, became wandering teachers and healers. Convinced that the world was about to end, with a strong inner sense of living in virtually another world already, they traveled about, preaching the "gospel" or "good news" that the Messiah of God had appeared on earth and all should repent of their sins. Like Jesus, they practiced healing and exorcism of demons (which were believed to cause some illnesses), and by healing people they demonstrated their power over the present evil world. Throughout the Roman Empire, from Asia Minor to Spain, they taught in or near synagogues and organized new communities of believers. This missionary impulse outlasted the first few generations. Even when Jesus did not return, Christians continued their evangelistic work, and the evangelical attitude became deeply ingrained in the Christian tradition.

Christian missions gradually succeeded in establishing the new religion throughout the Roman Empire, increasingly among non-Jews rather than Jews. The written documents of early Christians, especially the letters of Paul and the Book of Acts (by the same author as the Gospel of Luke), reveal many issues raised in the first generation about the admission of non-Jews, particularly how much of Jewish law they should observe. In the time of Paul's ministry (approximately 40–60 C.E.), after heated arguments, the churches dropped the requirement of circumcision and modified the dietary laws, making it easier for Gentiles to enter. Both Gentile and Jewish Christians undertook a lengthy period of study, usually almost a year, before baptism. They studied the Bible— that is, the Jewish Bible in Greek translation, known as the Septuagint. Presumably they learned the outline of the legends and records of Jewish history and the Christian interpretation of the Hebrew prophets. (Christians read the prophetic words about God's chosen king as referring to Jesus. Jews understood the same texts differently; in some cases they did not understand them to be messianic in meaning at all.) New Christians may also have learned secret or mystical interpretations of Jesus and of Christian rites.

The shift to a predominantly non-Jewish environment and membership of most churches, combined with their use of a Greek translation, led to the development of Christianity as a religion thoroughly independent from Judaism —truly a new religion rather than a variation on the parent tradition. First of all, Hellenistic interpretations deeply influenced the basic beliefs of the church. Even the basic assertion that Jesus was God's chosen was understood differently by non-Jews than by Jews. For example, many other Hellenistic religions believed in a savior figure, divine or semi-divine, who would save human beings from the evils of this world and transport them to a heavenly realm beyond the planetary spheres. As Christianity quickly spread away from Palestine (which itself was influenced by Greek culture), the Jewish messianic idea of a human king divinely chosen to rule on earth combined with, or gave way to, the Hellenistic view that "Jesus the Christ" was a divine savior from the heavens. In this view, belief in Christ as divine, together with repentance from sin and acceptance of the rites of the church, could bring assurance of "salvation"— eternal life in an otherworldly sense—when Jesus returned.

Early believers also developed new interpretations of the **Holy Spirit.** Tradition held that when Jesus' followers gathered in Jerusalem for the Jewish festival of Shavuot ("Weeks," being seven weeks after the beginning of Passover, and called Pentecost by Greek-speaking Jews), they received the Holy Spirit.

Tongues of fire seemed to appear over their heads, and they began prophesying or "speaking in **tongues**"—probably an outpouring of languagelike sounds or words in known or unknown languages. This outburst of ecstatic speech, not at all unusual in new, enthusiastic spiritual communities, marked in Christian tradition the occasion of God's sending his Spirit on the church to guide it until Jesus returned. The Holy Spirit became God's manifestation on earth, eventually regarded as part of the **Trinity** of Father, Son, and Holy Spirit, which were the three manifestations of God's self-revelation. The church itself as recipient of the Holy Spirit, and especially its leaders to whom authority had been given by **laying on of hands,** represented God's activity on earth. [See Judaism pp. 433, 440, 443–44 for discussion of Passover and Easter.]

Thus the early Christian churches constituted enthusiastic, often "spirit-filled" communities. Living in high expectation of a glorious world to come, blessed with gifts of healing and spiritual ecstasy, they often felt they lived in a new world already by their faith in the Christ. Originally a Jewish sect, they quickly developed their own new practices and gradually dropped many of the observances that made them distinctively Jewish. Of course, many elements inherited from Judaism remained in the **liturgy** and in theological attitudes. Keeping the Jewish Bible as a basic text ensured some continuity. Increasingly, however, Christianity followed its own way, cutting its ties to traditions of Jewish learning and, indeed, often turning against its parent tradition. Christianity's relative lack of success among Jews led some early writers to castigate the Jews for rejecting Jesus, wrongly accusing them of responsibility for Jesus' death. Also, Christians had to defend their faith against Roman misunderstanding: How could they claim to be carriers of the true Jewish faith (as they did in order to claim freedom of worship) while supplanting the practices of the ancestral religion? Together with the psychological difficulties of individuals who were departing from their mother religion, these factors planted in the writings that became part of the Christian Bible the seeds of antagonism that would later support Christian anti-Semitism. The great spiritual ecstasy and evangelical passion that characterized early Christianity thus had also a dark side in antagonism toward Jews.

Organization and Development

The period from about 150 C.E. until about 450 C.E. was crucial in shaping this diverse movement into an organized religion with its own institutions. We can trace the development in leadership, literature, forms of worship, and theology.

The first century of Christianity, until about 150 C.E., had seen the expansion of the earliest small, dedicated groups into larger groups of converted Jews and Gentiles—and eventually groups not identified as Jewish at all—dotted throughout the cities and larger towns of the Roman Empire. In Israel, where Christianity was important before 70 C.E., members were mostly villagers; outside that land, converts were mostly from the urban middle class. At first, wandering preachers led the congregations, but soon settled local leadership emerged. Early groups gathered in homes on Sunday mornings. Roles were assigned to keep order because of the great spiritual excitement in some churches and the debates and disputations in others. "Teachers" emerged as the primary local leaders, and evangelists continued traveling on missions. The **deacon** was one of the local leaders responsible for managing the ritual and perhaps for other administrative duties. This became the lowest priestly office (that is, an office requiring the laying on of hands by a **bishop**). Women were prominent as teachers in the early church but were not allowed to rise higher than the level of deacon; in later generations men appropriated even that role to themselves alone. The central figure in any community was the bishop, originally elected by all the Christians in a given city (as determined by the Roman city boundaries). The bishop, as spiritual head of the church, celebrated the ritual of bread and wine for the entire community until it became too large to gather in one building. He selected and ordained, by laying on of hands, priests to be his assistants, and as the community grew, priests celebrated the Eucharist for outlying churches. Gradually, a greater hierarchy emerged, in some respects parallel to that of the empire. The bishop of the capital city of a Roman province became the center of power for his province. By the third century there were four centers of power in the church: Jerusalem, Antioch (in Syria), Alexandria (in Egypt), and Rome. The bishop of each, called a **patriarch,** held authority coordinate with the three others. After the reign of Constantine and the establishment of Constantinople (formerly Byzantium; now Istanbul, Turkey) as the new capital in his name in the fourth century, that city and Rome began to move into prominence ahead of the others. By that time Christianity had a strongly organized government of municipalities with a great deal of power vested in the upper levels.

During the first three centuries the literature that eventually became the New Testament was written, copied, and shared among the churches. (All the early churches also used the Jewish Bible—Torah, Prophets, and Writings—which came to be known as the Old Testament.) The earliest Christian literature known to us is the letters of Paul, written during his missionary work between 40 and 60 C.E. Shortly afterward came the Gospels, which are stories of Jesus' life, and Acts, telling of the deeds of the early apostles.[2] The various other letters come from the late first or early second century, some of them written in the name of Paul to enhance their authority. The Book of Revelation, in the form of an **apocalypse,** probably was written down shortly after 100 C.E. Christian communities also produced other works not in the New Testament—other gospels, letters, acts, and apocalypses. But because of their small circulation, lack of apostolic authority, or late composition, the organized Christian church did not include them when, in the third and fourth centuries, it began to draw together its body of holy literature. [See Religions of Mesoamerica p. 179, Native Religions of North America p. 285, Judaism pp. 390–94, Islam pp. 635–37, 648–53, 665–72, Hinduism pp. 728–29, 738–43, 750–53, Buddhism p. 861, Religions of China pp. 995–96, 999–1000, 1031, and Religions of Japan pp. 1100, 1101 for discussion of Bible, scriptures, and religious texts.]

Also in the first three centuries Christian liturgy began to take shape. Originally Christians gathered on Sunday mornings for a common meal that included the rite of bread and wine, that is, the Eucharist or "thanksgiving." Soon this rite was separated from the rest of the meal, the *agape* or communal love-feast, which was more casual. The Eucharist took center stage; it became the primary Christian **sacrament,** a rite of great spiritual power that communicated **grace** by re-enacting the saving acts of Jesus himself. For most of Christian history this ritual has been regarded as a mysterious and indeed **mystical** sharing in the body and blood of Christ. In chapter 21, we will see in greater detail its significance; for now, it is sufficient to note that the Eucharist became the central act around which an entire liturgy evolved: prayers, hymns of glory and thanksgiving, Scripture readings, and sermons.

In many respects, then, the churches were moving toward uniformity in rite and literature and toward hierarchy in organization. Yet Christianity included a great deal of diversity well into the third century. The variety of literature circulated in the early years is one indication of differences among communities; also, Paul's letters show that each church had its own spiritual, theological, and organizational problems. From the second century onward, Christians tended to express their differences in debates over doctrine. In the philosophically oriented Hellenistic world, it was expected that any sophisticated religion would develop a body of correct, rational thought. However, in Christianity it was not always easy to agree on a single formulation of religious wisdom; so various Christian theologies emerged, some of which actually split the churches into hostile factions. It will be helpful for us to glance briefly at some of the important theological debates.

In the second century some groups of Christians claimed a special knowledge, or *gnosis,* apart from the written literature and traditions handed down to the bishops (presumably from Jesus' first apostles). Most of these Gnostics, as they were called, believed that the world was created by, and under the control of, an evil god. The true God was totally separate from any material creation and was known only through special spiritual revelation. Marcion, a Christian leader from Asia Minor who preached in Rome in the second century, argued, for example, that the church should not keep the Old Testament because it was the book of the evil creator God. In the middle of the third century, another leader arose in the East, the prophet Mani (d. 276), who called himself Apostle of Jesus Christ. Mani taught that the universe was divided into the forces of Light and Darkness and that the God of Light had sent many messengers to human beings, but the most perfect of these was Jesus, a truly divine being who only seemed to be mortal and material. Thanks to Jesus, the fragments of Light in the souls of humans could be caught up after death, distilled, and returned to the realms of Light.

Both Marcion and Mani gained many followers (even Augustine, later the great orthodox bishop and theologian, spent nearly ten years as a Manichee). Manichean churches were powerful up to the sixth century and in the eastern regions even to the year 1000. The Orthodox churches eventually succeeded in establishing their primacy, however. By the fourth century most Christians had come to agree that Jesus was both human and divine, the "son" of the good God who had created the world. Yet there were still arguments: How exactly was Jesus related to God? If he was divine, were there two Gods? Or was he less than God, as some statements in Scripture seemed to indicate (e.g., "My Father is greater than I").

Such questions led to another series of controversies, the most important one beginning in fourth-century Alexandria. There a church elder named Arius argued that Christ was different from God, indeed was created at a certain point in time by God. Christ was not a mere man—rather, he was the Logos, the first principle of the cosmos, a primary angelic being through whom all else was created—but he was clearly a creature. The bishop's secretary (later bishop himself), Athanasius, claimed that Arius's view threatened the idea of salvation through Christ. For if Christ were merely a creature, he might even turn evil (as angelic beings had been known to do). Therefore Christ was not created but begotten, generated, from God himself. Soon, bishops and elders in many churches lined up on either side of the argument.

Constantine, who did not well understand why his subjects were quibbling over such a point, called a council in 325, the Council of Nicea, to settle the dispute. The bishops decided in favor of Athanasius, but the Arians continued to win adherents—including later emperors. Over the next few decades, Athanasius would be exiled four times for his views. At one point when Arians were in control, missionaries were sent west who converted some of the warrior societies to an Arian version of Christianity—a fact that caused difficulties centuries later in their coming to terms with Rome. The controversy shows how fervently Christians argued about doctrine—and how each argument could send ripples through the entire empire.

Yet, despite such controversies, the Christian churches within the empire did remain conscious of their underlying unity. One important factor in creating this consciousness was pressure from outside. Competition with numerous religious groups—Judaism, Hellenistic mystery cults, the worship of traditional Roman gods—pressured each group to define itself clearly. Christians defined themselves in relation to Judaism by recognizing their parent tradition and tried to claim they should enjoy the protected status of an "ancestral religion" so that under Roman law they would be allowed freedom of worship. They never gained that status, however, because Rome saw them as rejecting much of Jewish practice.

In relation to other religions, Christians entered into encounters with them through dialogue and debate with the Greek philosophical tradition that dominated the educational system of the empire. In the second century Justin Martyr developed an **"Apology"** for Christianity as *the* true philosophy in the Greek sense. He claimed that Christ was the manifest Logos, known to the Greeks as the first principle of the cosmos, that is, Wisdom. Socrates, he said, had known the Logos, so in effect he had known Christ. This "Logos theology" was highly influential in defining Christian doctrine—as we have seen, Arius used the idea in his theology. Earlier, the great scholar Origen of Alexandria (c. 185–254) had argued that Christianity was the culmination of all civilized culture; Eusebius of

Caesarea (263–339), the first church historian, propagandized for Christianity among the educated public—including his friend the emperor Constantine. The apologists thus paved the way for Christianity to become acceptable and powerful in the empire by enlarging the philosophical scope of the religion. And though these thinkers were often engaged in internal disputes, they also helped weld the churches together by uniting Christian ideas with the best of current Greek thought.

Persecution was another factor in promoting Christian unity, although its significance has sometimes been exaggerated. Christians came under attack as early as Nero's reign (54–68 C.E.), but that persecution and most others in the first two centuries were local and short-lived. By the middle of the third century, however, Christianity had become strong enough to come into direct conflict with Roman imperial religion, and that was when serious and thorough persecution, as a matter of imperial policy, began. At that time, in the face of increasingly serious external threats, the empire had to inculcate at least a minimal patriotism to forge some unity among the diverse cultures of the Mediterranean. The worship of traditional Roman gods and of the emperor served this function, while bringing some added economic benefits through donations and sacrifices. New laws therefore required Christians to sacrifice to the emperor; if they refused, they were subject to imprisonment or death. Some did sacrifice; some illegally bought a certificate stating they had performed the ritual. Others, upholding the church's view that such a practice compromised their allegiance to God, were persecuted under Decius (249–251), Diocletian (284–305), and Galerius (305–311 in the eastern half of the empire).

The persecutions, especially Diocletian's, shook the churches badly. Yet at the same time they publicized Christian beliefs and added to the church's list of heroes, exemplars of true faith: the martyrs (from the Greek *martyros,* "witnesses"). The martyrs followed in the footsteps of Jesus and of the first apostles; their suffering, like his, renewed the spiritual power of the church. The authority of their teachings and writings increased, and they were believed to ascend directly to heaven at death—unlike the ordinary believer, who had to wait for the return of Christ. Together with the early apostles and church fathers, the martyrs became the great saints of Christianity. As we will see, their power after death, enshrined in their **relics,** helped sustain believers in their faith.

The Church in the Later Empire

As the churches gained more adherents and organized more effectively, two divergent developments occurred. On the one hand, Christianity became the religion of the empire; on the other, a new spiritual movement emerged to challenge this close relation to society, **monasticism.** These represent the inner tension in Christianity between being involved in the world and withdrawing from it. We will see this tension often in the history of Christianity.

By the late third century Christians still numbered a minority of the population of the Roman Empire. Nevertheless, they were respectable and their churches soundly established, having proven their staying power in the competitive world of late Roman religion. Especially in Syria and Asia Minor, the Christian cult had grown dramatically in the previous hundred years. When in the late second century barbarian invasions and plagues threatened many cities, Christians had provided for their own poor, for widows, orphans, and the sick; they offered social and economic security in a world that had become less stable. This intense communal orientation, partly an inheritance from Judaism, distinguished Christianity from other Hellenistic religions and made it more successful than, say, Manicheanism. Other religious movements also offered such benefits as life after death or protection from demons, but they gave far less support to their members during their earthly lives. In Christianity many people found a firm social grounding, a stimulating intellectual life, a rich and dramatic liturgy, able leaders dedicated to the spiritual life, heroes to admire and emulate, and a hope for a future life beyond the grave.

Shortly, events put the capstone on the growing power of the Christians. Hardly had the persecution of Galerius ended when, in 312, the new emperor, Constantine, took a highly favorable attitude toward the Christians. Having received help in winning a battle from a deity he referred to as the "Unconquerable Sun" (possibly the Roman god Mithra), he soon found himself persuaded by Christian apologists that indeed this deity had to be the one God in Christ. He agreed to patronize the Christian church, although he also continued to support temples of various gods. With this move he gained considerable support among the urban population, countering the strength of his Eastern rival, Licinius. The outcome was that Christianity came to occupy a far more powerful position in the empire. No great influx of converts occurred, but wealth and influence shifted so that, over the next several generations, Christian bishops gained the eminence that Roman senators had once had. Christian celebrations gradually edged out traditional Roman ones, and the power of the churches superseded that of the influential non-Christian families of the empire.

Nevertheless, at the same time a number of critics had begun to question the worldly success of the churches and their growing interest in honors and prestige. Those who sought a higher spiritual life, a greater closeness to God, began to look elsewhere. Elsewhere, it turned out, was away from the cities entirely, in the desert. In 269 an eighteen-year-old Egyptian named Anthony declared his intention of battling with the demons alone, first on the fringes of his village, then farther into the desert. From 285 until his death in 356 (at the age of 105) he lived weeks from the nearest town, braving the elements and the demonic forces that appeared to him in the most terrifying forms. Athanasius, patriarch of Alexandria, wrote a biography of Anthony that spread the legend of his trials and victories. Before long, Christians in Mesopotamia, Syria, Armenia, and Egypt were leaving the centers of Mediterranean culture to become hermits of various styles.

In Syria the new seekers tended to become wandering holy men, wild and startling in appearance and behavior but revered by the villagers. Some adopted special disciplines, like Simeon Stylites (296–359), who sat atop a tall pillar for thirty years. At times as many as two thousand people gathered at the base to be near such holiness. The Roman emperor finally had to ask him to come down, for the crowds were a public nuisance. But it was to Simeon and others like him that the people brought their prayers, their arguments to be settled, and their children to be blessed. In Egypt, by contrast, the new monasticism took a communal turn. A farmer named Pachomius (c. 290–347) created a community in the desert by linking monks' cells and providing a system of mutual support for the hermits. By the year 400 there were seven thousand monks living in Pachomius's establishment. Again, they were the object of veneration from the townsfolk, who admired their courage and religious dedication. [See Islam pp. 659–62, Hinduism p. 772, Buddhism pp. 915–21, 942–52, Religions of China pp. 1004–5, 1009, 1033–34, 1056, and Religions of Japan p. 1102 for discussion of monasteries and monasticism.]

The monastic movement and the emergence of holy men affected all of Christianity. Western bishops often distrusted the new movement, but a few leading churchmen—Ambrose in Milan (Italy), Martin of Tours (Gaul), and Augustine of Hippo (North Africa)—supported monastic developments in the late fourth century. In the East, the holy men were respected and feared by people of all social ranks. In effect, monks and hermits became the new models of martyrdom as the church conquered the Roman world. The battle against traditional Roman religions, exemplified in the martyrs, was over. Now a different battle began with less tangible forces of evil, namely, the demonic forces that infected people and threatened their souls. Wealth, sexuality, any kind of worldly appetite could become a great temptation. Monks exemplified their conquest of the world and their otherworldly power by being celibate, eating little and fasting frequently, and living an impoverished life without care for worldly comforts. Constantly before them stood the great goal: to persevere in the battle, to win the race, to overcome through great personal ordeals. Their persistence in the life of perfection, Christians believed, brought them closer to Christ and to God and assured them final victory on the Day of Judgment.

Monks brought spiritual power through their battles in the desert, and bishops and new Christian aristocrats brought it to the upper echelons of the empire, but another sort of holy personage extended the benefits of Christian power to all: the dead holy one, that is, the saint. Those who had died as martyrs or performed great miracles became available to Christians on earth as heavenly friends, as protectors or patrons. Their graves were holy sites and their relics—bones, teeth, or pieces of clothing—were holy remnants that still carried the personal power of the saint. The veneration of relics grew so popular that bishops even ordered tombs opened so that saints' remains could be transported to various parts of the empire; wealthy Christians would then build new shrines for the relics. Roman families had often held ritual meals at the graves of their ancestors; now bishops began to celebrate the **Mass** at the graves of saints—the honored spiritual "ancestors" of the Christian "family." Later, churches put relics under their altars as a kind of foundation stone for the holiness of the church itself, or encased them in jeweled boxes to be displayed behind the altar. Relics attracted devotion from people at all levels of society for hundreds of years.

Christian political power, the ascetic movement, and devotion to relics all signaled a gradual unification of fourth- and fifth-century Christianity. Roman religions lost ground, and dissenting Christian groups found it increasingly difficult to make headway against orthodoxy, as the "catholic" church became in fact the "universal" church of the empire. One of the landmarks of this development was the life and work of Augustine, bishop of Hippo in North Africa. First a follower of the philosophy of Plato and then of the religion of Mani, Augustine converted to Catholicism and became a political and intellectual leader of the first rank. In the early years of the fifth century he was influential in helping the orthodox defeat a competing African church, that of the Donatists, that claimed it was the true, pure church because its bishops had never given in to persecutors. Later he was involved in an important theological controversy over the extent to which human beings have free will in achieving salvation. Augustine held a doctrine of **predestination,** that God had determined the fate of each soul from the beginning; his chief opponent, Pelagius, argued that individuals are free to accept or reject God's grace.

From about 413 onward Augustine began writing his great work *De Civitate Dei (On the City of God)*, answering Roman charges that Christianity had weakened the empire. Augustine argued that all worldly states and empires, including Rome, are corruptible and ultimately will die; only the City of God is eternal. Christians therefore reside as aliens in this world; their true home is the eternal city that awaits them after this life. Followers of traditional Roman religions invest too much in this world, which, beautiful though it is, is transient and full of suffering, marred by the divine punishment of Adam's sin. Christians who long for the other world have as their protector and guard the church and its sacraments, for the church is a shadow here on earth of the true heavenly city. This attitude toward the church and the world was satisfying to Augustine's generation, troubled by the incursions of barbarians and the economic ups and downs of late imperial society. It also offered a basis for a continued critique of the world, and as such his work has been a resource for theologians down through the centuries. *The City of God* marked the unification of Christianity as a religion in this world, promoting good order on earth, but with aspirations that went far beyond the ordinary round of life.

Yet, at the same time, Christians were beginning to regard the state itself and the emperor as sacred; and the unity that Augustine expressed was melting away in the heat of the growing differences between East and West. Augustine himself could barely read Greek, the language of the eastern half of the empire and of many great thinkers of the time; and most Greek thinkers would never become interested in his doctrine of predestination. [See Religions of Africa pp. 24, 35, 60, Religions of Mesoamerica pp. 198–201, Native Religions of North America pp. 347–48, Judaism pp. 391–92, Islam pp. 632–33, Hinduism p. 748, Buddhism pp. 875–77, 952–53, Religions of China pp. 991–93, and Religions of Japan pp. 1095–96, 1105–6 for the relationship of religion to political leaders.]

Eastern and Western Branches of the Church

We might have expected a division in Christianity between those who supported king and empire and those who favored the monastic ideal. But this did not happen. Instead, the Christian world divided geographically.

While the links among Christian institutions—monasteries, shrines, churches —formed an interlocking network that crisscrossed the entire Roman Empire, still a rift was forming that would eventually undermine the broad cultural continuity of Mediterranean Christianity. Before 400 C.E. the most important boundaries seemed those between south and north, between the "civilized" Mediterranean world and the "barbarian" kingdoms of Europe. That border gradually eroded in favor of one between the East, centered in Constantinople (formerly Byzantium, where Constantine had moved his capital), and the West, centered in Rome, where the western patriarch kept his seat.

The West had been more recently Christianized, for the Roman senators and upper classes had long remained loyal to the worship of the Roman gods. Moreover, the West was threatened earlier by barbarians who wanted to enter the wealthy Mediterranean world. Christian leaders in the West therefore felt more precarious in their positions, and they built a strong organization of the elite that, much like the old Senate, sharply defined its own status. Wandering holy men and monks were not so welcome in the West, unless they submitted to the power of Rome. As for the martyred saints, they were, as historian Peter Brown has put it, safely dead, and the hierarchy could control their shrines. In general, holiness was more clearly the monopoly of the church hierarchy— priests, bishops, and the patriarch of Rome, who came to be called the pope (i.e., "father").

In the East, by contrast, there was still a strong emperor (Rome's last had been a boy, Romulus Augustus, in 476), and the Eastern emperor occupied a semi-priestly position. He could not perform sacraments or alter the **dogma** formulated by councils, but he could preach, hold the Eucharistic cup of wine in his own hands, and bring incense around the altar during the Mass. Other laymen as well were more powerful in the East, for they could participate in church councils. Thus lay power permeated the church, and religious power permeated all of society, for a variety of monks and holy men inhabited villages and towns throughout the countryside. Christian spirituality was more generally accessible, not primarily the possession of the elite. There could be direct human contact with the holy. Indeed, one of the teachings of the Eastern church was that "God became Man, that men might become God."

These differences made for different religious emphases and styles of spirituality. The West focused on the grandeur and awe of the work of God in the world, particularly in the sacrifice of himself, in Christ, for the sake of all humanity. A strong awareness of sin marked the distance between an ordinary human life and a life of true holiness. Yet, because of the great miracle of Christ's sacrifice, human beings could be freed from sin. The Eucharist repeated this most awesome act; it was to be performed with utmost correctness. The emphasis on sacrifice, on purification from sin, and on perfection in ritual created an atmosphere of deep dignity and reverence that has been the hallmark of the Western liturgy. Moreover, in the rest of human life perfection was the goal, to be achieved through discipline, order, and obedience in an attitude of humility. The West thus came to focus on church order, exemplified in the development of church law and legal interpretation of Christian doctrines. (The tradition of Rome itself contributed to this, of course, for the Roman legal system was unsurpassed in the ancient world.) Ultimately, the emphasis on personal discipline, purification, and correct action in ritual and the rest of life served the church well in its encounters with the non-Christian kingdoms to the north and west.

Such themes were by no means absent in the East, but the Orthodox church focused more on the mystical goal of Christian life: the knowledge of God, unity with Christ, unity with the divine. The accent was on deification more than purification. The whole people participated in the process of deification through the Divine Liturgy and the veneration of icons. The Eucharist in the Orthodox church was more than a sacrifice to cleanse from sin; partaking of Christ's body and blood enabled one to share his humanity united with his divinity. In addition, the celebration was conceived as a wedding feast, in which the church below joined with the holy assembly of saints above in a foretaste of the future transformation of the world when Christ returned.

The heavenly host themselves were present, represented in the icons—portraits of angels, Christ, the **Virgin,** and saints—that stood in the front of the church, between the people and the altar. The originals of many of these paintings were believed to be miraculous appearances; the paintings themselves had to be prepared according to precise ritual, as exact copies of the originals. The icon could be venerated by bowing and kissing because it was believed to be a faithful representation of a heavenly archetype, so true to the divine that it was an earthly reflection of God himself. Indeed, the entire theology of Orthodoxy could be said to be iconic in tone. Each person was believed to have an image or icon of God within him- or herself; the Bible, like an icon, was a faithful reflection of the heavenly "book" of God now made present in words accessible to the worshiper. God becoming human had meant the revelation of the divine energies throughout the world, concentrated with special intensity in the church, its liturgy, and its icons. The Eastern church thus nourished a sense of the continuing transformation of human beings through the divine presence, whereas the West encouraged human striving for perfection through discipline, humility, and sacrifice.

The differences between East and West sharpened as the centuries passed. On the one hand, their different structures of power led to competition between the Roman pope and the Eastern emperor. The pope believed that only he, as the highest churchman, should direct the goals and aims of Christian society; any king was to be the church's protector and the executor of the pope's policies. The emperor saw himself as part priest, part king, and in all ways suited to rule all of society, settling its policies and making its laws. The church should perform its special task of maintaining a proper relationship with God, but it should not rule. On the other hand, each branch of the church had to deal with very different problems. In the West the barbarian invasions took precedence: In the fifth and sixth centuries various societies on the perimeters of the empire attacked Rome, southern Italy, Africa, and Gaul (roughly equivalent to modern France). From then on, the popes and their missionaries had to deal with European societies that were, from their viewpoint, primitive and pagan, and in any case very different from urban, literate Christianity. The Eastern church faced Persia, a sophisticated society, with its mixture of Zoroastrian and mystical traditions, and then later confronted Islam. Both were literate, imperialistic societies with their own high theologies and ethics. As a result, differences between East and West grew; the two branches of Christianity maintained contact, but their interaction had little lasting significance until the time of the Crusades.

The Eastern church was part of an empire, the Byzantine, that went on continuously for many centuries after the decline of Rome; indeed, its government and economy functioned more effectively for a longer period of time (over seven centuries) than any other state in history. Thus, whereas some historians have seen a sharp break in Christian history after the fall of Rome, it is preferable to see the Eastern church as the continuation of imperial Christianity. Doctrinal controversy continued: The fifth through the seventh centuries saw the church preoccupied with the Arian issue, and then with a new heresy known as the Monophysite (from the Greek, meaning "one nature"). The Monophysites objected to the accepted formulation of the church (since the Council of Chalcedon in the fifth century) that Christ was of two natures: "truly human, truly divine." They held that he could only be divine, and his divine nature had absorbed the humanity in him. Later, in the eighth and ninth centuries, the church faced a great storm over the use of icons. Influenced by Muslim sentiments against images, the emperor Leo III ordered in 726 that all holy images of Christ, the Virgin, and the saints be destroyed. Opposition came from the monks, the people, and the Western pope. Icons were restored by the empress Irene in 787, but later emperors renewed Leo's order; only in 843 did the empress Theodora restore them again, finally ending the controversy.

These issues suggest the continuing tension in the Eastern church over the nature of divinity and the nature of holiness. The rise of the new and powerful religion of Islam in the seventh century accentuated such issues. For the prophet Muḥammad and his successors adopted a strongly Semitic view of these matters, not unlike that of the ancient Hebrew prophets: There was only one God; only he was divine. Human beings could not achieve divinity. Images of God were absolutely forbidden. Many Christians in Asia Minor had also held similar views, and they tried to reform their religion accordingly. Ultimately, the rich aesthetic and theological tradition of the icons prevailed, and the church upheld its views of the union of divinity and humanity. [See Islam pp. 625–29 for treatment of the rise of Islam and Muḥammad.]

The continuing strength of the Orthodox church after these controversies shows in the expansion that followed. In the ninth century the Bulgars, a strong empire in the Balkans, embraced Eastern Christianity. In the later ninth and tenth centuries the rest of the Balkan nations, the Slavs, and finally Russia came into its orbit. Byzantine culture influenced that of Arabs to the East, transmitting knowledge of the Greek language and Greek philosophers, artistic styles, and techniques of work. For example, the Mosque of Omar (Dome of the Rock), built in Jerusalem in the late seventh century, has a Byzantine dome and Byzantine-style mosaics. In return, Byzantine artists learned from Arabic ornamental styles. We find in Orthodox Christianity from the seventh through the tenth centuries a religion united with a rich Eastern imperial culture, often at war with its Islamic neighbors but also participating in an exciting cultural exchange that helped the younger Islamic empires to mature and reach their own heights.

This great period gave way to another, more difficult one, however. The eleventh century brought internal difficulties, invasions by the Seljuk Turks and the Normans, and controversies with the West. Already a number of incidents had increased difficulties between East and West. In the sixth century the Roman church, combating Arians in Spain, had added a clause to its **creed** stating that the Holy Spirit proceeded from the Father "and the Son." This usage became entrenched in the church and was approved by Western authorities without ever being presented to a whole council of the church; the Greek branch had theological objections. In the ninth century, the rivalry between pope and patriarch had erupted into direct political conflict as Pope Nicholas I tried to intervene in the appointment of the Eastern patriarch.

This Byzantine icon from the late thirteenth century shows the Madonna and Child on a curved throne. (Used by permission of the National Gallery of Art, Washington, D.C.; Andrew W. Mellon Collection.)

Finally, in the eleventh century the Normans conquered the Byzantine colony of southern Italy, and Pope Leo IX insisted that the Orthodox change their allegiance from patriarch to pope. Naturally, the patriarch, Michael Cerularius, protested. In 1054 the pope sent three legates, headed by the strong-willed Bishop Humbert, to Constantinople to assert Western rights, but Cerularius received them scornfully. They then entered the cathedral of Saint Sophia and deposited there a bull of **excommunication** against Cerularius and his supporters. Michael immediately convoked a council and in return excommunicated the legates. This event has traditionally marked the formal division between Catholic and Orthodox churches, for despite later attempts to heal the breach, the two never reunited.

As we will see, the West later launched crusades that were intended in part to help the weakened East, suffering the attacks of the Turks. They accomplished nothing lasting in its defense, however, and the behavior of the crusaders and their eventual attack on Constantinople itself destroyed relations between East and West. The disordered relations between the two branches weakened both civilizations when they had to face their enemies. The centuries of poor communication led to the West's losing touch with some of its original sources of spirituality, the great mystical and theological traditions of the East. On the other hand, the Eastern empire never recovered its strength after the onslaughts of Latin Christians and Muslims, and the Orthodox church, united as it was with its culture, suffered as well. Organizationally, the Eastern church divided into its various national branches—Greek, Russian, Serbian, Armenian, Syrian, and so on. The Russian church became so important that Moscow was given its own patriarch in the fourteenth century. These churches, however, regarded themselves as unified in tradition and never became competitive with one another as the later Western denominations would be.

Moreover, the Eastern church continued its creativity in the realm of spirituality, especially in the centuries before the Turkish conquest of Constantinople (1453). The monks of the Byzantine Empire developed a spiritual discipline known as "hesychasm," referring to the aim of the practice: tranquility or serenity. Their methods included specific postures and forms of breathing as well as mental concentration, similar in some respects to yogic or other forms of meditation. They repeated a prayer, usually the "Jesus Prayer" ("Lord Jesus Christ, Son of God, have mercy on me a sinner") as a kind of *mantra* or repeated verbal formula, aiming to achieve a state of ceaseless prayer. This would ultimately result in a vision of God, not with the ordinary eye or even with the mind, but through divine illumination of one's being. This illumination by God's "grace" did not mean, as grace did in the West, that something was added to human nature, but rather that the human, the created being, now participated in God's uncreated "energies," that is, the powers that God manifests (his essence always remaining hidden). This was the mystical and theological development of the idea of deification, which as we noted before was prominent in Eastern thought and liturgy for centuries.

While the Eastern church developed its inward spirituality in theological reflection, the Roman branch was developing the political allies it needed to ensure its survival. The pope sought the help of the Franks, who had converted to Christianity in 496 when their lord Clovis accepted baptism. Their leaders afterward helped Rome militarily against other societies (Arian Christian and non-Christian), and Rome sent, to both Gaul and England, Benedictine monks as missionaries and teachers. Irish monks also traveled into Frankish lands, and through these two sets of teachers Christianity began to penetrate Europe. After nearly two centuries of missionary work, however, many people had not accepted church discipline. A church council in 742 under the leadership of the great missionary Boniface ordered monks and priests to refrain from battle, insisted that priests give up their concubines, and forbade rites such as animal sacrifices and magical incantations in the churches. Christianity was still competing with many older customs and religious practices.

A few decades later when Charles the Great (Charlemagne) took the Frankish throne, he renewed Boniface's orders and added other measures to strengthen the church. He ordered that all altars without relics be destroyed, that all oaths be sworn on a relic, and that no new saints be introduced. These steps aimed at orienting the clergy more firmly toward Rome, while at the same time insisting that Christianity alone was the guarantor of bonds between men. Further, Charles instituted a program of education, decreeing that every monastery and bishopric should set up a school. The prior state of learning is suggested by the fact that one Bavarian priest had been found baptizing converts *nomine patria et filia,* "in the name of the nation and the daughter," (instead of *nomine patri et filio,* "in the name of the Father and the Son"). Under the new system priests had to learn Latin, chanting, and calculation and had to memorize the major parts of the Mass and some sermons. Some would begin to study Scripture as well. At Charlemagne's encouragement books began to be collected and copied, and the Latin liturgy took definitive shape and spread through the realm.

Charlemagne's devotion to the faith and to Rome were recognized in his famous coronation in the year 800, when Pope Leo III anointed him Emperor of the Romans, creating what came to be known as the Holy Roman Empire. The coronation was a statement of Rome's independence from Constantinople, where there was already a Christian emperor. But it also officially confirmed that the Frankish rulers had accepted Christianity fully as an important dimension of their society. In 745 Pope Zacharias had written to the Frankish clergy and aristocrats, urging them to accept the reforms of Boniface. It was, he said, because they had false and misleading priests that their enemies had won battles. If the priests would become pure, observing chastity and refraining from bloodshed, the non-Christians would fall before the Christian armies. Christianity, in short, would provide the support of God for the Frankish warriors; they in turn would protect the church. Undoubtedly it had helped the cause that a Christian leader, Charles Martel, had won a great battle only a short time before, turning back the advance of the Muslim armies at Tours (in modern-day France) in 732. In any case, by 800 the coronation of Charles cemented the pact between church and state. Moreover, like the Eastern emperors, the Western ones came to believe they had a priestly role to fulfill: If the king, now emperor, fulfilled his obligations to God and dispensed justice and peace, he would ensure the salvation of his whole people. The bishops, on their part, believed it was their duty to keep the king and princes in line, advising them as to their Christian duties.

Nevertheless, the West could not duplicate the stability of the Eastern empire. By the late 800s Europe was again the target of raids from peoples on the perimeters. Vikings from Scandinavia, Magyars from Hungary, and Muslims in Spain engaged the people in continuous wars, reducing much of the population to dire poverty. Monks' chronicles tell of famines and epidemics, mob violence and mass deaths, even cannibalism in desperate attempts to stay alive. In this situation, power passed from the hands of the kings to the lesser nobles, each

The military orientation of early medieval Christianity in the West is suggested by these scenes from the Bayeaux Tapestry, about 1095, portraying events of the Norman conquest of England: William the Conqueror and his troops approaching the Mont St-Michel, and the English resisting the attack of the Norman Cavalry. (Used by permission of Editions d'Art Albert Skira, Geneva.)

of whom built his own power base to fight the enemies, leading to a decentralized Europe and the social structure known as the feudal system. Power lay in the hands of the warrior class, the knights, who paid homage to their sire, the noble of a principality. This reorganization of European society marks the beginning of a new era following the general disorder of the previous centuries, after the fall of Rome and the gradual break with the East. But it was not, at first, an era in which the church could be confident of its strength.

The Western Middle Ages

It was in the period called the "Middle Ages" that Christianity became the primary force in European society in a political sense and gave birth to a number of significant spiritual movements. First the church hierarchy had to deal with the nobles, who held the key positions in the social structure.

Christianity in the eighth and ninth centuries had adjusted to being the religion of a warrior society, but it had firm attachments only at the higher levels of that society. The lesser nobles, who came to power in the debacle of the tenth-century invasions, did not always respect the traditional rights of the religious class as the anointed emperors had done. Struggles soon began between the lay aristocracy and the bishops and abbots of the church. Church councils made rules limiting the power of nobles, threatening them with excommunication if they did not obey. In the early eleventh century the church declared the "Peace of God" to forbid knights from destroying church property and killing unarmed peasants, monks, and priests. This was followed by the "Truce of God," which forbade the "joys of war" during Lent and urged Christians not to fight other Christians. Although many knights vowed to uphold these, the agreements did not succeed in controlling vendettas and the raids of armies.

Meanwhile, the nobles on their part were fighting back by simply appointing their own men to be bishops or abbots in their territory. Traditionally, a king consecrated to God's service could appoint a churchman by "investing" him with the symbols of his office—for example, ring, hat, and crozier (staff) for a bishop—but the church usually had a say in his election. The nobles, however, were taking this power into their hands with neither divine right nor church approval. In the late eleventh century a dispute of this sort disturbed all of Europe when Pope Gregory VII excommunicated one of the German kings, Henry IV, who was appointing his own church officials and opposing Gregory's reforms. Henry humbled himself before Gregory after a dramatic march through the snowy Alps—a wise political, as well as religious, move; Gregory had virtually no choice but to grant him forgiveness. After his return to Germany, however, Henry called a council of bishops that deposed Gregory from the papacy. The struggle, which came to be known as the investiture controversy, continued beyond the lifetimes of Henry and Gregory and was resolved only in 1122 at the Concordat of Worms, which set some limits on the power of church and state.

Despite the power of the lords, the church gradually gained political ground during the controversy. The religious punishments the church could use, its practical alliances, and the supportive system of bishops built by popes like Gregory yielded greater power than ever before. Moreover, Gregory's insistence on the independence of the church signaled the growing influence of a new movement in Europe: the monasteries of Cluny. Cluny had been founded in the tenth century by William the Pious, Duke of Aquitaine, under an unusual charter linking it to the saints Peter and Paul, and thus to Rome rather than to local powers, and permitting the monks to elect their own abbot without interference from duke or bishop. Cluny and the monasteries associated with it became famous for many things: their devotion to the life of prayer, their emphasis on music, and their encouragement of the great Romanesque architecture of the eleventh century.[3] But they also became centers of political power because of their fierce insistence on the independence of the church from secular control. Thus it is no accident that Gregory VII, educated at an Italian monastery influenced by Cluny, initiated an era of powerful popes.

The investiture controversy was only one aspect of a new spirit in the church that, we can see in retrospect, was preparing the ground for a new religious movement. The church had dealt effectively with the nobles and, by the last twenty years of the eleventh century, Christian ideals and expectations had permeated most of European society. The reputation of Cluny was setting a model of discipline and devotion, and the knights, who sought to participate in Christian society but whose lust for battle often burst the bounds of Christian discipline, had become a powerful class. The fuel, so to speak, was ready. The spark was lit in a dramatic address by Pope Urban II, speaking to a public session at the end of a council of bishops meeting in 1095 at Clermont, France. Urban appealed to those present to come to the aid of the Eastern church, which was suffering at the hands of its Muslim conquerors. He also sought aid for Jerusalem, appealing to his listeners' fascination with the holy sepulcher of Christ in Jerusalem and assuring them that any who died in battle would be forgiven their sins. Thus Urban launched the First Crusade.

Popular response was overwhelming. Soon nobles were leading armies of trained soldiers while popular visionaries led thousands of poorer men, and even bands of children, toward Constantinople and Jerusalem. Defeating "the infidel" (by which Christians meant Muslims, and usually Jews as well) became the watchword of Europe. Mobs began massacring Jews, especially in the Rhineland, where more Jews were killed than in Jerusalem. The peasants' branch of the movement, known as the People's Crusade, arrived disorderly and hungry in Constantinople in 1096. The Eastern emperor, shocked at the sort of help sent by the West, provided them with rations, but most soon met death in Asia Minor in battles with the Muslims. The serious armies, arriving a few months later, spent time arguing with the emperor but eventually went on and, after lengthy battles, captured Jerusalem in 1099. As a result, several small Christian states existed in the region for nearly a hundred years, until the Muslims retook Jerusalem in 1187. Succeeding crusades failed to establish any significant expansion of Christian power. Meanwhile, the professed goal of the Crusades, to help the Eastern church, had disappeared. In 1204, during the Fourth Crusade, Western warriors attacked Constantinople itself, incurring the wrath of the East.

Despite the violence of the Crusades, the spiritual revival that the West experienced in the eleventh century with the growth of Cluny and the reforms of Gregory came to fruition in the next several generations. The twelfth century has been called a time of renaissance, a proto-Reformation, or the beginning of modernity; the thirteenth is generally considered the peak of medieval European civilization. The components of these developments were numerous: the growth of learning in monasteries and cathedral schools; the first universities; greater church involvement in secular affairs; an upsurge of religious devotion, especially to the Virgin and the Eucharist, and an increase in pilgrimage; the rise of heresies and the establishment of the **Inquisition;** new monastic orders, the Franciscans and the Dominicans; the rise of mysticism; and a revolution in art that culminated in the Gothic cathedral. Throughout, we can see significant changes in the way people regarded the divine or spiritual realm in relation to the human or material. In this period humanity and materiality took on a higher value, and gradually people came to see holiness within the world as well as coming from outside it.

One of the clearest examples of this transformation was the new work in the world of the intellect. In the eleventh century scholars began to reexamine Christian faith, seeking to understand it in terms of human reason. This was the beginning of the movement known as scholasticism. After 1085, when Spanish Christians conquered Muslim Toledo, Christians with the help of multilingual Jewish scholars began retranslating into Latin the Arabic translations of ancient Greek philosophers, the most important being Aristotle. Scholars flocked to Toledo and brought back the manuscripts that would further transform Christian theology. Intellectual life began to move out of the monasteries and into the universities at Paris, Oxford, and elsewhere. In the monasteries, study had been preliminary to prayer, *lectio* (reading) merely a preparation for *contemplatio,* the soul's search for God. The universities began to take a different turn, valuing learning as a means of gaining clarity and understanding in one's approach to God and allowing learning to be sought for its own sake. Further, the new **friars,** Franciscans and Dominicans, who contributed much to the growth of learning, were also more involved in the world. An interest in human knowledge and the capacities of the human mind struck new chords in the twelfth century and afterward.

These developments came to fruition in the thirteenth century in the work of the greatest medieval theologian, also a popular teacher, the Dominican Thomas Aquinas (1224/25–1274). Aquinas came to the fore in the Aristotelian controversy, as Greek philosophy was being introduced into university curricula. Some thinkers influenced by the Greeks were proposing radical ideas, such as that all human minds were but parts of one great Mind, or that the world was eternal. Others feared such ideas might undermine the church, calling into question the doctrine that God was a personal deity, or that God created the world from nothing and would bring it to an end. As a result certain propositions related to Aristotle's thought were condemned in the 1270s. Thomas Aquinas, however, developed a form of Aristotelianism that was acceptable to the church. His *Summa Theologica* ("comprehensive theology"), though still incomplete when he died, continued to attract other theologians and provided the foundation for Roman Catholic theology up to the twentieth century.

Aquinas diverged from Augustine, the rock of Christian thought since the fifth century. Augustine had emphasized the dependence of human beings on God: By God's grace, the human will is enabled to do good; by his divine illumination, the human mind is enabled to reach truth. The purely human side—the body, the senses, the ordinary mind—is at best only a vehicle, not a source, of good or truth; at worst, it is an obstacle. Aquinas rejected Augustine's dualism and held, in harmony with Aristotle, that the spiritual and the material were related rather than opposed. True knowledge begins not with divine illumination but with basic sensory experience of the world, followed by reflection using the natural faculty of human reason. Through this process one arrives at knowledge of "universals"—what we might call ultimate concepts as to the essences of things—that, as with Augustine, were the supreme truths.

Aquinas's theory had important ramifications: Human reason, and indeed human nature generally, were in the image of God. They were flawed by sin but not, as Augustine had held, completely corrupted. Humans needed correction by God's grace, mediated by the sacraments as medicine mediates healing power. Once corrected, human faculties could achieve perfection and human souls reach their true goal of full likeness to God. God's grace, in short, enabled human efforts to cooperate in God's own divine activity: to bring all souls to himself. The material and the spiritual, the natural and the supernatural, reason and revelation, were intertwined in a grand system that existed in perfection in the mind of God.

This was radical thinking in the thirteenth century, but it was paralleled in many ways by the intertwining of the religious and secular worlds in practical action. As we have seen, papal power was growing in the late eleventh and twelfth centuries. As intellectual life became more important, the church's control of education meant greater social power. The church drew on a centralized and dependable source of wealth, the papal treasury, and possessed an efficient bureaucracy. By the early thirteenth century, Pope Innocent III (in office 1198–1216)—who once wrote privately of himself that he was "less than God but more than man"—could influence the politics of all Europe. By frequent use of interdictions to suspend masses and other church rites in a given region, he brought German, French, and English princes into submission to the church. He called the great Fourth Lateran Council in 1215, which became a significant event in unifying the church. He supported and integrated into the church the new Franciscan and Dominican orders, thus bringing many potential dissidents into the mainstream, while also centralizing the Inquisition (introduced in the late twelfth century) to deal summarily with others. Innocent's rule was the peak of papal power, and it indicated how human and spiritual power were joining forces in the Middle Ages.

The changes among the elite in thought and politics found a reflection in forms of religious expression among the laity. New monastic orders, lay organizations, or heretical groups appeared in almost every generation from 1100 to 1300. Within the mainstream of the church, lay confraternities devoted to the Eucharist emerged in the twelfth century, emphasizing the importance of

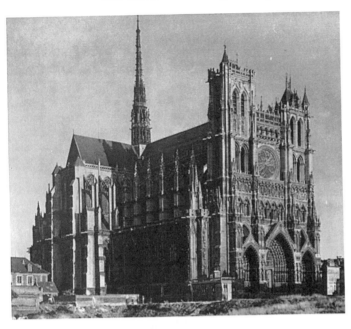

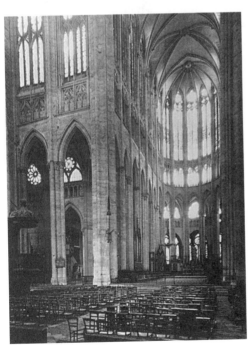

The artistic achievements of the Western Middle Ages culminated in the Gothic cathedral with its strong architectural construction, detailed sculptural design, stained glass windows, and effective use of interior light. Here, the Amiens Cathedral, France, built 1220–1288 (except for the towers, 1366–1420). (Photo used by permission of G. E. Kidder Smith, New York.) Below, the interior of Beauvais Cathedral, France (begun 1247). (Used by permission of Kresge Photo Study Archive, Department of Art, Oberlin College.)

communion and glorifying the moment of the **elevation of the host,** when the priest raised the bread for all to see. Innocent III officially declared the doctrine of **transubstantiation** (long an accepted church tradition): The wafer of bread and the wine actually became, in substance, the body and blood of Christ.

This was a shift from the attitude of the ninth and tenth centuries, when the Eucharist was regarded as more like a relic of Christ. Now the accent was on the transformation of ordinary material into the substance of Christ himself.

The twelfth and thirteenth centuries also saw a striking increase in expressions of devotion to the Virgin Mary, mother of Jesus. Previously local and regional saints and their relics had dominated popular devotion. Now there appeared numerous popular prayers to Mary (notably the *Ave Maria*), stories of her miracles, and portrayals of the Virgin in painting and statuary. Innocent III officially endorsed, despite the opposition of many scholastic philosophers, the popular feasts celebrating the **Immaculate Conception** of Mary (the notion that Mary was free of **original sin** from the moment of her conception). The movement of devotion centering around Mary was epitomized by the sermons of Bernard of Clairvaux, a leading figure of the twelfth century and a great mystic who organized a new monastic order (the Cistercians) and preached the Second Crusade. He urged all who were troubled to turn to Mary, to call out to Mary, in every kind of danger or hardship, for she was the guiding star for human life. Bernard and others gave impetus to the great movement of Marian piety that has continued in Roman Catholicism down to the present. It represented another reevaluation of the human world, specifically, of the feminine elements that, except for a few local female saints, had been ignored for centuries. The Virgin was the perfect woman, through whom one could approach Christ the king. That a woman should be so exalted was significant, when a few centuries earlier monks had debated whether women even had souls. Mary was unique, however, for she was chaste and sinless, unlike ordinary women who were tainted by the sin of sexuality like the first woman, Eve. "Alone of all her sex" as the phrase went, she could be glorified and venerated. Even with this qualification, however, the cult of Mary represented a shift in attitudes toward women and the feminine. Soon to follow was the more secular code of chivalry, glorifying the pure woman as the lady of love to whom every knight should bow and whose love was the most desired of all goals.

We have already mentioned briefly the new orders of friars, the Franciscans and Dominicans. Their members were not cloistered (i.e., confined to monasteries) but preached in the towns. Dominic (1170–1221), a Spaniard, saw his followers as primarily a teaching and preaching order, bringing religious knowledge to people while also battling the heretics. The Italian monk Francis (1182–1226) was more radical. He insisted on apostolic poverty—owning nothing, relying on no one but God for support—as the foundation of spirituality and taught his followers to travel about teaching, praying, and helping those in need. Church leaders were concerned about the potentially disruptive character of a movement that insisted that true followers of Christ should possess no property; thus a later leader, Bonaventura, who headed the order from 1257 to 1274, adjusted the ideals of poverty and itineracy to make the Franciscans more like the other monastic orders. Both Franciscan and Dominican orders are still part of the Roman Catholic church.

Other more marginal groups flourished as well. The Spiritual Franciscans, who wanted to keep Francis's original ideals, broke off from the main body and took up the ideas of an earlier mystical philosopher, Joachim of Fiore, who had taught that the age of the Father and the Son had passed and a new age of the Holy Spirit had arrived. The church promptly declared them heretics. A lay-women's movement emerged in the cities of France, the Netherlands, and the Rhineland: the Beguines, who dedicated themselves to a life of higher spiritual-ity together with work in the world. One of the great Christian heresies flour-ished in southern France in the 1200s, namely, Catharism, which adopted Gnostic ideas of extreme dualism, denying the goodness of the material world. These ideas had spread from the East, most recently from a teacher named Bogomil in the Bulgar Empire, where the Eastern church had been fighting such groups for centuries. The Cathars believed that the elect could subdue the body by per-fecting the spirit, not in itself an unusual idea. But they were heretics because they rejected the sacraments and practiced only the laying on of hands; more-over, they allowed women to act as priests. (Since the body was evil, however, procreation was discouraged, and pregnant women were denied the laying on of hands.) The Orthodox church acted vigorously to stamp out the Cathars by means of the papal Inquisition; still, it took nearly two centuries before their churches were effectively undermined.

As the church was becoming more worldly, such heresies as the Cathars offered an alternative, more otherworldly in orientation. So too did another movement within the church, namely, that of mysticism. Mysticism was not truly a popular movement, for only a few rare individuals were mystics; never-theless, it indicated a far-reaching interest in the interior life. Mystics adopted a more intense discipline in order to gain a direct experience of spiritual reality, ideally a vision of God. Their approaches differed considerably depending on their tradition and their own experience. Yet we may take as an example the approach developed by Bernard of Clairvaux.

Bernard taught that the spiritual life progresses by stages developed through disciplined control of one's action and prayerful devotion to God. He set them forth as follows: compunction, devotion, repentance, good works and prayer, con-templation, and love. Compunction meant recognizing one's evil ways followed by cutting away one's bad habits. Devotion was the first joyful turning to God, hoping for pardon. Repentance included fasting, keeping nighttime vigils, and other difficult tasks, while good works and prayer sustained the soul. Contem-plation was like a dream of God, beholding him as though in polished metal, but not yet face to face. Love was the perfection of the heart that warmed the soul. If one followed the stages faithfully, one could, over the years, come to a vivid and powerful experience of the love of God, which Bernard regarded as the ulti-mate attainment. Other mystics defined the stages slightly differently or described the goal in a different fashion—for example, as the union with God in knowledge of God. All, however, were turning away from involvement in events of the day toward a more intense experience of the inner life. Their creativity contributed another dimension to the rich culture of the twelfth through fourteenth centu-ries. [See Judaism pp. 422–27, Islam pp. 659–62, Hinduism pp. 752–53, Buddhism pp. 946–48, Religions of China pp. 1032–34, and Religions of Japan pp. 1102, 1121–27, 1151 for discussion of meditation and mysticism.]

In theology, in politics, in popular devotion, and in the search for higher spirituality these centuries were an enormously creative period. We should not imagine, however, that they were also a time of freedom or tolerance in our modern sense. The church, and most European Christians, remained on the defensive in regard to outsiders or those of divergent beliefs and practices. The Inquisition was on the alert for heresy; Abelard, a recognized French scholar, was declared a heretic, and a great mystic, Meister Eckhart of Germany, was accused of heresy. The church hierarchy regarded many of Francis's ideas as highly questionable. Moreover, this was the period in which perceptions of the Jews began to change: Instead of regarding them as resident aliens, accepted although not necessarily possessing the same rights as others, Christians began seeing them as demonic beings within the walls of Christendom itself (as Muslims were the evil forces outside). Attacks on Jews during the Crusades were part of this pattern. So were expulsions: In 1290 Jews were expelled from England, in 1305 from France, in 1492 and 1497 from Spain and Portugal, respectively. Intolerance and a fear of difference were part of the triumph of Christian culture in Europe. [See Judaism p. 430 and Islam p. 626 for persecution of Jews.]

European Religious Reformation

The gradual growth of lay devotional movements, mysticism, and dissidence reflected some dissatisfaction with traditional authority and a desire to modify religious practices in the Roman Catholic church. This mood would eventually lead some to break with the church or at least seek to reform it. We can see the seeds of reform in the fourteenth and fifteenth centuries. Even though scholastic theology was continuing to develop on what seemed to be a confident foundation of universal faith, radical leaders were beginning to challenge common practices of the church. In the late fourteenth century an English writer, John Wycliffe, called for vernacular translations of the Bible, lay communion with both bread and wine, the right of secular courts to punish clergy, and an end to the sale of indulgences. A group that took up his ideas, the Lollards, was implicated in uprisings against the crown a few years later. In Bohemia, John Huss of the University of Prague led a related movement based on Wycliffe's ideas, with the result that the Czech armies threatened to invade other parts of Europe. The Council of Basel in 1449 settled that particular dispute, but these movements foreshadowed the growth of large popular, sometimes nationalistic, movements for religious reform.

The conditions leading to the call for reform were manifold. Europe suffered a great deal of inner turmoil in the fourteenth and early fifteenth centuries. The Black Death beginning in 1348 destroyed one-third of Europe's population. The Hundred Years' War, a series of conflicts between England and France (1337–1453), directed a great deal of energy into military ventures. The church hierarchy became caught up in its own controversies and enmeshed in international politics. The papacy had allied itself with France and moved to Avignon from 1309 to 1377. At the end of this period, the **cardinals,** divided between French and Italian sympathies, elected one pope in April 1377, then another in September. The Great Western Schism in the papacy persisted through the reigns of several popes, and a complication was added when the Council of Pisa declared both popes heretical and elected a third. Not until the Council of Constance (1414–1417) was the schism healed. Such difficulties in the papacy, supposedly the central axis of Christendom, signified a profound unsettlement in all of Europe. Meanwhile, the beginnings of the Renaissance suggested new visions of humanity in art and literature. The recovery of interest in the human form, in human emotions, and in the various disciplines of human reason—often modeled on the culture of ancient Greece—was a source of inspiration and a challenge to medieval traditions.

The late fourteenth and fifteenth centuries were also an age of proliferation of religious observances, to the point that they became easy targets of criticism. Pilgrimages, devotions to the saints, and religious processions on holy days were important to the laity as religious expressions over which they had a great deal of control. But the learned accused them of being less matters of spiritual discipline and sacrifice than social occasions. Also, the endowment of masses for the dead had reached enormous proportions. Since ancient times it had been common to contribute money for masses to be said after one's own death or the death of a relative for the repose of the soul; the funds went to the proper support of priests. But now the number of masses had increased unreasonably.

The Renaissance saw a new humanizing of art and religion, as exemplified in Michelangelo's famous paintings on the ceiling of the Sistine Chapel (1508–1512). This scene, depicting "The Creation of Adam," shows even God in anthropomorphic form, and the human body is portrayed in its full glory. (Used by permission of SCALA/Art Resource, New York.)

In 1244 at Durham, England, the monks were supposed to say 7,332 masses a year. Henry VIII in the sixteenth century was said to have bought twelve thousand masses at sixpence apiece. The sense of proportion between spiritual exercises and monetary support was being lost in a changing economy, in which money was becoming increasingly the measure of value.

There were similar problems with indulgences, problems that generated much controversy. An indulgence was a papal decree that granted a person remission from punishment in **purgatory** for his or her sins. (It did not grant forgiveness, which came only from the sacrament of **penance.**) Originally indulgences might be granted in return for a spiritual service, as when Urban II promised indulgences to crusaders in 1095. By the fifteenth century, however, one could, at least unofficially, buy an indulgence for money, and other corruptions had ensued—as in 1476 when Pope Sixtus IV allowed people to obtain indulgences for their dead relatives suffering in purgatory. Buying and selling of church offices (the sin of simony) had increased, and many priests and bishops were known to be living with concubines. In some cases they were absolved of their sins on payment of fees—concubinage fees, "cradle fees" for illegitimate children, and the like. This naturally led to mistrust between people and priests. Though laypeople did not neglect the sacraments, they sometimes turned to itinerant priests who seemed more holy than their own parish leaders, and they continued to seek alternative forms of devotion.

In the late fifteenth and sixteenth centuries a number of learned men issued serious criticisms of the church. A Dominican friar in Florence, Italy, named Savonarola attacked corruption, gathered a large following, and prophesied a millennial upheaval that would bring thorough reform. The Dutchman Erasmus, one of the great Catholic humanists, wrote treatises expounding the need for reform and aimed humorous jabs at the church. Martin Luther, a friar and professor at the University of Wittenberg, Germany, had a distinctive religious experience that led him to reformulate the doctrine of **justification** and sharply criticize the church for its practices. Luther's preaching and writing sparked the Protestant Reformation and marked the beginning of the Lutheran church. Ignatius of Loyola in Spain, following his own inner experience, developed a kind of meditation that disciplined the will to obedience. Ignatius founded the highly disciplined and dedicated order, the Society of Jesus (Jesuits), whose teaching and missions deeply affected the Roman Catholic church. The religious scene in Europe would never be the same after the sixteenth-century reformers.

The changes came most dramatically and quickly in the areas that became Protestant, notably Germany and Switzerland. There the burghers—the lay citizens, nonaristocrats—had been gaining power for a century. Whenever possible, they had taxed church lands and tried to insist that clergy be part of the citizenry, not a separate estate. They had endowed preacherships for themselves to satisfy their need for learning. Much of Luther's support came from among these lay-endowed preachers. Thus, from the beginning Protestantism represented a new and strong option for the laity that was not just a weaker version of the ascetic piety of the monks. The Protestant reformers upheld the religiousness of the lay-person who was involved in the ordinary world of work, money, and sexuality.

The first reformers, led by Luther in Germany and by Ulrich Zwingli and then John Calvin in Switzerland, attacked the monastic ideal first of all. Whereas the monastic life created a separate state of holiness, Protestant thinkers emphasized that every profession was a "calling," not just the religious professions. Another important tenet was the "priesthood of all believers," meaning that every Christian was in charge of his or her relation to God without the mediation of a priest. Especially was this true of penance (as well as extreme unction, a form of penance for the dying), which most Protestant preachers attacked. By the fifteenth century penance had become a lengthy proving of the individual, as the confessor checked off long lists of major and minor sins. Protestants regarded this as improper both because it made the person dependent on the confessor and because it required the impossible feat of perfect memory and full knowledge of all possible sins. They argued instead that any Christian could confess to any other; all believers were in this sense "priests."

Protestants went on to do away with a number of important practices. The sacraments of penance and extreme unction were eliminated, as was the taking of monastic vows. Marriage and **confirmation** were no longer regarded as sacraments, nor was a priest's or a minister's **ordination.** Supplementary penitential practices such as the endowment of masses or the making of pilgrimages also disappeared. Baptism and the Eucharist remained, and different Protestants disagreed over the nature of each. Though most churches still baptized infants, some more radical reformers limited baptism to adults. As to the Eucharist, the Protestants did away with the multiplicity of masses and substituted an occasional celebration of the Lord's Supper. Some reformers, like Luther, continued to hold that Christ's body was present in the Eucharist; others, like Zwingli, saw the Supper as a memorial only. In either case, the significance of the Mass tended to diminish among most Protestants.

The substitute for the sacraments in virtually all Protestant churches was the preaching of "the Word," that is, the holy Scriptures, and the reception of that word by the believer, in faith. Luther's central new doctrine, the cornerstone of all reformers, was "justification through grace by faith alone." One became righteous in the eyes of God, not by any external works, whether the Eucharist itself or penitential pilgrimages, but only by one's faith in the saving acts of Jesus Christ. The preaching of the Word according to Scripture was the means provided for arousing faith. Thus *sola fide, sola scriptura*—by faith alone, by Scripture alone—became slogans of the Protestant movement. In addition, most Protestant thinkers held that Christians were so totally dependent on God that they could do nothing to create faith in themselves. God had predestined each soul to salvation (Calvin held that he had also predestined some to be damned). Thus the Reformation emphasized, in the style of Augustine, the direct sovereignty of God over the soul, the Christian's own responsibility for his or her relation to God, and the church as a vehicle of the Word by which faith was awakened and brought to maturity.

The Reformation spread quickly in Germany and Switzerland, though a number of areas remained Catholic (and political alliances played a considerable part in religious allegiances). In France the Huguenots represented a strong Protestant force at first but in the late sixteenth century experienced severe persecution. In England the Reformation began from royal initiative, when Henry VIII broke with the pope because he could not get his latest marriage annulled. Though the next ruler, Mary, was Catholic, Elizabeth followed and, from 1559 on, promoted a gradual Reformation that created the Church of England (later to be named, in the United States, the Episcopal church).

Many of the larger denominations of today came from the main branches of early Protestantism. Lutheran churches came from Luther's protest; the Reformed churches (German, Dutch, and so on) from the combined work of Calvin and Zwingli. Calvinism traveled to England and blended with other elements to become Puritanism, a movement attempting to "purify" the Church of England. From this came Presbyterian, Congregationalist, Baptist, and Quaker groups. A later reform of the Church of England produced, in the eighteenth century, the Methodist church. Of these, the Baptists and Quakers were the most radical. They were akin to another stream of reform, today called by scholars the "radical reformation." The groups it produced tended to be small and independent, but equally important.

The radical reformers held that the church should become perfect—according to some, by returning to the ideals of primitive Christianity, according to others, by following the immediate guidance of the Holy Spirit. Abolishing the monastic life and certain other rituals and doctrines was not sufficient. Most of the radicals insisted that the church should contain only voluntary believers, that is, those who joined as adults. Some therefore rebaptized their members (who had already received baptism as infants) and earned the name Anabaptists, or "baptized again." This practice especially aroused the furor not only of Catholics but also of mainstream reformers, for it suggested that all their churches were wrongly constituted. Some radicals were pacifists; others—early Baptists, Quakers, Mennonites—refused to be involved in secular government at all; still others were willing to use force to revolutionize society. Some groups were quiet and contemplative, emphasizing the inner work of the Holy Spirit within the believer—the Quakers are the best known example. Many believed that the millennium would arrive at any moment, with the Second Coming of Christ; thus it was important to separate from the world and create the perfect Christian church and society.

What united most of the radicals was their insistence on the freedom of the church from state interference. They believed that Catholicism had allowed the system of religious authority to be corrupted by entanglement in secular politics. In the Protestant Reformation as well, the new religious principles seemed to be gaining a foothold not because of purity of faith but by alliance with magistrates, town councils, or princes. The few who wanted to revolutionize society wanted only the saints to rule. In short, the radicals wanted no secular authority to have any influence over the religious life. Their unwillingness to compromise on this point preserved their autonomy as self-governing religious groups, but

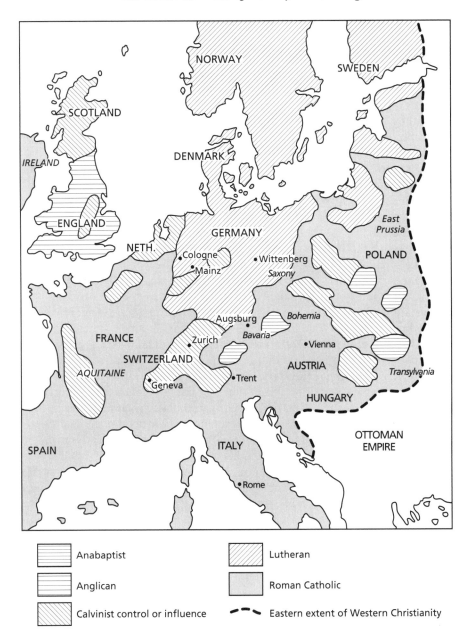

Anabaptist

Anglican

Calvinist control or influence

Lutheran

Roman Catholic

Eastern extent of Western Christianity

Divisions of European Christianity after the Reformation.

it also decreased their social power. As individual churches they simply could not command the influence that the Reformation as a whole possessed.

Meanwhile, however, Roman Catholic rulers in France, Spain, Austria, and the small states of Italy disliked all these reformations. Remembering the Hussite rebellion of the fifteenth century, they wanted to set their own house in order, create peace and unity among Catholics, and win back some of the ground they had lost to the new "heretics." Therefore the church called a great convocation, the Council of Trent, which met in three long sessions spanning the years from 1545 to 1563.

Trent represented a long process of coming to agreement in an age of confusion when many former certainties had become questionable. Later historians have often accused the council of being extremely conservative, simply restating old views. Such a judgment is not fair, however. The theologians and bishops who gathered at Trent spent hundreds of hours reexamining old statements and hammering out the Roman Catholic doctrines of original sin, of justification, and of the sacraments. Those in attendance often held diverse views. If some of the statements sounded traditional or conservative, that is because, first, the best Catholic minds of the age held them to be still correct and, second, those in attendance valued the unity of the church over their private divergent views. One cardinal refused to state his views of justification in public. It was later discovered that he agreed essentially with Luther, but he did not wish to contribute to the troubles of the church; therefore, he kept silent and submitted to whatever the council, as the agent of God's Spirit, would decide.

Ultimately, the Council of Trent offered important statements of doctrine that, though not substantially new, now clearly formulated what was to be taught. The council added a new emphasis on teaching: It provided for the education of the lower clergy in institutions called seminaries and encouraged the wider teaching of the **catechism.** Under Ignatius of Loyola's new order, the Society of Jesus, the missionary work of education would be carried out with great vigor. The Jesuits were largely responsible for returning Poland to the Catholic fold, as well as for the conversion of many Native Americans to the Catholic faith.

Further, the council reformed the structure of the church, giving the bishops greater responsibility for what happened in their domains and urging them to reside permanently in their own districts. A large number of the council believed that the difficulties in the church were due, not to wrong doctrine or practice, but to the fact that bishops and priests had become distant from their communities; they were no longer bringing to them the "bread of the gospel" and showing its power by their own holy lives. The Jesuit theologian Alphonsus Salmeron preached to the council that priests and bishops had come to desire honor and fear rather than love from their parishioners, that they were seeking mainly to satisfy their ambitions rather than to be "good shepherds" like Christ. Salmeron's sentiment was widely shared. Therefore the spirit of Trent moved to reinstate the authorities of the church but with a renewed concern for, and a genuine relationship to, those under their authority. By clarifying the responsibilities of the various levels of the church hierarchy, the council did what it could to encourage that development.

The Roman Catholic reforms, which became known as the Counter-Reformation, aimed to build up the church, to strengthen it at the core. So, too, the Protestants wanted a strong and healthy Christian church. The differences in their approaches, however, were crucial. The Catholics saw the church's core as being the ordained priests and bishops, those who held the power of the sacraments; if they were set on the right path the church would regain its health. The Protestants radically revalued the religious life of the laity, asserting that they represented the strength of the church. They therefore diminished the importance of special callings, such as the priesthood and the monastic orders, and the sacramental life which depended on priests. Instead, they emphasized the faith of the believer, which was a matter between the individual and God. In the Radical Reformation this emphasis on the inner life was sometimes exalted to a total dependence on the workings of the Holy Spirit. In the mainstream, however, the role of the church remained important: The church was the vehicle of the saving Word. Only through the church and its messengers, the preachers, could one have knowledge of Scripture and the basic gospel message that, in turn, could awaken faith. The ministry was therefore a special calling, but it was no longer set apart as especially holy. All vocations were callings, and all citizens could respect one another and provide mutual support within the church and society. The various views that emerged in the Reformation era represented different visions of society and of the church as an organic body; these would continue to shape the nature of each church through the following centuries.

Orthodox churches in Poland, Russia, the Balkans, and Greece were much less affected by these reform movements. Some local councils, to define the essentials of faith, developed "confessions" on the Protestant model, but these never achieved wide acceptance. The conflicts that fueled the Western Reformation—between church and state, between clergy and laity—were less pressing in the Orthodox churches where the liturgy and the worshiping community continued to be the focus of unity.

New Worlds

In the meantime, the era of the religious revivals known as Reformation and Counter-Reformation also saw one of the most revolutionary events in world history: European (re-)discovery and settlement of the American continents. Columbus and the seamen who followed him eventually discovered a way around the world and set the stage for a new era in Christianity. Beginning in the sixteenth century and continuing up to the present, Roman Catholic and Protestant missionaries transported their varieties of Christian doctrine and practice to the Americas, southern Africa, Asia, Australia, and the Pacific islands. At the same time the Russian Orthodox church sent missions to Asia, Japan, and Alaska. Each region contributed to the variety of Christian life, for each culture added its imprint to the underlying structure of Orthodox, Catholic, or Protestant faith. The resulting forms of Christianity ranged from direct transplants of European churches to fascinating amalgams of native and European religions, to new reform movements under the leadership of native prophets. It is impossible to survey them all; nevertheless it will be instructive to look at some of the contrasting styles and results just on the American continents.

In Mexico, for one example, Spanish Catholic missionaries (Jesuits, Dominicans, and Franciscans) encountered a highly civilized society that had been ruled by the Aztecs. The friars clearly held their own religion to be superior and accused the Mexicans of idol worship, but they also recognized in the native religion similarities to Christian or biblical practices. Some argued that Aztec religion was a degenerate form of a superior religion, that perhaps one of the apostles—mostly likely Thomas—had brought the gospel to Mexico, but after his death the truth had been lost and the Christian message corrupted. Mexicans sometimes identified Saint Thomas with Quetzalcoatl, a former king/god who was expected to return at the end of time. Similarly, the great goddess Tonantzin was translated into the Virgin Mary and became Our Lady of Guadalupe, later a symbol of Mexican nationalism. Thus in certain societies where Spanish Catholicism met a strong native religion, a kind of syncretism developed wherein new holy figures and new practices were superimposed on the local beliefs. [See Religions of Mesoamerica pp. 117–19, 121–22 for the European "discovery" of Mexico and the introduction of Christianity; see Religions of Mesoamerica pp. 223–26 and Native Religions of North America pp. 357–58 for discussion of the Virgin Mary and Guadalupe, and the relationship between Catholicism and native religion.]

However, not all missionaries were so tolerant as to allow old beliefs and practices to continue. Especially when in contact with Native American societies that they regarded as primitive, missionaries declared the people of these societies to be ignorant and depraved, with customs that were totally immoral. In such situations, Catholics and Protestants alike viewed their task as bringing civilization and Christianity to lands and people barren of human virtue. Still, the Catholic approach differed from the Protestant. The Spanish Catholics who ruled most parts of the Americas held to their religion and intermarried with the local inhabitants; the missionaries meanwhile instructed the people at least to a level at which they knew the catechism and had begun to move away from their former "superstitions." If possible, they tried to gather them into Spanish-style villages and towns where they would learn European ways more quickly. Over the generations the gradualist approach and intermarriage with Europeans created a hierarchical society of mixed ethnicities. Catholicism, the religion of the conquerors, became the religion of high-status citizens, thus unifying the church across national lines and adding to its wealth and power. Also, the church often saw itself as protector of the poor, trying to bring the lower classes and even the enslaved into the church. Nevertheless, Catholic attitudes were not uniform. In non-Spanish areas, such as French Canada and Louisiana, Catholics were tolerant of local traditions, but less open to intermarriage. Thus, a variety of Catholic societies developed in the New World.

The English Protestant colonies, most of which eventually became part of the United States, differed sharply in their pattern. Immigration styles were different: not friars and soldiers, explorers and traders (the latter often looking for female partners), but family groups focused on farming and village life. Protestants usually objected to intermarriage, viewing Native Americans and African slaves in a harsher light than did the Catholics. At first, very few settlers cared about the conversion of the Indians or of the black slaves. Moreover, Protestantism offered little of the ritual life or rich store of legends of the saints that could more easily integrate people from traditional societies into their communities. The Protestant missionary expected converts to learn to speak and read English, read Scripture, and attend a church highly focused on the verbal—indeed, centered on a long and complex sermon. A few members of the eastern tribes did assimilate into Protestant societies, but soon Indian wars took priority over Indian missions. When territorial expansion began after the American Revolution, relations were marked by wars and oft-broken treaties. Missionaries carried on their work, but only a few strong native churches emerged until after the Indians had been forced onto reservations, in the late nineteenth century.

Other difficulties arose in Christians' relations to African slaves. In South America, Africans were generally regarded as the lowest class; yet the possibility of intermarriage meant gradual change through the generations. In the Anglo-American world, however, slaveowners generally did not recognize their children by black concubines, and all blacks remained at the level of slaves. The slaves had come for the most part from the highly developed civilizations of West Africa. Yet, separated from their families and compatriots, they soon lost touch with the richness of their home cultures. Nor did slaveowners make strong efforts to integrate them into Christian culture. After the eighteenth-century religious **revivals** (to be discussed later), some slaveowners began instructing their slaves in the rudiments of Christianity, but in the nineteenth century slaveowners discouraged education for slaves, for they feared that teaching them to read the Bible might lead them to revolt. As a result, Black American Christianity took a form different from Native American, Protestant, or Catholic Christianity. Thanks to their ancient African heritage, blacks retained a preference for ecstatic religion, dance, body movement, and responsive chanting that still characterize some black churches. On the American scene, their religion developed primarily in the age of revivals, so it was highly evangelical; since slave masters discouraged education, blacks relied on oral tradition, song, and dramatic preaching styles. The result is a unique form of Christianity that only in recent times has begun to be recognized in its full richness. [See Religions of Africa pp. 55–56, 80–82 for a discussion of Christian influence in Africa.]

Modern Developments in Christianity

Amid the diversity that grew out of worldwide Christian missions, there were some additional developments that affected virtually all forms of Christianity. These stem largely from the religious awakenings of the eighteenth century and later, usually called revivals. England, Germany, and English-speaking North

America have been the primary sites for these awakenings, although most other Christian countries have been touched in some ways.

In the seventeenth century the American colonies and most European countries had settled into the church divisions already mentioned, coming from the Catholic and Protestant mainstreams and from the radical reformations. In the area that was to become the United States many denominations were represented; however, the dominant tradition was Puritanism, deeply rooted in New England culture and expressed through the Congregational and Presbyterian churches. Highly intellectual, yet deeply concerned about the individual's inner development in faith, the Puritan tradition maintained itself through a strong vision of the church as the center of society. In England the Church of England held a similar position, threatened only by the Puritan dissenters, who wanted to place their churches in the center. In Germany the Lutherans dominated. By the middle of the eighteenth century, however, in all three areas a movement developed that encouraged greater inward devotion, greater individual piety. Sometimes adherents formed a new sect; the Methodists, led by John Wesley, eventually were forced to break off from the Church of England, but in the Lutheran church, the Pietists were accepted without having to make a break.

The primary significance of this movement, however, was that it opened the way toward a greater role for emotions in Christian faith. Protestants, with their emphasis on the inward faith of the believer, and Catholics, with their strong mystical tradition, had always recognized that emotions had a place in Christian experience. The American Puritans had greatly developed their sensitivity in that direction, shaping their religious lives in an inward quest for peace, over against the continual Calvinist uncertainty about salvation. The question, Was I predestined to be one of the **elect?** created a dynamic of anxiety, terror, and hope that became a hallmark of Puritanism. But in the eighteenth century these and other emotions began to emerge into the open. They were no longer a matter merely of private communication between the individual and God but were visibly expressed in response to a minister's sermon. Great preachers like Jonathan Edwards, America's first original theologian, were startled to find their audiences deeply and openly affected, and then rather quickly converted to a profound love of Christ. Less publicly, the small circles of believers who were Methodists in England or Pietists in Germany shared their inner religious feelings and supported one another in developing a deeper Christian experience.

These beginnings heralded the emergence of a different type of Christianity, known often as revivalistic or, more broadly, evangelical. More properly, we should regard it as experiential (in the late eighteenth century the term would have been *experimental*) Christianity: a form of religious expression in which the believer's personal experience, testimony to that experience, and heartfelt expression of it in prayer or song became central. In the eighteenth century, these expressions were still largely contained within the orderly forms of the church, supplemented by prayer fellowships or an occasional extra meeting. In the nineteenth century, however, they exploded into a long era of revivals. Frontier revivals, known for their wild ecstasies; annual church revivals, in which the regular congregation gathered for an extra series of meetings; mass revivals in the larger towns and cities—all these were popular variations on a single theme, the religion of inward experience. Along with offering personal prayers aloud and sharing experience with others came a great rush of hymn writing by laypeople (in Britain and the United States, by large numbers of women). The "gospel hymn" (of the white middle-class culture, not the black) became the theme song of the new era. In modern times the great mass revivalists like Billy Graham and Oral Roberts have continued this tradition.

The late nineteenth century saw movements that aimed at an even more intense experience than did most revivals. The Holiness movement aimed at perfection in morality, simplicity in religion, and a deeper, heartfelt experience of God. The Pentecostal churches of the turn of the twentieth century went further: They sought a higher "blessing," usually the gift of speaking in tongues, a form of ecstatic speech attested in the New Testament. These different forms of a higher Christian life through inward experience continue to thrive today; Pentecostalism is popular not only among some Protestants but also in many Mexican-American Catholic churches, and the 1960s and 1970s saw it emerge among the white middle and upper classes, notably in the Roman Catholic and Episcopal denominations. [See Religions of Mesoamerica pp. 240–41 for a discussion of Chicano culture and religion.]

The inward turn of religious practice appeared in another, rather quiet, development of the nineteenth century: the growth of what we would today call meditative traditions. Often these combined the popular search for authentic experience with a more rational approach coming from the European Enlightenment and Romantic movements. In the United States, Transcendentalism, among the northeastern elites, was the intellectual side of that movement. Although the Transcendentalists are best known for their literary productions, their primary motivation came from a search for true inner experience, as in Ralph Waldo Emerson's "I become a transparent eyeball," or Henry David Thoreau's meditations on nature. Concurrently, at the popular level, the tradition of Spiritualism emerged in Europe and the United States. The Spiritualists were best known—and ridiculed—for their seances in which they tried to contact spirits of the dead as "scientific" proof that an afterlife existed, but they also shared a larger philosophy of which the seances were only a part. They held that the universe consisted of a harmonious unity of all things and that humans, by deepening their self-knowledge and their contact with other worlds, could live in greater harmony with God and with the All. This amorphous, loosely organized tradition began to achieve clearer definition in the latter part of the century, when New Thought and Christian Science (Mary Baker Eddy's Church of Christ, Scientist) appeared. Though these are in many respects independent movements—Mrs. Eddy insisted that hers had nothing to do with Spiritualism or other such popular traditions—they are clearly a part of the meditative tradition. Through specific practices of study and refocusing thought, Christian Scientists and New Thought practitioners attempt to bring the mind into harmony with the universal Mind, the power of healing in the universe, in order to gain power over material existence.

The growth of experiential Christianity went hand in hand with a voluntaristic emphasis: If each person's experience was valid, then each person could choose the appropriate church to suit his or her needs. This had dramatic effects on the churches. Where the eighteenth-century awakenings had produced temporary splits that healed (except for the Methodists), the nineteenth-century movements produced a rash of independent groups, especially in the United States. Literally hundreds of new denominations began in the century between 1825 and 1925—some small and short-lived, others, like the Disciples of Christ, becoming major churches. In some cases the freedom to follow one's own experience also gave rise to prophets with new revelations. For example, in the early nineteenth century Joseph Smith claimed he had been visited by an angel who revealed to him the location of a great holy book. This book, translated under Smith's inspiration, became the Book of Mormon, foundation of the Church of Jesus Christ of Latter-day Saints (or Mormons). In the same era Ellen G. White, a member of a millennial sect, began receiving messages that led her, with others, to establish the doctrines and practices of the Seventh-day Adventists. Despite the emergence of some strong new churches, however, the concept of the church in general grew weaker. The church, for most American Protestants, was no longer an organic body, but a company of believers, each with his or her individual experiences that constituted the center of the religious life. The church therefore faced the danger of becoming merely another social gathering place.

These trends affected even the strongest church in the West, the Roman Catholic. During the nineteenth and early twentieth centuries, when European and immigrant communities remained strong in themselves, the Roman Catholic church kept a firm, though in the United States defensive, attachment to its traditions and doctrines. By the mid–twentieth century, however, intellectual ferment and internal dissatisfaction had brought many people to question what seemed to be the antimodern position of the church. In response, Pope John XXIII called the great Second Vatican Council (1962–1965). The council adopted a declaration on religious freedom that urged tolerance of other religious ways and even other Christian churches; previously the church had regarded Protestants as heretics, outside the path of salvation. Major changes came in the liturgy: translation of the Mass into the language of each nation (previously it had been said wholly in Latin) and adaptations allowing greater time for congregational singing and for sermons. These changes reflected the Catholic church's support of the voluntary principle and a great willingness to allow for the importance of the worshiper's experience.

The experiential movement of the past two centuries has also led to an increase in missionary and reform activities. As often happens in a time of new religious movements, Christians with a strong inner sense of spiritual guidance have become newly concerned about the condition of their society, or at least about the unsaved souls of their fellow human beings. On the whole, most such work has gone toward preaching the gospel to non-Christians at home or in foreign countries. Significant energy, however, has been directed toward political and social action: alleviating poverty, fighting disease and improving aid in underdeveloped countries, attending to the needs of the poor and elderly in the growing cities. Around the turn of the twentieth century some theologians, particularly in the United States, articulated a theological rationale for this emphasis, developing what they called the Social Gospel. In recent times theologians have developed "liberation" theologies that express a Christian commitment to the freedom and human rights of the oppressed people of the earth. Some of these outreach movements have been politically and socially conservative, others more radical. In general these movements have also allowed a larger religious role for women, though conservative churches have limited the definition of that role, and the role of pulpit minister is still largely dominated by men. Women have played a considerable part in the spread of experiential religion in general, as well as in spearheading many reforms.

Of course, the more emphasis among Christians on outreach and social action, the less energy is likely to be devoted to inner spiritual experience. For brief periods it has seemed that "social Christianity" has become the major force in modern development. Yet the repeated waves of revivals, awakenings, Pentecostal experiences, and devotional movements focusing on Jesus or on being **born again** show that the experiential movement that began some two centuries ago continues to be the major force in modern church movements. Social Christianity, apart from these movements, is the provenance of a small though important liberal wing. Theology is not dead, but it is largely confined to the seminaries; only in the Fundamentalist critique of modern culture do we find popular interest in theology and the doctrines of traditional Christianity. As for the sacramental life, some churches in recent times have expressed new interest in ritual; the Eastern Orthodox traditions have once again become important resources in that area. Such developments are minor, however, compared to the experiential movement and its offshoots, which, over a span of two hundred years, have brought about major changes in Christians' understanding of themselves, their churches, and their religious lives as a whole. In the next chapter, we will look at these developments in a different perspective, considering how they are related to the enduring structures of Christianity. [See Religions of Africa pp. 25, 54–57, 79–82, Religions of Mesoamerica p. 240, Native Religions of North America pp. 287, 320–22, 357–58, Judaism pp. 427–31, 456–75, Islam pp. 698–700, Hinduism pp. 770–74, 828–31, Buddhism pp. 952–56, Religions of China pp. 998–1002, 1055–59, and Religions of Japan pp. 1132–33, 1163–72 for discussion of new religious movements.]

21

Structures of the Christian Life

LIKE ALL RELIGIONS, Christianity can be understood through its structures as well as its history—that is, through its symbols, rituals, and institutions. Central to the structure of Christianity is its basic symbol: the figure of Jesus the Christ, represented graphically by the crucifix and the cross, symbols of his death and resurrection. The New Testament stories of Jesus have become common currency in Christian culture, but even apart from this, the various aspects of the religion cannot be understood without a grasp of the centrality of Jesus. The meanings of Christian rituals are based on stories about him, and the churches often regard their organizational forms as springing from his commands. The writings that describe Jesus' life and death, his acts and words, thus provide the founding myths of Christianity. These documents are structurally equivalent to the creation myths of other traditions, for they are the pivot around which the religion turns and to which it returns. This myth or set of myths is the fundamental story, containing the meaning of the religion. The different versions may or may not be true in the factual or historical sense; indeed, different Christian interpreters themselves disagree over the historical truth the myths contain. But they are "true" in that they are true to a particular vision of life; they are the seeds from which germinate the essential Christian practices and attitudes. The stories of Jesus encapsulate the spiritual truth of Christianity. [See Religions of Africa pp. 36–37, 64–67, Religions of Mesoamerica pp. 129–35, 154–55, 163–68, Native Religions of North America pp. 288–95, 327–29, 333–42, Judaism pp. 380–84, Hinduism pp. 739–41, 743–46, Buddhism p. 890, and Religions of Japan pp. 1094–96 for discussion of myth and mythology.]

The Christian Story

The basic kernel of the stories is roughly as follows: Jesus was born in the reign of Herod the Great in Palestine, his birth being heralded by various signs of greatness even though his social status was humble (his father was a carpenter).

His full appearance in the world came at the age of thirty, when he received baptism at the hands of another Jewish religious figure, John the Baptist. John was executed not long after, and Jesus began his own independent ministry. Different versions of the myth emphasize different aspects of his character, but in general they agree that he was a teacher and healer. As to his ultimate nature, some stories present him as a prophet (spokesman of God), others as the Messiah (God's chosen king), still others as God himself. He was expected to bring redemption not only to the Jewish people but to all peoples.

The versions that came to be included in the Christian New Testament give great prominence to Jesus' death. They tell that Jesus anticipated his own death and celebrated a "last supper" with his twelve disciples shortly before the Jewish Passover holiday.[4] One of the disciples, Judas, betrayed him, and Jesus was captured by the Romans, tried as a political rebel (for claiming to be the new Jewish king), and executed by being nailed to a cross. His body was taken down and buried, but after three days the body had disappeared. Some of his followers reported that angels had appeared, saying Jesus had risen from the dead; others then reported seeing him in several bodily appearances. This is the story of the resurrection.

This basic myth has been the occasion for multiple interpretations throughout nearly two thousand years of Christian history. We cannot deal with them in depth, of course, but we must look at two important aspects of the way the story has been interpreted. On the one hand, Jesus has become a model for others to follow: The *imitatio Christi* (imitation of Christ) has become a guide for the Christian life. This is not unusual in religious traditions. The *imitatio Dei* (imitation of God) was and is a part of Judaism; Buddhists follow in the footsteps of the Buddha; and so on in many traditions. Later we will look at specific ways in which this has been true in Christianity. On the other hand, most Christian traditions have given special attention to the suffering, death, and resurrection of Jesus as a unique and miraculous event that brought about salvation for those who followed him. The story of Jesus is the story of salvation; it holds the keys to how to be saved. Salvation, then, is a central meaning of the myth. Here, the imitation of Christ becomes a participation in Christ, becoming a part of the great and mysterious events that, according to most Christians, transformed all of existence. [See Religions of Africa pp. 29, 55–57, Religions of Mesoamerica pp. 152, 163–68, Native Religions of North America pp. 266–67, Islam pp. 622–28, 698–99, Hinduism pp. 769, 770–72, Buddhism pp. 860, 861–68, 892–99, Religions of China pp. 993–95, and Religions of Japan pp. 1090, 1100, 1122–23 for discussion of religious founders.]

The accompanying diagram shows, in simplified form, the basic system of Christian salvation. In brief, it shows how human beings, living under the rule of "sin" and "death," can experience renewal and ascend to a higher form of life through the acts, objects, and holy personages of Christianity. In the discussion that follows, we will elaborate on the concept of salvation and the beliefs and practices associated with it, showing how it has been developed in the life of Christian communities and of individual believers.

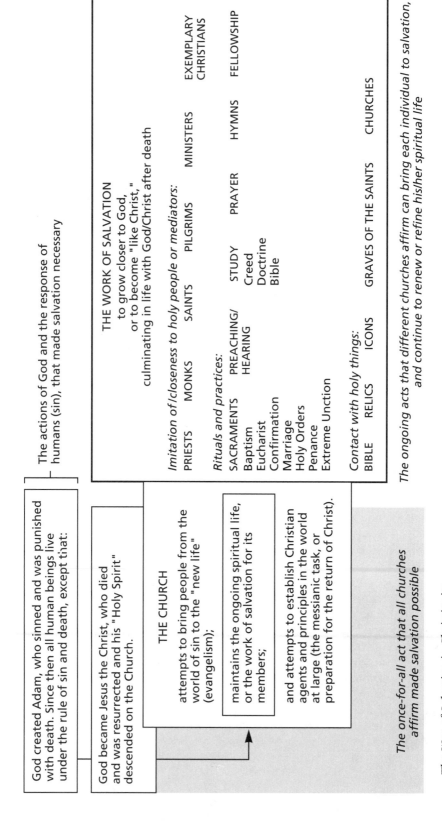

The actions of God and the response of humans (sin), that made salvation necessary

THE WORK OF SALVATION
to grow closer to God,
or to become "like Christ,"
culminating in life with God/Christ after death

Imitation of/closeness to holy people or mediators:
PRIESTS   MONKS   SAINTS   PILGRIMS   MINISTERS   EXEMPLARY CHRISTIANS

Rituals and practices:
SACRAMENTS   PREACHING/   STUDY   PRAYER   HYMNS   FELLOWSHIP
Baptism   HEARING   Creed
Eucharist   Doctrine
Confirmation   Bible
Marriage
Holy Orders
Penance
Extreme Unction

Contact with holy things:
BIBLE   RELICS   ICONS   GRAVES OF THE SAINTS   CHURCHES

God created Adam, who sinned and was punished with death. Since then all human beings live under the rule of sin and death, except that:

God became Jesus the Christ, who died and was resurrected and his "Holy Spirit" descended on the Church.

THE CHURCH

attempts to bring people from the world of sin to the "new life" (evangelism);

maintains the ongoing spiritual life, or the work of salvation for its members;

and attempts to establish Christian agents and principles in the world at large (the messianic task, or preparation for the return of Christ).

The ongoing acts that different churches affirm can bring each individual to salvation, and continue to renew or refine his/her spiritual life

The once-for-all act that all churches affirm made salvation possible

The Way of Salvation in Christianity.

The Meaning of Salvation

According to Christians, the fundamental divine miracle is the incarnation, death, and resurrection of Jesus; the church claims that this event had effects on the whole human race. Although different views of this miracle have appeared at different times in the history of Christian thought, most Christians would agree on a basic understanding of the event, briefly as follows: God became a human being in order to take on the state of sin, for sin constitutes the fundamental human condition since the fall of Adam and Eve, the first human beings according to the Bible. Yet although God-as-Jesus became human, he did not sin; nor (since he was God) did he have any stain of original sin inherited from Adam. Instead he suffered the punishment—namely, death—for the sin of the whole world. He was resurrected bodily from death, "redeemed" even from the world of the dead. From that time forward it would be possible for human beings also to be freed from the punishment for sin if they repented of sin, believed in Jesus as the Christ, and accepted the offer of salvation. "Repent and believe in the good news!" was the call of early Christian preachers. Correlatively, God offered to Christians and to the church as a body the gift of the Holy Spirit as a continuing divine presence in their lives making them more like Christ himself. [See Religions of Africa pp. 39–42, 64–69, Religions of Mesoamerica pp. 157–58, 186–89, Native Religions of North America pp. 274–76, 288–305, 330–32, Judaism pp. 414–15, Islam pp. 635–37, Hinduism pp. 739–41, 759–61, 780–84, Buddhism pp. 900–903, Religions of China pp. 1024–26, and Religions of Japan pp. 1112–27 for discussion of God, gods, and objects of worship.]

The experience of salvation is accordingly a rebirth to a new life. The seeker moves from repentance and forgiveness, through the sacrifice of Christ, to taking on a new life in Christ and receiving the Holy Spirit. Since earliest times Christians have understood salvation in its original sense: It meant being saved, rescued, safe in a fortress besieged by the enemy. The related term *redemption* expresses a similar experience—being "bought back" from the evil powers by the gracious acts of God. The sense of evil afoot in the world and rooted deep in oneself is part of the basic Christian experience. With the experience of salvation, Christians feel freed from their anxiety, inner guilt, and sin, and less subject to the demonic forces that seem to be bombarding them. That sense of freedom is the beginning; in addition, the experience of salvation brings a growing closeness to the divine and sometimes even ecstatic states, as if the Christian is being transported to higher levels of being. Salvation is thus a vividly real state of being connected to God, to the divine, which in a supportive Christian community may be an ongoing or a continually renewed experience.

Nevertheless, the state of present ecstasy sometimes diminishes in the churches. This should not surprise us. Often in new religious movements the early believers live in a high spiritual state of consciousness, with their positive experiences continually reinforced by the dedication of others around them. Later, however—especially in the second or third generation—the group's members may experience less of that ecstasy. Instead, if the group continues, they look to the future and emphasize the experience of hope. This happens in Christianity as well. One generation of Christians may have an immediate sense of the divine presence in their lives, whereas later ones, who no longer find that experience available to them, focus on future hopes. Such hopes come quite naturally to Christianity, which grew up among Jewish groups alive with the expectation of a Messiah and in a Greek environment filled with hopes of personal immortality after death. In this context, salvation has also come to refer to the state Christians would experience after death. As early as the writings of Paul (54–58 C.E.), we can see a tension between the present state of salvation and the even greater life that is promised when the Messiah returns: Now Christians are "justified," Paul writes—that is, they are put in a right relation to God—later they will be "sanctified," made perfectly holy. Christianity fluctuates between the two poles, sometimes becoming very otherworldly, at other times emphasizing the quest for spiritual experience in the present.

It is important to recognize that, whether salvation is conceived in terms of present experience or of future promise, the reality of salvation has almost always been mediated through ritual. In some varieties of Christianity the primary rituals have been the receiving of the sacraments; in others, the discipline of a life of prayer and contemplation has led toward the higher life. Preaching, singing, or personal interaction have been channels through which a person might experience salvation from sin or the blessings of the Holy Spirit. Salvation can be a highly personal, transcendent experience, an encounter of the individual Christian with the divine. But on the earthly plane it is expressed as an initiation, a ritual leading to new birth. The early church developed a series of rituals as vehicles of that transforming experience: a period of study and testing, the rites of baptism and confirmation, and the first partaking of the Eucharist.

Spiritual Knowledge: Creed and Doctrine in Christianity

As in most initiations, the candidate has to pass a test, and the testing in Christianity has revolved around knowledge of spiritual things, particularly the creed. People wishing to enter a Christian church had to be of good moral character, and the priest or bishop would watch them closely for their sincerity and willingness to lead upright lives. Study was central, however; in the early church they spent nearly a year learning the beliefs and rites of the church, particularly the meaning of the incarnation, death, and resurrection of Jesus. Before baptism the candidate would be asked questions, probably a triple question for the triple immersion. We do not have the exact text of any such examination, but it probably went something like the following: "Do you believe in God the Father, maker of heaven and earth? Do you believe in Jesus the Son, who suffered, died, and rose again? Do you believe in the Holy Spirit in the Holy Church?" The questioning was, of course, a formality; someone who had gone through the course of study was unlikely to answer no. Nevertheless, the examination symbolized an important aspect of Christian existence; belief in the appropriate creed was a crucial standard for belonging to the community. [See Judaism pp. 386–87, Islam pp. 612–13, 639–40, and Native Religions of North America pp. 267–68 for discussion of creeds.]

Yet against the background of other religions this is quite remarkable: No other major tradition puts so great an emphasis on belief, on correct thinking, on affirming the correct words. Most traditions emphasize practice far more than belief. Why did Christianity take this path? An important reason is that the culture in which Christianity came to flower, the Hellenistic culture of the Mediterranean, valued philosophy and, indeed, linked religion closely to philosophy. Philosophy itself had a religious aura—the philosopher was a lover of Wisdom, who often was portrayed as a semi-divine, usually feminine, being (Sophia in Greek, Chokmah in Hebrew). The great Roman orator Cicero regarded the faculty of reason as being the mode by which the soul could ascend to the divine. Hellenistic philosophies usually viewed the soul as essentially rational and held that God expressed himself through Mind. Thus Christianity, as it began its work of theology, of systematically elucidating the nature of God and his revelation to human beings, referred to similar concepts.

When the Gospel of John declared, "In the beginning was the Word [Logos]," the author was asserting that Jesus was to be understood as a revelation of the divine Mind. As we saw in chapter 20, Logos theology was prominent among the early apologists. Christians thus set out the path to God in terms of a path to wisdom, explicit in stating and reasoning out the things one had to know. Clarity of thought in matters of religion meant freedom of movement, a clear path to God. Incorrect understanding could lead to one's worshiping the wrong God, following the wrong savior or leader. Part of the responsibility that the church took on, one of the ways it became a vehicle of salvation, was to smooth the path by establishing right belief and right understanding.

This task came to a focus in the creeds of the churches. Creeds (from the Latin *credere,* to believe) are simply statements of belief. From very early, however, they became part of public worship: Part of paying homage to God was stating one's belief. This practice had precedent in Judaism, where the Shema (a statement of the Jewish covenant with God, beginning "Hear O Israel, the Lord is our God, the Lord is One") and its accompanying blessings contain some affirmations of faith. [See Judaism pp. 384, 435 for the Shema.] But the theological-philosophical emphasis of Hellenistic culture made the creeds of the daughter religion somewhat different. We can see the careful statement of issues by looking at samples of three early Christian creeds. The first example here is the Roman Creed as known from fourth-century texts.

Roman Creed

I believe in God the Father Almighty,
And in Jesus Christ, his only Son, our Lord,
Who was born by the Holy Ghost, of the Virgin Mary, was crucified
   under Pontius Pilate, and was buried.
The third day he rose from the dead,
He ascended into heaven and sits on the right hand of the Father;

From thence he will come to judge the quick and the dead.

And in the Holy Ghost, the Holy Church, the forgiveness of sins, the resurrection of the body.

The second example, the so-called Apostles' Creed, was generally used in the West from about the sixth century and is still used in many Protestant churches today.

Apostles' Creed

I believe in God the Father Almighty, Maker of heaven and earth, and in Jesus Christ, his only Son, our Lord, who was conceived by the Holy Ghost, born of the Virgin Mary, suffered under Pontius Pilate, was crucified, dead, and buried. He descended into Hell.

The third day he rose from the dead, he ascended into heaven and sits on the right hand of God the Father Almighty.

From thence he will come to judge the quick and the dead.

I believe in the Holy Ghost, the holy catholic church, the communion of saints, the forgiveness of sins, the resurrection of the body, and the life everlasting.

The third, the Nicene Creed, is in general use, with slight variations, in Eastern Orthodox and, since the Council of Trent in the sixteenth century, in Roman Catholic churches. The form given here is the current one, very close to the Constantinople formula of 381.

Nicene Creed

We believe in one God the Father Almighty, Maker of heaven and earth, and of all things visible and invisible.

And in one Lord Jesus Christ, the only begotten Son of God, begotten of the Father before all worlds,

Light of Light, Very God of Very God,

Begotten, not made, being of one substance with the Father, by whom all things were made,

Who for us men, and for our salvation, came down from heaven,

And was incarnate by the Holy Ghost of the Virgin Mary, and was made man.

He was crucified for us under Pontius Pilate, and suffered and was buried.

And the third day he rose again, according to the Scriptures, and ascended into heaven, and sits on the right hand of the Father,

And he shall come again, with glory, to judge the quick and the dead; Whose kingdom shall have no end.

And in the Holy Ghost, the Lord, and Giver of life;

Who proceeds from the Father, Who with the Father and the Son together is worshiped and glorified,

Who spoke by the Prophets.

And in one holy catholic and apostolic Church.

We acknowledge one baptism for the remission of sins, and we look for the resurrection of the dead, and the life of the world to come.

In these three creeds we can trace the evidences of numerous theological debates. The Roman Creed did not need to specify that God was "maker of heaven and earth," but both other creeds did, countering Gnostic assertions that the true God could not have created the evil material world. The Nicene emphasis that he made "all things visible and invisible" reflects the church's conflict with Manicheanism beginning in the late third century. The prophet Mani taught that the world was a battleground between good and evil and, like the Gnostics, that there was an evil god who had created the visible world and invisible demonic forces. The Apostles' and Nicene creeds emphasize the suffering of Jesus over against the Docetists, who claimed that Jesus' human form was not real. The fourth-century debate with Arius over the relation of Jesus' humanity to his divinity lies behind the careful statements of the Nicene: Jesus was begotten, not made (Arius claimed Jesus was a created being), and was of the same substance as God the Father (some theologians argued he was only of similar substance). One could go on; virtually every phrase is the result of untold hours of thought, argument, and reflection.

The creeds gave rise to dogma or doctrine (literally, "teaching"), for the faithful needed to have fuller instruction as to what the church affirmed and why. Not all branches of Christianity have given the same significance to doctrine and theological understanding, however. For the Orthodox churches, doctrine was essential, but truth was fully confirmed only by one's experience in the worshiping community. In the West, before the year 1000 education was a rarity; few learned even to read, let alone argue theology. From the eleventh century onward, however, theology emerged into prominence again, being regarded as "queen of the sciences," the capstone of knowledge, which unified all the partial truths of the various branches of learning. The Protestant Reformers used theology as one of their primary weapons against Roman Catholicism, arguing that many Catholic errors stemmed from theological misunderstandings. Therefore the Protestant churches reformulated many basic doctrines of the church and wrote lengthy catechisms like the Westminster Confession (Calvinist). For several centuries the rival Protestant groups thrived on theological argument among themselves. Even the nineteenth-century American frontier churches held spirited theological debates, although the people were poorly educated. The Protestant emphasis on Scripture gave people a concrete foundation for argument, so that even relatively unlearned persons could "theologize," so to speak, on the basis of specific passages in the New Testament. On the other hand, despite the high level of education in the twentieth century, theology has declined in importance again.

Yet, on the whole, creed and doctrine have been very important defining characteristics of a Christian; they are not merely traditional formulas but expressions of a deep acceptance of the faith. The implicit assumption is that the most profound acceptance requires the concurrence of the great human faculty of intellect: The mind itself must grasp the ideas of the faith if the person is to be truly bound to them. Indeed, the highest levels of mind are engaged—those levels that approach the divine. Once the mind is trained to spiritual things, then the individual can approach the great mysteries: the rites of the church.

The Drama of Transformation: From Baptism to Eucharist

Baptism is clearly the primary Christian rite of initiation. Sometimes it is highly dramatic; at other times it appears largely perfunctory. But in any case it is understood as a powerful reenactment of the death (through immersion) and resurrection (coming out of the water) of Jesus himself. Of course, baptism also imitates Jesus' baptism by John in the Jordan River. Further, Judaism already had a similar ritual of conversion: a long period of study and examination followed by immersion in a naturally constituted body of water. There, as in many other religions, immersion symbolized the death of the old person and rebirth of the new. For Christians it was appropriate to adapt this ritual to their new understanding of existence: as Jesus had died and been "reborn," so with every Christian. Thus Paul wrote in his letter to the church at Rome:

> Do you not know that all of us who have been baptized into Christ Jesus were baptized into his death? We were buried therefore with him by baptism into death, so that as Christ was raised from the dead by the glory of the Father, so we too might walk in newness of life. (Rom. 6:3–4, RSV)

The drama of baptism, which in the early church was usually on Easter morning after a fast and an all-night vigil, culminated with the new Christian

The dramatic event of baptism in the early church often took place in a specially designed baptismal font. The Baptistry of St. John Lateran in Rome, originally built in the time of Constantine, was rebuilt by later popes. (Photo used by permission of Hirmer Archive, Munich.)

donning white garments, a symbol of purity and new birth that is echoed in the white baptismal gowns of babies even today.

The next part of the initiation is confirmation—originally an anointing with consecrated oil, the "Christing" of the believer—for *Christos* meant "anointed one"—like a king. In this act the believer becomes like Christ and at this moment receives the gift of the Holy Spirit. Just as the Spirit descended on Jesus in the shape of a dove after he came up out of the Jordan, so the oil of anointing represents the descent of the Spirit on the Christian. The rite of confirmation is still practiced immediately after baptism in Eastern Orthodox churches; Roman Catholics and most Protestants perform it at a time when the person has reached an age of understanding. In churches where ecstatic experience is the goal, for example the Pentecostal, the gift of the Holy Spirit has again come into prominence as the mark of the true Christian, although it is not usually considered a ritual of confirmation.

After baptism and (usually) confirmation, the convert comes for the first time to the Eucharist, literally the thanksgiving service, the meal celebrated on Sunday mornings in honor of the Lord's Day by full members of the church. In the early church, candidates were excluded from this part entirely, even as observers; they could attend services only to the point where selections from the Bible were read and a sermon was preached. Their first communion after baptism therefore would have been a special event: At last they were part of the inner circle, the intimate community of the church. In the early decades this was indeed a small group, a dedicated band meeting quietly to avoid detection in times of persecution. Their meals, at which they ritually remembered Jesus and reenacted his last meeting with his disciples, would have been charged with tension, excitement, and joyous fellowship. Yet the meaning of the Eucharist did not depend on the feelings of the believers present; even when baptism and confirmation became less dramatic, the Eucharist remained powerful and mysterious. It continued as the heart of Christian worship for centuries.

We can develop some sense of the meaning of the Eucharist by looking at the way it was most likely practiced in the churches of the first hundred years of Christianity.[5] The rite began with a greeting from the bishop to the people: "Peace be with you." They responded, "And with your spirit." The congregation exchanged the kiss of peace, men to men and women to women. The laypeople brought their offerings, a small loaf of bread and a little wine in a flask. The deacons received them and laid them on the altar, pouring the wines into larger flasks. The bishop and the presbyters ("elders," primarily church administrators) rinsed their hands and then laid hands on the offerings. The bishop recited the Eucharistic prayer of thanks to God. The deacons or bishop broke the loaves, they partook, and then the bishop himself distributed it to the people, saying, "The Bread of heaven." Presbyters and deacons then distributed the wine, and also water, to the people, who came up in a row to receive three sips from each cup. At each sip the one who held the cup said, "In God the Father Almighty," "And in the Lord Jesus Christ," and then "And in the Holy Spirit in the Holy Church," with the recipient responding, "Amen." After this the vessels were washed and the communicants dismissed.

The ritual had three prominent dimensions, each of them important to the new Christian. The Eucharist was a joyous communal feast; it was a sacrifice; and it communicated great spiritual power. The communal nature would have been evident from the beginning, with the exchange of greetings and the kiss of peace; here was the goodwill and intimacy of a group of people who felt almost like a family. Moreover, each person had his or her role in an organic and interdependent society: The layperson brought an offering, the deacon presented and distributed the offerings, the bishop consecrated the ordinary bread and wine to be spiritual food. The community ate together, solemnly, affirming their unity, becoming more truly one in Christ. The Eastern church called the Eucharist a wedding feast, celebrating the union of Christ with his bride, the church. And as at a wedding, the community overcomes its differences and becomes one in rejoicing with bride and groom.

Second, the Eucharist was a sacrifice, with each member bringing something, a gift of his or her own substance in the form of bread or wine, to become part of the sacrifice. The form is reminiscent of the practice of sacrifice in many societies: The person who has sinned or who desires a spiritual benefit brings an animal or some loaves or fruit as offerings to the divine source of life. In giving over part of oneself, one participates in a vital exchange with the deity. In Christianity, this fundamental structure is amplified. The offering one brings becomes transformed into the body of Christ, who is God, who has sacrificed himself for the benefit of all. The food offered becomes divine through the cosmic miracle of Jesus' suffering and death; one eats not bread and wine but the body and blood of Christ.

In this miracle, the sacrifice releases great spiritual power, an infusion of spiritual nourishment for the Christian. For this reason some Christians have wished to partake of it often. The development of the "low mass," which requires only one other person to be present besides the priest, came from the wish of priests to commune daily for their spiritual nourishment. At the same time, the extreme holiness of the rite, the sense that it held enormous power, kept some away. About the fifth century the laity stopped communing each Sunday because they felt too impure to approach the altar; it also became the practice that only the priests would drink the wine, and the laypeople would take only the bread. Nevertheless, the meal remained the "bread of heaven" and the body of Christ. As Theodotus of Egypt (c. 160) wrote, "The bread is hallowed by the power of the name of God. It is transformed into spiritual power."

Because of the enormous power associated with the Eucharist, the awesomeness of the idea of God's sacrifice, and the sense of unity it generated in the church, Christians throughout the ages have entered into the ritual with humility, awe, and gratitude. The taking of holy food has been the spiritual nourishment of the church continually, week to week, in the celebration of the Lord's Day. As the culmination of the initiation of a new believer, the Eucharist has been a most powerful ritual; the seeker of salvation becomes a part of a holy community. [See Religions of Africa pp. 67, 88–89, Religions of Mesoamerica pp. 166–67, 177, 186, 237–38, Judaism pp. 399–40, Islam p. 646, and Hinduism pp. 743–45, 747–48 for description and discussion of sacrifice.]

The Church as Holy Community

From the beginning the churches conceived of themselves as a corporate entity; Paul called it "the body of Christ":

> For just as the body is one and has many members, and all the members of the body, though many, are one body, so it is with Christ. For by one Spirit we were all baptized into one body—Jews or Greeks, slaves or free—and all were made to drink of one Spirit. . . . Now you are the body of Christ and individually members of it. And God has appointed in the church first apostles, second prophets, third teachers, then workers of miracles, then healers, helpers, administrators, speakers in various kinds of tongues. (1 Cor. 12–13, 27–28, RSV)

The many roles mentioned by Paul devolved into three "orders," as we have seen—the laity, the deacons, and the bishops—with the presbyters, or elders, being the administrators. As more priests were needed, the priesthood became the order of which the bishop was the authoritative head (archbishops and cardinals appeared still later as the church needed a clear hierarchy of organization). The three primary orders each had their own role to play, interdependently, but the community fully affirmed its unity in the rites of the Eucharist. The bishops, further, understood themselves as continuing the intimate community of Jesus and his disciples; the pope regarded himself as the successor of Peter, who headed the disciples after Jesus' death. Moreover, a great spiritual event in the life of the church happened communally. Tradition as recorded in the Book of Acts tells that fifty days after the resurrection, probably on the Jewish holiday of Shavuot (Gk., Pentecost), the followers who gathered in Jerusalem experienced a gift of the Holy Spirit, including ecstatic behavior like speaking in tongues. They received a spiritual experience of unity; they were as one person at Pentecost. Like the Jews who together had seen the separation of the Red Sea as they left Egypt, and together had heard God's voice while standing at Sinai to receive the Ten Commandments, Christians now claimed to experience God's revelation not just to individuals but to the group as a whole. Similarly, the church fathers held that the church partakes of the Eucharist corporately, not as individuals. The community is one being.

This strong sense of community appears in the repeated attempts of various groups to purify the church. In the fourth century a major movement led by Donatus attempted to purify the church in Africa. He and his followers believed that no bishop who had given in to Diocletian's persecution (284–305) by handing over holy Scriptures or other church property should be allowed to hold office. The mainstream church, led by Augustine, concluded that the church on earth could not be expected to be so pure. As Augustine put it, the "invisible church," composed of the elect whom only God could know, would remain pure; the "visible church" here on earth would always include some sinners. Nevertheless, the presence of sinners—even among those who performed the sacraments —would not divert the church from its true course, or prevent the elect from gaining their salvation. Yet, despite the defeat of the Donatists, movements of purification appeared repeatedly. The Cathars of the twelfth century and the seventeenth-century Puritans of England and America are only two major examples of groups who believed they alone constituted the true or pure church. The ultimate recourse of such movements appears in the life of Roger Williams, founder of Rhode Island colony. He separated from the main body of Puritans to found his own Baptist church; then, finding its members were too impure, he eventually separated from them and would worship in company with no one but his wife—and sometimes not her.

Such movements illustrate a central conviction of Christians through the ages: The worshipers called the church are tied together in an intimate way. If they are one body, then the leg affects what the arm does, and both influence the liver and kidneys. The members of a Christian church are not independent; what each does affects the others. Moreover, the church should be as much like Christ as possible. Thus some Christians have believed that the presence of sinners would bring disastrous results on all, so they undertook to purify the church, making it more truly the body of Christ. A similar impulse arises among Christian groups who seek to minimize their contact with the world. By forming nearly self-sufficient communities, as in the villages of the Amish in Pennsylvania or Ohio, they can try to keep their group untainted. By adopting specific rules limiting interaction with others, as when some churches forbid marriage to nonmembers or some born-again Christian movements encourage buying goods only from other born-again Christians, they increase their consciousness of the holiness and purity of their own community.

The deep sense of interrelatedness in the church, the conviction that all are truly one body, can help us understand how priests or monks have sometimes functioned on behalf of the whole church. The various orders of the early church worked like different groups of organs within a body. As people pursued their spiritual quest more intensely, however, other "orders" emerged. The early church had an order of penitents (as we will see); later, the orders of monks, nuns, and friars emerged; and even pilgrims became a kind of unofficial "order" in the Middle Ages. Some of these people seemed especially holy because of their religious dedication, and the church at large came to regard them as a stream of spiritual power from which the whole body could drink. Those who were unable to or who preferred not to take on such religious tasks performed the more material work of sustaining the church. Thus from a group where all were "saints," as the early church called members, the church developed into an organization in which certain groups became higher-level specialists in the spiritual realm. The few who dedicated themselves wholly to God became the more spiritual organs, and as such came to represent the Holy Church itself. Thus at certain times the church regarded the monks' prayers as communicating with God on behalf of the whole church, and the priest could perform the Eucharist, the communal event par excellence, with as few as one other person communing with him.

Each of these specialized roles was an imitation of Christ (*imitatio Christi*) as well as being representative of the whole body. The bishop, for example, was leader of his flock in the same way that Jesus had led his band of disciples. According to an early tradition, Jesus handed the mantle of leadership to Peter (whose name means "rock"), saying, "On this rock I will build my church." This became an authoritative statement for one particular leadership pattern. The flock would have one shepherd, like Jesus and then Peter, as head of the apostles after Jesus' death. The bishop therefore was to take Jesus' place. He usually celebrated the Eucharist, distributing bread and wine to the people just as Jesus did at the Last Supper. He was also the teacher, as Jesus had taught. For example, in the fourth century, Jesus was portrayed on stone coffins as teaching a group of men from a book—a teacher of wisdom like the philosophers of the day. During that same period congregations expected their bishops to deliver learned lectures on Sundays, expounding the true wisdom as revealed in Christ. As a group, the bishops together became like another band of disciples who guided the church as a whole.

Secular leaders could take on the model of Christ as well. Eastern emperors regarded themselves as bearing the mantle of a Christly king and almost a priest, and when monarchy became the form of government in medieval Europe, the kings saw themselves as imitating the heavenly kingship of the resurrected Christ. The crowning of a monarch included the religious ceremony of anointing with oil. The king performed what were considered religious functions and had supernatural powers. Like Christ who would return to judge all, the king was judge; like Christ who sacrificed himself on behalf of humans, the king interceded between the people and God to protect them. Kings occupied a special place between the heavenly and earthly realms, like Jesus who was both human and divine. Some people even believed that kings could heal the sick and make crops grow. In short, the king was a religious personality like a bishop. One tenth-century chronicler, Bishop Otto of Freising, wrote after observing the coronation of a German king that

> On the same day and in the same church, the elected bishop of Munster was consecrated by the same prelates who had anointed the king . . . as a favorable presage for the future, since the same church and the same day witnessed the unction of the two persons who . . . are the only persons sacramentally anointed, each alike entitled *Christus Domini*.[6]

All kinds of leaders, whether religious or secular, thus took on holiness by making themselves like Christ.

Outside the regular leadership roles other manifestations of holiness revealed the *imitatio Christi*. For example, the martyrs of the early centuries took on the mantle of Christ; it was a great calling in times of persecution to die for Christ. This was not entirely new—Jews reckoned it an honor to die *al kiddush Hashem,* while sanctifying the name of God. Christians gave the martyr's death an additional value, however, because Jesus had died a violent death at the hands of persecutors. [See Judaism p. 407 and Islam pp. 673, 678–9 for discussion of martyrs.] To die in that way meant coming near to Christ, participating in his sacrifice, and partaking of his glory. The bishop of Antioch near the end of the first century C.E., Ignatius, looked forward with an almost sensuous

The emperor as the representative of Christ on earth is illustrated by the cross in the left hand and the scepter of rulership in the right. Here the Emperor Otto II is depicted on the Master of the Registrum Gregorii, *a book made in Trier, France, about 983. (Used by permission of Editions d'Art Albert Skira, Geneva.)*

delight to following in the footsteps of Jesus by becoming a martyr. He pleaded with his friends not to intervene in his behalf:

> Grant me nothing more than that I should be poured out as a libation to God, while there is still an altar ready. . . . I am God's wheat, and I am ground by the teeth of wild beasts, that I may be found pure bread. . . . Entreat Christ for me, that through these beasts I may be found a sacrifice to God.[7]

Ignatius got his wish: He died at the hands of the Romans, who threw him to the lions in 110 C.E.

The model of Christ has become an important motif in the ascetic movements of Christianity as well. Those who wanted to follow Jesus when there was no more outside persecution could engage in their own battles with the demonic forces that ruled the world. As Jesus had battled demons in his contest with Satan, the monks of the desert or the cloister could fight the evil forces within themselves. By conquering the temptations of the world, by giving up its luxuries and pleasures and instead devoting oneself to prayer and praise of God, one could be following Jesus' command, "Be ye perfect." Francis of Assisi in the thirteenth century offered another version of the model, vowing to be an itinerant, never having a roof over his head and never owning anything. Popular asceticism included even more dramatic examples, like the flagellants of the late Middle Ages who marched in procession, beating themselves with whips or thorns to symbolize their identification with the sufferings of Jesus. Thus monks, martyrs, bishops, and kings all represented an intensification of the imitation of Christ within the structure of the church, whether by asceticism, sacrifice, or the taking on of spiritual leadership. As religious specialists, they have helped to ensure the holiness of the community as a whole.

At various times some groups of Christians have criticized that sort of specialization, insisting instead that the church as a whole is holy, and no one in the church is any more holy than anyone else. The Protestant Reformation, as we saw in chapter 20, virtually erased the older structure of orders on behalf of the idea of the "priesthood of all believers." Any member could perform the specialized spiritual function, for example, of receiving another member's confession. Many small evangelical sects follow the principle that there should not be any ordained minister or preacher, that anyone who feels the call to preach may do so. The Quaker meeting is another version of that principle: All sit quietly until a person's "inner light" leads him or her to speak or pray. Nevertheless, the idea of spiritual specialization did not entirely die. The larger Protestant tradition maintained the requirement that those who would interpret Scripture—the clergy—must have specialized training. They are not inherently more holy, but their education represents their devotion and dedication, just as other special practices did for the monks. Even the idea that one should have a spiritual "calling" to preach (whether that calling is temporary or for a lifetime) suggests again the idea of spiritual specialization. In the popular mind missionaries and other dedicated Christian teachers have earned some of the status given to religious orders; they are regarded as possessing special grace that enables them to endure unusual hardships and trials. And even in Protestantism the reluctance of churches to pay their ministers high salaries indicates not the stinginess of congregations but the persistent sense that the Christian leader should be less tempted by worldly things, by the things that money can buy. Thus, on the one hand, there have been repeated movements for democratization of the church, emphasizing that all are equally holy; on the other, the holy community has always had leaders who, officially or unofficially, are the spiritual specialists—those who possess a special dedication or spiritual intensity that benefits the church as a whole.

The Life of the Church

Drawn together as a holy community, energized by its dedicated spiritual leaders, the church lives as a corporate being, an organic entity moving through time. It partakes of the Holy Spirit as regular nourishment, through the Eucharist or Holy Communion in most churches (though some celebrate it infrequently), and also through the preached word in the Protestant churches. Moreover, the church is the vehicle of the Holy Spirit in the world, the embodiment of the third person of the Trinity as Jesus embodied the second person. The church therefore aims to continue the work of Christ on earth: to bring salvation to humanity, to unite humanity with divinity. We can see this work as having three parts, each modeled on a different aspect of the life of Christ: first, evangelism, calling people outside the church to repent and believe; second, the work of salvation proper, enacted in the regular liturgies of the church; and third, the work of establishing the messianic kingdom under the rule of Christ. In each of these, the church as a body imitates Christ.

The first part of the church's work, evangelism, imitates the preaching of Christ. As the story of Jesus tells that he went about preaching the coming of God's kingdom, inviting people to enter, so the church has as one of its primary tasks the spreading of the gospel or "good news" to all people. Though Jesus preached to Jews, the church from early times has interpreted its mission far more widely. The apostles were to preach to all nations, to the ends of the earth. Among the various churches the message at its core has been nearly universal: All have sinned, but God has provided a remedy for sin in the work of Jesus the Christ; turn from sin and believe in Christ and you will receive the gift of salvation and eternal life. Usually the church has appointed special teachers or missionaries for the work of going out to the non-Christian world. Yet every believer also bears some responsibility for witnessing, that is, attesting to the truth of the Christian message in the presence of those who are not part of the church.

The evangelistic work, however, is only the beginning. The second part of the church's work, salvation, imitates the saving acts of Christ. As we have seen, the rites of baptism, confirmation, and the first communion introduce the convert into the community. But rituals are also essential to maintain the community and continue the work of salvation. The church as a body has, from early times, held that it was nourished by the regular weekly sharing of the Eucharist. For the Eastern church, as mentioned earlier, this rite embodies the union of humanity with divinity and is appropriately called the Divine Liturgy. In the setting of the church, the icons mirror the heavenly presence of Jesus, Mary, saints, and angels. The Eucharist itself is a wedding feast, uniting Christ with his church, his two "bodies" as it were, and presaging the great reunion that will take place when Christ returns at the end of time. As this holy union is repeated week after week, the church and its members, sharing in the feast, are continually reconnected with their divine source of life.

The metaphor that in the West dominates the Eucharist is that of sacrifice. According to Roman Catholic theology, each repetition of the rite actually reenacts the original sacrifice of Jesus (though not his physical death). In an awesome event, Jesus gives himself entirely to God, and God in Jesus gives himself to save human beings from eternal death. The sacrifice reflects an archaic structure: A part of the whole (for example one's crops or herds) is given to ensure continuing fruitfulness. Here, one death is given in order that all humanity may receive fullness of life. Partaking of the body and blood of the one sacrificed is the source of continuing spiritual nourishment of the Western church.

Protestant churches have deemphasized the Eucharist, many churches treating it only as a memorial rather than as a present and immediate spiritual event. Instead, they have turned to the preached word as the source of spiritual nourishment. The sermon based on Scripture offers a different kind of ritual experience for the church than does the Eucharist. Rather than the taking of food, which involves taste and texture combined with the visual drama of the priest's actions, the altar, and statues or icons, the sermon focuses on hearing and mental action, taking in with the ear and assimilating with the mind. The spiritual transformation in the ritual of the preached word takes place not through the tactile and visual senses, but from the top downward, so to speak, through ear and mind to the rest of the person.

Here, too, there are significant variations within the Protestant tradition. Some churches emphasize the learned discourse; others, the immediacy of spiritual calling that leads a person to preach spontaneously. The first emphasizes the rational mind: Scripture is given to the church as its source of spiritual guidance, and to grasp it Christians must use their minds. They must study, reflect, and think through carefully to unravel the mysteries of the holy Word. The second focuses on inspiration or intuition: Since Scripture is a mystery, only those possessed by the Spirit can understand it; study is less relevant. The one appeals to the rational mind and aims at a sense of satisfaction through convincing argument; the other appeals to the aesthetic and intuitive and aims at an experience of unity through congruence of scriptural passages with everyday experience. Most Protestant churches, of course, expect a mixture of the two. A learned lecturer without spirit or aesthetic quality sounds dead; high spirit without some thought about the content and some familiarity with the Bible is, as the saying goes, nothing but hot air. The two synthesize both poles of the Protestant worship experience, spirit and intellect, which then inspires the whole person and the whole church.

The life of the church involves more than the weekly partaking of the Spirit through word and sacrament. The church moves through time, repeating the work of Jesus himself by re-creating each year the cycle of the major events of his life and celebrating them in the round of the calendar. From the birth of Jesus and the visit of the wise men, to the resurrection and the descent of the Holy Spirit on the church, the yearly cycle recognizes the special times in Jesus' life. The church as the body of Christ acknowledges them and, by participating in them, experiences their power. In addition the Catholic and Orthodox churches celebrate feast days of saints—those who are closest to the model of Jesus himself. The saints' days are feasts of the church celebrating the Holy Spirit at work in the community, within the body of Christ—that is, the church —as it now lives, making the yearly round more nearly divine with the experiences of its own members. [See Religions of Mesoamerica pp. 159–60, 206–9, Native Religions of North America pp. 280–82, 351–54, Judaism pp. 431–33, Islam pp. 674, 707, Hinduism pp. 727, 793–94, Buddhism pp. 890–91, Religions of China pp. 1021–24, and Religions of Japan pp. 1141–46 for discussion of religious calendar and time.]

The major seasons of the Christian year begin with Advent (literally "the coming"), which looks forward to the birth of Jesus. Although the date of Christmas was not established until the fourth century (and Catholic and Orthodox still disagree), once a date was established it became a major festival with its own seasonal rites. From the Sunday nearest Saint Andrew's feast (November 30), that is, approximately four weeks before Christmas on December 25, special prayers and hymns appear in church services, and the priest or minister offers sermons appropriate for the occasion. The Western Christmas season itself does not end with the Nativity but goes on for twelve days more, culminating in the Epiphany on January 6, when according to tradition the three wise men from the East arrived to pay homage to the infant Jesus. For the church this represented the first manifestation of the Christ to the world at large. (January 6 is also the day established in Orthodox churches for Christmas.) For the church the entire season is one of joy and hope, full of the expectation of Jesus and the transformation he will bring. Like the birth of a child in a family, the Nativity brings excitement and happy fellowship as the church unites around the reenactment of the appearance of Jesus in the world. Nativity plays, popular among children and adults through the centuries, are a simple but profound expression of that special sort of joy.

The season is also, of course, that of the winter solstice, a time when many traditions express their hope and expectation of the renewal of the world as the days grow gradually longer and greater light returns to the earth. Christmas sanctifies that hope in a Christian light, and undoubtedly the presence of Roman religious celebrations at that time contributed to the final establishment of a winter date for Jesus' birth.

The next major season begins in late winter with the onset of Lent, forty days before Easter. This was originally the time for the final preparation of the candidates for baptism, with prescribed fasting and serious repentance, a final turning away from sin. When the sacrament of penance developed, the penitents often had to serve their special duties for the length of Lent. Gradually the whole church joined the **catechumens** and penitents in making Lent a period of self-examination, repentance, and abstinence (for example, abstinence from rich foods like meat). Thus the period became a somber and reflective one, looking forward toward the coming suffering of Christ.

The day before Lent begins, Shrove Tuesday, became in many countries a carnival day. First it was celebrated in Italy, then it spread to France and Spain; the French brought it to New Orleans as Mardi Gras ("Fat Tuesday"). In England, it was called Pancake Day, the day on which one should use up all one's fats and oils, which were considered rich and luxurious foods. The wild carnival atmosphere gives way to Ash Wednesday, so named because many would attend Mass and have ashes smeared on their foreheads as a sign of penitence.

Lent culminates in the services of Holy Week, the last week before Easter. Palm Sunday, the Sunday before Easter, reminds the church of Jesus' triumphal entry into Jerusalem and is a day of high spirit anticipating Easter. Afterward, however, the church becomes solemn again with Maundy Thursday, the day of the Last Supper of Jesus with his disciples, so called because at this time, tradition says, Jesus gave two commands (mandates, from which "Maundy" is derived): "Do this in remembrance of me" and "Love one another as I have loved you." The church remembers also the betrayal of Judas and Jesus' agony in the garden of Gethsemane as he faced his death. The next day, Good Friday, recalls his trial and crucifixion. Deep sadness penetrates the church, and altars and pulpits are often draped in black.

Easter, preceded in the early church by an all-night vigil on Saturday night, brings a total change of mood to joy and rebirth from the depths of despair. Even today, though the vigil is a rarity, sunrise services celebrate the renewal of life symbolized by the resurrection of Jesus from the tomb. One of the great festivals of the early church, Easter celebrates purity as well as joy; this was the time when new members were baptized, coming forth from the water to don their white robes. Easter is dated on the first Sunday after the first full moon following the spring equinox, and it coincides in northern latitudes with the beginning of spring, echoing at another level the gift of newness of life.

Forty days later, on a Thursday, is the traditional date of Jesus' ascension into heaven, a major feast in Catholicism and Orthodoxy. It anticipates the great festival of the "fiftieth day," Pentecost (always on a Sunday, for Easter is counted as day one). Here the church celebrates the gift of the Holy Spirit. This is also, of course, a festive holiday, but more than Easter's joy of newness Pentecost relives the endowment of spiritual power given to the church, the sense of transformation to another level of existence. It also looks toward taking up the work of the church, which is the successor to Jesus himself: announcing the good news to others and establishing God's kingdom on earth. One week later Trinity Sunday celebrates the oneness of God's three revelations as Father, Son, and Holy Spirit.

The importance of the round of the Christian year is accented in many churches by the use of special vestments and tapestries for each season. The pattern of Christ's life as model for the church is, in addition, repeated over and over again in Christian art. The architectural form of the church itself became, in the Middle Ages, an expression both of the spiritual reality of the church as image of Christ and of the heavenly world to which Christians looked forward. The floor plan followed the shape of the cross: Being in the church implied being within the "body" of Christ crucified and resurrected. The church's altar stood at the eastern wall, facing Jerusalem where the crucifixion had occurred; the western portal, the main entrance, was often decorated with a dramatic scene of Judgment Day or of Christ in triumph, suggesting the future destiny of the church. Scenes from the life of Christ have been painted, woven into tapestries, or portrayed in stained glass throughout the centuries, for Christian artists have never tired of portraying the great events that carry the meaning of Christian existence. As the year passed, the walls would tell the stories of the life of Jesus that had now become the ongoing life of the church.

Nevertheless, another element has always been present in Christianity that transcends the yearly cycle—namely, the expectation of the return of Jesus himself. Portrayals of Judgment Day and the popularity of scenes from the Book of Revelation suggest that someday, perhaps soon, this world will end and a "new heaven and a new earth" will be established by the hand of Christ himself. In the liturgy we find this in prayers—"Thy kingdom come!" in the Lord's Prayer, for example—and in the interpretation of the Eucharist as presaging a great banquet for the wedding of Christ and the church. At times this different sense of time has broken through the bounds of the regular, repeated ritual and exploded in **millenarian** movements (which, of course, Christianity itself was at the beginning). Groups of Christians take on new and intense religious practices in preparation for the Second Coming, often ignoring the regular work of the church. The great spiritual movements of Christian history—the monastic movement of the fourth and fifth centuries, the Crusades and related movements of the eleventh, twelfth, and thirteenth centuries, the Reformation of the sixteenth and seventeenth centuries, and the evangelical awakenings of the nineteenth and twentieth centuries have all been accompanied by millenarian expectations. Christians begin to feel that the time is short, the work is coming to a close, and God will soon bring the perfect world they yearn for into being.

Some churches, though not fully millenarian, have taken an intermediate position in which they leave behind the church calendar, relying on another sense of time altogether. For example, the American Puritans eliminated all the feasts except Easter (they did not celebrate Christmas at all, regarding it as a left-over from older, idolatrous religions) and the regular Sunday services, which featured a lengthy sermon. Instead of the traditional feasts, their magistrates, on the advice of the ministers, would proclaim feast days or fast days whenever it seemed appropriate: a feast of thanksgiving when the community had experienced a blessing or a fast day when they experienced troubles, which, they believed, were due to their sins and therefore required penitence. Their faith in God's providence was so strong that they attributed to him sovereign power over each day, to choose whether he would administer blessing or curse. The community, the Puritans believed, should respond to God's immediate action rather than to a repetitive calendar. This was the way in which as a community they chose to imitate Christ: in full obedience to God the Father. [See Religions of Africa pp. 74–75, Religions of Mesoamerica pp. 229–38, Native Religions of North America pp. 308–16, 351–57, Judaism pp. 439–45, Islam pp. 674, 677–79,

The millennium, or expected thousand-year reign of Christ, has at times been a major topic of Christian study and speculation. This illustration was the front cover of a medieval commentary on the Book of Revelation, Beatus of Liebana's Commentaries on the Apocalypse: The Coming of the End of the World *(France, mid–eleventh century). An angel trumpets and a third of the sun and moon are darkened, while an eagle cries, "Woe, woe, woe . . . !" (Rev. 8:13). (Photo used by permission of Bibliothèque Nationale, Paris.)*

Hinduism p. 829, Buddhism pp. 937–41, Religions of China pp. 1021–24, and Religions of Japan pp. 1140–46, 1153–62 for description and discussion of festivals and annual celebrations.]

The church, then, has acted out the way of salvation in a variety of manners, in different modes of worship, in different responses to God's action in the temporal world. In addition to evangelism and salvation, there is a third part to the work of the church: the messianic task, to transform the world itself. In this dimension of Christian existence, being a successor to Christ means continuing the work he began of actually establishing God's kingdom. If one is looking toward Christ's immediate return, this impulse is likely to be weak. But often Christians have acted to organize and literally to govern the world in accord with the norms of the church itself. The Christian emperors of Byzantium, the popes of the Middle Ages, the radical reformers who wanted the "saints" to govern society, all expressed the confidence that Christianity is not merely waiting for the Messiah to return, nor is it only concerned with ensuring the salvation of its members; rather, it transforms the world by direct action. We find many examples of this impulse in modern times as well: Christian efforts to end the slave trade and free black slaves in the nineteenth century; temperance movements to control liquor consumption; Christian lobbies and political parties; Christian peace movements or nonviolent movements; campaigns for laws against abortion or homosexuality, or in favor of prayer in the schools. Sometimes Christians appear politically liberal in these campaigns, sometimes conservative; but all express the conviction that the church has the duty to work toward the perfection of the world during this in-between time before Christ returns.

Thus the church in the various dimensions of its corporate life aims to be the body of Christ: as an organic entity with each of its members supporting the others and being supported; as an evangelistic organization, continuing the preaching of Jesus; as a keeper of the mysteries, reenacting the redemptive sacrifice of Christ and extending the pattern of his life into the yearly round; as a vehicle of the Holy Spirit in all realms; and as the executor of Christ's will for the world, establishing the perfect kingdom of God on earth. These have been the great strengths of the church through the ages, and they have given direction and purpose to innumerable individual lives. Yet there is also a strong personal dimension to Christianity, suggesting to every individual that he or she also can live in imitation of Christ. Not only by participating in the great body of the church, but also by sanctifying his or her personal life in Christ, can the Christian achieve spiritual fulfillment.

Jesus as Model of the Christian's Personal Life

Christianity sanctifies the great events of a person's life by bringing them under the umbrella of Christian ideals. These events are marked in virtually all societies by rites of passage: birth, puberty, marriage, death. They are times of critical change in biological and/or social status, and although modern American society has paid little attention to them, they are usually accompanied by profound psychological transformations. Christianity, in its work of transforming human beings toward divinity, uses rituals around these crucial events to aid in that process as well as to ease the transition for the individual and the community. [See Religions of Africa pp. 42–51, 76–79, Religions of Mesoamerica pp. 201–6, Native Religions of North America pp. 278–79, 295–98, 306–8, Judaism pp. 445–50, Islam pp. 677–78, 680–86, Hinduism pp. 747, 807–14, Buddhism pp. 915–17, 921, 931–37, Religions of China pp. 1019–21, and Religions of Japan pp. 1146–50 for description and discussion of rites of passage.]

Birth has attracted to it the rite of baptism and christening, a modified version of confirmation. Though some churches shun infant baptism, many have used it as a means of confirming the infant born into a Christian family as part of the organism of the church. The purity of the infant corresponds to the purification of baptism, so the two seem naturally to go together. Yet at the same time, many churches have held that, despite the appearance of innocence, the infant is already contaminated by original sin, transmitted down through its ancestors ever since Adam, so baptism is already necessary in order for the child to be a part of the church. Christening gives the child a Christian name; as Christ received his title, "the Christ," or Messiah, so the child receives the proper name—traditionally, the name of a saint. By this too the child becomes a social being in a Christian community of "saints." [See Religions of Africa pp. 45–46, 76, Native Religions of North America p. 307, Judaism pp. 385–86, 445–46, Islam p. 682, Hinduism pp. 810–11, Buddhism p. 932, Religions of China pp. 1019–20, and Religions of Japan pp. 1146–47 for description and discussion of birth rites.]

Puberty has received surprisingly little attention in the Christian liturgy considering that most religious traditions focus sharply on that crucial period of transition from childhood to adulthood. It is not quite so surprising, however, when we remember that puberty means the onset of adult sexuality, and in Christianity sexuality has been regarded as one of the great sources of sin. Most churches have interpreted the sin of Adam and Eve as primarily sexual, a sin of lust (though some churches have focused more on the sin of pride). The danger in sexuality has meant that puberty as a physical transformation has been largely ignored, and privileges and responsibilities of adulthood have been emphasized instead. Many churches have made the age of puberty an appropriate time for confirmation: final acceptance into the church as a full member. Also, to deal with rising sexual impulses, adolescents in earlier times were often encouraged to enter religious orders, where they would be taught celibacy, or to marry and be chaste within the marriage. Thus the taking of vows and weddings have superseded puberty rites. Both of these are marriages: In the religious order, one becomes married to Christ; in the wedding, one unites with one's spouse "in Christ," imitating the marriage of Christ to the church—an eternal, faithful union in which each mirrors the other in holiness. [See Religions of Africa pp. 48–51, 77–78, Judaism pp. 447–48, Islam pp. 683–84, Hinduism pp. 809–10, Buddhism p. 935, Religions of China p. 1020, and Religions of Japan p. 1148 for description and discussion of marriage rites.]

The rites of death in Christianity are designed to give comfort to the dying Christian; for, after all, he or she is going to an eternal life. In Roman Catholicism, for example, the rite of extreme unction offers the individual an opportunity for penitence, clearing the soul through a final confession, then for being anointed once again, as at confirmation, as in the biblical story of the descent of the dove of purity on Jesus. Death is a summation of life, and it looks forward to the next. We find in some forms of evangelical Christianity an expectation that the dying person may even be able to see the brightness of the light ahead, may have a vision of future joy immediately before death. The Christian is usually buried on the third day, expressing the identification with Christ who was resurrected on the third day. Tombs are marked with empty crosses, not crucifixes, thus symbolizing the resurrection: The soul of the person is no longer here. [See Religions of Africa pp. 42–45, 78–79, Religions of Mesoamerica pp. 144, 229–33, Native Religions of North America pp. 300–301, 307–8, 335–37, Judaism pp. 448–50, Islam pp. 684–85, Hinduism pp. 813–14, Buddhism pp. 935–37, Religions of China pp. 1021, 1041–44, and Religions of Japan pp. 1149–50 for description and discussion of death and funeral rites.]

Thus the major passages of the individual's life receive their distinctive Christian flavor, always pointing to Christ. More generally, however, the model of Jesus has stood out in the guides to personal piety through the ages as one that should be present in every moment of a person's life. Essentially, this has been a model of continual purification, leading toward sinlessness. Jesus was above all that human being who did not sin, who did not fall into temptation or error—for he was God. If human beings are to become like God, they must eliminate sin. This has required ritual, self-discipline, and continual self-examination in terms of Christian ideals.

Probably the most dramatic example of the process of purification has been the Roman Catholic rite of penance. Sometime in the second or early third century, churches began to exclude from the Eucharist those who had committed serious sins, at least for the period of Lent, sometimes for many years. Such persons requested admission to the order of penitents. They wore sackcloth and ashes or other special garments, sat in a separate section of the church, observed sexual continence, and devoted themselves to prayer and acts of charity. Some churches used public flogging or required penitents to prostrate themselves at the feet of the congregation. This series of rites, the early sacrament of penance, could be performed only once in a person's life. Afterward one would be restored to the church and thenceforth would live an upright, and it was hoped, perfect Christian life. Since it could be done only once, many people postponed it till late in life.

Penance acknowledges the quest for perfection in the face of the obvious fact that humans continue to be imperfect even after original sin is washed away; the phenomenon commonly known as "backsliding" is a universal occurrence. It is so widespread, in fact, that the churches found the original form of penance too strict. They had generally relaxed the punishments of penance by the fourth century, and in the sixth century a new form, introduced by Irish monks, spread through the churches. The sinner would have a private audience with a priest in which the priest, ideally without knowing the identity of the penitent, heard the sins that the sinner wished to confess and prescribed a correction, together with certain devotional acts, as a way of making amends in the person's relationship with God. This practice was repeatable. It became known as auricular confession, or simply confession. The acts prescribed tended to be positive practices, unlike the asceticism of earlier days. Fasting and self-flagellation were still modes of penance, but so were endowing masses (which gave financial support to the church), going on pilgrimage, and saying additional prayers and psalms.

In Protestantism confession became optional, a private matter, and any Christian could confess to any other. Occasionally, however, confession has risen again to become an important rite even in Protestant sects. The famous Shakers of the nineteenth century, led by Mother Ann Lee, practiced confession to the "saints," that is, the whole communal group, as a major ritual. More commonly, Protestants have substituted a process of self-examination, identifying and correcting one's own faults. Among the Puritans, such self-examination was a crucial part of the process of becoming a church member, and one shared it with one's pastor. However, the practice was not so much a confession of specific sins as a narrative account of the struggles of one's spiritual life. The importance of testimonials—that is, giving a public account of one's previous sinful life and one's experience of salvation—in some evangelical churches indicates the continuing presence of the same impulse; open examination of one's faults and errors is a crucial part of Christian spiritual development. In modern times, psychotherapy has often taken the place of self-examination and confession for Christians (and others) whose churches no longer provide a satisfactory ritual expression of that impulse.

The larger purpose of such rites is the purification of the soul, to abolish temptation to sin in order to live a more Christly life. What exactly was meant by the more Christly life has varied from one era to the next. At times the model has been an ascetic one, with the monk exemplifying the highest ideals. Jesus was conceived of as the one who left the world entirely behind—especially the worldly temptations of wealth, power, and sexual lust. Only the monk could fulfill this ideal, but laypeople could take on part of it while living family lives and working in the world. They could, for example, practice charity, giving away their wealth rather than accumulating it; they could spend extra time in prayer and worship, focusing their attention on the godly rather than the everyday realm. They could for a period of time take on vows of continence, fast regularly, or even spend short periods of time in a monastery or convent. They could go on pilgrimage—becoming for some months or a year wanderers like Jesus, living by the gifts and hospitality of others, seeking only God. Ordinary people could incorporate all these variants on the ascetic model of Jesus into their lives.

Another popular model of Jesus has emphasized more his inner character and ethical action than his ascetic life. Jesus was humble, kind, forgiving, charitable; outwardly he exemplified love toward his fellow human beings. This more humanized Jesus was drawn from sections of Scripture that told, for example, of his feeding the multitudes, forgiving the prostitute Mary Magdalene, calling the little children to him. The Sermon on the Mount ("Blessed are the poor . . . the meek . . . ," and so on) emphasized his humility; his telling a rich man how hard it was to get into the kingdom of God echoed the vow of poverty. This ideal has often appealed more to the laity and has grown increasingly strong since the Protestant Reformation. In this respect, Christians can take on the model of the loving person rather than the inner struggles of the ascetic to attain godliness. In place of the earlier image of Jesus battling Satan in the wilderness, recent Christians tend to favor the gentler view of Jesus reflected in the popular Protestant hymn "What a Friend We Have in Jesus."

Other portraits of Jesus have emerged at various times. We saw in an earlier section both Jesus the teacher of wisdom and Christ the king. Modern times have seen portraits of Jesus as social reformer, successful businessman, or revolutionary. The diversity of portrayals reflects the multiplicity of Christian communities and Christian ideals throughout history. The past century has seen scholars of early Christianity searching for the "historical Jesus" in an attempt to clarify who this person was, in the hope of constructing a firm model for the Christian life. The quest has not succeeded, however; the picture of Jesus in even the earliest Christian literature already was shaped by layers of tradition and the authors' own images of a holy man or Messiah. The amount that is incontestably authentic, if any, is too small and insignificant to build a rich model of human life.

Still, the ideal of Jesus continues to hold the imagination of Christians. He was the perfect man, the ideal of humanity (although some women in recent times have questioned whether the human ideal can be fully represented in a *male* figure). To rise above sin and error as Jesus did is, for Christians, to reach upward to God. Whether that means parting company with the material world as the ascetics did or becoming a loving person like the humanized Jesus, whether it means being impoverished or wealthy and charitable, it remains above the ordinary reach of life. To attain that ideal, to take on the *imitatio Christi*, requires continual self-examination, discipline, and practice. Whatever the specifics of the ideal, Christians have turned to the practice of purification of the soul to rise above ordinary human nature. Most Christian groups have held, of course, that this is not possible by human effort alone: God's grace, mediated through the saving acts of Christ's suffering, death, and resurrection, have made it truly possible to approach the divine life, the sinless life. Even when we look at human efforts to follow in Jesus' steps, we must remember that central assertion of the Christian myth: that God became man in order that human beings could return to God. For that remains Christianity's great mystery.

In this respect, the system of salvation discussed earlier in this chapter remains central to our understanding of Christianity. Even while modeling themselves on Jesus, Christians have sought through specific actions to place themselves in the stream of salvation—through the regular receiving of the sacraments, contact with holy personages, or the devout prayers of the heart. The ways and means developed by the churches—rites and relics, icons and sermons—have remained meaningful as vehicles through which Christians can be in direct contact with purity and holiness, in order to move from death to life

Different models of Christ have appeared in art and statuary. Here "Christ gives Peter the Law," from a fourth-century sarcophagus, suggests Christianity's connection with Judaism as well as Christ the teacher. (Used by permission of Hirmer Archive, Munich.) Below, the suffering Christ appears in Michelangelo's famous Duomo Pietá (Florence, Italy, mid–sixteenth century). (Used by permission of SCALA/Art Resource, New York.)

and to higher and higher levels of spiritual life. From reflection on their particular traditions of ritual and morality, saints and sinners, renewal and transformation, Christians in every era have formulated their highest ideals of service, devotion, knowledge, and leadership. Christianity in its many forms holds out the promise of bringing humans to the intersection of the divine and human worlds, where the spiritual and invisible touches the earthly and visible. In that encounter a new humanity takes shape—different for each place and time, affected by politics, economics, aesthetics, and the like—but a new vision of humanity nonetheless. In the next chapter we will look closely at the dynamics of such changes, in two widely separated examples.

22

Dynamics of Christian Life

WE HAVE LOOKED AT CHRISTIANITY as a historically developing religion, in overview, and we have examined some of its principal enduring features. Both the history and the structures can better be understood, however, if we look at specific examples in greater depth. For Christianity at any given time, in any particular place, is *both* a defined community with a set of beliefs and ceremonies held to be the foundation of the tradition *and* a community changing its thoughts and practices to grapple with new situations. How this can be, how change and continuity can be simultaneously present, will become clear as we look at particular examples.

We will consider two cases, far removed from one another in space and time, different in the kinds of source material they present for our consideration, and different as models of the basic Christian system of salvation. The first is a ritual: the pilgrimage to Saint James (Santiago) of Compostela in Spain, as it developed in the twelfth century. While pilgrimage never had the status of the official sacraments of the church, it was regarded with honor as part of a spiritual path for those who did not wish to take monastic vows but wanted to develop in their spirituality, to approach closer to God. The increasing popularity of the Compostela pilgrimage gave it the character of a mass movement, encouraged and guided by the elites of medieval Europe. Its story must be pieced together from fragments of legend, liturgy, and chronicle.

The second example is a pair of biographies: those of Lyman Beecher and Harriet Beecher Stowe, father and daughter, from the nineteenth-century United States. They left a considerable body of written work and personal material from which we can reconstruct their lives and thoughts, and the historical details of the period are well known. Since they are closer in time to us, some of the issues their lives raised will be more familiar than those of the twelfth century. In terms of the structure of the quest for salvation in Christianity, they exemplify the use of more personal vehicles of salvation rather than the ritual and hierarchical ones of medieval times. We will also be able to see across the centuries some common themes in the struggles of Christians to come to terms with the problems of their times.

The Pilgrimage to Compostela

Pilgrimage itself has a long history in Christianity as well as in other religions. Undertaking a journey to visit a holy place—the grave of a saint, the site of some famous religious event—has been almost universally regarded as good for the soul. Whether it is to obtain a blessing, to pay homage to authority, or to be purified of one's past errors, going on pilgrimage is an especially effective means of spiritual elevation. The physical and psychological effort of leaving home uproots people from their old habits and familiar environment, and that in itself can spur changes in their personal lives. In addition, travel, in all ages and places until the past hundred and fifty years, was difficult, burdensome, and unpredictable. The medieval Jewish commentator Rashi held that travel diminished one's wealth, one's fame, and one's fertility—an adage that in most cases probably held true. To take on a long and difficult journey, then, meant that one gave up a great deal of familiarity and comfort. Except for the rare lone adventurer, a person would have to feel considerable desire for change to enter upon a pilgrimage. [See Religions of Mesoamerica pp. 226–33, Judaism pp. 469–70, Islam pp. 645–47, Hinduism pp. 815–20, Buddhism p. 874, Religions of China pp. 1041–44, and Religions of Japan pp. 1154–60 for description and discussion of pilgrimage.]

In Christian history, those who went on pilgrimage were generally regarded as pious souls—less than the martyrs or monks, but certainly devout men and women worthy of praise. The favorite sites were Jerusalem, where Jesus himself had walked and where the church had begun, and Rome, where according to tradition Peter and Paul had died martyrs' deaths and where the papacy had its seat. Throughout the centuries, devout Christians would travel to these holy spots to pray, ask forgiveness of sins, or seek nearness to God. Yet in the early centuries pilgrimage was a voluntary, private devotion, usually practiced only by those wealthy enough to afford the journey.

In the sixth century the Irish missionary monks who crisscrossed Europe began to impose pilgrimages as penance for certain sins, especially sins that were openly scandalous. Nobles or priests who were found to have committed some crime often were assigned long pilgrimages. Over the centuries this motive for pilgrimage increased in importance. By the twelfth century many undertook pilgrimage whether a priest had imposed it as punishment or not; they believed they had accumulated so many sins, or such great ones, that they needed to satisfy some of the punishment due them by an especially holy act. (By this time the church held that the guilt of sin was absolved through confession, but the punishment still had to be paid, usually in purgatory, after death.) In the same period, the doctrine of indulgences grew in importance; the pope through the local bishop occasionally granted remission of part of the punishment to those who went on pilgrimage, those who gave alms, and/or those who were present at the consecration of a church. At first indulgences were few and far between and, in any case, remitted only a portion of the penalty. But from the late eleventh century onward, greater and more frequent indulgences were offered. The first certain record of a plenary indulgence—granting remission of all penalties for sin—was offered by Pope Urban II in 1095 to participants in the First Crusade.

Thus pilgrimage moved from the periphery of Christian devotion to near the center as the Christians of Europe became more concerned about purging themselves of sin. It was just at this time that the pilgrimage to the Spanish shrine of Saint James grew in popularity, and we will look later at the connection between the two developments. First, however, we might ask how it was that this shrine was known at all. There is no mention in the New Testament of the Apostle James in Spain; nor is there any other apparent reason for a shrine in the far northwest corner of that country. Rome and Jerusalem were the obvious goals for long pilgrimages, and if one needed a short trip, there were many holy churches scattered through the countryside of Europe.

The answer has many dimensions, but the most direct comes from the cult of relics. As we observed in chapter 20, people of the early Middle Ages defined their religiousness largely through devotion to relics. Relics were stolen, transported across land and sea, dug up, and invented. Whenever a new relic appeared or an old one was found in a new place, it attracted attention and prestige to a church or abbey; often it provided the site for a new pilgrimage. In the late eighth century Charlemagne's reforms forbade the addition of new saints to the roster while simultaneously requiring that every church altar have a holy relic. Thus any shift in the geography of holiness would necessitate finding an old saint to verify the power of a place.

This is precisely what happened at Compostela. We have no contemporary accounts of the discovery of the relics of Saint James. We do know that a legend circulated from at least the seventh century saying James had preached in Spain. By the early ninth century a cult of James had begun in northwest Spain, the region then known as Galicia. A later legend tells us the following story: A hermit named Pelayo,[8] together with some villagers and shepherds, noticed strange starlight and angelic voices in the vicinity of a wooded area. Pelayo informed the nearest bishop, Theodomir. He and his assistants fasted for three days, then searched the thick woods until they discovered a hut containing a marble coffin. Inside rested the bones of Saint James (one version adds that an attached piece of parchment gave the full description of how the bones had arrived there). Theodomir told King Alfonso II, who immediately constructed a church on the site. This was the beginning of the cathedral of Compostela—which, in one derivation of the name, means *campus stellae*, "field of the star." From that time the legend of James in Spain grew, and the Christian kings of northern Spain held James to be the protector of the country.

Nevertheless, Compostela remained of mostly local importance until the eleventh century. Then Europe, in the middle of the spiritual revival led by Cluniac reformers and culminating in the Crusades, began to find in Spain an interesting focus of pilgrimage. We will shortly look at the reasons why. But first it is important to understand what a pilgrimage involved. It was not a matter simply of packing one's bags and taking the next wagon for Compostela. Becoming a pilgrim in the twelfth century meant taking on a serious religious obligation;

it was almost like entering a religious order. Some traveled with the pilgrims for lighter reasons, to be sure—merchants to sell their wares, adventurers for the excitement of travel—but the true pilgrim was traveling to come closer to God.

The Route of the Pilgrim

Since pilgrims might be gone a long time, they would first set their affairs in order and make their wills. The latter was not a common practice—indeed, only pilgrims had the undisputed privilege of wills, of deciding how their property would be distributed in case of death. Then, whether going voluntarily or because of an imposed penance, the pilgrim would go to his or her priest to confess. The full confession of all sins was necessary before setting out on the holy journey that would satisfy some of the penalties. Pilgrims donned the symbols of their status: a tunic (often stamped with a cross), a staff, and a pouch for carrying valuables. These items singled them out, though unofficially, as religious personages, and would, it was hoped, attract alms and hospitality along the route. Pilgrims had to carry money for road tolls or religious donations, but otherwise they were expected to travel light, imitating the poverty of Jesus and relying on charity.

If they seemed materially impoverished, however, they could expect great spiritual richness. No matter which of the routes pilgrims took, they would be visiting the greatest and holiest spots of all Europe. For example, the pilgrim from Burgundy (eastern France) would go first to Cluny itself, which boasted relics of Saint Peter and Saint Paul. Next might be nearby Clermont, where Urban II preached the First Crusade and where the church of Notre Dame de Port had a famous tenth-century statue of Virgin and Child. Next would be Le Puy, an ancient pilgrimage center and possibly a holy site of the Druids in pre-Christian days. Le Puy was famous for its volcanic craters as well as its thorn from Christ's crown, donated by Saint Louis, and it had a special stone, the Pierre de Fièvres (the Stone of Fevers), on which the sick could lie while priests recited prayers to the Virgin. Next came the church of Sainte Foi at Conques, also a site of healing, especially for blindness and diseases of the eyes. It was well known that the monks of Conques had stolen the relics of Foi from another site, but this did not mar their holiness—after all, Foi would not have let herself be stolen if she had not wanted to move. Besides her own relics, including the famous crowned statue of her called the "Majesty," the church possessed the famous reliquary of King Pepin: a jeweled wooden chest containing relics of the Virgin and Saints Peter, Paul, Andrew, George, John the Evangelist, John the Baptist, Martin, and Hippolytus, plus the foreskin and umbilical cord of Jesus. Before reaching the Pyrenees Mountains, the pilgrim would also stop at Saint Peter of Moissac, a church believed to have been founded by King Clovis, the first Frankish convert in 496.

A pilgrim from north-central France would come to Orleans, where at the cathedral of the Holy Cross could be seen a chalice consecrated by Jesus and a

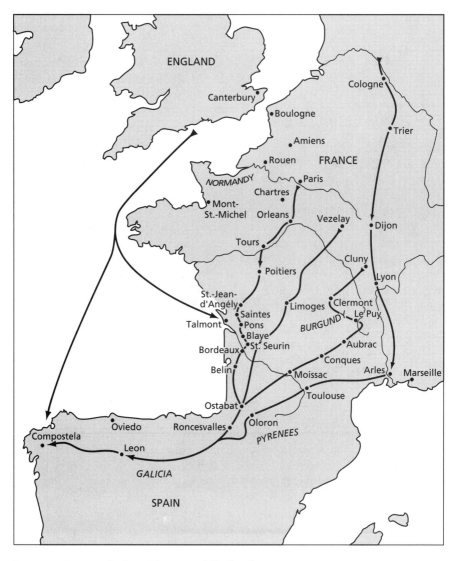

Routes to Compostela from France and England.

fragment of the cross. At Tours, the great basilica of Saint Martin contained relics of that saint, one of the patron saints of France. In Poitiers the pilgrim could visit the enshrined remains of Bishop Hilary, a famous upholder of orthodoxy in debates with the heretics. Poitiers was also the scene of the famous battle against the Muslims in 732, which Charles Martel had won, preserving Gaul for Christianity. At Saint-Jean-d'Angély was the head of Saint John the Baptist; and there too the pilgrim could hear a great liturgical choir of a hundred monks singing day and night. At Saint Romain of Blaye there was the body of the famous knight Roland; at Saint Seurin of Bordeaux, Roland's horn; at Belin, the tomb of Roland's compatriots. These warriors had died in battles against the Basques on returning from the First Crusade, but legend held that they had been fighting the Muslims. They were therefore treated as saints, martyrs in the war against unbelievers.

There were other routes from different parts of France and from Italy, plus many other supplementary roads through famous towns like Chartres or Amiens. The northern routes converged at the approach to the Pyrenees, and the climb into the mountains marked a high point in more ways than one. There the pilgrims came together in large numbers for the final approach to the holy site. At the pass at Ostabat, each planted a small wooden cross, imitating the large stone one that, it was said, had been erected by Charlemagne himself. They went on to Roncesvalles, where they could see the huge rock Roland had split with his sword. At other towns there were more relics including those of the famous scholar Saint Isidore at Léon. Some might take a side trip to the church of San Salvador at Oviedo, where King Alfonso VI had revealed a great casket

Pilgrims frequently stopped along the route to pay homage to relics of famous saints. This bejeweled statue, 33.5 inches high, stood atop the case said to contain relics of Sainte Foi, famous for her ability to heal the blind—hence the large, staring eyes. (From the Abbey Treasure, Conques; photo used by permission of Maurice Babey, Basel.)

of holy relics. Then finally, after a lengthy trek in the semi-arid plain, they approached Compostela.

The pilgrims immersed themselves in a stream two miles outside the city, just as their counterparts in the Holy Land would bathe in the Jordan. This was almost a second baptism, an initiatory purification. Each person picked up a stone from the limestone quarry and carried it to the city, thus contributing his labor to the building of the shrine. Entering the city itself, the pilgrims would pass through streets filled with merchants and minstrels, stopping perhaps to buy. Eventually most pilgrims would purchase a scallop shell, the insignia of Compostela. Their main purpose now, however, would be to find lodging and prepare to go to the basilica for services.

Most pilgrims would try to be at the church for an all-night vigil at least once during their stay. They would, of course, hear Mass in the church as often as possible, as they had in each church along the way. If possible, a pilgrim would have arranged the trip so as to be there on one of the feast days of Saint James, either July 25 or December 30. Then he or she could hear the great liturgy of the saint himself, which had developed by the twelfth century into a magnificent piece celebrating James and John as the "Sons of Thunder," called by Christ to do his work on earth. The glory of the processional the pilgrims would witness on one of the feast days was overwhelming:

> The King marched wearing his crown and royal robes in the midst of his many knights accompanied by the different orders of his counts and commanders. He held in his right hand the silver scepter of the Spanish Empire, embellished with gold flowers of various workmanship and studded with variegated gems. The diadem on his forehead, with which he was crowned for the greater glory of the Apostle, was of beaten gold, adorned with enameled flowers *niello*, precious stones and glistening images of birds and four-footed creatures. An unsheathed two-edged sword, decorated with golden flowers and glistening inscription, with golden pommel and silver hilt, was borne before the King. At the head of the clergy, preceding the King, the archbishop walked in dignity surrounded by the other bishops. He was vested pontifically with a white mitre and gilded sandals and in his right hand, with white gloves and a gold ring, he held a crozier of ivory. The clergy advancing before him were bedecked in venerable ornaments, the 72 canons of Compostela were vested in begemmed silken copes with silver brooches, gilded flowers, and everywhere resplendent fringes. Some wore silk dalmatics which were embroidered in gold from the shoulder down and of exquisite beauty.
>
> Others were adorned with golden necklaces studded with gems, bands laced with gold, the richest mitres, attractive sandals, golden cinctures, gold-embroidered stoles and maniples [armbands] inset with pearls. What more is to be said? The clergy of the choir of Santiago displayed every kind of precious stone and as much silver and gold as can be told. Some carried candlesticks and others silver censers; and others again crosses of silver-gilt. Some carried Gospel books with variously begemmed golden covers, others coffers with the relics of many saints; and others phylacteries [boxes inscribed with holy words]. Finally others bore gold or ivory choir batons, their tips deco-

rated with onyx, beryl, sapphire, carbuncle, emerald, or other gem. Others bore two tables of silver-gilt on silver cars which held the lighted tapers offered by the faithful.

The splendid sights, illuminated by hundreds of candles, and the sweet smells of incense must have been stunning to every pilgrim. The songs proclaimed the glory of James:

O James, Apostle of Christ, unconquered soldier of the eternal king, shining in the brilliant court of the apostles as the sun glittering amid the stars, you gleam in glory.

The prayers appealed to James to pray for the poor pilgrims, and guide them to salvation:

O helper of all the ages, glory of the Apostles, bright light of those who live in Galicia, protector of pilgrims, James the uprooter of lies, loosen the chains of our sins and lead us to the haven of salvation. You who assist those in peril who cry to you both on sea and land, help us now and in the danger of death, and lead us.[9]

Finally, after attending the morning service, the pilgrims grouped themselves around a priest, who would deliver to them the indulgences they had earned by making pilgrimage. They brought gifts of cash or jewelry to the altar, then venerated the relics of James—his chain, crown, hat, staff, knife, and stone. They then received the indulgences. They touched and kissed the saint's tomb, prayed earnestly there, and promised good works for the future. It was hoped they would also have the experience of feeling forgiven of their sins. After this, the rite of penance was complete. It was now that the pilgrims would buy scallop shells as the public sign of finishing the pilgrimage. Then, although they might tour the city, they were free to return home.

The Meaning of the Pilgrimage

From one point of view, the entire pilgrimage was a lengthy and elaborate preparation for the final purification, which took place when the pilgrim celebrated the divine service at the basilica and prayed at the saint's tomb. There, having achieved the goal of the journey, the pilgrim could feel cleansed, fully forgiven, renewed—indeed, set anew on the path of salvation. Yet that is a minimal account of what happened in these ritual acts; after all, sins could be forgiven and a life mended at any church. Why the multiplication of visits to churches and holy sites all along the way? Why the appeal to a distant saint like James rather than one close to home? A long journey might be a catalyst for change and renewal of one's life, but how are we to understand the elaborate ritual of the journey?

It might seem simply a yearning for greater holiness, expressed quantitatively: If one Mass is good, twenty are better. But that would miss the special quality of medieval piety. In fact, to the eyes of the pilgrim, each locus of holiness had its own special quality. The healing of fevers at Le Puy was different from the healing of blindness at Conques; the piety of John the Evangelist was different from that of Hilary the bishop. Christian holiness in that age was polymorphous; it had many facets, each of which could be touched in different places.

There were, of course, recurrent themes, and sometimes a pilgrimage route emphasized certain kinds of holiness more than others. That was certainly true in the case of Compostela. The legends recounted to the travelers on these routes spoke often about the warrior heroes: Charlemagne, Roland and his knights, Charles Martel, King Clovis. Part of this was nationalistic history and legend, integrated into the Christian framework. But part of it was new or newly popular, and it took on special significance in the context of the times. The story that Roland had battled Muslims rather than Basques is an example. The Muslims were figures of great contemporary significance; crusades had begun to oust them from the Holy Land, and Spain itself had long been the site of such conflict. Since the 800s, much of Spain had been under Muslim control, and Christians were struggling to regain territory. In 997 Christian armies had suffered terrible defeats at the hands of the great Muslim leader "Almanzor" as the Christians called him, or al-Mansur in Arabic, who had devastated northern Spain and razed Compostela itself. Afterward his kingdom fell apart in the hands of weaker heirs, and northern Spain rose again with the aid of the French. In this context, we can see Saint James connected with the rise of medieval martial spirit. The early stories of James, son of Zebedee, mentioned his nearness to Jesus; he was a brother of John the Evangelist. Some spoke of his preaching in Spain and the miraculous transport of his bones to Galicia in northwestern Spain. Later legends, however, viewed him as Matamoros, Moor-Slayer (killer of Muslims). A twelfth-century legend told the story of the battle of Clavijo, supposedly in 845, when Christian forces under King Ramiro were hard-pressed by the Muslims. In a dream, Saint James appeared to the king promising victory. When he told his warriors, they prayed together and then rushed on the enemy. In the sky at the head of the Christian legions appeared the Apostle James in shining armor, on a white horse, carrying a white banner with a blood red cross. He himself, said the legend, killed sixty thousand Moors. Afterward the army vowed that all Spain would pay tribute to Compostela. [See Islam p. 632 for discussion of Islam in Spain.]

The battle of Clavijo is fictitious; it was probably a reflection in legend of a later battle, in 939 under Ramiro II, the story of which was made famous in many chronicles of the time. It too was a battle by Christians of northern Spain against Muslims, where James appeared, together with another saint, riding a white horse into battle; it too resulted in a vow of tribute to Compostela. In either case, however, we find James linked with a military and nationalistic spirit, as Christians rose up against Islamic invaders. After the devastation wrought by Almanzor, James's prestige may have waned somewhat. But in the 1060s his legend rose again, and it was claimed that he helped King Ferdinand I and his famous warrior Rodrigo Diaz de Bivar—later known as El Cid—win the battle of Coimbra.

By the late eleventh century, then, Spain, Saint James, and the pilgrimage were linked in a particular set of legends that told, not only of James's great piety and closeness to Jesus, but also of his being an ally in Christian warfare. The next stage of development occurred under Alfonso VI, one of the sons of Ferdinand. Alfonso took a company of clergy and knights to the town of Oviedo, whose cathedral of San Salvador, since the beginning of the tenth century, had occupied a place of honor second only to Compostela. The church possessed a case of relics that no one dared to examine, for in 1030 some clergy had opened it and been struck blind by the dazzling light that burst out. Alfonso and his cadre fasted and did penance in preparation, and on the fourth Friday of Lent they opened it and saw what they claimed were fragments of the cross, drops of Jesus' blood, the napkin that had bound his head, crumbs of the Last Supper, and relics of Mary and the apostles. This ceremony became famous all over Europe, adding to Alfonso's prestige. He was confident enough to declare himself emperor of all Spain—in the same year that the reforming Pope Gregory VII (Hildebrand) declared that Spain was a province of the church.

The scene was set for a struggle between national pride and the universal church, and the outcome would deeply affect the pilgrimage to Compostela. Many of the Christians in Spain asserted their unique tradition over against the pope in a struggle over ritual. The ancient Spanish church, under the converted Visigoths, had developed a liturgy, called the Mozarabic rite, that was significantly different from the Roman. Alfonso VI, however, decided not to be narrowly nationalistic. Married to a French woman, Constance, the daughter of the duke of Burgundy, he was drawn to the universal church. He did not, therefore, use his prestige to support the Mozarabic partisans but chose to seek the aid of the monks of Cluny to popularize the pilgrimage to Compostela and thereby elevate Spain's role in the universal church. The men from Cluny were, as we saw in chapter 20, the great reformers and centralizers of the church, cementing the spiritual and political connections between France and Rome.

Now, as the twelfth century began, Cluny and the French extended their influence into Spain, once even putting a Cluniac monk into the archbishopric of Compostela. They were creating lasting connections between Spain, France, and Rome and, by extension, the whole church of Europe. The medium for this task of unification was the pilgrimage to Compostela. The work that most exalted the pilgrimage was the *Book of St. James,* attributed to Pope Calixtus but actually written, probably around 1130, by a monk or monks from Cluny. The book told the stories of James, the miraculous transport of his bones, their discovery in Galicia, and the miracles that had happened by James's intervention. Most significantly, however, the book also recounted the story of Charlemagne, his great archbishop Turpin, and the famous warrior Roland. The popular *Chanson de Roland,* as well as earlier legends, had already celebrated the saintliness of Charlemagne, and the fair Roland had become one of the great medieval heroes. The legend as rewritten by Cluny now made Charlemagne the first pilgrim to Saint James. In a vision he was instructed to lead an army into Galicia and capture the road that led to Saint James's tomb, whereupon he went beyond Compostela to the sea and met the miraculous boat carrying the body of James from the Holy Land. In other expeditions, he conquered more of Spain for the Holy Roman Empire, but the third time his rear guard was attacked by Muslims, and Roland and his knights were slain.

The transformation of the legends of Charlemagne and Roland reflected and enhanced the transformation of piety that centered on the pilgrimage to Compostela. James in Spanish legend had been a Christian knight, fighting with those who wanted to maintain Christianity in Spain against the Muslim on-slaught. He could have remained merely a local hero, but the alliance of Spanish royalty with Cluny to promote the pilgrimage gave him a larger role: He was the perfect figure to rouse the spirit of all of Christian Europe in the age of the Cru-sades. Cluny's effect on the spirituality of Europe was manifold. It upheld the monastic way of life as the true channel for proper devotion to God; it elaborated the liturgy as the pure expression of that devotion; it brought penance to the center of the Christian life even for laymen; and it taught the knights a religious discipline by focusing their martial energies on opposition to the Muslims. In the last task, the pilgrimage to Compostela served a dual purpose. It brought the pilgrim to the very border of a Muslim country, just as in the Holy Land, and it also brought him or her to the place where the spirit of holy war reigned supreme—the Tomb of Saint James. Moreover, at each step of the way, the relics of the saints, Mary, and Jesus were intertwined with the heroes of war. Paradoxi-cally, the penance that stemmed from the humility of encountering the most holy relics was mixed with the cultivation of heroic temperament from touching the bones of Roland or the stone cross of Charlemagne.

We can see from this example that the practice of a ritual may have many dimensions other than the most obvious. Pilgrimage as an expression of devo-tion and means of purification has had a long and venerable history in Chris-tianity; the pilgrimage to Saint James was a part of that tradition. Yet it was also much more. It grew out of the evolving spirit of the "church militant"—from the Spanish resistance to Muslim rule to the crusading spirit of the eleventh and twelfth centuries. For reasons that may remain obscure, James became the focus of Spanish resistance legends, and this in turn made him the perfect vehi-cle for the growing militance of the knights. Further, although Spain claimed him as a national saint, he was, like Peter and Paul, intimately connected to the church universal. He could reflect Spain's ties to Rome and be appropriated by the French monks of Cluny as a symbol for all Christians in their battles against the Muslims. Finally, he could be for the pilgrim a focus of penance and humil-ity and, at the same time, a model of the heroic warrior who was the exemplary figure of the age.

The story of the Saint James pilgrimage shows how a ritual ancient in its heritage and familiar in its form can be adapted to express the spirit of a particu-lar time and place, even the political attitudes and dreams of particular groups of people. Moreover, it shows how the vehicles of salvation are appropriated in different settings. The poor humble pilgrim, saint of ancient times, could take on the armor of a knight while still partaking of the Eucharist and practicing devotion to holy relics. Within the overall framework of spiritual purification, he was also transforming spiritual strength into temporal power. Similarly, the monk who had withdrawn from the world could now write legends celebrating the Christian conquest of Europe: a life of penance combined with a life of learning, as the church became an arbiter of politics as well as spirituality.

The ongoing work of salvation was, along one dimension, geared to individual spiritual rebirth and renewal: the purification of baptism and Eucharist, personal devotions to various saints. Yet these same rites could develop into an instrument of the messianic task, helping to spread the power and influence of the church throughout Europe. By making the strength of a warrior-knight part of a system of spiritual blessings, an individual of the knightly class could more fully participate in the system of rebirth and renewal. And as larger numbers of people, including politically minded monks as well as the laity, became conscious of the significance of the pilgrimage to Compostela, the church as a spiritual community came to encompass more and more of the temporal realm. Thus the changes in the pilgrimage reflected shifts of emphasis within the overall system of salvation, while maintaining its basic structure. [See Religions of Mesoamerica pp. 233–38 for description and interpretation of the Feast of Santiago (Saint James) among the Tzutujil Maya.]

In the next section, we will examine how Christian symbols and the meaning of salvation developed in another cultural context.

Lyman Beecher
and Harriet Beecher Stowe

The Beecher family represents a remarkably different version of Christian salvation. Heirs of the Protestant tradition, their vehicles of salvation were the study of theology, the church as a dedicated moral community, and an intense, inward personal search for a relationship to God rather than the impressive rites and the climb to sainthood characteristic of the medieval church. We will find the Beechers transforming their received tradition just as the knights and monks of Europe changed the pilgrimage tradition, but with different emphases and directions.

The Beechers were one of America's most famous families. Like the Adamses in politics and the Jameses in literature and philosophy, they made their mark in religion and culture. The Beechers' influence reached far, partly because there were so many of them. Lyman Beecher had three wives in succession, the first two bearing him eleven children who lived to adulthood. Of these, five achieved wide renown: Catharine was a pioneer in women's higher education; Edward, a minister and editor, became a college president; Harriet wrote popular stories and novels; Henry Ward was a nationally known minister; and Isabella was involved in the campaign for women's rights. Even some of the lesser known had significant achievements. William, the oldest male, was a minister in a number of cities; Charles, an influential liberal minister, became superintendent of public instruction in Florida and demanded higher education for blacks; Thomas, another minister, led his community in Elmira, New York, to break new ground in dealing with urban problems. Of the women, only Mary lived a wholly private life. George died at the age of thirty-four of a gunshot wound. James served as a minister for many years but suffered from poor health after being wounded in the Civil War in his thirties.

Of such a large and illustrious family, a father such as Lyman Beecher, himself a famous minister, could be rightly proud. And indeed he was; yet he was also greatly concerned for his family, for none of his children embraced the religion he preached: the traditional Calvinist creed. This makes the Beechers doubly interesting; not only can we study a large Christian family through their public writings and private letters, but we can also see within the boundaries of the family itself some of the dynamics of religious change. Since we cannot look in a few brief pages at the entire family, we will focus on Lyman and his third daughter, the sixth surviving child, Harriet. Lyman often said that Harriet was so bright and interesting, he wished she had been a boy. That set the tone for their relationship: a deep interest, pride, and love, but also the distance that in the nineteenth century could not be bridged between the world of men and the world of women.

The World of Lyman Beecher

Lyman Beecher wanted his sons to follow in his footsteps, to become ministers of the gospel (they all did), for religion was his ruling passion. He came from a heritage and a region—he was a seventh-generation New Englander—that still in 1800 could be called Puritan. Puritan did not mean and should never have meant "puritanical," that is, prudish about the personal vices of drink, sex, dancing, and the like (the proper adjective for that would be *Victorian*). Puritan did mean having a strong sense of religion and morality at the center of personal and social life. The church, generally Congregational or Presbyterian, was at the center of society, influencing government and regulating the behavior of citizens. Church attendance was a major part of one's duty to God and an important way of becoming learned in the faith, for the minister's sermons were erudite and carefully argued from Scripture and reason. Every intelligent man was expected to participate in theological discussions, and women also read treatises on God's providence, the nature of free will, or human depravity. Regular social occasions included afternoon tea, where the subject might be the previous Sunday's sermons.

Each Puritan underwent a process of self-examination and personal experience of God's grace before conversion, that is, before being accepted as a full member of the church. This was the inward part of Puritan piety, besides the outward devotion to the church, reverence to ministers, and upright moral behavior. Conversion began with a sense of **conviction** of sin, the intense recognition of oneself as truly a sinner. Then, over a stretch of time, often several years, the awakened sinner examined his or her heart, intentions, behavior, and relation to God to see whether he or she might have any hope of salvation.

In a theological system like Calvinism, all was predestined by God, but one could never know for sure one's future fate. Nevertheless, if one was sufficiently humble and received some signs of grace, of closeness to God, one might have hope of heaven after death. Men and women searched their souls in torment and eagerness, working to remove their sins, erase their self-deceit and pride, and put all their trust in God. Under the guidance of a minister, they analyzed their experiences, and if they and he felt that there were evidences of grace, they could be counted as converted—for this was the most one could know on earth about one's possibilities for salvation.

Lyman Beecher believed fully in this system. The sovereignty of God and his mysterious grace were pillars of his personal piety. Born in 1775 to a line of New Haven blacksmiths, he had forged his faith out of his own personal experience and learning. His father loved the world of ideas, but the only books in his aunt and uncle's home, where he actually grew up, were a Bible and a psalm book. His urge for learning and dislike of farm work motivated him to prepare for college, and he went to Yale. There he encountered the first challenges to his Christian faith in the thought of Thomas Paine, a deist, whose works the students were excitedly discussing. By the time he finished his studies and was ordained in 1798, he was already a fighter for Calvinist orthodoxy.

Beecher made a name for himself over the next thirty years as a champion of orthodox religion and morality over deism, freethinking, and Unitarianism. These rational forms of religion (to him irreligion) often denied the miracles of Jesus and diminished religion to those universal truths with which the reasoning mind could agree. To him, they denied God's great power and mystery. Moreover, he believed that their influence on the country was dangerous. Beecher feared that if people's sense of the sovereignty of God disappeared, if human beings thought they could decide what was true religion apart from what God had revealed, morals would decline and society would disintegrate. This, he thought, was what had happened with the French Revolution, in which liberal thinkers had wielded great influence.

In one of his most famous sermons, "A Reformation of Morals Practicable and Indispensable," Beecher argued that the only hope for the country was to return to the faith, laws, and institutions of the Puritan fathers. Even in his beloved Connecticut he saw signs of moral decline:

> Drunkards reel through the streets, day after day, and year after year, with entire impunity. Profane swearing is heard, and even by magistrates, as though they heard it not. Efforts to stop traveling on the Sabbath have, in all places, become feeble, and in many places . . . they have wholly ceased. Grand jurors complain that magistrates will not regard their information, and that the public sentiment will not bear them out in executing the laws. And conscientious men, who dare not violate an oath, have begun to refuse the office.[10]

The great society that the Puritans had built had kept this unrighteous behavior under control; now the controls were loosening, and human nature—with all its depravity, its urge to sinfulness—was creating moral devastation in the land. Lyman proposed several steps to correct the problems. First, the gospel ministers must call people's attention to the declining state of affairs. Then the better people in the community must take care to reform themselves. Attention should be directed to the education of the young and discipline within the family. Further, the existing laws against immorality must be enforced. Voluntary associations of citizens should form to pressure the magistrates to enforce the laws. Finally, the connection between sin and shame must be restored. The sinner must not be allowed to feel the approval or neutrality of his or her fellow citizens; on the contrary, they should express their disapproval so that the sinner might feel shame.

This was Lyman Beecher's call to the people of Connecticut, New England, and all the states to return to the ways of the civilization built by the founders of New England. Yet already in 1812 when he preached the sermon, the last pillars of that older society were shaking. Liberals and dissenting churches had begun to campaign for the separation of church and state in Connecticut and Massachusetts, the last fortresses of New England. Most other states in the new union had already disestablished their churches and proclaimed religious tolerance, but Connecticut and Massachusetts still held to the principle that the state should support religion. Taxes in these states went to support Congregational ministers, churches, and schools. Naturally enough, Lyman Beecher fought for the Standing Order, as it was called, the tradition of a connection between faithful Christianity and righteous government, but in 1818 Connecticut abolished state support of any church.

Surprisingly, after a brief period of dismay, Beecher changed his mind about seeing the event as a disaster. Soon he was saying that the separation of church and state was a good thing, for now people would have to come voluntarily to the church and would support it for heartfelt reasons rather than because of external pressures. He was in many respects right. Over the next twenty years, revivals and movements of moral reform—based on the voluntary associations Beecher had promoted—revealed the passion Americans could generate for their religion, and the evangelical churches grew successfully. But the change also meant subtle pressures on Calvinist theology. Society was no longer organized to execute God's commands, so that people should search their hearts to discover whether they were saved, whether they could enter society as full and upright Christians. Instead churches urged people to seek their salvation, so that religion appeared to be more a matter of the free agency of the individual.

This development would put Beecher in the middle of an interesting debate on free will, one that signaled the coming changes in American Protestantism. Beecher was already considered a partisan of the "new divinity," a slight adaptation of Calvinist theology that allowed some room for human free will. God was sovereign and had predestined each soul, and human beings were depraved sinners who without grace could do nothing—yet God in his grace had made it possible for them to make some moves toward him. As Beecher put it in his sermon on the reformation of morals, "The kingdom of God is a kingdom of means, and though the excellency of the power belongs to him exclusively, human instrumentality is indispensable."[11] Conservatives, or Old School Presbyterians, found this attributed too much power to humans. At the same time, more liberal ministers were emerging, such as the great revivalist Charles Grandison Finney, who allowed much more room than Beecher for the free will of human beings in seeking salvation. Thus Beecher, with his moderate position on free will, would find himself attacked by Finney in the late 1820s for his conservatism and tried by the Presbyterian church for heresy in the 1830s for his liberalism.

Nevertheless, Beecher was a man of battle, especially of moral and theological battle, and these opponents did not deter him. More important things remained for him, for his great passion was still the moral state of American society. After all, he was a child of the American Revolution; he had grown up immersed in the passion of his contemporaries for the great cause of the United States as a new, free, and even holy nation. By 1830 he saw the evangelical cause fairly well established in the eastern United States, but as he looked to the expanding West he became concerned again. In a famous essay, "Plea for the West" (1835), he described the land west of the Appalachians as full of promise, yet so untamed, so large, that it seemed as though nothing could govern it. Yet, he said, it was clear that men would control it, and the West in turn would affect the older part of the nation. Therefore the challenge was to tame the West in accord with the great traditions of the East. The great danger, as he saw it, was that Roman Catholic European immigrants and missionaries were moving rapidly into western cities and might soon dominate them, bringing with them all the flaws of European culture and the tyranny, as he saw it, of Roman Catholicism. Protestants must therefore move to the West, build up institutions of education, and thereby train westerners to govern themselves as a free, devout, and moral people.

When Lyman Beecher wrote this piece he was already practicing what he preached. In 1832, at the age of fifty-six, he had moved himself and many of his family (even though they were mostly grown) to the heartland of the new West, Cincinnati. There he had been invited to establish Lane Seminary, a school to train Orthodox ministers who would bring a faithful religious influence to the chaotic frontier. This became Beecher's last great venture. It had many difficulties. In the second year of its operation, the entering class included many radical thinkers led by Theodore Weld, a convert of Finney's. The group made abolition of slavery the chief issue facing the seminary, splitting the faculty and arousing the whole city—for Cincinnatians, though part of a free state, had many exchanges and cordial relations with slaveholders in neighboring Kentucky. Eventually the radicals departed to found a new school, Oberlin, in the north of Ohio. Beecher and the trustees were left with a damaged reputation among conservatives and had to search for funds to support the school and students to attend it.

The school did not fail while Beecher remained its president, but he gave it his last fruitful years. Then, in 1846, another controversy arose. Some of Beecher's opponents brought him to trial for improperly holding the presidency of Lane, an Old School seminary, when he was a New School Presbyterian (the two branches had officially split in 1835). Beecher won the case on the grounds that he could not be held responsible for the split in the denomination, and he had already been proved free of heresy. But the trial was taxing, and it clearly revealed the slippage of support for him at the seminary. In 1851, at the age of seventy-five, he resigned and returned to the East. The next twelve years were spent in gradual decline. He gathered his papers and occasionally preached, but his mind was no longer as keen as it once had been. He died in 1863.

The Christianity that Lyman Beecher represented can be summarized best not in terms of doctrine, even though that was often his field of battle, but in terms of values. Above all he held to a strong faith in a sovereign God whose gracious providence ruled all and a belief in the power of religion as transformative in people's lives. Equally important, however, was a belief in the importance of a society's relationship to God. The influence of religion in society, in the life of the nation, was as important as in the life of the individual; the nation needed righteous laws, righteous governors, and a responsible citizenry in order to stay on the right path. The soundest course, in his thought, was adherence to the proven tradition (namely, that of Puritan New England), combined with education, discussion, debate—in short, the use of reason and common sense—to produce a learned citizenry grounded in the heritage of the past. These were the best means of establishing religion and morals in the hearts and minds of people and in the society as a whole. To that end, the church, the ministry, and the seminary were absolutely central institutions, crucial to the health of American civilization as a whole. Lyman Beecher had a clear vision, then, of society—its ideal state, the dangers that threatened it, and the means to improve it—and a clear sense of the role of Christianity. For him, the salvation of the individual through God's grace, worked out in self-examination and development of right belief as well as baptism and church membership, was the cornerstone of the messianic task of the church. His vision guided him in New England and the West in struggling for the perfect society, the society that, he hoped, the United States was destined to achieve.

Lyman Beecher's children grew up in a home imbued with these values and energized by his passion for perfection. The atmosphere of the home, one of them once wrote, was charged with a kind of "moral oxygen" that made it exciting and stimulating virtually all the time. The practices of the family—daily prayers, churchgoing, learned theological discussions lasting long into the night—made the religion of Beecher a lived reality. Also, his great concern as a father for the fate of their souls came home to them at an early age, and sometimes weighed heavily on them. Yet, though they sustained some of his values, they all rejected traditional Calvinism and shaped different religious perspectives for themselves, even when they stayed within the framework of the established churches, as many of them did. Their changes reflected and shaped the ongoing transformation of American religion in the nineteenth century.

Harriet Beecher Stowe

Born in 1811, the sixth of Lyman Beecher's surviving children, Harriet Beecher felt somewhat obscured beside her older brothers and sisters. Yet she also attracted the interest of her father with her bright intelligence and her writing ability. As early as the age of seven she was receiving attention from her teachers for her written work. At twelve, competing in a school essay contest, she won first prize and the praise of her surprised father. As she grew up, Harriet was an avid reader, of both the theological works in her father's library and, increasingly, the romantic literature coming from England—Lord Byron and Sir Walter Scott were among those permitted by her father—and from women writers. When she was not busy with teaching in her sister Catharine's school, she experimented with stories and poems on her own. Neither her father nor her sister much encouraged her, however, for such work seemed frivolous compared to her other duties.

Meanwhile, in religion she seemed at first to stay close to tradition. She felt she had experienced conversion in early adolescence, and her account of it seemed to satisfy her father. But when she applied for membership in the church in Hartford, where she attended school, the minister questioned her so deeply as to arouse her doubts: If the whole universe were destroyed, he asked, would you be happy with God alone? She spent the next few years in doubt, sometimes experiencing morbid moods that may have been connected to religious questioning. This, indeed, would be natural in the Puritan tradition. But Harriet never brought this process to a resolution through a traditional conversion; she simply left it behind gradually. She married a man firmly in the tradition: Calvin Stowe, a professor at Lane Seminary in Cincinnati and a Bible scholar of the first rank. Despite his traditionalism, however, he had the curious faculty of falling into trance and experiencing visions from time to time.

Harriet Beecher married Stowe in 1836 at the age of twenty-five and bore seven children (beginning with twins) over the next fourteen years, of whom all but one survived past childhood. She was devoted to her children, yet she also wanted to write. In that desire Stowe supported her, so she wrote stories and magazine articles, often staying up late at night to work on them. From the early 1840s onward, she was publishing regularly and supplementing her husband's meager income as a seminary teacher. By the late 1840s she had begun writing some antislavery essays. In 1850 the Stowes moved to Maine, where Calvin was to teach at Bowdoin College. Harriet had never liked Cincinnati, so she was delighted to return to the East—and most of the other Beechers were back there too, with her father soon to follow in 1851. Harriet had even greater energy for writing after her last child was born in 1850.

Meanwhile, the controversy over slavery reached fever pitch with the congressional debate over the Great Compromise of 1850, which proposed to admit California as a free state, and New Mexico and Utah with the question open to decision by popular vote. Several Beechers, including Henry Ward who was always a strong influence on Harriet, were speaking out against slavery. Henry even brought a runaway slave into his pulpit and raised, on the spot, the money to buy his freedom. Harriet wrote a small piece of antislavery fiction for the *National Era,* whose editor immediately invited her to contribute more of the same. She came up against a blank wall, however: She could not seem to write anything more.

Then, in February 1851 while at communion services, she received what she later saw as her great inspiration: a vision of an aged black slave being beaten mercilessly by his white overseer while another white man egged him on, and then a vision of the same black man praying that God forgive his tormentors. She wrote down what she saw, and then the ideas started to flow. She decided to write a novel, which she would submit in serial form to the *National Era*. This was the beginning of the work that made her famous: *Uncle Tom's Cabin,* one of the great nineteenth-century American novels and one of the most popular books ever published. Published in book form in 1852, it sold three thousand copies the first day and three hundred fifty thousand in less than a year in the United States. Within two years it was published in seventeen other languages. Over the next fifty-eight years it sold between three and four million copies in the United States, one and a half million in Britain, and four million in other languages.

The power of the novel lay in Harriet's expression of a great moral vision. She portrayed in vivid detail slaves, hopeful, suffering, or rebellious; slaveholders and slave traders, some of them evil in nature, some feeling trapped helplessly in the system; operators of the "underground railroad" who risked their lives and reputations to save slaves; and above all, families, North and South, slave and free, showing how everyone was affected by the damaging effects of the institution of slavery. All who were touched by slavery felt suffering, loss, pain, grief; only those who had the moral courage to fight it could find some satisfaction. At the same time, the most dramatic characters in the book were not the rebels but those who most exemplified self-sacrificing Christian love: Uncle Tom, the aged slave she had seen in her vision, and little Eva, delicate child of a Southern gentleman, who died with prayers for everyone on her lips.

We can see in these figures something of Harriet's transformation of her father's religious vision. In place of the anxiety-ridden converts of Puritanism, we find soulful human beings, so close to God in their very nature that they have no doubts, living constantly the life of love for their fellow human beings. On the other hand, we find a vision of society as intense and clear as Lyman Beecher's, a society guided by moral passion and devotion to the cause of purging its sins. Yet where Lyman's guidelines were the laws and institutions of tradition, Harriet's were the sanctity of the home and the strength of love in the family. Hers was a feminized vision, in which women and children provided the deep religious grounding of society, in which the life of feeling was a surer guide than the exercise of reason and argument. Judging from the popularity of her book, many American readers were moved by such a vision.

Harriet herself explored this area consciously and directly in another work, *The Minister's Wooing* (1859), which many regard as one of her best works. Its theme is the exploration of the ground of true religion, set in terms of a love triangle. Dr. Samuel Hopkins, the middle-aged minister who clearly represents Lyman Beecher, falls in love with young Mary Scudder, a spiritual young woman of good New England upbringing. However, Mary already loves James Marvyn, an adventurous and irreligious young man who becomes a sailor. James is lost at sea until late in the story when he returns, a converted Christian, on the eve of the wedding of Dr. Hopkins and Mary. Mary probably is a composite of Harriet's ideas of herself as a young girl and of her mother, who died when Harriet was four. Thus the relationship between Mary, Hopkins, and James explores Harriet's own turn away from her father's religion, her attempt to find her own Christian way, and her attraction to the world of adventure—which she tames rather casually by making James a convert to Christianity.

The character of Mary is intensely feminine and spiritual. She was, Harriet says, "predisposed to moral and religious exaltation. Had she been born in Italy, . . . she might have seen beatific visions in the sunset skies." But as a child of New England, instead of lying "in mysterious raptures at the foot of altars, she read and pondered treatises on the Will." However, as she read or listened to Dr. Hopkins, she did not absorb information with the intellect alone. "Womanlike, she felt the subtle poetry of these sublime abstractions, . . . often comprehending through an ethereal clearness of nature what he had laboriously and heavily reasoned out." Hopkins, on the other hand, was the ideal righteous Christian man of Puritan times: humble, sincere, unselfconscious. He had in him "a perfect logic of life; his minutest deeds were the true results of his sublimest principles." He was not unemotional, but analysis prevailed: "Love, gratitude, reverence, benevolence—which all moved in mighty tides in his soul—were all compelled to pause midway while he rubbed up his optical instruments to see if they were rising in right order."[12] Ultimately, however, his great discipline had to face the test of passion. When James returned and a gossipy neighbor informed Hopkins that Mary and James had long loved each other, he had a great struggle to subdue his desires, to sacrifice his own happiness for theirs. Mary, for her part, was struggling to decide whether to keep her promise to the doctor or to tell him of her love for James; thanks to the intervention of the neighbor, she never had to make that decision.

Indeed, Harriet portrays the doctor's high ideals, his willingness to sacrifice "happiness" for "blessedness," as she puts it, as saving the situation. Mary is caught between her strong sense of duty and her deep passion for James, over which she has no control. Her own resolution comes only in her faith that life is merely transient, that beyond the grave there is a future life, and that love, which is immortal, will survive. She and James, in short, will be able to love each other after death, forever. She too would have sacrificed her earthly desires on behalf of her moral commitment, hoping for a future blessedness and happiness. Harriet clearly saw the struggle, accepted its dilemmas, and—though she gave her story a happy ending—recognized that often in this life there was no ideal resolution. One had to be true both to moral commitment and to one's deep feelings. Puritan tradition violated the feelings while upholding commitment; secular life threatened to lose the moral sense altogether. Harriet wanted both.

The outcome of the struggle for Harriet was that in 1864 she joined the Episcopal church. In this she followed her sister Catharine and her own twin daughters. Calvin Stowe's retirement from teaching at Andover Theological Seminary made the transition easier, as did Lyman's death in 1863. In a sense, Harriet was returning to her mother, Roxana, who was of Episcopal background. Though she barely knew her, she cherished her memory and the stories she heard from her older siblings. For Harriet the Episcopal church had a warmth and softness that the Puritan tradition lacked. She could express in it her appreciation for

Catholicism, which had grown during her travels in Europe in the 1850s and 1860s—an appreciation that her father could not have understood. Her new religion allowed for gradual growth in spirituality for those who chose such a path, the slow refinement of the soul climbing the ladder to God. The strenuous way of her father's tradition, as she saw it, was powerful in its discipline but left too many behind floundering in despair. Thus she freed herself to move to a church more of her own leanings. The aesthetic richness of the liturgy and the connection to a more congenial devotional tradition could combine with the Protestant spirit of free inquiry, flexible authority, and the centrality of the believer's relationship to God.

Harriet Beecher Stowe spent the remaining productive years of her life writing vigorously and traveling, usually to England and Europe, where she made contact with many of the leading literary lights. She wrote several more major works, the best being her novels of New England, and a large number of small pieces, publishing well into the 1870s. By 1880, however, her writing career was virtually at an end. She, like her father before her, spent her last years in quietude. Harriet died in 1896 and is still remembered as one of the century's great popular writers.

American Protestantism in a New Generation

Perhaps no generation between the Reformation and very recent times saw such dramatic religious change as that between Lyman Beecher's coming of age and that of his children. A number of writers have marked the year 1850 as a watershed in American religion, dividing the era of Calvinist tradition from the era of evangelical piety. This was precisely the time when Harriet Beecher Stowe and others of the Beecher clan were coming into their prime, while their father was retiring from active life. To be sure, there were agents of change before 1850: the growth of Methodism, the frontier revivals, the new revivalism of Charles G. Finney and others. But the issues concerning revivals were defined in Calvinist terms, though the new thinkers did not give Calvinist answers. After midcentury among the rising white middle class, the import of the old theological issues declined dramatically. Religion itself was being redefined.

Some have called the new evangelicalism sentimental—as indeed it was, some of the time. A better way of understanding it, however, is to say that the religious approach of the young Beechers and their contemporaries was rooted in feeling and sensibility rather than intellect and argument. The two generations shared an emphasis on moral character; but whereas the earlier generation saw character as the result of a rightly formed will, disciplined through careful education and the institutions of piety and law, the later generation saw character as a matter of proper feeling and sensitivity, shaped by loving nurturance and Christian friendship and association. The earlier aimed at clarity of thought and a vision of order, the later modeled itself after ideal figures of the imagination. That is why fiction, which was anathema to eighteenth-century Puritans, could become a vehicle of religion in the late nineteenth century. That is why Lyman Beecher argued for a reformation of morals in careful step-by-step reasoning, whereas Harriet Beecher Stowe portrayed characters who represented moral forces. In her world, dogma and argument could no longer teach well or engage people's support.

Lyman Beecher spoke of the government of God and urged his countrymen to preserve religion as the safeguard of the people. Harriet Beecher Stowe, never long doubting the government of God or the necessity of religion in American civilization, took issue with the mode of spirituality her father represented. For her, the moral character of the nation had to be ensured, not by preserving old laws and institutions, but by guarding the home and family and looking to the deep, feminine sensibility within to find guidelines for right action. Ultimately, she turned from her father's sense of right government to her mother's love and warmth and made self-sacrificing love the pivot of her religion.

This was indeed the right move in the context of nineteenth-century American Protestantism. For in fact people had rejected the old laws and institutions of Puritanism, however perfect they might have seemed, and no arguments of Lyman Beecher or anyone else could save them. People built their lives and relationships, not on the old system of ranks and statuses—no longer mindful of their family heritage—but on contemporary associations and friendships. The enormous changes brought by the Industrial Revolution and westward migration necessitated new ways of making relationships: friendships based on common feeling, associations based on common purposes. Deep, lasting relationships could be maintained only within the family circle; the rest depended more on changing circumstance. Puritanism had depended on a stable society. Lyman Beecher helped engineer the transition, in helping to form voluntary associations to accomplish certain tasks, but those associations outstripped him, becoming a new model of religious organization entirely.

By the late nineteenth century, then, morality began not in society but at home, and even the home was experiencing great stress. Thus Harriet Beecher Stowe's appeal to the sanctity of the family aroused great depth of feeling, and her sense that slavery poisoned all American families rang true. She had transformed the deep American concern for morality—indeed, for the "government of God"—into something that late nineteenth-century Protestants could grasp. Morality meant faith, love for one's fellow beings, and a deep inner sense of right action. Uncle Tom and little Eva were those saintly creatures born with that religious and moral sense. Those who worked for the freedom of the slaves were involved in the struggle to "feel right," as Beecher Stowe put it, and then act accordingly. Likewise, the characters of *The Minister's Wooing* were engaged in a struggle to feel right, to get their religion in tune with their feeling, and then to act rightly as well.

Harriet Beecher Stowe thus helped to articulate a transformation of religion for her time. Her father had focused on the moral and intellectual vehicles of salvation: the study of theology, which worked on the individual through the rational mind; and the discipline of a church community, which ensured right action in one's personal and social life and provided the foundation for a perfect society. To make these come about, the preaching and hearing of the holy word were central. Harriet Beecher Stowe developed a vision of Christian life that focused on exemplary moral figures such as Uncle Tom and little Eva, who affected people around them by the strength and sincerity of their feelings and by their self-sacrificing love. Personal ties, rather than the rational word, were the key element; right feeling rather than right thinking was the touchstone of spiritual growth and salvation. At the same time, inner experience became a source of authority, often complementary to (but sometimes in conflict with) the moral dictates of ministers and churches.

As the king of Spain and the monks of Cluny had helped transform Spanish nationalism and popular fervor for pilgrimage into a new ideal that welded Christian devotion to a knightly model, so Harriet Beecher Stowe and the other popular religious writers of her time transformed Puritan moral passion and popular experiential religion into a new ideal, welding Christian beliefs to a feminine mode of feeling and sensitivity. Placed next to one another, the contrast between the two is striking. How remarkable that these could both be Christian popular movements, so different in their contexts and their formulations of the Christian ideal! Yet a closer look reveals that the two, though certainly different, share a certain kinship. Whether consciously or not, the Cluniac monks were taming forms of energy new in their society: the power of the warrior class that, in its lust for the "joys of war," was a threat to the fragile Christian order of society; and the emergence of a kind of proto-nationalism in Spain, a pocket of independence from the Roman church that also could have threatened the fragile unity of religion in Europe. Honoring the Spanish legends of Saint James, they incorporated the Spanish spirit into the universal church, and simultaneously, they honored the knightly spirit by encouraging pilgrims to visit that Saint James who appeared in the midst of battles to help the Christian warrior. Both nationalism and the warrior spirit thereby submitted to the church and to the devotional ideals of Cluny and Rome. Indeed, the pilgrim ideal was just at that time developing into almost an order, a mildly ascetic discipline of its own.

Nineteenth-century America also faced the outpouring of enormous new energies—sometimes toward war and conquest, as in the Mexican War and the Indian wars. Contemporaries saw those energies, however, not as a dangerous military spirit but as the unruliness of freedom, throwing off old institutions that had become burdensome, expanding into new territory and experimenting with new ways of life. The dangers, as each followed his or her own opinion, came in religious splinter groups, factional strife, and political divisions that threatened to split the new nation. The great division that epitomized them all was between North and South. Harriet Beecher Stowe and others like her provided models for healing the spirit, for finding the deeper unity underneath the factions and divisions. For her, the model was the family, held together by the love of the woman. This represented the fusion of the ideal of the perfect society, which Americans all hoped to build, with openness to individual feeling, which could occur within the loving and supportive framework of the family. Moreover, the family was one place where common feeling could be shared. Harriet's work did not avert the great division, as she had hoped; soon the nation was embroiled in civil war. Yet it did help to bring people into a sense of shared purpose and, at the same time, a sense that in grounding themselves in their deepest, purest feelings they were submitting to God. The turbulent passions of the nineteenth century found a Christian ideal, a Christian place to rest, in the symbols of home, family, and self-sacrificing love.

The two examples we have considered, so widely separated in space and time, nevertheless both demonstrate ways in which Christians have brought human energies and drives into a religious framework. Moreover, they show how the system of salvation itself has been adapted to different situations. While the work of salvation in Christianity always has the same general goal—to grow closer to God, to become like Christ (see diagram, page 536), and some of the means may be the same (e.g., sacraments, prayer, study)—they take on different ramifications in different historical contexts while still retaining much the same structure. The humble pilgrim was often a person who pursued his or her quest for purification alone, distant from kin and friends. In twelfth-century Spain, however, the knight-pilgrim aimed to become more Christlike not only through traditional rites and relics but also by modeling himself on the warrior Saint James. Rather than retreating from the world, he became part of the conquest of the world over against the Muslims. Thus the vehicles of salvation—sacraments, relics, pilgrimages—that helped to purify and refine the soul also were identified with the heroes like Charlemagne and Roland who had come before, thus connecting spiritual with temporal power.

Lyman Beecher's approach to Christianity seems quite different in many respects; he had no interest in rites and relics. For him, spiritual strength came from learning and moral discipline; the pilgrim's journey (as in the popular Puritan work by John Bunyan, *Pilgrim's Progress*) was an inward one of struggles against temptation. Yet he too believed in establishing a Christian society over against the wrong-believers—in his case they were the Roman Catholics; and he fought battles too, though with words rather than swords. Where the medieval monks established sites of pilgrimage, Beecher encouraged his colleagues to set up Christian schools and voluntary associations to bring morality and right teaching to the world at large and to fight for Christian principles in the political arena. Beecher's daughter, Harriet, took over the Puritan focus on inwardness rather than ritual as the mode of spiritual development, but made it more emotional, aiming at the development of sensitivity rather than the internalizing of moral and doctrinal norms. Prayer and contact with exemplary models of kindness and love brought the Christlike strength one needed to fight the evils of this world (e.g., the slavery system). Yet the fight, while necessarily political at times, was more usually a matter of extending oneself in acts of love from the heart. Establishing the rule of God on earth did not mean constructing a Christian legal-political system so much as widening the circle of the loving family to include the whole world. This, of course, was far distant from the medieval model of extending the domain of Christendom; but it was not a model of withdrawal either. [See Religions of Africa pp. 45–51, 75–79, Native Religions of North

America pp. 318–20, Judaism pp. 457–69, Hinduism pp. 820–26, Religions of China pp. 1040–54, and Religions of Japan pp. 1163–72 for description and discussion of life histories and personal accounts.]

In each case we have considered, we find congruence with the basic system of salvation. It begins with the primary "work of salvation" that starts with repentance and baptism and then goes on to refine and enrich the Christian's spiritual life. In these established traditions, the act of baptism and the movement toward repentance are assumed; the personal work that continued is that of purification for the pilgrim, learning and discipline for the latter-day Puritan, coming to "feel right" for the evangelical Christian. These efforts at personal refinement lay the groundwork for the larger communal task of preparing the world for the Messiah. In the twelfth century the church could regard itself as the extension of Christ's work, bringing the dominion of the Holy Spirit into all of Europe by means of war if necessary—but the war of sanctified knights, devoted to the holy cause. By the nineteenth century such means were no longer acceptable in the society at large. But by preaching and establishing Christian institutions the battle could be carried on to secure a Protestant America, with the warriors being the dedicated ministers and devout parishioners of the churches. In Harriet Beecher Stowe's more feminized vision, politics and institution building were secondary; but still, following on one's inward exploration and development of one's feelings, the aim was to extend the blessings of Christianity in wider and wider circles, eventually to the whole world. Thus the Christian system of salvation repeats itself under different guises. Individuals aim at self-transformation and refinement, to achieve higher ideals and become "like Christ," using the ritual vehicles and social models of their tradition to do so. Then together in communally organized forms—whether by battle, persuasion, or gentle diffusion of influence—they aim to bring the world under Christian forms of life. Individual transformation in imitation of Christ, and societal reformation under the direction of Christian ideals, thus continue to constitute the system of Christian salvation in its many different historical contexts.

23
Conclusions

IN SOME WAYS, WE HAVE COME full circle. In our historical treatment of Christianity, we observed how an apocalyptic Jewish sect, expecting the return of the Messiah and living a high spiritual life, evolved into the religion of a great empire. In each succeeding period, some strove to bring religious commitment and belief to a higher level, to rise to greater holiness: the monks of fourth-century Egypt, the holy men of fourth- and fifth-century Syria, the battling iconoclasts and monks of the eighth-century Eastern empire, the Benedictines of eighth-century Europe, the Cluniac monks of the tenth to twelfth centuries— on to the Pentecostal churches of our own day. Whether within the established church or as critics of it, Christians have sought a higher life for themselves and, usually, for the Christian community and the society at large.

Even when we look at the enduring structures of Christianity we find the same movement toward higher levels of refinement. Baptism becomes of minor importance when it no longer marks a distinct separation between the Christian and the world. The Eucharist must be kept at some distance and adorned with ritual details to protect its holiness. Penance becomes a central sacrament when Christians feel too contaminated by the world; gaining forgiveness of sins becomes a constant preoccupation. To the Reformers of the sixteenth century, the entire system seems corrupt; there is too much emphasis on "works," on what the individual can do for him- or herself. They urge a return to the original purity, of the Book, and to the inward relationship of the individual with God. The inward quest becomes the new direction of purity and refinement in modern times.

We saw in detail how this dynamic operated in the two examples we examined in chapter 22, how each new burst of human energies was tamed and channeled, through a reimagining of Christian ideals, into a path of spiritual excellence. Even in times when the unity of Christianity seemed to have disintegrated, when the supposedly enduring structures no longer endured, the attempt to transform life in the direction of greater spirituality, greater perfection, continued. One of the central assertions of early Christianity was that, because Jesus died for the sins of humanity, salvation was possible. We understood this to mean that transformation was possible: One could live a higher life, a more nearly perfect life, approaching the divine.

Yet in emphasizing this transformative energy of Christianity, we might be in danger of losing some of the distinctiveness of Christianity. Many religions have this dynamic—perhaps all of them, to one degree or another. The quest for holiness, the yearning for perfection, the desire simply to live a "good life" in the midst of evil, are all aspects of a basic religious impulse. Christianity has the same motivation, but with its own peculiar character. The churches have asserted that what is involved in the transformation toward perfection is not only a change in one's behavior but a change in the quality of one's whole state of being. Particularly, it involves a divorce from the material side of one's nature and a turn to the spiritual. This appears most strongly in the ascetic strands of Christianity, but it is present throughout; unlike adherents of many religious traditions, Christians often enter into battle with the material, with the "flesh" that hinders the spirit. Moreover, such a divorce and such a transformation are possible, Christians have claimed, only because of the saving act of God in Jesus Christ. Left to themselves, people remain enmeshed in sin and temptation, deeply wounded in spirit by sin. In a great mystery, God acting in Jesus removed the effects of sin for those who believe, making possible a true and complete transformation—so that, as it were, not the least scar remains.

The basic religious quest in Christianity, therefore, has been intertwined with a belief in the necessity of Christ having come to earth, died, and been resurrected. The mystery is never resolved by rational attempts to understand it; it is simply believed. And the mystery becomes a model: Self-sacrifice, following in Jesus' steps, becomes prominent in many strands of the tradition. The idea and practice of sacrifice is significant in many religions, and in Christianity it is of course derived in part from the idea and practice of sacrifice in Judaism. But the image of personal sacrifice has dominated more than it has in other religions. The martyrs of the early centuries, the monks from Anthony to Francis, the pietists fascinated with the blood of Jesus, Harriet Beecher Stowe with her self-sacrificing, all-loving and forgiving characters—all these are dramatically Christian, with the figure of the crucified Jesus hovering in the background. Holiness in Christianity is most frequently intertwined with the idea of personal sacrifice—of property, of desires, of one's very life.

Yet Christianity has undergone enormous change over the centuries. One might question, for example, whether self-sacrifice is as important as it was a century, or five centuries, ago. Even more, one can ask whether people calling themselves Christians believe in the great mystery of the saving death of Christ, or do they instead see Jesus mainly as a great teacher? And if there is a quest for perfection, is there really one distinctively Christian way? It would seem that there are too many churches offering too many different versions of the Christian life. The problems facing modern Christianity thus require some discussion, at least to put the issues as clearly as possible. For in fact these issues are not entirely or necessarily unique to Christianity in modern times; we can find similar issues throughout Christian history.

Probably the most pervasive issue facing modern Christians is the fact of religious pluralism, within and outside the boundaries of Christianity itself. This is not new—diversity within Christianity is as old as the religion itself, and

Christianity grew up in an environment of many religions. What is new—essentially since the late eighteenth century—is the acceptance and tolerance of diversity within the ranks. Whereas Christians in earlier times fought desperately to assert the superiority of their version of the faith, to prove that theirs was the one true way, modern Christians have accepted the existence of a variety of Christianities. The outward framework for this has been the **ecumenical** movement, the association of churches to share ideas and cooperate on work where they can agree. Shortly after the turn of the century, a number of American denominations formed the Federal Council of Churches; later they reorganized as the National Council of Churches and gradually joined with churches in other lands to form the World Council of Churches. Not all denominations belong; indeed, some conservative groups who thought the council was too liberal have formed alternative organizations. Still, however, the ecumenical spirit is present, and the joint work has enabled the churches to accomplish social work and missionary efforts that would have been beyond the capacity of individual churches.

Nevertheless, the ecumenical movement skirts the issue that lies at the root of the problem of pluralism: the issue of truth. Is there one theology or way of thinking about Christianity? Is there one path to God that is better than the others? Are there a few basics, at least, that we can say Christians must agree on in order to consider themselves truly Christian? Particularly in a religion that traditionally has emphasized doctrine or belief, this would seem an important issue. Yet at present, neither theological faculties in seminaries nor bishops in council nor lay believers, with their involvement in daily practice, are moving toward any new agreement. Except in Fundamentalist churches, there has been a move away from relying on doctrine, so new developments may not come through great theological syntheses. Additionally, Christians have renewed their interest in ritual, especially since the Second Vatican Council (1962–1965); possibly the ancient sacraments may provide a new basis for unity. But nothing is certain; it is not even clear that most Christians feel any strong need for greater unification in the faith.

The issue is accentuated by the greater presence today of non-Christian religions in Europe and the United States. This larger pluralism has led Christians to learn more about other religions of the world. When in 1893 the World Parliament of Religions met in Chicago, most Christian leaders came away assured that Christianity was undoubtedly the most advanced religion in the world. Now, faced with a population intensely interested in other religions, encountering radically different assumptions about the nature of the universe, human nature, the goals of human life, and the means to achieve these goals, Christian scholars and teachers have had to take a different posture. It is not so easy to say, as Origen did in the third century, that Christianity represents the climax of civilization. Today the question must be asked whether Christianity—any of the Christianities—offers a way of salvation distinctive enough from other religions to make special claims on believers. Moreover, the modern attitude of tolerance makes it rather impolite to claim such specialness. Whereas Jews, Christians, and Muslims in the Middle Ages argued with intent to win, today Christians (and representatives of other religions) may prefer to take the attitude that people choose a religion according to their individual tastes. This does not accommodate well to the traditional belief that Christ came to save all humanity, that Christian claims are true universally, for everyone at all times. Yet it may be one of the advances—or casualties, depending on one's perspective—of modern times to see Christianity as one among many religious options.

Another problem, related to but separable from the problems of pluralism, is that of disbelief. As we observed earlier, Christianity has to a remarkable degree depended on belief as an integral part of faith—belief in a specific creed or doctrine, engaging the intellect in the act of faith. The past few centuries have brought developments in philosophy and the sciences that have called into question some of the fundamental doctrines that most Christians have held through the ages. Evolutionary theory in geology and biology have questioned the literal truth of the Bible, especially the story of creation, and archaeology and historical studies have strongly suggested that many of the accounts in the Bible are legendary, or at least that "history" has been greatly modified by the authors' points of view. Some of the sayings of Jesus appear not to be sayings of Jesus at all, but traditions of the church. The general scientific worldview, with its belief in laws of nature, has led many Christians to question the miracles of Jesus and special divine interventions like the virgin birth or the Immaculate Conception of Mary.

Again, intellectual challenges to the faith are not new. The introduction of Aristotle into the schools in the twelfth and thirteenth centuries created a furor not unlike the modern arguments over scientific theory. Greek ideas seemed to threaten the very foundation of Christian faith. The issues were resolved only by Aquinas's new, and for that time daring, synthesis, which preserved the doctrines while incorporating the philosophical strengths of Aristotle's position. Today it is a question whether a new philosophical strategy could also preserve the doctrines in their classic form. Doctrines themselves may have to be reinterpreted, using what scholars have learned about the deeper meanings of myth and legend, for example, or what psychological theories have to say about the work of religious symbols and rites in human consciousness. The advantage of the challenges is the same as in the twelfth century: A major work of education will likely be stimulated, both in the seminaries and among the lay believers in the churches.

There are many other issues we could consider, but we will content ourselves with just one more: the problem of experiential Christianity. We have observed that since the Reformation, and especially in the past two hundred years, Christians have focused increasingly on the individual's personal experience as the center, and sometimes the measure, of Christianity. This contributed to the breakdown of traditional communities and the corporate conception of the church and led to the voluntary choice of one's church affiliation; this in turn contributed to the growth of a pluralistic Christianity. These represent dangers to a traditional model of the Christian church. However, there is a problem with experiential Christianity itself. Experience, by its nature (excluding telepathic perception), cannot be shared directly; it must be communicated in language, gesture, or art. Deep feelings, profound religious experiences, are, as the great mystics have observed, very difficult to communicate. The religious experience and the stages of it tend to take forms, to become formalized, in a way that is diametrically opposed to the ideal of experiential religion—namely, that each person find his or her own way to God. Thus the stages of mysticism were formalized, the process of Puritan conversion became a rigid standard, the testimonials of nineteenth-century revivals became clichés. Some modern Christians, in reaction to such developments, have turned to ethics as the core of the religion. Others have simply ignored the problem, trusting that each individual will be sincere about his or her own faith.

Yet it is not a question of sincerity, but one of spiritual growth. One can be sincere about one's feelings and still not know what to do with them, or how to act on them, except to follow the prescriptions of one's group. This can result—in some cases has resulted—in a highly conformist religious practice and belief, even while the group continues to preach individuality. This, of course, is a problem in any religion that takes as its foundation the individual's experience rather than some common ritual or commonly experienced event. Other religions, for example Buddhism, have dealt with the problem by introducing another factor: the spiritual teacher. The teacher, involved intimately with the student yet far more experienced in exploring the inner life, can be a guide in development. In Christianity, the abbot often served this purpose for the monks; the mystics had their circles in which one person usually served as guide for the others; in Puritanism the pastor was supposed to play this role. (In secular life today the psychotherapist guides the person in inner development, though it does not always include spiritual development.) In most modern forms of Christianity, however, the individual is bereft of experienced spiritual leadership. Conformity, shallowness, and ultimately dissatisfaction are often the outcome. Modern Christianity sometimes covers this dissatisfaction with involvement in external affairs—missions, charitable work, social occasions for gathering together. It remains to be seen whether it will become a serious problem in the years ahead.

Christianity is not alone in facing these problems, of course. All religions face pluralism on a large scale; all must deal with hard questions of disbelief in a society immersed in rational philosophy, scientific culture, and critical historical studies. All, too, must face the issues of experiential versus externally grounded religion; each type has its own difficulties. Christians must face such issues in their own distinctive ways, reflecting on their traditions, returning to their resources in the Bible, religious thought, and practice, while at the same time developing as deep an understanding of each issue as possible. In that continuing dialogue of the Christian religion with its culture, in the ongoing struggle to define Christian existence, the Christian quest for perfection will continue.

Study Questions

Before you begin to read this part, pretend that you are asked to present a short talk on Christianity. How would you interpret the origin and development of Christianity? How would you set forth the unity of the beliefs, doctrines, and practices of Christianity? If you were limited to two major examples with which to illustrate religious life within Christianity, which two would you select? As you read this part, notice how your presentation compares with the author's.

CHAPTER 19

Introduction

1. What is the definition of Christianity given in the book? In this definition, what is the meaning of "Jesus Christ," "savior," and "believe in"?
2. Why does the book use the terms Christianities and churches in the plural?
3. Note the three approaches used in the book to study Christianity, focusing on history, basic structures, and specific examples of Christian belief and practice. How would you explain to another person the author's definition of and approach to Christianity?

CHAPTER 20

The Historical Development of Christianity

1. Interpret early Christianity as a Jewish sect. How did this "Jewish sect" develop into the Christian church?
2. Trace this Christian church from its informal beginnings to a more formal organization of practice and authority.
3. In what way was monasticism a reaction to the "success" of this more formal organization?
4. Compare and contrast Eastern (Orthodox) and Western (Roman Catholic) Christianity—focus especially on the "iconic" character of Orthodoxy and the "legal" character of Roman Catholicism.
5. What were the major factors leading to the "reform" in the Reformation?
6. What were the changes in "the church" within the Protestant Reformation (for example, in the sacraments)?
7. What was the reaction of the Roman Catholic church to the Protestant Reformation (the Counter-Reformation)?

8. What are the "modern developments in Christianity," especially in the New World and "experiential Christianity"?
9. How would you sum up the author's account of "the historical development of Christianity"?

CHAPTER 21
Structures of the Christian Life

1. What is "the central structure in Christianity"?
2. State in your own words "the Christian story."
3. What is "the meaning of salvation" in Christianity?
4. How did Christianity, much more than other religions, come to emphasize belief in creed? What is the gist of some basic Christian creeds?
5. In your own words describe and interpret the basic Christian rituals of baptism and the Eucharist.
6. What is the meaning of the church as "holy community" or "the body of Christ"?
7. What kinds of "orders" and roles of leadership developed in the church?
8. How did the model of Christ become a pattern for ascetic movements, and how is this contrasted with the "priesthood of all believers" in Protestantism?
9. Define the "work of the church" as evangelism, salvation, and establishing the messianic kingdom.
10. Trace the life of the church in the annual cycle patterned on the major events in the life of Jesus.
11. What is the meaning of "the expectation of the return of Jesus himself"?
12. How does Christianity sanctify birth, puberty, marriage, and death through the use of Christian ideals?
13. How is the model of Jesus a guide for personal piety (especially in penance and confession)?
14. How has the attainment of the ideal of Jesus (the *imitatio Christi*) been central to Christian life?
15. How would you sum up the author's interpretation of "structures of the Christian life"?

CHAPTER 22
Dynamics of Christian Life

1. What is the general definition of pilgrimage?
2. Where were favorite sites for Christians to go on pilgrimage, and what religious benefits did they receive from their pilgrimage?
3. How did Christian pilgrimage change from early centuries to the twelfth century?
4. What is the legendary account of the origin of the cult of Saint James in northwest Spain?

5. What preparations were involved in going on pilgrimage?
6. What were the religious attractions along the route of pilgrimage to Compostela?
7. What were the activities of the pilgrims at Compostela?
8. How were purification and holiness mixed with nationalistic history in the pilgrimage to Compostela?
9. Define "Puritan."
10. Describe the Puritan process of self-examination and the personal experience of God's grace before conversion.
11. How did Lyman Beecher see the United States as moving away from Calvinist Orthodoxy and what did he propose to correct the problems?
12. Why did Lyman Beecher oppose the separation of church and state, and how did he change his mind after their official separation?
13. How did the separation of church and state bring subtle pressures to bear on Calvinist theology?
14. How does this part summarize "the Christianity that Lyman represented"?
15. What was Harriet Beecher's relationship to Calvinism in her early life?
16. How did Harriet Beecher Stowe happen to write *Uncle Tom's Cabin?* What was the power of her novel, and how did it represent a transformation of her father's religious vision?
17. How do Harriet's later writings attempt to combine moral commitment and personal feeling?
18. What is meant by the statement "For Harriet the Episcopal church had a warmth and softness that the Puritan tradition lacked"?
19. How does the shift from Lyman Beecher's strict Puritan Calvinism to the "softer" religious life of his children represent a dramatic religious change in American Christianity?
20. What parallels of religious transformation are found in the life of Harriet Beecher Stowe and the pilgrimage to Compostela?
21. How would you sum up the two major examples of "dynamics of Christian life" in the pilgrimage to Compostela and in the religious life of the Beecher family?

CHAPTER 23

Conclusions

1. How does "greater holiness" represent the "transformative energy of Christianity"?
2. How does the life, death, and resurrection of Christ represent the "great mystery" of Christianity?
3. What is the meaning of "self-sacrifice" in Christianity?
4. How does religious pluralism present a problem for Christianity, and how is Christianity facing this issue?
5. How is Christianity facing the issue of "truth"?

Recall the talk on Christianity you were asked to present at the beginning of this part. How does your own presentation of history and system of Christianity differ from the author's? How do your own examples of religious life within Christianity compare with the author's choice of pilgrimage to Compostela and the faith of the Beecher family? In reading the author's treatment of Christianity, what did you find that was different from what you expected and what was most interesting? How has your understanding of Christianity changed as a result of reading this part?

Notes

Any effort to paint an overall portrait of so large a phenomenon as Christianity depends on the work of literally hundreds of scholars, past and present, known and unknown to me. I can only express my deep gratitude to my many teachers and colleagues, particularly those at the University of Chicago Divinity School and at Miami University. They helped me, by advice and example, to develop my skills in searching, seeing, sifting, thinking, and writing, and each was a special source of information as well. I wish to dedicate this work to two teachers in particular, my dissertation advisers Jonathan Z. Smith and Jerald Brauer. More than anything, they encouraged me to be fearless in taking on unusual projects and advancing new ideas. Without their inspiration and support in my intellectually formative years, I doubt I would have been so bold as to attempt to summarize Christianity in so few pages. Any errors of fact or bizarre interpretations are of course my own.

1. Our calendar is based on the Christian custom, introduced in the sixth century and formalized by Pope Hadrian I about 780 C.E., of dating from the birth of Jesus (the "year of our Lord," *anno Domini* in Latin, or A.D.). Scholars have recently introduced the abbreviation C.E. for "of the common era" or "Christian era," since other religions have their own calendars. B.C.E., or "before the common era," replaces B.C.

2. Paul's authentic letters are Romans, First and Second Corinthians, Galatians, Ephesians, Colossians, First (and possibly Second) Thessalonians, and Philippians. The Gospels were most probably written in the following order: Mark (c. 65–70 C.E.), Matthew (c. 85), Luke/Acts (c. 90–95), John (c. 90–100); the exact dates are disputed.

3. It seems likely that Cluny's emphasis on the *opus Dei* (the "work of God," i.e., the liturgy of the divine office) may have been encouraged by the influence of monks from the Eastern church. In the ninth, tenth, and eleventh centuries some Byzantine monks fled the Arab invasions of Sicily and Italy and went north, taking refuge in Western monasteries. The mystical emphasis of the East may thus have contributed to Cluny's focus on the proper worship of God: Cluniac monks were expected to spend as much waking time in collective prayer as in all their other activities combined.

4. Some Christian traditions have claimed that this meal was actually the Passover *seder*, the festive meal of the great Jewish holiday, celebrated on the first night. This is highly unlikely, as the courts would not have been in session to try Jesus on the following day; moreover, nothing in the nature of the meal mentioned suggests the elaborate Passover celebration. It is possible that Jesus was tried only by a Roman court, not a Jewish one, but that calls into question other parts of the New Testament accounts.

5. Originally the Eucharist was a regular meal, but its center was the repetition of the crucial acts of Jesus at the Last Supper. There, tradition records, Jesus blessed and broke bread according to Jewish custom while saying to his disciples, "Take; this is my body." On blessing the wine cup at the end of the meal he said, "This is my blood

of the covenant, which is poured out for many" (Mark 14:22–24). The church understood that this was to be repeated, as a powerful remembrance of Jesus; it re-called, invoked the very presence of Jesus in the bread and wine. This central part became the core of the Eucharist. The rest of the meal was separated off, becoming the *agape* or love-feast, a communal meal; eventually that part was dropped, leaving the drama of the Eucharist itself.

6. Georges Duby, *The Making of the Christian West, 980–1100* (New York: World Publishing Co., 1967), 25.

7. Ignatius, *Letter to the Romans,* 2.2, 4.1,2.

8. Pelayo was also the name of a nationalist Spanish hero in a battle against the Muslims in 718; this man was reputed also to live in caves and eat only honey, like the later Pelayo.

9. Quoted from *Codex Calixtinus,* Bk. 5, in Horton and Marie-Helene Davies, *Holy Days and Holidays: The Medieval Pilgrimage to Compostela* (Lewisburg, PA: Bucknell University Press, 1982), 213, 215.

10. Lyman Beecher, "A Reformation of Morals Practicable and Indispensable," in *Lyman Beecher and the Reform of Society* (New York: Arno Press, 1972), 22.

11. Ibid., 15.

12. Harriet Beecher Stowe, *The Minister's Wooing* (Ridgewood, NJ: Gregg Press, 1968; originally published, 1859), 23, 54.

Glossary

apocalypse A Jewish or Christian writing from the period 200 B.C.E. to 150 C.E. prophesying in vivid symbolism the imminent end of the world.

Apology A formal defense of the Christian faith.

apostle One of the earliest missionaries commissioned to preach the gospel; traditionally, twelve are counted (Jesus' twelve disciples), plus Paul, the "apostle to the Gentiles (non-Jews)."

baptize, baptism The rite of ritual immersion that initiated a person into the Christian church; it was held to cleanse a person from sin and begin a new, pure life. At first, full immersion was used as in Jewish conversions; later, pouring or sprinkling with water came into use in some churches.

bishop The rank in Roman Catholic and Eastern Orthodox churches above a priest, with authority to ordain priests as well as perform other sacraments. In the early church, an elected head of the church for an entire city; now, an appointed head of a diocese. (A few other churches, such as the Methodist and Mormon, also have the office of bishop.)

born again In modern Christianity, having experienced a true conversion and/or total dedication to Christ, usually in an intense emotional experience.

cardinal An official in the Roman Catholic church directly below the pope in the church hierarchy, appointed by the pope as a member of the "college" of cardinals that was formed in the Middle Ages to assist the pope and elect new popes.

catechism Originally, oral instruction in doctrine; catechism can mean any official summary of doctrine used to teach newcomers to the faith.

catechumen One receiving instruction in basic doctrines before baptism or, if already baptized as an infant, before confirmation or first communion.

circumcision A rite for males (usually infants) in which the foreskin is cut away; in Judaism, the sign of the covenant between God on the one hand and Abraham and his descendants on the other.

clergy The body of ordained men (and in some churches women) in a church, permitted to perform the priestly and/or pastoral duties.

communion The Christian sacrament of receiving bread and wine as the body and blood of Christ (or as symbols thereof).

confirmation A rite admitting a baptized person into full church membership, originally by anointing with oil.

conviction In modern Christianity, the state in which one recognizes one's sinfulness and guilt before God, preliminary to experiencing conversion.

creed A statement summarizing the essence of Christian belief, according to the particular church adopting the statement.

deacon The lowest ordained office in the Roman Catholic church (together with subdeacon), originally in charge of gathering and distributing the Eucharistic offerings, later a stage in seminary training. In modern Protestant churches, a deacon may be an official elected to a certain responsibility in worship or administration.

dogma A church's authoritative statement of belief; doctrine.

ecumenical Promoting a worldwide Christian unity or cooperation.

elect Those chosen by God for eternal life, according to theological systems that believe in predestination.

elevation of the host The priestly practice of raising the Eucharistic bread above the head at the moment of transubstantiation so that the laypeople behind the priest can see it.

eschatology A theory of the end of the world, how and when it will occur, and what the end times will be like.

Eucharist The Christian sacrament of receiving bread and wine as the body and blood of Christ. This term is more often used for the sacrament in the Catholic and Orthodox churches; *communion* is often used in Protestant churches.

evangelical, evangelizing Those churches or movements that emphasize preaching specifically aimed at repentance and conversion; in modern Christianity, their beliefs usually include salvation by faith and emphasis on scripture as well as a conversion experience.

excommunication The act of church authorities to deprive a person of church membership, specifically the right to take communion.

friars From the Latin word for brothers, members of one of the mendicant (begging) orders as distinct from the cloistered monks.

grace Unmerited divine assistance on one's spiritual path; often conceived of as a special blessing received in an intense experience, but also may include a sense of special direction in one's life.

Holy Spirit In Judaism, the presence of God as evidenced in the speech of the prophets and other divine manifestations; in Christianity, understood more generally as the active, guiding presence of God in the church and its members. See also Trinity.

icon A painted religious image—for example of Mary, Christ, or a saint—understood in Eastern Orthodoxy to be a copy of a heavenly image.

Immaculate Conception The doctrine asserting that Mary was free of original sin (the effect of Adam's sin) from the moment of her conception. Feasts celebrating her conception were popular in the Middle Ages, although the official doctrine was not declared by the pope until 1854.

Inquisition Roman Catholic tribunal for investigating and punishing heresy. The first papal Inquisitions began in the late twelfth century and were centralized under Innocent III; another famous tribunal was the Spanish Inquisition in the fifteenth and sixteenth centuries.

justification The state of being released by God from the guilt of sin.

kingdom of God The state of the world in which God's will is fulfilled; expected to be brought into being at the end of time when Christ returns.

laying on of hands A ritual in which spiritual power (for authority, healing, or other gifts) is transmitted by one in authority placing his or her hands on another person, usually on the head.

liturgy Rites of public worship, usually institutionalized in church tradition.

Mass The entire set of prayers and ceremonies surrounding the Eucharist.

Messiah Literally, the "anointed one" of God (*Christos* in Greek, Christ in English); God's chosen king, expected to bring peace, prosperity, and perfection to the world.

millenarian Having to do with the expected millennium, or thousand-year reign of Christ prophesied in Revelation, a time in which the world would be brought to perfection. Millenarian movements often grow up around predictions that this perfect time is about to begin.

monasticism The way of life or tradition of monks or nuns living in monasteries, that is, houses established to support a celibate, disciplined, and intensely religious way of life.

mystical, mysticism Aspects of religion that emphasize the individual's quest for union or direct communion with God.

ordination Ceremony of investing a person with ministerial or priestly office.

original sin The fundamental state of sin, inherited from the first man Adam, which according to most Christian theology infects all of humanity if not saved by Christ.

patriarch One of the bishops of the four major early Christian centers—Rome, Jerusalem, Antioch, or Alexandria, with Constantinople later added as a fifth. After the break with Rome, the term may refer to the head of any of the national divisions of the Eastern church.

penance The sacramental rite, in Roman Catholicism, consisting of repentance, confession to a priest, payment of the temporal penalty for one's sins, and forgiveness.

predestination The idea that one's eternal destiny is determined beforehand, from the beginning of time, by God's will.

purgatory An intermediate state after death, according to Roman Catholic theology, where one can finish satisfying the temporal punishments for one's sins and purify one's soul before being admitted to heaven.

relics Objects or parts of the body (e.g., clothing, teeth, bones) left behind after the decay of the corpse, which are venerated for saints of the Roman Catholic and Eastern churches.

resurrection Rising from the dead, with a restored bodily form.

revivals Events of spiritual awakening or high religious interest; specifically in modern Christianity, special meetings to encourage such awakening or interest.

sacrament A formal religious rite regarded as sacred for its perfect ability to convey divine blessing; in some traditions (especially Protestant), it is regarded as not effective in itself but as a sign or symbol of spiritual reality.

salvation Most generally, liberation from the power and effects of sin; often refers to an experience or series of experiences leading to a sense of liberation; sometimes refers to the expected liberation of a Christian after death.

sin A transgression or offense against God's laws or wishes; more generally in Christian belief, a continuing state of estrangement from God.

tongues An ecstatic utterance while in a state of religious excitation; sometimes regarded as a special spiritual language or ability to speak in different languages.

transubstantiation The change, during the Eucharist, of the substance of bread and wine into the substance of Christ's body and blood. According to Roman Catholic theology, the "accidents" (taste, color, shape) of the elements remain the same, but the substance changes into the holy elements of the sacrifice.

Trinity God the Father, Christ the Son, and the Holy Spirit in perfect unity, as three "persons" in one God. The nature of this union was much debated in the early church, and Western and Eastern understandings differ.

Virgin Mary, the mother of Jesus, held since early times to have conceived and given birth to Jesus without losing her virginity.

Selected Reading List

This list includes a sampling of surveys as well as interesting studies of specific topics but is by no means comprehensive. Most of the studies below include bibliographies to direct the student to other resources.

Ahlstrom, Sydney. *A Religious History of the American People*. New Haven, CT: Yale University Press, 1972.

Albanese, Catherine. *America: Religion and Religions*. Belmont, CA: Wadsworth Publishing, 1981.

Benz, Ernst. *The Eastern Orthodox Church*. New York: Doubleday, 1957.

Brown, Peter. *The Cult of Saints*. Chicago: University of Chicago Press, 1982.

———. *The Making of Late Antiquity*. Cambridge, MA: Harvard University Press, 1978.

Dix, Dom Gregory. *The Shape of the Liturgy*. New York: Winston Press (reprint), 1982.

Duby, Georges. *The Making of the Christian West 980–1140*. New York: World Publishing, 1967.

Foster, Lawrence. *Religion and Sexuality: Three Communal Experiments of the Nineteenth Century*. Chicago: University of Chicago Press, 1980.

Gager, John. *Kingdom and Community: A Social History of Early Christianity*. Englewood Cliffs, NJ: Prentice-Hall, 1975.

———. *The Origins of Anti-Semitism*. New York: Oxford University Press, 1983.

Knowles, David. *The Evolution of Medieval Thought*. New York: Random House, 1964.

Lossky, Vladimir. *The Meaning of Icons*. Boston: Palmer, 1956.

McKenzie, John L. *The Roman Catholic Church*. New York: Doubleday, 1969.

Male, Emile. *Religious Art from the Twelfth to the Eighteenth Century*. Princeton, NJ: Princeton University Press, 1982.

Marty, Martin. *Christianity in the New World*. New York: Winston Press, 1984.

Ozment, Steven E. *The Age of Reform*. New Haven, CT: Yale University Press, 1980.

Placher, William C. *A History of Christian Theology: An Introduction*. Philadelphia: Westminster Press, 1983.

Raboteau, Albert J. *Slave Religion: The Invisible Institution in the Antebellum South*. New York: Oxford University Press, 1980.

Sizer, Sandra S. *Gospel Hymns and Social Religion: The Rhetoric of Nineteenth Century Revivalism*. Philadelphia: Temple University Press, 1978.

Southern, Richard W. *The Making of the Middle Ages*. New Haven, CT: Yale University Press, 1953.

Ullmann, Walter. *A Short History of the Papacy in the Middle Ages*. New York: Methuen, 1974.

Williams, Georges Huntston. *The Radical Reformation*. Philadelphia: Westminster Press, 1962.

Zernov, Nicholas. *Eastern Christendom*. London: Reader's Union, 1963.

PART SIX

Islam

and the Muslim Community

Frederick M. Denny

Chronology of Islam

Dates	Major Cultural and Religious Features
to 610 C.E.	The *Jāhilīya* or "Age of Ignorance" in pre-Islamic Arabia
c. 570	Birth of Muḥammad
c. 595	Marriage of Muḥammad to Khadīja
610	Muḥammad's call to be a prophet and the beginning of the revelations of the Qur'ān
622	The *Hijra* or "Emigration" of Muḥammad and his followers from Mecca to Medina, which marked the founding of the Umma and the beginning of the Islamic lunar calendar
624	Battle of Badr
630	Muḥammad's conquest of Mecca and the rededication of the *Ka'ba* sanctuary as a purely Islamic worship center
632	Muḥammad's death
632–661	The period of the "Rightly Guided Caliphs" (Abū Bakr, 'Umar, 'Uthmān, and 'Alī) and the great conquests
661	The assassination of 'Alī and the rise of the Umayyad dynasty, which ruled from Damascus until 750
680	The massacre of Ḥusayn and his Shī'ite followers at Karbalā', Iraq
750	Fall of the Umayyads and beginning of the 'Abbāsid dynasty, which ruled from Baghdad until the Mongol conquest in 1258; the 'Abbāsid period witnessed the flowering of classical Islamic civilization; a separate Umayyad dynasty continued in Spain
1099	Crusaders conquer Jerusalem
1187	Saladin retakes Jerusalem for Islam at Battle of Hattin
c. 1500–1800	Major Islamic empires flourish: the Ottomans in the west, the Persian Safavids in Iran, and the Mughals in India; Islam gradually comes to dominate in the Malay-Indonesian regions and in parts of Africa

Dates	Major Cultural and Religious Features
1700s	The rise of the puritanical Wahhābi reform movement in Arabia, with strong influence beyond
1800s	Development of various Muslim reform movements and an increasingly strong Pan-Islamic, anti-Western consciousness
1900s	Continued renewal and reform of Islam, with emergence of many nation-states dedicated in various degrees to Islamic principles; Muslims experience challenges of modernity and science
1960s on	Muslim populations in Europe and North America increase dramatically through immigration and conversion

24

Introduction: The Islamic Umma—A Community Defined by a History, a Religious Way, and a Culture

THEY WERE JAPANESE, about twenty men and women, all dressed in white and standing in straight rows behind a stocky, older man with close-cropped hair. This leader recited the first chapter of the **Qur'ān*** in perfect Arabic with a resonant voice. The setting was Karachi, Pakistan's international airport transit lounge during the **Muslim** pilgrimage season, when believers from all over the world make their way to Mecca, in Arabia. The little group of Japanese Muslims was waiting to board the plane for the final leg of their long journey to Jedda, the Red Sea port of entry for the holy city of Mecca. The Japanese performed their prayers in a small **mosque** in the terminal, near duty-free shops and refreshment stands.

Japan does not have many Muslims, either of ethnic Japanese or other descent. However, the Muslims I saw at prayer in Karachi were clearly Japanese —in language, manner, and physical appearance—but they were also something else. That "something else" is a special style or pattern of behavior and comportment that sets observant Muslims apart from other people, regardless of ethnic, linguistic, cultural, or racial identity.

This work introduces the distinctive features of Islam as a religious tradition, while at the same time providing information on the varieties of Muslim peoples. Islam is a complete way of life embracing beliefs and devotional practices within a larger context of regulated social relations, economic responsibilities and privileges, political ideals, and community loyalties. Muslims inhabit at least two cultural spheres, the one they were born into and nurtured by and the one acquired as Islamic identity. Usually the two are closely connected, as in Muslim communities of long standing in the Middle East, Africa, southern Asia,

---

*Terms defined in the glossary, pp. 708–10, are printed in boldface type where they first appear in the text.

and Southeast Asia. But the cultures and subcultures of those vast regions also have very distinctive individual elements and characteristics that have been blended with Islamic beliefs, values, and behavior patterns. In regions where Islam is practically nonexistent or a small minority, there is a greater contrast between the general culture and what we will come to recognize as Islamic culture. Often, observant Muslims have to make difficult choices in such places as North America and Europe when it comes to social and family relations, economic behavior, food, clothing (especially for females), and entertainment, because of conflicts between what Islamic teachings prescribe and what the dominant culture considers the norm.

But even in countries like Indonesia, with dominant Muslim populations and great cultural complexity, several variations of Islamic culture operate in relation to other dimensions of national life. On the heavily populated Indonesian island of Java, for example, there are three generally recognized Muslim populations. The largest is the *abangan,* mostly working-class people who combine Javanese folk customs and beliefs with Islam in a syncretistic manner. Next are the *priyayis,* descended from the old Javanese court bureaucracy—they are Muslim but proud of the indigenous courtly tradition and at home with its symbols and tolerant style. Finally are the *santris,* the strictly observant Muslims who closely follow the Qur'ān and Muḥammad's teachings (the **Sunna**) and reject traditional Javanese cultural and religious beliefs and practices that they consider to be incompatible with pure Islam. There is much similarity and a strong sense of community between *santri* Muslims of Indonesia and strict Muslims in other regions. In my own travels to Muslim countries in the Middle East, southern and Southeast Asia, I have always been able to sense immediately when I was with *santri* types, regardless of their actual nationality, because of their strong orthodox faith and behavior patterns. [See Religions of Africa pp. 23–24, Religions of Mesoamerica pp. 117–19, Native Religions of North America pp. 261–64, Judaism pp. 389, 426, 456–75, Christianity pp. 492–94, Hinduism pp. 719–21, Buddhism pp. 853–55, Religions of China pp. 990–1015, and Religions of Japan pp. 1090–92 for discussion of the diversity and variety of religious traditions.]

The Islamic Religious Way

Writers on Islam have sometimes emphasized the doctrines of the religion to the exclusion of the human contexts in which they are believed and the practices by which they are confirmed and celebrated. The central beliefs and devotional duties of the religion of "submission" (*islām*) to God are easy to learn, in the way that the floor plan of an office building can be clearly comprehended by consulting a blueprint. But once the elementary, external features have been memorized, Islam as a living reality still remains undiscovered until one begins to perceive how the beliefs and practices are integrated into the fabric of social and personal life in specific cultural contexts. Muslims—those who have "submitted" to God—continually explain to interested outsiders that their religion is a "complete way of life" in which no distinction is made between religious and secular and all things are within the purview of Islamic authority and regulation.

Islam and Christianity have been conspicuously successful in spreading their doctrines among peoples of widely varying cultures and geographic contexts. Among religions of Asian origin, Buddhism has spread far and wide. Islam is the only Abrahamic tradition—like Judaism and Christianity, the great Hebrew patriarch figures in its myths and it is dedicated to belief in and covenant with the one God—that has had a major impact on Asia to the point of becoming dominant in some regions. Islam has maintained a more consistent system of fundamental beliefs and practices than any other world religion, including Judaism. Although there are sectarian divisions in Islam, they arose largely from political differences and do not include, except for minor details, differences in worship and devotional practices.

Because Islam is a religion of law and recognizes no sharp cleavage between religious and secular matters, it views all things as under God's legislation. Not all aspects of life are relevant to ritual, but they all have been assigned value by Islamic law on a scale from "forbidden" through "indifferent" to "obligatory." The holy law is known as **Sharī'a,** from an Arabic word that means "way," such as the way to the water hole. *Sharī'a* does not literally mean "law"; rather, it means God's ordaining of the right way for his faithful creatures, a way that includes actual law. It closely parallels the Jewish concept of Torah. [See Judaism pp. 387–89 for discussion of Torah.]

Muslims are fond of declaring that "humankind has no rights, only duties." This plainspoken conviction is foreign to the thinking of Americans, who are influenced by the Declaration of Independence and the Bill of Rights. But Islamic commitment to the way of submission to the one, sovereign God is not a grim totalitarianism. Muslims insist that the only proper relationship between humans and God is that of slaves to master. But God has created the world for just purposes, and he is both righteous and compassionate. God has given his human creatures freedom, along with other divine attributes such as intelligence, will, and speech.

Service to the Almighty must be a free act, which is then rewarded with responsibility in this world. The person who fears only God is raised above all other, lesser fears and enabled to carry on a free and active life as a **caliph,** or "vicegerent" of God. The duties of Islam, then, are entered upon freely and, in fact, are believed to bring actual freedom over against the slavery of human greed, anxiety, desire for personal status, and other things to which humans are prone as imperfect creatures. For Muslims, being in the service of God is not humiliating in the human sense; it is liberating and fulfilling. This conviction is shared by all three Abrahamic traditions, because of their common concern for a life of worship and obedience under their one true deity.

Islam and History

Muslims are defined not only by a religious way and by the cultural forms in which they live, but also by the historical development out of which they emerged. Just as Jews and Christians find in the understanding of their own history a model for their religious lives, so Muslims see in the understanding of the history of Islam an exemplary model that helps sustain both their personal and communal identities. Life is lived on the historical plane, where God is believed to have revealed his will definitively through prophets, signs, and mighty acts. Change and flow are natural, but people cannot merely fatalistically accept whatever happens; their behavior must be intentional and will involve crucial decisions. Opportunities come and sometimes pass by, never to be repeated. Responsible living requires making hard choices. History in the biblical and Islamic traditions is an irreversible process in which fateful consequences are decided, either in close covenant relationship with God or, perilously, outside of it.

Muslims study their history in order to adjust their present course in conformity with its teachings about God's providential acts. To become a Muslim is to submit to this history and be formed by it. As in Judaism and Christianity, there is also a forward-looking attitude that believes that the goal of history is in God's hands. History thus becomes a way of proceeding in life, suspended between the definitive events of the religious community's original constituting and development and its ultimate goal, "Judgment Day," when God gathers all people to a final reckoning and holds individuals responsible for their acts.

The Dome of the Rock, Jerusalem. This is the oldest surviving Islamic monument, dating from 691–92 C.E. Although used as a mosque and sometimes called the "Mosque of 'Umar," the Dome marks the traditional location of Muhammad's miraculous "Ascension" to heaven. It also marks the place where the Jewish Temple stood and thus brings together meaningful symbols and historical memories of Jews and Christians, as well as Muslims.

According to all three Abrahamic religions, revelation in the form of scriptural guidance has come down from God. Although natural life contains certain cycles and patterns of repetition, such as the seasons and the recurring generations of plant, animal, and human life, historical existence is essentially one-directional and "linear" and thus full of novelty and suspense. The cumulative history of the past provides crucial indicators and lessons as well as reassurances. Islamic sacred history contains some of what the Bible also preserves, such as memories of Abraham, Moses, Solomon, Mary, Jesus and other exemplary persons. In all the Abrahamic religions historical events are remembered and interpreted as revelatory of God's Providence and purposes for humankind. The record of Islam's origins and development contains, for Muslims, the wonderful story of the people of God in a language and with persons, events, and places of their own. That history will be reviewed in the next chapter.

The Umma

The Islamic community is known as the **Umma,** an ancient Arabic religious communal term that spans the range of religion, shared values, and common concerns. Umma sometimes has a cultural meaning, but it does not denote nationality, kinship, or ethnicity, at least in its fully developed meaning as the Muslim community. According to the Qur'ān, every religious community is an Umma. The Muslim Umma is the totality of Muslims in the world at a given time, as well as the sense of shared history of the Islamic venture inherited from the past. This latter sense is similar to the Christian notions of the "communion of saints," a "cloud of witnesses," and a "noble army of martyrs," all existing in a mysterious manner both in the historical past and present until the final judgment.

The Umma is not any particular Islamic culture, even though it has always exhibited strong Arabic influences. Rather, the Umma is the shared and mutually compatible, complementary family of cultures belonging to Muslim peoples in many places. This transcultural Islamic "culture" unites and preserves the Umma even as it draws strength and specific qualities from its many distinct, component cultures.

There are important synonyms for Umma. One is the Arabic word *jamā'a,* "community" in the sense of dominant group. Related Arabic words from the same root include *jāmi',* "congregator," "collector," which in conjunction with *masjid* ("mosque") means congregational mosque for the performance of Friday noon worship, which must be performed in congregation. Another word is *ijmā',* "consensus," which is one of the major sources of Islamic jurisprudence. Its relation to Umma can be seen in the famous declaration of Muḥammad, "Indeed my Umma shall never agree together on an error." The consensus of the Umma, according to that statement, is infallible.

Another major synonym for Umma is **Dār al-Islām,** "the Abode of Submission," meaning the lands and peoples under Islamic law and rule. There is an administrative and legal dimension to this term that Umma by itself lacks. The paired opposite of *Dār al-Islām* is *Dār al-Ḥarb,* the "Abode of Warfare," meaning the non-Muslim lands and peoples. *Warfare* refers both to the presumed quality of such places from the perspective of Muslims (namely, that they lack the security and order of the *Sharī'a* and are therefore lands where everyone is at war with everyone else) and to the necessity for **jihād**—"exertion" in spreading the true faith, an activity that may include armed conflict. It is one thing to force conversion, which the Qur'ān forbids; but it is another to conquer territory in the name of God and—from the Muslim vantage point—for the welfare of peoples who stand to benefit from imposition of the holy law. Religious minorities, especially Judaism and Christianity, have their place under the *Sharī'a* as protected groups, but they are under certain constraints, one of which forbids their members to proselytize.

Islam as Orthoprax Religion

It has been common in recent years for scholars of comparative religion and Islamic studies to characterize religions as either "orthodox" or "orthoprax." Those two terms derive from Greek compound expressions of *ortho* ("correct") plus *dox* ("opinion") or *praxis* ("practice"). All religions, of course, are concerned with both teachings and practices: matters of doctrine, such as concepts, symbols, creeds, and theologies, and matters of action, such as ritual, law, and devotional life. So when we describe a religion as either orthodox or orthoprax, we are describing its particular emphasis.

Judaism and Islam are orthoprax religions to the extent that each places fundamental emphasis on law and the regulation of community life, the Jews according to the Torah, the Muslims according to the *Sharī'a,* parallel institutions based on revelation and interpreted by respected specialist scholars. Christianity, in contrast, is orthodox because it has traditionally placed greater emphasis on belief and its intellectual structuring in creeds, catechisms, and theologies. The antilegalistic bias of Christianity, particularly as enunciated by the Apostle Paul in his Epistle to the Romans, led to a much less centrally regulated system of worship and communal life in Christianity, in spite of the mighty and sustained efforts of Catholicism, especially in its Roman form, to impose order on both doctrine and practices. The orthodoxy of Christianity extends also to worship and the common life, but doctrine takes precedence as the main formulation of the experience of revelation. The orthodox Jewish and Islamic traditions are also vitally concerned with correct thinking and clear formulation of belief, but knowing the truth without doing it is vanity. In fact, the truth cannot be merely known, in the sense of being brought into mental awareness; it must be fully known through realization in action.

Orthodoxy and orthopraxy are really only analytically distinct from each other, and for that reason should be used only for generalization. In every religion, belief and practice and their community context are integral dimensions of the total system of symbols and actions. Yet it is instructive that Judaism and

Islam both lack universally accepted creedal statements while they exhibit remarkable liturgical and legal uniformity within themselves. Christianity has generated various creeds, one of which (the Apostles' Creed) is still today recited by Christians in extremely differing institutional and liturgical contexts: Roman Catholic, Eastern Orthodox, and Protestant. [See Judaism pp. 386–87, Christianity pp. 538–42, and Native Religions of North America pp. 267–68 for discussion of creeds.]

The Muslim World Today: An Overview

Today, sizable Muslim populations exist in Africa, the Middle East, and central, southern, and Southeast Asia; in many of these areas Muslims constitute a majority of the population. In the West, especially in North America, there has long been an assumption that the Islamic world is composed mainly of Arabs, although Turks and Iranians are now generally included too. It is true that Arabic language, history, and culture have played definitive roles in Islamic history (to be reviewed in the following chapter), but Islam is a world religion that rivals, if it does not surpass, Christianity in its ability to spread to highly diverse cultures and regions.

By far the largest national Islamic population is in Indonesia, where approximately 90 percent of the 191 million people are Muslim. The second largest national Islamic population is in Pakistan, with about 97 percent of 113 million; the third is Bangladesh, with 85 percent of 118 million; and the fourth is India, with 11.5 percent of 850 million. Other large Muslim populations exist in the former Soviet Union (around 45 million), and China (which has been estimated at 14 million, probably much lower than the actual number). [See Religions of China pp. 1015, 1057 for mention of Islam in China.]

One object of this summary is to illustrate how very widespread and numerous Muslims are in Asia, well outside the Arab, Turkish, and Iranian Middle East. Arabs are people who speak Arabic as their first language and not just those people who live in the Arabian Peninsula. They live in countries throughout the Middle East and North Africa. There are more than 160 million Arabic speakers, of whom well over 90 percent are Muslim. Iran's 55 million people are at least 93 percent Muslim, and Turkey's 55 million are no less than 98 percent Muslim. Similar percentages can be found in most other Middle Eastern and North African countries. Sub-Saharan Africa contains at least 100 million Muslims.

It is difficult to arrive at an accurate figure for the world Muslim population, but there is general agreement that it is around one billion.[1] Only Christianity claims more adherents. However, statistical figures of religious populations are hampered by inconsistent measuring tools and lack of agreement on membership criteria.

A very significant factor in current and future Muslim populations is the annual rate of growth. Among the twenty-five fastest growing nations in the

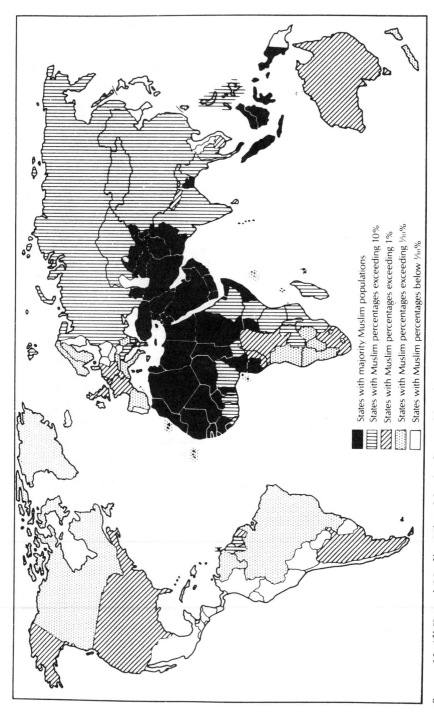

States with majority Muslim populations

States with Muslim percentages exceeding 10%

States with Muslim percentages exceeding 1%

States with Muslim percentages exceeding ¹/₁₀%

States with Muslim percentages below ¹/₁₀%

Source: M. Ali Kettani, Muslim Minorities in the World Today (London and New York: Mansell, 1986; reprinted with permission), with addition of Central Asian independent republics.

world, eleven have majority Muslim populations (e.g., Pakistan, Bangladesh, Saudi Arabia, Syria, Egypt, Iran, Morocco, and Iraq), while others have very substantial minorities (e.g., Nigeria, Tanzania, Niger). Other predominantly Muslim nations, notably Turkey, Chad, and Indonesia, have growth rates well above the world average of 1.7 percent.

For the first time, Islam is becoming a significant minority religion in Western nations, especially France (2 million +), Britain (2 million +), West Germany (2 million +), Canada (½ million), and the United States (c. 5 million). There has long been a 10 percent Muslim population in Yugoslavia and Albania has traditionally been almost entirely Muslim. Although most Muslims in the West have roots in traditional Islamic countries, an increasing number are indigenous converts.

Islam as a History, a Religious Way, and a Culture

Islam is a religion marked by a powerful concern for community. The Umma may be compared to a triangle with one angle representing history, one angle religious way, and the third angle culture.[2] This triangle can be drawn in many forms, representing the relative prominence of one or another of the three angles. For example, at times and in certain places Muslims have emphasized doctrine and ritual over culture and history, as in some expressions of scriptural **fundamentalism.** At other times, cultural identity within particular regions has been foremost. At still other times, Muslims have emphasized the ideal of certain historical eras of Islam, perhaps in the hopes of restoring former strength and glory. But all three dimensions are essential to the Umma and exist, finally, as mutually supporting elements of the mysterious reality that Muslims know is their strongest bond: the Umma in covenant with God.

Our introduction to Islam as a complete way of life will begin in chapter 25 with a survey of its rise and historical development. Of central importance in Islam's history is the original and continuing power of Arabic traditions, symbols, personages, moral ideals, and social attitudes. All of these have been maintained through the Arabic language and in the migrations of Arabs. We shall see that, with the coming of Islam into the Arabian Peninsula, old Arabic ways were in some cases rejected, but in others transformed for service in the new religion. At the center of the rise of Islam and inspiring and regulating its continued vitality and development to the present day are the Prophet Muḥammad and the message Muslims believe was divinely revealed to him, the Noble Qur'ān. So, Islamic history has been definitively shaped by its Prophet and Scripture. Muḥammad is thought to be the perfect embodiment of the ideal human life, and the Qur'ān is considered to be a perfect message expressed in the purest Arabic speech, which is believed by Muslims to be the language of God and the angels.

Following our survey of the historical dimension of Islam, we shall examine in chapter 26 the religion's formal beliefs and practices, which provide the structures of Muslim life. Both aspects have been definitively commanded and regulated by the Qur'ān and the closely associated teachings and example of Muḥammad. The Qur'ān teaches Muslims what God requires of his faithful servants and in the process reveals much of his nature as Creator, Sustainer, Lord, and Judge of the universe. The teaching and example of Muḥammad, known as his Sunna, exemplify the ways in which humans are to receive, ingrain, and apply the message of God. In a real sense, then, the Qur'ān tells humans *what* to believe, and the Sunna instructs them in *how* to believe and act.

The chapter on the doctrines and practices of Islam will go beyond simple description of basics by treating ways in which they have been structured and applied in law, theological reflection, and the interrelated spiritual disciplines known as **Sufism.** We shall see that the sacred law dominates Muslims, especially in its protection and regulation of the all-important communal aspects of life. But intellectual definition and clarification have also been important activities, both in jurisprudence and systematic theology. Even more important, to the point of rivaling the religious law for the loyalties of Muslims, has been Sufism, the mystical path of Islam. Sufism, as we shall see, is personal and spontaneous. It emphasizes love and a warm, intimate relationship with God and one's fellow Muslims. Sufism has taken on enduring institutional forms in regional as well as international orders, each with its distinctive emphases in pursuing spiritual enlightenment and mystical union with God.

In fact, Islam is, in addition to being a history and a religious way, a culture. Muslims constitute a great *variety* of cultures, all of which conform in one way or other to the ideals and practical requirements of the *Sharī'a,* especially its two most authoritative sources, the Qur'ān and Sunna. There is an Islamic culture that transcends local cultures. In the process, local cultural influences, which always exist, contribute greatly toward making the Umma the richly diverse yet spiritually unified community that it is. Throughout this work, attention will be paid to cultural aspects of the Umma, whether by describing specific Muslim peoples and their customs or demonstrating the occasional tensions that arise when orthodox-orthoprax Islam is juxtaposed with regional forms and practices, which sometimes include folk beliefs and behavior. In any case, a religion as deeply involved in all aspects of the human condition as Islam is will inevitably have strong cultural dimensions, some of which we will examine in chapter 27, on the dynamics of selected Muslim institutions.

This introduction to Islam closes with a chapter on Islam and Muslims in today's world. The themes that we shall have come to recognize as being central to the tradition—such as the primacy of the Qur'ān, the exemplary model of Muḥammad as guide for the faithful, Arabic language as both medium of revelation and Umma-wide force for community and shared concepts, the *Sharī'a* as God's legislation for Muslims everywhere, and strong Muslim commitment to justice and social order in a harmonious and disciplined community that knows no distinction between religious and secular realms—these themes and others will be seen still to inspire and regulate the ways in which today's Muslims believe, behave, interact with others, and anticipate their destinies as servants of God. At bottom, the story of Islam is a story of enduring commitment to a transcendent ideal—God's gracious ordaining of humankind's way on earth and into the hereafter—and the working out in history of that vision.

25

The Rise and Historical Development of Islam

IN THIS CHAPTER, we shall survey the Arabian setting into which Islam was born, a setting that has continued to exert considerable influence on it to this day. Then we shall survey the major events in the origin and early development of Islam, with special emphasis on the biography of Muḥammad and the role of his key followers who founded the caliphate and established a powerful Islamic international order in the Middle East and North Africa. The spread of Islam to many regions of the world is described next, followed by a consideration of the decline of Muslim political strength as the West rose to global prominence.

Arabia

The Islamic movement arose in Arabia in the seventh century C.E. and declared itself to be a restoration of the original monotheism of the Semitic patriarch Abraham, who was, as the Qur'ān states, a righteous person and a prophet who established the proper worship of God at the **Ka'ba** sanctuary in Mecca. In Islamic teaching, Abraham was neither a Jew nor a Christian, but a person of pure faith and a Muslim (Qur'ān 3:68). The Qur'ān affirms its spiritual pedigree in unmistakable terms: "We believe in God, and that which has been sent down on us, and sent down on Abraham and Ishmael, Isaac and Jacob, and the Tribes, and in that which was given to Moses and Jesus, and the Prophets, of their Lord; we make no division between any of them, and to Him we surrender" (3:85). According to the Qur'ān, the Jews and Christians received true guidance from God and sometimes followed it in a mode of authentic surrender—islām—but more often they split up into sects and corrupted the messages of their prophets. Thus God, in his mercy, restored his original message in the Qur'ān, the "Recitation," which he revealed to Muḥammad in plain Arabic speech. Not only the Jews and Christians but other descendants of Abraham, the pagan Arabians— who had forgotten their true spiritual roots—would be called back to the original religion of Islam, which, according to Islamic doctrine, God had established in archaic times for his faithful servant Abraham and his descendants. To understand the rise and historical development of Islam, we must first look into the region known as Arabia and the beliefs and customs that were followed there before Islam.

→ "The Arabian Island," as the Arabian Peninsula is known in Arabic, is a vast area approximately equal in size to the United States east of the Mississippi River. Most of it is uninhabited desert similar in appearance to arid regions of Utah, Nevada, and Arizona. However, a minimal amount of moisture and pasture has made it possible for humans to live in parts of Arabia since prehistoric times.

The southern part of the Peninsula, Yemen, was known in biblical times as the Land of Sheba. This region was once a flourishing civilization, with rich agriculture made possible by irrigation, and a complex and interrelated social, political, and religious life that resembled that of Mesopotamian civilizations. The western region of Arabia is rugged and mountainous, with ancient overland north-south routes linking Yemen with Egypt, the Holy Land, and the Mediterranean Sea. Although most of the people of western and central Arabia since early times were pastoralists, by Roman and early Christian times there were also significant permanent settlements, especially in Hijāz, the region in west central Arabia that extends from Mecca in the south to north of Medina.

Hijāz is the cradle of Islam. Before Muḥammad's time, Mecca arose as an important trading town and regional sanctuary and attracted merchants and pilgrims in great numbers. There was, by the sixth century, a growing merchant class that had left behind the old pastoralist way of life. Caravans passed through Mecca going north to Palestine and south to Yemen with valuable cargoes. The close interrelationships between the town and desert Arabs put the Hijāzīs (people of Hijāz), especially those living in Mecca, at a distinct advantage in conducting long-distance trade. The camel drivers, rough men with great fighting skills, were masters of the trade routes: They were capable of passing through inhospitable territories by using sheer force or tactical finesse. When necessary, clever merchants could forge alliances and treaties with tribes along the routes, guaranteeing safe passage and shared profits. Outsiders (i.e., non-Arabs) did not stand a chance in Hijāz business or warfare, because they lacked both the camel-based techniques of long-distance transport and the crucially important kinship and cultural advantages that united specific Arab groups in closed communities. Outsiders had to have the cooperation and protection of Arabs to be successful.

Before Muḥammad's revolutionary impact on Arabia, it had never known any kind of political unity. The most that had been achieved were temporary federations for specific purposes, such as mutual defense. Now and then a strong leader dominated a limited region, but there was no form of large-scale political unity. Certain essential ingredients for unity were present, such as a common Arabic language, similar social structure and customs, common traditions (especially pertaining to Abraham as father of the Arabs), and mastery of the difficult mode of life in desert and steppe regions, but these were not marshalled in the service of any kind of political unity before Muḥammad.

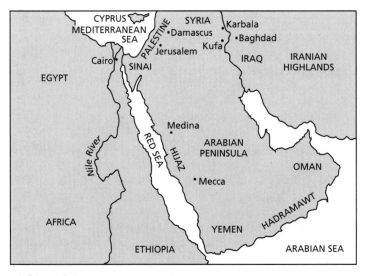

Arabia and the Near East in early Islamic times.

Before the rise of Islam, the values of the Arabs centered in the honor of the family, clan, and tribe—honor that was to be defended at all costs. This honor was maintained within a context of manliness that expressed itself in martial skills and acts of valor. Manliness was also a kind of nobility of character, evidenced in hospitality and generosity. It was a combination of physical strength, moral courage, and a sense of one's own genealogical superiority. Another characteristic that some Arabs had was known as *jahl.* This term literally means "ignorance," but its connotation is "barbarism," especially in performing violent and cruel acts against others with no motive except delight in wreaking havoc. Barbarism could be overlooked or at least forgiven in a young and impetuous man, because it might be an early sign of unusual potential as a fighter and leader. But if a person's life were continuously characterized by unreasoning violence and wanton destruction, he became a threat to society and had to be subdued or eliminated. Because there was so much lawlessness and violence in pre-Islamic Arabia as well as the absence of a strong religious ethic, later Islamic generations came to call the period before the rise of Islam *Jāhilīya,* the "Age of Barbarism," when people were ignorant of the peace and blessings of true religion. Pre-Islamic Arabia did have a loose tradition of religious beliefs and practices, connected with tribal values and maintenance. In fact, Mecca's central sanctuary housed some 360 idols representing the spirits and divinities found in Hijāz. Chief among them was an image in human form representing the god Hubal, who seems to have had some relation to Mars, the war god. Three "Daughters of **Allāh**" were also worshiped, called Al-Lāt, Manāt, and 'Uzza.

Before the rise of Islam, Arabs also believed in a deity called Allāh, but the pre-Islamic conception of Allāh was significantly different from the notion of Allāh in Islam. Allāh was acknowledged as a creator god, but because he was perceived as transcendent and abstract like the "High Gods" of many ancient traditions, the pre-Islamic Allāh was not worshiped formally on a regular basis. The power of Allāh was recognized, and there is evidence that some ancient Arabs focused on him to the exclusion of lesser deities; however, for most Arabs, Allāh was not the center of a monotheistic movement until this was promoted by Muḥammad's prophetic career. Allāh is a contraction of the Arabic definite article *al-,* "the," and *ilāh,* "god"; thus *"al-ilāh"* equals "Allāh." *Allāh* in Islam is the corresponding term for "God" in Judaism and Christianity.

↩ Old Arabian religion recognized the sacred character of places like springs, wells, groves, and unusual rock formations. Often such sanctuaries contained the graves of tribal ancestors, long maintained and guarded as a matter of honor by generations of descendants. The holy character of clan genealogy is apparent in such places. Certain deities had unique relations with particular family and regional shrines, and sacrifices and offerings were made periodically at their altars. This pattern resembles the religious practices of the ancient Israelites as recorded in the Bible, especially those of the patriarchs Abraham, Isaac, and Jacob.

The ancient Arabs practiced circumambulation of their shrines, especially shrines connected with sacred stones. This walking around a sacred site came to be incorporated into Islamic worship in the ritual during which pilgrims circle the holy *Ka'ba* at Mecca. The pilgrimage to Mecca was an important element in the religion of Hijāz long before Muḥammad's time. Pilgrims coming into Mecca presented many opportunities for trade and commerce, and many Meccan families became wealthy just from the concessions that served the pilgrimage. The close alliance between commerce and religion was a key ingredient in Mecca's prestige and power as the dominant city of western Arabia at the time of Muḥammad. When Muḥammad preached the end of idolatry in Mecca, the leaders there saw him as a real threat to their livelihoods.

We do not know as much about the details of pre-Islamic religion in Hijāz as we would wish. We do know that fatalism characterized much of the people's outlook on life. There was no belief in an afterlife, in a just recompense after suffering, or in punishment after sinning in this life. The ultimate power appears not to have been a specific deity, but rather "Time," an impersonal and indifferent process of change that rolls on despite humankind's hopes or fears. Death was widely believed to be final, so people had to make the most of life now. There is archaeological evidence for afterlife beliefs, but these seem not to have included resurrection.

There was considerable satisfaction in raising children and in strengthening family size and quality, for in kinship relations were realized the most important goals of wealth, prestige, and power. Outsiders were not important, because all personal values were in closed community life within the kinship group. Altruistic arrangements were a matter of strict calculation of benefits for one's own group. If someone from one kinship group injured or killed a member of another family, clan, or tribe, there would be a vendetta against the offending kinship group until balance was restored by exacting a life or some equal recompense for the crime. Such feuds could continue for a long time.

The most influential people in ancient Arabia in a religious sense were the *kāhins,* shamanistic seers who could enter a trance state and through visionary means locate lost relatives, camels, or other objects. *Kāhins* uttered sacred formulas in a rhymed prose. Poets were also considered to be repositories of sacred power because of their inspiration, which was thought to be caused by invisible spirits, *jinn* (sing., *jinnī,* from which the English word *genie* derives). Poetic utterance was entertaining as well as edifying. The Arabic language of poetry transcended the dialects of separate tribes and united the widely dispersed Arabs in a remarkable manner at the level of shared symbols, ideas, and aesthetic sensibilities. Poetry was the major art form in *Jāhilīya* times. At the same time, it contained much of historical and descriptive value for the collective memory of the past. Poetic contests were held periodically and the greatest honor was to have one's verses engraved on sheets and hung in the *Ka'ba* sanctuary at Mecca.

Muḥammad: Messenger of God and Founder of the Umma

Muḥammad was born after the middle of the sixth century C.E., when Hijāz was enjoying its period of greatest economic progress and growth. A main reason for this prosperity was the diversion of much east-west trade south along the Arabian routes because of a protracted war between the Byzantine and the Sassanid (Persian) empires, the great powers of the age. The lucrative overland trade routes of the Near East and Central Asia were effectively shut down much of the time, so that merchants were forced to look elsewhere for ways to transport goods to and from distant east and west markets and sources. The Arabs had long been preeminent traders, of course, but the impetus brought about by increased use of the Hijāz and other Arabian routes enabled this area, especially Mecca, to become rich. This development was very influential in the social system, promoting the movement of more and more people to Mecca and changing tribal and clan patterns of mutual support and leadership. The religious dominance of the Meccan sanctuary, especially at pilgrimage time, also generated substantial revenue for those individuals and groups that owned a share in the concessions around the holy *Ka'ba.*

There is evidence that during this period of increased population in towns or even urban settings, the weaker and poorer members of the society suffered neglect. The older tribal system included a loose kind of protection and welfare for less fortunate members such as unmarried or divorced women, widows, orphans, and old persons. But with the shift from rural to urban life the social system deteriorated and social welfare declined. Town and city life tended to produce relative indifference and anonymity. Lucky entrepreneurs were able to make fast money in the caravan trade or in the pilgrimage concessions, but the majority of ordinary folk were left out. Nor was there any widespread religious consciousness of ethical character strong enough to combat the degenerative social and economic effects. Political unity, except in limited contexts, was unknown. It was a matter of people being out for themselves in a highly competitive, heartless race for wealth.

The leading tribe in Mecca was the **Quraysh.** Many of its members enjoyed considerable wealth, prestige, and power within the oligarchical system that had arisen in Mecca during the sixth century C.E. The tribe was divided into two major groups, known respectively as the Quraysh of the "inside" and the Quraysh of the "outside." The former were the influential and wealthy members; the latter were people of more humble station. But the tribal system was still strong enough to guarantee that even a "poor cousin" Qurayshī could depend on the strength and dignity of the entire Quraysh tribe for protection if confronted by an outside threat.

Muḥammad's Birth and Early Life

The precise year of Muḥammad's birth is unknown, but it was probably around 570 C.E. Muḥammad's early life was inauspicious—his father died before he was born and his mother died when he was six; he was raised by his loving grandfather who died when the boy was eight. From that time Muḥammad's uncle looked after him and continued to provide indispensable tribal protection even when Muḥammad was in his forties and had become a controversial religious reformer.

Muḥammad's clan within the Quraysh tribe was Banū Hāshim, a dignified but less influential or wealthy clan than Banū Umayya, which was chief among the Meccan oligarchy. (The later Umayyad dynasty would rise from that clan and rule the young Islamic empire from Damascus.) Muḥammad grew up a poor orphan and worked as a shepherd in the environs of Mecca. He did benefit from being sent out to live among the desert Bedouin in that it enabled him to learn the pure Arabic language and to become trained in basic techniques of desert travel, survival, and self-defense. Even when many Arabs had settled down in towns and cities, they continued to send their sons off to nomadic tribal relatives for training in the lore and skills of the traditional Arabian way of life, which was considered to be essentially superior to sedentary life on the land.

We do not know much about Muḥammad's youth, except that he developed a reputation as a trustworthy person with unusually good sense about human relationships. In his twenties Muḥammad went to work for Khadīja, a widow who owned a caravan business. Because Muḥammad succeeded so well in helping his employer make a profit and because of his appealing personal qualities, Khadīja proposed marriage, and the two were wed when Muḥammad was about twenty-five and Khadīja perhaps as much as fifteen years older. This marriage provided Muḥammad a secure livelihood, because Khadīja was well off and happy to be the source of Muḥammad's good fortune. Several children were born of the marriage, including Fāṭima; she and her husband, 'Alī, would become two of the greatest personages of early Islam. During Muḥammad and Khadīja's long and fruitful marriage, which lasted from 595 to 619 C.E., Muḥammad had no other wife. It appears that the marriage was a very strong and satisfying one. Muḥammad had the greatest affection and respect for Khadīja, who did so much to support him during difficult times in his life, especially when he first began receiving his prophetic revelations around 610; at this time he was already forty and she fifty-five.

Muḥammad's Prophetic Career

We do not know much about Muḥammad's life between the time of his marriage to Khadīja and the beginning of his prophetic career, a period of fifteen years. We do know that Muḥammad increasingly took to private religious meditation, including protracted retreats in a mountain cave outside Mecca. Muḥammad's religious practices seem to have had much in common with a wider spiritual movement within Arabian society. During the time Muḥammad lived, other serious and sensitive individuals were seeking a deeper spiritual experience. The name **ḥanīf,** which occurs in the Qur'ān, refers to persons of monotheistic convictions who were neither Jews nor Christians. Abraham is called by the Qur'ān a ḥanīf and also a "muslim," that is, one who is submissive to God (3:67). The Qur'ān proclaims that Abraham had established the original ethical monotheism in Arabia, but that it had gradually degenerated after him into the polytheistic idolatry that prevailed in Muḥammad's time. Yet there were still a few persons remaining as ḥanīfs, "rightly inclined" (as the term means) toward the correct way. Muḥammad was among these ḥanīfs.

One day when Muḥammad was meditating in a cave on Mt. Hira, a voice declared to him that he was the messenger of God. Muḥammad was frightened by this experience, which was followed by the command "Recite!" or "Read!" Muḥammad said that he could not (i.e., read). After a repetition of the command accompanied by a heavy pressing down on his body by the unknown, mysterious presence, Muḥammad was then told: "Recite! 'In the name of your Lord who created, created humankind from clotted blood.' Recite! 'And your Lord is the most noble, who teaches by the pen, teaches humankind that which they did not know'" (96:1–5). Muḥammad believed that he saw the source of the command to recite as a gigantic figure on the horizon. Muslim tradition has considered that figure to have been the archangel Gabriel, the angel of revelation of the Qur'ān.

Muḥammad hurried to his wife, Khadīja, to tell her of his experience. She received the news in a serious and positive manner and soon became the first to believe and submit to the new revelation as a Muslim. Soon others followed suit, both within the Prophet's family and outside. After a hiatus the revelations continued until the end of Muḥammad's life. Muḥammad sometimes experienced discomfort during the coming of the revelations, but over the years he became accustomed to the visitations of Gabriel. Even so, his receiving of the divine message by means of **waḥy,** a kind of verbal inspiration, was never to be dull routine. The accumulated revelations were known as qur'āns, "recitations," both because they were first revealed to Muḥammad in recited form and because they were in turn recited by Muḥammad and his fellow Muslims. The emerging Scripture of Islam was known as the Qur'ān, "The Recitation," the collection of the individual recitations revealed by means of *waḥy*.

The call of Muḥammad to be a prophet occurred in 610 C.E., when he was about forty years of age. In the ensuing years Muḥammad built up a loyal following in Mecca composed mainly of rather humble citizens. The center of the faith that Muḥammad preached by means of the revelations was submission to the one true God, who had spoken before to Abraham, Moses, Jesus, and other prophets known in the biblical record of Judaism and Christianity. The name of the new religion was to be Islam, which means "submission," and one who submits is called a "Muslim."

The early years were relatively calm, enabling the Muslims to develop their characteristic devotional practices centering in a prayer service of several complete prostrations. The emerging Qur'ān was taught to the believers, many of whom memorized it and used it in their own devotions and meditations. The Muslims worshiped at the *Ka'ba,* which they believed was originally dedicated to Allāh by Abraham. As the new movement became more energetic, especially over against the idolatry of the main *Ka'ba* cult, difficulties increased.

Muḥammad's early years of preaching in Mecca constituted a period of gradual growth of the Muslim community, but increasingly Muḥammad came to be at odds with many of the leaders of the Quraysh, who saw in him a potential threat to their economic and religious system. Muḥammad preached against the idolatry of the *Ka'ba* cult, which was a primary source of income in the pilgrimage system. There was also apprehension on the part of the Meccan oligarchy that Muḥammad was a threat to the established social system, which had held the people together since ancient times. It was disrespectful as well as dangerous for Muḥammad to question the ways of the ancestors, whose memory and nobility were preserved in honored genealogical traditions.

As persecution of Muḥammad and his followers became severe, Muḥammad sent a number of Muslims across the Red Sea to the Christian kingdom of Ethiopia. Muḥammad and some of his followers enjoyed the protection of powerful clansmen in Mecca, but other followers did not have such security. Those were the ones who participated in Islam's first *hijra,* or "emigration." The Meccan leaders sent a delegation after these Muslim emigrants, ordered to return them to Arabia and "submission," not to God, but to the Meccan establishment. The Ethiopian king, however, refused to turn over the religious refugees and gave them hospitality and protection in his realm. But emigration to Ethiopia was not practical for the entire community, nor did Muḥammad want to leave his native land.

Muḥammad realized that the Muslim movement could not continue in Mecca, so he looked around for a new base of operations. He attempted to negotiate with the leaders of the not-too-distant mountain town of Ta'if, but the residents there drove the Prophet away with abuse and stone throwing. This occurred near the end of the first decade of Islam, about 620 C.E. During that critical period Muḥammad's beloved wife, Khadīja, and his uncle and protector, Abū Tālib, died.

A delegation from the agricultural oasis town of Yathrib, nearly three hundred miles north of Mecca, met with Muḥammad and asked him to move to Yathrib and serve as arbitrator and counselor to lead that bitterly divided community. Two Arab tribes, the Aws and the Khazraj, were at odds with each other, while the long-standing Jewish community of Yathrib was caught uneasily in between. Muḥammad grasped this opportunity to move his following to Yathrib. He concluded a pact with the delegation, and it was agreed that the Muslims could emigrate with him and that the people of the town would submit to God as Muslims and respect Muḥammad not only as leader but Prophet, that is, God's messenger and guide for the new religion. Although the natives of Yathrib did not immediately become Muslims in the fully devout sense, they did recognize that it was in their interest to give the new arbitration plan a chance for political, economic, and social purposes. An outsider, although not welcome by all parties, could at least claim neutrality.

Muḥammad did not insist that his fellow Muslims move to Yathrib, although almost all of them chose to do so. The emigration was achieved without fanfare, with groups moving north at different times, partly to avoid alarm in Mecca. Muḥammad, his close companion, Abū Bakr, and his son-in-law ʿAlī were the last to leave. Just before Muḥammad planned to depart, the Meccans attempted to assassinate him while he slept. But the cautious leader had foreseen this and arranged to have ʿAlī occupy his bed that night. No harm was done to ʿAlī; Muḥammad and Abū Bakr hid in a cave. The patrolling Meccan leaders, thwarted by ʿAlī's ruse, also passed by the mouth of the cave. Legend says that a spider web across the entrance made it look unoccupied.

Muḥammad and Abū Bakr traveled to Yathrib by a circuitous route. On reaching the outskirts of the oasis, the emigrants, along with the curious natives, gathered to greet their leader. Muḥammad thus had a proper reception, which was to prove auspicious for his and Islam's future success. Yathrib came to be called al-Medīna, "The City," because of Muḥammad's move there. (The full name is Medīnat al-Nabī, "The City of the Prophet.") The **Hijra,** or "Emigration," took place in September of 622 C.E. July 1 of that year came to be the beginning of the Muslim calendar[3], because it was with the *Hijra* that the Muslim Umma began.

Several distinct groups came into being as a result of the *Hijra,* both within and outside Islam. Those who made the *Hijra* became known as *Muhājirūn;* they have a special place of honor in Islam. The Medinan supporters of Muḥammad were known as the *Anṣār,* or "helpers." Tradition came to refer to the equivocal or recalcitrant Medinans as *Munāfiqūn,* "hypocrites." Added to these three main groups were the Meccans, who were now the enemy, and the Jews, who occupied a difficult position as monotheists who were skeptical about Muḥammad's religious authority but for a time cooperated with and even worshiped alongside the Muslims. Eventually the Jews would be eliminated from Medina, because of a breach caused by their failure to support Muḥammad against an invading Meccan force. The men were executed and the women and children deported. [See Judaism pp. 409–10, 430 and Christianity pp. 514, 520 for persecution of Jews.]

In Mecca, Muḥammad had organized a religious cult, but in Medina he became the political and military leader as well as the spiritual guide of a far wider movement. The *Hijra* resulted in the founding of the Umma, the Muslim "community," which from that moment has ideally been a union of "church" and state, with no essential distinction between religious and secular life. The revelations of the Qur'ān during the Meccan years emphasized God's absolute unity, sovereign will, justice, and compassion; there was ample warning for humans to repent and submit before an awful judgment would come and divide people into those destined for heaven and those condemned by their wicked ways to hell. Many stories of prophets and their peoples of old were revealed in the Meccan years. In Medina, however, in addition to the themes of judgment and warning, there was much Qur'ānic revelation about communal, ritual, and legal matters. The developing theocracy of the Umma needed guidance of a more mundane, practical sort.

The emigrants experienced difficulty finding their niche within the economic life of Medina. They had been traders in Mecca, but Medina was agricultural. Muḥammad organized his fellow emigrants into raiding parties and gained much booty from attacks on Meccan caravans. In 624 (2 *Hijra*), a large Meccan force rode north to protect a homecoming caravan from the Muslim raiders. The two forces, approximately 950 Meccans and 300 Muslims from Medina, met in a bloody battle at the wells of Badr, near Medina. The outnumbered Muslims routed the Meccans and gained an enduring sense that day that God had sent his angels to fight on the side of Muḥammad. This "Day of Discrimination" has remained in Muslim memory and sentiment a providential sign of God's special favor.

Even though the Muslims suffered serious defeats in two later engagements with Meccan punitive expeditions, the Umma continued to grow and thrive. Muḥammad as a charismatic prophet succeeded in forging pacts and agreements with a great variety of tribal leaders all over Arabia, so that by 628 he and his followers were strong enough to plan an attack on Mecca. Instead a pilgrimage was substituted and Muḥammad and the Meccans established a tenyear truce, which was broken a couple of years later by Mecca. Muḥammad thus mounted another military expedition in 630 but finally relented and simply demanded the evacuation of Mecca and its conversion to Islam from idolatry. Muḥammad entered the city as conqueror without bloodshed. He proceeded to destroy the idols in the *Ka'ba* and rededicated the ancient shrine to Islam.

The main characteristics of Islamic belief and practices were developed largely in the Medinan period. By the time of Muḥammad's death in 632, the ritual and symbolic dimensions of the new religion had incorporated many elements of the Arabian mythic past, as well as specific ritual practices and customs. Certain continuities from the past were considered to be part of Muḥammad's restoration of the primeval Arabian monotheism of Abraham and included aspects, for example, of the later Muslim pilgrimage to Mecca known as the **Ḥajj.**

Muḥammad's personal life was filled with drama and people. Of the Prophet's numerous marriages after Khadīja's death, that with the young, vivacious

The Holy Ka'ba in the Grand Mosque, Mecca. The black covering contains
Qur'ānic passages embroidered in silver and gold. (Photo used by permission of
Abdulaziz A. Sachedina.)

'Ā'isha (Abū Bakr's daughter) proved most satisfying. Muḥammad never became
personally wealthy, but he did give much to others over the years. His home in
Medina was also the site of the main mosque of the community. Muḥammad
often had to meet with petitioners there as well as judge disputes, just as Moses
had done with the Jews in the Sinai wilderness. The Qur'ān draws parallels
between the two prophets. [See Religions of Africa pp. 29, 55–57, Religions of
Mesoamerica pp. 152, 163–68, Native Religions of North America pp. 266–67,
Christianity pp. 495–97, 531–32, 534–35, Hinduism pp. 769, 770–72, Buddhism
pp. 860, 861–68, 892–99, Religions of China pp. 993–95, and Religions of Japan
pp. 1090, 1100, 1122–23 for discussion of religious founders.]

Muḥammad's great political acumen enabled him to extend the prestige of
the Umma throughout Arabia by the time of his death. Not all tribes that concluded agreements with him or submitted to his power actually became Muslims at the time, but Muḥammad did require that all who entered into covenants
with him pay the **Zakāt,** or "alms." According to old Arabian custom, all pacts
were automatically dissolved on the death of a great leader. What was different
about the Umma was that the pact was essentially between the parties and God,
who is eternal; therefore the pact was permanent. After the death of Muḥammad the outlying tribes especially had to be convinced of the enduring nature
of the agreements they had prudently, if sometimes hastily, made with the Arabian Prophet. The wars of apostasy, known as the Ridda, which broke out in Arabia after the Prophet's death, restored and strengthened the incomplete Arabian
unity first achieved by Muḥammad based on a single idea of governance and
belief. That is, Muḥammad's successors compelled recalcitrant groups to return
to Islam and the Umma. Much of the old tribal system continued into Islamic
times—and still does—but faith rather than blood relation became the uniting
principle of the Umma and remains so on a global scale today.

The Caliphate

The Rightly Guided Caliphs:
Abū Bakr, 'Umar, 'Uthmān, and 'Alī

Muḥammad's closest and staunchest companions moved quickly after his death to ensure a smooth and stable succession. Abū Bakr, one of the chief converts from the Meccan days, was selected by a small group to be **khalīfa** ("caliph"), or "deputy," of the Prophet. The caliphal position was political and military, but not religious, at least in the sense that Muḥammad had been a religious authority. Muḥammad was declared by the Qur'ānic revelation to be the "Seal" of prophecy, which means both the final prophet and the validation of earlier prophets from Adam through Jesus.

Abū Bakr ruled during a brief but critically important period from 632 to 634 when many groups had pulled away from the Umma. He presided over the struggles that brought the Arabs back into the Islamic fold. His successor was the redoubtable 'Umar, one of the greatest additions to the Muslim cause during late Meccan times, who as caliph masterminded and led the great Arab-Islamic conquests in Palestine, Syria, Egypt, North Africa, Iraq, and the Iranian highlands and beyond. 'Umar was the first caliph to bear the title "Commander of the Faithful." He was both respected and feared. His personal integrity was legendary and his frugality extreme. 'Umar ruled an ever-increasing territory until he was killed by a servant in 644.

Abū Bakr and 'Umar and others who had been at the Prophet's side from Meccan times comprised a sort of Islamic aristocracy, distinguished from the Qurayshī elite of wealthy and influential individuals like the Banū Umayya. After 'Umar's untimely death, the Muslim leaders settled on a compromise candidate, 'Uthmān. 'Uthmān was a member of the Banū Umayya clan and the only representative of the Meccan oligarchy to have converted to Islam during the difficult Meccan years. He was a pious and personally upright man, but as caliph he earned the censure and disrespect of many by his weakness and nepotism. His major achievement was the commissioning of a group of experts to collect all the known copies and variants of the Qur'ān and establish a standard text, which would be used by all Muslims. 'Uthmān came to a tragic end when dissidents stormed his residence in Medina and killed him even while he was standing on the pulpit and holding the Qur'ān in his mosque. The killing of 'Uthmān would continue as a bitter memory in many future events of the Islamic community, dividing the Muslims politically and spiritually.

'Uthmān's successor and the last of the line of so-called "rightly guided" caliphs was 'Alī ibn Abī Tālib, who was both cousin and son-in-law of Muḥammad and thus a member of "The People of the House," as the Prophet's exalted family were called. 'Alī became leader of a significant faction called the **Shī'a,** which literally means "party." 'Alī and his followers (called Shī'ites) claimed that Muḥammad, before he died, had designated 'Alī as his rightful successor. As it turned out, the majority of Muslims (who would later be called **Sunnīs**) rejected this claim. 'Alī, however, had felt frustrated each time a new caliph was chosen instead of him. In 656, upon 'Uthmān's death, he finally came into his own as caliph. By that time, the spread of Islamic power and peoples had reached to distant Khurasan in eastern Iran and Afghanistan. The entire Fertile Crescent (the "cradle of civilization" composed of Palestine, Syria, and Mesopotamia) and the nearer reaches of North Africa were also part of the *Dār al-Islām*. 'Alī moved the capital from Medina to Kufa, a new garrison settlement at the desert's edge near the Euphrates River in Iraq. This was a more central location, making possible swift communications with the new Muslim provinces east and west.

However, 'Alī's rule was filled with problems. Although he appears not to have instigated or even condoned the killing of 'Uthmān, neither did he punish the guilty party after he ascended to the caliphate. The still powerful and perennially proud Umayya clan (of which 'Uthmān had been a member) resisted 'Alī's rule and ultimately brought it to an end. Mu'āwiya, nephew of 'Uthmān, who had been installed in Damascus as governor of Syria by the great 'Umar, challenged 'Alī's right to the caliphate. 'Alī's and Mu'āwiya's armies met at Siffin on the upper Euphrates in 657. After protracted skirmishing and fruitless negotiations, the Umayyad side, prompted by the conqueror of Egypt, 'Amr ibn al-'As, raised Qur'ān pages on their spears and called for a deliberation in which God would decide the matter of who should rule. 'Alī agreed against the wishes of his staunchest supporters. The deliberation, conducted by respected experts on both sides—but with the partisan 'Amr arguing the case for Mu'āwiya—resulted in a decision against 'Alī. 'Alī rejected the unfavorable decision, but he had made the mistake of agreeing to arbitration in the first place. After three more years of attempting to rule a thoroughly fractious Umma split between Umayyads and Shī'ites, 'Alī was finally assassinated by a rebellious member of the new Khārijite faction in 661.

The "Arab Kingdom" of the Umayyads, 661–750

Mu'āwiya became the first caliph of the Umayyad dynasty, which ruled about ninety years from its capital in Damascus. The old Qurayshī aristocracy was now in control of the political fortunes of the Umma. The humiliation of 'Uthmān's assassination was somewhat relieved, although the deed would continue to rankle for generations. Opponents and successors of the Umayyad dynasty derisively referred to it as the "Arab Kingdom," with the word "Arab" signifying ethnic particularism and old *Jāhilīya* habits and "Kingdom" symbolizing haughtiness and worldliness (because God alone is true king of the Umma).

Despite such criticism, the Umayyads succeeded in building a powerful state apparatus. They were, for the greater part, responsible Muslims who took seriously the duty to declare holy war against the Christian Byzantine Empire, with its capital in Constantinople (later Istanbul). The Umayyads also greatly extended the borders of the Islamic world, across North Africa and through Spain into France in the west, and to the Indus and as far north as the Jaxartes River in south and central Asia.

Damascus did not turn out to be the best center for the expanding Islamic empire, although it was certainly central, given the extent of the domains east and west. As mentioned, 'Alī had moved his government to Iraq, and his followers continued to be active there and farther east in the Iranian highlands and Khurasan. In 680, when the Umayyad caliph Mu'āwiya died, his son Yazīd ascended the throne. But in Iraq a movement favoring Ḥusayn, the son of 'Alī, gained strength. The Iraqi Arabs resented Syrian rule and they persuaded others in their region to support the grandson of the Prophet. Ḥusayn and his family and some loyal Shī'ites (those loyal to 'Alī and his line as true caliphs) traveled to Iraq to join with the movement there, but they were intercepted by stronger caliphal forces and Ḥusayn and his men were annihilated at **Karbalā'**, northwest of Kufa. The tragedy occurred on the tenth of the Muslim month of Muḥarram, a traditional day of fasting, which ever since has been the Shī'ite day of mourning for its blessed martyrs. The Shī'ite movement, favoring a caliph descended from the Prophet's family through 'Alī and Fāṭima, has ever since the Karbalā' disaster had a tragic cast in its worldview in which redemptive suffering is a major theme. Shī'ite hagiography later elevated Ḥusayn to restorer of the original Islam of his grandfather, sinless intercessor for his people, and infallible guide (***imām***).

The International Islamic Order of the 'Abbāsids

The Umayyads ruled until 750, when a Shī'ite-inspired revolution toppled the Damascus caliphate and installed a new dynasty in Iraq known as the **'Abbāsids,** after 'Abbās, the father of the first 'Abbāsid caliph 'Abd Allāh. The 'Abbāsids came to power proclaiming a new order of egalitarianism and brotherhood based on the old Medinan community of Muḥammad and the "rightly guided" caliphs. By 750 the Umma was composed of many different ethnic, linguistic, and cultural groups that had gradually converted to Islam. During Umayyad times Islam was largely an Arab affair. But the religion could not be ethnically contained, for spiritual as well as material reasons. To be a Muslim brought privileges and status. At first, non-Arabs became Muslims by becoming attached to an Arab tribe as a client. Soon there were many clients who provided ready recruits for the revolution against the Umayyads. After the 'Abbāsids had been in power for a short time, however, they began to behave like pre-Islamic oriental despots in traditional Mesopotamia, whether of Babylonian, Assyrian, or Persian times.

During the 'Abbāsid centuries, from 750 until the Mongols brought the dynasty to a decisive end in 1258 with the destruction of Baghdad, the greatest accomplishments of Islamic civilization were achieved. Art and architecture flourished, as did crafts, trade, military tactics, and strategy. Scholars made great strides in mathematics, medicine, geography, astronomy, philosophy, and the systematic study of languages—especially Arabic, because it is the language of Qur'ānic revelation. The religious sciences of law, theology, Qur'ānic exegesis, and scholarly criticism of Prophetic traditions (***Ḥadīth***) came to maturity in the ninth and tenth centuries.

New waves of people came to dominate in the central 'Abbāsid territories, especially Turkish groups that had migrated from the steppes and mountains of inner Asia. In Baghdad, a round, fortified city built early in the dynasty's history on the Tigris, the caliphs declined in actual political and military power from about 900, although they continued until the end to wield immense symbolic and moral influence. Practical affairs of state and warfare were in the hands of strongmen, who took such titles as *amīr*, "commander," and *sultān*, "ruler."

The caliphate provided at least symbolic unity for the vast Muslim domains of 'Abbāsid times. As early as the first century of 'Abbāsid rule, however, an independent Umayyad dynasty was established in Spain by the sole remaining member of the royal family, 'Abdul Rahmān. Spain developed a brilliant Islamic civilization of its own, with arts, commerce, sciences, letters, and religious scholarship that did not suffer in comparison with the achievements of the central Islamic lands from Egypt to Afghanistan. Muslims remained in Spain, known in Arabic as al-Andalus (Andalusia), for nearly eight centuries, although their political dominance declined steadily from around the eleventh century, when the Umayyad dynasty there ended. In 1492, the remaining Muslims were forcibly ejected from Spain, and the Christian reconquest of the Iberian Peninsula was achieved under King Ferdinand and Queen Isabella. [See Christianity pp. 570–71 for discussion of Islam in Spain.]

After the invading Mongols' sack of Baghdad in 1258, attempts at restoring the caliphate were made, most notably in Egypt, but the office never regained real power, in spite of attempts to assume it by occasional strongmen up to recent times. It is a tribute to the integrity of the Umma that the title "caliph" could not be easily assumed. Over the centuries, certain prerequisites had come to be accepted for the office, not the least of which was Qurayshī descent. The sacredness of the position of caliph seemed to increase with its political weakening. As recently as the post–World War I period, a "khilafatist" (from *khilāfa*, "caliphate") movement was active in the Middle East and southern Asia, but the final disestablishment of what was left of the caliphate under the Ottomans by the new Turkish and westernizing dictator Mustafa Kemal Ataturk (1881–1938) dashed the khilafatists' last hopes.

The spread of Islamic political power and the development of an international civilization were not the achievements solely of the mainline caliphs introduced above. Islamic rulers and thinkers, traders and artisans, succeeded in many other places as well. Tenth-century Egypt was the arena for the development of a remarkable Shī'ite caliphate, the Fāṭimids, which was quite independent from Baghdad. The Fāṭimids (named after the Prophet's daughter, Fāṭima, who married 'Alī) founded Cairo in 969 and later established the Azhar University, the Umma's greatest center of religious learning up to the present. Islamic empires arose in Iran, central Asia, Southeast Asia, and the Indian subcontinent. The Turkish Ottoman Empire came to greatness in the fifteenth century and succeeded in dominating not only the Arabic-speaking countries of the Near East and North Africa, but also the Black Sea lands, southeastern Europe, and the Danube territories to the doorstep of Vienna. Farther east, a great

Persian Shī'ite empire was established under the Safavids, while in the subcontinent Bābūr founded the Mughal dynasty, which would rule India until the early eighteenth century. [See Religions of Africa pp. 24, 35, 60, Religions of Mesoamerica pp. 198–201, Native Religions of North America pp. 347–48, Judaism pp. 391–92, Christianity pp. 503, 505, Hinduism p. 748, Buddhism pp. 875–77, 952–53, Religions of China pp. 991–93, and Religions of Japan pp. 1095–96, 1105–6 for the relationship of religion to political leaders.]

The Ways in Which Islam Spread

There is a long-lived myth that the great Arab conquests spread Islam by the sword throughout the Near East and North Africa. The conquests in fact were not primarily religious, but economic and political, enabling the newly united Arab tribes to continue their momentum as a politically and economically feasible community. Religious faith was certainly the most important element in uniting the varied Arab tribes in the grand venture upon which they engaged. But in the early conquests, there was a clear distinction made between the Muslim Arabs and the subject peoples. Only gradually did non-Arabs embrace Islam, and for a variety of reasons, not the least being a share in the benefits of the Islamic empire. Christians, Jews, and other religious communities with a Scripture—"People of the Book" as the Qur'ān calls them—were accorded "protected" status and required to pay a poll tax. The tax was levied in return for protection and government. Muslims did not pay it, because they already had to pay the religious tax, *Zakāt,* which is a specified proportion of various forms of property.

Within Arabia, particularly, conversion to Islam was forced on idolaters, but not on People of the Book. Motivated more by national pride, even fanaticism, than by fear of annihilation, pagan Arabs flocked to Islam. This strong group feeling, called *'aṣabīya,* was known long before Islam on the clan and tribal levels. But it was not until Muḥammad and the Qur'ān came along that a faith and identity strong enough to transcend kinship and regional particularities enabled the Arabs to coalesce into a nation, in fact an Umma 'Arabīya, "Arabian Community."

Throughout the Near East and North Africa, conversion was generally a voluntary affair, but at times non-Muslims suffered persecution, discrimination, and other indignities. Gradually the Christian communities diminished in size and vigor in countries where they had been strong before Islam. In sub-Saharan Africa, Islam entered through Ethiopia and the Sudan in the east and from the Berber regions in North Africa in the west. Trade was an important means of Islam's spread, but military conquest was also significant. In the subcontinent of India, Muslim military invasion from early times was important in spreading Islam and converting Hindus. But force was not always used. Immigration from the northwest added many Muslims to the population, as did the conversion of Hindus. [See Hinduism pp. 766–68 for discussion of Islam in India.] Southeast

Asia, the lands that today hold Malaysia, the southern Philippines, Indonesia, and Brunei, began to convert to Islam at least by the twelfth and thirteenth centuries, when Marco Polo passed through north Sumatra and reported Muslim towns there. From Sumatra, Islam spread across the Straits of Malacca to the Malay Peninsula, and then down to the north coast of Java. Merchants and traders of mystical Islamic bent were most prominent in spreading Islam peacefully throughout the Malay-Indonesian archipelago, so that today half of Malaysia, virtually all of Brunei, and 90 percent of Indonesia are Muslim. There are also sizable Muslim populations in the southern Philippines and in southern Thailand.

In this century, Islamic missionary activities and the migration of Muslims from the Middle East and southern Asia, especially, have brought Islam to Western Europe and the Americas.

Muslim Political Weakening and the Rise of the West

International Islamic political power reached its height during the fifteenth through the seventeenth centuries, when the Ottoman Turks, the Iranian Safavids, and the Indian Mughals ruled vast empires stretching from North Africa to Bengal. But that period saw also the rapid accumulation of political and economic power in Europe, especially in connection with the development of new trade routes around Africa and across the Atlantic and Pacific oceans. Western nations, especially Britain, France, and the Netherlands, colonized and exploited extensive Muslim territories in North Africa, India, and Southeast Asia. By the nineteenth century, the Ottoman Empire was retreating from its eastern European enclaves and effectively giving up real power in some of its Middle East countries such as Egypt, Libya, Tunisia, and Algeria. The Anatolian Peninsula was the last outpost of the Ottoman Empire, but it was transformed into the modern nation-state of Turkey after World War I and was never colonized. Turkey has continued to be staunchly Muslim.

During this century, European colonialism has nearly disappeared from the world, but the effects of it are still apparent. However, as early as the late eighteenth century, significant Muslim reform movements arose in Egypt, Arabia, and India that started the slow process of winning back Muslims' sense of confidence and ability to govern themselves. The aftermath of World War II included the independence of many Muslim countries all over Eurasia, Africa, and the Indonesian archipelago. In predominantly Muslim countries such as Pakistan, Bangladesh, Egypt, Indonesia, Iran, and Algeria independence in the political sense has been closely associated with strong Islamic faith and practice. The old Islamic triumphalist and success attitudes have returned in strength and, more than satisfying Muslims' desires to live independent of outside control, have increasingly found expression in vigorous missionary activities both at home and abroad, especially in non-Muslim regions. These and related matters will be treated in chapter 28.

26
The Structures of Muslim Life

IMPORTANT AS THE BASIC ELEMENTS of the history of Islam's rise and development are for historical analysis and interpretation, they do not provide an adequate sense of what the structures of Muslim belief and life are for the believers.
In this chapter, we will consider the basic "story" of Islam from an Islamic viewpoint and the claims the religion makes about the human condition and the
ways in which it seeks to realize them at the individual and communal levels.

The Central "Story" of Islam: Good News and Warning

Muḥammad is the centrally important human figure in the drama of Islam's rise
and early development into a comprehensive and successful system of religious
beliefs, devotional practices, and community ordering. But Muḥammad is not
the basic cause of Islam's coming into the world. That fundamental cause is the
conviction among his people that God was entering definitively into the Arabian
scene and commanding their attention in novel ways.

The Arabic Qur'ān, that remarkable collection of recitations revealed to
Muḥammad, was collected after the Prophet's death and circulated among the
Muslims in all the places they came to inhabit. This urgent message called the
early generations of Muslims to reflect on the old ways of Arabia, so as to realize
the chasm between them and the new dispensation of Islamic monotheism.
But, more important, the Qur'ān continues to command and instruct people in
the present as it challenges them to consider their futures as obedient servants
of God.

The story of Islam as understood by Muslims is grounded in the Qur'ān. The
Qur'ān teaches that God created the heavens and the earth, that he is One and
untouched by his creation, that his angels carry out his decisions and communicate with humans through prophetic inspiration. God has entrusted prophets of

old with his message of justice, mercy, and a final judgment, with salvation in paradise for believers and fiery damnation in hell for infidels. God's justice, tempered by compassion, requires that he communicate this message to all people. The Arabs were the last human community to receive the message, and through their transformation into the Muslim community they were entrusted with the task of calling all people to Islam. The Qur'ān calls the Muslim community, the Umma—which in the time of its revelation meant the Arabian monotheists who followed Muḥammad's way—a "mid-most community," marked by balanced moderation and awareness of its responsibility to serve as the model for the Muslim community in its ever-expanding future development beyond Arabia.

The Qur'ān often calls people to reflect on God's providential signs: in the natural world, in the seasonal round of plant and animal life and the regular courses of the heavenly bodies; and in history, in the wonderful deliverances of upright people and the deserved punishment of wayward folk in the Arab, Jewish, and Christian traditions. A recurrent theme is humans' ingratitude for the blessings they have received. The Qur'ānic term for "infidel" is actually shaded more toward meaning one who lacks thankfulness, rather than one who disbelieves merely as an act of the mind. There is something fundamentally wrong with a person who fails to acknowledge with wonder and gratitude all that he or she has received without effort or asking. Such a person ignores, or, as the Qur'ān says, "covers" or "hides" God's blessings and thus fails to enjoy the close linkage with the Creator that is his or her birthright. [See Religions of Africa pp. 39–42, 64–69, Religions of Mesoamerica pp. 157–58, 186–89, Native Religions of North America pp. 288–305, 330–32, Judaism pp. 414–15, Christianity pp. 537–38, Hinduism pp. 739–41, 759–61, Buddhism pp. 780–84, Religions of China pp. 900–903, 1024–26, and Religions of Japan pp. 1112–27 for discussion of God, gods, and objects of worship.]

At the core of this notion of gratitude versus ingratitude is the Qur'ānic good news that humans have been created with a sound nature and provided by God with a true religion that enables them to have fullness of life through close communion with God in this world and the next. Each human is a religiously grounded person, created and endowed with a *fiṭra,* a "sound constitution" that acts as a kind of internal guidance system and way to God. That is our "natural" birthright. But humans also are cultural beings, in that God has permitted, indeed commanded, them to participate in the creation of meaning in this life and to be lords over all other aspects of creation. The Qur'ānic word for such a human "lord" is *caliph* (Arabic *khalīfa*), which means "deputy" or "vicegerent" of God on earth. The religio-political rulers of the Islamic empire in its first centuries thus received their title of caliph from the Qur'ān. They and their institution failed in the long run, but the notion of God's caliphate has persisted, with its deepest meaning being each Muslim's own commitment to ruling for God in this life by means of the opportunities that are available and through the abilities and knowledge one has been granted.

Mystically inclined Muslims have always been captivated by a saying Muḥammad attributed to divine inspiration that God was a "Hidden Treasure," who wanted to be known and so he created the world of sentient beings for community with himself. We humans, according to this story, are endowed with the divine nature to the extent that God is pleased to contemplate himself through our own being and devotion, in a kind of mirroring of his glory and goodness.

To be satisfied with our lower selves and to stray from what God has provided in the way of our natural capacities, on the one side, and from our privileged access to revelation in the form of the Qur'ān and the Scriptures that preceded it, on the other, is to be guilty of both moral and intellectual error. Islam provides the way back to God, through a vital process of living in this world in God's presence by means of faith, obedience, and abiding hope. If we persist in our individual, straying paths, satisfied with ourselves and blinded by feelings of self-sufficiency, we shall, the Qur'ān warns, be doomed.

In summary, the Qur'ān provides the good news of what we are, where we came from, and where we are bidden to go as faithful servants of God. But the Qur'ān also warns us of the "awful journey's end" for those who fail to return by repentance to the "Straight Path" of submission and faith—whether by outright refusal by hardness of heart and opaqueness of reasoning or by placing our individual egos ahead of God's service. To reject God is to reject our true nature and to refuse to realize our true nature, our *fiṭra,* is to be astray and bound for loss. We cannot destroy our *fiṭra,* but we can fail to be fulfilled by it, because God has provided along with it the freedom for us to imagine and to choose. Free will, not fatalism, is at the heart of Islam's teaching about the human condition, but this freedom is not license nor is it by itself a guarantee of success. Rather, free will is the necessary condition of success, whereas God's will and power and compassionate relenting are its final cause. [See Religions of Mesoamerica p. 179, Native Religions of North America p. 285, Judaism pp. 390–94, Christianity pp. 497, 499, Hinduism pp. 728–29, 738–43, 750–53, Buddhism p. 861, Religions of China pp. 995–96, 999–1000, 1031, and Religions of Japan pp. 1100, 1101 for discussion of Bible, scriptures, and religious texts.]

The Goal of Islam:
"Success" in This World and the Next

Most religions have some sort of doctrine of salvation, in the sense that they envision the possibility of attaining a better state than the one that comes about in the normal, this-worldly course of events. Of course the word *salvation* is not universal, but the concept is found in most traditions. However, the term *salvation* is native to Islam. For example, it may mean a literal deliverance, as when the Qur'ān tells of Jonah having been delivered from the belly of the great fish, a story that it shares with the Bible. But the most characteristic word that Muslims use to express their final religious goal, although it is sometimes translated as "salvation" even by Muslims, is best rendered as "success." A typical Qur'ānic definition of this notion is contained in a passage that sets forth the virtue of the revealed Word:

This is the Scripture whereof there is no doubt, a guidance unto those who ward off evil. Who believe in the unseen, and establish worship, and spend of that We have bestowed upon them; And who believe in that which is revealed unto thee (Muḥammad) and that which was revealed before thee, and are certain of the Hereafter. These depend on guidance from their Lord. These are the *successful*. (2:2–5)

Muslims believe that God alone is able to bring about his servants' success, but the efforts of the Muslims are essential, too. Faith and works both procure God's blessings and reward, but the very faith that uplifts the Muslim is itself God's gracious gift, too.

God saves the repentant sinner who mends her or his ways sincerely, but God will not accept the repentance of the inveterate infidel who is at the verge of death. There must have been an established pattern of repentance and good works, even if it was preceded by a life of evil-doing and unbelief or marred by occasional lapses. But there is nothing in humans that is essentially—that is, fundamentally and irrevocably—evil. At their core, recall, humans are constituted according to the *fiṭra*. Therefore no doctrine of salvation ever developed in Islam—at least in the dominant Sunnī majority—that required an atoning, or substitutionary, sacrifice in which wayward and sinful humans are "bought back," *redeemed* and rendered acceptable to God through sheer grace, as in Christian salvation doctrine.

Muslims do acknowledge sin and its ravages, but they consider God's guidance in the Qur'ān and his constant presence and goading compassion to be all that humans need to direct them aright, bringing them, because of their good center, back to the truth. Far from being alienated from God, humankind's own thirst for justice and balance, which can be witnessed even among secular, atheistic persons, is testimony to the Divine Justice, which has determined our deeply ethical natures from our creation. Not to recognize the source of our ethical yearnings and convictions is not to display a corrupt nature per se; it is to be guilty of identifying a false ultimate: ourselves or some other aspect of the created world. Recognizing a false ultimate, known by Muslims as **shirk,** is the one unforgivable sin according to the Qur'ān.

The greatest danger to humankind is, thus, *shirk,* idolatrous association of something with God. The Islamic doctrine of *shirk* and its unforgiveableness is harsh, to be sure, but in application the doctrine means that a *habitual,* unrelenting pursuit of what the modern Protestant Christian theologian Paul Tillich calls an "idolatrous ultimate concern" carries with it its own death sentence. Idolatry, at bottom, whether it is a credulous worship of an actual graven image or the crazed pursuit of wealth, power, pleasure, or fame is like betting on the wrong horse or investing in a bankrupt cause. *Shirk* is the refusal to recover the divinely appointed and life-giving *fiṭra* in our inmost being. *Shirk* is denying the truth about *ourselves* just as much as it is a literal focus on something other than God. Our lower selves, our greedy and vain feelings of self-sufficiency, are actually not the most real parts of us. To act as if they were is to cut ourselves off from God by denying his ground within us. *Shirk,* then, is not so much a matter leading to God's refusing to forgive us as it is our refusal to acknowledge him. How can he forgive that, and even if he "can," why, in a universe established according to justice, *should* he? Do people, who have been invested with intellect enough to conceive of the divine nobility and nature, want to end up with a God who overlooks and in the act ignores our stupidity? Our perverse failure to be our true selves is damnable, Islam argues.

The success that Muslims hope for in this world runs the gamut from ordinary physical and emotional well-being—like the biblical Job's blessed existence before his trials: a large, happy family, many cattle, and the admiration and respect of his associates—to more inward states marked by serene joy, steadfast patience, faith in adversity, honest dealing in the face of treachery and defeat, and intelligent regard for the wondrous gifts of this life, be they pleasant or painful. In fact, the greatest success in this life seems for Muslims to be blessed with the faithful, accepting patience that endures all misfortunes and seeks the final outcome only in God's justice and reward. Success in this sense is itself believed to be proof of God's abiding presence. It is not an obvious kind of worldly good fortune but a kind of spiritual poverty of total resignation to God.

The success of the life to come is eternal and sublime beyond the ability of human words to describe. The Qur'ān speaks of heavenly gardens, with sheltering trees, pure brooks and rivers, beautiful serving maidens, and continual joyful praise of God. But thoughtful Muslims of all periods have also discerned in the vivid Qur'ānic depictions of paradise deeper, symbolic levels that ultimately transcend worldly physical description and the life of the senses.

The Realization of the Goal of Islam in Faithful and Observant Communal Life

Muslims believe that they have been called by God to establish a righteous human political and social order on earth. The only way to live gratefully as God's caliphs is to make full use of what he has bestowed on humankind. The fundamental Islamic doctrine of the divine unity requires a unified human religious community as well. *Tawhīd* is the Islamic name for this unity. But it is not a matter of mere number, in the sense that one is different from two and three and so forth. Rather, *tawhīd* means "unification"; it has verbal force. Muslims declare God to be One and reinforce, indeed *embody*, that declaration with strenuous efforts at unity in their doctrinal, ritual-devotional, and communal lives, which are regulated by the Qur'ān and Muhammad's teaching and example as contained in his Sunna.

Faith

The elements of Islamic faith, known as **imān,** can be briefly summarized, even though there has never been anything like a universal uniform creed in the sense of a formal statement that Muslims have been required to recite and endorse. The closest thing to such is the **Shahāda,** the "witnessing" both to the unity of God and the messengerhood of Muḥammad. But this two-part utterance does not have sufficient specific detail to be a comprehensive creed; rather it provides a crisp summary of the two vast areas of theological awareness and reflection: God and humankind, the vertical dimension being belief in no god but God and the horizontal dimension being the recognition that Muḥammad has been chosen to be God's messenger on the human historical plane. But nothing is said in the *Shahāda* about the Qur'ān, or about the Last Judgment, or other central elements of Islamic faith.

The first basic doctrine of Islam is the belief in the divine unity, *tawḥīd.* This belief is easy to declare but difficult to understand and apply; indeed, the whole edifice of Muslim religion is dedicated to realizing *tawḥīd.* The second great doctrine is belief in angels as the divinely appointed agents of God's revelatory activity and helpers in myriad other tasks. The third is belief in prophecy and sacred books that have been revealed to prophets in the past and, especially, acceptance of Muḥammad and the Qur'ān as the final "seal" of the cycle of prophecy in history. The fourth belief is in the Last Day, when all the dead will be raised and humankind shall be gathered before the Judgment Seat of God, the righteous to be saved in eternal heavenly bliss and the unbelievers to be cast down guilty into hell. The final doctrine is the Divine Decree and Predestination. Its workings are a mystery to humans, who nevertheless are given sufficient freedom and responsibility to make genuine moral and spiritual decisions.

The Pillars of Islam

In chapter 24 we considered Islam to be a religion with an emphasis on orthoprax issues; that is, the *acting out* of basic beliefs and attitudes is central. This orthoprax character of Islam can best be seen in the five basic devotional-ritual duties called the **Pillars of Islam,** required of every Muslim; these work together to form a potent inner structure for the Umma and at the same time demarcate it from and defend it against outsiders.

Muslims have a strong sense of distinction between themselves and non-Muslims. The universal Islamic greeting *as-salāmu 'alaykum,* "Peace be upon you!" is normally used only between Muslims. It is forbidden for female Muslims to marry outside the faith and male Muslims who do are restricted to monotheistic spouses, and children of such a union are considered Muslim and must be brought up so. The closed community of the Umma is not inhospitable to outsiders in the sense of being cold or indifferent to common human needs and problems. Rather, the Umma is closed in the sense that it does not permit its members to stray outside the fold and still be considered Muslim.

SHAHĀDA   As far as welcoming outsiders into the fellowship of faith is concerned, the gates are wide open at all times and there is always hearty rejoicing when a person responds to the call of Islam, pronounces the *Shahāda,* and becomes a brother or sister in the faith. It is necessary only to perform the first pillar of uttering the *Shahāda* ("I bear witness that 'There is no god but God'; I bear witness that 'Muḥammad is the messenger of God.'") once, with sincere conviction, to become a Muslim.

Once, in a university class on Islam, one of my students was inspired to utter the *Shahāda* in the middle of my lecture. He had evidently been thinking about his potential commitment to Islam for some time, but when he felt the call of God in the classroom, he could not resist. Two Muslim students in the class embraced the student and together the three performed a joyful prayer prostration while the class looked on in surprise, awe, and respect lightened by cheerfulness.

ṢALĀT: WORSHIP The Pillars of Islam begin with the *Shahāda,* which is both a doctrinal declaration and an act of public witnessing. As soon as this brief confession has been uttered, the appropriate next expression is formal worship, known as **Ṣalāt.** This act of worship is the most frequently performed and pervasive of Islam's devotional duties; it is required five times daily and also at other times such as funerals and eclipses. The *Ṣalāt* is highly formalized and minutely regulated in its precisely observed cycles of spoken formulas and bodily postures. Prescribed in the Qur'ān and developed by Muḥammad for the earliest Muslims, the *Ṣalāt* has bound the Umma together across the ages and geographical frontiers of Islam at a more nearly uniform level of performance than the practice of any other world religion. There is no priestly clergy in Islam, so all adult Muslims must know the *Ṣalāt* and be able to lead it if called upon.

Worshipers prostrating during the Friday Ṣalāt *in an overflow congregation at the Masid Jame (Friday Mosque) in the heart of Kuala Lumpur, Malaysia.*

Muslims learn early how to perform the *Ṣalāt* as they are trained to form straight rows behind the *imām,* the prayer leader who serves as a pattern and pacer for the series of standings, bowings, prostrations, and sittings that make up a cycle within the service. All eyes are directed straight ahead, with the heart and mind focused on precisely what is to be done during the service. The entire congregation faces in the direction of Mecca and the sacred *Ka'ba* there. The *Ṣalāt* is observed at dawn, at noon, during the mid-afternoon, just after the sun has set, and in the evening. A prescribed number of cycles is required at each of these times, but each worshiper may also perform additional ones.

A prime prerequisite for performing the *Ṣalāt* is ritual purification for every individual; usually (unless there is major impurity) purification is achieved by means of simple washing of the face, head, ears, mouth, nostrils, hands and arms to the elbows, feet, and ankles, while uttering certain invocations for purity and guidance. However, if the individual has experienced what is considered a major impurity, such as sexual intercourse or contact with foul substances such as pigs or dog saliva, then she or he is obliged to perform a major ablution in the form of a ritualized full bath of the entire body. Purification is of such great importance for Muslims that they constantly distinguish between a pure state and an impure state. This distinction stems from the closed nature of the Umma and protects it. Closely associated with purity and avoidance of impurity is the legal division of the world and human actions into the basic categories of permitted and forbidden. Not only is it forbidden to perform the *Ṣalāt* without first becoming purified, it is understood that if one observes the *Ṣalāt* while impure, the performance is invalid. The *Ṣalāt* is both an individual and a communal ritual act that strongly symbolizes the specialness of the Muslim community and sets it apart from profane and impure objects and associations. "Cleanliness is next to godliness" is as pervasive an ideal among Muslims as it has been among pietistic Protestants.

The English word *mosque* is based on an Arabic word (*masjid*) that simply means "place of prostration." A mosque, then, is not primarily a building, but a ritually dedicated space. The exclusive nature of the Umma is sometimes symbolized in some countries by forbidding non-Muslims to enter a mosque (e.g., Morocco, Iran). Even Muslims must leave their shoes at the door and in all ways deport themselves fittingly.

Muslim religious and aesthetic inspiration have come together in two supreme expressions in the art of Qur'ānic Arabic calligraphy and sacred architecture. The mosque as a building has reached heights of symbolic expression in testimony to the divine unity by means of its simplicity, spaciousness, and manner of drawing the eyes, ears, and hearts to meditation on God. Sometimes mosque architecture has symbolized the vision of the garden of the afterlife in heaven, with pillars resembling tree trunks, and fountains and pools bubbling and spreading out as cool invigorating streams under the trees and domed heavens of the mosque as a miniature paradise.

The first requisite for a mosque is proper placement: The location should be free from pollution (e.g., not next to a tannery or brewery) and the main prostration area must be situated so that the worshipers face toward Mecca (Indonesian Muslims face west, whereas Syrians face south, and so forth).

Mosques always have a niche (or other suitable marker) in the wall that faces Mecca, indicating the proper direction of prayer. The niche may be plain and unadorned or lavishly decorated, but the ritual purpose is unvarying. Next to it is a raised pulpit, with a stairway leading up and a canopy over the top. This pulpit is used whenever a sermon is preached, as at Friday congregational *Ṣalāt,* when Muslims are required to assemble together in a major mosque. The floor must be clean and clutter-free. There are no chairs or benches in mosques; the worshipers perform their services on carpeted or matted floors. Usually there are lamps, a clock, and a library corner with copies of the Qur'ān and other religious books available for study. Adjacent to the worship area is a properly outfitted ablution area, one for males, another for females, with running water (ideally), toilets, and privacy. Usually there is a minaret next to or atop the mosque, from which the call to prayer is chanted. The minaret, in fact, is a universal symbol of Islam. The word comes from the Arabic word for "lighthouse" and the symbolism is obvious—it guides people to the Straight Path of Islam. The call that comes from this lighthouse is God's summons to righteousness and truth: "God is most great! I bear witness that there is no god but God. I bear witness that Muḥammad is the Messenger of God. Hasten to *Ṣalāt!* Hasten to success! God is most great! There is no god but God!"

ZAKĀT: ALMSGIVING   The third Pillar of Islam is legal almsgiving, called *Zakāt.* *Zakāt* is a kind of religious tax on certain types of property and wealth, provided a minimum level is already owned. It is believed that *Zakāt* purifies the remaining property for the giver.

Interior of the mosque at the tomb of the Prophet Abraham, considered to be the patriarch of Judaism, Christianity, and Islam; Hebron, West Bank. The niche marking the direction of Mecca is to the left of center, while the pulpit is to the right.

This almsgiving is rendered at the end of each year for the support of various people: for poor Muslims, for converts who need help getting on their feet (in many societies, leaving a religious community for another has entailed a radical break, sometimes even social and economic "death"), for Muslim debtors of necessity, for Muslim wayfarers in dire straits, for Muslim prisoners of war, for Muslims engaged in the defense of or propagation of Islam, and for those whose job it is to collect *Zakāt.*

Zakāt is not considered charity. Rather, it is a religious obligation and placed right alongside the *Ṣalāt* as a primary act of service to God. The *Ṣalāt* strongly symbolizes the total submission of the Muslims to the one, almighty God; the *Zakāt* symbolizes the solid communal-mindedness of the Muslims, who support each other with their wealth and thus increase not only the cohesiveness and security of the Umma but also render it purer. The Qur'ān likens the *Zakāt* to a good loan paid to God, which he will repay multifold. God thus enjoins the Muslims to participate with him in sustaining the righteous community of faith. Human caliphal activity is a real responsibility and possibility, exercising stewardship of earth's resources. God has endowed his creatures with wealth, and humankind is asked to return it through works enhancing the community. To support the community by *Zakāt,* then, is to worship God.

ṢAWM: FASTING Fasting, known to Muslims as **Ṣawm,** the fourth Pillar of Islam, is also prescribed for Muslims for the whole month of **Ramaḍān,** one of the lunar months of the Muslim calendar lasting either twenty-nine or thirty days. No food, drink, medicine, smoke, or sensual pleasure may be taken from dawn until dark. In the evening it is permitted to eat and enjoy marital relations, and before dawn a meal is eaten to provide sufficient strength for the coming day's activities. The ill, children, the aged, and certain other classes are excused from the fast, although those who can should make it up later.

Ramaḍān is the month in which the Qur'ān first came down upon Muhammad and it is considered auspicious for other reasons, too. Muslims try to improve their spiritual and ethical lives during this holy month. Evenings are spent in special prayer gatherings in mosques, where cycles of pious exercises are recited, some twenty in all. There is congregational recitation of the Qur'ān, as well as increased individual recitation. Some people observe a retreat during the last ten days of Ramaḍān by residing in the mosque.

Ramaḍān is a time of sober reflection and, depending on the season and region, it can be a difficult discipline. But experienced fasters soon get into the rhythm of the observance and testify to physical as well as spiritual benefits of fasting. One of the major benefits is a shared feeling of common humanity, with differences of rank, status, wealth, and other circumstances that distinguish people from each other minimized. With all the effort that the fast entails, Ramaḍān is not a sad or anxiety-ridden period. Evenings are usually joyful occasions and people strive to be at their best at all times and to be especially aware of the dangers of crossness and hasty, angry words. There may be weariness for some, but there is also keenness of perception and self-scrutiny.

At the close of the Ramaḍān fast comes one of the two canonical festivals of the Muslim year, the "Feast of the Fast-Breaking," when Muslims send greeting cards to each other, enjoy special foods, and travel to be with family. A special *Ṣalāt* service opens the festival. [See Religions of Mesoamerica pp. 159–60, 206–8, Native Religions of North America pp. 280–82, 351–54, Judaism pp. 431–33, Christianity pp. 551–53, Hinduism pp. 727, 793–94, Buddhism pp. 890–91, Religions of China pp. 1021–24, and Religions of Japan pp. 1141–46 for discussion of religious calendar and time.]

THE *ḤAJJ*: PILGRIMAGE   The fifth and final Pillar of Islam is the pilgrimage, or *Ḥajj,* to Mecca during the special month established for it. This is the only Pillar that is not absolutely obligatory. It is to be performed only if personal, financial, and family circumstances permit. Completing the *Ḥajj* confers on the pilgrim the honorific title *Ḥajjī,* which may then be attached to the person's name for the rest of his or her life.

The *Ṣalāt* is a continuous exercise in worship and communal strengthening, with ritual concentration directed toward Mecca. The *Ḥajj* permits the worshiper to travel in body to the sacred center, where Muslims believe that Adam and Eve lived, where Abraham and his son Ishmael erected the *Kaʿba* as the first house of worship of the One True God, and where Muḥammad often raised up the *Ṣalāt* and led his fellow believers, even when they were persecuted cruelly as they prostrated in prayer and praise. Prostration was ridiculed as craven by the proud pagan Arabs, but it became a new symbol of pride for Muslims in submission before their Lord.

Pilgrims experience the thrill of seeing, hearing, and meeting fellow believers of all races and languages and cultures from the corners of the globe. Male pilgrims are required to don a two-piece, white, seamless garment, symbolizing their entry into the ritually pure and consecrated state of **iḥrām.** Women may also wear a white garment that covers their entire body and head, but they are also allowed to wear clean, modest clothing in their national styles. When men wear the *iḥrām* garment and women their national dress, Muslims rejoice at this dual symbolism of Muslim unity and equality alongside rich and creative cultural diversity. The Umma, thus, is both strongly focused in its common dedication to God, and brilliantly diffuse in its variegated cultural forms, all of which are turned toward the common task, which God commanded in the Qur'ān, of "enjoining the right and forbidding the wrong."

Although Islam knows no rite of passage into the Umma, the *Ḥajj* can be compared to a ritual of passage marked by separation from one spiritual status and movement to a higher one. The first step in this separation is formal leave-taking and the writing of one's last will and testament. In Mecca, the dedicated state of *iḥrām* requires abstention from sexual relations, from shaving the beard or cutting one's head or body hair, wearing scent or precious ornaments, hunting animals, and uprooting vegetation. The pilgrim is thus separated from everyday life and placed in a special ritual state, a common feature of rites of passage the world over. The actual time of the pilgrimage rites, in Mecca near the *Ka'ba* and in several locales outside, includes ritual reenactments of primordial spiritual events: Pilgrims pray where Abraham prayed; they run in frantic search of water like Hagar did for her defenseless son Ishmael, when they were cast out into the wilderness; they circumambulate the *Ka'ba* seven times on three occasions, just as the monotheistic worshipers of old were believed to do and as Muḥammad prescribed by his example; and they perform a blood sacrifice of consecrated animals in commemoration of Abraham's sacrifice of a ram when God had tested his faith and then released him from the awful command to sacrifice his son (who the Qur'ān identifies as Ishmael).

The climactic event of the *Ḥajj* is a standing ceremony on the Plain of Arafat, several miles from Mecca, near the Mountain of Mercy, where Muḥammad sat astride his camel as he delivered his farewell sermon to the assembled pilgrims in the last year of his life. The standing ceremony begins at noon with a special *Ṣalāt* and continues until sundown. The pilgrims observe a reflective afternoon, seeking God's forgiveness of their sins and resolving to spend the remainder of their lives in renewed and more intense service of God and the Muslims. There may be as many as three million pilgrims gathered in the vast plain for the standing ceremony, ample witness to the great worldwide community of Muslims. If one misses the standing ceremony, for whatever reason, the entire pilgrimage is thus rendered invalid and must be repeated in another annual season. Notice that the standing ceremony focuses on the individual pilgrim's own recommitment, which is renewed in light of the reenactments leading up to it. In ritual studies terminology, this is a "betwixt and between" time when a spiritual transformation and the graduation to the new status occur definitively, the status of *Ḥajjī*.

After the standing ceremony comes the blood sacrifice that extends symbolically back to Abraham. This sacrifice—of sheep, goats, camels, cattle—is of double significance. Not only is it a high point of the pilgrimage, a sort of liturgical release just as it was for Abraham and Ishmael; it is also the one point in the *Ḥajj* when Muslims around the world also participate by means of a Festival *Ṣalāt* and animal sacrifices at home. This observance is known as the Great Feast and with the Feast of Fast-Breaking completes the annual canonical observances of Muslim festivity. The performance of the sacrifice is done by pointing the animal's head toward the *Ka'ba* in Mecca, saying "God is great" and "In the Name of God," and then slitting its throat quickly and cleanly. The blood is thoroughly drained before the meat is butchered, in a way similar to the Jewish practice of koshering meat. Again, this is a kind of ritual separation and believed to render the flesh pure as well as wholesome. The meat is divided into portions, at least in the case of Muslims not on pilgrimage, and usually given to the needy, and to neighbors, with the third portion remaining for the use of the sacrificer and his or her family. Only males may perform the slaughter; females have it done on their behalf by a male relative or special agent. [See Judaism p. 452 for discussion of kosher; see Religions of Africa pp. 67, 88–89, Religions of Mesoamerica pp. 166–67, 177, 186, 237–38, Judaism pp. 399–400, Christianity pp. 543–44, 550, and Hinduism pp. 744–45, 747–48 for description and discussion of sacrifice.]

During the final days of the *Ḥajj* and after the sacrifice, the pilgrims gradually emerge from the state of *iḥrām* by having their hair cut and beard shaved, by donning everyday clothes, and by beginning to focus on the tasks ahead beyond Mecca. Sexual relations are still forbidden until after certain final rites have been completed, like the ritual stoning of the devil and a farewell circumambulation of the *Kaʿba*. If they have not done it before the *Ḥajj*, pilgrims usually try to visit Medina, the City of the Prophet, some 280 miles to the north. Medina, like Mecca, is a forbidden city, open only to Muslims. Although the visit to Medina is not obligatory, it is meritorious and always deeply meaningful, because it provides an opportunity to pay respects at the Prophet Muḥammad's tomb and to visit other holy places nearby in this oasis city where the Umma was first organized under the guidance of the Qurʾān and God's Prophet.

Emergence from the pilgrimage, symbolized by the lifting of the requirements of *iḥrām,* departure from Mecca, and being welcomed home by relatives and friends (there is typically a large crowd of greeters at airports and seaports) marks the return to normal life in a new status, which ritual studies experts call "reincorporation." Not only is the *Ḥajjī* permitted to bear that title before his or her name, but in some places there are additional marks of the new status. In Egypt, for example, it is common for pilgrims to have special *Ḥajj* paintings applied to the exterior walls of their homes. Typically, these paintings depict scenes of the journey—a steamship, airplane, camel, or horse with rider (some traditionalists like to enter Mecca as Muḥammad did, on a mount)—and they always contain a representation of the holy *Kaʿba* and usually also the Prophet's tomb in Medina. Such *Ḥajj* art can be interpreted at various levels, but the main meaning, according to recent field analyses, centers in Egyptian ideas of saintly persons and the blessings and spiritual power that they provide in a community. The returning pilgrim is, as it were, a living saint who resides in a sacred house marked by the symbols of the supreme centers of Islamic sacral power, Mecca and Medina.[4] [See Religions of Mesoamerica pp. 226–33, Judaism pp. 469–70, Christianity pp. 562–73, Hinduism pp. 815–20, Buddhism p. 874, Religions of China pp. 1041–43, and Religions of Japan pp. 1154–60 for description and discussion of pilgrimage.]

JIHĀD The five Pillars of Islam—witnessing to God's oneness and Muḥammad's messengerhood, worship through the *Ṣalāt* service, almsgiving, fasting in Ramaḍān, and pilgrimage to Mecca—constitute only a minimum structure of Muslim orthopraxy. There are also many additional practices both at the individual and communal levels that make up the total way of life that is Islam. The Muslim term for worship is *ʿibāda,* a word that literally means "service," in the same sense Christians mean it when they say worship service. God is *served* through worship, and worship is reserved for God alone. One additional form of service to God in Islam is *jihād,* whose meaning must be carefully explained. *Jihād* is often mentioned in news releases from the Middle East in which Muslims have proclaimed "holy war" against evil and Islam's enemies, whether Western countries or fellow Muslims with whom they disagree (the extremist

"Islamic *Jihād*" movement in Lebanon is an example). But *jihād* properly speaking means "exertion" in the way of God. It may mean fighting against Islam's enemies or even attempts to spread the religion by force (although Muslim opinion on the latter differs sharply); but a famous teaching of Muḥammad's holds that the "greater *jihād*" is the spiritual struggle each individual has with her or his own faith and need for repentance, whereas *jihād* as armed conflict is called the "lesser" exertion. Whatever the prevailing opinion or practice, *jihād* has sometimes been considered a sixth Pillar of Islam, and thus a form of worship, or service according to specified rules.

Guidance for the Umma in the Form of Holy Scripture and Prophetic Example

The twofold structure of the *Shahāda*, focusing first on God's unity and second on Muḥammad's prophetic role as messenger, is embodied within the Muslim community by the Qur'ān, which for Muslims contains God's revealed guidance, and by the Prophet's Sunna, which contains Muḥammad's "custom," as recorded in reports telling of his teachings and actions. These reports are regarded by Muslims as supremely worthy of learning, obeying, and, where appropriate, imitating.

The Qur'ān

The Qur'ān was revealed to Muḥammad by a mysterious process of verbal inspiration, believed to have been mediated by the archangel Gabriel. Muslims insist that the Qur'ān contains only God's words and nothing of human admixture, whether from Muḥammad or from other sources (such as other scriptures, like the Bible). Muḥammad received and transmitted the Qur'ānic recitations as they came down to him. The accumulating body of revelation came early to be used by the Muslims as their prayer book and source of guidance. In fact, one of the several synonyms for the Qur'ān is "The Guidance." Another is "The Criterion"—between good and evil, truth and falsehood.

After Muḥammad's death, his companions collected the Qur'ānic materials and eventually succeeded in arranging them in written, book form to the satisfaction of the knowledgeable of the day who had been at Muḥammad's side, recited the material with him and other reliable companions, and knew it well. Thus, the Qur'ān, both as live recitation and as book, came into being in the full light of history and was declared valid before a qualified representative grouping of Muslims of the Prophet's circle. That is a remarkable pedigree for a sacred Scripture when compared to other holy books; most holy books tend to emerge from diverse origins and develop gradually into their eventual canonical form.

The complete Qur'ān is almost the length of the Christian New Testament. A chapter is called a **sūra** and there are 114 of them, arranged more or less from longer in the beginning down to shorter ones toward the end. The first *sūra* is a short prayer, which, like the Lord's Prayer of Christianity, stands as the model of prayer for Muslims. It reads, in translation from the original Arabic:

> In the Name of God, the Beneficent, the Merciful.
> Praise Belongs to God, the Lord of all Beings,
> The Beneficent, the Merciful.
> Master of the Day of Judgment,
> You alone we worship, You alone we ask for help.
> Guide us on the straight path,
> The path of those to whom You have been gracious,
> Not of those with whom You are incensed
> Nor those who are straying.[5]

This prayer, known as "The Opening," is uttered in each cycle of the *Ṣalāt* and on many other occasions, too, and is learned very early in a Muslim's life.

The second *sūra* is called "The Cow" because of the occurrence of that word in connection with the story of Moses and the people of Israel who were commanded to sacrifice a yellow heifer (vss. 67–71). It is sometimes also called the "Qur'ān in Miniature," because it contains all the main features of the message and was revealed after the *Hijra* of Muḥammad from Mecca to Medina, when the main elements of the religion had been established. Certain passages dealing mainly with legislative matters are from quite late Medinan times.

The question of when the *sūras,* or in some cases individual verses or groups of verses, were revealed raises the issue of the relationship of the message to its historical setting. Muslim scholars have always recognized a chronological order of *sūras,* divided into those produced in Muḥammad's Meccan period as Prophet and those revealed in Medina when the Umma had been founded and Muḥammad was responsible also for the leadership of a complex political, social, military, and religious order. The Meccan *sūras* are characterized by warnings of a coming divine judgment, when sinners will be punished with hellfire and believers rewarded with heaven. The language is vivid and passionate, with dramatic oaths, bold metaphors, and oracular outbursts. God's "signs" in nature and historical happenings are frequently emphasized as evidences of his providential relationship to the world and humankind. Stories of religious leaders of old, prophets like Abraham, Moses, and Jesus, are cited as antecedents to the Qur'ān and Muḥammad's prophetic activity among the Arabs. The Medinan *sūras* contain many of the same themes as the Meccan ones, but they are also definitively marked by a concern for legal and practical communal matters that reflect the founding and early development of the Umma as a social and political order.

A typical example of a Meccan passage of the Qur'ān is the following, about how the individual will be made to know his or her status on the Last Day:

> When the sun shall be covered up,
> And when the stars swoop down,
> And when the mountains are set moving,
> And when the pregnant camel is abandoned,

And when the wild beasts are herded together,
And when the seas are made to overflow,
And when the souls shall be joined (to their bodies),
And when the buried-alive infant is asked
   For what sin she was put to death,
And when the pages are spread out,
And when the firmament shall be pulled down,
And when Hell shall be set blazing,
And when the Garden is brought near,
Then shall a soul know what it has produced. (81:1–4)

This dramatic passage, from the early Meccan *sura* called "The Darkening," achieves its impact through symbolic reversals. The sun shines much of the time in Arabia; the stars were traditionally believed to be constant in their courses; the mountains were called by the Old Arabian poets "tent pegs" of the firmament; the pregnant camel was never abandoned in tribal society, because it was the most valuable type of property; and infant girls were sometimes put to death by being buried alive, so as to prevent dishonor to the father and other male relatives if the girl should stray when grown up. Muḥammad and other morally sensitive Arabs of his time considered female infanticide to be the ugliest evidence of a generally decaying social, criminal, and ethical order in their day. The coming of Judgment Day is to be accompanied by the near approach of blazing hellfire and a cool, shady heaven. All secrets will then be known and all acts weighed for their merit or demerit.

Typical Medinan passages of the Qur'ān, in contrast, read as follows:

The adulterer and the adulteress, scourge each one of them with a hundred stripes. And do not allow pity for the two to keep you from obeying God, if you believe in God and the Last Day. And let a party of believers witness the punishment. (24:2)

O believers, Do not enter houses not your own without first announcing your presence and invoking peace on their occupants. (24:27)

And marry off the spouseless among you, also the upright among your male and female slaves; if they are poor, God will enrich them of His bounty; God is comprehending and aware. (24:32)

Note the practical, community-oriented content. The first passage, about people taken in adultery, goes on to prescribe four witnesses to the act. This has remained part of Islamic law, as have many other passages treating specific social, criminal, and ritual matters.

It would be misleading, however, to cite only Medinan passages that have a practical purpose and subject matter. Some of the most memorable and operative spiritual and ethical passages in the Qur'ān were revealed in the busy, conflict-filled Medinan period of Muḥammad's prophetic career. One is the "Throne Verse," which is often copied out and worn as an amulet.

God: there is no god but He, the Living, the Eternal; slumber overtakes Him not, nor sleep. To Him belong whatever is in the heavens and whatsoever is in the earth. Who is there that will intercede with Him except by His permission? He knows that which is in front of them and what is behind them, while they comprehend nothing of His knowledge except what He wills. His throne includes the heavens and the earth, and He is never weary of preserving them. He is the Sublime, the Mighty. (2:255)

Another Medinan verse that expresses something of the mysteries of God's nature is the "Light Verse," which Sufi mystics have especially applied to their meditation practices:

God is the Light of the heavens and the earth. His light is like a niche in which is a lamp, the lamp in a glass and the glass like a brilliant star, lit from a blessed tree, an olive neither of the East nor of the West whose oil would almost give light even though no fire did touch it; light upon light; God guides to His light whomsoever He wills; God coins parables for the people, and God knows everything. (24:35)

Our final example of a Medinan verse that transcends the immediate situation of the Umma in those days is found in "The *Sūra* of the Cow." Whereas the previous two passages tell about God, this one sets forth what it means to be truly pious as a believing servant of God:

Truly pious conduct is not turning your faces to the east or to the west; truly good is the one who believes in God and the Last Day and the angels and the Book and the prophets; and gives his wealth, for love of Him, to relatives, and orphans, and the poor, and the one along the way [who suffers because of conversion to Islam], and to set captives free; who observes the *Ṣalāt* and pays the *Zakāt;* those who fulfill their covenant when they have entered into one, who endure steadfastly under adversity and hardship, and in time of trouble; these are the ones who have spoken truth, they are the truly devout. (2:177)

Muslims preserve and learn and apply their Scripture because of the guidance it contains in the way of information about God and his commands for Muslims individually and collectively. This may be called the "informative" level of Qur'ānic use, because it emphasizes knowledge. But Muslims also preserve and receive spiritual guidance from the Qur'ān through carefully regulated ritual recitation, which ideally must always be done in as beautiful a manner as possible by means of chanting. This level of Qur'ānic use in the community may be called the "performative" level, because it centers in the utterance of and listening to God's sacred words. Surely Muslims strive both to understand the Qur'ān's message even as they enjoy its beautiful recitation as an aesthetic blessing, but the very sounds of Qur'ānic Arabic, when properly chanted, bring people to high planes of spiritual experience and delight. This is experienced even among Muslims who have little or no comprehension of Arabic, at least at the informative level. They may, it is sometimes admitted, "know"

the Qur'ān at its deepest, most moving level, even though they do not understand what is literally being said. Most Muslims try to learn the general gist
of what they hear of recitation, whether by means of translations or summaries. But ritual performance of the highest caliber does not absolutely imply
literal understanding of the text, even by quite skilled reciters who have learned
by rote.

The Qur'ān is the central reality of Islamic existence without which the tradition would not have come into being. Scholars have compared the Qur'ān in
the Islamic context to Christ in the Christian religion—each is considered to be
God's holy Word. In the Christian message the Word is believed to have come
down into the world of history as a human being, Jesus of Nazareth. Muslims
believe that God sent his Word into the world as a living recitation and a written
book, the two being complementary aspects of the central phenomenon of
God's presence through sacred speech. Christians partake of the body and blood
of Christ symbolically through the sacrament of Communion. Muslims, it may
be said, "partake" of the nature of their Lord by means of reciting the Qur'ān.
When the Qur'ān is recited properly, God's presence, in the form of his **sakīna,**
is believed to descend upon the reciter and hearers. This *sakīna* is a "tranquility,"
literally, which includes the sense of a protecting and guiding spiritual presence.
(Compare this with the Jewish notion of *shekhinah,* "the Presence of God in the
world.")

Just as all mindful Muslims know how to perform the *Ṣalāt* and observe the
other Pillars of Islam, most also know how to recite the Qur'ān, at least at a
rudimentary level. Short of that, they know how to respect their holy book and
how to listen to its recitation properly. Muslims handle the physical copies of the
Qur'ān only in a ritually pure state (because the text itself contains such a command). They honor it by always placing it in a clean and exalted place, never
under anything else. And they do not write in the pages of the text, although it
is permissible to make notations in a commentary of the Qur'ān.

It is considered to be a specially meritorious achievement to memorize the
entire Qur'ān and such a person is honored as "guardian" of the revelation. The
Qur'ān was first revealed orally to Muḥammad, who in turn mastered the text
and recited it to his companions. Since that time, the Qur'ān has been transmitted orally as well as in written form through the generations.

The ritual recitation of the Qur'ān can be performed and appreciated by
most Muslims, but its scholarly interpretation is a task reserved for the relatively few who have the intelligence, training, and time to master the difficult
sciences connected with exegesis: Arabic grammar and rhetoric, the history of
the text and its dialectal variants, the principles of interpretation (*hermeneutics*
is the modern term), the history of interpretation, and other matters. Qur'ān
interpretation is known in Islam as **tafsīr,** "explanation." There have been different types of *tafsīr,* but the main ones are: literal interpretation, using ancient
traditions handed down from the early scholars; rationalistic interpretation,
which has a strong theological bias and prefers to treat the Qur'ān as a self-
consistent, endlessly revealing spiritual sourcebook not at all limited by traditional views; and allegorical exegesis, preferred usually by mystical types who

Qur'ān reciters at the shrine of Sunan Ampel, Surabaya, East Java, during the saint's mawlid or birthday festival. Many other Muslim personages are also buried in the cemetery adjoining the Sunan Ampel mosque.

discern various levels of symbolic meaning in the text, each appropriate to a different plane of spiritual insight and understanding.

The Prophet's Sunna

Muḥammad's success as Prophet to the Arabs rested in no small measure on his charismatic personality, which was expressed in wise teaching and balanced judgment on a great variety of matters. Like Moses, he led the people as military commander, preached to them as spiritual counselor, and judged them according to God's law. Muḥammad married and had a large, active family. He was constantly in the public eye, yet he also cultivated a thoroughly disciplined private spiritual life of prayer, meditation, fasting, and retreat. In his own life, people came to regard his words as infallible and his acts and gestures as worthy of imitation. The ancient Arabs called by the term *sunna* any established "way," whether it was a way of living, a procedure, or an actual physical "beaten path" to someplace; it contains an implicit imperative, in that it is a recommended way. After Muḥammad died, the Muslims continued to seek guidance from him by remembering his words and acts. These were preserved in verbal reports, or traditions, called *ḥadīths* (collectively referred to as Ḥadīth). If, after consulting the Qur'ān on a matter of importance, nothing could be found to guide individuals or the community on a particular problem or decision, then Muḥammad's Sunna was recollected in hopes of finding a solution. The Muslims who initiated this practice were succeeded by generations of increasingly scholarly collectors and authenticators of *ḥadīths* of the Prophet. There eventually came into being a full-fledged science of Ḥadīth, which coexisted and served as a kind of complement to the evolving scholarly disciplines connected with interpretation of the Qur'ān as well as with jurisprudence and historical studies.

Abū Bakr Abī Shaybata and Abū Kurayb reported: They said "Wakī related to us from Mis'ar, [who got it] from Waṣīl, from Abī Wā'īl, from Hudhayfa, that the Messenger of God (May God bless him and give him peace) met him [i.e., a certain companion named Abū Hurayra] and he was sexually polluted, and he turned away from him and performed the major ablution. Then he came and said: 'I was sexually polluted.' And he [i.e., Muḥammad] declared: 'A Muslim is never polluted.'"[6]

This *ḥadīth,* like all such reports, is in two main parts: The first part is the chain of transmitters, which is traced back as completely as possible to an eyewitness of the Prophet's teaching or gesture; the second part is the actual story or report containing the information about what Muḥammad said or did. It is essential that a properly authenticated *ḥadīth* have a sound chain of transmitters, and a special "science of men" was developed to collect and verify biographies of people whose names feature in the transmission of *ḥadīth.* [See Judaism p. 411 for chains of authorities.]

The interesting *ḥadīth* quoted above contains an important detail about the interpretation of ritual impurity. Muḥammad's intent in his sweeping denial of "pollution" attaching to a Muslim was that such a committed person is rightly guided and properly attuned to his *fiṭra;* although sexual intercourse still renders him or her unfit for *Ṣalāt* and other rites, there is no *essential* pollution of the person who is a Muslim. That is, the *person* is not polluted; rather the person is in an impure state, which is transitory. It is not difficult to imagine a rich and detailed discussion arising over this matter, and Muslim legal experts have traditionally been as probing and comprehensive as Jewish rabbis in their devotion to and even love of extended debate on legal and religious topics.

A number of reliable collections of *ḥadīth* were achieved by the third Islamic century, with six being especially well regarded. Of those six, two collections, one by al-Bukhārī (d. 870) and another by Muslim ibn al-ḥajjāj (d. 875), stand out for their high standards, which earned each collection the name "sound." There are many *ḥadīth*s common both to Sunnī and Shī'ite Muslims, but there are also separate Shī'ite collections that contain much about the Prophet's family. Many thousands of *ḥadīth*s were finally collected by scholars—as many as 600,000 by al-Bukhārī alone. However, a certain percentage of these are the same report, but with differing chains of transmitters. And a large number of *ḥadīth*s discovered by such severe judges as al-Bukhārī and Muslim were found to be fraudulent or to suffer from lesser defects. Nevertheless, al-Bukhārī's collection contains about 2,600 different reports and Muslim's a bit over 3,000 (not counting repetitions with differing chains of transmitters).

The Ḥadīth cover a multitude of subjects and comprise a sort of summation, alongside the Qur'ān, of all that can and should pertain to the Islamic religion and the Muslim way of life. Ḥadīth collections contain sections on such topics as God, faith, eschatology, worship (detailed instructions on the Pillars, for example), warfare, marriage and family life, divorce, inheritance, proper deportment and etiquette, food, clothing, toilette (e.g., cutting the nails, growing a moustache, dressing the hair), bodily functions and hygiene, travel, conversation, trade, funerals, Qur'ān recitation and proper procedures for handling the Qur'ān, interpretation of specific Qur'ān verses, details of Muḥammad's life and biographies of his family members and companions, and other things.

Sunna and Umma

A major reason why the Muslim community enjoys such a high degree of uniformity across vast and diverse cultural, geographic, and linguistic boundaries is the Sunna of Muḥammad. The Sunna has provided specific guidance on what a Muslim must believe and do to preserve the Umma's distinctiveness, which is a mark of the people of God. There is something soteriological or "saving" about being part of the Umma, and the Sunna, passed down from parent to child over the generations, preserves something of the genius and temperament of the Prophet in the hearts and life patterns of the Muslims. Just bearing the name "Muḥammad" is believed by most Muslims to lead toward paradise. The *imitatio Muḥammadi* (comparable to the imitation of Christ in Christianity) has constituted a deep structure in the life of the Umma since the rise of Islam. It would be as difficult to imagine Islam without Muḥammad as without the Qur'ān.

It should be apparent that, far from being learned only from books, the Ḥadīth are learned from *living* examples and *living* teaching, by persons who themselves have striven to be at home on the "Muḥammadan" path by internalizing his Sunna. When we consider the crucial importance of the study—in fact the actual memorization—of the Qur'ān and also take into account the Muslims' practice of all the key elements in Muḥammad's Sunna, we realize how the *Shahāda* becomes internalized in a thorough and concrete fashion. We must remember that the Qur'ān and Ḥadīth do not guide the Muslims primarily as books, that is, as *written* texts; rather, the Muslims themselves become, as it were, "textualized" and activated in such a way as to be in turn a living guide for others. The Umma as community of faith is sustained and its peculiar identity secured by the Qur'ān and Sunna as they are incorporated through intimate and indelible processes of personality formation and imprinting and habits of the mind, body, and heart.

Although the Qur'ān is considered by Muslims to be the true words of God and the Sunna to contain the record of Muḥammad's human life and teaching, there is nevertheless a close relationship between the two. Muslims know that the heart of their beloved Prophet can be discerned in every verse of the Qur'ān. They also believe that in the Sunna they have a veritable living commentary on the scriptural revelation.

There is also a third level—beyond Qur'ān and prophetic Ḥadīth—of sacred guidance for the Muslims in the form of the "Divine Saying" (*ḥadīth qudsī*) couched in Muḥammad's words but purporting to be inspired by God. Divine sayings take as their subject matter spiritual and ethical issues and have thus been especially influential in Muslim piety, particularly of the mystical Sufi sort. Some examples: "My mercy prevails over My wrath." "I was a hidden treasure and desired to be known; therefore I created the creation in order that I might be known." "My Earth and My Heaven contain Me not, but the heart of My faithful servant contains Me." In the Divine Saying we see the closest possible identification between the mind and will of God and the spiritual consciousness of Muḥammad. Indeed, Muḥammad is reported once to have declared: "He that hath seen me hath seen God."[7] Although this declaration would be considered idolatrous by very strict Muslims, it does reveal something of the Prophet's functional divinity at the popular level. So respectful are Muslims of their beloved Prophet that they customarily say "Peace Be Upon Him" after each mention of his name, whether oral or written.

The Sharī'a: *God's Legislation for the Umma*

The solid community structure of the Muslim Umma is informed and regulated by the *Sharī'a,* the "way" that has been ordained by God and set forth in the Qur'ān and Sunna. But Scripture and Muḥammad's teaching are not, by themselves, capable of application without a form and method. These have been developed in the various schools of Islamic jurisprudence (*fiqh*) that arose over the first three centuries of Islam. *Sharī'a* as a concept is similar to the Jewish notion of Torah, the "law" or "instructions" governing Jewish teachings and practices. It includes actual law, but transcends law by defining the whole reality of how God relates to humankind in a covenant relationship of Lord and servants. Humans are God's servants but they also are privileged as God's caliphs with the charge to manage affairs aright on earth and in historical existence. The *Sharī'a,* then, is a noble idea and firm conviction about the way of the universe, which is in God's hands. The *Sharī'a* is the instrumentality by which the Muslim community persists through the generations in a close bond among its members, which in turn is made possible only by the close bond each Muslim has with God. The rule of the *Sharī'a* among the people of God is the essence or heart of Islam. "Let there be one Umma of you, calling to goodness, and enjoining the right and prohibiting the wrong. Those are the successful ones" (3:104).

Fiqh: *Islamic Jurisprudence and Theology*

Islamic orthopraxy has always emphasized law over theology, the consequences of actions over the merely theoretical dimensions of intellect. Intellect is essential, but it should be cultivated only in the service of "enjoining the right and prohibiting the wrong." Learning beyond the practical needs of the faith has very often been suspect among Muslims. This suspicion applied largely to intellectual theorizing about God of a purely speculative, academic and ruminative kind. The useful sciences—medicine, astronomy, geography, tactics and strategy, mathematics, chemistry, and so forth—have enjoyed distinguished careers in Islamic civilization, as have music, literature, fine arts, and philosophy. But systematic theology, in the sense that it is cultivated in Christianity, is decidedly secondary in importance to jurisprudence in Islam and is in fact only a subcategory under it. Known as "the science of discourse (*kalām*)," its use has generally been restricted to specialists who have cultivated it for the defense of Islam.

The two greatest sources of jurisprudence in Islam are the Qur'ān and Sunna. Most issues can be treated using a teaching from one or the other or both in consort. And even when it is not possible to find specific guidance in the Qur'ān or Sunna, Muslim legal experts have traditionally been able to proceed by means of analogy. In the early generations, when *fiqh* (the term literally means "understanding") was emerging in response to the practical needs of Muslim communities extending over an increasingly large empire, scholars applied the revelation and example of Muḥammad, and indeed of other worthies of his time, along with their own considered personal opinion. Gradually, however, there came into being a limited number of legal schools that were recognized as authoritative, whether by Sunnīs or Shī'ites. Four principal sources of *fiqh* came to be standard for Sunnīs: Qur'ān, Sunna, community consensus, and analogical reasoning. The third source, consensus (**ijmā'**), is followed only by Sunnīs, who have a strong belief in the infallibility of the Umma, based on the famous *ḥadīth* attributed to Muḥammad: "Truly, my Umma will never agree together on an error." In practice, consensus has prevailed in Sunnī law schools as the most influential of the sources of *fiqh,* because by means of it the Muslims have been able to relate all important matters to what was believed to have been the earliest consensus concerning the Qur'ān, Muḥammad's teachings, and the positions of the pious forebears in the first generations. Consensus is a very conservative force and has often come to block new ways of thinking about and applying both Qur'ān and Sunna to new developments and needs.

The conservatism of Islam has been both a blessing and a bane for the Umma. Traditional Muslim scholarship considered that all major questions of belief and law had been aired and settled by around the fourth century after the *Hijra.* Up until then, Muslim jurists, known throughout the Umma by the collective term **'ulamā'** ("learned"), had exercised their professional right of independent legal decision making, called **ijtihād.** This technical term derives from the same root as *jihād* and thus carries the meaning of "exertion," too, but in the intellectual sense. An independent Muslim jurist is known as a *mujtahid.* Consensus, at least among Sunnī Muslims, came eventually to regard the "gate" of *ijtihād* as closed. Henceforth, legal scholars and judges would be guided by "imitation" of the ancient and sound worthies in the field of jurisprudence. This imitation eventually proved exceedingly burdensome to alert legal specialists who discerned alternate valid ways of interpreting the Qur'ān and Sunna in matters of law. A number of them, such as the great Damascus legal expert and theologian Ibn Taymīya (d. 1328), continued to claim the right of *ijtihād* and in the process moved Islamic jurisprudence ahead creatively, although such legal specialists sometimes suffered censure and persecution from those who were more conservative, who usually were in the majority. Since the eighteenth century C.E., more and more Muslims have been calling for reopening of the gate of *ijtihād* so as to update and extend in rationally sound ways the *Sharīʿa* in the modern world, which has presented unforeseen and complex challenges to the Umma.

Shīʿites and Sunnīs

Shīʿite Muslims have never ceased exercising *ijtihād*. They have persisted in their different subcommunities in maintaining an honored place for independent legal reasoning, in the belief that God guides them through the divine light descending from Muḥammad through ʿAlī and several *Imāms* or divinely guided "leaders" of Shīʿism. Shīʿite *fiqh*, consequently, has been considerably more flexible and adaptive than Sunnī jurisprudence, although there are also certain areas where the two inevitably and willingly overlap and mutually reinforce each other; that is, Sunnīs and Shīʿites are equally Muslim, and the two divisions of the Umma, even though the former numbers around 85 percent, do consider each other to be members of the same tradition of faith, order, and community. Their sometimes pronounced (and tragic) differences over rule and political theory as well as other matters nevertheless did not result in anything as drastic as the theological, liturgical, legal, and denominational divisions that Christianity experienced. Thus, although such comparisons are perilous, Shīʿites and Sunnīs are closer to each other in liturgical, legal, and even theological essentials than such Christian groups as Episcopalians and Baptists. In the liturgical dimension—which includes the Pillars, and especially the *Ṣalāt* and the *Ḥajj*—Shīʿites and Sunnīs are virtually identical.

Sunnī Islam has dominated in most periods and places, at least politically. The great ʿAbbāsid dynasty (750–1258 C.E.), although it was launched with the help and ideas of Shīʿism, soon revealed its Sunnī basis and suppressed Shīʿite movements during its long history. But in Iraq, and later even more in Iran, Shīʿism continued to maintain loyal followings. By the fifteenth and sixteenth centuries, Iran came increasingly to be dominated by Shīʿite principles and figures, thus establishing its character up to the present, when Shīʿite religious scholars and judges are in complete control of the revolutionary Islamic regime in Iran, established under the leadership of the late Ayatollah ("Sign of God") Khomeini. Khomeini ruled as a *mujtahid* and as the sole contemporary representative of the last divinely guided *Imām*, who disappeared in the early Islamic centuries and is believed to be preserved by God in an occult state of concealment until the time comes for him to return in judgment at the end of time.

Although the *Sharīʿa*, theoretically, rules all of Muslim life, in the present only a few countries are earnestly applying it—Saudi Arabia, Iran, and Pakistan are the most noteworthy. It is difficult to govern by the medieval *Sharīʿa* in the complex world of today, when all countries depend to some extent on an international economic, political, and military order, with the great powers forcing alliances, if only by default, and a host of peoples and societies not governed by

Islamic principles impinging on the Umma in countless ways. Aspects of these problems, especially when faced by Muslims in the contemporary West, will be considered in chapter 28.

The Ṭarīqa: *Personal Piety and the Quest for Union with God*

As crucially important and pervasive as Muslim regard for the *Sharī'a* and its right ordering of life in service to God is, to the extent that Islam fully deserves the characterization of "orthoprax" that we have given it throughout this work, Muslims also know another major way of being religious. This way is known as the **Ṭarīqa,** an Arabic word that, like *Sharī'a,* also means "way," but includes the sense of a spiritual discipline or path, rather than God's legislation in the external sense of law and correct procedures for the Umma as a whole. The *Ṭarīqa* is the interior way of mystically inclined Muslims. Unlike the *Sharī'a,* it is not in any sense official or required to be maintained and applied. Rather, Muslims follow the *Ṭarīqa* because of inward urgings and personal questings for a more intimate religious life of closeness to God and to like-minded spiritual seekers.

Because of the interior aspect of the *Ṭarīqa,* its forms of expression and institutionalization have been many and varied. The name that is given to these forms of personal spirituality is "Sufism," a term with a fascinating history. In early Islamic times, after Muslims had succeeded in conquering and coming to dominate many regions of the Middle East and North Africa, there came into being a kind of spiritual reaction to the wealth and ease that people were enjoying in various centers of the Umma. The formal ritual observances of *Ṣalāt, Zakāt,* fasting in Ramaḍān, the *Ḥajj,* and related acts continued to be the center of orthoprax Islam, to be sure, but increasing numbers of Muslims wanted also a more intimate and informal dimension to their religious lives. And a good number also considered the wealth and pleasures of this world to be a trap, tempting them to lose sight of their obligations and the life of the world to come. There were some who took to wearing patched woolen frocks as a sign of renunciation of the world and reliance on God's grace alone. Before long, this woolen garment gave to the new fashion of ascetic piety the name of *ṣūfī,* from the Arabic word *sūf,* "wool." [See Christianity pp. 502–4, 510, Hinduism pp. 772, Buddhism pp. 915–21, 942–52, Religions of China pp. 1004–5, 1009, 1033–34, 1056, and Religions of Japan p. 1102 for discussion of monasteries and monasticism.]

The Muslim mystics came to express their religious convictions in many new ways and with distinctive forms of ritual and communal etiquette. Sufism did not, except for some extremist exponents, depart from the universal religious duties of Muslims; rather it may be understood to have intensified them and augmented them with new rites and ceremonies. These last centered in remembering God by mentioning in prayerlike formulas his "Most Beautiful Names," as the Qur'ān calls them, which are believed to number ninety-nine.

The "mentioning" of God often is commanded of all Muslims by the Qur'ān, but the Sufis came to focus on this practice more than all others. This practice of mentioning is known as **dhikr** and it took on a variety of forms, from plain voiced repetition of Qur'ānic words and phrases in a rhythmic manner, to silent forms of inner meditation with elaborate breathing exercises, to enraptured dance to the music of flutes and drums until the performers fell down in swoons of ecstasy in union with their Lord.

From its beginnings, Sufism emphasized the place of the spiritual master, or **shaykh,** who was always believed to have received esoteric doctrine through a line of spiritual guides traceable back to the Prophet Muḥammad, whom all Muslims consider to be the perfect human master, imbued with God's blessing and wisdom. Although many different doctrines and practices developed in an unregulated and translegal environment of Ṭarīqa cultivation, there was the governing conviction among Sufis that God through the Qur'ān and Muhammad through his Sunna were the ultimate authorities and sustaining power of their diverse institutional modes of doctrine and meditation. The charter event of the Ṭarīqa and of all the individual orders that embodied it in most parts of the Muslim world was the mysterious Night Journey and Ascension of Muḥammad from Mecca to Jerusalem and up through the seven heavens to the presence of God. This meeting of Muḥammad with his Lord provides unlimited inspiration to Sufis, as well as other Muslims, who see it as the completion of the relationship between God and his Prophet: First God sent down his Word in the form of the Qur'ān, then he lifted his servant Muḥammad up to his own abode. God condescended to earth so that his faithful creature could ascend to heaven. Just as Jesus' life, passion, and resurrection are seen by Christians to be moments in a great redemptive epic, whereby all those baptized in Christ believe that they will inherit eternal life with him and the Father in heaven, so Muslims consider Muḥammad's Ascension to be crucial proof of God's promise of success in a blessed afterlife with him. Muḥammad was raised up to heaven in this life, and the Sufis especially have deduced important religious principles from Muḥammad's Ascension.

The main deduction of Sufism with regard to Muḥammad's Ascension is that others, too, may experience God directly and definitively in this life. The aim of Sufi meditation, then, came to be the gradual purifying of the lower self of all things pertaining to this world, until the higher self could experience annihilation and unification with God. Once the Sufi experiences loss of his or her own ego, then God takes over indeed and transforms the person into a being intimately entwined with him- or herself. The precise way in which this is believed to occur inspired various theories and forms of expression, all of which admittedly are imperfect as such, but nevertheless attempt to characterize in words what is finally beyond human ability to verbalize. The experience, the actual "tasting" of union with God, is the important thing, whether or not mere human intellect can grasp it.

Sufism took on institutional form as doctrines and schools first and later as actual organizations, "brotherhoods" which came to spread from country to country. The earliest Sufis, like the great theologian and legal scholar Ḥasan of

Baṣra (d. 728), tended toward asceticism and a very sober and often sad view of life, which included weeping for one's sins and despairing of salvation. Although an ascetic mode has continued to inspire and inform Sufis up to the present, before long it was more love than sorrow that came to characterize the *Ṭarīqa.* A remarkable woman saint, Rābi'a al-'Adawīya (d. 801), discovered in her solitary vigils with God, often lasting all night, that love was at the core of the universe; not to reflect and relate this love to those around us and back to God was to renounce our highest privilege. Rābi'a's conviction that the love in the believer's heart is itself a response to God's prior love was expressed memorably by a later saint, Jalāl al-Dīn Rūmī (d. 1273), whose thousands of Persian rhymed couplets contain the entire spectrum of Sufi emotion and reflection.

> Never, in sooth, does the lover seek without being sought by his beloved.
> When the lightning of love has shot into this heart, know that there is love in that heart.
> When love of God waxes in thy heart, beyond any doubt God hath love of thee.
> The soul says to her base earthly parts, "My exile is more bitter than yours: I am celestial."
> The body desires green herbs and running water, because its origin is from those;
> The soul desires Life and the Living One, because its origin is the Infinite Soul.
> The desire of the soul is for ascent and sublimity; the desire of the body is for self and means of self-indulgence;
> And that Sublimity desires and loves the soul: mark the text *He loves them and they love Him.*[8] (translator's emphasis)

This last line is the favorite passage in the Qur'ān for Sufis—5:59.

There have been different kinds of Sufis as well as Sufi organizations and meditation paths. Sufis have sometimes divided themselves into three types: "sober," "antinomian," and "intoxicated." The first type of Sufis are really normal pious Muslims, but they have a capacity to experience the depths of what the *Sharī'a* prescribes by way of ritual worship practices. In fact, every Muslim should be a Sufi in this sense. And very many are, without using the title "Sufi," because of the strong conviction that God's friends, those whom he loves, are all who submit to him and love him, too. Muḥammad and his companions, as well as members of the Prophet's family, are considered to be the soberest of Sufis, if Sufis they are considered to be at all, for they lived before the term *Sufism* was coined.

The antinomian type of Sufi is a type of religious person known in other traditions, marked by resistance to moral and ritual rules as hampering spiritual spontaneity. He or she may go to extremes, even violating certain commands of the *Sharī'a,* (e.g., refusing to perform the *Ṣalāt*), or one of these types might simply not exhibit any obvious piety, for fear of being praised and thus placed in danger of prideful self-esteem and thus, eventually, damnation. The antinomian Sufis want to bring blame upon themselves, following a Qur'ānic passage (12:53) that has been interpreted to mean that it is required for true believers to blame their own carnal selves so as to prepare the higher self for union with God. Various opinions, from highly laudatory to vituperative, have been held about the antinomian Sufis, but the type persists.

The third type are the intoxicated Sufis who delight in the ecstatic transport they experience in close union with God. These "drunken" Sufis did not gain their reputation by drinking actual alcoholic beverages (intoxicants are forbidden in Islam); rather, they expressed their brimming joy mostly by means of beautiful poetry, often centering on the theme of wine and taverns of a heavenly character. This wine is God's love, which inspires, intoxicates, and transforms the true seeker, just as in paradise there will be a delightful drink that thrills like earthly wine but has no negative effect or hangover.

Sufism makes for a fascinating and rewarding study, but to go further into the subject here would require considerable additional historical, doctrinal, and literary discussion. Suffice it to say that Sufism has often been called the "heartbeat" of Islam, in that it provides the inner dynamic and delight of being a Muslim, whereas the *Sharī'a* provides the external regulating structure for Muslims in community. Working together, the *Sharī'a* as the exoteric and the *Ṭarīqa* as the esoteric dimensions of Islam, the Umma enjoys a balanced and inspired life. The *Sharī'a* enables the Umma to proceed securely through history by regulating matters of common faith and order, while the *Ṭarīqa* convinces its followers that God is very near, indeed, and in close communion with his special friends (**walīs**), as the Sufis like to characterize themselves. As the Qur'ān declares: "Surely God's friends—no fear shall be on them, neither shall they sorrow" (10:63). [See Judaism pp. 422–27, Christianity pp. 500, 507, 519, Hinduism pp. 752–53, Buddhism pp. 946–48, Religions of China pp. 1032–34, and Religions of Japan pp. 1102, 1121–27, 1151 for discussion of meditation and mysticism.]

This chapter has described the main structures of Islamic belief and practice, within the context of the strong community that is the Umma. This treatment of Islam can be expressed in abbreviated form in the following diagram. In brief, it shows the basis for Islam in belief in Allāh and in recognition of humans as deputies of Allāh. The message of Allāh was received by a long line of prophets beginning with Abraham and ending with Muḥammad, who received the revelations of the Qur'ān and established the Muslim community. The Umma as the Muslim community attempts to realize a unified religious community and to establish Islamic principles in all areas of life and culture. The spiritual life of the Islamic community is expressed in patterns for spiritual life, rituals and practices, and contact with spiritual power. In the next chapter, we shall consider some of the dynamics of Muslim faith and order by describing and analyzing representative institutions in greater detail.

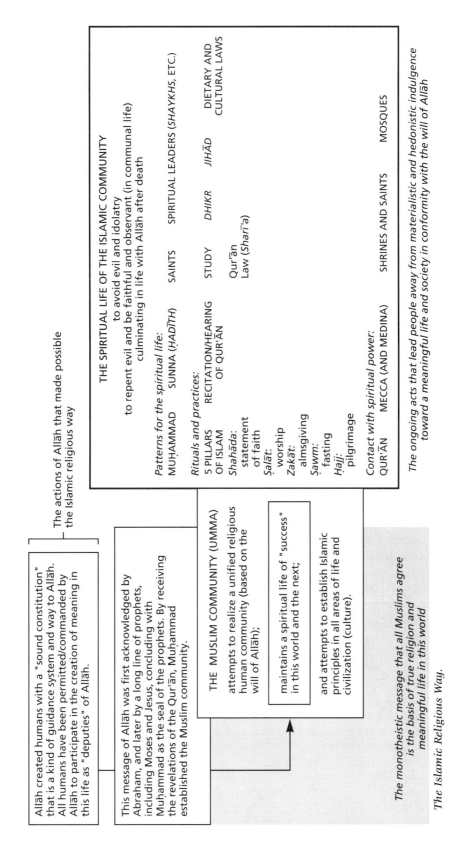

The actions of Allāh that made possible the Islamic religious way

Allāh created humans with a "sound constitution" that is a kind of guidance system and way to Allāh. All humans have been permitted/commanded by Allāh to participate in the creation of meaning in this life as "deputies" of Allāh.

This message of Allāh was first acknowledged by Abraham, and later by a long line of prophets, including Moses and Jesus, concluding with Muḥammad as the seal of the prophets. By receiving the revelations of the Qur'ān, Muḥammad established the Muslim community.

THE SPIRITUAL LIFE OF THE ISLAMIC COMMUNITY
to avoid evil and idolatry
to repent evil and be faithful and observant (in communal life)
culminating in life with Allāh after death

Patterns for the spiritual life:

| MUḤAMMAD | SUNNA (HADĪTH) | RECITATION/HEARING OF QUR'ĀN | SAINTS | SPIRITUAL LEADERS (SHAYKHS, ETC.) | STUDY | DHIKR | JIHĀD | DIETARY AND CULTURAL LAWS |

Qur'ān
Law (Sharī'a)

Rituals and practices:

5 PILLARS OF ISLAM
Shahāda: statement of faith
Ṣalāt: worship
Zakāt: almsgiving
Ṣawm: fasting
Ḥajj: pilgrimage

Contact with spiritual power:

| QUR'ĀN | MECCA (AND MEDINA) | SHRINES AND SAINTS | MOSQUES |

THE MUSLIM COMMUNITY (UMMA)

attempts to realize a unified religious human community (based on the will of Allāh);

maintains a spiritual life of "success" in this world and the next;

and attempts to establish Islamic principles in all areas of life and civilization (culture).

The ongoing acts that lead people away from materialistic and hedonistic indulgence toward a meaningful life and society in conformity with the will of Allāh

The monotheistic message that all Muslims agree is the basis of true religion and meaningful life in this world

The Islamic Religious Way.

27

Representative Muslim Institutions and Their Dynamics

THE KNOWLEDGE OF ISLAM'S STRUCTURES of faith and practice, Scripture and tradition, law and spirituality is in itself insufficient for gaining a rounded appreciation of the quality of Muslim life. The Qur'ān is of central importance for all dimensions of Islamic belief and life, and we know that its appropriation by the believers is both intellectual (aimed at understanding the message's meaning) and practical (devoted to spiritual power and guidance by means of ritual recitation). But the actual human institutions by which the Qur'ān is mastered also need to be described. The description provided in this chapter on dynamics will be an aid to understanding some of the ways in which the Qur'ān is received, enjoyed, and applied among Muslims. Our focus will be on recitation.

The second major dimension of Muslim life to be treated in this chapter is somewhat different from the appropriation of the Qur'ān. Qur'ān-based education is universal and provides most of the formal matter by which Islam is authenticated as true, but there is another way in which Muslims in many but not all regions cultivate their religious lives beyond the study of their sacred book. Muslims also recognize the importance of sacred persons whom they venerate and from whom they seek guidance, boons, and intercession with God. They do this principally by means of specific cults that have grown up around the burial places of holy persons, "saints." Even with the immeasurably great guides of the Qur'ān and Sunna to regulate and inspire them, Muslims prove by their beliefs and practices related to the veneration of saints that it is impossible for most people to be generic Muslims, that is, detached from specific, local, often folk cultures that antedate, coexist with, and sometimes even compete with scriptural, "official" Islam.

The third and final dimension to be examined in this chapter is the Muslim life cycle, the stages of life from birth to death that mark each person's progress in the Muslim way. Like Qur'ānic education, it is universal. And like the practice of the veneration of saints, it also has many local variants and associations. However, unlike saint veneration, it is part of orthoprax Islam in that it is considered by all to be required.

Recitation of the Qur'ān

Qur'ānic Education in Indonesia

As we learned earlier, the recitation of the Qur'ān with at least a minimum level of proficiency is done in all Muslim locales. Initially, native Arabic speakers have an obvious advantage, because although Qur'ānic Arabic is archaic and highly idiomatic compared with modern colloquial dialects of Arabic, it is nevertheless the same language, with many points of convergence and identity with modern spoken and written Arabic. And Arabic-speaking nations have many radio and television programs featuring classical and Qur'ānic Arabic recitations, Friday sermons, theological lectures, and religious discussions.

But Muslims living in non-Arabic-speaking countries also strive to master Arabic well enough for worship and meditation, including reading and recitation of the Qur'ān. In Indonesia, where the Malay-based national language, Bahasa Indonesia, has no linguistic connection with Semitic languages, Indonesian nonetheless contains around two thousand words derived from Arabic, especially in the religious fields. Nearly all the terminology of ritual and religious concepts is based on Arabic words, mostly from the Qur'ān and the Ḥadīth. Since the coming of Islam to the Indonesian archipelago, beginning in the twelfth and thirteenth centuries and increasing to major proportions by the fifteenth and sixteenth centuries, converts have worked hard to learn Arabic. At first, in Java, for example, recitation of the Qur'ān seems to have been performed in Javanese, using traditional themes and symbols to communicate the story of Islam to a population steeped in aboriginal Javanese as well as imported Hindu and Buddhist lore antedating the coming of Islam.

Centuries ago, Muslim teachers (traditionally male) began establishing small schools on Java and Sumatra. Such a religious teacher in Indonesia is called a **kiai**, which is roughly equivalent to the Arabic *shaykh,* "master." The center of the *kiai's* teaching has traditionally been the text of the Qur'ān, both read and recited. In addition, to the extent that the *kiai* was able to master the materials himself, Ḥadīth materials and other religious texts were included in the curriculum. The Islamic school came to be known as a *pesantren,* the place where *santri,* "orthoprax," Muslim students learn. Thus the institutions of *kiai* and *pesantren* formed the ongoing educational nucleus of Indonesian *santri* Muslim society, introduced in the opening chapter of this part. *Pesantrens* have always been mainly local affairs, to which students go during certain hours of the day or evening for instruction, prayers, and fellowship with other young folk, boys with boys and girls with girls. But there are also many residential *pesantrens,* especially in traditionally minded East Java, where students ranging from eight to eighteen years of age or older comprise a cohesive community. A residential *pesantren* is called a **pondok pesantren,** from the Arabic word *funduq,* meaning "hostel" or "inn."

Pondok pesantrens today continue to make the Qur'ān and Arabic education the center of the curriculum, but in some cases additional subjects like math,

"Pondok Modern," in Gontor, near Ponorogo, East Java, Indonesia. This famous pon-dok pesantren for boys and young men emphasizes modern subjects but maintains a strong commitment to Islamic learning and values in its communal life and co-operative self-government. Students and faculty together built the mosque and minaret at the center of the campus, shown here. Many of Indonesia's most impor-tant Islamic leaders of recent times were educated here.

social studies, science, history, and practical arts are also included. Instruction in the Qur'ān and Arabic begins as early as feasible, with students writing on slates or paper tablets, pronouncing the letters, then groups of letters, and short Qur'ānic phrases. Recent years have seen the introduction of a wide range of instruction manuals covering principles of recitation and related matters of eti-quette and doctrine. Regional and national Qur'ānic education societies cooper-ating with Indonesia's Department of Religious Affairs have also developed graded curricular materials for Qur'ānic instruction. Such textbooks are used in *pesantrens* and other, more modern types of schools.

Although the Qur'ān is the backbone of traditional *pondok pesantren* educa-tion, the close community of students and *kiai* and other instructors serves as a human laboratory for the socializing of Indonesian youth in habits and pat-terns of cooperation and consensus that are considered essential to Indonesian personal and communal identity. Indonesians have a strong sense of loyalty to the society as a whole and prefer to subordinate their individual wills and ambi-tions and blend them into the collective whole of shared values and mutually beneficial disciplines. The close fit between traditional Indonesian social cus-toms and convictions and Islamic doctrines and communal values is fortuitous for both and a major factor in Islam's phenomenal success in being embraced by 90 percent of Indonesians.

Indonesian Muslims, especially the *santri* types who cultivate Qur'ānic literacy and pure *Sharī'a*-based devotional practices and social relations, enjoy a combination of close social and cultural identification with their local group and with Javanese, Acehnese, Maduran, or some other ethnic subcommunity along with a transcending Muslim identity, which extends to the whole nation and to all parts of the Muslim world. The ability to read the Qur'ān carries with it the ability to read widely also in the classics of Islamic legal, theological, historical, and devotional literatures. But although most Indonesian Muslims do not possess sufficient Arabic literacy to delve into such classical sources, the minimal Qur'ānic Arabic comprehension they do have permits them to experience a deeply satisfying ritual incorporation into certain patterns and processes of Muslim awareness and intimacy with God and fellow believers that enliven and sustain Muslims everywhere.

Although the *kiai* provides the fundamental instruction for the *pesantren,* he in fact is as often an imposing, serene eminence as he is a constantly or overtly active leader. That is, his leadership consists in large part in setting an example of a wise, virtuous, and commanding personality. He actively teaches, but much of the time the older students work with the younger ones, passing on their superior knowledge and ability, especially in Qur'ānic recitation. Beyond the formal instruction, which may take only a few hours of each day, the students occupy themselves with such household and personal chores as cleaning the premises, tending vegetable gardens, washing clothes, and preparing meals. The *kiai* certainly maintains order and decorum within the *pesantren,* but he also acts as counselor and inspiration to the wider community outside the walls of the *pondok.* Sometimes a *kiai's* fame spreads far, even outside of Indonesia, resulting in parents sending their children to be enrolled for their whole period of adolescent coming of age as Muslims and proper citizens.

In general, the more traditional the *pesantren,* the better the mastery of Qur'ān recitation and Arabic literacy. In some establishments, this includes also the memorization of the Qur'ān, a demanding task that takes a candidate with suitable aptitude and disciplined study habits about three years to achieve. One of the most important factors in memorizing the Qur'ān is a supportive, similarly dedicated community of fellow reciters. And once the Qur'ān has been memorized, it must be kept in memory through continuous review and practice. As the Prophet Muḥammad is reported to have said, "Keep refreshing your knowledge of the Qur'ān, for I swear by Him in whose hands my soul is that it is more liable to escape than camels which are tethered."

A typical *pondok pesantren* has both individual and group Qur'ān recitation as a daily activity. The youngest students are typically taught by older students, beginning with rudimentary instruction in the writing of individual Arabic letters and practicing their sounds. Little groups can be heard pronouncing series of letters until, when the pronunciation is satisfactory, they are assigned Qur'ānic words, and then whole phrases to recite. The teacher intones the passage and then the students repeat after him, back and forth, sometimes for long periods. The teacher will often mark time, either with hand clapping or by rapping a stick on the desk (the stick is also used for occasional disciplinary measures).

In Indonesia, instruction in recitation is essentially a mimicking process, whereby the teacher's tones and inflections become replicated in the recitation of the students. When the time for recitation of longer Qur'ānic passages comes,

Advanced student reciting the Qur'ān at the Institute of Qur'ānic Studies, Singosari, East Java, Indonesia. The students concentrate on Qur'ānic education at the residential pondok pesantren *but attend public school for modern subjects.*

an introduction to the quasi-musical elements of true chanting is begun. Such performance is beautiful to the ear, and individuals who come to excel in it achieve a special status in each school. In one respected *pesantren* in East Java, the "head boy," who is around twenty, is entrusted with teaching recitation to a large gathering of adults, more than three hundred, who come for a weekly training session. It is impressive to hear the assembly, which is divided by sex into separate but adjoining groups, practicing in unison the ancient Qur'ānic words and phrases as made fresh and vibrant by the mellifluous baritone voice of the preceptor. The *kiai* presides and gives formal instruction, but his student assistant provides the crucially important vocal demonstration and model phrases according to their proper melodies and rhythms. The teaching of eager and grateful townspeople is an example of this particular *pesantren's* Islamic outreach to ordinary folk. The joyful receiving of recitation training by the people is evident in the expressions on their faces and the respectful manner with which they greet and say good-bye to the *kiai* and his assistant. The unison chanting, even of practice phrases, is a thrilling expression of heartfelt praise of God by a class that also considers itself to be a congregation.

One way by which modern Indonesian Qur'ān students maintain high standards of recitation and enjoy the process as well is through contests. For more than twenty years the authorities have sponsored local, regional, provincial, and national Qur'ān chanting competitions that cycle over a period of two years, normally, and end in the recognition of individual male and female reciters as the best in the country in youth, adult, and handicapped categories. Awards are made for high achievement in artistic chanting, in memorization of the Qur'ān, and in knowledge about the Qur'ān and its proper uses in piety and the religious sciences.

Wherever the national Qur'ān reciting tournament is held, the host city takes special pride in preparing itself for the many contestants and visitors who spend upward of two weeks participating in and attending daily and nightly sessions and enjoying Islamic fashion shows, book and cultural exhibits, and other special events. The process preserves high-caliber Qur'ānic competency among succeeding generations of Muslim students, and also unites Indonesian Muslims in the common cause of Islamic mission and revival, both among the believers and in outreach to others.

I observed a national Qur'ān chanting tournament held in 1985 in Pontianak, the capital of the Indonesian province of West Kalimantan, on the island of Borneo. Before the opening ceremonies there was a parade of around a hundred colorful floats through the city streets; teams from all over the country and local organizations and clubs were represented. The floats were decorated with Qur'ānic calligraphy. The formal opening ceremonies were presided over by President Suharto and officials from the Ministry of Religion and Islamic organizations. A large sports stadium had been transformed into a recitation arena by the erection of a special pulpit of recitation in the center of the playing field.

The opening ceremonies included recitation by the previous winners in the male and female categories, who reigned over the events as a kind of king and queen, complete with crowns. Then, after speeches from dignitaries, the official tournament flag was presented by the president of Indonesia to a special Islamic drill team, which then raised it at the end of the field, next to the flag of the Republic of Indonesia. A large brass band marched briskly around the track leading the twenty-seven provincial recitation teams, each in its regional dress, as they passed in review before the president and gathered officials. After these formalities were over, the second half of the program was introduced, featuring a dance performance by eleven hundred brightly costumed men and women, who spilled out onto the playing field and went through a number of intricate formations including prayer postures, and closing with the spelling out of the logo of the tournament, like an American football band's halftime show. Music was provided by a five-hundred piece orchestra and a Chinese Catholic choir of several thousand men and women. Pontianak, which has a non-Muslim, mostly Chinese, ethnic majority, extended its warmest hospitality to the visiting Muslims and joined in the spirit of the chanting tournament, which in Indonesia is viewed as a "national discipline" as well as Islamic piety. The Indonesian national Qur'ān chanting tournament is covered extensively on the national media, with a daily televised recap of events in the evening as part of the national and world news.

Qur'ān recitation competitions are held in other Muslim countries, too, notably Egypt, Saudi Arabia, Brunei, and Malaysia. This last country sponsors the prestigious international Qur'ān reciting contest, which attracts the best reciters from all over the Muslim world. Very often non-native-Arabic-speaking reciters win top honors. Such persons typically have received the kind of intensive exposure to the Qur'ān and specialized training in its recitation that the Indonesian *pondok pesantren* system provides.

Qur'ānic education is available to Indonesians outside *pondok pesantrens,* too, in neighborhood mosques, after-school institutes, and through tutors. Recitation instruction is also available through tape cassettes and accompanying workbooks. Both radio and television carry recitation frequently, and it is common for the final moments of the broadcast day to be devoted to the recitation of Qur'ānic passages before sign-off.

In the large East Java port city of Surabaya, I was present in a studio audience in the provincial television station where a regional Qur'ān recitation competition was held. Each contestant knelt on a raised platform; the open Qur'ān was mounted on a stand in front of him or her. Three lights—green, amber, and red—marked the time in which the performance had to occur; red meant stop, the end of the recitation. The same procedure marks the national tournament. In between groups of reciters, special entertainment was provided by a Muslim rock band of young men and women from the nearby Islamic teachers' college. Performers played guitars, drums, and other instruments, and singers swayed back and forth with fingers snapping and eyes flashing in a wholesome display of youthful exuberance. Both sexes were properly dressed; the women wore glitzy ensembles that nevertheless covered both hair and body without concealing a brimming enjoyment of being young and "with it." As I watched, I was led to compare the show with American parallels of rock gospel groups and squeaky-clean evangelistic pop music. Not all Muslim leaders would approve of combining Qur'ān recitation with popular entertainment, whether on the same program or in the same stratum of society, but their integration in a common Muslim youth culture in Surabaya seems not to be too controversial.

It is not unusual for persons of means in Indonesia to endow an institute for Qur'ānic instruction. I once met a medical school professor from North Sumatra who established such a school for very small children, complete with a special building and a full-time teacher. I asked my friend why he went to such lengths when there were already mosques, *pondok pesantrens,* and other opportunities for learning the Qur'ānic message and the skills of recitation. He replied that he himself had been greatly blessed in his life by the Qur'ān, not only with professional success—which he had surely achieved—but also with the satisfaction of becoming a very accomplished Qur'ān reciter himself. This physician had developed his own approach to recitation training, with which he had had great success with university students in the large city of Medan. His institute for young children was his way of promoting his successful method, which was designed especially for people whose native language is not Arabic. When I was about to say good-bye to my host and fly across the Malacca Straits to Malaysia, a difficulty was discovered concerning my ticket and my credentials. The doctor inquired and, with a combination of humble patience and savoir-faire, succeeded in smoothing out the difficulty. When I thanked him profusely, he said not to think that he had done anything; rather, as he put it, I had experienced "something of the blessings of the Qur'ān." His meaning seemed to be that anyone pursuing knowledge of the Qur'ān—even a Western anthropological fieldworker—could not fail to be rewarded by God in his or her search.

Scriptural Piety

The contemporary Islamic revival has brought Muslims back to their spiritual roots in the Qur'ān and Sunna. In Cairo, Egypt, for example, one can find Qur'ān recitation training going on in groups of people of very diverse backgrounds and occupations. Recitation teachers, some old and venerable, make the rounds of mosques and homes to provide individual and group instruction. One class that I came to know over the course of several months included a middle-aged computer programmer, a retired banker, a young woman student of religion, and a janitor. Another was made up of a retired government official from the department of textiles, a young professor of veterinary science, a stockbroker, a retired military officer, a teacher of religion, a laborer or two, and others. One of the attractions of the classes, both of which were taught by the same highly revered elderly recitation master, was the privilege of being in frequent contact with him, thereby receiving blessings. Another was the satisfaction of trying to improve one's spiritual life by means of the considerable application that Qur'ānic recitation requires. One person confided that he had not been brought up with religious training and now that he was middle-aged and beginning to ponder his own mortality he thought that the Qur'ān would provide a badly needed sense of security and purpose.

There are a number of technical Arabic terms connected with Qur'ān recitation. One, often used as an overall term for the oral performance aspects of recitation, is **tilāwa.** This term also means "reading" and the root includes in addition the sense of "to follow." I was told by the recitation master mentioned above that *tilāwa* is the most meaningful term for recitation, because it includes the essential element of "following," in the sense of *obeying,* God's message. Without such faithful commitment, beautiful sounding recitation is devoid of spiritual benefits; it is simply musical entertainment.

The Qur'ān has been the main ingredient in providing Muslims security and purpose in all times and places. Although its scientific interpretation and application in ritual and social-legal contexts is a matter for specialists, the Qur'ān overflows the banks of professional boundaries into all areas of personal and communal Muslim life, from popular religious television programs in Indonesia to gatherings of pious folk in Egypt bent on revitalizing and preserving their spiritual and moral lives. The dynamics of Qur'ānic religion are the lifeblood of Islam without which the tradition would eventually vanish. It is significant that, although Muslim theological and legal schools have often been rigid and unable to adapt to changed situations, the Qur'ān and its related piety structures, above all recitation, have continued to motivate, challenge, comfort, and sustain Muslims through the multitude of trials and temptations that their successes as well as their calamities have brought them through the generations.

The Qur'ānically grounded Muslim—and that is the only true Muslim—is grateful to God for whatever he ordains, serene in the conviction that the steadfast patience he or she is able to muster is itself a sign of God's guidance. To "seek the Face of God," as the Qur'ān characterizes the ultimate quest of Islam, requires approaching him first and last by his Word. Reading the Qur'ān in Arabic is a special experience unmatched by any other for Muslims. The power of its sounds and cadences, coupled with its striking expressions, grips readers and listeners, often rendering them helpless to resist its sacred "magic." The Qur'ān itself contains many statements and examples of religious experience. The performative aspect of Qur'ānic recitation, introduced earlier, is securely rooted in the text itself. That is, the Qur'ān *does things* to people beyond merely providing an informational message. What it does to readers and hearers through the medium of oral performance is itself a main part of the message. The Qur'ān is like a living, breathing reality, fully aware of itself and its power to inspire.

> The skins of those who fear their Lord shiver from (hearing) it, then their skins and hearts soften at the remembrance of God. (39:23)

There comes a moment in the reading of the Qur'ān, as for example in personal study focused on understanding the meaning, whether reciting out loud or reading silently, when readers start feeling an uncanny, sometimes frightening presence. Instead of reading the Qur'ān, the reader begins feeling the Qur'ān is "reading" the reader! This is a wonderfully disturbing experience, by no means requiring a person to be a Muslim before it can be felt. This expression of the Qur'ān's inherent power has been a major factor in the spread of Islam, as well as Muslims' continuing loyalty to the Straight Path, as the Qur'ān itself characterizes the religion.

Islamic legal and theological schools have risen, prospered for a time, then vanished. In today's complex and cosmopolitan world, certain traditional aspects and institutions of Islam, such as rule in accordance with the *Sharī'a,* have been called into question by Muslims and even set aside. But throughout all the change and ferment of modern times, the Qur'ān has continued to provide the central source of meaning, values, and spiritual power for Muslims everywhere. It is one thing for Muslims to study the Qur'ān's literal message and apply it to life. But when difference of opinion and confusion reign and when Muslims find it difficult if not impossible to agree on interpretations and applications of the Qur'ān in actual situations, then the pious recitation of it can still serve as a uniting and empowering force. A colleague once told me about a gathering of Muslim religious experts traveling together on a long bus trip. A violent theological argument broke out, one no one could stop until someone started reciting the Qur'ān. Gradually, the others realized that they were shouting and bickering in the presence of God's manifest speaking. Silence returned and the men repented in the renewed fellowship of receiving God's "tranquility," that *sakīna* which descends when the Word is recited.

Muslim "Saints" and Their Veneration in Popular Islam

Christians have always placed great emphasis on the sanctity of persons. This practice is rooted in the Bible itself. The greatest of all Christian saints is, of course, Jesus, in whom Christians believe that God himself was pleased to have come into human historical life for the redemption of the race from sin and death. But Jesus is really more than a saint; for Christians, he is the incarnation of God. The church developed an elaborate doctrinal and institutional structure for the recognition and, it could be said, the regulation of sainthood. There even developed a theory that the saints, through their abundant spiritual virtues, provide a treasury of merit that can be dispensed by the pope to penitent sinners who purchase indulgences. The selling of indulgences became one of the main controversies leading to the Lutheran Reformation in the sixteenth century, but the theory of saintly merit and its availability for the remission of punishment in purgatory still stands in Roman Catholicism.

A saint, at least in Christian understanding, is a holy person who is exemplary in conduct and able to perform miracles, or a martyr, or the center of cultic veneration, or all of these. Usually it takes a considerable time after the death of a candidate for sainthood before the official ecclesiastical machinery of canonization produces a certified saint. This has been true especially since around 1000 C.E. Next to Jesus, the Blessed Virgin Mary has been the leading saint of the church. [See Judaism p. 407 and Christianity pp. 502, 547–48 for discussion of martyrs.]

The Qur'ān, unlike the Bible, never speaks of the holiness of persons, so, strictly speaking, it does not recognize "saints." The word *saint* derives from the Latin *sanctus,* meaning "holy." According to the Qur'ān, God alone is holy, and even there the Arabic word expressing holiness is not often encountered. (Other terms concerning sacrality are, of course, abundant in the Qur'ān.) The Qur'ānic term rendered in English as saint is *walī,* which actually should be translated "friend." We were introduced to this term at the end of the preceding chapter, in connection with Sufism, which has always placed emphasis on the warm, intimate relationship between God and his human friends.

But, Qur'ānically based arguments notwithstanding, Muslims have in fact considered certain persons to be specially endowed with spiritual power and blessings, which they believe can be bestowed on others. Such potent *walīs* may indeed be recognized for their sanctity during their lifetimes, but most often it is after their deaths that a cult grows around their memory and their mortal remains, represented in burial shrines humble and grand found in most Muslim regions.

In Egypt, for example, the cult of Muslim saints exists alongside the veneration of Christian saints, and the two sometimes overlap and mingle at certain seasons and in special places. There is a cultural dimension in Egypt that exhibits great sensitivity toward persons and objects believed to contain spiritual power, known in Arabic as **baraka**. Upper and Lower Egypt have each had distinct cultural identities since prehistoric times. But both regions, the long, narrow Nile Valley extending upstream from Cairo toward the lakes of Central Africa and the low lands of the Delta, where the branches of the Nile meander until they reach their Mediterranean mouths at Damietta and Rosetta, enjoy exuberant growths of saint cults in hamlets, towns, and cities everywhere.[9]

There is something in traditional Egyptian attitudes that considers a human habitation without a resident saint as somehow lacking an essential element for full life. As noted earlier, returning Egyptian pilgrims who have made the Meccan *Ḥajj* often have the outside walls of their houses painted with *Ḥajj* scenes and sacred texts. A *Ḥajjī* is a kind of living saintly presence in an Egyptian village. But most Egyptian saints, whether Christian or Muslim, are spiritual beings who have lived on after their biological deaths. In some cases, appropriate burial edifices have been erected to their memories because of uncanny post-death events such as visitations to the living in dreams and visions. Not all such saints are pleasant or beneficial; sometimes they are threatening and disposed to carrying out destructive acts if suitable recognition of their cultic demands is not forthcoming.

The greatest Egyptian Muslim saint is Sayyid (a title borne by descendants of Muḥammad) Aḥmad al-Badawī, a thirteenth-century Sufi master originally from Morocco, who settled in the Delta city of Tanta and built a large, loyal following there. He is remembered principally through major celebrations held several times a year at the mosque, tomb, and educational complex dedicated to him in downtown Tanta. The most colorful and famous of the annual celebrations is the autumn **mawlid** or birthday festival, attended mostly by working-class Egyptians, especially farmers, from all over the country. [See Religions of Africa pp. 74–75, Religions of Mesoamerica pp. 229–38, Native Religions of North America pp. 308–16, 351–57, Judaism pp. 439–45, Christianity pp. 551–55, Hinduism p. 829, Buddhism pp. 937–41, Religions of China pp. 1021–24, and Religions of Japan pp. 1140–46, 1153–62 for description and discussion of festivals and annual celebrations.]

It is noteworthy that Sayyid al-Badawī's biggest celebration is held according to the pre-Islamic solar and not the lunar Muslim calendar. Ancient Egyptians worshiped the sun and gave a religious interpretation to the agricultural round of the seasons, which marked not only the progress of the heavenly bodies through the skies but also the waxing and waning of the life-giving Nile River, whose yearly inundation brought the essential silt and water upon which Egypt's life depended absolutely in premodern times. The solar (rather than the Islamic lunar) dating of the greatest of the saint's celebrations suggests a pre-Islamic antecedent for the festival, as do the folk practices long associated with the autumn *mawlid,* which include magical charms to induce fertility in women. Also, the autumn event features extensive market activities centering in agricultural products and related goods.

Sayyid Aḥmad al-Badawī lived during the period when Sufi brotherhoods, *ṭarīqas,* were being established throughout the Umma. As a youth, Sayyid al-Badawī had been a famous pugilist and horseman, but after a period of residence in Mecca, he took up serious studies in Islamic sciences and went on to advanced Sufi meditation in his travels to visit Sufi masters in Iraq and Syria, together with his brother. Arriving at Tanta, he was at first resisted by the local Sufis, but after a while he established a secure place and a reputation for strange and unsettling spiritual exercises. Sayyid al-Badawī's former renown as a martial arts expert continued to color the perceptions of his followers as well as his cautious detractors, so that his cult developed into a following of the more humble, down-to-earth levels of society. This saint is a sort of god among Egypt's saints, and the common folk sense Sayyid al-Badawī's presence everywhere and are thus extremely careful about how they refer to him in conversation.

Although the Badawī complex of veneration and lore contains large amounts of folk material unrelated to either Qur'ān or Sunna, let alone to official theological and legal interpretations, there is a strong connection with Sunnī orthopraxy through the respected theological school attached to the mosque-tomb complex in Tanta. The great Egyptian Muslim theologian Muḥammad 'Abduh (1849–1905) was educated at the Tanta institute, as have been other prominent Islamic leaders.

Egypt's tolerance toward folk beliefs and practices among its Muslim multitudes indicates a confident attitude toward life's complexities, a national trait that can be traced to ancient times when the Nile people worshiped all kinds of deities and incorporated them into a harmonious if, to modern people, baroque hierarchy of animals, monsters, hybrid creatures, divinized humans, elemental forces, and moral virtues. Muslim saints in Egypt continue the old pattern of hierarchy by the popular practice of seeking intercession with God through them.

Intercession is believed by Muslim scholars to be permitted through the Prophet Muḥammad when Judgment Day comes; that is, Muḥammad will intercede on behalf of Muslims directly with God for their forgiveness. But most official Muslim authorities agree that there is little if any scriptural basis for the intercession of saints. Nevertheless, people do in fact seek such intercession in many ways. They do not consider this to be idolatrous in the least. Rather, they view the friendly help of a holy personage as a natural link between humans and God, a sort of exemplary proof of God's providence and continuous working in the world for their ultimate good. The holiness of Muslim saints thus does not inhere in persons as such, but in the blessings and power bestowed on them by God, which are then mediated outward to needy human devotees.

Since the stern puritanical reforms of the **Wahhābi** movement got under way in Arabia more than two hundred years ago, saint veneration has been outlawed in the Hijāz and all regions under the authority of the Sa'udi dynasty. But neighboring Yemen has continued to maintain extensive saint cults at the popular level of culture. And in southern Asia, North Africa, the Fertile Crescent, and Indonesia, varieties of saint veneration are found, sometimes in profusion.

In North Africa, saint veneration is closely linked with family lineages and political power. Each major tribal grouping expresses its prestige and cohesion as a potent sociopolitical entity through its sacred sites, where its saints, called marabouts, are buried. Not all marabouts are dead, whether in Egypt or Morocco; they serve as sacred resources for people seeking intercession, boons, healing, and other blessings. A marabout is a saint who has been identified because of wonder working, descent from the Prophet Muḥammad, or both. The word marabout itself has a relationship with military defense of the Muslim community, because *murābiṭs* (the Arabic source of "marabout") were medieval warriors who guarded the frontiers of the Islamic lands in fortified positions. The word *murābiṭ* means "one who is bound" to something; in the case of Moroccan holy men with this title, they are bound to God.

The phenomenon of saint veneration in Morocco and North Africa is generally linked with Sufism, as well as with tribal, clan, and family groupings. Sufism and sainthood are also closely tied in other Muslim countries, such as Pakistan and India. However, way over at the other end of the Islamic world from Morocco is a major Muslim region where Sufism has less influence, but where the veneration of God's friends is nevertheless practiced, too. Let us look at Indonesian saint veneration.

The "Nine Saints" of Java

Java was Islamized, according to legends, by nine holy men who brought the teachings of the Qur'ān to that island in the fifteenth and sixteenth centuries. They are known collectively in Javanese as the *wali songo,* or "nine saints." Although these heroes are historically connected in some respects with Sufism and although Sufi merchants and travelers were prominent in spreading Islam peacefully throughout the Malay-Indonesian archipelago, the *wali songo* tradition is not limited to Sufism. In fact, Sufism of the *ṭarīqa* variety, with established brotherhoods and extensive lineages and linkages throughout the islands, never became as firmly entrenched in Indonesia as in Egypt, Iraq, North Africa, and the Indian subcontinent, where it has sometimes dominated. In Indonesia the indigenous tradition, deeply influenced by pre-Islamic Javanese, Hindu, and Buddhist beliefs and practices, was already so profoundly mystical in orientation that Islam in Sufistic forms made easy headway as a familiar kind of phenomenon. The Javanese especially were converted to Islam not as to the strange new worldview of Semitic monotheism, but as to a familiar path of shared mystical convictions already held in essence by pre-Islamic Indonesians. Many Javanese Muslims continue to be more "cosmocentric" than "theocentric," as one scholar has put it.[10]

One of the nine Indonesian saints was Sunan Ampel, who established Islam at Ampel in East Java near the modern city of Surabaya. This *walī's* original name was Raden ("Prince") Rahmat, the son of an Arab missionary in Champa. After his successes as a missionary on the north coast of East Java, he came to be venerated as the leading Muslim saint of Java and was given the title by which he has been remembered in his cult: Sunan Ampel, "Prince of Ampel." The large mosque-tomb complex dedicated to the memory of Sunan Ampel and a number of other great *walīs* in the old quarter of Surabaya is the scene of a variety of religiously oriented activities, such as Arabic and Qur'ānic instruction, Friday congregational worship, religious education, community services, and youth activities. The surrounding streets are residential and commercial with religious bookstores, sellers of incense, perfumes, souvenirs, and other items standard near Friday mosques in all parts of the Muslim world. There are many old Arab families in the Ampel district and the casual stroller can hear Arabic as well as the native Indonesian and Javanese being spoken in conversation in some of the shops, especially those catering to buyers of classical Islamic texts in Arabic. In fact, the "feel" of the Ampel district is very much like the atmosphere of the medieval Azhar district in Cairo, with its venerable mosque and university, kiosks, religious bookstores, and bazaar. Women dress with modest

Islamic covering of the hair, arms, and legs, while men often wear caps such as those found in other Muslim countries of southern and Southeast Asia.

The most notable times at Ampel are when religious festivals are held, as in the fasting month of Ramaḍān, when evenings are given over to joyful group recitation and people fill the narrow streets shopping and socializing in family and neighborhood groups. A very special time is when the saint's birthday is celebrated with a *mawlid,* just as in Egypt and other places. Religious organizations parade through the streets with flags and banners, and men and boys chant sacred songs in honor of Sunan Ampel. The old walled-in graveyard next to the main mosque fills with pilgrims and local pious people, the men and boys at one end and the women and girls at the other, both groups facing the central area where the saint reposes in a fenced-in plot together with a number of fellow saints. The *imām* of the mosque and other officials and dignitaries spend periods leading a multitude in reciting long litanies together, calling down blessings on the Prophet Muḥammad and recalling the heroic work of Sunan Ampel and other Muslim missionaries to Java.

On one of the days of the *mawlid* there is a group circumcision of little boys, a standard feature of saint festivals in Java, commemorated in modern times by a "class" photo. Circumcision is a genuine rite of passage when it occurs near adolescence, as it often does in Southeast Asia. The boys are first brought to a clinic and given a medical examination. Later they are operated on, with their parents and relatives seated nearby under a canopy. There is much joy and children running around, except for those about to be circumcised. They are set apart and have some dread of the ordeal, but their new status afterward

Members of Muslim men's society parading in the streets of Rawalpindi, Pakistan, in celebration of the Prophet Muhammad's birthday. The poster calls for Muslim unity with a verse from the Qur'ān: "And hold fast, all together, to Allāh's lifeline, and do not become divided" (3:102).

normally more than makes up for the pain and anxiety suffered both during the operation and in the time leading up to it. [See Religions of Africa, p. 76, Judaism pp. 385–86, 445–46, and Christianity p. 496 for discussion of circumcision.]

The *mawlid* of Sunan Ampel in Surabaya is a major Indonesian saint day, but it does not compare with the Tanta *mawlid* of Sayyid Aḥmad al-Badawī either in scale or prestige or in the variety of folk-magical associations and practices around its fringes. Sunan Ampel is still a major Indonesian Muslim saint, but other regions of Java venerate other of the nine *walīs* so that in Tuban, west of Surabaya, there is a *mawlid* in honor of Sunan Ampel's son, the great *walī* Sunan Bonang, and in nearby Gresik the people visit the hill where Sunan Giri, the great warrior saint who defeated the Hindu armies in the name of Islam, is buried. And there are still other saints in Kudus, Demak, and other Javanese locales who command the respect and veneration of continuing cults. Nevertheless, Sunan Ampel does attract visitors from afar. One night, while we were listening to Qur'ān recitation in the graveyard of the Ampel mosque, a teenager with a pack came and sat next to me and my friend and, before falling asleep in that holy place, told us that he had just arrived from central Java after walking and hitchhiking for two days. He had come especially to pay his respects to Sunan Ampel during his *mawlid*.

Shī'ite Saint Veneration

The saint veneration activities described so far are taken from Sunnī contexts and traditions. The Shī'ites have their own holy personages connected with the Prophet's family and the lineage of *Imāms* and their associates. Unlike Sunnī Islam, Shī'ite tradition accords the visitation of the burial places of its sacred heroes a central place within the total belief and practice system. That is, although Shī'ites consider the *Ḥajj* to be one of the Pillars of their religion along with their fellow Sunnī Muslims, they also universally recommend pilgrimages to Karbalā' and the tomb of the martyr Ḥusayn; to Najaf, where the grave of 'Alī, the first *Imām*, is; and to other places like Mashhad in eastern Iran, the burial place of the eighth *Imām*, 'Alī Riḍā. A linkage between Shī'ite visitation of the graves of the *Imāms* and the Meccan *Ḥajj* is the practice of visiting the tomb of 'Alī, in Najaf, before continuing on to Mecca for the *Ḥajj*.

There are many features surrounding the Shī'ites' visits to their holy places that are like saints' festivals among Sunnīs, such as popular local practices, Qur'ān chanting in the evenings, buying and selling of things (particularly religious goods), special foods, gatherings of Sufi brotherhoods, and the like. But the Shī'ites have an additional observance that occurs on the fateful tenth day of the month of Muḥarram, the anniversary of the tragic martyrdom of Ḥusayn, son of 'Alī and grandson of the Prophet, in Karbalā', back in 680. Remember that Ḥusayn, together with his close kin and supporters, was on the way to Iraq to accept leadership of the Shī'ites there, in preparation for an attempted recovery of rule of the Umma from the Damascus-based Umayyad dynasty. Ḥusayn was intercepted by the caliphal forces at Karbalā' and, after being warned to desist from his course, upon refusing was cut down along with his followers. The women and children were transported in bonds to the capital, Damascus.

Ta'zīya performance in a special theater designed for the Shī'ite "passion play" in Shiraz, Iran. The mounted actor represents the Imām Ḥusayn, *just before his martyrdom at Karbalā' in 680 C.E. (Photo used by permission of Peter J. Chelkowski.)*

The commemoration of this black day in Shī'ite sacred history is a "passion play," called **ta'zīya,** "consolation," which recounts the events and their meaning. *Ta'zīya* productions are mounted in Iran, Iraq, Pakistan, India, and wherever Shī'ites live. Sometimes they are held in special theaters, sometimes in town squares or other places. In small villages storytellers unfurl cartoonlike paintings of the Karbalā' story while singing and reciting the episodes as the gathered audience shares in all the emotions generated by the tragedy and becomes, in a sense, part of the long-ago saga as it is ritually recalled and incorporated into the ongoing experience of Shī'ites. For example, when a Shī'ite soldier falls on the field of battle, he is identified with Ḥusayn. At the end of the year, when Shī'ites in Iran remember their dead of the year, a close, intentional identification with Ḥusayn is made. In the case of women, the identification is often with Ḥusayn's mother, Fāṭima, who also died young.

Ḥusayn long ago became the prototype of the suffering righteous person, whose wounds would be used by God to redeem the Shī'ites if they sustained their faith and dedication to what they consider to be true Islam. The martyrdom of Ḥusayn and the ritual repetitions of it by means of the *ta'zīya* sacred drama are finally not tragic at all; rather, they are a persistent showing forth of victorious faith in God's ultimate vindication, similar to the expression of the battered and humiliated Old Testament figure Job, who declared during his lowest point, "I know that my Redeemer lives, and that on the latter day he will stand upon the earth."

According to tradition, the severed head of Ḥusayn was first transported to Damascus, the capital of the Umayyads. Later it was moved, according to another tradition, to Cairo by the Shī'ite Fāṭmids who founded the city in 969. There is a large mosque dedicated to Ḥusayn near the Azhar University in Cairo and it is believed that among its treasured relics is Ḥusayn's head. Many miracles have been attributed to Ḥusayn, as well as marvels associated with his birth, death, and accomplishments. His head is said to have emitted a wonderful perfume in one legend, and in another to have recited Qur'ānic passages.

During the *ta'zīya* performance Ḥusayn is always dressed in a green tunic that is worn under his white grave shroud, the latter symbolizing martyrdom. Green has always been associated with Muḥammad and is thus the Islamic color par excellence. Descendants of the Prophet are permitted to wear green turbans, symbolizing their status as **sayyids.** The Umayyad commander in the *ta'zīya* wears red, symbolizing conflict and bloodshed, the color of the enemies of the Shī'ites.

The Muslim Life Cycle: Rites and Processes

We have seen how Qur'ān recitation and saint veneration work to reinforce and integrate Islamic beliefs and values, the first by constant reminding of God's transcending authority expressed in a message and a powerful spiritual presence, the second through sanctification of specific persons in particular places, showing divine providence percolating, as it were, through the soil of ordinary life. In this final section we shall see how Islamic beliefs and values are expressed in the behavioral patterns associated with the major transitions of human life.

Islamic behaviors, whether the official practices prescribed as the Pillars of Islam or variable rituals of social relations and etiquette, comprise a complex code regulating individual and communal life at different levels. This code sets Muslims apart from other peoples and religions. Although Muslims warmly welcome and embrace new members into the Umma, they do so with the utmost regard for those individuals becoming new kinds of persons with Islamic convictions and habits.

The Lawful (ḥalāl) and the Prohibited (ḥarām)

Although this section focuses on stages in the life cycle, it should be understood that Muslims are concerned foremost with the ongoing flow of life, which ceremonies and rites of status—such as circumcision, marriage, and funerals—punctuate and help regulate. To guide Muslims in making Islam a complete way of life is a general dualism that guides orthopraxy in evaluating both behavior and matter: *ḥalāl*, namely that which is lawful, and *ḥarām*, that which is prohibited. The Qur'ān and Ḥadīth contain the essential information about what God has permitted and what he has forbidden. Muslims also use summaries of these things, such as the enormously popular and influential contemporary work *The Lawful and the Prohibited in Islam,* by Yusuf al-Qaradawi, which has been translated from Arabic into several languages spoken widely by Muslims.

Among the most common *ḥalāl/ḥarām* concerns of Muslims on a daily basis is food. The Qur'ān and Ḥadīth contain commands and specifications about what is permitted and what forbidden. Most foods are permitted, but the following are forbidden: pork, blood, intoxicants, carrion, and food dedicated to idols (Qur'ān 6:145; 5:4, 93–94). Also forbidden is any flesh rendered *ḥarām* by the way it was killed; Islamic slaughtering rules must be followed. Many consider other foods to be forbidden as well, although legal specialists sometimes differ and consider them to be merely "detestable" (*makrūh*), and thus not strictly forbidden. Examples of these are insects and animals with canine teeth and birds with talons (both predators). Interestingly, and in contrast with Jewish dietary rules that are otherwise similar, most Muslims consider all marine animals to be lawful as food, provided that they cannot survive out of water (this includes whales but excludes amphibians). Law books cover the fine points of prohibited and permitted foods in considerable detail, but enough has been given here to suggest the main outlines of the topic. In an emergency, even *ḥarām* foods may be consumed by Muslims to preserve life, but such a decision is not made lightly.

Ḥalāl and *ḥarām* considerations also apply to worship, as well as to marriage and divorce, sexuality, clothing, the use of jewelry and perfume, etiquette and social relations, proper use of the lavatory, sports and recreation, business dealings, relations with non-Muslims, and many other things.

Life-cycle stages are points at which both the structure and dynamics of Muslim life intersect. All cultures have rites of passage from one stage to another, whether they occur primarily in the religious sphere, along social, civil, military, or political lines, or combinations of these, as is most common. For example, an Australian aboriginal puberty rite of coming of age included spiritual and social dimensions in an integrated whole: To be considered mature and responsible enough to share in the sacred wisdom of the tribe's origins carried with it a significant portion in the guardianship of the wisdom in the future. The knowledge of sacred origins in Australian aboriginal society was a principal element in being a complete human and thus a trusted member of the community as well as a spiritually fulfilled person. [See Religions of Africa pp. 42–51, 76–79, Religions of Mesoamerica pp. 201–6, Native Religions of North America pp. 278–79, 295–98, 306–8, Judaism pp. 445–50, Christianity pp. 542–43, 555–57, Hinduism pp. 747, 807–14, Buddhism pp. 915–17, 921, 931–37, Religions of China pp. 1019–21, and Religions of Japan pp. 1146–50 for description and discussion of rites of passage.]

Islam does not have a formal rite of passage for entry into its ranks. An individual desiring to become a Muslim has only to utter the *Shahāda* ("There is no god but God; Muḥammad is the messenger of God") with a sincere heart to join the Umma. Normally the witnessing is done in the presence of other Muslims, and that is recommended, but one may submit alone in the presence of God. By the time one actually joins his or her fellow Muslims, for example in the performance of the *Ṣalāt,* one will again utter the *Shahāda* periodically. The witnessing in the *Shahāda* is not itself the conversion, but the public expression of it.

However, once a person has become a Muslim, then all of the duties as well as privileges of membership in the Umma are immediately in force. It is normal for an uncircumcised adult male convert to Islam to undergo circumcision. Most converts also take an Islamic name, which may simply be added to previous names or used as a replacement name. In either case, a significant statement is made about the person's new identity as a Muslim. Preferred names among Muslims are 'Abdullāh ("Servant of God"), 'Abdurraḥmān ("Servant of the Merciful"), Muḥammad, 'Alī, 'Ā'isha, Fāṭima, Khadīja, Ḥasan, Ḥusayn, 'Umar, and other names associated with the Prophet's family and companions. Two well-known Americans adopted Muslim names upon conversion: Boxer Cassius Clay became Muhammad Ali and basketball player Lew Alcindor became Kareem Abdul-Jabbar.

Birth and Childhood

Islamic rites of passage begin at birth and continue to death and even beyond. When a Muslim couple engage in marital relations, they first utter the **Basmala,** "In the Name of God, the Merciful, the Compassionate." Upon the birth of a child, someone recites the call to prayer in the infant's ear. The seventh day is the traditional time for naming, as well as a related ceremony consisting of the sacrifice of an animal and the shaving of a tuft of the baby's hair. When a child begins to talk, simple Islamic words and phrases are taught, like the *Basmala.* As soon as possible, training in reading and reciting the Qur'ān is begun. Young boys and girls may play together, but unrelated males and females are separated as puberty approaches. [See Religions of Africa pp. 45–46, 76, Native Religions of North America p. 307, Judaism pp. 385–86, 445–46, Christianity p. 556, Hinduism pp. 810–11, Buddhism p. 932, Religions of China pp. 1019–20, and Religions of Japan pp. 1146–47 for description and discussion of birth rites.]

Puberty and Circumcision

Coming of age rites among Muslims vary considerably from region to region, but circumcision of boys, although it often is performed long before puberty, is a universal symbol of Muslim male identity. In some regions, girls are "circumcised," too, by scarring or even excision of the clitoris, but this operation is largely a pattern of culture and not a religious rite. Circumcision of boys is often performed in infancy, but many undergo the operation around age seven, and significant numbers experience it at the onset of puberty. In the last case, circumcision is sometimes associated with a first complete recitation of the Qur'ān. A double potency is thus proclaimed: knowledge of God's teaching, which enables the person to distinguish between right and wrong, and biological as well as cultural male potency as a full-fledged Muslim and "citizen" of the

Umma, with full enjoyment of its privileges and responsibility for its defense and propagation.

To return to the observation that Islam requires no rites of passage into its ranks, it is sufficient simply to cite the rites surrounding birth, childhood, and puberty to discern a processual dimension to a person's development as a complete human being within the Islamic scheme of things. That is, Muslim life is a dynamic, developmental process of *becoming*. Because Islam is a complete way of life, as Muslims so often emphasize, there have to be accompanying rites that mark and reinforce the *natural* cycles of human life in Islamic ways. All humans typically are born, develop, mature, pass through a marriageable phase when reproduction is a possibility, grow old, and die. All societies have rites marking these transitions. Islam puts its special stamp on each of these natural passages and thus consecrates them to God in a manner that recalls our discussion of the original constitution or *fiṭra* of human existence as a good creation, made from the beginning for the service of God. We turn now to two of the greatest transitions in human life: marriage and death.

Marriage

Islamic marriage is a time for great rejoicing and celebration. In traditional settings, which are dominant still in most Muslim regions, the parents serve as matchmakers. Young women are not allowed to go out looking for a husband, although they may express their preferences and they have the right to refuse someone selected for them. A man may initiate the matchmaking, but he normally does not approach a prospective bride directly. Propriety and custom require indirect negotiations with the woman's father or other male guardian. The betrothed pair are not permitted to be alone together before marriage, although they may sometimes enjoy each other's company in the presence of other responsible adults such as parents.

Islamic law has strict regulations concerning relations between the sexes. The concept of **mahram** refers to the permitted degrees of close blood relationship within which males and females may not marry and thus may associate socially with each other. A proper Muslim woman never associates socially with a non-*mahram* male. Even in cases of necessity there is usually another close adult relative in attendance, such as in visits to the doctor or other places where outside contact with the opposite sex is unavoidable. In modern settings such as Western universities it is generally acceptable for Muslim female students, for example, to confer with their male professors one on one in the professional setting of a faculty office. But such a situation is an exception, bowing to the custom of the host country; all other Islamic standards of deportment are otherwise observed.

There are no prohibitions regarding socialization between females with each other or males with other males. This leads to a two-sided, but not divided, society among Muslims. For example, when unrelated Muslims meet for a meal, the custom is for the women to occupy separate rooms and eat together, while the men associate only with each other. Proper Muslim men do not normally inquire about female members of a non-kinsman's family, although it is expected that a general inquiry about the well-being of the *family as a whole* be offered. Thus, the society is not divided, essentially; it is simply most fully artic-ulated at the *family* level where the division of roles, labor, and responsibility between husband and wife, boys and girls, uncles and aunts, and so forth exhibits a basic complementarity rather than opposition.

The Qur'ān permits Muslim men to marry up to four wives concurrently, provided all are treated equally. Since this is a practical difficulty—many would say impossibility—there is a wide consensus that marriages should be monoga-mous except in special circumstances (as, for example, in early Islamic and other times when there was a surplus of women, because of high death rates of men in battle). Women are permitted only one spouse at a time. Divorce is allowed for both partners, but it is generally easier for the man to dissolve the marriage. Muslim men may marry non-Muslim women, so long as they are from the People of the Book, that is Jews or Christians, but Muslim women are not permitted to marry non-Muslim men. Conversion of the male to Islam is always a possibility; however, if it is done solely to remove the legal disqualification such conversion is disapproved.

The marriage ceremony is a simple affair of writing up and signing a con-tract between the partners. There is no specific ritual connected with the cere-mony, at least as a requirement, although it is customary for someone to recite a passage of the Qur'ān and to deliver a brief inspirational speech. At the signing of the contract, the groom meets with a male representative of the bride. An official from the government often supervises the proceedings, although he does not do so in any sense like a cleric; his responsibility is strictly legal.

It is after the legal ceremony of signing that the real marriage festivities begin. These celebrations vary widely according to region, but all Muslims con-sider it important to launch the marriage with a happy time for relatives and other guests to the extent that means and circumstances permit. This typically includes special and abundant food, new clothes, Qur'ān recitation by a hired professional, music, dancing (folk types prevail, with each sex dancing together), bright lights and decoration, dramatic performances (e.g., shadow puppetry in Java), and other activities. Sometimes the festivities continue for days. There may occasionally be mischievous snooping on the newlyweds, but in good fun. In Middle Eastern societies there is still found the ritual exhibition of a bloody sheet after the marriage has been consummated, thus certifying the propriety of the union and preserving the honor of the virginal bride's family as well as demonstrating the virility of the groom. [See Religions of Africa pp. 48–51, 77–78, Judaism pp. 447–48, Christianity p. 556, Hinduism pp. 809–10, Buddhism p. 935, Religions of China, p. 1020, and Religions of Japan p. 1148 for description and discussion of marriage rites.]

Death and Its Rites

At the approach of death, the dying person should turn her or his face toward Mecca and say, "There is no god but God," in preparation for the ques-tioning that is believed to occur in the tomb by the angels of death. The thirty-sixth *sūra* of the Qur'ān is often recited to the dying person, after death, and at funeral and memorial observances, because it summarizes so vividly the end of life and the passage to the hereafter. "Who will revive these bones when they have rotted away? Say: He will revive them Who produced them at the first, for He is Knower of every creation" (36:77–78).

After death the deceased's body must receive its final ablution, which is a complete ritual bath performed according to precise rules. No embalming is permitted, but the body may be scented before it is wrapped in a plain white grave cloth that completely enfolds the corpse. It is not necessary to place the corpse in a coffin. Islamic law requires that the burial be performed the same day as the death if possible, but burial may not take place after sundown.

It is a communal obligation to follow the funeral procession to the burial place, but it is sufficient that only a representative group actually do it. The funeral *Ṣalāt,* consisting of four parts in each of which "God is most great!" is uttered, is performed at the gravesite with all standing throughout. It is even possible to perform the *Ṣalāt* in the absence of the corpse. When the burial party arrives at the gravesite, the first *sūra* of the Qur'ān is recited. If it has not been done earlier, the person presiding at the burial whispers the *Shahāda* into the ear of the deceased just before beginning to fill in the grave, so as to remind the departed one of the true religion and the correct answer to the questioning angels waiting to receive the dead soul. The traditional and recommended grave is four to six feet deep, with a shelf hollowed out on one side. The corpse is placed on its side on this shelf, with the head turned toward Mecca.

There is strong testimony in the Ḥadīth that excessive mourning and loud lamentation cause the deceased to suffer in the grave. The best expression of grief and respect for the dead is recitation of the Qur'ān, whose merit redounds to the benefit of the deceased. After the day of burial there is usually a reception in commemoration of the death. In Egypt, for example, an observance is held on the fortieth day after the death, where people express their condolences, sign a guest book, and stay a while to sip coffee and listen to Qur'ān recitation.

The Muslim martyr does not need to receive the final ablution because his or her wounds are purification in the sight of God, who rewards the fallen warrior with immediate admission to paradise. Nor is the funeral *Ṣalāt* said over the martyr's remains. It is interesting to observe that persons considered martyrs are not limited to those who die in battle defending Islam. The pilgrim who dies while making the *Ḥajj* is a martyr, as is one who perishes while reciting the Qur'ān or engaged in other pious acts. [See Religions of Africa pp. 42–45, 78–79, Religions of Mesoamerica pp. 144, 229–33, Native Religions of North America pp. 300–301, 307–8, 335–37, Judaism pp. 448–50, Christianity p. 557, Hinduism pp. 813–14, Buddhism pp. 935–37, Religions of China pp. 1021, 1041–44, and Religions of Japan pp. 1149–50 for description and discussion of death and funeral rites.]

Conclusions

We have reviewed only the bare essentials of Islamic rites of passage connected with the life cycle. Other rites of passage attend initiation into a Sufi brotherhood, which typically culminates in the bestowing of the patched frock, symbol of the spiritual poverty of the Sufi mendicant. Other symbols may also accompany the status change from novice to adept on the Sufi way, such as the gift of a cap or the placing of the disciple's hand into that of the master so that the latter's *baraka* may be transmitted, thus extending the lineage one link further.

Titles are also part of status changes in Islam. The title of *Ḥajjī*, "pilgrim," has already been mentioned. The title *shaykh* is applied to various types of Muslims, from the youth who has just completed memorizing the Qur'ān to any older man who is respected for devotion and religious learning, even if not as a professional scholar. In Iran, the title *ayatollah*, which literally means "sign of God," has in modern times been bestowed on exceptionally pious and learned religious scholars with significant followings. The famous Ayatollah Khomeini, late leader of Iran's Islamic revolutionary government, was but one of thousands of venerated religious guides in Iran today who bear the title of *ayatollah*.

In Java many Muslims observe Islamic rites of passage such as circumcision and marriage by sponsoring the performance of a classical shadow-puppet play. The traditional stories that are dramatized by the manipulation of leather puppets against a white screen are taken from Hindu myth and epic, but they are thought to have enduring meaning and power within the Javanese worldview as interpreted in an Islamic framework. In such classical Javanese regions as Yogyakarta and Solo in central Java the majority of guests, particularly of more well-to-do hosts, expect a marriage especially to be celebrated by a suitably opulent expression of traditional high culture such as shadow plays and accompanying gamelan music provide. It is relevant, also, that the puppet master is a person of high ritual status within the Javanese value system. Thus, a proper Islamic marriage—which, remember, does not in itself require anything beyond the basic contract signing—when joined to a traditional Javanese festive structure produces a dynamic that fulfills both what God has commanded and what the Javanese themselves have inherited as an ancient legacy of the way things are done.

Islam as a Dynamic Reality

The preceding chapter focused on structures of Islam and the Muslim life, with special emphasis on the Pillars, the Qur'ān and Sunna, the *Sharī'a*, and Sufism. This chapter has examined dynamics of Muslim life beyond the formal structures of orthoprax prescription and precept. The Arabic word *islām* is itself a noun containing within its meaning a dynamic sense of "submitting," not an objectified sense of "submission" as a kind of static entity; that is, Muslims must *intend* submission and all the accompanying attitudes and acts that make up being Muslim in the world, each day. Just as a single act of repentance, for Muslims, is not a once-for-all guarantee of success, so also must surrender to God be that lifelong process of becoming that was described in our discussion of life cycle. Muḥammad, when asked whether he, a great prophet, had ever felt the need to repent, to turn again toward God, declared once that he repented seventy times each day. Likewise, Islam is a constant turning again in submission to God, requiring the patterns and structures of doctrine and devotion as a clearly marked path for what, after all, is a journey through life in which human will in history is progressively harmonized with that preexisting, life-sustaining *fiṭra* that is humankind's birthright.

Although this chapter has attempted to show how the Qur'ān contributes to the dynamics of Muslim individual and community life, nothing has been said about the Prophet's Sunna. But Muḥammad's teaching and example are of fundamental importance in the teaching of Qur'ānic interpretation and recitation, as well as the learning of how to enjoy and follow the Qur'ān in life's varied situations. Similarly, the veneration of saints derives much from the anciently developed practices surrounding the veneration of Muḥammad. The Prophet's birthday is celebrated in most Muslim countries by colorful festivities, thereby serving as a universal saint's day, which then is mirrored in multifarious forms by the *mawlids* of saints from Morocco to Java, all of which pay respects in some manner to Muḥammad, the greatest saint of all.

The Muslim life-cycle rites are all in some way also based on Muḥammad's or the Qur'ān's teaching. For example, circumcision is not prescribed in the Qur'ān, but it is mentioned in the Ḥadīth literature, from which it received its high status among the marks of Muslim identity. In general, it should be remembered that the Qur'ān teaches Muslims *what* to believe and do, whereas the Sunna prescribes and describes *how* faith is to be incorporated into all dimensions of life. As in life Muḥammad and the Qur'ān were practically indistinguishable, so also since has the Prophet's charisma become progressively transferred onto the Muslim community itself. Thus the Umma is also a charismatic reality, bearing both God's message and his Prophet's exemplary teaching not primarily by means of written records, but through the ingrained convictions, attitudes, and habits of persons in a strong communal bond. Islamic structure and dynamics come together when Qur'ān and Sunna are thus internalized by Muslims.

28
Islam in Today's World

THE RECENT EMERGENCE of a renewed and vigorous Islam was noted toward the end of chapter 25. The strength of Islam in today's world may be witnessed in several areas: political expression, economics, the rejection of Western and materialistic values, the acceptance of science and technology, and widespread missionary activities on a global scale.

Muslim Rejection of the West

It may seem contradictory to mention together the rejection of Western values and the acceptance of science and technology, because the latter have been dominated by Western peoples or at least most of the approaches and patterns of inquiry have been developed in the modern West. Nevertheless, Muslims share the memory that in earlier times their civilization made great progress in science, especially in such fields as mathematics, medicine, astronomy, geography, and optics. For various reasons, the Islamic world fell behind in scientific inquiry. The fact that the West succeeded in developing modern science in no way suggests that it was because of a better religion or more intelligent human resources. Rather, historical, political, economic, and geographical circumstances permitted the West to monopolize science and industrial technology.

The problem with the West's domination of science and technology according to Muslim critics is that underneath it is a rationalistic and materialistic worldview that denies the sovereignty of God and any covenant responsibility from his human creatures. What is more, Muslim reformers agree that Western materialism seduces people into a blind consumerism based on satisfaction of sensual desires. In the contemporary world of global communications and markets, non-Western peoples are also victimized by Western commercial exploitation of universal human cravings of a hedonistic sort. Thus, we find in stricter Islamic circles a rejection of rock and other popular music, alcohol, social mixing of the sexes, motion pictures, Western television series, bank interest, pornography, and other things.

But Muslims endorse many other products of Western technology such as automobiles, airplanes, medicine, industrial manufacturing, computers, electronic media, and especially technical education, as well as Western marketing strategies. North American and European universities and technical institutes have large enrollments from Asian and African countries, including significant numbers of Muslim students from such nations as Saudi Arabia, Kuwait, the Gulf Emirates, Pakistan, Egypt, Iran, Lebanon, Syria, Malaysia, and Indonesia.

The rejection of Western materialism on the part of many vocal Muslim critics is not shared by all or even most Muslims. For one thing, the characterization of the West as "materialistic" needs to be placed in perspective, because there is much religious belief and ferment in Western countries, too. And Western criticisms of materialism are strong and sophisticated, extending beyond consumerism to assessments of and attacks on ideological materialism, whether Marxist or capitalist. Religious people everywhere—Muslim, Christian, Buddhist, Jewish, Hindu—share important insights and convictions about the human condition and the permissibility of attachment to material goods and the proper disciplining of human passions. In the Islamic case, rejection of what are regarded to be Western values and ways has less to do with the West than with forming and maintaining Islamic allegiances. The memories of Western colonialism and imperialism are bitter, and the descendants of the colonized peoples, including many of those in Muslim countries, are committed to ensuring that foreign domination does not recur, whether in political and economic or in more subtle symbolic, cultural, and social ways. Islamic convictions and ordering principles are believed by many to be the strongest bulwark against foreign domination.

The traditional separation of the world into the *Dār al-Islām* and the *Dār al-Ḥarb* may be seen in today's world in the rejection of the West as a religious duty. Materialism and consumerism are regarded by staunch Muslims as forms of idolatry. But exploitation of the natural world by means of science and technology is considered not only permissible but encouraged by God, so long as it is done according to Islamic principles that are adumbrated, if not specifically detailed, in the Qur'ān and Sunna. *Ijtihād* becomes once again an important method of relating God's Word to the world in the present day when so many new developments and discoveries need to be evaluated.

More extremist Islamic revolutionary movements call for a total removal of Western and especially American interests and influences from Islamic nations. This rejection sometimes takes the form of *jihād*, in the sense of actual holy warfare, which may include terrorism. Although most Muslims do not endorse terrorism, powerful emotions are stirred among them when extremist groups carry out their aims in the name of Islam. Islam thus serves both as religion and ideology, that is, a means of relating to God in faith and service and a means of mobilizing fellow humans for political and social ends. Islam is co-opted for many reasons in this process, but overall Islam may serve as a symbol for otherwise highly diverse peoples who have in common a deep-seated aversion to outside agencies thought to be responsible for their current plight, whether injustice and revolution in Lebanon, the Israeli occupation of Palestine, a pro-Western government in Egypt, or the former Soviet occupation of Afghanistan. In revolutionary Iran, where Western influences have been systematically uprooted, the West nevertheless continues to serve as the primary symbol of satanic evil, partly because this helps the rulers maintain a grip on their people.

Islam and Muslims in the West

We have witnessed conflicting opinions on what results from close contacts with Western peoples and institutions. On the one side is the view that exposure to Western ways corrupts and turns Muslims from the Straight Path. It is true, for example, that Muslim youth who attend Western universities find them-selves in strange social situations with little or no reinforcement of their accustomed social patterns, which include close family ties, no mixing of the sexes, and well-imprinted patterns of ritual observance. Western daytime work and class schedules do not immediately make way for prayer times, nor is the Ramaḍān fast thought to be conducive to efficiency and productivity. But often foreign Muslim students in the West seek each other out, if not for religious, then for cultural and language reasons: Malaysians, Indonesians, and Bangla-deshis tend to form support systems, as do Arabs and Iranians. (Often Muslim students of diverse nationalities cooperate in forming student associations and observing Ṣalāt and other duties.) In our experience, Muslim visitors to the United States, for example, sharply distinguish their own values and customs from the prevailing ethos and adjust accordingly, accepting what they can and maintaining their own ways as far as possible.

Muslim visitors in the West tend to become stronger Muslims rather than straying into alien ways. For one thing, North American and European societies have free presses and a high degree of freedom of association and expression that tolerates dissenting and even radical viewpoints. Muslims and others from the East are able to form associations and express opinions that would be forbid-den and even severely punished in their native countries. So, ironically, while Muslim students in the West benefit from its superior scientific and technologi-cal education, they also discipline themselves in religious ways, including wit-nessing to their convictions through **daʿwa,** the missionary "call" to outsiders to enjoy the benefits of Islam.

There is no question but that Muslim degree earners, when they return to their countries, carry with them a wide range of reactions and attitudes con-cerning Western and non-Muslim ways. But a significant number of Muslims remain in Western countries, for economic betterment, professional opportuni-ties, and other reasons. The presence of these people has brought about the first significant development of Islamic institutions in the West. Muslims comprise the second largest religious community in France now, way behind the Roman Catholics, but ahead of the Protestants. There are significant Muslim communi-ties in Germany and the United Kingdom, too, as well as in the Netherlands. In

Canada, the Muslim population is well established, especially in major cities. And in the United States there may be as many as five million Muslims now. Very significant is the increase of Muslim conversions, especially of African-Americans, so that gradually Western Muslim communities will cease to be largely ethnic enclaves but will increasingly become native to their regions, peacefully coexisting with other religious communities, especially Christians and Jews. The following case study illustrates what can happen when a Muslim community has developed a long-term tradition in an American setting.

The Islamic Center of Greater Toledo

The American manufacturing city of Toledo, Ohio, has attracted many peoples from foreign countries to its factories. Among these people were Syrian and Lebanese Muslim immigrants who started arriving around the turn of the century. In the late thirties, a number of families from the Middle East established the Syrian-American Muslim Society. In 1954 Toledo's first Islamic center was erected to provide a place for community worship and other activities. The late sixties and early seventies witnessed an influx of many more Muslims into the Toledo area and immigration continues. The center thus needed much more space, so it was decided to purchase a sizable tract and erect a major building. The site chosen was a pastoral setting at the crossing of two interstate highways, several miles outside Toledo in suburban Perrysburg. The late Turkish-born Toledo architect Talat Itil designed the new structure, which features a large white dome flanked by two 135-foot-tall Turkish-style "pencil" minarets. The two-story building has an octagonal prayer room under the dome, a large lecture hall adjacent, plus more than a dozen classrooms, a well-stocked and staffed library, offices, a medical clinic, a mortuary, a professional-level kitchen, and a spacious dining hall. Seventy-two custom-designed stained glass windows adorn the building. They feature calligraphic designs drawn from the Qur'ān, written in different styles. The plot of forty-five acres sets off the center nicely, as do the lawns, flower beds, and decorative shrubs and trees. Travelers on the interstate highways are often strongly impressed by the beautiful Indo-Turkish–style mosque. Many of them stop for visits, so many that the center has instituted special tours ending with a first-class Middle Eastern luncheon of roast lamb, vegetables, hummus with tahini, tabbouleh and green salads, flat Syrian bread, olives, baklava, and other tasty treats, all at a modest charge. Hospitality is important to Muslims, and the extending of it tells more than words can something of the friendliness and goodwill of the Toledo Muslim community.

Activities of the Toledo Islamic Center focus on education, health, social services, youth and recreation, publications, outreach through tours and hospitality, and, most important, worship. The center is open to all Muslims. A council directs the affairs of the center assisted by a board of elders and a ladies' auxiliary. Chief officers include a president, a vice-president and general counsel, a secretary, and a treasurer. Administrative and spiritual direction of the center is in the hands of an *imām*-director, who reports to the council. The current *imām* is an Egyptian with thorough classical Islamic training at Cairo's

Islamic Center of Greater Toledo, near Perrysburg, Ohio.

famous Azhar University as well as an advanced degree in social sciences from a Canadian university. He is fluent in English as well as his native Arabic and helps the community maintain a healthy balance between orthodox Islamic training and conduct of life and necessary as well as desirable contacts with American society and values.

There is much that is traditional about the Toledo Islamic Center. The mosque is open daily for prayer, there is a large congregation on Fridays for communal worship, Arabic is taught to some 250 enrolled students, close ties are maintained with other Islamic communities both here and abroad, and the architecture of the main building itself makes a strong statement about origins, aesthetic/symbolic commitments, and pride.

But there are also striking differences between the Toledo community and Muslim communities elsewhere, especially in traditional Islamic societies of the Middle East and Asia. The Umma has never known a parish model for religious association. Rather, in Islamic countries, at least, mosques have been made available where needed by the government in cooperation with ministries of religious endowments. Individuals and groups have also erected mosques, but their governance has not been ecclesiastical in style, nor have there been memberships as in Christian parishes. The Islamic Center of Toledo has adapted to the dominant North American pattern of religious sociology by instituting membership, with annual dues that are called *Zakāt*. Moreover, the *imām* of the center is not the highest authority. Rather, he is technically an employee of the council, which is the legally incorporated authority for all center activities and property. The membership as a whole has the privilege of voting on important issues, but the council has supreme authority over the center's affairs.

The Islamic Center's peculiar governance structure has not escaped criticism from traditionalist Muslims, mostly from outside America. When outside groups have visited the *imām* and complained about the "un-Islamic" arrangements, he has had to refer them to the council. So far, such confrontations have ended amicably, with deepened understanding of ways in which a community can be truly Islamic and at the same time responsible and successful citizens of an American community. Thus, the Islamic Center of Greater Toledo's innovative approach to polity and governance is considered by its members to be a **bid'a** *ḥasana,* a "good innovation," and not the type of *bid'a* that is condemned as heresy.

Another unusual aspect of the center's life is the social mixing of the sexes, whether in Sunday school classes (religious education is on Sundays, another common North American Muslim innovation) or at frequent communal luncheons and dinners. When we visited the center and were honored with a special evening dinner, we were frankly amazed to be chatting and laughing around a table with wives, husbands, parents, grandparents, children, and guests from near and far. It was very much like a typical American church supper, except that the food was above average because of the large number of good Lebanese and Syrian cooks. The center's membership includes both Shī'ites and Sunnīs from such countries as Egypt, Lebanon, Syria, Palestine, Turkey, Iraq, Saudi Arabia, Pakistan, India, and twenty other countries. Occupations include teachers, professors, merchants, doctors, lawyers, realtors, scientists, engineers, contractors, factory workers, laborers, homemakers, and students.

The center members appear to enjoy each other's company greatly through religious education classes, communal meals, worship, special events, and frequent visiting of each other's homes. It appears to us that, whereas in traditional Middle Eastern and Asian countries, Muslim social life centers in constant rounds of visits between members of extended family groups, in the Toledo area members of the Islamic Center extend this circle to include fellow Muslims in mixed social life. Traditional practice of course encourages friendly social visiting outside the family, but it restricts it to groups of the same sex occupying the same social space. For example, when a couple goes to visit unrelated friends in a traditional Muslim setting, the men sit and eat in one part of the house and the women in another. The non-*mahram* visiting woman may greet the host, but there will be no social interaction beyond that. The same is true of the hostess and the non-*mahram* male visitor.

What has just been described is the most conservative practice. In actuality, one may encounter Muslim social situations in Pakistan, Indonesia, Malaysia, Egypt, Turkey, and other places where there may be some social mixing of the sexes outside the *mahram* boundaries. Muslims who mix socially in this way in dominantly Muslim countries are almost always Westernized and on the upper social and economic levels. They may be Muslim in the nominal sense only, although it is possible to find modernized (i.e., "Westernized") Muslims of deep conviction who nevertheless have a liberal social lifestyle with circles of friends of both sexes beyond the extended family and beyond the confessional boundaries of Islam.

The striking difference about the Toledo and some other North American Islamic communities is that liberal social mixing is enjoyed within the context of the "parish." In coeducational Sunday school classes, Muslim teenagers discuss the same sorts of issues that Christian and Jewish youth are concerned with: drugs, rock music and its effects, commitment to God in a world of conflicting values and secularism, growing up, and other things. One of the things that American Muslim youth have to resolve is the tension between wanting to be accepted as normal Americans and at the same time observant Muslims who, with all their liberal habits when compared with traditional Islamic societies, nevertheless cannot in good conscience share in certain aspects of American social life, like dating, dancing, and, at the college level and beyond, drinking alcoholic beverages and choosing an independent sexual lifestyle.

Another problem faced by all North American Muslims is dietary. Pork is absolutely forbidden and permitted meats must come from animals slaughtered in the proper manner, which, remember, is similar to the Jewish method of koshering food. It is sometimes difficult to avoid pork and pork products in American food, especially prepared varieties, where pork enzymes may be used. Muslims share a strong repugnance to pork in the American diet. This avoidance is based on divine prohibition, but it has come also to include revulsion at what is believed to be unclean. People who eat pork—the majority of Americans—are in this regard separate from Muslims and somewhat alien. But the same is true of conservative and orthodox Jews, who have an ancient prohibition against pork that extends back long before the coming of Islam.

It is necessary to distinguish among different types of Islamic communities in North America. The Toledo Islamic Center is a diversified community of multiple national backgrounds and contains both Sunnīs and Shī'ites. It is largely middle- and upper-middle class and comfortably situated in Middle American life. The members blend into the greater Toledo ambience with their late model cars, suburban homes, American-style clothing, and typically American occupations. The women, by and large, do not cover their hair, a mark of Islamic revival that is seen in the behavior of Western converts as much as longstanding Muslims. At a celebration of the anniversary of the erection of the center and mosque, Muslim guests from other American cities stood out in their traditional Islamic garb when compared to the Toledo Muslim women especially, who dressed conservatively, but no more so nor different than well-bred and devout American Jewish or Christian women would in a similar setting. By contrast, at the mosque in Boulder, Colorado, a university city with many international students, Muslim mosque gatherings are strictly separated by sex, and the women (whether from abroad or American) cover up completely, leaving only the face and hands exposed.

We do not wish to appear to harp on the dress issue, but it is symbolically significant. The Toledo community seems to be saying by its style that Muslims can and should participate in the dominant American lifestyle, so long as that does not entail forsaking truly Islamic principles of belief, practice, and comportment. The Boulder Muslim community (and many others like it in North America) appears to be saying by its traditionalist style of community life, including female dress code, that Muslims have a duty to be different when it comes to adhering to their true principles, even if that means significant separations and differences from the dominant social and personal patterns of behavior and dress. There is survival value in maintaining strict Islamic customs. But it may also be true that such pattern maintenance is more easily sustained by a constantly shifting mosque population in a university setting, where

Saudis, Kuwaitis, Pakistanis, Malaysians, and other foreign nationals of Muslim belief continually cycle in and out of the community as degrees are earned and new matriculates arrive. Such an Islamic community can maintain over time "pure" Islamic patterns of life and in the bargain provide a comforting and familiar context for foreign Muslim students and others who find American life lonely, bewildering, in some respects disagreeable, and just plain alien.

It is natural for Muslims to gather together wherever they may be. What is more, it is prescribed by their religion to observe the Friday congregational *Ṣalāt,* to come to each other's aid, and to struggle always to maintain a moral environment. Muslim university students, for example, sometimes find their faith and home ways of life threatened and severely tested by the material wealth and social and intellectual freedom that they experience in the West. Campus Christian groups as well as evangelically minded individuals often seek to convert Muslim students. Proselytization attempts rarely if ever occur in Muslim countries, because they are outlawed by Islam; only *Islamic* missionary endeavors are legal under the *Sharī'a.* Muslims in the *Dār al-Ḥarb* often experience severe disorientation at the sight of a dominant religious presence that is other than Islamic.

As the North American Muslim community grows, it is becoming more diverse and experimental. Whereas foreign student populations of Muslims tend to maintain strict traditional behavior patterns, immigrant Muslims and their children are becoming aware that to be citizens requires some degree of assimilation and participation in the political, social, and educational institutions and processes of their new home countries. The increasing numbers of indigenous converts are also having an effect on what one Muslim scholar has called the "domestication" of Islam in North America. Most Muslims are understandably anxious about the possibility of becoming assimilated to the point of losing their own Islamic distinctiveness. But there is growing awareness that radical separation from the dominant society has its costs as well. Muslims are beginning to explore and evaluate a wide range of options as they take their place as a religious minority in North America. Large-scale organizations are gaining adherents in the quest to establish an Islamic environment here. The most prominent organization is the Islamic Society of North America, an umbrella organization for a number of cooperating societies and organizations aimed at realizing Islamic goals in education, scholarship, finance, youth and college student affairs, *Sharī'a* applications, and helping Muslims find suitable spouses.

Islamic Activism: "Fundamentalist" or "Islamist"?

The term *fundamentalism* was coined early in this century in an American conservative Protestant framework to characterize a Scripture-based doctrine embracing five key points (the virgin birth of Jesus, his physical resurrection, the infallibility of the Scriptures, the substitutional Atonement, and the physical

Second Coming of Christ). The only corresponding point with which Muslims agree concerns the infallibility of Scripture—in the Islamic case, of course, the Qur'ān. In recent years it has become popular, especially in the media, to refer to conservative militant Muslims as fundamentalists. The name does not quite apply, when taken at its original meaning. But the spirit of Christian fundamentalism is certainly paralleled in Muslim convictions concerning the infallibility of the Qur'ān, literally interpreted; the authentic prophethood of Muḥammad as chief and last of the long series of prophets to appear in history; Muḥammad's Sunna as impeccable example for human behavior; and the authority of the *Sharī'a* for a closed community of true believers, the Umma. Furthermore, Muslims, like evangelical fundamentalist Christians, strenuously apply themselves to the missionary task, believing that it is God's will to convert unbelievers to the true way.

Having demonstrated that there is some justification in applying the idea, if not the term *fundamentalist* to Muslims, it should immediately be added that there is no organizational structure or universally subscribed to creedal statement that binds Muslims together in any formal manner. Nor is there in Protestant Christianity, although for a time some denominations of Baptists and Presbyterians did contain zealous and disciplined members who adhered to the fundamentalist principles and applied them to their coreligionists as a standard for orthodoxy. This led to serious splitting and new denominational arrangements.

There is a fairly wide range of interpretations and temperament among Muslim individuals and groups that might be content to be called, if not fundamentalist, then **Islamist**, as is the case in Egypt and some other countries. Some Islamists express themselves politically, supporting revolutionary and even terrorist methods, whether against supposed enemies from outside—the West is a frequent target—or against what are deemed to be false or weak individuals and institutions within the Umma—Egypt's Anwar Sadat and his regime is a recent example. Other Islamists express themselves through preaching, teaching, and other forms of communication, in organizations, schools, universities, mosques, and in print and other media—among which audiocassette tapes are prominent, because they are easily copied and disseminated, even in countries where the radio or television appearances of certain fundamentalist leaders are outlawed.

A third, broad group of Muslims is found in every region of the world. These are the rank-and-file believers who are concerned with maintaining and handing down as pure a version of the faith as possible. Some of this type are militant in temperament, but not necessarily organized into specific political or cultural groups. Most are moderate, tolerant, and devoutly observant without being especially Islamist. However, they can be aroused mightily when a threat to the Islamic community and way of life is perceived. I prefer to call this large, centrist group by a name other than Islamist or fundamentalist. Perhaps the best label is simply "devout Muslim." They all unite around the central beliefs and practices of Islam as contained in the Qur'ān and Sunna. This group contains people of all educational levels and occupational groups, rich and poor, men and women, young and old.

Again, all Muslims inhabit at least two cultural spheres, the one providing them with an identity as part of a nation or local ethnic grouping (as Egyptians, or Pakistanis, or Indonesians, or Americans, or whatever) and the one providing them with Islamic identity. Sometimes the two are highly contrasting, as in the American context; at other times, as in Arabia, the native cultural context and Islam are closely aligned, because they have coexisted and indeed produced each other. Islamist or simply devout Muslims—and I do not mean to suggest that the latter is equivalent to the former, although the former surely embraces the latter in significant ways—reflect their cultural backgrounds. The more strongly activist type of Islamists generally try to minimize their own cultural idiosyncrasies in favor of a Pan-Islamic style of presentation of self, for example, favoring simplicity of clothing and lifestyle and sometimes verging on asceticism. There is constant mindfulness of following the strict letter of Qur'ān and Sunna and avoiding any compromise of either on the basis of specific cultural background. Such Muslims can move easily from country to country and enjoy a high level of uniformity of comportment, convictions, and goals among their fellow fundamentalists. This unity does not always extend beyond central beliefs, practices, and approved social and personal habits, however. Political and ideological differences can be sharp and the methods preferred to pursue goals can diverge radically.

The key to Islamist awareness was forcefully expressed by a Muslim student in a large university class on the Abrahamic religious traditions. When invited to comment on a point the lecturer had made concerning *jihād,* "exertion" in the way of God—which sometimes includes holy warfare—the Malaysian student declared to the class that true Islam is always *jihād,* in every way. He explained that Muslims could not be true to their faith if they did not see themselves as constantly alert and militant, both as to inward disposition and outward behavior. Both the "lesser" *jihād*—warfare and struggle in the world —and "greater" *jihād*—the continuing exertion against the straying tendencies within us—are absolutely essential to Islam, according to the student. I would say that his focused concern for *jihād* is a mark of Islamism everywhere among Muslims.

Some think that Islamism is a view of the world that is generally fearful of change, of newness, specifically of modernity. Recall that the traditional Arabic word for what in English is called "heresy" is *bid'a,* "innovation," in doctrines and practices. But I think that the characterization of Islamism, often caricatured as Muslim fundamentalism, as fearful of change is too negative. It is also misleading, because Islamists, or many of them, want radical change: from following Western ways and depending on Western products; from what are perceived to be irreligious and impure "Muslim" leaders and regimes—Sadat and the Shah of Iran are dramatic cases; and what are thought to be idolatrous practices among Muslims, such as visiting saints' tombs for blessings and intercession, paying allegiance to a spiritual guide as in Sufism, and other things.

Backgrounds of the Islamic Revival

Contemporary Muslim activism has appeared on the world stage in the past few years partly because of the transportation and communication revolutions that have brought the peoples of the earth closer together, both in the various media and in actuality. But the global Islamic revival, which features Islamism as a major expression, began well before the current era. The revival can be traced to nineteenth- and twentieth-century reform movements in India, Indonesia, Egypt, Iran, and other places. Even before these movements there was a radical reform in the Arabian Peninsula in the eighteenth century launched by the puritanical preacher Muḥammad ibn 'Abd al-Wahhāb (c. 1703–1787) and enforced by his protector and collaborator, Ibn Sa'ud, ancestor of the present Sa'udi dynasty in Arabia. The Wahhābi movement, as it came to be called, was fanatically opposed to idolatry in any form—physical, symbolic, or psychological. Particularly loathsome was the popular cult of saints in Arabia and elsewhere. It was eradicated from the domains where the Sa'udis and Wahhābis came to dominate, which embraces contemporary Saudi Arabia. Tomb structures were pulled down and all but the plainest and smallest grave markers in cemeteries removed, lest they come to occupy an intermediary place in people's affections and reverence between them and the One God.

Wahhābi reforms spread to Iraq, India, and Africa. One of the key points, in addition to the stamping out of idolatrous practices and beliefs, was the exercise of *ijtihād,* independent legal decision making. For centuries, Sunnī law especially had operated within the context of **taqlīd,** following the decisions and procedures of the early legal experts in a blindly imitative manner. The Wahhābis realized that the Muslims needed to return to the basic sources of inspiration and governance that had created the Umma in the beginning and nurtured it during its most creative centuries. This return to Qur'ān, Sunna, and the ways of the early legal experts was a sort of Islamism, which has served as a model for subsequent reformers, who have nevertheless not usually followed Wahhābism in all its features, especially its puritanism.

The later nineteenth century saw the rise of Muslim reformers who continued the themes of return to Qur'ān and Sunna, and the repudiation of *taqlīd,* "blind imitation," in law. But certain reformers added something new: a rejection of Western colonialism and a summons to the faithful to rise up and throw off the rule of infidels. The greatest of these revolutionary reformers was Jamāl al Dīn al-Afghānī (1838–1897), a learned and charismatic writer, teacher, orator, and political activist who spread ideas of Islamic reform and liberation from India to Europe. He was especially influential in Egypt, where his assistant, the Egyptian scholar Muḥammad 'Abduh (1849–1905) continued aspects of Afghānī's work after his death. 'Abduh went on to exert his own long-lasting influence in education, theology, Qur'ān commentary, and legal decision making. 'Abduh reformed the medieval Azhar University in Cairo by liberalizing the curriculum and improving teaching procedures. He urged his fellow Muslims to exploit modern science for Islamic ends, seeing no essential contradiction between scientific method and what is taught in the Qur'ān about the nature and scope of human reason and mastery of the things of the natural world.

'Abduh has had strong impacts outside of Egypt, but nowhere more than in Indonesia, where, not long after his death, the young Javanese religious teacher Kiai Hajji Ahmad Dahlan founded a new Muslim movement based on 'Abduh's and modernist Indian teachings. The movement is called **Muhammadiyah** and it was established as an organization in Yogyakarta in 1912. Muhammadiyah has never been political in focus; rather, it has emphasized educational and social welfare concerns. Many schools were established by the organization, publications launched, and both a women's organization, known as 'Aishiya, and a boy scout movement have been successfully developed. In Indonesia today, Muhammadiyah is still strong, with a substantial membership throughout the archipelago. Other, non-Muhammadiyah Indonesians sometimes have characterized the organization as "fundamentalist," and I have heard the term used approvingly by members. This is not done in a critical fashion. It simply refers to the strong emphasis among Muhammadiyah Muslims on the Qur'ān and Sunna and the strict observance of the core devotional practices. Traditional Indonesian folk beliefs and practices are rejected in favor of a purified Islam that strives to be in harmony with like-minded Muslims in the rest of the Umma. But if fundamentalism connotes rejection of modernity, especially scientific method, technology, and rational thought, then Muhammadiyah is not fundamentalist. I would prefer to call it "moderate Islamist." My point in selecting Muhammadiyah as an Indonesian version of Islamic revivalism is to demonstrate how flexible and varied Muslims can be in the pursuit of a purified Islam.

Indonesians are traditionally very tolerant of other Muslims as well as non-Muslims in the interests of harmony, courtesy, and above all, "togetherness," a supreme virtue of these close-knit people, where consensus and mutual responsibility are crucial. In chapter 24 I introduced the Indonesian *santris,* who are strictly observant Muslims. The Muhammadiyah people are *santri* in orientation, while the vast majority of Indonesians, especially on Java, are *abangan,* Muslim to be sure, but also dedicated to many aspects of traditional beliefs and practices that existed before the coming of Islam. In fact, most Indonesians are mixtures of different elements, both traditional indigenous and strict Islamic.

In Bangladesh also are "fundamentalists," as they call themselves, who are sincere Qur'ān and Sunna Muslims, but who also pursue philosophical, mystical, and scientific thought. When I first visited Bangladesh, I was told by Western informants that some Muslim scholars I was going to meet were fundamentalists. This was said with a certain foreboding, because of the connotations that militant Muslims have in the press, especially in non-Muslim eyes. But after I had spent some time with the scholars, I soon realized that they had much in common with the rather liberal Muhammadiyah people in Java and other devout Muslim intellectuals in Egypt, Pakistan, Iran, and other places. [See Religions of Africa pp. 25, 54–57, 79–82, Religions of Mesoamerica p. 240, Native Religions of North America pp. 287, 320–22, 357–58, Judaism pp 427–31, 456–75

The Faisal Mosque, Islamabad, Pakistan. This national mosque was a gift from Saudi Arabia. Designed by a Turkish architect and dedicated in the 1980s, it is the largest mosque in the world.

Christianity pp. 529–33, Hinduism pp. 770–74, 828–31, Buddhism pp. 952–56, Religions of China pp. 998–1002, 1055–59, and Religions of Japan pp. 1132–33, 1163–72 for discussion of new religious movements.]

Whither Islam?

Islam and the Muslim community are thriving in the present age. Their current strength has not been achieved overnight, nor has it been made possible simply by oil wealth in some Muslim nations, although that wealth has had important consequences in aiding the Islamic revival, especially its missionary and educational dimensions. The Wahhābi reform movement, still powerful in its native country, was an entirely indigenous Islamic phenomenon unrelated to Western and non-Muslim concerns and influences. The nineteenth- and early twentieth-century movements did sometimes have rejectionist aspects, but they too relied most heavily on internal resources of Qur'ānic conviction and a strong loyalty and willingness to defend the religion against both internal and external enemies.

The Islamic revival was also greatly extended through the development of new nations in the present century, especially after World War II. Along with *national* identity—in places like Jordan, Morocco, Libya, Algeria, Pakistan, Indonesia, Malaysia, and other countries—being *Muslim* has also been of critical importance, with different styles and intensity of application in different places. Thus, Pakistan was founded in 1947 as an Islamic state, and Islam has continued to be the most important principle in the development of that nation's institutions. Indonesia, 90 percent Muslim, nevertheless achieved independence from the Netherlands after World War II through an independence movement that carefully balanced religious, nationalistic, and ethnic issues in a pluralistic manner. It was decided that the Republic of Indonesia should be composed of citizens who believe in the one true God, but although the Muslims enjoy a vast majority, the monotheistic traditions of Buddhism (according to the Indonesian interpretation), Hinduism, and Christianity should be included fully in the national idea too. Even so, there has continued in Indonesia a strong Muslim sentiment among many to require the Muslims to be ruled by the *Sharī'a*.

The Islamic revolution in Iran, characterized by powerful Shī'ite convictions, considered itself to be returning its people to a sort of divine right rule of the religious scholars, who in Iran are known as *mullas* as well as *'ulama'*. Although Shī'ites and Sunnīs have long been at odds with each other, they also realize their common Islamic roots and shared beliefs and rituals. They are, in fact, much closer in these and other respects than Protestants and Catholics are within Christianity. The Iranian leaders, especially the late Ayatollah Khomeini, have preached Islamic unity and condemned sectarian differences and disagreements as fatal in the continuing struggle to preserve Islam from infidel Western ways and to extend the borders of the Islamic community through missionary efforts.

Islamic revivalist strength in many places does not mean that there is a coordinated monolithic organization and structure. The tendency of Muslims to take strength from each other and to close ranks for the common good is as old as the religion. The high level of uniformity in worship and social regulations without clerical class or hierarchical government is a product of profound convictions and thoroughly ingrained spiritual, social, political, and cultural habits. The influence of Qur'ān and Sunna and their proper interpretation and application through legal schools, both in Sunnī and Shī'ite Islam, is at bottom what makes Muslim unity and group loyalty strong. The great variety and wide geographic distribution of Muslim peoples is proof of the religion's appeal and ability to accommodate many different cultures into its vision of faith and order. A monolithic system never could have had such success in winning the allegiance of so many peoples, most of whom had no previous close relations with each other or reason to develop a shared identity at the religious level.

The American anthropologist Clifford Geertz has studied Islam and Muslims in two highly contrasting geographical and cultural contexts, Morocco and Indonesia. The title of his book, *Islam Observed*,[11] is meaningful. Geertz realizes that it is very difficult to define Islam as a social and cultural reality, because of the great differences that exist in different regions at the levels of symbols, folk behavior, historical traditions, and general religious temperament. Moroccans are vigorously competitive, intensely motivated people with a rugged desert and mountain heritage, strongly influenced by Arabism, which arrived early in Islamic history. They possess a narrow scope as a cultural tradition in which Islamic faith and observance combine forcefully with native Moroccan social relations—especially the tribal structure of authority and prestige—to exert a definitive, regulating influence on life. Indonesia, on the other hand, has a very wide cultural scope with tolerant and syncretistic habits, which thus decrease the force of purely Islamic ideals. Old Javanese, Hindu, and Buddhist symbols and customs continue to exert gentle but firm influences, to the extent that stricter Muslims from outside—activists of the Wahhābi type especially—are often critical of Indonesian Muslims for accommodating so much that is considered un-Islamic by a strict *Sharī'a* attitude. But Indonesian Muslims defend their own ways, and insist that regional customs, known as *adat,* are fully acceptable in combination with scripturally based Islamic values, attitudes, and practices.

Geertz's challenging comparative analysis is a warning against trying to understand a religious tradition as old and broad as Islam by applying book definitions and categories. This viewpoint underlies the title, *Islam Observed.* The author does not attempt to *define* Islam before examining it as a complete cultural system in the two countries. Rather, he wants the data to be drawn out and then carefully studied in their proper contexts, before raising the question of what constitutes "Islam" and what lies outside that category. In general, Geertz holds that if people call themselves Muslim, it is then up to the investigator to discern and understand what that may mean in any situation. It is sometimes a complex task, especially when Muslims themselves can be divided on the question, as when theological definitions—based on Scripture and traditional authoritative positions—are invoked.

"Islamic" and "Muslim"

Mohammad Koesnoe, a leading Indonesian specialist on the relationship between Islam and regional folk law (*adat*), distinguishes the terms *Islamic* and *Muslim* when referring to different aspects of Indonesian religious life.[12] *Islamic,* for Koesnoe, means that which is based on the Qur'ān and Sunna as interpreted by the major schools of jurisprudence (*fiqh*). More often than not, it is an ideal more than a reality. *Muslim,* on the other hand, means that which is produced essentially by human intellect and is therefore subject to critical rational investigation and alteration, if necessary. Koesnoe holds that much of what people call "Islamic" is really just "Muslim," in that it does not have the authority of the scriptural bases of the religion, but only human consensus and provisional utility backing it up. Koesnoe further contends that even jurisprudence is essentially Muslim rather than Islamic and is thus subject to continual evaluation, reexamination, and improvement. This position allows for considerable flexibility in determining how Muslims may relate the enduring sources of their religious doctrines and laws to actual situations in a historically dynamic world. Koesnoe's position, obviously, favors continual independent legal decision making (*ijtihād*).

Conclusion

Muslims are enjoying greater global unity and accord than have been possible in recent centuries, even though they lament serious divisions and difficulties that plague the Umma, such as the Iran-Iraq war, challenges to certain regimes (for example, those in Egypt, Algeria, and Saudi Arabia) by militant and extremist Muslim groups, and sectarian strife such as erupts often in Iraq, Syria, and Lebanon between Shī'ites and Sunnīs. But the overall picture is one of progress, with successes in missionary work, charitable endeavors on the part of the wealthier Islamic nations for those less fortunate, and a regained sense of pride and strength that has largely replaced the feelings of weakness, backwardness, and humiliation of the colonial period. As was remarked early in this chapter, however, there are still problems concerning how Muslims view the Western scientific and technological world, among which is a feeling of being in a neo-colonial situation.

One of the most noteworthy aspects of contemporary Islam, as was noted, is its increasing presence in Western countries: Europe, the Americas (especially the United States and Canada), and Australia. Christianity, the dominant religion of the West and of the former colonial powers, never became securely established in Muslim countries except the Balkans and Spain—where it was a matter of reconquest in the presence of a large continuing Christian population—and certain African countries where both religions have often competed openly for converts. Christianity, since the rise of Islam, has not been successful, in spite of sporadic, sometimes intense, attempts at missionary activity, in becoming widespread in the Arabian Peninsula, Turkey, North Africa, Iraq, Iran, Pakistan, Malaysia, or Bangladesh. Until recently, Islam had at most a very weak presence in urban areas of Europe and North America. But now, Islam is enjoying considerable acceptance in these places, so that in some regions, of England and France, for example, the call to prayer can be heard alongside church bells, and the atmosphere of whole neighborhoods is being palpably transformed. Christianity is not making headway in the Islamic world, but Islam is certainly prospering in countries that have a strong tradition of Christian dominance in the religious sphere.

As we observed earlier in this chapter with reference to the Islamic Center of Greater Toledo, as Islam becomes domesticated in the West, especially in North America, it will inevitably take on many aspects of Western culture and society in the process. In an open field for missionary activities, almost anything can happen. Islam's inherent capacity to adapt to and accommodate different cultures and societies, both changing them and being colored by them, is a great advantage in parts of the world that are highly secularized and lukewarm if not indifferent or even hostile to religion. Muslims can freely call their fellow humans to Islam in a great variety of ways, both in strongly Muslim countries and in most other nations as well, especially in the West.

We have included these remarks on Islam in relation to other faiths because the issue is important to Muslims. The Qur'ān itself contains many references to other religious ways, especially Judaism and Christianity, and teaches that Islam is the fulfillment in history and God's plan of both. It is no wonder, then, that Muslims true to their calling should continue to invite others to the Straight Path and to hope for the day when all humans will celebrate together their brotherhood and sisterhood in a worldwide Umma, reflecting God's Unity in human religious unity and harmony, which for Muslims is the culmination of *tawḥīd,* the Divine Unification.

Study Questions

Before you begin to read this part, take a mental inventory of what you know and think about Islam. What images do you have of Islam? What countries, cultures, and peoples do you associate with Islam? What would you imagine Islam to be like? Keep these images and things in mind as you read this section and develop new notions about Islam.

CHAPTER 24

Introduction: The Islamic Umma—A Community Defined by a History, a Religious Way, and a Culture

1. How does the author define Islam and characterize it as a religion?
2. What are the three Abrahamic traditions, and what do they have in common?
3. How does Islam compare with other world religions?
4. What is the contrast between orthoprax and orthodox religions?
5. What are the roles of the Qur'ān and Sunna in Islam?

CHAPTER 25

The Rise and Historical Development of Islam

1. What is the role of Abraham in Islam?
2. How are Jews and Christians viewed in the Qur'ān?
3. What were the major features of religion in Arabia before Islam?
4. Describe the role of the *Ka'ba* before Islam.
5. What was the pre-Islamic notion of Allāh, and how did the Islamic notion of Allāh differ?
6. What is the meaning of the Arabic term *jinn*?
7. Relate the major facts of Muḥammad's life, and his first revelation.
8. What was the content of Muḥammad's preaching?
9. What was the early reaction to Muḥammad's message, and why did he go from Mecca to Medina?
10. What did Muḥammad do when he conquered Mecca?
11. How did Muḥammad's Islamic community differ from pre-Islamic society?

CHAPTER 26

The Structures of Muslim Life

1. How does the author introduce the central story of Islam?
2. What are some of the key concepts of the Qur'ān?

3. How does the author present the major teachings of Islam?
4. How does Islam view the human condition, especially regarding free will, sin, and salvation?
5. What are the main elements of Islamic faith?
6. What are the essentials of worship in Islam?
7. What are the necessary conditions for a mosque?
8. Identify the five Pillars of Islam.
9. How do Muslims view the Qur'ān?
10. Describe the Qur'ān—its length, composition, and use in ritual.
11. How are Sunna and Ḥadīth central to Islam?
12. What is the significance of law (*Sharī'a*) for Islam?
13. What are the similarities and differences between Shī'ites and Sunnīs?
14. How did Sufism arise and what is the role of Sufism within Islam?

CHAPTER 27
Representative Muslim Institutions and Their Dynamics

1. How does the author use Qur'ān recitation in Indonesia as a way of illustrating the dynamics of Islam?
2. What does this example tell us about the Qur'ān, Islam, and Indonesian culture?
3. How does the author use veneration of saints in Egypt as a way of illustrating the dynamics of Islam?
4. What does this example tell us about saints, Islam, and Egyptian culture?
5. Identify and describe the major rites of passage in Islam.
6. Why is circumcision so important in Islam?

CHAPTER 28
Islam in Today's World

1. How does the author portray Islam today as an interaction between Islam and the West?
2. What Western values have Muslims criticized and rejected?
3. How does the author use the Islamic community near Toledo, Ohio as an example of contemporary Islam?
4. What does this example tell us about Islam today and American culture?
5. How does the author use the term "fundamentalism" in relation to Islam?
6. How does the author assess the situation and prospects of Islam today?

Recall the mental inventory of images about Islam that you made before reading this part. What is there in Islam that is most like your own religious tradition? What in Islam is most different from your own tradition? What is most interesting? How has your understanding of Islam changed as a result of reading this section? Can you now imagine yourself participating in Islam?

Notes

I am very grateful to Byron Earhart, who invited me to write this work in his series. My students in "World Religions—West" at the University of Colorado, Boulder, provided valuable feedback to the emerging manuscript over several semesters. Neither my editor nor my students are to be held responsible for any errors in fact or interpretation or infelicities of style that remain in this work.

Some of the material for this work was gathered in research visits to Muslim countries over a period of years. Grateful acknowledgment is made to the following agencies and institutions: the National Endowment for the Humanities for a senior fellowship in Egypt in 1976–1977; the Council on Research and Creative Work of the Graduate School, University of Colorado, Boulder, for two Grants-in-Aid and a Faculty Fellowship for field work in Indonesia in May–June 1980 and for nine months in 1984–1985; the council for International Exchange of Scholars and the United States Information Service for a Fulbright Islamic Civilization Grant in Indonesia in 1984–1985; the State Islamic Institute (Institut Agama Islam Negeri) "Sunan Ampel," Surabaya, Indonesia, for sponsoring my 1984–1985 research on Qur'ān recitation and providing much guidance and assistance; and the Indonesian Institute of Sciences ("L.I.P.I.") for research permission. My 1976–1977 Egypt fieldwork was greatly facilitated by the sponsorship of the Center for Arabic Studies of the American University in Cairo, as well as by the American Research Center in Egypt, which made me an honorary fellow and permitted me to use its library and other resources.

Many individuals have helped me, in one way or other, to write this work. In Egypt, Dr. Galal Nahal guided me to the *mawlid* of Sayyid Aḥmad al-Badawī in Tanta in 1976. The Cairene Qur'ān recitation masters Shaykh Muḥammad Ismā'īl Yusuf al-Ḥamadānī and Shaykh 'Amer Uthman taught me much about Qur'ān recitation in 1976–1977. During 1980 and in 1984–1985, my Indonesia research was greatly enhanced by the advice and guidance of many persons, but especially by Rector Drs. Marsekan Fatawi, Prof. Dr. H. Mohammad Koesnoe, Dr. H. Rachmat Djatnika, Drs. H. Muhammad Ghufron, Drs. Abd Syakur Thawil, Mr. Achudiat, Drs. H. Syamsudduha, Drs. Bisri Affandi, and Drs. Zein al-Arifien of I.A.I.N. "Sunan Ampel," Surabaya; by Kiai H. M. Bashori Alwi, director of the Institute of Qur'ānic Studies, Singosari, East Java, and his fellow recitation master Kiai H. Achmad Damanhuri, of Malang, who permitted me to observe their instructional techniques and kindly received me into their homes; and by Dr. Yahya Lubis and Dr. A. Y. Hasibuan, University of North Sumatra. My discovery of the Islamic Center of Greater Toledo was made possible by S. Amjad Hussein, M.D., President. He and the Center's *imam* and Director, Abdel-Moneim Khattab, and other members of the Toledo Muslim community provided much hospitality, information, and insight during my October 1985 visit. The ways in which data from Egypt, Indonesia, and Toledo have been selected and presented for this work are entirely my responsibility, of course.

My wife, Alix, and our son and daughter Josh and Sydney, once again patiently endured the writing of this work in their midst, for which they deserve to be canonized.

Finally, I dedicate this work to my honored teacher, colleague, and friend Fazlur Rahman (1919–1988).

1. The Islamic Center, Washington, D.C., estimates that there are approximately one billion Muslims in the world. A region-by-region global survey of Muslim populations is contained in M. Ali Kettani, *Muslim Minorities in the World Today,* Institute of Muslim Minority Affairs, Monograph Series Number 2 (London and New York: Mansell, 1986), which estimates the global Muslim population at one billion thirty million. See the tables on pp. 238–243. Other sources for population statistics of Muslim peoples are *The Statesman's Year-Book,* ed. John Paxton (New York: St. Martin's, 1991–1992 and revised annually); *Worldmark Encyclopedia of Nations,* 6th ed., 1984 (New York: Wiley); and United Nations publications. A useful reference work on characteristics of different Muslim societies and regions is Richard V. Weekes, ed., *Muslim Peoples: A World Ethnographic Survey,* 2d rev. ed., 2 vols. (Westport, CT: Greenwood, 1984). There are valuable appendices with population estimates for all Muslim ethnic groups.
2. I am indebted to Professor Yusuf Ibish, of the American University of Beirut, for this model, which I have adopted.
3. The Muslim calendar is reckoned by the phases of the moon and is divided into twelve months of twenty-nine or thirty days, with a total year of around 354 days. Because of the lunar reckoning, the Muslim year falls behind the solar year by about eleven days annually. The Qur'ān forbids intercalation—adding extra days periodically—to make up for this discrepancy. The Muslim calendar governs religious observances, but most Muslim countries also use the common solar calendar without attaching any spiritual significance to it. Conversion charts are available for comparing Muslim and Western historical dates.
4. For a detailed, sophisticated analysis and interpretation of domestic pilgrimage murals, see Juan Eduardo Campo, *The Other Sides of Paradise: Explorations into the Religious Meanings of Domestic Space in Islam* (Columbia, SC: University of South Carolina Press, 1991), 139–165, 170–191.
5. Translations from the Qur'ān in this section are my own, although I am indebted to the following recommended translations, which have been consulted: A. J. Arberry, *The Koran Interpreted* (New York: Macmillan, 1964); Mohammed Marmaduke Pickthall, *The Meaning of the Glorious Koran* (New York: New American Library and Mentor Books, n.d.); and 'Abdullah Yūsuf 'Alī, *The Holy Qur'ān: Text, Translation and Commentary* (Brentwood, MO: Amana Corp., 1409 A.H., 1989 A.C.).
6. *Ṣaḥīḥ Muslim* (Beirut: Dār al-Fikr, 1398/1978), I:282, no. 116. (An English translation of this important *ḥadīth* collection by Abdul Hamid Siddiqi has been published in four vols. by Sh. Muhammad Ashraf, Lahore, Pakistan, 1976.)
7. As quoted in A. J. Arberry, *Sufism* (New York: Harper & Row, Torchbooks, 1970), 28.
8. Reynold A. Nicholson, trans., *Rumi: Poet and Mystic, 1207–1273* (London: Allen and Unwin, 1950), 122–123.
9. See Joseph Williams McPherson, *The Moulids of Egypt* (Cairo: N.M. Press, 1941).
10. Prof. Mohammad Koesnoe (see n. 11). A very detailed examination of Javanese religion, both Islamic and indigenous and their interrelations, is Koentjaraningrat, *Javanese Culture* (Singapore: Oxford University Press, 1985; pb 1989), ch. 5, "Javanese Religion," 316–445, and ch. 6, "Javanese Symbolic System and Value Orientation," 446–464.
11. Clifford Geertz, *Islam Observed: Religious Development in Morocco and Indonesia* (New Haven, CT: Yale University Press, 1968).
12. Professor Koesnoe outlined his views in a series of class lectures in the Department of Religious Studies, University of Colorado, Boulder, Spring Semester 1986.

Glossary

'Abbāsid Muslim dynasty (750–1258 C.E.) centered in Iraq (Baghdad) under which Islamic civilization achieved maturity.

Allāh Arabic word for "God"; literally, *al-ilāh,* "the god."

baraka "Blessing" or "spiritual power" believed to reside in holy places and persons.

Basmala The name for the sacred Islamic invocation "In the Name of God, the Merciful, the Compassionate" (*bi'smillāh al-rahmān al-rahīm*) uttered frequently by pious Muslims, as before meals, before writing something down or making a speech, before conjugal relations, before reciting the Qur'ān, and at other times.

bid'a Literally, "innovation," but a term that came to mean "heresy."

caliph (*khalīfa*) Literally, "successor," "deputy," "vicegerent"; in the Qur'ān it refers to people who submit in voluntary service to God and are thus empowered to carry on a free and active life as God's vicegerents on earth. In the early history of Islam, caliph is the title for the military/political leaders of the Umma functioning as Muhammad's "successor" in all but the prophetic role.

Dār al-Islām "The Household of Submission," meaning the territories governed by Muslims under the *Sharīʿa.* The term's opposite is *Dār al-Harb,* "The Household of Warfare," those lands lacking the security and guidance of God's law.

da'wa The "calling" of people to the religion of Islam; thus, "missions."

dhikr "Remembering," "mentioning" God by means of his names and his words in the Qur'ān; the central practice of Sufi meditation.

fiqh Literally, "understanding" in matters of religious law; Islamic jurisprudence.

fitra The original framework or nature of humans as created by God, considered good.

fundamentalism A term originally applied to conservative Protestant Christians, but more recently applied to religiously conservative Muslims who interpret their Scriptures literally and in general favor a strict adherence to their doctrines and practices. The term *Islamist* is increasingly replacing *fundamentalism.*

hadīth "Report," or "account"; a tradition about Muhammad—what he said or did on a particular occasion. The *hadīths* were collected and they came to be a record of the Prophet's Sunna, which is second only to the Qur'ān in authority for Muslims. (Collectively referred to as Hadīth.)

Hajj The pilgrimage to Mecca, and one of the five Pillars of Islam.

hanīf Pre-Islamic Arabian monotheists whose beliefs are thought to have descended from the time of Abraham.

Hijra The "Emigration" of Muhammad and the Muslims from Mecca to Medina in 622 C.E.; the Muslim lunar calendar dates from that year.

'ibāda "Service" to God through worship by means of the five Pillars.

ihrām The state of ritual purity and dedication entered into by the pilgrim on *Hajj* to Mecca.

ijmāʿ "Consensus," one of the four sources of Sunnī jurisprudence.

ijtihād Intellectual "effort" of Muslim jurists to reach independent religio-legal decisions, a key feature of modern Islamic reform; one who exercises *ijtihād* is a *mujtahid.*

708

imām "Leader," specifically of the Ṣalāt prayer service; in Shī'ite Islam, *Imām* also refers to one of the revered early leaders of the community who both ruled in the political sense and also interpreted doctrine with infallible, God-given wisdom.

imān "Faith"; one who has faith is a *mu'min*, "believer."

islām "Submission" to God, the name of the true religion, according to the Qur'ān; one who submits is a Muslim.

Islamist A term used by some Muslim activists instead of fundamentalist. There is a wide range of types, but Islamists as a whole have a strong allegiance to Qur'ān and Sunna and want to see them applied to contemporary life.

Jāhilīya The pre-Islamic Arabian age of "ignorance," marked by barbarism and unbelief; Islam came to end this evil age, according to its view.

jihād "Exertion" in the work of God, including, sometimes, armed force.

Ka'ba The sacred cubical shrine in Mecca, toward which Muslims face in prayer; legend says the *Ka'ba* was built by Abraham.

Karbalā' The place in Iraq where Ḥusayn, grandson of Muḥammad and son of 'Alī and Fāṭima, was ambushed and killed on his way to assume leadership over the Shī'ites in Iraq, a tragic event commemorated each year by Shī'ites on the tenth of the Muslim month of Muḥarram.

khalīfa See caliph.

kiai An Indonesian term for a religious teacher of high status.

maḥram The bounds of close blood relationship within which it is unlawful to marry and thus lawful for members of the opposite sex to associate socially (as between brothers and sisters, aunts and nephews, and so forth).

mawlid "Birthday" celebration, most often used in connection with Muḥammad and the saints of Islam.

mosque English corruption of the Arabic word *masjid*, "place of prostration" for performing the Ṣalāt.

Muhammadiyah Twentieth-century Indonesian Islamic reform movement emphasizing purity of faith and practices and service to fellow Muslims, especially through education.

Muslim One who has submitted to God by Islam; literally, "submitter."

Pillars of Islam The five basic devotional-ritual duties of Islam: *Shahāda*, testifying that "There is no god but God, and Muḥammad is the Messenger of God"; *Ṣalāt*, five daily prayer services; *Zakāt*, almsgiving; *Ṣawm*, fasting during daylight in the month of Ramaḍān; *Ḥajj*, pilgrimage to Mecca.

pondok pesantren An Islamic boarding school in Indonesia with a traditional curriculum based on the Qur'ān.

Qur'ān Literally, "recitation"; the Islamic Scripture, believed to have been revealed to Muḥammad orally through the angel Gabriel.

Quraysh The leading Meccan tribe to which Muḥammad belonged.

Ramaḍān The holy month of fasting, during which the Qur'ān was first revealed.

sakīna A divine "tranquility" that is believed to descend when the Qur'ān is recited.

Ṣalāt The obligatory Muslim prayer service held five times daily, one of the Pillars of Islam.

Ṣawm "Fasting" during the month of Ramaḍān, one of the Pillars of Islam.

sayyid A title borne by descendants of the Prophet Muḥammad.

Shahāda Literally, "witnessing" that "There is no god but God, Muḥammad is the Messenger of God," a kind of minimal creed for Muslims and one of the Pillars of Islam.

Sharī'a The "way" of Islam, including law and governance, according to the Qur'ān and Sunna.

shaykh Arabic word meaning an old man with grey hairs, a term that came to mean a respected leader and in Islam a religious teacher or person learned in religion or respected for piety.

Shī'a Literally, "party," of 'Alī; the Shī'ites believe that Muḥammad designated his son-in-law, 'Alī, to succeed him as leader of the Umma of Islam; the Shī'ite community numbers up to 20 percent of the total Muslim community today.

shirk "Association" of something with God, thus "idolatry," the one unforgivable sin according to the Qur'ān.

Sufism The mystical path of Islam.

Sunna The "custom" of the Prophet Muḥammad, that is, his words, habits, acts, and gestures as remembered by the Muslims and preserved in the literary form of the Ḥadīth reports. The Sunna is second only to the Qur'ān in authority for Muslims.

Sunnīs The majority of Muslims, who believe that any good Muslim can be leader; they prefer to reach agreements by means of consensus and do not recognize special sacred wisdom in their leaders as Shī'ites do.

sūra A chapter of the Qur'ān, of which there are 114 in all.

tafsīr Interpretation of the Qur'ān, of which there are various types.

taqlīd Adoption and imitation of traditional legal decisions. Criticized by reform-minded legal thinkers as blind imitation—the opposite of *ijtihād*.

Ṭarīqa Literally, "way" of Sufism as a whole as the mystical path of Islam in contrast to the *Sharī'a*, the religious law; *ṭarīqa* also refers to a specific Sufi organization or method of meditation.

tawḥīd The divine unity, Islam's central doctrine.

ta'zīya Literally, "consolation"; a Shī'ite passion play commemorating the tragic death of the third *imām*, Ḥusayn, at Karbalā', in 680 C.E.

tilāwa Ritual recitation of the Qur'ān.

'ulamā' Scholars "learned" in Islamic law, the top class of religious officials in Islam.

Umma The Muslim "community" worldwide.

Wahhābism Puritanical Muslim reform movement that arose in Arabia in the eighteenth century under Muḥammad ibn 'Abd al-Wahhāb (1703–1787).

wahy "Revelation" of the Qur'ān to Muḥammad by a kind of verbal/mental process of inspiration.

walī "Friend," "client," "kinsman," "patron"; in English *walī* most often means Muslim "saint" or "holy person."

Zakāt Legal almsgiving required as a Pillar of Islam.

Selected Reading List

Abdalati, Hammudah. *Islam in Focus.* Indianapolis, IN: Islamic Trust Publications, 1977.

Arberry, A. J., trans. *The Koran Interpreted.* New York: Macmillan, 1964.

Beck, Lois Grant, and Nikkie Keddie, eds. *Women in the Muslim World.* Cambridge, MA: Harvard University Press, 1978.

Cragg, Kenneth. *The Event of the Qur'ān: Islam in Its Scripture.* London: Allen & Unwin, 1971.

———. *The Mind of the Qur'an: Chapters in Reflection.* London: Allen & Unwin, 1973.

Cragg, Kenneth, and R. Marston Speight, eds. *Islam from Within: Anthology of a Religion.* Belmont, CA: Wadsworth, 1980.

Denny, Frederick Mathewson. *An Introduction to Islam.* New York: Macmillan, 1985.

Denny, Frederick Mathewson, and Abdulaziz A. Sachedina. *Islamic Ritual Practices: A Slide Set and Teacher's Guide.* Asian Religions Media Resources, vol. 7. New Haven, CT: Paul Vieth Christian Education Service, Yale Divinity School, 1983.

Encyclopaedia of Islam, new ed. Leiden: Brill, 1954–. An essential reference. An abridgment of the first edition, containing articles on religion only, is *Shorter Encyclopedia of Islam,* edited by H. A. R. Gibb and J. H. Kramers. Leiden: Brill, 1953. See the Register of Subjects, pp. 663–65, for help in finding technical entry words, most of which are Arabic.

Gätje, Helmut. *The Qur'ān and Its Exegesis.* Translated by Alford T. Welch. London: Routledge and Kegan Paul, 1976. Translations of representative *tafsīr* works.

Geertz, Clifford. *Islam Observed: Religious Development in Morocco and Indonesia.* New Haven, CT: Yale University Press, 1968.

Gerholm, Tomas, and Yngve Georg Lithman, eds. *The New Islamic Presence in Western Europe.* London and New York: Mansell, 1988.

Gilsenan, Michael. *Recognizing Islam: An Anthropologist's Introduction.* London and Canberra: Croom and Helm, 1983.

Guillaume, Alfred, trans. *The Life of Muhammad: A Translation of Ishāq's Sīrat Rasūl Allāh.* London: Oxford University Press, 1967.

Haddad, Yvonne Yazbeck. *The Muslims of America.* New York: Oxford University Press, 1991.

Haddad, Yvonne Yazbeck, and Adair T. Lummis. *Islamic Values in the United States.* New York: Oxford University Press, 1987.

Haneef, Suzanne. *What Everyone Should Know About Islam and Muslims.* Chicago: Kazi Publications, 1982.

Hodgson, Marshall G. S. *The Venture of Islam: Conscience and History in a World Civilization.* 3 vols. Chicago: University of Chicago Press, 1974.

Khan, Muhammad Zafrullah, trans. *Gardens of the Righteous: Riyadh as-Salihin of Imam Nawawi.* London: Curzon Press, 1975.

Koentjaraningrat. *Javanese Culture.* Singapore: Oxford University Press, 1985; pb 1989.

Lewis, Bernard. *The Arabs in History.* 4th rev. ed. New York: Harper & Row, 1966.

Momen, Moojan. *An Introduction to Shī'ī Islam.* New Haven, CT, and London: Yale University Press, 1985.

Nasr, Seyyed Hossein. *Ideals and Realities of Islam.* Boston: Beacon Press, 1972.

Pickthall, Mohammed Marmaduke, trans. *The Meaning of the Glorious Koran.* New York: New American Library and Mentor Books, n. d.

Qaradawi, Yusuf al-. *The Lawful and the Prohibited in Islam.* Indianapolis: American Trust Publications, n.d. [c. 1980].

Qutb, Sayyid. *Milestones.* Indianapolis: American Trust Publications, 1990.

Rahman, Fazlur. *Islam.* 2d ed. Chicago: University of Chicago Press, 1979.

————. *Islam and Modernity: Transformation of an Intellectual Tradition.* Chicago: University of Chicago Press, 1982.

————. *Major Themes of the Qur'ān.* Minneapolis and Chicago: Bibliotheca Islamica, 1980.

Schacht, Joseph, and C. E. Bosworth, eds. *The Legacy of Islam.* 2d. ed. Oxford: Clarendon Press, 1974.

Schimmel, Annemarie. *Mystical Dimensions of Islam.* Chapel Hill: The University of North Carolina Press, 1975.

Watt, W. Montgomery. *Bell's Introduction to the Qur'ān.* Edinburgh: Edinburgh University Press, 1970.

————. *The Formative Period of Islamic Thought.* Edinburgh: Edinburgh University Press, 1973.

Waugh, Earle H., Sharon McIrvin Abu-Laban, and Regula Burckhardt Qureshi, eds. *Muslim Families in North America.* Edmonton: University of Alberta Press, 1991.

Weekes, Richard V., ed. *Muslim Peoples: A World Ethnographic Survey,* 2d rev. ed., 2 vols. Westport, CT: Greenwood, 1984.

Wensinck, Arendt Jan. *The Muslim Creed: Its Genesis and Historical Development.* Cambridge: Cambridge University Press, 1932.

Wiebke, Walther. *Women in Islam.* Montclair, NJ: Abner Schram Ltd., 1981.

Woodward, Mark R. *Islam in Java: Normative Piety and Mysticism in the Sultanate of Yogyakarta.* Tucson: University of Arizona Press, 1989.

PART SEVEN

Hinduism

Experiments in the Sacred

David M. Knipe

Chronology of Hinduism in South Asia

Date	Event
	PREHISTORY AND THE INDUS VALLEY CIVILIZATION
c. 6500 B.C.E.	Beginnings of agriculture west of the Indus River
c. 3000 B.C.E.	Emergence of pastoral nomad societies in the Deccan
c. 2500 B.C.E.	Emergence of urban societies along the Indus River
c. 2200–2000 B.C.E.	Harappa at its height
c. 2000–1500 B.C.E.	Decline of the Indus civilization; migrations of Indo-Iranian pastoral nomads from Central Asia onto the Iranian plateau and into northwest India
	THE VEDIC PERIOD
1500–1000 B.C.E.	Continuing Indo-Aryan migrations into northwest India
c. 1200 B.C.E.	Composition of the hymns of the *Rigveda*
c. 1200–900 B.C.E.	*Yajurveda, Samaveda, Atharvaveda*
c. 1000–800 B.C.E.	*Brahmanas*, early *Shrauta Sutras*; Indo-Aryan migrations eastward across North India; emergence of urban societies along the Ganges River
c. 900–600 B.C.E.	*Aranyakas*, early *Upanishads*
c. 600–200 B.C.E.	Later *Upanishads*, other *Sutras* dependent on the *Vedas*
c. 500 B.C.E.	Indo-Aryan migrations southward into Sri Lanka
	THE EPIC PERIOD AND CLASSICAL INDIAN CIVILIZATION
c. 483 B.C.E.	Traditional date for the death of Siddhartha Gautama, the Buddha
c. 468 B.C.E.	Traditional date for the death of Vardhamana Mahavira, twenty-fourth and last great sage of Jainism
400 B.C.E.–400 C.E.	Composition of the epic *Mahabharata*

Date	Event
c. 327–325 B.C.E.	Invasion of northwest India by Alexander the Great
c. 324–185 B.C.E.	Maurya dynasty begun by Chandragupta; Ashoka, patron of Buddhism, ruled 272–242
200 B.C.E.– *200 C.E.*	Composition of the epic *Ramayana;* respective consolidation of Buddhist and Jaina schools
c. 150–300 C.E.	Early *Dharma Shastras:* Manu (Manava), Yajnavalkya
c. 300–500	Early *Puranas:* Markandeya, Matsya, Vayu, Narasimha, Vishnu, Devi
c. 320–550	Gupta dynasty, India's golden age
c. 450	Tamil epic *Cilappatikaram*
c. 500–700	Early *Tantras*
c. 500–900	Nayanmar Shaiva poets of Tamil South India
c. 550–750	First Chalukya dynasty of South India
c. 600–930	Alvar Vaishnava poets of Tamil South India
c. 650	Tamil Shaiva Siddhanta schools

THE MEDIEVAL PERIOD

Date	Event
c. 711–715 C.E.	Arab Muslims invade northwest India
c. 750–1000	Later *Puranas:* Vamana, Kurma, Linga, Varaha, Padma, Agni, Garuda, Skanda, Shiva, Bhagavata, Bhavishya, Brahma, Brahmavaivarta, Devibhagavata
c. 788–820	Traditional dates for Shankara
c. 800	Manikkavachakar, Tamil Shaiva poet-saint, author of *Tiruvachakam*
c. 850–1279	Chola dynasty of South India
c. 900–1200	Great temples of Khajuraho, Bhubaneswar, Thanjavur, Konarak, and so on
c. 1021	Ghaznavid (Turkish) Muslim capital at Lahore; beginning of the decline of Buddhism in India, disappearance by 1550
c. 1056–1137	Traditional dates for Ramanuja
c. 1150	Kamban's *Iramavataram,* a Tamil *Ramayana*
1192	Ghorid Muslim capital at Delhi
c. 1200	Jayadeva's *Gita Govinda;* Virashaivas in South India; early orders of Sufis in North India

Date	Event
1210–1526	Delhi sultanate
c. 1238–1317	Madhva, founder of the Dvaita school of Vedanta
c. 1300–1350	Muslim conquest of peninsular India; Deccan sultanates established
c. 1336–1565	The Vijayanagara empire of South India
c. 1398–1448	Kabir, North Indian devotional poet
1399	Destruction of Delhi by Timur, ruler of Central Asia
c. 1400	Villiputtur Alvar's Tamil version of *Mahabharata*
c. 1469–1539	Guru Nanak, founder of Sikhism
c. 1479–1531	Vallabha, founder of sect devoted to Krishna
c. 1483–1563	Surdas, North Indian Hindi devotional poet
c. 1485–1533	Chaitanya, Bengali mystic
1498	Vasco da Gama lands on west coast of India
c. 1498–1546	Mirabai, Rajasthani devotional poetess
1526–1707	Mughal empire, Muslim emperors Babur to Aurangzeb
c. 1532–1623	Tulsidas, author of *Ramcaritmanas* (Hindi *Ramayana*)
1542–1605	Akbar, greatest of Mughal emperors
1608	British East India Company in Surat
c. 1608–1649	Tukaram, poet-saint of Maharashtra
1666–1708	Gobind Singh, tenth and last Sikh Guru
c. 1700	Kalki, last of the major *Puranas*
1739	Destruction of Delhi by Nadir Shah, king of Iran
1757	Battle of Plassey, defeat of Muslim rulers in Bengal by the British East India Company

THE MODERN PERIOD

Date	Event
1772–1833 C.E.	Ram Mohan Roy; Brahmo Samaj founded 1828
1824–1883	Dayananda Sarasvati; Arya Samaj founded 1875
1836–1886	Ramakrishna, Bengali mystic
1858	British viceroy officially replaces Mughal rule in India
1861–1941	Rabindranath Tagore, 1913 Nobel laureate for *Gitanjali*
1863–1902	Vivekananda; Ramakrishna Movement founded 1897
1869–1948	Mohandas Karamchand Gandhi
1872–1950	Aurobindo Ghose, philosopher, teacher, founder of religious center in Pondicherry

Date	Event
1876–1948	Muhammad Ali Jinnah, president of Muslim League; separate states for Muslim majority areas proposed 1940
1877–1938	Muhammad Iqbal; separate Muslim state proposed 1940
1879–1951	Ramana Maharshi, mystic of South India
1893	Vivekananda at the World Parliament of Religions in Chicago; Vedanta societies spread in the West
1896–1977	A. C. Bhaktivedanta Swami, founder of International Society for Krishna Consciousness, based in Los Angeles
1926–	Sathya Sai Baba
1947	British grant independence to India; migrations of seventeen million Hindus, Muslims, and Sikhs; more than a quarter of a million killed during partition of India and the creation of the Islamic Republic of Pakistan
1948	Sri Lanka (Ceylon) granted independence from British rule
1950	Republic of India; Jawaharlal Nehru, first prime minister, 1947–1964
1960s	Maharishi Mahesh Yogi, Bhaktivedanta, and other Indian gurus establish eclectic movements in the West
1970s	Hindus in Europe, United States, Canada begin building temples
1971	East Pakistan becomes separate state of Bangladesh
1975	Birendra crowned as tenth Shah ruler of Nepal, the last Hindu kingdom of South Asia

29

Introduction

UNDERGRADUATE STUDENTS WHO are fortunate enough to travel and study in South Asia are almost invariably transformed by their experiences. Typical of most of them, if perhaps more articulate, one such student wrote this testimony following a junior-year study tour.

> In my travels in South Asia I was exposed to things emphatically different from what I had known in the West. Some of the differences were obvious—skin color, language, climate—and some subtle—metaphysical beliefs, perceptions, worldviews. In Asia I saw the most abject poverty imaginable, and became friends with begging lepers; I saw beautiful tropical forests, and shared my lunch with Sherpa children in the Himalayas; I drank tea with Buddhist monks, and discussed the caste system with wandering ascetics. My experiences in Asia unsettled me, and changed the way I see myself, my culture, my society. And of course, these experiences immeasurably altered my view of South Asia.
>
> Oddly, in many ways I feel I know even less about South Asia than I did before I left, for with each new experience emerged layer upon layer of meaning, layer upon layer of understanding. I don't find this at all daunting, for although I know that there are an infinite number of things about South Asian culture I do not know, I also know that there are an infinite number of things I can know. The journal entry for the day I left South Asia consists of a single sentence: "My head is a jumble of possibilities."

We might well employ this enthusiastic undergrad's final phrase as a subtitle for an introductory chapter, for Hinduism does seem to present itself as "a jumble of possibilities," including also the probability that no definition of "Hinduism" will prove satisfactory to all insiders and outsiders. So elusive is this ancient and cumulative religious tradition that some scholars have despaired of definition and suggested that Hindus are identified simply as the religious remainder after one subtracts all Muslims, Jainas, Buddhists, Christians, Jews, Parsis, and tribals from the religious landscape of South Asia. That observation is challenged in this introduction and in the following chapters with a portrayal of the character, extent, and significance of experiences and expressions that have been the dominant feature of South Asian religion for most of the past

South Asia.

thirty centuries. [See Religions of Africa pp. 23–24, Religions of Mesoamerica pp. 117–19, Native Religions of North America pp. 261–64, Judaism pp. 389, 426, 456–75, Christianity pp. 492–94, Islam pp. 607–8, Buddhism pp. 853–55, Religions of China pp. 990–1015, and Religions of Japan pp. 1090–92 for discussion of the diversity and variety of religious traditions.]

Let us begin with the territory, South Asia. According to those who study plate tectonics and the geological history of our planet, South Asia includes the triangular area that detached itself from southern Africa and sailed off until it crunched into the belly of Asia, forming the Himalayan massif with the impact and becoming what is known as the Indian subcontinent. Historically speaking, South Asia is the equivalent of India, that is, the land the ancient Greeks and Persians declared to be east of the river known in Sanskrit as the Sindhu. Politically speaking, modern South Asia is the large nation of India, which occupies most of that subcontinent, and the several smaller nations immediately adjacent, including Pakistan, Tibet, Nepal, Sikkim, Bhutan, Bangladesh, and the island country off the southeast tip of India, Sri Lanka. One additional modern nation not adjacent but historically and culturally linked to India is Afghanistan.

With reference to South Asia today this region is distinguished from West Asia (the Mediterranean coast to Iran), Central or Inner Asia, East Asia (China, Taiwan, Korea, Japan), and Southeast Asia (Burma [Myanmar], Thailand, Cambodia, Laos, Vietnam, Malaysia, and Indonesia). From prehistory to the present the region of South Asia has had significant historical and cultural exchanges with all of these other areas—West, Central, East, and Southeast Asia.

Where religions are concerned, South Asia harbors three dominant faiths, Hinduism, Islam, and Buddhism, and a number of minority religions, including Christianity, Jainism, Parsism (Zoroastrianism), and Judaism. Hindus are to be found in all the nations of South Asia, comprising the dominant tradition of India and Nepal (more than 80 percent in each), roughly one-fifth of the population of Sri Lanka, and only tiny minorities in Pakistan and Bangladesh, where Islam is the state religion. There are also thriving Hindu communities outside of South Asia. In Southeast Asia there were large populations of Hindus in the medieval period, but after the advent of Islam only certain enclaves of traditional Hinduism remained, the Indonesian island of Bali being one prominent example. The modern era has witnessed the growth of Hindu populations in many cosmopolitan urban centers in Southeast Asia, including Singapore and Kuala Lumpur on the Malay peninsula, as well as Hong Kong on the south coast of China. Substantial communities of Hindus live in eastern and southern Africa, in the thriving Persian Gulf states, on the island of Fiji in the South Pacific, on the northeast coast of South America, on islands such as Trinidad in the Caribbean and, as the active temples in Pittsburgh, Chicago, Houston, San Francisco, London, and elsewhere may suggest, in many major cities of North America and Europe.

However far-flung these medieval and modern migrations might have been, it remains true that Hinduism is not a multicultural religion to the same extent as Buddhism, Christianity, or Islam. India, the source, remains India, the heartland. In fact, so deep is this identity of a people and a faith that the modern nation of India often finds its credibility tested when declaring itself a religiously plural secular state.

Important for an understanding of a people is a recognition of the land they inhabit and in many respects revere. The great variety of natural regions of the subcontinent explains in part the tremendous cultural and linguistic diversity within the South Asian area. A brief survey of the terrain from north to south is in order.

Separating the subcontinent from Central or Inner Asia is the world's greatest system of mountain peaks and glaciers, the Himalayas, extending west-east for fifteen hundred miles. In the inhabited plateaus, valleys, and foothills of these mountains are many regions, including the whole of Nepal, where Hinduism, Buddhism, and indigenous folk religions have interacted for many centuries. South of the Himalayas, between the Indus River system in the west and the jungles of Assam in the east, stretch the North Indian or Gangetic plains. This is a zone of intensive cultivation along the rivers Ganges and Jamuna with dense populations in numerous cities and thousands of villages. It is in this region that Hinduism received much of its basic character. In fact modern cities such as Varanasi (also known as Kashi or Banaras), Allahabad (ancient Prayaga), Gaya, and Hardwar remain sacred centers for Hindu pilgrims today, just as they were in ancient times nearly three thousand years ago.

Farther to the south the relatively low-lying Aravalli, Vindhya, and other mountain ranges provide another border declaring a third distinctive region, peninsular India or the Deccan plateau. This vast triangular area is largely savannah bordered by two additional mountain systems, the Western Ghats running along the west coast on the Arabian Sea and the Eastern Ghats fronting the east coast on the Bay of Bengal. The deep south of this peninsular region generated a classical culture and literature quite independent of the north. Already in the early centuries of the Common Era many southern sacred centers became pilgrimage goals on a spiritual chart known throughout the subcontinent. Such a Pan-Indian map included the cities known today as Thanjavur, Kanchipuram, Madurai, and other sites such as the ancient temple at Sri Shaila.

In addition to the Indus, Ganges, Jamuna, and Brahmaputra rivers in the north, several great southern rivers cross this Deccan plateau. The Narmada flows west into the Arabian Sea; the Mahanadi, Godavari, and Krishna all run eastward to the Bay of Bengal. Historically, agricultural settlements developed along all of these rivers, and such migration routes linked together the diverse subcultures of South Asia. Furthermore, the rivers themselves became sacred entities and therefore sites of distinguished temples, calendrical festivals, personal rituals, and human transformations.

The physical borders provided by mountains, rivers, forests, and deserts of course had much to do with the historic emergence of intangible borders declared by languages. The subcontinent displays four distinct linguistic families: Indo-European, Dravidian, Tibeto-Burman, and Austro-Asiatic. During the second millennium B.C.E., speakers of Indo-Aryan migrated into northwest India, thereby extending an eastern branch of the Indo-European language family into South Asia. In North India today Hindi, a descendant from ancient Indo-Aryan, is spoken in a variety of dialects as a mother tongue or second language by more than three hundred million people, as well as by others in South India. Additional languages of the north include, among others, Marathi, Gujarati, Sindi, Punjabi, Rajasthani, Bengali, and Nepali.

In peninsular India to the south, the Dravidian family has been dominant from prehistory; it includes four major languages: Malayalam, Kannada, Telugu, and Tamil. Each of these four dominates a linguistic state of contemporary India (Kerala, Karnataka, Andhra, and Tamil Nadu, respectively), just as the northern states of India from Gujarat to Bengal, plus the separate nation of Nepal, are essentially language zones. Most of the Hindu minority on the island nation of Sri Lanka speaks Tamil rather than Sinhala, the official language and that of the Buddhist majority.

The other two language families of South Asia are much smaller considering the number of speakers. The Tibeto-Burman family is represented by languages spoken in the Himalayan and northeastern areas—Newari in the Kathmandu valley, for example, or Lepcha in Sikkim and elsewhere, or Manipuri in the northeast. Austro-Asiatic languages are still spoken by the many tribal peoples of central, eastern, and northeastern India, including the Mundari, Santali, Kherwari, and others.

English, established by the British in the eighteenth and nineteenth centuries as the language of commerce, government, and higher education, is today the language of only about 2 percent of the population of India. That figure sometimes surprises Americans and Europeans who regularly encounter many South Asians who have been fluent in English since childhood.

It may be noted here that the vocabulary of Hinduism is primarily Sanskrit, a "perfected" or "refined" speech, that is to say, a classical form of ancient Indo-Aryan that became, via the learned Brahman elite, the language of the oral traditions of Hinduism. Eventually the ancient oral texts became written texts and inscriptions (as well as continuing oral literatures) after the introduction of various scripts from West Asia late in the first millennium B.C.E. However, it was not until the early medieval period—about the seventh or eighth century C.E.— that one of the later scripts, *devanagari,* was widely employed in North India. Never a mother tongue, always a second or third language of the learned, Sanskrit is still spoken today by many priests and scholars. From the Vedic of the *Rigveda* to present-day recitations of medieval *Puranas* by priests in temples and homes, Sanskrit has remained the fundamental sound of Hinduism. The glossary at the end of this part provides a brief note on Sanskrit pronunciation and transliteration.

The peoples and cultures of India, ancient or modern, have always been celebrated for a diversity quite as rich as that of their terrain and its varied climates: multiple economies, diets, habitats, clothing, lifestyles; today, sixteen official languages, each with multiple dialects, and hundreds of minor tongues; a mind-boggling array of castes, subcastes, tribes, clans, and kinship designations; half a dozen major religions, each with a battery of sects, and tens of thousands of localized cults; nonliterary traditions that, for lack of knowledge and imagination, outside observers sometimes dismiss as "animism." And yet, through all of this vigorous display of geographic, historic, cultural, and linguistic diversity there remains a religious entity, Hinduism, that can in fact be identified and explored.

Hinduism can be seen to develop over a period of more than three thousand years, with significant contributions entering the tradition continuously. Such a breadth of historical experience in addition to multicultural and regional diversity might excuse the Hindu tradition from any concise or simple definition. Nevertheless, a pattern of beliefs and practices emerged over time on which both ancient and modern Hindus might agree.

One concise statement appeared about the beginning of the Common Era in what came to be an authoritative text of classical Hindu law, the *Laws of Manu,* or *Manava Dharma Shastra.* Traditionally this Sanskrit text was compiled by the sage **Manu** as one of several digests concerned with religion, law, right conduct—all that is encompassed in the Sanskrit word ***dharma.**** Manu declared

---

*Terms defined in the glossary, pp. 838–40, as well as concepts and names that appear on the list of Deities, Powers, and Diefied Heroes, pp. 841–43, are printed in boldface type where they first appear in the text.

that a person may concentrate on liberation from the world of continuous rebirths only after paying off three debts. Manu's statement is a good working definition of Hinduism because it focuses upon the central concerns of the ongoing tradition.

The flow of existences is known in classical Hinduism as transmigration (**samsara**), a dilemma to be solved by release (**moksha**) from bondage to this world brought about by the consequences of action (**karma**). *Manava Dharma Shastra* 6.35 reflects the historical development of Hinduism, as well as its powerful conservatism. Manu's phrase combines the individual's three debts, a belief that was already a thousand years old in Manu's day, with the notion that an individual experiences continuous cycles of births and deaths in this world, a more recent doctrine.

Turning first to the older belief, the three debts—to the ancient sages, the gods, and the ancestors—are first described about 1000 B.C.E. in sacred texts known as the *Vedas*. Three obligations are said to be incurred at birth by everyone in the elite class of priests and scholars known as Brahmans, and they should be paid to the mythical sages who first transmitted the *Vedas*, to the gods, and to the ancestors or collective "Fathers" as they are known. A Brahman becomes free of this natal liability by learning and reciting the eternal *Vedas* (thereby passing them on as the ancient sages did in the beginning), by sacrificing to the gods (thereby continuing the world that was created by sacrifice in the beginning), and by producing a son (thereby perpetuating a lineage as the Fathers did in the beginning). Freedom from such debts was a spiritual fulfillment, an emancipation from the routine of a householder reciting the three sacred texts and tending his three sacred fires.

By the time the *Laws of Manu* were compiled, however, several significant transitions had occurred to provide a new context for this belief in three basic obligations. For one, the notion of three debts at birth applied to all three "twice-born" classes—the Brahmans, the warriors, and the producers. In other words, the whole of the three-level society was involved as a unit distinguished from an alien world outside the authority of these sacred texts and rituals. Second, the worldview in Manu's time was radically altered from the one that had prevailed in 1000 B.C.E. Attention now focused upon release from bondage to this painful world of *samsara*, upon an adequate means of dealing with the consequences of action, karma, a cosmic impersonal accounting that causes rebirth. And third, the *Laws of Manu* suggest in this same passage that a Brahman householder may transcend domestic life by incorporating his three sacred fires within himself in order to take up the renunciant ascetic path in the forest.

Thus all the ingredients by which classical Hinduism is defined are present in this *Laws of Manu* segment. *Samsara* and karma are basic facts of the human condition, and *moksha* the ultimate aim of the spiritual life. The path toward liberation from the round of births and deaths involves recognition of the eternal *Vedas* and the ancient sages (**rishis**) who made them available, worship of the gods (**devas**) who created this universe, and responsible regard for the Fathers (**pitrs**) with continuation of their lineage into the future. But the path also involves an idealized fourfold program for life that proceeds from study of the sacred texts—the student (***brahmacarin***) absorbs sacred knowledge (***veda***) —to the life of the married householder (with children, civic responsibilities, and sacred tasks such as worship of the family deities), to the chaste simplicity of the forest-dwelling stage and intensification of the spiritual quest. The fourth and final stage is that of the ***samnyasin,*** the renunciant who interiorizes his sacred fires and is detached from actions that bind.

Matching this fourfold program of life stages, known as ***ashramas,*** is a set of four goals of life for every Hindu, also sequential: the pursuits of sexual love (*kama*), wealth or material gain (*artha*), spiritual conduct or duty (*dharma*), and liberation (*moksha*). *Moksha* transcends the preceding three pursuits as the *samnyasin* transcends his previous three life stages.

In the two millennia that separate such classical texts as Manu's from the Hinduism of regional South Asia today a great deal has transpired. Attention shifted from the great body of texts known as *Vedas* to equally huge collections of epic recitations and performances, as well as other new genres of oral mythology and tradition. The focus on sacrifice in the Vedic mode gradually gave way to worship of and devotional expression to a powerful set of deities including the older gods **Vishnu** and **Shiva** and newer goddesses such as **Durga** or **Kali.** The structure of society became increasingly complicated as the class hierarchy gave way to a regionally varied and more intensely stratified caste system. And along the way Hinduism was frequently threatened and then benefited by encounters with other faith traditions, including Jainism and Buddhism, and subsequently Christianity, Zoroastrianism, and Islam.

In sum, if we were to identify a Hindu in India, Nepal, or elsewhere in South Asia today, he or she would no doubt believe in karma and *samsara,* revere certain sacred texts and certain deities (usually without naming a single text or deity as requisite), accept the obligation of satisfying his or her older ancestors with progeny and with more or less regular offerings and prayers, declare class and caste status within a social structure that most Hindus would recognize, demonstrate certain ascetic tendencies in the form of fasts and vows, and describe certain progress or intentions in life goals and pursuits toward an ultimate release (although for many the ideal of *moksha* is a remote target at the far end of an inevitable series of rebirths).

In other words the broad definition of Hinduism today is very nearly what it was more than two millennia ago in the classical period. Two important changes might be registered here, however. One is the deepening base of Hinduism in the folk and tribal traditions of every region of the subcontinent. Those who were "alien" in the period of the early *Vedas* and "excluded" in the time of Manu have in many respects come to be the dominant forces in the currents of Hinduism over the millennia, and their traditions are now mingled irreversibly into the mainstream. The other change is to the gender base. We noted that the debt to the Fathers is paid by producing a son (not just a child) according to this male-dominated tradition, and everywhere in Vedic, classical, medieval, and modern Hinduism the paradigms in myths, rituals, doctrines, and symbols are masculine. But just as goddess traditions encroached successfully on the territory of masculine deities, so too has the impact of women's religious activity, the ritual life in particular, been of increasing significance in the overall scale of Hindu tradition. To put this another way, in traditional life the unlettered folk have always shaped Hinduism, and half of them have been women. It is not feminine roles in Hinduism that have been lacking but rather the acknowledgment of such in literature, the arts, and institutions such as the priesthood and temple and monastic administrations. Only now, in a world rapidly changing because of educational opportunities, are such institutions and media beginning to reflect accurately the total picture of Hindu class, caste, gender, and regional life.

In the following exploration of Hinduism past and present the extraordinary diversity of regions and locales, cultures and subcultures, languages and dialects, sects and cults must be kept foremost in mind. Illustrations cannot be drawn equitably or convincingly from every region or tradition or period, from Nepali-speaking Shaivas in the Himalayas to Tamil-speaking Vaishnavas in Sri Lanka, from Nambudiri Brahmans in Kerala to tribal ritualists in Orissan temples. Therefore a few selected voices must be asked to attempt the impossible, that is, to speak for the many.

30
Hinduism and History: Prehistoric and Vedic Periods

Time ripens all beings by itself, in itself. But no one here on earth knows one whom Time has fully ripened.
   Mahabharata 12.231.25

HINDUISM AS A LIVING TRADITION today has a long and exacting but quite selective memory. It is a tradition that remembers the cumulative experience of ages rather than specific events of a decade or century. Only the Greeks recalled that Alexander and his armies once invaded South Asia, and it was Chinese travelers who retained important details about early Buddhism in India. It is a tradition that prefers to live on cosmic time, not human social calendars. To this day there is often uncertainty about the beginning times of major festivals: The proper moment is eventually divined from the movements of celestial bodies and communicated from the specialists to the public. It is a tradition that seldom remembered the names of its ancient poets and rarely recorded political details, but generated the longest known epic poem about a war that may never have happened. Today many people who routinely recite 108 names of a goddess or a god cannot recall the name of any Hindu ruler before Jawaharlal Nehru became prime minister of India in 1947. [See Religions of Mesoamerica pp. 159–60, 206–9, Native Religions of North America pp. 280–82, 351–54, Judaism pp. 431–33, Christianity pp. 551–53, Islam pp. 674, 707, Buddhism pp. 890–91, Religions of China pp. 1021–24, and Religions of Japan pp. 1141–46 for discussion of religious calendar and time.]

   Immediately there is a problem of communication. The contemporary West is a historically minded civilization with a legacy of tough-minded critical inquiry and analysis. "Myth" is depreciated into that which is not true; lines are drawn between past, present, and future; the stuff of human experience is ordered and conclusively paginated, bound, and covered, with HISTORY embossed on the spine. Who wrote this, when did that happen, what happened next? Is this true, or just a myth or legend? When responses to queries such as these tend to collapse time and space, or apply some other frame to the picture, or worse, regard these organizing habits as interesting but irrelevant, it is not unusual for the outsider to lose all bearings.

The following conversation, an illustration, took place in North India when a villager pointed outside his village to an ashen stretch of land where nothing would grow: "A great fire swept through here," he explained. "When did this happen?" asked his American student guest. "Oh, long ago." "How long ago? In the past century?" persisted the American. "Oh, no, much further back, in the time when **Rama** was king." "But isn't Rama a god?" asked the student, who had read a book on Hinduism. "Yes, yes, but here he was also our great king."

How should one consider the countless "long agos" of Hinduism, the timeless tides of mythology, ritual, and symbolism that wash over the outlines outsiders try to impose upon them? Communicating with India is a demanding process, and one that favors procedure. A first step is to declare what the tradition says about itself. Second comes an organization of what the tradition says into components that make sense to us as observers, students, and investigators, even if inadequacies are recognized in such organization. And third, the meaning of these components is highlighted within the tradition as a whole.

For example, the *Vedas* are the foremost texts of ancient Hinduism. Vedic tradition says they are a unity existent from eternity and without human origin. That religious fact must be declared first and stated clearly. But outside scholarly curiosity has applied itself to these texts as it has to Aristotle, Shakespeare, and the Bible, and on linguistic and literary grounds determined them to have been composed variously between something close to 1200 and 200 B.C.E. That organizational and text-critical view must also be provided before moving on to questions of meaning. What is the immediate religious significance of this unity and eternity attributed to the *Vedas?* What does the Hindu tradition over the long haul do with such notions? Can outsiders learn something by valuing the traditional perspective as much as the analytic one, in other words by allowing space for reflection and dialogue?

The title of this chapter, a prefiguration of dialogue, is not "The History of Hinduism," but "Hinduism and History." A division of Indian experience into historical periods does not come with the territory. There are no sequential dynasties, as in Egypt, Assyria, or China, for example, that are particularly meaningful to the Hindu tradition, and no historical records on the order of Chinese classics such as the *Book of History* or the *Spring and Autumn Annals.* Nor are there powerful establishers like Gautama Buddha, Vardhamana Mahavira, or Guru Nanak, all of them historically grounded shapers and transmitters of traditions in South Asia outside Hinduism. Most of the usual textual, institutional, and biographical criteria are missing until fairly late in the stream of time.

Certain features do present themselves from the collective Indian experience, however, and it is these we may designate historical breaks in an overview. One of these is the emergence of full-scale urban societies along the Indus River, societies that formed the first cohesive civilization in South Asia in the third and second millennia B.C.E. A second is the appearance of the *Vedas,* providing a Vedic age, the period when these great oral traditions were dominant paradigms and unchallenged sacred utterances for large segments of the populace.

The third feature is also an oral-literary one, a period when new post-Vedic texts and accompanying traditions surfaced to establish the classical definitions of Hinduism. The earliest of these post-Vedic texts were oral compositions, like the *Vedas,* eventually transmitted into writing. The *Dharma Shastras,* such as the *Laws of Manu* employed in chapter 29 as a link midway between ancient Vedic Hinduism and medieval regional Hinduism, were among them. But the two most important post-Vedic works were the great Sanskrit epics, the *Mahabharata* and the *Ramayana.* These vast collections of verses became classical storehouses of Hindu mythology, folklore, and doctrine. So encompassing of tradition were these Sanskrit epics, and so thoroughly did they dominate cultural life in the first several centuries of the Common Era, this third period might well be labeled an epic age. Its last phase witnessed the growth of towns with temples that served as ceremonial centers for extensive areas of the subcontinent, regions that also embraced other pilgrimage goals focused on sacred mountains and rivers. These centers in turn generated still more texts and traditions, including the classical treatises of **Yoga** and other philosophical schools, additional collections of mythology known as "old stories" or *Puranas,* and esoteric texts known as *Tantras* that focused on special techniques for liberation. The final phase of this epic age also displayed the flowering of ancient Indian culture and its most creative genius in literature, music, the arts, and philosophy.

Finally, subsequent to this formation of classical Hinduism in a post-Vedic age, two additional periods can be identified as medieval and modern. In the fourth or medieval age—median, that is, between classical and modern—several forceful minds and personalities came to identify and synthesize the philosophical, theological, and devotional bases of the faith. Shankara and Ramanuja were the most significant voices of this age. From the sixth to the seventeenth centuries regional poet-saints grew immensely popular when they countered traditional Sanskrit by employing their local languages as the medium of devotional songs.

In the fifth or modern period Hinduism has undergone—and is undergoing —a series of comprehensive and affective reforms. Two particular challenges called for responses from the Hindu tradition during the last eight centuries. One of these, largely a feature of the medieval period, was the encounter with Islam as an intrusive and innovative cultural entity in South Asia. The other, largely a feature of the modern period that continues today, is the encounter with the political, religious, and cultural force of the West.

Thus we may examine five segments of the Hindu experience. A rough chronology and set of comparative timelines might serve for the purposes of this overview:

The Indus Valley Civilization c. 2500–1750 B.C.E.

A Vedic Age c. 1200–200 B.C.E.

An Epic Age c. 400 B.C.E.–800 C.E.

Medieval South Asia c. 750–1750 C.E.

Modern South Asia c. 1750–the present

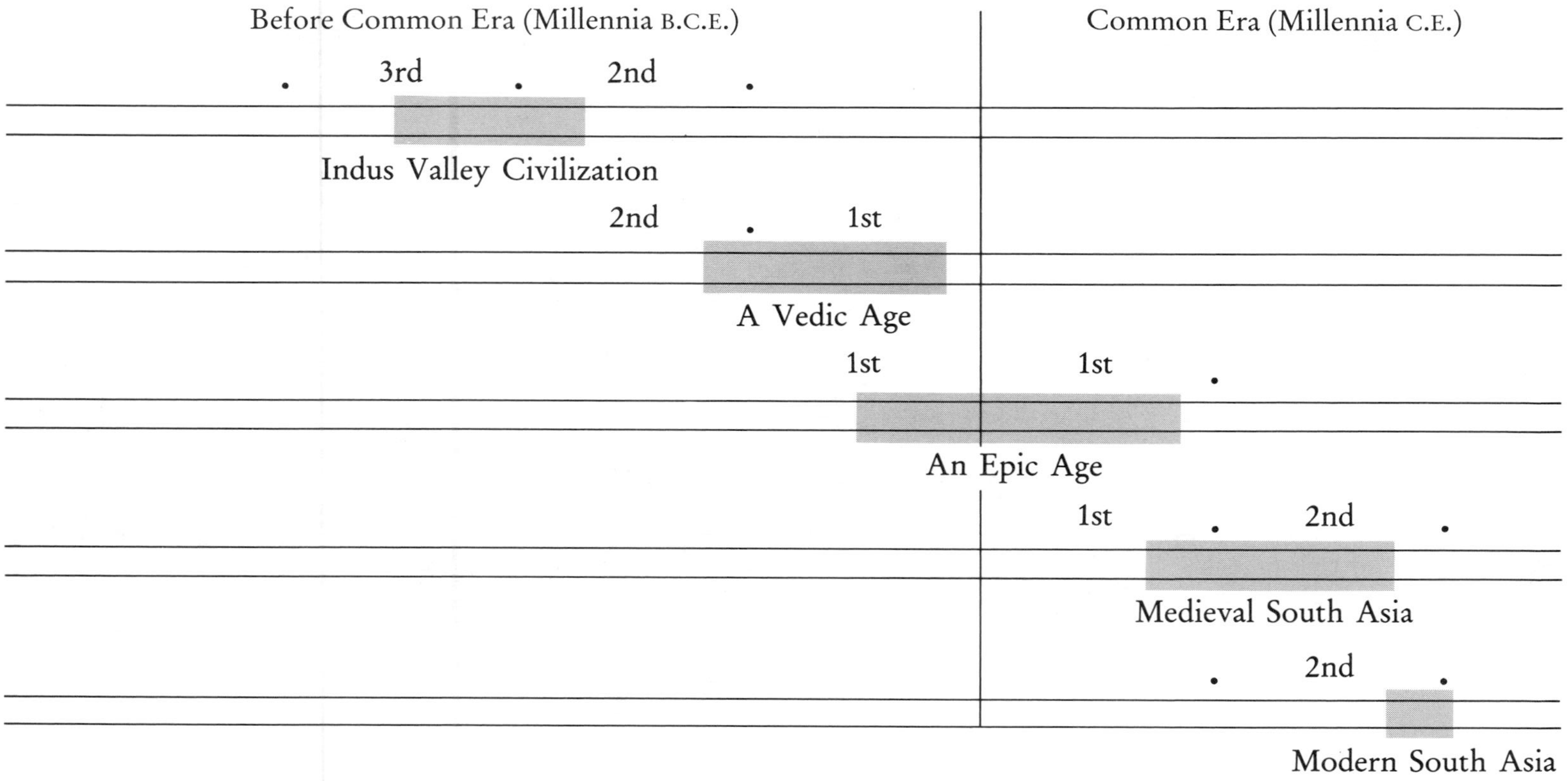

Before Common Era (Millennia B.C.E.) Common Era (Millennia C.E.)

3rd 2nd 1st 1st 2nd

Indus Valley Civilization

A Vedic Age

An Epic Age

Medieval South Asia

Modern South Asia

Table 7-1. History and Hinduism: Comparative Timelines of Significant Eras and Their Millennia.

If these five periods are situated in rough millennia (thousand-year eras), something of their duration as well as overlap is seen in the context of South Asian history at large (see table 7-1).

From the outsider's historical point of view, essential experiences and expressions have been mixed into the rich Hindu synthesis in each of these periods. From the insider's traditional point of view, however, the enduring features of Hinduism have remained unaltered by the flow of history, "time ripening," or any circumstance of linguistic, ethnic, social, or political change. The marvelous thing about the faith is that both of these seemingly contradictory points of view are true, each in its own way, and both must be heard by the student of Hinduism.

Important to remember, therefore, is that this segmentation of human experience into ages and periods, while familiar to Western experience, is largely absent from Hindu tradition. These divisions are a search for organization, chronology, continuity, and development. In chapters 32 and 33 we will look through and beyond these divisions in order to focus on interactive worldviews and the dynamics of Hinduism. By and large these take scant notice of our five periods, or any other schedule of historical episodes, even while their expressions are concrete evidence of cumulative memory and changing experience.

Earliest Civilization: The Indus Valley

The Indus, one of the world's greatest river systems, flows from southwestern Tibet eighteen hundred miles before it empties into the Arabian Sea. Its earliest known name is the Sanskrit—Sindhu—which provided through ancient Greek and Persian both "India" and "Hindu" as designations for the land beyond the river and its people. The northwest region of India, known as the Punjab ("land of five rivers"), takes its name from five large tributaries of the lower Indus. And now in our time the river has lent its name once again, for lack of an ancient one, to what appears to have been a coherent urban civilization, one that developed in the middle of the third millennium B.C.E. and lasted for about eight centuries. A string of cities, the largest of them about one mile square, reached from Harappa on the Ravi tributary in the north down through Mohenjo-daro to Lothal in the delta on the sea.

This civilization resulted from the discovery of rich arable soil in the Indus flood plain (just as earlier urban societies developed along the Nile and along the Tigris and Euphrates, and a later one on the alluvial plain of North China). Smaller, pre-Indus settlements can be traced by archaeologists back into the seventh millennium B.C.E. in Baluchistan and Afghanistan. Those early settlers— seminomadic pastoralists, sedentary cultivators, and some who combined cattle herding with small-scale wheat-barley agriculture—provided a technological heritage many thousands of years old, one that blossomed dramatically when transferred eastward to the Indus River system in the third millennium B.C.E. About four thousand years ago the civilization may have been at full strength, with upward of two hundred villages and towns and half a dozen cities, a common system of weights and measures, uniform building supplies and techniques, granary systems to store harvests, and established trade routes that aimed westward by sea into the Persian Gulf and northward by land into Central Asia.

From seventy years of archaeology a great deal has been learned about the material culture of the Indus sites. It is surprising therefore that the religious life remains largely hidden. One may only speculate. For starters, there are over two thousand brief inscriptions, and more coming to light every season, but scholars cannot agree on the reading of their signs. Second, the inscriptions are on a startling array of finely carved steatite stamp "seals," square or rectangular, about two inches wide, with what appear to be sacred figures of humans and animals in mythic and ritual scenes. But the myths and rituals are absent, and the "humans" could be deities, royalty, heroes, heroines, sacrificial victims, or devotees.

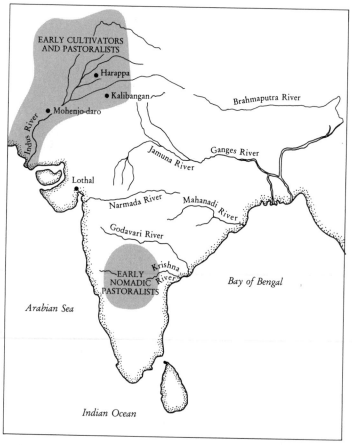

Early Cultivators and Pastoralists (3000–2500 B.C.E.).

With about four hundred graphemes—and no decipherable inscription—even the purpose of this seal-writing remains unknown. Third, there is nothing clearly identified as a shrine or a temple in any excavated site. If Mohenjo-daro or Harappa became established ceremonial centers for their regions, perhaps they resembled ancient Chinese cities more than the temple-centered urban societies of Egypt, Mesopotamia, and Anatolia in that they relied more on cosmic images and symbols than upon the building of impressive dwellings for deities. [See Religions of Africa p. 59, Religions of Mesoamerica pp. 114–15, and Religions of China p. 986 for discussion of early cities.]

Having stated how much information is lacking, we may proceed to some of the more useful speculations concerning religious life along the Indus River about 2000 B.C.E. We have the benefit of hindsight, of course, and often expect features of today's Hinduism to be at least four thousand years old. It may be imprudent to second-guess a culture that left us, thus far, few clues concerning its social structure, few significant works of art or institutional architecture, no literature of any kind, and only a disputed supposition that its language or languages were "Proto-Dravidian." (The Dravidian family is confined, as it is known historically, to four languages of South India and the remnant Brahui now spoken by a quarter of a million pastoralists in Pakistan.)

But second-guessing is an established academic tradition, a tantalizing one, and quite frequently instructive. If some of the peoples of Pakistan and northwestern India still today plow their fields in the patterns of ancient furrows or make wooden carts that resemble toy miniatures found in levels of Harappa, then perhaps something of their spiritual ethos may have survived four or five thousand years as well.

First, the overall impression from surveying the excavated Indus sites is one of urbanity, sophistication, well-being, and ordered existence. From the huge wheat and barley storage systems down to the presence of household and public drainage works, there is visible an overarching hand of authority and urban planning. From the uniformity of material culture across hundreds of miles and a great many centuries there is felt the weight of tradition. It is not difficult to imagine a centralized religious authority corresponding to, or perhaps superseding, the obvious political and economic authority.

Second, if major cities such as Harappa, Mohenjo-daro, and Kalibangan did serve as ceremonial centers, several features in their layouts are worth remarking on. They are axially oriented north-south with streets in a grid and raised, brick-walled mounds dominating the western quarter. Burials in cemeteries frequently also reveal a common north-south alignment, head to the north, a direction that remains to this day an auspicious one in South Asia. On top of Mohenjo-daro's mound, at the center, is a tank that archaeologists have labeled the "great bath." It has wide steps at each end and resembles the ritual bathing tanks of Hindu temples that began to appear in the subcontinent in the first few centuries C.E. If there were constructions of steps descending into the river for ritual bathing, as is the case with every riverside town or city in India today, these have long since disappeared without a trace.

New excavations in the Harappa cemetery, 1987. (Photo by J. M. Kenoyer, courtesy of the University of California at Berkeley Project at Harappa, an ongoing project with the Department of Archaeology and Museums, Government of Pakistan.)

Third, as we might suspect from a long-established agrarian tradition, there appear to have been prominent feminine images and symbols in the deepest strata of the region, going back to the pre-urban seventh millennium. Small, distinctive terra-cotta females, of a popular, perhaps votive type, are abundant in village sites and common in the larger settlements. And many of the most intriguing motifs on the Indus civilization seals include feminine powers, frequently linked with symbols of vegetation or of animals, including real animals and composite or mythic creatures. After the Indus cities withered, nude female figurines maintained their importance in village cultures; later there were to appear the voluptuous life-size figures, the **yakshis** of classical Hinduism, Jainism, and Buddhism. And the presence of the tiger among the animals associated with females depicted on the seals reminds us again that tigers and lions were the favored mounts of later Hindu goddesses, and the goddess as lion or with lion, leopard, or panther was a familiar motif in ancient Egypt, the Aegean, Asia Minor, and the whole of West Asia.

Fourth, these animal symbols in their own right are graphically powerful expressions and immediately call to mind the significance of zoological symbols, both wild and domestic, in the history of Hinduism. With the exception of composite creatures and serpents, not easy to sex, the prominent animals are horned males—the bull, water buffalo, ram, and others. The buffalo (*bubalus*) and two distinct species of cattle, one the humped zebu (*bos indicus*) and the other a humpless relation to the *bos primigenius* of West Asia, had been domestic animals in South Asia for several thousand years. All three appear to have gained sacred status in pre-Indus religion, often in association with vegetation —the pipal tree or its leaves, to take one example.

Certain Indus seals and impressions show a humanlike male seated in "yogic" posture, wearing what may be a buffalo mask as well as buffalo horns, and surrounded by animals both wild and domestic. Mistakenly identified several decades ago as a "proto-Shiva," with reference to the later Vedic-Hindu god, this commanding and obviously significant figure seems now to be even older than the Indus civilization and may be related to a similar figure from Elam, a more ancient culture to the west that was closely linked to adjacent Mesopotamian urban societies.

Perhaps this figure should be studied in connection with the goddess-and-male-consort known in West Asia. The comparative study of ancient urban cultures from the Danube to the Aegean area (Old European civilization) and from Anatolia across West Asia to Iran reveals a striking association: A timeless Great Goddess, who guarantees the fertility of plants, animals, and humans, is depicted either with or as trees or pillars, in sacred groves, with serpents, lions, and a wide variety of animals known for powers of regeneration. Her subordinate male consort, on the other hand, is frequently identified with the victim of blood sacrifice, a virile horned animal such as the bull, for example. It is the male of the pair who is subject to time via sacrificial death, sometimes

Seal 420 from Mohenjo-daro, the most widely discussed object from the Indus Valley civilization. A horned animal–masked male figure of apparent cultic significance sits surrounded by a number of powerful wild animals. (Photo courtesy National Museum, New Delhi.)

dismemberment, and then regeneration at the hands of the goddess. Whether or not the Indus civilization based much or any of its religious traditions upon such a pairing, with the buffalo at times in the role of the bull (as suggested recently by one scholar), remains to be seen and will probably be known only from decipherment of the script.

At this point what is most exciting about the religion of the Indus in the third and second millennia B.C.E. is not what we know but what we may be about to learn in the coming decades. Many of the essential features of this vaguely appreciated but decidedly formative era may at last be visible as studies in ethnoarchaeology, philology, and the history of religions converge on the material evidence brought out by new excavations and new technologies.

What caused the demise of the Indus urban civilization is at this point as mysterious as the Indus script and the subject of as many interpretations. About 1750 B.C.E. declining standards in construction and the appearance of different types of pottery signal a break in the Indus timeline. Whether immigrations of new peoples, droughts, deforestation, floods, or alterations in the course of the life-giving river were causes or contributing factors cannot be determined from current evidence. In any case, while the great urban sites decayed, some village areas, particularly those to the east of the river, maintained their traditions for a time, although without benefit of the former great commercial and ceremonial centers and what must have been vivid cosmopolitan traffic. It is these areas to the east in the second half of the second millennium B.C.E. that may well have served as links to preserve and disperse age-old Indus traditions.

Nowhere else on the subcontinent were there urban complexes to rival the Indus cities, but other cultures did leave their traces. For example, in the Deccan of South India there were seminomadic pastoralists who penned their cattle in large corrals and quartered themselves within similar stockades. These structures were burned periodically, perhaps at the times of seasonal grazing migrations, leaving behind distinctive cow-dung ash-mounds that date from c. 3000 B.C.E. on. The notion of a cattle pen associated not only with human sustenance but also with kinship, that is, the connected human generations, may indeed be very old in India, and possibly multicultural. In later Hinduism an individual's *gotra* or clan-descent is an important aspect of identity; the Sanskrit word literally means "cow pen."

Other early cultures of North and peninsular India are known from their surviving pottery; their stone tools or metalworking in copper, bronze, or gold; and their agrarian or pastoral means of subsistence. Once again, little is known of religious life, but certain phenomena are recurrent in widely separated sites: the long-horned humped bull, either in terra-cotta figurines or in rock art; distinctive female figurines, thought to be popular goddesses; burials and grave-goods, sometimes in urns beneath the floors of dwellings or between them. Other artifacts are unique: a copper anthropomorph, possibly for ritual use, and a remarkable find of large animals cast in solid copper—a rhino and a water buffalo, each on axled wheels; an elephant on a pedestal fashioned to hold wheels; and a rider on a light two-wheeled chariot behind two yoked oxen, all from the second half of the second millennium B.C.E.

The contributions to the growth of Hinduism of these bygone cultures, their responses to the sacred in the symbols of animals, plants, rivers, earth, fire, and the other elements can only be the subject of speculation, since they left us no inscriptions, literature, or sacred architecture. We know only from the literatures of invading peoples who later encountered and generally subjugated them that the newcomers themselves were gradually and indelibly transformed in major and minor ways by a vivid new religious pluralism and had to devise means of separating, incorporating, or explaining alternate worldviews, rituals, beliefs, and practices.

A Vedic Age

> With the sacrifice the gods sacrificed to the sacrifice. . . . These were the first cosmic laws. (*Rigveda* 10.90.16 [concluding verse of the hymn of Purusha])

Returning to the upper Indus in the northwestern area of the subcontinent, we confront one of the major intrigues of South Asian history. In the same early centuries of the second millennium B.C.E. as the decline and demise of the Indus cities, there arrived new peoples whose dynamic religious expressions structured ancient Hinduism for more than a thousand years. These people—or peoples more precisely, since they probably arrived in serial migrations that lasted for many centuries—were nomadic pastoralists from Central Asia and the Iranian plateau entering the subcontinent through passes in the mountains of what is now Afghanistan and Pakistan. As noted in the preceding chapter, these nomads spoke dialects of Indo-Aryan, the easternmost of all the dozens of Indo-European languages.

Indo-Aryan had descended from Proto–Indo-European speech current perhaps two or three thousand years earlier. Comparative religious studies and linguistics, with recent assistance from archaeology, have permitted speculation not only about languages but also about the worldview and symbol system of the Proto–Indo-Europeans who may have inhabited the lower valleys of the Ural, the Volga, and the Don where these rivers reached the Caspian and the Black seas. These cattle and horse herders supplemented a pastoral economy with limited agriculture in the fifth millennium B.C.E.—almost seven thousand years ago—before their Eurasian dispersal to the west, east, and south to establish regional languages and cultures from Iceland to India.

One great set of Indo-European migrations was eastward into Central Asia, the Indo-Iranian one, so called because a split occurred, perhaps some time after 2000 B.C.E., between those peoples who moved with their herds south and then westward onto the Iranian plateau and those Indo-Aryan speakers who negotiated high mountain passes to cross over into India. Eventually these two separated nomadic groups composed religious poetry as the earliest literature of all the migrant Indo-Europeans. Comparative studies of the ancient Indian *Vedas* with the scarcer remnants of an ancient Iranian text—the *Avesta*—

indicate that religious traditions in these two distinct areas of Asia appear to have developed along parallel lines for some centuries after the division. Basic mythologies, community and domestic rituals, social classes, priestly functions —even the nomenclature of myth and cult—are illuminative one of the other, and many key names and terms are cognate.

Eventually, however, the religious reforms of Zarathustra and others in Iran yielded a major new religion, Zoroastrianism, about the same time that India produced a set of remarkable philosophers who transformed the religion of ancient Vedic Hinduism into classical Hinduism. After that, Indo-Iranian parallelism continued only in echoes from the distant past, for example in the perpetuation of mythic themes in long, oral epics about ancient heroes and kings. A remarkable event more than a thousand years later, however, allowed Zoroastrian refugees from medieval Islamic persecutions in Iran to migrate to western India. Today, bracketed by their ancient cousins, descendants of these refugees live as Parsis ("Persians") in the land of the Hindus.

The degree of contact between waves of Indo-Aryan nomads and the settled cultivators and herders of the Indus cities is the subject of considerable speculation. Early Vedic literature celebrates repeated conquests of forts, including those labeled "triple forts," but describes nothing like the cities of the archaeological record. It is possible that the migrants who produced Vedic poetry, ritual, and speculation were but one of several Indo-Aryan-speaking cultures mobile in the second millennium B.C.E. In any event, they were the ones who impressed and altered South Asian history with their formidable culture.

The Vedas

The Vedic religion of ancient India takes its name from, and is dependent upon, the *Vedas,* books of "knowledge" (*veda*). As already noted, these oral texts, regarded as unitary and eternal, are understood to have no human or divine origin. They have always been a sacred sound, **brahman,** a foundational cosmic utterance. Somehow this sound was intuited by ancient seers, the *rishis,* an aggregate of seven sages who then transmitted the *Vedas* for the benefit of the world. The **mantras** or verse formulas of the *Vedas* always had and still have today an aural destiny. Buddhist canonical texts were committed to writing in India late in the first century B.C.E., but many centuries later, when portions of some *Vedas* were written on birch bark or palm leaves or eventually printed on paper by European scholars, they were still learned by hearing and expressed by recitation. The whole corpus of Vedic texts is known as **shruti,** what is heard, since those who transmit it from generation to generation learn the *mantras* a lesson at a time by listening. This unitary revelation is thus a sacred verbal power employed in one or another liturgical composition—such as an invocation, a hymn in praise of a deity, a directive for an offering—in the entire ritual system that structures Vedic religion.

This vast body of *shruti* included in antiquity as many as several scores of separate texts. Over the centuries many were lost, but the extant corpus is still enormous, with some of the survivors reaching more than a thousand pages each in contemporary printed editions. From the nontraditional, text-critical point of view this corpus is a series of genres that required a full millennium to complete. It extended from the four early collections known as *Samhitas*—the *Rigveda, Yajurveda, Samaveda,* and *Atharvaveda,* all composed between about 1200 B.C.E. and 900 B.C.E.—down through genres known as *Brahmanas* and *Aranyakas* to the last of the *Upanishads* and ritual *Sutras* about 200 B.C.E. Let us examine briefly each of these Vedic literary assemblies, keeping always in mind their nature as oral texts.

First and foremost of the *Samhitas* (and of all the *Vedas*) is the *Rigveda.* It is a large hymnal, a collection of 1,028 metrical hymns to all the deities revered in the late second millennium B.C.E. **Indra, Varuna, Agni, Soma,** the **Ashvin** twins, **Vayu, Rudra,** and Vishnu are among the many whose basic mythologies can be pieced together from these songs of reverence, praise, awe, and occasionally fear. Some deities, **Dyaus,** for example, associated with the masculine Sky or Heaven, had already lost favor by the time of the editing of the hymns; his consort **Prithivi,** however, lived on as a feminine power in Earth.

Indra, the hard-drinking, chariot-driving warrior god with an invincible thunderbolt weapon, is celebrated in more hymns—almost a quarter of the total—than any other deity. He is known as a heroic conqueror of enemies of the Vedic nomads, as well as of assorted demons, including the infamous **Vritra.** By piercing the belly of Vritra—a powerful cloud-serpent being who had withheld the life-giving waters and light—Indra released the rains and allowed creation to

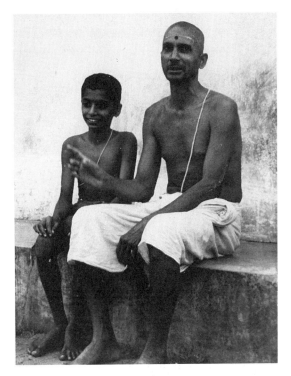

Learning to recite, phrase by phrase, from a portion of the Vedic oral tradition. This boy will spend eight or more years committing to memory a particular branch of the Vedas. If capable he will then go on to another branch for several more years.

resume. As patron of warriors, king of the gods, and drinker of the sacred juice of *soma,* Indra has the most dynamic personality of all the pantheon.

Varuna is guardian of cosmic order (**rita,** a word replaced in later texts by *dharma*). Also a sovereign deity, he is universal monarch by virtue of his transcendent character as a sky god. Since he is known to discipline those who break his cosmic laws, many hymns address him in petitions for mercy and hopes that he will not inflict disease as a punishment. Frequently this god of occult powers is invoked together with Mitra, another ancient celestial deity, and one who is a protective, mediating figure.

Agni is the mysterious sacred fire, at once the sacrificial element and the interior energy of the universe and each of its beings. Known for his multiple births, he is resident in all three levels of the cosmos. Agni is addressed in the opening verse of the *Rigveda,* and as both primordial sacrificer and fulfiller of every priestly function he is the oblation-bearer to the gods and the divine messenger to humans. The hidden, covert, secret nature of Agni is a constant reference in the *mantras.* He is lord of every household (in the hearth), eater of corpses (in the cremation pyre), born anew every day (from the kindling sticks), and yet omniscient (as fire in the sun, lightning, waters, and plants).

Soma is, like Agni, simultaneously substance and mystery. Plant, juice, king, sacrificial victim, and god are among the roles assigned by Vedic faith to this being. Stolen from the highest heaven by an eagle, the plant and its essence (ritually pressed juice) bestow upon the divine or priestly drinkers both poetic

Indra, king of the gods, on his white elephant Airavata (thirteenth-century temple relief, Somnathpuram, Karnataka).

insight and immortality. Indra, the warrior deity, becomes invincible in battle through *soma*-intoxication; the ecstasy it induces in poets allows them supernatural vision.

The Ashvin twins are a good example of pastoral deities. Identified as horsemen, they are celestial charioteers, an auspicious sight in the early dawn behind their golden chariot. Connected with the fertility of herds, crops, and humans, they are also healers of diseases and rescuers of those in danger.

Vayu was the first of the gods to drink *soma*. Closely associated with Indra, Vayu is a god of wind and warfare and one also connected with fate and cults of the dead.

Rudra is an outsider god, a howler (as his name implies) in the wilderness. More paradoxical and unpredictable than "insider" deities, he may either burn with his fierce heat of destruction or heal with his cooling remedies. His sons are a collection of storm deities known either as the **Maruts** or the Rudras. Euphemistically called Shiva, "auspicious," in later literature, he lives on in classical Hinduism as one of the two major male deities.

Vishnu is the other preeminent male deity of classical Hinduism; like Rudra, he is a relatively minor figure in the *Rigveda*. The god who crosses the universe in three great strides, Vishnu is sometimes involved in Indra's exploits.

Without going into much further detail it is worth noting that our knowledge of some of these deities and their cults is more or less enhanced by comparative Indo-Iranian and Indo-European studies. The mythology and cult of *haoma* in ancient Iran, for example, reveals multiple parallels to the Vedic *soma* tradition. The Ashvins have their mythological counterpart twins in the Dioskouroi of ancient Greece and Gemini of ancient Rome, as **Yama** (whose name in fact means "twin") has a match in the Iranian Yima. One of Indra's correlates is Thor, the hard-drinking, chariot-driving warrior deity of ancient Scandinavia.

There are scores of other gods and collective powers addressed or extolled in the *Rigveda*. **Surya** and Savitr are solar gods, Yama is a primal being who is the first to die and therefore lord of the dead, and Pushan, another pastoral deity, is patron of travelers and a bringer of prosperity. Although there are numerous feminine powers in the *Rigveda*, some of them connected in a vague and shadowy way with fate and destiny, the pantheon had few places of prominence for goddesses. **Ushas** is the dawn, celebrated by the poets for her splendor. **Aditi,** the primordial "boundless" goddess, is mother of a class of sovereign deities, including Varuna. And **Sarasvati,** associated with the ancient river of that name, has nurturing and healing functions similar to those of the Ashvins.

Turning now to the three later *Samhitas*—the *Yajurveda, Samaveda,* and *Atharvaveda*—*mantras* from the *Rigveda* were employed in all three of these collections. Specific purposes were in mind, and certain modifications or additions to the Rigvedic text were performed, including in some cases prose additions. The *Yajurveda* became a manual of directions for the performance of sacrifices and included the *mantra* formulas chanted in them. The *Samaveda*, an index to melodies required in the great *soma* sacrifices, set specific *mantras* to a seven-note musical scale. The last *Samhita*, the *Atharvaveda*, not concerned with the priestly sacrificial system, drew together certain domestic rituals and the religious concerns of popular culture, including charms, spells, incantations, and India's earliest medical and pharmacological lore.

From two to five branches of each of these *Samhitas* survive today. In antiquity each of them generated discourses about the procedures of the sacrifices and the meanings attributed to them. Such traditions when assembled as oral texts were called *Brahmanas*, and they were followed by other texts known as "forest books" or *Aranyakas*, with both of these commentarial genres fully developed about 1000 B.C.E. to 700 B.C.E. By 800 B.C.E. certain directives for each of the great sacrifices began to appear, and these were assembled and edited as ritual manuals known as *Shrauta Sutras* (**shrauta,** concerned with *shruti*). And by 600 B.C.E. still another genre surfaced, this one philosophical, esoteric, and radical in its substitution of knowledge of the eternal Self for knowledge of the sacrifice. This genre was known as *Upanishads*, the subject of the final segment of this chapter.

To take an example from this confusing array of texts within branches, schools, and genres of the *Vedas*, consider the Brahman boy in the photo on page 739. He was born into the Taittiriya branch of the Black Yajurveda, so he must begin his Vedic instruction by learning a set sequence of Taittiriya texts: the *Taittiriya Samhita, Taittiriya Brahmana, Taittiriya Aranyaka, Taittiriya Upanishad,* and the *Apastamba Shrauta Sutra,* a kind of handbook of the great sacrifices of the Taittiriyins. This will require some eight to twelve years of daily effort on his part. If he is successful in his examinations he may then begin another *Samhita,* the *Rigveda,* for example, and proceed with it daily, followed by the *Aitareya Brahmana,* and so on to the *Ashvalayana Shrauta Sutra.* If his memory is sufficiently agile his instructor or **guru** will also train him to recite portions of the same text in recitation patterns far more complicated than the direct word-by-word order with which he begins. [See Religions of Mesoamerica p. 179, Native Religions of North America p. 285, Judaism pp. 390–94, Christianity pp. 497, 499, Islam pp. 635–37, 648–53, 665–72, Buddhism p. 861, Religions of China pp. 995–96, 999–1000, 1031, and Religions of Japan pp. 1100, 1101 for discussion of Bible, scriptures, and religious texts.]

As an illustration of the relationship of these texts and the way in which this boy may learn them, table 7-2 provides a structure for just two of the four *Samhitas* and their total of eleven branches.

TABLE 7-2. *The Sequence of Texts in Two Branches of the* Vedas

	Yajurveda	Rigveda
Samhita	Taittiriya branch	Shakala branch
Brahmana	Taittiriya	Aitareya
Aranyaka	Taittiriya	Aitareya
Upanishad	Taittiriya	Aitareya
Ritual *Sutra*	Apastamba	Ashvalayana

There is much more to "the *Vedas*" than this brief discussion allows. Other components of Vedic and related post-Vedic textual traditions will be discussed further under the rubric of the worldview and the systematic ritual.

The Early Vedic Worldview

In order to understand the significance of the *Vedas* and Vedic Hinduism several related concepts are worth reviewing. One might say that the seeds of each were carried into South Asia with the migrant Indo-Aryans and then planted and nurtured in the specific soil and climate of India, that is to say in the territory of the Indus and the Ganges rivers where indigenous religious traditions had long been fertile.

These related notions are the following: First, the universe is a projection of a primordially sacrificed body of a cosmic being. The myth of this cosmic Self, **Purusha** (literally, "man, person"), who is also known in later Vedic texts as **Prajapati,** Lord of creatures, is a primary creation myth.

Second, it is a human responsibility to refabricate and sacrifice anew that cosmic body. This is a continuous process that regenerates the world through human spiritual knowledge and effort (karma). The myth of Purusha announces what was done in the beginning; the ritual accomplished by the priests assumes responsibility for a continuing world. [See Religions of Africa pp. 36–37, 64–67, Religions of Mesoamerica pp. 129–35, 154–55, 163–68, Native Religions of North America pp. 288–95, 327–29, 333–42, Judaism pp. 380–84, Christianity pp. 534–35, Buddhism p. 890, and Religions of Japan pp. 1094–96 for discussion of myth and mythology.]

And third, there are two mysterious cosmic substances—fire and plant—that must be identified and made available through ritual work. One, Agni, pervasive sacred fire, is life maintaining and reveals sustaining correspondences between cosmic and human energies. The other, Soma, immortal sacred plant, is life transcending and reveals visions to humans of the other world, the realm that is not created and therefore is not subject to change. [See Religions of Mesoamerica pp. 195–98 and Native Religions of North America pp. 269, 275 for discussion of cosmic tree or World Tree.]

These three concepts structured a faith that endured in South Asia for over a thousand years until the unveiling of new spiritual emphases in the classical Hinduism of a post-Vedic age. A few significant details of each of these notions might be pursued here, and because this early Vedic worldview is foundational, later chapters will expand upon them further.

First, existence is understood as a process of projection and assimilation. There is unity in the macrocosm (the world of the unmanifest) and multiplicity in the microcosm (creation, the world of phenomena). Each, however, is divided into three parts, each is hierarchic (that is, the three parts are ranked one above another in authority and power), and each is organically interdependent (that is, the parts work together as one being with three separate functions). It is an extraordinary system, at once tidy and complex. For example, an individual human body has three components (identified later in the classical medical literature as *doshas,* humors), the essential human social body has three eche-lons (identified as **varnas,** "colors" or classes), and the world itself has three characteristics (identified later in the philosophical texts as **gunas,** "threads" or qualities)—all because these layered bodies are replications of the divine tripar-tite cosmic being. The process of projection and assimilation, of creation and reintegration, is a continuously sacrificial one. The world in its multiple forms, human society with its varied classes, and an individual with diverse bodily parts are all the result of the sacrifice and dismemberment of an original unity, the sacrifice Being, just as the death of a world or an individual is an assimila-tion—by sacrifice—of multiple parts back into the tripartite whole.[1]

The Purusha hymn cited at the head of this segment, *Rigveda* 10.90, is the oldest documentation for such an Indo-European sacrificial cosmogony. And Vedic texts subsequent to the *Rigveda* continue to authenticate these correspondences of the upper three social classes and the individual sacrificer with the house-holder's three-fire ritual system and the return of a sacrificer at death—by means of his three fires—to the three-level cosmos. Table 7-3 portrays the continuity of such projection and assimilation.

A second imported concept concerns human responsibility for this continu-ous sacrificial process. Since the projected world is a result of a divine sacrifice (*yajna*), the continued existence of the world is dependent on repetitions of that primordial, cosmogonic event. As the Purusha hymn declares, the original cos-mic laws were laid down by sacrifice. Once created, the world is thus constantly re-created by sacrifice. But now the ritual action is accomplished by human agents, namely the godlike Brahmans who take upon themselves the work of the dei-ties. The sovereign power of the priestly Brahman class becomes apparent in two astounding tasks: Brahmans, not gods, perpetuate the eternal sacred utterance, *brahman,* in the form of *mantras* that are, in their totality, *veda,* sacred knowl-edge. And Brahmans, not gods, perpetuate the world through sacrifice. This sacrifice or ritual work (karma) proceeds on two separate but interactive scales. One is the communal, *shrauta,* world-regenerating schedule with staffs of as many as sixteen or seventeen priests. The other is a familial, domestic (**grihya**) one accomplished by the householder with or without a family priest. Each of the Vedic schools transmitted *Sutras* for both of these schedules of sacrifice, the *Gri-hya Sutras* in general later than, and similar in outline to, the *Shrauta Sutras.* [See Religions of Africa pp. 67, 88–89, Religions of Mesoamerica pp. 166–67, 177, 186, 237–38, Judaism pp. 399–400, Christianity pp. 543–44, 550, and Islam p. 646 for description and discussion of sacrifice.]

For example, with reference to table 7-3, procedures for the cremation of a deceased householder-sacrificer are described in the *Shankhayana Shrauta Sutra* of the Kaushitaki branch of the *Rigveda.* His offering fire is placed at his head, his southern fire on his right side, his cooking fire close to his belly and genitals, his two fire sticks on his thighs, and the entire body is thus returned by the god Agni, the sacred fire, to the threefold cosmos as a "last sacrifice." Such an offer-ing is accomplished by his oldest son as the new and continuing householder-sacrificer.

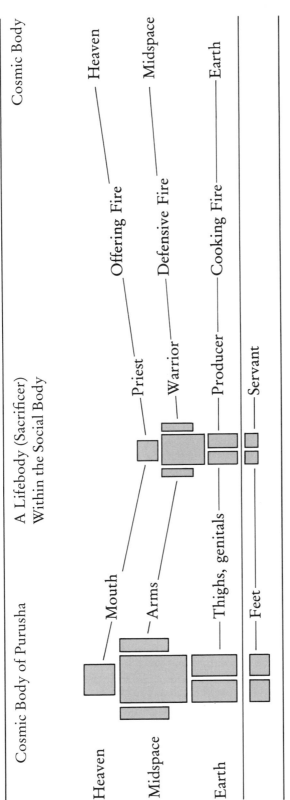

Cosmic Body of Purusha	A Lifebody (Sacrificer) Within the Social Body	Cosmic Body
Heaven — Mouth	Priest — Offering Fire	Heaven
Midspace — Arms	Warrior — Defensive Fire	Midspace
Earth — Thighs, genitals	Producer — Cooking Fire	Earth
— Feet	Servant	

Table 7-3. The Continuous Vedic Sacrifice.[1]

[1] A lifebody, like the social body of four classes and the householder's system of three fires, is first a projection from the cosmic body of Purusha, then an assimilation back into the cosmic body. (The servant class, like the feet of Purusha, is subordinate and outside the ritual system that—like the cosmos—must be tripartite.)

The third Indo-European concept brought into India some thirty-five hundred years ago involves an interaction of both myth and cult focused on concepts of sacred fire and sacred plant. There is a life-maintaining fire that pervades all and translates mutable existence to immutability, and there is a life-transcending plant of celestial origin that provides mortals with poetic inspiration and immortality. Like Purusha these two substances are divisible, macro-microcosmic, and obtainable by the ritual use of a special knowledge, that of operational correspondences between the divine/human and the unmanifest/manifest realms. As noted in the survey of Vedic deities, Agni is the god within the sacred element of fire, resident in every household and in the body of every living creature. Nomadic pastoralists of the late second millennium B.C.E. attached special importance to constructing settlements with hearths. Vedic texts emphasize repeatedly the notion of being grounded, established, and connected by assembling a hearth, by situating Agni. The significance of course transcended any economic concern or architectural detail regarding the transport of fire. What is established by a sacred presence is the self within the family within the community within the cosmos, and the constructive event is again an echo of the original sacrifice, the original creative event. As the Vedic poet-philosophers elaborated their doctrine of sacrifice, Agni became identified with Purusha-Prajapati and thereby with the transcendent self of the sacrificer. Fashioning the simplest domestic hearth or the year-long construction of a gigantic fireplace of 10,800 enormous bricks was necessary ritual work, an integrative cosmogonic act.

As for the cult of a divine plant, an elaborate sacred drama was already in place, probably for many centuries, among the Indo-Iranian nomadic pastoralists. Their descendants perpetuated this sacred drama that focused on *soma* in India and *haoma* in Iran. Acquiring the plant from mountain tribal peoples, proceeding with this *soma* on a special cart onto the sacred field of fire, royally enthroning it, ritually immolating it along with one or more animal victims, then pressing it to obtain the elixirlike and probably hallucinogenic juice—all these and other ritual stages preceded the offering to the gods and the priestly sharing of this sacred essence. This drama of transformation became the focal point of institutional Vedic religion, as it remains to this day among the tiny remnant of authentic Vedic Brahman communities in South India. Both fire and plant were therefore simultaneously gods and divine substances that could be collected through the combined spiritual technology and physical labor of Brahman priests acting as agents in the necessary work of sacrifice and world-maintenance. In the great synthesizing text known as the *Brahmana*-of-the-hundred-paths, the *Shatapatha Brahmana*, these two, Agni and Soma, were brought together as principals in the cosmic mystery of the fire altar.

Thus three notions—the universe defined as a projection of the primordially sacrificed body of Purusha, the application of precise spiritual technique in the great work (karma) of renewing worldly life from cosmic resources, and the identification of sacred fire and plant as liaisons in the sacrificial scheme of transcendent time and space—became the ground structure for a thousand-year tradition that was dominant in South Asia until the appearance of post-Vedic classical Hinduism.

A Systematic Ritual

As noted above, the Vedic sacrificer maintained his household system for both routine and extraordinary rituals. In the full-blown domestic schedule as described in the *Grihya Sutras,* a single fire received the dawn and evening twilight milk libations known as the *agnihotra* (oblation to Agni), or the offering known as *ishti* of grain cakes or butter porridge and milk, or the fortnightly offerings on the days of the new and full moon. Particularly important were offerings made to the ancestors on the new-moon day succeeding the "dark" or waning moon fortnight of each lunar month, since the dead required sustenance on a regular basis from their living descendants. At the outset of three significant cosmic transitions—the seasons of spring, rains, and autumn—there were "four-month" sacrifices. Aside from such daily, fortnightly, and seasonal schedules certain other rituals were occasional. The animal sacrifice, for example, included optional versions. The arrival of a special guest might call for the slaughter of a cow or goat, for example, to feast the visitor after invocation and feasting on the part of the gods, or meat as well as rice, grain cakes, and vegetables might be offered in the dark halves of three successive months to nourish the ancestors.

An entirely personal schedule of rituals concerned the life cycle of every family member. The rituals of marriage, including that of conception of a new offspring as the final act of the wedding ceremony, rituals for the production of a male child and for safe delivery, for the birth of an infant, for the naming ceremony and first feeding with solid food some months later, for the child's first tonsure, for thread-investiture in youth as initiation into Vedic texts and sacrifices, for the opening and closing of instructional terms for the Vedic student as well as his ritual bath at the conclusion of study, for cremation of the dead, and for offerings to the ancestors (**shraddha**) in the form of rice balls (*pinda*)—all of these were important rites of passage occurring in the household. A **purohita** or domestic priest could be employed for many or all of these, but in most cases the male head of the household could act as the family's priest. Essential in all rituals was the participation of the householder's wife, although the *mantra* recitations and most of the offerings were the husband's obligation.

All of these rituals served the household in the domestic scheme outlined in the *Grihya Sutras.* A magnified scale of sacrifice existed for those who aspired to a system governed by the *Shrauta Sutras.* The *soma* tradition, the most advanced of all *shrauta* rituals, called for a priestly staff divided not only by specialized functions but by texts as well. Four major priests were responsible for the four Vedic *Samhitas.* The *hota* or invoking priest recited from the *Rigveda,* the *adhvaryu* or executive priest directed the entire sacrifice and proclaimed from a recension of the *Yajurveda,* the *udgata* or chanting priest sang from the *Samaveda,* and finally, transcending this trio the *brahman* or supervisory priest, possessing skillful knowledge (*vidya*) of all four *Vedas,* silently audited and surveyed the entire drama. Each of the four could employ three assistants for designated functions, a full staff thus being sixteen (occasionally seventeen for special rituals requiring an additional acolyte for the *brahman*).

The power and scope of the Vedic *shrauta* ritual enterprise, one of the most complex known in the history of religions, is not easy to grasp. At its very heart is the creative murder known as sacrifice, that is to say, the ritually controlled violence done to the divine Soma and the animal victims following the pattern of Purusha-Prajapati's self-inflicted violence. Death, dismemberment, and dispersal are one side, regeneration, reintegration, and transcendence the other, all reflective in the continuity of sacrifice. The whole elaborate structure is cemented by the notion of ritual control.

Only a married householder skilled in *mantras* could extend his single household fire into the three sacred fires for the *shrauta* schedule (the offering, defensive, and cooking fires in table 7-3). The *agnyadheya* ritual established a three-fire domestic hearth employed for many of the same calendrical and other rituals accomplished in the one-fire domestic schedule, although on a grander scale of preparations, offerings, and *mantras.*

But the highest aspiration of the *ahitagni,* the householder maintaining three fires, was the *soma* sacrifice. The *agnishtoma,* a five-day ritual with three separate *soma*-pressing ceremonies on one day, was always the initial *soma* rite, and for most remained the pinnacle of religious life. The sacrificer (*yajamana*) underwent a period of consecration (*diksha*) in order to be eligible for the role of *soma* and animal offerer. Six other great *soma* rituals lay beyond the *agnishtoma,* with many variations regarding the number of *soma*-pressing days and the number and types of animal victims. Among the greatest of *shrauta* rituals were the *agnichayana* (the piling of the fire altar in five layers of a thousand or more huge bricks, often in the form of the eagle who stole *soma* stalks from heaven), and the *vajapeya* (the *soma*-drink of power, with its emphasis on Prajapati's sacred number, seventeen). Some were royal sacrifices, such as the *rajasuya* or consecration of a king, involving chariot races, enthronement, and symbolic dice games, and the famous horse sacrifice, the *ashvamedha.*

The last named, with comparative evidence from the ancient Celtic, Roman, and Scythian horse sacrifices, was a sacrifice performed (rarely) by kings in India up until the seventeenth century C.E. A successful performance of this demonstration of universal kingship required two years, the assembly of nearly seven hundred animals, a cast of four hundred warriors and four hundred women, and a virtual king's ransom in cows, land, and gold. The monarch as sacrificer was identified with the stallion-victim—who was permitted to wander freely for a year of territorial conquest—as well as with Purusha-Prajapati as the year and the world as newly integrated "king-dom." The smothering of the horse and channeling of its vital breath (**prana**) into the queen in symbolic sexual union was the climax of the rite in the middle of three *soma*-pressing days, and the expected fruition of this creative murder of the horse/king was of course a prince, a new king for the new kingdom. [See Religions of Africa pp. 24, 35, 60, Religions of Mesoamerica pp. 198–201, Native Religions of North America pp. 347–48, Judaism pp. 391–92, Christianity pp. 503, 505, Islam pp. 632–33, Buddhism pp. 875–77, 952–53, Religions of China pp. 991–93, and Religions of Japan pp. 1095–96, 1105–6 for the relationship of religion to political leaders.]

Bound up in all the complexity of ritual activity on both major and minor scales was the fluid cosmic/human power of fire and plant, Agni as life maintaining, and Soma as life transcending. The mysterious entity known as sacrifice itself—identified with the elusive being of Purusha-Prajapati—expresses a simultaneity of life-maintenance and life-transcendence. Congruent with the regeneration of the entire world-as-it-is occurs the promotion of a single lifebody, the sacrificer, to life-as-it-might-be. That is to say, the individual accomplishing the ritual becomes "immortal," no longer material for assimilation and reprojection. In the synchronous mystery of sacrifice a solitary individual becomes destined to return to the unmanifest, not to die, while the unitary world at large becomes destined to die precisely because it has been created all over again.

Obviously such notions, developing in multiple schools over centuries of time in the several regions of India, allowed for generous increments of speculation on human and world destiny. The concept of world-abandonment or renunciation was certainly among those speculations. A significant moment in Vedic rituals was designated **tyaga**, "abandonment," a turning over to the invited deities not only the offered substance, but the benefits of the ritual itself, a notion that developed later into the concept of renouncing the fruit (**phala**) of all action.

A Three-Plus-One Society

Already remarked upon is the triadic principle of ordering in the Vedic worldview, one inherited from an apparent Proto–Indo-European threefold hierarchy of functions—priestly, warrior, and productive. The created universe, eternal *Vedas,* ranks of the gods, ritual fires, priesthood, and classes of human society are all tripartite and hierarchic according to function. With reference again to table 7-3 it may be seen that the three twice-born *varnas*—**Brahmanas, Kshatriyas,** and **Vaishyas**—are derived respectively from the mouth, arms, and thighs of Purusha. The **Shudras**, a subordinate fourth estate, are outside this triadic, interdependent society, excluded from both *mantras* and rituals, cosmically destined to serve the upper classes.

The notion of a subordinate fourth that "doesn't count" is an important one and is already there in the multivocal Purusha mythology. Three quarters of Purusha remain unmanifest during his sacrificial self-distribution; only one quarter becomes manifest in the created world. It is a way of saying that Purusha (Supreme Being, *Brahman,* the absolute) remains whole and undiminished by the act of creation, a way of expressing simultaneous transcendence and immanence of divinity. But it also says that this created world "doesn't count."

The essential triadic nature of the unmanifest and manifest worlds continues to be maintained by Vedic Hindu ritualists and philosophers, even when the symbol system becomes quite busy with variant numerologies. Fabrication of the Vedic fire altar in the *agnichayana* proceeds with five layers of bricks representing five levels of the world and the surrounding matrix, the body, of the constructed **atman** of the sacrificer. The interior triad, however, remains its skeleton. Still later there are expansions of the hierarchy to seven and nine, but the basic triad remains in play. It is a three-plus-other numerology. In chapter 32 some of these later themes will be discussed further as Hindu expressions of classifying the universe.

For now it is important to consider the basic four *varnas* and the three-plus-other society first represented in the late *Rigveda* and assumed to be normative throughout the Vedic age. Brahmanas, responsible for the transmission and application of *mantras,* the directing of *yajnas,* and acceptance of those gifts (*dakshinas*) that provide ritual closure to sacrifices, were the dominant *varna.* Rajanyas or Kshatriyas, whose *dharma,* like that of their patron deity, Indra, was defense of the populace against enemies and demons, were the median rank. The warrior class was also the source of political sovereignty, namely kingship. And Vaishyas, the bulk of society, were those responsible for animal husbandry, agriculture, crafts, and trade, all of the activities that comprise the *dharma* of productivity.

In the course of their migrations across North India, Indo-Aryans encountered hundreds of varied indigenous societies. Many were subjugated or embraced as a part of Vedic civilization, added on at the bottom of the social scale under the rubric of Shudra. By the middle of the first millennium B.C.E., when the *Upanishads* and ritual *Sutras* were concluding genres of Vedic textual activity, Vedic civilization was no longer the simple three-plus-other *varna* system. There were powerful occupational guilds (*shrenis*) with significant impacts in social ranking. Many of the most essential artisans, as well as the great pool of agriculturalists, came from the Shudra class. There were elaborate strictures regarding ritual purity and impurity, and certain activities considered to be defiling were designated for communities who were then by definition unclean. The "other" *varna,* the Shudras, were broadly divided into those who were an actual component of society and those who were literally outside, a fifth class, later to be labeled Untouchables or outcastes (today's "Scheduled Castes").

By the time of the *Dharma Shastras* in the early centuries of the first millennium C.E. these codes of law (*dharma*) were forced to explain how scores of separate communities (**jatis,** kinds of "birth") had come about. A traditional explanation was the mixing or confusion of *varnas,* that is, improper marriages between the original four classes. Thus the *dharma* of class came to be applied more rigidly in the post-Vedic period to the hierarchy of scores of separate communities (today known as castes[2]), separated by sacred laws that prohibit intermarriage and interdining. Appearing in the next segment of this chapter will be the Upanishadic formulation of the doctrine of rebirth, still another factor added to the many explanations for the variations and apparent inequities within human society, and the relative ranking of humans within the larger company of gods, animals, and demons.

The Upanishads *and a New Worldview*

Most of the Vedic branches or schools included in their chains of texts a genre of "forest books," *Aranyakas,* and short prose or verse works concerning mystical "correspondences," *Upanishads.* Some schools edited these texts as fused versions: The *Shatapatha Brahmana,* for example, concludes with an *Upanishad* known as the *Brihad* (Great) *aranyaka,* one of the most important of all late Vedic texts. The "forest" denoted territory outside the village, private space where esoteric, hidden doctrines could be revealed to each new student. More than a dozen of these Vedic *Upanishads* evolved over a period of several centuries from about the eighth century B.C.E. Together they constituted a reformation—a reassessment of the sacrificial worldview and a redirection of religious energies inward toward salvation by insight and knowledge rather than reliance upon ritual action alone.

Their significance extended far beyond the Vedic tradition. This new vision, enlarged by non-Brahman as well as Brahman transmission, and linked with energetic ascetic movements (the **shramanas,** wandering renunciants) and the ideologies and techniques of salvation known later in the schools of Yoga and Samkhya, were crucial in the formation of new religious communities such as the Jainas, Buddhists, and Ajivikas. The flow of speculation in the period of the *Brahmanas, Aranyakas,* and *Upanishads* culminated in a radical new interpretation of sacrifice and its consequences; because this interpretation forced clarification of the doctrines of *samsara* and karma, the *Upanishads* became a watershed for South Asian thought. In the final centuries of the first millennium B.C.E. there was for the first time in South Asia a clear and distinct plurality of religious traditions, each with texts, doctrines, and institutions. What was to become "classic" and enduring in Hinduism emerged from gifted poet-philosophers in a four-hundred-year period of Upanishadic inspiration.

The point of departure for the *Aranyakas* and *Upanishads* remained the sacrifice, just as previously in the *Yajurveda* and *Samaveda Samhitas* and all the *Brahmanas.* The *Brihadaranyaka Upanishad,* for example, begins with an accounting of the parts of the *ashvamedha* sacrificial horse and their cosmic correspondences (eye = sun, breath = wind, and so forth), an indexing reminiscent of the notion of bodily parts returned to their respective origins in the sacrifice person Purusha. Basic to the Vedic sacrificial worldview, as noted above, is a synchronous construction of a world (the unmanifest Purusha-Prajapati) and of a self for the sacrificer. In ritual terminology the word for the body or self constructed in the center of the fire altar for *shrauta* performances is *atman.* This word became the key to a new vision of human destiny when it was declared to be ultimate reality, the unmanifest, *brahman.*

The *Chandogya,* an early *Upanishad* linked by tradition to a lost *Brahmana* of the *Samaveda,* is a good example of how the *Upanishads* could remain embedded in traditional sacrificial thought processes while inventing radical new expectations. It begins by exploring the mystical connection (*upanishad*) between the chant and the essence (*rasa*) of all cosmic entities, including the elements, speech, syllable, breath, mind, and so forth. It is of course the responsibility of the *Samaveda* chanter (*udgata*) to know these infinite identities and to involve himself with knowledge, faith, and insight into the inner workings of the *soma* sacrifice.

The *Chandogya Upanishad* never lets go of the significance of the chant (*saman, udgitha*) in the context of world-maintaining sacrifice. But quickly another agenda surfaces: Study, meditation, and concentration upon the infinite identities arrives at the point of ultimate breakthrough, that is, a recognition of the eternal, universal, absolute Self (*atman*) and its identity with *brahman*. The *atman-brahman* homology is the ultimate correspondence, beyond which no further search is possible.

It is revealing to note that in these discourses on the character of the *atman* the essential threefold and fivefold structure of the Self is a constant subject, involving a functional division of fires, breaths, and senses within one body, as well as in the processes of digestion, speech, and breathing. Abstraction is the language, the sacrificial terminology referring constantly to the offering of mystical substances. And in this fashion the sequential passage known as transmigration (*samsara*) comes under scrutiny. Transmigration according to *Chandogya* 5 is nothing other than a series of offerings into five successive cosmic fires, the fifth being woman, from whom the embryo (*garbha*) is born as the soul passes by ritual labor into yet another embodiment following the offering up of a previous one.

The link between the rebirth of a lifebody and ritual action (karma) is explained further by this same *Upanishad*. After death the soul ascends on one of two paths. The souls of those who perform rituals and good works go on the "path of the Fathers" to the world of the ancestors and then to the moon to become food (*soma*) for the gods. When the results of their previous actions (note that karma is now not limited to ritual action) can no longer maintain them in heaven they rain down into the earth, grow as vegetation, and become food once again, this time for humans and animals. And again dependent upon the fruits of previous action, the eaten becomes like the eater, blessed or burdened with rank, from that of the Brahman, Kshatriya, or Vaishya down to rebirth as a Chandala (the lowest of human outcastes, beneath the Shudras), or a dog or a pig. By contrast the souls of those with knowledge—not of the rituals but of the imperishable *atman*—go by the "path of the gods" to *brahman* and immortality; they do not return, they have achieved *moksha,* release from the cycle of birth-death-rebirth. Knowledge of the *atman-brahman* identity wins over knowledge of the world-recycling ritual.

The sixth chapter of the *Chandogya,* reminiscent of the Purusha hymn in its division into sixteen parts, places all of this in proper perspective. The chapter concerns Svetaketu, who takes his father's advice and follows *brahmacharya,* the Vedic student's life, from age twelve to twenty-four. Having mastered the Vedic texts and rituals he is chagrined to discover—from his father, who had encouraged him to learn the *Vedas*—that he is quite ignorant of what is supremely important, knowledge of the Self. And so his father instructs him in sixteen lessons about the highest truth. Each of the last nine lessons ends with a famous refrain, *tat tvam asi svetaketo iti* ("YOU are that, Svetaketu!" YOU are *brahman,* the absolute, the highest Self).

Like many reformations the Upanishadic one returns to religious roots (the Purusha hymn, basic sacrificial procedures, correspondences between the manifest and unmanifest realms). But also like many reformations a reshaping of basic religious expressions for a new era is in order. The static teaching of the

Vedas and the mindless performance of rituals (Svetaketu's twelve-year education, useless from the perspective of salvation) are subordinated to the inner quest, mystical insight into transcendent selfhood, and an interior or meditational form of sacrifice. [See Judaism pp. 422–27, Christianity pp. 500, 507, 519, Islam pp. 659–62, Buddhism pp. 946–48, Religions of China pp. 1032–34, and Religions of Japan pp. 1102, 1121–27, 1151 for discussion of meditation and mysticism.]

The *Upanishads* also reintroduce the gods to center stage of Indian religious experiences. They have been there all the while, invited to the sacrifices and dismissed from them by the chants of the priests, but not since the powerful hymns of the *Rigveda* have they been so prominent in Vedic experience. The ritual work and godlike workers were always in the spotlight. A section of *Chandogya Upanishad* 3 describes the *atman* in strongly devotional language: The *atman* in the heart is *brahman,* and "on departing [this lifebody] I shall enter into him."

But it is the later verse *Upanishads* that introduce a theistic, even a sectarian note, moving from the Purusha-Prajapati and *atman-brahman* identities to embrace Ishvara, the Lord, as supremely worthy of meditation and praise. The *Shvetashvatara Upanishad* quotes extensively from the hymn of Purusha (*Rigveda* 10.90) and identifies him with Rudra, also called Shiva ("auspicious"). He is eternal, the one god without a second who lives in the hearts of all beings and brings cessation of birth to those who truly know him. The poetry of the *Katha Upanishad* also reveals this theistic trend. One who reins in with *yoga* his body, senses, and mind as a charioteer controls his horses and chariot will attain the highest abode of Vishnu.

Alongside the clarification of *samsara,* an expanded definition of karma, the interiorization of sacrifice, an emphasis on techniques of *yoga,* and the reintroduction of theism, the *Upanishads* were innovative in several other ways. They were now teachings with a more open transmission, primarily but not exclusively Brahman and masculine. Kshatriyas, women, and others became "knowers" and teachers of the mystical connections because access to knowledge was no longer a birthright. Meditation, effort, striving, exertion—all of the experiences of Prajapati working toward creation or the renouncer working toward salvation—became hallmarks. References also were made to the careers of the student, householder, and mendicant-renunciant or forest hermit, later to be arranged as a program of life stages or *ashramas.* Finally, it might be said that the genre itself was an innovation, for post-Vedic "*upanishads*" continued to be composed over succeeding centuries until eventually more than a hundred were known.

Most of the significant developments in the religions of India in the classical or epic age, and the following medieval and modern periods, have partial or substantial bases in the *Upanishads,* from the all-encompassing themes of devotion (**bhakti**), to traditions of Tantra with esoteric attempts to establish divine androgyny, to the philosophical schools of Advaita Vedanta developed by Shankara, Ramanuja, and their successors.

31
Hinduism and History:
The Epic Through Modern Periods

RAVANA (the demon king who has abducted Sita, wife of Rama, and carried her off to his palace in Lanka): *"O beautiful one! Wherever on your body I set my eyes, there they remain fixed and immovable. Accept me and enjoy all the pleasures of the world."*

SITA: *"How can I become your wife when I am the wife of another? Do not violate dharma. I belong to Rama as the Veda belongs to one who has reverently mastered it. Even now I hear the twang of Rama's bow. You cannot escape him."*

RAVANA: *"Change your mind. Be my wife and come to my bed. If you refuse you will be sent to my kitchen and cooked for my meal. Beware!"*

Valmiki's Ramayana[3]

FOR NEARLY A MILLENNIUM and a half the *Vedas* were the dominant sound and authority of northern India. By the early centuries of the Common Era, however, two huge Sanskrit epics had begun to command the religious imagination and energy of Hinduism. Although eventually classified as **smriti,** tradition—and therefore subordinate to the *Vedas* in authority—these two verse dramas soon eclipsed all Vedic texts in popular religious life. To this day almost every Hindu knows the basic outline and scores of major and minor episodes in both the *Mahabharata* and the *Ramayana.* Frequently, this familiarity is doubled. Not only are portions of the Sanskrit epics known from local recitations, temple iconography, traveling performers, radio, film, and now television productions, but also from regional versions in the many spoken languages of India, popularized in the same versatile range of media.

One region—Tamil Nadu in South India—produced a classical civilization to rival that of the North and of Sanskrit. And one of its many assets was an epic tradition, displayed for example in the most famous of Tamil literary epics, the fifth-century *Cilappatikaram,* as well as later in the medieval period in Kamban's twelfth-century version of the *Ramayana,* and Villiputtur Alvar's *Mahabharata* composed about 1400 and completed by another poet in the eighteenth century.

Classical Indian Civilization

The lengthy period in which the Sanskrit epics were in the process of formation in North India ushers in the classical age not only of Hinduism but of Indian civilization at large. Epics were not the only extra-Vedic expression to emerge in the final centuries of the first millennium B.C.E. Legal, ethical, ritual, medical, philosophical, grammatical, astronomical, and many other interests were served textually, with classical Sanskrit the medium for an astonishing range of disciplines and schools. As noted previously, the various branches of Vedic tradition produced *Sutras* for both domestic and priestly ritual schedules. These were soon supplemented by law codes known as *Dharma Sutras* with instructions about proper conduct in all aspects of life. Few *Dharma Sutras* survived, but their subjects were later codified in verse in texts known as *Shastras,* and the *Dharma Shastras* remain today an established genre for Hindu religious life in general. The *Laws of Manu,* or *Manava Dharma Shastra,* cited in chapter 29, is among the most significant.

More specialized, but also an outgrowth of the Vedic schools and their textual or ritual requirements, were the *Vedangas,* "limbs of the *Veda.*" One concerned a combination of astronomy and astrology, a result of the obligation to match celestial and sacrificial precision and publish an exact ritual calendar. Another grew from a demand for textual precision, and grammar, etymology, lexicography, phonetics, and metrics were all initially born from this need for exactitude in the transmission of *shruti.*

In addition there were the beginnings of philosophical schools such as Mimamsa—adhering closely to analysis of Vedic ritual—and others such as Samkhya, Yoga, and Nyaya with agendas of speculation far removed from Vedic textual or ritual interests.

In this same period the unsystematized traditions of mantric healing known in the *Atharvaveda* gave precedence to new schools of medicine. Physicians grounded their practice on the theory that the human body functions with three humors in active correspondence with cosmic entities. The Sanskrit texts of *Charaka* and *Sushruta,* plus later works from the medieval period, are still today the basis of traditional medicine known as the *veda* of long life, Ayurveda.

In other words, the building blocks of classical Indian civilization were laid in relatively short order in the late first millennium B.C.E. and the early centuries C.E. The Gupta dynasty, under four successive rulers from about 320 to 454, was able to unify politically most of the small kingdoms of North India and to influence both politically and culturally several regions of the South as well. At this time, in the fourth and fifth centuries C.E., Indian culture reached its high point, a golden age of productivity in literature, philosophy, art, architecture, music, dance, drama, and—evident in all of these—religion.

By the middle centuries of the first millennium C.E., after the compilation of both Sanskrit epics and with classical Indian civilization at its zenith, two important new types of Sanskrit texts emerged. One was the *Puranas,* collections of "old stories," that is, myths, folklore, temple legends, and details on everything from the creation of the world and the genealogies of gods and heroes to the significance of *dharma,* class and caste, asceticism, rituals, pilgrimages, and other acts of devotion to deities. Of course, the related concepts of *samsara,* karma, and *moksha* were never out of focus. Aside from their contents an important factor in the development of the *Puranas* was a regional one, as urban temples, festivals, pilgrimages, and localized mythologies, legends, and folklore gained prominence by the publicity of a *Purana.* Eventually a standard list of eighteen great *Puranas* surfaced, but the genre, once established, continued with hundreds of minor textual traditions.

There was another Sanskrit textual tradition that incorporated "old" material in a new form during the middle centuries of the first millennium C.E. The *Tantras,* esoteric texts promoting liberation by radical beliefs and practices, were produced by Buddhist and Hindu schools alike. After the destruction of Buddhist monasteries in the medieval period Buddhist Tantrism survived as the "diamond vehicle," Vajrayana, in the Himalayas. Hindu Tantrism, on the other hand, became a significant element on the more provocative and experimental wing of Hindu tradition. A remarkable spiritual discipline evolved centering on mystical identification with masculine divine power, particularly the heroic form of the god Shiva, in order to unite with and be liberated by feminine cosmic energy (**shakti**). Various yogic techniques of long standing in South Asia were combined with erotic mysticism—partly traceable in the *Upanishads,* but mostly non-Aryan in origins. The emergence of goddesses into devotional prominence coincided with these practices, and eventually two paths were declared for Tantric devotees. One is the right-hand, safe path of the conventional *yogin* or *bhakta,* the other the left-hand, dangerous and radical path of one who breaks the code of *dharma* in order to be liberated from all constraints. Typical of the latter is the practice of a ritual set of "five M's," community worship involving men and women employing five items that begin with the letter *M* in Sanskrit: eating meat, fish, and parched grains; drinking an alcoholic beverage; engaging in sexual intercourse as heroic Shiva and as Goddess or Shakti in order to attain a transcendent, genderless unity.

Some of the prominent themes of Yoga, the *Puranas,* and the *Tantras* will be pursued in chapter 32. It was the Sanskrit epics that left the strongest mark on the period subsequent to the major *Upanishads.* The two together—the *Mahabharata* and the *Ramayana*—identify an age.

The Mahabharata

A popular tradition points to Vyasa, the "Arranger," as compiler of the larger of the two Sanskrit epics, the *Mahabharata* or Great Bharata. But the epic as it is known to scholars in eighteen long books and a total of nearly one hundred thousand verses was probably in a continuous state of composition and reformulation for many centuries between the fourth century B.C.E. and the fourth century C.E. Some scholars propose that key themes of the *Mahabharata,* including some with counterparts in other Indo-European epic traditions, may have been brought to India early in the first millennium B.C.E. by a later Indo-

Aryan–speaking culture, one substantially different from that of the earliest Vedic period.

Bharata is the name of an ancient hero. It is also an area of North India between the Himalaya and the Vindhya mountain ranges and the scene of a gripping drama, a land contested by two powerful sides of one family. One side includes the sons of Dhritarashtra; they are known as the Kauravas. Their cousins on the other side are known as the **Pandavas,** sons of Pandu, the younger brother of Dhritarashtra. While the Kauravas number a hundred heroes, with Duryodhana as their champion, the Pandavas count five brothers as principals: Yudhisthira, the eldest; **Arjuna,** the noblest warrior; Bhima, a rough-hewn guerrilla fighter; and the amiable twins Nakula and Sahadeva.

The opening book of the epic establishes a bad guys versus good guys plot, with the horde of Kauravas cast as demons and instigators of disorder. The Pandava heroes, on the other hand, are projections of specific functions of the foremost Vedic gods, and together they fight on the side of *dharma.* Arjuna, for example, was actually fathered by the great warrior god Indra, and the twins are the transposition into heroic form of the divine twins of Rigvedic mythology, the Ashvins. Like gods and demons, however, the heroes on both sides are not always predictable, and in true epic fashion they display the full range of human emotions and actions, not omitting valor and treachery.

In the city of Hastinapura the two sets of cousins are drawn into a game of chance. Yudhisthira, in a fit of gambling addiction, dices away his kingdom, his brothers, and even **Draupadi,** the common wife of all five Pandava heroes. They are forced into exile in the forest for thirteen years, after which Duryodhana reneges on his promise to return the Pandavas' portion of the kingdom. The middle books of the epic detail the great war that ensues, culminating in the slaughter of Duryodhana and most of his army, then a retaliatory night raid in which the carnage now embraces the children of the Pandavas and their troops. Only the five Pandava heroes survive among the lamentations of the women. Yudhisthira becomes universal emperor by the performance of the horse sacrifice (*ashvamedha*), and eventually the five heroes journey up into the Himalayas in an "ascent to heaven," the title of the final book.

The third episode of the sixth book is a Hindu classic known as the *Bhagavad Gita.* It serves not only as a condensation of themes in the epic itself, but also as a distillation of the Hindu worldview in the emergent classical age. The setting is a dramatic one of the moment before battle. **Krishna,** a counselor to the Pandavas, serving here as Arjuna's charioteer, instructs him about the eternal Self that cannot be killed, about the three paths (*margas*) to salvation— devotion, action, and knowledge (*bhakti,* karma, *jnana*)—and about the performance of one's own duty (*dharma*). In one powerful scene Arjuna asks Krishna to reveal himself as he really is, and Arjuna is able to experience, briefly, the awesome splendor of the transcendent god Vishnu.

The whole of the *Mahabharata* defies analysis. It has been aptly labeled a library rather than a text, since it includes a vast range of materials composed over a period of eight or more centuries. It contains even a version of the other epic, the *Ramayana.* And like epics in other cultures it is rich territory for scholarly interpretation. The great themes of Vedic mythology and ritual, some of them transparently Indo-European, have been transposed from the mythic to the epic sphere. The god Vishnu appears in the form of Krishna to assure the triumph of *dharma* and the defeat of chaos. The nature of deity—sometimes detached, sometimes immanent—is ambiguous, however, and the price of victory is heavy and includes, like sacrifice, death and destruction as a prelude to regeneration. Although renunciation and asceticism have their place, the *Bhagavad Gita* and the epic in general put an enduring stamp of approval on proper human activity in this world, including selfless devotion to God and selfless action in accord with *dharma*.

The Ramayana

The *Ramayana* shares a number of features with the *Mahabharata:* dynamic opposition of good and evil, exile in the forest, heroic combat, the victory of *dharma* over *adharma* ("nondharma"), even a performance of the horse sacrifice near the close of the epic. And both achieved extended popularity with versions in regional languages in the medieval period. On the whole, however, they are substantially different. The *Ramayana,* only one-fourth the length of the *Mahabharata,* is tighter in focus as it unfolds its core narrative about the adventures of Rama and his wife **Sita.** Ascribed by tradition to the poet Valmiki, it is considered to be the first structured literary work in Sanskrit, crafted with metaphor, simile, and elaborate ornamentation that typify the poetic genre known as *kavya.*

The scene of this epic is well to the east of the Pandava-Kaurava kingdoms, in the city of Ayodhya. Rama, eldest son of King Dasharatha, wins the hand of the beautiful Sita by stringing the ponderous bow of the god Shiva. Court

A Ramayana *panel sculpted on the wall of a Hindu temple compound about 900 C.E. on the island of Java in Indonesia. An army of monkeys hurls boulders into a monster-filled sea, building a causeway to rescue Sita from Lanka.*

intrigue among the wives of Dasharatha forces the king's hand and, reluctantly, he satisfies a boon granted to his youngest wife and sends Rama and Sita into forest exile for fourteen years. After numerous adventures **Ravana,** a demon king of Lanka, falls in love with Sita, disguises himself as an ascetic, and contrives to carry her off to the South to his fortress in Lanka. A long campaign to retrieve Sita from the ten-headed Ravana ends in the siege and defeat of Lanka and the death of Ravana. In the war Rama and his brother **Lakshmana** have valuable assistance from Sugriva, the monkey king, and **Hanuman,** his champion. Rama is crowned king in Ayodhya with Sita restored to his side.

The citation at the head of this segment sets the tone of this romantic drama: Ravana lusts after his captive princess, but the damsel in distress resists and furthermore shames him by preaching about *dharma* and the *Vedas.* Sita retains her virtue until the rescue. However, the seventh and final book, considered by most scholars to be a later addition, rewrites the ending. The people of Ayodhya do not believe that Sita resisted the ten-headed demon. Rama accedes to their protests and reluctantly banishes his queen. A distraught Sita beseeches the earth goddess to validate her innocence (her name, *Sita,* is the plowed "furrow," and she was born from the earth mother). The earth swallows her forever.

The characters are ideal types, Rama being the heroic, vigorous, princely figure, Sita the beautiful, virtuous, loyal wife. Their divinity is established only in the first and last books. It is in the regional versions that the transformation of hero to god, heroine to goddess is complete. In the vernacular epics Rama is an incarnation of Vishnu, Sita an incarnation of Vishnu's consort **Lakshmi.** Hanuman, the monkey ally, plays another ideal role, that of supreme devotee, and his enormous strength and devotion are always in the service of Rama. By extension he too became the center of human devotional attention and has his own *bhaktas.*

The medieval epics based on the Sanskrit or Valmiki *Ramayana* include the *Iramavataram,* composed in the twelfth century in Tamil by Kamban; the *Ramcaritmanas,* composed in Hindi by Tulsidas; the Telugu *Ranganatha Ramayana;* and the Krittivas *Ramayana* in Bengali. Episodes from the *Ramayana* (and *Mahabharata*) also were the material of the sacred shadow puppet dramas (*wayang kulit*) of Javanese tradition.

Vishnu, Shiva, and the Goddess

More than a millennium separates the period of the major *Upanishads* and the medieval period of Indian civilization. During these many centuries the two epics were composed, shaped, and reshaped, gradually incorporating a synthesis of Hindu tradition. The classical civilizations based on Sanskrit in the north and Tamil in the deep south reached their full productivity; *Puranas* and *Tantras* developed as new genres alongside the older *Dharma Shastra* and epic texts. It was in this period that Hinduism achieved its classical, that is to say, definitive guise.

With the reemergence of theism in the late centuries B.C.E. came the opportunity for *bhakti,* the devotional tradition, to achieve status not only as one among several options for religious expression, but as the dominant path toward salvation. Two figures emerge, Vishnu and Shiva, each with a full range of expressions that continue essential elements of myths, rites, and symbols of the past—Vedic and non-Vedic—and each in position to move on this new tide of devotional energy across the subcontinent. They are joined by an array of local, regional, and pan-Indian goddesses who achieve equal status and in some cases (village goddesses, Tantric circles) higher prominence in popular affection.

The two Sanskrit epics include key figures who become in the course of the epic age the two most prominent ***avataras,*** "descents" or incarnations of the great deity Vishnu. Krishna of the *Bhagavad Gita* and Rama of the *Ramayana* indicate the priority of these two *avataras.* Eventually lists of ten or more *avataras* appear, and Vishnu becomes almost a pantheon in his own right. In the process of assembling this system of *avataras* several regional deities were incorporated. Active sects in the last centuries B.C.E. included the Bhagavatas, worshipers of Bhagavan, the Lord (Vishnu), originating in the area of Mathura in North India. Another that appears eventually to have merged with the Bhagavatas was the Pancharatras, a sect centering on Narayana. The twelfth book of the *Mahabharata* contains a section extolling Narayana-Vishnu. Still another early movement seems to have focused on a clan deity, Vasudeva, later identified with Krishna. One of the principal doctrines to emerge in these centuries was that of *vyuhas* or emanations of Vishnu, five manifestations of God that correspond to the five regions of the macrocosmos and the five aspects of the human microcosmos. In the Tamil south between the seventh and tenth centuries C.E. there developed a tradition of Vishnu *bhaktas* known as the Alvars. Eventually twelve in number, these poet-saints, mostly non-Brahmans, deepened the basis of devotional Hinduism into all strata of Hindu society.

The twelve Alvars complemented a traditional medieval list of sixty-two or sixty-three poet-saints expressing devotion to Shiva in their Tamil verses composed between the sixth and ninth centuries. Perhaps the earliest of these Nayanmars, as they are known collectively, was a woman devotee of Shiva, Karaikkal Ammaiyar. Earlier than the Nayanmars of the south, however, were the Pashupatas, worshipers of Pashupati, Lord of Creatures, identified with Shiva. These communities, mentioned in the *Mahabharata,* developed distinctive ritual patterns and ascetic traditions until the medieval period. By then numerous Shaiva sects were active in both north and south, including Shaiva Siddhanta in Tamil Nadu, the Virashaivas or Lingayats throughout the Deccan, and Kashmiri Shaivism in the far northwest.

Already mentioned are the epic heroines Draupadi of the *Mahabharata* and Sita of the *Ramayana.* Both may be seen in the long-term development of devotional tradition as incarnations of Vishnu's consort Lakshmi or Shri, although Sita demonstrates possibly much older characteristics as an earth or agrarian goddess. It is in the *Markandeya Purana,* however, that the Hindu goddesses are finally recognized and synthesized in all their power. The *Devi Mahatmya* section, probably sixth century C.E., celebrates Durga as the invincible slayer of the buffalo-headed demon **Mahisha,** who has threatened the world. Vishnu, Shiva, and all the other gods are powerless before him, but the inexhaustible interior strength of the goddess prevails, and Durga mounted on her lion is victorious. Durga's lion (sometimes tiger) mount (***vahana***) brings into focus animal associates of the deities. Interestingly, her wild feline does not become an independent being in the fashion of **Nandi**, the bull mount of Shiva, or **Garuda**, the hawk *vahana* of Vishnu, or even the other mount associated with Vishnu, the precosmic serpent coil, **Shesha**, upon whom the deity sleeps.

The mythologies and rituals of Krishna, Rama, **Narasimha,** and other *avataras* of Vishnu; of Nataraja, Bhairava, and other forms of Shiva; and of Durga, Kali, **Parvati,** and other manifestations of the Goddess, will be further explored in chapter 32. [See Religions of Africa pp. 39–42, 64–69, Religions of Mesoamerica pp. 157–58, 186–89, Native Religions of North America pp. 274–76, 288–305, 330–32, Judaism pp. 414–15, Christianity pp. 537–58, Islam pp. 635–37, Buddhism pp. 900–903, Religions of China pp. 1024–26, and Religions of Japan pp. 1112–27 for discussion of God, gods, and objects of worship.]

Medieval South Asia

The Chandogya Upanishad can describe the various components of the sacrifice of breath only by way of such imaginary correspondences as "the chest is the sacrificial area, the hairs are the sacrificial grass, the heart is the cooking fire, the mind is the defensive fire, the mouth is the offering fire."

Shankara, Commentary on the Brahma Sutra *of Badarayana*

> Feet, navel, hands,
>   chest, eyes, and lips
> red-rayed jewels
>   set in a blue glow,
> and golden silks round his waist,
> my lord is all blaze and dazzle:
> I do not know how to reach him.
>   Nammalvar, Tamil poet[4]

In this overview of history and Hinduism, *medieval* ("middle age") refers to a thousand-year period midway between the classical age in which the Sanskrit epics were formed and the modern age shaped by contact with the Western world. The time frame for this epoch is roughly 750 C.E. to 1750 C.E.

Two great synthesizing minds stand out during the early medieval period. Shankara opens this age and Ramanuja appears about three centuries later. Both were Brahmans born in South India, both were scholars and writers of influential Sanskrit commentaries on the classic Sanskrit texts, and both were strong-willed institution builders responsible for much in the patterns of Hindu thought and practice today.

And two significant events are prominent in the later centuries of the medieval period. Islam made its presence known in the subcontinent only gradually between the seventh and twelfth centuries, then more impressively with the Delhi sultanate in the thirteenth century. Almost the entire region was unified politically by 1600 after the conquests of Akbar, third and greatest of the Mughal emperors to rule India. Although the Mughal empire began to unravel in the eighteenth century, from Akbar's reign until the present day Islam has been an effective religious and cultural force in many areas of the subcontinent; it is the state religion in both Pakistan and Bangladesh. The Hindu-Muslim encounter is one of the definitive events of medieval South Asia.

The other late medieval phenomenon was a remarkable new surge of devotional theism throughout India, together with the wider appearance of vernacular languages as voices of revitalized Hindu faith. *Bhakti,* openly declared in the Sanskrit *Bhagavad Gita* and the Tamil poems from devotees of Vishnu and Shiva, established itself permanently in each of the multiple tongues of India.

Shankara and Advaita Vedanta

Reflection on the past is appropriate as a person begins middle age; and Shankara, more than anyone, was the reflective mind of Indian civilization as it approached its own middle years. A review and assessment of classical thought is precisely what he accomplished for medieval India.

Although Shankara is recognized as one of the two most creative Hindu thinkers subsequent to the period of the *Upanishads,* his life is so buried under saintly legends that nothing can be said about him without the preface "according to one tradition." Not even the century in which he lived is certain, but the eighth is most probable, and Kerala is generally accepted as his birthplace. He is said to have taken vows of *samnyasa* already as a child and then to have traveled throughout India, first as student and later as teacher and founder of monastic centers (**mathas**). If the tradition that he lived for only thirty-two years is correct, then his genius flowered early and splendidly. In an effort almost mythic in scope, he is said to have established monasteries in each of the four corners of India: Badrinath, source of the Ganges in the Himalayan north; Puri on the Bay of Bengal in the east; Sringeri and possibly also Kanchi in the Tamil south; and Dvaraka on the west coast. And tradition accords more than three hundred Sanskrit works to him, making Shankara a close rival to the legendary Vyasa as best-selling author—if only in honor and respect.

The most influential works that are authentically Shankara's were his commentaries on the *Brahma* (or *Vedanta*) *Sutras* of Badarayana and on certain major *Upanishads.* Since the *Brahma Sutras* (possibly a first-century B.C.E. work) are themselves terse commentaries on the major *Upanishads,* it is those works —about eight centuries old in Shankara's day—that command attention. Some of the later *Upanishads* used the term *vedanta,* "end of the *Veda*," with reference to their doctrines as a distillation of Vedic knowledge. This term became the name of a leading philosophical tradition among the six systems of Indian thought known as **darshanas,** or points of view. It was Shankara who shaped Vedanta, and the nondualistic or Advaita Vedanta tradition in particular.

By focusing on speculations in the *Upanishads* as scriptural authority (*shruti*) and linking those speculations to selected texts in tradition (*smriti*), Shankara was able to develop a coherent "point of view." It included the following observations. The *Upanishads* (and therefore the eternal *Vedas*) reveal a paramount instruction: Only *brahman* is real. Since *brahman* is without duality (**advaita**), no distinctions are real. And *brahman,* the true Self, is not subject to *samsara.* A self caught in *samsara* makes distinctions, sees multiplicity, takes qualities for real because it is bound by ignorance (**avidya**) and illusion (**maya**). Enlightenment or liberation (*moksha*) of the self from *samsara* occurs through replacement of the wrong knowledge (*avidya*) with knowledge of the highest *brahman.* The object on the ground that was thought to be a snake turns out, on closer inspection, to be a rope. Likewise, said Shankara, where the self is concerned, the acquisition of true knowledge supplants ignorance and *samsara,* and the sole reality of *atman-brahman* as Self is recognized.

As an illustration of Shankara's scholarship and of the complicated interaction of textual and scholastic traditions in his day, consider the passage cited on page 761. It is from the third lesson of his lengthy commentary on the work of Badarayana written perhaps seven or eight centuries earlier. Shankara's (and Badarayana's) concern is a passage in the *Chandogya Upanishad* (5.19.2) composed perhaps six centuries or so before Badarayana. Note that the subject is sacrifice, the central doctrine of the *Vedas.* But the attention of the *Upanishad,* Badarayana, and Shankara is not on the actual performance itself in all of its details. For that we should consult the *Samhitas* and *Brahmanas,* which Shankara refers to as the ritual (karma) portion of *shruti,* as distinct from the knowledge (*jnana*) portion of *shruti,* the *Aranyakas* and *Upanishads.* Nor is the attention of the *Chandogya Upanishad,* the *Sutras,* and Shankara's commentary on the mythic power of the cosmic person (Purusha) whose members and organs have become—in a set of correspondences as old as Proto–Indo-European tradition—world parts, including the sacrificial fires. Instead the focus is a symbolic sacrifice, an interior offering of breath within the absolute Self (*atman*), the world soul that is independent of any need of human offerings or acts of any sort whatever.

Shankara's position is even further removed from the condensed symbols of sacrifice in the *Upanishad.* He reviews the ancient set of sacrificial members not out of belief, but only to demonstrate their unreality; they are effective only by "imaginary correspondences," the result of *maya,* illusion. The highest *brahman* is devoid of qualities (chest, hair, heart, mind, mouth, and so forth), and Shankara is convinced that both *shruti* and *smriti* are agreed upon this fundamental truth. Quite simply put, the Vedic sacrificers appreciated, even revered, the correspondences between the creative unmanifest and the created world, including human bodily parts in particular. Shankara dismissed these correspondences as a mistaken point of view.

For a parallel to this gradual theological march away from the graphic realities of blood sacrifice and a parallel also to this telescoping series of scriptural
discourses and commentaries (*Samhitas, Brahmanas, Upanishads, Sutras*, Shankara's Advaita Vedanta), consider biblical tradition. There is considerable distance between animal sacrifice described in the Torah of ancient Israel, the
symbolic interpretation of sacrifice in postexilic Judaism, its further extension
in early Christianity in the letters of Paul, and finally the theology of Thomas
Aquinas commenting on scripture and the Greek and Latin church fathers. This
lineage moves from ancient Hebrew to Hellenistic Greek to medieval Latin,
whereas Shankara's Sanskrit is not far removed from Vedic Sanskrit. In terms of
religious expression, however, the gradual abstraction of sacrifice is not dissimi-
lar, there are parallel strategies to align scripture and subsequent "tradition," and
the textual time span is more than two millennia in both situations.

Ramanuja and Developing Bhakti

The other giant of the early medieval period was also a South Indian Brahman, learned traveler, teacher, and administrator. Educated in the Vedanta traditions at Kanchi, Ramanuja became a much-sought-after teacher in Tamil Nadu,
probably in the early twelfth century. Like Shankara he was well versed in
Vedic texts, and eventually he wrote commentaries, again like Shankara, on
the major *Upanishads* and the *Brahma Sutras,* as well as a separate one on the
Bhagavad Gita. His intense devotion to Vishnu, however, led him on a path that
was different both intellectually and spiritually from that of his eighth-century
predecessor.

Ramanuja was initiated into the Shri Vaishnava movement, a sect that
looked for authority not only to the *Vedas* but also to the devotional songs of the
Tamil Alvars. The Alvars were twelve poet-saints of the popular southern *bhakti*
tradition. Perhaps the most famous of them was Nammalvar, whose verse in
praise of Lord Vishnu is cited above (after the quote from Shankara, p. 761). Written only a century before Ramanuja's time, this verse celebrates precisely the
qualities of God discounted as unreal by Shankara's nondualism. Nammalvar's
god is "all blaze and dazzle" and has a chest, eyes, and mouth like his devotee,
or the *yogi* in concentration, or the meditating sacrificer who encompasses the
world in his inner offering of breath, or the divine Purusha who becomes this
world in sacrifice. Without performing sacrifices Nammalvar is doing what the
Vedic sacrificers did, revering correspondences. But even with all of these
divine/human mediations the poet still laments "I do not know how to reach
him."

Ramanuja's Vedic upbringing and training in Vedanta were tempered by
exactly this kind of popular theism. The result was his intellectual contribution
to a school of "qualified" nondualism, Vishishtadvaita Vedanta. The point of
departure for this tradition is *brahman* as Brahman, that is, as God, Ishvara, the
Lord, a Supreme Being with attributes and personality. Whereas Shankara maintained *brahman* as impersonal and without qualities (*nirguna*), Ramanuja and
his school of Vedanta insisted upon *brahman* as personal and with qualities

(*saguna*). *Brahman* is truth, knowledge, infinity. And yet Ramanuja, too, upheld the oneness, the nonduality of *brahman*.

Two additional features of Ramanuja's theology signaled his departure from the position established by Shankara. First, whereas Shankara maintained that both a lower knowledge (of rituals) and a higher knowledge (of *brahman*) were revealed in the *Upanishads,* Ramanuja understood the instruction of the *Upanishads* to be uniform and undivided. The world in which rituals are performed is real, and therefore a source of knowledge and truth; positive results from worship and devotion are to be recognized in this world. Second, Shankara taught that the revelation of the *Upanishads* concerning the identity of *atman-brahman* meant the merger of the individual soul into the absolute soul. Since distinctions prevail only in *samsara* and are due to illusion and ignorance, *moksha* reveals the supreme truth: There is no individual self. Ramanuja, on the other hand, taught that the individual self is a distinct personality, eternal even after liberation.

Like Shankara before him Ramanuja founded *mathas* in various locations. Legend credits him with establishing seventy-four Vaishnava centers in a lifetime of 120 years. Equally important was his effort in the reform of temple ritual. As a temple priest at Kanchi, and later as head priest of the huge staff of the Ranganatha temple at Srirangam, he had ample opportunity to insert his interpretations of *shruti* and *smriti* into the daily liturgies. Many of his reforms are both visible and audible today in the great Vaishnava temples of the south.

In sum, Ramanuja effected a compromise that became the Hindu mainstream. He reconciled the Sanskrit textual tradition of the Brahmans, including

Part of a swiftly moving crowd of nearly one million pilgrims of all castes on the way to the temple of the god Vithoba in Pandharpur in western India. They walk barefoot for fifteen days, following the route of medieval saints and singing their devotional songs.

both the *Vedas* and the post-Vedic Sutras and epics (the *Bhagavad Gita* in particular) with the Tamil textual tradition of popular non-Brahman poet-saints. Ramanuja provided authoritative philosophical and liturgical voices for the devotional tradition that he himself—through personal experience in the worship of Vishnu and Lakshmi—valued as deeply as the Upanishadic-Vedantic tradition of nonduality. In this respect his efforts resembled those of al-Ghazzali, the great Muslim teacher and writer who provided—also from intense personal experience—theological credentials for the popular devotional and mystical traditions of Sufism in twelfth-century Baghdad. Interestingly enough, Ramanuja and al-Ghazzali—separated by religion, culture, and geography—were contemporaries, and their respective reforms would meet one another in India only a few generations later.

Early in the fourteenth century Ramanuja's school of Vedanta became divided over issues of divine grace and human action. Both were agreed upon *bhakti* as the path of release. Their differences, however, were popularized in the Tamil country by reference to two animal mothers saving their young in crises. When a kitten is in danger the mother cat springs to it, picks it up by the scruff of the neck, and carries it to safety. A baby monkey in danger jumps onto the chest of the mother, clasps her neck, and is carried to safety. The "cat's way," as it came to be known, is the way of divine salvation by God's grace alone. Like the kitten dangling in the air, an individual soul can do nothing to earn release from *samsara* and must therefore surrender and become absolutely dependent. The "monkey's way," by contrast, teaches cooperative effort alongside grace; like the baby monkey's act of holding on, human action as well as God's grace is essential, and initiative does count as merit toward eventual release.

Islam and Hinduism

All four of the great religions that emerged in West Asia—Zoroastrianism, Judaism, Christianity, and Islam—were established in South Asia during the first millennium C.E. Whereas Jews and the Parsis (Zoroastrians) remained tiny regional minorities on the west coast of India, Christians and Muslims were part of multiform traditions that gradually spread throughout South Asia. Of the four, however, only Islam became a state religion, and this occurred in the Mughal empire in the late medieval period. [See Religions of Africa pp. 24, 31, 60–61, Religions of Mesoamerica pp. 112–14, 215–21, Native Religions of North America pp. 320–21, 325, and Religions of China pp. 988–89 for discussion of invasion and colonization.]

Already within a century of the death of the Prophet Muhammad in 632, Arabs raided outlying settlements in the northwest of India. From the eighth to the fifteenth centuries successive waves of ethnic Muslims—Arabs, Turks, Afghans, Persians, Mongols—entered the subcontinent. Raiders came to loot the palaces, treasuries, and temples, but it was the settled merchants and other colonists who slowly spread the new religion. A confessional faith, Islam presented itself as the mirror opposite of Hinduism: a strict monotheism with a sacred book, the word of Allah in an Arabic Qur'an, revealed through his messenger, the Prophet Muhammad; a single community with a single law and the notion of an abode of Islam (*Dar al-Islam*) in which religion and polity are one; a doctrine of the unity of God that has no place for iconography, let alone myths, symbols, and rituals celebrating the dynamic multiplicity of the divine. This vigorous new faith was presented lucidly and aggressively.

By the thirteenth century political control came into the hands of the Muslims of the Delhi sultanate. With Arabic the language of religion, and Persian the language of government, literature, and the arts, the Sanskrit base and Brahman hegemony of North Indian civilization were seriously challenged. By the sixteenth century Islam stretched from Europe to China and Indonesia and surpassed Buddhism as the most extensive world religion in Asia. The Mughal dynasty in South Asia surfaced as the easternmost of three great empires alongside the Ottomans in southeastern Europe, Anatolia, North Africa, and West Asia, and the Safavids in Iran and Afghanistan. By 1600 the military genius of Akbar, third Mughal emperor, brought political unification to the subcontinent, and by 1700 that control was virtually total. Aurangzeb, the last great Mughal, was a ruler by confrontation as far as non-Muslims were concerned. Hindus were forced to pay the poll tax for the unbelievers; destruction of Hindu *mathas*, temples, pilgrimage sites, and iconography was at its height. But by 1800 the Mughal empire had all but collapsed, and with it the dream of a *Dar al-Islam*. (Only after independence from the British in 1947 did the partition of India create the modern Islamic state of Pakistan; eventually, East Pakistan became Bangladesh, also an Islamic state.)

The net result of this event of Islam that occupied the entire medieval period is informative. Hindus who did not convert were liable to the more or less restrictive poll tax known as *jizya*, but by and large they went on as before. As a tradition, Hinduism was apparently not impressed by any of the six statements of belief or the five practices, those straightforward articles of faith that make Sunni Islam—of all world religions—one of the most lucid and declarative. On the other hand, Islam found itself drawn ineluctably into a process of South Asianization, a series of minor modifications already evident by the end of the medieval period. Such modifications—significant only in aggregate, and variable by region—still continue today in the nation of India, where Islam is a minority faith. They include observance of castelike hierarchies and restrictions, complete with a continuum running between those peoples regarded as pure or clean and those regarded as polluted or unclean; recognition of guru like preceptors with great spiritual powers and of yogi-like or sadhu-like mendicants with special skills or roles; particular expressions in prayers and devotions; tantra or yoga-like techniques of meditation; life-cycle rituals similar to Hindu **samskaras;** participation in local or pan-Indian pilgrimages and festivals; and above all, worship at the tombs of saints and reliance upon the powers of saints for personal needs such as childbirth, healing, release from demons, and so forth. Despite the presence of one or several of these special features of South Asian Islam, the average Muslim continued to subscribe to most of the requisite articles of belief and practice in Sunni custom.

It was the Sufi mystics in several orders established in India between the thirteenth and sixteenth centuries whose spiritual quests and recognition of divine immanence were most in tune with the experimental, eclectic, and individualist modes of Hinduism. [See Islam pp. 659–62 for discussion of Sufism.] Among the half dozen major orders were the Chishti brought from Afghanistan, the Suhrawardi from the area of Baghdad, and later the Shattari and Naqshbandi. It was not only spiritual guidance proved by the *pir* or *shaykh* and initiation onto the path and into the order that found a match in Hindu traditions of guru, disciple, path, and order. There were also discussions of the proper recipe of divine grace and guided human action, the reality or unreality of the world and of the self, and the union with God as partial or complete. All these discussions were similar to debates among followers of various schools of Vedanta, Yoga, and Samkhya. And Sufis spoke of a choice between spiritual modes, a hazardous and a safe mode, for example, parallel to traditions of Tantric Yoga with its left- and right-hand paths. Certain techniques on the path such as breath-control and devotional, even ecstatic, recitation of the divine names found a ready reception. And just as Sufi teachers were effective in vernaculars elsewhere, so also in rural South Asia. Urdu, Bengali, Telugu, Marathi, and other regional languages of the late medieval period became the medium of expression to those without knowledge of the scriptural language, Arabic, or the official language, Persian. [See Islam p. 613 for discussion of Islam in India.]

One Chishti holy man so impressed the Mughal emperor Akbar that he moved his capital into a city newly constructed near the saint's remote residence. Fascinated with the diversity of active religions, Akbar built there a House of Worship in which debates were held. Invited were not only Sufis from the Chishti and other mystic orders, as well as Shi'a and Sunni Muslims, but also Vaishnava, Shaiva, Jaina, Jesuit, and Parsi authorities. Akbar later instituted a reconciling "religion of God" (*din-i ilahi*) in his court. Although short-lived, it was one more sign of the remarkable religious pluralism of the late medieval period in which Islam, intent on domination, was reluctantly caught in a struggle for self-definition and an eventual compromise position as an influential minority faith.

Late Medieval Bhakti

Already mentioned were the impact of the *Bhagavad Gita* segment of the Sanskrit *Mahabharata*—in which *bhakti* is taught by Krishna-Vishnu as one of the three paths to release—and the devotional hymns of the Tamil poet-saints in praise of both Vishnu and Shiva. By the time the first southern expressions of *bhakti* emerged in the sixth and seventh centuries, the Sanskrit *Puranas* were well established as a genre of mythology, folklore, and regional tradition. Collections known as *Puranas* continued to form throughout the medieval period until eventually there were eighteen Sanskrit texts rivaling the epics for prominence.

Some were Vaishnava, some Shaiva, some a mixture, and all found space for traditions of the regional and pan-Indian goddesses.

From the thirteenth to the seventeenth centuries great poet-saints to match the Alvars and Nayanmars of the south achieved fame in the west and north of India. Jnaneshvar (also known as Jnandev) brought Krishna-*bhakti* into regional prominence in the late thirteenth century with his popular treatise on the *Bhagavad Gita*, the *Jnaneshvari*, written in Marathi, the language of Maharashtra in western India. In the following centuries Namdev, Eknath, and Tukaram all composed their songs in Marathi in praise of great deities, temples, and pilgrimage traditions. Tukaram, a Shudra by birth, became the most celebrated of the western poet-saints.

In North India the prominent Hindi devotional poets included Tulsidas (author of the Hindi *Ramayana* mentioned earlier); Surdas, devotee of Lord Krishna and a poet-singer who, according to tradition, was blind; Mirabai, a Rajput princess and another devotee of Krishna who sang as a renunciant itinerant of her marriage to the dark Lord; and Raidas, a Chamar (Untouchable leatherworker). The religious pluralism of late-medieval North India allowed for syncretic devotional traditions. Although born into a Muslim weaver family, the fifteenth-century saint Kabir often referred to God as Ram (Rama); his iconoclastic verses were always quick, however, to reject any divine qualities, or any faith in images, rituals, or scriptures as means to salvation. Guru Nanak, credited with establishing the Sikh tradition in the late fifteenth century, and Dadu, founder of the Dadu Panth ("tradition") in the late sixteenth century, were two additional North Indians whose *bhakti* generated innovative followings.

In Bengal in the northeast, where Jayadeva composed in Sanskrit his famous love-song of Radha and Krishna known as the *Gita Govinda*, there were also great poet-saints composing in their native language, Bengali. Chandidas is the signature on many popular Bengali poems of the late medieval period, and Vidyapati, who wrote in the Maithili vernacular, was equally well loved in the late fourteenth and early fifteenth centuries. Mention should also be made of the sixteenth-century mystic and saint Chaitanya whose inspired devotion to Krishna was a stimulus to Vaishnava traditions throughout northeastern India. Although these centuries witnessed the decline of Buddhism, in Bengal the Tantric traditions in Buddhism as well as Hinduism continued to flourish, and the erotic mysticism of many Vaishnava and Shaiva devotional poems reflects a Tantric presence. Ramprasad Sen was an eighteenth-century Bengali poet celebrating the divine essence as *shakti*, feminine energy.

In sum these many poet-saints were key regional figures in the late medieval period. Instrumental sometimes in establishing regional variants of selected Sanskrit or Tamil classical traditions, they were even more effective in the spread of new institutions of followers who perpetuated their passionate celebration of the immanence of deity, the community of the faithful, and the ease of the divine-human encounter through music and song instead of priestly rituals, remote texts, and divisive laws. They also stimulated the growth of vernacular literatures in each major language region of the subcontinent.

Modern South Asia

> This ashram has been created . . . not for the renunciation of the world but
> as a center and field of practice for the evolution of another kind and form
> of life. (Aurobindo [1872–1950])[5]

In the ancient period the demise of the Indus civilization was closely followed by the expansion of energetic new immigrants to the subcontinent—the Vedic pastoralists. Likewise, a five-century-old Muslim hegemony in South Asia gave way to vigorous new immigrants—the European colonial powers of the eighteenth century. The Portuguese, beginning with the navigator Vasco da Gama who opened the sea trade routes from East Africa in 1498, Dutch, French, Danes, and Germans all established colonies along the coasts of the peninsula. But it was the British with the East India Company who proved most capable in appropriating and consolidating territory. By the late eighteenth century, only a generation after the collapse of the Mughals, the British Raj was the new empire for the shaping of India over the next period of nearly two hundred years. The post–World War II era of dismantling colonial systems in Asia and Africa included India, and on Independence day, January 26, 1947, a new constitutional government succeeded England's rule.

The British Raj—a substantial period of modern political history although brief in South Asia's long memory—was an era of changes as rapid as they were radical. One shift was to a new language that remains to this day the language of commerce, government and the civil service, higher education, and large segments of the media, cultural institutions, and the arts (although an estimate is that only 2 percent of the total populace of India today speaks English). The Raj also introduced new social, political, and economic institutions. Eventually these would transform the many self-sufficient regional Hindu and Muslim kingdoms into clusters of viable economic areas connected physically by road, rail, and sea and linked ideologically by a common world language and a dynamic technology from the European industrial revolution. Great cities such as Bombay, Calcutta, and Madras arose from humble origins, and others like Delhi and Hyderabad were transformed by the urban style of the new rulers. Transformations in rural India and the bulk of the Hindu, Muslim, and tribal population were slower and less visible, but there too the effects of Western education, social reform, law, medicine, religion, literature, and the printing press were gradually evident. With the creation of an English-speaking, British-educated, often Christian-influenced elite, the stage was set for the appearance of several charismatic personalities in the nineteenth century.

Reformers and Traditionalists

Two imposing personalities stand out in the middle decades of the nineteenth century, each the founder of a society (*samaj*) concerned with redesigning Hinduism for a new age, each convinced that "the *Vedas*" were the proper basis for a renascent faith, each with an eye toward a pan-Indian reformation.

But their experiences and agendas were substantially different. Ram Mohan Roy (1772–1833)—a Bengali Brahman intellectual who founded the Brahmo Samaj (Society) in 1828—traveled in England, was influenced early in life by the faith of Islam and by Christian missionaries, and thought of the Hindu tradition as unnecessarily burdened by image worship, polytheistic myths, vulgar festivals, knotty regulations of caste behavior, and limiting doctrines such as *samsara*. In other words, all the things in Hinduism that puzzled Western observers began to appear to Ram Mohan Roy as extraneous to the real Hindu faith. He proposed the *Upanishads,* which he had already translated from Sanskrit into both English and Bengali, as the essence of the *Vedas,* and a rationalist, humanist basis for renovation. The society's meetings were in fact recognizable Protestant services with sermons based on *Upanishads* as scripture, hymn singing, and prayers addressed to the one supreme God revealed in the *Upanishads.* Debendranath Tagore (1817–1905), father of the Nobel prize–winning poet Rabindranath Tagore, and Keshab Chandra Sen (1838–1884) were later overseers of the society and one of its offshoots. The society's narrow regional base in Bengal and its elitist membership of upper-caste intellectuals rendered the movement ineffective in terms of its immodest goal of overturning some twenty-five centuries of the Hindu worldview.

A Gujarati Brahman named Dayananda Sarasvati (1824–1883) also preached a back-to-the-*Vedas* movement, but for him it was not the *Upanishads* but the *mantras* of the *Rigveda* that held the key to Hindu reform. His interpretation of the *mantras* was entirely idiosyncratic, for he found in them one supreme God only, as well as the doctrines of karma and *samsara.* Equally inventive was his notion of what was not in the *mantras,* and that included any connection with the performance of sacrifices. The Arya Samaj that Dayananda founded in 1875 was for decades centered in another regional base, the Punjab, until it spread gradually through the Hindi-speaking north and became more successful than the Brahmo Samaj not only in geographical breadth but also in outreach to the several *varnas* as well. This new society became notorious, in fact, for investing untouchables with the sacred thread. Like the Brahmo Samaj, however, the Arya Samaj splintered into ineffectiveness over complicated issues of social reform and militant politics.

Quite different from these two reformers—each with an ideology intentionally undermining Puranic Hinduism in favor of a universal theism—were three other vigorous personalities—Ramakrishna, Vivekananda, and Aurobindo, founders of another pair of institutions still active in modern Hinduism in India and the West. Ramakrishna (1836–1886) was a Bengali Brahman temple priest and devotional mystic whose spiritual trek through Yoga, Tantrism, Vedanta, Vaishnava theism, Christianity, and Islam never took him far from the feminine power (*shakti*) he worshiped as the goddess Kali. His principal disciple was Vivekananda (1863–1902), founder of the Ramakrishna Mission and order of devotees who today are more in accord with the philosophy of Advaita Vedanta than of Ramakrishna's eclectic mysticism. An event that every Indian child assimilates with pride in school is the 1893 assembly of the World Parliament of Religions in Chicago where Vivekananda "astounded the West" by his discourses on Hinduism, then went on to establish the Vedanta societies of New York, San Francisco, and other cities. The Ramakrishna Mission is still an influential force in towns and cities throughout India, with a significant charitable and educational outreach in medical clinics, pharmacies, publishing houses, and forums in their *mathas* for religious discourse. The compelling combination of Ramakrishna, the visionary-saint, and Vivekananda, the missionary-orator, accomplished more for the Hindu self-image in the community of world religions than any other movement until Gandhi.

Aurobindo (1872–1950) was another visionary of self-realization and interior harmony, well traveled and educated, versed in the full range of Vedic and Sanskrit classics and, like Ramakrishna, experienced in Tantric Yoga and imbued with reliance on the divine *shakti*. His three-volume *The Life Divine* became a modern classic with its optimistic program of progression from primal matter to perfect being, consciousness, and bliss. He lived in the French colony of Pondicherry in South India for most of his adult life; his place of residence grew into an *ashram* for his disciples and eventually into an international center for spiritual transformation. Subsequent to his death the *ashram* and its acolyte institutions were led by Aurobindo's companion of thirty years, Mir Richard, a French woman known to devotees as the Mother. [See Christianity pp. 502–4, 510, Islam pp. 659–62, Buddhism pp. 942–52, Religions of China pp. 1004–5, 1009, 1033–34, 1056, and Religions of Japan p. 1102 for discussion of monasteries and monasticism.]

These modern voices—Ram Mohan Roy, Dayananda Sarasvati, Ramakrishna, Vivekananda, Aurobindo—as well as many others like them might be described as reforming traditionalists or traditional reformers. Many were Bengalis; most were educated in British academies and spoke and wrote in English. Each maintained his personal perspective about what is enduring in Hinduism and what components should be promoted or eliminated in the ongoing experience and expression of the faith. All of them spoke of "self-realization," and in that sense they identified common ground in both the *Upanishads* and the traditions of Yoga. Each had a sphere of influence in the shaping of contemporary Indian thought and yet, so remote and sheltered is life in the world of village India that few of their names and fewer of their ideas evoked much response in their day, and villagers of the next century may forget them altogether. [See Religions of Africa pp. 29, 55–57, Religions of Mesoamerica pp. 157, 164–68, Native Religions of North America pp. 266–67, Christianity pp. 495–97, 531–32, 534–35, Islam pp. 622–28, 698–99, Buddhism pp. 860, 861–68, 892–99, Religions of China pp. 993–95, and Religions of Japan pp. 1090, 1100, 1122–23, for discussion of religious founders.]

One name, face, and figure of twentieth-century India, however, is known to all, as indeed he is instantly recognized, as few humans are, throughout the world. Mohandas Karamchand Gandhi (1869–1948), the Mahatma or "Great Soul," a lawyer from a Vaishya family in western India, became one of the architects of Indian independence, a champion of *svaraj* (self-rule) through *satyagraha* (a grasping of the truth), of nonviolent resistance to evil and oppression. The *Bhagavad Gita* and its doctrine of detached action became his spiritual guide, and a life of simple self-sufficiency and chastity (*brahmacharya*) his well-publicized lifestyle. But even the powerful personality of Gandhi with his demonstrative *dharma* could not prevent the Hindu-Muslim mutual slaughter that accompanied independence and the 1947 partition of the subcontinent into the nation of India flanked by a divided Pakistan. Gandhi himself was murdered by a Hindu extremist. His program of nonviolence (**ahimsa**), simplicity, and economic self-sufficiency in a casteless society is but dimly remembered today, but the man himself has passed into sainthood. Any sizable Indian town boasts dozens of white- or silver-painted plaster statues and busts guarding its crossroads like gaunt ghosts, the Mahatma striding out with his wooden staff or just seated calmly in familiar pose surveying the traffic from under his godlike canopy of serpent hoods. Always freshly garlanded by some invisible hand, he now belongs to a mythic past, a time prior to the bloody partition of Mother India that wrecked his dream and well before today's mindless terrorism, communal strife, and population floods that threaten the well-being of all.

The half-century since independence has witnessed a different balancing act, the world's largest democracy attempting to maintain a secular state with freedom for religious pluralism. Minorities such as Muslims, Christians, Sikhs, Jainas, or Buddhists feel the pressure of conformity to the dominant Hindu faith in an environment that assumes the identity of "Indian" and "Hindu." For their part the majority Hindus feel threatened by a government that chips away at hallowed traditions, replacing the eternal *dharma* with constitutional laws pertaining to untouchability, polygamy, divorce, inheritance, property division, *sati* (widow burning), widow remarriage, dowries, and temple maintenance and revenue.

A common sight in every part of India is a crossroads statue of Mahatma Gandhi, staff in hand, guarded by Lord Vishnu's multiheaded cobra.

Finally, it should be noted that the modern period also witnessed the largest expansion of Hinduism outside Asia. Unlike Buddhism, which originated in India but began its spread throughout the rest of Asia within its first few centuries, Hinduism proved to be a stay-at-home faith until the medieval trading colonies were established in Southeast Asia. In the nineteenth and twentieth centuries, however, millions of Indians migrated throughout the world, as colonies of indentured laborers, merchants, physicians, engineers, and teachers creating new communities in England, Canada, the United States, the West Indies and South America, South and East Africa, Southeast Asia, and Pacific islands such as Fiji. These migrations continued in the 1970s and 1980s with burgeoning Hindu populations in several Persian Gulf states. Although Brahmans and a normal range of castes were frequently absent from new Hindu enclaves abroad, certain essentials of faith and practice remained intact. Recent temple-building activities in several second- and third-generation Hindu communities in the West are a sign of current vitality.

A separate aspect of Hinduism in the West is the development of communities and institutions ranging from the Vedanta Societies in the early twentieth century to the movements of the 1960s and 1970s, such as the International Society for Krishna Consciousness (Hare Krishna Movement), Transcendental Meditation, the *ashram* of Rajnish, Swami Rama, Meher Baba, the Divine Light Mission, and others. [See Religions of Africa pp. 25, 54–57, 79–82, Religions of Mesoamerica p. 240, Native Religions of North America pp. 287, 320–22, 357–58, Judaism pp. 427–31, 456–75, Christianity pp. 529–33, Islam pp. 698–700, Buddhism pp. 952–56, 998–1002, Religions of China pp. 1055–59, and Religions of Japan pp. 1132–33, 1163–72 for discussion of new religious movements.]

We will return to contemporary Hinduism in chapter 34. In sum, the period of the last two and a half centuries has been an era of momentous change for Hinduism as it has been for every long-lived religious, philosophical, or political system in modern global history. Hinduism as a multicultural and multiregional amalgam of traditions has been forced into a juggling act in order to keep its modernizing pan-Indian (and now worldwide) audience involved. Festival calendars; temple rituals; pilgrimage schedules; individual meditations and vows; competing Vedic, epic, Puranic, and philosophical textual traditions; *mathas; sadhus;* and myths must all somehow keep circulating in the air at once if Hinduism as it has been defined for the past two millennia is to continue intact into the twenty-first century.

32

Dimensions in a Worldview

IN THE PRECEDING BRIEF SKETCH of Hinduism and the history of South Asia many details were omitted and some complex movements and traditions, many centuries in the making, were condensed to a few words of passing description. To provide a fuller treatment, this chapter will examine some of the "stuff" of Hinduism—deities, myths, texts, doctrines, rituals, sects, personalities, symbols —from the perspective of worldview, that is, a particular way of looking at and thinking about the world of human experience. Since Hinduism is rich enough in expression to afford multiple perspectives, not incompatible but interactive ones, there is opportunity to identify and explore in this chapter five different dimensions within this single worldview. In fact, Hinduism is so diverse that it may be seen as a multidimensional tradition not easily reduced to a simple code or neat system, but one that nevertheless constitutes a living whole. The term *dimension* suggests a particular extent of the tradition through the historical periods just surveyed, a range that has established enduring and essential aspects of the faith. Each of these dimensions is intrinsically Hindu, and each is dependent upon the others for its viability and coherence. Listening to the universe, mythologizing the universe, classifying the universe, recycling the universe, swallowing the universe—these are five modes of expression and therefore five zones of exploration in which to consider revelation and recep- tivity; myth and the significance of gods, goddesses, God, and assorted powers; being, order, function, and notions of transcendence; ritual and sacrifice; and finally, soteriology or the meaning of salvation. Throughout this fivefold discus- sion we should recognize that the diversity of Hinduism revealed in these dimensions finally gives way to coherence within a single, integrated worldview.

Listening to the Universe

There are two Absolutes, Sound and Silence . . . Inundated by the Absolute- that-is-Sound, one arrives in the Absolute-that-is-Silence. (*Maitrayaniya Upani- shad* 6.22)

If one knows when and where to be, the chanting of the *Vedas* may be heard daily in certain major temples, at the sites of great festivals, in Vedic schools, or in Brahman hamlets scattered about India. Brahmans who specialize in different *Vedas* and styles of recitation chant what they have laboriously committed to memory, one line at a time, for some eight to twenty years. Sometimes the recitant is part of a temple staff and chants to please the god during daily service. But often these Vedic Brahmans have little or nothing to do with the daily temple functions for the resident deity; they are employed by temple authorities to recite, usually between 7 and 11 A.M., simply because the *Vedas* should be heard in such sacred spaces.

The essential components of the *Vedas* are the *mantras,* timeless sounds believed to be universal and eternal. Human agents, the Brahmans, both perpetuate the *mantras* and enable others to tune in to the universe. Through them others can somehow apprehend the knowledge whose essence is *brahman,* the sacred utterance. Vedic *mantras* were and are believed to have the power to transform those who place faith in them. Since their power is cosmic they can in fact transform all the phenomena of the world. In a phrase familiar in every language of India, profound changes occur "by means of the *mantra."*

However, as we have already noted, more than two thousand years ago the great textual tradition of the *Vedas* began to give way to *smriti*—the *Shastras,* epics, *Puranas, Tantras,* and other texts of classical Hinduism. At the same time the great Vedic sacrifices became less important than temple and household **puja,** the worship of deities in a non-Vedic mode. Nevertheless, a sensitivity to the powers of sacred sound remains today among the most precious assets of living Hinduism. This is reflected in the continued priority of an oral over a written tradition and a reliance upon the power of *mantras*—even Tantric *mantras* and epic or Puranic verses (*shlokas*) drawn from post-Vedic sources.

➤ During the transition from *Veda* to *smriti* the philosophers of the *Upanishads* sought to identify links between universal sound—the sacred utterance declared to be *brahman*—and the silence beyond in the realm of the unmanifest where change and distortion have no place. Such cosmic connections, they said, are revealed to one who knows. Without conscious reflection, Hindus today still express, in both individual and collective life, a variety of ways of realizing these mysterious bonds.

For comparative illustration in a single scene we are invited on a time-lapse walk for three blocks down one lane of a small town. As we begin our stroll at dawn we hear the low voice of a Brahman who recites the Gayatri *mantra* (*Rigveda* 3.62.10) in a prayer to the sun seeking wisdom and inspiration as he sips water from his palm. Later he will repeat this daily personal ritual at the other "joint" of time, twilight, as day gives way to night. Across the street another man, a shopkeeper beginning his day, reads aloud from the *Ramayana,* his daily practice. He sits on a footstool to chant the sacred text from a handsome bound volume once owned by his grandfather, who taught him to read Sanskrit. On the floor beside him sits his wife, who spends this recitation hour listening and writing over and over the name of Rama in the tiniest possible letters, filling each day the pages of a school copybook until it is completely covered with God's holy name and may then be deposited prayerfully in his temple. In midblock are two small shrines, each five feet in height and lighted by a single, bare bulb. One houses a green painted Hanuman, the other a garish orange **Ganesha.** Both are the recipients of mumbled prayers throughout the day and evening as people from every caste and social level pause before them with clasped hands.

Ahead of us at the first corner is a billboard with an improbably fashionable woman smoking a cigarette and apparently reciting Sanskrit *shlokas.* As we pass the billboard, however, we discover behind it the office and tenor voice of a law-yer who is far more involved in reciting than in disturbing any of the dusty piles of legal papers scattered about his quarters. While the other early risers have been all but inaudible, this sonorous voice would appear to be known in every corner of heaven. He hails us good morning, identifies the text that was inter-rupted, and says cheerfully of the list of gods and goddesses in his litany, "They are *all* good medicines and I take them every day!"

Somewhere a devotee is blowing a conch shell, either to scatter evil spirits with the sound sacred to Lord Vishnu or to awaken a deity for morning worship. As the echo of the conch fades, the heavy beat of a drum is heard from a distant lane, signaling the passing of a funeral procession on its way to the burning-ground by the river. It is the beat of Lord Shiva's drum of destruction, the end of a single human body or the end of an era of cosmic time.

In late afternoon we pass a large, old house with a group of people seated in the inner court grouped about the family priest (*purohita*), who recites a portion of the *Garuda Purana.* A member of the household has died, and the familiar lines about the journeys of the soul beyond this world of *samsara* are welcome sounds in this house of death and impurity. The mourners have heard the text before but do not know Sanskrit, so when the Brahman finishes his reci-tation he explains in the local language.

At dusk we come to the second corner and the busy temple of Shiva where a heavy traffic of devotees, three-fourths of them women, is mobile through the narrow entry gate and down the long, open corridor to the inner shrines con-taining the **linga,** the generative phallus of Lord Shiva, and its flanking god-desses. Accompanying the crowd, we take on a barrage of sensations: wild, lamp-lighted colors set off against the dark corners and outer hallways; splash-ing water; sudden cold marble against bare feet; overpowering smells of freshly spilled coconut oil and milk; thousands of fresh flowers; smoking incense; and the constant clanging of brass bells of every size, rung by each devotee to alert the many gods and goddesses of her or his arrival for worship. The bells momen-tarily overcome the sound of shuffling feet in the pushing throng and the mur-mur of prayers, but they cannot compete with the voices of priests belting out *mantras* and *shlokas* from the tiny chambered shrines. These echoing sounds are the essence of *puja,* Vedic and post-Vedic verses in a blend of praise, devo-tion, and ritual attendance upon Lord Shiva, his neighboring goddesses, and all the many deities enshrined in the outer hallways. After prayerful attention to the three interior shrines the crowd is diffused in several directions according

Near the conclusion of a thirteen-day funeral the chief mourner holds the tail of a cow on behalf of his deceased father and listens carefully as the priest on his left recites verses describing the cow pulling his father across the terrible river Vaitarani that separates our world from the world of the departed. Another priest pours water from the Ganges.

to personal preference for continued devotions, each worshiper carrying away **prasada,** some portion of an offering now graced and transformed by the touch of a deity.

Small groups may be seen pressing toward any one of the thirty-odd acolyte shrines. One large shrine of Krishna and his consort Radha, here within the temple compound of Shiva, has a group of twenty-five women of all ages seated in an oval before it. They are reading aloud from the *Bhagavad Gita,* forcefully, rapidly, in a continuous presentation of the eighteen chapters. Young girls who have not yet learned the text sit among them, absorbing the mellifluous sounds of Sanskrit until they too may add their voices to the Song of Lord Krishna. As we leave the outer courtyard we see a large, pillared hall filling up with more than a hundred Brahmans and another hundred spectators, men on one side and women on the other, all gathering for a three-hour Vedic assembly to listen as learned pandits debate topics of revelation, sacrifice, *dharma,* merit and demerit, and the attainment of heaven. The pandits lace their speeches with *mantras* and *shlokas,* addressing the crowd with the assurance of those who well know the meaning of existence and the authority of the cosmos.

It is now after midnight on our time-lapse promenade, and all the people who rise before the sun have been in bed for hours. But the deserted street is lighted by a brilliantly sparkling Hanuman temple, and the night air is bombarded with music and singing. A dozen men sit on the floor with cymbals, drums, stringed and metallic instruments, and lusty voices shouting the night away in praise of Hanuman, recounting his heroic deeds on behalf of Rama and Sita.

It is morning again, Sunday morning, as we reach the last corner of our three-block promenade, where stands a comfortable house packed with neighbors and friends crowded in to sit on the floor beside the family members. Leaving their sandals outside the door they sit reverently facing a television set garlanded with fresh flowers, incense burning, bananas and coconuts offered before it, and a lamp waved as if in the face of a god. It is time for the *Ramayana* to be seen and heard, an episode in a year-long presentation that employs the newest medium for the continuation of an age-old sacred drama.

Our short walk enabled us to hear a few of the many sacred sounds of Hinduism. Listening to the universe, as well as passing on the sacred utterances, the infinite guises of *brahman,* is a powerful form of devotion, and we realize that *shruti* and *smriti, Veda* and *Purana,* are inextricably blended in the *brahman*-that-is-Sound. As we noted with the woman writing the name of Rama as she listened to his cycle of tales, the passing on may also employ visual media. In fact, Hindu *mantras* may be perpetuated in a variety of written, even iconographic forms. The Tantric tradition turned not only to esoteric sounds, mostly monosyllables, for its *mantras* but also elaborated ritual diagrams known as **mandalas** and **yantras** in which meditating devotees could immerse themselves as in a newly created universe. Even more common in Hinduism generally is the popular practice of writing *mantras* on tiny bits of paper to be inserted in silver tubes or inscribing them on small copper plates. The tubes or plates are then tied with a black thread around the neck, waist, or wrist of a child or adult, even at the throat of the household cow or buffalo, for protection against the evil eye, for curative purposes, or simply as an act of devotion. In talismans and amulets the oral *mantra* continues to exert its cosmic force, usually undergirded by the shamanic powers of the religious specialist who prescribes and ties it on, just as medical practitioners from traditional Ayurvedic physicians to village spirit-healers pronounce their *mantras* for therapeutic purposes. In their own simple, unassuming way these popular and widespread mantric techniques are accomplishing the transition declared by the philosopher-poet of the *Upanishads,* the passage from sound to silence.

Mythologizing the Universe

The gods entered man . . . all the gods are seated in him. (*Atharvaveda* 11.8)

Whenever one sits down to talk to people in the villages or small towns of South Asia or in the many pocket villages that try to ignore the burdens of civilization by hiding in the depths of every city, a story or two is usually forthcoming. If you are a newcomer you will need to be informed about the important events that happened on this spot to which you have journeyed. The story you hear may feature local gods and goddesses, bygone kings and heroes, power-hungry demons, weird ascetics and the beautiful women who tempted them. Everyone loves a story, particularly an old one, and *Puranas,* literally "old stories," are the fabric of Hinduism. It is usually difficult to separate a local tale with local characters from the vast corpus of Sanskrit *Puranas.* For a far-fetched parallel we must imagine dropping into an Israeli kibbutz today and hearing an old resident narrate the story of "the king's fiery furnace and Shadrach, Meshach, and Abednego, who lived in this kibbutz long ago when our ancestors were hassled by corrupt rulers." Yes, that's from the Book of Daniel in the Hebrew Bible, we say, but the narrator contradicts, "No, that's another story, not our story!"

There were, of course, "old stories," myths, legends, and folktales, already at the time when the *Vedas* were compiled. Their narrative force was diminished by the all-absorbing sacrifice, the attention given to compiling gigantic manuals for ritual performances and treatises probing into the meanings of sacrifice. But the good stories were never forgotten. In such great sacrifices as the royal horse sacrifice, the *ashvamedha,* an entire year of storytelling was demanded of the bards and singers who never failed to notice all the ways in which their king matched or exceeded the virtues and deeds of all the famous kings and heroes of past ages. It was no doubt many of these recitals, and others like them circulating in ancient India, that surfaced in the compilations of the two great Sanskrit epics and the major *Puranas* that were to become Hinduism's treasure house of mythology.

It is revealing that the Vedic Brahmans who recite professionally the *Vedas* today tell lots of good stories, but almost always they are from one of the *Puranas* and usually concern their special heroes, one might even say their divine prototypes, the *rishis.* These learned Brahmans—and people in every class, caste, and stratum of Hindu society, literate or illiterate—are at home in the same universe, and that universe is thoroughly mythologized, loaded with old yet living stories.

It is the deities and demons who have long occupied center stage in Hindu mythology. The *Rigveda* and *Atharvaveda* describe on several occasions the number of gods as 33, distributed among the three levels of the universe. At the other end of the Vedic textual tradition, a passage in one of the *Upanishads* accounts for 33 or 303 or 3,003 gods, although the poet-theologian manipulates a clever dialogue to establish that there is in reality only one. As for the demons, the **asuras** who are presented in Hindu mythology as adversaries of the gods, these were in origin of the same order of being as the gods. A confrontation of cosmic proportions and significance between gods and demons, creation and chaos, order and disorder, righteousness and unrighteousness—in other words all that makes up the world of *dharma* against the world of *adharma*—is demonstrable in the mythology of South Asia, as it is in other Indo-European–speaking areas, and it remains vivid in every phase of South Asian religious history from the Vedic to the epic and Puranic periods. That gods and epic heroes can be miscreant, treacherous, even morally reprehensible, while the demons can at times be powerfully attractive, even serving as divine models for human devotees (Ravana, for example, the demon of the epic *Ramayana,* is a devout worshiper of Shiva), is one of the many intriguing features of Hindu mythology.

In the period of the late *Upanishads* and early epic poems, the Vedic deities who had once dominated spiritual life in ancient India—Indra, Agni, Varuna, the Ashvins, and the others—were being upstaged by just two of their number, Vishnu and Rudra-Shiva, each one of whom in time became a complex pantheon, an umbrella godhead for dozens of regional deities and cults. But the old gods did not disappear; they slipped into the background of myths, iconographies, and liturgies. Even today one finds sculptures of the ancient **lokapalas**— guardian deities at the eight compass points of the world (**loka**)—protecting temples from their rooftop posts, although the priests, when asked, may not always be certain which is Soma, Yama, Vayu, or Agni. **Brahma,** the successor of Vedic Purusha-Prajapati, is remembered in countless myths as the grandfather of the gods, a kind of elder statesman among them, although one with but a single important temple active today in the whole of India. Varuna still is invoked on occasion for relief from drought, and the Ashvins for certain personal ailments, but scarce is the memory that one was once king of the gods and the twins were a first recourse in times of distress.

The sharper focus of Hindu mythology stays, as we have seen in the preceding chapter, with Vishnu and his *avataras* (Krishna, Rama, and Narasimha in particular); with Shiva, the classical Hindu extension of Vedic Rudra; and with the many goddesses visible either as independent powers or as loyal wives of the male deities. When considering these three sets of divine manifestations centered on Vishnu, Shiva, and **Devi** (one generic name for the goddess in her multiple presences), we should not construe them as disconnected religious communities or allegiances, as for example, in the distinction between Christians who are Greek Orthodox, Roman Catholic, and Seventh-Day Adventists. It is true that a *"shaiva"* worshiper pays particular attention to Shiva, a *"vaishnava"* is a devotee of one or another aspect of Vishnu (such as Krishna or Rama), and a *"shakta"* acknowledges *shakti,* feminine cosmic energy, as the motivation of the cosmos. But each pays attention to other major deities in festivals and special occasions if not also in daily prayers and rituals, and a great many Hindus express strong devotional allegiance across vaguely sectarian lines.

The very success of Vishnu, Shiva, and several powerful goddesses in Hinduism of the last fifteen to twenty centuries calls for comment. These options for the devotion of hundreds of millions of people are no arbitrary array. Instead they represent basic stirrings in the late Vedic period that coalesced in the epic and Puranic eras as tendencies to experiment with every dimension of spiritual, mental, and physiological experience, to redirect Vedic authority and institutions, and to reconceive the meaning of sacrifice and of human action in every respect. Above all, as a corrective to centuries of preoccupation with knowledge of the sacrifice as world-maintaining performance, there came into prominence a set of fundamental recognitions: This world is the realm of *samsara* or bondage to the cycle of existences; beyond this world is the state of *moksha,* release or liberation from bonds to *samsara;* though gods and God exist in the transcendent, unmanifest, unconditioned realm beyond *samsara,* they are nonetheless active *in samsara;* and the paramount means of obtaining the freedom that is *moksha* is devotion to those deities capable of rescuing the faithful.

One who seeks Krishna, who celebrates his childhood exploits, heroic battles to ward off demons and catastrophes, romantic escapades with adoring

gopis (milkmaids), or mystical union with Radha, his chosen one, is able to enter and relive the life cycle of Krishna through worship and meditation. And one who recounts the deeds of the ideal warrior king and hero, Rama, whose rule remains to this day the paradigm of the kingdom of righteousness and truth, participates in the mythology of another great manifestation of the same god. As Rama is the presence of Vishnu in this world, so is his wife, Sita, the feminine ideal of beauty, loyalty, and chastity, a projection of the goddess Lakshmi into this life. And again, one who sees transcendent power in Shiva, patron of wandering ascetics and *sadhus,* employer of both passion and renunciation, lord of the cremation-ground, and one whose body is smeared with ashes of the dead, is able to reconcile in the dynamic character of one deity the ambiguities and polarities of transient human as well as transient cosmic life. And the Tantric devotee who sings ecstatically his praise of the goddess and ritually elevates himself to the status of the hero, like Shiva, able to unite with her, is still another who lives out the myths and symbols spoken in a thousand ways throughout the subcontinent.

Hindu mythology is so densely forested with deities and assorted powers and so singularly lacking in discrimination about who is an age-old standby and who is a recent upstart that one comes to a simple recognition that all of these deities and powers are available to anyone who wants one. An Indian anthropologist has reported from southwest India a conversation as amusingly honest as it is revealing about the changing emotional relationships between devotees and deities. Some elders had gone to the oldest temple in their village to ask

Ten-armed Durga, riding her lion mount, grasps the hair of the demon king Mahisha and thrusts her spear into his side (Durgapuja festival in Banaras).

the resident deity, Basava, the bull, about possibilities for rain in their drought-stricken area. Sandalwood paste, wet flowers, and bilva leaves (sacred to Shiva, whose mount is the bull) had been stuck all over the face and neck of a stone image of the reclining Basava. The elders anticipated the bull's response to their queries in a form of divination, a flower or leaf falling as a sign from the right side of his body as a "yes," from the left side as a "no." One elder stood up and addressed the deity:

> "You are famous. . . . Do you wish to retain your reputation or not? Please give us a flower. We have not performed your feast because of lack of water. . . . It has rained all around us [in the other villages]. Why has it not rained here? Tell us if you are angry. Why should you be angry with us? We have seen to it that you do not lack anything."
>
> A second elder contributed: "Give us your order, why do you torture us? Give it early."
>
> The first elder, now irritated, continued: "Give us a flower on the left side if you so wish. Why do you sit still? Are you a lump of stone or a deity?"
>
> Someone chimed in: "He is only a lump of stone; otherwise, he would have answered."
>
> The first elder remonstrated, "We will say that there is no god in the temple and that you have left the village."
>
> Someone else took a different line: "We are not entirely dependent upon you. On June tenth, canal water will be released by the government. . . . Even if it does not rain, we won't starve. . . . So give us a flower."

Later the anthropologist asked the villagers whether if it rained that evening (after the deity's silence), they would conclude that Basava had given the rain. They said "no." The anthropologist then asked the elders what the next step was. They said they would visit the temple on the next morning to ask for a stale flower. The priest would stand outside the door and wave lighted camphor before the deity, and everyone would wait for a flower to fall. If no flower came down then it meant that the deity had left the village.[6]

There is no doubt that the villagers believed that this deity, like all supernatural powers, could come and go in his own good time. Fields of force in this world are never stable. And in the shifting realms of multiform powers not even the line between the divine and the demonic is secure: In many of the languages of India the same word is employed for deity and demon. Nevertheless, certain figures do stand out from the crowd, as we have seen. Every village has its special deities, like Basava in the account just noted. These might be local goddesses, guardian deities, or former heroes, saints, and holy persons. Within a caste or clan there may also be gods or goddesses shared by all in the kinship group, often over an area embracing several villages, towns, or cities. Families also may consider one or another deity their special concern. Finally, at the individual level there is the particular or chosen deity, the **ishtadevata,** one among all the gods and powers with whom a spiritual bond is established, perhaps as the result of a vow or some occurrence in the vicinity of a shrine or temple of this deity. In the preceding segment, "Listening to the Universe," we noted that devotees in the Shiva temple paid attention first to the *linga* of this great god, then to personally preferred deities, perhaps those who had granted specific favors on earlier occasions, either to the devotee or someone known to her or him. In the next chapter we will observe further some of these devotional links between an individual, a family, a caste, a village, and a particular deity.

A large part of day-to-day Hindu faith and practice is spent enlisting the aid of available powers, for example, such helping or protective deities as Ganesha, Hanuman, Lakshmi, Narasimha, or Durga. Less frequently, and perhaps only through the mediation or guidance of a specialist entrusted with ominous spiritual enterprises, would there be invocations of their dangerous, often uncontrollable and malevolent counterparts, for example, the goddess Kali of the cremation- or burial-ground. But aside from pan-Indian or regional gods and goddesses, Hinduism has profound concerns for other personal powers active in a thoroughly mythologized universe, and these must not be neglected in our overview. Among them are the vaguely departed but still powerful dead, a host of amorphous demons and evil spirits, and visible or invisible celestial bodies. These too make up the everyday world of Hindu experience: ancestors, demons, and the inescapable planets.

Taking a cue from one of the earliest Vedic texts, the *Laws of Manu* remind all twice-born Hindus that they have three debts to pay in this life: Study of the *Vedas* removes the debt to the *rishis,* performing sacrifices takes care of the debt to the gods, and having sons satisfies the ancestors, the collective "Fathers," as they are known in Sanskrit. This third debt illustrates an outstanding feature of virtually all traditional societies, the powerful links, continuities, even symbiotic exchanges between the living and the dead, who are known to exist in more or less vaguely connected realms of the same universe.

Hinduism has not only vivid funerary rituals and symbols but also one of the most elaborate traditions of rituals for ancestors known to the history of religions. Those advanced into other realms from which they will later be reborn (until eventual liberation from *samsara,* the round of births and deaths) are dependent upon the living for offerings of *mantras,* food, and water. In turn, these "Fathers," including female ancestors, look out for the needs of the living. Precisely because of great detail in these ancient, still universal ceremonies, there is widespread popular concern over their absence or erroneous performance, since a troublesome spirit or ghost, possessing and otherwise interfering with the living, is the expected result if the deceased is not properly promoted and satisfied. Particularly liable to haunt the living and make special demands are all those who have died "untimely" deaths because of accidents, murders, snakebites, or other unnatural causes. Cremation- and burial-grounds, banyan trees, and other haunted places are therefore dangerous to the unwary; and the crow, who alone is able to see the formless ones, is a bird of signs and portents.

The hungry, often angry dead are not the only class of powers that threaten the living and stir caution into day-to-day existence. In fact they blend into hosts of baleful creatures that hang about the village borders, crossroads, hills, rivers, ponds, and forest tracts. In modern as in ancient India they go by many

names and have almost unnumbered regional guises. Everyone knows about
the night-prowling **rakshasas,** the corpse-eating **pishachas,** the mysterious
nagas who are sometimes benevolent, sometimes deadly serpent spirits, and
the fearsome haglike demoness with her feet turned backward who comes to
steal away a child from the village. Humans require divine protection from
things that go bump in the night, which is why every village has its guardian
deity and every hamlet or city block has a Hanuman standing by with a trusty
club at his side. One of the favored tales of the *Puranas* is stated iconographically
in sculptures, paintings, and household lithographs as a seated figure with a
limp body draped across its lap, looking from a distance like a *pietá* scene of the
sorrowful Mary and lifeless son. On closer inspection it is the fierce lion-headed
Narasimha tearing out the guts of the helpless demon Hiranyakashipu, who
once threatened his own son, **Prahlada,** for worshiping Vishnu. Such is the fate
of a terrible demon, declares the icon, when he endangers the life of a true devotee of God. And such is the nature of a demon, the icon also states, that like Prahlada his good side may triumph over evil.

➤ In another appeal to available powers, virtually everyone in India today—
Hindu, Muslim, Christian, Jaina, Parsi, or even that rare new breed, the agnostic
—is directly and articulately concerned with his or her relationship to the planets and their influences upon life experience. This is a matter of long tradition
in the subcontinent. Offerings to the twenty-seven constellations in the lunar
path are documented in the early Vedic period, and recognition of the important
group of "nine planets," the **navagrahas,** is also ancient. Two of the nine planets,
Rahu and Ketu, exist only in the realm of Hindu mythology, for they are connected with lunar phases and eclipses of both the moon and the sun. The
others—the sun, moon, and five visible planets (a septad that provides, as it does
for the Western calendar, the names of the days of the week)—are strongly
mythologized, their personal influence a matter of belief quite apart from their
actual appearance in the heavens. (This point also is shared with folklore and
astrology in the West: Most of the readers of this page know the "signs" in the
zodiac, but few could locate them among the stars.) An example of the powerful
hold that planets exert upon people is a pan-Indian belief in Shani, the sinister
and malevolent planet Saturn. Almost every Hindu has at some point in life
blamed the influence of Shani for specific failures, whether minor ones such as
flunking an exam or missing a raise in pay, or such major traumas as loss of a
child, a business, or sound health. And therefore virtually everyone has found
time to make offerings in a shrine of the nine planets, whose images stand in
a strange cluster, none facing any other, inside the compounds of temples.

One of the last of the Vedic texts, a handbook of directions for domestic
rituals, concludes with a cautious reference to the nine planets: "Being revered,
they revere us, but if ignored they torment us," a phrase that might be employed
for *all* the named and unnamed supernatural powers of Hinduism, including
most of the major deities. A person today, just like a person in India two or
three thousand years ago, steps carefully into this shape-changing world, paying due respect, even worship including material offerings with prayers and

mantras, to the major and minor expressions of mystery, power, and the sacred. The prayerful hope is that malign powers will stand aside or be thwarted and that benevolent beings—those who reward and protect—will not abandon the village, or one's person. As the *Atharvaveda* stated long ago, the gods are all in man—or so they should be.

Classifying the Universe

> Goodness, passion, inertia:
> the three qualities found in material nature
> bind the changeless self in the body.
> Transcending these three qualities . . .
> the self, freed from birth and death,
> old age and sorrow, attains immortality.
> (*Bhagavad Gita* 14.5, 20)

Before they retire at night or in the early morning darkness, millions of women throughout India may be seen barefoot before their houses, bent over dampened earth or pavement, creating intricate designs of white rice or lime powder. This daily feminine artistry provides order of the space that gives access to the family living quarters and protection of the threshold with an auspicious pattern. It is a symbolic, and therefore largely unconscious means of keeping back the "outside," the inauspicious, the impure. The designs at the borders of space are particularly important and increasingly more elaborate in the month of the winter solstice, at the borders of time as the waning half-year gives birth to the strengthening one. Nowadays mothers and daughters frequently study booklets containing designs favored in other regions of India and compete along their lanes and streets for the most spectacular continuous line drawings. These ritual diagrams are but a single example of the many ways in which Hindus organize the world of space, of time, and of all the subtle nuances of human experience.

Where space, time, and the quality of being itself are concerned the auspicious and inauspicious, male and female, inside and outside, pure and impure, hot and cool, bright and dark may all be seen as categories within a larger process of classification. Every *thing* in the universe has its niche in the great scheme of *things;* it belongs to a kind of being, separate from all other kinds of being, with certain qualities, knowable relationships, and a defined place in the hierarchy, above, equal to, or below any other specific thing.

What are the marks of this attempt to classify the universe? They are too numerous and complex to document here, but one momentous expression, older than the *Vedas,* has already been noted. That is a threefold hierarchy of functions—priestly, warrior, productive—evidently belonging to a Proto–Indo-European legacy refined over many centuries by Indo-Iranian nomadic pastoralists and then carried into South Asia with those who produced the Vedic tradition. This archaic principle of ordering established a determinative worldview for India: the eternal *Vedas,* created universe, ranks of gods, ritual fires,

A daughter of the household creates an auspicious design of circular green parrots at the front gate. The New Year is just beginning as she finishes.

classes of humans, even humors within the human body, are all tripartite and hierarchic according to function. Any one of these phenomena presents itself as a unity divisible into three hierarchic but interactive constituents, that is, one supreme, one relatively devalued or even debased, and a third in mediation, active midway between the high and the low of this triadic unity.

The most famous example of this worldview is the hymn to Purusha in the tenth book of the *Rigveda* discussed in chapter 30. Purusha established the world as we know it in a definitive, cosmogonic act of self-sacrifice by projecting the dismembered parts of his person into hierarchical being. Among the parts of the world derived from this creative self-murder is human society, imagined with its classes ranked literally from head to toe as the body of God.

The quotation at the head of this segment is a continuation of this belief in the world as triadic unity. It is part of a well-known teaching of divine Krishna to the warrior hero Arjuna, one known as the *Bhagavad Gita* or Song of the Lord (Vishnu manifest as Krishna), found in the sixth book of the *Mahabharata*. Recited here is the important concept of three *gunas,* literally "threads" or "strands" of matter—constituents or qualities woven together to represent the material world. Instead of the *yin/yang* duality discussed in ancient China, a triad of qualities was perceived as "natural" by the philosophers of India: *sattva,* goodness, brightness, intelligence; *rajas,* activity, passion, transformation; and *tamas,* darkness, inertia, dullness. The point of Krishna's teaching is direct: These *gunas* that bind the embodied self in various combinations are all subject to change, even such apparently terminal changes feared by Arjuna and others on the battlefield, the destruction of human lives in warfare. But there is something other than these three *gunas,* beyond them, unaffected by "time" and

impervious to "killing." That which Arjuna—the Indian Everyman of this sermon—must discover is the eternal *atman,* the Self identical with infinite spirit
that cannot be killed.

Here the Sanskrit poetry of the *Bhagavad Gita* reflects not only the deep heritage of Vedic ritual and speculation, including the Upanishadic *atman-brahman*
correspondence, but also the gradually maturing legacy of certain schools of
philosophers that blossomed in the first four centuries C.E. The classical systems of Vedanta, Samkhya, and Yoga actively debated metaphysics, for example,
in the relationship between the world of three *gunas,* that is, nature, **prakriti,**
and that which is immaterial, namely spirit or consciousness, **purusha.** Samkhya and Yoga also debated the question of a personal being or "Lord" beyond
both nature and consciousness.

Appearing in the same period as the *Gita* and the developing philosophical
systems was a post-Vedic medical tradition. The texts of Charaka, Sushruta, and
earlier writers at the close of the first millennium B.C.E. noted that the human
body had three interactive humors, *doshas;* this triad essentially related to the
hierarchic *gunas,* as well as three ranked cosmic elements: wind/air, bile/fire,
and phlegm/water. This ancient tradition of medicine—Ayurveda, the *Veda* of
longevity—is still practiced widely today throughout the subcontinent. It recognizes a healthy body as one with the three humors in balance, an unhealthy
body as one reflecting imbalance. The task of this traditional medicine, and
therefore of every physician, is to correct by therapy, pharmacy, diet, and advice
on well-being any apparent dysfunction or disharmony among these three entities. The physician focuses upon the immediate realm of qualities, humors, and
changes, with an eye toward a healthy "long" life in this world of *samsara.* But
always there is the hint of something more. Alongside details of the gross symp-
toms of disease there is mention of transcendence, immutability, immortality,
something beyond the constant changes of the three humors, attainable perhaps
by *soma,* the ultimate pharmaceutical, or perhaps by special knowledge.

Thus the mind-set of Vedic Hinduism and the early philosophies of South
Asia was prone to see the world as triadic unity. But tripartition by no means
exhausted the desire to classify the universe. The number three was not the only
sacred number in the spiritual calculator, nor could we expect this from the
civilization that recognized 108 names of a god (not to mention 3,003 gods) and
invented the digit zero in its ancient science of mathematics. Many numbers
gained special status, and for many reasons. Certain integers stand out, and
many of these are susceptible to hierarchic analysis.

For example, four is significant in orientation symbolism, four quarters or
cardinal directions (east and west, north and south) appearing as primary components of space in the symbol systems of most world cultures. In South Asia
four is also three-plus-one, gained by the addition of a subordinate or a transcendent fourth to the hierarchic triad. Thus four *Vedas* or four human classes, to
take two prominent examples, are disclosed in the appendage of one that is both
different from and less important than the original and basic three. The threefold body of the cosmic person, Purusha, is completed by the addition of feet
meant to serve the upper triad of head, torso, thighs. From these feet, according

to the *Rigveda,* came the Shudra class meant to serve the three twice-born *varnas,* the Brahmans, Kshatriyas, and Vaishyas who were created respectively from the mouth, arms, and genitals of Purusha. Alternatively, a transcendent fourth is declared by superimposition of that which is above and beyond the original triad—*moksha,* for example. From the point of view of any individual in this triadic world, *moksha* deserves ultimate consideration and recognition as the designated fourth goal of human endeavor beyond *kama, artha,* and *dharma* (respectively, the pursuits of passion, wealth, and religious knowledge). Another example is the transcendent fourth stage (*ashrama*) of a lifebody beyond the *ashramas* of student, householder, and mendicant forest-dweller. In other words, one who has abandoned worldly goals transcends all three stages by taking a vow known as *samnyasa* and becoming a *samnyasin* (see table 7-4).

There are other important examples of this correspondence between the hierarchic design of the cosmos and a kind of spiritual hopscotch that is human progress. Every Vedic householder was responsible for maintaining three sacred fires that corresponded to earth (the circular domestic or preparatory fire), midspace (a semicircular defensive fire to the south), and heaven (a square fire for the essential daily offerings into the mouths of the gods). However, they are all summarized and transcended by Agni, the divine unmanifest Fire as cosmic totality. And today twice-born Hindus still make offerings to ancestors in the manner of the late Vedic era, that is, to a sequence of three generations of deceased plus a fourth assembly of remote ancestors who are envisioned now as gradually melding into the unmanifest from which they came and from which they will come again to birth and death.

Hinduism (and Indian thought in general) experiments endlessly with systems of classification. Instructive in this particular example is a lesson about the one and the many, transcendence as totality, and an Absolute discovered through perception of the twin efforts of projection and reintegration. From the unmanifest there is divulged a world—a world of qualities and experiences,

TABLE 7-4. *Examples of Subordinate and Transcendent Fourths in Vedic-Hindu Classifications.*

Worlds	The Vedas	Purusha	Varnas	Gunas	Life Goals	Ashramas
4	THE UNMANIFEST		Purusha	*atman*	*moksha*	*samnyasa*
3 Heaven	*Rigveda*	head/mouth	Brahmana	*sattva*	*dharma*	*vanaprastha*
2 Midspace	*Yajurveda*	torso/arms	Kshatriya	*rajas*	*artha*	*grihastha*
1 Earth	*Samaveda*	thighs/genitals	Vaishya	*tamas*	*kama*	*brahmacarya*
[4]	*Atharvaveda*	feet	Shudra			

ranked yet intertwined like the strands of a rope. The notion of a transcendent fourth points toward a collapse of the many and a return of tripartite creation to the primordial unity that preceded manifestation. Therefore even as the body of Purusha descended from the unmanifest as a result of the first sacrifice and the *Vedas* and *brahman*-as-sacred-utterance descended from silence, so is it possible for a created individual to ascend through careers of a self and the stages of a lifebody in *samsara* to the point of transcendence. Such a journey is a return to the unmanifest, the totality of being. Both the supreme identity declared in the *Upanishads*—that the individual *atman* is in reality *brahman*—and the later statement of *bhakti*—that the individual by devotion may become deity—are disclosed in this blueprint for cosmic and human experience.

All of this proceeds from the single illustration of the symbol of four as three-plus-one. In a similar manner classifications based on the numbers five and seven become powerful expressions in South Asian thought, that is, not only for Hinduism but also for Jainism, Buddhism, and most of the religions and philosophies that flourished on the subcontinent. The ritual reintegration of the cosmos in Vedic sacrifices focused upon a five-layered altar with its triadic skeleton and an *atman* as nucleus. This notion of a pentadic world body sacrificed to obtain a new and immutable body for the sacrificer (to which we will return in the next segment of this chapter) was to live on in the Upanishadic concept of five sheaths embracing the *atman* and in the important Buddhist concept of five aggregates or constituents presumed to make up an individual. The brace of cosmic elements also extended to five, namely, earth, air, fire, water, and space. Time was recognized as divisible into five seasons, gods became manifest in five successive emanations or faced in five directions, and so forth.

The extension of a triadic to a septadic symbol system was equally pervasive in Indian thought. Vaisheshika philosophy recognized not three but seven *gunas* intertwined in nature. Some Puranic cosmographies detailed seven levels in each of the three hierarchic strata of the universe and a plan of the cosmos with seven concentric continents separated by seven seas. Yoga perceived the human body as cosmos and therefore a replication of seven levels each with its point of reference, a "circle" or "lotus" as a milestone toward spiritual reintegration. Ayurveda enjoyed having it all ways: The human body is a single unit composed of three humors, five elements, five breaths, and seven substances.

Nowhere does the experimental nature of Hinduism become more apparent than in such numerological speculation. This symbolic process began with the Vedic doctrine of correspondences and an effort to connect and universalize by means of sacrifice, to regenerate every phenomenon until eventually the mysteries, the codes of creation and annihilation, could be broken and the devastating transformations of existence short-circuited. And this speculation continued with the post-Vedic philosophies, mythologies, sciences, and other symbol systems that reckoned, classified, and ranked the constituents of being and experience. The fact that both the created world and the human body undergo perpetual transformation and are simultaneously threefold, fivefold, and sevenfold poses no problem; that is no more astonishing than the fact that the two—cosmos and body—are ultimately one.

Thus we see in this third dimension explored by the Hindu tradition a recognition of enormous variations in the structure of the universe and a concomitant desire to understand and pigeonhole them. The original body of the cosmic person, Purusha, is variegated, head to toe. The world derived from his dismemberment must necessarily also be so arranged; and rank, function, order, and interdependence of members are basic facts of this world of planets, gods, humans, demons, animals, plants, and other kinds of being. The cosmos is ordered in ways accessible to the eye of faith, and knowledge of order, *dharma*, is essential for life in the world. Knowledge of the real self, *brahman-as-atman*, is essential for the ultimate task of summarizing and transcending the world, achieving the release from *samsara* known as *moksha*. A worldview that is forever classifying finally pinpoints synthesis and then transcendence in a category beyond all categories. "The self, freed from birth and death," according to Krishna, "attains immortality."

Recycling the Universe

... the sacrifice becomes the sacrificer's Self in the other world, and the sacrificer who knows this and sacrifices in redemption obtains a new body in the other world. (*Shatapatha Brahmana* 11.1.8.6)

No doubt the most striking feature of Indian *society* is the class and caste system with its hundreds of isolated yet interdependent *jatis* distributed hierarchically within and beneath the classical four *varnas*. But the first distinct impression made by Indian *thought* upon the mind of the outside observer concerns the concepts of karma and *samsara*. In this dimension—the notion of recycling the universe—we explore further these two linked concepts that became molded into doctrines in the middle of the first millennium B.C.E. and remained as the keystone of the South Asian worldview in every century down to the present.

The oral (eventually written) traditions that first clearly presented teachings on karma and *samsara* were, as noted in chapter 30, late Vedic ones, namely, the *Aranyakas* and *Upanishads*. They moved on the age-old theme of a sacrificially motivated universe, one that is perpetuated by the human work (karma) of *yajna*. But their authors' language was new, even radical, and their eyes were trained on a newly discovered prize unconsidered by early Vedic poets and ritualists. These new generations of poet-philosophers became a spiritual elite and vanguard of seekers of release from all births-and-deaths, not for final rebirth in the other world. What was their message and what effect did it have as Hinduism developed through successive periods of South Asian history? It is a fascinating story: The expression of "recycling" that the Upanishadic poets sought to escape has, like all things Indian, several versions.

First, we have already noted that the concepts of karma and *samsara* may be seen gradually evolving from the basic tenets of the Vedic worldview. Vedic faith presumed human responsibility for the ritual action (karma) of sacrifices that recycled cosmic energies and resulted simultaneously in continuous renewal of the world and personal regeneration of the sacrificers. An example was the famous kingship ceremony, the *rajasuya,* a great *soma* sacrifice that regenerated the principle of sovereignty and its personification on both cosmic and human scales. Order or *dharma* was directly dependent upon such renewal, and no sooner was this year-long royal consecration completed than preparations were begun to perform it all over again. The law of karma at that point was concise: Ritual work was incumbent upon human beings, and it obtained immediate and apparent cosmic, social, and individual results. For that reason the remnant Vedic Brahman communities today still perform sacrifices. If, to take but one example, there is too little or too much rain, human and world survival hang in the balance, and among all the karmani (plural of karma) an appropriate ritual action must and can be found that is restorative.

But little in the early Vedic worldview prepares us for recognition of two notions that conjoin by the sixth century B.C.E. First, karma takes on the meaning of all action—not just ritual effort—as causal and productive of results. Second, the notion of continuing and prosperous long life in this world is no longer a worthy goal but a dilemma from which escape must be sought, a bondage to be slipped not by knowledge of the mysteries of sacrifice but by insight into the nature of a real Self that transcends this pain-filled world.

This about-face of late Vedic ideology has called for explanation from historians of culture. Were indigenous peoples—whose ritual and symbol systems can be tracked as influential upon Indo-Aryan traditions early in the Vedic period—bearers of a concept of transmigration of the soul along with individual consequences of prior actions? Does a period of North Indian political, social, and economic turmoil harbor the secret of this shift from an optimistic worldview—in which an ideal life was "a hundred years and a hundred sons" and an ideal afterlife was more of the same—to a negative worldview—in which this life was defined as a burden of sorrow, a problem to be solved by a spiritual quest for release into something completely "other"?

There are no clear answers to these questions. What is obvious, however, is the lasting and commanding authority of an ideology of cycles, recycles, and earned escape from the bondage of time. Let us consider the power within this dimension by examining three motifs: the continuous sacrifice, deaths and rebirths for worlds and humans, and the eternal dance of the gods.

We begin with our previous theme of classifying the universe. The world and all its ordered categories of life are the result of a killing, the self-sacrifice of Purusha whose dismembered pieces were projected into hierarchical being and whose self-immolation became the exemplary action and destiny for all creatures who followed. The world (nature, life) itself is a temporary entity always proceeding toward its own destruction. Vedic religion was and is nothing less than a series of programmatic reintegrations and creative killings that remains continuous. Mysterious sacrifices perpetuate life as it must be in all of its diversity and multiplicity, torn limb by limb from an original unity. Systematic dismantling is not only a way of life, it is the explanation of life.

Classical post-Vedic Hinduism marks down ritual on the scale of Vedic sacrifice but it does not lose sight of the central problem: Both the world and the individual human lack permanence because they are created to die. Worlds, gods, demons, humans are all mutable: Only the discovered Self is without change. Does *samsara* apply to a "world"? It would appear so. The *Puranas* are always unfolding stories of the ages, the **yugas,** and we now live in the fourth and most wretched of ages, the Kali *yuga* (another subordinate fourth). When a world's fated time has run out, a pause will ensue and then repetition will occur "from the top," from perfection, proceeding once again down through the three hierarchic *yugas* until goodness and truth have run thin and another Kali *yuga* becomes enforced. From one point of view, therefore, world time and space are always degenerating, deteriorating, worsening. From another point of view there is "time out," a great time beyond the *yugas,* in which no thing is valued or devalued. Measurement can be only on the scale of the god Brahma himself (in the *Puranas'* mythic mode of semipersonalization) or on the scale of the inexhaustible unmanifest (to revert either to the *Upanishads'* impersonal *brahman* or the earlier sacrifice-being, Purusha-Prajapati). The time that is renewable and recyclable is the time of *samsara* for the cosmos or *samsara* for an individual lifebody in process.

But how can one make sense of *samsara* for the world? The *Puranas* do it quite well by opening up the mystery of "time" for mythic inspection. They display ridiculous quantities of time in myths so engaging that infinity and cyclicity seem not only plausible but entirely natural. In some *Puranas* a human year is but a day and a night for the gods; in others a day in the life of the god Brahma lasts for a thousand cycles of the four *yugas,* and his night is of equal duration. Since a sequence of four *yugas* lasts for 4,320,000 years, someone with an eye on the human calendar might calculate a day and a night for this geriatric deity to be 8,640,000,000 years. Brahma's relationship to the three worlds is equally fantastic, for his night is the time when an ocean overwhelms and destroys his creation, his day is the time of re-creation. In other metaphors the universe exists when he exhales or opens his eyes, and it is withdrawn when he inhales or blinks. Some *Puranas* employ Vishnu as creator and re-creator, Shiva as destroyer and redestroyer, with Brahma calmly balanced between, essentially above the process and yet actually the process itself. Whatever the version recited from the *Puranas,* the point is not lost on the devotee who listens: The world itself, like the body of Purusha endlessly collected and dismembered in the sacrifice, is a victim. And that is the glory and the peril for the human inhabitant who has yet to discover the Self that is *not* of this world.

Such accounts of astronomical time spans lead one to think of sameness in eternal recurrence. But repetition, recycling, does not always mean sameness. The ancient Vedic sacrificer (or his modern counterpart) sacrificed every day, that is, he offered milk into the household fire in the ritual known as *agnihotra* at dawn and twilight, at the joints of time as it were. Occasionally, however, he also performed extraordinary sacrifices, rituals that required as much as a year or two to complete. By the same token the modern Hindu may bathe every day in the river at Allahabad (formerly Prayaga, one of a triad of Hinduism's ancient sacred cities including Kashi [Banaras] and Gaya), where three great rivers are joined, namely the Ganga, Yamuna, and the invisible subterranean Sarasvati. But on a certain day he or she will be accompanied by a million others because of a particular joint in time, that is, a special astrological conjunction. Like the Vedic sacrificer who achieves exceptional status from performing a great *yajna,* this simple pilgrim of today is spiritually transformed in the presence of uniquely auspicious temporal and elemental mergers. Literally "things have come together" for the bather, as indeed for the sacrificer, and life can proceed with new momentum.

The modern cosmopolitan view of human existence declares on its best current evidence that we are mobile organisms on a spheroid spinning on its axis while it orbits a much larger spheroid that itself is a speck inside a vast gaseous mass traveling at vertiginous speed away from an unknown point in the cosmos. It is a story upon which few can focus for more than a couple of minutes at a time; we are, after all, busy being mobile organisms. Hindus have trouble focusing on *their* myths of *samsara* for the world or the individual: They too are preoccupied mobile units inside families, clans, castes, villages, and regions. It is common belief, however, that each lifebody is engaged in a long sequence of births-deaths-rebirths in this world. In the next chapter we have occasion to track an individual lifebody along a unique passage through a shared series of events in one episode between conception and death.

The notions of what happens between death and conception in another womb, however, call for discussion here, since they illustrate key articles of Hindu belief. Like birth/rebirth, death is a dangerous period of transition and therefore one of significant impurity for the entire family. One emergent from a womb enters this world like an immigrant; one who exits from a lifeless body is therefore like an emigrant off on a journey . . . once again. Classical texts attempting to capture this thought of a soul traveling from body to body employ such metaphors as a caterpillar crawling from leaf to leaf or a person changing old for new clothes. But it is ritual manuals that provide us with many intriguing details about the transitions and how they are accomplished. As in other traditional cultures, India reveals not only continuities between the living and the dead but also symbiotic duties, that is, mutually beneficial actions. It is the living who promote the deceased with food, water, and *mantras,* while the advancing ancestors look out for their descendants from the vantage points of their otherworldly station. And again, as in other traditional cultures, there is constant concern over proper procedures lest the deceased linger on as a **bhuta,** a troublesome, disgruntled ghost liable to possess people and disrupt their lives.

One who dies must be established ritually as an ancestor, a *pitr,* literally, a deified "Father," for such powerful status does not happen automatically with the loss of a body. Traditionally this requires ten days of rituals, representing, perhaps, like the ten days of rituals immediately after childbirth, the ten lunar months of developmental residence in the womb, growth and acclimatization in a new environment. One is not fully human at birth, one is not fully ancestral at death: In both cases ritual efforts are necessary to refine a being and eliminate its defects. Part by part a temporary and invisible body is fashioned in ten days, enabling the deceased spirit to cross over and join the safe company of preceding ancestors of the lineage. Frequently, shortened versions of these rites prevail, but in any case the ancestors—including this newly arrived member—require continued attention, particularly on new moon days and death anniversaries. That attention is primarily in the form of cooked rice ritually offered.

The sense that after three generations ancestors begin to dissolve into vaguer zones from which they are eventually reborn is present in the texts discussed today by priests and scholars. In the *Upanishads* two celestial paths for the dead were distinguished, one of the gods and another of the Fathers (ancestors). The former path leads by way of the moon to the world of *brahman,* the Absolute, and is for those who do not return to terrestrial births. The latter path, linked to a schedule of sacrifices, recycles beings to the world of rebirths. As noted, the *Chandogya Upanishad* describes the return journey by way of the moon back into earth in rain, growth as a plant that is soon eaten, and then rebirth from the womb of the eater, human or animal, according to the karma of the eaten. Even older texts such as the *Shatapatha Brahmana* related the mystical development of a cosmic self-body by meditative means and ascetic techniques (**tapas,** the practice of creative austerities), both as expressions of sacrifice. In this way mind, speech, breath, vision, hearing, action (karma), and fire are successively generated by knowledge. It is important to note that despite all the changes Hinduism has undergone in the past twenty-five or twenty-eight centuries since those texts were composed, the connection between human ritual activity and the recycling of the dead has never been broken.

But other concerns intersect with this ancient and still pervasive ritual one. For example, since the Vedic period the deceased is said to return to the elements in a reversal of creation, that is, the original projection of Purusha-Prajapati's body into cosmic being is turned about. Breath returns to wind, the eye to the sun, hair to the trees, and so on, the assumption being that after an interval the elements will once again be reassembled in the form of a human body. We are reminded that Prajapati is exhausted after his effort of creation, that the three worlds are exhausted each time the curtain comes down on the Kali *yuga;* it would seem that an individual self too has the right to be exhausted between births, between "actions." For the individual, karma is not dissolved but carried along to remain effective—even determinative—as long as existence in *samsara* is continued. The remarkable point is that from the time of the *Upanishads* Hinduism's stated target for the self is *moksha,* that termination of all future rebirths and location of the self on a path of the gods from which there is no return. And yet replenishment and reconstitution come in the form of food from the living in order to promote and recycle, not to liberate, those emigrant dead.

Here is one of the fundamental paradigm shifts of Hinduism. The ancient Vedic desire to "hold on" to the dead, the forefathers, as recorded in the citation at the head of this segment is a natural human one: A new, ritually created and therefore immutable body awaits the deceased in the other world. Continuing anxiety about "redeath" and dissolution of that self-body, however, reflects not a lack of faith in ritual action, but rather an uncertain belief in the efficacy of sacrifice *in the other world,* that is, the world of the Fathers. In the logic of karma as ritual work/action, recycling the dead for yet another chance would satisfy both the human need to keep one's Fathers and the ethical requirement to improve the Fathers' spiritual report cards, even to the point of divine graduation. And so an ambiguity that remains to this day was written into Hindu faith and practice in the middle of the first millennium B.C.E.: The living feed their forefathers as if they were gods in heaven in order to bring them back to earth as humans.

Another item on the agenda of this committee of the living and the dead has to do with debts to be paid. As we noted previously in the segment on mythology, it is believed that everyone enters the world carrying three debts, one to the *rishis,* to be paid off by reciting *mantras* (*Vedas*); a second to the gods, to be settled by offerings to them; and a third to the ancestors, to be reckoned by bearing children and thereby continuing the lineage. Those three are identified already in early Vedic texts. But throughout India today many Hindus wish to select their parents from the collective ancestors and assign to them a special payment, often in the form of a long pilgrimage to a sacred city such as Gaya or Nasik, where lengthy rituals may be performed on behalf of this recently departed pair.

A final point regarding this complicated journey of the emigrant, soon-to-be-immigrant dead is that of reward and punishment in other realms. Descriptions of heavens—such as Vishnu's, named Vaikuntha—and hells—the stratified Narakas—are famous in Hindu mythology, and the *Puranas* delight in lurid details, sometimes with more precision on the side of torment than bliss. The symbolic sacrifice-gift of a cow during postcremation rites, for example, has a precise purpose. The deceased's spirit may then grasp the tail of this beneficent creature as she swims across the dread river Vaitarani, a thick stream of pus, blood, and sweat into which the soul might otherwise descend in suffering because of past evil deeds (see photograph on page 778). The karma system of automatic retribution might appear to be a just and sufficient reading of the balance sheet of an individual's accumulated merit and demerit during each successive rebirth. But a series of temporary residences in situations of pleasure or pain becomes an added guarantee of attention to action on the part of the living, lest they too sink in the Vaitarani River with no cow's tail to the rescue.

There is another intriguing aspect of cyclicity revealed in the mythologies and iconographies of gods and goddesses who dance—Krishna, Ganesha, Virabhadra, Kali, and others. Like musicians, dancers keep time and expose the fluidity of past, present, and future. Nataraja, "Lord of the Dance," is an epithet of Shiva, and earlier we listened to the beat of a funerary drum that served as reminder of Shiva's cosmic dance of destruction. At his temple in Chidambaram in Tamil Nadu a multi-armed Shiva can be seen dancing on one foot within a ring of fire, his matted locks flying, the drum in his upper right hand balancing a flame of destruction in his upper left hand, a lower hand pointing toward his foot that has risen gracefully free of this world, and an opposite hand gesturing peacefully "fear not" to the worshiper. A devotee's eye cannot escape being drawn through this energetic symmetry to the serene and meditative face of the divine. The Lord's dance has been going on for eternity, according to a local

Purana concerning this temple, and is praised in the *Vedas*—although even they do not understand its significance. When the forest could not withstand the awful vibrations of his dance, Shiva continued to the beat of his drum within the great hall of Chidambaram. His mysterious "space *linga,*" also at the heart of this temple, is one of the five elemental Shiva *lingas*—earth, water, wind, fire, space—distributed in five famous temples of South India. Thus the "outsider" god became an "insider" where he may be worshiped in the invisible form of his powerful generative phallus and where he points the way to liberation from the world that his dance is even now destroying.

In many cases it is not the god alone who dances but a human possessed by the god. God-dancers, exorcists, or shamanlike healers can be possessed by Shiva, for example, or by one of his terrifying *avataras* such as Bhairava or Vira-bhadra, and dance ecstatically for many hours. In such cases channels are open to that otherness frequented by Shiva, including the realms of demons and ghosts of the untimely dead.

Another well-known dancer is Krishna, whose **lila** ("sport, play") with the cowherd girls (*gopis*) in the moonlit forests of Vrindavana by the Yamuna River is one of the most cherished episodes in all of South Asian literature. Celebrated by medieval poets, painters, sculptors, and musicians, this dance—a circular one, like time—is another world-abandoning one, although the Krishna *lila* is nuanced not with fire and destruction but by all the charming interplay of romantic love, even erotic detail, the bliss of union, sexual jealousy, and the anguish of separation. In the tenth book of the *Bhagavata Purana* the Sanskrit

Stacked here to conclude a hundred-day ritual for Nataraja (Shiva as Lord of the Dance) in his temple at Chidambaram, Tamil Nadu, are 2,016 clay pots. Half the pots are white, representing Shiva, and half are red, for his consort, the goddess Shivakamasundari. A hundred priests conduct fire sacrifices at nine surrounding altars. (Photo by John Loud.)

poet reveals the scene: Amorous *gopis* have forsaken their household duties, including their husbands and infants and, lured by the magic of Krishna's flute, have run off to the forest to seek him. To assuage the competitive jealousies of the *gopis,* Krishna extends his divine grace to these souls who have renounced *dharma* out of devotion to and desire for him and multiplies himself so that each may dance with the god in a great whirling circle of bliss.

This Gopala (cowherd) Krishna theme of the Sanskrit *Puranas,* the Sanskrit *Gita Govinda* (in which Krishna's favorite *gopi* is identified as Radha), and the vernacular poets of *bhakti* in nearly every region of India continues by means of the motif of *lila,* an important earlier article of faith. In the third chapter of the *Bhagavad Gita,* Krishna declares to Arjuna that he has nothing whatever to accomplish in the three worlds, nothing that he should attain. "And yet I continue to act," admits the god, so that "these worlds will not perish." In other words, Krishna's karma is like that of the Vedic sacrificer insofar as it is action that regenerates cosmic energies. But from the wider context of the *Bhagavad Gita* his counsel is clear: His action is a model for Arjuna and therefore all humans, for it is detached action, with no thought for personal rewards or the fruits of action. This is of course the meaning of play or sport, the *lila* that has no end in view, the dance in the moonlit forest that is freedom from the world of contingencies and the ordered, classified world of *dharma,* not to mention the continuous sacrifice.

And again, there is another dark dancer, the fearsome goddess Kali, black as night, her blood-red tongue lolling, the dismembered limbs of human victims jangling at her waist as she prances on the pallid, inert form of her consort Shiva. She is *shakti,* feminine cosmic energy, dancing another message, a lesson on the transient nature of everything and everyone, including even Mahadeva, the great god Shiva. Hers is the power of creation, and in the bowl of food she offers with one hand she proves that she is the Mother of all life. Raised in her other hand, however, is the bloody sword of decapitation, and there she discloses the incontestable brevity of life for all her creatures in this world.

Thus three dancers, varied as their choreographies and rhythms may be in myths, poems, and iconographies, perform on the same stage of world and human experience.

In the previous segment, "Classifying the Universe," we noted that one of the many ways of ordering experience that is meaningful to Hindus is the separation of that which is pure from all that is impure or polluted. The interplay of purity and pollution, like that of harmony and disharmony or projection and assimilation, is yet another example of the Hindu cyclical view. To the outside observer of the overpopulated Indian landscape many rivers are sewers choked with refuse, feces, industrial effluents, and not infrequently the corpses of animals and humans. To the Hindu insider every river is sacred and eternally pure, the element of incorruptible power in which one is cleansed inside and out by drinking from and bathing in this fluid goddess. How can this be when Hindus are so concerned with the pollution of bodily wastes, hair, animal skins, and everything reminiscent of death? The answer must lie somewhere in the profound recognition that cosmic energies and elements are renewable resources, that the universe is driven by perpetual regenerations, and that in the final analysis it is a process of necessary and repeated dying that mysteriously provides new being for the world, its elements, and its inhabitants of every species.

By tracking a fourth dimension in this chapter we have located another way in which Hinduism has been constantly innovative yet consistent with its earliest sense of direction. The sacrifice that provided "the first cosmic laws" is still in action and continuous. The cosmic dance of the god and goddess is still in action and continuous, "lest these worlds perish." And the births and deaths of each of us are still in action and continuous. We are in fact defined by our actions, all of them, until the final bonds of ignorance and attachment are broken and the sacrifice-dance of these worlds is absolutely of no consequence.

Swallowing the Universe

> The true yogi meditates, realizing
> . . . I am a stranger to this world,
> there is no one with me!
> Just as the spume and the waves
> are born of the ocean then melt back into it,
> so the world is born of me and melts back into me.
> (*Yoga Darshana Upanishad* 10.6)[7]

The cartoon stereotype of an Indian ascetic portrays an emaciated fellow in a loincloth lying flat out on a bed of spike nails. Occasionally at festivals or pilgrimages in the carnival-like atmosphere outside renowned temples, one may see this and other bizarre examples of self-mortification. The true ascetics of Hinduism, however, are not performers and claimants of small coins but large-scale explorers, dedicated and intrepid seekers, occasionally solitary, usually social, often pushing out the limits of human endurance in body, mind, and soul. Asceticism can take the form of the ordinary housewife who decides to fast for two days as a particular vow (**vrata**); a wandering mendicant who for decades walks from village to village as a holy man; or the *yogi*, practitioner of *yoga*, who works toward the cessation of normal thought processes by first altering normal respiration, blood pressure, diet, and other physiological routines, and then pursuing a program of **dhyana,** systematic meditation.

Paleontologists and marine biologists inform us about "minimal organisms" that dominated the fossil record of life on earth half a billion years ago and still exist today as tiny animals—brachiopods and stalked crinoids, for example—in the depths of the oceans. Their consumption of oxygen in relation to body weight is the smallest of all animals, and this low metabolic rate makes them the most efficient of organisms. If we were to imagine a model for the *yogi* we might suggest such minimal organisms who are in, but not of, this world, barely functional in the eye of busier, more ambitious creatures but destined nevertheless to survive the changes that signaled extinction for millions of species. The

*A Tantric yogi in red garments medi-
tates deep underground in a tomblike
shrine of the black goddess Kali.
Flanking her jeweled image are human
skulls and the wooden sandals of
former gurus on the Tantric path.*

brachiopod and the *yogi* are survivors because they have conquered the dangerous process of change; each has perfected a technique of absorbing an entire
world of change.

The *yogi* is an outward sign of a final dimension taken by Hindu tradition,
one demonstrated time and again over three millennia of myths, rituals, doctrines, and symbols until it has become one of the fundamental components of
the worldview. It is a reflection of the physiological and mental experimentation, spiritual audacity, profound intuition, stubborn courage—and even sporadic
humor and incredulity—that enabled certain movements in South Asia to promote and to realize in spirit so immodest a goal: the swallowing of the universe.

In a Vedic *soma-yajna* known as the *vajapeya*, the sacrificer swallows the
drink of strength (*soma*), places his foot on the sacrificial pole that connects the
three worlds, and in triumph announces "I have become immortal." Clearly,
spiritual modesty was not the medium of Vedic faith. Even a student of the
Vedas, proclaims the *Atharvaveda*, seizes the three worlds and brackets the seas,
repeatedly fashioning them. As knower of *Vedas* and as future sacrificer the student will transcend change by identifying the precise ritualized killing that
extinguishes imprecise dying. And the *Upanishads*, as we have seen, make a
quantum leap with a discovery that even the killing can be sacrificed, that is, forfeited. Indeed it must be given up, because the animal or *soma* sacrifice itself is
action that binds the sacrificer. The Upanishadic poet-philosopher locates the
ultimate liberating audacity: "Everything is *brahman, atman* is *brahman*, I am
brahman."

This aggressive spirituality of Vedic tradition was not limited to the sacrificer and his cohorts. There is an equally bold legacy of the heroic warrior, from mythologies of an intrepid Indra in the *Rigveda* to the militant energies of Kshatriyas, who taught the new Upanishadic mysteries to educated but unenlightened Brahmans. The notion of action as courageous, heroic physical force that defined the Indo-European warrior lived on in the Indian epics, classical and medieval. More important, it endowed South Asian spirituality at large with this enduring concept: Transformation occurs in the mediating, connecting midspace or midtime. That passionate midspace is the liminal realm not only of Indra, Arjuna, and other heroic warriors of mythic and epic fame, but also of the *avataras* who appear as saviors in times of human and cosmic crisis. Again, it is the territory of *rajas,* the connecting link in the triad of the *gunas.*

Midspace is thus the pause in the laborious process of creation, but also the pause in an equally stressful return journey, a process of reintegration that is world-and-self-destructive, but Self-locative. The "heroes" (*viras*) of Tantrism see themselves as bold warriors of the middle ground, between the trenches, as it were, of domesticity and bondage behind, transcendent unity still ahead. Examples of such mediation are found outside Hinduism as well. There are the *bodhisattvas* and *buddhas* of Mahayana Buddhism, those who postpone their earned *nirvana* and challenge *samsara* until it is defeated for all beings. And there are the *tirthankaras* or *jinas* of Jainism whose conquest of the self is one of cosmic proportions.

There were and still are many figures on this no-man's land, those who followed the beat of a different drummer: Long-haired ascetics who ride on the wind, go naked or clad in dirty red loincloths, and drink with Rudra a cup of "poison" are described in the *Rigveda.* Their traditions date at least from the late second millennium B.C.E. and could well be much older, but since they left us no texts, of such ascetics we know only what little the Vedic poets and ritualists cared to relate. Other communities such as the Vratyas, ancient bands of pastoral nomads known in the *Atharvaveda* for their special vows, sacrifices, sorcery, and prowess in ritualized warfare—all apparently at variance with the norms—may have generated certain legacies of ascetic techniques.

The middle of the first millennium B.C.E. brought greater visibility to ascetic traditions and linked them to concepts of renunciation already evident in Vedic articles of faith, for example, in the vows of the Vedic student, the *brahmacarin;* in the ritual consecration, **diksha,** undertaken by the sacrificer; and in the formula of *tyaga* or renunciation pronounced by the offerer who abandons to a deity the fruits or results of sacrifice. A common rubric for certain counter-Vedic communities of this period—the Ajivikas, Jainas, and Buddhists who rejected the authority of the *Vedas* and the *dharma* of class, caste, and sacrifice —is *shramana* movements. The *shramana* is a "striver," one who exerts himself or herself as a renunciant mendicant on the path to liberation from *samsara.* Early on these movements established monastic orders of monks and nuns. While the Buddhists emphasized a middle path between rigorous ascetic techniques and self-indulgence, the Jainas were steadfast adherents to progressively severe regimens of self-mortification (*tapas*) and maintained, even to the present day in its conservative sect, the vow of nudity for monks.

The *Upanishads* synthesized and to a certain extent institutionalized renunciation in the schedule of four *ashramas*. As we have noted, an ideal triadic program—student, householder, forest dweller—is capped by a transcendent fourth life-stage entered through the vows of renunciation taken by the *samnyasin*. In abandoning the three worlds the renunciant virtually swallows the three ritual fires, that is, interiorizes them and discontinues all prescribed external offerings. One who has taken *samnyasa*, a vow that ideally eliminates all the principles by which the world of *dharma* is classified, including class, caste, and ritual status, is transcendent yet still involved. That is a powerful but necessarily ambiguous model. The renunciant is one deserving of liberation but still living, and in that respect is a Hindu counterpart to the *bodhisattva* of Mahayana Buddhist tradition. Pointing toward a difficult but not impossible ideal, the role is there as a measuring stick; in practice there are few who embrace entirely the renunciant path. The *sadhu*, *yogi*, holy person, and realized saint all take their cue from this concept of liberation from *dharma* typified by the *samnyasin*. And all are burdened by the ambiguity of the Vedic sacrificer who "abandons" what is sought and the *samnyasin* who keeps what was abandoned. Still continuing today is the institutional process begun twenty-five centuries ago by the establishment of the third and fourth *ashramas* and by the counter-Vedic *shramana* movements. In 1987 a pan-Indian society of *sadhus* decided to publish a "national directory of eminent holymen of the country," thus assuring a continuing professionalization of such figures who presumably have renounced worldly professions.

Their expressions are manifold. In chapter 31 we have already seen two examples in Yoga and the *Tantras*. The *Bhagavad Gita* disparages the idea of asceticism but stamps with approval a special kind of renunciation. Inaction is not possible, says Krishna to Arjuna, with reference to asceticism, for a *yogi* in transic concentration, like a tortoise with limbs drawn inside its shell, is still an actor bound by the activity of being. But sacrifice or abandonment of the fruits of action—that, says Krishna, is the correct path. Detached action is thus a compromise, a legitimation of the householder's lifestyle over against the renunciant who abandons family and society. The *Bhagavad Gita* thus adds its teaching to a long-time tension in Indian culture between the abandonment of desire for the world and the desire to conquer the world by embodying it.

Another aspect of this same tension between abandonment and conquest involves gender symbolism. As in other areas, India has it all ways: The female is both elemental matter (*prakriti*) that traps masculine spirit (*purusha*), and therefore a negative force, or exactly the reverse, a positive force as intelligence or wisdom that liberates. Similarly, the human soul can either be female in love with the male deity (Krishna) or male in self-sacrificing submission to the female deity (Durga or Kali). Either way the deity wins and the world, including its two temporary genders, loses. Deities are frequently manifest in what the world labels inappropriate gender—Siva as the god who is half female, Siva incarnate as a female Vishnu (Mohini), the goddess Durga as heroic lion-riding warrior, the renowned warrior Arjuna disguised as a transvestite—and in the end the deity may often declare both genders and also genderlessness. And so we are turned back by these myths, iconographies, and rituals upon the inexpressible and qualityless *brahman* as Absolute.

In a remarkable way the traditions of the *Tantras* in the middle of the first millennium C.E. perpetuate a discovery declared a thousand years earlier in one of the *Upanishads:* The world can be absorbed and dismissed by the union of the two genders, and feminine cosmic energy or intelligence is an active, liberating force. Thus the goal of world abandonment was eventually declared attainable by a dangerous path, that of indulgence rather than renunciation.

The Tantric schools of *yoga* evolved as secret counterascetic communities bent on release by extreme actions. These actions included, as we have seen earlier, ritual performance of the "five M's," one of them, *maithuna,* being either symbolic or actual sexual union. From one point of view the Tantric *yogi* embracing his young, low-caste, female-as-goddess partner is performing the most outrageous breach of religious law in this adharmic behavior, overturning Hinduism's traditional display of celibacy as spiritually meritful. From his point of view, however, he has left *dharma* behind and is pushing the limits toward androgynous union and a genderless territory of origins/conclusions. In fact he insists that for him, a *vira* (hero) like Shiva, the sexual act is not a lack of continence but precisely a demonstration of cosmic self-control. Unlike domesticated, nonheroic creatures who procreate and die, he does not suffer semen loss. Like the Vedic sacrificer reversing Purusha-Prajapati's dismemberment/creation and returning to the moment before creation, he intends by his counterascetic action to reverse time and locate the moment of primordial unity. His recognition of the goddess as *shakti* is multiform: He worships her, is empowered and liberated by her, and finally embodies and transcends her.

He tells us all of this in his cryptic texts and vivid practices. For example, according to Hindu physiology semen is life-essence and properly belongs at the top of the head. In Tantric Yoga the top of the universe and the top of the head are one, as indeed *soma* and semen are one. *Soma* descends in time and space, and worlds are continually born anew; semen descends in the body and is lost in the procreative act that perpetuates birth and death in the world. The Tantric *yogi* reverses this natural, worldly, human flow: Semen is not ejaculated but directed upward through the channels of the body, even as feminine cosmic energy, *shakti* or **kundalini,** roused from its coiled and serpentine sleep on the feminine earth, ascends from its locus beneath the navel. Unity of these two—white masculine essence and red feminine energy, deified respectively as Shiva and Shakti—is achieved in the thousand-petaled lotus in the crown of the body-become-universe.

In the words of the text cited at the head of this segment "the world is born of me and melts back into me." The creation, absorption, then re-creation of the cosmos, a cycle detailed so well in the *Puranas,* has become an interior event for this *yogi* who reports about **samadhi,** his state of total reintegration, fulfillment, and interiorization. The three main channels within his body are ruled, he says, by Shiva, Vishnu, and Brahma, while such Vedic gods as Prajapati, Varuna, Vayu,

Soma, Pushan, and Viraj protect other conduits for vital breaths and fires (just as these Vedic gods are found today in the concrete form of strategically placed guardian deities in Hindu temple architecture). The courses of the sun and moon, as well as their eclipses, and the changes of the seasons all take place within the *yogi's* body, and therein are the meetings of the holy rivers, the cosmic mountain Meru, and the sacred city of Banaras. No need for a pilgrimage to Banaras if it is embodied, no need to offer to the gods if they are within, no need for a clock or a calendar if world time as well as world space are the Self.

Obviously the dimensions of Hinduism discussed above are all encompassed by this new one: The world that is listened to, mythologized, classified, and recycled is also the embodied world, the swallowed world. In the eleventh chapter of the *Bhagavad Gita* there is a famous theophany in which Arjuna's charioteer reveals himself to be not only Lord Krishna but the transcendent Vishnu, godhead behind all gods. Krishna supplies heroic Arjuna with a divine eye so that he may bear, if only briefly, the splendor and terror of this vision with the light of a thousand suns. "The whole universe," announces Krishna-Vishnu, "is united inside my body." And Arjuna, witness to the very process of reintegration, is struck dumb at the sight of gods, sages, demons, ghosts, humans, and animals all in a great white-water river rushing into the multiple flaming mouths of this awesome god as if to the sea. The sea is Krishna is Vishnu but yes we now know it as Purusha as we recognize through Arjuna's eye the raging torrent of *samsara*. All one body we. Food for the god.

But what of swallowers today, what of the living *sadhus,* saints, god-men, *samnyasis, yogis,* who challenge the comfortable norms or quietly pass on their traditions in *mathas, ashrams,* or the million roads of India? Clearly they have multiple roles and are as diverse a lot as the strivers and questers of ancient times.

From the same region of South India come two opposite examples, one the passive, silent, lonely seeker, like the tortoise with all its limbs drawn in, said to have renounced not only society but also food. He was Bal Yogi, who lived in a cave near the remote coastal village of Mummidivaram until his "death" in 1985. Believers swear that he emerged on only one night of the year, Shiva's night in February, to eat in silence a modest ball of cooked rice offered to him by a devotee. If they are correct, then he was even more efficient an organism than our example of the brachiopod. In any event, today tens of thousands of believers still gather at his *samadhi* each Shivaratri to experience his continuing presence.

The other is Sathya Sai Baba, one of India's best-known god-men, easily recognizable on calendars and posters all over India by the Afro hairstyle framing his smiling, well-fed face. In no way does he resemble a traditional *yogi,* and he is certainly no brachiopod. Born in 1926, he continues to dispense holy ash (*vibhuti*) and the sight (*darshana*) of his person as a living, breathing *avatara* of the divine to hundreds of thousands of devout believers and fascinated onlookers every year. Having cured himself publicly in 1963 of an incapacitating illness (described variously by the faithful as a heart attack, paralytic stroke, or tubercular meningitis), Baba is seen by many to have miraculous healing powers for any believer who is ill or disabled. Locally, in the Telugu-speaking vicinity of his *ashram* at Puttaparthi, Andhra Pradesh, he is known by all classes and castes, but his pan-Indian appeal is particularly to those of the urban middle class who have followed his cult in newspapers and magazines for four decades as he flies from Bangalore to Delhi, Bombay, or Madras, or tolerates the reverent Americans and Europeans who sit at his feet.

Like the Tantric *vira* (hero), Sathya Sai Baba identifies with Shiva, and like the *yogi* in the *Yoga Darshana Upanishad* he embodies all gods and goddesses as well as the cosmic unison of Shiva and Shakti. Tantrism and ascetic *yoga*, however, have no place in this cult that highlights a guru-as-god. Baba explains his relationship to this world in the traditional mode of the *avatara*, that is, as a god who engages with the world in times of crisis and need. In fact, he claims to be a tripartite *avatara* of past, present, and future. First he was the famous Sai Baba of Shirdi in Maharashtra, western India, dispensing Shiva's holy ash until his "death" in 1918; now he is Shirdi Sai Baba's reincarnation in Andhra; and he will come again a third time as Prem Sai, in yet another state of modern India, Karnataka.

In Sathya Sai Baba and similar figures today we see a demonstration of the deity-become-human, the being who is as free to return to the world as he is to swallow it. For the many devotees who see him as Bhagavan, the Lord, and as omniscient, clairvoyant miracle worker, he is the God of our time and our place. The fact that these believers are involved in education, social service, medicine, disaster relief, and other varieties of institution building indicates they intend neither to abandon the world nor to identify with Baba. He is an *avatara*, a sufficient manifestation, and a relevant ideal in an imperfect age. More than this, he is a target of devotion, and it is precisely because he has entered the world and transformed their lives that his followers cannot imagine leaving it.

Not all are believers who see or hear about Sathya Sai Baba's favorite act of pulling packets of sacred ash or wristwatches out of thin air. Some are scoffers, and they also represent a tradition of Hinduism. Many ascetics, *sadhus*, self-proclaimed gurus, and divinely realized saints have a hard-core following of disbelievers, those who dismiss them as charlatans, snake-oil salesmen, or just false-faces for a degenerate age. But many, on the other hand, would accept the statement of a government clerk in response to a scholar's query about ascetics today: "A *sadhu* has a deep understanding of life's philosophy and believes in god. *Sadhus* are the force that keeps society going."[8]

Swallowing implies eating, digesting, and the processing of food, and these are among South Asia's favored metaphors. The *Taittiriya Upanishad* contains a famous passage concluding with the chant *aham annam aham annam aham annam* (I am food I am food I am food). It reminds the hearer of the chain of being in which each individual in *samsara* has been recycled to earth in rain, emergent as plant, eaten as someone's food, born as embryo, grown into eater of food, but only for a moment until the eater is once again the eaten—*aham annam*.

Revealed in the five dimensions explored in this chapter is a diversity that is astonishing given that all of our probing has been within a single religious tradition. Listening, mythologizing, classifying, recycling, swallowing the universe—these appear like experimental balloons sent up to try the currents of the wind and determine possibilities. No doubt other balloons have soared well enough across the early *Vedas, Upanishads, Yoga Sutras,* epics, *Puranas, Tantras,* medieval devotional poets, and beyond. Finally, however, the diversity of Hinduism disclosed by these experimental flights appears to give way to coherence within a single worldview.

It is as if each experiment were able to intuit the mobility of all the others and locate a common flight pattern. As we have seen, a tendency to effect compromises has assisted in this remarkable coordination. When ascetic movements contest the standards, asceticism is given latitude and legitimacy. When indulgence is proposed as an alternative to austerity, it is ritualized and declared a gateway to liberation. The message is, strive to perform one's proper duty in society, but also strive to abandon the world—or at least the fruits of action. In the same period in which Shankara extols absolute nonduality and *brahman* without qualities, Manikkavachakar praises and confesses, laughs and weeps before his Lord sweet as honey. All gods, one God, no gods, multiple solutions. The inexhaustible *Vedas,* compact *Sutras,* favorite *Puranas,* dynamic epics, poems of local saints in the local language—all are sacred, all are essential, and no one of them is sufficient for everyone. Thus the paradox of Hinduism: Experiments appear to have no limitation, yet none is so radical as to fracture the mold.

The five dimensions surveyed above do express this seemingly limitless yet coordinated participation in the Hindu worldview. Taken in the order in which they were discussed they provide a summary of Hinduism: The oral tradition is mythology concerning classifications in a world of *samsara* that can be transcended.

In chapter 29 a typical Hindu was identified as one who would accept karma and *samsara* in the belief system, uphold certain sacred texts and deities, honor ancestors with a continuing lineage and with offerings, admit to class and caste status within a broader social system, express certain overt or symbolic ascetic practices such as fasts or vows, and consider important the pursuit of goals toward ultimate release. In the process of reviewing five dimensions of the Hindu worldview we see that all of these aspects of identification are between twenty-five and thirty-two centuries old. It is the task of the next chapter to engage with some of the dynamics of contemporary faith and further probe the range and effectiveness of this singular worldview.

33
The Dynamics of Hinduism

SO FAR HINDUISM AND HISTORY have been surveyed as well as some of the many ways in which Hindus view the world and themselves in relation to faith and tradition. This chapter focuses on a few features selected from this rich history and complex worldview. Three different topics will be considered in order to look more closely at Hinduism as it is lived today.

First, Hinduism in its long history has held out a program for individual advancement. Such progress not only takes many forms and occurs over a great series of sequential rebirths, but also occurs by various means, including rituals, education, and the direct acquisition of spiritual knowledge and power within a given lifetime. As a first topic of living Hinduism a traditional set of rituals may be examined, one that extends from conception to funeral, an individual bracketing known as the *samskaras,* which highlights progressive stages in the journey of a lifebody. A survey of *samskaras* reveals one of the oldest and most enduring ritual structures of South Asia. It also illuminates important aspects of Hindu physiology, family coherence, and social structure.

Second, an entirely different sort of journey may be reviewed by considering the traditions of pilgrimages, vows, donations, and other devotional activities that occur beyond the household and, in many cases, outside the village or hometown. Again this is the realm of ritual action, as in the first topic, but this time the pan-Indian structure is far more subtle: There are no precise manuals descended from Vedic texts, no Brahman authorities hovering as essential guides, and even the definition of "ritual" at times seems stretched. The action here takes us out of house and temple to the elemental forces and rhythms of life. We could, of course, track a Hindu of either sex at these devotional tasks that, with a few exceptions, are not gender specific. But it seems appropriate to observe a woman engaged in her portion of what amounts to a great network of fasts, offerings, and journeys long and short, because this life-support system—a lifelong devotional exercise—is primarily undertaken by the women of Hinduism. Therefore Sita's Mother is followed in a day devoted to religious duties that take her away from her family but by no means apart from its welfare. In the process of this glimpse of a few hours in the life of a woman of North India we will discover, just as with the life-cycle rites, several unifying features that assist in answering the recurrent question: What holds Hinduism together?

Third, we take up a life history, that of a forty-year-old man in South India. Whereas Sita's Mother's experiences, as related here, are typical of a North Indian woman of the twice-born castes, Krishnayyas's life may only in some respects be called normative. His story is selected to illustrate the regional character of Hinduism noted in passing throughout these chapters. Hinduism does seem to pop up in an endless series of guises, and some of the most prominent ones carry regional tags. Here a personal history offers an opportunity to explore the area of the Godavari River delta on the Bay of Bengal coast in the Telugu-speaking state of Andhra. This subject also previews the final chapter of this part in that this life is accomplished with one foot in traditional Hinduism and the other in modern, upwardly mobile, secular India.

Thus this chapter will consider three different sorts of passage: the life cycle, a woman's devotional routine, and a man's spiritual-academic odyssey.

The Journey of a Lifebody

On the fourth night after the marriage and prior to first intercourse the groom addresses the bride with the verse: "May Vishnu prepare the womb, may Tvashtar mould the embryo's form, may Prajapati emit seed, may Dhatar place the embryo. Place the embryo, Sinivali, place the embryo, Sarasvati! May the Ashvins garlanded with lotuses provide the embryo, the Ashvins with their golden fire-churning sticks, the embryo that I now place for you to bear in ten months." (*Jaiminiya Grihya Sutra* 1.22)

Hindus recognize multiple sources of power in the world about them, sacred forces in rivers and rocks, in village temples and on hilltop shrines, even in holy women and men. It has been noted that time, like physical space, also reveals an abundance of spiritual meanings and events. There is the time of nature, a cosmic time of seasons and universal changes, measured by celestial bodies and monsoon winds, and evident in the alternations of light and darkness, warmth and cold, rain and drought, growth and decay. But there is also the time of an individual in the hoped-for span of a hundred years between birth and death. Like cosmic time, carefully segmented into memories of important events of the seasons and the deities, so too personal time is ritually marked. The marks are called *samskaras*, rites of passage and transformation. [See Religions of Africa pp. 42–51, 76–79, Religions of Mesoamerica pp. 201–6, Native Religions of North America pp. 278–79, 295–98, 306–8, Judaism pp. 445–50, Christianity pp. 542–43, 555–57, Islam pp. 677–78, 680–86, Buddhism pp. 915–17, 921, 931–37, Religions of China pp. 1019–21, and Religions of Japan pp. 1146–50 for description and discussion of rites of passage.]

Some ritual manuals consider as many as forty *samskaras* to be worthy of performance, but a more traditional set of ten to eighteen is characteristic. A *samskara* is literally an accomplishment, perfection, or refinement, and therefore the ritual advancement of a lifebody from its moment of conception to the moment just beyond its bodily death. Since many of the symbols are agricultural, the metaphor of ripening is often employed: A single cycle of life proceeds from seed planting to harvest sacrifice and beyond to rebirth in the succeeding cycle. Therefore food and its transformation, both material—in processes within the body—and spiritual—in ritual exchanges—remain dominant expressions.

Every culture, every religion, pays ritual attention to the life cycle. Not all of them, however, place as great an emphasis as Hinduism does upon the substantive transformations that occur in such procedures. There are several significant features of Hinduism to keep in view during a survey of the *samskaras*.

First, because of unquestioned acceptance of the concept of transmigration, the personal journey from conception to cremation or burial is not a singular one. Rather, each life is one of a great number of rebirths for that self until the achievement of its final state of liberation from the birth-and-death cycle.

Second, this personal journey of a lifebody is not a lonely one. It begins, obviously, as an extension of an existing parental family with all of its remembered forebears. It ends, ideally, with a living son, one further extension of the lineage, acting as performer of the last rites, the final sacrifice of the used-up body. If our own cultural image of the family tree is a great spreading oak or chestnut with many branches, the Hindu image is a slender bamboo, tall and undeviating, with regularly spaced joints (*vamsa*, "lineage") to represent an unbroken descent from father to son. The masculine character of this lineage is one of the central features of Hindu ritual and kinship: Every attention is given to producing a son to keep the lineage and its ritual structure intact. A daughter is only a temporary member of the family, since she will be assumed into her husband's lineage, first during the marriage ceremony itself, and then, after her life in *his* village or town, again at death when she may join the company of his ancestors. From the point of view of the personal journey of each lifebody, however, it is important to remember this wider community that is involved in every ritual. It is composed not only of all the visible relatives, but the invisible ones as well. The participant presence of the deceased, both male and female, is never forgotten, and offerings of food with accompanying *mantras* are invariably shared with them, as with the living.

Third, there is in the series of *samskaras*, to borrow a current media expression, an apparent front-loading. The majority of the rites occur before the age of six months and, in fact, several are accomplished before the severance of the umbilical cord. Since a dominant concern of the *samskaras* throughout a lifetime is refinement, that is to say, the elimination of impurities, attention is drawn once more to the previous career of this self, including its dangerous passage from body to body. What follows is the orderly sequence of *samskaras*, the ritual passage from conception through childhood, initiation, marriage, death, and beyond.

From Conception Through Childhood

Vedic manuals for domestic rituals begin the life cycle with marriage procedures. It is on the fourth night of the wedding ceremony that consummation should occur, and sexual union is actually the rite of impregnation. According to the *mantras* of a famous wedding hymn in the *Atharvaveda,* the bride is earth and the groom is heaven. This notion of woman as crop field and man as provider of seed remains throughout Hindu myth and experience. Furthermore, the embryo that grows in the bride as a consequence of the marriage rite is itself a new being composed partly of the father's semen—the source of bones, teeth, bodily channels, and semen—and partly of the mother's uterine blood—the source of blood, flesh, and internal organs. If the father's contributing substance predominates, the new being will be male; if the mother's is stronger, then female. [See Religions of Africa pp. 48–51, 77–78, Judaism pp. 447–48, Christianity p. 556, Islam pp. 683–84, Buddhism p. 935, Religions of China p. 1020, and Religions of Japan p. 1148 for description and discussion of marriage rites.]

The next *samskara,* however, performed in the third month of a woman's first pregnancy, is the "generation of a male." This indicates that ritual action may still determine the sex of the fetus. Beans, barley, berries, or banyan tree shoots may all play a part in the ritual. In the fourth or a later month is the ritual "parting of the hair" in which the father-to-be parts his wife's hair three times upward, from front to back, using for a "comb" a porcupine quill, tufts of sacred grass, or a full spindle. Ripening fruits are also employed in this ceremony that, like the others, takes place at the hearth fire of the home and involves special *mantras.* In some parts of India the mother-to-be looks at cooked rice, envisioning the child yet to be born.

The ritual of birth itself is performed immediately upon delivery, before the umbilical cord is severed. The first part of this *samskara* concentrates on the "production of wisdom" in the newborn; the father touches the baby's lips with a gold spoon or ring dipped in honey, curds, and clarified butter. The name of the goddess of sacred speech, **Vach**, is whispered three times into the infant's right ear. The second part of the rite includes *mantras* for "long life." After the cutting of the cord the infant may be given a secret name, known only to the mother and father, before being placed at the mother's breast. [See Religions of Africa pp. 42–45, 76, Native Religions of North America p. 307, Judaism pp. 385–86, 445–46, Christianity p. 556, Islam p. 682, Buddhism p. 932, Religions of China p. 1019–20, and Religions of Japan pp. 1146–47 for description and discussion of birth rites.]

In the Vedic period several mysterious feminine powers were in attendance during birth, functioning as midwives of the child's destiny as well as its physical arrival into the world. Worship of the goddess Shasthi ("Sixth") on the sixth day of life is a contemporary survival of such ancient feminine guardian figures.

Ten or twelve days after delivery (or in some areas, one year later), the baby undergoes the name-giving *samskara* and receives an everyday name, often that of an astrologically appropriate deity, by which she or he will be known. This name serves as a "cover" or distraction from the real one, still a secret from the evil eye or other dangerous elements. Amulets, black threads around the wrist, lampblack marks on the body, and other devices may also guard the child from now until puberty or later.

Some time in the fourth month the newest addition to the family may be taken out of the house for the first time. That event, witnessing the sun and the moon, is a *samskara,* as is the moment of first feeding with solid food (cooked rice), usually in the sixth month. A month or so later is the ear-piercing ceremony, the earlobes being ringed with wire, the right ear first for boys, the left one first for a girl. Ritual shaving of the head and direct removal of impurities held by the hair is an important procedure throughout life in Hinduism and is often connected with special pilgrimages and vows as well as standard rites of passage. Thus the first such tonsure is the forerunner of a continuing voluntary ritual. When the hair is shaved away a small lock is left at the back of the bare skull, a twist of hair as a visible reminder of this consecration. Incidentally, the first tonsure rite is the only *samskara* that may be performed in a temple, often an ancestral goddess temple, as well as in the home. A secondary tonsure for males in their sixteenth year is sometimes considered a *samskara,* this one including the first shaving of facial hair as well as the scalp.

Education, Marriage, and Adulthood

The most powerful of *samskaras* between birth and marriage is certainly the initiatory thread-ceremony known as the **upanayana,** the ritual "leading near" of a student to his guru for religious instruction. Nowadays only the most exacting Brahman families request such a performance for a son; more frequently an abbreviated version serves as a preliminary to the marriage vows.

Through the Vedic era and on into classical Hinduism the *upanayana* was the indispensable second birth for all twice-born classes, that is, the Brahmans, Kshatriyas, and Vaishyas, who received their threads at the ages of eight, eleven, and twelve, respectively. Being "born again," bound for lifetime by a sacred thread worn over the left shoulder, was a transition of great community as well as personal significance. An initiate was not merely introduced to the Vedic tradition, both textual and sacrificial, when he heard from his guru the first *mantra* (the **gayatri,** which is *Rigveda* 3.62.10) and learned from him the procedures for offering into the sacrificial fire (the standard **homa**). At that moment he became a link in the ageless transmission of knowledge and assumed his part of human responsibility for maintaining cosmic truth and order. No small step was that.

The elaborate ritual itself opened the door to the first stage of life, that of the student "living according to *brahman,*" the *brahmacarin,* receptive to his guru and all that this spiritual father would turn over to him in this lengthy birthing process. The *Atharvaveda* speaks with awe of the Vedic student more powerful than a thousand suns. Still today a few Brahman boys from special families follow the ancient tradition, living in the home of the guru for a period of years, learning daily the Vedic texts, orally, one line at a time, reciting the line back until the entire *Veda,* or significant parts of several *Vedas,* are committed to memory.

Another *samskara* marked the other end of the *brahmacarin's* career, the "return" to the parental home after a ritual bath signifying graduation. The second stage of life, that of the married householder, became the focus of ritual attention. The ancient student received his entire education during the years with his teacher; nowadays, of course, a Brahman boy will normally be in public schools like everyone else. Today the tradition has been trimmed down to a symbolic studenthood of the religious life: the investiture with the thread, whispering of the *gayatri mantra*, instructions in domestic sacrifice, and the ritual bath and "return" all occur on the same day in the boy's own home, usually on the day before his departure for the marriage ceremony that takes place in the village or town of the bride.

The marriage arrangements, for all castes, are the responsibilities of parents, and preparations may take a great many months. The ceremony proper, a *samskara* transforming both bride and groom, occurs at night in the house of the bride's father. It is embedded in a wide range of other rituals and local practices that may go on for several days and usually have all the traits of a community festival. One preliminary ritual of significance, done in the privacy of the respective bride's and groom's homes well in advance, is the anointing of their bodies with an oil of turmeric, the yellow root known for its powers of fertility.

Already in the ancient period there were many variations of procedures and levels of symbolism in this union of two individuals, two cosmic principles, male and female. Modern India has even greater diversity in this universally observed *samskara*, but a number of features have carried over from the Vedic manuals and may be recognized in most parts of India and the wider Hindu world today. These include construction of a ritual booth of auspicious banana

A twelve-year-old Brahman boy in a North Indian village undergoing initiation (upanayana) into sacred mantras and offerings on the day before his marriage. He is instructed here in the art of writing. The day-long ritual proceeds facing the ritual fire and a sacred tree with a large decorated pot representing the goddess. The boy wears an antelope skin and holds his sacred staff, symbol of the Vedic student. On this day he receives the sacred thread that he will always wear over his left shoulder.

and mango leaves, tying of a thread around the wrist of the bride, first gazing of the couple at one another after the removal of a separating cloth, placing the bride's foot three times on the family grinding stone as a vow of fidelity, the important seven steps northward from or around the ritual fire, and an initial offering into the hearth of the new home. The *homa* that the boy learned in his initiation is now performed with the bride as the pair assumes the role of house-holders in the community. Together they observe the pole star, Dhruva, and the nearby star, Arundhati (wife of the sage Vasistha), who is, like Dhruva, a model of loyalty and steadfastness. Usually there is a ritual marking of the part in the bride's hair with a stroke of vermilion, a signal to all of her marital status but also the symbol and promise of her powerful new role as mother-to-be.

Death and Beyond

The last *samskara* in the journey of a lifebody is the ritual disposal of the material body after death, either by cremation or by burial. This is a "final offer-ing," as the *samskara* is named. Cremation and burial are both known from the time of the *Rigveda,* and both are widely practiced in Hinduism today (although the tendency for higher caste groups is to burn, for lower caste groups in South India to bury the dead). Funerary rites highlight once again Hinduism's claim that death is a continuing experience in the long course toward liberation, while the self in process remains indestructible.

This *samskara* declares the same ends as all the previous ones. It celebrates the completion of a stage of life, in this case, the end of the lifebody. It refines, by eliminating impurities and rendering the entire material body into ashes or earth. And it promotes, by liberating the subtle body for another birth in the long course. Again, this set of rituals, like the preceding ones, is subject to wide variation, but the traditional ritual sequence includes preparation of the body in or just outside the home; a procession to the burning-ground or cemetery, both usually found together at a river bank in or just outside the village or town; a ritual lighting of the pyre or placing of the body in the grave; circumambula-tion of the pyre or grave by the chief mourner, usually the eldest living son, who is the "offerer" of his father's body; the breaking of a large ceramic pot of water over the fire or grave; ritual bathing by the mourners along with shaving and tonsure of the men; the symbolic or actual gifting of a cow. If cremation is the means of disposal, a bone-gathering ceremony follows; later these fragments are dispersed in a sacred river.

More or less elaborate preparations, depending upon the ritual and finan-cial status of the mourners, are immediately begun to promote the deceased on to a new journey. No longer technically *samskaras,* these *shraddhas,* as they are called, constitute a whole ritual enterprise in itself and an important dimen-sion of Hindu life and thought, as already noted in chapter 32. [See Religions of Africa pp. 42–45, 78–79, Religions of Mesoamerica pp. 144, 229–33, Native Religions of North America pp. 300–301, 307–8, 335–37, Judaism pp. 448–50, Christianity p. 557, Islam pp. 684–85, Buddhism pp. 935–37, Religions of China pp. 1021, 1041–44, and Religions of Japan pp. 1149–50 for description and discussion of death and funeral rites.]

To summarize and reflect upon what can be learned from this review of a life cycle according to Hinduism, a number of insights into the tradition as a whole become available. For example, there are correspondences between cosmic time and personal time, as well as an apparent symmetry of generation and regeneration. The seed of a lifebody is ritually placed in the field-womb, where it germinates after ten lunar months ("days"). After death the used-up body is ritually devoured by the funeral fire or the earth and a new temporary body is ritually begun, one that also germinates after ten days, then functions to carry the self to the company of ancestors. The clustering of essential rituals at the points of birth and death-rebirth is best understood in this light.

Throughout these rituals there are strong continuities with the oldest layers of Hinduism. It is perhaps in the *samskaras* and ancestor rites that India best remembers its ancient Vedic heritage. Basic *samskaras* have endured through centuries of changes in doctrine and practice. They proved to be an all-Indian template, a unifying pattern that countered the regional diversities and popular innovations that inevitably sprang up across the subcontinent. Of course not every householder today performs the entire set of *samskaras*, but everyone knows the system, participates in the most essential ones, and attempts, even if the scale is abbreviated or several rites are telescoped into a single performance, to accomplish as many as possible on the oldest surviving male child. Here, too, we learn of the ritual need for a continuing lineage, a link in the living present to connect the ancestors to those not yet born, a link who must by long tradition be male provider of seed. And as noted more than once, in these rituals there is an underlying spiritual basis for Hindu physiology.

Above all, a lifebody does not begin, nor does it remain, whole, pure, or safe. It requires ritual prescriptions in a lifelong process of ripening and refinement. This process is accomplished within the context of the family and its sacred hearth. Household deities may be invoked or mentioned, but no one of them is credited with these mysterious transformations. The male head of the household or an invited Brahman priest is the outward visible performer, but it is the ritual "work" itself that succeeds in refining, shaping, perfecting the ongoing lifebody and advancing it on yet another step on the path toward ultimate liberation.

Beyond the Household:
A Woman's Devotions

A town incorporates the ruins of a twelfth-century fort. Pilgrims passing from a regional temple to the train station are led aside by a local self-appointed guide, who halts the troop before a gaping hole, a partially collapsed tunnel at the base of the fort, and tells them grandly that if they dare to enter, and persevere, they will eventually emerge in Kashi. The troop gazes at the hole appreciatively and that is sufficient. One of them presents a coin to the guide and all of them turn toward the railway and the next temple town, reassured that Kashi, the holy city of Banaras, a thousand miles off by rail, is really just the other side of the hole they have now witnessed. (Rajahmundry, October 1980, from author's journal)

There is a marvelous way in which Hinduism—and India—shake down space and time into absorbable bits. Not far from the fort in the preceding passage, in an isolated hamlet curled about a broad circular pond, villagers will tell you of the most remarkable event within memory: "Not so very long ago" an elderly villager, now deceased, rose earlier than usual and went to the pond to bathe. There in the predawn mist he discovered the famed seven *rishis* engaged in their morning ablutions, the very sages who long ago at the dawn of time first heard the *Vedas*.

Duplicates or complements of these examples could be collected from virtually any region of India. The vivid spiritual imagination of Hinduism naturally and consistently fashions links to places and periods enriched by formative events (in these samples, the powerful locus of Kashi, where the *rishis* lived, and the time when the *Vedas* were apprehended and made available to humankind). Established by links to these great events, and the recounting of them, local time and space are therefore resonant with their sacred force. The village, river, hilltop, or anthill is not in isolation but directly connected to cosmic models of ultimate authority.

But interestingly, at the same time that each puzzle piece stresses its continuities with the grand subcontinental picture, each local element is also quick to promote its uniqueness, its Hinduism-found-nowhere-elseness. It is not surprising, of course, to note innumerable special claims to authority in the vastness of Hindu mythology, legend, and ritualism. What is remarkable is the modest self-image of each of these special claims that allows it to be just a piece in the overall design and not a whole puzzle among many other puzzles. How does that work?

For example, the preceding chapters have shown that Hinduism values the Goddess under an extraordinary range of local names (as if all the female saints of Christianity from Brigid to Teresa were to be seen as manifestations of a single feminine power). Illustrating this theme of unity and diversity is one well-known myth of the dismemberment of the goddess **Sati,** wife of Shiva, by the discus-weapon of Vishnu. Shiva, grief-stricken over the fiery suicide of Sati, abandoned his celestial duties and flew wildly about in the heavens with her body over his shoulder. To restore him to normalcy Vishnu hurled his discus skyward. Each time the discus struck the lifeless body a piece of Sati fell to earth, until finally more than fifty portions of the self-sacrificing Goddess descended. From the oneness of Goddess Sati came multiple parts that returned to the oneness of Goddess Earth. Today Hindu pilgrims proceed with reverence into temples and shrines that incorporate each unique fragment—the left little finger, the genitals, the tongue, the right breast—as if the pilgrimage map of

India were an interstate highway of relics. India itself is in this way the immortal
Goddess. But the pilgrim devotee, while affirming the unity of the Goddess tradition, pays particular attention to each site, with its special claim and its own
story to relate.

With this remarkable notion of unity and plurality in mind a second topic
may be examined for some of the themes of devotion that occur outside home
and family. Although less formal than the routines of worship in temples and
home shrines, the activities of vows, fasts, pilgrimages, and local shrines are
among the oldest and most significant of Hinduism. Unlike the *samskaras*, they
have little or no basis in Vedic religion, and yet their roles are so integral within
Hinduism that they seem always to have been its basic territory.

These rites may be examined by following a woman who lives in a cluster
of villages in eastern Uttar Pradesh, a Hindi-speaking state of North India. Since
the birth of her first child, Sita (a daughter named after the heroine-goddess of
the *Ramayana*), she has been called by her husband and relatives Sita's Mother.
A day on which to observe her and listen to her thoughts is selected: the first day
of the bright half of the lunar month of Jyestha and also a Sunday.

Sita's Mother disentangled herself from the grasp of her four-year-old son,
rose from the rope-bed in the courtyard of her house, made her way through the
mud-walled lanes by starlight to the field to relieve herself, then quickly departed for the river. She bathed rapidly in her sari (garment), then composed
herself standing waist-deep in water, enveloped in mist. Of all the moments in
the day this was the finest: She was alone with the dark cleansing purity of the
river, cool before the sun burned off the mist, filled with love and gratitude for
Being. She raised her hands—palms together, fingers widespread, thumbs to her
bowed forehead—and recited her morning prayers with her eyes closed.

On the bank she wrapped herself in a clean sari and slipped out of the wet
one. She emptied from a corner knot of her sari a handful of rice grains onto the
spread cloth of a *sadhu* who sat in silence on the top step of the riverbank. Other
bathers were approaching as she took the familiar path home; it was too dark to
recognize faces, but one acknowledged her in passing with "Jai Ram" and the
blessing of Lord Rama, and she knew the voice. She carried a small brass pot of
river water in her right hand, and halfway home she circled a banyan tree three
times, then poured half the water at the roots where a slab of stone carved with
twined serpents was leaning. Someone had already lighted a tiny mustard-oil
lamp on the stone. Two more stops were also routine, one to touch the raised
mace of a crude stone statue of Hanuman splashed with vermilion paint, the
other to acknowledge the whitewashed square of stones that represented the Dih
Baba, the guardian deity on watch here midway between the hamlets of the village cluster. For all three—the banyan and serpent tree, Hanuman, and the Dih
Baba—she had special verses in the Bhojpuri dialect of Hindi she had learned
as a child. Crossing the threshold of the house she recited another couplet, this
one in Sanskrit, a *mantra* taught to her by her husband, invoking the god Shiva,
the goddess Gauri, and other deities. Then she touched the little image of
Ganesha on the kitchen shelf, said a prayer as she started the hearth-fire, and
set the rice to boil. Daughters Sita and Priya were awakened and prompted to

their task of creating auspicious rice-flour designs on the ground outside the front door. By now it was 4:30 A.M., and her husband had returned from his river bath. She followed his sonorous prayers from the other room and knew, as from a clock on the wall, the time remaining before her departure.

Entrusting the serving of food to the girls, and allowing her youngest to sleep until dawn, she was packed and on the path toward the crossroad bus stop, exhilarated, despite a forty-eight-hour fast, excited as she focused on her journey. By sunup the bus arrived and lurched off toward the nearby town and its railway station. The train was an hour or so behind schedule. As she sat on the platform a small, whiskered man with large, liquid eyes came and stood silently before her. Sita's Mother bent over her belongings and unpacked the nested set of steel containers she had brought from home. The old man's companion, a young, nearly naked fellow with one arm missing at the shoulder, joined him, and the pair squatted before their benefactress, tin bowls gradually filling with scooped handfuls. A little girl of five expanded the pair to a trio and the one-armed man began to empty his bowl into her bucket. The hot rice moved from canister to bowl to bucket under appreciative smiles. All retired in different directions, the child to divide her blessing with her mother, the men to sit and be joined by other men who silently spread dirty cloths on the platform to receive a share of a share. All ate rapidly, then washed bowls, hands, and mouths at the railway water faucet, elbow to elbow with Sita's Mother who was scouring the empty canisters. Two scruffy dogs went after the remnants in the drain as their portion of the feast. Not a word was spoken throughout the ceremony.

By the time she descended from the train at her stop it was nearly noon, and Sita's Mother faced a strenuous walk in dreadful heat. From the experience of

A line of women pilgrims walking barefoot along the Ganges River in a five-day, fifty-mile circumambulation of Kashi (Banaras). They carry food, bedding, and a supply of small coins and grains to toss to beggars and ascetics as well as to offer to the deities of 108 shrines and temples along the path.

previous pilgrimage fasts she knew how to conserve strength, not just for getting there, but also for the endless return journey to a ritual bath in the river before food. This pilgrimage was a first for her, one long planned as she learned its details from other women in the village. Unlike a pilgrimage to a famous temple or a celebrated river during its festival season, her goal this time was a tree. It was, in fact, another banyan tree, just like the one at home by the river. But this one was unique: It was regarded locally as the very tree under which a man was restored to life, not by his own merit, not by the grace of Vishnu, Shiva, or Durga, but by the quick-wittedness and persistent devotion of his wife. Sita's Mother told the story to her children every year at this time when she performed, usually at the banyan tree by the river, the Vow of Savitri. Here is a consideration.

> One day long ago the king's son, Satyavat, was collecting wood in the forest when he collapsed beside a great banyan tree. Yama, Death, appeared with his terrible noose to carry off another soul. But Satyavat's wife, Savitri, came just in time and pursued them. Yama repeatedly insisted that she go home and let him do his godly work. With each remonstrance Savitri became even more determined, impressing Yama so deeply with her eloquent loyalty to her husband that at last he granted her a series of three wishes. For the third wish Savitri requested many sons, forcing the hand of Death to relinquish Satyavat and allow him to father sons with this faithful and resolute woman. Satyavat came to under the banyan tree, remembering nothing of this ordeal, and together they returned to the village where eventually they raised many fine sons.

Now Sita's Mother could see this renowned tree and at last she entered its canopy of shade, a vast space of incredibly cooling relief from the heat of the 120-degree plain. More than a hundred people, mostly women, were within its multitrunked shade, but altogether they filled only part of this living arena. It was the largest tree she had ever seen and as magnificent as any temple. After a brief rest she deposited a coin on the shrine set up by a self-appointed priest, then took a large spool of cotton thread from her bag and began to circle the central trunk, slowly adding her white thread to hundreds of others. With the tree always on her right, she prayerfully wound her thread the sacred number of times, 108, and for the hour that it required kept in mind, as she had been instructed, the health, prosperity, and longevity of her husband, her desire for a second, perhaps even a third son, and a plea for herself to avoid widowhood.

In tracking Sita's Mother for this portion of a day we observe something of the diversity and surprising subtlety of Hindu ritual life. Both the tenor of women's rituals and the importance of minor details of ritual performance are deserving of comment here. First, the significance of rituals performed by women in Hinduism cannot be overestimated. Although largely unrepresented in published manuals in Sanskrit, underrepresented in the more available ritual booklets in regional languages, and not generally discussed by the male priests of village or urban institutions (shrines, temples, *mathas,* monasteries), women's religious activities are nevertheless understood to be the cement that holds together Hindu society at its basic level, the family. Like married women throughout the Hindu world, Sita's Mother accomplished the Vow of Savitri in accord with a version of this popular tale. It is found in one of the epics (the *Mahabharata*), several of the *Puranas,* and illustrated devotional tracts in every language of India. Her renewal of her marriage vow to be a steadfastly loyal wife was no mere statement of conjugal duty; it was, and continues to be, in the annual performance of this vow and many others of a similar character, a recognition of her sacred obligation and role of protectress of her family. The Savitri Vow and certain others are directly concerned with the physical and spiritual well-being of males—husbands, sons, brothers. They are accomplished entirely without them. And they can be performed only by an auspicious woman, one whose great powers of fertility, prosperity, wealth, abundance, and long life (all the powers, that is, of the goddess herself) are properly directed to continue the patriarchal lineage. In other words, her powers must be properly channeled by traditional marriage.

Sita's Mother displays the marks of such an auspicious woman: the vermilion mark in the part of her hair, first placed there by her husband as the binding act in the marriage ritual; a spot of color on her forehead; bangles on her arms; rings on her toes; red paint on her bare feet. Her prayers while circling the banyan tree included a plea to avoid becoming a widow. In traditional India the condition of a widow is proverbially labeled a "fate worse than death." It is a painful deprivation not only of the colorful, opulent display of the above symbols of auspiciousness, but even of basic physical needs and liberties. However, the main reason for such a plea to Savitri is that widowhood is a direct signal of failure to protect a husband. Some lapse in her devotion, chastity, or dutiful performance can allow fate to take his life before hers. A widow must live with a dual reproach as one who failed her husband and one for whom the marriage ritual no longer directs her considerable powers into safe and benevolent rewards. However, for the family of Sita's Mother all is well, even as it was for the family of Savitri, and credit for present well-being is as clear as it was in the model of long ago.

The focus has been on a particular type of women's rites in Hinduism, a minor pilgrimage, a one-person journey by a family protectress. A pilgrimage, even a short one to a regional site with its local myths, legends, and procedures, is a fairly obvious example of religious observance. It has a journey to and a journey from the sacred site framing the actions performed there. But there are many other details of ritual in the day of a Hindu woman or man that might escape the outsider's attention were it not for verbal and nonverbal clues, the grace, reverence, even affection that attend such everyday actions (karmas) as entering or crossing a river, watering a plant or tree, preparing food.

For example, handouts to beggars might easily be dismissed as an occasional response to the circumstances of poverty, but such a view loses sight of several definitive aspects of Hinduism. Giving, *dana,* whether a wealthy patron's gift of a new temple to his town or the casual tossing of food remnants to ants, ghosts, or "beings" in the most generic and anonymous of senses, is ritual activity. Of the five prescribed daily "sacrifices," all involve reverent giving to other beings, and one in particular is directed to other humans in acts of hospitality or donation. Also, in sacrifice or giving, whatever the scale and duration, the sacrificer or the giver is altered, the merit of the event being added on to the life-body of the sacrificer.

In this sense, the incidental beggars on the railway platform were just one more group in the large, amorphous company of ritual recipients of Sita's Mother's activities on this day, as she herself, consciously or unconsciously in the ritual routine, was the recipient of merit and spiritual advancement. And such merit as she obtained was of course extended to her family, whose nourishment was her constant selfless duty. The beggars blended in with the *sadhu* on the riverbank, the would-be priest at the famed tree, the village deities, the household gods who first received the food she prepared in the predawn darkness, and indeed the trees at home at the sacred site and the Ganges River into which she had prayerfully tossed a coin as the train rattled over the long railway bridge. [See Religions of Mesoamerica pp. 226–33, Judaism pp. 469–70, Christianity pp. 562–77, Islam pp. 645–47, Buddhism p. 874, Religions of China pp. 1041–44, and Religions of Japan pp. 1154–60 for description and discussion of pilgrimage.]

A Region, a River, and a Life

One dew-wet morn, here, I unfolded my life, and practiced my songs on a harp. This harp of my life's entirety I know I must leave behind—but their airs, filling my heart, I shall take with me. (Rabindranath Tagore [1861–1941])[9]

The forty years after independence in 1947 witnessed changes in India that rival those of the previous forty centuries. For example, the rapid spread of television in the 1980s brought the immediacy and concrete, specific awareness so characteristic of video imagery to many remote areas of the subcontinent. More available than the automobile, more personal than radio, more versatile than the fantasy-world cinema, a single television set in a village suddenly opens that small society to alternate realities and presents to its people entirely new options. Life in the smallest village in Kerala is linked visually, and thereby realistically, to life in Bombay and Delhi, or to rural Assam or Madhya Pradesh.

Individuals in the complex of Indian civilization have experienced twentieth-century changes in different ways and to varying degrees; most have had to adapt to new economic, political, social, and religious realities, and many have had to devise a more or less fluid stance between the poles of traditional and post-traditional lifestyles. A closer look at one individual may instruct about certain aspects of Hinduism today. It would be impossible to find in so diverse and multicultural a subcontinent as India a "typical" Hindu. In some ways the life history we are about to survey is atypical, particularly in the last two decades. But his roots are traditional, and characteristic of his region, and his experiences are not at all remote from those of his countrymen in other regions. M. V. Krishnayya[10] is selected for this chapter because he is open, reflective, and

India's Eastern Seaboard.

articulate about his life and also because his life as a whole represents a composite—familiar throughout the long history of Hinduism—of several modes of being a Hindu.

Krishnayya has lived all but a year of his life on the southeastern coast of India in the Telugu-speaking state of Andhra Pradesh. He was born in 1946 in the village of Dowleshvaram on the left bank of one of India's greatest rivers, the nine-hundred-mile-long Godavari. His family belongs to the Golla or Shepherd caste of the *Shudra varna*; in the ordering of castes in the region Gollas are in the median ranks. As is the case with many castes with occupational names, Gollas in contemporary India are involved in a wide variety of trades and professions outside the traditional one.

Dominating Krishnayya's childhood memory is the vast expanse of the river, considered auspicious at Dowleshvaram where a forty-mile-long delta begins. Morning baths, riverside ceremonies, immersion of household and festival images, all link human and riverine cycles as the Godavari changes from monsoon ferocity to dry season docility. Overlooking the river from a Dowleshvaram hilltop is a temple of Vishnu (who is here called Janardhana) with its great carved wooden festival cart housed in a shed just across the street from

Krishnayya's house. And down the street, almost at the center of the village, is the temple of Shiva.

On the outskirts, where the crop fields begin, are half a dozen small shrines of disease goddesses, but closer to Krishnayya's street are two more substantial goddess centers, one a temple of Ankalamma, the other a shrine for Mutyalamma, both of them recipients of chickens sacrificed at their altars. Mutyalamma is the village guardian deity and Sister to everyone in Dowleshvaram. Her shrine on its square base includes a Nim tree and numerous stones. Krishnayya remembers his parents saying, "Mutyalamma is not in the shrine, so we [the village] are going to bring her here from her mother-in-law's place." In Mutyalamma's honor, each house has a fresh yellow turmeric patch on one interior wall, with three dots and two stripes representing the goddess. And an earthen pot containing water from the daily washing of rice is allowed to ferment slowly; in Krishnayya's house it is kept by his mother on a bed of leaves; it represents Mutyalamma's presence in the house, providing health, well-being, and coolness. It was quite a different presence, Krishnayya recalls, from that of the little images of Lakshmi and Krishna that were worshiped in the household shrine. The local Washerman, shrine priest for both Mutyalamma and Ankalamma, became possessed by one or the other goddess whenever she needed to express her anger to the villagers. Krishnayya remembers a terrible smallpox epidemic when he was ten or eleven; hundreds died, including someone from nearly every household.

"According to my parents," says Krishnayya, "we are Vaishnavas, in the tradition of Ramanuja. But we went more often to the Shiva temple, and our family priest was a Shaiva." More influential upon Krishnayya in his early years than temple traditions were the many rituals performed by his mother. Krishnayya was the fourth child born in the family, but the first to survive, and he remained exceptionally close to his mother. He remembers circling with her the "Tulsi Fort," a basil plant sacred to Vishnu, while she performed her daily *puja* with a lamp of oil. Among the many women's rituals called *nomus* in Telugu he particularly recalls one in which he accompanied his mother in house-to-house distribution of green chick-peas, soaked in water, to all the village. "Don't you want to have a sister?" he was asked repeatedly, for the ceremony, his mother's vow, was to gain another child.

Krishnayya also remembers absorbing "what everybody knows," for example, about the many objects hung from doorways, gates, and rooftops to ward off the evil eye or about the *mantras* recited, especially to Anjaneya (Hanuman), to frighten demons while walking at noon and midnight, or about all the things that are auspicious or inauspicious for first "sight" at the start of the day or any important undertaking.

Krishnayya has seen a photo taken on the day when, at six months, his ears were ritually pierced and ringed. But the first of the *samskaras* that he remembers was his initial tonsure at the age of five years, on a memorable day for him when the family journeyed over the immense Godavari River to the temple of Lord Venkateshvara in "little Tirupati." There Krishnayya had his head shaved while his eleven-month-old brother underwent the *samskara* of first feeding with solid food. Back in Dowleshvaram the ceremonies were repeated by the family priest and then, shortly after, came the ritual that began Krishnayya's formal education. The schoolteacher and the family priest both came to the house, and Krishnayya observed closely as the priest wrote a prayer to Shiva in rice grains spread on a great brass tray. Verses to Sarasvati, the goddess of learning, were taught and then a new slate received *pujas,* and on it were written first "OM" and then the letters of the Telugu alphabet, beginning with "A." Krishnayya made the ritual presentation of gifts to the priest and the teacher, as well as new slates and chalk to all the students in his new class.

A significant part of Krishnayya's education took place outside home and school. A Brahman widow with shaved head lived next door, and Krishnayya spent considerable time with her. His mother would lift him over the garden wall to the widow, who called him "Gopalam" and read to him stories from the *Ramayana,* the *Mahabharata,* and the *Bhagavata Purana.* Krishnayya was repeatedly cautioned never to touch her, as she was a Brahman. From her he learned not only the great tales of gods, demons, and heroes, but also of India's famous cities, Banaras, Calcutta, Puri. She would periodically go on pilgrimage to one of these mysterious places, then return to tell him more about *samsara,* karma, and *moksha,* about heaven and hell, and even of the Buddhist doctrine of emptiness.

Gradually, with his family increased by two brothers and two sisters, Krishnayya came to know the temples and towns of his region, and horse- or bullock-carts, busses, and trains took them all to the great festivals. After his initial tonsure Krishnayya had his head ritually shaved another dozen times in twenty years, in connection with various vows, school examinations, and diplomas. One such tonsure was in the Satya Narayana temple on the hill at Annavaram, another at the temple of Venkateshvara in greater Tirupati, India's wealthiest temple, situated far to the south in the Seven Hills. At twelve years Krishnayya traveled for the first time outside Andhra, experiencing briefly a new language, Tamil, and a bewildering urban culture in the city of Madras. The year before this his world had already begun to widen when he started his studies in both Hindi and English. Krishnayya was the first in his family to learn English. As a child he heard not only the multiple dialects of Telugu, but also Urdu, Oriya, Marathi, Tamil, Kannada, Hindi, and English, but only as he started to travel did he begin to link language with region, religion, class, and education. Krishnayya tried also to start Sanskrit but was removed from the roster. "It will be difficult for you," said the teacher. In other words, says Krishnayya, "I was not a Brahman."

Krishnayya's father was not able to work for a time, and the family suffered considerably. When the priest came to inform them that the third anniversary funerary observance for Krishnayya's deceased grandfather was due, and would cost ten rupees, there was no money. Krishnayya sold his books for that amount, a gesture that left him uneasy; in his twelve-year-old thoughts it was like selling the goddess Sarasvati.

After finishing high school in Dowleshvaram, Krishnayya received a modest scholarship to study in the Government Arts College in Rajahmundry, where he followed his father's wishes and pursued a science degree. He was also introduced to the ways of life in a large town. Mathematics courses he found trying, and he spent several years on the degree, with interruptions of employment as a government clerk in a forest area of central Andhra, and then for three years in the city of Vijayawada. His religious life in these years away from home was intense, with numerous *pujas* at the Shiva temple or up on the hillside at the ancient temple of Durga in Vijayawada. As part of his early morning *puja* each day he worshiped the *navagrahas,* or nine planets, including Surya, the sun; he also had special reverence for Ganesha, Sarasvati, and Lakshmi. To his mother he gave a framed lithograph of Venkateshvara, Lord of the Seven Hills, which she incorporated into the home shrine in the kitchen at Dowleshvaram. Frequently he heard religious discourses at the Ramakrishna Matha in Vijayawada, and once he asked a visiting swami from Kanchipuram for his blessing in anticipation of an exam; receiving it, Krishnayya felt exhilaration that his boldness had brought him within the aura of a holy man.

When he was accepted at Andhra University to begin, at age twenty-five, a degree in philosophy, he was drawn back across the wide Godavari to Waltair, on the coast of northern Andhra. There was money for tuition only, so he slept at first outside the door of the student hostel. At times in that initial year, perhaps because of a necessary asceticism, the religious life seemed powerfully attractive to him. He began to reexamine his religious experiences and think about the "logic" of Hinduism. He was aware that he was going to temples less for *vratas* or personal problem solving, more for aesthetic and religious enjoyment. He also reflected on what the Brahman widow had taught him about the *atman,* about the importance of self-discovery ahead of self-gratification.

His university studies in both Indian and Western philosophy led him through an M.A. degree program and appointment as a research scholar and candidate for the Ph.D. in philosophy. His close friends among foreign students at the university included Russians and Americans, and he absorbed from them ideas, attitudes, language, everything that aroused his abundant curiosity. Russian became his fourth language, and he earned an interpreter's certificate, Russian-English-Russian. A research fellowship to work in the National Library in Calcutta took him out of Andhra for a year and led not only to a fifth linguistic fluency, in Bengali, but also to a friendship with a fellow student, resulting in 1975 in the unusual step of a self-chosen marriage. The union was against outraged protests on both sides; although of the same caste, their different regions were seen by the elders as an insuperable barrier. The bride's father refused to attend and perform the important giving-away ceremony, so that was done by her mother. "Bengalis think we are another race," scoffs Krishnayya, "an inferior race!"

The intensity of his research program, coupled with a degree of self-consciousness in the company of foreign friends, had gradually curtailed some of his personal religious activities, and for some years he gave up his morning devotions. But as the years stretched out and his future job prospects remained unpromising, he resumed worship of the nine planets each morning and undertook, on the advice of a friend, a lengthy recitation from the *Puranas,* a **japa** by which the sage Markandeya overcame death. Every morning for two months in 1978 he did this at home, as there was no money for a service in the temple. But the verses had no appreciable result and, despite the arrival of a daughter to the new household, Krishnayya's worries were magnified by a marriage turned quarrelsome.

By 1980 Krishnayya's position was increasingly insecure. His degree program was stalled, he had not had a job for seven years, and he had a wife and daughter to support. His mother was convinced that the village astrologer could help, and the tall, gaunt Brahman with the musty Sanskrit manuscripts and brass zodiac dials was consulted. In the mail Krishnayya received a large packet of horoscopes: The standstill, according to the astrologer, resulted from the long-time evil influence of Saturn and Mars, two of the nine planets in Hindu astrology. After some resistance Krishnayya acceded to his mother's request that he make ritual presentations (*danas*) to a special Brahman designated by the astrologer. He took the train from Waltair to Rajahmundry, then a rickshaw (pedicab) to the village. The *puja* arranged by the family priest was brief: Krishnayya sat opposite a Brahman brought from outside the village, one of a special class willing to assume, for a fee, the misfortunes of others. Under the instructions of the family priest, Krishnayya transferred from a brass tray to this Brahman a bag of black chick-peas, two iron nails, sesame seeds, cotton threads, and some raw sugar, along with the invisible but dangerous effects of Saturn and Mars, which the visiting Brahman would in turn remove from his own person at home by means of another ritual expiation.

Krishnayya was reluctant to credit the ritual, but he readily admitted that his fortunes showed marked improvement from that point on, as did those of his brother, who performed about the same time a similar rite to remove the unfavorable effects of the planets Rahu and Ketu. Eventually his dissertation

Krishnayya (left) consults a roadside fortune-teller in Rajahmundry, 1985. A parrot selects a card from the deck and gives it to the fortune-teller, who interprets its signs for the client.

was completed and accepted, and Krishnayya received an appointment on the faculty of the Department of Philosophy at the university. This brought relief from painful economic worries and eased some of the tensions in the family. Krishnayya's horizons continued to expand: In 1985 he was invited abroad and traveled to London and throughout the United States, then returned to Waltair to teach and begin work on a book. As he examined his fortieth year he reflected on the constant changes that occur in a life—like those that stir the depths and surfaces of the Godavari River—although apparent all the while is the unity of the life—like the oneness of the river.

At a distance from the region of Andhra and the nation of India one may observe in the details of this life many features of contemporary Hinduism, including some of the more elusive ones. Though Krishnayya's name and family are traditionally Vaishnava, Shiva and various goddesses play an important part in their faith and practice. This kind of balance is typical of Hinduism. Belief systems are personal, subdued, flexible, and subordinated to practical expressions of faith in vows, devotions, prayers, life-cycle rituals, festivals, and pilgrimages. While these traditional family and community stepping-stones dominate, their importance fluctuates according to the period of life and specific challenges of that period.

This survey of Krishnayya's experiences, a tiny fraction of them at best, is instructive in another way. It undercuts the "classical"/"folk" dichotomy that is sometimes used to discuss Indian tradition. The Brahman widow telling stories from the Sanskrit *Ramayana* and the untouchable priest possessed by the goddess of smallpox are both vital parts of living Hinduism in a single village and are equally important components in the faith of one individual. Krishnayya, no longer a villager, never having been a "peasant," is at ease in modern India, travels frequently, and is well acquainted with contemporary innovation and change, yet he carries in his experience those and many other parts in the composite of his Hindu background. He has ventured onto paths totally unknown to his parents, but he still is shaped by his origins and, like great numbers of his countrymen and women, must nurture a lifestyle that engages simultaneously in the old world of tradition, both "folk" and "classical," and the new world of cosmopolitan, television-viewing India. [See Religions of Africa pp. 45–51, 75–79, Native Religions of North America pp. 318–20, Judaism pp. 457–69, Christianity pp. 573–86, Religions of China pp. 1040–54, and Religions of Japan pp. 1163–72 for description and discussion of life histories and personal accounts.]

34

Hinduism Today

ON SEPTEMBER 4, 1987, Roop Kanwar, an eighteen-year-old woman in the village of Deorala in Rajasthan, burned to death as she sat upright, enclosed in the logs of her husband's funeral pyre. The practice of *sati,* widow burning, is an ancient one in northwest India, although without sanction in any Hindu text. Condemned by nineteenth-century reformers such as Ram Mohan Roy and prohibited by ordinances beginning in 1829, it has survived in sporadic instances in the last two centuries, one of many graphic illustrations of the manner in which India and Hinduism appear to inhabit multiple time frames.

The nationwide debate generated by the Deorala *sati* is instructive for those who seek to understand the destiny of Hinduism at the close of the twentieth century. The government of India, as a modernizing secular state under constitutional law, was swift and unanimous in passing a bill providing for life imprisonment or the death sentence for abetment of *sati.* Vigorous condemnations of this cultural anachronism appeared in the press, along with denunciation of those who would glorify *sati* by citing scriptures on women's loyalty to their husbands, even to the point of self-sacrifice. But little was said about the thousands of active shrines throughout the subcontinent that commemorate *sati* events of the past. Some prominent Hindu sectarian leaders even came out in support of "voluntary *sati*" and "*sati dharma*." One of their arguments was that the ideal of feminine loyalty demonstrated throughout Hindu mythology, folklore, ritual, and symbolism is upheld by only a few women, just as the ideal of renunciation is maintained by only a few *samnyasis.* Still others resisted taking a stand on the issue on the grounds of freedom of religious expression guaranteed by the constitution.

A few weeks after Roop Kanwar's death, which some witnesses stated was physically enforced by her male in-laws, a poll was conducted in thirty-two towns and villages in fourteen districts of Rajasthan.[11] A majority (63 percent) of those interviewed were women. Of those interviewed, 86.6 percent knew of the *sati* cult, 80.7 percent knew of Roop Kanwar, and 63.4 percent approved of the act in her case. Only 3.65 percent of those interviewed felt that the young woman had been forced to commit *sati.* A number of respondents declared that she had become a goddess (Sati Devi).

The forceful debate on this single event, and the public opinion of Rajasthanis, remind us of the dangers of easy generalizations about contemporary Hinduism. From a corner of a high-rise apartment complex in Bombay, Kanpur, or Hyderabad there may be no temples or shrines visible, no traditional dress, festival activities, or outward evidence of caste. By contrast, at a crossroads in a traditional town or village there may be two or three temples and half a dozen shrines and statues in sight, a local goddess procession going by, a colorfully clad *sadhu* or traditional beggar making his rounds of doorways, and ample evidence of caste distinctions in dress, occupation, and behavior. But the degree of religious faith and practice, the measure of "being a Hindu," often cannot be determined by appearances. It would be a mistake to assume that modernization and Westernization, so apparent in urban India, have erased essential Hindu traditions. Personal and family patterns of worship, participation in temples, *mathas,* and other religious institutions, and visits to pilgrimage sites or ancestral shrines, although often modified or abbreviated by the exigencies of urban life, go on just as they do in villages and traditional towns.

Hinduism throughout its history has had a limitless capacity for absorbing events into its symbol system, and it continues to do so in modern times. Indira Gandhi, prime minister of India until her assassination in Delhi in October 1984, is now visible in the guise of plaster busts in every village and town. Like a goddess, she is usually at crossroads, garlanded, with a fresh red dot on her forehead, and is often revered by a largely illiterate populace that recognizes in her statue a power to see, touch, borrow. It remains to be seen whether an actual Indira cult will emerge, but already the myths are in process, translating a secular political life into a new hagiography, an illustration of Hinduism's perpetual drive for self-renewal.

One indicator of vitality and experimentation in Hinduism has been described by scholars as a process of Sanskritization, whereby Brahmanic faith and practice, and Sanskrit texts, become increasingly more significant to non-Brahman strata of society. This is, of course, a process already documented in early Vedic religion, and one that is apparent in every subsequent phase of the history of Hinduism. The Brahmans, once the educated and educating elite, protected the Sanskrit language, the *Vedas,* and the *shastras* and limited access to the law codes, great temples, *tirthas,* and monastic institutions. In modern India they have seen their power base eroded by the secular state, upwardly mobile caste groups, and political institutions. Education is open to all. Untouchables, tribal peoples, "backward classes," and "weaker sections" are given special catch-up privileges and positions in affirmative action programs. Temples may no longer exclude Hindu untouchables; some Vedic schools and even major temples are administered by state governments, and the *Vedas* and Sanskrit devotional *shlokas* can be heard by all at public bathing facilities, fairs, and festivals. Radio and television broadcasts democratize the faith. *Mantras* are recited by women and recorded on cassettes, and the epic *Ramayana* has been serialized for Sunday morning television. A Brahman recitant is not required if the Sanskrit classics are available on a personal videocassette recorder.

Along with the decline of Brahman hegemony and the increase in universal education has come a slowly increasing affluence in the middle and lower classes that enables many to enrich their spiritual lives by a variety of means: travel to sacred sites and regional fairs and festivals; adoption of new and more elaborate rituals; religious education in *mathas* and societies; donations for shrines or temples; devotional allegiance to a god-man or living goddess; purchase of religious books, tracts, and posters. [See Religions of Africa pp. 74–75, Religions of Mesoamerica pp. 229–38, Native Religions of North America pp. 308–16, 351–57, Judaism pp. 439–45, Christianity pp. 551–55, Islam pp. 674, 677–79, Buddhism pp. 937–41, Religions of China pp. 1021–24, and Religions of Japan pp. 1140–46, 1153–62 for description and discussion of festivals and annual celebrations.]

As an illustration, consider a middle-aged South Indian man named Raju whose caste in the Shudra *varna* places him outside the traditional three twice-born classes and Sanskrit learning. A spiritual conversion in his late twenties and economic independence, the result of a successful blue-collar job, propelled him into prominence as the most resourceful religious personality of his neighborhood. Essentially he has two spiritual careers that now increasingly absorb his time, one visible to the community, the other private and personal. He is a faith healer who provides sacred ash (*vibhuti*), lime juice, and *mantras* as cures for ailments such as boils, rashes, or the bites of centipedes, scorpions, or snakes. Mothers bring to him children affected by the evil eye or by malevolent winds and spirits. He also treats adult "body weakness" caused by the influence of dark planets, and he is knowledgeable about charms, amulets, gemstones, and talismans for a variety of purposes. At certain local festivals he is an ecstatic god-dancer, one who is routinely possessed by a powerful and dangerous deity. Well known as a benefactor of religious institutions, he has personally constructed goddess shrines in different parts of his city, one for example housing the pan-Indian Durga, another for a particular epidemic disease goddess. Recently he has taken up sponsorship of a local haven for wandering *sadhus*, regularly supplying them with brass bells and begging bowls, daily leaf plates, and even pampering them with cash to assure them of what he regards as a balanced diet.

The invisible side of his religious life is more astonishing. Although a Shudra, he wears a sacred thread, and his daily meditations and rituals in a fluent Sanskrit would rival the procedures of the strictest Brahman. Following his dawn bath in the river he meditates upon the *linga* he wears always around his neck—a grey agate surrounded by minute figures of Ganesha, Lakshmi, Durga, Parvati, and Sarasvati, all enclosed in a great silver egg. One of the three small rooms in the city apartment he shares with his wife and two children is entirely devoted to minishrines and altars, and here he performs *pujas* in Sanskrit for two hours, followed by another hour of meditation, all before starting the day's work. Raju diets on milk and fruits, observes celibacy (*brahmacarya*), allows his long, matted hair to grow into Shiva's locks. He describes his goal as the Upanishadic quest: knowledge of the Supreme Soul, *brahman*.

The spiritual life of this man is a good illustration of a conscious and deliberate program of Sanskritization. It is also a corrective to the outsider's tendency to separate the shaman or faith healer of non-Sanskritic "folk" religion from the high-caste Hindu Sanskritic tradition. Riding about the city on his motor scooter, his matted locks flying in the wind, Raju seems happy to include the entire range of Hindu phenomena within his own expansive embrace.

Another process in modern India might be labeled "acharyization." This is the tendency of urban, educated classes to simplify Hinduism by reducing it to selected pronouncements of a few great teachers (**acharyas**) and divesting it of all aspects perceived to be communal, parochial or rural, divisive, and "superstitious." A standard list of *acharyas* might begin with such medieval synthesizers as Shankara and Ramanuja, then jump to one or more recent reformers such as Ram Mohan Roy, Dayananda Sarasvati, Ramakrishna and Vivekananda, or Aurobindo. A more generous list might add Gautama Buddha, Jesus Christ, Guru Nanak, and Gandhi, and those exposed to regional swamis and gurus who have gained national or international followings might mention Sathya Sai Baba, Ramana Maharshi, Maharishi Mahesh Yogi (or Rajnish, who died in India in 1990, under the name of "Osho," after his deportation from the United States). Note here one incongruity demonstrated in back-to-back discussions of Sanskritization and acharyization: While Raju wears on his person the images of four goddesses (along with Shiva and Ganesha) and daily worships several other goddesses, the standard lists of respectable *acharyas* are all male.

Like Sanskritization, this phenomenon centering on *acharyas* is related to the process of democratization of the faith at the expense of the Brahman elite, as well as to increased exposure to Western values, widening educational opportunities, and the expansion of modern mass communications. (As in the United States, the media hold the power to turn religious figures into national celebrities in relatively short order.) Behind an eclectic and often dogmatic acharyized Hinduism is the desire to modernize, to demonstrate that the dominant faith of India is effective and up-to-date not only for South Asians, but for humankind, a universal faith, eternal and seminal for human spirituality. It is in effect Hinduism without warts.

Acharyized Hinduism ignores or dismisses impediments to universal acceptance of the faith. In this view the pandits' distinctions between *shruti* and *smriti*, the caste hierarchy, untouchability, concerns for purity and pollution, magic and witchcraft, astrology, faith healing, "barbarisms" such as *sati*, child sacrifice, ritual possessions by the dead, fire walking, or the offerings of chickens, pigs, goats, sheep, or buffalo to local goddesses, even the profusion of gods and goddesses in Puranic myths are all left behind in the program of evolution for modern Hinduism. Emphasis is upon self-realization after the example of the self-realized teacher. The program is usually strongly egalitarian and devotional-meditative, moralizing, with emphasis on overt monotheism or the Upanishadic, Vedantic identification of the self with the divine world Soul. Frequently there is a focus on "modern scientific principles" harnessed not for pleasure and material gain (as in "the decadent West"), but for those spiritual ends manifest in the eternal *dharma* and represented by the *acharyas*.

Seldom apparent in village India and still rare in traditional towns, achary-ized Hinduism is familiar in English-speaking urban sectors throughout India and has had considerable success as an export to the West, from the Theosophical Society and Ramakrishna Mission to the more recent Transcendental Meditation movement and Divine Light Mission. It is worth remarking that alongside the guru-establishments purveying *yoga* and hybrid, updated Hinduism to the West, Hindu temples and *mathas* have been steadily appearing all over Europe and America. They are built by traditional Indian masons and sculptors, dedicated and staffed by Hindu *pujaris* and pandits, and serve the large immigrant communities who now establish roots in major cities of the West. Westerners fortunate enough to visit these new institutions are treated to authentic Hindu rituals and discourses previously not seen outside India, although here too the general tendency is to foster a faith acceptable morally and intellectually to Western societies and to Hindus who have chosen to live in them.

For the vast majority of Hindus in South Asia the adjective "modern" before Hinduism holds no particular meaning. Even dynamic new movements—striking to long-time observers of South Asian religions—are perceived by the faithful as age-old, normative expressions. The sudden appearance of a popular goddess such as Santoshi Mata or the huge increase in pilgrim attention to the goddess Vaishno Devi in northwest India are phenomena readily absorbed into the patterns of classical Hindu goddess traditions. And when hundreds of thousands of black-clad, exuberant young men mobilize all over India in the burgeoning cult of **Ayyappan** and travel by chartered trains and busses, then on foot up Kerala's Sabari Hill to his shrine, they are after all traditional pilgrims displaying a standard repertoire of vows, devotional fervor, fasting, celibacy, and recitation

Devotees from different castes, drawn together in the cult of the bachelor god Ayyappan, son of Shiva and Mohini, a feminine incarnation of Vishnu. These young men undergo a forty-one-day penance and five-hundred-mile pilgrimage every year.

of the divine name. In fact, the curious result of the endless experimentation of Hindu tradition is that true innovation is virtually impossible: It seems that in one or another age everything has already been done many times over!

As the world moves into the twenty-first century and India overtakes China as the most populous nation on earth, South Asia faces more pressing challenges than at any previous point in history. South Asia is riddled with communal violence—Hindu-Muslim, Sikh-Hindu, Tamil Hindu–Sinhalese Buddhist, tribal-nationalist. Despite the "green revolution" of the 1970s, oppressive poverty and malnutrition burden half the population with no relief in view. Two-thirds of the people are illiterate, and the democratic institutions of India and Sri Lanka, plus the liberal Hindu kingdom of Nepal, sandwiched between the changing regimes of neighboring nations, seem always to be targets for anarchy. But Hinduism as a dominant faith in the region of South Asia exhibits little concern for the turn of a century, of an economy, of a dynasty. Its age-old ways of listening, mythologizing, classifying, recycling, and swallowing the universe look at the world and its ills with a relative eye. This is, after all, the Kali *yuga,* the worst time, and one to be succeeded by a long rest. Then a perfected age will dawn, truth and *dharma* will be restored to fullness and plenitude, and the universal order will prevail once again—for a time.

Epilogue

ON THE WALL BESIDE MY DESK is a photo taken many years ago of a darkly gnarled tree. From its branches hang half a dozen heavy burlap packages, blackened with mildew from the rains. Together they are an awesome, mysterious image. They provide no clue as to what they are, although one suspects they may either be offerings to some local deity, ancestor, or power—named or nameless to the one who took the trouble to place them there—or bundles to draw away attention of the evil eye and therefore protect the area. As for the photo, it hangs here as a reminder of how much of Hinduism I do not understand.

Study Questions

Before you begin to read this part, take a mental inventory of what you know and think about Hinduism. What do you know about India, its people, culture, way of life, music, and art? What would you imagine Hinduism to be like? Keep these images and things in mind as you read this section and develop new notions about Hinduism.

CHAPTER 29

Introduction

1. How does the author use the notion "jumble of possibilities" to introduce Hinduism?
2. What are the major religious traditions in South Asia, and in what ways is Hinduism understood apart from these traditions?
3. How old is the tradition of Hinduism, and what are its major beliefs and practices?

CHAPTER 30

Hinduism and History: Prehistoric and Vedic Periods

1. How does the author compare the notions of "time" or "history" in Hindusim and in the contemporary West?
2. What are the dates and hallmarks of the Indus Civilization?
3. What are the dates and major features of the Vedic Age?
4. Summarize the Vedic worldview and its major concepts.
5. How do the Vedic *Upanishads* represent a reformation of the sacrificial worldview of the *Vedas*?

CHAPTER 31

Hinduism and History: The Epic Through Modern Periods

1. Define *Vedas* and *Puranas* as religious texts.
2. Compare and contrast the *Mahabharata* and the *Ramayana* as epics.
3. What is *bhakti* and why is it important in the development of Hinduism?
4. Compare and contrast the religious thought of Shankara and Ramanuja.
5. How did Islam interact with Hinduism?
6. What was the role of poet-saints in late medieval Hinduism?

CHAPTER 32
Dimensions in a Worldview

1. What is the relationship between written and oral tradition in Hinduism?
2. How does the author use the notion of "listening to the universe" to interpret Hinduism?
3. How does the author use the notion of "mythologizing the universe" to interpret Hinduism?
4. After centuries of emphasis on physical sacrifice, what became more important in Hinduism?
5. How does the author interpret the existence of a great number of deities in Hinduism?
6. How does the author use the notion of "classifying the universe" to interpret Hinduism?
7. How are karma and *samsara* central to all Indian thought?
8. How does the author use the notion of "recycling the universe" to interpret Hinduism?
9. What is the significance of rites for ancestors in Hinduism?
10. What is "cyclicity" in Hindu mythology?
11. What is the role of the *yogi* in Hinduism?
12. How does the author use the notion of "swallowing the universe" to interpret Hinduism?
13. How does the author relate the five dimensions of listening to, mythologizing, classifying, recycling, and swallowing the universe?

CHAPTER 33
The Dynamics of Hinduism

1. Identify and describe the major rites of passage in "the journey of a lifebody."
2. What is the significance of the Goddess in Hinduism?
3. Trace the movement and action of "Sita's Mother" in her pilgrimage—what is the significance of this pilgrimage as an example of Hindu ritual life?
4. Trace the religious events in the life history of Krishnayya—what does this one life tell us about religious life in contemporary India?

CHAPTER 34
Hinduism Today

1. In what ways do such incidents as the 1987 death of an eighteen-year-old Rajasthani widow inform us about religion in contemporary India?
2. What is the process of "Sanskritization" and how does the South Indian man named Raju illustrate this process?
3. What is "acharyization" and to what social group does it appeal?

Recall the mental images and facts about Hinduism that you made before reading this part. What is there in Hinduism that is most like your own religious tradition? What in Hinduism is most different from your own tradition? What is most interesting? How has your understanding of Hinduism changed as a result of reading this section? Can you now imagine yourself participating in Hinduism?

Notes

To my daughters Nicola, Viveka, and Jennifer, and to my wife Susan, warm thanks for sharing the enchantments, conundrums, and gentle hazards of life in Kashi and Rajahmundry.

1. See Bruce Lincoln, *Myth, Cosmos and Society: Indo-European Themes of Creation and Destruction* (Cambridge, MA: Harvard University Press, 1986), chs. 1, 2, 6.
2. The English word *caste* comes from the Portuguese *casta,* a word the sixteenth-century explorers used to render the local Indian word *jati.*
3. Translated from Sanskrit by Chakravarti Rajagopalachari, *Ramayana* (Bombay: Bharatiya Vidya Bhavan, 1952), 219–21; condensed and cited with modifications.
4. Translated from Tamil by A. K. Ramanujan, *Hymns for the Drowning: Poems for Visnu by Nammalvar* (Princeton, NJ: Princeton University Press, 1981), 30.
5. From a pamphlet, "Sri Aurobindo Ashram, Delhi Branch" (Delhi: Matri Press, 1986), i.
6. M. N. Srinivas, *The Remembered Village* (New York: Oxford University Press, 1976), 326–28; cited with modifications.
7. Translated from Sanskrit by Jean Varenne in his *Yoga and the Hindu Tradition;* translated from French by Derek Coltman (Chicago: University of Chicago Press, 1976), 221–22.
8. David M. Miller and Dorothy C. Wertz, *Hindu Monastic Life: The Monks and Monasteries of Bhubaneswar* (Montreal-London: McGill-Queen's University Press, 1976), 103.
9. Rabindranath Tagore, *A Flight of Swans: Poems from Balaka,* translated from Bengali by Aurobindo Bose (London: John Murray, 1962), 107.
10. His real name, used with his approval following interviews 1980–1987.
11. *Times of India,* New Delhi, December 11, 1987.

Glossary

Names and terms in the text have been simplified at the expense of accuracy in transliteration and pronunciation. For example, the *sh* in Vishnu and Shiva are not the same sounds and letters in spoken and written Sanskrit, and the vowels in Sita are long whereas in Indra they are short. In this glossary and accompanying list of Deities, Powers, and Deified Heroes the standard diacritics have been added as a guide to pronunciation and for ease of recognition in further studies of Hinduism. All terms and names, with the exception of the South Indian deities Ayyappan and Murukan, are Sanskrit, the language of religion and philosophy for classical and modern Hinduism.

Macrons over vowels lengthen them: *ā* as in "father," *ī* as in "teen," *ū* as in "boot." Vocalic *ṛ* is close to the *ri* of "ring." The sibilant *s* as in "sow" is distinct from both *ṣ* and *ś* as in "sure" or "shine." A *c* is always *ch* as in "church." All aspirated consonants contain a crisp following *h* as in "goat-herd," "hog-head," "head-hunter," "up-hill," "knob-hill." Other diacritics distinguish among additional variations in sounds and letters, but they are minor and need not detain us here. Contemporary languages in South Asia frequently drop the final "a" of terms that derive from Sanskrit, as for example, *āśram, darśan, maṭh, yug.*

ācārya A spiritual teacher or preceptor; learned scholar of religious traditions. See also guru.

advaita Nonduality; the philosophical premise made prominent in Vedānta by Śankara that only *bráhman* is real.

ahiṃsā Noninjury to any life form.

āśrama One of the four stages of life; a tranquil place suitable for the third and fourth stages; a retreat or hermitage.

ātman The Self, Soul, Spirit that is eternal, surviving successive mortal bodies until *mokṣa* provides release.

avatāra A descent, manifestation, or incarnation of a deity, Viṣṇu, for example.

avidyā The wrong knowledge, worldly wisdom, that is, ignorance.

bhakti Devotion to a deity, the most popular path to salvation. A devotee is known as *bhakta.*

brahmacārin Vedic student who lives according to *bráhman* in the first of four stages of life (*āśramas*).

bráhman The eternal essence of the sacred word; later, ultimate reality, the imperishable absolute without *guṇas;* the *Upaniṣads* identify *ātman* with *bráhman.* The *brahmán* is a supervisory priest for Vedic rituals.

Brāhmaṇa varṇa Highest of the three twice-born classes, the traditional priestly rank of society; Brahman and Brahmin are common spellings.

darśana Sight of a deity, sacred site, holy person; such vision transforms the seer.

dharma Spiritual duty in accord with cosmic law and order; perhaps the closest Sanskrit word for "religion," *dharma* replaces the Vedic term *ṛta.*

dhyāna Meditation; in classical *yoga,* the state of awareness prior to *samādhi.*

dīkṣā Ritual consecration, initiation.

gāyatrī The initiatory *mantra* of a twice-born Hindu (*Ṛgveda* 3.62.10).

gopi One of the cowherd girls in love with Kṛṣṇa; in devotional poetry, songs, paintings, and instrumental music she is the human soul longing for God.

gṛhya The household, domicile.

guṇa "Strand," "thread," quality, attribute; the three strands of nature according to certain philosophies are purity or brightness (*sattva*), passion (*rajas*), inertia (*tamas*); a distinction often made is one between the impersonal absolute (*bráhman*) without qualities (*nirguṇa*) and a personal Absolute or supreme being with qualities (*saguṇa*).

guru A teacher, spiritual guide. See also *ācārya*.

homa An offering to a deity, especially one into a sacred fire.

iṣṭadevatā Chosen deity, a god or goddess with whom a devotee maintains a special relationship.

japa The repetition of divine names, *mantras*, or prayers.

jāti A "kind" of being; a caste or caste-group in the social hierarchy. See also *varṇa*.

jñāna Knowledge, particularly spiritual knowledge acquired by insight, the grace of a deity, or other nondiscursive means.

karma Action; in the *Vedas*, ritual work; later karma comes to mean not only all action but the personal consequences or destiny that accrue from action. See also *saṃsāra*.

Kṣatriya varṇa Second of the three twice-born classes, traditionally the warrior nobility of society.

līlā The divine play or sport of a deity, Kṛṣṇa, for example.

liṅga The phallus, major symbol of Śiva's regenerative powers.

loka World-space.

maṇḍala A diagram of circles and squares representing the cosmos for ritual and meditation. See also *yantra*.

mantra An essential sound or phrase from *śruti*; later, any oral formula of sacred power.

mārga Path, way, discipline leading to salvation.

matha A study hall, sectarian school, monastery, or all three, often part of the institutional structure of an important temple.

māyā The creative magic powers of a deity, Varuṇa or Kṛṣṇa, for example; cosmic illusion.

mokṣa Release, freedom, liberation of the *ātman* from its bondage to *saṃsāra*.

phala Fruit, consequence, result of sacrifice; in post-Vedic Hinduism, the fruit of all action, not ritual action alone.

prakṛti Nature, primal matter, the phenomenal world with its three *guṇas;* the feminine complement/opposite of masculine *puruṣa*.

prāṇa Breath, both cosmic and human; *prāṇāyāma* is yogic control of breathing.

prasāda Grace, favor of a deity or holy person; the consecrated ritual remnant, the coconut, for example, broken before a goddess as offering, then returned to the offerer as food transformed by her grace.

pūjā Worship of a deity, person, or object representing the sacred.

purohita Domestic priest.

puruṣa "Male," spirit; consciousness, the complement/opposite of feminine *prakṛti*.

ṛta Cosmic order. See also *dharma*.

sādhu A world renouncer, a wandering mendicant on a spiritual quest.

samādhi A state of release, transcendence; eighth and highest stage in the process of classical *yoga*; also the burial site of a holy person.

saṃnyāsa Renunciation, the fourth and highest stage of life; one who takes a vow is a *saṃnyāsin*.

saṃsāra This-worldly realm of rebirths; transmigration. See also karma.

saṃskāra Perfection, rite of passage, life-cycle ritual.

smṛti Tradition, memory, the total human recall of spiritual values; distinct from and dependent on its basis, the eternal *śruti*.

śrāddha Funeral rites and subsequent offerings to ancestors.

śramaṇa "Striver," non-Vedic ascetic or renunciant.

śrauta See *śruti*.

śruti, śrauta Both from the verb "to hear," *śruti* being "that which is heard," that is, the Vedas, and *śrauta* being those rituals that maintain human-cosmic links according to *śruti*, the ultimate authority. See also *smṛti*.

Śūdra varṇa Fourth of the social classes, not among the twice-born; in many regions of India *śūdras* and the still lower Scheduled Castes and tribes are the majority of the population.

tapas "Heat," austerities, ascetic techniques that are spiritually creative.

tyāga Abandonment, relinquishment; a Vedic ritual term that came to mean a letting go of the fruits of action.

upanayana Initiation by investiture with a sacred thread and instruction in Vedic *mantras* and offerings.

vāhana An animal, bird, or other mount of a deity.

Vaiśya varṇa Third of the three twice-born classes, traditionally concerned with productivity (domestic animals, agriculture, certain crafts), but today calling to mind the merchants.

varṇa One of the four classes of humans in the social hierarchy; each includes numerous *jātis*.

veda Sacred knowledge, collection of revealed texts made known to the ancient seers.

vrata Personal vow, often connected with fasting, pilgrimage, donations, particular *pūjās* or austerities.

yajña Sacrifice, the ritual work (karma) of Vedic priests on behalf of the sacrificer and the world.

yantra Mystical diagram of cosmic powers. See also *maṇḍala*.

yoga, yogi Yoking of the self by spiritual discipline (*yoga*) creates of an ordinary human a spiritually disciplined one (*yogin*). Yoga is one of the six great systems of philosophy.

yuga One of the four ages of cosmic timekeeping: Kṛta, Tretā, Dvāpara, and the (present) Kālī *yuga*.

Deities, Powers, and Deified Heroes

Aditi Vedic goddess, boundless mother of the gods, especially of the eight or twelve Ādityas, including Mitra, Varuṇa, and Indra.

Agni The Vedic sacrificial fire and god of fire.

Arjuna Warrior hero of the *Mahābhārata* epic; celebrated for his dialogue with Kṛṣṇa in the *Bhagavad Gītā*.

asura An early Vedic term for sovereign deity or "lord"; in subsequent mythology the *asuras* are collective demonic powers opposed to the *devas*.

Aśvins Twin "horsemen" in the *Vedas*, divine physicians, comparable in some respects to the Greek Dioskouroi.

Ayyappan A son of Śiva and a female incarnation of Viṣṇu; related mythically to Skanda and Kārttikeya; popular in South India, where his principal locus is the Sabari Hill (Sabarimala).

bhūta Ghost, particularly a troublesome or malevolent spirit of the dead, likely to possess people.

Brahmā The creator, grandfather (that is, the oldest) of the gods; perpetuates in epics and *Purāṇas* only a shadow of the supreme being Puruṣa-Prajāpati of the early Vedic texts.

deva "God"; generic name for Vedic and later deities.

devī Feminine form of *deva* and generic name for "goddess"; regional names and forms are countless; in the epics and *Purāṇas* Cāmuṇḍā, Durgā, Gaurī, Kālī, Lakṣmī, Mahādevī, Pārvatī, Sarasvatī, Śrī, and Umā are prominent, among others.

Draupadī Heroine-goddess of the *Mahābhārata* epic and wife of the five Pāṇḍava brothers.

Durgā A fierce, aggressive goddess, celebrated for her killing of Mahiṣāsura; worshiped in two great annual festivals.

Dyaus The masculine Sky or Heaven, paired in early Vedic myths with Pṛthivī.

Gaṇeśa Also known as Gaṇapati, "lord of the hosts (of devotees)," or Vināyaka; the elephant-headed remover of obstacles, he is a son of Śiva and Pārvatī.

Garuḍa The eagle or hawk mount of Viṣṇu; enemy of the *nāgas*.

Hanuman or **Hanumat** Monkey hero and ally of Rāma in the *Rāmāyaṇa* epic; popular for his demonstrative devotion and loyalty, as well as courageous guardianship.

Indra Heroic warrior god, most dynamic of Vedic deities, drinker of *soma* and slayer of Vṛtra; king of the gods in pre-epic mythology.

Kālī Terrible goddess, black in color and bloodthirsty in action, provider and taker of all life-forms; recipient of blood sacrifice—goats, for example.

Kṛṣṇa The dark blue or black god, celebrated in mythic episodes as mischievous child, heroic slayer of demons, lover of the cowgirls (*gopis*), king; an *avatāra* of Viṣṇu and principal figure in two of the most popular of texts, the *Bhāgavata Purāṇa* and the *Bhagavad Gītā*.

kuṇḍalinī A specific type of *śakti* in Tantric Yoga, a feminine serpent power coiled at the base of the spine, but raised by yogic techniques through the seven levels (*cakras*) of the human-cosmic body.

Lakṣmaṇa Younger brother of Rāma. Kṛṣṇa also has an older brother, Balarāma.

Lakṣmī Goddess of good fortune, wealth, prosperity; wife of Viṣṇu.

lokapāla Guardian of the universe; four, sometimes eight, are stationed at the directions, for example, Indra (east), Kubera (north), Varuṇa (west), Yama (south).

Mahiṣa or **Mahiṣāsura** The buffalo god/demon slain by Durgā (*Devī*); possibly a pre-Vedic deity, he is still worshiped in South India, as Pōtu Rāja, the Buffalo King, for example.

Manu Progenitor of humankind; the *Purāṇas* elaborate on each of the Manus to appear in the successive periods (*manvantaras*) of cosmic time.

Marut One of the storm gods, militant troops of Rudra. See also Rudra.

nāga Serpent god/demon; mythically related to autochthonous peoples of South Asia.

Nandin The bull mount of Śiva; celebrated for his devotion and guardianship.

Narasiṃha The "man-lion" *avatāra* of Viṣṇu, a fierce form of this otherwise benign deity.

navagraha One of the nine planets: Sūrya (Sun), Candra (Moon), Maṅgala (Mars), Budha (Mercury), Guru or Bṛhaspati (Jupiter), Śukra (Venus), Śani (Saturn), and the mythical invisible planets of eclipses, Ketu and Rāhu; all are males; the last three are dark and dangerous; shrines, temples, calendars, horoscopes, talismans, and rings reflect their significance.

Pāṇḍava Any one of the five sons of Pāṇḍu, heroes of the *Mahābhārata* epic: Yudhiṣṭhira, Arjuna, Bhīma, and the twins Nakula and Sahadeva.

Pārvatī Goddess-daughter of the mountain, chaste wife and passionate lover of Śiva.

piśāca A flesh-eating demon, one of the hordes that haunt cremation and burial grounds.

pitṛ "Father," that is, an ancestor, one of the community of the departed, male and female, who receive offerings of food, water, and *mantras*.

Prahlāda Famous devotee of Viṣṇu rescued from his murderous demon-father Hiraṇya-kaśipu by the Narasiṃha *avatāra* of Viṣṇu.

Prajāpati "Lord of creatures," the Vedic creator-god who perpetuates in the *Brāhmaṇas* the self-sacrificing creation of Puruṣa in the *Ṛgveda;* his ascetic fervor (*tapas*) is the origin of beings.

Pṛthivī The female Earth; paired in early Vedic myths with Dyaus, the masculine Sky or Heaven.

Puruṣa The primordial sacrifice-Person (*puruṣa*, literally, "male"); he projects his dismembered parts into cosmic phenomena and also the four human classes, derived respectively from his mouth, arms, thighs, feet; *Ṛgveda* 10.90 is a famous hymn known as the Puruṣa-sūkta. See also Prajāpati.

rākṣasa A terrible demon opposed to gods and heroes.

Rāma Hero of the epic *Rāmāyaṇa*, king of Ayodhyā, husband of Sītā; considered the model of masculine virtue and power; an *avatāra* of Viṣṇu.

Rāvaṇa Captor of Sītā and enemy of Rāma in the *Rāmāyaṇa* epic; a demon in the Sanskrit texts, he is considered a powerful deity in parts of South India.

ṛṣi A "seer" or sage; the seven great sages who first apprehended the *Vedas* include the well-known Bharadvāja, Bhṛgu, Dakṣa, Kaśyapa, and Vasiṣṭha. *Rishi* is a common spelling.

Rudra Vedic god, a "howler" in the wilderness; his late-Vedic epithet Śiva, "auspicious," becomes his best-known name. The Rudras are the eight or eleven troops of Rudra, including the major epithets of the classical god Śiva. See also Marut.

śakti Feminine cosmic energy. See also *kuṇḍalinī*.

Sarasvatī Goddess of wisdom and patroness of musicians, poets, artists, scholars; wife of Brahmā.

Satī Daughter of Dakṣa and wife of Śiva; she immolated herself in a self-created sacrificial fire to protest her father's insult to Śiva; her name is also wrongly applied to the practice of widow self-immolation on the husband's funeral pyre.

Śeṣa The cosmic serpent on which Viṣṇu lies asleep.

Sītā Heroine-goddess of the *Rāmāyaṇa* epic, wife of Rāma; as Rāma is the ideal male, so is Sītā the model of feminine chastity, loyalty, devotion.

Śiva The epic and Purāṇic deity Rudra-Śiva, also known as Bhava, Hara, Iśānā, Mahādeva, Maheśvara, Naṭarāja, Paśupati, Śambhu, Śaṅkara; two of his terrible forms are Bhairava in North India and Vīrabhadra in South India.

Skanda Also known as Kārttikeya, Kumāra, Subrahmaṇya; a bachelor son of Śiva, portrayed in iconography with six heads; in Tamil Nadu he is identified with the popular deity Murukaṉ, and throughout South India shares certain aspects with Ayyappaṉ.

Soma Sacred Vedic plant of poetic visions and immortality; a divine king immolated and sacrificed in the most exalted of Vedic rituals; his pressed juice (*soma*), offered to the gods and drunk by the priests, was said to produce ecstasy.

Sūrya The Vedic god of the sun; Savitṛ is another name for the sun.

Uṣas Vedic goddess of the dawn.

Vāc Vedic goddess of speech, the sacred word.

Varuṇa Vedic sovereign, celestial deity; king of the gods before Indra; often invoked along with Mitra, god of contracts.

Vayu Vedic god of wind and warfare.

Viṣṇu Vedic god connected with the all-pervasive cosmic pole, creative order, and the energy of the sacrifice; in post-Vedic mythology he is known by many names, including Bhagavan, Hari, Nārāyaṇa, and Vasudeva; his manifestations (*avatāras*) include powerful independent deities such as Kṛṣṇa, Rāma, Narasiṃha, and the boar Varāha.

Vṛtra The cosmic serpent who withholds creative waters; slain by Indra in a famous cosmogonic combat described in the *Ṛgveda*.

yakṣa, yakṣī Respective male and female powers of fertility and abundance; Kubera, god of wealth and one of the *lokapālas,* is chief of the *yakṣas.*

Yama First human, born before his twin sister Yamī; the first to die and therefore lord of the dead and, later, judge of the dead.

Selected Reading List

LITERATURE IN ENGLISH TRANSLATION

Dimmitt, Cornelia, and J. A. B. van Buitenen, ed., tr. *Classical Hindu Mythology: A Reader in the Sanskrit Puranas.* Philadelphia: Temple University, 1978.

Edgerton, Franklin, tr. *The Beginnings of Indian Philosophy.* Cambridge, MA: Harvard University Press, 1965.

Miller, Barbara Stoler, tr. *Love Song of the Dark Lord: Jayadeva's Gitagovinda.* New York: Columbia University Press, 1977.

O'Flaherty, Wendy Doniger, tr. *Hindu Myths: A Sourcebook Translated from the Sanskrit.* Baltimore, MD: Penguin, 1975.

————, tr. *The Rig Veda: An Anthology.* Baltimore, MD: Penguin, 1981.

————, ed. and tr. *Textual Sources for the Study of Hinduism.* Manchester: Manchester University Press, 1988.

Ramanujan, A. K., tr. *Hymns for the Drowning: Poems for Visnu by Nammalvar.* Princeton, NJ: Princeton University Press, 1981.

Sources of Indian Tradition. 2 vols. 2d ed. New York: Columbia University Press, 1988. Vol. 1, *From the Beginning to 1800,* edited by Ainslee T. Embree. Vol. 2, *Modern India and Pakistan,* edited by Stephen Hay.

Van Buitenen, J. A. B., tr. *The Bhagavadgita in the Mahabharata: A Bilingual Edition.* Chicago: University of Chicago Press, 1981.

GENERAL SURVEYS

Basham, A. L., ed. *A Cultural History of India.* New York: Oxford University Press, 1984.

————. *The Origins and Development of Classical Hinduism.* Edited by Kenneth R. Zysk. Boston: Beacon, 1989.

————. *The Wonder That Was India.* New York: Grove, 1954.

Brockington, J. L. *The Sacred Thread: Hinduism in Its Continuity and Diversity.* Edinburgh: Edinburgh University Press, 1981.

Hopkins, Thomas J. *The Hindu Religious Tradition.* Encino, CA: Dickenson, 1971.

Kinsley, David. *Hinduism: A Cultural Perspective.* Englewood Cliffs, NJ: Prentice-Hall, 1982.

Sivaraman, Krishna, ed. *Hindu Spirituality: Vedas through Vedanta.* New York: Crossroads, 1989.

Zaehner, R. C. *Hinduism.* New York: Oxford University Press, 1962.

SPECIAL TOPICS

Allchin, Bridget, and Raymond Allchin. *The Rise of Civilization in India and Pakistan.* New York: Cambridge University Press, 1982.

Alper, Harvey P., ed. *Mantra*. Albany: State University of New York, 1989.

Babb, Lawrence A. *The Divine Hierarchy: Popular Hinduism in Central India*. New York: Columbia University Press, 1975.

Blackburn, Stuart H., and A. K. Ramanujan, eds. *Another Harmony: New Essays on the Folklore of India*. Berkeley and Los Angeles: University of California Press, 1986.

Carman, John. *The Theology of Ramanuja*. New Haven, CT: Yale University Press, 1974.

Courtright, Paul B. *Ganesa: Lord of Obstacles, Lord of Beginnings*. New York: Oxford University Press, 1985.

Daniel, E. Valentine. *Fluid Signs: Being a Person the Tamil Way*. Berkeley and Los Angeles: University of California Press, 1984.

Das, Veena. *Structure and Cognition: Aspects of Hindu Caste and Ritual*. New York: Oxford University Press, 1977.

Dasgupta, Surendranath. *A History of Indian Philosophy*. 5 vols. Cambridge: Cambridge University Press, 1922–1955.

Deutsch, Eliot. *Advaita Vedanta: A Philosophical Reconstruction*. Honolulu: University of Hawaii Press, 1969.

Dumont, Louis. *Homo Hierarchicus: The Caste System and Its Implications*. Translated by Mark Sainsbury. Chicago: University of Chicago Press, 1970.

Eck, Diana. *Darsan: Seeing the Divine Image in India*. 2d ed. Chambersburg, PA: Anima, 1985.

Eliade, Mircea. *Yoga: Immortality and Freedom*. Translated by Willard R. Trask, 2d ed. Princeton, NJ: Princeton University Press, 1969.

Gonda, Jan. *Visnuism and Sivaism: A Comparison*. London: Athlone, 1970.

Gupta, Sanjukta, Dirk Jan Hoens, and Teun Goudriaan. *Hindu Tantrism*. Leiden: E. J. Brill, 1979.

Hardy, Friedhelm. *Viraha-Bhakti: The Early History of Krsna Devotion in South India*. New York: Oxford University Press, 1983.

Hawley, John S. *Krishna, the Butter Thief*. Princeton, NJ: Princeton University Press, 1983.

Heesterman, J. C. *The Inner Conflict of Tradition: Essays in Indian Ritual, Kingship, and Society*. Chicago: University of Chicago Press, 1985.

Hiltebeitel, Alf. *The Ritual of Battle: Krishna in the Mahabharata*. Ithaca, NY: Cornell University Press, 1976.

————, ed. *Criminal Gods and Demon Devotees: Essays on the Guardians of Popular Hinduism*. Albany: State University of New York, 1989.

Jayakar, Pupul. *The Earthen Drum: An Introduction to the Ritual Arts of Rural India*. New Delhi: National Museum, 1980.

Kane, P. V. *History of Dharmasastra*. 5 vols. 2d ed. Poona: Bhandarkar Oriental Research Institute, 1968–1975.

Khare, Ravindra S. *The Hindu Hearth and Home*. Durham, NC: Carolina Academic Press, 1976.

Kinsley, David. *Hindu Goddesses: Visions of the Divine Feminine in the Hindu Religious Tradition*. Berkeley and Los Angeles: University of California Press, 1986.

Kramrisch, Stella. *The Hindu Temple*. 2 vols. Calcutta, 1946; rpt. New Delhi: Motilal Banarsidass, 1976.

Lincoln, Bruce. *Myth, Cosmos, and Society: Indo-European Themes of Creation and Destruction*. Cambridge, MA: Harvard University Press, 1986.

Lingat, Robert. *The Classical Law of India*. Translated by J. Duncan M. Derrett. Berkeley and Los Angeles: University of California Press, 1973.

Marriott, McKim, ed. *India Through Hindu Categories*. New Delhi and Newbury Park, CA: Sage Publications, 1990.

O'Flaherty, Wendy Doniger. *The Origins of Evil in Hindu Mythology*. Berkeley and Los Angeles: University of California Press, 1976.

————, ed. *Karma and Rebirth in Classical Indian Traditions.* Berkeley and Los Angeles: University of California Press, 1980.

Pocock, D. F. *Mind, Body, and Wealth: A Study of Belief and Practice in an Indian Village.* Oxford: Basil Blackwell, 1973.

Schwartzberg, Joseph E., ed. *A Historical Atlas of South Asia.* Chicago: University of Chicago Press, 1978.

Shulman, David D. *Tamil Temple Myths: Sacrifice and Divine Marriage in the South Indian Saiva Tradition.* Princeton, NJ: Princeton University Press, 1980.

Singer, Milton. *When a Great Tradition Modernizes.* New York: Praeger, 1972.

————, ed. *Krishna: Myths, Rites and Attitudes.* Chicago: University of Chicago Press, 1969.

Smith, Brian K. *Reflections on Resemblance, Ritual, and Religion.* New York: Oxford University Press, 1989.

Staal, Frits. *Agni: The Vedic Ritual of Fire.* 2 vols. Berkeley, CA: Asian Humanities Press, 1983. Vol. 2 edited by Staal.

Stevenson, Margaret Sinclair. *The Rites of the Twice-Born.* London: Oxford University Press, 1920.

Varenne, Jean. *Yoga and the Hindu Tradition.* Translated by Derek Coltman. Chicago: University of Chicago Press, 1976.

Waghorne, Joanne Punzo, and Norman Cutler, eds. *Gods of Flesh: Gods of Stone: The Embodiment of Divinity in India.* Chambersburg, PA: Anima, 1985.

Welbon, Guy R., and Glenn E. Yocum, eds. *Religious Festivals in South India and Sri Lanka.* Delhi: Manohar, 1982.

Zelliot, Eleanor, and Maxine Berntsen, eds. *The Experience of Hinduism: Essays on Religion in Maharashtra.* Albany: State University of New York, 1988.

Zimmer, Heinrich. *Myths and Symbols in Indian Art and Civilization.* Edited by Joseph Campbell. New York: Bollingen Foundation, 1946; rpt. Princeton, NJ: Princeton University Press, 1972.

Zvelebil, Kamil V. *The Smile of Murugan: On Tamil Literature of South India.* Leiden: E. J. Brill, 1973.

PART EIGHT

Buddhism

The Path to Nirvana

Robert C. Lester

Chronology of Buddhist History

Western Dates	Major Events
563–483 (624–544) B.C.E.*	Life of Siddhartha Gautama, the Buddha
563 (624)	Birth at Lumbini (southern Nepal)
534 (595)	Renunciation
528 (589)	Enlightenment at Bodh Gaya; Founding of the Sangha
483 (544)	Death at Kushinara
468 B.C.E.	Death of Vardhamana Mahavira, founder of Jainism
327–325 B.C.E.	Invasion of northwest India by Alexander the Great
322–185 B.C.E.	Mauryan dynasty; Buddhism spreads throughout northern India
269–232 B.C.E.	Reign of Ashoka Maurya, patron of Buddhism
247 B.C.E.	King Tissa of Sri Lanka officially adopts Buddhism
202 B.C.E.–220 C.E.	Han dynasty rules China
200 B.C.E.–200 C.E.	Rise of the Mahayana; Buddhism spreads throughout South India, to Central Asia and to China
140–115 B.C.E.	Reign of Greek king Milinda (Menander)
29 B.C.E.	Portions of *Tripitaka* committed to written form in Sri Lanka
50–200 C.E.	Kushana dynasty rules northwest India and central Asia
78–101 C.E.	Rule of Kushana king Kanishka, patron of Buddhism
200 C.E.	Nagarjuna, founder of Madhyamika school of Mahayana thought
300–500	Buddhism introduced to various parts of Southeast Asia; Buddhism rises to prominence in China; Pure Land and Chan (Ch'an) (Zen) Mahayana established c. 500
320–540	Gupta dynasty rules India; rise of Buddhist centers of learning patronized by Gupta kings
399	Buddhism introduced to Korea from China

*Dates in parentheses are those respected by Theravada Buddhists.

Western Dates	Major Events
400	Asanga and Vasubandhu, founders of Yogacara school of Mahayana thought; Buddhaghosa produces interpretive texts on Theravada *Tripitaka* in Sri Lanka
402–411	Fa-xian (Fa-hsien), Chinese Buddhist pilgrim, visits Indian Buddhist centers
538	Buddhism introduced to Japan from Korea
630–644	Xuan-zang (Hsuan-tsang), Chinese Buddhist pilgrim, visits India
740–798	King Khri-srong officially establishes Mahayana Buddhism in Tibet
750	Construction of the great Borobudur *stupa* on the island of Java (Indonesia)
760–1142	Pala dynasty rules northeast India, patronizes Buddhist centers of learning
1044–1077	King Anawrahta establishes Theravada Buddhism in Burma
1133–1212	Honen, founder of Pure Land (Jodo) sect, in Japan
1141–1215	Eisai, founder of Rinzai Zen sect, in Japan
1150	Construction of Angkor monastery and temple in Cambodia
1173–1262	Shinran, founder of True Pure Land (Jodo Shinshu) sect, in Japan
1200	North India comes under Muslim rule; Buddhist centers destroyed; rise of Pure Land and Zen in Japan
1200–1253	Dogen, founder of Soto Zen sect, in Japan
1222–1282	Nichiren, founder of Nichiren sect, in Japan
1275–1317	Rama Khamheng, Thai king, recognizes Theravada Buddhism
1327	King Jayavarman Parameshvara of Cambodia establishes Theravada Buddhism in his kingdom
1360	Fa Ngum establishes Theravada Buddhism in Laos
1880	American Henry Steele Olcott spurs Buddhist revival in Sri Lanka
1881	Pali Text Society founded for editing and translation of the Theravada *Tripitaka*
1893	World Parliament of Religions meets in Chicago; speeches by Japanese Zen master and Theravada monk stir American interest in Buddhism

Western Dates	Major Events
1931	Buddhist Society of America (Zen) founded in New York City
1937	Tsunesaburo Makiguchi founds Nichiren Shoshu Soka Gakkai, in Japan
1944	Buddhist churches of America organize, uniting North American temples of Pure Land Buddhism
1950	World Fellowship of Buddhism inaugurated in Sri Lanka
1956	Celebration of twenty-five hundred years of Buddhism; B. R. Ambedkar's revival of Buddhism in India
1960	Founding of a chapter of Nichiren Shoshu in California
1968	Tarthang Tulku, Tibetan Buddhist master, begins propagation of Buddhism in United States
1970	Chogyam Trungpa Tulku (d. April, 1987), Tibetan Buddhist master, begins propagation of Buddhism in United States

Prologue

THIS WORK IS A brief introduction to a large and complex subject. Buddhism is more than twenty-five hundred years old and was defined not only in its native India but also in China, Japan, Tibet, and the several countries of Southeast Asia. Choosing what to include here and what to highlight was, to say the least, a painful process. Nonetheless, I believe that the result is a reasonably reliable entrée to the origin, development, and major traditions of the Buddhist religion.

In our study of Buddhism it is necessary to become familiar with a certain number of non-English terms. The ancient and authoritative accounts of the life and teachings of the Buddha are written in two languages: Sanskrit and a dialect of Sanskrit known as Pali. Some of the terms useful to our study are the same in both languages; others are slightly different, for example: ***Tripitaka****** (Sanskrit)/ *Tipitaka* (Pali), **Dharma**/Dhamma, **nirvana**/nibbana. To avoid unnecessary confusion, I have used the Sanskrit terminology throughout. In chapters 37 and 38, where we are considering specific aspects of the practice of Buddhism in Thailand and Japan, the technical terms are appropriately Thai and Japanese.

The *pin-yin* romanization system is used for spelling out the sound of Chinese characters as approved by the Chinese government. Wade-Giles spelling appears in parentheses for more familiar names, as "Daoism (Taoism)."

---

*Terms defined in the glossary, pp. 964–67, are printed in boldface type where they first appear in the text.

35

Introduction

ITS LONG HISTORY, large number of followers, and global distribution mark Buddhism as one of the major religions of the world. Buddhism arose in India twenty-five hundred years ago, inspired by the life and teachings of Siddhartha Gautama, a wandering monk who came to be known as the **Buddha,** "the Enlightened One." Today the way of the Buddha has more than five hundred million followers, concentrated in Asia, but also found in significant numbers in Europe and North America. It is the majority tradition of the Asian countries of Sri Lanka, Burma, Thailand, Laos, Cambodia, Vietnam, Tibet, Bhutan, and Japan. By reason of its historical prominence in India, China, Korea, and Indonesia, it has left its mark on cultural values throughout Asia, influencing the behavior of what is today more than two-thirds of the world's population.

I speak of Buddhism as if it were one system of beliefs and practices, everywhere understood and practiced in the same way. This, of course, is no more true of Buddhism than it is of other world religions such as Christianity or Islam. After twenty-five hundred years and adaptation to many different cultural contexts and individual needs, Buddhism encompasses a wide variety of beliefs and practices. There are two major traditions: **Theravada** ("the Way of the Elders") and **Mahayana** ("the Great Vehicle"). The latter is divided into numerous sects, each with a distinctive emphasis. Even within the Theravada tradition there are significant differences of practice from one country to another. The Mahayana is not only divided into sects, but each sect takes a variant form in each of the societies in which it is practiced. There is a wide gamut of belief and practice among individuals of the same sect and society. The gap is so wide in some cases that one may wonder how the variants can all belong to Buddhism. Some Buddhists emphasize self-understanding through meditation, others good deeds, and still others the worship of the Buddha. There is no one single Buddhism but many Buddhisms. [See Religions of Africa pp. 23–24, Religions of Mesoamerica pp. 117–19, Native Religions of North America pp. 261–64, Judaism pp. 389, 426, 456–75, Christianity pp. 492–94, Islam pp. 607–8, Hinduism pp. 719–21, Religions of China pp. 990–1015, and Religions of Japan pp. 1090–92 for discussion of the diversity and variety of religious traditions.]

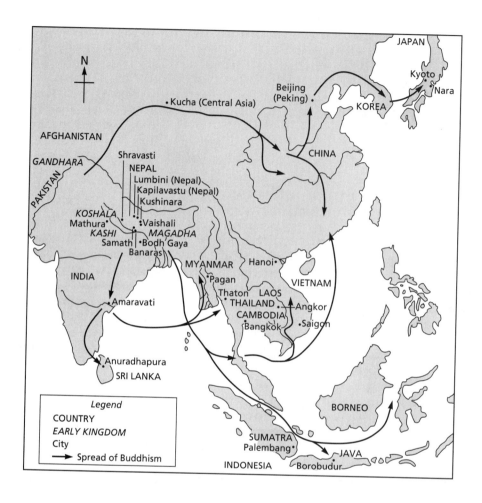

JAPAN

Kyoto
• Nara

Beijing
(Peking)
• Kucha (Central Asia)
KOREA

AFGHANISTAN

CHINA

GANDHARA

PAKISTAN

Shravasti
NEPAL
Lumbini (Nepal)
Kapilavastu (Nepal)
Kushinara

KOSHALA
Mathura•   •Vaishali
KASHI   *MAGADHA*
Samath •Bodh Gaya
Banaras

Hanoi•

INDIA

MYANMAR
•Pagan   VIETNAM
Thaton LAOS
•Amaravati   THAILAND   •Angkor
CAMBODIA   •Saigon
•Bangkok

•Anuradhapura
SRI LANKA

BORNEO

Legend
COUNTRY
EARLY KINGDOM
City
→   Spread of Buddhism

SUMATRA
Palembang•   •JAVA

INDONESIA   Borobudur•

Nonetheless, all Buddhisms are Buddhism. There is a common framework for all these variants, a framework that distinguishes Buddhism among the religions and, at the same time, permits and inspires a number of adaptations. Let us begin with an overview of this framework.

Religion is the product of humanity's struggle with finitude, its struggle to overcome suffering and death, to find stability and lasting satisfaction in a world of change. It was the Buddha's perception that instability is inherent in human existence. Reflecting intensely on his body, his feelings and thoughts, and the processes of his mind, he concluded that the human person as well as the natural environment is constantly in flux—from moment to moment arising and decaying—without a permanent substratum.

That is to say, in contradiction to popular belief, there is no unchanging soul or God underlying change, only moments passing, each giving rise to the next by its own demise. His reported last words were, appropriately, "To everything that arises, there is cessation; work out your salvation with diligence." He meant, "Be alert, awake; life is passing as quickly as it arises." In this circumstance, according to the Buddha, it is people themselves who cause suffering by trying to hold on to what is incessantly changing—their own life and material possessions. Indeed, humans' belief in a soul and/or a supreme being persisting through time is self-delusion, a feverish attempt to protect themselves in the face of change and death. To be free of suffering, one must renounce all attachments and break through the illusion of permanence by rigorous discipline of body and mind. Self-denial (refusing to lie or steal, commit violence, or engage in sexual misconduct) and meditation will result in enlightenment (***bodhi***)—waking up to life as it really is—and the cessation of suffering (nirvana).

Since it is people themselves who, by desire for self-aggrandizement, cause suffering, it is people who must conquer suffering by self-control. The Buddha's prescription for happiness was self-reliance, strict morality, cool rationality, and meditation. He lived the life of a monk, encouraged others to join him in monastic self-denial, and founded a monastic order.

At this point, readers may wonder how Buddhism became a popular religion. The answer lies in the fact that, while the Buddha advocated monasticism, he nonetheless encouraged a lay following and urged the monk to interact with society rather than radically withdraw. He conceived of the layperson as well as the monk as pursuing nirvana, the two at different levels of intensity and in a relationship of mutual dependence. He called his path to nirvana "the Middle Way," a way defined in rejection of both a life of unbridled sensuous enjoyment (hedonism) and a life of extreme self-denial (asceticism). The Path emphasized mental discipline accompanied by physical restraint, not punishment of the body, and it envisaged a progressive discipline beginning with a morality of self-denial practicable in the lay life. Monks were to live in proximity to society as inspiration, examples of liberating self-discipline, and as teachers. Laypeople were to cultivate self-denial by honoring the monks and giving of their wealth in material support of them.

Furthermore, in time, the Buddha, the order of monks, and even the Buddha's words of teaching became objects of veneration for the laity. The laity came to believe that the self-denial of the Buddha and his disciples created a reservoir of power that could be tapped by prayer and by the recitation and hearing of the Buddha's words, as well as by practicing the teaching and materially supporting the monks. And they believed that this power could effect worldly prosperity as well as progress toward nirvana.

Let us expand on this generalization, leading finally to a compact guideline for understanding Buddhism. The ultimate goal of Buddhism is nirvana—freedom from suffering. Its message begins with the recognition of the fact of suffering in human existence. It characterizes the human person—subject to constant change, pain, and ultimately death—as fundamentally ill-at-ease, full of anxiety, endlessly striving, and never satisfied. According to the Buddha, the cause of suffering is not the natural environment, human society, or the actions of a supernatural force, but humans themselves. More specifically, the cause of suffering is **karma**—the force of a person's thoughts, words, and deeds. Indeed, karma is the cause of life itself. People are self-creating; their physical form is the expression of a mental disposition, shaped and driven by desire—the desire for life, for pleasure, for power, for possessions, and for freedom. Within certain limits, whatever a person wills, that is what he or she becomes.

Desire results in thoughts, words, and deeds that have consequences (karma), either for happiness or suffering. Consequences are basically of two kinds: meritorious (*punya* karma, or "good" karma) or demeritorious (*papa* karma, or "bad" karma). Merit makes for happiness—good health, long life, high status, wealth, power, rebirth in a heavenly realm of great pleasure—and, if sufficient, it results in total freedom from suffering (nirvana). Demerit makes for unhappiness—poor health; lack of wealth and status; untimely, perhaps violent, death; and rebirth as a subhuman being. The law of karma necessitates belief in more than one life, indeed, a series of lives, ended only by the cessation of desire. A person is presently living as the result of karma from previous lives as well as the karma so far accumulated in the present life. And accumulated karma at the end of this life will cause yet another life, perhaps several. Further, future lives may be experienced in other than human forms. In the Buddha's worldview, there are numerous levels of life-forms, such as god forms, animal forms, and ghostly forms, as well as human forms. Below the earth are realms of punishment; above it are realms of pleasure (see chart on p. 874).

What, then, is the path to merit, to relative happiness, and eventually nirvana? Demerit is the result of action motivated by selfishness, merit the result of action motivated by unselfishness. Selfishness is characterized by lust and hatred and is ultimately rooted in delusion, in ignorance of the true nature of the self and the world. Unselfishness shows itself in sexual restraint, nonviolence, nonpossessiveness, and deeds of charity. Moral virtue leads to tranquility and clarity of mind, qualities conducive to meditation. By meditation, one may attain a state of selflessness or self-negation and know the self and the world as they really are. This is enlightenment (*bodhi*), the result of which is nirvana.

The moral perfection and insight necessary for the achievement of nirvana may take many lives to acquire. Because suffering beings exist at many different levels of ignorance and selfish attachment, they require different levels of discipline to alleviate suffering. Ancient Buddhism offered a progressive cure for the selfishness that causes suffering, a progression from good deeds (**dana**) to morality (**sila**) to meditation (**samadhi**). Good deeds, especially deeds of respect and service to holy monks, develop moral character and allow the giver to participate in the merit of the recipient. A morality that precludes violence, lying, stealing, and sexual misconduct cultivates selflessness. Such generosity and morality are appropriate to the lay life—life in family and society. They will eventuate in the ability to live the monastic life, a life of renunciation suitable to full moral purity and meditation. Failing this achievement in one lifetime, the layperson may enjoy rebirth in one of the pleasure realms as a god, and then again return to the human realm in more favorable proximity to the monastic life and nirvana.

Monks withdraw from society to strive for the ultimate perfection and insight. Their greater purity and wisdom permit them to see the suffering of others and give them responsibility to spread Buddha's teachings. They may also exercise the power of their merit and the power of Buddha's teachings on behalf of those who suffer in the world as humans or as wandering hungry ghosts, or those beneath the world, agonizing in hell.

Ancient Buddhism conceived of the lay life and the monastic life as mutually beneficial. The laity shared their goods, giving food, clothing, and housing to monks and thereby permitting the monks a life of strict morality, study, and meditation. Monks shared their merit, their holiness, by receiving offerings from the laity, preaching to them, and performing rituals of healing, protection, and blessing on their behalf. Monks were a "field of merit" from which society could harvest blessings.

The path to enlightenment and nirvana begins with faith and proceeds with charity, moral discipline, and meditation. Faith is confidence in the **Three Jewels/Treasures,** the three valued resources for human fulfillment: the Buddha, the Dharma, and the **Sangha.** This faith is expressed by means of an ancient and still commonly invoked formula, the **Threefold Refuge:**

I take refuge in the Buddha.
I take refuge in the Dharma. (way of Buddha)
I take refuge in the Sangha. (community of Buddhists)

The Buddha, "the Enlightened One," is the historical person Siddhartha Gautama, who lived c. 563–483 B.C.E. He is also a symbol of the realization of truth and the conquest of suffering and an enormous accumulation of power for suffering beings. According to traditional accounts, Gautama left his home and possessions in mid-life to wander as a monk. He turned inward, subduing all desire and clarifying his mind. After six years of rigorous physical and mental discipline, after intense self-analysis and success in destroying all lust, anger, and delusion within himself, he clearly and definitively realized the cause of and cure for human suffering.

The Dharma, "the Doctrine and the Path," is Gautama's teaching. In simple form it is the **Four Noble Truths:**

1. That there is suffering;
2. That suffering is caused by desire;
3. That the cessation of suffering (nirvana) is possible; and
4. That the **Eightfold Path** is the way to the cessation of suffering.

The Dharma is more than Gautama's teaching; it is Eternal Truth, manifested through Gautama; it is powerful by mere invocation, apart from the meaning of the words in which it was spoken.

The Sangha is the community of monks founded by the Buddha and continuing to the present day. In a narrower sense, it is all the saints who through the ages have attained enlightenment. In a wider sense, it is the accumulated holiness and power achieved in a long and continuing tradition of renunciation.

"Taking refuge" in the Buddha, the Dharma, and the Sangha has two levels of meaning. It means following the example of the Buddha by practicing the Dharma as a member of the Sangha. It also means relying on the power of the Buddha, the Dharma, and the Sangha, which is actualized by prayer, ritual incantation, and offerings. The Buddha, Dharma, and Sangha are resources for both worldly prosperity and the attainment of nirvana, and worldly prosperity is itself necessary to the achievement of nirvana. The Buddha is the great teacher and example of one who attains nirvana for those treading the path that he revealed. At the same time, by his meritorious deeds, purity, wisdom, and compassion, he is a reservoir of power for those in need of protection and healing. The Dharma is a pathway to nirvana; it is also the power of the Buddha in words, which, when chanted, control and channel the forces of nature, transfer merit from the living to the dead, and protect against disease and the attack of wild animals. The Sangha is the community of saints and monks striving for nirvana; at the same time, its actual and intended purity and wisdom and its command of the Dharma are power to heal, protect, and bless those who are yet mired in worldly affairs.

In compact generalization, Buddhism is the pursuit of worldly prosperity, rebirth in heaven, and ultimately nirvana by making and sharing merit (good karma). Nirvana is freedom from rebirth, freedom from suffering. Karma is the force or energy produced by thoughts, words, and deeds. It causes pleasure and pain and rebirth in heaven, on earth, or in hell. Good karma or merit is the result of deeds of charity, moral discipline, meditation, prayer, chanting, and preaching. Making and sharing merit is ultimately for the sake of achieving nirvana—the transcendence of time and space; it is also for healing the sick, channeling the forces of nature, facilitating harmonious family and community relationships, easing the burden of life's transitions, protecting the village, city, and nation, relieving the misery of souls suffering in hell or as wandering ghosts, and attaining a favorable rebirth.

The resources for making and sharing merit are the Three Jewels/Treasures: the Buddha, the Dharma, and the Sangha. They are both the inspiration to the making of merit and the source of merit. The Buddha is "the Enlightened One," the heroic trailblazer of the path to nirvana and an enormous store of merit for suffering beings. The Dharma is the teaching or word of the Buddha that shows the way to nirvana, and it is the expression of the merit of the Buddha, which has power to protect, heal, and give prosperity. The Sangha is the community of monks founded by the Buddha, and it is a store of merit for the world.

Our goal is to understand living Buddhism, Buddhism as an existing and ongoing way of life, one of the important value systems of our world. To do so, we shall first have to consider how it came to be and how it developed to become what it is today. Like a person, Buddhism is a product of its history. It has its own karma, the marks of the accumulated effects of past events. We shall consider this karma in chapter 36. Having traced out its development in space and time in chapter 36, having taken it apart, so to speak, we shall then put it back together in chapter 37, looking at it as a unified system of beliefs and practices. Our emphasis will be on the enduring and characteristic features of Buddhism, its essential logic as a worldview and as a way of life. With this broad context established, we shall be prepared for chapter 38 in which we shall consider some concrete examples of the living religion.

In conclusion, in chapter 39, we shall briefly identify some recent trends in Buddhism worldwide and the major features of American Buddhism.

36

The Historical Development of Buddhism

SIDDHARTHA GAUTAMA (563–483 B.C.E.) lived in a time of rapid social change resulting in the disintegration of old tribal values. His quest for meaning led to the renunciation of all worldly pursuits and the adoption of the life of a mendicant; as such he was one of many inhabiting the forests of northeast India. He was influenced by the prominent religions of the time, especially **Brahmanism** and **Jainism,** but, in the end, forged his own way. Through rigorous moral discipline and meditation he achieved an insight by which he became known as the Buddha, "the Awakened One." After his awakening, he continued to wander as a monk-teacher, encouraging others to follow the path he had discovered to nirvana, the cessation of suffering. He gave shape to an order of monks (Sangha) supported by lay charity. Highly charismatic, he inspired devotion to his person as well as adherence to his teaching. [See Religions of Africa pp. 29, 55–57, Religions of Mesoamerica pp. 152, 164–68, Native Religions of North America pp. 266–67, Christianity pp. 495–97, 531–32, 534–35, Islam pp. 622–28, 698–99, Hinduism pp. 769, 770–72, Religions of China pp. 993–95, and Religions of Japan pp. 1090, 1100, 1122–23 for discussion of religious founders.]

The Sangha, charged with a mission to preach the Dharma (the Buddha's teaching) "out of compassion for the world . . . for the welfare of gods and men" and supported by wealthy merchants and rulers, steadily grew, to become a distinctive, highly structured, and powerful institution in Indian society. Lay Buddhism continued to derive its fundamental inspiration from the Sangha, but progressively a cult of devotion to the Buddha was formed that in time significantly altered the whole tradition.

The movement developed harmoniously for the first two hundred years. After 300 B.C.E. distinctive schools of thought began to appear in the Sangha. Increasingly, both lay and monastic Buddhism were influenced by Hinduism and the influx of Greek and Iranian ideas. By the beginning of the Common Era the Sangha was effectively divided into schools adhering to either Great Vehicle (Mahayana) Buddhism or Little Vehicle (**Hinayana**) Buddhism, the latter self-styled as the Way of the Elders (Theravada). The **elders** held to the old ways; the Mahayana set forth a new vision.

After nine hundred years of prosperity, 250 B.C.E.–650 C.E., Buddhism slowly declined to extinction in India. But long before that, Buddhist monks and merchants carried the Way of the Buddha to Sri Lanka and Southeast Asia, through central Asia to China, Korea, and Japan, and to Tibet. The Theravada came to dominate in Sri Lanka and on the mainland of Southeast Asia, the Mahayana in China, Korea, Japan, and Tibet. In modern times all of these traditions have come west to Europe and North America, where they thrive, becoming progressively Westernized.

The Buddha and His Times

The Record

The chief source of our knowledge of the Buddha and early Buddhism is the authoritative or sacred literature of the Buddhist movement known collectively as *Tripitaka*.

Tripitaka, "Three Baskets" or "Three Collections," is made up of *Sutra* ("Discourses"), discourses attributed to the Buddha and embodying his general teachings; *Vinaya* ("Disciplines"), the Buddha's specific pronouncements on the rules of the monastic life; and *Abhidharma*, ("The Further or Higher Teachings,"), teachings formulated by the Buddha's disciples. The oldest portions of this literature, the *Sutra* and *Vinaya*, as we now have them date from about four hundred years after the death of the Buddha. They are based on memories of the Buddha and his teachings, preserved in the monastic community and transmitted orally for two hundred and fifty years (there is evidence that there were written records about 250 B.C.E. but they are not extant). During the oral period, the events of the Buddha's time were reviewed, supplemented, and interpreted again and again as the movement progressed, each addition and interpretation being attributed to the Buddha. This has resulted in a record that reflects two hundred and fifty years of development and in which we cannot clearly distinguish the original teaching from what was added later. [See Religions of Mesoamerica p. 179, Native Religions of North America p. 285, Judaism pp. 390–94, Christianity pp. 497, 499, Islam pp. 635–37, 648–53, 665–72, Hinduism pp. 728–29, 738–43, 750–53, Religions of China pp. 995–96, 999–1000, 1031, and Religions of Japan pp. 1100, 1101 for discussion of Bible, scriptures, and religious texts.]

The life story of the Buddha found in this record is an interpretation of the Buddha by his followers over a long period of time and in the light of their belief that he was an extraordinary, wondrous being, an archetype of heroic human existence. We shall consider this archetypal life in chapter 37 as a key element in Buddhism as a unified system of beliefs and practices. It portrays Gautama as a prince, conceived and born under extraordinary circumstances, married to Yashodhara at the age of sixteen, and productive of a son, Rahula, just prior to renunciation at the age of twenty-nine. If we view the existing record in the light of what critical historians can tell us about the Buddha's period in Indian history, we can conclude only that the Buddha lived during the late sixth and early fifth centuries B.C.E., that he belonged to the Gautama clan of a people known as the Shakyas, that he came to prominence in the kingdoms of Koshala and Magadha as a wandering monk whom many believed to be enlightened, and that he founded a monastic community supported by lay devotees.

Background

Northeast India in the time of the Buddha was divided into small kingdoms and republics according to tribal affiliation. Gautama's tribe, the Shakyas, inhabited the Himalayan foothills along what is today the border between India and Nepal. Gautama wandered the lands of the Koshala, Magadha, Vrijji, and Kashi tribes, spending much of his time in and around their capital cities. The Shakyas were governed by a council of elders, possibly including Gautama's father. They lived on the edge of and paid tribute to the more prosperous kingdoms to the south (Koshala and Magadha) that controlled the fertile lands along the Ganges River and its tributaries.

The economy of the area was based on agriculture. Iron technology had permitted not only more effective weapons of war but also the clearing of the previously forested areas along the Ganges and the development of an increasingly prosperous rice culture. Agricultural prosperity, growing trade, and centralized rule had given rise to large towns and cities—the centers of government, commerce, and guilds of artisans. With the cities and increasing commerce came the mixing of peoples and cultures and the consequent breakdown of old tribal ties and values. One response to this crisis of shifting values was renunciation, withdrawal into the forest for meditation. Gautama was one of many who made this response.

The religious life of the time was dominated by **brahmanas** (priests) and *samanas* (wandering monks). The *brahmanas* were officiants of a religion of fire rituals that developed in northwest India beginning c. 1500 B.C.E. among a people known as the Aryans. Brahmanism was an elite religion with worldly goals, based on an ancient revelation called *Vedas*. This revelation, effectively known only to the priests, was the instrument for the performance of rituals believed to maintain harmony between humans and a hierarchy of forces (the gods) in the natural world. The offering of food to the gods in fire rituals ensured health, wealth, and good offspring in this life and abode in heaven after death.

Brahmanism fostered a highly structured social order, with the priest (*brahmana*) at the top, followed by the warrior/ruler (*kshatriya*), then by the herdsman/farmer (*vaishya*), and at the bottom by the laborer (*shudra*). This hierarchy was believed to be ordained from the beginning of creation and was consistent with the hierarchy of gods and levels of the natural world—sky, upper atmosphere, and earth. As in the natural world the sky directed the activities of the atmosphere and the earth, so in human society the priest ordered the activity of the three lower classes. The high status and power of the priest were guaranteed by his knowledge of *Veda* and his performance of the rituals by which ordered, prosperous life was maintained.

In renunciation, Gautama joined the *samanas* (literally, "strivers"), homeless wanderers—monks who rejected the settled, worldly life, preferring to live on the fringe of society. They inhabited the forests, living on alms and seeking wisdom through physical renunciation and meditation. By the time of the Buddha a monastic thrust had taken shape within Brahmanism, but it was not well integrated; the *brahmana* and the *samana* essentially represented two different ways of life. The *brahmana* was concerned with ritual purity and social order; the *samana* was concerned with individual moral purity and self-knowledge. The *brahmana* was concerned with worldly prosperity; the *samana* rejected the world in hope of release from the struggle for wealth and power. The *brahmana* was oriented outward, concerned with social structure and rituals by which to worship divine powers; the *samana* turned inward on the self. *Samanas* renounced all function in society and sought a new vision of reality through monastic discipline and meditation; they sought to cut through the illusions and suffering of wealth and power and, as the Buddha put it, "see things as they really are." Having renounced all means of sustenance, the *samanas* relied on householders—rulers, merchants, artisans, and farmers—for food, clothing, medicine, and temporary housing. In exchange they offered their wisdom and healing powers, their blessing to the affairs of their patrons.

Among the *samanas* contemporary with the Buddha was the teacher Vardhamana, known as Mahavira ("Great Hero") or Jina ("The Conqueror"). His disciples were called Jains ("Followers of the Conqueror"), and this tradition is known as "Jainism." Vardhamana taught the attainment of release of the soul from the material world by extreme asceticism and nonviolence. He went about naked, subjecting himself to discomfort and showing his total rejection of worldly possessions. He taught strict vegetarianism and the rigorous avoidance of the taking of life in any form.

Gautama's Innovation

According to traditional accounts, Gautama studied under two masters of *yoga*, a discipline of body and mind whereby one systematically withdraws from all ordinary sensory/mental experience and passes into a succession of trance states. He also tried the extreme asceticism of the Jains, punishing his body by fasting. Finding no lasting satisfaction in these disciplines, he turned to the practice of what he called "mindfulness" (**smriti** or *sati*), a kind of self-analysis in which, rather than trying to subdue or cut off sensory/mental experience, he simply sat, watching his feelings and thoughts as they arose and reflecting on causal patterns.

He realized that his existence was an aggregation of physical and mental states conditioning one another and endlessly arising and passing: "This arising, that arises; this ceasing, that ceases." He realized that his experience of pleasure and pain was conditioned by mental states—states of desire. He felt pleasure when his desire was satisfied and pain when it was not. He knew that a certain amount of pain is inevitable in physical existence, which is constantly subject to change and decay, but he realized that his very physical existence was the result of the force of desire, that desire was merely the surface phenomenon of a complex mental construction—the ego or self-concept. He saw that the mind controls the body, indeed brings it into existence as an instrument of ego satisfaction. The ego patterns or energies that gave rise to present existence were themselves the product of a former existence, the resultant energies of which are called karma. Through the practice of intense mindfulness, aided by certain disciplines of concentration that quiet and purify the mind, Gautama was able to review his karmic stream far into the past. He saw how one life stream gave rise to another, again and again. Having realized this causal pattern, he then saw that since it was desire—the whole ego complex—that caused existence and therefore the physical and mental suffering inherent in existence, subduing and finally extinguishing this ego would result in the cessation of suffering (nirvana). Gautama is portrayed as recounting his enlightenment experience as follows:

> With the mind concentrated, purified, cleansed . . . I directed it to the knowledge of the remembrance of my former existences. I remembered many former existences. . . . There I was of such and such a name, clan, color, livelihood, such pleasure and pain did I suffer, and such was the end of my life. Passing away thence I was born elsewhere. . . . This was the first knowledge that I gained in the first watch of the night. Ignorance was dispelled, knowledge arose. . . . (Then) I directed my mind to the passing away and rebirth of beings. With divine, purified, superhuman vision I saw beings passing away and being reborn, low and high, of good and bad color, in happy or miserable existences according to their karma. . . . This was the second knowledge that I gained in the second watch of the night. . . . (Then) I directed my mind to the knowledge of the destruction of the binding influences [sensual desire, desire for existence, and ignorance]. I duly realized (the truths) "This is suffering. . . . This is the cause of suffering. . . . This is the destruction of suffering. . . . This is the way that leads to the destruction of suffering." As I thus knew and thus perceived, my mind was emancipated. . . . I realized that destroyed is rebirth. . . . There is nought for me beyond this world. . . . Ignorance was dispelled, knowledge arose. Darkness was dispelled, light arose. So is it with him who abides vigilant, strenuous, and resolute.[1]

In common with Brahmanism and Jainism, the Buddha taught that life is conditioned by karma—"the force of deeds." The Law of Karma stipulates that what a person is and does is significantly the result of his or her past deeds, that the circumstances of life—a person's mental and physical capacities, the social and economic situation into which a person is born, and the ongoing events of life—are not accidental or caused by some outside force but are the fruit of a person's own past lives as well as the present one. Karma implicates all living beings—animals and insects as well as human beings—in a series of births and deaths (**samsara**), the present life being the fruit of past lives and, in turn, contributing to the shape of future lives. The Brahmanas and Jains called this process "transmigration," believing that living beings possess an eternal, unchanging soul (*atman*) that "crosses over" from one body to the next at death.

The Buddha rejected the idea that any such eternal, unconditioned entity—soul *or* God—exists. His self-analysis revealed that everything that makes up a living being, as well as everything that makes up the natural world, is constantly changing, arising and decaying moment by moment. Inasmuch as one complex of fleeting elements decays, at what is commonly called "death," and gives rise to an initial complex of elements that shapes another body, we can speak of "rebirth"—but not transmigration; nothing unchanging carries over. This same rebirth is occurring every moment in what we call life.

Indeed, according to the Buddha, it is the belief in the fact of or possibility of permanent soul/selfhood (*atman*) that causes all human suffering and dissatisfaction. The core of the Buddha's discovery in becoming enlightened was the realization that life is a mass of suffering and this suffering is caused by desire—desire for life, for pleasure, for status, for possessions—which is rooted in belief in self. His prescription for the good life—freedom from suffering—was moral and mental discipline leading to insight into the true nature of life and therewith the extinction of desire. The desireless state, the goal of his teaching, he called nirvana, "extinction" (of the flame of desire).

Brahmanism, Jainism, and Buddhism respected the same moral principles (nonviolence, sexual restraint, and prohibitions against stealing, lying, or drinking alcohol), but in Brahmanism morality was secondary to ritual purity, that is, ritual correctness based on knowledge of *Vedas.* Jainism and Buddhism emphasized knowledge of the self through meditation. They parted company on the degree of rigor in moral discipline.

The Buddha offered his insight as "the Middle Way," defined by the rejection of a life lived simply and solely for the satisfaction of sensory desires and a life of extreme asceticism—the total denial of sensory satisfaction. He rejected the *brahmana's* claim to superiority by reason of his knowledge of *Veda* and performance of the fire rituals. He rejected the *brahmana's* concern with worldly riches. Instead he preached the simple life that renounced attachment to worldly goods and was concerned for moral character and self-knowledge through discipline. He did not reject the gods of Brahmanism but subordinated their power to the one who has conquered all desire. At the same time, he rejected the extreme asceticism of the Jains, which he considered "painful, ignoble, and useless." For the Buddha, the goal of self-discipline was not the punishment and death of the body, but the serenity of mind and body through the extinction of desire.

The Formative Period: 500–250 B.C.E.

Monks and Laity

According to the record, the Buddha wandered for forty-five years after his enlightenment, teaching and gathering both lay and monastic disciples. He is portrayed as teaching the laity the merits (good karma) of giving alms to those who have taken up the homeless life and of keeping the five moral precepts—

abstention from taking human life, lying, stealing, engaging in illicit sexual activity, and drinking alcohol. He taught charity and morality as the means to harmony and prosperity in this life and a favorable rebirth in the next.

To those he perceived ready, he taught "the higher Dharma," the truths of suffering, its cause, its cure, and the monastic path leading to nirvana.

In general, *samanas* avoided contact with society as much as possible. The Buddha instructed his monks to "wander alone, like a rhinoceros," to have no refuge but the Dharma. But this did not mean that they were to avoid all contact with society. The Buddha rejected the life of extreme asceticism—total withdrawal and the practice of physically punishing disciplines; he instructed the monks to teach the Dharma, "for the welfare of the many." Most important of all, he encouraged both lay and monastic disciples and taught them a life of mutually beneficial dependence. We might say that the Buddha made a virtue of necessity. Monks, whose discipline prohibited them from working to provide the necessities of life, would benefit by the laity's gifts of food, clothing, medicine, and temporary housing. But the monks were not to be seen as an unproductive drain on society. The laity would benefit by the teaching of the monks and by the good karma they would accumulate as the result of giving. This karma would result in a more favorable rebirth and eventually a life in which the layperson would be ready for the monastic pursuit of nirvana.

> They pay you great service, O monks, the Brahmins and the householders who give you clothing, alms, seats, couches, and medicines. You also pay them great service when you teach them the Good Doctrine and the pure life. Thus it is through your mutual help that the religious life, which causes the crossing over beyond rebirth and puts an end to suffering, can be practiced. Each relying on the other, householders and homeless cause the Good Doctrine to prosper. The latter are protected from need, since they receive clothing and the rest; the former, having practiced the Doctrine in this world, the Path which leads to good forms of rebirth, delight in the world of the gods possessed of the blisses.[2]

> In five ways should the clansman minister to recluses: by affection in act and speech and mind; by keeping open house to them, by supplying their temporal needs. Thus ministered to recluses . . . show their love for the clansman in six ways: they restrain him from evil, they exhort him to good, they love him with kindly thoughts; they teach him what he had not heard, they correct and purify what he has heard, they reveal to him the way to heaven.[3]

Monks, by their purity and wisdom, were a reservoir of goodness, a "field of merit" for society.

> The Lord's order of disciples [Sangha] is of good conduct . . . worthy of alms, worthy of hospitality, worthy of offerings, worthy of reverence, it is a matchless field of merit for the world.[4]

The laity were eager to provide for the monks. They saw them not only as a source of wisdom and an example of purity of life, but also as possessed of special powers by reason of their wisdom and purity. They believed that the very presence of a monk would subdue forces of misfortune and disease and create an air of prosperity. The Buddha is portrayed as dispelling malicious spirits who had brought disease to the city of Vaishali and as subduing wild animals. It is said that he gave his disciples verses called **paritta** ("protection"), by the pronouncement of which they could avert danger and create an auspicious environment.

Early Disciples

A wide variety of persons, women and men, responded to the Buddha's message. The first sixty he received into the monastic life were five *samanas* and fifty-five merchants "of prominent families." These sixty are said to have quickly attained the status of **arhat**, "holy one," in whom all desire was extinguished and for whom there would be no further birth. The Buddha then sent them forth to "wander, for the gain of the many, for the welfare of the many, out of compassion for the world," to preach the Dharma and "proclaim a consummate, perfect, and pure life of holiness."[5] Many *brahmanas* joined the Sangha, among them Sariputra and Maudgalyayana, who became the Buddha's chief disciples. Sariputra was known for his great wisdom and Maudgalyayana for his supernormal powers (e.g., superhuman hearing and sight, to be discussed later).

After an initial ministry in Magadha, the Buddha returned home to Kapilavastu, the chief city of the Shakyas, and there received his son, Rahula, two cousins, Ananda and Devadatta, and one of their attendants, Upali, a barber, into the monastic life. Ananda became the Buddha's companion and valet in later life. Devadatta, brother-in-law as well as cousin to Gautama, endeavored to rival the Buddha for leadership of the monastic community but was not successful. He is portrayed as bearing resentment toward the Buddha in spite of his monastic vows for the Buddha's having left his wife (Devadatta's sister) in renunciation. Upali, the barber, was one of several persons of the lower social classes who joined the Sangha; Upali and Ananda were remembered as the two who rehearsed the entire teaching of the Buddha before a great assembly of monks just after the master's death.

The Buddha agreed (reportedly, with strong reservations) to allow women to undertake the monastic life. Mahaprajapati, the second wife of the Buddha's father (his first wife, the Buddha's mother, died a few days after giving birth to Gautama), became the first nun. The record of early monastic life pays very little attention to the nuns but it does show that a significant number of women ·were attracted to the order, many of them widows without children.

The prominent lay disciples of the Buddha came from the merchant and ruling classes—the father, mother, and wife of Yasa, a wealthy merchant who himself became a monk; King Bimbasara of Magadha; the Buddha's father; and Ambapali, a wealthy courtesan. This is only to identify those who, it is said, made a formal commitment to the way of the Buddha. The laity that played a crucial role in the early development of Buddhism included householders in general. Even those who had no particular knowledge of or commitment to the teachings of the Buddha were drawn to respect and support these new *samanas* in hope of being blessed by such contact.

Those who entered upon the homeless life committed themselves to a highly demanding morality and daily regimen. They were not to take life in any form; they were not to lie, steal, engage in sexual activity, drink alcoholic beverages, participate in any form of entertainment, use comfortable seats or beds, handle money, or eat more than one meal per day. They were permitted a minimum of possessions: inner and outer robes, a belt, a food bowl, a water strainer, a toothpick, a razor, a needle, and a staff. At first, they followed a way of life common to all *samanas:* wandering, dwelling, and meditating in the forest; wearing castoff rags; begging for their food; and using only cow's urine for medicine. In time, the Buddha permitted *samanas* to dwell near a village for ease of access to food, to accept gifts of robes from the laity, to accept invitations to eat in the homes of the laity, and to use a variety of medicines depending upon their need. Some, who came to be called "forest dwellers," continued to keep the old rule; the majority became "village dwellers." This distinction persisted and exists today in Theravada Buddhism. Whether forest dwellers or village dwellers, their discipline was intended to promote good health and strong control, rather than to punishingly deny physical existence.

Monks wandered, then entered a village for food, rested, meditated, and received and instructed lay visitors; they left the village to sleep outside of it at night, then moved on the next day. This was their pattern except during the rainy season, a period of approximately four months from mid-June to mid-October, when it was difficult to move about and customary for *samanas* to take shelter. Some of the monks constructed temporary housing in the forest and kept largely to themselves in study and meditation. Most followed the Buddha's example and sought shelter in close proximity to a populated area where they could conveniently beg for food.

It is recorded that, among others, the king of Magadha, the wealthy merchant Ananthapindika, and the courtesan Ambapali each donated pleasant groves for the use of the Buddha and his monks. During the rains, the monks gathered in such places, especially where they might be with the Buddha. This kind of **rain-retreat** fostered the development of a communal life among the monks and encouraged more than the usual contact between monks and laity.

After Buddha

In the course of time, with the approval of the Buddha, the monks fashioned an elaborate code of behavior and an administrative structure for communal living. They also developed a number of community rituals, in some of which the laity were invited to participate. After the Buddha's death, the monks intensified their communal life in mutual support and in preserving the teaching and way of life. In the absence of the charismatic leader, solidarity gave authority to the teaching and tended to maintain the purity of the lifestyle; regularized ceremony heightened the sense of authenticity and power of the monastic way. The laity strongly encouraged such developments by providing more and better amenities for the monks' sojourn during the rains. Desirous of the opportunities for merit making afforded by the continuous presence of monks, the laity were just as concerned about the welfare and purity of the monks as the monks were themselves. The monks tended to return to the same places year after year. The laity constructed more and more permanent and elaborate dwellings and ceremonial halls, until what had begun as informal, temporary gatherings had become more or less settled monastic communities, each with a defined boundary and a particular membership.

The first two hundred years of the Sangha was a process of gradually settling and formalizing the monastic life. After the death of the Buddha, there was no centralized authority. The Buddha did not appoint a successor; rather, he instructed his followers to be governed by the teaching (Dharma). Nevertheless, under the guidance of senior monks, uniform rules, regulations, and rituals evolved and were generally respected. According to the *Vinaya* (the section of the *Tripitaka* dealing with the rules of the monastic life), immediately following the death of the Buddha, five hundred monks gathered in rain-retreat jointly confirmed the teaching as recited by Ananda and Upali. A similar council one hundred years later again reaffirmed the authoritative teaching. Monastic rule and ritual as practiced today were fully formulated by 250 B.C.E. Each community was autonomous and self-governing by consensus of the gathered body under the guidance of elder monks.

> So long, O mendicants, as the brethren meet together in full and frequent assemblies—so long as they meet together in concord, and rise in concord, and carry out in concord the duties of the order—so long as the brethren shall establish nothing that has not been already prescribed, and abrogate nothing that has been already established, and act in accordance with the rules of the order as now laid down—so long as the brethren honor and esteem and revere and support the elders of experience and long standing, the fathers and leaders of the order, and hold it a point of duty to hearken to their words . . . so long may the brethren be expected, not to decline, but to prosper.[6]

The elders (senior monks) gathered the Buddha's remarks on what was prohibited in the monastic life into a code of discipline called the **Pratimoksha,** (literally, "that which is preparatory to freedom from desire"). In the first two or three centuries of Buddhism, this code functioned as an identifying mark of the monastic followers of the Buddha and an indication of their essential unity as Buddhists. It includes 227 prohibitions in order of seriousness of offense and beginning with what the Buddha called "The Four Things Not to Be Done." A monk

> 1) Ought to abstain from all sexual intercourse even with an animal; 2) ought to abstain from taking what is not given to him, and from theft, even of a blade of grass; 3) ought not intentionally to destroy the life of any being down to a worm or ant; 4) ought not to attribute to himself any superhuman condition.[7]

Offense against these four prohibitions resulted in expulsion from the order. Offense against the other prohibitions entailed one degree or another of penance and forfeiture of privileges, to be determined by the gathered community, or simply confession of the offense to another monk.

The elders set forth a separate *Pratimoksha* code for nuns, containing more than double the number of rules for monks. It is said that when the Buddha permitted women to join the Sangha, he did so only with the stipulation that nuns be strictly subordinate to monks. He specified, for instance, that women, regardless of age, spend a minimum of two years probation as novices before full ordination; that they be ordained by an assembly of monks as well as by an assembly of nuns; that nuns reside only in an area in which there are monks; that they honor all monks as their seniors; and that they accept criticism from monks without the privilege of giving it. In placing such special restrictions on women, the Buddha reportedly had a twofold concern: that women not be encouraged to renounce their household responsibilities in order to join the Sangha, and that, should they do so, their presence must not corrupt the order.

Inspired by a Brahmanical practice of purificatory rites on the day before the new-moon and full-moon fire sacrifices, the Buddhist elders prescribed that the *Pratimoksha* code should be jointly recited in each monastery on these days each month. This "Observance" (*uposatha*), as it was called, came to be a time when monks would confess any infraction to a fellow monk before engaging in the communal recitation. Lay devotees were invited to spend this day at the monastery, observing a discipline of fasting and keeping the basic precepts of the monastic life. Following the recitation, the laity were permitted to sit in the presence of the monks to hear a sermon by one of the elders. Observance days became a vital link between monk and laity, in importance second only to their daily contact in the giving and receiving of food.

Ordination

The Buddha reportedly received those desirous of undertaking the monastic life with a simple invitation:

> Come, O monk. Well taught is the Dharma; lead a holy life for the sake of the complete extinction of suffering.[8]

After his death, reception into the order became a formal act of ordination, increasing in complexity as the order grew in size and became more and more formally constituted. Concerned that the new initiates, especially young men in their teens, might not be prepared for the full rigor of monastic life, the elders instituted a probationary or novitiate ordination (*pravrajya*). The novice had to be at least fifteen years of age and was assigned a preceptor, or "big brother," and a teacher, who supervised his conduct and learning throughout the probationary period. The ordination procedure was as follows.

> Let him first have his hair and beard cut off; let him put on yellow robes, adjust his upper robe so as to cover one shoulder, salute the feet of the monks

with his head, and sit down squatting; then let him raise his joined hands and tell him to say: "I take my refuge in the Buddha, I take my refuge in the Dharma, I take my refuge in the Sangha."[9]

Following the recitation of the Threefold Refuge three times, he was instructed in the **Ten Precepts:**

1. Not to take life;
2. Not to lie;
3. Not to steal;
4. Not to engage in sexual activity;
5. Not to drink alcohol;
6. Not to take food from noon to the next morning;
7. Not to adorn the body with anything other than the three robes;
8. Not to participate in or be spectator to public entertainments;
9. Not to use high or comfortable beds;
10. Not to use money.

It was determined that the candidate for full or higher ordination (*upasampada*) had to be at least twenty years of age, free of serious illness, and free of any social obligation (e.g., debt or obligation to military service). He had to have the permission of his parents or wife, as the case may be. His ordination required the presence of at least ten monks and committed him to the full *Pratimoksha* rule.

Ordination was a special occasion for the laity, especially the parents and relatives of the candidate, to receive merit. They attended the ritual, bearing small gifts for the monks. Ordinations most frequently occurred just prior to the rain-retreat, thus affording the new initiate a time of intensive training under close supervision. It was likely also that, at an early time, the laity believed that the merit-force created by the act of renunciation by virile young men would stimulate rainfall for the crops. No formality was prescribed for entrance into rain-retreat, but the retreat was to be concluded with a ritual "invitation" (*pravarana*) by each monk to the gathered body to inform him of infractions he may have committed during retreat.

As noted above, the Buddha permitted the monks to receive robes as a gift from the laity. The opportune time for this giving was at the end of the rain-retreat when the monks prepared to wander. Thus, the elders prescribed a ritual called Kathina (*kathina* means "rough cloth") at which the laity formally presented cloth and the monks prepared and distributed new robes. Kathina became another special link between monk and laity.

The monk was permitted few personal possessions. The daily regimen of the monk, whether residing in a monastery or wandering, became quite standardized. He was to rise early, well before dawn, cleanse himself, and sit quietly in meditation until the time (dawn) to enter the village for food. In the village, he was to walk without speaking, with his gaze downward, receiving food in his bowl at random, wherever it was offered. He was permitted to receive certain kinds of meat, as long as he was not aware that it had been specially prepared for him. Returning to the monastery or his place outside the village, he was to eat in silence, taking the food from the bowl in whatever order it had been placed there and reflecting to himself on food as medicine for a wound. According to the precepts he had to finish eating before noon. Thereafter, if a novice, he would receive counsel from his preceptor or instruction from his teacher; if a senior monk, he would engage in instructing others. Midafternoon was a time for quiet sitting and/or napping, after which he received guests. In the evening he returned again to study or instruction before retiring for the night.

The early monastic communities were self-governing units. Each had a specified geographical boundary and a certified membership, in accordance with the commonly accepted monastic code. The code was generally respected by secular authority. Adherence to the discipline was policed by fellow monks (peer pressure), laity, and, when necessary, by a formally constituted meeting of the entire monastic community. Important issues were settled by consensus. Seniority, determined by the number of years since ordination, was respected and seniors consulted, but senior monks had no formal authority. The gathered community appointed a senior monk as chief administrator and he, in turn, appointed other functionaries—overseers of buildings, robe and room distribution, and so on, as the community had need.

Early Appeal

In the early centuries of the movement, Buddhism had greater potential for mass support than either Brahmanism or Jainism. In Brahmanism the concern for ritual purity, expressed in a well-defined class structure, set the priests apart from the people. The sacred knowledge of Brahmanism, the *Vedas,* was transmitted in an elite language and was known only to the priests. The Buddha's words were carried in the vernacular languages and freely shared. Class status was of no concern to the Buddha; moral character rather than ritual purity was the basis for status. Jainism, although it developed a strong lay following, separated the monk from the laity more sharply than Buddhism by its extreme asceticism. This extreme posture was confrontational rather than conciliatory. The Buddha's Middle Way rejected both asceticism and worldliness and strongly encouraged lay participation and the close proximity of monks and laity. The monastic communities were visible and available to the people. His teachings were accommodating rather than confrontational; they subordinated and reinterpreted most existing religious beliefs and practices rather than pushing them aside.

The monastic life appealed to a significant number of persons, both female and male, especially those in need of security. As members of the Sangha, they enjoyed not only the necessities of life but enormous prestige. To warrant this status they had to maintain a somewhat demanding way of life, but the discipline was not onerous once the initial adjustment had been made.

The settled, well-ordered Sangha pursuing a nonviolent lifestyle also appealed to local rulers and the general populace. Not only was the Sangha a peaceful influence, but also, the laity desired to benefit from the merit of the monks. The more they invested in the monks and monasteries, the greater the merit for them. With the provision of permanent, well-furnished dwelling places, the monks wandered less. In any event, there were always some monks present, appointed to maintain the monastery.

The laity had opportunity for daily contact with the monks in providing them with food. The monks were readily available and anyone could give alms. This became a ritualized act of great merit. The laity had opportunity to consult with the monks at the monastery and on Observance days to receive instruction and blessing at their feet. Participation in an ordination by provision of amenities to the ordinand and the order of monks or simply by presence at the ceremony came to be seen as an opportunity for great merit, especially for the parents and friends of the new monk or nun.

The early lay practice of Buddhism was dependent upon the monastic community, with one important exception. The laity initiated the practice of venerating the remains of the Buddha and his most renowned disciples. According to the *Tripitaka,* the Buddha himself authorized the burial of his cremation remains in a mound at a crossroads, where travelers might honor his memory and thereby be assured of rebirth in heaven.

> And as they treat the remains of a king of kings, so, Ananda, should they treat the remains of the **Tathagata** ["the One Thus-come" or "Thus-gone"]. At the four cross roads a *thupa* should be erected to the Tathagata. And whosoever shall there place garlands or perfumes or paint, or make salutation there, or become in its presence calm in heart—that shall long be to them for a profit and a joy. . . . At the thought, Ananda, "This is the *thupa* of that Blessed One, of that Arahat-Buddha," the hearts of many shall be made calm and happy; and since they there had calmed and satisfied their hearts they will be reborn after death, when the body has dissolved, in the happy realms of heaven.[10]

A *thupa* (San., **stupa**) is a mound of earth. The practice of building a mound over the remains of great persons as a place of remembrance and worship (marking the remains or a **relic**) is very old in India, predating the Buddha. The Buddha instructed Ananda that the cremation and enshrinement were not to be performed by the monks but were to be left to the laity. Reportedly, the bones and ashes of the Buddha were divided into eight portions and distributed to eight parties of the laity who enshrined them in various locations. Whether or not this actually occurred immediately after the Buddha's death, such memorialization of the Buddha is very old and quite understandable. From all accounts, the Buddha was a highly charismatic personage, an imposing and compassionate presence. Furthermore, he himself urged the laity to respect and benefit from the power of holy monks. The development of *stupa* worship was based on the belief that the great merit and compassion of the Buddha continued to radiate from his remains. In effect, the *stupa* marked the continuing presence of the Buddha.

In time, the practice of erecting *stupas* became a hallmark of Buddhism. With the development of brick and plaster construction techniques, multi-leveled, relatively permanent, and sometimes quite large structures replaced the simple mound of earth. The most powerful *stupas* were those erected at places believed to have been frequented by the Buddha, and worship at *stupas* came to be closely associated with the practice of pilgrimage. Pilgrimage to the birthplace, the place of enlightenment, the place of the first sermon, and the place of the death of the Buddha is authorized in the same discourse in which the Buddha speaks of the *stupa*. As with *stupa* worship, great merit results from pilgrimage:

> And they, Ananda, who shall die while they, with believing heart, are journeying on such pilgrimage, shall be reborn after death, when the body shall dissolve, in the happy realms of heaven.[11]

[See Religions of Mesoamerica pp. 226–33, Judaism pp. 469–70, Christianity pp. 562–73, Islam pp. 645–47, Hinduism pp. 815–20, Religions of China pp. 1041–44, and Religions of Japan pp. 1154–60 for description and discussion of pilgrimage.]

Early Buddhism assimilated the gods and spirits of Brahmanism and popular folklore, interpreting their nature and existence in terms of karma—merit and demerit. They are conceived as part of a hierarchy of life-forms running a gamut from existence in extreme pain to existence in great pleasure as the result of good and bad deeds.

THE SIXFOLD HIERARCHY OF BEINGS

I. The Realms of the Gods—twenty-two levels, above
the earth, for example:

Sublime Gods
Richly Rewarded Gods   *increasing*
Radiant Gods   *pleasure*
Great Brahmas
Satisfied Gods
The Thirty-three Gods (of Brahmanism)

II. The Realm of Humans—mixed pleasure and pain

III. The Realm of Demons, in the atmosphere, near
the earth
IV. The Realm of Hungry Ghosts, on the earth   *increasing*
V. The Realm of Animals   *pain*
VI. The Realm of Hell-dwellers, below the earth

Human existence is the middle tier of this hierarchy, a realm of mixed pleasure and pain. Merit and demerit (good and bad karma) are created only in the human realm. Its effects are experienced, appropriately, in one or another of the six realms. Gods, demons, ghosts, animals, and hell-dwellers do not produce karma; they only live out the effects of karma produced in the human realm. Demerit earned as a human leads to rebirth as a demon, a hungry ghost, an animal, or an inhabitant of hell; merit leads to rebirth as a god or, again, as a human being. Those who grasp for power are condemned by such karma to a life as a powerful demon. Those who are unduly attached to family, money, and possessions are reborn as hungry ghosts—invisible beings that roam and haunt the earth suffering insatiable hunger. Preoccupation with food and sex leads to life as an animal, and a life dominated by violence, hatred, and anger leads to the most extreme punishment—life beneath the earth, in hell. On the other hand, generosity, morality, and meditation result in rebirth in the happy realms as a god or return again to the human realm in a position more favorable for the achievement of nirvana. These nonhuman forms of existence may last millions of years; still, like human existence, they are temporary. When a being's store of merit is exhausted as a god, he or she returns again to the human realm with another opportunity for merit and nirvana; or, perhaps, if there is sufficient demerit remaining from the former human existence, he or she falls to a realm of punishment to work out this demerit. Likewise, when demerit is exhausted, a hungry ghost, for instance, may revert to human form or rise to a realm of pleasure.

The activities of the various nonhuman beings may impinge upon life in the human realm for good or ill. The actions of malicious spirits may be curbed or warded off by the power of the monks and recitation of words of the Buddha; the power of the Buddha, the Dharma, and the Sangha is far greater than that of gods or demons. Certain of the gods have power over certain forces of nature or malevolent spirits and may be invoked for protection or blessing on special occasions. Furthermore, just as the monk can share merit with the laity, so human beings can share merit with those languishing in one of the realms of punishment, some of whom may, indeed, be their relatives.

From Ashoka to the Guptas: 250 B.C.E.–300 C.E.

The spread and prosperity of Buddhism in India was greatly assisted by the patronage of kings. Magadha was the heartland of Buddhism. The Magadhan kings Bimbasara and Ajatasatru, contemporaries of the Buddha, patronized the Sangha. Their successors gradually rose to power over all India. In 327 B.C.E. the Greeks conquered northwest India under Alexander the Great. Alexander crossed the Indus River and then gave up the campaign and returned to Macedonia, leaving governors in charge of the conquered area. His brief entrance and exit created a power vacuum such that, shortly thereafter, under the leadership of Chandragupta Maurya (reigning 322–297 B.C.E.), the Magadhans extended their rule all across northern India. Chandragupta's successors conquered to the south. Magadhan pacification and unification of the subcontinent encouraged the spread of Buddhism.

Ashoka Maurya (reigning 269–232 B.C.E.), the third emperor of the dynasty, left a record of his activities and ideals in edicts written on rocks and pillars. The edits show that, in remorse after a conquest in which several hundred thousand people were killed, Ashoka declared that henceforth he would rule by Dharma. His *dharma* emphasized:

> ... abstention from killing animals and from cruelty to living beings, kindliness in human and family relations, respect for brahmanas and samanas and obedience to mother, father and elders. . . .[12]

The declared reward for living in accord with this *dharma* is peace and prosperity in this world and abode in heaven after death. Ashoka declared himself to be a lay follower of Buddhism; his edicts note that he made pilgrimages to the Buddha's birthplace at Lumbini, the place of the great enlightenment near Gaya (Bodh Gaya), and the place of the first sermon at Sarnath. Edicts at Sanchi and Sarnath show that he exhorted monks to study the Buddha's teaching and adhere to it without schism in their ranks. Although himself a follower of Buddhism, his official policy recognized and supported all religions.

> My officers charged with the spread of Dharma are occupied with various kinds of services beneficial to ascetics and householders, and they are empowered to concern themselves with all sects. I have ordered some of them to look after the affairs of the Sangha, some to take care of the Brahmin . . . some to work among the Nirgranthas [Jains]. . . .[13]

According to a chronicle compiled in Sri Lanka by Buddhist monks in the fifth century, Ashoka's rule was the archetype of Buddhist kingship. The chronicles say that he constructed eighty-four thousand monasteries and *stupas*, and

Pillar-capital of King Ashoka, at Sarnath, where the Buddha preached his first sermon. The Buddha's preaching of the Dharma, symbolized by the wheel, came to be referred to as "the lion's roar." The animals accompanying the Dharma wheel around the midsection of the capital—an elephant, a bull, a horse, and a lion—are taken to symbolize the conception, birth, renunciation, and first sermon of the Buddha.

that to purify and preserve the Sangha, he convened a great council of monks at his capital, Pataliputra (modern-day Patna). The council dismissed some sixty thousand monks who had deviated from the monastic code and then dispatched missionaries to various parts of Asia. According to this account, Ashoka's own son, who had become a monk, was dispatched to Sri Lanka; his daughter, a nun, followed shortly thereafter. Ashoka's edicts say nothing of a council of monks or the monastic involvement of his son and daughter, but even if the chronicle account is exaggerated, Ashoka certainly set a precedent for the relationship between government and Sangha.

The fall of the Mauryan dynasty in 185 B.C.E. did not greatly affect the fortunes of Buddhism. The Shungas, who succeeded the Mauryans in the northeastern heartland of the empire, were not positively disposed toward Buddhism, but neither did they cause significant disruption. Under the Satavahanas, who succeeded the Mauryans in the south, prosperous centers of Buddhism arose at Amaravati and Nagarjunikonda. By the third century C.E., Nagarjunikonda was a complex of twenty-seven monasteries and twenty *stupas;* inscriptions here record the gifts of members of the royal household as well as those of wealthy merchants. These centers were influential in spreading Buddhism to Southeast Asia.

The Greek kingdoms that succeeded Mauryan rule in the northwest supported Buddhism. King Menander (reigning 140–115 B.C.E.), the most famous of the rulers, is featured in the *Milinda-panha (Questions of Milinda)*, a text on basic Buddhist teachings important to the Theravada tradition. In the text, Menander (Milinda) engages in a lengthy dialogue with a monk, Nagasena. At the end it is said that the king not only urged support for the Sangha, but he abdicated in favor of his son and became a monk. [See Religions of Africa pp. 24, 35, 60, Religions of Mesoamerica pp. 198–201, Native Religions of North America pp. 347–48, Judaism pp. 391–92, Christianity pp. 503, 505, Islam pp. 632–33, Hinduism p. 748, Religions of China pp. 991–93, and Religions of Japan pp. 1095–96, 1105–6 for the relationship of religion to political leaders.]

The Greek kingdoms were succeeded by the rule of the Sakas and the Kushanas, invaders from Bactria (northeast Afghanistan) and Parthia (eastern Iran). The Kushanas, whose rule in the first and second centuries C.E. extended from north central India into central Asia (Afghanistan, Uzbekistan, and Chinese Turkestan), were avid patrons of Buddhism. During this period Buddhist monks and merchants established the tradition in central Asia and western China. King Kanishka (c. 78–101 C.E.) built *stupas* and monasteries; his coins bear the image of the Buddha. Fa-xian (Fa-hsien), a Chinese monk traveling in India around 400 C.E. remarked that the *stupa* built by Kanishka at Peshawar was the most magnificent of all the ones he saw on his journey. Images of the Buddha appear in the first century C.E., fashioned by artists at Mathura and in the Gandhara region, centers of Kushana rule. Traditional accounts say that Kanishka called a council of monks who recited and authorized a version of the *Tripitaka.*

Archaeologists have uncovered the remains of monasteries and *stupas* dating from the second century B.C.E. The monasteries were either freestanding fired-brick structures or rock-cut caves. Typically, they consisted of cells for the monks surrounding a ceremonial hall. More than a thousand cave monasteries have been found, chiefly in western India, their construction dating from the second century B.C.E. to the ninth century C.E. A complete cave monastery consisted of a series of small rooms with rock beds and pillows, a pillared ceremonial hall, and a sanctuary, at the back of which was a *stupa* or *caitya* (a mound without a relic). The remains of great complexes of monasteries have been discovered at Sarnath, Kushinara, and Nalanda in the northeast, Sanchi and Mathura in central India, Peshawar and Taxila in the northwest, and Amaravati and Nagarjunikonda in the south.

The laity, especially wealthy merchants and rulers, built up monasteries in their desire for merit, not only the merit of financing construction, but also the whole range of merit-making opportunities made possible by the presence of a community of monks. From the Ashokan period on, the Sangha was drawn more and more into society. Rulers supported the monastic establishments as centers of culture and conveyors of blessing and protection to the state. Rulers and merchants' guilds as well as the common people made donations. Individual monks as well as monasteries received grants of land and/or portions of the income of a village to provide for their temporal needs. Along with the land they received the services of the tenants who worked the land. While laypeople were engaged to administer these properties, the senior monks in charge of monastery affairs in effect became landlords. In cases where the income from land and the donations of goods and money exceeded the needs of the monks, the monasteries built up a reserve of wealth that was then loaned to support local farmers or merchants.

The monasteries became centers of learning. The monks increasingly turned to scholarship and spent less time in meditation. They studied and taught a whole range of secular subjects as well as the Dharma. Some practiced medicine and gave astrological consultations. Even though Brahmanism had developed a whole range of life-cycle rituals (birth, marriage, death, and so on), which the priests performed for members of the upper classes, Buddhist monks were often called upon to bless these occasions by chanting words of the Buddha. Very likely, they also performed funerals, memorial services, and house-blessing rituals for the lower classes. From ancient times to the beginning of the eighteenth century, the lay practice of religion in India was not exclusivistic; that is, people often participated in various aspects of different religions at the same time. We should not think of the laity of Brahmanism, Buddhism, and Jainism as competitive, or even clearly distinguished. King Ashoka is a good example of the laity in general. He declared himself a lay Buddhist, but he respected and supported the leadership of all sects and, on occasion, probably sponsored the performance of a Brahmanical fire ritual.

The *stupa* became a standard feature of the monastery environment, necessary to a sacred complex. Monks and nuns as well as laity contributed to the construction and upkeep of *stupas* and regularly walked around them and made flower offerings in prayer and meditation. Sanchi and Bharhut, in central India, were major complexes from 200 B.C.E. to 200 C.E. Inscriptions indicate that the remains of many renowned monks were enshrined at Sanchi. The gateways to the large *stupa* at Sanchi are elaborately decorated with sculptures depicting scenes from the life of the Buddha. Prior to the first century B.C.E., there were no anthropomorphic portrayals of the Buddha. His presence was indicated by an empty space, footprints, a Dharma wheel (see photograph on page 876), or the tree of enlightenment. Buddha-images originated at Mathura and Gandhara in northwest India and soon came to adorn the ceremonial hall of the monastery as well as the *stupas*.

The Rise of the Mahayana

The five hundred years from the fall of the Mauryan dynasty to the reunification of India under the Guptas was marked by the rise of Mahayana, "Great Vehicle" Buddhism. The Mahayana was defined by the monks and grew out of doctrinal disputes rather than differences in monastic practice.

The monastic code was likely fully formulated by 300 B.C.E. and thereafter, apart from the differences of lifestyle between the minority forest-dwelling monks and the majority village-dwelling monks, there was general uniformity in monastic practice. Variant interpretations of the Buddha and his general teachings circulated from the earliest times; several schools of thought grew up in the Sangha without great consequence until the second century B.C.E. Then new **sutras** ("discourses") appeared, purporting to be the "higher" teachings of the Buddha, hidden for a time and rediscovered. These *sutras* forced the drawing of doctrinal lines and the eventual division of the monks into adherents of either the Mahayana tradition or the more orthodox Theravada ("The Way of the Elders") tradition.

The Theravada (senior) monks held to the view, represented in the early *sutras*, that the goal of the monastic life is *arhatship*, a goal achievable only by monastic discipline and not through the lay life. (The layperson may achieve heavenly bliss for a time but will have to be reborn again in the human realm to pursue the monastic path.) The *arhat* is one who has attained nirvana, that is, has extinguished all suffering by means of moral purity and insight and will not experience rebirth at the end of the present life. The elders believed that Buddhahood was unique to Gautama, at least within the present age of time, and that Gautama had, in addition to *arhatship*, attained perfect knowledge by which to teach others the way to nirvana.

Mahayana monks submitted that the goal of the monastic life, a goal that could also be achieved in the lay life, is full Buddhahood. They criticized the pursuit of *arhatship* as a selfish pursuit and submitted that the complete extinction of suffering could only be achieved with the mental disposition of a **bodhisattva.** Bodhisattvas, "beings striving for enlightenment," strive on the monastic path or the lay path not for themselves, but for the welfare of others. They deny all self-interest, most of all interest in achieving nirvana. Even if they could have nirvana, they would refuse it to be born again and again for the sake of releasing others from suffering. *Bodhisattvas* are a force of compassion for the world. This ideal is clear, they argued, from the Buddha's own career, if not his early teaching. As the Buddha reveals in the "new" *sutras,* he has been on the *bodhisattva* path for eons and eons, striving to save other beings. And he will continue that striving—one should not think that with the death of Gautama, he became extinct. This apparent passing to nirvana, indeed also the achievement of enlightenment earlier, was only an appearance, an illusion to motivate others.

This Mahayana vision makes the "historical" Buddha a manifestation of a cosmic force, a transcendent principle and power. This principle and power is the pure Dharma, Dharma as the True Reality, that which pervades all, and is the true nature of every thing and being that exists. The Buddha of the new *sutras* reveals numerous other Buddhas, manifestations of Dharma, who preside over other universes in a vast reality and whose power radiates even into our world. The Buddha reveals countless *bodhisattvas,* striving in one state or another toward *bodhi* (enlightenment). What is important in this, according to the *sutra,* is not only that the way of the *bodhisattva* is the true way, but that the power of *bodhisattvas* is available to those in need. The *bodhisattva* ideal is double-edged—those who are ready should strive on the *bodhisattva* path; those who are not can call on the *bodhisattvas'* power. This ideal may have been influenced by developments in devotional Brahmanism/Hinduism, but most of all it is an elaboration of the early Buddhist teaching that the monk is a merit-field for others and of the lay Buddhist belief in the power of relics of the saints. [See Hinduism pp. 760–62, 764–66, 768–69 for devotional Hinduism.]

This vision of the Buddhist way is called Great Vehicle, both because the ideal (Buddhahood) is great and because it is a way open to all (not just to monks), either by pursuing the *bodhisattva* path or by calling on the merit-power of the *bodhisattva* through prayer. Adherents of the Mahayana disparaged the Way of the Elders by calling it Hinayana, "Little Vehicle."

The emergence of Mahayana is marked by the appearance of a number of new scriptures between 100 B.C.E. and 200 C.E.: *The Sutra of the Lotus of the True Dharma* (*Sad-dharma-pundarika Sutra*), the *Vision of the Pure Land* (*Sukhavati-vyuha*), and *The Sutras of the Perfection of Wisdom* (*Prajna-paramita Sutra*). The *Lotus Sutra* reveals the Buddha as a cosmic being unbounded by time and space who exercises many skillful devices by which all beings may be saved and lauds the way of the *bodhisattva* over the one that leads to *arhatship.* The *Vision of the Pure Land* reveals the *bodhisattva* vows of the monk Dharmakara and describes the **Pure Land** paradise that Dharmakara establishes as the result of eons of striving. Dharmakara becomes known as **Amitabha Buddha,** "the Buddha of Endless Light." According to the *sutra,* his paradise in the western sphere of the cosmos can be reached by good deeds and meditation on Amitabha and his paradise or simply by praising his name over and over with full faith in his power.

The *Perfection of Wisdom sutras* set forth the higher wisdom of the Buddha, the wisdom of the accomplished *bodhisattvas* and transcendent Buddhas. This wisdom builds on the Buddha's teaching of "no-self." The so-called human person, which in reality is an aggregation of energies and processes arising and decaying every moment, is said to be "empty" (**shunya**), that is, empty of self, having no enduring nature. The same may be said of the entire phenomenal world; it is everywhere and completely in process and therefore devoid of an unchanging core. *Bodhisattvas* seek to realize the emptiness (*shunyata*) of self and world. They seek to dissolve the self that separates and alienates them in the life-flow. To dissolve self is to dissolve the distinctions that separate things and persons and cause suffering; it is to be one with each moment of life-flow as it occurs and, therefore, it is to experience the essential unity of life, the bliss of oneness. In the light of emptiness, *samsara*—the world of individual existence in bondage to karma—and nirvana are the same, that is, this very phenomenal world is nirvana when emptiness is realized.

These doctrinal differences did not notably alter the pattern of life of the Mahayana monks. They were no doubt reflected in their meditations, but Mahayana monks aspiring on the path of the *bodhisattva* did not become aggressive in social action. The *bodhisattva* saves by accumulating a store of merit that can be drawn on by others.

In the propagation of the Mahayana, its interpretation and transmission by individual masters took on more importance than in the Theravada. The most important of the early masters were Nagarjuna, c. 200 C.E., and the brothers Asanga and Vasubandhu, c. 400 C.E. Nagarjuna founded the Madhyamika ("Middle Way") school of interpretation and Asanga and Vasubandhu developed the Yogacara ("Practice of Yoga") school.

Monasteries came to be identified as either Mahayana or Theravada. They coexisted without strife, sometimes in the same monastery complex, and were equally appealing.

Xuan-zang (Hsuan-tsang), a Chinese Buddhist pilgrim to the major Buddhist centers in India from 630 to 644 C.E., estimates that in these centers there were a total of 115,000 Theravada monks in 2,000 monasteries and 120,000 Mahayana monks in 2,500 monasteries.

With the formulation of the Mahayana vision, the laity had more centers of power (the transcendent *bodhisattvas* and Buddhas) to appeal to in their prayers. Amitabha did not become popular in India, but rose to prominence in Chinese Buddhism. One of his close associates, the *bodhisattva* **Avalokiteshvara,** "The Lord Who (Kindly) Looks Down," the *bodhisattva* of infinite mercy, became an object of widespread appeal, in India as well as China, Korea, and Japan.

Final Flowering and Decline in India

The Gupta dynasty, 320–540 C.E., unified India once again and ushered in the classical age of Indian culture. The Gupta kings were committed to Brahmanism/Hinduism, but they also patronized Buddhist institutions. A prime example is their construction of Nalanda, a great monastery complex, near their capital, Pataliputra. Nalanda became a full-fledged university offering a wide range of secular subjects as well as Buddhist studies; it attracted scholars from all over Asia. Construction began in the early fifth century. Xuan-zang (Hsuan-tsang) describes its glory in the early seventh century:

Six kings built as many monasteries one after the other, and an enclosure was made with bricks to make all the buildings into one great monastery with one entrance for them all. There were many courtyards, and they were divided into eight departments. Precious terraces spread like stars and jade pavilions were spired like peaks. The temple arose into the mists and the shrine halls stood high above the clouds. . . . Streams of blue water wound through the parks; green lotus flowers sparkled among the blossoms of sandal trees, and a mango grove spread outside the enclosure. The monks' dwellings in all the courtyards had four stories. The beams were painted with all the colors of the rainbow and were carved with animal designs, while the pillars were red and green. . . . In India there were thousands of monasteries, but none surpassed this one in magnificence and sublimity. Always present were 10,000 monks, including hosts and guests, who studied both the Mahayana teachings and the doctrines of the 18 Hinayana schools as well as worldly books such as the *Vedas* and other classics. They also studied grammar, medicine, and mathematics. . . . The king gave them the revenues of more than 100 villages to support them, and each of the villages had 200 families who daily offered . . . rice, butter, and milk. Thus the students could have the four requisites (clothing, food, shelter, and medicine) sufficient for their needs without going to beg for them. It was because of this support that they had achieved so much in their learning.[14]

Relic worship grew to major proportions in the Gupta period in both monastic and lay Buddhism. The Chinese traveler Fa-xian (Fa-hsien; c. 400 c.e.) reports that at Peshawar the Buddha's begging bowl was enshrined. At Nagara, he found shrines for the Buddha's shadow, tooth, the flatbone of his skull, his sandalwood staff, and his robe. The Buddha's toothpick was found growing out of the earth where, it was said, he stuck it after cleaning his teeth. Fa-xian found senior monks paying reverence at *stupas* for Sariputra, Maudgalyayana, and Ananda, and novices honoring a mound for Rahula (Gautama's son). There were *stupas* enshrining portions of the *Tripitaka*. He observed rulers making daily offerings at such shrines. At Shravasti, Fa-xian viewed a sandalwood image of the Buddha that he was told had been fashioned to symbolize the Buddha's presence when he went to the heavens to preach the Dharma to his mother. He was also informed that this was the pattern for all other iconic representations of the Buddha.

Beginning in the late fifth century, invading Huns sacked and burned many of the great monasteries of northwest India. They attacked the monasteries for their considerable wealth—donations of supplies, money, and images made from precious metals that had accumulated beyond the daily needs of the monks. Xuanzang reports that some of these centers of Buddhism had been partially restored, but they would never return to their former status. Gupta power disintegrated in the mid–sixth century and the country returned to warring factionalism. King Harsha briefly (606–647 c.e.) reunited North India, renewing support to traditional institutions, but thereafter the area was divided again into small monarchies. The Palas, who came to power in northeast India around 750 c.e., strongly supported Buddhist institutions. They restored Nalanda, which had

been destroyed at the death of Harsha, and built up two more monastery universities: Odantapura and Vikramasila. The Palas had extensive relations with kingdoms in Southeast Asia.

During the Pala period, a third "vehicle" of Buddhism, the **Tantrayana** ("the *Tantrayana*
vehicle of [specialized] ritual"), came to maturity at Nalanda. Philosophically,
the Tantrayana is consistent with the Mahayana and may be considered an
offshoot. Its distinctiveness lies in its introduction into Buddhism of very old
ritual techniques and Yoga practices. Numerous texts were produced by adherents of Tantrayana, but the true wisdom of the vehicle was known only to masters called *siddhas* ("Perfected Ones"). In contrast to the open transmission of
knowledge in the Mahayana and Theravada traditions, the wisdom of the *siddha*
was transmitted only in an intimate, one-to-one relationship with a carefully
prepared disciple. *Siddhas* from Nalanda and the far northwest of India were
responsible for the development of Buddhism in Tibet.

The monastic centers of Buddhism all across North India were utterly
devastated by Muslim invaders in the late twelfth century. They were never to
rise again. The wealth and power of their patrons was usurped by Muslim rule.
With the death or dispersion of the monks, lay Buddhism could not sustain itself. Lay devotionalism was easily absorbed into Hinduism. Buddhism lingered,
especially in South India, but by 1500 had passed from the Indian scene.

Beyond India

The Spread of Buddhism

As we have noted, the Buddha instructed his monastic disciples to go forth
and preach the Dharma, "for the welfare of the many." The Sri Lankan chronicles record that following a great council of monks during the reign of Ashoka
(269–232 B.C.E.), missionary monks were dispatched to various outlying areas of
the Indian subcontinent, Sri Lanka, and Southeast Asia. Even so, Indian Buddhism was not an aggressively proselytizing religion. By and large, Buddhism
spread by the casual wanderings of monks and the travels of Buddhist merchants. Monks wandered eight months of the year in accordance with their discipline. The merchant class was strongly supportive of Buddhism from early
times.

As in India, the growth and prosperity of Buddhism outside India was significantly the result of official patronage. Buddhism spread to the island of Sri
Lanka off the southern tip of India in the latter half of the third century B.C.E.
It may be that a diplomatic mission sent to the island by King Ashoka c. 247
B.C.E. encouraged its king to patronize Buddhism. If we accept the word of
chronicles compiled in Sri Lanka in the fifth century C.E., missionary monks
(including Ashoka's son) dispatched from Ashoka's capital converted King Tissa
of Sri Lanka. According to the chronicles, Tissa built monasteries for monks and
nuns ordained by the mission, enshrined the collarbone relic of the Buddha in

a great *stupa,* and planted a slip of the *bodhi* tree (the tree under which the Buddha achieved enlightenment) brought to the island from Bodh Gaya by the nun Sanghamitta, Ashoka's daughter. The chronicles also indicate that at the same time monks were sent to Sri Lanka, some were dispatched to Suvarnabhumi in Southeast Asia—probably what is today southern Myanmar (Burma) and Thailand and the island of Sumatra. Indian traders established colonies across Southeast Asia as far as Vietnam and the islands of Indonesia beginning in the first century C.E. These colonies led to the rise of Indianized kingdoms in which Brahmanism as well as both Mahayana and Theravada Buddhism gradually rose to prominence.

Buddhism spread from northwest India into central Asia in the first century C.E. and from there "trickled" into western China. Kushana rule (first and second centuries C.E.) came to encompass the area from Banaras (northcentral India) west to include northern Afghanistan and north and northeast to include Uzbekistan and Chinese Turkestan (eastern China). The Kushana ruler Kanishka (c. 78–101) patronized Buddhism extensively. In the relative peace and prosperity of the Kushana period, monks and merchants carried Buddhism to central Asia and China along the trade routes. The remains of impressive *stupas,* cave monasteries, and freestanding brick monasteries, and inscriptions and numerous Buddhist texts show that Buddhism thrived along the silk route for ten centuries. It was officially recognized in the kingdoms of Kashgar and Khotan (Chinese Turkestan) c. 150 C.E. Xuan-zang (Hsuan-tsang), the seventh-century Chinese traveler to India, reports finding a hundred monasteries and five thousand monks at Khotan. Central Asian Buddhism provided most of the texts and scholars that spurred the development of Buddhism in China, 300 to 600 C.E. Declining prosperity, the rise of Islam, and the declining fortunes of Buddhism in India and China led to its disappearance in central Asia by 1000 C.E. [See Religions of China pp. 1005–9 for the coming of Buddhism to China.]

Chinese monks and diplomatic missions, perhaps on the model of Ashoka's "Dharma missions," carried Buddhism to Korea in the late fourth century C.E. Korean diplomatic missions introduced Buddhism at the Japanese court in the mid–sixth century. Thereafter, direct contact between Japan and China spurred the development of Japanese Buddhism. Buddhism reached Tibet from China in the seventh century. It was officially established by the Tibetan King Khri-srong (740–798), who invited a Mahayana monk from Nalanda to his court. [See Religions of Japan pp. 1096–99 for Chinese and Indian influence on Japanese religion.]

Integration

Except in the case of China, Buddhism was welcomed throughout Asia as the religion of a superior civilization. For Sri Lanka, Southeast Asia, and Tibet, the superior civilization was Indian civilization; for Korea, Vietnam, and Japan, it was Chinese civilization. Throughout Asia, Buddhism was accommodated to already established religions—spirit cults in Southeast Asia and Tibet, Confucianism and Daoism (Taoism) in China, and Shinto in Japan.

Buddhism appealed to a select few as a way of self-discipline and learning en route to nirvana. Its chief appeal to rulers as well as to the common people was as a religion of power in worldly affairs. Buddhist monks had a reputation not only for great learning, but also for extraordinary power over nature. It is said, for instance, that Ashoka's son, Mahinda, and his monastic companions flew through the air to Sri Lanka. The worship of the image of Buddha and his relics was considered a source of power for the present life as well as a means of gaining merit for the next life. The Buddha-image itself was believed to have power inasmuch as it was patterned after an image made during the lifetime of the Buddha and therefore qualified as a relic. Legend has it that the Chinese emperor Ming (ruling 58–75 C.E.) sent envoys of inquiry to India as the result of a dream in which he perceived a great golden Buddha. According to Japanese chronicles, in 538 C.E. a Korean ruler sent a mission to the Japanese court requesting military aid. The envoys presented the Japanese emperor with a gold-plated image of the Buddha, several Buddhist texts, and an exhortation that worship of the Buddha would result in prosperity in his kingdom. The Tantrayana *siddha* Padmasambhava (eighth century) was invited to Tibet in part for his reputation in exorcising evil spirits.

Initially, both Theravada and Mahayana traditions were practiced in Sri Lanka, Southeast Asia, and China. In time, the Theravada died out in northern Asia but came to be officially established in Sri Lanka and across the mainland of Southeast Asia (except in Vietnam) to the exclusion of the Mahayana. Tantric Mahayana developed as one of the several sects in Chinese and Japanese Buddhism; in Tibet, it eventually came to dominance.

Monks of Sri Lanka codified Theravada Buddhism by committing their traditions of what the Buddha taught to final written form during the first four centuries C.E. This authoritative text, written in a language called Pali, came to be known as the *Tipitaka* (San., *Tripitaka*). Around 400 C.E., a monk named Buddhaghosa compiled and completed commentaries to the *Tripitaka* and a definitive summary of the teachings entitled *Visuddhimagga*, "The Path of Purification." After Buddhaghosa, the *Tripitaka*, his *Visuddhimagga*, and the *Milinda-panha* became the recognized standard of Theravada teachings and practices. Between the eleventh and the fourteenth centuries this Buddhism became officially established in the kingdoms of Burma, Thailand, Cambodia, and Laos.

The practice of Buddhism in Sri Lanka and Southeast Asia followed essentially the patterns established in India, with the exception that from its beginning in Sri Lanka, from the eleventh century in Burma, from the thirteenth in Thailand, and from the fourteenth in Cambodia and Laos, official patronage forged an intimate relationship between Sangha and government and led to the gradual disappearance or assimilation of other religions and the appearance of majority Buddhism. The Sangha prospered and at times significantly influenced the course of government but was also subject to close scrutiny and control by government.

Sri Lanka adopted the Indian caste system, and eventually casteism affected the Sangha as well as Sri Lankan society, dividing the Sangha into three distinct ordination lines. As the result of periods of South Indian rule and migrations from South India a large Hindu minority accumulated on the island and lay Buddhism gradually assimilated certain Hindu practices.

In Southeast Asian Theravada, ordination came to be seen as a rite of passage, an initiation into adult society, expected of all young men. Large numbers became monks for a short period of time; only a few undertook the monastic life as a lifelong commitment. Buddhism assimilated local spirit cults, just as it had assimilated the gods and spirits of popular religions in India.

In China, Buddhism had to compete with Confucianism and Daoism (Taoism), highly sophisticated and long-established religions. These religions were world affirming. Confucianism emphasized the family and harmonious relationships of loyalty and consideration—loyalty of son to father, wife to husband, subject to ruler; consideration of father for son, husband for wife, and ruler for subject. Buddhist monasticism devalued the family and placed loyalty to the discipline and the monastic community above that to the ruler and society in general. Daoism fostered introspection and nonconformism but in favor of light-hearted, easy flowing communion with nature rather than rigorous mental discipline. At the same time Confucianism valued learning (sageliness) and Daoism attributed extraordinary powers to one who lived in harmony with nature. Since learning and magical powers were key attributes of the accomplished Buddhist monk, the Chinese could appreciate the monk in spite of other areas of conflict. Furthermore, since the goal of Confucianism and Daoism was harmony in this world, the Buddhist belief in a heavenly rebirth gained by merit and the ultimate attainability of nirvana added new dimensions to Chinese religious life.

Confucianism was the established religion of the Han dynasty (202 B.C.E.–220 C.E.). In the period of disunity and disfavor toward Confucianism following the fall of the Han (300–600), monastic Buddhism gained general acceptance and official support. A census of 517 C.E. indicates that there were then thirty thousand monasteries and two million monks and nuns. The pattern of monastic life was much like that of Indian Buddhism with the major exception that the monasteries were self-sustaining through land grants and the monks had much less daily intimacy with society because they did not go out for food. Also, the monastic communities largely arose focused on individual master monks; each community was made up of a master and his disciples. This arrangement, which was a tendency in Indian Mahayana Buddhism, was accentuated in China by the Confucian and Daoist (Taoist) ideal of sageliness. By way of contrast, in Theravada Buddhism the focus was on the community itself, in which each monk had a common status.

Mahayana Buddhism in India tolerated great diversity of thought without dividing into distinct sects. In China, from the sixth century on, a variety of sects took shape, each appealing to one or another of the Mahayana *sutras*. The two sects that gained the greatest popularity and came to have the largest impact on Japanese as well as Chinese Buddhism were the Chan (Ch'an; Jap., **Zen**), or "Meditation" sect, and the Jing-tu (Ching-t'u; Jap., Jodo), or "Pure Land" sect.

The early monks of China, influenced from India, emphasized scholarship and were perhaps somewhat lax in keeping the ancient monastic code. Chan

(Ch'an) monks downgraded concern with textual learning and translation and emphasized discipline and above all meditation. They withdrew into the mountains, where they developed a variety of new techniques for achieving insight. They also innovated by introducing manual labor as part of the monastic discipline. Following Mahayana teaching, particularly *The Sutras of the Perfection of Wisdom,* they taught that this very concrete world is the realm of enlightenment. Influenced by Daoism, they taught that ordinary, mundane activity could be the occasion for enlightenment.

Other Chinese monks had discovered the *Vision of the Pure Land sutras,* which praised Amitabha Buddha (Chin., *A-mi-duo-fo* [*A-mi-to-fo*]) and his Pure Land paradise. Amitabha and his Pure Land were the object of meditation in Indian Buddhism. The Chinese master Tan-luan (T'an-luan) (476–542) interpreted the Pure Land scriptures to say that one could attain the Pure Land after death simply by reciting the name of Amitabha in the manner: *nă-mō ă-mī-tō-fo,* "Reverence to Amitabha Buddha." He taught that by such recitation alone, without meditation or any particular discipline, and by Amitabha's grace, one could gain the Pure Land paradise; once in the Pure Land, nirvana would be easy to attain. In a relatively brief time, this teaching attracted thousands of persons, both monks and laity, to faith in Amitabha Buddha in the hope of being reborn in his paradise.

Along with Amitabha Buddha, the *bodhisattvas* Avalokiteshvara and **Maitreya** also became popular objects of worship in China. Avalokiteshvara (Chin., Guanyin [Kuan-yin]) was accommodated to pre-Buddhist religion by identification with a goddess who, like Avalokiteshvara, was believed to have power over fertility. Lay Buddhism in China did not develop in close collaboration with the life of the monks, as it did in India, Sri Lanka, and Southeast Asia. It came to consist largely of merit making by gifts to the monasteries and worship of Buddhas and *bodhisattvas* alongside of the worship of pre-Buddhist gods and spirits. [See Religions of China pp. 1002–9 for the development of Buddhism in China.]

Japanese Buddhism developed on the Chinese model, with the notable exception that, from the thirteenth century on, Pure Land (Jap., Jodo) Buddhism gave up monasticism and began functioning with a married clergy. In Japan, Buddhism interacted with Shinto, the native Japanese tradition. A division of labor developed making Shinto priests responsible for worldly affairs, such as consecrating marriage, and Buddhist monks responsible for funeral rites.

Had Buddhism not become established outside India, it may well have died out after the destruction of the great monastic centers in India around 1200. Sri Lankan monks preserved the texts and traditions of the Theravada, and Chinese and Tibetan monks preserved the literature and traditions of the Mahayana.

In Tibet, Buddhism took shape primarily under the influence of Indian Mahayana masters and at the height of the popularity of Tantric Mahayana. As in other parts of Asia, monks and monasteries played a key role in its establishment and growth. However, both traditional Mahayana monk scholars and Tantric wonder-working *siddhas* were instrumental in this process, and some of the *siddhas,* like Padmasambhava, were householders (noncelibate). Tantric *siddhas* did not necessarily adhere to the monastic code followed by Mahayana and Theravada monks; their teachings were passed to disciples in a private relationship rather than through ordination by a body of monks. Tantric practices came to dominate Tibetan Buddhism under the leadership of both monastic and nonmonastic masters (*lamas*). The recognition of different lineages of masters divided its practice into six distinct schools or sects.

Tibetan Buddhism developed two unique features: first, the institution of the reincarnation of *lamas,* based on the belief that each successive head *lama* in a given lineage is a reincarnation of the previous head *lama* in that lineage, and second, *lama* rule over Tibet. The Mongol ruler of China in the thirteenth century appointed a *lama* as regent over Tibet. In 1656, Tibet came under the direct rule of a *lama* with the title of **Dalai Lama** or "Ocean Lama." The current Dalai Lama lives in exile in northwest India.

Beyond Asia

European presence in Asia from 1500 on brought Buddhism to note in the West. Western scholars, some of whom became devotees, assisted in the revival of Buddhism in Sri Lanka and its reintroduction into India and founded Buddhist societies in England, Germany, and the United States. Chinese and Japanese immigrants transplanted the faith in Hawaii and the western United States. An influx of Japanese and Tibetan monks and scholars in this century has produced sizable communities of Buddhists throughout the United States (see chapter 39).

Buddhism as a Unified System of Beliefs and Practices

WE HAVE SEEN HOW Buddhism developed from the life and teachings of Siddhartha Gautama into a religion practiced worldwide. Now let us look at this religion as a fully developed system functioning in the modern world. As in the historical survey, our focus will be Asian Buddhism, both Theravada and Mahayana. With respect to the Mahayana, we shall specifically consider the Zen and Pure Land Buddhisms of Japan.

> All that we are is the result of what we have thought: it is founded on our thoughts, it is made up of our thoughts. If a man speaks or acts with an evil thought, pain follows him, as a wheel follows the foot of the ox that draws the carriage. If a man speaks or acts with a pure thought, happiness follows him, like a shadow that never leaves him.[15]

The "*result* of what we have thought" is karma. Buddhism defines the world in terms of karma. Karma manifests itself as a multitude of life-forms, each with its distinctive characteristics and potential, each in its appropriate sphere or environment according to its merit-status. Karma causes suffering; it causes relative happiness; and it causes ultimate happiness—release from suffering, nirvana.

The resources for shaping good karma, which results in worldly prosperity, favorable rebirth, and nirvana, are the Buddha, the Dharma, and the Sangha. These Three Treasures are the source of self-power to those who actualize them through a life of self-discipline. They are power to be shared with those who respect them, have confidence in them, and worship them. The Buddha is a heroic example for those who seek self-power. He is a reservoir of merit for those who need to rely on the power of another. The Dharma is wisdom-power or enlightenment-power to those who comprehend it. It is a force of healing, protection, and blessing to those who invoke it. The Sangha is an instrument of enlightenment and nirvana to those who commit themselves to its discipline. It is a reservoir of merit for those who respect and materially support it.

The Theravada and Mahayana interpretations of the Three Treasures, each in its own way, give emphasis to both foci of the Buddha's life and teaching—self-power through self-discipline and shared power by the conjunction of compassion and devotion. Charity, moral discipline, meditation, and worship are the means of actualizing the power of the Three Treasures, that is, making and sharing merit in the production of good karma and the attainment of worldly prosperity, enlightenment, and nirvana. These means dictate a ritual ordering of individual, familial, and community life.

The World as Constituted by Karma

There is no story of the first or primal creation in the annals of Buddhism. Buddhists, like Hindus, taking their cue from the repeating phases of the sun and moon in relation to the earth and the ever-repeating cycles of growth and decline in nature, think of time and space as without beginning or end and incessantly pulsating in lesser and greater cycles. The material universe repeatedly issues forth from a state of latency, expands to a peak, and then declines to a state of rest once again, much as the moon appears, phases from new to full, and then goes back to new. Of course, the life span of a manifest universe, 432 billion years (a *maha-kalpa*), is enormously greater than the twenty-eight day cycle of a moon. Within the great span of time of the *maha-kalpa,* the universe pulsates in lesser phases of 432 million years (a *kalpa*), each of which is constituted of four ages (*catur-yuga*). A universe is made up of one billion world systems, each of which consists of an earth with heavens above and hells below. [See Religions of Africa pp. 36–37, 64–66, Religions of Mesoamerica pp. 129–35, 154–55, 163–68, Native Religions of North America pp. 288–95, 327–29, 333–42, Judaism pp. 380–84, Christianity pp. 534–35, Hinduism pp. 739–41, 743–46, and Religions of Japan pp. 1094–96 for discussion of myth and mythology.]

While they recognize these great cycles of time and the numerous world-cycles, the teachings of Buddhism focus on the repeated cycling of life-forms (*samsara*) in this world system by reason of karma. Karma, the force or energy created by human thoughts, words, and deeds, causes the various life-forms that inhabit our world system—their physical and mental capacities, sex, and social circumstances. There are gods who reside in heavens above the earth; humans, demons, hungry ghosts, and animals who live on or near the earth; and hell dwellers whose abode is below the earth. Karma is of two kinds: meritorious (*punya,* or "good," karma) and demeritorious (*papa,* or "bad," karma). Merit results in pleasure, demerit in pain. Merit and demerit are accumulated in human existence. Their effects must be experienced, if not in the present life, then in another. Human beings who die with greater merit than demerit are reborn as gods or again as humans. Those with greater demerit than merit are reborn as demons, hungry ghosts, animals, or inhabitants of hell. The life of a god is one of great pleasure; that of a human, mixed pleasure and pain; and that of demons, hungry ghosts, animals, and hell dwellers, great pain. Thus, it is desirable to gain heaven, or at least rebirth in a human form of high status and potential. But, even heavenly existence comes to an end when merit is exhausted; these beings must then revert to human status, or if they carry sufficient demerit from their former human existence, a lower form where they experience the results of this demerit. Therefore, the ultimate goal of the practice of Buddhism is freedom from karma and rebirth, freedom from suffering. [See Religions of Mesoamerica pp. 159–60, Native Religions of North America pp. 206–9, 280–82, 351–54, Judaism pp. 431–33, Christianity pp. 551–53, Islam pp. 674, 707, Hinduism pp. 727, 793–94, Religions of China pp. 1021–24, and Religions of Japan pp. 1141–46 for discussion of religious calendar and time.]

The resources for merit and through it for the attainment of heaven and nirvana are the Three Treasures or Jewels: the Buddha, the Dharma, and the Sangha. Faith or confidence in the Three Jewels is the foundation of the practice of Buddhism. It is expressed by the chanting of the Threefold Refuge:

> Reverence to the Lord, the Holy One, the Perfectly
> Enlightened One!
> I take refuge in the Buddha!
> I take refuge in the Dharma!
> I take refuge in the Sangha!

Full faith in Buddha, Dharma, and Sangha is the mark of conversion, the assurance that one will never again be born in a form of life lower than human. The content of this confidence is defined in an early formula:

> The elect disciple is in this world possessed of faith in the Buddha—believing the Blessed One [*bhagavan*] to be the Holy One [*arhat*], the Fully-enlightened One [*sammasambuddha*], Wide, Upright, Happy, World-knowing, Supreme, the Bridler of men's wayward hearts, the Teacher of gods and men, the Blessed Buddha.
>
> He (the disciple) is possessed of faith in the *Dharma*—believing the truth to have been proclaimed by the Blessed One, of advantage in this world, passing not away, welcoming all, leading to salvation, and to be attained to by the wise, each one for himself.
>
> And . . . he is possessed of faith in the *Sangha*—believing the multitude of the disciples of the Blessed One who are walking in the four stages of the noble Eightfold Path, the righteous, the upright, the just, and law-abiding—believing this church of the Buddha to be worthy of honor, of hospitality, of gifts and of reverence; to be the supreme sowing ground of merit for the world. . . .[16]

"Taking refuge" in the Buddha, Dharma, and Sangha has two levels of meaning. It means following the example of the Buddha by practicing the Dharma—giving gifts (*dana*), cultivating morality (*sila*), and striving for wisdom (***prajna***) through meditation (*samadhi*). It also means relying on the power (merit) of the Buddha, Dharma, and Sangha, which is actualized by prayer, offerings, and ritual incantations. The Three Jewels are resources for worldly prosperity as well as for the achievement of nirvana.

The Buddha

The Buddha is the great teacher and example of one who attains nirvana for those treading the path that he revealed. At the same time, by his meritorious deeds, purity, wisdom, and compassion, he is a reservoir of power for those in need.

The Buddha is the Holy One (*arhat*)—he has conquered all lust, anger, and delusion, dispelled all sensuous desire, all yearning for personal existence, and all ignorance. He is the Perfectly Enlightened One—he has knowledge of his former lives, knowledge of the sufferings of other beings, knowledge of anything he wishes to know.

> Now, someone, in things never heard before, understands by himself the truth, and he therein attains omniscience, and gains mastery in the powers. Such a one is called a *sammasambuddha*.[17]

By his holiness and perfect enlightenment, he is the Blessed One, the Lord and Teacher of all beings—he has power over all realms of life and the compassionate skill to deliver all beings from suffering. He is

> abounding in wisdom and goodness, happy, with knowledge of the worlds, unsurpassed as a guide to mortals willing to be led, a teacher for gods and men, an exalted one, a Buddha. He, by himself, thoroughly knows, and sees as it were face to face, this universe—including the worlds above of the gods, the Brahmas, and the Maras [forces of death]; and the world below with its *samanas* and *brahmanas,* its princes and peoples—and having known it, he makes his knowledge known to others.[18]

He is the Tathagata, the one "Thus-come" or "Thus-gone." He has come and gone the way of a Buddha: He has come, accumulating great merit through many lives; he has gone beyond the physical and mental characteristics that define and limit other beings:

> In the world with its devas [certain of the gods], Maras and Brahmas, amid living beings with recluses and Brahmins [Brahmanas], devas and mankind, the Tathagata is the victor unvanquished, the absolute seer, self-controlled. Therefore is he called Tathagata.[19]

A Tathagata has ten powers by which he comprehends all causes and effects, the nature and destiny of all beings. A *brahmana,* seeing the footprints of the Buddha with their thousand-spoked wheel markings, exclaimed: "Indeed, how wonderful and marvelous—it cannot be that these are the footprints of a human being." Coming to the Buddha he inquired, "Is your Lord [Are you] a god, an angel, a demon, or a human being?" The Buddha responded that he was none of these; rather he was a Buddha. All the characteristics by which he would be a god, an angel, demon, or man had been extinguished.

> Just as a . . . lotus, although born in the water, grown up in the water, when it reaches the surface stands there unsoiled by the water—just so, brahmin, although born in the world, grown up in the world, having overcome the world, I abide unsoiled by the world. Take it that I am Buddha. . . .[20]

Buddha in the enlightenment posture at Polonnaruva, Sri Lanka.

Great Events

The story of the Buddha, as it came to be told from the second century B.C.E., is a story of heroic conquest, compassionate service, and the exercise of impressive power.

Representing the Buddha as an example of perfection in self-control and self-knowledge and the magnificence and power of a perfected being, the story is an inspiration toward faith, charitable deeds, and morality and a model for the monastic life. It portrays a wondrous being who is supremely confident, completely in control not only of himself but of the physical environment and all of the gods, spirits, and powers honored and feared by the people of the Buddha's time. The great events of the story are the birth of Gautama at Lumbini, his renunciation of worldly things at the age of twenty-nine, his enlightenment at Bodh Gaya six years later, his first sermon at the deer park near Banaras—"setting in motion the wheel of the Dharma"—and his death at Kushinara at the age of eighty. These events are the final effects of long strivings—the strivings of more than five hundred lives.

The Buddha's pilgrimage to enlightenment began "one hundred thousand cycles vast and four immensities ago," when Sumedha, a wealthy and learned *brahmana*, happened upon a Buddha by the name of Dipamkara (one of more than twenty Buddhas of former ages, mentioned in the *Tripitaka*).

Sumedha, dissatisfied with life and overwhelmed by the serenity of Dipam-kara, vowed to undertake the discipline by which he too would become a Buddha. Thereafter, he was known as a *bodhisattva*, "a being striving for enlight-enment."

When Sumedha died, the force of his deeds and his vow to seek enlighten-ment caused the birth of a new form—a body and consciousness appropriate to these accumulated life-energies. In this form and again and again in hundreds of rebirths, sometimes human form and sometimes nonhuman, the *bodhisattva* strove to achieve ten perfections: perfection in morality, renunciation, courage, patience, truthfulness, resolution, goodwill, equanimity, wisdom, and charity. For example, as a rabbit, he showed supreme charity by offering his body on the fire to provide food for a hungry *brahmana:*

> There came a beggar, asked for food;
> Myself I gave that he might eat.
> In alms there's none can equal me;
> In alms have I perfection reached.[21]

As a great bull elephant, he was pierced in the navel by a hunter's poisoned arrow but showed no antagonism toward the hunter. Indeed, as he slowly died, he graciously assisted the hunter in removing his tusks. Finally, as Prince Ves-santara, the *bodhisattva's* next to last life, he manifested supreme perfection in charity, giving away not only his material wealth, but also his beloved wife and children.

The Magnificent Conception and Birth

At the death of Prince Vessantara, the *bodhisattva* was born among the gods where he reflected on the circumstances of his upcoming final birth. Concur-rently, on the earth in the Shakya capital city of Kapilavastu, Queen Mahamaya, sleeping, dreamed of being carried off to a golden mansion on a silver hill some-where in the Himalayas. There, laid out on a couch, assisted by several angelic beings, she experienced the arrival of a great white elephant. The elephant, bearing a lotus in its trunk and trumpeting loudly, circled her couch three times and entered the side of her body. Thus was Gautama conceived, and the entire cosmos responded:

Now the instant the Future Buddha was conceived in the womb of his mother, all the ten thousand worlds suddenly quaked, quivered, and shook. . . . An immeasurable light spread through ten thousand worlds; the blind recovered their sight; . . . the deaf received their hearing; the dumb talked; . . . rain fell out of season. . . . In the mighty ocean the water became sweet. . . . [22]

Having awakened and reported her dream to King Suddhodana and the wise men of the court, she was informed by the wise men that she would bear a son who would either become a universal monarch or a Buddha.

When pregnancy was nearing its term, Queen Mahamaya set out for the home of her parents, there to give birth. Labor pains came upon her en route, near the village of Lumbini. Withdrawing to a grove of Sal trees blooming out of season, she gave birth to the child while standing, holding onto a branch of a tree. The child emerged from her side, pure and sparkling, and fell into a receiving net held by several of the gods. Bouncing up from the net, the well-formed child came down on the ground and, taking seven steps, shouted, "I am the greatest of all beings. This is my last birth!"

Prince Gautama was born on the full moon of the month of Vaisakha (April–May). (His renunciation, awakening, and death will all occur on this same day of the year.) His body bore the thirty-two marks of greatness, some of which were golden skin with a hair to each pore and so smooth that dust would not cling to it, webbed hands and feet, and thousand-spoked wheel designs on the soles of his feet. Asita, a wandering ascetic, wept upon seeing the child because he realized that the child would become enlightened and teach others, but only after his (Asita's) own death. Queen Mahamaya died seven days after Gautama's birth and was reborn in one of the heavens of the gods.

Still a baby, the child was left seated beneath a great tree during a plowing festival; there he entered upon meditation and experienced successively four states of trance. He will reflect back on this incident as he sits just prior to final awakening.

The Great Renunciation

The young Gautama showed skill in all the martial arts and great promise toward becoming a ruler. He married Yashodhara at age sixteen. However, even though he was surrounded by lovely female servants and enjoyed all the physical comforts, he was unhappy. According to the biographies, at age twenty-nine, riding near his father's palace, Gautama saw persons suffering from disease and old age; then, he happened upon a funeral procession. Informed by his charioteer that disease, old age, and death are common to all people, he became despondent and returned to his room for deep reflection. Upon observing a serene wandering monk, he vowed to renounce his princely status and go forth into the homeless life in search of a cure for suffering and death. Not long before this decision, Yashodhara bore him a son, Rahula (literally, "fetter").

Late one night, sitting surrounded by the exhausted bodies of dancing girls and servants with spittle running from their mouths as they slept sprawled on the floor, he experienced utter revulsion. Kissing his sleeping wife and child, he took his horse and favorite servant and started for the gate of the city. The Great Renunciation had begun! The gate to the city was securely locked, but the "spirits," cheering on Gautama's renunciation "for the welfare of gods and men," opened it with ease. Going forth, he stopped near the river, cut his hair with his sword, exchanged his princely attire for the simple clothing of a passing hunter, and dismissed his horse and servant.

Gautama joined the *samanas* (wandering monks) inhabiting the forests of Koshala and Magadha. He practiced *yoga* successively under the guidance of two well-known *samana* masters but found no deep satisfaction. He then spent several years with five companions practicing severe asceticism, attempting to starve the body into submission by extreme fasting. On the verge of death and having only enhanced suffering rather than having conquered it, he again wandered alone, finally settling in a grove near the village of Gaya.

Seated beneath a great fig tree, his body glowing with a golden aura, he received the first solid food since breaking his fast. A young woman, Sujata, who believed she had been blessed with a good husband and a male child as the result of a prayer beneath the great tree, came to make an offering of fine food to the tree. She made her offering to Gautama, thinking him to be the spirit of the tree. Gautama took the food; he bathed at the river, ate, and cast the food bowl into the river where it floated upstream, a sign that he was destined that day to become a Buddha. At nightfall, the night of the full moon in Vaisakha (April–May), the same night on which he was born, he seated himself again beneath the tree facing east, determined not to rise until he had achieved true insight:

The bodhi *tree—tree of enlightenment—at Bodh Gaya in northeast India; believed to be the tree under which Gautama attained final awakening. The Mahabodhi temple in the background dates from the twelfth century. The* stupas *in the foreground enshrine relics of saints.*

Let my skin, and sinews, and bones become dry, and welcome! And let all the flesh and blood in my body dry up! But never from this seat will I stir, until I have attained the supreme and absolute wisdom![23]

Then came **Mara,** the Lord of Death, and his hosts of demons—personifications of all the desires and ego-ridden satisfactions of human life. Exclaiming, "Prince Siddhartha is desirous of passing beyond my control, but I will never allow it," Mara arrayed his army for battle.

Mara's army extended in front of him for twelve leagues, and to the right and to the left of him for twelve leagues, and in the rear as far as to the confines of the world, and it was nine leagues high. And when it shouted, it made an earthquake-like roaring and rumbling over a space of a thousand leagues. And the god Mara, mounting his elephant, which was a hundred and fifty leagues high and had the name "Girded-with-mountains," caused a thousand arms to appear on his body, and with these he grasped a variety of weapons.[24]

Mara tempted Gautama with lovely women and positions of wealth and power. Failing to dissuade him from his discipline, Mara showered fierce storms upon him—rain, hot rocks, flies, and wind. Each successive shower was transformed into harmless flowers as it came near the pure and powerful *bodhisattva.* Finally, in desperation Mara questioned Gautama's perfection, taunting him as being alone and without a witness to his achievement. Gautama shifted the fingers of his right hand to point to the ground and silently called upon the earth itself to witness to his perfection. Mother Earth bellowed forth, "I bear you witness," and Mara and his hosts were utterly dismissed. The entire cosmos of non-human beings—gods, spirits, snakes, birds, and so forth—acclaimed his victory:

The victory now hath this illustrious Buddha won!
The Wicked One, the Slayer, hath defeated been![25]

The Setting in Motion of the Wheel of the Dharma

The Buddha remained seven weeks in the vicinity of the great tree, savoring his insight and pondering whether it would be profitable to try to teach others what he had discovered.

> Through painful striving have I gained it,
> Away with now proclaiming it;
> By those beset with lust and hate
> Not easily is this teaching learnt.
> This teaching, fine, against the stream,
> Subtle, profound, and hard to see,
> They will not see it, lust-inflamed,
> Beneath the mass of darkness veiled.[26]

Seeing that the Buddha was "inclined to remain in quiet," Brahma himself, lord of the gods of the Brahmanical pantheon, came down to persuade him to go forth and teach:

Lord, may the Blessed One preach the doctrine! May the perfect One preach the doctrine! There are beings whose mental eyes are darkened by scarcely any dust; but if they do not hear the doctrine, they cannot attain salvation. These will understand the doctrine. . . . The Dhamma [Dharma] hitherto manifested in the country of Magadha has been impure, thought out by contaminated men. But do thou now open the door of the Immortal; let them hear the doctrine discovered by the spotless one! . . . Look down, all-seeing One, upon the people lost in suffering, overcome by birth and decay. . . . Arise, O hero; O victorious One! Wander through the world, O leader of the pilgrim band, who thyself art free from debt. May the Blessed One preach the doctrine; there will be people who can understand it![27]

Receptive to Brahma's plea and encouragement, the Buddha decided to go to Banaras. He had first thought to enlighten his former teachers, but the gods informed him that they had died. He then saw, with his "divine, clear vision" his former companions in asceticism, dwelling at a deer park near Banaras. He decided that they should be the first to hear his teaching, and so proceeded to Banaras. There, his former companions greeted him with great respect, and he delivered his first sermon, called "The Setting in Motion of the Wheel of Dharma." In it he taught the Middle Way consisting of the Four Noble Truths:

1. The truth of the existence of suffering;
2. The truth of the cause of suffering;
3. The truth of the cessation of suffering; and
4. The truth of the path that leads to the cessation of suffering.

One after the other, the companions, "having understood the Dharma, . . . having dispelled all doubts, . . . having gained full knowledge," asked the Buddha to receive them as disciples. In a short time, all five attained the status of *arhats*—those free of all attachment to the world.

Feats of Ministry

Many extraordinary feats are attributed to the Buddha. He exorcised disease-causing spirits from a city; he preached while walking in the sky. He instantaneously quieted a mad elephant; he outwitted the great magicians of his time. In one of the more spectacular events of his ministry, the Buddha ascended into the heavens to preach the Dharma to his mother where she resided among the gods. After three months he descended to the earth triumphantly on a jeweled staircase accompanied by the Brahmanical gods Brahma and Indra. According to Buddhist tradition, when the Buddha goes into the village for alms

. . . gentle winds clear the ground before him; the clouds let fall drops of water to lay the dust in his pathway, and then become a canopy over him; other winds bring flowers and scatter them in his path; elevations of ground depress themselves, and depressions elevate themselves; wherever he places his foot, the ground is even and pleasant to walk upon, or lotus flowers receive his tread. No sooner has he set his right foot within the city gate than the rays of six different colors which issue from his body race hither and thither over palaces and pagodas, and deck them, as it were, with the yellow sheen of gold, or with the colors of a painting. The elephants, the horses, the birds, and other animals give forth melodious sounds; likewise the tom-toms, lutes, and other musical instruments, and the ornaments worn by the people.[28]

The Great Decease

In his last year, traveling north from Rajagriha, the Buddha fell ill with dysentery. A short time later, this condition was aggravated by a meal of dried boar's flesh he received from Cunda, a blacksmith. He retired to a grove near the village of Kushinara. There, lying on his side, he gave final instructions to Ananda about the monastic life, authorized the ordination of one last disciple, and received the Malla people of Kushinara who had come to pay their respects. As he lay dying, flowers fell from the sky and heavenly music sounded; the area was crowded with the gods—for twelve leagues around the grove "there was no spot in size even as the pricking of the point of the tip of a hair which was not pervaded by powerful spirits." Finally, with the words: "To everything that arises, there is cessation; work out your salvation with diligence!" he passed in and out of a series of states of deep concentration and expired.

> When the Blessed One died there arose, at the moment of his passing out of existence, a mighty earthquake, terrible and awe-inspiring; and the thunders of heaven burst forth.[29]

Chieftains of a local tribe prepared the body for cremation. They were unable to move it or to set it afire without first apprehending the will of the spirits. When the cremation was completed, the fire was extinguished by a flow of water from the sky. After some debate, the remains were distributed to eight parties who, upon returning to their native places, enshrined them in memorial mounds (*stupas*).

The great events of the Buddha story are well known to every devotee. The Buddha's former lives, especially the one as Prince Vessantara, are remembered when Buddhists perform acts of charity. His birth, enlightenment, and death are celebrated as events of great power by festivals, pilgrimages to Lumbini and Bodh Gaya, and the building of *stupas*. The Great Renunciation is reenacted at every ordination to the monastic order. Various mishaps of life are commonly referred to as due to the attack of Mara, and they are faced with the confidence of knowing that the Buddha conquered Mara. The incident of the Earth Goddess witnessing to the Buddha's merit is appealed to in every act of transferring or sharing merit in the Theravada tradition.

The whole story of the Buddha concretely illustrates the integration of gods and spirits into the Buddhist worldview and the subordination of these powers to the power of the Buddha. The gods honor and serve the Buddha and the spirits are vanquished by his power; these episodes provide inspiration for many of the rituals of daily life.

Two Views of the Buddha

Theravada Buddhism and Mahayana Buddhism share the story of the great events of the Buddha's life but develop from it two distinctive views of the Buddha. Theravada Buddhism affirms the Buddha as a unique being of the present age of time (indefinite in length). He stands in a line of Buddhas, the enlightened ones of other times (Dipamkara, for instance), each of whom brought the Dharma. He has achieved a status that will not be achieved by others in this age. He has come and gone, leaving the Dharma as a guide by which others may attain *arhatship,* the extinction of suffering but not full Buddhahood. This view is exemplified by remarks attributed to the Buddha just after his great awakening. On the road to Banaras, Gautama met an ascetic, Upaka, who, noticing his serenity and pure and bright complexion, asked what teacher and doctrine the Buddha followed. The Buddha replied:

> I have overcome all foes; I am all-wise; I am free from stains in every way; I have left everything; and have obtained emancipation by the destruction of desire. Having myself gained knowledge, whom should I call my master? I have no teacher; no one is equal to me; in the world of men and of gods no being is like me. I am the holy One (*Arhat*) in this world, I am the highest teacher, I alone am the Perfectly Enlightened One (*sammasambuddha*); I have gained coolness and have obtained nirvana. To found the kingdom of truth (*Dharma*) I go to the city of the Kashis (Banaras).[30]

The Buddha foretells the coming of Maitreya, the Buddha for the next age, who now resides in the Tusita heaven (a god-realm just above the human realm) awaiting his time for birth in the human realm. Theravada Buddhists occasionally appeal to the power of Maitreya as well as to that of the Buddha Gautama. Maitreya, of course, is "alive" in the world system and may be prayed to directly; even so, residing as he does in another realm, his presence is distant and his power not particularly related to everyday matters of human life. Gautama has come and gone, but his power is close at hand and can be easily brought to bear on mundane affairs. It resides in the Dharma, which is mediated by the monks, and in the *stupas, bodhi* trees, and images, which are still "hot" by their association with the Buddha or his remains.

In the Theravada, the concept of *bodhisattva* ("A Being of [i.e., destined for] Enlightenment") is not central to the doctrine of Buddhahood. It is applied to the many lives through which the Buddha strove toward Buddhahood. The designation does not especially emphasize striving for the sake of others, nor is it applied to anyone other than the Buddha, former Buddhas, and Maitreya, the one to come. It is not used in reference to the Buddha's disciples. It is significant to the Theravada that the Buddha proclaimed the Dharma for the world, but this is not the central purpose of his striving as a *bodhisattva.* The Buddha's power for others, like that of the monk, is incidental to his striving for nirvana.

The Mahayana view of the Buddha is distinctively different from the Theravada view. In the Mahayana the concept of the *bodhisattva* is central and has the meaning (as, in fact, exemplified by the lives of the Buddha) of a being striving toward enlightenment not for his or her own sake, but for the sake of others. It also has the meaning of a being who has attained enlightenment but foregoes nirvana in order to deliver others from suffering. A Buddha, for eons prior to perfect enlightenment (Buddhahood) and thereafter, that is, even as a Buddha, is essentially "A Being for Others." Further, he has not come and gone, but exists eternally, emanating merit (goodness and truth) throughout the cosmos.

In the Mahayana discourse known as *The Sutra of the Lotus of the True Dharma,* the Buddha reveals his transcendent nature as everlasting: "Father of the world, the Self-born One, Healer, Protector of all creatures," who attained perfect enlightenment eons and eons ago, but out of compassion for his children takes form again and again to educate them and bring them to nirvana. Like a father who offers his children splendid bullock-, deer-, and goat-drawn carts to lure them out of a burning house, to which they are oblivious by their play, the Tathagata offers people various vehicles (teachings) by which each of them, according to his or her capacity, may attain to nirvana. Like a father who, separated from his son for many years, employs various skillful devices by which to bring his son to an awareness of his inheritance, the Tathagata, Father of the world, exercises various means by which to save suffering beings. Since their parting, the father has become rich and powerful, the son poor and destitute. The father remembers and longs for his son; the son has long since forgotten his father. When the father happens to see his son, his impulse is to run to him and embrace him as a son, but he realizes that the son, in his destitute state, would be unable to comprehend that he is really the heir to great wealth. Instead, the father sends servants to offer the son work in the stables. After a time, the father disguises himself and works alongside of his son, getting acquainted and encouraging the son to look upon him as if he were his father. Eventually the father bestows his wealth upon the son, revealing to him his true nature.

As the father in the parable disguises himself to work alongside of his son, so the Tathagata makes appearances among people as **Shakyamuni** ("The sage of the Shakya Tribe"—a title for Gautama Buddha preferred in the Mahayana) and skillfully plays out the drama of renunciation, the attainment of enlightenment, the wandering teaching, and final decease:

> The force of a strong resolve which I assumed is such . . . that this world, including gods, men, and demons, acknowledges: Now has the Lord Shakyamuni, after going out from the home of the Shakyas, arrived at supreme, perfect enlightenment . . . at the town of Gaya. But . . . the truth is that many hundred thousand myriads of kotis [ten millions] of eons ago I have arrived at supreme, perfect enlightenment. . . . I . . . created all that with the express view to skillfully preach the Dharma. . . . Without being extinct, the Tathagata makes a show of extinction, on behalf of those who have to be educated.[31]

The transcendent, formless Tathagata is called the *dharma-kaya,* the "Dharma body" or "Dharma principle." Shakyamuni is the *nirmana-kaya* or "Appearance body," the Dharma temporarily taking form in the phenomenal world. The Dharma principle also manifests or takes form in celestial realms or

Buddha-lands. This is the *sambhoga-kaya*, "Enjoyment body"—the form by which various Buddhas enjoy themselves and are enjoyed by the happy beings who inhabit their realms.

The Mahayana envisages an enormous cosmos made up of numerous universes, many of which are "Buddha-fields," paradises, each presided over by a Buddha whose merit assists suffering beings. Also inhabiting these realms are countless *bodhisattvas* striving to relieve suffering and enjoying the vision of the Buddhas and the hearing of the Dharma that constantly emanates from these Buddhas. To understand this phenomenon of numerous Buddhas and *bodhi-sattvas*, we must have in mind not only that the one Buddha-truth or Dharma principle takes many forms, but also that the goal of the practice of the Mahayana is not *arhatship*, in the sense of individual extinction, but *bodhisattva-hood* and Buddhahood.

Mahayana Buddhism emphasizes belief in a host of *bodhisattvas* and Buddhas. Amitabha Buddha (Chin., A-mi-duo-fo [A-mi-to-fo]; Jap., Amida Butsu), "The Buddha of Endless Light," presides over Sukhavati, "The Pure or Happy Land," in the western region. Eons ago he was the monk Dharmakara who, like the Buddha Shakyamuni, heard the preaching of a Buddha and vowed to strive as a *bodhisattva* to achieve full Buddhahood. He vowed to strive to accumulate the merit necessary to create the most magnificent paradise, a land "prosperous, rich, good to live in, fertile, lovely, . . . rich with manifold flowers and fruits, . . . adorned with silver and gold gem trees," a land rich with every conceivable food, to be consumed simply by the thought of it. There would be no physical or mental pain and only gods and humans would reside there. By Dharmakara's vow, men and women could be reborn in this paradise by good deeds and meditating on Amitabha; they may even be received there by simply hearing Amitabha's name and keeping it firmly in mind for one night. Having arrived in the Pure Land, they may remain there indefinitely or, if they wish, pass easily to nirvana. Striving for many eons, Dharmakara attained his goal and now resides in Sukhavati as Endless Light and Endless Life (Amitayur).

Other Buddhas have no personal history like that of Amitabha; they are essentially personifications of characteristics of enlightenment, ruling the spheres of the cosmos. Akshobhya, "the Imperturbable," presides in the east. Vairocana, "the Illuminator" (Jap., Dainichi, "Great Sun"), reigns in the center. Ratnasambhava, "the Jewel-born," presides in the south, and Amoghasiddhi, "the Unfailing Success," reigns in the north.

Among the celestial *bodhisattvas*, the most powerful and gracious is Avalokiteshvara, "the Lord Who (Kindly) Looks Down from Above." Originally male, he is designated female in China and Japan. He resides in Amitabha's Pure Land as chief attendant of the Buddha. Having strived on the *bodhisattva* path for hundreds of eons, he

> possesses the perfection of all virtues, and beholds all beings with compassion and benevolence, he, an ocean of virtues, Virtue itself, . . . is worthy of adoration.

He saves those in dire trouble, who merely think of Him:

If one be thrown into a pit of fire, by a wicked enemy, . . . he has but to think of Avalokiteshvara, and the fire shall be quenched as if sprinkled with water. . . . If a man delivered to the power of the executioners, is already standing at the place of execution, he has but to think of Avalokiteshavara, and their swords shall go to pieces.[32]

He grants the wish of women who pray to him for children. [See Religions of Africa pp. 39–42, 64–69, Religions of Mesoamerica pp. 157–58, 186–89, Native Religions of North America pp. 274–75, 288–305, 330–32, Judaism pp. 414–15, Christianity pp. 537–38, Islam pp. 635–37, Hinduism pp. 739–41, 759–61, 780–84, Religions of China pp. 1024–26, and Religions of Japan pp. 1112–27 for discussion of God, gods, and objects of worship.]

The Dharma

Dharma has the dual sense of "the doctrine" and "the path" taught by the Buddha, and the latter is most important. Doctrines merely point to that which is to be realized experientially. The power or merit of Dharma lies in the practice and realization of it in one's life. It also resides in the mere sound of the Dharma, the energy of the Buddha-word, when ritually chanted. The word of the Buddha, like the Buddha-name (e.g., Amitabha, above), is charged with the merit of the Buddha and is powerful simply as sound, apart from the meaning of the word.

The Dharma to Be Realized

The core of the Dharma is the Four Noble Truths:

1. There is suffering (*duhkha*);
2. Suffering is caused by desire;
3. The cessation of desire results in the cessation of suffering (nirvana); and
4. There is a path that leads to the cessation of desire.

These truths are not theories—the result of philosophical speculation—nor are they the content of a divine revelation. They were realized experientially by the Buddha through moral discipline and meditation—rigorous self-analysis. They are the conclusions of a physician, rather than the reasonings of a metaphysician or the visions of a mystic. The physician experienced disease (suffering), experientially isolated its cause (desire) and therefore its cure (cessation of desire), and took the medicine (the path) by which he definitively conquered the disease. Buddhism takes a psychological approach to reality, describing the world in terms of a depth analysis of personal experience. It begins with an existing state of affairs—the personal experience of physical and mental suffering—and looks for a solution to this undesirable state of affairs not in manipulating the natural environment or human society, but in examining the feelings and thoughts of the sufferer. The fact of suffering is to be comprehended; the cause of suffering is to be abandoned; the cessation of suffering is to be realized; and the path that leads to the cessation of suffering is to be practiced.

A man asked the Buddha a series of abstract questions: "Is the world eternal or noneternal? Are the soul and the body the same or different?" and the like, saying that if he could answer these questions satisfactorily, the man would become his disciple. The Buddha replied that the questioner was like a person wounded with a poisoned arrow who wanted to know who shot the arrow, the assailant's village, caste, family, and so on, before being willing to have his wound attended to. The Buddha's point was that the wounded man's questions, like philosophizing about life in general, draw attention away from the existential, brute fact that there is suffering, that it has a cause and a cure. The Dharma is not a general theory about life but a practical and personal discipline by which one may realize the nature and extinction of suffering.

1. SUFFERING

This is the Noble Truth of Suffering: birth is suffering; decay is suffering; illness is suffering; death is suffering; presence of objects we hate is suffering; separation from objects we love is suffering; not to obtain what we desire is suffering. In brief, the five aggregates which spring from grasping, they are suffering.[33]

All religions wrestle with the finitude—the impermanence and imperfection of human existence. In a word, Buddhism describes this problem as suffering (*duhkha*). Being born is suffering; growth is suffering; experiencing disease is suffering; growing old and dying is suffering. Subtler than physical pain is the suffering of dissatisfaction, the unhappiness occasioned by not having what we want and having what we do not want. There is anxiety (mental suffering) even in the experience of pleasure and satisfaction—the knowing or at least apprehension that it will not last. There is fear of failure, loss of status, loss of self-worth, loss of loved ones, loss of property. Deep down, there is a vague and gnawing anxiety about death—not only the prospect of life ending but of ultimate meaninglessness. It is anxiety about death that motivates human striving, that makes the world run.

To describe existence as suffering implies more than simply physical pain. *Duhkha* signifies a state of being "ill-at-ease, insecure, unsatisfied." It identifies life as impermanent and characterized by no-self (**anatman**) or constantly changing personal identity. Everything that exists is transitory, momentary, subject to constant change. With respect to the natural world, this is a fact confirmed by modern science. We used to speak of particles in motion—matter and energy; now, we speak of energy fields. What is functionally a solid object is, in fact, a process identified by reference to molecules, electrons, and protons, and so on, which themselves are not solid, but processes, patterns of interacting energies.

What is true of nature at large is also true of human existence. Buddhism identifies the human being as interacting moments of material form, sensations, consciousnesses, perceptions, and volitions (acts of will). These energy patterns are called the Five Aggregates. These aggregates are no more solid than molecules and electrons. Everything that a person is or experiences can be described in terms of the interaction of these five phenomena.

The material sense organs (eye, ear, nose, tongue, body, and mind) come into contact with sense objects, giving rise to sensations, which are either pleasant, unpleasant, or neutral.

From sensation arises consciousness, awareness of an object;

From consciousness arises perception, the identification of the object;

From perception arises volition, an act of will with reference to the object.

I touch a finger to a table; a sensation (smoothness, hardness, or whatever) arises from material contact. From the sensation a consciousness arises: the awareness of the object that is smooth and hard. This touch consciousness causes the perception of a table and stimulates a decision to sit on the table. As there are six organs of sense and six kinds of sensory objects—sight, sound, smell, taste, touch, and thought—so there are six kinds of sensations, perceptions, consciousnesses, and volitions. They are all momentary, incessantly rising and passing.

There is no unchanging personal identity, no self (*atman*) apart from the constantly changing aggregates. This is the teaching of "no-self" (*anatman*)— not no self at all, but no permanent, underlying selfhood or soul. The interplay of the aggregates creates the illusion of a permanent self—an agent underlying and experiencing materiality, sensation, consciousness, perception, and volition—just as, from a distance, a point of light moving in a circular pattern creates the illusion of a solid circle of light. In fact, there is no such self—a person is process, a constant becoming.

> In the absolute sense, beings have only a very short moment to live, life lasting as long as a single moment of consciousness lasts. Just as a cart wheel, whether rolling or whether at a standstill, at all times only rests on a single point of its periphery: even so the life of a living being lasts only for the duration of a single moment of consciousness. As soon as the moment ceases, the being also ceases. For it is said: "The being of the past moment of consciousness has lived, but does not live now, nor will it live in future. The being of the future moment has not yet lived, nor does it live now, but it will live in the future. The being of the present moment has not lived, it does live just now, but it will not live in the future."[34]

The aggregate energies arise and decay in serial succession, the cessation of one moment causing the rise of the next, the self being born and dying from moment to moment.

2. DESIRE Thus, life is impermanent; in particular it is without unchanging personal identity and characterized by the experience of physical and mental suffering. Having identified a condition, the physician/psychoanalyst inquires into the cause of that condition. He or she asks, "What is the cause of suffering?"

> This is the Noble Truth concerning the Origin of Suffering: verily, it origi-
> nates in that craving which causes rebirths, is accompanied by sensual
> delight, and seeks satisfaction now here, now there; that is to say, craving for
> pleasures, craving for existence, craving for nonexistence.[35]

It is easy to see how desire or craving causes mental suffering. If a person
wants something that cannot be attained, there is mental stress. If something or
someone a person is emotionally attached to is taken away, there is the anguish
of loss. We can understand how desire causes physical suffering, if craving leads
a person into a situation in which injury occurs. It is not so easy to understand
how desire causes the physical suffering inflicted by, say, an earthquake or by
another person where one is an innocent bystander. Much of the suffering of the
human condition is inherent in the impermanence of that condition. But Buddhism submits that desire is the cause of the very existence of a human being.
There are no innocent bystanders. This is explored and explained by what is
called the Wheel of Becoming—the wheel of life based on the principle of
dependent origination.

The wheel identifies causal patterns, factors linked in dependence, one giving rise to another. Together they constitute what is called *samsara,* an "endless
cycling," marked by birth, death, and rebirth. *Samsara* is symbolized by the
demon Mara (literally, "death") holding the wheel in his grasp. In general, three
factors of ill—greed, hatred, and delusion, symbolized by the cock, the snake,
and the pig at the wheel's center—perpetuate *samsara.* They cause humans to
be reborn in realms of punishment—as demons, animals, hungry ghosts, or den-
izens of hell. Those who strive to conquer the three ills are reborn again as
humans or in heaven as gods. The outer ring breaks down the twelve factors that
characterize human life from moment to moment and in the past, present, and
future.

Reference to desire is only a simple, convenient way of referring to a whole
complex of continuously arising and ceasing states discovered by meditative
self-analysis. Desire (8) arises in a person dependent upon sensations (7), which
arise from contacts (6)—physical and mental impressions occasioned by the
existence of sense organs and mind (5). The sense organs and mind are the
instrumentalities of a body (4) that has come to exist as the result of a life-force
called consciousness (3). This life-force is what we associate with the interaction
of sperm and egg, which then is to be thought of as materializing itself, "growing
itself" a body with a brain, nervous system, and sense organs in the mother's
womb. Such an organism, through contact with itself, other organisms, and
physical objects, experiences sensations (7) that give rise to desires (8). Desires
lead to clinging (9)—attachment to things and persons—which perpetuates and
progressively complicates ongoing life or the process of becoming (10). It is
desire for sensory pleasure, desire for life, or even desire for death that perpetuates life.

These eight factors (3–10) describe present life, but they do not arise out of
nothing. Life does not begin at birth or even at conception. The life-force of
birth-consciousness (3) is the result of acts of will (karma) (2) that occurred in

The Wheel of Becoming.

a previous existence. These acts of will arose as the result of ignorance (1) of the true nature of reality.

Thus, two factors in the past (ignorance and karma) gave rise to the eight factors that characterize the present. Likewise, the eight factors of present life result in the life-force of yet another, future life—birth (11) (rebirth) and more growing old and dying (12).

Thus, desire is bound up with a fundamental delusion that continually expresses itself as an individual personality, with body and mind interacting with sense objects, striving for satisfaction of desires. Desire gives rise to attachment or grasping—a clinging to life, to self—which causes continued becoming, rebirth, and from birth decay and death. These twelve elements in a causal chain of dependent arising may be taken to describe any one moment in a person's life (a moment of ignorance, volition, consciousness, and so on) or the progression from past life (life essentially characterized by ignorance and volitions) to present life (life in the Five Aggregates, characterized by desire, clinging, and constant becoming) to future life (birth and continued growing old and dying).

The first two noble truths, then, describe the common human situation—suffering as the result of desire. If one asks, "Whence did desire, ignorance, birth, and selfhood begin?" the answer is both that a beginning is imperceivable and the inquiry is not fruitful. It is imperceivable because a being caught up in becoming is unable to see beyond his or her own creation. It is not fruitful to so inquire, because the question is abstract, purely speculative, and does not effectively relate to the existential situation of suffering, its cause, and destruction. Seeking an answer to such a question is, again, comparable to a man wounded by a poisoned arrow who demands to know who shot it before he will have his wound attended to. Dharma addresses itself to the immediate human predicament—there is suffering, it has a cause, it can be destroyed, and there is a path by which to destroy it.

If one asks, "If there is no self, no soul, what is reborn? What experiences desire and the rest?" the answer is that it is simply the Five Aggregates that are constantly arising and ceasing, like a flickering flame. Each flicker is momentary, arising out of the previous flicker and giving rise to the next by its own extinction. Birth and death occur every moment in what we call life; the final flicker of the present gross body is no different from any one moment in the life of this body.

3. THE CESSATION OF DESIRE

This is the Noble Truth concerning the Cessation of Suffering: verily, it is passionlessness, cessation without remainder of this very craving; the laying aside of, the giving up, the being free from, the harboring no longer of, this craving.[36]

Stated simply, the third noble truth is that if desire (the whole complex chain of becoming) is the cause of suffering, then the cessation of desire is the cessation of suffering. Cessation of suffering is nirvana, "blowing out," "extinction" of the flame of greed, hate, and delusion.

Enraptured with lust (*raga*), enraged with anger (*dosa*), blinded by delusion (*moha*), overwhelmed, with mind ensnared, man aims at his own ruin, at the ruin of others, at the ruin of both, and he experiences mental pain and grief. But if lust, anger and delusion are given up, man aims neither at his own ruin, nor at the ruin of others, nor at the ruin of both, and he experiences no mental pain and grief. Thus is nirvana visible in this life, immediate, inviting, attractive, and comprehensible to the wise.[37]

Nirvana is freedom from future rebirth, old age, and death. It may be said to be blissful, but not in any sense of worldly pleasure or, for that matter, any pleasure defined by other than the absence of suffering. The aggregates may linger, but not with any sense of self, and when one's accumulated karma finally flickers totally out, one cannot be said to have gone anywhere—to a heaven, for instance. The aggregates simply cease, go out, not to arise again.

> Mere suffering exists, no sufferer is found; The deed is, but no doer of the deed is there; Nirvana is, but not the man that enters it; The Path is, but no traveler on it is seen.[38]

4. THE PATH   Nirvana is to be realized by treading the Eightfold Path:

> This is the Noble Truth concerning the Path which leads to the Cessation of Suffering: verily, it is this Noble Eightfold Path, that is to say, right views, right intent, right speech, right conduct, right means of livelihood, right effort, right mindfulness, and right concentration.[39]

The Eightfold Path consists of three dimensions:

Wisdom (*prajna*), which consists of right views and right intent;

Morality (*sila*), which consists of right speech, conduct, and livelihood;

Mental Discipline (*samadhi*), which consists of right effort, right mindfulness, and right concentration.

Wisdom as right views is, to begin with, an intellectual acceptance of the Four Noble Truths. In the end, it is the full realization, the full penetration of these truths. Right intent is intent free of sensuous desire, ill will, and violence. Positively stated, it is goodwill (*maitri*) toward all living beings, compassion (*karuna*) for all suffering beings, sympathetic joy (*mudita*) in the success and happiness of other beings, and equanimity (*upeksha*) in all states of affairs.

Morality may be summarized by the **Five Precepts:** not to lie, not to kill, not to steal, not to engage in illicit sex, and not to partake of intoxicating drink. Right speech is abstaining from lying, slander, harsh or malicious talk, and idle gossip. Right conduct is abstaining from taking life, stealing, and unlawful sexual activity. Right livelihood is abstaining from making a living by activities that bring harm to other beings—trafficking in weapons or alcoholic drink, the killing of animals, engaging in prostitution, and the like.

In the Buddhist ethic and in accordance with belief in the law of karma, concern for the welfare of others is essentially concern for one's own welfare. Wrongdoing is not sin in the sense of being subject to judgment and punishment by another being; it is self-inflicted punishment by the fact of its bringing suffering upon oneself, if not immediately, in later life or some future existence. This is not to say that some immoral acts are not subject to punishment under civil or monastic law; but it is to say that the motivation for behavior should come from within rather than from fear of punishment by society.

A monk is walking along the narrow embankment that separates the muddy rice fields. He is pushed off into the mire by a careless man hurrying to pass him. The man rushes on without saying anything or stopping. Another man, seeing this incident, runs up to help the monk out of the muddy field. Back on the embankment, the monk quietly proceeds, without comment to or about either of the other men's actions. When asked about his behavior by the second man, who desires praise for his assistance, the monk calmly replies, "I have learned to be even-minded in all circumstances; you and the other man have your reward."

Mental discipline must proceed hand in hand with morality to produce right views and right intent. Right effort is essentially the exertion to rid oneself of unwholesome states of mind and to cultivate wholesome states of mind.

It, like all other dimensions of the path, critically depends upon right mindfulness:

> This is the sole way, monks, for the purification of beings, for the overcoming of sorrow and lamentation, for the destroying of pain and grief, for reaching the right path, for the realization of Nirvana, namely the four Foundations of Mindfulness. What are the four? Herein (in this teaching) a monk dwells practicing body-contemplation on the body, ardent, clearly comprehending the mindful, having overcome covetousness and grief concerning the world; he dwells practicing feeling—contemplation on feelings, . . . mind-contemplation on the mind, . . . mind-object—contemplation on mind-objects. . . . [40]

Mindfulness is the heart of Buddhist meditation. It is practiced by giving close attention to the functioning of the body, the feelings, the mental processes, and conceptual patterns like those found in the teachings of the Buddha (e.g., the Four Noble Truths). In practicing mindfulness of breathing, for example, one should sit with the body erect and mind alert and simply watch one's breathing:

> Breathing in a long breath, he knows "I breathe in a long breath"; breathing out a long breath, he knows "I breathe out a long breath"; breathing in a short breath, he knows "I breathe in a short breath"; breathing out a short breath, he knows "I breathe out a short breath."[41]

By directing the mind solely to the breathing over longer and longer periods of time, one becomes more and more keenly aware of this bodily process, calming the body and objectifying the process so as to depersonalize it—to strip it of any sense of ego or selfhood.

We may see more clearly how mindfulness affects ego if we consider the mindfulness of feelings, such as a feeling of anger. Turning one's attention to the anger feeling itself and away from its object or activity that might follow from anger, one "defuses" or depersonalizes the feeling by seeing it for what it essentially is—just another psychophysical process that now disperses as quickly as it has arisen. This practice of mindfulness is to be extended to all bodily functions, all feelings (pleasant as well as painful), all states of mind, and all particular ways of thinking about body and mind (e.g., the twelve factors of the Wheel of Becoming). Once the mind is trained in solitude, one is able to practice mindfulness in the course of ordinary daily activity—mindfulness of walking, sitting, eating, and so on. In every activity one undertakes one should carefully consider and clearly comprehend its purpose relative to one's goals and its suitability or potential effectiveness toward achieving those goals; then one should apply mindfulness to the action while engaging in it, gradually stripping it of all sense of self, all personal attachment.

> In looking forward, or in looking round; in stretching forth his arm, or in drawing it in again; in eating or drinking, in masticating or swallowing, in obeying the calls of nature, in going or standing or sitting, in sleeping or waking, in speaking or in being still, he keeps himself aware of all it really means.[42]

Mindfulness enhances one's capacity to live in accord with the five moral precepts. It builds insight toward wisdom (right view and right intent) by allowing one to more and more thoroughly realize the impermanence, suffering, and impersonality of life, the cause of suffering, the cessation of suffering, and the path that leads to the cessation of suffering—in short, to realize the Four Noble Truths and to see things as they really are.

The capacity for mindfulness may be enhanced by developing right concentration. The purpose of practicing concentration is to quiet or tranquilize the mind by experiencing radically altered states of consciousness, states of deep absorption. To accomplish this one focuses the mind on one or another of some forty recommended objects suitable to one's ability and personal disposition. For instance, a beginner sitting quietly may take a circle of light red clay the size of a dish as an object. By focusing upon it intensely, the person produces a mental image, which then becomes the object—one that he or she may hold before the mind even while interrupting the sitting for some other activity. By occupying the mind entirely with this mental object, one excludes all other sensory-mental awareness and enters the first of a series of trance states:

> Detached from sensual objects, detached from unwholesome states of mind, the monk enters the first absorption, which is accompanied by thought-conception and discursive thinking, concentration, rapture and joy.[43]

With the passing away of thought-conception and discursive thinking, the person enters a second absorption characterized by concentration, rapture, and joy. The third absorption is characterized by only concentration and joy, and the fourth simply by equanimity. One dismisses each successive absorption by practicing mindfulness on its contents—seeing there impermanence, suffering, and impersonality. By the insight of this mindfulness, one may gain special powers:

> Being one he becomes many; having become many, he again becomes one; he appears and disappears; unhindered he goes through walls, fences and mountains as through the air; he submerges and emerges in the earth as in water; without sinking he walks on the water as on the earth; cross-legged he flies through the air like a winged bird; he touches and strokes with his hand the sun and the moon. . . .[44]

The Buddha discouraged his disciples from using these powers, even though much is made of them in the literature and the Buddha himself is portrayed as having used them on several occasions. The experience of such power should serve only to confirm the level of attainment in concentration. They are incidental to the progress toward enlightenment; exercising them may lead one astray from insight to nirvana; they should not be employed by way of impressing others as to the validity of the teaching.

There are other powers that are directly instrumental to cessation of desire and the attainment of enlightenment. Having attained the highly rarefied levels of consciousness through concentration, one may experience superhuman hearing and sight: the divine ear, the capacity to hear other persons' thoughts, and the divine eye, the ability to perceive one's own former lives and the sufferings and births of other beings. Finally, through applying mindfulness to each of the four absorptions, one may attain the knowledge-power by which to extinguish the three cankers (asavas): sensuous desire, the desire for existence, and ignorance. This is nirvana, deliverance from birth and death.

The progress from mindfulness to nirvana is described as a sevenfold attainment: The attainment of mindfulness leads to the investigation of reality, to the rise of extraordinary energy, rapture, tranquility, fixation, and finally equanimity.

The state of equanimity is a state totally lacking desire and therefore a state without suffering, a state of freedom from rebirth. Progress on the path is also described as gradually overcoming ten binding obstacles: the belief in self, doubt, attachment to rules and ritual, sensuous craving, ill will, the craving for rebirth among the gods of subtle form, the craving for rebirth in the formless realms, conceit, restlessness, and ignorance. The one who has overcome the first three obstacles has become a Stream-entrant, that is, one who has definitively entered the stream flowing toward nirvana. A Stream-entrant dying at this level of attainment will never again be reborn in a realm lower than the human. A disciple who is nearly free of obstacles four and five—sensuous craving and ill will—becomes a Once-returner, that is, one who will return to this world only once more and in that life attain nirvana. The disciple who is totally free of the first five obstacles is a Non-returner, that is, one who will be reborn in a realm higher than human and will reach nirvana from that realm. One who conquers all ten obstacles attains nirvana in this very life; he or she becomes an *arhat,* a holy one.

THE PATH IN VARIOUS TRADITIONS The Mahayana elaborates and develops the Buddha's original teaching of "no-self." To say that there is no unchanging personal identity is to say that a life-form is empty (shunya), devoid of an essential nature; it is incessant process or energy flow. This is true of things as well as persons. To see the world (of things and persons) as it really is, the goal of the Eightfold Path, is to realize its emptiness (shunyata). This does not mean to see that the world does not exist; it means to see that everything that exists does so in a relation of dependence and, therefore, in an essential unity.

Nirvana is not a negation of the world, but a seeing of the world such as it is, without the imposition of personal selfhood upon it. The unity of the world is called Buddha-nature; thus, it is said that everything has Buddha-nature and to realize unity is to realize Buddha-nature. This is the perfection of wisdom (**prajna-paramita**).

Logically, emptiness is the necessary implication of the dependent origination of all phenomena. If, in a series of factors identifying a phenomenon (e.g., the twelve factors of the Wheel of Becoming), the first factor causes the second, the second causes the third, and so on to the last factor, which causes the first, then the existence of any factor depends upon another factor—it has no existence of its own, no existence apart from relationship; it is empty of self-nature; it has only relational nature.

The larger implication is that the existence and well-being of a life-form is dependent upon the existence and well-being of every other life-form. A life-form has true existence only by existing in harmony with and for the welfare of other life-forms. A *bodhisattva* exists solely for the sake of others.

The *bodhisattva* strives on the same Eightfold Path as those who seek *arhat-ship*. The key difference is twofold: first, the *bodhisattva* strives for the perfection of wisdom that is the perfect enlightenment of a Buddha and not simply the *arhat's* goal of the cessation of suffering (nirvana); second, the *bodhisattva* vows to strive for the release from suffering of all beings and vows to forego personal nirvana in order, life after life, to share his or her merit with others—the *arhat* acts only for his own nirvana. The hallmark of the *bodhisattva* is compassion.

Monks striving on the Theravada path are a field of merit for others, although their intent is the conquest of suffering in their own lives. *Bodhisattvas* realize that in a universe in which life-forms are totally interdependent there is no release for one without the release of all. They see also that the means must be compatible with the end. If the end is selflessness, then the means must be an emptying of self for others, existing only for others. Those who strive only for their own happiness will never attain selflessness.

Bodhisattvas strive for six perfections (*parami*): perfection in giving, morality, patience, vigor, meditation, and wisdom. It is the same path as that taken by Theravada monks, but the intention is different. After many lives of deeds of charity, they give without any thought of self or reward. Their giving is informed by the realization of the emptiness of self and others and, therefore, their identity; their giving is perfected. Then they are able to arouse "the thought of enlightenment" (*bodhi-citta*), from which they will never thereafter lapse. They vow to strive for perfection in morality, patience, and so on, for the sake of all beings. It is the force of this vow that distinguishes their striving from that of those striving to become *arhats;* indeed, their energy is the much greater because they strive for others and not for self.

> The *bodhisattva* is endowed with wisdom of a kind whereby he looks on all beings as though victims going to the slaughter. And immense compassion grips him. His divine eye sees . . . innumerable beings, and he is filled with

great distress at what he sees, for many bear the burden of past deeds which will be punished in purgatory, others will have unfortunate rebirths which will divide them from the Buddha and his teachings, others must soon be slain, . . . others have gained a favorable rebirth only to lose it again.

So he pours out his love and compassion upon all those beings, and attends to them, thinking, "I shall become the savior of all beings, and set them free from their sufferings."[45]

The Mahayana develops distinctive techniques for mental discipline. In the Soto Zen tradition, for instance, simply sitting (Jap., *zazen*) without focusing the mind anywhere is the basic technique:

To study the way of the Buddha is to study your own self. To study your own self is to forget yourself. To forget yourself is to have the objective world prevail in you. To have the objective world prevail in you, is to let go of your "own" body and mind as well as the body and mind of "Others."

In the pursuit of the Way the prime essential is sitting. . . . Just to pass the time in sitting straight, without thought of acquisition, without any sense of achieving enlightenment.[46]

This sitting is intended to have the same result as mindfulness meditation —a progressive emptying of the mind resulting in immediacy with the flow of life. Rinzai Zen advocates a more active meditation, active both in the sense of focusing the mind on an object rather than simply sitting passively and in the sense of doing such meditation in the course of ordinary daily activity as well as in formal sitting. The meditation object, called a *koan,* is a riddle or puzzling story given the student by the master that defies intellectual solution. Persistent meditation upon its meaning produces mental exhaustion and occasions a sudden, intuitive insight—a disjunction in the flow of ordinary, purposeful thought. Solving the *koan* may be assisted by a well-timed shout or blow of the hand or a stick administered by the master.

The Power of Dharma as Sound

Every word of the Buddha is charged with merit. Certain of his discourses, by reason of the occasion on which they were given or by the fact that they summarize the essence of the teaching/truth, are considered to be especially powerful. In the Theravada tradition, these are called *parittas,* "protective blessings." In the Mahayana, they are called **dharanis,** "those (words) which hold (power)."

In the *Vinaya* collection of the *Tripitaka,* there is report of an occasion on which a monk was bitten by a snake and died. The Buddha reportedly said:

I allow you, O monks, to make use of a safeguard [*paritta*] for yourselves for your security and protection, by letting your love flow out over the four royal breeds of serpents. And thus, O monks, are you to do so:

I love live things that have no feet, the bipeds too I love. I love four-footed creatures, and things with many feet. . . . Let no footless thing do hurt to me, nor thing that has two feet. . . . Infinite is the Buddha, infinite the Dharma, infinite the Sangha. Finite are creeping things. . . . Made is my safeguard, made my defense. Let living things retreat, whilst I revere the Blessed One. . . .[47]

This authorization of the use of *paritta* applies only to protection from wild animals and it assumes that the one using the formula is, indeed, full of love (*maitri,* goodwill). That is to say, the power of the exhortation lies in the merit of the exhorter and not simply in the formula as a magical spell or charm. These and other words of the Buddha came to be used in a variety of circumstances (to promote general prosperity as well as specific protection) and only by persons who were assumed to be highly meritorious. In the Theravada tradition the *paritta* is chanted by monks or ex-monks, and in the Mahayana, the *dharani* by monks or masters, whether monastic or lay.

The Mangala Sutra, "The Discourse on Auspiciousness," is the *paritta* most frequently used in Theravada practice. In it the Buddha summarizes the moral principles of lay Buddhism. This *paritta* is invoked on all occasions in which there is merit making and sharing between monks and laity. The *Angulimala paritta,* on the other hand, is used to allay the pain of childbirth. It is the word of the Buddha to the monk Angulimala, who was desirous of easing the pain of a woman giving birth:

Go to the place and say, "I have never knowingly put any creature to death since I was born; by the virtue of this observance may you be free from pain."[48]

In the twenty-second chapter of the Mahayana *Sutra of the Lotus of the True Dharma,* it is said that anyone who hears this *sutra* "will produce an accumulation of pious merit the term of which is not to be arrived at even by Buddha-knowledge." *The Sutra of the Heart of the Perfection of Wisdom,* which summarizes the wisdom on emptiness, is also considered a most powerful *dharani.*

The Sangha

In the Theravada, the Sangha is the community of monks. It may also have the more limited sense of "the community of saints"—all those who, through the ages, achieved *arhatship* and are, like the Buddha, fit objects of prayer and meditation.

Those who undertake the way of the monk are ordained to a life of poverty and strict discipline. Theravada monks are ordained by a body of senior monks, a minimum of five for the novitiate ordination and ten for the higher ordination.

They vow to keep the Ten Precepts:

1. Not to take life;
2. Not to lie;
3. Not to steal;
4. Not to engage in sexual activity;

5. Not to drink alcohol;
6. Not to take food from noon to the next morning;
7. Not to adorn their bodies with anything other than the three robes;
8. Not to participate in or be spectator to public entertainments;
9. Not to use high or comfortable beds;
10. Not to use money.

In addition, those of the higher ordination commit themselves to keep the 227 rules of the monastic code (*Pratimoksha*) and to regularly (twice monthly) recite these rules and confess any infraction thereof in the company of other monks. They are to keep to themselves in study and meditation, except when they go into the village or city to receive food offerings or perform a merit ceremony for the laity.

The preferred and usual time for ordination is in June and early July, just prior to the rainy season. On the Theravada mainland of Southeast Asia, it is customary for all young men to receive the lower or novitiate ordination and many also undertake the higher ordination. Monks are free to leave the monastic life at any time. The great majority of those ordained spend only a short period in the order, typically the four months of the rainy season. In Sri Lanka, fewer take ordination and the expectation is that those who do will remain in the order for life.

Ordination is an option for any male at any age. It, of course, serves as the mode of entrance into the monastic life; but typically it is undertaken between the ages of ten and eighteen. It is then like the Christian confirmation or the Jewish *bar mitzvah*, a rite of passage from youth to adult responsibility. The ordinand ritually dies and is reborn; he gives up family and friends and all

A young man being escorted to a monastery in Bangkok, Thailand, by friends and family for ordination. Dressed like a prince and "riding" a friend as his "horse," he follows the example of the Great Renunciation of Siddhartha Gautama.

*Thai monks reciting the monastic code (*Pratimoksha) *in the ceremonial hall of the Marble Temple, Bangkok.*

former associations; he casts off his old clothes, has his head shaved, undergoes a ritual bath, and receives a new name.

Ordination is not an option for women. As we noted in chapter 36, the Buddha authorized the formation of an order of nuns. This order flourished for several centuries but later declined for unknown reasons. In the mid–fifth century C.E., for want of sufficient nuns to perform the ceremony (a minimum of ten is required), the Theravada ordination line lapsed. Women in Theravada are permitted to take novitiate vows, wear the monastic robe, and live in or near a monastery, but such persons are not considered to be full-fledged nuns and are not given the respect that is given to monks. The few who take this option are usually older women without family. They live in relative seclusion and perform menial tasks for the monks.

Ordination is a communal act. Above all, it brings merit to the community in which it occurs, especially to the parents of the ordinand and those of his ancestors who may be suffering in hell or as hungry ghosts. It is commonly said that the lower ordination benefits primarily the mother, the higher ordination the father. The ordinand is a sacrifice for society. He renounces all worldly pleasures, particularly sexual pleasure, thereby becoming a storehouse of spiritual power for others to draw upon. In some communities, it is believed that the renunciation of sexual activity releases energy or adds to the total fertility potential in the environment, so as to stimulate rainfall. This is one reason for performing ordinations just prior to the rainy season.

The monastic practice of Buddhism is ultimately aimed at the attainment of enlightenment for individuals. But in both the Theravada and the Mahayana traditions, the monk is seen to have an obligation to society. In Sri Lanka, Myanmar (Burma), Thailand, Laos, and Cambodia, the great majority of the people adhere to Theravada Buddhism. Most monasteries are an integral part of local communities. Theravada monks have extensive contact with the laity, in receiving daily food, at ordinations, on Observance days, in receiving new robes during the Kathina festival, in giving blessings at funerals, birthday celebrations, occasions of the start of new business ventures, and public celebrations.

The way of the laity as practiced in Theravada Buddhism consists of keeping the Five Precepts (to the extent possible in pursuit of the lay life), showing respect for and supporting the monks, spending Observance days at the monastery under the strict **Eight Precepts,** and generally taking every opportunity to gain merit at the hands of the monk. The farmer inevitably takes the life of small insects and animals in tilling the fields and protecting his crop. Laypeople take the life of animals for food. Husband and wife necessarily engage in sexual relations to produce children. The demerit of such acts is outweighed by the merit of offering food to the monks and producing a son who becomes ordained as a monk. The lay man or woman may attain the status of a Stream-entrant even in the lay life and someday or in some later life be able to join the Sangha. In the short run, he or she looks to a harmonious and prosperous life and a more favorable rebirth, perhaps in one of the heavens of great enjoyment.

Theravada Buddhism essentially "works" by the mutual dependence of Sangha and lay society. Monks most exemplify the ideal of self-discipline, enlightenment, and nirvana. They are holy persons; their renunciation makes for purity and wisdom; their self-control gives them power over the forces of disease, the destructive forces of nature, and the physical and mental forces that make for pain and stress in human life. At the same time, the monastic life of moral purity and meditation is not possible without gifts of food, clothing, and housing from the laity. These gifts, essential to the material well-being of the monks, are the vehicle by which the laity benefit from the monks' purity and power. The mere presence of the monks is inspiring and auspicious. They are worthy of reverence and gifts. Their reception of gifts conveys merit to the givers. Their ritual chanting of the Buddha's word generates power to heal and protect the laity, to stimulate rain for the crops, and to dispel malicious spirits. The monks' power is a by-product of their striving toward nirvana. The laity provide material support to the monks; the monks exercise their power to bring prosperity to the laity so that they may provide material support. Buddhism is the path to nirvana; it is also the path to the material prosperity that makes the pursuit of nirvana possible.

The community of monks is the central and essential feature in the practice of Theravada Buddhism. In the Mahayana, the way of the *bodhisattva* is open to everyone; the Sangha consists of all those who are striving in the way of the Buddha, lay devotees as well as monks and nuns. Unlike the Theravada, where there is essentially one tradition, the Mahayana is practiced in accordance with numerous, sectarian definitions. Some of these sects have a monastic dimension and others do not; and, even where monastic discipline is practiced, it is the individual master and lineage of masters rather than a community of monks that is the center of attention. Let us consider, for example, two sects of Japanese Mahayana: the Zen and the Jodo. The distinctive focus of Zen is meditation and this may be practiced in the lay or monastic mode, in a monastery, in a local temple, or in one's home or workplace. Every Japanese community—village, group of villages, town, or city—has at least one temple. Each of these temples belongs to one or another sectarian tradition, has a priest or priests, and functions primarily as a place for sermons on the Dharma and the performance of funeral and memorial rituals. In the Zen tradition, those who serve the temple as priests receive their training for priestly functions under the head priest of a local temple. Typically, if not always, a young man preparing for the priesthood will withdraw to one of several Zen monasteries for two years of intensive training in meditation. Upon completion of this training, he will return to his local temple, marry, and take up priestly duties. If he is sufficiently accomplished, he may choose to offer his parishioners instruction in meditation as well as sermons on the Dharma and rituals for the dead. Thus, there are two main centers of Zen activity—the local temple and the monastery. The monastery essentially functions to provide the intensive, short-term training in meditation. Its life centers on a **roshi,** "venerable teacher/master," a man or woman who is recognized as highly accomplished in insight, having been designated so by his or her master, in a lineage of masters extending back ultimately to the Buddha Shakyamuni. Those who enter the monastery for training do so by the *roshi's* choice and thereby become the *roshi's* disciples. They are not ordained to the monastic life, as in the Theravada, but while in training must observe a Rule of Purity (*shingi*), less elaborate but very much like the monastic code adhered to by Theravada monks (see chapter 38). Some few of the *roshi's* disciples will receive the *roshi's* recognition as having attained a certain level of mastery, and a few of this number will continue in training to eventually themselves become *roshis.* Most of the trainees will return to their local temple to serve as priests. Zen monasteries are somewhat self-sustaining in that working a garden and maintaining the monastery properties are part of the daily discipline of the monks and nuns. Nonetheless, there is also a merit-sharing dimension to the monastic life, albeit less intense and less important than that of the Theravada monastic community. Zen monasteries have patrons, dispersed among the general population, from whom the monks and nuns receive food and for whom they perform blessing ceremonies. The monastery trainees also, periodically, make rounds in communities near the monastery to receive food from anyone who desires to give. [See Religions of Japan p. 1102 for discussion of Zen.]

In the Pure Land branch of Mahayana (Jap., Jodo and Jodo-shin), there is no monastic Sangha. The way is faith in the power of Amida Buddha who has stored up tremendous merit over the course of eons of time as a *bodhisattva* and who founded the Pure Land. Since Amida has accumulated enough merit for the salvation of the whole world and this merit is available directly to any devotee, there is no need for monks. One has assurance of being admitted to the Pure Land after death by surrender to Amida, expressed by chanting his name with all one's heart. This chant, called the **nembutsu,** is *namu Amida Butsu,* "Reverence to Amida Buddha." Pure Land Buddhists strive to keep the Five Precepts, earnestly desiring to live a life of compassion, but not as a means of making merit. The pure and compassionate life is to be lived simply in gratitude for what Amida has done.

The practice of Jodo is centered in the home and the local temple. Those who serve as temple priests are trained in seminaries and regularly perform services of worship to Amida Buddha as well as performing funeral and memorial rites. [See Religions of Japan pp. 1101–2 for discussion of Pure Land in Japanese Buddhism.]

The Rituals and Festivals of the Buddhist Life

Daily and Periodic Rituals

Merit is made and shared through daily, periodic, and special rituals and yearly festivals. Morning and evening services of chanting or worship take place in every monastery, temple, and home. With the placing of flowers and the lighting of candles and incense before a Buddha-image or some other symbol of the presence of the Buddha, monks chant together and the lay family offers a prayer. The flowers, beautiful one moment and wilted the next, remind the offerers of the impermanence of life; the odor of the incense calls to their mind the sweet scent of moral virtue that emanates from those who are devout; the candle-flame symbolizes enlightenment.

A lay devotee offers incense and prayer before a Buddha image. The Buddha's uplifted hand is in the gesture of "do not fear."

The central daily rite of lay Buddhism is the offering of food. Theravada laity make this offering to the monks. Mahayana laity make it to the Buddha as part of the morning or evening worship. In both settings merit is shared.

The weekly Observance Day rituals at the Theravada monastery are opportunities for both laity and monks to quicken faith, discipline, and understanding, and make and share merit. On these days, twice each month, the monks chant and reaffirm the code of discipline. On all of these days, they administer the Eight Precepts to the gathered laity—the laity repeating them after the monks—and offer a sermon on the Dharma. The monks pour water to transfer merit to the laity; the laity pour water to share this merit with their ancestors.

Zen monks twice each month gather in the Buddha-hall of their head temple and chant for the welfare of the Japanese people. Pure Land Buddhists congregate at the temple once each week to praise Amida.

Rites of Passage

There are special rituals to mark, protect, and bless the occasions of major life transitions. They publicly mark and protect times of passage from one status to another—times of unusual vulnerability such as birth, birthdays, coming of age, marriage, the entering into a new house, and death. Monks preside over ordinations, funerals, and death commemoration rites. In the Theravada tradition, ordination is a puberty or coming-of-age rite. Theravada monks also preside over birthday and new-house blessing rites. Ex-monks—elders in the lay community—perform the rituals for childbirth and marriage.

In Japanese Pure Land, the lay priest presides over rituals of the first presentation of a child at the temple, confirmation of boys and girls at the age of puberty, and death. Japanese Buddhists undertake marriage at the Shinto shrine, presided over by Shinto priests.

Yearly Festivals

Buddhists everywhere celebrate the New Year and the Buddha's birth, enlightenment, and death. The beginning of a new year is, generally, a time for "taking stock" of one's karma, cleansing, and well-wishing. In Theravada communities the New Year is celebrated in mid-April on the lunar calendar and lasts for two or three days. The laity ritually bathe the Buddha-images and sprinkle water on the monks and the elders, showing respect and offering good wishes. The monks chant blessings on the laity, and together they share the merit of the occasion with the dead. The New Year appropriately begins at the end of the dry season and the beginning of new life in nature. The pouring of water is not only an honoring of the Buddha, the monks, the elders, and the dead but also an offering for plentiful rain and prosperity in the days to come. In Thailand, Laos, and Cambodia, the laity build sand mounds (*stupas*) at the monastery or on the bank of the river. Each grain of sand represents a demerit, and placing the grains in the monastery or letting them be washed away by the river symbolizes a cleansing from bad deeds. Bringing sand to the monastery also serves to renew the floor of the compound.

Zen and Pure Land Buddhists celebrate the New Year on the Western calendar. This is an occasion for Zen monks to publicly read large volumes of sacred *sutras,* thereby sending out cleansing and enlivening sound waves for the benefit of all beings. Pure Land Buddhists hold special services at the temple twice daily in praise of the Buddha Amida.

Theravada Buddhists celebrate the birth, enlightenment, and death of the Buddha on the same day—the full moon of May, called Vaisakha. In Sri Lanka, it is a festival of lights, and houses, gardens, and streets are decorated with lanterns. It is not a major festival in other Theravada countries, but, occurring on an Observance Day, it is at least an occasion for special food offerings to the monks and more than the usual devotion to keeping the moral precepts.

Japanese Buddhists celebrate the Buddha's birth, death, and enlightenment on different days of the year: the birth on April 8, the enlightenment on December 8, and the death on February 15. The birth celebration, Hanamatsuri, is a flower festival and time for ritually bathing images of the Buddha. Enlightenment Day (Bodhi) and Death Day (Nehan [Nirvana]), are simply occasions for special worship.

Lao monk receiving food offerings on a festival occasion.

Theravada Buddhists mark the beginning and end of the rain-retreat, which generally coincide with the beginning and end of the rains. They conclude the year with a harvest festival. Theravada monks enter rain-retreat on the full moon of either June or July. The three- or four-month period is a time of relative austerity for both laity and monks.

The monks remain in the monastery, spending more than the usual time in study and meditation. No marriages or public entertainments occur in the lay community and the laity are more devout in their attendance of Observance Day ceremonies and in their daily food offerings. The Observance Day on which rain-retreat commences is generally occasion for the entire lay community to offer food and many more than usual undertake to spend the day at the monastery, keeping the monastic precepts.

The full-moon Observance with which the rain-retreat ends is much like that with which it begins, with the exception that the monks gather privately and invite each other to point out infractions of the monastic code during the retreat period. The mood of this Observance is a happy one—the rains have ended (usually), the monks may again move about, and public celebrations are in order. The month that follows, mid-October to mid-November, is the time for Kathina, the offering of cloth from which the monks prepare new robes. Kathina offerings are typically a group effort—of an entire village, a lay association for merit making, a government agency, or the employees of a prominent commercial establishment. Typically, the group approaches the monastery in joyful procession. Upon arrival, the presiding monk administers the Five Precepts to the laity, receives the cloth, and declares the great merit of such offerings. The monks jointly chant a blessing verse and the laity pour water, symbolically transferring a portion of the merit to the ancestors.

Theravada Buddhists honor and transfer merit to their ancestors on every occasion of merit making and sharing. Japanese Buddhists give special honor and merit to their ancestors three times each year: on the spring and autumn equinoxes in March and September and during the month July 15–August 15. The equinox festivals, called Higan, "Other Shore," mark times of transition in nature and therefore are occasions to reflect on the passage of time and the progress of beings toward enlightenment—the "other shore."

In the next chapter, we shall consider the practice of Buddhism in concrete detail and will be able to compare and contrast specific, living examples of the Theravada and the Mahayana. Here let us appreciate that, at the level of ideals, the Theravada and Mahayana are not two distinct systems of Buddhism but choices of "vehicles" within the same system. Indeed, as we saw in chapter 36, this is historically how these traditions functioned in India from their origin to the end of the twelfth century. Both viewpoints are inspired by the Three Treasures—the Buddha, the Dharma, and the Sangha—and both respect these Treasures at two levels: as guides to self-achievement and as merit-power to be shared. If we consider the Mahayana as a whole, represented by Zen on the one hand and Pure Land on the other, we can see that both Theravada and Mahayana offer opportunity for accumulating merit through monastic self-discipline and for dependence upon the merit of others.

Through desire and ignorance there is
life in the six realms, characterized
by one degree or another of suffering,
except that:

The human predicament of suffering
that calls for a resolution

THE WAY OF MERIT-MAKING AND ENLIGHTENMENT
to bring about world prosperity,
favorable rebirth, and nirvana

Imitation of/appeal to holy beings:

PRIESTS MONKS ARHATS/BODHISATTVAS BUDDHAS

Rituals and practices:

ANNUAL/	PREACHING/	RECITING	FIVE/TEN	MEDITATION	OFFERINGS/
SEASONAL	HEARING	THREE	PRECEPTS		CHARITY
(New Year)		REFUGES			
for Buddha					
(birth,					
renunciation,					
death)					
rites of passage					
(ordination,					
marriage,					
death,					
memorials)					

Contact with holy things:

| SUTRAS | STUPAS | BUDDHIST | ANCESTORS | DEITIES | SPIRITS | TEMPLES |
| | (RELICS) | STATUES | | | | |

The Buddha, through his life and teachings
(the Dharma), provided the model and
power for human-form beings to achieve
freedom from suffering (nirvana), through
the Threshold Refuge (Buddha, Dharma,
Sangha) by which they may realize Three
Noble Truths (suffering, its cause, and its
cessation) by entering upon the Eightfold
Path (the fourth Noble Truth).

THE SANGHA

consists of all those who have
entered upon the Middle Way
of the Buddha, through: moral
living, charity, meditation,
and prayer.

*The ongoing practices of Buddhist groups that help individuals
on the path to merit and enlightenment*

*The realization/discovery that made
merit-making/enlightenment possible
for all humans*

The Way of Merit-Making and Enlightenment in Buddhism.

In the Theravada these two foci are equally emphasized in a relationship of reciprocity. In the Mahayana each is the central emphasis of distinct sects. The Mahayana belief in perfected celestial Buddhas and *bodhisattvas* obviated the necessity of reliance on the imperfect, earthly Sangha and, thus, encouraged the development of devotional lay Buddhism independent of the Sangha. Even so, as we see by the existence of Zen Mahayana, not all Mahayana Buddhists turned away from meditation and monasticism.

38

The Dynamics
of the Buddhist Life

WE HAVE TRACED the history of Buddhism from its beginning with a charismatic teacher and his disciples, through its twofold definition as Theravada and Mahayana and its spread throughout Asia, to its emergence as a world religion. By interpreting authoritative texts and generalizing a knowledge of Buddhism as it is articulated and practiced in various parts of the world, we have defined the Theravada and Mahayana as unified systems of belief and practice.

But this generalized Buddhism never existed nor does it exist today as such; it is only a guideline or framework by which we may understand the living Buddhism of a variety of particular cultural settings. As a system of values, itself a product of a particular time and place, spreads to other cultural settings, it is actualized by interplay with the existing beliefs and patterns of behavior, the social system, and the climate and geography of each of these different contexts. The teachings of the Buddha were first offered and received in the context of northeast India c. 500 B.C.E. They were transformed again and again in different times and places in a constantly changing civilization. Carried to other parts of Asia at a particular stage of ongoing development in India, they were again transformed by actualization in the natural and cultural settings of these areas.

Our task now is to give concreteness to Buddhism by considering some examples of Buddhist life in particular settings. We shall consider two Buddhisms of Asia, one Theravada, the other Mahayana, one showing us a total pattern of village life, the other a distinctive feature in the life of one sect among several functioning in the same environment. These examples, of village-Theravada in Thailand and monastery-Zen in Japan, should give us a sense of the range of practiced Buddhism as well as the peculiarities of two types. As we have seen in the chapters on history and beliefs and practices, the two foci of practical Buddhism are self-discipline (self-power) on the one hand, and merit sharing (other-power) on the other.

Each of the varieties of Buddhism centrally emphasizes one or the other of these foci: In the case of village-Theravada it is the sharing of merit and in the case of monastery-Zen it is self-discipline.

Making and Sharing Merit
in Phraan Muan

The Buddhism of the village of Phraan Muan in northeast Thailand is typical of that of villages throughout the country and in many ways of those in neighboring Burma, Laos, and Cambodia. Theravada Buddhism is the established religion of the Kingdom of Thailand. It is a way of life for 95 percent of the country's fifty million people. The Sangha, consisting of approximately two hundred and sixty thousand monks residing in twenty-four thousand monasteries, is nationally organized under a supreme patriarch (San., *sangha-raja*) appointed by the king and a council of senior monks and is officially patronized and regulated through the Department of Religious Affairs in the Ministry of Culture. The administrative structure of the Sangha parallels that of the government, and monastic and government officials work hand in hand in matters of national development.

The Village and Monastery

The village of Phraan Muan in 1961 consisted of 182 families, a total population of 932.[49] The people of Phraan Muan are relatively poor. Their chief occupation, like that of most of the people of Thailand, is rice farming. Because they are without irrigation systems, their prosperity is heavily dependent on timely and adequate rainfall. The houses of Phraan Muan, built on stilts to protect against flood and wild animals, are clustered together so as to permit the greatest use of the surrounding farmland. The village is a tightly knit community; of married couples in the village, 90 percent of the wives and 64 percent of the husbands were born in Phraan Muan and all of the monks of Phraan Muan are kinsmen of the villagers.

The village monastery or *wat* stands apart from the clustered houses, yet it is the hub of village life. Built by the villagers themselves, it consists of living quarters for the monks, a ceremonial hall for rituals pertaining to the monastic discipline, and a preaching hall that serves not only as a place of worship and religious instruction, but also as a primary school and a place for public meetings.

The Inhabitants of Phraan Muan

Just as the world as conceived by classical Buddhism is populated by a variety of beings, so is the world of Phraan Muan villagers. The cast of characters in the life drama of Phraan Muan includes gods and spirits as well as human beings.

The most authoritative and powerful person of the village is the monk of long standing and extensive learning. All monks are revered for their merit and wisdom; the longer their tenure and the more extensive their learning, the more revered. The abbot (head monk) of the Phraan Muan *wat* has been a monk for eight years, six as a novice and two under higher ordination. He has passed all three levels of examinations concerning knowledge of the Thai language, the life and teachings of the Buddha, and the rules of the monastic life. Most of the monks of Phraan Muan at any one time are short-term members of the Sangha; they will have memorized the important chants and sermons and learned how to conduct a basic merit-making rite, but they will not have significant knowledge of the Buddha or the Dharma.

Second to the monks in authority and merit-power are ex-monks who, by the merit of having been monks and by the knowledge of language and ritual texts gained as monks, have become respected elders of the community. There are two ex-abbots among the elders of Phraan Muan.

Also inhabiting and exercising power in the world of Phraan Muan are gods (Thai, *thewada;* San., *devata*) and spirits (*phii*). The gods are described as in classical Buddhism (see pp. 874–75), but they are believed to reside permanently in certain of the heavens, rather than being subject to karma, as is so in classical Buddhism. The gods are benevolent toward humans but exercise their power only upon proper invitation. Generally, they are ritually addressed as a category, rather than as individuals. The one notable exception is Nang Thoranee, the goddess of the earth, who witnesses merit and mediates in the transfer of merit from the living to the dead. This office is based on her role in the conquest of Mara by the Buddha just prior to his enlightenment.

The *phii* are the spirits of the dead and may be benevolent or malevolent. They are "touchy" but usually malevolent only when their prerogatives are encroached upon. The spirits of humans who died untimely and/or violent deaths, such as women and children who die in childbirth or those who die in an accident, tend to be malicious; they resent the fact that their opportunities for merit were cut off prematurely and/or violently. The most prominent spirits of Phraan Muan are Tapubaan, the "owner/guardian of the village," and Chao Phau, "Respected Father-monk," the guardian of the *wat.* Tapubaan is the spirit of the original owner of the village and dwells in a miniature house at its edge, where the farmland joins the forest. Chao Phau is the spirit of a very devout servant of the *wat.* His presence there is indicated by a statue placed near the Buddha-image. He is also represented as dwelling with Tapubaan in the shrine at the village edge. These guardians look after the interests of the village and *wat* and uphold certain moral values.

When properly honored and fed, Tapubaan exercises his power to bring rain and good crops; Chao Phau, when his permission is sought for ceremonies and festivals at the *wat,* protects and blesses these occasions. Tapubaan punishes those who go to live in another village without his permission and those who cut down trees near his house. Chao Phau inflicts stomachache on those who urinate in the *wat* compound and makes the abbot ill when merit-making rituals are held without his permission. Both spirits discipline those who engage in certain physical labor on the Observance days. Appropriate to their context and function, Tapubaan eats meat, while Chao Phau is a vegetarian. Closely associated with these spirits are other *phii* who guard the rice fields. They are honored regularly with food offerings and are given special attention just before plowing and after the harvest.

Generally, the spirits of kin who died natural deaths are not bothersome to humans. Those of kin who died violently and untimely deaths and those unknown, neglected spirits who may dwell in trees along the roadside or on mountaintops inflict illness on humans by attacking them or by possessing them.

The Monks of Phraan Muan: Their Life and Services

The monks of Phraan Muan are native to the village. It is a Thai ideal that every young man spend some time as a monk, not with the hope of attaining enlightenment, but to bring merit to his parents and community and to mature in preparation for marriage and adult responsibility. Fifty years ago, it was typical for a boy to spend his daytime hours at the *wat,* serving the monks and receiving his basic education under the tutelage of monks. At the age of twelve or thirteen, he would receive the novitiate ordination and remain a monk until receiving the higher ordination at the age of twenty. One of the elders of Phraan Muan village had, in general, followed this pattern, serving as a temple boy for two years, ages ten to twelve, receiving novitiate ordination at age eighteen, and the higher ordination at age twenty. He remained a monk to age twenty-seven, serving as abbot of the *wat* for the last three years. Today it is more usual that, without prior experience of monastery life, a young man will receive the novitiate and higher ordination successively at the age of twenty, just prior to marriage. Countrywide, upward of 75 percent of the eligible males undergo ordination, but less than 40 percent of those ordained remain monks for life. The great majority stay in the order for only one to three rain-retreats. There is no stigma attached to giving up the vows, even after only a few weeks. It is also acceptable to leave the order for a time and return again later.

In Phraan Muan, there is a very high turnover rate in Sangha membership. At any one time during the 1961–1966 period, there were as few as two monks and as many as fifteen. From 1961 to 1964 a total of twenty-six young men, ages twelve to twenty-four, received either the novitiate or higher ordination; most remained for only a short period. In 1966, there were eleven monks in rain-retreat, nine of whom had been ordained just prior to the retreat. Continuity is provided by two or three long-termers, such as the present (1966) abbot, who at the age of twenty-two has been a monk for eight years. Of the 182 families in the village, more than half of their male heads have spent some time as novices or fully ordained monks.

DAILY ROUTINE   The monks of Phraan Muan rise at 4:30 A.M., chant together in the ceremonial hall, clean their rooms, and then go into the village to receive their morning food. They move about without design, quietly receiving food wherever it is offered. Only women present food to the monks and they must do so quietly and with reserve. After consuming the food upon return to the *wat,* the monks engage in study and the learning of *sutras,* which they must chant in various ritual performances. Lunch is at 11:00 and is brought to the *wat* by women of the village. This food must be finished before noon according to monastic rule. Before and after lunch the monks take care of personal matters such as washing clothes and bathing and cleaning up the food dishes. Some may nap in the afternoon. Evening chanting takes place in the ceremonial hall at 6:00, after which there is again a period of study before retiring for the night, around 9:00.

On the Observance days or "moon days" (Thai, *wan phra*), which occur four times each month, the monks do not go out for their morning food. Women of the village bring food to the *wat* in both early and late morning. Novices must sweep the public hall, light the candles, and spread mats in preparation for the chanting of the *Pratimoksha* code. The villagers of Phraan Muan frequent the Observance Day rites only during the rain-retreat months. Some, especially elderly women, will commit themselves temporarily to the monastic precepts and remain at the *wat* throughout the day. The monks may preach to the gathered laity before breakfast and in the evening.

HOME RITUALS   The Phraan Muan monks are frequently invited to individual homes of the village to perform a merit-making ritual. The occasion may be a birthday or a death anniversary. Less frequently, they are invited to bless a new house, to chant for the cure of illness or the granting of long life, or to bring blessing to those on their death bed.

Thai monks chanting the words of the Buddha in a home-blessing ceremony. The string held by the monks and wound around the silver bowl (right foreground) is connected to the Buddha-image of the domestic altar and passes around the house and the laity who are gathered for the blessing. The water in the silver vessel becomes "charged" or "holy" water during the ceremony and is the means of conveying merit to the dead and to the gathered laity.

The form of these rituals is basically the same. A string, which will act as a "hot-line," is stretched out around the house; it is attached to the domestic Buddha-image, passed through the hands of the abbot or chief officiating monk, wound around a bowl of water, and finally passed through the hands of other monks. The laity sit within the area marked off by the string. The monks then chant the *paritta* called "The Auspiciousness Sutra" (*Mangala Sutra*), during which the abbot drops wax from a burning candle into the bowl of water. As the chant ends, he immerses the candle in the water, extinguishing the flame. The *sutra* speaks of the great merit of the Buddha, the Dharma, and the Sangha. This merit is symbolically infused into the water. The extinguishing of the candle suggests the power of extinguishing all desire. After this chanting, the monks are fed as sumptuously as possible. Having eaten, they chant the "Victory Blessing" *paritta* and the "Received-with-Satisfaction Blessing" *paritta* and conclude by sprinkling the charged water on the householders and/or around the house as may suit the occasion. In chanting for the cure of illness, a portion of the "hot-line" string is tied around the wrist of the patient to seal in the power radiated by the ceremony.

The "Victory Blessing" *paritta* lauds eight victories of the Buddha over malevolent forces. After each verse of praise, it commends or transfers the power of the Buddha to those who hear the *sutra*. For example:

> The Buddha, through his ten Perfections, beginning with charity, has conquered Mara the Evil One who, having created a thousand hands all armed, came riding on his war elephant Girimekhala, together with his army. By this power, may you be endowed with conquests and blessings.
>
> . . .
>
> The Buddha, through the exercise of his psychic power, has conquered the formidable robber Angulimala who, brandishing a sword, had covered a distance of three Yojana in pursuit of Him. By this power, may you be endowed with conquests and blessings.[50]

The "Received-with-Satisfaction Blessing" is a chant by which the monks transfer merit as an expression of gratitude for food. A portion of the chant is as follows:

> May all evils vanish, may all diseases disappear, may danger not come to you. May you have happiness and old age.[51]

After the monks have blessed the householders, the latter in turn pour water onto the floor, transferring a portion of the merit to the dead, the gods, and to all beings.

RITES OF PASSAGE The important times of transition and change of status in life—birth, puberty, marriage, and death—are times of great vulnerability. At these times there is need for blessing and protection for the affected parties and recognition of these changes by the community. In Phraan Muan, the monks officiate at ordinations (the puberty or youth-to-adult passage rite for males) and funerals. Former monks, respected elders of the community called *paahm* (San., *brahmana*), officiate at pregnancy and childbirth rites and marriages. (This title is a carryover from a time when Brahmanism and Buddhism shared authority in the life of the Thai people.) [See Religions of Africa pp. 42–51, Religions of Mesoamerica pp. 201–6, Native Religions of North America pp. 278–79, 295–98, 306–8, Judaism pp. 446–50, Christianity pp. 542–43, 555–57, Islam pp. 677–78, 680–86, Hinduism pp. 747, 807–14, Religions of China pp. 1019–21, and Religions of Japan pp. 1146–50 for description and discussion of rites of passage; see Religions of Africa pp. 45–46, 76, Native Religions of North America p. 307, Judaism pp. 385–86, 445–46, Christianity p. 556, Islam p. 682, Hinduism pp. 810–11, Religions of China p. 1019–20, and Religions of Japan pp. 1146–47 for description and discussion of birth rites.]

ORDINATION   Entering upon monastic life is a stage in the pilgrimage toward nirvana. In the Theravada practice of Buddhism, its immediate importance is as a rite of passage for young men. The preferred time of year for ordination is June or early July, immediately prior to the rain-retreat. Since the rain-retreat is a time of relative seclusion and intense study, it is an ideal time for the new novice to be properly instructed and encouraged. In addition, ordination at this time is associated with a rocket-firing festival, the Bunbangfai, "Merit of (Firing) Rockets," the purpose of which is to stimulate rainfall. The merit of ordination is shared with the guardian spirit-forces who control the rains.

It is customary for candidates for first-time ordination to spend the week prior to ordination at the *wat,* learning the words to be vocalized in the ceremony and "getting a feel" for the monastery environment. The candidate is called a *nag,* or "snake," to signify his potency and to commemorate an occasion in the time of the Buddha when a snake gained admission to the Sangha by magically assuming human form. When the Buddha discovered the snake, he forbade it from the monastic life but promised that it would be remembered on every future occasion of ordination.

The parents of the *nag* consult an astrologer to set an auspicious time for the ordination ceremony. During the morning of the day before ordination, assisted by relatives and friends who wish to enjoy some of the merit of the occasion, the parents gather together eight requisites for their son's life as a monk: two robes, an umbrella, a food bowl, slippers, a lamp, a razor, and a spittoon. They also prepare food and gifts for the monks. A girlfriend of the *nag,* who perhaps will eventually become his wife, may provide a pillow for his sojourn at the *wat.*

While family and friends make ready, the *nag* goes to the *wat* where the abbot shaves off his hair and eyebrows. Body hair is considered dead matter; its removal signifies the renunciation of the old life. It signifies, specifically, renunciation of concern with personal appearance and sexuality. Thereafter, the candidate returns home to don a red or green loincloth and a fine white shawl. This clothing identifies him with Prince Siddhartha prior to his renunciation. The white shawl also signifies the *nag's* entrance upon a liminal or neutral state, in transition between his former life and the one to come.

CALLING THE VITAL FORCES On the afternoon of the same day, the *nag,* his relatives, and friends, particularly the elders of the community, gather at the public hall of the monastery for a *sukhwan* ceremony. This ritual strengthens the young man for his ordeal of entering upon the monastic life by "calling (his) life-forces" (*sukhwan*) together and symbolically sealing them in his body. The ceremony is performed by a former monk who is a respected elder of the community.

The *sukhwan* or "calling the vital forces" ceremony is included in all rites of passage except the funeral. It is the essential element of pregnancy and childbirth rites and in the marriage ceremony. It is also performed for the monks when they enter retreat and for any villager before and after a trip or military service and during illness.

The ceremony begins with invocation of the gods and recognition of the power of the Buddha:

Reverence to the Blessed One, the Holy One, the Perfectly Enlightened One!

The gods are invited to attend the *sukhwan* and give blessing to the occasion—they are, in a sense, channels for the flow of Buddha-power. A central element of the ceremony is a tiered, conical structure built up on a tray and bearing a boiled egg, bananas, flowers, and a lump of rice. The purpose of this centerpiece is to attract the *khwan* (life-forces). Near the cone are placed the eight requisites of the monk's life (robes, food bowl, and so on). A candle the length of the circumference of the *nag's* head is attached to the cone. It is believed that a person has thirty-two *khwan* or vital forces, the most important of which is that of the head. These forces tend to wander out of the body in search of enjoyment and, therefore, must be called together to ensure a safe, healthy, and powerful transition from one status to another. The head-candle signifies the *khwan* of the head and when lit marks the living presence of this *khwan.*

Another candle, the length of the *nag's* body from shoulder to waist, is placed in association with the eight requisites. It signifies that the *nag's* body is to become committed to these articles through ordination. The *nag* sits on one side of the cone and requisites, the elder officiant on the other. They are united by a string, called "the thread of good fortune," which is attached to the cone, then passed through the hands of the *nag* and to the officiant. The officiant lights the candles and then reads a standard text that reminds the *nag* that his mother sacrificed and cared for him as a child and that now it is appropriate that he bring merit to her through his ordination. Next, the officiant calls the *khwan* into the food offerings and candles. He then prepares "holy" water by adding liquor or perfume to the water in a small bowl and sprinkles the *nag.* Placing rice, banana, and egg from the cone into the *nag's* hands, he transfers the *khwan* to the *nag* and then binds it in the body by tying a piece of white thread around the *nag's* wrist. Parents and other elders of the community then also tie strings. The ceremony concludes with a blessing upon the *nag* chanted by the monks. They chant the *Mangala Sutra,* the Buddha's words invoking prosperity.

On the morning of ordination day, parents and other villagers take food to the monks at the monastery and then, at the sound of a drum, assemble for the procession of the *nag* to the monastery. The *nag,* the monk who will officiate at the ordination, and the two monks who will act as the *nag's* companion and teacher are carried on palanquins at the head of the procession. The parents and others of the community follow, bearing the *nag's* requisites and gifts for the monks. The procession circles the public hall three times—once for each of the Three Jewels—and then proceeds to the ceremonial hall, where the monks await. Before the *nag* is carried into the hall, parents and relatives wash his feet with perfumed water, symbolically removing the last taint of his old life.

The ordination plays out the Great Renunciation of Gautama, the Buddha. The *nag's* peers act the part of Mara's army and playfully attempt to waylay his progress to the ceremonial hall. Before entering the hall, the *nag* throws a handful of coins to the crowd as a final gesture of renunciation of worldly goods.

Valid ordination requires the presence of at least five monks of higher ordination. At times when sufficient monks are not available in Phraan Muan, others are invited from nearby villages and towns. A former abbot of Phraan Muan is now (1966) serving at the district level and frequently returns to the village to officiate at ordinations.

The ordaining monks are gathered on a platform at one end of the hall. The parents stand behind the *nag* with his requisites, the father holding his robes. The *nag* prostrates himself before his father and requests his robes. Giving him the robes, the father then leads the *nag* before the head monk. The *nag* bows before the monk three times, each time reciting the Threefold Refuge and requesting permission to be ordained. The officiating monk takes the *nag's* hand, instructs him as to the meaning of the Three Jewels, and recites a *sutra* on the impermanence of the body. The officiant then calls upon the *nag's* companion and teacher to assist him (the *nag*) in putting on the robes and to administer the Ten Precepts, which the *nag* repeats after them. The parents then present the *nag's* food bowl and the gifts they have brought for the monks. The officiant places the bowl's carrying-sling on the *nag's* shoulder and concludes the novitiate ordination by giving the *nag* a new name—the one by which he will be known as long as he is a monk.

Those *nags* who are twenty years of age or more at the time of first taking ordination will receive the higher ordination on the same occasion. This involves the *nag* properly answering a series of questions about his health and status (as classically defined, see p. 871). Thereafter the officiant requests that the gathered monks duly admit the novice to full ordination. Their silence indicates assent. The officiant then instructs the new monk concerning his responsibilities, the monks chant the Victory Blessing *sutra* while the new monk pours water, symbolically transferring merit to his parents and other members of the community, and the parents pour water to transfer a portion of this merit to the souls of their dead parents and other ancestors. The ordination concludes with a feast, first by the monks and afterward by the whole community.

MARRIAGE   In Phraan Muan, the dominant pattern in marriage is one in which the groom comes to live with the bride in the home of the bride's parents. Later, with the marriage of a second daughter or with the coming of children, the first daughter and her husband will move into a separate house in the same compound or initiate a new compound with land given by the daughter's parents. The wedding ceremony is, appropriately, held in the sleeping room of the bride's home. It begins with the arrival of the groom and the performance of a *sukhwan*.

The basic elements in the *sukhwan* rite for marriage are the same as those for the *sukhwan* in ordination. The conical structure of offerings to the *khwan* is preferably made by older married women. Widows and divorced women do not attend, since their presence would be inauspicious. The bride and groom and the ex-monk elder (the officiant) sit on opposite sides of the ritual cone. Several young men sit with the groom and several young women with the bride, completing a circle with the officiant. The *sukhwan* string passes from the cone through the hands of the women attendants, bride, groom, and men attendants and ends with the officiant. The ceremony begins when the officiant places bamboo rings with pieces of cotton fluff attached to them on the heads of the bride and groom. After lighting a candle, he chants, inviting the gods to come and witness the ceremony and bless the couple. Thereafter, he calls the *khwan* to come from wherever they may be and reenter the bodies of the bride and groom. In reciting this call, he states that the marriage is approved by the parents, the elders, and the gods. Then he instructs the couple as to their proper behavior in marriage, in relation to each other and to the parents on both sides. The officiant then prepares "charged" water by adding liquor or perfume to a vessel of water and sprinkles the couple. Placing a portion of the *khwan* food in the hands of the groom, he transfers the *khwan* to the groom's body and then ties a piece of white string around his wrist. After he has done the same for the bride, the elders and then the younger persons attending add strings to the wrists of the couple and present them with gifts of money. Following the *sukhwan*, there is a brief ceremony in which a bowl containing candles and flowers is offered to the elders by the couple through the elder-officiant, and the latter lectures the couple, at more length than previously, on their behavior toward each other and the elders in marriage. The lecture concluded, an older married woman leads the couple to view their sleeping quarters on the other side of the room. The officiant distributes candles and flowers to all those present, thereby marking them as witnesses to the marriage. The parents then provide food for the guests and the new couple. [See Religions of Africa pp. 48–51, 77–78, Judaism pp. 447–48, Christianity p. 556, Islam pp. 683–84, Hinduism pp. 809–10, Religions of China p. 1020, and Religions of Japan p. 1148 for description and discussion of marriage rites.]

DEATH RITES   The funeral rite is the most important rite of passage. Facilitating the transition of the spirit of the deceased from one life to another is a delicate matter; failure in proper performance of the rite may bring great harm to the spirit and to the villagers. Soon after death, the immediate relatives of the deceased bathe the body and dress it in new clothes. Then they ritually bathe the corpse by pouring water on the deceased's hands, herewith showing respect for the person and asking his or her forgiveness. The body is laid out face up, the head toward the west; the feet are tied together with a thread; and the hands are placed in a prayerful posture on the chest and tied together. A coin is placed in the mouth and flowers, candles, and paper money in the hands. The money is said to be for buying entry to heaven and the flowers and candles for worshiping the Buddha. The mouth and eyes are then sealed with wax.

The entire village community assists in the funeral arrangements. Women prepare food, cigarettes, and betel nut chews. The men construct a coffin and gather wood for the cremation. Everyone contributes small amounts of money to defray the expenses of the funeral.

The body is placed in the coffin along with several articles used by the deceased, a basket of food, and a vessel of water. It is believed that the deceased will use the personal articles in heaven and the food and water are for his or her spirit. When all is made ready, the monks come to the home, take food, and afterward chant near the body. The intent of the Buddha-words chanted is to call together the elements and spirit of the deceased, which tend to disperse at death, to increase the merit of the deceased, and to show the spirit the way to heaven.

The chanting concluded, the coffin is carried from the home in procession to the cremation ground near the *wat*. Before they lift the coffin, the coffin-bearers are given flowers and candles with which they will later pay respects to the deceased so that his or her spirit (*phii*) won't attack them. The monks lead the procession, holding a string that is attached to the coffin. This keeps the deceased within their merit-field during the journey. Upon reaching the prepared pile of firewood, the coffin is carried around the pile three times, signifying the hope that the deceased will be reborn as a human being, will have a spouse and children, and will lead a good life. The coffin is placed on the ground, the monks chant, then receive gifts of tobacco, betel nuts, and money, and again chant a blessing in response for the gifts. Monks and relatives "cleanse" and "beautify" the corpse by pouring coconut juice and scented water on the face. Their sentiment in this act is that the deceased may fare well in rebirth. After further chanting, the coffin is placed on the pile of wood and both monks and laity ignite the fire. The monks chant while the body burns.

On the way home, the villagers go first to the *wat* to rid themselves of any bad effects resulting from association with death. On the evening of the day of cremation and again the next two evenings, monks perform a blessing rite at the home of the deceased. They chant holding onto a string attached to a Buddha-image, a bowl of water, and the collected items belonging to the deceased or items used in the funeral proceedings. The effect of these rites is to purify or neutralize the latter objects and again bring merit to the family and friends of the deceased. On the morning of the third day after cremation, a party of monks and villagers collect and wash the bones of the deceased and place them in a pot. The pot is covered with a cloth secured by a string, one end of which is left dangling. The pot is then placed on the "chest" of a human figure fashioned on the ground with the ashes of the funeral pyre. The monks chant first near the pot and then while holding onto the string. This concluded, the cloth covering of the pot is pierced to allow the spirit of the deceased to depart and the pot is buried. It is believed that the spirit is now on its way to heaven. In some parts of Thailand, a portion of the ashes and bones of the deceased are enshrined in the home or in a *stupa* constructed in the *wat* compound.

Following this ceremony, villagers and monks gather at the *wat,* the women present food to the monks, and close relatives make food offerings to the spirit of the departed and offer to the monks a palanquin of gifts that had been prepared by the community the day before. The gifts are items of use to the monks, such as a robe, a flashlight, or a pillow. One of the monks responds with a sermon, the import of which is that life is impermanent and that those who perform funeral rites gain great merit for their deeds. [See Religions of Africa pp. 42–45, 78–79, Religions of Mesoamerica pp. 144, 229, Native Religions of North America pp. 300–301, 307–308, 335–337, Judaism pp. 448–50, Christianity p. 557, Islam pp. 684–85, Hinduism pp. 813–14, Religions of China p. 1021, 1041–44 and Religions of Japan pp. 1149–50 for description and discussion of death and funeral rites.]

The Yearly Round of Communal Rites and Festivals

Family merit-making rituals and rites of passage take place at various times, appropriate to the changing circumstances of families and individuals. Certain collective or all-village rites and celebrations take place every year, at the same time each year, and are ways of marking time and focusing power for the whole community. The events of this yearly cycle are determined with reference to the key moments of agricultural endeavor, the great events of the life of the Buddha, and the major points of transition in the life of the Sangha. For the most part, the events of these three patterns are coordinated with each other to make for a harmonization of all of the life resources operative in the village environment.

NEW YEAR　The lunar year begins April 15, which is seasonally at the end of the dry period when the villagers look forward to the rains. It is a time for cleansing, sharing merit with the dead, and invoking rain. The New Year is celebrated on three successive days: The first marks the end of the old year, the second is a day of transition, and the third is the actual New Year's Day. On these days women take food to the *wat* in the early morning as well as the late morning, and each evening the monks chant *parittas* of blessing. The last day of the old year is a time for ritually bathing the Buddha-image and sprinkling water on the monks. By this act the laity cleanse themselves of the bad karma accumulated during the past year and symbolically refresh the Buddha and the Sangha for the year to come. The second day of the celebration is a time for remembering ancestors and transferring merit to them. During the day, the monks chant at the cemetery, some of the laity build and decorate sand *stupas* (Thai, *pagodas*) in the *wat* compound, and young people ritually bathe their elders with perfumed water, asking their forgiveness and blessing. In the evening, monks and laity gather near the sand *stupas* and the monks chant the Victory Blessing *paritta*. New Year's Day is a time for reveling; characteristically the young playfully shower each other with water.

BUDDHA DAY In May the rains begin and the fields must be plowed and planted. The full-moon day is a time to remember and celebrate the birth, enlightenment, and death of the Buddha.

In Phraan Muan, the day is marked by the laity taking food to the monks early in the morning and in the evening processing three times around the ceremonial hall of the *wat* with lighted candles and incense. Visakha Puja, as the day is called, is a national holiday in Thailand. Many towns and villages celebrate it more elaborately than the people of Phraan Muan. Usually, for instance, following the candlelight procession, monks and laity gather in the public hall of the *wat* for a lengthy recitation of the life of the Buddha, displaying this life as a paradigm for all life and a paragon of power for the new year.

THE ROCKET FESTIVAL In mid-July the monks enter the rain-retreat. Leading into the retreat, ordinations are performed and the village holds a rocket-firing festival (Bunbangfai, literally, "Merit of [Firing] Rockets"). This is the time of year when the young rice plants are growing and there is need for plentiful rain. The merit-power of ordination and the festival of rockets are addressed to the village guardian deities who are believed responsible for rain. The rocket festival begins the day after ordination day. A number of rockets—as many as the villagers can afford—are constructed at the *wat* with the help of the monks several days prior. Two special rockets, one called "rocket for paying respect" and the other "wishing rocket," are made for honoring Tapubaan, the village guardian spirit.

On the first day of the festival, the rockets are carried in procession to the dwelling of Tapubaan at the edge of the village. The participants have been drinking and there is much boisterous reveling. The procession proceeds from the *wat* and, arriving at the spirit dwelling, circumambulates the dwelling three times. After a prayer by a villager believed to be in special communion with the spirit, in which rain, good health, prosperity, and health for the livestock are requested, the "paying respect" rocket is fired, and the procession returns to the *wat*, circumambulating the public hall three times.

In the evening, the villagers enjoy dancing, folk opera, and the like in the *wat* compound and the monks chant to bless the remaining rockets. The next morning, the monks are feasted at the *wat*, and thereafter monks and laity gather near the rice fields and one after the other fires the rockets. The "wishing rocket" is fired first. If it flies straight and high, it is believed that there will be prosperity. The firing of the other rockets is a time for much "horseplay," for monks and laity alike. Those whose rockets do not fly well are pelted with mud.

ENTERING RAIN-RETREAT The revelry of the rocket festival is followed by the solemnity of entering into the rain-retreat. The day is the full moon of July. In the morning, the laity make merit by feeding the monks. Then, the lay elders perform a *sukhwan* ceremony for the monks, calling and binding in their vital forces in preparation for retreat. Following the *sukhwan,* the monks are presented with bathing cloths for use during retreat and the monks respond with a blessing and a short sermon on the merit of the occasion. In the evening, there is a candlelight procession like that of Visakha Puja day and the monks chant a final blessing *paritta.*

HONORING THE DEAD   In the month of September, when the rice is in a critical growing stage, the villagers celebrate Bun Khaw Saak, the festival of "making merit with puffed rice." This is a time when the spirits of the dead visit the earth, as they do on the day before New Year. If they and the guardian spirit of the rice crop are fed and offered merit, they will protect the crop. After offering food to the monks and listening to a sermon, the laity place packets of puffed rice and vegetables on the ground near the ceremonial hall of the *wat* while the monks chant and pour water, transferring merit to the dead. At the same time, puffed rice is placed in the paddy fields, so that the rice spirit and the ancestors, coming there for food, will be pleased by the fact that the fields have been well kept. Puffed rice, which is rice that will not grow again, or "dead rice," is the preferred offering to the dead. By contrast, raw rice, which suggests life and fertility, is offered in the marriage ritual.

CONCLUDING RAIN-RETREAT AND KATHIN   On the full moon of October, the monks conclude their retreat. They have been "growing" by discipline and study as the rice has been growing and now emerge from relative seclusion as the rice grains are coming to maturity. Early in the morning the monks perform the invitation rite in the ceremonial hall, inviting each other to point out infractions of the discipline during the retreat. Afterward the laity bring food and gifts to the monks and themselves take a communal meal at the *wat.* When the meal is finished, the elders listen to a sermon and the young people frolic, lighting firecrackers and throwing puffed rice on the Buddha-image. In the evening there is a candlelight procession.

The end of the rain-retreat is marked in a grand way by the festival of Bun Kathin "the merit of giving robes," which occurs sometime between the full moon of October and that of November. The festival lasts for two days. On the morning of the first day the public hall of the *wat* is decorated and gifts for the monks are assembled on a wooden palanquin. It is customary in Thailand that the gifts for Kathin should be provided by donors from another village; failing this, they are provided locally. The palanquin is elaborately decorated to look like a palace. It is said to signify the hope for a heavenly rebirth. Carved serpents on the roof ends represent the Buddha's conquest of desire, and pincushions hung from the four corners of the roof signify the hope for rebirth with sharpness of mind. On the evening of the first day, a blessing by the monks is followed by dancing and folk opera in the *wat* compound.

The next morning the villagers gather for a procession of the "palace" of gifts around the public and ceremonial halls. The procession is led by an ex-monk bearing a Buddha-image on his head. Behind him are monks holding onto a yellow string attached to the palanquin. Between the monks and the palanquin are men of the village, bearing money trees—branches on which are hung paper money and small gifts for the monks. These trees are said to imitate the great wishing tree that stands in the Tusita heaven and grants all wishes. Other participants carry flags bearing the image of Nang Thoranee, the Earth Goddess, and aquatic animals. (According to Thai legends, the Earth Goddess, when witnessing to the perfection of the Buddha, wrung a flood of water and aquatic creatures from her hair, thereby dispersing Mara's army.) After the procession has entered the public hall, another yellow string is tied around the hall to mark the boundary within which merit will be received. The ceremony begins with a lay elder requesting one of the monks to administer the Five Precepts to the gathered laity. Then, an elder presents new robes to the abbot, another presents the money trees, and the ceremony is concluded with a blessing chant.

THE HARVEST FESTIVAL Appropriately for an agricultural community, the climactic merit ritual of the year occurs in February after the harvest. The festival is called Bun Phraawes, "The Merit of the Venerable Wes (Vessantara)." The next to last birth of the Buddha was that as Prince Vessantara, who showed perfection in charity. The recitation of the life story of Vessantara is one of the central acts of the festival. The festival brings together the powers of nature, the gods, and human beings, in order that all may share in the merit of the Buddha.

On the first day of the festival, monks sit, together with a Buddha-image, in a grand pavilion constructed for the occasion. There they receive gifts of unmilled or rough rice. Late in the afternoon, monks and elders lead a procession to a pond near the village, where they invite the serpent (*naga*), lord of the waters, to the *wat* to hear the story of Vessantara. The spirit-lord of the waters is believed to have power over Mara—the power to protect the activities of the festival from Mara's onslaught. He is enticed to the festival with gifts, which include a food bowl, robes, other requisites of the monk's life, flowers, puffed rice, and cigarettes. After an elder chants the invitation to the spirit, guns are fired and drums are beaten and the monks chant the Victory Blessing. A kettle of water is then taken from the pond; this water is the spirit. Two small Buddha-images are placed in the kettle of water, completing the harnessing of the spirit's power to the Buddha and the blessing of the festival. The kettle is carried in procession back to the *wat* and placed on a high shelf in the public hall, where the story of Vessantara will later be told. In the evening, the monks chant blessings and a fair is held at the *wat*. On the afternoon of the next day, the villagers gather for a special sermon concerning a virtuous monk who preached to both the inhabitants of hell and those of the heavens.

Very early the next morning (2:30 A.M.) the villagers gather at the public hall to invite the gods to the festival. Older men and women carrying flowers, candles, and balls of rice process around the hall three times, each time dropping some of these offerings in baskets attached to flagpoles at each corner of the hall. When the procession is concluded, the elders take the baskets, which are now the residence of the gods, into the hall and place them near the pulpit. After the presentation of flowers, candles, and incense before the Buddha-image and the recitation of the Five Precepts, the story sermons begin. The first tells of the Buddha's renunciation, the second tells of his victory over Mara, and the third is the story of Vessantara. The recitation lasts throughout the day. [See Religions of Africa pp. 74–75, Religions of Mesoamerica pp. 229–38, Native Religions of North America pp. 308–16, 351–57, Judaism pp. 439–45, Christianity pp. 551–55, Islam pp. 674, 677–79, Hinduism p. 829, Religions of China pp. 1021–24, and Religions of Japan pp. 1140–46, 1153–62 for description and discussion of festivals and annual celebrations.]

Making and Sharing Merit

The central feature of life in Phraan Muan is making and sharing merit. Making and sharing are inseparable. Life goes on by exchanges of merit. Young men renounce worldly enjoyments to bring merit to their parents and community. They, of course, earn merit for themselves by their moral discipline and study; but the emphasis in their becoming monks is on service to the community. In turn, they are fed, clothed, and housed by the community. They enjoy the highest respect of anyone in the village and are free from labor in the fields. They have opportunities to travel. They are the beneficiaries of the merit of the laity. The fruits of labor are the merit of the laity. Sharing it, by feeding, clothing, and housing the monks and by bearing the cost of sponsoring ordination and honoring the gods and spirits whose power provides prosperity, they gain greater merit. The ex-monk, by the fact of his previous service and study, has merit second only to that of the monk and enjoys high status in the community. He shares his merit by mediating between the monks and the lay community and by facilitating the times of transition (marriage, childbirth, illness, entering rain-retreat, and so on) in their lives. The living make merit for the dead in reciprocation for the merit that the dead relatives brought to their lives while they were alive. Human beings share their merit to empower the guardian spirits of the village, *wat,* and crops.

The villagers give highest priority to the merit of financing the building of a *wat.* This act is reserved for only the very wealthy. But second priority is given to the merit of becoming a monk or having a son become a monk. Although this is costly due to the fact of the expenses incurred for ordination and the loss of the labor of the one ordained, the entire village joins in sharing the expenses (and therefore the merit) of ordination, and the loss of a field hand is more than compensated for by the services performed by a monk. In order of priority, the merit of contributing to the repair of the *wat,* giving gifts to the monks at Kathin time, giving daily food to the monks, observing moon days, and adhering to the Five Precepts rank below building a *wat* or sponsoring or undergoing ordination. Everyone can participate at some of these levels of merit making and sharing. The preparation and offering of food to the monks is the special province of the village women; repair of the *wat* is the province of the men. The elderly, who do less of the field work, are free to observe the moon days; their merit is shared by their family members. Adherence to the precepts, a pillar of the lay life as defined in classical Buddhism, gets a low priority, perhaps because it is just assumed as basic to the Buddhist life and its performance is the least spectacular or publicly displayed. Every communal merit-making ritual begins with the recitation of the precepts under the administration of one of the monks.

Zen Training

Our second example of Buddhism in practice concerns intensive training in the Rinzai sect of Zen Buddhism.[52] The Zen tradition in Japanese Buddhism is centrally a tradition of seeking enlightenment through meditation (Jap., zen; San., *dhyana*). This tradition is preserved and perpetuated by masters who, through years of arduous practice under other masters, have mastered the Dharma and have become recognized as enlightened. The master (*roshi,* literally, "venerable teacher"), may be male or female, married or single. The master resides in a monastery where he or she offers intensive training in meditation to those deemed ready to receive it. Most of those who come for training are young men preparing to serve or already serving as priests in local Zen temples. [See Religions of China pp. 1033–34 for description of meditation in a Chan (Zen) monastery.]

The large monastery temples of the Rinzai sect offer two training terms per year: the summer or rain term from May through October and the winter or snow term from November through April. During the first three months of each term (May–July and November–January), the trainees are expected to remain in the monastery, observing a rigorous discipline. These periods are comparable to the rain-retreat period in Theravada monastic practice. During the second portion of each term the trainees may continue their sitting-meditation practice, but they are free to go on pilgrimage, return to their home temple, or engage in such things as gathering vegetables for the monastery in the countryside.

A priest learns his temple duties from the head priest of a local temple. What he must learn at the monastery is self-discipline, humility, and a special kind of awareness. Discipline begins before he departs his home temple. He must dress in a formal robe, cotton leggings, straw sandals, and a large bamboo hat; he must carry food bowls and a small box containing a robe, a razor, books, and enough money for his funeral rites lest he meet with an accident. Ideally, he travels to the monastery, however far, on foot.

The large monastery typically consists of seven buildings of varying size: an entrance or reception hall, a Buddha-hall for formal chanting or prayer services, a Dharma hall for lectures on the *sutras,* a meditation hall (*zendo*), a latrine, a bathhouse, and a refectory storehouse. These structures are enclosed by a high wall with an imposing gate. In a typical scenario, arriving at the monastery, the would-be trainee passes through the gate, knocks on the door of the entrance hall and, bowing deeply, requests permission to enter for training. Now begins his first lesson in humility and perseverance. He is turned away by a monk at the entrance and told that there is no space available. If he earnestly desires to enter, he remains bowed outside the door, supplicating for admission. The guard then pushes him outside the main gate and firmly shuts the gate. There the traveler sits throughout the day and into the evening. As it begins to grow dark, humbled and tested by his ordeal, he is finally invited to spend the night in the guest room of the entrance hall. Inside, he is given a cup of tea and a sleeping mat and is instructed to sit facing the blank wall of the room until bedtime at 9:00.

The next morning, he is given breakfast and directed to return outside the gate, to spend the day crouched down in a posture of submission. If he perseveres in this, at evening he is again invited to the guestroom and instructed to meditate, simply sitting crossed-legged, facing the wall. After breakfast each day for five days he must visit the quarters of the administrative head of the monastery and pay his respects, then return to his room for sitting meditation. During this time, he is under surveillance. If he is perceived to be serious in his solitary sitting, he is invited to join the other monks in the meditation hall and thus becomes "a novice in training" (*unsui*). From then on for the next three months he will spend most of his time in this hall meditating, chanting, and sleeping. The *zendo* (meditation hall) is a large rectangular hall twice as long as wide, with a door for formal entrance and exit at one end and one for informal entrance and exit at the other. There is a raised platform along each of the long walls, where the monks meditate and sleep. Just inside the formal entrance is the altar of Manjushri, the *bodhisattva* of Wisdom.

The new novice must bow in respect to Manjushri upon entering the hall. Then he is shown to his mat on the platform, a space about four feet wide and seven feet long, where he will spend much of his training time. Behind the mat, on the wall, is a shelf for his meager belongings and his sleeping mat. The rules of conduct during training are posted outside the informal entrance to the *zendo*, but the elder monks, especially the ones who supervise behavior in the hall, take care to instruct the novice as activity proceeds.

In a few days, the novice is summoned to his first meeting with the *roshi*. He must prostrate himself three times at the entryway to the master's quarters and, upon entering, present incense sticks or incense money to show his submission to training under this master. The two have tea and the master kindly inquires about the welfare of the novice, his name, and hometown. Future meetings with the master, part of the training, will not be so cordial, as it is the master's task to awaken the novice to his Buddha-nature and this will require severe questioning and harsh treatment.

The Daily Routine

The monks are awakened at 3:30 A.M. by the tinkle of a small bell. They use the toilet and wash face and hands with a few cups of water. Although there is plenty of water available, they are admonished to conserve. At the sound of a gong, they adjust their robes and walk quickly and quietly to the Buddha-hall for the morning service. Entering the hall, each monk bows before images of the Buddha and certain of the great masters such as Bodhidharma and Eisai that adorn the altar. Then follow thirty minutes of chanting from the *sutras* from memory. Monks who are slow waking up are encouraged by a slap with a stick, administered by an elder monk. The service ends with the chanting of the four vows of the *bodhisattva:*

> However innumerable beings are, I vow to save them;
>
> However inexhaustible the passions are, I vow to extinguish them;
>
> However immeasurable the Dharmas are, I vow to master them;
>
> However incomparable the Buddha-truth is, I vow to attain it.

A similar evening service of chanting takes place in the Buddha-hall late in the afternoon.

After the morning service, the main body of monks returns to the *zendo* for chanting of reverence to Manjushri, followed by a cup of tea. This is not a "tea break." The tea is served and drunk in a very meticulous manner as part of a total program of cultivating heightened awareness. The chanting for Manjushri, the *bodhisattva* of Wisdom, "awakens" and "enlivens" this patron of the meditation hall and, most of all, creates an appropriate mind-set among the monks for their daily striving after wisdom. While this is taking place, the monks who have been appointed to administrative duties for the term are chanting to the guardian spirit of the monastery, who is enshrined in the monastery office. The monks attribute a living spirit to the monastery, which is indicative of a deep humility and respect toward nature. The emphasis in honoring Buddha, *bodhisattvas,* former masters, and spirits is on the state of mind created thereby, not on the objective existence of such beings.

A Zen monk engaged in a tea ceremony.

Breakfast follows the morning services. The monks eat three meals a day; early morning, at 10:00, and in the evening. Breakfast is a small quantity of rice, pickled plums, and vegetables; lunch is a heavier meal, consisting of rice mixed with wheat, soup, vegetables, and pickles. Since it is recognized that the evening meal is contrary to the rules of the ancient Indian monastic code, this meal is simply leftovers from the midday meal and is called "medicinal food."

All food is prepared by monks in the monastery kitchen. The monks do go into the town to receive donations eight times a month—on the first, third, sixth, eighth, eleventh, thirteenth, sixteenth, and eighteenth days—but the donations are raw rice and money rather than cooked food.

The monks walk the town for about three hours in sets of three, their eyes shielded by their large bamboo hats. As they walk, they chant over and over, "*Ho . . . u*," "rain of Dharma." They receive the donations in a bowl without seeing the donor and respond with a bow and a short recitation. In addition to these begging rounds, which convey merit to the laity in general, once a month monks walk to the homes of lay patrons of the monastery to receive more sizable donations of rice. At the end of October each year the monks gather nonmarketable radishes from the farms surrounding the monastery. All of this food is supplemented by a harvest within the monastery itself. As an important part of their total discipline, Zen monks work a monastery garden. Pai-zhang (Pai-chang), an eighth-century Chinese master, introduced the rule: "A day of no work is a day of no eating." The monks eat at the refectory, sitting on the floor at low benches. The food is served ceremoniously by the monk on duty, each course beginning at the signal of the head monk. Before eating, the monks chant *The Sutra of the Heart of the Perfection of Wisdom* (*Prajnaparamita-hridaya Sutra*), which gives the essence of the teaching on emptiness (*shunyata*). It begins:

> When the *bodhisattva* Avalokiteshvara was engaged in the practice of the deep Perfection of Wisdom, he perceived that there are the five aggregates; and these he saw in their self-nature to be empty. . . . Form is emptiness, emptiness is form. . . . The same can be said of sensation, perception, volition, and consciousness.[53]

Following this *sutra,* they invoke ten Buddhas and *bodhisattvas:* Vairocana, Shakyamuni, Maitreya, Manjushri, Avalokiteshvara, and others. At breakfast, there is a verse accompanying the rice gruel:

> The gruel-meal has ten advantages
> Whereby the yogins are benefited;
> The results accruing from it are boundless,
> Finally leading them to eternal happiness.[54]

At lunch, the *sutra* and Buddha-invocation are followed by a fivefold vow:

> Let us think on how much we have accomplished and how this food
> has come to us.
> Let us accept this prepared food only because we have now
> performed good deeds.

> Let us take only enough food to satisfy our needs, leaving our
>   hunger not quite satisfied.
> Let us partake of this food as medicine in order to aid our thin
>   bodies.
> Let us accept this food so that we may establish our way.[55]

Eating begins with a verse to the first three morsels:

> The first morsel is to destroy all evils,
> The second morsel is to practice all good deeds,
> The third morsel is to save all sentient beings—
> May we all attain the path of Buddhahood.[56]

The food is taken thereafter in silence and with care not to make biting or chewing sounds. When the meals are finished, short verses are again chanted recognizing that the body is strengthened as an instrument of realizing enlightenment. The monk on duty carefully cleans up any particles of food left on the bench. Outside the eating hall, he first offers these particles to the hungry ghosts (see pp. 874–75) and then sets them out for the birds.

After breakfast there is a tea ceremony in the meditation hall. Periodically, tea is taken with the master, who then delivers an address exhorting the trainees to study and work hard in all that they do. Hanging outside the *zendo* entranceway, there is a wooden board that is struck three times daily to mark dawn, evening, and bedtime. The sentiment of the master's exhortation is hereon capsulized in verse:

> Matter of life and death is great.
> Time runs quickly; nothing remains;
> It waits for no man.
> You should not waste your time.[57]

Every morning following tea, each trainee must meet individually with the *roshi*. In accord with what he senses to be the disciple's state of mind, the *roshi* may give the disciple a *koan* (literally, "a public case or legal precedent"), one of several hundred problem-sayings formulated by Zen masters over the centuries. The problem appears nonsensical and usually consists of a statement such as, "Listen to the sound of one hand clapping" or a question and answer:

Q: Has a dog the Buddha-nature?

A: *Mu!* ("Nothing," "none")

The *koan* is to be reflected on at all times—in sitting meditation, at work, and at night before sleep. It is meant to break open the mind, to cause a disjunction in the ordinary way of thinking and sensing, and thus to occasion a moment of egoless clarity or immediacy with life (*satori* or *kensho*, "seeing into one's own nature," "seeing things as they really are"). Each successive time that the disciple has a consultation with the master, he must show by word or deed his progress in "solving" the *koan*. The master may be harsh, shouting at the disciple or striking him with his hand or a stick. He strongly rejects the disciple until a breakthrough has occurred. Having solved one *koan,* the master gives the disciple another and another. [See Judaism pp. 422–27, Christianity pp. 500, 507, 519, Islam pp. 659–62, Hinduism pp. 752–53, Religions of China pp. 1032–34, and Religions of Japan pp. 1102, 1121–27, 1151 for discussion of meditation and mysticism.]

Every day there are periods of sitting meditation and work in the garden. On certain days each month (as above), the monks must make the food-collection rounds. Every fifth day of the month—the fourth, ninth, and so on—is a cleaning day. The monks shave each others' heads; bathe, assisted by others; and clean the monastery halls and sweep the compound. These activities are occasions for selfless service and the cultivation of humility. Menial tasks are frequently found to provide unexpected moments of clarity. The bathhouse and latrine each have a guardian spirit, enshrined therein, who is given special respect on cleaning days. The fourteenth and last days of the month are days of rest. The monks are permitted to sleep late, to enjoy wrestling or simply lounging about, and to partake of special food at lunchtime.

Sharing Merit

Frequently on food-collecting days, monks are invited to take a meal in the homes of lay patrons. These occasions are understood to bring merit to the patrons and their ancestors. Unlike the Theravada practice, where food offerings pass only from the laity to the monk, several times each year the Zen monks prepare and serve food to their patrons at the monastery. On the first and fifteenth day of every month, the monks visit the head temple of the sect and there chant in the Buddha-hall for the welfare of the nation. These dates are consistent with those on which Theravada monks chant the *Pratimoksha* or code of monastic discipline.

Sesshin

One week each month during the retreat portion of the term, the monks engage in daylong sitting and walking meditation (*zazen* and *kinhin*), punctuated by discourses (*teisho*) by the master and individual and group consultations with the master (*dokusan* and *sosan*). This special training week is called *sesshin* (literally, "to collect thoughts"). During *sesshin* the monks take their meals in the meditation hall. They leave the hall only for consultations with the master, to attend the master's discourses in the Dharma hall, and to go to the latrine. The laity are also welcome at these *sesshins,* as long as they are willing to follow the same rules as the monks.

Sitting meditation (*zazen*) is performed in forty-five minute segments, the time of the burning of an incense stick. It is begun and ended by the tinkle of a bell or the clap of woodblocks. There are fifteen-minute intervals between sittings. The practice is akin to the mindfulness meditation practiced in the

Theravada tradition, but in *zazen* it is simply sitting in a correct posture and intensely holding the *koan* before the mind. The posture of the body is described by an early master as follows:

> When one wishes to begin *zazen,* he places a thick cushion in a quiet place, wears his robe and belt loosely, and puts all things about him in good order. Then he sits with his legs crossed in the lotus position. First, one places the right foot over the left thigh, then the left foot over the right thigh; or, one may sit in a half-crossed sitting position, in which only the left foot rests upon the right thigh. Secondly, one places the right hand on the left foot, palm facing upward; then the left hand on the right palm so that the faces of the thumbs push against each other. Then, gradually, one raises the body, moving it backwards and forwards, to the left and to the right, to secure a balanced sitting posture for the body. . . . Keep ears and shoulders, nose and navel parallel to one another. The tongue should touch the upper jaw while both the lips and teeth are kept closed; the eyes should remain slightly open so that one avoids falling asleep. . . . Once the physical posture has been well-ordered, one should regulate the breath by pushing forward the abdomen.[58]

The sitting progresses in complete silence and ideally without any breaking of posture. A senior monk walks along the rows of meditators carrying "the encouraging stick" (*keisaku*), which he applies to the shoulders of those who are experiencing sleepiness or muscle soreness. He administers three whacks to each shoulder with the flat side of the stick. This is usually done by the request of the meditator and with compassion. The monks bow to each other before the stick is applied.

Four times each day there is opportunity for individual consultation (*dokusan*) with the master. This is voluntary but strongly encouraged, especially for beginners. The consultation is for encouragement, but often the master is

*Zen monk receiving a blow with "the encouraging stick" (*keisaku*) during meditation.*

rather harsh if no progress is notable and those who have not experienced what they consider an insight are hesitant to approach him. There are times of high tension, when senior monks physically force a junior to approach the master and receive his rebuke. Periodically, the master enters the *zendo* for an inspection and thereafter holds a group consultation (*sosan*). Each monk, in order of his time under the master, must approach and receive comment in the presence of the other monks. Every three hours the monks shift from sitting to a short period of walking meditation (*kinhin*). They walk slowly with the hands on the top of each other held tightly at the chest and their minds still working with the *koan*. Walking serves the purpose of stimulating the body as well as continuing the meditation. Now and then during the *sesshin,* the *roshi* will give a discourse on a text (*teisho*) to show its inner meaning. At the sound of the Dharma drum, the monks gather at the Dharma hall. After they are seated, the master enters with his attendants and offers incense to the founder of the monastery and to his own master (if he is no longer living). With each offering he prostrates himself three times, while the monks chant adoration to the *bodhisattva* Avalokiteshvara and recite the admonitions of one of the great past masters. When these preliminaries are concluded, the *roshi* seats himself in a high chair facing the Buddha-altar and reads a text. He then comments on the text with reference to his own experience. At the end of the discourse, the monks recite the "Four Great Vows" of the *bodhisattva* (as above).

In December, for one week prior to the Buddha's enlightenment day—celebrated in Japan on December 8—an especially rigorous *sesshin* is held in the Zen monastery. The monks sleep only for an hour or two each night and in a sitting position. It is considered particularly auspicious to attain insight (*kensho*) during this period.

Each three-month retreat period ends with the examination of each trainee in the quarters of the master. If the disciple is hoping to return for the next term, the *roshi* reviews his conduct thoroughly. In some cases, entrance to the next term is denied and this is effectively the end of the monk's training. No other monastery is likely to accept him once he has been turned away.

Periodic Observances and Celebrations

The monks change their robes twice a year, on July 1 and October 15. There is no particular ceremony associated with this act, such as the Kathin festival of the Theravada tradition. October 15 is also memorial day for Bodhidharma (in Japanese, Daruma), the great master who, according to tradition, brought Zen from India to China in the sixth century C.E. Monks as well as laity purchase Daruma dolls and the monks honor the sage with special chanting at the monastery. During the weeks of the autumn and spring equinoxes (September 20–26 and March 18–24), called Higan, some Zen monks undertake long begging tours to various parts of the country. Many of the great masters consider travel a good stimulant to heightened awareness. On the night of the winter solstice (December 21), monks have a sometimes wild party. Lay patrons bring food and wine to the monastery and there is singing, dancing, and general frivolity.

From July 15 to August 15, Japanese Buddhists celebrate Bon, a festival in which food is offered to the ancestors. The festival is believed to be inspired by an act of Maudgalyayana, the great disciple of the Buddha. According to the *Ullambana* (Jap., *Ura-bon*) *Sutra,* by his special powers Maudgalyayana was able to perceive that his mother was suffering as a hungry ghost. He gathered a large number of monks and together they offered bowls of rice to the mother to relieve her suffering. Zen monks are invited to the homes of their patrons to chant *sutras* to transfer merit to the family's ancestors. In addition, each day they chant in the Buddha-hall of the monastery and throw water in the air, inviting the spirits of the dead to come for food. On August 15, they offer large quantities of food and scatter rice and water. A tablet marked as dedicated "to all the departed spirits of the triple world" and flags bearing the names of Buddhas, *bodhisattvas,* gods, and demons are set up on the altar of the Buddha-hall, and all these beings are invited to the feast by the chanting of *dharanis (parittas)* and a prayer:

> It is desired that all the hungry ghosts inhabiting every corner of the worlds, filling the ten quarters, come to this place and partake of the pure food offered to them. You be filled with it, and when you are fully satisfied, you come here, and see to it that all sentient beings in turn are fed by you. It is also desired that by virtue of this magic food you shall be delivered from the pain you are suffering and be born in the heavens and visit as you will all the Pure Lands in the ten quarters; that you come to cherish the desire for Enlightenment, practice the life of Enlightenment, and in the life to come attain Buddhahood. It is again desired that you protect us days and nights so as to let us attain without hindrances the object of our lives. Whatever merit that is productive of this deed of feeding the hungry ones—let it be dedicated to the universal realization of the Supreme Enlightenment and let every being come speedily to the attainment of Buddhahood. This prayer is offered to all the Buddhas and *bodhisattvas* of the past, present, and future in all the ten quarters, and to Mahaprajnaparamita [The Great Perfection of Wisdom].[59]

At the start of the new year (January 1), Zen monks take three days rest from their normal discipline, but they also create auspicious vibrations for all beings by "reading" the entire corpus of *The Sutras of the Perfection of Wisdom* (six hundred volumes). They accomplish this over three days by reading the title of each *sutra* and the first and last few pages and then turning the volumes several times to the right and left between their hands. This is called *tendoku,* "reading by turning." The texts are written on a continuous sheet of paper, folded back on itself again and again to make pages. Thus they can be opened like a fan. With several monks at the same time chanting loudly and fanning texts back and forth in front of them, it is an impressive performance.

Japanese and Thai Monasticism: A Comparison

We can see a number of similarities and a number of differences between the practice of Rinzai Zen monks and that of the Theravada monks of Phraan Muan.

Zen monks do not pay formal attention to the ancient monastic code; even so, they live a highly disciplined style of life. They are celibate, live with a minimum of possessions—more or less the eight requisites—and cultivate a nonviolent reverence for life. As vegetarians, they practice a form of nonviolence that is not a concern of Theravada monks. They do not honor the prohibition against alcoholic drink or that concerning labor in the fields.

Zen monks give more serious attention to meditation than their Theravada counterparts. It should be noted, however, that significant numbers of the monks and laymen of Thailand and the other Theravada countries do engage in serious meditation, even if it is not so in Phraan Muan.

Although the Zen monks have fashioned a much more self-sufficient way of life than the monks of Phraan Muan, there is still significant dependence upon and interaction with the laity. They continue, in a variant form, the tradition of begging for food; indeed the large monasteries could not exist or survive without reliance on lay giving. The Zen monks' garden work is more significant as part of a self-discipline than as a way to provide food.

Within worldwide Buddhism, it is unique to Zen that the entire life activity of the monk is interpreted as meditation. Rather than separating sitting meditation from other aspects of the monk's life, all activities of the Zen training are conceived of and practiced as meditation—eating meditation, gardening meditation, sweeping meditation, and so forth. This is consistent with the Buddha's ideal of applied mindfulness, but it is not so thoroughly worked out in the Theravada tradition.

Zen monks share merit by the same instrumentalities and with the same understanding of the world of beings as the Theravada monks. Apart from the reference to all beings becoming Buddhas—a teaching peculiar to the Mahayana—the sentiment of the above-quoted prayer for Bon is fully shared by Theravada Buddhists. By the fact of less daily contact with the laity, there are fewer occasions for the Zen monk to share merit. And, of course, consistent with the Mahayana teaching that the way to enlightenment is equally open to laity and monks, there is less concern in Zen with sharing merit among human beings. [See Christianity pp. 502–4, 510, Islam pp. 659–62, Hinduism p. 772, Religions of China pp. 1004–5, 1009, 1033–34, 1056, and Religions of Japan p. 1102 for discussion of monasteries and monasticism.]

39
Conclusion

Trends in Twentieth-Century Buddhism

WE HAVE CONCENTRATED on long-established forms of Asian Buddhism. In closing, let us note some new developments in Asia and the current shape of Buddhism in America. Generally speaking, the main trend in twentieth-century Buddhism worldwide has been toward a more vigorous lay Buddhism. Buddhism has been revived in India with an essentially lay emphasis. Theravada monastic and lay leaders of Burma and Thailand have recently come to encourage the lay practice of meditation. In Japan, the laity have founded so-called New Religions. Buddhism in America, although inspired by Asian monks, is essentially a lay Buddhism.

India

Buddhism was revived in India in the late nineteenth century by a Sri Lankan monk, Anagarika Dharmapala, who in 1892 founded the Maha Bodhi Society for the restoration of the Buddhist shrines at Bodh Gaya. Dharmapala's society, headquartered in Calcutta, attracted attention to Buddhism but did not gain many converts. It was mainly an instrument for channeling gifts from around the Buddhist world for the renewal of Bodh Gaya.

According to the 1971 census of India, there were then almost four million Buddhists in India. Most of these were former Hindus belonging to the "untouchable" social classes. Three hundred thousand untouchables were converted to Buddhism in 1956 under the leadership of B. R. Ambedkar (1891–1956). Thereafter, although Ambedkar died within two months of his successful leadership, more than three million other untouchables joined the movement through mass conversions. Ambedkar, himself an untouchable, had managed nonetheless to get a college degree and a scholarship to Columbia University in New York, where he completed a Ph.D. As Minister of Law in the first government of India after independence, he chaired the committee that drafted the Indian constitution. Frustrated in his efforts to significantly change the Indian civil code, he left his government post and began organizing untouchables to throw off their social disabilities as Hindus by conversion to Buddhism. Ambedkar's Buddhism, informed by Theravada teachings and set forth in a book, *The Buddha and His Dhamma* [Dharma], emphasized a rational approach to life and striving for moral order and social equality. He argued that the Buddha and many of his disciples were non-Aryans and that Gautama was essentially a social reformer. The movement is largely a lay movement, although a Burmese Theravada monk initiated Ambedkar and today several Theravada monks are active in the community in teaching roles.

Southeast Asia

Historically, Indian monks were known for their scholarship as much or more than their achievements in meditation. The concern with scholarship was accentuated in Sri Lankan, Southeast Asian, and early Chinese Buddhism, with a corresponding deemphasis on meditation (in the case of Chinese Buddhism, one of the factors that prompted the rise of the Chan [Ch'an] or Meditation sect). Early in the twentieth century, monks of Burma (Myanmar) rediscovered and began propagating what they called "the simplified method" of mindfulness training taught by the Buddha. They encouraged lay as well as monastic disciples. Two of the lay disciples of Ledi Sayadaw (Burmese, *sayadaw;* Sanskrit, *maha-thera,* "most venerable elder monk") founded meditation centers.

The International Meditation Center at Rangoon, founded in 1952 by U Ba Khin, has come to attract foreigners as well as Burmese Buddhists. Here, lay men and women enroll for intensive, short periods of training, much like the *sesshins* of Zen practice in Japan. The Sasana Yeiktha Center of Rangoon, founded by the monk Mahasi Sayadaw in 1949, has also come into prominence as a center for lay as well as monastic meditation. This center has spawned more than one hundred branches in Myanmar, Sri Lanka, and Thailand.

Jinarakkhita Thera, an Indonesian monk and disciple of Mahasi Sayadaw, was responsible for the revival of Buddhism in Indonesia in the late 1950s. The small but active movement continues to grow, taking inspiration not only from the Theravada but also from the ancient Mahayana (especially Tantrayana) Buddhism that built the great Borobudur *stupa* on the island of Java in the ninth century.

Japan

The most notable of the New Religions or rather, in the case of specifically Buddhist developments, the "re-newing" religious movements of Japan is the Nichiren Shoshu Soka Gakkai, "The Value Creation Society of the Nichiren True Sect." Founded in 1937 by an elementary school principal, Tsunesaburo Makiguchi, Soka Gakkai appeals to the teachings of the thirteenth-century monk Nichiren (1222–1282). Nichiren taught that the *Lotus Sutra* (*The Sutra of the Lotus of the True Dharma*) embodied the only true Buddhism and that simply praising the *sutra* by chanting its name in faith would result in power and prosperity for worldly life as well as the realization of Buddha-nature. Makiguchi advocated the daily worship of the *Lotus Sutra* by chanting the formula (*daimoku*) *Namu Myoho Renge Kyo,* "Homage to the Sutra of the Lotus of the True Dharma," before a scroll bearing the name of the *sutra* (*gohonzon*). Soka Gakkai came to prominence shortly after World War II, under the leadership of its second president, Josei Toda, and with appeal especially to people of the working classes. In the spirit of Nichiren, who declared all other religions, including other forms of Buddhism, to be false, Toda encouraged aggressive proselytization toward the eventual conversion of the world with a united Nichiren Buddhist Japan as its center. Its membership grew rapidly. Under the leadership of Daisaku Ikeda from 1960, it spawned a political party, the Komeito, "Clean Government Party," in Japan and founded propagation centers in other parts of the world, most successfully in North and South America. Today, Soka Gakkai claims more than sixteen million members in Japan and several hundred thousand in other countries. Its great temple center, Taisekiji, south of Tokyo near Mount Fuji, is the object of pilgrimage by several million devotees each year. Its emphasis on the power of the word of the Buddha is characteristically Buddhist; its aggressive style and heavy emphasis on power for worldly prosperity are innovative.

Buddhism in America

All of the major traditions of Asian Buddhism—Pure Land, Zen, and Nichiren Mahayana; Theravada and Tibetan Tantrayana—have a following in the United States. Indeed, one can find a list of "Buddhist churches" in the yellow pages of the telephone directories of most major cities. It is estimated that there are about five hundred thousand American Buddhists, mostly of non-Asian descent, active in more than three hundred places of worship and meditation.

Pure Land

Pure Land Buddhism was brought to Hawaii and the west coast of the United States by Chinese and Japanese immigrants in the late nineteenth century. Missionaries from Kyoto, Japan, brought the True Pure Land (Jodo Shinshu) Buddhism, founded by the followers of Shinran Shonin (1173–1262), to prominence among the Japanese-American population in the early 1900s. In 1944, the temples of this sect organized as the Buddhist Churches of America (BCA) with headquarters in San Francisco. This was the beginning of a gradual separation from the head temple in Kyoto. The clergy of the American Pure Land continued to receive their ministerial education in Japan until 1966, when the Institute of Buddhist Studies was established in Berkeley, California. The BCA has a current membership of approximately fifty thousand, consisting mostly of Americans of Japanese descent.

As in Japan, Pure Land in America is a lay movement led by nonmonastic clergy. Unlike the practice of Pure Land in Japan, where worship of Amida is centered in the home and the temple is the locus only for special memorial rites and festivals, American Pure Land worship is centered around weekly (Sunday morning) congregational services at the temple. These services consist chiefly of chanting the *nembutsu,* singing hymns in praise of Amida's power and grace, and listening to a sermon.

Zen

Zen Buddhism was first brought to note in the United States by the Japanese *roshi* Soyen Shaku, who spoke to the World Parliament of Religions, which met in Chicago in 1893 in conjunction with the World's Fair. Impressed by the number of Americans who expressed interest in Zen, upon return to Japan, Soyen dispatched several of his disciples to propagate Zen in the United States. Two of these disciples established Zen centers in San Francisco. A third, D. T. Suzuki, went to work for Open Court Publishing Company in Illinois and published numerous books on Zen. Suzuki's writings and lectures paved the way for a number of other Japanese masters to visit the United States, some of whom remained long enough to gather a significant number of disciples and establish strong meditation centers. There is no accurate count of the number of American Zen centers or their total membership. They belong to both the Rinzai and Soto traditions; some have farms and mountain monasteries in addition to their city meditation halls; some have branches, but they are not nationally organized. They exist primarily to teach meditation, and for the most part, they follow the traditional Japanese method and chant in Japanese. Older centers under the leadership of teachers or *roshis* of non-Japanese descent, such as the Zen Center of Rochester, New York, founded by Philip Kapleau in 1966 and the Shasta Abbey in California, founded by the British-born woman Jiyu Kennett, are beginning to fashion an "American Zen"; for example, they require less rigorous discipline and permit chanting in English and the use of knives and forks rather than chopsticks.

Nichiren

A chapter of Nichiren Shoshu Soka Gakkai, under the leadership of its third president, Daisaku Ikeda, was established in California in 1960. Initially its appeal was chiefly to Japanese Americans. In the late 1960s, under the Japanese leadership of Masayasu Sadanaga, who changed his name to George M. Williams, the American chapter reorganized independent of the Japanese center, as Nichiren Shoshu of America, and began aggressively seeking converts among Americans generally. Today, there are more than three hundred chapters throughout the United States, with a combined membership of more than three hundred thousand. The focus of Nichiren Shoshu of America is on promoting self-respect and material well-being through recitation of the *daimoku,* a formula paying homage to the *Lotus Sutra.* The "church" has emotional but no formal ties to the parent society in Japan and its members are encouraged to be patriotic Americans. [See Religions of Africa pp. 25, 54–57, 79–82, Religions of Mesoamerica p. 240, Native Religions of North America pp. 287, 320–22, 357–58,

Judaism pp. 427–31, 456–75, Christianity pp. 529–33, Islam pp. 698–700, Hinduism pp. 770–74, 828–31, Religions of China pp. 998–1002, 1055–59, and Religions
of Japan pp. 1132–33, 1163–72 for discussion of new religious movements.]

Theravada

Theravada Buddhism has not attracted a significant following in the United
States. Since 1966, Sri Lankan and Thai monks have been active in the country
and have established meditation centers and temples in several U.S. cities, but
the number of supporters of these centers is small and consists mostly of recent
refugees from Southeast Asia. Nonetheless, the number of Cambodian refugees,
most of whom are Theravada Buddhists, is significant and still growing.

Tibetan Mahayana

In 1950 the Chinese army occupied Tibet, pursuing a policy in strong opposition to the traditional way of life. Revolt and suppression in 1959 led to the
flight of some eighty thousand Tibetans into Nepal and India. A number of these
refugees emigrated to Europe and the United States, among them several
learned and accomplished Buddhist masters. Two of these masters, Chogyam
Trungpa Tulku and Tarthang Tulku, have gathered a large number of disciples
in the United States and have established several centers for study and meditation. Chogyam Trungpa's largest center is in Boulder, Colorado. One of its
branch organizations, the Naropa Institute, has recently become accredited to
offer graduate degrees in Buddhist studies. Trungpa died April 4, 1987. Tarthang
Tulku is based in Berkeley, California. Both of these masters have published
extensively and have built strong organizations emphasizing study and meditation as cornerstones of the lay life.

The future of Buddhism in America is uncertain. Pure Land Buddhism
appeals mainly to Americans of Japanese descent. Meditation Buddhism—Zen
and Tibetan Mahayana—has had appeal to a relatively small number of highly
educated Americans. Nichiren Buddhism has attracted a mixed clientele largely
of persons who are "down and out" or who feel disenfranchised or alienated
from the mainstream of American life. It is clear that the teaching of the Buddha, viewed as a highly rational approach to life, and one or another of several
varieties of meditation are appealing to many Americans. The very presence of
Buddhist meditation centers and temples and the availability of a large literature
on Buddhism have influenced American Christians and Jews to search their
own heritage for resources by which to encourage the contemplative life. In the
past few years, Christian and Buddhist leaders have initiated a lively dialogue on
meditation and prayer. In terms of sheer numbers of adherents—the three hundred and fifty thousand of a total of five hundred thousand Americans involved
in Pure Land and Nichiren Buddhism—it is also clear that devotional Buddhism
appeals to many Americans. Pure Land and Nichiren have the potential by their
simplicity, and as shown by their success in Japan, of engaging the working
classes.

Concluding Reflections

In its more than twenty-five hundred years Buddhism has become many things to many people. With a few exceptions such as Nichiren Buddhism, it is a notably tolerant, flexible, inclusive religion. It has assimilated spirit cults in Southeast Asia and Tibet, accommodated to highly sophisticated traditions (Confucianism and Daoism) in China, and established itself as a complement to Shinto in Japan. It has permitted a wide gamut of belief and practice under its banner. Zen and Theravada, although part of two different cultural streams (Chinese-Japanese and Indian) and two different traditions of Buddhism, are not far removed from each other. On the other hand, one may wonder how Pure Land and Zen could be part of the same religion, let alone of the same tradition within that religion.

In general, the inclusivity of Buddhism is rooted in the Buddha's emphasis on practice rather than correct belief, morality rather than formality, and non-violence. It is rooted in the Buddha's emphasis on subjectively constructed rather than objectively given reality. He considered the merit or demerit of a belief or practical method in terms of psychological function rather than consistency with an objective norm. The teaching that the world is a product of karma places the onus of behavior ultimately on the individual.

The wide variance of belief and practice within Buddhism is permitted by the dual focus of Buddhism from its beginning: on self-power through self-discipline and reliance on other-power through offerings, invocation, and worship. The Buddha "married" these foci in teaching the mutual dependency of monk and society. This marriage remained intact in the Theravada tradition. The bond was loosened in the Mahayana by its advocacy of the career of the *bodhisattva*—a being for others—and therefrom, by its projection of a store of merit into the heavens in the form of celestial Buddhas and *bodhisattvas*. Belief in a store of merit, unconditioned by the exigencies of time and space with direct and simple access to all believers, took some of the onus of merit making and sharing off of the monk. And, it permitted the development of lay Buddhisms independent of the Sangha.

Each of the varieties of Buddhism has defined itself by emphasis on one or the other of these foci, in some cases to the exclusion of the other of the two poles. We may consider this in terms of their use of the Three Treasures. Pure Land Buddhism focuses on the Buddha not as a guide but as a savior. Zen focuses on the Dharma as essentially meditation—an instrument of enlightenment. Nichiren appeals to the Dharma as power not as the result of practice but by simple invocation. Theravada Buddhism centers itself on the Sangha.

We began this study with the observation that Buddhism is the pursuit of worldly prosperity, rebirth in heaven, and ultimately nirvana by the making and sharing of merit. Early Western scholars of Buddhism characterized the religion as world denying, essentially pessimistic toward life. Working solely from texts rather than with an awareness of living Buddhism, and even then failing to see the full import of the texts, they generalized from the Buddha's central emphasis on renunciation (monasticism) toward the goal of nirvana. We can see that this is a distortion of Buddhism in theory as well as practice. In both theory and practice, and from its very beginning, Buddhism is, in fact, strongly world affirming. Indeed nirvana, the ultimate goal, is the negation of worldly existence conditioned by karma. But worldly existence for Buddhism is the instrument for the achievement of nirvana as well as the context of suffering. Specifically, in the Buddha's path to nirvana, worldly prosperity and the opportunity for rebirth, along with renunciation, are the means; they are the short-range goals and, indeed, the effective functional goals of most Buddhist striving. Social harmony and the accumulation of wealth are strongly and positively motivated by the fact that their existence is indicative of past merit and the foundation for present merit making. For most Buddhists, meditation as well as morality are effectively motivated by the desire for wealth, status, and social harmony. This is inspired by the Buddha's teaching concerning the mutual dependency of monk and society; it is not simply the way Buddhism came to function because nirvana was an abstraction—a too-distant goal—for the average person.

The Mahayana enhanced a positive attitude toward the world with its restatement of the goal as the realization of emptiness, the realization of unity—oneness—through compassion apprehending the world as itself, Buddha-nature. Zen Mahayana, influenced by the naturalism of Daoism (Taoism) as well as this Mahayana interpretation of the Dharma, came to see the mundane world as, in every respect, the arena of meditation. In Zen, enlightenment is easy, egoless flow or harmony with nature; it is here and now and does not look beyond this world. By reason of the Mahayana emphasis on merit-for-others of those who have realized emptiness, Pure Land Buddhists strive in life-affirming works of compassion out of gratitude for Amida's assurance of release from suffering by rebirth in the Blessed Land. Nichiren Buddhists push the nirvana of world negation into the background in unabashed favor of worldly prosperity through the power of the Dharma.

While the great majority of present-day Buddhists follow a devotional path, the distinctiveness of Buddhism among the world's religions lies in its psychoanalytical/meditative approach to the solution of human problems. Indeed, Pure Land and Nichiren Buddhism would make no sense apart from the assumption of the Buddha's conquest of suffering and accumulation of merit by means of meditation. It is significant to the survival of Buddhism through the centuries that meditation and monasticism, the traditional context for the practice of meditation, have always been part of the tradition. Likewise, the current emphasis on lay meditation in Theravada Asia and the popularity of Zen in various parts of the world are important to the survival of Buddhism in the future.

Study Questions

Before you begin to read this part, take a mental inventory of what you know and think about Buddhism. What images do you have of Buddhism and Buddhist practices? What countries, cultures, and peoples do you associate with Buddhism? What would you imagine Buddhism to be like? Keep these images and things in mind as you read this section and develop new notions about Buddhism.

CHAPTER 35

Introduction

1. Why does the author say "There is no single Buddhism but many Buddhisms"?
2. What is the common framework for all the variants of Buddhism?
3. What is the relationship between monks and laypeople in Buddhism?
4. How are suffering, karma, and nirvana related in the Buddhist worldview?
5. What are the Three Jewels/Treasures in Buddhism?
6. How do the Four Noble Truths sum up the Buddhist insight into human life?
7. On the basis of reading chapter 35, how would you explain Buddhism to a friend?

CHAPTER 36

The Historical Development of Buddhism

1. What were the general social and religious trends at the time of Siddhartha Gautama?
2. What was the "Gautama's innovation" in religion? What did Gautama hold in common with Brahmanism and Jainism, and how did Gautama's religious teaching differ from Brahmanism and Jainism?
3. How did "monks and laity" follow the religious teachings of the Buddha?
4. What kinds of people became "early disciples," and how did they practice Buddhism"?
5. How did monks fashion an elaborate code of behavior and an administrative structure for communal living?
6. What were the conditions of ordination in early Buddhism?
7. How did early Buddhism have "greater potential" for mass support than either Brahmanism or Jainism? How did Buddhist practices give these early followers "power"?
8. What was the relationship of Buddhism to political authority from 250 B.C.E. to 300 C.E.? How did monasteries and *stupas* become developed during this time?

9. Compare and contrast Theravada Buddhism (especially the *arhat* ideal) and Mahayana Buddhism (especially the *bodhisattva* ideal).
10. What were the conditions of the "final flowering and decline (of Buddhism) in India"?
11. What kinds of persons were responsible for the spread of Buddhism?
12. How was Buddhism accepted by most Asian cultures? How did China present an exception to the general Asian acceptance of Buddhism?

CHAPTER 37
Buddhism as a Unified System of Beliefs and Practices

1. Identify/define each of the forms of power Buddhism offers people. How do each of the Three Treasures—Buddha, Dharma, and Sangha—represent the power of Buddhism?
2. How does Buddhism interpret "the world as constituted by power"? What does it mean to have faith or "take refuge" in Buddha, Dharma, and Sangha?
3. List the various terms by which the author describes or identifies the Buddha; how would you sum up all these terms?
4. What are the "Great Events" of the Buddha's life? Retell each of the great events in your own words.
5. Compare and contrast the Theravada and Mahayana visions of the Buddha.
6. Why does the author say the Four Noble Truths are not theories or divine revelation but experiential realization?
7. How does Buddhism interpret the problem of life as suffering?
8. How does Buddhism interpret desire as the cause of suffering?
9. How does Buddhism interpret the cessation of desire as nirvana?
10. How does Buddhism employ the Eightfold Path as the means of realizing nirvana?
11. Compare and contrast the path of the *bodhisattva* in Mahayana and the path of the *arhat* in Theravada.
12. What is "the power of Dharma as sound"?
13. What is the significance of the precepts and ordination in Theravada? Compare and contrast Theravada monks and Zen monks.
14. In Buddhism, what does it mean to say that "merit is made and shared" through ritual?
15. What are the yearly festivals of Buddhism, how are they celebrated, and what are the religious benefits of these celebrations?

CHAPTER 38
The Dynamics of the Buddhist Life

1. What are the general conditions of life in the village of Phraan Muan?
2. Who are the major human and spiritual inhabitants of Phraan Muan?

3. How is monastery life central to all young Thai men, and how does monastery life penetrate the village and home? How do women relate to monks and the ministry? What are the roles of string and water in the rituals?
4. Identify the key symbols and actions in the ordination of a Thai young man —how does ordination benefit the family and village?
5. Compare the marriage rite with the ordination rite.
6. Identify the key symbols and actions in death rites.
7. Note the three patterns (agricultural endeavor, great events, and major transition points in the Sangha) in the yearly round of communal rites and festivals. What are the main symbols and actions in these rites/festivals?
8. Now that you have read this section on Thai Buddhism, interpret the statement that "the central feature of life in Phraan Muan is making and sharing merit."
9. What are the general conditions of religious practice in the training of a Zen monk?
10. Trace the daily routine of a Zen monk, both in ordinary matters and in meditation.
11. What are the requirements for participating in *sesshin?*
12. What are the periodic observations and obligations performed by Zen monks?
13. Compare and contrast Japanese and Thai monasticism.

CHAPTER 39

Conclusion

1. Summarize the practice and vitality of Buddhism in India, Southeast Asia, Japan, and America.
2. How does the author handle the unity and diversity of Buddhism through twenty-five hundred years and many cultures? How does he balance:

   self-power and other-power

   renunciation and world affirming

   emptiness and prosperity

   devotion and meditation?

Recall the mental inventory of Buddhist images and practices that you made before reading this part. What is there in Buddhist religion that is most like your own religion? What in Buddhist religion is most unlike your own tradition? What is most interesting? How has your understanding of Buddhism changed as a result of reading this part? Can you now imagine yourself participating in Buddhism?

Notes

This work is dedicated to my wife, Donna, my first-level editor. I thank her for putting up with and graciously helping me through the moments of frustration and lack of clarity. I am also grateful to H. Byron Earhart, the general editor of this book and my second-level critic, for his patient and penetrating critique and kindly advice. I commend the several editors at HarperSanFrancisco for their careful, well-informed work in finalizing the manuscript for publication.

1. *Majjhima Nikaya* I.247–49, as found in Edward J. Thomas, *The Life of the Buddha as Legend and History* (London: Routledge & Kegan Paul, 1949), 67–68.
2. *Itivuttaka* 111, as found in Heinz Bechert and Richard Gombrich, *The World of Buddhism: Buddhist Monks and Nuns in Society and Culture* (New York: Facts on File, 1984), 53.
3. *Digha Nikaya* iii.191, in *Dialogues of the Buddha,* trans. T. W. and C. A. F. Rhys Davids, vol. 4, *Sacred Books of the Buddhists* (London: Luzac, 1965), P. III, p. 183.
4. *Majjhima Nikaya* 1.37, in *The Collection of The Middle Length Sayings,* trans. I. B. Horner, Pali Text Society Translation Series, no. 29 (London: Luzac, 1976), vol. 1, p. 47.
5. *Vinaya Pitaka, Mahavagga* I.11, in *Vinaya Texts,* trans. T. W. Rhys Davids and Hermann Oldenberg, vol. 12, *Sacred Books of the East* (London: Clarendon, 1881), P. I, pp. 112–13.
6. T. W. Rhys Davids, trans., *Buddhist Suttas,* vol. 11, *Sacred Books of the East* (Oxford: Clarendon, 1881), 6–7.
7. *Vinaya Pitaka, Mahavagga* I.78, *Vinaya Texts,* 235–36.
8. Ibid., I.6.32, 99.
9. Ibid., I.54.3, 209.
10. *Buddhist Suttas,* 93–94.
11. Ibid., 91.
12. N. A. Nikam and Richard McKeon, ed. and trans., *The Edicts of Asoka* (Chicago: University of Chicago, 1959), 58.
13. Ibid., 34.
14. D. D. Kosambi, *Ancient India* (New York: Pantheon Books, 1965), 176–77.
15. *The Dhammapada* I.1, trans. F. Max Müller, vol. 10, *Sacred Books of the East* (Oxford: Clarendon, 1898), 3–4.
16. *Buddhist Suttas,* 26–27.
17. *Puggala-pannatti* VI.1, in *Designation of Human Types,* trans., Bimala Charan Law, Pali Text Society Translation Series, no. 12 (London: Luzac, 1979), 97.
18. *Dialogues of the Buddha,* Pt. I, p. 289.
19. Ibid., Pt. III, p. 127.
20. Edward Conze, et al., eds., *Buddhist Texts Through the Ages* (New York: Harper & Row, 1964), 105.
21. Henry Clarke Warren, trans., *Buddhism in Translations* (New York: Atheneum, 1984), 35.
22. Ibid., 44.
23. Ibid, 76.
24. Ibid., 76–77.

25. Ibid., 81.
26. Thomas, *The Life of the Buddha,* 81.
27. *Vinaya Texts,* Pt. I, pp. 86–87.
28. Warren, *Buddhism in Translations,* 92.
29. *Buddhist Suttas,* 116.
30. *Vinaya Texts,* Pt. I, p. 91.
31. H. Kern, trans., *Saddharma-Pundarika or The Lotus of the True Law,* vol. 21, *Sacred Books of the East* (Oxford: Clarendon, 1884), 298–302.
32. Ibid., 413–16.
33. *Vinaya Texts,* Pt. 1, p. 95.
34. Thera Nanamoli, trans., *The Path of Purification* (Columbo: Semage, 1956), 256.
35. *Vinaya Texts,* Pt. I, p. 95.
36. Ibid.
37. *Anguttara Nikaya* III.55, in *The Book of the Gradual Sayings,* trans. F. L. Woodward, Pali Text Society Translation Series, no. 24 (London: Luzac, 1973), 79.
38. Nanamoli, *The Path of Purification,* 587.
39. *Vinaya Texts,* Pt. I, pp. 95–96.
40. Thera Nanaponika, *The Heart of Buddhist Meditation* (New York: Weiser, 1971), 117.
41. Ibid., 118.
42. *Dialogues of the Buddha,* Pt. I, p. 70.
43. Thera Nanaponika, *The Heart of Buddhist Meditation,* 130.
44. Ibid., 164.
45. William Theodore De Bary, ed., *The Buddhist Tradition* (New York: Modern Library, 1969), 81–82.
46. Ibid., 371.
47. *Vinaya Texts,* Pt. III, p. 75–77.
48. S. J. Tambiah, *Buddhism and the Spirit Cults in North-east Thailand* (Cambridge: Cambridge University Press, 1970), 222.
49. This account is based on Tambiah, *Buddhism and the Spirit Cults.* Tambiah's study of the village of Phraan Muan spans the period 1961–1966; all references to the present are to 1966.
50. Tambiah, *Buddhism and the Spirit Cults,* 216.
51. Ibid., 208.
52. This account is based on Daisetz Teitaro Suzuki, *The Training of the Zen Buddhist Monk* (New York: University Books, 1965) and Bardwell Smith, ed., *Unsui: A Diary of Zen Monastic Life* (Honolulu: University Press of Hawaii, East-West Center, 1973).
53. Daisetz Teitaro Suzuki, *Manual of Zen Buddhism* (New York: Grove Press, 1960), 26.
54. Suzuki, *Training of the Zen Buddhist Monk,* 145.
55. Smith, *Unsui,* no. 28.
56. Suzuki, *Training of the Zen Buddhist Monk,* 146.
57. Smith, *Unsui,* no. 11.
58. Ibid., no. 53.
59. Suzuki, *Training of the Zen Buddhist Monk,* 81–82.

Glossary

Amitabha Buddha (Chin., Ami-duo-fo [A-mi-to-fo]; Jap., Amida Butsu) "The Buddha of Endless Light," founder of the Pure Land heaven, which may be reached by faith.

anatman "No-self," no unchanging soul or self-nature; one of the three characteristics of existence: impermanence, suffering, and no-self.

arhat "The holy one," one who has conquered all lust, hatred, and delusion; one who has conquered suffering and rebirth by following the Eightfold Path.

Avalokiteshvara (Chin., Guan-yin [Kuan-yin]; Jap., Kannon) "The Lord Who (Kindly) Looks Down," the *bodhisattva* of endless compassion who protects those who call on him in circumstances of great danger or when desirous of childbirth. Originally male, this celestial being is female in Chinese and Japanese Buddhism.

bodhi "Enlightenment," seeing things as they really are, the full realization of the Four Noble Truths that results in nirvana.

bodhisattva "A being striving for enlightenment"; in the Theravada, the term applies to the Buddha during his many lives preceding enlightenment and to Maitreya, the one who is yet striving and who will appear on earth as a Buddha at some future time. In the Mahayana, the term applies to all those earthly and heavenly beings who are striving toward enlightenment and, most significantly, who are striving for the welfare of other beings, that is, those who are dedicated to sharing their merit with others.

brahmana Priest of ancient Aryan religion and later Hinduism, a member of the highest caste; in Buddhist scriptures the term sometimes refers to any morally upright and learned person who is, therefore, worthy of respect and gifts.

Brahmanism An ancient religion of India, under the leadership of priests (*brahmanas*) who believed that their performance of fire rituals maintained the world and brought prosperity to human life; Hinduism is largely based on Brahmanism.

Buddha "Awakened One," "Enlightened One," the title of the historical founder of Buddhism—Siddhartha Gautama; the Theravada tradition recognizes Gautama Buddha as the one and only Buddha for the present age and as one who has come and gone; the Mahayana recognizes numerous living Buddhas and uses the title "Shakyamuni" (sage of the Shakya Tribe) to distinguish Gautama from other Buddhas, such as Amitabha and Vairocana.

Dalai Lama "Ocean Lama," in the Tibetan tradition a spiritual teacher who is an "ocean" of wisdom and compassion; the spiritual leader of Tibetan Buddhists, once also the ruler of Tibet.

dana "Giving/charity"; good deeds.

dependent origination The phrase designating the causal connection between moments arising and decaying in the endless process of life; the formula of dependent origination explains the cause and effect pattern of twelve factors that characterize ego-ridden existence.

dharani "That which holds (power)," words spoken by a Buddha that, when invoked, have the power to bless and protect the invoker. The Mahayana equivalent of *paritta.*

Dharma "That which is firmly established," the Doctrine and Path taught by the Buddha.

duhkha "Suffering, unsatisfactoriness, the state of being ill-at-ease," one of the three factors or characteristics of existence (impermanence, suffering, being without self).

Eight Precepts The moral precepts to be kept by the laity on Observance days; in addition to the Five Precepts (see below): not taking food after noon, not watching or participating in public entertainments, and not adorning the body.

Eightfold Path The middle path between worldliness and asceticism taught by the Buddha; the discipline of morality and meditation by which one gains the wisdom that results in nirvana.

elder (*Thera*) senior monk; when used in reference to the laity, it designates an older, respected member of the community.

Five Precepts The five moral precepts to be kept by all Buddhists, although with different levels of rigor for the laity than for the monks and nuns: no violence, no sexual misconduct, no stealing, no lying, and no partaking of alcoholic beverages.

Four Noble Truths The basic and essential teaching of the Buddha: (1) that there is suffering; (2) that suffering is caused by desire; (3) that the cessation of suffering (nirvana) is possible; (4) that the Eightfold Path is the way to the cessation of suffering.

Hinayana "The Little Vehicle, the Narrow Path," the term used by Mahayana (Great Vehicle) Buddhists to designate traditions of Buddhism such as the Theravada, which teach monasticism as the only way to nirvana.

Jainism A religion of India founded by Mahavira, a contemporary of the Buddha; Mahavira taught that nonviolence and asceticism were ways to overcome suffering and death.

karma "Action," the consequence or residual energy created by action—particularly, human thoughts, words, and deeds. Karma may be meritorious or demeritorious and causes desirable or undesirable rebirth.

lama A master or spiritual guide in Tibetan Buddhism, usually, but not always, a monk.

Mahayana "The Great Vehicle, the Wide Path," the Buddhist tradition emphasizing that the way to enlightenment and nirvana is open to all, by means of the merit of Buddhas and *bodhisattvas* as well as monastic discipline.

Maitreya "The friendly one, the benevolent one," the celestial *bodhisattva* who now resides in a heaven, whence he blesses those who call upon him; he will come to earth as the Buddha of the next age.

Mara "Death," the name of the personification of desires that lead to repeated suffering and death; Mara was definitively subdued by the Buddha as the latter came to enlightenment beneath the great tree near Gaya.

nembutsu "Thinking of the Buddha" (Jap.), the formulaic chant or thought—*namu Amida Butsu*—by which Japanese Pure Land Buddhists express devotion to Amida Buddha.

nirvana "Blowing out" (the fires of lust, hatred, and delusion), the cessation of suffering, freedom from rebirth.

paritta "Protection (-formula)," words spoken by the Buddha and later by monks that, when invoked, have the power to bless and protect. The Theravada equivalent of *dharani.*

prajna "Wisdom," the wisdom that results from moral and mental discipline and leads to enlightenment and nirvana.

prajna-paramita "The perfection of wisdom," in the Mahayana, the wisdom sought by *bodhisattvas* and possessed by Buddhas, by which they see all, know all, hear all, and shed compassion on all beings. This wisdom is the subject of the *Prajna-paramita Sutras* ("Perfection of Wisdom Discourses").

Pratimoksha "That which is preparatory to freedom from desire"; code of unity, code of discipline, the code of rules to be kept by monks and nuns of the higher or full ordination. In Theravada Buddhism, the monks are committed to recite this code in unison on the new and full moons of each month.

Pure Land (San., Sukhavati; Chin., Jing-tu [Ching-t'u]; Jap., Jodo) The paradise established by Amitabha Buddha by reason of his great merit and out of his compassion for suffering beings, who, by faith, may enter his paradise at death. Also, the name of one sect of Mahayana Buddhism that, in Japan, has two major sub-sects: Jodo and Jodo Shinshu ("True Pure Land").

rain-retreat The four months (mid-June to mid-October) of the rainy season when Theravada monks remain in the monastery and intensify their discipline and study. Lay Theravadins are more devout in giving and more rigorous in attendance of Observance Day rituals during this period.

relic The ashes, bones, or personal effects of the Buddha or an *arhat,* impounded in a *stupa.*

roshi "Venerable teacher/master," (Jap.), a Zen master.

samadhi The term is used in both a narrow and a general sense; designating one of the eight elements of the Eightfold Path it means "concentration"; collectively designating one threefold dimension of the Eightfold Path—right effort, right mindfulness, and right concentration—it means "mental discipline" or "meditation."

samsara "Wandering through (lives)," the round of repeated births and deaths caused by karma.

Sangha "Community"; in ordinary usage, the term designates the order or community of monks following the way of the Buddha.

Shakyamuni "The sage of the Shakya Tribe." See also Buddha.

shunya "Empty, devoid of"; the fleeting phenomenal world is said to be empty—devoid of any substantial, unchanging self-nature. The Mahayana uses the term to emphasize both the lack of self in beings and the lack of substantiality in the natural world. Enlightenment is the realization of the emptiness (*shunyata*) of the self and world.

sila "Morality," the term designating the threefold dimension of the Eightfold Path including right speech, conduct, and livelihood.

smriti (Pali, *sati*) "Mindfulness"; the clarity of mind attained through meditation that leads to the cessation of desire and the achievement of nirvana.

stupa A memorial mound or monument, ideally encasing a relic of the Buddha or an *arhat,* and therefore a place where a devotee or meditator may experience the power of the one commemorated by the mound.

sutra "Discourses"; a text embodying the words of the Buddha.

Tantrayana "The vehicle of (specialized) ritual," a subdevelopment of the Mahayana in which highly technical rituals are the special means to enlightenment. A *tantra* is a ritual manual and, by extension, the term designates the rituals prescribed in the manual.

Tathagata One who has "Thus-come" or "Thus-gone" the way of a Buddha; a perfectly enlightened being. This is the way that Gautama referred to himself after his enlightenment.

Ten Precepts The precepts undertaken by a novice upon ordination to the monastic life; in addition to the Eight Precepts (see above), a novice vows not to use a high, comfortable bed and not to use money.

Theravada "The Way of the Elders," the tradition of Buddhism whose followers believe they are following the original ("Elder's Way") Buddhism and in which senior monks (*theras*) hold primary authority in matters pertaining to the Buddha's way.

Threefold Refuge The formula recited by Buddhists to affirm their commitment to the Three Treasures.

Three Jewels/Treasures The Buddha, the Dharma, and the Sangha, the three valued resources of Buddhist belief and practice.

Tripitaka (Pali, *Tipitaka*) "The Three Baskets," the threefold text embodying the Buddha's teachings and authoritative interpretations of these teachings; the canon of Buddhist sacred writings.

Zen (Sanskrit, *dhyana;* Chin., Chan [Ch'an]) "Meditation"; the term designates the Japanese meditation sect of Mahayana Buddhism.

The Scriptures of Buddhism

The earliest written accounts of the life and teachings of the Buddha were formulated in both Sanskrit and a dialect of Sanskrit that came to be known as Pali. Monks of the Mahayana tradition used Sanskrit and those of the Theravada tradition used Pali. The Sanskrit version is called *Tripitaka* and the Pali version *Tipitaka*, both terms meaning "The Three Baskets." The baskets, or collections, are called *Sutra/Sutta, Vinaya,* and *Abhidharma/Abhidhamma.* The content of the first two baskets in the two versions is very much the same; that of the third baskets significantly differs, reflecting the differing doctrines of the two traditions. The quotations from "The Three Baskets" in this part are taken from translations of the Theravada *Tipitaka,* which is outlined below.

In addition to the *Tipitaka,* the Theravada tradition recognizes the *Milinda-panha* and the *Visuddhimagga* as authoritative treatises on the Buddha's teachings. The Mahayana recognizes a large number of texts besides the *Tripitaka,* some of which Mahayana Buddhists consider of greater importance than the early threefold collection. The more important of these are detailed below.

THE THERAVADA TEXTS

Tipitaka ("Three Baskets")

Sutta Pitaka ("Basket of Discourses")

1. Digha-nikaya ("Division of Long Discourses")
2. Majjhima-nikaya ("Division of Middle-length Discourses")
3. Samyutta-nikaya ("Division of Connected Discourses")
4. Anguttara-nikaya ("Division of Gradual Discourses")
5. Khuddaka-nikaya ("Division of Little Discourses")

Vinaya Pitaka ("Basket of Discipline")

1. Sutta-vibhanga ("Division of Rules")—this is the *Patimokkha* (Sanskrit, *Pratimoksha*)—the Code of Discipline
2. Khandhaka ("Sections")
   a. Mahavagga ("Great Group" of disciplines for the monastic life)
   b. Cullavagga ("Small Group")
3. Parivara ("Summaries")

Abhidhamma Pitaka ("Basket of Higher Teachings")

1. Dhamma-sangani ("Enumeration of Dhammas")
2. Vibhanga ("Divisions")
3. Dhatu-katha ("Discussion of Elements")
4. Puggala-pannati ("Designation of Individuals")
5. Katha-vatthu ("Subjects of Discussion")
6. Yamaka ("The Pairs")
7. Patthana ("Activations")

The entire *Tipitaka* may be found translated in the two multivolume sets, *Sacred Books of the Buddhists* (London: Luzac Co.), and *Pali Text Society Translation Series* (London: Luzac Co.). Selections from the *Tipitaka* may be found in H. C. Warren, *Buddhism in Translations*, Harvard Oriental Series, vol. 3 (Cambridge, MA: Harvard University Press, 1922); *Milindapanha* ("Milinda's Questions"), translated by T. W. Rhys Davids as *The Questions of King Milinda*, The Sacred Books of the East, vols. 35, 36 (Oxford: Clarendon Press, 1890, 1894); and *Visuddhimagga* ("The Path of Purification"), translated by Bhikkhu Nanamoli as *The Path of Purification* (Colombo: A. Semage, 1964).

SELECTED MAHAYANA TEXTS

The Prajna-paramita sutras ("Perfection of Wisdom Discourses")

There are more than a dozen of these texts, varying in length from 100,000 lines to fourteen lines. The two of these that have had the greatest impact on Mahayana life and thought are *Prajna-paramita Hridaya Sutra* ("The Sutra on the Heart of the Perfection of Wisdom") and *Vajracchedika Prajnaparamita Sutra* ("The Sutra of the Diamond-cutting Perfection of Wisdom"), translated by Edward Conze in *Buddhist Wisdom Books* (London: Allen and Unwin, 1958).

Sad-dharma-pundarika Sutra ("The Sutra of the Lotus of the True Dharma")

Translated by H. Kern as *Saddharma-Pundarika or The Lotus of the True Law*, The Sacred Books of the East, vol. 21 (Oxford: Clarendon Press, 1884).

Sukhavati-vyuha ("Vision of the Pure Land")

Translated by E. B. Cowell, F. Max Müller, and J. Takakusu, in *Buddhist Mahayana Texts*, The Sacred Books of the East, vol. 49 (Oxford: Clarendon Press, 1894).

For selections from the whole Mahayana literature, see Edward Conze, *Buddhist Texts Through the Ages* (New York: Harper & Row, 1954).

Selected Reading List

Bechert, Heinz, and Richard Gombrich, eds. *The World of Buddhism: Buddhist Monks and Nuns in Society and Culture.* New York: Facts On File, 1984.

Bharati, Agehananda. *The Tantric Tradition.* Garden City, NY: Anchor Books, 1970.

Blofeld, John. *The Tantric Mysticism of Tibet: A Practical Guide.* New York: Dutton, 1970.

Ch'en, Kenneth K. S. *Buddhism in China.* Princeton, NJ: Princeton University Press, 1964.

Conze, Edward, et al., eds. *Buddhist Texts Through the Ages.* New York: Harper & Row, 1954.

————. *Buddhist Thought in India.* Ann Arbor: University of Michigan Press, Ann Arbor Paperbacks, 1967.

Cowell, E. B., F. Max Müller, and J. Takakusu, trans. *Buddhist Mahayana Texts. The Sacred Books of the East,* vol. 49. Edited by F. Max Müller. Oxford: Clarendon Press, 1894.

De Bary, William Theodore, ed. *The Buddhist Tradition.* New York: Modern Library, 1969.

Dumoulin, Heinrich. *A History of Zen Buddhism.* Translated by Paul Peachey. New York: Pantheon, 1963.

————, ed. *Buddhism in the Modern World.* New York: Macmillan, 1976.

Dutt, Sukumar. *Buddhist Monks and Monasteries of India.* London: Allen & Unwin, 1962.

Foucher, Alfred. *The Life of the Buddha According to the Ancient Texts and Monuments of India.* Abridged translation by Simone Brangier Boas. Middletown, CT: Wesleyan University Press, 1963.

Govinda, Anagarika Brahmacari. *The Psychological Attitude of Early Buddhist Philosophy.* London: Rider, 1961.

Kapleau, Philip. *The Three Pillars of Zen.* Boston: Beacon Press, 1968.

Kern, H., trans. *Saddharma-Pundarika or The Lotus of the True Law. The Sacred Books of the East,* vol. 21. Oxford: Clarendon Press, 1884.

Lamotte, Etienne. *History of Indian Buddhism.* Louvain: Publications Universitaires, 1988.

Lester, Robert C. *Theravada Buddhism in Southeast Asia.* Ann Arbor: University of Michigan Press, 1973.

Ling, Trevor O. *A Dictionary of Buddhism.* New York: Scribner, 1972.

Morgan, Kenneth William, ed. *The Path of the Buddha: Buddhism Interpreted by Buddhists.* New York: Ronald Press, 1956.

Murti, T. R. V. *The Central Philosophy of Buddhism.* London: Allen & Unwin, 1955.

Nanamoli, Thera, trans. *The Path of Purification (Visuddhimagga).* Colombo: Semage, 1956.

Nanaponika, Thera. *The Heart of Buddhist Meditation.* New York: Weiser, 1971.

Prebish, Charles S., ed. *Buddhism: A Modern Perspective.* University Park: Pennsylvania State University Press, 1975.

Rahula, Walpola. *What the Buddha Taught.* New York: Grove Press, 1974.

Reynolds, Frank E. *Guide to Buddhist Religion* (Bibliography). Boston: Hall, 1981.

Rhys Davids, T. W. *The Questions of King Milinda. The Sacred Books of the East,* vols. 35, 36. Oxford: Clarendon Press, 1890, 1894.

————, trans. *Buddhist Suttas. The Sacred Books of the East,* vol. 11. Oxford: Clarendon Press, 1881.

Sangharakshita, Bhikshu. *A Survey of Buddhism.* Bangalore: Indian Institute of World Culture, 1966.

Smith, Bardwell L., ed. *Unsui: A Diary of Zen Monastic Life.* Honolulu: University Press of Hawaii, East-West Center, 1973.

Suzuki, Diasetz Teitaro. *Introduction to Zen Buddhism.* New York: Grove Press, 1964.

———. *The Training of the Zen Buddhist Monk.* New York: University Books, 1965.

Suzuki, Shunryu. *Zen Mind, Beginner's Mind.* Tokyo: John Weatherhill, 1973.

Tambiah, S. J. *Buddhism and the Spirit Cults in North-east Thailand.* Cambridge: Cambridge University Press, 1970.

Thomas, Edward J. *The History of Buddhist Thought.* London: Routledge & Kegan Paul, 1963.

———. *The Life of Buddha as Legend and History.* London: Routledge & Kegan Paul, 1949.

Warren, Henry Clarke, trans. *Buddhism in Translations.* New York: Atheneum, 1984.

Wright, Arthur F. *Buddhism in Chinese History.* Stanford, CA: Stanford University Press, 1959.

PART NINE

Religions of China

The World as a Living System

Daniel L. Overmyer

"If we dance, it will rain."

> (Shang dynasty oracle bone inscription,
> about 1300 B.C.E.)

Chronology of Chinese History and Religion

Dates	Dynasties and Major Cultural and Religious Features
c. 6000 B.C.E.	Prehistory: beginning of agricultural village life; grave objects buried with the dead; bone divination (without writing)
c. 1500 to 1040 B.C.E.	Shang dynasty: rule of a large area by powerful kings; bone and shell divination with written inscriptions; huge tombs with many offerings; rituals by king and priests for ancestors and nature gods
1040 to 256 B.C.E.	Zhou (Chou) dynasty: China's feudal period; one king with many separate states; ritual feasts for ancestors; "Decree of Heaven" as source of king's authority; first records of shamans and spirit-mediums; search for immortality; rise of philosophy and skepticism about religion for a few scholars
202 B.C.E. to 9 C.E.	Han (or former or Western Han) dynasty
221 to 207 B.C.E.	Qin (Ch'in) dynasty
9 to 23 C.E.	Xin (Hsin) dynasty
25 to 220 C.E.	Later Han (or Eastern Han) dynasty: beginnings of Chinese empire and imperial state religion; Confucianism established as official teaching; rise of popular religious movements; Buddhism enters China
220 to 280 C.E.	Three Kingdoms era: Wei (220 to 266); Shu Han (221 to 263); Wu (222 to 280)
266 to 316	Jin (Chin) (or Western Jin) dynasty
316 to 589	Era of North-South division: Sixteen Kingdoms (301 to 439); Northern and Southern dynasties (317 to 589): collapse of empire; China divides into separate states again; beginnings of Daoist religion; Buddhism becomes established at all levels of society

Dates	Dynasties and Major Cultural and Religious Features
581 to 618	Sui dynasty
618 to 907	Tang dynasty: China reunified; Buddhism and Daoism reach a peak of development, with many monasteries and temples; development of Chinese Buddhist philosophy; formation of Pure Land and Chan (Zen) Buddhism; Confucian reaction and the suppression of Buddhist monasteries in the ninth century
907 to 970	Five Dynasties era: another period of political disunity
916 to 1234	Northern Conquest dynasties: Liao dynasty (916 to 1125); Jin (Chin) dynasty (1115 to 1234): China reunified once again, but with threats from other kingdoms to the north; revival of Confucian philosophy; spread of Buddhist devotional societies among the people; Chan becomes the major form of monastic Buddhism
960 to 1127	Song (Sung) (or Northern Song) dynasty
1127 to 1279	Southern Song dynasty: North China ruled by the Jurchen (Jin) dynasty; continued development of Confucian thought; popular religion takes shape as a tradition in its own right
1264 to 1368	Yuan dynasty, Mongol: all of China conquered by the Mongols; popular religious sects take their characteristic form
1368 to 1644	Ming dynasty: Mongols driven out and replaced by a Chinese emperor; Roman Catholic missionaries in China
1644 to 1912	Qing (Ch'ing) dynasty, Manchu: Manchus rule China; continued development of Buddhism, Daoism, and popular religious sects; gradual suppression of Catholicism; invasion of China by European powers in the nineteenth century; Protestant missionaries arrive and Catholics return

Dates	Dynasties and Major Cultural and Religious Features
1912 to 1949 (on mainland) *1945 to the present (in Taiwan)*	Republic of China
1949 to the present	People's Republic of China: collapse of the Qing empire and the rise of a new China; invasion by Japan; civil war between Nationalists and Communists; Communist victory in 1949, Nationalists retreat to Taiwan; popular religion flourishes in Taiwan; suppression of religion during the Cultural Revolution in China, 1966 to 1976; restoration of some religious activities after 1978
1980s	Gradual revival of some traditional practices

Prologue

THIS WORK ATTEMPTS TO explain some basic ideas and practices of Chinese religions in direct and simple language, with lots of examples. Its basic assumption is that religion is best understood as an aspect of everyday life, as something that makes sense to those who practice it, even if outsiders might be puzzled at first. Most religious activities and feelings are special forms of things many people—even if they are not religious—do and feel, so all have an opportunity to understand if they wish. Of course, someone who does not practice a particular religion can't feel about it the same way as a person who does, but with careful study we can go a long way toward understanding and appreciation. In the beginning, we should try to let the religion speak for itself without bringing in our own ideas and reactions too soon. Once we better understand what is going on, and why, then we are free to accept, reject, or just enjoy without getting involved. The best approach to a different religion or culture is the same as the way we try to relate to another person: polite, attentive, and sympathetic, but still having our own point of view. Just as we can learn from friends and teachers, so we can learn from other human traditions, even if it is only to decide that we prefer our own.

The *pin-yin* romanization system is used for spelling out the sound of Chinese characters as approved by the Chinese government. Wade-Giles spelling appears in parentheses for more familiar names, as "Daoism (Taoism)."

Since this work is focused on traditional China before the twentieth century I tend to use the past tense, but in fact many of the beliefs and practices described are still alive, at least in some Chinese communities. So, past tense here does not necessarily mean no longer present.

40

Introduction: Beliefs and Values of One of the World's Oldest Living Cultures

THE *FENG-SHUI** MASTER, followed by the oldest son of the Liu family, walked up the wooded hillside, pausing now and then to look at the view below. They went over a ridge, and there below them was a small meadow with a creek running across its lower edge. The meadow, facing south, was bathed in sunshine. The master paused and looked back along the ridge; the point where they stood was the end of a long series of hills connected to the mountains in the distance. He went down to the meadow and dug into the soil with a trowel; the soil was dark and crumbled in his hands, and it was covered with grass and wildflowers. He looked down the slope; the view was beautiful and made him feel peaceful and comfortable within. Behind him, the ridge blocked the north winds, which would soon be turning cold. He turned and said, "This is the spot"; this was the place to bury the young man's father. Here his spirit would be at peace.

Back in the village, the son consulted a fortune-teller to decide on a good day for the funeral. The fortune-teller asked him the date and hour of his father's birth in order to calculate which cosmic power was strongest then and to choose a day when that power would be strong again. The best time for the funeral would be *ji-mao* day of the sixty-day cycle, the fourteenth of the next lunar month. Burial then would reinforce the power of Mr. Liu's spirit and make him even more inclined to bless his family. The master laid out the horseshoe-shaped tomb facing south down the hill, set to catch and hold the fertile powers of the meadow. On the fourteenth day, the funeral procession arrived, and the coffin was aligned with the auspicious direction of the year, symbolized by the constellation Mao, the Pleiades. A rectangular wooden tablet about a foot long was laid on its top as a place for the soul to reside. When the ritual was finished and the soul tablet blessed, the Liu family took it home, put it on the altar, and feasted before it to celebrate their new **ancestor.** They felt satisfied. They had

---

*Terms defined in the glossary, pp. 1070–72, are printed in boldface type where they first appear in the text.

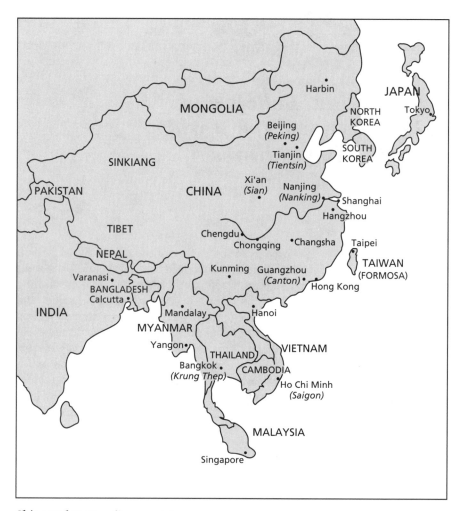

China and surrounding countries.

done their job; death had been put in its proper place, and life could go on, guided by memories of the old man and his ancestors many generations before.

This is a story of *feng-shui,* "wind and water," the art of locating graves and houses so that they benefit from cosmic forces in the sky and landscape. Scenes like this have been repeated millions of times in China for the last two thousand years and can still be observed in Taiwan, Hong Kong, and some places in China. *Feng-shui* puts in practice an ancient Chinese way of looking at the world, a way that assumes that the world is a living system in which everything is connected by shared rhythms and resonances, like instruments in a symphony orchestra. These rhythms are discussed as the cold, dark forces of **yin** and the hot, bright forces of **yang,** together with the **five powers** of wood, fire, earth, metal, and water. These forces are modes of **qi (ch'i)**, "vital substance," which interact within the rhythms of the living system to produce all things in the world.

From about 100 B.C.E. until the mid–twentieth century, most Chinese assumed that this system was simply the way the world was, just as we today assume it is composed of atoms, molecules, electrical forces, and gravity. In China, from an even earlier time, it has been taken for granted that human beings are a natural and necessary part of the world around them; hence, what they do influences nature, and nature in turn is full of significance for them. So, on the longest night of the year in December the emperor would sacrifice a red (*yang*) bullock on an outdoor altar south of the capital to make sure that the *yang* force of warmth and life would revive. When spring came, he wore green robes to encourage the growth of plant life. Executions had to be reserved for autumn, the time of harvest and cutting down; otherwise the seasons would be disrupted. Peasants, too, offered sacrifices: to gods symbolizing fertility, for example, or for power over diseases caused by cosmic forces out of balance. Most Chinese religions and philosophies have been based on this lively view of the world, whatever else they have taught. They assume that the world itself is a sacred place of power and mystery, and that to human beings belongs the important task of cooperating with this power and making it operative within society. They shared this understanding with other traditional cultures, such as that of Japan and those of the native peoples of America, Africa, and Australia. In China, however, philosophers and religious leaders wrote sophisticated books about these ideas long ago, books that have continued to be studied up to the twentieth century. In recent decades scholars all over the world have been studying traditional Chinese religion and philosophy more than ever before. This work is an introduction to what they have learned.

Along with India, China is the oldest literate civilization that has continued to exist into the twentieth century. Though there were preliterate tribes in the area of what we now call China many thousands of years ago, the first sophisticated civilization in that part of the world was the Shang kingdom, which appeared about 1500 B.C.E. Properly speaking, history begins with written records, and this was the beginning of Chinese history. Since the Sumerians and Egyptians developed comparable civilizations about fifteen hundred years before that, China is not the oldest culture; it has just lasted a long time. It is as if the Babylonian kingdom established by Hammurabi in 1750 B.C.E. were still active today, with its ancient language and social ideas still largely intact. One of the factors that helped Chinese culture survive was religious beliefs teaching that the world makes sense and that human beings have an important responsibility to help hold it together. Many of these beliefs go back to prehistory but have been developed by centuries of thought and writing—writing that millions of people can still read today (more easily than Westerners can read Latin or Old English).

China was attacked by the British in 1839 and invaded by France, Russia, Germany, and Japan later in the nineteenth century. Since that time, China's economy and society have been changing under foreign impact. A revolution in 1911 overthrew the last emperor and established a republic. The Japanese invaded again in 1931 and 1937, and then came the devastation of World War II. After the war, China was torn apart by a civil war between Communists and Nationalists, a war that the Communists won. They established the People's Republic of China in 1949, and the Nationalists retreated to Taiwan, an island ninety miles off the South China coast. In both China and Taiwan there has been even more rapid change since 1949, both because of communism and because of the impact of modern knowledge and technology. And yet, despite one hundred fifty years of change, many of the basic values of Chinese life have remained. Religious beliefs have been strongly criticized on the China mainland for more than forty years, and many **temples** and images have been destroyed; yet even there a strong sense of family loyalty remains, and ancestor worship and traditional rituals have been making a comeback since a period of liberalization began in 1978. In Taiwan, not only are the old religions thriving, but many new religious sects have sprung up, with their own books of scripture and brightly painted temples. There, people who work in factories and offices during the day, drive automobiles, and watch television still worship the old gods and venerate the teachings of **Confucius,** who lived twenty-five hundred years ago, just as modern people in North America and Europe still read the Bible and believe its teachings.

Our deepest hopes and fears are expressed in our religious beliefs and activities. So it is that a study of Chinese religions tells us much about the fundamental attitudes and values of the Chinese people. Through such study we also learn of different points of view, challenging us to think more clearly about our own values. For example, one important Chinese characteristic is remembering and honoring ancestors through simple acts of worship, such as offering sticks of burning incense before wooden tablets bearing ancestors' names at the family altar. Many Chinese have also kept records of their families for generations, records that are read to young people to remind them of what their ancestors did and stood for. In this way, each generation is taught to be grateful and loyal to the family tradition and to work hard to keep it going. This emphasis may have contributed to the economic success today of such countries as Taiwan, Japan, and South Korea, where the traditional family loyalty is still strong. In such cultures many young people have a sense that they are working for something bigger than themselves; therefore, they study hard and strive to succeed. Of course, sometimes an individual is prevented by the demands of family

A home altar. Vertical inscription on the left says: "May the ancestors long aid their descendants"; on the right: "May the power of Buddha forever support the peace and prosperity of the family."

from doing what he or she wants to do, as in the case of a university graduate who wants to study art but is expected to take over the family's business instead. On the whole, however, the Chinese-style family has worked well for a long time. Perhaps we can learn something from the gratitude and mutual support among family members that keep this system strong. At the least, thinking about it gives us a fresh perspective on the more individualistic tradition of the West.

Another potential contribution to our own thinking is the Chinese sense of the world itself as a holy place, a place that human beings should honor and protect. For example, in a popular religious book called the *Earth Mother Scripture* (*Di-mu jing*), the earth is considered a goddess, who says,

> All the **Buddhas** of the three worlds arise from me,
> and **bodhisattvas** do not depart from the body of the Mother.
> All the gods are not separate from me;
> if they left me, where would they rest?
> The four directions, continents, and seasons were all created by me.
> Rivers, lakes, and seas do not exist apart from me.
> I produced all states and continents. . . .
> I created mountains and forests,
> and produced the five grains and six kinds of rice. . . .
> When people are alive they eat me,
> and when they die they return to my bosom.
> Prefectures and counties do not exist apart from me;
> temples and monasteries are formed of my body.

After bewailing the fact that people have forgotten their debt to Mother Earth, the text continues with passages like the following:

> If every household will reverence Mother Earth,
> there will be an abundant harvest of the five grains,
> and peace and joy [will come].
> [For them] there will be no great disasters or calamities,
> and pious men and women will enjoy health and tranquility.
> However if they do not listen to Mother Earth's instructions,
> there will be no harvest, and not enough to eat. . . .

This sort of reverence for the earth has obvious parallels with modern ecology; both ecology and Chinese religion understand the world to be a product of delicately balanced forces. To interfere with these forces is to interfere with our own well-being, since we are ourselves a part of the world. The Bible, also, teaches that the world is created and loved by God and is to be properly cared for by human beings, but sometimes Christians and Jews have forgotten this. A study of Chinese religions can help remind us of important emphases in our own tradition.

The chapters that follow discuss the history of Chinese religions and some of their distinctive ideas and themes. We also look at how Chinese people actually practice religion today. The basic concerns of this work are, first, to understand Chinese religions in their own right, and then to see how they constitute a worldview or living system.

41

History: The Development
of Chinese Religious Traditions
over Time

TO UNDERSTAND CHINESE religion we must trace its development through time. For the most part, Chinese culture and religion developed on their own terms, the products of centuries of village agricultural life. This historical treatment will enable us to see both the regional differences and some changes over time, but in general all Chinese assumed the same worldview: Everyone venerated ancestors, practiced *feng-shui,* carried out funerals, and enjoyed the same annual festivals. It is because of this common tradition that we can discuss points of unity among Chinese religions. China has been one of the world's largest and most populous countries for more than two thousand years. By 100 C.E., China's population of sixty million equaled that of the entire Roman Empire. Today, the People's Republic of China is second only to Canada in area with a population of more than one billion—about one-fifth of the world's population. The People's Republic of China extends from the Pacific Ocean to India and Afghanistan, and from Myanmar, formerly Burma, in the south to Siberia in the north (see map, p. 980). Many different climatic regions are contained within such a large area. The Yangtze River, which horizontally divides China into halves, is a climatic boundary between the dry, cold north and the wet, warm south. Beijing (Peking), the capital, is surrounded by a vast plain, on which the most important crops are wheat and millet. In the more temperate south, which has more rivers and lakes, the most important crop is rice, which requires large quantities of water. Western China presents a sharp contrast, a desert area with minimal rainfall and vegetation.

A Summary of Chinese History

The area now known as China has been inhabited for at least five hundred thousand years; we have evidence of many different tribes by 6000 B.C.E., some of which had begun to grow grain and vegetables and to raise domestic animals such as chickens, pigs, and dogs. These people lived in small, mud-brick villages, surrounded by their fields. As time passed, some of these villages grew larger and constructed perimeter walls, houses on earthen platforms, pottery factories, and markets. The existence of some more elaborate houses and graves within these villages leads us to conclude that wealth was not evenly distributed, which in turn suggests the presence of a chief. Perhaps the walls built around these villages were built as defensive safeguards against attacks led by neighboring chiefs.

About 1500 B.C.E., tribal chiefs on the northern plain had amassed sufficient power to impose a new form of social organization, a powerful state led by hereditary kings, called the Shang dynasty. This state, ruled by land-owning aristocrats, supported an army that controlled the population and attacked neighboring groups for territory, treasure, and prisoners to be used as slaves or as sacrificial offerings. The Shang elite developed writing to record their petitions to their ancestors and gods and also devised a sophisticated method of casting bronze, which they employed in the manufacture of elaborate bowls, swords, and spearheads, along with many other objects. These developments occurred in cities, now composed of much larger buildings and city walls. Still, the majority of the population continued to farm in small communities, using the same sorts of stone tools that their ancestors had used for thousands of years. [See Religions of Africa p. 59, Religions of Mesoamerica pp. 114–15, and Hinduism pp. 732–33 for discussion of early cities.]

The Shang area was bordered on the west by the Zhou (Chou) tribe, with whom the Shang had alternately fought and traded for centuries. The Zhou continued to gain strength in their military exploits against the Shang, finally overpowering them completely about 1040 B.C.E. With the Shang defeated, China entered a feudal period many centuries before similar developments in Europe. At the head of the feudal system was a king, who ruled over nobles who maintained semi-independent territories of their own. Nobles and king held inherited power, which was usually passed from fathers to eldest sons. Nobles vowed loyalty to the king, traveling each year to his court, bearing gifts. In return, the king was responsible for settling disputes between lords and protecting them from non-Zhou attacks. Although some of the common people moved to urban areas to practice a trade, most remained propertyless farmers, serfs who worked the land of a noble in exchange for a place to live and a portion of the crops they harvested.

This early Zhou feudal system lasted for about three hundred years, but in the eighth century B.C.E. some of the lords started to become more independent. A Zhou king was assassinated in 771, after which real power passed into the hands of the lord who was strongest at any given time. Soon civil wars broke out among the many small states, which formed alliances for protection. The Zhou kings continued to rule their own little domain, but not much else. The period of competition and warfare between independent states lasted for several hundred years. Many of the smaller states were swallowed up, so that by 300 B.C.E. only seven large ones were left. One of these was Qin (Ch'in), in the far west, which was very well organized and had been steadily growing in power. In

256 B.C.E. Qin took over the royal domain, thus ending the Zhou period, and by 221 it had conquered all the remaining states and set itself up as an empire that included much of what we now call China. Our name *China* comes from the word *Ch'in.*

The first emperor of Qin worked very hard to control China by unifying laws and ways of writing, building the Great Wall, and raising large armies to attack non-Chinese tribes. But many people still remained loyal to the customs of their old states, which were now just provinces run by governors appointed by the emperor. In addition, Qin public work projects and military campaigns caused a lot of dislocation and suffering, so that just a few years after the Qin empire was founded, rebellions broke out against it. The eventual victor in this new civil war was a former village head named Liu Bang (pron. "Bong"), who set himself up as emperor of a new dynasty, the Han, in 202 B.C.E. Except for one fourteen-year break, the Liu family ruled China for the next 408 years. The Han rulers were less harsh than the Qin but continued many of their innovations, such as abolishing feudal principalities in favor of provinces run by appointed officials. They also took over much of the Qin law code, which was supposed to apply to everybody, including former nobles, and they continued to let people buy and sell their own land. It was during the early Han period that China settled down and became the large, semicontinental state it is today. It is no accident that when Chinese refer to themselves as an ethnic group, they use the name *Han-ren,* "people of the Han."

Han rule was relatively stable for a long time, certainly a big improvement over the civil wars that preceded it. Between 9 and 23 C.E. the Liu line was temporarily displaced by a rebellious prime minister, but the Han dynasty was reestablished in 25 C.E. However, in the second century C.E. the government started to lose its power because of weak emperors who neglected their business and because of quarreling among groups of officials at court. Protests and rebellions broke out, culminating in a huge uprising by a religious sect called the **Yellow Turbans** in 184 (to be discussed later). By this time the imperial army was too disorganized to defeat the Yellow Turbans, so the emperor encouraged provincial governors to raise militia armies to do the job. This policy worked, and the uprising was put down in a few months, but when the dust settled there were several victorious provincial armies that the governors wanted to hang on to. The result was civil war between these provincial warlords, which led to the fall of the Han dynasty in 220 C.E. From then until 581 China was politically divided, first among three kingdoms in the north, southeast, and southwest that immediately succeeded the Han. Now, however, each state claimed the right to reestablish the empire, the unity of which always remained an ideal.

China had long been threatened by nomadic tribes from inner Asia, which was too dry and cold for agriculture. In 311 and 317 C.E. two northern Chinese capitals were captured by one of these peoples, while similar tribes were attacking the Roman Empire at the other end of Asia at the same time. As a result of this conquest non-Chinese clans ruled North China for about 250 years, and many of the Chinese elite fled south across the Yangtze River, where Chinese states held off the invaders. Of course, there were not many nomads in comparison with Chinese, and the nomads were illiterate and not organized to rule a large farming economy, so the inner Asian rulers in the north had no choice but to learn Chinese and administer with the help of Chinese officials. Before long they became culturally Chinese themselves, and Chinese religions continued to develop in the north as well as the south during this "period of disunion."

In the late sixth century a northern ruler named Yang Jian conquered the south and reunified China in the Sui dynasty, beginning in 581. However, Sui rule was too abrupt and harsh, as the Qin had been centuries before, so it lasted only until 618. By then there had been another long period of rebellion and civil war; the victors, a family named Li, set up a new dynasty, the Tang, in 618. Just as the Han rulers had done, they strengthened the unity enforced by their predecessors and established the foundation for a long period of peace and prosperity. From then on, China alternated between periods of political unity and disunity and rule by Chinese or central Asian peoples. After the Tang there was half a century of disunity between north and south (see the chronology, p. 976), and then China was reunited again by the Song (Sung) dynasty, from 960 to 1127. The north was then taken over again by peoples from what are now Manchuria and Mongolia. In the thirteenth and fourteenth centuries the country was united for ninety years by the Mongols under Chinggis Khagan (Genghis Khan), who by that time had an empire stretching all the way to Europe. However, by 1368 several Chinese rebel armies had driven out the Mongols, and the victorious general set up a new dynasty, the Ming, which established a period of unity that lasted until the revolution of 1911. From 1644 to 1912, the unified China was again ruled by a non-Han people, the Manchus, who called their dynasty the Qing (Ch'ing). So it was that imperial Chinese history ended with rulers of non-Chinese origin on the throne, although the Manchus had become quite Chinese in their language and customs.

Chinese Society

Thus, for the first 1700 years of their history the Chinese ruled themselves in the Shang, Zhou, and Han. They had contacts with other people and traded with them, but foreigners had very little impact on Chinese culture, which pretty much developed by itself. Beginning about 300 C.E., central Asian peoples began what became a long history of occasionally ruling part or all of China. These tribes were originally illiterate and technologically and socially less developed than the Chinese, though superior at horse-mounted warfare. However, despite their military power, they had little influence on Chinese culture and ideas. Instead, after the tribal peoples took over, they were assimilated into China and sometimes even forgot their own language and dress. The most important exceptions to this pattern of assimilation were the coming of Buddhism from India beginning in the first century C.E. and the invasions by Europeans in the nineteenth century. In both cases, Chinese culture was slowly influenced by foreign ideas.

Village agricultural life formed the basis of Chinese culture, religion, and society. Social divisions appeared between men and women, rich and poor, aristocrats and commoners, but these divisions evolved locally out of the same peasant base. For the first 1800 years of its history China was never successfully invaded by foreigners whose nobility took over the country as happened in such places as India, Britain, and Mexico. Even later invaders, such as the Manchus, relied on Chinese officials. This means that at a cultural level the split between rulers and people, aristocrats and peasants, was not as sharp as it was in some other countries. [See Religions of Africa pp. 24, 31, 60–61, Religions of Mesoamerica pp. 112–14, 215–21, Native Religions of North America pp. 320–21, 325, and Hinduism pp. 766–67, 770 for discussion of invasion and colonization.]

In China even the elite who lived in cities usually had family farms in the countryside; the people all shared similar views of the world. Other factors influenced this relatively high degree of cultural integration. One was printing, which was used to publish books in China as early as the ninth century C.E., six hundred years before the first printed book in Europe. In China printing spread rapidly, particularly after the twelfth century. This meant that knowledge was not confined to a tiny elite but was available to anyone who could read, and until the nineteenth century a higher percentage of Chinese could read than could Europeans.

Another integrating factor was written civil service examinations, which were first established in the sixth century C.E. There were several levels of these examinations, from the county to the capital city. Those who passed received degrees as well as government offices when they were available. This was important because in old China, government service was the main route to power and prestige. Except for a few categories, such as beggars and criminals, all Chinese men were eligible to take these examinations and progress as far as they could. Small schools were set up in most towns to help them prepare. To be sure, the sons of rich families often did better because they could afford private tutors, but the examination system was still a big change from the days when aristocrats passed government offices around among themselves and their sons. This change meant that there was more opportunity for men to move up or down within the social system, depending on their wits, energy, and luck. The civil service examinations were based on a set of Confucian books that everyone had to study, usually in the form of preparation manuals similar to those Americans use for college entrance examinations. This meant that ideas and values supported by the state were memorized by people throughout society, further contributing to cultural integration.

At another level this integration was fostered by the network of outdoor markets in villages and towns to which people came from a wide area to shop, get haircuts, worship at temples, go to popular operettas, listen to storytellers, and exchange news. In larger markets there would be people from other parts of China, or even foreign merchants. Through these market networks people learned that they were part of a larger society with many common customs, values, and religious traditions. All of this makes it possible for us to discuss points of unity among Chinese religions.

Of course, there were many differences and tensions as well. In the past, as now, each local area in China had its own dialect, which people from other areas often could not understand, though everyone who could read and write used the same written language. Each area also had its own particular customs and food and special gods and heroes. Even after the civil service examination system took effect, those who passed looked down on those who did not, and there were sharp differences between rich and poor. Most of the people had to struggle every day just to survive, and they were often oppressed by high taxes and rents, greedy landlords, and corrupt officials. Educated religious leaders tended to despise the beliefs and rituals of the common people, even though members of their own families usually practiced them. Such leaders sometimes criticized one another's religions as well. Any kind of popular religious sect was outlawed by the state, particularly after the thirteenth century, and there were laws as well against **spirit-mediums** and some forms of **divination.** In sum, there were enough differences to provide variety, but enough common ground so that China may be discussed in general terms as one culture.

As has been true for many traditional societies, in China the family was the basic unit of ownership, economic activity, and prestige. Individual differences were recognized, but for the most part individual interests were subordinated to those of the family. Fathers had the highest authority, and families were known by their surnames. Sons were to continue the family line, and often followed their fathers' occupations. Women had some rights, but they were basically in an inferior position and didn't become full-fledged members of society until they married and had sons. Since the family was so central (and still is), it is not surprising that the single most important religious activity was ancestor worship, the veneration of predecessors in the father's line of descent, beginning with his parents. The spirits of ancestors were believed to live on and had power to bless or curse their descendants, depending on how they were treated. Living and dead were connected together in one stream; the living were to uphold the family traditions, bring honor to their ancestors, and prepare for becoming good ancestors themselves—to be remembered for their work and example. Descendants were expected to offer food and incense regularly before wooden tablets inscribed with the names of their parents, grandparents, and earlier predecessors. These offerings revived the power of the spirits and encouraged them to aid their families. Such ancestor worship is reflected in the earliest records of Chinese religions and is a fundamental connecting point in the Chinese view of the world. Once the realms of the living and dead were understood to be so intimately related, relationships with the gods were easy to accept as well.

A Brief History of Chinese Religious Beliefs and Activities

The history of religion in China is quite long and extremely varied, stretching from prehistoric times to the present and including both a number of indigenous developments as well as several imported traditions. As we have seen with Chinese history and society in general, we can best understand the history of Chinese religious beliefs and practices as a gradual development into more formal patterns, which then came to interact with foreign traditions, in turn resulting in the formation of distinctively Chinese traditions. The overall unity of religious life in China that has guided this process is the understanding of the world as a living system, an understanding that was implicit in early centuries but fully expressed in written texts from the second century B.C.E. on. [See Religions of Africa pp. 23–24, Religions of Mesoamerica pp. 117–19, Native Religions of North America pp. 261–64, Judaism pp. 389, 426, 456–75, Christianity pp. 492–94, Islam pp. 607–8, Hinduism pp. 719–21, Buddhism pp. 853–55, and Religions of Japan pp. 1090–92 for discussion of the diversity and variety of religious traditions.]

Prehistory and the Early Period

Our knowledge of the earliest form of the religious system of the Chinese is fragmentary, gleaned from the prehistoric material that archaeologists have unearthed. Although we do not have a complete picture of the earliest Chinese religion, we know that the outlines of this tradition included notions of worship, ancestors, fertility, and divination that provided the basis for later Chinese religion. Archaeologists have found some evidence of prehistoric religious activities, predating the Shang dynasty. Most tombs included offerings such as tools, pottery vessels, and jade ornaments, which indicate belief that the dead could use such objects in some form of afterlife. Graves were often located in clusters and lined up in rows near villages, suggesting a special relationship between the living and the dead. Some people buried deer in fields, presumably as offerings to the power of fertility in the soil. Divination was also practiced by heating dried shoulder bones of sheep or deer and reading answers to yes-or-no questions through the patterns of the cracks. In the light of later practices we know more about, it looks as if prehistoric Chinese already venerated their ancestors, tried to discover their will through divination, and made offerings to powers of nature.

For the Shang period (c. 1500–1040 B.C.E.) we have evidence for the religion of the king and aristocracy but not for the common people, except for grave objects, as mentioned before. The king was the chief priest and diviner of the realm, and the results of his bone-cracking divination were often inscribed on the bone after the process was completed (the bottom shells of turtles were also used). For example, on the right and left sides of a shell there might be such inscriptions as "The king's toothache is caused by Ancestor Jie," and "Perhaps the king's toothache is not caused by Ancestor Jie," with an indication of which alternative was suggested by the cracks and which came true. It was usually ancestors who were consulted, but sometimes nature gods of rivers or mountains, and in a few cases, **Shang-di,** "The Ruler on High," the chief god of the Shang state. ("Shang" in Shang dynasty is written with a different character than "Shang" in Shang-di.)

Shang diviners also inquired about the weather, harvests, warfare, and many other topics. The king and his priests offered regular sacrifices to ancestors and to gods believed to live in the water, the earth, and sky. Such offerings included jade thrown into rivers, wine poured out on the earth, and flesh and grain burned on open-air altars. It was assumed that if the offering was properly made, the god or ancestor had to respond. Shang kings were buried in huge pit tombs several yards wide, with all sorts of grave offerings, including not only implements of bronze and jade but also dogs, horses, and decapitated human beings. It was believed that at death kings could enjoy the same luxuries they had in life, perhaps in heaven with their ancestors and Shang-di. Of course, we know of similar royal tombs all over the world, from ancient Egypt, Africa, Persia, and many other places.

For the religion of the early Zhou period we have more detailed records, such as the *Shi-jing*, "The Book of Poetry," which was composed by 600 B.C.E. From these materials we know that Zhou nobles honored their ancestors with great feasts in which the ancestor was represented by a nephew or grandson who had to dress and act in a very formal manner. First, petitions to the ancestor were read, then everyone ate and drank to the full; they believed such ritual meals should be joyous occasions. The Zhou continued to offer sacrifices and to divine much as the Shang had done, but they had a better developed understanding of their High God, whom they called **Tian (T'ien)**, meaning "Heaven." The Zhou founders proclaimed that Tian had chosen them to replace the Shang because the last Shang kings were corrupt and no longer took proper care of the people, who were really the "people of Heaven." This new theory was that of the "Decree of Heaven" (Tian-ming): Every ruler was given authority by Heaven, but only so long as he was compassionate and just. If he failed, the divine right to rule could be transferred to someone else. The "Decree of Heaven" idea has been important in Chinese history ever since because it imposes an ethical and religious check on the king's behavior and provides a basis for criticism of him by officials and the people. Over the centuries many rebellions have been led by men who claimed the "Decree of Heaven" for themselves.

The Zhou kings had a religious title, "Son of Heaven" (Tian-zi, T'ien-tzu), which indicates how important their task was; they were Heaven's representatives on earth. As such, they were responsible both for the people and for the powers of nature as they affected human life. A large part of the king's time was spent performing rituals to make sure that the ancestors and gods were satisfied, that rains would come and crops would grow. The king had a vital role in the balance of cosmic forces; failure to perform the proper ritual at the right time could bring disaster, as could bad laws or cruelty by royal officials. So it was that the king appointed officers to report on any unusual happenings in the realm, such as earthquakes, comets, epidemics, or rebellions; any such disturbance could mean that things were out of balance because the king was doing something wrong. If he was, then he had to repent before Heaven and do something to make up for it, such as freeing prisoners or reducing taxes. [See Religions of Africa pp. 24, 35, 60, Religions of Mesoamerica pp. 198–201, Native Religions of North America pp. 347–48, Judaism pp. 391–92, Christianity pp. 503, 505, Islam pp. 632–33, Hinduism p. 748, Buddhism pp. 875–77, 952–53, and Religions of Japan pp. 1095–96, 1105–6 for the relationship of religion to political leaders.]

Some Zhou court officials had special responsibility for assisting with rituals and divination, but there was no separate organization or "church" for priests. However, other religious specialists—shamans or spirit-mediums, persons who believed they could be possessed by gods or ancestral spirits—were sometimes brought to court. It was thought that spirits temporarily came down into their bodies, spoke through them, and gave them special knowledge of the future or of how to heal illness. Most illness or misfortune was believed to be caused by demons (**gui [kuei]**) or ancestral spirits angry because their graves had been neglected or because they were not receiving enough sacrificial offerings to sustain their energy. Because shamans could talk to such spirits, they could identify the cause of a problem and suggest what to do about it, such as rebuilding a grave. These shamans were not aristocrats, but commoners with special skills, much in demand by both the court and ordinary folk. By the fifth century C.E., shamans were gradually forced out of court rituals by officials, who thought they were too emotional and hard to control, but they continued to be active among the general population and still are in Taiwan and the Chinese countryside. They are folk psychiatrists and healers who try to cure illnesses that do not respond to other forms of medical care.

In the early Zhou period, all the feudal domains had their own rituals and priests, centered on the ancestors of the ruler and on mountains and rivers, imposing natural forces that were believed to control rainfall. During the long period of civil war that began in the eighth century B.C.E., many of these domains or states were destroyed, and with them their ancestral temples and shrines to deities of mountains and rivers. The ancestors and deities were supposed to protect the state, but clearly many of them failed. The same could be said of Heaven, which was expected to preserve prosperity and peace for those who ruled properly. Thus, for a few intellectuals, destructive civil warfare led to questions about the gods and spirits. Maybe they weren't so powerful after all. Were there natural explanations for storms and earthquakes? Were demons just imagined by people when they were really afraid? Questions such as these helped prepare for a new way of thinking that concentrated more on human beings and less on the spirit world. The first well-known representative of this new approach was Confucius (551–479 B.C.E.).

The Rise of Philosophy

Confucius was the son of an obscure family in the small state of Lu, a state in northern China in which the old Zhou cultural traditions were strong but that had been repeatedly upset by invasions and by struggles between local clans. Confucius was concerned about restoring peace and order and studied old books, rituals, and legends to look for guidelines for the present. He came to realize that what was needed were moral principles that applied to everyone— principles such as justice, honesty, and love, that could be followed in all situations. He believed that these principles were the will of Heaven for human beings, in particular for the ruler and his officials, who were supposed to rule for the benefit of the people.

The highest goal for such leaders was to develop an inner sense of ethical commitment, *ren* (*jen*), deep empathy and compassion for others. This inward power of concern was to be expressed in everyday life as reverence for parents, loyalty to friends, and care for the common people, all carried out in a balanced harmonious way (*li*). Ethically educated persons were to be honest, frugal, and hard-working, always trying to improve society and government.

Confucius never did obtain a high office in Lu from which he could put his teachings into practice, but he soon gathered a small group of disciples whom he taught to be "superior persons" (*jun-zi*), educated men with high principles who would be good government officials. For him, what counted was intelligence and dedication, not inherited aristocratic status. Confucius claimed he was just restoring old ideas, but actually he was a reformer who introduced new ethical concepts and a new type of education and reinforced the policy of appointing good men to office whether they were aristocrats or not. [See Religions of Africa pp. 29, 55–57, 152, Religions of Mesoamerica pp. 164–68, Native Religions of North America pp. 266–67, Christianity pp. 495–97, 531–32, 534–35, Islam pp. 622–28, 698–99, Hinduism pp. 769, 770–72, Buddhism pp. 860, 861–68, 892–99, and Religions of Japan pp. 1090, 1100, 1122–23, for discussion of religious founders.]

There were two sides to Confucius's religious views. On the one hand, he paid no attention to such practices as shamanism and divination, which he thought were beneath the dignity of a "superior person." On the other hand, Confucius had a deep personal sense of loyalty to Heaven (Tian), which he felt had given him a mission to reform the world. After he died, Confucius's disciples remembered his teachings and eventually put them together into a book, the *Discourses and Sayings* (*Lun-yu*). In this book we read that on a few occasions when Confucius's life was in danger he fell back on his faith in Heaven to keep his confidence and sense of destiny.

For example, once a powerful official named Huan Tui tried to have Confucius assassinated, probably because the philosopher had criticized his policies. When Confucius was warned, he said, "Heaven begat the power that is in me. What have I to fear from such a one as Huan Tui?"

Because he was never appointed to an important position, Confucius felt that no one appreciated his ability, but here also his sense of mission from Tian gave him confidence. As he once said, "The truth is no one knows me. . . . I do not accuse heaven nor lay the blame on men. But the studies of men here below are felt on high, and perhaps after all I am known; not here, but in heaven."[1]

After Confucius, many other thinkers taught methods of saving the world from warfare and disorder. Most of them also had disciples whom they trained to obtain government office and put their ideas into practice. Since most of the rulers of the mid-Zhou period were corrupt and power hungry, this was no easy task, but the philosophers kept trying. Most of them retained the ancient sense that the world should be ordered and peaceful, but their teachings became more and more practical in order to catch the attention of rulers. In the process, most language about Heaven, the gods, and rituals dropped out of sight; these philosophers were concerned almost entirely with human society and government. One group of thinkers, the Authoritarians, simply talked about how the ruler could become more powerful by centralizing and organizing his administration.

The Confucians, however, kept their sense of Heaven's will, as did a philosopher named **Mo-zi** (**Mo-tzu,** fifth century B.C.E.), who taught that Heaven had created the world, loved its people, and wanted them to be prosperous and at peace. In practice, Heaven's love meant material and social benefits for the people, such as food, land, and mutual caring for one another. Several of Mo-zi's disciples obtained government positions during his lifetime, worked hard to follow his teachings, and reported back to him what they had accomplished. Mo-zi's belief in Heaven's love is well expressed in the following passage:

> Moreover, I know for the following reason that Heaven loves the people generously: it sets forth one after another the sun and moon, the stars and constellations, to lighten and lead them; it orders the four seasons, spring, fall, winter, and summer, to regulate their lives; it sends down snow and frost, rain and dew, to nourish the five grains, hemp, and silk, so that the people may enjoy the benefit of them. It lays out the mountains and rivers, the ravines and valley streams, and makes known all affairs so as to ascertain the good or evil of the people. It establishes kings and lords to reward the worthy and punish the wicked, to gather together metal and wood, birds and beasts, and to seek the cultivation of the five grains, hemp, and silk, so that the people may have enough food and clothing. From ancient times to the present this has always been so.[2]

In the fourth and third centuries B.C.E., some thinkers appeared who tried a different approach, that of noninterference (*wu-wei*), letting things be in their natural state. This approach was first discussed in two books, called the **Lao-zi** (**Lao-tzu**) and **Zhuang-zi** (**Chuang-tzu**), which were written by disillusioned intellectuals who thought that all the various theories of improving the world only made things worse, because they all depended on telling other people what to do. These books teach that everything in the world is produced by the cosmic Way (**Dao [Tao]**), which also provides harmony and balance. Because of this Way, things are just fine in their natural state and should be left alone, from plants and animals to people. The eternal Way of the universe is far wiser than any person could possibly be, so it is always a mistake for us to try to change things around. All we are doing is asserting our own egos and trying to substitute our own limited knowledge for the wisdom of the universe. So it was that the writers of the *Lao-zi* and *Zhuang-zi* taught that the best rulers were those who left the people alone, because they could prosper by themselves. They know how to act even without being taught such high-sounding moral principles as righteousness and respect for elders. Indeed, advocating such principles shows that one probably does not have them!

The *Lao-zi* and *Zhuang-zi* have very little to say about gods or rituals, but they do have a strong sense of the mystery and power of the universal Dao that is present everywhere for those who know how to look. These books are thus important sources for Chinese cosmic mysticism, a sense of personal identification with the basic forces of the universe. We can get an idea of this sense of mystery from such passages as the following:

> There was something undifferentiated and yet complete,
>> Which existed before heaven and earth.
> Soundless and formless, it depends on nothing and does not change.
> It operates everywhere and is free from danger.
> It may be considered the mother of the universe.
> I do not know its name; I call it Tao [Dao].
> If forced to give it a name, I shall call it Great.
> Now being great means functioning everywhere.
> Functioning everywhere means far-reaching.
> Being far-reaching means returning to the original point.
>
> The Great Tao flows everywhere.
>> It may go left or right.
> All things depend on it for life,
>> and it does not turn away from them.
> It accomplishes its task,
>> but does not claim credit for it.
> It clothes and feeds all things
>> but does not claim to be master over them.
> Always without desires, it may be called The Small.
> All things come to it and it does not master them;
>> it may be called The Great.
> Therefore (the sage) never strives himself for the great,
> and thereby the great is achieved.[3]

The Dao in this passage sounds a bit like Jewish or Christian concepts of God, but unlike God, Dao has no consciousness or will. This use of the term *Dao* is a way of talking about the world itself as something sacred. The term *sage,* in the second passage, refers to the wise ruler who imitates the Dao or way of nature in his administration. He works to help everyone else find peace and prosperity but does not claim credit for himself. Because he doesn't harass the people with military service and high taxes they accomplish much on their own, and so "the great is achieved."

By the fourth century B.C.E. there were also philosophers who taught that the universe had developed through the interaction of natural forces such as *yin, yang,* and the five powers or phases. They were the first formulators of the distinctive Chinese worldview described in chapter 40. One thinker, **Xun-zi (Hsun-tzu,** d. 215 B.C.E.), taught that Tian, or heaven, was not divine at all but was simply a general name for what we would call the laws of nature. It was orderly, but had no will or purpose and had nothing to do with human morality. For Xun-zi, gods and spirits were not real, but just products of human imagination. Rituals and music might be beautiful and inspiring but were not a matter of pleasing the gods. Xun-zi's skepticism about religion went much further than that of Confucius and helped establish a skeptical tradition in Chinese philosophy that has persisted to today. His views are well illustrated by the following passage:

You pray for rain and it rains. Why? For no particular reason, I say. It is just as though you had not prayed for rain and it rained anyway. The sun and moon undergo an eclipse and you try to save them;* a drought occurs and you pray for rain; you consult the arts of divination before making a decision on some important matter. But it is not as though you could hope to accomplish anything by such ceremonies. They are done merely for ornament. Hence the gentleman regards them as ornaments, but the common people regard them as supernatural. He who considers them ornaments is fortunate; he who considers them supernatural is unfortunate.[4]

In other words, Xun-zi taught that the educated person should understand religious rituals to be a kind of decoration, not literally true. This was always a minority view in China but had much influence on how intellectuals looked at religion, especially that of the common people. It was considered vulgar and uneducated to be too enthusiastic about religious beliefs and practices.

The Search for Immortality

While a few philosophers were ignoring religion or redefining it in a more abstract way as identification with "heaven" or the "Dao," the great majority of the Chinese people continued to practice rituals and divination as they always had. By the fourth century B.C.E. a set of beliefs appeared that had been developing for a long time, beliefs that there were ways for human beings to escape death, either by living for a very long time or by being reborn in a new form after what only appeared to be death. Methods for attaining such immortality were developed by men called *fang-shi*, "technique specialists," who tried to gain influence and positions in state governments just as the philosophers did. They claimed they had learned techniques for overcoming death from beings who had attained immortality long ago and now lived in paradises on distant mountaintops or islands. These methods were all based on refining and strengthening the *qi*, or "vital substance," of which we are made. One method involved deep breathing to circulate the breath (*qi*) in the body; others were exercises based on the movements of such long-lived animals as cranes and tortoises. Some *fang-shi* advocated special vegetarian diets; others advocated drinking compounds of gold and other minerals to make the body as firm and changeless as they were. Chinese religions of this period did not have a very well developed idea of an afterlife; at best, souls of the dead continued to exist for a time in the ancestral tablet, in the grave, or in a dark underground area called the Yellow Springs, which was not very pleasant. Going to Heaven's court was reserved for the royal family; others who wanted to survive death in a more satisfactory way had to work at it and spend a lot of time and money learning immortality techniques. Nonetheless, the search for immortality became quite widespread; there are even stories of whole families ascending to paradise together after they were daubed with an immortality potion by a *fang-shi*.

---

*In ancient China it was believed that eclipses were caused by a great doglike monster in the sky who was eating the sun and moon. Hence, during an eclipse people made a lot of noise to scare the monster away. Xun-zi rejects this practice.

During the Qin and Han dynasties (221 B.C.E.–220 C.E.) several emperors tried to attain immortality themselves and even sent expeditions to look for island paradises. They summoned shamans and *fang-shi* to court from all over China. In this first period of the Chinese empire, official rituals of all sorts were made more elaborate, and emperors periodically toured the realm, climbing sacred mountains and performing sacrifices to important local deities. They did this both because they believed in divine powers and because they wanted to impress on everybody that all the gods in China were on their side, and therefore the government should be obeyed.

The Beginnings of Daoism (Taoism): Popular Movements in the Late Han (Second Century C.E.)

In 3 B.C.E. there appeared in China a popular religious movement based on faith in a mother goddess, **Xi Wang-mu** (**Hsi Wang-mu**), the "Queen Mother of the West." Many people believed that if they worshiped her and wore charms with her name on them they would not die. This is what some old Chinese history books have to say about the movement:

[Chien-p'ing], fourth year, spring. There was a severe drought [in the first lunar month: February to March]. In the area east of the passes, the people were exchanging tokens in preparation for the advent of the Queen Mother of the West. They passed through the commanderies and kingdoms, moving west to within the passes and reaching the capital city. In addition persons were assembling to worship the Queen Mother of the West, sometimes carrying fire to the roof-tops by night, beating drums, shouting and frightening one another.

In the first month of the fourth year of Chien-p'ing, the population were running around in a state of alarm, each person carrying a manikin of straw or hemp. People exchanged these emblems with one another, saying that they were carrying out the advent procession. Large numbers of persons, amounting to thousands, met in this way on the roadsides, some with disheveled hair or going barefoot. Some of them broke down the barriers of gates by night; some clambered over walls to make their way into [houses]; some harnessed teams of horses to carriages and rode at full gallop, setting up relay stations so as to convey the tokens. They passed through twenty-six commanderies and kingdoms, until they reached the capital city.

That summer the people came together in meetings in the capital city and in the commanderies and kingdoms. In the village settlements, the lanes and paths across the fields, they held services and set up gaming boards for a lucky throw, and they sang and danced in worship of the Queen Mother of the West. They also passed round a written message, saying "The Mother tells the people that those who wear this talisman will not die; and let those who do not believe Her words look below the pivots on their gates, and there will be white hairs there to show that this is true."[5]

This movement died out a few months later. We know little of its origins, though the Queen Mother of the West is mentioned in earlier Chinese stories. What is most significant for our understanding of the history of Chinese religions is that here a single, powerful deity promises an easy and simple means of salvation to ordinary people. This is the first such popular religious movement we know of in China. It helped prepare the way for the rise of **Daoism,** China's earliest organized religion, with its own special priests, rituals, and scriptures.

As the Han dynasty started to fall apart in the second century, several popular religious leaders appeared who claimed to have received revelations from gods and immortals, all intended to restore peace and prosperity in China. At first they appealed to the court, but the emperors were not interested, so before long some of these leaders began to proclaim that they had a divine commission to replace the Han with new kingdoms of their own in which everyone would be secure and happy. Since the government considered this treason, several of these men were executed, but others kept on trying. During the decade of 180–190 C.E. a man named Zhang Jue organized a huge popular movement called the Way of Great Peace and Prosperity (Tai-ping dao) and announced that at the beginning of the next sixty-year cycle of time (184 C.E. by our calendar) the cosmic force of earth would become dominant and replace that of the Han. In that year several thousand of Zhang's followers rebelled in provinces all over North China in an attempt to set up their own utopian kingdom. They came to be called Yellow Turbans, because of the colored cloths they wore to symbolize the power of earth, which has a yellow hue in North China. Their leaders were both priests and military officers at the same time. They taught that illness could be cured by confessing the sins that caused it, and they performed rituals to enlist the aid of the gods in bringing immortality to the souls of their ancestors. Their chief deity was the Lord Lao, the legendary author Lao-zi worshiped as a god and believed to be the creator of the world. The Yellow Turbans also had a sacred book, the *Scripture of Great Peace and Prosperity (Tai-ping jing)*, some of which still survives.

The *Tai-ping jing* proclaims itself to be a "celestial book" revealed by a "divine man" to save humankind. This is to be done by restoring good government, which will encourage peace and cooperation in society. To make sure he is on the right track, the ruler is to collect suggestions and complaints from the people, placed by them in the sealed boxes he has scattered throughout his kingdom. By setting a good example, he is to transform the people so that they will support one another and help those in need. Those who live in this noncompetitive and noninterfering way are promised good health and long life.

The moral teachings of the *Tai-ping jing* are summarized in the following list of six serious sins and their results:

1. To accumulate Dao, the source and order of the universe, to keep it for oneself, and to refuse to teach it to others for their salvation. Those who commit this fault interrupt the Celestial Dao of life and bring the wrath of Heaven upon them.

2. To accumulate De [inner vitality] and to refuse to teach it to others so that they may nourish their vital principle. This is to interrupt the nourishing De of Earth and to arouse her wrath.

3. To accumulate riches and refuse to help the poor, letting them die of starvation and cold. These goods belong to the Central Harmony, that is to say, to mankind, and they are the means through which Heaven and Earth lavish their blessings. . . . They must circulate so that everyone has what he needs. Those who interrupt this circulation and who hoard what does not belong to them are enemies of the Harmonious Breath of Heaven and Earth.

4. To know that Heaven has a Dao and nevertheless to despise that Dao, to refuse to study it to prepare for one's own salvation and obtain long life. This comes to treating with contempt the body that was bequeathed by the ancestors, that is, to be a man without Dao and to be fated to die.

5. To know that it is good to practice De but to make no effort toward the good, to do evil in contempt of oneself. This is to revolt against Earth, which loves De.

6. The person whom Heaven has provided with muscles and physical strength so that he may nourish and clothe himself and who lives in idleness and becomes the parasite of the rich commits a deadly sin, because Heaven and Earth produce the riches necessary for man, who has to draw from them according to his strength and within the limits of his needs. If he does not make any effort and if he cannot obtain from others what he lacks, he will go so far as to seize the goods of others. Then he will be an enemy of the Central Harmony.[6]

The ideal government promoted by the *Tai-ping jing* was never put into practice, but the teachings of this book influenced many generations of Daoists in the centuries that followed. [See Religions of Mesoamerica p. 179, Native Religions of North America p. 285, Judaism pp. 390–94, Christianity pp. 497, 499, Islam pp. 635–37, 648–53, 665–72, Hinduism pp. 728–29, 738–43, 750–53, Buddhism p. 861, and Religions of Japan pp. 1100–1101 for discussion of Bible, scriptures, and religious texts.]

The Yellow Turban uprising was defeated in 184, but there was a similar group in West China at the same time that lasted much longer, The Way of the Celestial Masters (Tian-shi dao). This religious sect set up its own state ruled by a "Celestial Master," Zhang Lu (Chang-lu), who was assisted by priest officials. (The Yellow Turbans were similarly organized.) The Way of the Celestial Masters also worshiped Lao-zi as a god and recited the book attributed to him as a scripture text. Since members were required to contribute five bushels of rice each year, the nickname for this group was The Way of Five Bushels of Rice. The Celestial Master state lasted until 215 C.E., when it was incorporated into the state of Wei in the north, one of the three kingdoms that later succeeded the Han dynasty.

These popular movements in the late Han marked an important new development in the history of Chinese religions, the beginning of religious sects, with their own gods, beliefs, scriptures, rituals, leaders, and organizations, separate from the state and family. Their priests were commoners, yet they claimed to have direct revelations from celestial deities and powers that earlier were supposed to be available only to the emperor and court officials. Thus, these groups marked the beginning in China of a type of religious organization that is still very active all over the world today. They were parallel in time and structure to early Christianity and other sects in the Roman Empire.

The Yellow Turbans and the Way of Five Bushels of Rice were also the fore-runners of Daoism, which was the most important religious tradition founded in China (next to the ritual system supported by the government).

With the decline of the Han dynasty in the second century C.E., law and order in many areas were not enforced, and state-supported rituals not per-formed. Some officials, *fang-shi,* and literate farmers responded to this decline by creating their own systems of administration and religion. The Celestial Mas-ter state in West China was divided into twenty-four administrative districts, each led by a "libationer," a priest who was also in charge of all local affairs. These priests performed rituals modeled on those of the old imperial religion. After their state was taken over by Wei, some of these libationers served the Wei court and promised it divine support. At the same time they were the chiefs of religious congregations whose members were promised health and long life. Such benefits could be obtained partly through proper diet and exercises and partly with the help of gods who cooperated with the libationers. So it was that the Celestial Master movement became an established religion in North China.

When the north was invaded by nomadic tribes in the early fourth century C.E., many Chinese aristocrats fled south and took the Celestial Master religion with them. There, around what is now Nanjing (Nanking), they encountered southern religious leaders who had long practiced alchemy and worshiped gods of their own. The southerners were influenced by the Celestial Master religion, but before long a few of them began to have visions of gods who were higher and more mysterious than those of the Celestial Masters. These deities revealed scriptures that were written down in a beautiful flowing script: scriptures that spoke of immortals and star gods who would share secrets of health and per-petual life with those devoted to them. Some of these devotees were appointed by the gods as their special intermediaries or priests and told to warn people that although before long the world would end, a special few could be saved.

At about the same time, other intellectuals were writing books about alchemy, and mixing herbs or chemicals that could bring long life for someone who was a good person and who prepared them properly. Daoism developed out of the combination of these new revelations with alchemy and the older tradi-tion of the Celestial Masters. By the late fourth century it had priests who initi-ated novices to succeed themselves, elaborate rituals, scriptures in classical Chinese, and scores of gods with different levels of power. The scriptures were supposed to be studied only by the priests and those instructed by them; they contained the names of gods and secret chants for bringing the power of the gods down from the stars and into the body of the priest. Different organs of the body were believed to be residences for these gods. Priests were supposed to

A Daoist priest conducts a ritual.

repare for rituals by meditating on the gods and abstaining from sex, wine, and strong-tasting foods. After several months of such preparation, their bodies would be charged with star power, which they could transmit to earth through ritual chants and movements. Thus they could drive away demons, heal illness, and renew the forces of life and fertility in the community that sponsored the ritual. The Daoist priesthood thus provided a means of religious expression and status for educated people and also made cosmic life-power available for ordinary villagers. However, real knowledge of Daoist beliefs and techniques was limited to priests and their initiated disciples. They did not preach sermons to explain things to the people. This shows that Daoism was still elitist.

There were still millions of people in China, educated or not, who were not sure what happened after death, and not sure that in the long run a moral life made sense and was worth the effort. What these people did not have was a religion that provided an organized path of life for everybody, with clear teachings about the fate of the dead, whether good or bad. Many Chinese found this sort of egalitarian universal religion in Buddhism. [See Religions of Africa pp. 25, 54–57, 79–82, Religions of Mesoamerica p. 240, Native Religions of North America pp. 287, 320–22, 357–58, Judaism pp. 427–31, 456–75, Christianity pp. 529–33, Islam pp. 698–700, Hinduism pp. 770–74, 828–31, Buddhism pp. 952–56, and Religions of Japan pp. 1132–33, 1163–72 for discussion of new religious movements.]

The Coming of Buddhism

Up to this point, we have seen the ancient Chinese worldview as it was presupposed in various beliefs and practices, and as it came to be elaborated in explicit systems such as the thought of Confucius and in the *Lao-zi* book and even in the rather skeptical ideas of Xun-zi. With Buddhism we encounter the first significant "foreign" tradition in China.

Buddhism was founded in northeastern India in about 500 B.C.E. by a man named Siddhartha Gautama from the Shakya tribe in the mountains near what is now Nepal. Later on, he came to be called Shakyamuni (Chin., Shi-jia-mou-ni), "the Sage of the Shakyas," and Buddha (Chin., Fo), "the Enlightened One." Gautama studied with a number of spiritual guides, or gurus, to look for a religion that had sensible and satisfactory teachings about suffering, life, and death, but he found them all too one-sided in one way or another. Finally, after years of searching and meditating, he found the answers he wanted in his own mind; he was "enlightened" and immediately started to tell others what he had discovered. What Gautama believed he had found is the way life really is, always changing and full of suffering, yet offering hope to those who accept things as they are and do their best to live a moral life. Most other religions teach that there is something solid and eternal behind the changes of life, something they call God, or Dao, or Brahman (the cosmic soul of Hinduism). But for the Buddha such solidity is an illusion: It is just something we want to believe in order to feel secure and to assure ourselves that we can live forever too. He thought it was better to accept the fact that life is basically impermanent and to stop trying to deny the inevitable, ever-changing character of life and death. In his experience such acceptance eventually brought a new peace of mind and a new sense of compassion for other living things, all of which are caught in the same situation. [See Buddhism pp. 860–88 for the historical development of Buddhism.]

The Buddha believed that the reason most people are anxious and fearful is that underneath they are egocentric; that is, they tend to have a narrow and selfish point of view that sees everything as threatening or promising, victory or defeat, just for themselves. So they are always trying to build up their egos, to make them permanent and free from injury or even death.

Of course, since the world is always changing, this is an impossible task; our false sense of ego is always threatened and thus makes us a lot more nervous than we need to be. The answer is to meditate on life and affirm its impermanence and change as just the way things have always been. We can thus come to realize that we too are part of the movement of everything else, and so there is really no isolated and fearful ego to fight for. Life just is, and we might as well relax and enjoy it. Of course, there was more to it than that, because the Buddha also believed that life moves according to regular patterns of cause and effect that the human mind can understand. There is a cause or reason for everything that happens, and every result or effect of one cause in turn becomes the cause of something else. Eventually, everything is related. This was a very advanced idea for 500 B.C.E.; we would even call it scientific. But the Buddha was more interested in psychology than physics; for him, the point was that our feelings and actions also operate according to laws of cause and effect, which he called **karma,** an Indian word meaning "act" or "deed." For example, if I shout angrily at someone, he or she is likely to shout back; my anger causes another's reaction. Buddhism teaches that all human acts set in motion a chain of reactions, and that sensations such as desire can never be completely satisfied because there is always a greater or different desire. Whatever the sensation, it springs from changing desires, and those desires in turn arise from an ego that is always grasping for more in an endless quest for self-assurance. For the Buddha, all such emotions have reasons and results; our task is to meditate upon them to understand how they rise and fall and thus be free from their power. He taught that applying such "scientific" thinking to oneself helps get rid of illusions and brings a new sense of clarity and self-control. Eventually one reaches a point at which the old sense of ego has disappeared, and one acts simply in response to situations as they arise, without any concern for gain. Done in such a state of mind, actions are spontaneous and natural, without any "load," so they do not create reactions. Hence one breaks the cycle of cause and effect and becomes completely free. In other words, it is the intentions of action that cause its effects; if there are no selfish intentions, there are no effects.

In the Buddha's day most Indians believed (and still do) that all animals and humans live many lifetimes, not just one, with the form of each life shaped by how one lived in the last. Good living leads to a happy rebirth as a prosperous person or even a god; evil deeds lead to rebirth as a beggar or insect, usually after being punished in hell first. The Buddha accepted this idea and made it part of his karma system of cause and effect. According to Buddhism, what we do now has effects that last beyond death to shape our next life, one way or another. For ordinary people, this means one should be compassionate and fair, to build up good karma for a better rebirth; for religious specialists, it means that if one meditates long enough one can reach a level at which one's actions leave no reactions or residues, and thus one will not be reborn again but instead will enter a state of perfect peace called **nirvana.** Nirvana is a wonderful state, not a place, and is difficult to define; it is usually characterized as nonattachment (to things of the world), acceptance of one's life, and a peace that goes beyond mere sensual gratification.

The Buddha traveled around northeastern India for about forty years after his **enlightenment,** preaching and instructing small groups of disciples. To ordinary people he taught a life of discipline, compassion, and devotion to spiritual leaders, but to his closest followers he taught a path of **meditation,** mind control, and intense discussion. It was through months and years of inward-looking, seated meditation that one could train the mind in the Buddha's way of seeing. Such meditation demanded a quiet lifestyle free of worries about money, success, and family, so the Buddha's disciples left their families, did not marry, and were forbidden to engage in business, farming, or military service. At first they followed the Buddha on his preaching tours, but eventually they settled down in small groups in villas or gardens donated to them by wealthy merchants who also admired the Buddha. During his lifetime the Buddha emphasized that his followers should test his teaching for themselves, not just believe what he said, so that when he died there were a number of experienced disciples who could continue his message. Those who had "left the household life" lived in monasteries (for monks) and nunneries (for nuns) and devoted themselves to meditation and study, sharing the work of cleanup and repair, and begging every day for food in nearby villages. They were not allowed to raise their own food, because such labor could distract them from meditation, and furthermore it involved killing insects and animals, which creates bad karma. Those who joined the monasteries gave up all they owned, took new religious names, and wore simple robes. At first the Buddha's teachings were recited orally to keep the memories alive, but eventually they were written down in books, which became Buddhist scriptures known as *sutras*.

The Buddha's teachings were eagerly received by many people in India partly because they seemed sensible and direct and did not involve elaborate and expensive sacrifices to the gods. They were adapted to individual needs, could be followed by anybody, and could be practiced anywhere, at home or on the road, if one were a traveling merchant. Within one hundred fifty years of the Buddha's death, his movement was well established in monasteries across northern India and began to move south to Ceylon (now Sri Lanka), east to what are now Myanmar (Burma) and Thailand, and northwest toward modern Afghanistan. By the second century B.C.E., Buddhism was active in central Asia, particularly in oasis kingdoms along the main trade routes between India, China, and the Mediterranean world. Wherever it went, Buddhism was accepted by many people as a new, liberating religion that had something for everybody; simple morality for peasants and sophisticated philosophy for intellectuals, all based on scriptural texts and interpreted by literate monks. As has happened with the founders of other religions, the Buddha came to be venerated as a superhuman being whose teaching was eternally true, even though one suspects such veneration would have made him uneasy.

Sometime in the first century C.E. the first Buddhist merchants from India or central Asia reached China, which controlled trade routes far to the west. By the next century there were Buddhist monks in several Chinese cities, preaching and translating scripture texts from Indian Sanskrit into Chinese. Many Chinese were interested; Buddhism offered some religious ideas and practices they had not known of before, such as karma and rebirth, hell or purgatory, meditation, monks and monasteries, and a well-developed philosophy of mind and knowledge. By this time Buddhists in India worshiped images of the Buddha as symbols of his wisdom and compassion, using simple offerings of incense and fruit. Such images were also convenient objects of meditation, to remind meditators of who the Buddha was and what he had discovered. These images were also very popular in China, which had never seen anything like them before.

By the end of the second century C.E., there were several centers of Buddhism in China, and Buddhism grew rapidly from then on. The collapse of Han control made it easier for a foreign religion to get started, because people were freer to believe what they wanted. By the third century some aristocratic clans supported Buddhist missionaries and even produced a few young monks of their own. In 260 the first Chinese Buddhist pilgrim went to a kingdom in central Asia to study the faith and bring back scriptural texts to translate. He was the first of scores of such hardy pilgrims in the centuries to come, but early Chinese Buddhism depended heavily on monks from other lands who took the trouble to come to China and learn the language. The trip from India was very difficult and dangerous and could take as long as two years; most of these missionaries never made it back home. Buddhist thought was quite different from Chinese philosophy, so it took the Chinese a long time to understand it. Buddhism was more individualistic and psychological than the family-centered Chinese tradition, with its emphasis on agriculture, government, and a long, happy life in the midst of the world. But by the eighth century Chinese thinkers had developed forms of Buddhist philosophy and practice that fit the Chinese scene, the most important of which were **Pure Land** and **Chan** (which was later called Zen when it reached Japan).

Buddhism Becomes Chinese: Pure Land and Chan (Zen)

We have noted that Indian Buddhists came to regard the Buddha as a superhuman being whose teachings are eternally true. Since they believed that every person had lived many lifetimes in different places, it was natural to believe that Shakyamuni had been through many life cycles before the rebirth in which he attained enlightenment. Some Indian thinkers had long maintained that our universe is just one of many, and that each universe has a history of birth, growth, and decline, a view quite similar to that of modern astronomy. So it was that Buddhists began to say that in fact there were many Buddhas, one for each of the myriad universes, yet all preaching the same basic wisdom. As each universe went through cycles of death and rebirth, new Buddhas appeared to resume the teaching anew, because it too declined in power and had to be revived. They said that even in their time it was becoming more difficult to communicate Shakyamuni's teaching because people are ignorant and stubborn, and a new Buddha-to-be—Maitreya (Chin., Mi-le Fo), the future Buddha—is waiting in heaven to come to earth and start Buddhism all over again.

The combination of these ideas led to the belief that even in our universe there are many Buddhas, each in his own land or realm, each representing a particular Buddhist virtue, such as wisdom or compassion. Though Shakyamuni is the Buddha of our particular historical cycle, these other celestial Buddhas are available to help reinforce his teaching. The most popular of them is **Amitabha** (Chin., A-mi-tuo Fo), the Buddha of compassion who presides over a paradise, or "Pure Land," (Chin., Jing-tu) far to the west. Those who believe in him, meditate upon him, and pray for his aid will be saved and go to his paradise at death. There they will be surrounded by the Buddha's influence and teaching and easily attain enlightenment. This belief was appealing to many people because it promised a better afterlife than going to purgatory or just being reborn on earth. It was also more specific than nirvana and gave people more to look forward to.

Indian scriptures describing Amitabha's paradise were translated into Chinese by the third century C.E., and by the sixth century some Chinese monks began to base their whole message on this belief, telling people that if they just called out Amitabha's name in faith they would be saved. There was no need for meditation or studying philosophy, or even being able to read; just faith and devotion were enough. These Buddhist evangelists traveled about preaching and organizing groups of Amitabha worshipers, and people responded by the tens of thousands. By the seventh century Pure Land was the most popular form of Buddhism in China, and it remains so to this day in both China and Japan (which it reached in the ninth century). The appeal of this hope for paradise is easy to understand, because the Pure Land is described in Buddhist scriptures as a wonderful place indeed. In one book the Buddha tells his disciple Ananda that the Pure Land (San., Sukhavati), is

> the world system of the Lord Amitabha, rich and prosperous, comfortable, fertile, delightful and crowded with many Gods and men. And in this world system, Ananda, there are no hells, no animals, no ghosts, no Asuras [demons] and none of the inauspicious places of rebirth.
>
> . . .
>
> And that world system Sukhavati, Ananda, emits many fragrant odours, it is rich in a great variety of flowers and fruits, adorned with jewel trees, which are frequented by flocks of various birds with sweet voices. . . . And these jewel trees, Ananda, have various colours, many colours, many hundreds of thousands of colours. They are variously composed of the seven precious things, in varying combinations, i.e., of gold, silver, beryl, crystal, coral, red pearls or emerald.
>
> . . .
>
> And many kinds of river flow along in this world system Sukhavati. There are great rivers there, one mile broad, and up to fifty miles broad and twelve miles deep. And all these rivers flow along calmly, their water is fragrant with manifold agreeable odours, in them there are bunches of flowers to which various jewels adhere, and they resound with various sweet sounds.

[See Buddhism pp. 886–87, 919–20 and Religions of Japan pp. 1101–2 for discussion of Pure Land in Japanese Buddhism.]

In this paradise people get whatever they wish for, be it music, fine food, clothing, jewels, or palaces. They look and live like gods. But most important, in the Pure Land they constantly hear the Buddha's teaching, so that it is easy for them to attain enlightenment, never more to be reborn on earth. Believers are assured that nowhere in this wonderful place

> does one hear of anything unwholesome, nowhere of the hindrances, nowhere of the states of punishment, the states of woe and the bad destinies, nowhere of suffering. Even of feelings which are neither pleasant nor unpleasant one does not hear here, how much less of suffering! And that, Ananda, is the reason why this world-system is called the "Happy Land" [Sukhavati].[7]

All this is available to those who sincerely believe in the Buddha and his power.

Pure Land Buddhism was fine for ordinary people, but it became a mass movement that did not attract some of the more individualistic and intellectual. They were concerned for enlightenment now in this life and argued that however beautiful a Pure Land was, it was still not nirvana, the ultimate peace and clarity of mind. Some of them also felt that by the seventh and eighth centuries (in the Tang period) Buddhism had become *too* successful. There were thousands of monasteries, many of them wealthy, with lots of land, servants, and golden images donated by rich merchants and officials. By this time there had been several Buddhist emperors who gave money and official status to monasteries and expected the monks to support them in return. Buddhism was becoming a new form of Chinese state religion, which some more dedicated monks thought distracted people from the real point of their faith: finding a new level of awareness and acceptance within their own lives.

By the seventh century some reforming monks began a movement back to quiet meditation as the central practice of Buddhism. This movement developed gradually, and by the Song period (960–1127) these monks were considered to be the founders of a new school of Buddhism, the meditation school, or Chan, a word that in Japanese is pronounced "Zen." This school became quite popular among pious officials and merchants, but it never had the mass appeal of Pure Land, because the Chan path to salvation took more time and hard work. In part it was a return to the self-enlightenment that had been advocated by Shakyamuni himself a thousand years earlier. Some Chan leaders, feeling that Buddhism had become too worldly and materialistic, rejected images and scriptures and spent their lives meditating in small isolated monasteries, but most Chan people felt that images and scriptures were useful reminders of Buddhist truth as long as one did not become attached to them and remembered that the potential for enlightenment was inside every person. Their slogan was: "Become a Buddha yourself by realizing your own inner potential" (*jian-xing cheng-fo*). It is not surprising that it is this form of Buddhism that has had the most appeal in North America and Europe, because it sounds similar to our own ideas of self-development. Listen, for example, to some passages from the teachings of the Chan masters:

> Within your own natures the ten thousand things will all appear, for all things of themselves are within your own natures. Given a name, this is the pure . . . Buddha.
>
> . . .
>
> Good friends, when I say "I vow to save all sentient beings everywhere," it is not that I will save you, but that sentient beings, each with their own natures, must save themselves. What is meant by "saving yourselves with your own natures"? Despite heterodox views, passions, ignorance, and delusions, in your own physical bodies you have in yourselves the attributes of inherent enlightenment, so that with correct views you can be saved. If you are awakened to correct views, the wisdom of *prajna* will wipe away ignorance and delusion and you all will save yourselves.
>
> . . .
>
> Good friends, each of you must observe well for himself. Do not mistakenly use your minds! The *sutras* say to take refuge in the Buddha within yourselves; they do not say to rely on other Buddhas. If you do not rely upon your own natures, there is nothing else on which to rely.[8]

[See Buddhism pp. 919, 942–50 and Religions of Japan p. 1102 for discussion of Zen Buddhism.]

Prajna is a Sanskrit term for the wisdom of the enlightened mind, which sees things as they really are, without fear or illusion. It is this wisdom that makes a Buddha a Buddha; since we can also attain such enlightenment, we can become Buddhas too. All the potential for salvation is in our own minds.

Even though various forms of Buddhism became very popular during the Tang dynasty (618–907 C.E.), there were always some Daoists and Confucians who did not like it and who several times convinced rulers to make Buddhism illegal, confiscate monasteries, and force monks and nuns to return home. Most of these persecutions did not last long, but finally, in 844–845 C.E., a Daoist emperor forced thousands of monasteries to close and made most of the monks and nuns give up their religious vocations. This suppression of Buddhism was the most devastating of all. Then as now the Chinese government claimed complete authority over religion as well as politics and society. As a result of this nationwide persecution, many of the most important monasteries were ruined, and, with them, the schools of Buddhist study and philosophy they supported. In a few years the law was changed again, and Buddhism was allowed to rebuild, but by then there were only two schools left, Chan and Pure Land, both of which survived because of their popular support. Since then, they have been the dominant forms of Buddhism in all of east Asia. The most important reason for their success in China is that they both were developed there by Chinese monks who knew what their people wanted—a religious hope that was simple, direct, and practical, and that in the case of Pure Land could be carried out in the midst of ordinary social life. Even Chan monks developed forms of meditation that could be practiced by merchants and officials at home. Chan leaders also taught that the eternal truth of Buddhism was the same as the cosmic Dao, so that one could seek enlightenment amid the beauties of nature. [See Christianity pp. 502–4, 510, Islam pp. 659–62, Hinduism p. 772, Buddhism pp. 915–21, 942–52, and Religions of Japan p. 1102 for discussion of monasteries and monasticism.]

Buddhism started out in China as a foreign religion imported from India, but in the process of mutual influence with the Chinese tradition, it became more thoroughly "Chinese" than any other religion to enter China. So it was that Buddhism found its place in the Chinese view of the world.

A Revival of Confucianism

During the Han dynasty Confucianism became the official state philosophy; so when the Han dynasty fell, Confucianism lost prestige with it. After 220 C.E. it continued to exist as a conservative moral and social tradition but no longer produced many philosophers. For several hundred years the best philosophers in China were Buddhists, not Confucians. But eventually a reaction set in: Some officials and scholars began to worry that China was going to become so Buddhist that it would forget its own customs and culture, so they wrote articles and pamphlets attacking Buddhism as a foreign religion that the old Chinese sages had never heard of. By the eleventh century a few thinkers started to put together a new form of Confucian philosophy that was intended to provide a theoretical basis for all of life, from individual enlightenment to ruling the country. In so doing they borrowed ideas from Daoism and Buddhism, but combined them in a new system dominated by Confucian values, with Confucius venerated as wisest of all. The best-known of these new Confucians was **Zhu Xi (Chu Hsi,** 1130–1200), who taught that everything in the world is composed of "vital substance" (*qi*), which is shaped into different forms according to "ordering principle" (*li*). Though at one level every type of thing has its own ordering principle, at a higher level all things are united by the supreme ordering principle of the whole universe, which Zhu Xi called the *tai-ji,* "the great ultimate." Of course, human beings are put together in this same way, although for most humans their *qi* is so dark and thick that it obscures their *li.* That is, their physical needs and psychological desires block their potential for intelligence and moral concern. To become better people they must meditate on the ordering principles within themselves and in the world around them, so that they gradually become more mature, rational, and in control of themselves. *Li* are patterns that make sense of life; these patterns should be discerned in Confucian books, in society and government, and in nature. Wherever one finds harmony and order, there are principles that can be understood and followed, such as loyalty between friends, the fairness and honesty of a good judge, or the structure and flexibility of a stalk of bamboo, which keeps springing back no matter how hard the wind blows. When one has studied and thought long enough on such things, *li* is strengthened and one eventually becomes a wise and mature person who can help bring order to family, society, and government.

This Confucian combination of individual development with social responsibility appealed to many people who thought that even Chan and Pure Land Buddhism still placed too much emphasis on finding salvation outside the ordinary world, in a monastery or paradise. The government liked the new Confucianism too, because it affirmed that the existing social system would be fine as long as everyone lived according to the *li* of his or her position, for example, wife, father, or official. The principles of these social rules involved obedience to superiors, which, of course, was approved of by an authoritarian government. In the fourteenth century the government ordered that Zhu Xi's interpretations of the Confucian classics become the basis of civil service examination questions, so from then on every educated person had to study them.

Zhu Xi accepted ancestor worship and the veneration of the spirits of Chinese heroes, but he was opposed to Daoism, Buddhism, and the gods of popular religion and specifically denied that there was a supreme creator deity. The world simply came into existence through the interaction of *li* and *qi,* which are impersonal natural forces. This meant that after the new Confucianism was established many educated people became more skeptical about religion, or at least certain kinds of more personal and emotional religion. So it was that in China the religion of ordinary people had to develop on its own, without much help from intellectuals like the theologians of Christianity and Judaism. In China there was training for Buddhist monks and Daoist priests, but there were no seminaries that taught them to go out and preach to the people in a rational and orthodox way, and indeed, there were no churches for people to go to. So, though the Chinese have always practiced some forms of religion and divination, for the past thousand years religious thought and institutions in China have not had the same high profile they have had in Europe and North America. Religion has been more a part of ordinary life and always ultimately under government control.

Popular Religion

Nevertheless, even if some intellectuals did not place much emphasis on religion, various kinds of rituals and beliefs continued to be important for the vast majority of the population. As far back as the records go, we read of a variety of religious activities practiced by all except a few of the more strict scholars, priests, and monks, including ancestor worship, sacrifices to spirits of sacred objects and places, belief in ghosts and demons, **exorcism,** divination, and the use of spirit-mediums. By the eleventh century (Song period) these practices had been blended together with Buddhist ideas of karma and rebirth and Daoist teachings about many levels of gods to form the popular religious system common from then on.

Chinese popular religion is carried out in the midst of ordinary social life, in family, village, and city neighborhoods. It has no full-time specialists but is led by people who have other jobs, such as a farmer who may serve on a temple managerial committee, or a mechanic who works as a spirit-medium at night. There are popular religious temples where the gods are believed to live, but they usually have no resident clergy, just a caretaker or two. They are run and paid for by local people, who hire Daoist priests or Buddhist monks to perform special rituals. Worship in these temples is by individuals or families in the area who bring food offerings and incense to pray for blessings whenever they feel the need, though most come on the first or fifteenth of the lunar month or on festival days. In such temples there are no congregations or group worship, and usually no reciting of scriptures. In any event, most popular rituals are done at

A temple of popular religion.

home before the family altar or at the shrine of the locality god who is responsible for just one field or neighborhood.

The gods of popular religion are almost all the spirits of former human beings who have been deified, unlike the star gods of Daoism or the natural powers worshiped in the state religion. Since these gods were once human, they understand the needs of their worshipers, and furthermore they need their offerings and recognition if they are to keep their position as gods. Under Daoist influence popular gods were organized into a system like offices in a bureaucracy, each responsible for a specific function, such as healing smallpox, bringing up children, or protecting fishermen. This system is ruled by the **Jade Emperor** in heaven, parallel to the emperor on earth. The Jade Emperor appoints the spirits of virtuous people to divine offices, which they hold temporarily until they are promoted for doing well or demoted for not being effective. In fact, if people feel their prayers are not being answered, they can abandon a god, or even a temple, and look for aid somewhere else. The offices remain much the same, but gods to fill them appear and disappear.

These gods of popular religion are symbols of order, and many of them are believed to be equipped with weapons and celestial troops, as are some Daoist deities. Such force is necessary because beneath the gods is a vast array of demons, hostile influences that bring disease, suffering, and death—in a word, disorder. Ultimately the gods are more powerful, but these demons are violent and unruly and can be subdued only through repeated commands and dramatic rituals of exorcism. Most demons, or *gui,* are the spirits of the restless dead who died unjustly or whose bodies are not properly cared for; they cause disruption in order to draw attention to their problems. Other demons represent natural forces that can be dangerous, such as mountains and wild animals. Since these harmful spirits are believed to cause most illnesses, fires, and destructive weather, much effort is devoted to keeping them under control. A common method for driving them away is for a spirit-medium or Daoist priest to write out a charm in the name of a powerful god, a charm that is really a command such as might be issued by an emperor. Such a charm says something like, "I, the Jade Emperor, hereby order the evil and crooked forces causing this illness to leave immediately. This order has the power to smash and drive away all demons." The priest reads the charm aloud, then burns it so that its message is communicated to the sky through the smoke. There is a dramatic split in popular religion between the forces of good and evil. Most people in China had to struggle just to survive every day, so they easily felt threatened and did all they could to fight back, from working hard in their fields and protesting against unfair landlords to hiring a spirit-medium to heal a daughter's fever. This spirit of struggle has a lot to do with the success of Chinese people today.

There is another kind of Chinese popular religion, organized as sects or denominations similar to Protestant Christian groups in North America and Europe that are led and supported by ordinary people. These sects, still active in Taiwan, have their own books of scripture, which they chant or sing from in group worship. People join these associations as individuals looking for their own religious satisfaction, whereas in general popular religion there are no members, just families who worship in a village temple because they happen to live there. The sects go back in Chinese history to groups like the Yellow Turbans at the end of the Han dynasty, but they took their present shape in the thirteenth century under Buddhist influence. Some evangelistic monks started organizing groups of followers outside the monasteries, teaching them Buddhist beliefs in simple form, mostly about Amitabha's paradise. These groups grew so rapidly that more conservative monks became jealous and reported them to the government, which outlawed them because it was uneasy about any organized associations among the people. Once the sects were declared illegal, it was difficult for orthodox monks to work with them, so they were left on their own. They picked up a lot of ideas from Daoism and popular religion and tried to protect themselves by forming communes to raise their own food. When they were attacked by police or troops, some of them resisted with weapons, and even raided towns themselves; the government considered them just bandits or rebels. Perhaps because of this pressure, some sects started emphasizing Maitreya, the future Buddha, whom they said was coming soon to bring in a new world where they would be safe and happy. In the fourteenth century a few sects rebelled against the Mongols in the name of Maitreya, which confirmed their bad reputation with the government.

However, for the most part the sects were peaceful and provided a way for some people to be more religious if they wanted and to go directly to paradise at death, without going through purgatory first. By the sixteenth century the

Women reading scriptures and praying at a popular temple.

beliefs of most of these groups were centered on a great mother goddess who created the world and humankind and loves everybody as her own children. Unfortunately her children have forgotten the Mother, their real parent, and where they came from, and so they lead sinful lives and get into trouble through sex, drinking, dishonesty, and stealing. Sectarian scriptures were regarded as having been revealed by the Mother or her messengers to remind people of who they are, how they should live, and how they can be saved. Those who believe the message should join the sect and share the good news with others. These scriptures were passed on from one sect leader to the next and used as the basis of preaching, ritual, and discussion. Sect members were supposed to be more pious and good than their neighbors; their perception of themselves was very different from that of the government.

Foreign Religions in China Besides Buddhism

During the Tang dynasty (618–907 C.E.) China was again open to trade with foreign countries, so there was opportunity for foreign religions to come as well. In the seventh century some Christians reached China from what is now Syria, and many thousands more came in the thirteenth century during the period of Mongol rule. These Christians, called Nestorians after the name of the founder of their denomination, built churches in several Chinese cities and at one point had up to thirty thousand members, but for the most part their members were non-Chinese who had been brought in by the Mongols to help with administration and trade. They disappeared when the Mongols and other foreigners were driven out in the fourteenth century. There were a few Italian Catholic missionaries in China during the thirteenth and fourteenth centuries who also built churches, but their work too disappeared without a trace. The third time Christians tried to gain a foothold in China they were more successful, due primarily to the work of Italian Jesuits who arrived in the sixteenth century. They were intelligent and well educated, learned Chinese, and eventually were given permission to preach and build churches. By that time European astronomy and mathematics were superior to Chinese (though this was not true earlier), so a few of the Jesuits were appointed as court astronomers and mathematicians in Beijing. The Jesuits did a good job of communicating Christian teachings in language aristocratic Chinese could understand, though they played down Jesus' miracles and crucifixion. They accepted ancestor worship and agreed that Confucius was a very wise man. Before long, other Roman Catholic missionaries were admitted to China as well, and the church grew rapidly. However, some of the more conservative priests thought Jesuit attitudes went too far toward the acceptance of ancestors and Confucius, and they complained to the pope. After several decades of debate, Pope Clement XI in 1704 and 1715 ordered the Jesuits to change their approach and forbid ancestor worship, which disgusted the Chinese, who sent a lot of missionaries home and closed their churches. It was made illegal for Chinese to become Christians, but some did anyway; although the church was weakened it still survived. When a new wave of Roman Catholic missionaries came to China after 1840, they found several thousand Chinese Christians already there, but just a handful of priests.

A few Protestant missionaries from Europe and America first came to China in the early nineteenth century, and many more were permitted to come as a result of the treaties the Chinese were forced to sign when they lost wars with Britain and France. The Protestants translated the Bible into everyday spoken Chinese, brought in modern printing presses, and established schools and hospitals as well as churches, so they had an important impact on Chinese culture. However, not many Chinese actually became Christians, a pattern that continued into the twentieth century. Before 1949 Chinese Christian churches were still heavily dependent on foreign missionaries and financial support. At present there are about thirteen million Christians in a population of more than a billion Chinese.

The other major foreign religion in China is Islam, which was brought there by Arab and central Asian Muslims in the eighth century. Many more Muslims came during the Mongol period, when China was wide open to the rest of the world, and settled in cities all over the country, but mostly in the western provinces. There are now about thirty million Muslims in China, more than in Saudi Arabia. Though they have intermarried with other Chinese, they have kept their religion and taught their children Arabic so they can read the Qur'ān (Koran), the holy book of Islam. [See Islam p. 613 for mention of Islam in China.]

Before the new wave of Christian missionaries in the nineteenth century, the only foreign religion to have much impact on Chinese culture was Buddhism. By contrast, Islam has always been the religion of a large central Asian immigrant group and did not become an integral part of Chinese culture; earlier Christian efforts failed to make a dent in the religious life of China, and even more recent Christian missionary work did not convert more than a few million Chinese. The relative lack of success of these foreign religions in converting large numbers of Chinese is an indication of how Chinese culture has continued to be strong and self-contained.

42

Types of Beliefs and Activities in Chinese Religious Life

NOW THAT WE HAVE LOOKED briefly at the historical development of Chinese religions, we can use that knowledge to better understand the unity of Chinese religions as the expression of a comprehensive worldview. The members of every religion believe that its teachings are special and reveal basic truths about life and the world. Our task is neither to dispute nor to support these claims but to try to understand them in as objective and balanced a way as we can. We must also remember that living religion is as much what people do as what they think, so in this chapter we will discuss rituals, buildings, and types of leaders as well as beliefs.

Once a religious tradition has assumed its definitive shape, it operates as a religious system that can be analyzed and interpreted in terms of all the interrelated aspects that fit together to express and maintain the system. Key aspects of the Chinese religious tradition are its general understanding of how the world fits together, as well as related features such as sacred space, sacred time, symbols of superhuman power, rituals, divination, exorcism, meditation, leadership and organization, and ethical teachings. Worldview is the overall picture of what the "world" (or universe or reality) is. Sacred space and sacred time are those places and occasions within the world that help members of that tradition orient themselves. Symbols of superhuman power are the forces beyond and even within the world that come to the aid of humans. Rituals are the actions that relate humans to these divine powers. Divination is a special ritual for anticipating the future, while exorcism is a ritual of driving out evil powers. Meditation is a form of self-development practiced by individuals. Leadership and organization refer to the individual figures and the social structures that maintain, guide, and transmit particular religious forms. Ethical teachings are the principles of proper behavior by which individuals and groups regulate their lives. All these aspects of the Chinese religious tradition interact and interrelate to express a unified worldview.

Worldview

In chapter 40 we saw the traditional Chinese understanding of how the world is and how it came to be as an interrelated living system. Such an understanding is a set of basic assumptions about the origins and nature of life. These assumptions shape everything else people do or say. As Chinese religions became more highly organized and formally thought out, these assumptions were codified in explicit statements. Although particular statements may appear rather different because of their respective emphases, they still express the basic Chinese worldview. Good examples are two famous statements by Confucian philosophers of the eleventh century C.E., Zhang Zai (1020–1077) and Zhou Dun-yi (1017–1073):

> Heaven is my father and Earth is my mother, and even such a small creature as I find an intimate place in their midst.
>
> Therefore that which fills the universe I regard as my body and that which directs the universe I consider as my nature.
>
> All people are my brothers and sisters, and all things are my companions.
>
> The great ruler (the emperor) is the eldest son of my parents (Heaven and Earth), and the great ministers are his stewards. Respect the aged—this is the way to treat them as elders should be treated. Show deep love toward the orphaned and the weak—this is the way to treat them as the young should be treated. The sage identifies his character with that of Heaven and Earth, and the worthy is the most outstanding man. Even those who are tired, infirm, crippled, or sick; those who have no brothers or children, wives or husbands, are all my brothers who are in distress and have no one to turn to. (Zhang Zai, "The Western Inscription")

> The Ultimate of Non-being and also the Great Ultimate (Tai-ji)! The Great Ultimate through movement generates *yang*. When its activity reaches its limit, it becomes tranquil. Through tranquility the Great Ultimate generates *yin*. When tranquility reaches its limit, activity begins again. So movement and tranquility alternate and become the root of each other, giving rise to the distinction of *yin* and *yang*, and the two modes are thus established.
>
> By the transformation of *yang* and its union with *yin*, the Five Agents of Water, Fire, Wood, Metal, and Earth arise. When these five material forces [*qi*] are distributed in harmonious order, the four seasons run their course.
>
> The Five Agents constitute one system of *yin* and *yang*, and *yin* and *yang* constitute one Great Ultimate. The Great Ultimate is fundamentally the Non-ultimate. The Five Agents arise, each with its specific nature.
>
> When the reality of the Ultimate of Non-being and the essence of *yin*, *yang*, and the Five Agents come into mysterious union, integration ensues. *Qian* (Heaven) constitutes the male element, and *kun* (Earth) constitutes the female element. The interaction of these two material forces engenders and transforms the myriad things. The myriad things produce and reproduce, resulting in an unending transformation.

It is man alone who receives (the Five Agents) in their highest excellence, and therefore he is most intelligent. His physical form appears, and his spirit develops consciousness. The five moral principles of his nature (humanity or *ren*, righteousness, propriety, wisdom, and faithfulness) are aroused by, and react to, the external world and engage in activity; good and evil are distinguished; and human affairs take place. (Zhou Dun-yi, "An Explanation of the Diagram of the Great Ultimate")[9]

These statements show that the world came into being through natural processes, and how everything we know is part of this universe and therefore related to all the other parts. This includes human beings and gods as well; we are all united in one big system, with nothing outside it. In the first document the cosmos is likened to a huge social system under the parentage of father Heaven and mother Earth; in the second document the universe is presented as the balanced interaction of physical and metaphysical forces. But these documents are just two examples of a distinctively Chinese worldview that is expressed in many particular forms, from ancient times through the present. There are some creation stories in China, but in them the basic physical stuff of the world already exists at the beginning; the gods or culture heroes just organize it into the forms we know. This view of the world is similar to that of many other cultures, such as the Hopi or the Sioux in North America, but it is quite different from the traditional teachings of Judaism, Christianity, and Islam. In these religions there is just one God, who exists outside the world, which he then decides to create: It is really God that is sacred, not the world itself. The Chinese approach tends to give more religious meaning to life in the midst of the world and does not emphasize a higher spiritual reality that individuals should try to attain. Of course there are high-level symbols in China like Tian and the Daoist star gods, and, on the other hand, in Christianity, Jesus Christ is a symbol of God's involvement with the world, but the basic difference between the two worldviews is still clear. In each case the tradition is shaped by its fundamental understanding of reality. What is distinctive of the Chinese worldview is its conception of the world as a living system. [See Native Religions of North America pp. 267–68 for comparison with Native American religions.]

Sacred Space

All religions have special places—such as certain churches, synagogues, shrines to saints, or towns where the founder lived—where people believe the real truth of things has been revealed. Worshipers visit such places regularly to come into contact with the power of these special places, to be reminded of who they are and to be inspired by the ideals represented by these places.

What is distinctive about sacred places in Chinese religions (as in Native American religions) is that the world itself is a sacred place. Therefore, the Chinese have always understood their world to be full of holy mountains, caves, and landscapes that particularly reveal the power and beauty of the earth. Even today Chinese vacationers go in groups to visit beauty spots, especially those that have been praised by a poet or painter. Daoism and the state religion organized China's geography into areas controlled by sacred mountains. Shrines and altars were built on these mountains where sacrifices were offered to petition for rain. The landscape was organized into smaller areas as well, with a locality god (earth god) for each neighborhood or field and city gods for county-seat towns. Lower in status than the locality gods were deities of the household bed, stove, and doorway, each with a little niche for a paper image and incense.

Buddhist monasteries and the temples of Daoism and popular religion provided parallel sacred places, as did little shrines along the roadsides for the spirits of the dead who, because they had died violently, were believed to have special powers. People regularly visited these places to ask for healing or for children, or to report deaths and weddings to the gods; some people in Taiwan and Hong Kong, and even in parts of rural China, still do. In China the whole world was potentially sacred, from crossroads, wells, and old trees to the highest mountain ranges. The most direct evidence for this is the *feng-shui* discussed in chapter 40. *Feng-shui* assumes that the earth is alive with lines of force; those living where such lines come together will have vitality and good fortune. People in Hong Kong may have no choice in the location and orientation of their apartments, but many of them still arrange their furniture on *feng-shui* principles, with a sofa facing south along a north wall or a cabinet set to block potentially hostile lines of force from across the street. The result can be a pleasant arrangement satisfying both religion and art. From the larger outlines of the universe to the smaller confines of one's home, the Chinese have always been concerned with sacred space. By properly observing local sacred places, Chinese people helped preserve the balance of the living world, and thereby were able to benefit from the power of a harmonious universe.

Sacred Time

Just as there are special places in Chinese religions, so are there special times set aside. Within the Chinese worldview there are particular seasons and particular occasions in a person's life that are seen as sacred, providing a continuing orientation within the passage of the years and the course of one's life. [See Religions of Africa pp. 42–51, 76–79, Religions of Mesoamerica pp. 201–6, Native Religions of North America pp. 278–79, 295–98, 306–8, Judaism pp. 445–50, 542–43, Christianity pp. 555–57, Islam pp. 677–78, 680–86, Hinduism pp. 747, 807–14, Buddhism pp. 915–17, 921, 931–37, and Religions of Japan pp. 1146–50 for description and discussion of rites of passage.]

Some of the sacred times in Chinese religions focus on individuals and others on groups. Because of the well-known Chinese emphasis on the family and group, individual celebrations were not so important as they are for Westerners. The birth of a male child was a cause for rejoicing, but there were no religious rituals associated with it, and not much attention was paid to individual birthdays until one reached sixty. The real birthday for everyone was New Year's Day, when the powers of cosmic life were renewed and everyone was counted a year older. [See Religions of Africa pp. 45–46, 76, Native Religions of North America pp. 307, 385–86, Judaism pp. 445–46, Christianity p. 556, Islam p. 682, Hinduism pp. 810–11, Buddhism p. 932, and Religions of Japan pp. 1146–1147 for description and discussion of birth rites.]

The most important celebrations in a lifetime were at marriage and death, but even then family interests were central. Marriage was essentially a contract between two families, arranged by the parents through professional "go-betweens." The wishes of the couple involved had little influence; they were often betrothed to each other when they were small children and may not have seen each other before the wedding. Marriage rituals consisted of exchange of gifts and agreements between the families, culminating in a great feast at the groom's home on the day the bride was brought there in a sedan chair, together with her furniture for the new family unit at her in-laws' house. No priests were involved, no exchange of vows by the couple. The Chinese equivalent was introducing the bride and groom to each other's families. The first time the couple was alone was in their bedroom at the end of the first wedding day (the whole process took about three days). Rituals we might call religious were involved with marriage at only two points, the first before betrothal when a diviner was consulted to see if the horoscopes of the couple were compatible. The second point was on the first wedding day; when the bride first entered the groom's house they both bowed briefly before the tablets of his ancestors. [See Religions of Africa pp. 48–51, 77–78, Judaism pp. 447–48, Christianity p. 556, Islam pp. 683–84, Hinduism pp. 809–10, Buddhism p. 935, and Religions of Japan p. 1148 for description and discussion of marriage rites.]

Hired dancers in a funeral procession.

Funeral rituals were very complex and took days to complete. Their essential point was to prepare a peaceful afterlife for the deceased and ensure that he or she would become a cooperative ancestral spirit who could help the family later on. The rituals included placing the open coffin in the main room of the house, offering food to the spirit of the dead, praying to the gods for safe passage to the underworld, and a procession to the grave, with sedan chairs, orchestra, and mourners wearing sackcloth. At the grave site, chosen through *feng-shui,* there was a ritual to place the spirit in its ancestral tablet, followed by a last ceremonial feast. After the coffin was buried the family returned home with the tablet, placed it on the family altar, and inaugurated it with a second feast, some of which was brought back from the tomb. Death was accepted, but the real emphasis in funeral rituals was on strengthening the continuing life of the family, through such practices as throwing beans and nails on the bottom of the coffin to symbolize a desire for many sons. (The word for nail is *ding,* pronounced the same as another character meaning male person.) [See Religions of Africa pp. 42–45, 78–79, Religions of Mesoamerica pp. 144, 229–33, Native Religions of North America pp. 300–301, 307–8, 335–37, Judaism pp. 448–50, Christianity p. 557, Islam pp. 684–85, Hinduism pp. 813–14, Buddhism pp. 935–37, and Religions of Japan pp. 1149–50 for description and discussion of death and funeral rites.]

Centuries ago there were initiation rites for young men and women in China, consisting essentially of giving a new adult name and cap to a man, and giving a special hairdo and new clothes to a woman. Over the years, however, these rites came to be celebrated just before marriage, which was the real coming of age for the young person as a producing member of society. It is interesting to realize that in China what we now think of as individual celebrations were primarily devoted to the well-being of the group. This has a lot to do with the sense of mutual dependence and relatedness that characterized the Chinese view of life.

Some of the sacred times in Chinese religions focus on special occasions of power and revelation for the group. Just as Christianity celebrates Easter and Judaism observes Yom Kippur, so too in Chinese religions are there "holy days" for every season of the year, and for saints and founders as well. China observes festivals throughout the year, from New Year's to the winter solstice, forming an annual cycle that is repeated every year. These celebrations have a broad significance that is more than just "religious." Because in traditional China there were no weeks or weekends, these festivals had economic as well as social and religious functions; they gave people time off from work, time to be with family and friends and to eat good food. For the poor, festivals usually were the only days they ate meat.

The major festivals of the annual cycle are traced here from New Year's to the end of the year. Most of them are determined by a lunar calendar. The most important annual festival is New Year's, which is celebrated for more than a month. According to traditional customs the festival begins in the twelfth month with a ritual to send the household gods to heaven, where they report on family activities during the preceding year. Then the house is cleaned to get rid of old

A woman offering incense at a popular temple.

dirt and bad influences, to start the new year fresh. Debts are paid off for the same reason. On the last night of the lunar year, families gather for a big feast, which is first offered to the spirits of the ancestors, who are believed to eat the invisible essence of the food. The house is sealed to keep out the last old *qi* of the year, and the family stays awake all night, talking and playing games, with everyone being sure to mention only good things and not say words that sound like those for death and disease. What one does that night influences good or bad fortune for the whole year. At dawn the doors are opened to let in the powerful, fresh, vital breath of the new year. The household gods are welcomed back with new paper images, and the oldest man in the family offers food and incense outdoors to the gods in heaven. During the next few days people visit one another with gifts of money or food, make offerings at local temples, and watch parades of paper lions and dragons. In China, New Year's Day is also everyone's birthday (though people have individual birthdays too), which further contributes to a strong sense of starting afresh.

In the spring there is the Pure and Bright (Qing-ming) Festival, one hundred six days after the winter solstice, in early April. Also known as the **Spring Festival,** it began as a kind of continuation of the New Year's Festival, so it emphasized the importance of taking baths in flowing streams to wash away the dirt, disease, and harmful forces that had accumulated in the previous year. Closely related to this washing was the Cold Food Festival for the renewal of fire, celebrated at about the same time. All old fires were put out for three days, while people ate cold food that had been prepared beforehand. At the end of this period, new fires were started in the ancient way, by rubbing sticks together, to symbolize the rebirth of *yang* power in the new spring season.

One theme in the old Spring Festival was worship of ancestors, and as time passed this element became more and more important; eventually the festival became a time of honoring the family dead by cleaning their graves and offering food to their spirits as part of a big picnic. In this way the dead are reintegrated into the life of the family, making the Spring Festival a time of both sadness and joy. (There is a detailed description of a Spring Festival ritual picnic in the next chapter.)

Another exciting time for people in old China was the Midsummer Festival, celebrated on the fifth day of the fifth lunar month at the summer solstice, the longest day of the year. On this day, the power of *yang* has reached its peak, and the power of *yin* is about to be reborn. People were ambivalent about this. On the one hand, too much of anything is bad, so one did not want to do things that encouraged *yang* any more. Hence, no big fires were lit, and boys born during this time were considered potentially dangerous. (Boys usually have enough *yang* already; too much will make them too aggressive.) On the other hand, the revival of *yin* leads eventually to the cold and darkness of winter. *Yin* was associated with disease, death, and demons; at the Midsummer Festival, people went up into the hills to collect medicinal herbs to ward off disease. The power of such herbs comes from *yang,* so this is the time they are most charged with the ability to hold off *yin* diseases. People also hung up protective charms at this time, made of *yang* symbols like red paper and peachwood.

The other major festival of the Chinese sacred year is the Feast of Souls on the fifteenth of the seventh lunar month (late August). This festival is influenced by Buddhist ideas of purgatory and rebirth. Purgatory is a place where the souls of the dead go to be purged of their sins before they are reborn in a new life. The Chinese believe that such souls need help from their living relatives, so pious and responsible families have Buddhist monks read scriptures and burn incense to encourage the souls as they are being punished for their sins in one court of purgatory after the next.

However, there are many lost souls in purgatory with no families to pray for them, and Buddhist compassion demands that these desperate, hungry souls be cared for as well. The belief developed that in the seventh lunar month the gates of purgatory open for a time, and all the lost souls can fly back to earth to receive food offerings and hear scriptures read for their salvation. So the Feast of Souls is a time of rituals for the dead, both by individual families and in temples and monasteries. For their own relatives, Buddhist families sometimes have monks burn elaborate paper houses full of paper furniture, food, and ritual money, all to be transferred to purgatory through the flames for the comfort of the dead.

The Chinese celebrate other festivals as well, such as a midautumn harvest festival in honor of the moon. At this time of year one can still buy moon-cakes in Chinese bakeries around the world. Another type of festival that is not directly tied to the seasonal cycle is held in honor of the birthday of the god in a local temple. Such birthday rituals involve hiring priests to recite scriptures and make offerings, entertaining gods and worshipers with popular operas on outdoor stages, and taking an image of the deity on a tour of its district to drive out harmful forces and renew good ones. [See Religions of Africa pp. 74–75, Religions of Mesoamerica pp. 229–38, Native Religions of North America pp. 308–16, 351–57, Judaism pp. 439–45, Christianity pp. 551–55, Islam pp. 674, 677–79, Hinduism p. 829, Buddhism pp. 937–41, and Religions of Japan pp. 1140–46, 1153–62 for description and discussion of festivals and annual celebrations.]

These Chinese festivals and rituals have much in common with the observance of "sacred time" in other traditions. All religions have a sense that sacred power periodically runs down and has to be renewed; similarly, all religions emphasize that individuals need to be "recharged" occasionally by contact with sacred power, particularly at crucial stages in their lives such as birth, marriage, and death. Chinese religions share this universal concern for sacred time but express it in a distinctively Chinese form. From ancient times in China there was an emphasis on the rhythm of the days, (lunar) months, and seasons as a kind of regularity within change that assured the balance and harmony of the cosmos. As we saw earlier, offerings must be *yang* or *yin* to correspond with the "cycle" of the cosmos. This is just one of the ways in which the Chinese felt they had to participate in and contribute to the ongoing rhythm of the universe. By participating in seasonal festivals and observing rites of passage (birth, marriage, death) the Chinese helped preserve the rhythm of the world as a living system. [See Religions of Mesoamerica pp. 159–60, 206–9, Native Religions of North America pp. 280–82, 351–54, Judaism pp. 431–34, Christianity pp. 551–53, Islam pp. 674, 707, Hinduism pp. 727, 793–94, Buddhism pp. 890–91, and Religions of Japan pp. 1141–46 for discussion of religious calendar and time.]

Symbols of Superhuman Power

In Chinese religions power is gained through harmonious relationship to sacred space and sacred time, but there are also symbols of higher power or special beings believed to be superhuman, or even gods. In the Western traditions of Judaism, Christianity, and Islam there is a range of such figures as in Jesus, Muḥammed, and the God of the universe. We have already seen that there are Chinese parallels to this kind of superhuman figure. However, in the Chinese worldview there is not such a sharp distinction between gods and humans as found in the Western traditions. In China, humans, special beings, and gods are all parts of the same system: Humans are potentially divine, and gods often take human form. People can live forever or even be resurrected from the dead if they know the correct rituals and alchemical drugs. So it is that most gods of popular religion are deified humans, venerated for their courage, strength, or compassion. The Buddhas too were once human, so they also can understand the needs of their worshipers. The cosmic gods of Daoism are provided with images and titles, and even mountains and rivers can respond to human pleas. After all, are not they too made of the same vital substance?

A good example of a popular Chinese deity is **Ma-zu (Ma-tsu)**, the goddess of fishermen and sailors, who is supposed to have begun her divine career as a pious young woman who lived on an island off the southern coast in the eleventh century C.E. This girl, who never married, was believed to be able to calm typhoons and to be able, while she was in a trance, to send out her spirit to rescue people drowning at sea. She died young, with lots of life energy left over and no husband or children to worship her restless spirit. Before long, local people began to worship her, claiming that their prayers had been answered, children healed, and fathers brought home from the sea. The spirit's fame spread and came to the attention of officials. Sailors on imperial naval expeditions turned to her for aid, and some claimed she had saved them from storms and pirates. On one such expedition, it was a crown prince who was saved, and when he became emperor, he had a temple built in her honor and gave her a new, more exalted title. In this way the girl became a goddess, with ever-widening fame and several titles, but she is popularly known today in Hong Kong as Tian-hou, "Queen of Heaven," and in Taiwan as Ma-zu, "Grandmother."

Here is a folktale about Ma-zu as a young girl that illustrates how she was understood by ordinary people:

Although the girl was only seven years old she already possessed supernatural powers. Her father and her two brothers were merchants, and each time they were overtaken by a storm during the sea crossing, she rescued them from the waves without anyone's being aware of it. One day her father and brothers were once more on the sea when a terrific storm sprang up. She felt very troubled at their great danger, and her soul immediately left her body and hurried to their assistance. Being half-immortal, she arrived in an instant at the sea, where the waves were breaking as high as the sky.

The ship was pitching and tossing in all directions, and the passengers, pale with terror, thought that their last hour had come. The daughter grasped her brothers in her arms and her father in her mouth and flew over the sea. It made no difference to her whether the sea was deep or shallow. The three castaways saw only a little girl appear through the winds and the waves to save them, and they thought that she was an immortal; they had no idea that she was their own little girl.

Before leaving she had been talking with her mother, who was frightened out of her wits when her daughter broke off in the middle of a word and her body became stiff and cold. The mother thought she had fallen ill, and began to sob and weep, but the girl lay as though she were dead.

After she had called and fondled her for a long time, the girl suddenly said, "Yes." "Wake up, child," said the mother, "I nearly wept myself to death." "Father is dead." "What are you saying?" cried the mother. "Father and my two brothers were overtaken by a terrible storm on the sea, and the ship sank, but my soul hastened over the water to save them. I grasped my brothers in my two hands, and caught my father's clothes in my mouth. But you wept and called for me, until my heart was touched, and I had to answer 'Yes,' whereupon my father dropped out of my mouth. I would otherwise have saved him, but immediately after his fall he was hidden by the waves, and I could find no trace of him. I managed to save my brothers, but, alas, father is dead!" "Is that really true?" asked the mother. "Yes." "Oh, woe is me, woe is me!"

Soon the brothers came home. Weeping, they clasped their mother in their arms and told her how first their father had been saved and later drowned. The daughter reproached her mother, saying, "You are to blame for the death of my father. Look, my feet and hair are still moist." The mother embraced her children again.

The daughter was sorry for her mother's widowed state and swore an oath never to marry. She tied her hair together and waited on her mother till her death. After her death she became an immortal. She became protectoress of merchants and ships on the rivers, and is particularly worshiped by them.[10]

Deities such as Ma-zu have special abilities and limited powers, but Ma-zu is just one example of the many symbols of superhuman power in China. When all these superhuman powers are linked together they are believed to be capable of doing anything that a single, supreme god can—from helping an army win a battle to healing a sore on a child's neck. In Chinese religions, it is all a matter of knowing what temple to visit to meet one's needs. All the gods have names and life stories comparable to those of Ma-zu to help people know what they can do: a deified general for a son at war; an ancient physician for healing illness. Popular operas portray the gods on stage, so even illiterate people know these figures. Beliefs concerning some deities are based on hero stories in novels; others are discussed by storytellers and spirit-mediums. Everyone in China has knowledge of and access to symbols of superhuman power to help him or her avoid misfortune and seek good fortune. [See Religions of Africa pp. 39–42, 64–69, Religions of Mesoamerica pp. 157–58, 186–89, Native Religions of North America pp. 274–75, 288–305, 330–32, Judaism pp. 414–15, Christianity pp. 537–38, Islam pp. 635–37, Hinduism pp. 739–41, 759–61, Buddhism pp. 780–84, 900–903, and Religions of Japan pp. 1112–27 for discussion of God, gods, and objects of worship.]

Rituals: Actions That Relate Us to Divine Power

Rituals are the religious behavior or action that bring human beings into meaningful contact with divine power. The basic theme of Chinese ritual is *reciprocity:* a mutual exchange of gifts and favors between gods and worshipers, so that both gain from the transaction. In China the most common way of forming a reciprocal relationship is through sharing a meal; when guests eat, they recognize that they owe the host a favor. Most ritual offerings consist of food—

cooked for gods and ancestors, uncooked for ghosts. Cooked food is usually left on an altar or table for a while until the gods have eaten its inner essence; then their worshipers take it home and eat it as food blessed with divine power, a Chinese form of Holy Communion. Food offerings are a shared meal; the god, as a guest, is expected to grant a favor in return, a favor requested through a prayer in the ritual. Chinese gods are treated with formality, particularly those in higher positions, and those honored in elaborate Daoist or state rituals. But even in Daoism, the priest is believed to have the powers of a god during ritual; after all, he has prepared himself for years and can call divine powers down upon himself. The Buddhist nun too knows that the Buddha image before her represents a potential for wisdom and compassion she has within herself. At the popular level, gods are treated as important guests, as divine officials, but nonetheless worshipers know that the gods need them too, so there can be a kind of familiarity in worship that is different from the solemnity of services in a Confucian temple or a Presbyterian church. There are some parallels between these Chinese deities and the saints of popular Roman Catholicism, who also represent special virtues and powers, easily available to their devotees.

Reciprocity also governs the rituals of state religion. In addition to ancestor worship, the oldest and most formal Chinese rituals that we know of in any detail are those of the imperial state religion. One took place at the winter solstice, on the longest night of the year, when the dark force of *yin* is at its peak. The emperor and his officials rose before dawn to offer sacrifice to Heaven and the power of *yang* to support the rebirth of light and warmth in the middle of winter, to make sure that spring would come again. Dressed in an embroidered

Offering food at a popular temple.

robe, the emperor climbed to the top of a great round stone altar south of the city, the direction of *yang*. There, officials called out to the royal ancestors and Heaven in a loud, slow monotone, asking for their aid and assuring them of the ruler's devoted support. The ancestors, and deities of the sun, moon, stars, planets, wind, and rain were represented by inscribed tablets. Food was offered before these tablets: soup, vegetables, and fruits, together with fish, beef, and pork. A young red bull without a blemish (a symbol of *yang*) was offered to Heaven. Its flesh was burned on a special altar. Wine, incense, and silk were also presented, all accompanied by the music of bells and drums. If all went smoothly and well, and the weather was clear, the emperor was confident that he had done his part and that the ancestors and Heaven would do theirs as well. The spirit and intention of such rituals is well illustrated by prayers offered to the "Ruler on High" (Shang-di; in the following passage called Shang-te or Te) by the emperor:

> Of old in the beginning, there was the great chaos, without form and dark. The five elements had not begun to revolve, nor the sun and the moon to shine. In the midst thereof there existed neither form nor sound. Thou, O spiritual Sovereign, camest forth in Thy presidency, and first didst divide the grosser parts from the purer. Thou madest heaven; Thou madest earth; Thou madest man. All things with their re-producing power, got their being.
>
> O Te, when Thou hadst separated the *Yin* and the *Yang* (i.e., the heavens and the earth), Thy creating work proceeded. Thou didst produce, O Spirit, the sun and the moon and the five planets, and pure and beautiful was their light. The vault of heaven was spread out like a curtain, and the square earth supported all on it, and all things were happy. I, Thy servant, venture reverently to thank Thee, and, while I worship, present the notice to Thee, O Te, calling Thee Sovereign.
>
> Thou hast vouchsafed, O Te, to hear us, for Thou regardest us as a Father. I, Thy child, dull and unenlightened, am unable to show forth my dutiful feelings. I thank Thee, that Thou has accepted the intimation. Honourable is Thy great name. With reverence we spread out these gems and silks, and, as swallows rejoicing in the spring, praise Thine abundant love.
>
> The great feast has been set forth, and the sound of our joy is like thunder. The Sovereign Spirit vouchsafes to enjoy our offering, and my heart feels within me like a particle of dust. The meat has been boiled in the large caldrons, and the fragrant provisions have been prepared. Enjoy the offering, O Te, then shall all the people have happiness. I, Thy servant, receiving Thy favours, am blessed indeed.[11]

The use of animal flesh in state rituals has continued in popular religion but is prohibited in Buddhism and some branches of Daoism. Though there are sticks of incense and bowls of fruit on Buddhist altars, characteristic Buddhist rituals are more verbal and personal, with group readings of scripture, recitation of the names of Buddhas, and quiet prayers. Rituals performed by Daoist priests are the most elaborate of all, with clouds of incense smoke; a small orchestra of Chinese violins, clarinets, bells, and drums; stately dances; complex hand movements; and the chanting of invocations and commands. But despite their differences, all these rituals are united by a common theme: the forming of a temporary relationship with gods or Buddhas through offering them gifts of food and incense, along with a kind of ritual money used in popular religion. Such relationships oblige the gods to respond in some way, even though it may not be exactly the way the worshiper has in mind.

Of course, such reciprocity is expected by ordinary worshipers in all religions, although some theologians maintain that the proper attitude toward the highest gods is reverence with no expectation of reward. Underneath, however, most people feel that if they perform the proper rituals and act decently, God should take care of them, and they complain if things go wrong. Popular religion in Western culture means expecting specific, positive answers to our prayers. Here again, religious attitudes are a special form of ordinary social interaction, in which we assume that a favor done is a favor due. Society is built on the reciprocity of such obligations, some of which we make into legal requirements, so it is not surprising to find religious rituals operating in the same way. What is distinctive about Chinese religion is the emphasis that this reciprocity occurs within the balance of sacred places, sacred time, and superhuman powers that preserves and maintains the world as a living system. [See Religions of Mesoamerica pp. 201–2 for a discussion of reciprocity.]

Divination and Exorcism

Most people would like to be able to anticipate and therefore exercise some control over the future, so they make plans, have medical examinations, invest their money, and listen to weather reports. Chinese religion is full of such concern to control the future, expressed at a much more intense level than most Westerners feel today. In the first place, there are many auspicious words in Chinese that are repeatedly invoked or written to bring about the promise they imply. Fancy rice bowls are inscribed with such phrases as *Wan-shou wu-jiang* "[May you have] ten thousand long lives with no limit," and such characters as *xi* ("joy") and *lu* ("good salary") are hung on walls on red paper scrolls or form designs on clothing. Symbolic puns are used as well, such as pictures of fish, pronounced *yu*, the same pronunciation as another character meaning "abundance."

In old China, and still today in Taiwan and Hong Kong, there were almanacs listing what was good or bad to do on every day of the year; people consulted such almanacs before they decided to do anything significant, from taking a trip to getting married. For more important events they also consulted fortunetellers, who calculated their fate on the basis of which natural forces were strongest at their time of birth, as we saw in the *feng-shui* story in chapter 40. There were also specialists who predicted the future of individuals from the shape of their faces and the lines on their hands.

In Chinese religion, two special forms of ritual—divination and exorcism—were emphasized in an effort to control the future. Divination was carried out as part of temple rituals to determine how the gods would respond to offerings. After praying for aid, worshipers would throw wooden blocks on the floor in front of the altar, blocks shaped like half-moons, one side flat and the other round. A round and flat side up together is a yes answer to a prayer, because it expresses *yin* and *yang* in balance; the same sides up mean no. Another common method of divination was to shake numbered, two-foot-long sticks out of a round canister. The first stick to fall out was taken to an attendant in a little booth at the side of the temple sanctuary, who matched its number with one of a row of paper slips hung on the wall behind him. Each slip had an obscure verse that the attendant read and interpreted to the worshiper as his or her fortune for the day. This practice continues today.

The oldest form of divination was a more complex procedure based on reading the significance of sets of six horizontal lines, broken and unbroken. These sets, called hexagrams in English, were formed by sorting out fifty dried plant stalks, with certain numerical values assigned to groups of stalks, values corresponding to types of lines, which were written down one at a time as the stalks were counted off. The whole process was controlled except at one point: the first random division of the bunch of stalks into two. The Chinese believed that at that point one's existence was partially open to cosmic influence, so the rest of the process was the spelling out of what one's destiny was at that moment.

Chinese archaeologists have recently discovered similar sets of lines on prehistoric pottery, so this form of divination is very old indeed. Over the centuries traditions developed about the significance of lines and hexagrams, which were understood to include different mixes of the two basic forces of life, the male (which initiates) and the female (which completes), like *yang* and *yin*, represented respectively by solid and broken lines, ———— and — —. Specialists in line divination tried to include every possible life situation in the six-line sets, so that eventually there were sixty-four hexagrams, composed of eight different groups of three lines (trigrams). Each hexagram was assigned a certain meaning, ranging between good fortune and bad fortune, or a mix of the two, depending on the circumstances. So, for example, the hexagram *fu* (returning) is a good sign because it portrays the rebirth of *yang* power coming up from below, just when it seemed that the dark forces of *yin* had taken over.

The following six lines constitute the hexagram *fu*.

$$
\begin{array}{cc}
\text{—} & \text{—} \\
\text{—} & \text{—} \\
\text{—} & \text{—} \\
\text{—} & \text{—} \\
\text{—} & \text{—} \\
\text{———} &
\end{array}
$$

This is what the commentary says about *fu*:

Returning. Good fortune
One can go out and come in without distress

. . .

There is advantage in having a place to go.

From this one can see that *fu* is a positive and encouraging indication. One meditating on it could get a fresh perspective on an important decision, such as whether to take an examination or go on a trip. It takes time to cast a hexagram with the stalks, and the whole process is approached reverently and slowly, like a religious ritual. This is so that one has time to meditate, to think more deeply about the implications of decisions, to project one's feelings out onto the hexagrams and then read them back in a more ordered way.

The hexagrams were believed not only to capture the structure of the present moment, but its potential for the future. Properly understood, the lines are always moving, just like life, slowly changing into their opposites, then back again. The collection of commentaries on the lines came to be called the **Yi-jing** (*I-ching*), "the Classic of Change," a book that developed layer after layer of explanations over hundreds of years from the seventh to the first centuries B.C.E. The result is a handbook of wisdom and personal guidance that has inspired generations of Chinese and is now used by many in the West as well.

We have noted that divination is really a form of ritual, an attempt to deal with the unseen forces that influence our lives. Another special type of ritual is exorcism, the use of dramatic words and gestures to drive out demons believed to be causing problems. In China exorcism was carried out chiefly by spirit-mediums and Daoist priests, both in the name of gods with whom they had special relationships. We have seen in chapter 41 that gods represent order and demons disorder, so exorcism consisted essentially of the priest asking for a directive from the gods, which he in turn communicated to the demons, commanding them to leave. The commands could be oral, written, or both. Spirit-mediums in a state of possession by a god sometimes cut themselves and wrote with the divine blood to give more power to their orders or charms. Demons are manifestations of *yin* force, which can be driven away by symbols of *yang,* such as the blood of a cock, firecrackers, swords, and mirrors. Reciting books of scripture and philosophy also helps, because such books describe the moral order of the world, which demons cannot tolerate. In other words, the structure of Chinese exorcism is very similar to Christian exorcism, in which demons are believed to be driven away by the power of God invoked by a priest armed with prayers and a cross.

Here is an example of an exorcism ritual used by a Daoist priest in Taiwan to cure a sick child:

> Having put mother and child at ease with the gentle ringing of the handbell and the quiet chanting of purificatory incantations, the Daoist next summons the spirits at his command, namely the exorcistic Pole Star spirits, the local Cheng Huang deity, the spirit of the soil, the virgin goddess Ma-zu, and the patron of Lu Shan, Chen Nai Ma. On a piece of yellow paper he draws a *fu* talisman (the model for which can be bought in book-shops) and signs it with a special talismanic seal at the bottom. The Daoist then lights a candle at the altar and recites an exorcistic mantra, or conjuration, such as the following:

> *I command the source of all pains in the body—*
> *Muscle pains, headaches, eye sores, mouth sores*

Aching hand and aching feet
[insert the particular ailment of the child]—With the use of this magic of mine,
Here before this Daoist altar,
May all demons be bound and captured,
May they be cast back into Hell's depths.
You are sent back to your source!
Quickly, quickly obey my command!

He then casts the divination blocks, i.e., two crescent-shaped pieces of bamboo with one side rounded and one side flat. The flat sides down (*yin* in ascendancy) is a negative answer. The flat sides up (*yang* in ascendancy) means "the gods are laughing." One flat side and one round side up (*yin* and *yang* in balance) is an affirmative response, an indication that the proper spirit has been exorcised. Once an affirmative answer has been received, the talisman is burned, and a few of the ashes are mixed in a glass of boiled water. A teaspoon of the water is given the child as an exorcistic cure. The Daoist then recommends aspirin, antibiotics, or whatever Chinese herbal medicine he judges an appropriate remedy for the natural cause of the illness.[12]

All the exorcism themes we have mentioned are included in this description, in addition to the use of medicine to cure the natural causes of the illness. So the exorcist functions as priest, psychologist, and doctor all at once, a convincing package for those who still believe the old Chinese view of the world. Divination and exorcism are dramatic expressions of the Chinese understanding of life as an arena where human beings constantly interact with cosmic forces. In some form such activities are practiced by most religions. Whatever our beliefs, when something goes wrong we still tend to look for someone or something to blame. The next step is accusations, prejudice, or even attack. So the spirit of exorcism still lives among us.

Meditation

Another way that Chinese religion observes the interaction between people and superhuman powers or cosmic forces is through meditation, quiet contemplation by individuals of the gods, Buddhas, or their own inner nature. All Chinese religions assume that self-development depends basically on individual effort, though figures such as Amitabha provide important aid as well. Meditation provides a method for this development and accompanies scripture study and group rituals. The assumption of meditation is that by training and concentrating the mind one can attain a new level of consciousness and become a different kind of person. For Daoist priests this means a new awareness of cosmic power within one's own body, power to be shared with the community through ritual movements and chants. For Buddhists, meditation is a means of calming the mind and controlling the ego, so that one can see things as they really are and find peace in a new level of acceptance. Confucians contemplate life's patterns of order (*li*) to strengthen their sense of dedication to the moral order of society. Popular sectarians meditate on the Eternal Mother in her paradise to purify their conduct and go to heaven at death. Daoists, Confucians, and sectarians may all sit in quiet rooms on low stools; Buddhists sit cross-legged on floor mats or low platforms. Meditation can be done either alone or with a small group of other people.

Meditation has been an important part of most religious traditions. Christian monks and nuns have been meditating for centuries, as have Jewish and Islamic mystics. Meditation has long been practiced as well in Hinduism. In Native American cultures, young men went off to lonely hillsides to seek a vision that would indicate their adult name and role in the tribe. The earliest meditators may have been shamans calling down the gods to give them new knowledge and power. These parallels remind us again that Chinese religious practices are part of the world history of religions, a history that includes Western traditions as well.

In China it is the Chan (Zen) Buddhists who place the most emphasis on meditation. Chan meditation is focused on emptying the mind of all ego-centered thoughts in a context of group support. Monks usually meditate side by side on low platforms around a large room in a monastery, watched by a senior monk who makes sure they do not talk or go to sleep. The meditators concentrate on a puzzling statement, such as "Where were you before you were born?" given to them by an experienced master. After weeks or months of concentrating on this question, the meditator finally realizes it cannot be answered; that normal logical thought by itself cannot lead to enlightenment. If the meditator keeps trying long enough perhaps he or she will realize that the deepest truths of life and death are not intellectual problems to be solved but facts to be accepted.

The following passage is a description of a Chan meditation session in a Chinese monastery in the 1940s, part of a day that began at 3:00 A.M. After reciting scriptures and names of Buddhas in morning devotions, the monks have a breakfast of rice and vegetables. They eat in silence, reflecting on the debt they owe those who prepared the food. At 7:00 A.M. they go to the sitting benches:

> In a well-run hall the monk should be able to forget his body and let it be guided like an automaton by the bell and board. He sits erect on the narrow bench, his eyes fixed on a point no further than the third and no nearer than the second row of tiles on the floor. He tries to keep his spine perfectly straight and to control his respiration. Talking is forbidden. The silence must be absolute. If a monk in the east makes a sound, the precentor goes over and beats him then and there with his incense board—and beats him hard. If it is a monk in the west, the blows are administered by the senior instructor present. But the blows may not be struck with the sharp edge of the board, nor is boxing the cheeks allowed, as it is outside the hall.
>
> Those who are new at meditation usually sit cross-legged with only one foot up. Even then it may be so painful that they cannot sleep at night. Some lose courage and flee the monastery. According to one informant, "The pain

is cumulative. It hurts until the sweat pours from your body. Some people try to cheat by uncrossing both legs under cover of their gowns, but eventually the precentor will catch them at it and give them a beating. The loss of face is one reason why so many run away." How many? "About 30 percent in the first week or two of each semester."[13]

After meditating for an hour, the monks run slowly around the hall in a circle and have tea and a snack. Then they resume seated meditation. So the day goes, with seven periods of running and seven of sitting, a total of about nine hours' work, interspersed with meals, short naps, and discussions with the chief monk. The day ends at 10:00 P.M.

This closer look at Chan (Zen) meditation gives some idea of the concentration and intensity required to "meditate." Zen Buddhist masters teach that this meditation can lead to the goal of enlightenment, a relaxed and open mind that enables us to appreciate life more fully. As in Western religious traditions of meditation, in China, too, there have been a number of "paths" of meditation. Whatever the "path" in China, whether Daoist, Confucian, sectarian, or Buddhist, it has emphasized a greater personal fulfillment, self-development, or consciousness by the ordering of one's own life through contact with a greater power. [See Buddhism pp. 942–50 for description of Zen training; see Judaism pp. 422–27, Christianity pp. 500, 507, 519, Islam pp. 659–62, Hinduism pp. 752–53, Buddhism pp. 946–48, and Religions of Japan pp. 1102, 1121–27, 1151 for discussion of meditation and mysticism.]

Leadership and Organization

Chinese religions, like religions in other parts of the world, are characterized by the kinds of leaders and organizations that guide people and structure activities. There have been many organized groups in Chinese religions, as has been noted above. One form of such organization is the group of government officials responsible for performing rituals at court and at officially sponsored temples in towns and villages. Beyond the state religion, the Daoist priesthood is organized as a self-perpetuating professional guild that trains new members in ritual, scripture texts, and hand signs. Some of this material is kept secret within the priesthood. Most Daoist priests marry and live at home, performing rituals in local temples at the invitation of village elders. However, there are some Daoist temples and a few monasteries.

Buddhist monasteries and nunneries range in size from small temples with two or three resident monks or nuns to large compounds with several buildings in which scores or even hundreds of monks live. There are usually separate buildings for sleeping, eating, meditating, and worship, with rooms for visitors as well. Each monk is assigned a task or office, such as cook, firewood gatherer, treasurer, librarian, or manager of guests. Their life together is directed by a chief monk, or abbot, who is usually a chosen disciple of his predecessor. The monastery grounds are owned by the group as a whole; the monks own only a few personal items: clothing, toothbrush, and books. The abbot usually makes important decisions in consultation with senior monks, who decide such matters as when to hold intensive meditation sessions or a series of lectures on a scripture text, or how to redecorate the main altar.

Temples of popular religion are managed by leading men of the community who are chosen every year by lot. These men solicit funds for renovation projects, hire custodians and attendants, and decide when to have special rituals and pilgrimages or which touring opera troupe to hire. Smaller temples are single buildings, sometimes with the front side open, with images of the gods on altars along the back wall. More important temples are built as rectangular compounds, with a wall surrounding several buildings. Ideally, the main gate of the compound faces south in accordance with the principles of *feng-shui*. As one enters there are niches for guardian deities on each side, then a wide courtyard, in the middle of which is a large, covered platform with altars and images for the chief deities of the temple. Continuous rows of rooms are built along the inside of the compound walls. At the back is another platform for additional altars. Whatever the size of the temple, there is an incense burner in the courtyard on a stand, about three feet high and a foot and a half wide. Here every worshiper places burning sticks of incense and prays to the gods. The incense burner is the holiest place in the temple because it is the key point of communication between worshipers and deities.

Larger sectarian temples in Taiwan are arranged much the same way, as they may have been years earlier on the China mainland, in times when it was safe for them to operate in public. However, the typical sectarian worship center is a small shrine in a storefront or home, with an altar and images at one end

Worshipers at a storefront chapel of a popular religious sect, the "Compassion Society."

of a room. Here people pray and recite scriptures together and sometimes listen to sermons by sect leaders. Sectarian organization can include several levels of offices, from flower arranger to congregation chief, with scripture recitation groups usually composed of women. There is a job for just about everybody, to keep people interested. Some sects in contemporary Taiwan use **spirit-writing;** that is, they believe the gods can come down, take possession of a writing implement, and write Chinese characters on paper or a tray of sand. Such a possessed implement can be called a "phoenix," or "flying phoenix" after a divine bird in Chinese mythology. A list of officers for such a group can include such titles as General Supervisor, Hall Chairman, Good Works Manager, Manager for Guests, Service Men, Phoenix Affairs Manager (in charge of spirit-writing), Chief Wielder, Chief Copyist, Assistant Copyist, Music Director, Scripture Manager, Cantor, Master of Rites, Fruit Bearer, Mistress of Incense, and Bellringer and Drumbeater.[14]

From this list we can see that Chinese sects are organized in ways similar to Christian and Jewish congregations in North America and Europe, where there are also many organized tasks and positions to provide a sense of belonging and to keep the group going.

Leadership and organization of Chinese religions are quite varied, from the formal state rituals to the rather informal (but highly organized) popular movements with lay officers. A particular movement may have a bewildering array of such officers, but the general thrust is the same as the formal state rituals: to bring the worshiper into meaningful contact with superhuman powers.

Ethical Teachings

All religions have some principles of proper behavior, even if the source and nature of these principles differ from culture to culture. Judaism and Christianity, based on faith and a commitment to God, teach their followers to act in love, honesty, and justice. The ethical teachings of Chinese religions, which are expressions of the order of the universe itself, are quite similar. Confucian ethics are based on love and respect within the family; young people are supposed to obey their parents, and parents to care for their children. Once this foundation is established, one is to respect social superiors, such as teachers and officials, be loyal to friends, and kind to people in need. In all situations one should be polite and dignified, basically honest, but not to the point of rudeness. Confucius taught his followers to constantly examine and correct their own conduct, to make sure they have been diligent as students or fair as administrators. They were to seek out friends who were good people and learn from them. To Confucius, religious rituals did not mean much if one was not an ethical person to begin with.

The basic ethical value of the *Lao-zi* and *Zhuang-zi* books is noninterference: letting things follow their natural course, without trying to "improve" them. The ethics of Daoist religion are similar to Confucianism in that Daoism too stresses that those who seek immortality or act as priests need to be pure themselves. Buddhism brought in some new principles because of its emphasis on compassion for all living creatures, including animals. According to the law of karma, every action brings its own appropriate reward, so it is obviously important for people to act in good ways. Buddhism stresses that giving support to monks and nuns is good karma, as is providing food and medical care for the poor and distributing scriptures free of charge. In this way people can be honored now and have a better rebirth the next time around.

In general, Chinese ethical teachings are pragmatic, conservative, and patriotic. They teach that good acts will eventually be rewarded, that people should be content in their social position and support the government. Here are lists of standard ethical instructions from two popular religious texts:

Officials: "bring about good order for all the people; do not covet wealth, or injure others."

The wealthy: "aid the poor," remembering that the "spirits are three feet above your heads."

Scholars: "study industriously; there are rooms of gold in books; don't worry about being poor. If you study with all your might for ten years why fear that your name will not appear on the notice board [with the names of those who have passed the civil service examinations]? Look at the son of the Yang family who gained great merit and a position at court."

Merchants: "be fair in business transactions, and you will become rich. Just devote yourself to your business; doing good does it no harm."

Young people: "be filial and obedient to your parents. Filial children always obtain a good reward."

Old wives: "if you have children, you must teach them the correct principles of behaviour, and must not allow them to idly roam around."

Young wives: "record in your hearts the 'three obediences' [to father, husband, and son] and the 'four womanly virtues' [right behaviour, proper speech, proper demeanour, proper employment]. Be obedient to your parents and in-laws; you also want to become a mother-in-law. If your husband doesn't act properly, you should urge him [to change his ways]."

Unmarried daughters: "read the *Classic of Female Sages* (*Nü-sheng jing*); obey your parents, study needlework, never go outside to stand in front of the gate. Look at the girl in the story who followed these precepts and married the son of the [wealthy] Yang family."

The licentious: "never reap any good rewards, but just sorely harm their bodies and minds" (here the example is given of an evil man who goes to purgatory).

Those who go out to work in the world (lit., "go out the gate"): "to seek wealth, profit and fame; they just bring calamity on themselves."

The specific moral acts that bring rewards are conveniently listed on the first page of another book. They are to:

- print morality books to exhort the multitudes
- collect paper with writing on it
- respect the five grains

- repair bridges and roads
- provide vegetarian food for Buddhist monks
- repair temples
- give money to the poor
- buy and release living creatures in the spring
- provide cold tea for travelers in the summer
- provide aid for orphan souls in the autumn
- give wadded clothing in the winter, thus forming good karma
- maintain a vegetarian diet and diligently recite the Buddha's name
- concentrate with one's whole mind on attaining Buddhahood or immortality[15]

Many of these practical ethical teachings are similar to those in other traditions, while some are peculiar to China. What is important to remember is that in China, both broad principles and specific practices emphasize the conformity of the individual to the whole of society and the course of the universe.

Some Related Cultural Activities

Many non-Chinese first learn something of Chinese culture through food, martial arts, landscape paintings, or acupuncture, all of which are indirectly related to Chinese religions through the worldview they share. We have already seen that food was the main form of offering to the gods and ancestors; sacrifice was really a shared meal. In addition, foods were understood to be related to the five powers: sour tastes with wood, bitter with fire, sweet with earth, and so forth. The ideal meal is a blend of these flavors, with peppery dishes balancing the more bland, fish alternating with poultry, vegetables, and pork. The typical Chinese dish does not consist of chunks of meat and vegetables on separate plates, but small pieces of several ingredients, each contributing to a harmonious taste.

The physical movements known as *tai-ji quan* (*t'ai-chi ch'uan*) or *gong-fu* (*kung-fu*), originated as exercises to help vital energy (*qi*) flow freely through the body and to concentrate it where it is needed to heal an infection or strike a blow. It is interesting that many *tai-ji* movements are named after those of animals they resemble, because there are references from the fourth century B.C.E. to people who imitated the movements of long-lived animals in order to seek longevity for themselves. However, *tai-ji* as we know it developed much later, so the connection is not clear. In any case, *tai-ji* is based on the same concern for harmony and balance that informs much of Chinese religion, so it is no accident that there are many references to Buddhist monks and Daoist priests practicing such exercises and to sectarian leaders who also taught martial arts. It was assumed that religion involved the whole person; that real piety should lead to good physical health, that the body was the place where gods could descend and enlightenment be realized.

Acupuncture and herbal medicine are direct expressions of the Chinese worldview, for all the organs of the body are correlated with the five powers and *yin* and *yang.* Good health is the balance of these forces; illness reflects their imbalance. For example, the kidneys are associated with the power of water, so an infection of the kidneys can mean too much water. Since earth overcomes water in the five-power cycle, the cure is to stimulate an organ associated with earth, such as the heart. This can be done with acupuncture needles because it is believed that all the bodily organs are connected to one another and to points on the skin by conducting lines. So, a needle inserted at the proper spot can activate the earth power needed to cure the kidneys. Herbal drugs are believed to operate the same way, by restoring lost balance and harmony to the body. So it is that traditional Chinese medicine and religion operated side by side, based on the same understanding of how things are.

In landscape painting too, the key is balance between mountains, sky, and water, with human beings, plants, and animals integrated in the whole. Mountains are *yang,* water is *yin;* one could say that such paintings are the Chinese worldview in art; their organizational principles are similar to those of *feng-shui.* Painting is considered a form of meditation, with the vital energy of the artist attuned to that of the scene. In effect, then, activities such as eating, painting, exercising, and the practice of traditional medicine are alternate expressions of the same understanding of life that motivates Chinese religions. From specifically religious places, times, actions, and objects to a variety of "cultural" activities, China presents a remarkably unified worldview.

43

Dynamics: Chinese Religions Lived and Practiced

TO UNDERSTAND WHAT a religion means to people we must study not only formal beliefs, but also the way in which people experience and express religion
in practice. In surveying the history and the system of Chinese religions we have
already seen some examples of this tradition as it is practiced. In this chapter
we will look at four examples in greater detail, drawing materials from the work
of modern observers and anthropologists. There is an endless array of customs,
celebrations, rituals, and other practices that might be offered here; these four
were chosen because they represent important forms of Chinese religious
activity and because detailed descriptions are available in English. Each illustration demonstrates the interrelated worldview basic to Chinese religion.

The first example describes a family trip to a mountain graveyard to clean
the graves of ancestors and to offer food and incense to them as a sign of respect.
This is done as part of the annual Spring Festival (Qing-ming) in early April, a
festival expressing the Chinese worldview through reunion of the living and the
dead (as was discussed in chapter 42). The Spring Festival expresses the close
relationship within families between the living (descendants) and the dead
(ancestors). Ancestors are worshiped because memories of them strengthen the
family and give it a greater sense of continuity and permanence. All family
members benefit from participating in these rites, because they know that when
they die they will be treated in the same way; their influence will continue.

The second example is the enlightenment experience of a young Buddhist
monk who finds a spiritual peace he never knew before. In his enlightenment
experience this monk realizes the Chinese worldview in a highly personal manner. He believes he is in communion with the spirit of his dead friend, who tells
him, "I am one with you and with all living beings." The monk comes to understand the basic unity behind all apparent opposites. As he says, "I can perceive the latent beauty behind all that is ugly and the ugliness which lies behind
the beautiful. Winter and summer, youth and old age, sickness and health,
activity and passivity—all these are but names we give to aspects of the one,
eternal Truth."

The third example is a village exorcism ritual to drive away frustrated ghosts believed to have drowned a young boy. The excited activities of the exorcism ritual contrast with the calm insight of the young Buddhist monk, but the exorcism is based on the same basic sense of the world as a living system. Harmful ghosts are spirits that have not been properly cared for by their descendants. Since it is assumed that they are connected both to living persons and to the gods, these spirits can communicate their discomfort, and offerings can be made to them to calm them down. If such offerings fail to solve the problem, more drastic means can be used, such as asking a spirit-medium to be possessed by a god who can identify the unruly spirit and order it to cease its activity and go away. Because in the Chinese religious system a ghost is less powerful than a god (has, in fact, very low status), it eventually has no choice but to obey the commands of its superior, the god.

The fourth example is the story of a young woman who becomes a spirit-writer for a popular religious sect in Taiwan. In spirit-writing the gods are believed to descend into a pen or stick and write moral instructions for their worshipers. This case of spirit-writing demonstrates a connection between the living and dead similar to the example of exorcism. The spirits who write are the spirits of dead human beings who have been venerated for so long that now they are considered gods. They still have consciousness and are concerned about what is going on in the world of the living. As gods, they are responsible for morality, social order, and healing, so in their messages they exhort people to do good, give wise advice about how to solve disputes, and reveal prescriptions for medicines. The gods formerly were people, and good people may be promoted to the status of gods after death; so gods and people understand one another, and it is only natural for them to communicate.

These four examples provide us with interesting concrete expressions of how Chinese religions operate in the lives of the people. The first example is the spring family picnic at the grave, a time more of joy than sadness, because it brings together the living and the dead in a setting of fresh air and plenty to eat.

The Spring Festival

The following Spring Festival trip to a family graveyard is described by an anthropologist who accompanied the family. A group of eighteen relatives walked about six miles from their hometown to the mountains, accompanied by a pack mule that carried the food, pans, firewood, and blankets they needed for the offering ritual.

> We walked in three groups: the family head, two male clan members, and myself formed one, the three helpers and the mule formed a second, while the ladies formed the last group. . . .
>
> Upon arrival at the graveyard the family head took out the blankets and spread them in an open space. He, the male clan members, and I sat down

on the blankets, while the three helpers and the ladies started to work. The
ladies first carefully put the flowers, which they had gathered on the way up,
in front of the two main tombs. Each tombstone was covered with a large
straw hat, which most of the unmarried girls wore for the occasion. Almost
simultaneously the helpers kindled a fire, while the ladies prepared for the
cooking. The helpers did the rough work, such as carrying water from a
spring and gathering large pieces of firewood. The ladies first made some tea,
which the two boys served to the men on the blankets. They then proceeded
to shell the peas, cut up the meat, and wash the vegetables.

The graveyard was not a big one, but it conformed in every respect to the
best of West Town standards. It had three terraces, hacked from the slope of
the mountain. On both sides of each terrace were two pine trees, and on both
sides of the lowest terrace were two engraved stone pillars marking the front
entrance to the graveyard. Below the plot was a heavily wooded slope. Flanking this particular height were two larger mountain ridges, which nearly
joined each other, but just failing to do so, left a narrow gap between them.
Viewed from the family graveyard, these ridges were like outer walls with the
gap serving as a gateway. Through that gateway a person standing in front of
any tomb could see part of the lake.

While the ladies cooked and the helpers hacked wood, our group, sufficiently rested, began to visit some other graveyards scattered at various
points on the same mountain. At all of them were signs of activity and cooking. Some families had just arrived; others were beginning to eat. We visited
one graveyard which occupied several hundred *mu* (one acre equals 6.6 *mu*)
of space and in which several hundred individuals were grouped near the
tombs of their own lineages. We visited a humble graveyard in which the
tombs were mere heaps of earth, by which only a few living members of the
family were gathered. We discussed the merits and demerits of the various
graveyards. When we came upon a group which was just sitting down for the
grand meal of the day, we were offered some wine and food.

Upon our return to the Y. graveyard, the meal was ready to be served. All
the dishes prepared, together with warm wine, were neatly arranged before
the two main tombs, which were those of the family head's parents. The family head then took some burning incense and wine and made a ceremonial
offering, first before one tomb, then before the other. He kowtowed [pros-
trated himself] nine times before each. As he did so, paper money was
burned. The other male members of the gathering followed suit, one by one.
As a guest, I made my incense offering according to the custom, but when
I offered to kowtow, the family head prevented me from doing so, saying that
I did not have to be so polite. When the men had finished, the ladies went
through the same procedure. When each person had had a turn, some dishes
were taken to the tomb on the lower terrace, which was that of the younger
brother of the wife of the family head. There a simpler ritual offering was
made, only by the family head, his wife, and all the women.

In the meantime, the young female relative who was pregnant left the
group and went to visit a small graveyard about fifty yards away. There were

two tombs, both very humbly constructed. One was that of her mother, and the other was that of an aunt. This young relative made some incense offering, sat leaning against the front part of her mother's tomb, and wept deeply for a long while. Later, other female members of the party with great difficulty persuaded her to desist and to leave the tomb.

With all the offerings completed, everyone sat down to the hearty meal. The men sat in one group, the women in another. There was ample wine, meat, deliciously cooked vegetables, and a portable fire pot similar to those used in North China during the winter months. This outdoor meal was thoroughly enjoyed by everyone in the party.

After the meal came tea and pipes. When the two groups felt that time enough had elapsed, the women and the helpers began to clear away the food and wash the dishes. At about three o'clock in the afternoon the party started on a leisurely return to West Town. En route to the graveyard, as well as on the way back, we met hundreds of other travelers on the same mission.[16]

The Spring Festival focuses on one of the central features of the Chinese worldview—the crucial relationship between the living and the dead—more precisely, between the family and its ancestors. The basic questions of social and religious identity are determined in China by membership in the family and worship of ancestors. The family ancestral cult constitutes the one universal religious structure in China; not to belong to a family and worship ancestors is, in effect, to be a nonperson or nonreality. The Spring Festival demonstrates the ancestral cult in a happy seasonal celebration. As was seen in the account of the *feng-shui* master and the oldest son of the Liu family at the beginning of chapter 40, the location of a grave site is a matter of serious concern and calls for the assistance of religious specialists who can analyze the terrain so that the grave benefits from cosmic forces in the sky and landscape. In the case of the Spring Festival celebrated by the Y. family, the grave site was selected and established long ago; the occasion for visiting the site is the annual spring rite for honoring spirits of the family dead. As the Y. family travels to its own graveyard it passes other graveyards on the mountain, an indication that this mountain generally is considered a sacred place. The trip to the mountain graveyard is both a pilgrimage to a sacred place and a seasonal family rite. In other words, the annual spring rite links a sacred place with a sacred time. Family ancestors are the symbols of superhuman power for this rite. The heart of the ritual is the offering of incense, wine, and paper money to the spirits of the ancestors, with all family members kowtowing (prostrating themselves) before the main tombs. This renews the harmonious relationship between the living and the dead, assuring the flow of blessings from ancestors to the family. This is a good example of reciprocity, the mutual exchange between gods or spirits and worshipers: The ancestors benefit by being honored with the offerings; the family benefits both by being blessed by the ancestors and by being united in the meal that culminates the celebration. The Spring Festival is but one instance of the pervasive concern for the ancestors in Chinese religions. [See Religions of Mesoamerica pp. 226–33, Judaism pp. 469–70, Christianity pp. 562–73, Islam pp. 645–47, Hinduism pp. 815–20, Buddhism p. 874, and Religions of Japan pp. 1154–60 for description and discussion of pilgrimage.]

Buddhist Enlightenment

The central concern of Buddhism has always been personal enlightenment—the realization of a new way of thinking and feeling. Through such an experience, Buddhists hope to become more open and compassionate persons who have spiritual peace within. The following account is of the enlightenment experience of a young monk named Fa-bao who had just been through three years of illness and spiritual uncertainty. Now his best friend, Tang Jin-nung, had died, and he was alone before his friend's portrait on the altar after the funeral. Below is what Fa-bao told an English Buddhist named John Blofeld. The "Path" here, of course, refers to Buddhism. "Universal mind" means the wise and compassionate way the Buddhas see the world, a perspective that can be shared by all beings.

As was discussed earlier, this new, objective way of accepting the world as it really is has always been the basic point in Buddhism. Such acceptance is possible only when one has stopped seeing things in the usual anxious and self-centered way, a way that inevitably judges what helps me as good and what harms me as bad. Such a point of view breaks up experience into all sorts of dichotomies, such as joy and sadness, love and hate, success and failure, life and death. Life becomes a constant struggle to seize the good side of things and avoid the bad. The problem is that there is no end to the struggle; as soon as something good is obtained (a love relationship, for example), one must start defending it, developing it, and worrying about whether it will change.

Buddhism tries to solve this problem of constant struggle by saying that it originates with the passions and desires of self-centered egos. If we can get beyond these desires, then we can relax and realize that life does not need to be a struggle, just a process that flows. In Fa-bao's story, we read that emotions such as grief and joy are dangerous to one's peace of mind, and that birth and death inevitably go together. One who really understands life and the world realizes that ultimately all things are related to one another and, in the long run, work themselves out in harmonious ways. Realizing this can bring a deep peace of mind that Buddhists call enlightenment.

Of course, a similar sense of the ultimate oneness of things can be found in other mystical traditions, though it may be called God, or Dao, or Brahman (the highest level of reality in Hindu philosophy) and each tradition may explain the experience in a different way. In all these traditions, one needs to come to a moment of awakening, of personal realization of how things really are underneath all the surface changes and differences. One who has such an awakening or conversion can become a very different person inside, even though on the outside he or she may look much the same as before. The reason is that one feels as though one has a new self and a new set of goals for life. These goals may be to "do God's will" or "practice Buddhist compassion," but the end result is often a more integrated, peaceful, and loving person. This certainly seems to have happened to Fa-bao. Now let us look at what he said about his experience:

> I think I must have spent more than an hour communing with the departed spirit. No one disturbed me, except one of the family who came in silently to renew the candles and incense on the altar and slipped out again without a word. I don't think I can explain this strange communion in words that anyone would understand, but it was as if Tang Jin-nung had taken my hand in his and said to me: "Why should you grieve on my account? Do you not understand anything of what I taught you? Do you not see that excessive grief is as dangerous to your progress along the Path as excessive joy or foolishness? True happiness lies in perfect stillness. Let your mind remain unmoved by joy or sorrow as the mountain remains unmoved by the winds which howl among its peaks. Birth and death are as inevitable as the awakening which takes place after sleep and the sleep which follows wakefulness. Where is there cause for grief in this? Since nothing exists except mind, and as the individuality of each human being is but a delusion which hides his oneness with the Universal mind, the living man at your elbow is no nearer and no further from you than the being who lives at a distance of eighty-four thousand universes from you. I have not gone from you, because 'I' was never there. The underlying reality which animated the appearance of my living body has not moved or diminished. On that ultimate plane I am one with you and with all living beings. Thus there is no coming or going, being born or dying, loving or being loved. All these are but empty forms. Why allow yourself to be moved by them? In the silence and the stillness you will find peace and the end of sorrow."
>
> I think [continued Fa-bao] that a lot more entered my mind as I knelt before the portrait of my friend, but all of it can be summed up in the words, "in the silence and the stillness. . . ." That night I returned home feeling much lighter of heart than ever before, and from then onwards I have found myself making good progress in the practice of meditation. That, again, is something which I cannot describe; I can only say that my life is full of peace and of that true happiness which is to be distinguished from the empty pleasure of desire fulfilled. In the silence and stillness of my own mind I find the answers to all the riddles of life. I can perceive the latent beauty behind all that is ugly and the ugliness which lies behind the beautiful. Winter and summer, youth and old age, sickness and health, activity and passivity—all these are but the names we give to aspects of the one, eternal Truth. All the sounds in the Universe add up to silence and all movements have their beginning and end in stillness. This was the message of my friend. This is the sum of my own experience and this is the Law expounded for the guidance of posterity by our Original Teacher, Sakyamuni Buddha.[17]

The Spring Festival and Fa-bao's experience both deal with death and the dead, but in rather contrasting fashion. The Spring Festival illustrated a group ritual related to family ancestors, but Fa-bao's experience is an individual encounter with the death of a friend. The atmosphere of the Spring Festival is a peaceful, rather matter-of-fact celebration, accepting death as a natural part of life. The mood of Fa-bao's reflection is more philosophical or existential, questioning the meaning of life or existence and the cessation of the same—death. Fa-bao draws on the more sophisticated teachings of Buddhism to soothe the personal loss of the death of a friend and to probe for the meaning of life in a more universal sense. In fact, Fa-bao's experience can be seen as an example of enlightenment in the Chinese context. The diversity of Chinese religions is demonstrated by the range of options for dealing with death—on the one hand, familial, seasonal, and festive; on the other hand, individual, existential, and reflective. [See Religions of Africa pp. 45–51, 75–79, Native Religions of North America pp. 318–20, Judaism pp. 457–69, Christianity pp. 573–86, Hinduism pp. 820–26, and Religions of Japan pp. 1163–72 for description and discussion of life histories and personal accounts.]

Exorcism of a Harmful Ghost

In Chinese popular religion it is believed that when people die their souls continue to exist, either as ancestral spirits or as ghosts. What makes the difference is whether or not their souls are properly cared for by the living: If they are adults provided with proper funerals they can become ancestors, but if they die violent deaths far from home, or before they are married, or if their funerals or graves are neglected, they can become wandering ghosts who frighten or injure people to draw attention to their needs. Similar ideas about ghosts can be found all over the world. In the following account from Taiwan, a child has drowned in a fish pond right after the image of the chief god of the village, King Guo, has been taken away in a religious procession to another town. People think that perhaps in his absence an angry ghost became braver than usual and took out its frustrations on the child, whose death leaves another ghost. An exorcism ceremony has been arranged, centered on a small chair held by two spirit-mediums. It is believed that gods can descend into these chairs and make them move, or even trace Chinese characters on a table with one of the chair's arms. The presence of the gods drives away the child's ghost, and in this way order is restored in the village. The following description is by an anthropologist:

> No sooner had King Guo left than a child drowned in the fish-pond in the center of Bao-an, causing no small consternation to all who lived in the village. It seemed strange to me that he should have drowned, for people said that he could swim a little, and the pond is shallow and often used for bathing. One man told me: "He was pulled in by a ghost. Someone died there before, and when someone dies, his ghost often wants to pull a second one after him. . . . A lot of people have died there. I don't know how many." Another speculated that the ghosts to the north had somehow managed to get into the village.
>
> The dead child left behind a malign ghost, which, it was feared, would do untold harm if permitted to remain in the village. Properly it would have

been called a "water ghost" . . . , but so dangerous was it that this term could not be spoken. (After my repeated inquiry one man wrote the word for me, but would not speak it.) Instead it was referred to merely as a "bad thing. . . ." Such beings appear to have caused alarm on the Fukienese* coast at the end of the last century as well as in modern Taiwan. Groot (1892–1910) writes of them: "The common opinion in that part of China is that those . . . 'water-spectres' mostly are souls of the drowned. Having spent their time in their wet abode in the bondage of the water-gods, they may be redeemed from this servitude by substitution, and therefore they lie in ambush for victims to draw into the water and make them take their place. Thus they are a constant lurking danger for people on the waterside, fishers, boatmen, and washer-women."

People in Bao-an were less explicit about the workings of a "bad thing" in the village, but it was clear it ought to be removed. The death took place on July 22 (the fifteenth day of the sixth moon). The twenty-seventh (that is, the twentieth day by the lunar calendar) was chosen as a calendrically appropriate day for the exorcism.

A little past noon two altar tables were placed on the porch of the temple, and the instruments of divination were placed by them so that the gods might provide instructions on how to perform the exorcism. These instruments I have called "divination chairs. . . ." [This] is a small chair, with arms and a back, that measures about thirty centimeters from the top of the back to the bottom of the legs. It is held by two bearers, who are said to "support" . . . the chair. The [chair] is used to provide a seat for the divine presence, and the descent of a god into it results in a bouncing motion . . . and sometimes in violent lateral movements as well. In divination the chair traces characters upon a tabletop with one of the protruding arms. . . .

The first god to appear was His Highness Chyr . . . , the patron of the Jang families in the village and a frequent visitor in séances. He advised that people should desist from speaking "bad words" to one another; that is, scolding or arguing. The death had disrupted the "harmony" of the village, and the village people were being instructed not to make matters worse by adding interpersonal disharmony, but to create as harmonious an atmosphere as possible. His second word of advice was that people should keep their children away from the fish-pond and watch them. He himself had business to tend to other than watching village children every minute. All of this was interpreted from the characters traced upon one of the altar tables by the divination chair. The second chair was now possessed by King Guo. He reiterated the same advice offered by His Highness Chyr, and then proceeded with instructions for the exorcism of the water ghost (or rather of the "bad thing"!). The two gods, represented by the divination chairs, would go in person to the pond and drive the "bad thing" from it. The bystanders must be very careful that it not lodge in their bodies, and to this end women and children were not to approach the pond, and those men who chose to do this work were to carry with them one

---

*Fukien is a province on the southeast China coast, across from Taiwan.

sheet apiece of spirit money* on which His Highness Chyr would write a protecting charm. His Highness now caused the arm of his divination chair to be dipped in ink, and with the ink he made a blot on each of twenty sheets of spirit money laid out on the altar before the chair. The men stuffed these into their pockets and left in a great hurry for the fish-pond, following the two wildly swinging divination chairs, which fairly dragged their wielders along the road.

Upon arrival at the pond the chairs ran madly about the perimeter of the pond, then hurled themselves and their bearers into the water, where they circled the pond several times more swinging up and down into and out of the water to drive out the "bad thing." At the same time the onlookers shouted high-pitched shouts, hurled burning firecrackers over the pond, and threw handfuls of sesame seeds into the water. The shouting, the rain of sesame seeds, and the continual and ubiquitous explosions of firecrackers were all calculated to terrify the ghost, and added to this were the chairs of the gods ploughing through the water, hot on the trail of the startled ducks. When the gods climbed out at one bank, they would leap in wildly elsewhere and beat the water with renewed vigor. Had I been the water ghost, I should surely have fled.

The body of the drowned child had been encased in an unpainted wooden box, and in the afternoon of the day on which the exorcism was held it was carried out of the village to the cemetery and buried.[18]

This exorcism of a potentially harmful ghost illustrates death in a very different context than the seasonal and familial celebration of the Spring Festival and Fa-bao's individual and existential reflection on the death of a friend. In this case exorcism is necessary because the death of the drowned boy represents an unnatural death that upsets the harmony of the village. In other words, the passage from life to death is violent, and this upsets the "living system" in the village; the rite of exorcism restores the world of the village to an orderly and harmonious state.

A number of facts persuade the villagers that this death is caused by ghosts and calls for special rituals: Drowning is always an unnatural death, the boy (who could swim) should not have drowned in such a shallow pond, and the fact that someone had died there before gives credence to the notion that a ghost might have pulled the boy in. The absence of the chief god of the village, King Guo, whose image had been taken in procession to another town, may have provided the ghost with the opportunity to act against the child. This gave rise to the fear that the boy might have left behind a malign ghost or water ghost, and such ghosts attempt to pull in other persons and cause them to drown, thereby taking the place of the ghost. Therefore the ghost of the drowned boy had to be exorcised, or driven out.

As is usual with all such rituals, a favorable date must be chosen according to the calendar. After the date was selected, divination chairs were used to come into contact with superhuman powers who had the ability to properly diagnose

---

*Spirit money is crudely printed paper money used as an offering to gods and spirits.

the spiritual situation. Two deities possessed the chairs and "wrote" messages on the altar tables with the legs of the chairs. The diagnosis of the two deities was that the harmony of the village had been disrupted, and in addition to the usual precaution of minding the children more carefully, the second deity prescribed an exorcism for removing the ghost and restoring the harmony of the village. The ghost was driven out by the more powerful presence of the two deities (represented by the chairs carried into the pond). Bystanders were protected from being invaded by the spirit with protective charms of spirit money that had been blotted with ink by a leg of a divination chair. Firecrackers, a standard Chinese device for driving out demons, and sesame seeds (a *yang* force that drives out the *yin* force of ghosts) helped finish the driving out of the ghost. The successful conclusion of the ritual is marked by the burial of the body of the drowned child. In this fashion, a death that disrupted the living system of the village is the occasion for restoring order and strengthening this system.

Spirit-Writing:
The Religious Vocation of Qiu Su-zhen

Spirit-writing has been popular in China for centuries as a way of obtaining direct communications from gods and spirits. At first it was used to tell fortunes, write verse, predict the results of civil service examinations, or reveal medical prescriptions. Later on, more of the messages were short sermons from the gods to their devotees, exhorting them to be good and be kind to others. By the seventeenth century, collections of these short revelations were being published as books of moral instruction. The spirit-writing tradition is still very much alive in Taiwan today, where hundreds of revelation books have been published by religious sects as their scriptural texts. The spirits are believed to descend into a Y-shaped stick suspended above an altar and write in a shallow tray of sand.

The story that follows is of a young woman in Taiwan named Qiu Su-zhen who gradually became involved in spirit-writing at a local branch of a religious sect called the Dragon Palace. The name of the branch was the Dragon Well Hall. From this account, we see that participation in the sect gave Su-zhen not only religious assurance but a sense of social worth as well because she now had the opportunity to write and teach. This was particularly important to her because her father had prevented her from completing her university education, on the grounds that a girl did not need it. This is her story as told to an American anthropologist, David Jordan:

> Qiu Su-zhen was born at the end of World War II. Her father worked as a cart puller, and her family lived in the countryside outside Tainan City, where Su-zhen tended a few family animals. She had two older sisters, as well as one younger sister, and two younger brothers, and she summed up her memory of the period as being one in which there were more mouths to feed than could be managed on the money available.

Su-zhen went to public school and did very well. In her same class was the son of the district head. When the teacher rated Su-zhen first in her class, and above the son of the district head, Su-zhen's father came to the district head's attention, and the two eventually became friends. The family participated in Taiwan's post-war prosperity, and eventually began operating a small general store on the outskirts of the city. Their tiny store was located not far from the site of the Dragon Palace Temple, and when this building was constructed in 1965, members of the Palace would stop by to make small purchases. Sometimes Su-zhen would make deliveries to the temple for her parents, or her mother would take her along to make a delivery, and the two would stop and worship in the Palace before returning home. Su-zhen's mother, probably because the temple was closer than others and therefore more convenient, developed the habit of visiting it more and more often, against the suspicious opposition of Su-zhen's father, who particularly opposed presenting New Year offerings to the Palace. His opposition was softened when he was eventually visited by a delegation of sect members, who persuaded him not only to permit his wife to visit, but even to visit the Palace himself. Years later, he became a member of the group. Initially, at least, there was probably nothing about the Dragon Well Branch Hall that seemed to make it very different from any other temple in Su-zhen's family's eyes. It was apparently simply the local spot where one could pray and divine, as one could at almost any temple. Her mother took Su-zhen there to inquire about her health when the girl was sick. And her two older sisters went to the Dragon Palace to receive an oracle about when Su-zhen might marry.

What Su-zhen remembered as most unhappy about her childhood was not poverty or hard work; it was her father's attitude toward education. Su-zhen's father, like many older Chinese, did not believe that girls benefitted from education, let alone required it. He did not mind her attending school as a child, and even took pride in her accomplishments. On the other hand he could not see any point in spending good money for additional schooling for her or her sisters beyond what the state required and provided. [As Su-zhen said:]

> *Everybody valued boys and not girls. That was the old rural society. I went to school on my own. My father said that if I went he would cut off my legs. I went myself. I walked every day. "I'm earning money myself; I'm not spending your money!" [I told him]. . . . My older sisters finished only primary school. He said: "Girls don't go to universities. Your sisters didn't study; why should you?" But still I wanted to go. If they didn't study, that was their business. . . . I used to go to bed very late in those days because it was very late at night [after work] that I could do my lessons. . . .*
>
> *My brothers wanted to study and so did I. He wanted his sons to study, but not me. He wanted me to give my money to them for school. I didn't want to. He said girls should get married. . . . My brothers got into a private university, but he wouldn't let me go; he said I had to make it into a public school [with higher admission standards] to save money. The more he used to oppose me, the more I wanted to study.*

In the end, however, Su-zhen's father prevailed. She did manage to begin in a university, where she studied accounting and statistics. She had completed two years of college and was in her third and last year when the conflict about the suitability of education for women came to a head. Her father had begun to worry that with a college degree she would be unmarriageable. He ordered her to stop her studies, to turn over her money to her brothers, and to come home to be married. Faced with a direct order, she complied.

The man to whom she was promptly affianced was named Huang Jinchun. His father owned the large plot of land on which the Dragon Palace stood. Suddenly Su-zhen's life became involved with the Dragon Palace in a way far less casual than it had been before. She was not really opposed to this. Even before she married, Su-zhen had begun to feel an attraction to the group and its activities. As she said:

> At that time it was not the way it is today. Lots of people did a kind of martial arts [here, a form of ritual exercise]. It seemed very queer to me: how could it be that everybody could do this but I could not? My mother told me to do it, and I tried, but other people could all do it and I could not. When they did it, if, say, their . . . stomachs hurt, they would pat their stomachs; wherever it hurt, they would pat themselves there. They really could do this sort of martial arts; it was as though they were practicing shadow boxing.

Were you afraid?

> I wasn't afraid; I envied them and wished I could do it too. . . . . I brought some classmates, but my classmates weren't at all interested in it.

Her mother had wanted her to learn to chant scriptures as well, but, although she began studying the art, she abandoned it after a time.

As a new bride, Su-zhen had some continuing contact with her father-in-law's group. Her name is among the contributors who helped finance the publication of a book of Dragon Palace revelations in 1968. Shortly, however, children arrived, and her activity was confined to the household. Although she had occasionally helped in the family's small factory, it was a small place, with few employees, and she remembers this period as a lonely one. By 1975 the children were old enough for her to be away from them, and she took to attending once more.

> It's strange. It was as though some kind of power was making me interested and making me think about going. If I didn't go in the evenings, I would go in the daytime. On the first and fifteenth of the lunar months I would take the three children and burn incense.

With three children, eight, six and three years old, attendance was still difficult, but there was little family opposition, since her father-in-law was the chairman of the group. On the 29th day of the second lunar month (March 29) in 1976, seven months after she began attending regularly, and about a month before Jordan's first interview with Su-zhen, the chief deity of the sect, the Golden Mother, speaking through a spirit-writing stick, commanded her to try acting as a spirit-writer.

How did you decide you wanted to become a writer?

> *I didn't say that I wanted to become a writer. I was divinely appointed to be. At the time I was really afraid, and at the altar itself my husband and father-in-law both strongly remonstrated [with the Golden Mother]. But it was the Golden Mother's command and could not be opposed. Whether or not I could succeed in it was the problem. . . . There is a secret, a spell that is chanted, which cannot be transmitted [to you], but [even though that helps] it also takes real determination.*

How did you feel that evening?

> *I was happy and frightened both. I really envied those who could help people heal illness and change bad to good [i.e., spirit-writers].*

How did the others feel about it?

> *They all get along really well with me. When they heard I was to become a writer, they all said the Golden Mother had chosen well. . . .*

And thus was Qiu Su-zhen launched upon her career as "Phoenix Pencil," spirit-writer of the Dragon Well Branch Hall, a religious name and status she acquired by command of the Golden Mother a few days later. Taiwan sectarians do not routinely keep track of which messages are received through which medium; the medium is only the agent of the revelation, which comes from a god, and it is the god whose name is carefully recorded.

Su-zhen was indeed well chosen for this role. She was much better educated than most of the members, and she also had an interest in the literary pursuits of the group.

> *[In college] I studied accounting and statistics, but I wasn't at all interested in that. I was more interested in the liberal arts. When I got into the Dragon Well Branch Hall, I saw a stick wielder writing characters that I didn't understand at all [because the text was in Classical Chinese], and I became really enthusiastic. My father-in-law wanted me to "help" [in reading them], but everybody gradually slipped away till I was left alone with it. There was no way to stop. Now I have grown accustomed to it, and I've made a lot of progress.*

Su-zhen rapidly became the fastest and most accurate reader in the group, a position which she attained even before the memorable night when she was asked to take command of the instrument itself. When she does not act as a wielder now, she is still the best reader. Often she is able to guess a character from the first couple of strokes, as though she already knew what the pen would have to write, and awaited only the confirmation of it by the writing itself.[19]

In Qiu Su-zhen's story there is much that can be found in the experience of members of other religious groups. She first became acquainted with the sect's temple because it was in her hometown near her family's shop, and her mother went there. She was an intelligent person whose love of study and reading had been frustrated by her father's old-fashioned opposition and her early marriage and motherhood. But she never forgot her earlier interest in books and study, and as her children grew older, she found a new opportunity in the Dragon Well Temple to study and even to help compose books herself. Furthermore, the members of the congregation supported her and gave her a sense of worth and ability that had been denied to her before. Beyond all this, she had been raised in a village and family in which most people believed in the power of the gods and accepted the idea that deities are interested in the human world. Su-zhen believed too, and eventually came to feel a special calling from the Golden Mother to become a spirit-writer. Her belief and level of activity intensified, and she became an important member of the sect. In one sequence of decisions she thus solved several important life problems: her inferior status as a woman in a male-dominated society, her concern for study and reading, her religious salvation, and her need for a supporting group of friends who could help her feel more useful in society. In fact, religions everywhere tend to succeed when they are able to meet just such a complex set of human needs, when they give people more to live for than they have been able to generate on their own.

Qui Su-zhen's story is a good example of how the worldview of Chinese religions can provide religious fulfillment for an individual, in this case a woman with three children. She was brought up in a traditional setting that respected the deities and their interaction with humans but was only casually related to the worship at the Dragon Well Branch Hall. Only later, after she gave up her education for marriage, and her children were older, did she come to participate more actively in this moment and was "appointed" by the Golden Mother to be a spirit-writer. For Qui Su-zhen, the Dragon Well Branch Hall is a kind of reconstruction of the traditional worldview. The branch hall constitutes sacred space while the ritual meetings are sacred time. The Golden Mother represents a symbol of superhuman power, and the rituals act out the reciprocity that is central to Chinese religions. Spirit-writing is a form of divination that Qui Su-zhen participates in directly, as one of the leading figures in this religious organization.

It is no accident that the first three examples in this chapter have something to do with death and the dead, because death is a central issue for religion in China, as for other religions. Some sociologists have argued that the real purpose of religious beliefs and rituals is to help people deal with situations beyond normal means of control, such as severe illness, the collapse of a business or marriage, and death. Through their faith, people find comfort in situations that are otherwise inexplicable and unbearable. There is certainly some truth in this interpretation, but there are aspects of religion that this sociological interpretation does not explain, particularly the sense of joy and commitment some religious people have.

In the Chinese cases discussed here there is healthy affirmation of life in the face of death, particularly in the enlightenment of the young monk and the peaceful family picnic around the graves of the ancestors at the Spring Festival.

In all these accounts there is a sense of close connection between the living and the dead, a sense of cooperation more than of fear. Chinese religion has provided meaning for every aspect of existence and has reminded people that they are not alone, even when they die. These four examples provide glimpses into the living system of Chinese religions as it is experienced in the actual practices of the people.

44
Chinese Religions Today

IN THE SIXTEENTH and seventeenth centuries Chinese from provinces on the southeast coast began migrating to Taiwan, the Philippines, and Southeast Asia. In the nineteenth century many more migrated after China's ports were forced open by Britain and France. Thousands of Chinese merchants and laborers moved to such countries as Indonesia, the United States, and Canada. At first they intended just to make some money and then go home, but eventually most stayed and settled down. Despite discrimination against them, the Chinese opened shops and restaurants in many towns and cities all over the world, worked hard, and survived. In cities such as New York, San Francisco, and Vancouver there were enough Chinese to form "Chinatowns," and here they continued many of their customs and religious practices and established Chinese newspapers, theaters, clubs, and temples. These organizations are still flourishing today. In Vancouver, for example, there are three Chinese Buddhist temples, one a beautiful building in a suburb, complete with a resident monk. Walking inside it makes one feel one has suddenly returned to Taiwan! There is also a spirit-writing sect in Vancouver, and many Chinese families there continue some form of ancestor worship. The New Year's festival is a colorful time, with feasts, parades, lion dances, and firecrackers.

Taiwan

Since 1950 Taiwan has steadily become more prosperous, and the people have had more freedom of religion than ever before in Chinese history. A few sects are still prohibited by law, but this is a continuation of imperial prohibitions that began centuries ago. The combination of better education and religious freedom with more leisure time and money has given a big boost to popular religion. There are shrines and temples in every town and neighborhood, many with elaborate and colorful roof decorations, carved pillars, and large images of deities with black or gold faces. The large incense pots in front of the altars smoke with offerings all day; people come and go, praying, throwing divination blocks, seeking their fortunes for the day through shaking numbered sticks out of a bamboo tube. In a side room there may be a spirit-medium shaking in trance, speaking the words of a god in a high falsetto voice, surrounded by devotees who need healing or advice for life's problems. On festival days a Daoist priest might be brought in to perform his powerful rituals, assisted by a scripture-chanting group, perhaps with a popular opera portraying gods and heroes on a stage outside the temple. If it is the birthday of a god, there will be a big potluck feast of roast pork, vegetables, and steamed pastries, and a parade around the neighborhood with an orchestra and the god's image carried in a fancy sedan chair.

Sectarian temples have all this, plus scripture study and spirit-writing sessions in which new divine revelations are prepared. Sectarian denominations flourish all over Taiwan, some with scores of congregations, all with an active sense that the gods and spirits are nearby, easy to contact, and interested in what people are doing.

There are Buddhist monasteries and nunneries in Taiwan also, some staffed by people who went there from the China mainland after the civil war of 1945–1949. In a well-run monastery the monks are awakened at 4:00 A.M. every day by the sound of a huge drum and bell: boom . . . dong, boom . . . dong. They dress, wash their faces, and go to morning devotions before a great golden image of the Buddha, chanting scriptures and the names of Buddhas and *bodhisattvas.* The monks alternate standing, kneeling on padded stools, and circling the image. After forty-five minutes of worship, they file silently into the dining room for a breakfast of rice gruel, salted vegetables, and tea. After they say grace, one monk takes a few grains of rice and offers them on a stone altar pillar outside the door, for the benefit of all the spirits of heaven and earth. After breakfast, the monks take off their outer robes to devote themselves to the work of the monastery: weeding the garden, painting window frames, sweeping walks, buying vegetables and incense, and settling accounts with rice merchants. Some of the monks may study scriptures in the library, while others show a family a niche inside the monastery pagoda where their grandmother's ashes will be placed after her funeral.

After lunch there may be a meditation session or a lecture on a *sutra* (Buddhist scripture text) by a visiting scholar monk. In the evening there is a more elaborate vegetarian meal featuring bean curd (tofu) prepared to look and taste like chicken or fish or pork, served with plenty of rice and steaming vegetables. At 7:00 P.M. all return to the main worship hall for evening devotions. By 9:00 P.M. lights are out, and the monks rest until the bell and drum wake them again.

Many families in Taiwan still observe the old festivals; visiting tombs in the spring is still done much as described in the example in the last chapter. Mothers continue to offer incense every day before ancestors' tablets on the family altar, and family members are expected to pay their respects at the community temple. However, since public school education is secular, many young people are neglecting the old ways, particularly in the cities. They prefer to go to movies, ride around in cars or on motorcycles, and chat with friends in coffee shops. To some, religion is just old-fashioned and unscientific, so it can no longer be followed.

In addition to secular education, another force for change in Taiwan religion is Christianity, represented by a large number of missionary groups: Roman Catholics, Presbyterians, Mormons, Pentecostals, and many others. Many

Buddhist monks at worship.

of these denominations were active in mainland China until 1949, when missionary work there was forbidden by the new Marxist government under Mao Ze-dong (Mao Tse-tung). At that time missionaries from China scattered all over the world; a large number chose to remain as close as possible to China, especially Taiwan (and Hong Kong). As a result, in Taiwan, Christian churches are in abundance and their related activities are conspicuous: schools, hospitals, and universities, as well as widespread distribution of the Christian message in the Chinese language—free copies of Christian books and tracts, and radio and television programs. It is common now for Chinese in Taiwan to be Christians; to some, Christianity seems like a more modern religion and has the advantage of being associated with Western industry and science. Also, it has become easier for Chinese to become Roman Catholics now that the church has recognized a modified version of ancestor veneration.

There are some Islamic mosques in Taiwan now too, supported by Chinese Muslims who came from the mainland. In fact, the first Islamic worship service I ever attended was in a beautiful new mosque in Taipei, the capital of Taiwan. We knelt on a rug with our shoes off and listened to an *imām* (worship leader) recite the Qur'ān in Arabic. The women were at one side of the sanctuary, separated from the men by a curtain.

The China Mainland

In Taiwan, Chinese and foreign religions are doing well; much the same could be said about Hong Kong, and Chinese communities in Singapore, Malaysia, and Thailand. But, of course, the center of Chinese culture is mainland China, and there religion has had a more difficult time, particularly since 1949. For hundreds of years Chinese governments have assumed the right to control, or even suppress, religions they do not like.

There has been destruction by rival religious movements as well, such as by the Taiping tian guo, "The Heavenly Kingdom of Great Peace and Prosperity," which arose in the mid–nineteenth century. This movement, strongly influenced by Protestant Christianity, became so active that the government sent troops to break up its meetings and arrest its leaders. By 1851, this resulted in a vast civil war over all of central China. The Taipings were eventually defeated in 1864, but not before they had established their own government in areas they controlled. This government carried out a number of revolutionary policies when it could, such as distribution of land to peasants and equality for women in the army. Another of their policies was to attack non-Christian temples and destroy their images in the name of the biblical God who wanted no rivals. The histories of many Confucian, Buddhist, and Daoist temples in China show that they were rebuilt in the 1860s after being destroyed by the Taipings. After the 1911 nationalist revolution there were sporadic attacks on temples and churches by radicals who believed that religion had to be done away with to make way for a new China. In the turmoil of warfare many religious buildings were either destroyed outright or turned into barracks for soldiers.

After the Communist victory in 1949, government pressures on religion became more systematic. Missionaries were expelled, and some church property was turned over to government-run factories, schools, and hospitals. Land owned by monasteries and temples was given to groups of peasants to farm for themselves, and the monks and priests were put to work in the fields like everyone else. People were taught that popular religion was just superstition and was to be replaced by Marxist teachings, better medical care, and modern methods of farming and water control. Many temples or shrines were neglected or pulled down.

However, until 1966, religious activities continued throughout China, protected by the Chinese constitution, which provides both for freedom of religion and for criticism of it. In 1966 China began a new phase called the Great Proletarian Cultural Revolution, an attempt by Mao Ze-dong and his followers to start the revolution of 1949 all over again by getting rid of old customs, ideas, and forms of leadership. Mao stirred up millions of young people to revolt against teachers and bureaucrats, and to attack everything that looked like a remnant of the "bad old days" before the revolution. All over China people suspected of opposing the government's policies were driven from their jobs, forced to make public confession of their sins against the revolution, exiled to rural villages, or even killed. Many factories, offices, and universities were closed because no one was left to run them. Groups of people called "Red Guards" roamed about denouncing supposed reactionaries, burning old books, and even destroying antique furniture. Religion, of course, was attacked as well, as an outdated "feudal superstition." The remaining Christian churches were closed or turned into factories, temples were ransacked and their images destroyed, and all but a handful of ministers, priests, and monks were forced to give up their religious positions and work at manual labor.

Mao Ze-dong died in 1976, and within a short time the Cultural Revolution ended. But when I studied in China in 1981, the effects of this devastating revolution on religion were visible everywhere in empty altars, churches used as machine shops, and stone inscriptions in temples laboriously scraped off. Near the end of my stay, I visited a mountain in Hunan province—Nan-yue, the "Southern Peak," one of the five old sacred mountains of China—where our family had spent some summers when I was a boy. There have been Daoist temples and Buddhist monasteries on Nan-yue for fifteen hundred years; scores of buildings still remain. Yet when I visited them in 1981, not one image of a deity or Buddha was left, just bare stone altars, a few with fresh incense ashes before them. The monks and priests were all gone, and the buildings abandoned or used as residences by several families each. When I asked what had happened, I was told that most of the destruction had taken place during the Cultural Revolution when groups of young "Red Guards" from the plains below climbed the mountain to wreck every "feudal remnant" they could find. One Chinese hiker told me, "You have no idea of the madness of those days."

During the Cultural Revolution almost all outward expressions of religion disappeared. No rituals were chanted in the monasteries; Christians kept their Bibles hidden under their beds and gathered secretly in little groups in one another's homes. The remaining popular religious sects were closed down, their leaders humiliated, imprisoned, or worse. Scholars no longer dared write about the history of Chinese religions, or if they did, only to ridicule them. Buddhist images all but disappeared from the National Museum of History in Beijing, as if Buddhism in China had never existed. For about a fifth of the human race, traditional religion dropped out of sight, though for a time there was a cult of Mao Ze-dong in which some people revered him almost as a god and spent a lot of time reading and reciting his teachings. But by the mid-1970s that was fading too, and "Mao buttons" and his "Little Red Book" gradually lost popularity.

A short time after Mao's death, his wife and other top leaders ("The Gang of Four") were removed from power, and China entered another new phase, one of more relaxed and practical programs. Since then, China has been changing rapidly once again; group agriculture is returning to the old pattern of individual farmers working their own land, leased from the government. After handing in a certain quota to local officials, farmers can keep the rest of the profits for themselves. This incentive has stimulated agricultural production to record levels. Factory workers are being paid bonuses for better work, and merchants, artisans, and physicians are being encouraged to go into business for themselves, once their work quotas for government units have been filled. Scholars are back at work again; the universities are full; and many foreign companies, with their technical and commercial expertise, are being invited to help China modernize.

Just as policies toward agriculture, industry, and society are changing from the Marxist model, so too are policies toward religion being liberalized. Hundreds of churches and temples have reopened, and their ministers and priests have returned. A few theological seminaries and other religious study centers have started up again, and scholars have resumed writing about religion in any way they like. The government is even paying back rent for religious buildings that were confiscated. There is some evidence as well for the revival of popular religious practices like ancestor worship, funeral rituals, and offerings at temples, though spirit-mediums and sectarian groups are still strictly forbidden. Of course, it is too early to tell how far this liberalization will go, and in any event, religious activities in China today are on a smaller scale than in the past. The government is still led by Marxists who believe that ultimately the government should control everything. Most people simply do not seem interested in religion anymore; they are concerned about having good jobs and working conditions, modern appliances, and education for their children, and about helping develop China's economy.

Nonetheless, many traditional attitudes that were for centuries reinforced by religion are still powerful in China, attitudes such as respect for the family and for older people, loyalty to the nation, and gratitude for being born Chinese. Chinese still assume that reciprocity is the basic rule of human relations: that one should do unto others what one would like them to do in return. So people give gifts and invite friends to dinner in restaurants, hoping that eventually their friends will help them out too. A favor given is a favor received; the first records of this principle are from Shang dynasty offerings to the spirits of ancestors in 1300 B.C.E.! Another ancient tendency that is still alive is that of interpreting human problems in moral terms—as a struggle between good and evil, between public order and private greed—a theme first clearly expressed by Confucius twenty-five hundred years ago. One can see this tendency in 1977 newspaper articles from Beijing concerning the campaign to get rid of the last echoes of the Cultural Revolution.

In these articles Madame Mao and her supporters are portrayed not just as political opponents but as evil heretics acting only for personal gain. One ditty about them read:

Overthrow the "Gang of Four"
Seize the fiendish devils.

And a headline said,

Utterly drive away the four harmful things.

Some of these terms are the same as those that have been used in exorcism rituals for centuries.

This moralizing tendency is alive in Taiwan as well, as can be seen in 1984 newspaper accounts about a police campaign against organized crime. The chief remedy suggested is increased teaching of morals in the public schools. Consumer protection groups argue that the reason companies make dangerous or unreliable products is that there is too much greed in modern society, greed that can be reduced by more and better teaching. This same approach can be seen in scripture texts from modern popular religious sects; for them, the fundamental illness of society is moral ignorance, which can be cured by preaching and good example.

There is evidence for the continuing influence of other old religious attitudes as well, even if they are not recognized as such. Special human beings are still held up as models for the whole country, either good or bad. The struggle between good and evil is personified; individuals become symbols of larger forces in society, just as were the gods of popular religion. Mao Ze-dong, for example, was long venerated as the savior of China, the bringer of light and hope to all, whereas his rivals were fiercely criticized as evil reactionaries. The Chinese press praises workers who exceed production quotas or invent new machines; they are held up as examples for all to imitate, as are heroes who give their lives to rescue others from drowning or being run over by trains. Virtuous death for the good of all is a common theme in many religions, illustrated in China by the famous deity Guan-gong, a symbol of loyalty and courage. Guan-gong began his career as a valiant general of the third century C.E. who died in battle against the evil rival of a good emperor. Guan-gong is no longer officially venerated in China, but the spirit he represented lives on. In China, as elsewhere, old religious attitudes still have power even for those who have forgotten their origins and who may not be religious themselves. From this perspective, studying the history of religions, including our own, helps us better understand the background of today's ideas and feelings.

Some Lessons of Chinese Religions for Today

Chinese religions have many lessons for us today, beginning with loyalty and cooperation within families and a strong sense of being responsible for the order of society. This social concern is the basis for an important form of immortality in China, the immortality of influence, which, in practice, means to act now so that one "leaves behind a fragrance for a hundred generations." Chinese are convinced that what counts in an individual life is its contribution to family and society, through education, hard work, and ethical integrity. Society keeps on going after we die, so by strengthening it our own influence continues; we have not lived for nothing.

This concentration on life in society is related to another Chinese conviction: that it is a rare opportunity to be born a human being. In Buddhist teaching there are six paths or forms of existence, ranging from gods to animals to demons in purgatory. All living beings rotate throughout these paths, reborn according to their karma, or moral worth. Human life is just one of these options, hard to attain, particularly rebirth in a civilized country like China. Therefore, once we are here we should make the most of it, try to be worthy of our good fortune and live a moral life so that we might be reborn as humans again.

At the highest philosophical level, some Chinese thinkers have taught that humans are to be "the mind of the universe." We are the universe being aware of itself, the only such intelligence we know of. Hence, our role is to think on behalf of everything else that cannot, to complete the development of the world through our culture and moral concern. For Chinese philosophy, humans "form a triad with heaven and earth"; we have an equal part to play, so that without us, nature is unfinished. To use Western language, the human role in evolution is to think, to continue the ancient process of natural development through society, government, economic activity, cultural life, and education; it is these that make up our part of the "triad." This is indeed a profoundly important responsibility; if we do not do it, it will not be done.

Another Chinese contribution is religious egalitarianism: a conviction that the potential for enlightenment is universal, that "the man on the street can become a sage." Confucian philosophers have long taught that we all have the seeds of goodness within us and need only encourage them to grow. They also teach that the real worth of a human being is his or her moral character, something that can be developed by anyone through dedication and hard work. The Daoists believe that cosmic energy and rhythm are present in all of us as the basis of our life, even if we have forgotten it. All we need to do is return to this Dao (Way) within us to find a new sense of peace and harmony with all things. Buddhists proclaim that everyone has the basic ability to understand life in a completely objective and unselfish way. This understanding was first consciously discovered by the Buddha, which means that we all have the capacity to become Buddhas ourselves. For the Chan (Zen) school, such enlightenment is possible right now for everyone who really tries. Thus the three major streams of Chinese religion agree that all of us have the potential to become better persons, psychologically secure, understanding, and compassionate.

There are many other valuable themes one could mention: harmony with the landscape in *feng-shui,* the Confucian concern for learning as a lifelong process, the conviction that life is fundamentally an arena for moral choices, choices that can change our destiny. This latter conviction in turn is rooted in the belief that in the long run the universe is on the side of order and goodness. If we persist, eventually we or our families will obtain the rewards that are due. As the Confucian philosopher Mencius said in the fourth century B.C.E., "Those who accord with Heaven will live; those who oppose Heaven will die." Our list could continue, but all these themes are united by the assumption that the world is a living system in which everything depends on everything else. It is this deep sense of mutual dependence and relationship that makes the study of Chinese religions so relevant today. Modern science, economic life, and history teach the same lesson, a lesson we still need to learn.

What might happen to Chinese religions in the future? Of course, no one can be certain, but it seems likely that as modernization advances, some forms of Chinese religious activity will continue and others will become less popular, depending in part on which are still perceived to have personal meaning and a useful role to play. Because death, families, and the changes of the seasons will always be with us, ancestor worship and funeral rituals will continue to be important, as will the New Year and other festivals. There are always some people who want a stronger and more personal sense of religious assurance through joining a group or congregation, so popular religious sects will probably be around for a long time. In modern societies people move from place to place and have to survive as individuals in new surroundings far from their families and hometowns. One way of settling into a new situation is to become part of a social group with specific purposes and activities, open to any interested person. Taiwan's popular religious sects have this role for individuals who need a sense of belonging, moral certainty, and a promise of salvation after death. The sects also offer meditation and scripture study, which appeal to those who want more direct personal knowledge of the gods and their teachings. Of course, the mainland Chinese government still opposes religious sects, so they may not reappear there.

Buddhist monasteries have not been strong in China for a long time; the major Buddhist activities of the future will probably be scripture study and meditation sessions for laypeople, along with rituals in honor of the Buddha Amitabha. As with the popular religious sects, the forms of Buddhism that will continue will probably be those that promise the most "power to the people." People want to have control over their own religious destiny, to know what is going on and find assurance for themselves. Chanting Amitabha's name to secure rebirth in his paradise fits right in with this need.

Another form of religion that will probably continue to grow in China and Taiwan is Christianity. Christianity has several advantages, the chief of which is its association with the science and modernity of Europe and North America. Most Chinese want to become more modern themselves, and so if they are inclined toward religion, Christianity might look attractive. The old rejection of Christianity because it is un-Chinese no longer has much force, because China is becoming more Westernized, and many of its people have drifted away from their traditional religious practices. This process is reinforced by the fact that the churches in China have been independent of foreign support since 1949 and are therefore no longer accused of representing foreign religion and interests.

In both China and Taiwan, Christianity has been accepted as a legitimate religion for people to join. It offers good organization, seminaries, scripture study, strong ethical teaching, and a promise of salvation. Christian schools and hospitals have long had a strong impact on China and are still active in Taiwan. Furthermore, in China much of the local competition has been eliminated through government suppression of popular religion. If people want a religion with coherent teachings, Christianity is an obvious alternative. In Taiwan the popular sects are very active, but Christianity has prestige, money, high-profile institutions, and trained leaders, due in part to outside support from North American and European churches. Most people in China do not practice any religion at all, but it seems likely that some of those who are still interested will look to Christianity as a way to be religious and modern at the same time. The same is true to some extent for Taiwan as well, though there is more religious competition there, and Christianity still depends on foreign support.

In sum, the kinds of Chinese religion that are most likely to survive are those that deal with basic problems, like death, and those that give meaning to the lives of individuals in modern, changing society. At least for now many traditional beliefs and rituals remain, and some are reviving, both in China and on Taiwan.

Of course, the continuing influence of Chinese religions is not limited to China, Taiwan, and Chinese communities overseas, because traditions such as *tai-ji quan* exercises, Chan (Zen) Buddhist meditation, and Chinese medicine are well established in Canada, the United States, and Europe. There are probably more practitioners of the ancient divination text, the *Yi-jing,* in America than in China; for us, it is new and interesting; for them, it is old stuff. The interrelated worldview of Chinese philosophy and religion has been known in the West since the sixteenth century, and new books about it are frequently published. In all this Chinese material some people sense a kind of wholeness and interconnection that is missing in their own beliefs. Chinese medicine, for instance, emphasizes the importance of preventing illness through good diet, exercise, and moderate life habits. When something goes wrong in one part of the body, it is understood to be due to an imbalance in the total system, from liver function to one's family situation and work habits. A persistent sore throat may be treated not only with an antibiotic but with herbal drugs to restore proper blood circulation and with instructions to rest and adopt a more relaxed lifestyle.

One of the lessons that traditional Chinese religion and philosophy can teach us is that we are a part of an interdependent world and need to take responsibility for it. This basic assumption is well stated by the philosopher **Wang Yang-ming** (1472–1529), who wrote:

> The great man regards Heaven and Earth and the myriad things as one body. He regards the world as one family and the country as one person. As to those who make a cleavage between objects and distinguish between the self and others, they are small men. That the great man can regard Heaven, Earth, and the myriad things as one body is not because he deliberately wants to do so, but because it is natural to the humane nature of his mind that he do so. Forming one body with Heaven, Earth, and the myriad things is not only true of the great man. Even the mind of the small man is no different. Only he himself makes it small. Therefore when he sees a child about to fall into a well, he cannot help a feeling of alarm and commiseration. This shows that his humanity forms one body with the child. It may be objected that the child belongs to the same species. Again, when he observes the pitiful cries and frightened appearance of birds and animals about to be slaughtered, he cannot help feeling an "inability to bear" their suffering. This shows that his humanity forms one body with birds and animals. It may be objected that birds and animals are sentient beings as he is. But when he sees plants broken and destroyed, he cannot help a feeling of pity. This shows that his humanity forms one body with plants. Yet even when he sees tiles and stones shattered and crushed, he cannot help a feeling of regret. This shows that his humanity forms one body with tiles and stones. This means that even the mind of the small man necessarily has the humanity that forms one body

with all. Such a mind is rooted in his Heaven-endowed nature, and is naturally intelligent, clear, and not beclouded. For this reason it is called the "clear character."

. . .

To manifest the clear character is to bring about the substance of the state of forming one body with Heaven, Earth, and the myriad things, whereas loving the people is to put into universal operation the function of the state of forming one body. Hence manifesting the clear character consists in loving the people, and loving the people is the way to manifest the clear character. Therefore, only when I love my father, the fathers of others, and the fathers of all men can my humanity really form one body with my father, the fathers of others, and the fathers of all men. When it truly forms one body with them, then the clear character of filial piety will be manifested. Only when I love my brother, the brothers of others, and the brothers of all men can my humanity really form one body with my brother, the brothers of others, and the brothers of all men. When it truly forms one body with them, then the clear character of brotherly respect will be manifested. Everything from ruler, minister, husband, wife, and friends to mountains, rivers, spiritual beings, birds, animals, and plants should be truly loved in order to realize my humanity that forms one body with them, and then my clear character will be completely manifested, and I will really form one body with Heaven, Earth, and the myriad things.[20]

It is views such as these that demonstrate the continuing value of traditional Chinese religion and thought for today.

Study Questions

Before you begin to read this part, take a mental inventory of what you know and think about China. What images do you have of China and Chinese people? Make a mental list of Chinese "things" that you know—chop suey, chopsticks, Chinese lanterns, and so on. What would you imagine religion in China to be like? Keep these images and things in mind as you read this part and develop new notions about China.

CHAPTER 40

Introduction: Beliefs and Values of One of the World's Oldest Living Cultures

1. What do you learn about Chinese religion from the story of "wind and water"? How does this story illustrate the Chinese assumption that "the world is a living system"?
2. How would you interpret "the Chinese sense of the world itself as a holy place"?

CHAPTER 41

History: The Development of Chinese Religious Traditions over Time

1. Frame in your mind a picture of the origin of what is China or "Chinese"—its ancient beginnings, its geographical boundaries, its people, its culture, and its religion.
2. What is the role of Confucius in Chinese history, and how did he and his followers help develop Chinese philosophy? What is the role of the two books *Lao-zi* and *Zhuang-zi* in Chinese history, and how did the followers of these books help develop Chinese philosophy?
3. What is the Dao (Tao), and how is it central to Chinese thought and religion?
4. What is "the search for immortality"?
5. How did early Daoism rise out of earlier popular religious movements? What are the moral teachings of the *Tai-ping jing*? Why did elitist Daoism and dry, formal state religion not satisfy most people?
6. Who was Siddhartha Gautama, and how did he found Buddhism?
7. How did Pure Land Buddhism become the most popular form of Buddhism in China?
8. What is the Chan (Zen) goal of enlightenment through meditation?
9. How did Confucianism redefine itself over against Buddhism?
10. What characterizes "popular religion" in China, and how would you distinguish it from other religions?
11. What are the major objects of worship and the major practices of popular religion?

CHAPTER 42

Types of Beliefs and Activities in Chinese Religious Life

1. How does Chinese religion define a worldview of sacred space, sacred time, and "symbols of superhuman power"?
2. Interpret the statement (p. 1026) that "The basic theme of Chinese ritual is *reciprocity. . . .*"
3. What are the general principles of divination and exorcism in Chinese religion?
4. Identify the basic ethical teachings in Chinese religion. Compare and contrast the list of "standard ethical instructions" (pp. 1037–38) with what you consider to be standard ethical teachings in the United States or Canada.

CHAPTER 43

Dynamics: Chinese Religions Lived and Practiced

1. Is the Spring Festival primarily a social gathering, a picnic, a nature outing, or a religious event?
2. How would you describe the enlightenment experience that Fa-bao had in front of his dead friend's portrait?
3. When does a dead person become a ghost, and what are the key features in an exorcism ritual? (Can you compare and contrast this event to "exorcism" films in the United States?)
4. In your own words, describe how Qiu Su-zhen became a spirit-writer.

CHAPTER 44

Chinese Religions Today

1. How do you account for the fact that Chinese religion is so active in areas outside mainland China (Hong Kong and Taiwan), while in mainland China there has been great persecution and indifference with regard to religion?
2. What have you learned in your study of Chinese religion—how does this compare with the "lessons of Chinese religions for today" suggested by the author? Do you agree or disagree with the author's forecast of future developments of religion in China—how and why?

Recall the mental inventory of Chinese images and things that you made before reading this part. What is there in Chinese religion that is most like your own religious tradition? What is most interesting? How has your understanding of China changed as a result of reading this section? Can you now imagine yourself participating in Chinese religion?

Notes

1. Arthur Waley, trans., *The Analects of Confucius* (New York: Vintage Books, n.d.; orig. pub. 1938), 127, 189. The quoted passages are *Analects* 7:22 and 14:37. (*Analects* is an obsolete word meaning selected parts of a book.)
2. Burton Watson, trans., *Mo Tzu: Basic Writings* (New York: Columbia University Press, 1963), 88.
3. Wing-tsit Chan, trans., *The Way of Lao Tzu (Tao-Te Ching)* (Indianapolis, IN: Bobbs-Merrill, 1963), 144, 160. These passages are from chapters 25 and 34 of the *Lao-zi* book. Chinese tradition attributes this book to a man called Lao-zi ("Venerable Philosopher"), but in fact we don't know who wrote it.
4. Burton Watson, trans., *Hsun Tzu: Basic Writings* (New York: Columbia University Press, 1963), 85.
5. Michael Loewe, *Ways to Paradise: The Chinese Quest for Immortality* (London: George Allen & Unwin, 1979), 98–99.
6. Max Kaltenmark, "The Ideology of the *T'ai-p'ing ching,*" in *Facets of Taoism,* ed. Holmes Welch and Anna Seidel (New Haven, CT: Yale University Press, 1979), 33–34.
7. Edward Conze, ed., *Buddhist Texts Through the Ages* (New York: Harper & Row, 1964), 202–6.
8. Philip P. Yampolsky, *The Platform Sutra of the Sixth Patriarch, the text of the Tun-huang manuscript with translation, introduction, and notes* (New York: Columbia University Press, 1967), 142–46.
9. Wing-tsit Chan, ed. and comp., *A Sourcebook in Chinese Philosophy* (Princeton, NJ: Princeton University Press, 1963), 497, 463.
10. Wolfram Eberhard, ed., *Folktales of China* (Chicago: University of Chicago Press, 1965), 79–80.
11. James Legge, *The Notions of the Chinese Concerning Gods and Spirits* (Hong Kong, 1852), 28.
12. Michael Saso, "Orthodoxy and Heterodoxy in Taoist Ritual," in *Religion and Ritual in Chinese Society,* ed. Arthur W. Wolf (Stanford, CA: Stanford University Press, 1974), 329–30. A Cheng Huang is the god of a county seat town; Lu Shan is a sacred mountain in Jiangxi (Kiangsi) province; a *fu* is a paper charm inscribed with written commands to trouble-making demons.
13. Holmes Welch, *The Practice of Chinese Buddhism* (Cambridge, MA: Harvard University Press, 1967), 64.
14. David K. Jordan and Daniel L. Overmyer, *The Flying Phoenix: Aspects of Chinese Sectarianism in Taiwan* (Princeton, NJ: Princeton University Press, 1986), chap. 8. Women can hold all of these positions, which give them more status in a sect than they would usually have outside it.
15. Daniel L. Overmyer, "Values in Chinese Sectarian Literature: Ming and Ch'ing *Pao-chuan,*" in *Popular Culture in Late Imperial China: Diversity and Integration,* ed. David Johnson, Andrew J. Nathan, and Evelyn S. Rawski (Berkeley and Los Angeles: University of California Press, 1985), 244–45.
16. Frances L. K. Hsu, *Under the Ancestors' Shadow: Kinship, Personality and Social Mobility in Village China* (Garden City, NJ: Doubleday, Anchor Books, 1967), 180–83.

17. John Blofeld, *The Jewel in the Lotus* (London: Sedgwick & Jackson, 1948), 82–84.

18. David K. Jordan, *Gods, Ghosts and Ancestors: Folk Religion in a Taiwanese Village* (Berkeley and Los Angeles: University of California Press, 1972), 56–59.

19. Jordan and Overmyer, *The Flying Phoenix,* chap. 8.

20. Chan, *Sourcebook,* 659–61.

Glossary

Amitabha Buddha of a paradise called the Pure Land of the West. Those who pray to him and call out his name in faith can be reborn there at death.

ancestors The spirits of the dead in the male line of the family who have been transformed by funeral and memorial rituals into sources of blessing for descendants.

bodhisattva One who has vowed to seek enlightenment and attain Buddhahood by developing wisdom and compassion. Many *bodhisattvas* who began their quest long ago are now the saints and heroes of Buddhism.

Buddha A person who has attained complete enlightenment through many lifetimes of moral and spiritual development. As a symbol of objectivity, selflessness, and compassion, a Buddha is a model for all. Each world and era has a Buddha; ours is Siddhartha Gautama, who lived in India during the sixth and fifth centuries B.C.E.

Chan (Ch'an [Jap. Zen]) A Buddhist school that emphasizes that one can attain enlightenment in this life through meditation. First developed in China in the eighth century C.E.

Confucius The first Chinese philosopher and teacher (551–479 B.C.E.), who advocated the moral reform of society through training men to become honest and compassionate government officials.

Dao (Tao) Literally, "a road, path, or way." In Confucianism the proper way of life for a "superior person," based on the will of Heaven. For Daoism, Dao is the source and order of the universe, formless, yet profoundly effective.

Daoism (Taoism) A priestly or theological religion that developed in China beginning in the second century C.E., with its own rituals, scriptures, and organizations. Emphasizes the revival of life power through contact with cosmic forces in the body of the priest.

divination The use of ritual to find out the will of ancestors or gods, through, for example, reading cracks in heated bones, drawing long and short sticks, or throwing moon-shaped blocks on the floor. In all these rituals it is assumed that divine powers influence the process in a mysterious way.

enlightenment The goal of Buddhism; to attain a completely objective and egoless understanding of life. Such egolessness is believed to bring about peace of mind and compassion for all beings.

exorcism Driving away demons through rituals performed by a spirit-medium or a Daoist priest, who represents the power of the gods.

feng-shui **(geomancy)** The art of locating graves and houses so that they benefit from cosmic forces in the sky and landscape. The best site is on the south face of a hill, above a pond or lake, so that it benefits from the warmth of the sun (*yang*) and is protected from the cold winds of the north (*yin*).

five powers A classification of modes of energy in the universe in an attempt to explain how different forces influence one another. The five are wood, fire, earth, metal, and water; all are forms of *qi* (*ch'i*), the one basic substance of which all is made.

gui (kuei) Demons or ghosts; usually spirits of the dead who are angry because they died unjustly or their graves have been neglected. *Gui* can cause illness, insanity, and other problems.

Jade Emperor The supreme deity of popular religion, ruler of all the other gods. He first became well known in the eleventh century C.E.

karma In Buddhism, karma means intentional action and its results, united as cause and effect. Whatever one does, good or ill, is always repaid, either in this life or the next. By such actions we create the form of our lives, present and future.

Lao-zi (Lao-tzu) Also called the *Dao-de jing/Tao-te ching.* The name of a book about how to live gracefully and successfully in accord with the Dao (Tao), the cosmic life-force. This book first appeared in about 300 B.C.E.; its author is unknown, though in Chinese legend it was ascribed to a person named Lao-zi, which means "venerable philosopher."

li The ordering principles of all that exists. *Li* are patterns of organization that shape *qi,* the basic stuff of which all is made.

Ma-zu (Ma-tsu) The goddess of fishermen and sailors, who began her career as a pious girl of the eleventh century C.E. She is still popular in Taiwan and Hong Kong.

meditation A process of concentrating and calming the mind, usually done while seated in a quiet place. The characteristic Buddhist way of attaining enlightenment.

Mo-zi (Mo-tzu) A philosopher of the fifth century B.C.E. who taught that people should love and care for one another in practical ways because that is Heaven's will.

nirvana A Buddhist term meaning how the world looks to one who has attained enlightenment. It is characterized by nonattachment, acceptance, and peace.

Pure Land A paradise presided over by a Buddha whose preaching and example make it easier to attain enlightenment. Some Buddhists pray to be reborn in such a paradise at death, which became the basis for a popular form of Buddhist devotion. See also Amitabha.

qi (ch'i) The one basic substance and energy of which all is made, from gods to rocks. Differences in things are due to different density, clarity, and form of their *qi,* and to different patterns of *li.*

Shang-di (Shang-ti) The "Ruler on High," supreme god of the Shang dynasty at the beginning of Chinese history, who later was equated with Tian and continued to be important in state rituals.

spirit-medium A man or woman whose body can be taken over by a spirit or god during a ritual. In such a possessed state, the person temporarily becomes a god and speaks the god's instructions or uses its power to drive out demons.

spirit-writing Writing on paper or a tray of sand by a spirit or god whose power moves the pen. A popular Chinese way of receiving revelations, moral instructions, and answers to prayers.

Spring Festival (Qing-ming) A festival in early April, a time to celebrate the unity of the living and dead in a family by having a picnic at the grave.

temple The residence of a god or gods, who are represented by statues on top of altar platforms. Temples are rectangular compounds, facing south, designed like old Chinese palaces.

Tian (T'ien) Tian, "Heaven," was the supreme god of the early Zhou people, superior to ancestors and other gods. Heaven's approval was necessary for rulers, who could lose it and their position if they were cruel or unjust.

Wang Yang-ming A Confucian philosopher and official (1472–1529 C.E.) who taught that the potential for goodness is already in the human mind. This goodness is to be expressed in love for all things.

Xi Wang-mu (Hsi Wang-mu) The "Queen Mother of the West," a powerful goddess in Daoism and popular religion. She presides over a paradise in the west, and promises immortality to those who believe in her.

Xun-zi (Hsun-tzu) A political philosopher of the third century B.C.E. who taught that Heaven (Tian) has no consciousness or will but is just a way of talking about the order of nature.

Yellow Turbans (Way of Great Peace and Prosperity) A popular religious movement that tried to take over China in a military uprising in 184 C.E.; a forerunner of Daoism.

Yi-jing (I-ching) An ancient Chinese book of divination and wisdom, based on sixty-four sets of six horizontal lines, broken and unbroken. By counting off short sticks, one can form such a hexagram for oneself and read in the book what it means.

yin/yang Modes of energy in the universe, symbolized by polarities of night/day, winter/summer, moon/sun. *Yang* represents heat and light, the power that starts things; *yin* symbolizes cold and dark, the power that completes them. See also *five powers* and *qi*.

Zhu Xi (Chu Hsi) A Confucian philosopher (1130–1200 C.E.) who taught that all things are composed of "ordering principles" (*li*) and "vital substance" (*qi*). His interpretations of Confucius were made official state teaching.

Zhuang-zi (Chuang-tzu) A philosopher of the fourth century B.C.E. who sought spiritual freedom through unity with the cosmic Dao present in all things. Also a book attributed to him. Unlike "Lao-Zi," we know that Zhuang-Zi really existed.

Selected Reading List

Chan, Wing-tsit, trans. and comp. *A Sourcebook in Chinese Philosophy.* Princeton, NJ: Princeton University Press, 1963.

Ch'en, Kenneth K. S. *Buddhism in China, A Historical Survey.* Princeton, NJ: Princeton University Press, 1964.

——. *The Chinese Transformation of Buddhism.* Princeton, NJ: Princeton University Press, 1973.

Creel, H. G. *Chinese Thought from Confucius to Mao Tse-tung.* New York: New American Library, 1960.

Hsu, Immanuel C. Y. *The Rise of Modern China.* 3d ed. New York: Oxford University Press, 1983.

Hucker, Charles. *China's Imperial Past.* Stanford, CA: Stanford University Press, 1975.

Jordan, David K. *Gods, Ghosts and Ancestors: Folk Religion in a Taiwanese Village.* Berkeley and Los Angeles: University of California Press, 1972.

Maspero, Henri. *Taoism and Chinese Religion.* Translated by Frank A. Kierman. Amherst, MA: University of Massachusetts Press, 1981.

Overmyer, Daniel L. *Folk Buddhist Religion: Dissenting Sects in Late Traditional China.* Cambridge, MA: Harvard University Press, 1976.

Robinson, Richard H., and Willard L. Johnson. *The Buddhist Religion, A Historical Introduction.* 3d ed. Belmont, CA: Wadsworth, 1982.

Smith, D. Howard. *Chinese Religions.* London: Weidenfeld and Nicolson, 1968.

Smith, Richard J. *China's Cultural Heritage: The Ch'ing Dynasty, 1644–1912.* Boulder, CO: Westview Press; London: Francis Pinter, 1983.

Thompson, Laurence G. *Chinese Religion, An Introduction.* 4th ed. Belmont, CA: Wadsworth, 1989.

——. *Chinese Religion in Western Languages.* Tucson: University of Arizona Press, 1985. (A bibliography)

——. *The Chinese Way in Religion.* Belmont, CA: Dickenson, 1973.

Waley, Arthur. *Three Ways of Thought in Ancient China.* New York: Doubleday, 1939.

Wolf, Arthur P., ed. *Religion and Ritual in Chinese Society.* Stanford, CA: Stanford University Press, 1974.

Yang, C. K. *Religion in Chinese Society.* Berkeley and Los Angeles: University of California Press, 1961.

Yu, David C., with contributions by Laurence G. Thompson. *Guide to Chinese Religion.* Boston: G. K. Hall & Co., 1985. (Annotated bibliography, by topics)

PART TEN

Religions of Japan

*Many Traditions
Within One Sacred Way*

H. Byron Earhart

Chronology of Japanese Religious History

Historical Periods and Western Dates	Cultural and Religious Features
	RELIGIOUS CUSTOMS IN EARLY JAPAN
Prehistoric (to sixth century C.E.)	Transition from hunting-gathering culture to rice agriculture and small villages and development of Japanese religious practices—ancient Shinto and *kami,* seasonal festivals and agricultural fertility—spirits of the dead; divine descent of imperial family
	CHINESE AND INDIAN INFLUENCE ON JAPANESE RELIGIONS
Taika (645–710) *Nara (710–784)*	Formal Chinese cultural influence (especially from the sixth century): development of written language, centralized government, first permanent capital at Nara; introduction of Confucianism, religious Daoism, and Buddhism; Shinto becomes more formally organized, and all traditions interact
	THE FLOWERING OF JAPANESE BUDDHISM
Heian (794–1185) *Kamakura (1185–1333)*	Capital moves from Nara to Kyoto, and elegant life develops among court and nobility; Shingon and Tendai sects of Buddhism founded during Heian period; rise to power of military dictator and warriors from new center of power at Kamakura; during Kamakura period Pure Land, Nichiren, and Zen sects of Buddhism founded; Shinto becomes more highly organized and develops eclectic teachings
	RELIGION IN MEDIEVAL JAPAN
Muromachi (1333–1568) *Momoyama (1568–1600)* *Tokugawa (1600–1867)*	Much civil war and strife until Tokugawa government gains control, unifying and stabilizing the country; development of cities and merchant class; Buddhist denominations develop from earlier sects, and Shinto refines systems of eclectic teachings; Christianity (Roman Catholicism) is introduced and enjoys brief success before being banned; Confucian teachings provide the social rationale for the Tokugawa ruling system, and families are required to belong to Buddhist temples

Historical Periods and Western Dates	*Cultural and Religious Features*
	JAPAN ENTERS THE MODERN WORLD
Meiji *(1868–1912)* *Taisho* *(1912–1926)* *Showa* *(1926–1989)* *Heisei* *(1989–)*	Transition from feudal rule to modern nation-state, end of rule by military dictators with new parliamentary government at Tokyo; rapid development of education and industry; in Meiji times required membership in Buddhist temples dropped, ban on Christianity lifted (and Protestant and Catholic Christianity reintroduced), Shinto made a state religion and New Religions become significant movements; after 1945 and Japan's defeat in World War II, development of more democratic policies, including a new constitution and complete religious freedom; Shinto's role as a state religion is removed, with all religions enjoying complete freedom; Japan rebuilds and becomes a major economic and political power; Shinto and Buddhism slowly recover strength after World War II, New Religions become the most rapidly developing religious force, and there is widespread secularism and religious indifference.

Prologue

FOR MORE THAN thirty years I have enjoyed my professional field of specialization, studying Japanese religion. Some of this time has been spent in Japan doing research on specific aspects of Japanese religion; much of the rest of the time has been spent teaching and writing on this subject. The present work is an attempt to share with others my fascination for its amazing variety. The rich treasury of religion in Japan makes it difficult to limit this work to those aspects that can be treated in a few chapters. But this essay is intended as a brief introduction to Japanese religion, not a comprehensive interpretation. I have therefore tried to explore whatever is of greatest help and interest to the person first reading about Japanese religion. To the extent that these chapters help the reader appreciate the richness of the Japanese tradition, my purpose is fulfilled.

Included in this treatment are several features to assist the reader in becoming acquainted with Japan and Japanese religion. The map on page 1081 shows the location of the Japanese islands in relationship to Asia and identifies major cities and some religious centers mentioned in the text. The chronology on pages 1077–1078 provides a convenient overview of Japanese religious history that can be used in at least three ways: first, before reading this part, to get a bird's eye view of the subject; second, while reading it, to place particular materials in historical context; and third, after reading it, to review and unify all the materials.

Chinese terms in the text and the glossary are given in the *pin-yin* romanization, with the Wade-Giles equivalent in parentheses.

45

Introduction: Japan and Japanese Religion

PEOPLE OUTSIDE OF Japan know more about recent Japan and its technological achievements—automobiles, cameras, and electronics—than about its traditional culture and religion. But as proud as the Japanese are of their technological and commercial success, they have not become completely "Westernized," for Japanese culture dates back several thousand years, and Japanese people are equally proud of the distinctive culture they inherit from the past—its language, national identity, arts, and religious traditions. This work will focus on the distinctively Japanese religious heritage (which will be called Japanese religion), introducing the individual religious traditions and interpreting the general worldview created by all these traditions together.

In order to treat Japan's religious heritage, it is necessary to deal with some other aspects of Japan as well. In this chapter we will look primarily at the two elements of the term *religions of Japan*—what defines Japan as a national and cultural unit and what religious traditions are found in Japan. Chapter 46 will describe how Japanese religion developed historically from the earliest times to the present. Chapters 47 and 48 will interpret how Japanese religion is organized into a total way of life, providing not only objects of worship but a complete understanding of the human career. The next chapter shows how Japanese religion has functioned concretely, giving two examples of the dynamics of Japanese religion in action, and the final chapter looks more closely at religion in contemporary Japan.

What Is Japan?

Japan has many aspects, some concrete and visible, some more abstract and intangible. Japan is the land that is the living space of the country; it is the people who live in the land and constitute its citizenry; it is the economic activity sustaining the life of the people individually and collectively; it is the nation as a political entity, both as the government forming the state and as the loyalty of

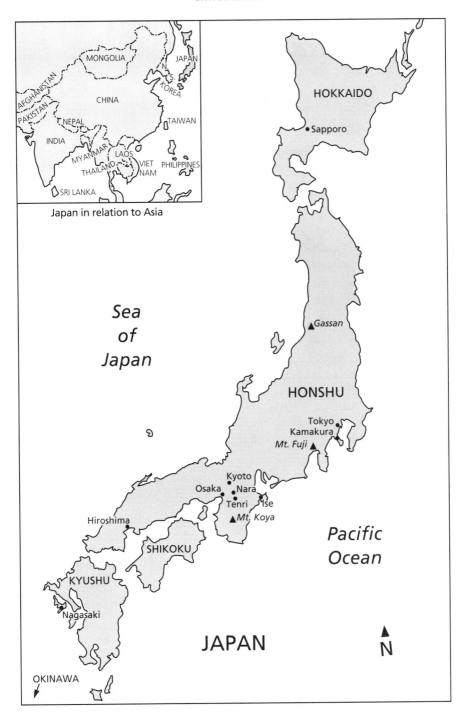

Japan in relation to Asia

MONGOLIA
JAPAN
N.
S.
KOREA
AFGHANISTAN
CHINA
PAKISTAN
NEPAL
TAIWAN
INDIA
MYANMAR
LAOS
THAILAND
VIET
NAM
PHILIPPINES
SRI LANKA

HOKKAIDO

Sapporo

Sea
of
Japan

Gassan

HONSHU

Tokyo
Kamakura
Mt. Fuji

Kyoto
Osaka
Nara
Tenri
Ise
Mt. Koya

Hiroshima

Pacific
Ocean

SHIKOKU

KYUSHU

Nagasaki

JAPAN

N

OKINAWA

the people supporting the state; it is the language, spoken by no other people in the world; it is the many art forms and the aesthetic sensibilities that characterize Japanese culture; and it is the pattern of individual religions and beliefs and practices that make up the Japanese religious tradition. All of these aspects are closely related parts of the total experience of Japan. For convenience we will view each of them separately, looking first at the components of Japan and then turning to the religious dimension of the Japanese experience.

When we look at a map, the first thing we notice about Japan is that it is a curved semicircle of islands off the coast of the Asian continent. This geographical situation of Japan in relation to Asia has played a great role in the formation of a distinctive Japanese culture and a separate national experience, because Japan was close enough to receive periodic influences yet far enough away to mold those influences into a peculiarly Japanese way of life. Some traditional accounts view the beginning of the Japanese nation as the creation of the Japanese islands six millennia ago by the **kami*** (deities), but most modern historians consider Japan to date from a little more than two thousand years ago.

From about two millennia ago, there began to emerge a distinctive group of people (the Japanese people), a particular way of life (Japanese culture), and a specific national identity (the Japanese nation). Throughout the centuries, many borrowed elements have entered Japan from the outside, and many changes have taken place within Japanese society, but underneath all these changes has been a strong sense of the continuity of Japan as an ongoing tradition.

The most concrete aspect of Japan is a number of islands: At present, Japanese territory includes four major islands (from south to north—Kyushu, Shikoku, Honshu, and Hokkaido) and numerous smaller islands (such as Okinawa). In earliest times, there were no clear-cut boundaries, but the people and culture that came to be known as Japanese formed first in the areas close to Korea, on the islands of Kyushu and southwest Honshu. Gradually the people of southwestern Japan came to control all the Japanese islands, and their lifestyle formed the basis for the culture found in these islands today.

Although today the Japanese people are viewed as a single nationality, they share a common ancestry with other Asian peoples. Early Japan was probably inhabited by people who entered from the northern Asian continent and from the areas south of Japan. The Japanese people, however, see themselves as much more than merely Asians who inhabit a particular place. From ancient times the Japanese have perceived themselves in terms of their mythology, which views the Japanese islands and the Japanese people as being created by the *kami;* the Japanese people see themselves as the descendants of these first people who inhabited the Japanese islands. Although this mythology is not always taken so literally today, there remains in the people of Japan a strong sense of identity distinct from all other people.

---

*Terms defined in the glossary, pp. 1184–86, are printed in boldface type where they first appear in the text.

To "be Japanese" means much more than to be born of Japanese parents and to learn Japanese customs. It means also to be part of a family system. By contrast with the sense of individualism in Western countries like the United States, Japanese people tend to view themselves and to behave as members of a family more than as individuals. Generally speaking, in Japanese society there is a greater sense of belonging to social groups than there is in Western countries, whether family, university, or company. And this sense of belonging is not just an abstract notion but is channeled through specific relationships: children's loyalty to parents, a student's respect for a professor (even long after graduation), and the cooperation with fellow workers in a particular division of a larger company.

Some scholars think that the present emphasis in Japan on large extended families and on social cooperation (rather than individualism) is closely linked to the pattern of rice agriculture in Japan. The economic life of the earliest inhabitants of the Japanese islands was a combination of hunting and gathering, especially collecting shellfish along the ocean shore. More than two thousand years ago, this hunting-gathering pattern gradually gave way to agriculture; in Japan rice became the staff of life, as it did in many other Asian countries. Rice has been an extremely important feature of the Japanese economy, closely related to social life and an important symbol of the blessings of nature. Rice requires large amounts of hand labor but also gives rather large yields. It was especially rice that allowed the Japanese people to develop more permanent large-scale settlements, and on the basis of this rice agriculture, a form of feudal government emerged, with nobility and wealthy landowners at the top of the society and relatively poor farmers and tenants at the bottom. The poorest farmers did not always have rice to eat (eating instead foods not so valuable as a cash crop), but they had to pay taxes in rice, which was almost the same as money. Many of the seasonal rituals in Japan are marked by the various seasons and events connected with the growing and harvesting of rice.

Japan is well known for its rapid technological and commercial development after World War II, but the foundations for this success go back at least several hundred years, when widespread trade arose between urban centers and rural regions. Not only foods such as rice, rice wine (*sake*), and soy sauce, but also textiles and fertilizer were important in this large trade network and its large-scale banking system. From the late nineteenth century, Japan deliberately set out on a course of promoting education, technology, and industry in order to compete with the West. Since World War II Japanese business has combined imported technical information and management techniques with native ingenuity and innovation to create one of the most competitive industrial-commercial forces in the world, emphasizing high quality at low prices. A few decades ago Japan still suffered the bad reputation of being a "borrower" of everything, from culture to technology, but nowadays Western countries ask how they can borrow technical breakthroughs and management practices from Japan.

The system of government has gone through many significant changes in Japanese history. In the earliest times, the clan, or large family, was an important social and political unit, and the most revered family line was that of the imperial family, thought to be descended from the divine creators of the Japanese islands. Some of the earliest records of Japan are Chinese writings that describe rule by empresses; however, rule by empresses soon gave way to a hereditary line of emperors. These emperors were the symbolic heads of state and national ceremonies but did not rule directly. Cabinets and ministries administered governments; as Chinese influence dominated Japan after about the sixth century, Chinese models of centralized government were adopted, but gradually the Chinese models were replaced by Japanese adaptations.

Until the twelfth century, a lively imperial court and a wealthy nobility ruled the country and presided over an aristocratic lifestyle that is still remembered with nostalgia today. Power gradually shifted to the military. In the twelfth century the military gained control of the country and, for all practical purposes, became the rulers, replacing the symbolic figure of the emperor and also the nobility. Much blood was shed in the quest for military supremacy among competing feudal powers, and finally in the seventeenth century, the country was unified by a military ruler (**shogun**) who received allegiance and tribute from regional feudal lords. Gradually the feudal way of life was weakened by internal changes in the Japanese economy and society and by external pressures of foreign governments that sought to open Japan to trade. These forces combined to help bring an end to the feudal style of government in 1867, when the modern nation-state of Japan was formed: Feudal domains and social class divisions were abolished and there came to be truly national control over regional prefectures (divisions similar to states in the United States). Some democratic ideas were developed during the early twentieth century, but major democratic changes in Japanese society were brought about after 1945 following Japan's defeat in World War II. Today, the emperor is still respected as a symbol of the nation, but Japan is a democratic country with a parliamentary government headed by a prime minister.

One of the most distinctive features of the Japanese heritage is the Japanese language. The earliest origins of Japanese are lost in history, much as are the origins of the Japanese people. Whatever the ancient influences upon the Japanese language, it is not spoken by any other people. Unlike the closely related Romance languages such as Italian, French, and Spanish, the Japanese language is not so closely related to languages of neighboring countries. For example, Japanese is quite different from Chinese: Spoken Japanese does not feature a distinct pattern of tones, as does spoken Chinese. One of the most interesting characteristics of Japanese—and one quite difficult for Westerners to learn—is the many levels of politeness expressed. The Japanese language is "hierarchical," in the sense that different verbs, verb endings, nouns, and other forms must be used depending on the hierarchical social relation between speaker and listener. A professor will use quite different language to speak to a student than the student will use to speak to the professor.

Japanese was not a written language until Chinese writing symbols ("characters" or "ideographs") were borrowed after the introduction of Chinese culture about the sixth century C.E. These Chinese symbols or characters are identical (or slightly abbreviated) in Japan (and in Korea). But in Japan, two phonetic systems were used to retain the structure and grammar of spoken Japanese while borrowing elements of written Chinese. Although some key elements are shared with languages using Chinese characters, a person must learn the phonetic system and grammar of Japanese in order to understand the relations between these elements and written Japanese. This language may be seen as an isolated pocket by outsiders, but to the Japanese people it is a proud expression of their national heritage. The Japanese have translated extensively, so that today they can read in their own language a wide variety of materials—from the Western classics to recent writing in science and social science. Japanese art has absorbed considerable outside influence but still expresses an aesthetic sensitivity that is peculiar to Japan. The seventh-century poetry anthology *Manyoshu* displays some of the same themes—love of nature and appreciation of subtle human emotions—that are found in poetry and literature even today. Nature is a major subject in poetry and also in graphic art. Nature is not depicted, as it often is in the West, as the creation of God—rather, nature itself is practically divine. Landscape painting is one of the favorite forms of graphic art: Mountains, rivers, trees, waterfalls, and other natural scenes grace paintings, folding screens, fans, and woodblock prints. Even popular decorative art from the sixteenth century selected natural phenomena, such as beetles or the cicada, for small carvings.

Not only does art praise nature, but it also focuses attention on the shifting seasons and subtle emotional responses to nature. In fact, the role of poetry in Japan contrasts sharply with the Western pattern in which God inspires poetry and art; in Japan it is poetry that moves the deities. The tenth-century *Kokinshu* (*Collection of Ancient and Modern Poetry*) states that Japanese poetry "moves heaven and earth, and stirs to pity the invisible demons and gods."[1] The twelfth-century *Tale of Genji*—sometimes considered the world's first novel—is an artistic chronicling of the life and loves of the nobility and the imperial court. In this novel, equally important as the message of a love poem is the paper on which it is written and the fragrance of the perfume on the paper. These aesthetic nuances live on today, for the *Manyoshu* and the *Tale of Genji* are not historical curiosities but are loved for their intrinsic artistic imagery and are still models for contemporary works.

It is difficult to capture the "essence" of Japanese art, which, like all cultural forms, has changed considerably through time. But one theme that has endured from prehistoric ages down to the present is an emphasis on the natural qualities of artistic materials. More often than not the texture of clay, the grain of wood, and the fibers of paper are not covered up but are valued as an integral part of the artistic creation. This is seen in prehistoric and ancient pottery; it is also reflected in great architectural achievements such as the **Shinto shrines** of Ise, where natural (unpainted) wood and thatch roof complement each other in stark simplicity against the background of a pebble-filled courtyard and majestic evergreen woods. Others may prefer the abstract quality of **Zen** gardens with raked sand and stones, where a person may meditate on these monuments of permanence contrasting with the impermanence of human life. These examples have been taken mainly from aristocratic and elite culture, but even folk toys are often made out of natural materials. One of the great contrasts in Japanese art is between the more refined and subdued traditions already mentioned and the more gaudy and bright colors associated with some shrines and temples and much of popular culture. There is no room here to explore the variety of art forms and their different moods—from the various forms of theater and puppetry to the art of the tea ceremony and other distinctive Japanese creations.

Japan has a whole treasure house of its own art forms, of which the Japanese people are quite proud. But we should recognize that modern Japanese artists are cosmopolitan, from woodblock print artists to painters and architects. Modern Japanese novels have been praised throughout the world, and in 1968 Yasunari Kawabata became the first Japanese novelist to win a Nobel Prize in literature.

What Is Japanese Religion?

Now that we have looked briefly at Japan itself—its land, people, economic activity, government, language, and arts—let us turn to the religions of Japan. Japanese religion is the general term we will use to refer collectively to all of the following religious phenomena: the half-dozen religious traditions found in Japan and their component parts, various beliefs and practices observed by the Japanese people, and the overall worldview that is shared by these organized religions and in which these beliefs and practices are grounded. We will look at these various phenomena one by one, starting with the more easily recognizable traditions. Many religious traditions are found in Japan: the formal religions of Shinto, **Buddhism, Christianity,** and numerous **New Religions**; the less formal traditions of **Confucianism** and **Daoism (Taoism)**; and the practices and beliefs of **folk religion.**

Shinto is the most ancient of all Japanese religious traditions, having grown out of prehistoric Japanese beliefs and practices—especially those revering nature. Shinto means, literally, "the way of many *kami* (spirits or deities)," and usually these *kami* either helped create aspects of nature or are themselves expressed in natural forms. Families, and villages as groups of families, worshiped local *kami* as the source of blessing for agriculture (especially rice) and their group life. The power of the *kami,* as the force behind and within life, was seen to reside within natural objects.

One of the chief characteristics of Shinto is the close and intimate relationship between humans and *kami.* (*Kami* can refer to one or many deities.) In fact, *kami* may even merge with human beings, such as, for example, the "divine" emperor and the "holy" founders of religious movements. *Kami* are also quite comfortable in the home: The traditional house still contains a Shinto-style altar for *kami,* and offerings of food are presented at this altar by the family members. *Kami* are everywhere, filling the landscape and inhabiting the home.

Generally the Japanese people have seen *kami* to be the source of life and blessing and have approached *kami* to pray for blessings and give thanks. In Shinto great emphasis is placed on cleanliness and purification; Shinto shrines provide water for people to purify their hands and mouths before coming into contact with *kami*. Most Shinto rituals begin with an invocation of the presence of *kami* and with a "sending off" of *kami*. Most of the occasions for such rituals are seasonal festivals, often linked to the agricultural work cycle. This direct appreciation of nature and sincere acceptance of the blessing of *kami* is favored, rather than the development of complicated doctrine and abstract philosophy. Leading a pure and sincere life under the blessing of many *kami* is at the heart of Shinto ideals.

Shinto arose gradually within Japanese culture, but Buddhism was founded in distant India by the Buddha and had to cross both China and Korea to arrive in Japan. The **Buddha** founded a way of life aimed at eliminating suffering through the realization of **enlightenment**—an awakening to a higher peace beyond human suffering. By the time of Buddhism's entry into Japan in the sixth century C.E., about a thousand years had passed since its founding. During that millennium, Buddhism had developed an elaborate monastic community, had come to serve as the religious rationale for the state, and had practiced rituals for the funerals and memorials of the dead.

In Japan, Buddhism exists on a number of levels for various groups of people. For example, the philosophical tradition of Indian Buddhism is preserved mainly by and for scholars, whereas the monastic tradition has gradually given way to a hereditary system of married priests. However, for most people today, the primary significance of Buddhism lies in the rituals for memorializing spirits of the family **ancestors** and the secondary significance in seasonal and special visits to **temples** for various blessings.

In Japan, Buddhism presents an interesting variety of institutional and popular forms. The goal of Indian Buddhism, enlightenment (**nirvana**), is well known in Japan through the Zen sect's quest for awakening (*satori*): Zen emphasizes meditation in order to still the mind and bring both mind and body to a state of serenity and peace. A number of other sects were also transmitted from China to Japan or developed in Japan. Generally, people are less concerned with enlightenment than with the safe passage of themselves (and their ancestors) to Buddhist paradise. Two practices are especially important in assuring passage to paradise: reciting praise to **Amida** (one of the chief Buddhist saints) during one's lifetime, and, after one's death, the family's performance or supervision of funeral and memorial rites for the spirit of the deceased.

On the popular level, the most important role of Buddhism is in memorializing the spirits of the ancestors in the home. In recent times almost every main family (headed by a first son) has had a Buddhist altar, a kind of cabinet in which are enshrined the wooden memorial tablets representing the transformed spirits of the family dead. On the anniversary of a family member's death, the family made offerings to the ancestors and might have called in a Buddhist priest to recite scriptures. The lofty notion of enlightenment and other complex doctrines dominated the monasteries, while more popular notions of entering paradise and venerating ancestors flourished in the home.

Daoism and Confucianism both developed in China and are less formal traditions than Shinto and Buddhism. Daoism and Confucianism are the two major philosophical and religious traditions arising in China, but we will be concerned mainly with their role within Japanese culture. Daoism means literally the "Way" (Dao or Tao in Chinese), in the sense of the Way of the universe or nature. The Daoist tradition is best known in the form of a Chinese philosophical and semimystical writing, the *Dao-de jing* (*Tao-te ching* or *Lao-zi*). Contrasted with philosophical Daoism are the many practices related to the calendar (indicating days of good and bad luck), divination, and other folk beliefs that came to be known as religious Daoism. [See Religions of China pp. 998–1002 for discussion of Daoism (Taoism).]

In Japan it was mainly this loose collection of beliefs and practices called religious Daoism that had greatest influence. Although Daoism never existed as a separate religious tradition in Japan, by the eighth century a Bureau of Divination was patterned on a similar bureau at the Chinese court. Gradually these Chinese notions of interpreting the workings of nature and harmonizing human life with nature came to be linked to Japanese notions about the *kami,* nature, and rituals. For example, most Japanese rituals are performed in accordance with the Chinese calendar, which incorporates many of the features of religious Daoism. The Japanese Bureau of Divination quickly passed out of existence, but many of the notions of religious Daoism about lucky and unlucky days and means of divining fortunes became part of popular culture and are still practiced today (though many Japanese people do not know their Daoist origins). In this sense, Daoism is more an indirect influence on Japanese culture than a formal religious tradition. Probably no Japanese person would call him- or herself a Daoist, even though Daoist notions may have unconsciously been used in selecting a proper day for a wedding or a funeral.

Confucianism has a much more definite origin and development than does Daoism. Daoism grew out of various writings and popular beliefs and practices, but Confucianism was based on the ideas of the historical man **Confucius** (551–479 B.C.E.). Confucius was a Chinese teacher who set forth his ideas about the nature of human virtue and the kind of human relationships that should be found in a harmonious society. Although he was not successful in persuading rulers of the many smaller kingdoms of his time to follow his teachings, once China was unified in the Han dynasty (202 B.C.E.–220 C.E.), the ideas of Confucius were elaborated and systematized into a rationale for society and government. Confucianism is the name given the philosophy of life and ethical system first taught by Confucius and later systematized by followers and the government. He emphasized a return to virtue and an overall social harmony based on proper relationships among people in terms of their social roles. Two of the most important of these hierarchical relationships are father-son and ruler-citizen: The father and ruler should be benevolent; the son and citizen should be obedient. In Japan, Confucianism as a philosophy of life served to legitimize society as a whole (reinforcing loyalty to a hereditary imperial line) and basic social units (especially the family). In some periods, forms of Confucian teachings tended to dominate Japanese society (particularly in the Tokugawa period, 1600–1867). Confucian ideas continue even today to influence Japanese notions of family and society. [See Religions of China pp. 993–94 for discussion of Confucius.]

Christianity, the dominant religion of Europe, spread to other lands, such as India and China, even within the first few centuries after it was founded. But Christianity did not reach Japanese shores until the Spanish Jesuit missionary Saint Francis Xavier arrived in 1549. For about the next hundred years, Catholic missionaries overcame tremendous obstacles—language difficulties and political turmoil—to convert an estimated 2 or 3 percent of the Japanese population to Christianity. During the seventeenth century the government banned Christianity and subjected Christians to one of the most cruel persecutions the church has ever suffered. It was thought that Christianity had been completely stamped out, but some Christians continued to practice some Christian rituals in their homes in secret. In the middle of the nineteenth century, when Japan again opened its doors to outside trade and culture, Catholicism once more entered Japan, as did Protestantism for the first time.

Christianity has played a relatively minor role in Japanese religion, partly because it entered Japan so much later than other traditions, and partly because Christianity has tended to remain a "foreign" tradition rather than blending freely with other Japanese traditions. In many crucial features Christianity differs from Japanese religion: Christianity emphasizes worship of one true God, whereas Japanese religion accepts many deities (both *kami* and Buddhas); Christianity preaches forgiveness of sins, whereas Japanese religion practices purification of defilement; Christianity demands total commitment to one religion, whereas Japanese religion accepts simultaneous participation in a number of religious traditions. The sharp differences between Christianity and the Japanese religious heritage help explain why less than 1 percent of the Japanese population today are members of Christian churches. But although membership is low, Christianity has had considerable influence in Japan through widespread reading of the Bible and through pioneering social reform programs.

Folk religion is less easily identified than these other traditions, which are either formal religions (with priests, buildings, and rituals) or at least written traditions (with texts, commentaries, and scholars). In fact, folk religion can best be characterized as the religious beliefs and practices that occur outside institutional religion, apart from written traditions. Folk religion often incorporates parts of the more formal traditions in its practices but continues them apart from an institutional religion or written tradition. Many of the beliefs and practices of folk religion are part of the oral tradition handed down in families and carried on by villages in seasonal observances and village festivals. For example, in traditional Japan many rituals connected with the growing of rice were performed by families and villages as part of their local culture. Sometimes Buddhist priests and Shinto priests participated in these ceremonies; at other times the villagers were able to carry out the festivals themselves. The celebration of the New Year in the home is a good example of folk religion; families observed many folk practices without any assistance from institutional religion. They placed pine boughs at their gate, set up special decorations within the home, and even cooked special New Year's foods. Even today much of the dynamics of Japanese religion takes place in terms of such folk religion.

In addition to the traditions that appeared in Japan from prehistoric times to several centuries ago, many New Religions have risen during the past century and a half. These New Religions are new in the sense of being new arrangements of elements from most of the other traditions. Usually a New Religion was founded by a charismatic individual who had a revelatory experience or rediscovered the power of earlier teachings and practices and arranged (or rearranged) such experiences, teachings, and practices into a separate religious group after a sufficient number of people had been attracted to the founder and the founder's message. These New Religions have been very active in seeking members and have been successful also through use of publishing and other mass media.

The earliest New Religion to gain a widespread following, **Tenrikyo** (literally, "the religion of divine wisdom"), was founded in 1838 by Miki Nakayama. She was possessed by a creator deity while she participated in a healing ceremony for her son, and this experience led to a lifelong commitment to teach the message of this divinity; she taught people to remove the impurities or "dust" from their souls and return to this deity in order to lead a joyous life. Tenrikyo developed a nationwide system of religious branches, and its headquarters at the city of Tenri (near Nara) is a famous pilgrimage site for Tenrikyo members.

Probably the most powerful New Religion today is **Soka Gakkai,** which was founded shortly before World War II. It was refounded about 1950 and attracted millions of followers in the space of about ten years. Soka Gakkai focuses on the power in the **Lotus Sutra,** a traditional Buddhist scripture of the **Nichiren** tradition. According to Soka Gakkai, members who commit themselves exclusively to practices of this tradition are able to solve all problems by placing their faith in the Lotus Sutra and chanting the title of the Lotus Sutra.

Tenrikyo and Soka Gakkai are two examples of the larger New Religions, of which there are several dozen. Including the smaller New Religions, there are several hundred such movements in modern Japan, making them one of the most conspicuous forces on the contemporary religious scene.

Many Traditions Within One Sacred Way

We have now looked at seven major areas of Japanese religion—the individual traditions of Shinto, Buddhism, Daoism, Confucianism, Christianity, folk religion, and New Religions. However, Japanese religion cannot be understood simply by separating it into individual components, because Japanese people do not "belong" exclusively to just one religion. It is common for a Japanese person to be active in several traditions, which may be combined in one religious activity or relied on individually for specific purposes. For most Westerners this is difficult to understand, because in the West religion is usually a matter of exclusive affiliation: A person identifies as Protestant, Catholic, Jew, or another religious persuasion but does not participate in two, three, or more religions. How is it possible for a Japanese person to be part of so many religious traditions? [See Religions of Africa pp. 23–24, Religions of Mesoamerica pp. 117–19, Native Religions of North America pp. 261–64, Judaism pp. 389, 426, 456–75, Christianity pp. 492–94, Islam pp. 607–8, Hinduism pp. 719–21, Buddhism pp. 853–55, and Religions of China pp. 990–1015 for discussion of the diversity and variety of religious traditions.]

When I first began to study Japanese religion in graduate school, something that both puzzled and amazed me was its diversity. How could so many traditions coexist in the same country? Japanese people usually have not chosen one "faith" exclusively but instead have participated in most of these traditions simultaneously or alternately. One of the reasons that I came to specialize in the study of Japanese religion was this challenge of trying to understand the unity of Japanese religion.

One cannot study Japanese religion simply by individual traditions, and then "add up" the seven or more traditions; this will not yield the "total." For Japanese religion is not a mathematical addition of individual components, it is a way of life that is constructed and supported by most of the individual components. A Japanese person does not have to "join" one religious tradition and thereby reject all others. Rather, this person comes to participate in a number of separate traditions as they form an integral part of his or her way of life. This can be illustrated for each of the seven traditions and will be seen at greater length in later chapters.

It is not necessary to formally join Shinto in order to venerate *kami*. *Kami* may be venerated daily at the household Shinto shrine (**kamidana**), or *kami* may be honored in seasonal festivals and as part of the rituals associated with agriculture. Any member of a family or any farmer may venerate *kami* as a natural part of being a family member or a farmer. Similarly, it is not necessary to formally "join" Buddhism in order to worship Buddhist divinities. Such "Buddhas" may be honored daily at the household Buddhist altar (**butsudan**), or Buddhas known for granting special requests may be prayed to when one wants to make this request. Buddhist divinities are worshiped as a natural part of family devotions and in the process of resolving personal requests.

Daoism is not a separate tradition in Japan, but various "Daoistic" beliefs about the calendar and good fortune have become an integral part of the Japanese way of life. People may not be "Daoists" but may still rely on the calendar to choose a proper day for a wedding or funeral. Confucianism is not a separate tradition in Japan, but Confucian ideals of proper social conduct—especially loving obedience of children to parents and loyalty of citizens to rulers—have become part of Japanese thought and practice. People do not consider themselves "Confucians" when they behave this way, but simply good children and good citizens.

Christianity is a special case, because a small number of Japanese do practice Christianity much in the same fashion as it is practiced in the United States and Europe: They belong exclusively to Christianity and reject other traditions. But there are many more Japanese who read the Bible and draw inspiration from it without becoming members of Christian churches and without giving up other traditions.

Folk religion is so loose and informal that a person could not even think of becoming a "member." A family puts up New Year's decorations, not because the family belongs to any special group, but because it is the folk custom to do so at this time of year. Members of New Religions are in a somewhat different category, because few people participate in two or more New Religions simultaneously. But members of New Religions do participate in various other Japanese traditions. And as we shall see later, New Religions contain many traditional notions, such as the worship of *kami* and ancestors.

Each of these seven traditions can be considered as a separate religious line, but a better approach to understanding is to see these traditions as they fit into the pattern of religious life as it has formed and as it is practiced. When we study Japanese religion as it is acted out in daily life, most of these traditions become blended into a unified worldview of belief and action. This worldview enables the Japanese to define their identity and find their place in the world, living a rich and meaningful life. Various traditions have been used as ingredients to form the total worldview for a culture and a comprehensive philosophy of life for individuals. This composite worldview provides the Japanese with the inspiration and spiritual power to guide them through life. In this sense we may say that Japanese religion is characterized by many traditions within one sacred way.

What are the procedures for studying a "sacred way"? The most commonly accepted approach for studying any religious or cultural subject is to treat it historically, tracing it from its first appearance to its present form; chapter 46 treats the historical formation of Japanese religion, or the sacred way. Subsequent chapters will treat Japanese religion as a total system and provide examples illustrating the dynamics of this sacred way.

46

The Historical Development of Japanese Religion

ONE OF THE BEST ways to discover the distinctiveness of Japanese religion is to trace its emergence from diverse traditions into one national heritage. In this historical panorama, Japanese religion arises out of prehistoric practices and mixes with influences from China and India, eventually forming peculiarly Japanese institutions and practices and contributing to and being influenced by more recent changes in Japanese national life. In this chapter we will follow the historical development of Japanese religion from prehistoric times to the present. This historical overview will provide the background for understanding the organization and dynamics of Japanese religion treated in subsequent chapters.

Early Religious Customs

As we have seen in our discussion of Japanese culture, including the origin of the Japanese people and the beginnings of the Japanese language, some of the earliest aspects of Japanese life are not known to us. The origins of religious customs, too, are rather vague. In prehistoric times there were many local customs and practices, but there was no single organized religion—even Shinto did not exist as a separate tradition during this early period. Some of the prehistoric religious picture must be pieced together from archaeological information. For example, archaeologists in Japan have unearthed prehistoric female figurines and human burials within urns. From evidence such as this, they have concluded that people living in the Japanese islands more than two thousand years ago were concerned with agricultural fertility (the female figurines were probably used in rituals related to fertility); the burials show a concern for the afterlife of family members. It is difficult to trace a clear link from these prehistoric materials to the later stages of a more unified Japanese culture, but the similarities are too close to neglect. From studying the earliest written records about Japanese culture, we realize that ancient religion was closely related to both agricultural fertility and veneration of family ancestors.

The link between prehistoric evidence and later practices is illustrated also by the prehistoric remains of stone circles surrounding central vertical pillars. These stone circles may represent a kind of sundial that was also a means of paying religious respect to the sun. According to Japanese mythological writings (**Kojiki** and **Nihongi**), the first emperor is descended from the **Sun Goddess**; even today numerous folk practices include greeting the rising sun with a prayer.

One of the most important developments of the prehistoric era was the gradual shift from a hunting and gathering economy (including fishing) to one based on the growing of rice. This began more than two thousand years ago, and it marked the development of permanent villages and the kind of social and religious life that has been characteristic of Japan until very recent times. Rice agriculture requires a great deal of manual labor on rather small fields but yields large amounts of rice that can support a large population. This pattern of small farming villages dependent on the income from agricultural goods—especially rice—has been very important for the development of the Japanese lifestyle. Usually a farming family was an economic unit that worked together to till, plant, weed, and harvest. A number of these families formed small villages that cooperated in many ways—not only in agriculture and politics, but also in social events and seasonal celebrations.

The picture of religion in early Japan is not completely clear, but it seems to involve a triangle of social life organized around families, economic life centered around small farms (especially rice agriculture), and religious life concerned with family units revering the spirits of the natural world for blessings of children and bountiful crops. This is the informal, loose tradition of beliefs and practices out of which Shinto eventually emerged. The recorded prayers (**norito**) of ancient Shinto, which preserve the religious beliefs and practices of prehistoric times, abound with prayers for rice agriculture. To this day, the rhythm of most Shinto shrines revolves around the two key seasons of spring (when rice is transplanted) and fall (when rice is harvested). Even the all-important enthronement ceremony for a new emperor (after the death of the previous emperor) is delayed until the fall because it is patterned after the harvest festival.

From as far back as we have reliable evidence, families appear to have been unified in their worship of local *kami* for agricultural blessings. Apparently *kami* were thought to dwell within remarkable forms of nature, for example, a tall tree or a large boulder or mountain; the families of the nearby village cooperated in the celebration of seasonal festivals just as they cooperated in social life within the village and in economic life to grow rice. There was no clear membership in a specific religion; in fact, probably there was no clear conception of "religion" apart from social and economic life: All aspects of life must have blended together.

This interaction of social, economic, and religious life gradually developed into a more complex cultural pattern, with some families owning more land and controlling more wealth. About the beginning of the common era, when Japanese culture was becoming more complex, the influence of continental Asian culture entered Japan by way of Korea.

This new influence included advancements such as metal crafts, armed horsemen, and elaborate burial mausoleums (reserved for leading families). Gradually this pattern of social, economic, and religious life developed into a more highly centralized and organized national identity that has come to be known as Japan. One of the key features of the emerging national identity was the respect paid to one leading family as the imperial line of the national heritage. The traditional accounts of the origin of the imperial line are recorded in some of the earliest written documents, the *Kojiki* and *Nihongi*. These writings begin with a mythological account of the creation of Japan and then describe legendary emperors and chronicle historical emperors. A brief summary of the mythological parts of these documents helps us better understand traditional Japanese notions about the creation of Japan and the sacred origin of the imperial line. [See Religions of Africa pp. 24, 35, 60, Religions of Mesoamerica pp. 198–201, Native Religions of North America pp. 347–48, Judaism pp. 391–92, Christianity pp. 503, 505, Islam pp. 632–3, Hinduism p. 748, Buddhism pp. 875–77, 952–53, and Religions of China pp. 991–93 for the relationship of religion to political leaders.]

The *Kojiki* and *Nihongi*, completed in the early eighth century but recording myths and legends much older, gives similar account of the "age of the *kami*," when creation took place. According to these records, "At the time of the beginning of heaven and earth," there came into existence many *kami*. The world was not completely formed—a mixture of water and land—and the various *kami* produced other *kami*, eventually giving rise to a divine couple, Izanagi and his spouse, Izanami. Looking down from heaven on the still unformed earth, they dipped a jeweled spear into the ocean, and from this action the first islands—solid land—were formed. This is the mythological precedent for the sacred character of the Japanese islands as created by *kami*.

The divine couple gave birth to other mythological figures, the most important of whom is the Sun Goddess (**Amaterasu**). Later the Sun Goddess ordered her grandson, Ninigi, to descend to earth and rule it; as signs of this right to rule, she gave him a necklace, a mirror, and a sword. These three objects are still respected today as the symbols of imperial power. According to Japanese tradition, the subsequent emperors of Japan down to the present emperor constitute an unbroken line of hereditary descendants from the divine parents. This is the mythological background for the sacred character of the Japanese emperor as descended from these central *kami*. Even the Japanese people are thought to be descended indirectly from *kami*, making them a sacred people distinct from other people. [See Religions of Africa pp. 36–37, 64–67, Religions of Mesoamerica pp. 129–35, 154–55, 163–68, Native Religions of North America pp. 288–95, 327–29, 333–42, Judaism pp. 380–84, Christianity pp. 534–35, Hinduism p. 743, and Buddhism p. 890 for discussion of myth and mythology.]

These mythological accounts show us that from early times there was a clear notion of Japan as a divine country led by a sacred emperor and inhabited by a people who had a special relationship to *kami*. This early combination of sacred origin for the Japanese islands, the emperor, and the Japanese people provided the foundation for a distinctively Japanese religious tradition. In

Japan, as in any tradition, the interpretation of such mythological origins has ranged from a completely literal to a rather figurative interpretation. Most Japanese today do not hold a completely literal view of their sacred origins. However, unconsciously, the notion of the land, people, and culture of Japan as a distinctive tradition persists—and the emperor remains the symbolic head of the nation. These early Japanese beliefs and practices formed the background for the development of a more highly organized religious heritage in connection with "foreign" traditions.

Chinese and Indian Influence

The history of Japanese religion begins with the informal tradition of customs, beliefs, and practices from prehistoric Japan, but Japanese religion formed and developed in close relationship with influences from relatively nearby China and distant India. One of the crucial events in Japanese history was the introduction of Chinese culture, starting from about the sixth century C.E.

Prior to this time, Japanese culture was not highly developed—there was no written language, little graphic art, no complex philosophical systems, and no government unified around a central state. Chinese culture was abundantly rich in all of these: a sophisticated writing system (including poetry and literature); elaborate art forms, especially painting (and thanks to Buddhism, magnificent statues); grand philosophical systems; and highly efficient governmental structures. It was only natural for Japan to adopt and adapt much of Chinese culture and religion at a time when Japanese forms of culture and government were becoming more highly organized. This is not to say that Japan borrowed everything and does not have a distinct culture of its own. It may be more appropriate to say that China is a cultural watershed for Japan, much as Greece and Rome are cultural resources for Europe and America.

China has been a transmitter, not only of native Chinese culture, but also of distant Indian culture. Buddhism, which was founded in India in the sixth century B.C.E. by the Buddha, was introduced to China about the beginning of the Common Era and became increasingly influential. Buddhism had already become part of Chinese culture when, several centuries later, both were formally transmitted to Japan.

The formal introduction of Buddhism into Japan occurred in the sixth century C.E., when a ruler from a Korean kingdom solicited military help from Japan and included Buddhist writings and statues as part of his tribute. According to the account in the *Nihongi*, at first the Japanese were afraid to worship these Buddhist statues, fearing that native *kami* would be jealous of "foreign *kami*." But they did worship the Buddhas, and when an epidemic broke out, it was considered a bad omen. Therefore, the statues were thrown away—until another omen showed that the epidemic was not due to the acceptance of Buddhism, and the Buddhist statues were worshiped once more.

This early incident is significant for understanding the development of Japanese religion. For one thing, foreign religions such as Buddhism were accepted for the power and blessings they were able to grant. Later, more abstract and philosophical aspects of Buddhism were interpreted by scholars, but to this day one of the major attractions of Buddhism is its power to provide blessings to people in their daily life. Another important aspect of this incident is that acceptance of Buddhas and Buddhism did not mean rejection of the native religion and *kami*. Rather, both Buddhas and *kami* were worshiped, often side by side. This is a good example of the kind of interaction among religious traditions that is so important in the development, organization, and dynamics of Japanese religion.

Chinese culture had its impact on almost every aspect of Japanese culture, and in every instance when Chinese elements were borrowed, they were also modified to fit Japanese culture. As we have seen with Japanese language, Chinese writing forms were used to write the Japanese language, but Japanese language retained its grammatical structure and used special phonetic signs to link the written Chinese characters. The written and spoken forms of Chinese and Japanese differ considerably, with Japanese retaining its own characteristics. China was the grand model to be followed in many plans of developing Japan. Even Japan's first permanent capital city, Nara (established in 710), was laid out after the fashion of the Chinese capital at the time. The governmental bureaucracies and systems of ranks for people were adopted from Chinese precedents. Later these Chinese patterns were modified or even abandoned, but the stamp of Chinese culture had been permanently imprinted on the Japanese scene.

Two examples of religious and philosophical influence from China are Confucianism and Daoism. Confucianism emphasized the principle of social harmony through a set of hierarchical relationships in which the subordinate person (such as a son) is obedient and loyal, and the higher person (such as a father) is benevolent and protective. In Japan, family units and social cooperation had been important before the introduction of Confucianism, but the new teaching provided a systematic means of reinforcing family loyalty, cooperation among groups, and even support for the state. Respect for the emperor as head of the leading family was further stimulated by the Confucian teaching of loyalty of subjects to rulers. The Japanese imperial tradition differed from the Chinese imperial system in one fundamental sense, however. The Japanese imperial line had the right to rule by hereditary descent from the founding *kami;* the Chinese imperial system was based on a "mandate of heaven" according to which heaven not only selected emperors but also could remove bad emperors (against whom the country might rebel). On this fundamental issue, the Japanese retained their traditional notion, rejecting the Chinese notion that leadership could shift from one family to another. In this case, as in other instances, Japan adopted a "both-and" stance, *both* accepting the Chinese Confucian notion to reinforce the authority of the emperor *and* retaining the Japanese tradition of the imperial line's traditional descent from the *kami.*

Daoism's influence in Japan was first formalized in the Bureau of Divination (Onmyoryo), which the government adopted after the Chinese bureaucratic model. This bureau was the official means of incorporating Daoistic practices into the government. The Bureau of Divination, in Japan as in China, had as its major task the determining of auspicious timing for governmental events and the interpretation of good and bad omens appearing in nature (especially unusual phenomena). The Bureau of Divination was adopted in the early eighth century, when the Japanese government was being remodeled after Chinese patterns. As in Confucianism, in Daoism, too, there were earlier Japanese notions and practices that made it easy to accept the basic principles of the new tradition. The prehistoric Japanese heritage of veneration for nature and the many *kami* inhabiting the natural world formed a receptive context for Daoism, with its emphasis on harmony with nature. Even if the Japanese did not have a philosophical system to express it in abstract principles, they were actually living out a way of nature in their worship of the *kami*. Gradually Daoism became part of the Japanese religious heritage. The Chinese calendar taken from Daoist practice filtered into both Shinto and Buddhism. Popular practitioners (*hijiri*) of Daoistic techniques wandered among the people and spread these teachings throughout the country. Eventually Daoist beliefs and practices became so thoroughly "Japanized" that most Japanese people would have difficulty identifying Daoist features within Japanese religion.

Although India is a continent away from the Japanese islands, and even though it was a long time before any Japanese traveled to India, nevertheless the Indian religion of Buddhism made a greater impact on the Japanese tradition than any other foreign religion. We have already seen that Buddhism, a religion founded in sixth century B.C.E. India as a teaching of enlightenment, was first transformed within Chinese culture and then brought through Korea to Japan about the sixth century C.E. When Buddhism entered Japan, it brought more than just the basic philosophy of enlightenment: It included powerful magical rituals and rites for ancestors and the prosperity of the nation, as well as elaborate art forms such as statues. When Buddhism was accepted in Japan, it was more than just a set of principles or a religious faith—it was part of a total way of life or civilization. [See Buddhism pp. 860–88 for the historical development of Buddhism.]

The many facets of Buddhism were first accepted in Japan by the imperial family and the nobility at court. From the start of its successful career in Japan, Buddhism was viewed as a powerful means of obtaining practical benefits in association with native *kami*. The power of Buddhist divinities was quickly associated with the imperial line and *kami*. Buddhism became so much a part of life at the court that it even provided rituals for safe childbirth for the empress, as well as other healing rituals. By the early eighth century, a Buddhist priest and an empress had set the Japanese precedent by having their bodies cremated, following Buddhist ritual. Buddhist memorial rites for the dead became important for the court.

In the eighth century, an emperor ordered the building of a kind of national cathedral for Buddhism, housing a large statue of the Sun Buddha. According to tradition, messengers were sent to the most important of all Shinto shrines, Ise, to consult the oracle there about the propriety of erecting this statue of the Sun

Buddha. The answer was that the Sun Buddha and the Sun Goddess (enshrined at Ise) were identical. This shows how Buddhism rapidly entered the life of Shinto and the nation. At about the same time as the building of this great cathedral, every province in Japan was ordered to build a monastery and a nunnery, where monks and nuns studied Buddhist scriptures and performed rites for the sake of the nation.

Buddhism was patronized by emperors personally and by the state as a matter of policy. Some of the imperial court may have been attracted to the more doctrinal and philosophical aspects of Buddhism, but the majority of the court and nobility were drawn directly to the ritual power and aesthetic richness of Buddhism. State support for Buddhism enhanced the role of the emperor as an enlightened Buddhist ruler and helped ensure a peaceful and prosperous reign.

Because the state used Buddhism partly as a means to reinforce its rule, it did not encourage the spread of Buddhism to the people. (In fact, at this time the state prohibited the teaching of Buddhism to the masses.) In this early period Buddhism existed mainly among the court and nobility. A variety of philosophical teachings from Indian Buddhism were transmitted to Japan in Chinese translation, but development of a distinctively Japanese Buddhism and its spread to the people came later.

Chinese and Indian religion made a permanent impact on Japanese religion through various influences—Daoism, Confucianism, and Buddhism. However, Japanese religion has retained a distinctive tradition, based on the prehistoric heritage and Shinto, and has influenced the "foreign" traditions accepted in Japan.

The Flowering of Japanese Buddhism

One of the remarkable features in Japanese religious history is the rapid development and extensive spread of Buddhism. The career of Buddhism in Japan is an interesting example of the power and flexibility of Buddhism and the adaptive and innovative character of Japanese culture. Indian Buddhism possessed a wide variety of doctrine and ritual, which was further enriched by its relationship to each new culture it encountered. China, Korea, and Japan accepted and transmitted Buddhist teachings and practices, and in the process, each country adapted Buddhism to its particular culture. Buddhism flowered in Japan especially from the ninth to the fourteenth centuries, developing the sects that have attracted the largest numbers of followers from that time to the present.

This expansion of Buddhism occurred especially during two major periods of Japanese history, the Heian (794–1185) and the Kamakura (1185–1333). During the Heian period, Japanese culture began to absorb and refine in a more independent fashion the heritage accepted from China. Early in the Heian period, two great Japanese Buddhists founded their own sects, each patterned after Chinese models but also formed in close relationship to Japanese culture.

These two founders, Kukai (774–835, known posthumously as Kobo Daishi) and Saicho (762–822, known posthumously as Dengyo Daishi), went to China to bring back to Japan a more authentic Buddhism. Kukai was most attracted to the Chinese form of Buddhism known as Zhen-yan (Chen-yen) (Jap., **Shingon**), whereas Saicho was drawn to the Chinese form of Tiantai (T'ien-t'ai) (Jap., **Tendai**).

Zhen-yan Buddhism is the Chinese form of esoteric Buddhism transmitted from India. (A similar form of esoteric Buddhism was transmitted from India to Tibet.) It is called esoteric because it focuses on complicated doctrines, rituals, and paintings as the means for gaining enlightenment, that is, realizing these esoteric truths in one's own life. Kukai brought back from China especially the Buddhist scriptures (in Chinese translation), ritual tools, and secret teachings that conveyed this esoteric realization of Buddhism. Kukai founded his new Buddhist sect, Shingon, on remote Mount Koya, partly in order to separate his new Buddhism from the older Buddhist schools at the former capital of Nara. He also stressed blending Buddhism with native practices and venerated the local *kami* of the mountain together with Buddhist deities. Esoteric Buddhism caught on rapidly at the court, especially because of its elaborate rituals (for example, the fire ritual, which burns up defilements and drives out demons). The impressive statues and mysterious magical formulas transmitted by Shingon Buddhism have become part of Japanese culture generally, accepted by most people whether or not they belong to the Shingon sect. Kukai is fondly remembered by the Japanese as an important literary figure, and he is the hero of many traditional folktales.

Saicho brought back from China the Tiantai form of Buddhism and continued most of its practices in the Tendai sect he founded in Japan. Tendai Buddhism is based especially on the *Lotus Sutra,* using its teachings to draw all other aspects of Buddhism together into a grand vision of the unity of all existence. The *Lotus Sutra,* one of the most widely known Buddhist scriptures in east Asia, is popular among the common people for its easily understood parables, which illustrate that every person can attain enlightenment through simple acts of devotion. Another aspect of Tendai practice is faith in the Buddhist divinity named Amida and meditation on Amida or recitation of faith in Amida as an act of piety. Saicho set up his sect headquarters on Mount Hiei, near Kyoto, the new capital (moved there from Nara in 794). He developed close ties with the faith and worship of *kami* on this mountain, which he established as a center of meditation and study. This sect and its mountain headquarters were extremely important as sources of inspiration for other sects that spread and popularized Buddhism.

In the Kamakura period (1185–1333), power shifted from the imperial court and nobility to a military dictator and warriors located at Kamakura. As feudal lords fought to control and conquer territory, there was widespread warfare and an atmosphere of uncertainty that influenced the entire culture, even religion. The three new sects founded during the Kamakura period helped resolve the sense of uncertainty, providing simpler techniques of faith and practice and making direct contact with the common people. These three new sects are the

Pure Land, Nichiren, and Zen. The founders of these sects had studied at the Tendai headquarters on Mount Hiei but developed different strands of Buddhism into major sects.

The Pure Land tradition in Buddhism was developed in China as the practice of faith in the Buddhist divinity Amitabha (Jap., Amida), which enabled a person to be reborn in the heavenly paradise, or "pure land," of this Buddhist divinity. This faith was present in Japan earlier, but not until Honen (1133–1212) made it the basis of his teaching did it become a separate tradition. Honen stressed faith in Amida and preached to the masses this very simple means of using Buddhist power to be reborn in the pure land (somewhat different from other notions of "enlightenment"). Reciting *namu Amida Butsu* is a way of invoking and taking refuge in Amida; in popular practice it means placing one's faith in Amida. This phrase is so short that anyone can recite it, even while working. Later there were disagreements among Pure Land leaders about whether the essence of this recitation's power was in its constant repetition, or in the total faith of just one recitation. But in spite of these theoretical differences, faith in Amida became very popular among the common people. [See Buddhism pp. 886–87, 912–20 and Religions of China pp. 1006–8 for discussion of Pure Land Buddhism.]

The denominations of the Pure Land developed strong parish organizations, and Pure Land priests are credited with setting the precedent of a married Buddhist priesthood. (Formerly, there was a celibate priesthood.) This was important for the development of "household Buddhism" in Japan, a pattern in which all sects eventually accepted the custom of married Buddhist priests controlling local temples (almost like family businesses). The influence of the Japanese family is reflected in this development of "household Buddhism."

The Nichiren sect is named after the man Nichiren (1222–1281), one of the most forceful personalities in all Japanese religious history. He concentrated on the *Lotus Sutra* as the embodiment of absolute truth and lived his life according to it. He rejected all other forms of Buddhism and called for the state to eliminate them, in order to establish the state on the foundation of the true Buddhism of the *Lotus Sutra*. Nichiren's technique for practicing faith in the *Lotus Sutra* was to recite *namu Myoho Rengekyo* ("I place my faith in the *Lotus Sutra*"). This enabled every person to resolve any worldly problem, benefiting not only the individual, but also the Japanese state. The denominations of Nichiren Buddhism are the most nationalistic of all Japanese Buddhist groups, a good example of how the universal message of Buddhism can be made into a highly particular national expression. Nichiren faith is exclusivistic (rejecting all other forms of Buddhism), and Nichiren's aggressive missionary style (sometimes compared to the Salvation Army in the West) has been an important model for recently developed New Religions (such as Soka Gakkai). [See Religions of Mesoamerica p. 179, Native Religions of North America p. 285, Judaism pp. 390–92, Christianity pp. 497, 499, Islam pp. 635–37, 648–53, 665–72, Hinduism pp. 728–29, 738–43, 750–53, Buddhism p. 861, and Religions of China pp. 995–96, 999–1000, 1031 for discussion of Bible, scriptures, and religious texts.]

Zen is a form of Buddhism emphasizing meditation, which developed in China into a separate tradition (called Chan or Ch'an in Chinese). Some Buddhist meditation had been practiced in Japan earlier, but not until Eisai (1141–1215) and Dogen (1200–1253) made their trips to China was Zen practiced in Japan as a separate tradition. Zen claims to be the continuation of the meditation practiced by the Buddha to gain enlightenment, but it was also influenced by Daoist ideals (such as the love of nature) and developed in China into highly formal meditation techniques. In formal Zen meditation, monks sit in a special hall for a number of hours each day, continuing this practice for months or even years until each monk is enlightened. Eisai and Dogen each brought back a particular form of this meditation. Zen priests also brought refined Chinese culture to Japan, which helped attract members of the ruling class to Zen as much as the meditation practices did. Gradually, the strict meditation of Zen, mixed with other devotional practices and memorial rites, attracted members of the warrior class. [See Christianity pp. 502–4, 510, Islam pp. 659–62, Hinduism p. 772, Buddhism pp. 915–21, 942–52, and Religions of China pp. 1004–5, 1009, 1033–34, 1056 for discussion of monasteries and monasticism.]

Zen's acceptance by the common people was made possible especially by Zen providing practical memorial rites for the family. In Japan the notion of sudden enlightenment blended with the Japanese love of nature so well that Zen teaching of enlightenment, or awakening, was interpreted as knowing one's own heart and being in tune with nature. The insights of Zen as a way of life have penetrated Japanese culture so thoroughly—from the fine arts to the martial arts—that it is sometimes identified with the spirit of Japan. In the present century, Zen has become popular in the West as a means of disciplining the body and mind to a more enlightened, peaceful way of life. [See Buddhism pp. 919, 942–50, and Religions of China pp. 1008, 1133–34 for discussion of Zen (Chan) Buddhism.]

These new Buddhist sects, from Shingon and Tendai in the Heian period to the Pure Land, Nichiren, and Zen in the Kamakura period, are solid evidence of the extent to which Japanese religion has been influenced by Buddhism. However, the process by which these sects were accepted also shows the features of Japanese culture that made it possible to accept foreign traditions and mold them to Japanese custom.

Whenever Japan has borrowed, the result has been both adoption and adaptation. Buddhism once was a "foreign" religion for Japan, but it quickly became naturalized as "Japanese Buddhism."

Medieval Religion

From the fourteenth through the eighteenth centuries, Japanese religion continued to develop in a number of ways. Buddhist sects split into competing denominations and spread throughout most of Japan. Shinto shrines became more highly organized and came to develop more systematic teachings in reaction to Buddhism. Toward the end of this medieval period, Christianity, another "foreign" tradition, entered Japan and enjoyed brief success before it was banned. A strong feudal society emerged with a comprehensive Confucian rationale.

Shinto grew out of the native tradition of early Japanese religion, especially the beliefs and practices related to the *kami,* but Shinto also freely accepted Chinese and Buddhist influences. Eventually Shinto incorporated ethical notions from Confucianism, a religious calendar and associated beliefs from Daoism, and philosophical systems and ritual practices from Buddhism. As with other Japanese borrowing, Shinto retained its original character but added these foreign elements, creating a more complex tradition.

Buddhism was the most prominent influence incorporated by Shinto, on both the theoretical and the practical levels. The best example of Buddhist influence on the theoretical level is the idea of Buddhist divinities and *kami* as counterparts, almost as if the two were opposite sides of the same coin. Throughout Southeast Asia as well as East Asia, Buddhism tended to blend with other religions and honor local deities (rather than rejecting the other religions and replacing local deities with Buddhist divinities). Japanese Buddhist scholars used a Chinese Buddhist theory to develop their notion that Buddhist divinities represent the original substance of reality, whereas *kami* represent the worldly "trace" or counterpart of the original substance. In this theory, Buddhist scholars valued Buddhist divinities as the primary or higher reality. However, as Shinto scholars began to form their own systems of thought, borrowing from other traditions, they began to assert the primary value of Shinto. One change Shinto scholars made was to reverse the counterpart theory, claiming that *kami* represent the original substance of reality and Buddhist divinities the worldly "trace" or counterpart of *kami.* This was an important precedent for Shinto priests and scholars in beginning to reclaim their position in Japanese religion and society.

For most people the interaction of Shinto and Buddhism was more important at the concrete level in local Shinto shrines. The interaction was so complete that Shinto shrines enshrined both Buddhist divinities and *kami,* and Buddhist temples and Shinto shrines were built next to each other as part of the same religious center. The common people prayed to both *kami* and Buddhist divinities and did not seem to concern themselves with the subtle differences between the Shinto and the Buddhist versions of the counterpart theory. These religions became interrelated to the point that Shinto prayers (*norito*) were read before Buddhist divinities and Buddhist scriptures were read before Shinto *kami.* This pattern of interrelated Shinto and Buddhist practices was transmitted to distant areas of Japan as Shinto shrines were built there. Sometimes the same priest served in both Shinto and Buddhist capacities, although generally Buddhist priests held more powerful positions. Gradually Shinto priests and scholars began to work for a stronger role for Shinto in the life of the nation.

The blending of Buddhism with Shinto shows how a foreign tradition gradually became naturalized as a Japanese tradition. Christianity first entered Japan much later than Buddhism and up to the present is still considered by most Japanese to be a foreign religion. Saint Francis Xavier first brought Christianity (Roman Catholicism) to Japan in 1549, arriving on Portuguese trade ships. In spite of the basic differences between Catholic Christianity and Japanese religion, Christianity experienced a brief but remarkable success before it was suppressed about a hundred years later. This "Christian century" is a good example of the meeting of two different cultures and religions.

The basic principles of belief and practice are quite different for Christianity and Japanese religion. Christianity is based on faith and worship of one true God, whereas Japanese religion is based on belief in and worship of both local *kami* (gods) and various Buddhist divinities. Christianity claims the exclusive attention of believers, not allowing participation in another religion; in Japanese religion, the usual practice is for a person (or family) to participate in several religious traditions. These and other differences between the two traditions made it unlikely that Catholicism would succeed in Japan, but the Catholic missionaries overcame these differences to convert a small percentage of the Japanese in a relatively short time.

One political factor that initially helped Catholicism gain support was the government's attempt to limit the power of Buddhist organizations (such as the monasteries on Mount Hiei): The state apparently allowed Christian missions into Japan in order to offset Buddhist strength. Eventually the government gained complete control over Buddhism and began to suspect political motives of the Catholic missionaries, all of whom came from Europe. The Japanese rulers also feared that if Japanese Christians were loyal to the foreign Catholic priests and a foreign God, they might side with Europeans against Japan in a war. Early in the seventeenth century, the government began to move against Christianity and by 1640 had almost totally eliminated Christian missionaries and Christianity from the Japanese islands.

The total ban on Christianity was enforced with policies that had a lasting effect on the organization of Japanese religion. In order to make sure that no Christians remained in Japan, the government required every family to belong to a local Buddhist temple and report all births, marriages, deaths, and changes of address to this temple. Family affiliation with a Buddhist temple became a hereditary custom: Funeral and memorial rites for family members were performed by a local Buddhist temple.

It was the Tokugawa family line of military rulers that unified Japan in a form of feudal order, gaining control over the powerful Buddhist temples and then suppressing Christianity. The Tokugawa period (1600–1867) was a time of centralization of power and stability, with foreign influence excluded. The feudal order, headed by the Tokugawa family, controlled most aspects of life and used the local Buddhist temple almost like a census office to register families.

The Tokugawa government also relied heavily on the rationale of Confucian teachings to support a hierarchical society with four classes: Warriors were the highest class, followed by farmers, then workers, and, in the lowest position, merchants. Warriors were considered highest because they protected the state, and farmers were relatively high in position because they produced the wealth (such as rice and other agricultural goods) that supported the society. Workers were next because they provided services; merchants were lowest because they simply profited from others' wealth and did not produce any wealth or service.

Some of the basic assumptions of the Confucian thought behind this system are an economy based on agriculture, a hierarchical society with little movement from class to class, and the duty of all to work within their respective classes for the good of the entire society. Loyalty to superiors and to the state was stressed. Although some of these ideas originated with Confucius and later followers, they blended with Japanese notions of life and morality.

During Tokugawa times a comprehensive philosophy of life took shape in which people felt indebted for the blessings of nature and *kami*, expressed gratitude to parents and ancestors for the gift of life, and were loyal toward their political superiors. As in any social or political system, there were abuses, and occasionally the farmers and townspeople protested against unfair policies. But the occasional protests did not seek a revolution to overturn the government and reject this comprehensive philosophy of life. There have been many changes in Japan since Tokugawa times (which ended in 1867), but many of the values developed during the Tokugawa period still influence Japanese life today.

Religion Enters the Modern World

There are two major turning points that separate traditional Japan from modern Japan and traditional Japanese religion from modern Japanese religion. The first is the end of the feudal government in 1867 and the beginning of a national government in the Meiji period (1868–1911); the second is the end of World War II in 1945 and the blossoming of many democratic freedoms. Religion helped bring about these dramatic changes, and in turn was affected by the changes.

The Meiji era marks the end of the more than two hundred years of Japan's relative isolation from the rest of the world during Tokugawa times. Because of changing internal conditions (especially the dominance of commerce over agriculture), the feudal system of government weakened, and foreign powers increasingly demanded the opening of Japan to trade. In the end, the feudal government was abolished and replaced with a national government symbolically headed by the emperor; power was held by a form of parliamentary government. One result of this change in government was the opening of Japan to political and commercial relations with other countries.

A main support for this new government was Shinto, which for centuries had been trying to reassert itself as a central factor in national life. From medieval times, Shinto had claimed that the worship of *kami* (rather than the "foreign" Buddhism) was the true national heritage of Japan, and that the emperor (rather than the military ruler) was the true ruler of Japan. Even study of the Chinese tradition of Confucianism, through its encouragement of scholarship in classical literature, promoted study of the ancient Japanese writings *Kojiki* and *Nihongi*, as well as Japanese mythological and historical writings honored within Shinto. In this complex sequence of events leading out of feudal times and into the modern age, Shinto was a force that helped bring about the formation of the new government in 1868 and influenced government policies in the following decades.

In the development of a national form of government, feudal forms—lords, their territories and armies, and the class system—were abolished. Henceforth, people were considered citizens of Japan as a nation, and national institutions were set up: national taxes, a national army, provinces (similar to states) under a national government, and a national parliament and cabinet holding actual power. The general effect of these changes was to harm Buddhism (which had been identified with the feudal government) and to benefit Shinto (which had supported the change in government and the greater role of the empire).

Families were no longer required to belong to Buddhist temples, and there was some persecution of Buddhist temples. But Buddhism was so close to the hearts of the people that the persecution quickly died out. Part of the rationale for forming a new government was to "restore" the emperor as the true ruler and Shinto as the true national heritage, but it was difficult to implement these ideals in practice. The emperor was a very important symbol around which the nation could be unified, but he held little actual power. Although there were many attempts to make Shinto a central feature of the government, eventually Shinto was used more as a patriotic rationale than as an established religion.

One factor that helped bring about relative freedom of religion was the effect of the government's policies toward Christianity. At the beginning of the Meiji era in 1868, when the ban on Christianity had not been lifted, it was discovered that some Japanese families had secretly continued their practice of Christianity for two hundred years. These hidden Christians were severely punished by the Japanese government, and this news traveled rapidly to Western countries. When representatives of the Japanese government toured Western countries in order to study modern social and political conditions in these countries and develop better ties with them, they encountered hostility because of the recent suppression of hidden Christians. This helped persuade the government to remove the ban on Christianity in 1873; in 1889, the Meiji constitution formally gave Japanese citizens relative freedom of religion "within limits not prejudicial to peace and order, and not antagonistic to their duties as subjects." However, until 1945 this formal freedom of religion was severely restricted by government and police. The change in government policy did allow Christianity to officially reenter Japan, through both Catholic and (for the first time) Protestant missionaries. Christianity gained a small number of converts and made some important contributions to Japanese society, especially in education and social welfare. But from about 1890, with the heightened nationalism accompanying the Sino-Japanese war (1894–1895) and the Russo-Japanese War (1904–1905), the Japanese turned more to their native traditions and did not enter Christianity in significant numbers.

Japanese society changed rapidly during the Meiji era (1868–1911), and even during the late Tokugawa times (1600–1867) some new religious movements had appeared. During Meiji and thereafter, other New Religions appeared, and all these movements continued to attract followers in spite of government efforts to hinder and suppress them. From the 1920s through the end of World War II in 1945, Japanese society and politics were increasingly dominated by nationalism, and the same held true for Japanese religion. Although the Meiji constitution officially granted freedom of religion, actual government policies made it difficult to practice religion freely.

The state had declared Shinto to be "nonreligious," in the sense that it was the patriotic duty of all Japanese as citizens of the state to pay their respects at Shinto shrines (honoring the foundation of the country); schoolchildren, for example, were required to visit and "pay respects" at Shinto shrines. Many shrines and Shinto priests were directly subsidized by the state. There was a law against teaching "religion" (such as Buddhism or Christianity) in the schools; but "national ethics" was required—a mixture of Shinto and Confucian teachings about the sacred character of the Japanese nation and Japanese people by virtue of their creation by the *kami* and the ethical responsibility of the people to be loyal to the emperor and the state. These teachings helped unify the country and mobilize it for war before and during World War II. Shinto was at the forefront of this effort, but there was remarkable unity in the support for national and military goals by Shinto, Buddhism, and even Japanese Christianity.

The end of World War II in 1945 marked not only the defeat of Japan and a disruption of the national government, but also considerable change for Japanese religion. The Allied Occupation of 1945–1952, led by the United States, helped establish a new constitution, with greater political and individual freedom and complete freedom of religion. Shinto had been disestablished; formally, the government could neither favor nor discriminate against any religion, and indirectly the compulsory teaching (or indoctrination) of "national ethics" was stopped. All religions were allowed to exist freely (including Shinto), supported by voluntary membership, with no coerced attendance and no financial subsidy from the state. However, the principle of separation of church and state is a delicate issue in many modern countries, and there are still unresolved issues in Japan today. For example, the emperor is a symbolic figure representing the nation; his involvement in key Shinto rituals has been interpreted as a "private" affair, but because he receives money from the state, does this mean that the state indirectly helps finance these rituals?

Two other examples of the problem of the separation of religion and state are the Ise Shrine and the Yasukuni Shrine. The Ise Shrine is considered the most important Shinto shrine for the Japanese nation as a whole, because tradition holds that the Sun Goddess (from whom the imperial line descends) is enshrined there. The Yasukuni Shrine is a special shrine in Tokyo for the war dead. After World War II, government subsidy of these shrines was stopped, on the grounds that the new constitution prohibits the establishment of any religion or the financial support of any religion. But many people seek to change the constitution, arguing that these shrines represent national traditions and qualify for national support (like the Tomb of the Unknown Soldier in Arlington, Virginia); others think that if the government renews financial support for these Shinto shrines, it could also renew the nationalism and militarism that led to Japan's involvement in World War II. These issues still generate heated discussion.

Shinto suffered most from the people's demoralization after defeat in World War II. Many stopped attending and contributing to Shinto shrines. Some of Shinto's problems were the result of gradual changes over the past century, such as the move away from a rural, agricultural lifestyle to a more urban, industrial lifestyle and greater concern for economic and secular matters. These changes, and the high degree of social mobility that accompanied them, were forces that tended to shift people away from participating in the seasonal festivals and local shrines of Shinto. Nevertheless, Shinto lives on in the hearts of many people as a continuation of the belief in *kami,* the celebration of seasonal festivals and city festivals, and a general blessing for the Japanese people.

Buddhism, too, had supported the war effort, but people did not link it so closely to war and defeat as they did Shinto. Also, Buddhism was not affected so much by social mobility. Buddhism's financial foundation was more secure, because it was based mainly on the fees for funerals and memorial rites for ancestors through hereditary affiliation. More families retained the hereditary family connection to a parish Buddhist temple than to participation in a local Shinto shrine (where affiliation traditionally was to the shrine near the family residence). A similar pattern held true for the home, especially in city apartments: The tendency was for families not to install Shinto-style altars but to retain Buddhist-style altars for family ancestors. One reason for retaining Buddhist altars has been the strong sense of family loyalty, which is expressed through veneration of ancestors at the Buddhist altar in the home. In general, both large Buddhist temples and Shinto shrines with income from rented land were hurt by the government's postwar land reform, which distributed the large holdings of landlords (including temples and shrines) to tenants.

Christianity suffered severely from the war, because most Christians and Christian churches were located in cities and thus felt directly the death and destruction of bombing focused on cities. There was some rise in church membership after World War II, but Christians (baptized members) still represent less than 1 percent of the Japanese population.

One of the main results of the complete religious freedom after World War II has been the flourishing of many New Religions (such as Tenrikyo and Soka Gakkai), which had been suppressed and persecuted before 1945. Hundreds, even thousands, of these movements sprang up: Some died out; some remained small; some grew in membership to hundreds of thousands, or even millions. Today Japan is a mixture of old and new. Some of the old traditions, like the belief in *kami,* go back to ancient times; others, like the New Religions, are relatively new. (In chapter 50 we will consider the significant changes in Japanese religion throughout history and their implications for the prospects of religion in contemporary Japan.)

This historical overview of Japanese religion shows us the manner in which many traditions emerged, took shape, and interacted to form "one sacred way." Tracing the course of religion's development in Japan, we recognize both continuity and discontinuity within the historical panorama of this sacred way: For example, in the history of beliefs and practices related to the *kami,* contemporary practices are continuous with those of prehistoric times, and yet they have been blended with other traditions, such as Buddhism. The course of Buddhism, too, represents both continuity and discontinuity. When Buddhism entered Japan it was a foreign religion encountering the native Japanese culture and therefore a kind of discontinuity; but as it was adapted to Japanese culture (providing blessings for the state and memorial rituals for family ancestors) it came to form a continuity with the Japanese heritage.

This historical overview also helps us to pinpoint the general features shared with other religions and the features more distinctive of Japanese religion. For example, throughout the world, religion is concerned with purification and rituals for the dead, and Japanese religion shares this concern. But in Japan, beliefs and rituals related to purification and the dead are raised to a much higher level of importance. In Japan purification is more than just a preparation for other rituals, it is practically a sacred state; the dead members of a family are so highly valued that they are honored as sacred sources of power. This is one of the distinctive aspects of the Japanese religious tradition we have discovered in tracing its historical development. To view the distinctive character of the "sacred way" more directly, we will shift from the historical perspective of the present chapter to a perspective that sees Japanese religion's unified worldview in the next chapter.

47
The World of Worship

THERE ARE SO MANY aspects to religion, and religious life is so closely related to other areas of life, that a number of approaches can be used to study a particular religious tradition. The philosophical aspect of religious thought can be treated separately, for example. Or the relation of religious life to social conditions and psychological states can be taken as a special area of investigation. But these specialized approaches are by their very nature limited; they tend to focus on just one aspect of a religion or on the relationships of religious life to other areas of life rather than the nature of a religion as a distinct tradition. If we set aside these specialized approaches and look at the nature of a religious heritage as a whole tradition, there are basically two perspectives: studying a religion from the viewpoint of its historical development and studying it as a unified world-view. The historical perspective is so widely used and well known that it needs little explanation. As seen in the last chapter, the historical approach traces a subject (the life of a person, the course of a nation, or the development of a religion) from its earliest beginnings through its various changes to its present form. Studying religion as a worldview is not so widely understood and thus requires some explanation.

Studying Religion as a Worldview

In contrast to the historical perspective that studies a subject as it occurs or develops through time, approaching the subject as a worldview means to study it as a unified system apart from its development through time. In other words, historical study traces how something continues and changes through time, whereas the focus on worldview examines the nature of a person, nation, or religion at any given moment. From this perspective, a person is studied not in terms of chronological development but as a whole person or organized personality, in terms of major ideas and practices that are expressed by the mature person. In fact, a person can be considered as a "world," in the sense of a world of ideas or an artistic world—as in the world of Shakespeare or the world of Beethoven. A culture is studied from the perspective of worldview, not in terms of historical development, but through the overall pattern of ideals and practices that are characteristic of this culture. For example, "the classical world," or "the world of ancient Greece," refers to the entire world or civilization of an age or culture. Similarly, a religion is studied as a worldview, not by tracing its gradual growth, but by interpreting it as an interrelated system of distinctive beliefs and practices. The worldview approach, like the historical perspective, can be used to study almost any human or cultural subject.

There are disagreements about exactly how these two approaches are best used, but it is obvious that some balance between the two is necessary. We cannot trace historical development through time unless we have some notion of the totality of the system we are tracing. And we cannot analyze the unity of a system without some idea of how that unity took shape. The balance between these two approaches becomes apparent from the biological example of studying an oak tree. The developmental or historical study of an oak follows the growth of an acorn into a seedling and sapling until the mature tree is formed. An oak can also be studied as a mature, unified form constituting a world of its own. This kind of study examines a cross section of the oak, analyzing such features as the layers of bark, the rings of the tree, and the characteristics of the wood. This helps determine the nature of an oak tree, as distinguished from tracing its development. These are two different ways of looking at the same tree: Both are needed for a more complete understanding of the oak tree. The same kind of balance is necessary for the successful study of religion and other human subjects. To simplify matters, I have called these two approaches historical development and worldview.

To study religion as a worldview is to focus on the basic pattern of beliefs and practices that is distinctive for a religion. For example, in Europe and America, religion is centered around the belief and worship of God, especially as practiced in regular services at local churches and synagogues attended by individuals and families. This is only a quick glimpse of the nature or "world" of European and American religion, but it illustrates what is meant by looking at religion as a worldview. And, by contrast, we know from the previous chapters that this pattern is quite different from the pattern of Japanese religion.

To discuss Japanese religion as a worldview, it is essential to specify the religion of a general time span. For the purposes of this treatment, we will concentrate more on recent and modern religion, from the late Tokugawa period (about 1800) to the present. As shown in chapter 46, during the Tokugawa period the various traditions interacted to form a definitive heritage that continues—with modifications—even today. Where necessary, differences in religious belief and practice over this range of several hundred years will be noted.

The religious worldview of Japan consists of at least five smaller "worlds." These five subworlds can be understood as providing responses to five questions about religious life: what, who, where, when, and how. In other words, these five questions are (1) what are the objects of worship? (2) who are the individuals and social groups involved in these worship activities? (3) where do these rituals of worship take place? (4) when does worship take place? and (5) how are the acts of worship related to human life? This chapter will discuss the Japanese religious worldview by focusing on the what of Japanese religion—the objects of worship. The next chapter will discuss the religious worldview in terms of who (society), where (space), when (time), and how (human life).[2]

The Sacredness of Kami

First we will look at the what of Japanese religion, the objects of worship. Every religious tradition is oriented around a cluster of objects of worship or principles that define what is real or at the heart of life and the universe; by living one's life in harmony with these objects of worship and/or principles, a person experiences a meaningful, rich career and realizes the fulfillment of unity with the essence of the universe. In Japanese religion at least four major objects of worship (or sources of power) can be singled out: kami, Buddhas, ancestors, and **holy persons.** These four sources of power are closely interrelated both conceptually and in actual practice, just as parts of the human body—the skeleton, muscles, internal organs, and nervous system—are inseparably connected. For the convenience of analysis, the four objects of worship will be treated separately, but frequently the interconnection among them will appear, both in the following four sections and in chapter 48, which treats other aspects of the worldview of Japanese religion. Further illustrations will appear in chapter 49, which gives concrete examples of the dynamics of Japanese religion.

One object of worship and set of principles in Japanese religion is the sacredness of *kami,* an ancient and persistent feature of the Japanese tradition. Beliefs and practices related to *kami* have changed considerably, especially in contemporary Japan, but the traditional perception of *kami* is described here because it is so distinctive of Japanese religion. The notion of *kami* is very flexible—it includes whatever is extraordinary both within and beyond the world, in the sense of being sacred and providing the abundance of life. The term *kami* can be either singular or plural and may be translated as "gods," "spirits," or "the sacred" in general. Examples of *kami* are the mythological deities found in the early writings *Kojiki* and *Nihongi,* emperors as "manifest *kami,*" specific *kami* of larger shrines, **tutelary *kami*** (guardian deities) of small local shrines, sacredness as represented by natural phenomena (trees, boulders, waterfalls, mountains), and even living persons (such as founders of New Religions).

The Japanese notion of *kami* is so different from the doctrine of God in Judaism and Christianity that it is helpful for Westerners to keep in mind the contrast between the two. In the Judeo-Christian tradition, the formal teaching about God emphasizes the transcendent character of the one and only true deity (more than the immanent presence of God within the world and human life). Generally, in both Judaism and Christianity, the relationship between a human being and God involves a formal act of faith, an acknowledgment of the existence of God and a conscious decision to accept God and live in obedience to him. By contrast, *kami* are many, and although they may hover above the earth, they are also within the forces of nature and within the lives of people. *Kami* are considered to be everywhere, and traditionally, the Japanese assume the presence of *kami* as naturally as they see beauty and fertility in nature—no conscious act of faith is needed.

From ancient times, as seen in the *Kojiki* and *Nihongi,* it is recorded that there are myriad *kami,* and these *kami* are woven into the fabric of the life of the Japanese nation and its people. As mentioned briefly in chapter 46, mythological accounts tell of the *kami's* gradual creation of the Japanese islands, their formation of the imperial line through descent from the Sun Goddess, and their responsibility for the Japanese people. In this fashion, traditionally *kami* are the force behind both the Japanese landscape and the political entity of the nation and the people. In Japanese religion, people are expected to respond to *kami* with sincerity and gratitude. *Kami* also represent the essence of Shinto as the continuation of the beliefs and practices from ancient times. In fact, the term *Shinto* is written with two Chinese characters that can also be pronounced *kami no michi,* "the way of *kami.*" In other words, Shinto is literally the way of life according to *kami.* In Shinto, *kami* are characterized not only by sacredness but also by purity, and humans must carefully purify themselves before approaching *kami.*

Ceremonies for *kami* can occur in a natural setting, in shrines, or in the home. Pilgrimages to sacred mountains and waterfalls are examples of religious rites in a natural setting. Often a massive boulder or a tall tree will be singled out as a site of prayers by placing a rice straw rope around it. The rice straw rope indicates that the natural object is set apart as special or sacred, in the sense

A woman bows her head and joins her hands as she prays before a small shrine of the **kami** *Inari within the grounds of a Buddhist temple in Tokyo. An offering box in front of the woman is where worshipers may drop coins; the small white objects placed against the shrine are porcelain foxes, offered here because Inari is associated with the fox. Inari traditionally was related to agriculture and food, but in cities people generally pray to Inari for good luck and protection.*

of being the place where *kami* dwell or can be ritually called down. Simple prayers or more elaborate rituals are performed here. In ancient times probably all religious celebrations were performed in such natural settings, but eventually buildings came to be used as Shinto shrines.

Even within a shrine, there is usually no physical representation of *kami* (such as a statue). The presence of the *kami* is assumed, and for special occasions, Shinto priests use formal prayers (*norito*) to call down *kami* and convey the blessing of the *kami* to the assembled people. At the conclusion of the ceremony, priests "send off" the *kami*. When there is no special occasion, people may approach the shrine as individuals. Usually they purify themselves first by rinsing their hands and mouths with water provided inside the shrine grounds; then they walk to the front of a shrine, make a small offering of money, ring a bell, bow their head, and clap their hands several times before saying their prayers silently. Such prayers can be simple requests for safety and blessing or thanks for previous blessings.

Perhaps the most important ceremonies for *kami* occur in and around the home. In traditional Japan (especially before the Meiji period, 1868–1912), almost every home was considered affiliated with a local shrine. This local shrine was the sacred site of the local tutelary *kami,* and people participated in festivals and other ceremonies by virtue of their living within the territory of this local shrine.

Families paid visits to the shrine especially at the New Year and for the shrine festivals (such as the spring and fall festivals). Often these local shrines were quite small, too small for many people to enter; such shrines were not intended as congregational gathering places as are churches and synagogues. It was customary for parishioners to say their prayers in front of the shrine without entering. Such simple visits to the tutelary *kami* took place at important times in a person's life.

The home itself is a sacred place, partly due to the presence of *kami*. Traditionally, in the central room of the house there was a special shelf called *kamidana* (literally, "*kami* shelf" or "*kami* altar," sometimes translated as "god shelf"). This shelf or altar usually held a miniature Shinto-style shrine, and offerings of food were presented there morning and evening. Paper amulets or charms from major shrines, such as the Ise Shrine, as well as from important regional and the local tutelary deity shrines, were placed on this altar. This was a symbolic means of enshrining these *kami* in the home and requesting their protection and blessing. In Japan the home has been a much more important center of religious activities than it is in contemporary Christian cultures.

The preceding discussion of the sacredness of *kami* is written in the past tense, describing "traditional" Japan, because these beliefs and practices are not so widespread and faithfully observed today as they once were. From the Meiji period (1868–1912) on, significant changes took place in Japanese society, especially the rapid move from a rural and agricultural lifestyle to a more urban and industrial-commercial one. As these changes took place, many practices related to *kami* came to be considered less important or were completely neglected. For example, the movement of families from the countryside to cities and from area to area greatly weakened the traditional pattern of families being affiliated to a local tutelary *kami* shrine. And with the increasing emphasis on an industrial-commercial society, the agricultural rhythms so important to the honoring of *kami* have been replaced by the cycle of the work week. In addition, many homes today do not have an altar and do not observe regular ceremonies for *kami.*

Although traditional observances for *kami* have declined, they still represent a venerable ideal and are still practiced by many people and actively encouraged by some groups, such as New Religions, thus demonstrating the significance of *kami* from ancient religion to contemporary times. What are some of the general features of the traditional notions about *kami?* One of the characteristics of *kami* that may surprise the Western viewer is the closeness and intimacy of *kami.* Something extraordinary and awe-inspiring, such as Mount Fuji or a majestic waterfall, or even a nearby hill or stream, can be considered a *kami* or viewed as expressing the sacredness of *kami.* And occasionally human beings, such as founders of New Religions, are considered "living *kami.*"

One of the general principles behind these notions is the ideal of close harmony among humans, *kami,* and nature. The desired human behavior in relationship to *kami* shows gratitude for the bounty of nature and thanks for the blessing of the *kami.* In this fashion, there is an intimate and harmonious relationship among the three that benefits all: The purity and sacredness of *kami* are honored, the rhythm and bounty of nature are preserved, and the sincerity and fullness of human life are enhanced.

Viewed negatively, if humans approach *kami* in an impure or insincere fashion, the purity of the *kami* is violated, destroying the harmonious relationship and endangering the blessing of *kami* and the bounty of nature. Living in tune with *kami* means to maximize this purity and sacredness and to minimize impurity and insincerity. As in any religion, an absolutely pure and sacred state is almost impossible to attain—there is a constant tension between the relatively sacred-pure and the relatively profane-impure. Shinto provides rituals both for regular purification and for special cases of purification. This makes it possible to restore the ideal relationship of harmony among humans, *kami,* and nature: This sacred harmony is the essence of the world of *kami.*

The Power of Buddhas

A second object of worship and set of principles in Japanese religion is the power of Buddhas. In some instances the power of Buddhas conflicts with the sacredness of *kami,* but in most cases the two complement and reinforce each other.

In fact the two are so closely interrelated that there is a term in Japanese for "*kami* and Buddhas" that can be pronounced two ways: The modified Chinese pronunciation is *shin-butsu;* the Japanese pronunciation is *kami-hotoke.* The term is used when referring to both traditions—for example, when speaking of protection by both *kami* and Buddhas, or "divine" protection. As we have seen in chapters 45 and 46, Japanese religion combines Shinto and Buddhism, along with other traditions, to construct a total worldview. Buddhist scholars and Shinto scholars have had their own theories about the relationship between *kami* and Buddhist divinities. However, in popular practice, people do not distinguish sharply between help from *kami* and help from Buddhas.

In Japan, Buddhism became an integral part of Japanese religion, but we must remember that Buddhism is a distinct tradition, possessing its own historical development and specific notions. It may be helpful first to distinguish between the historical Buddha (Gautama) and the many Buddhist divinities loosely called Buddhas. The historical Buddha was a prince named Siddhartha Gautama, who lived in India during the sixth and fifth centuries B.C.E. and developed the path of enlightenment. He taught that the power of enlightenment was available to all people, in the sense of living life meaningfully, especially overcoming human deficiencies (such as desire and greed), and achieving a peaceful, tranquil state. Thus, Gautama is considered the founder of Buddhism and is called the Buddha, which means "the enlightened one."

After the death of Buddha, his followers organized his teachings into the religion later called Buddhism. This religion came to include many divinities who express not only the power of enlightenment but also the power of many practical benefits. These benefits range from being reborn in heavenly paradise to the healing of sickness and even the granting of children to women. There are a number of technical terms for such Buddhist divinities granting these benefits, but in general they can all be called Buddhas.

It may seem strange that although the historical Buddha was the founder of Buddhism, in Japan there are fewer statues and less direct worship of this Buddha than there are statues and direct worship of the many Buddhist divinities, or Buddhas. One reason for this apparent contradiction is that the various divisions of Buddhist sects and denominations developed around specific teachings and particular Buddhist divinities. Another reason is that rather few people follow the difficult path of the historical Buddha to the power of enlightenment; many more seek out the specific powers of practical benefits granted by Buddhist divinities.

The elaborate statues of Buddhas within Buddhist temples create a different atmosphere from that of the rather "empty" space of Shinto shrines. Within Shinto shrines there are usually no statues, and one has to sense the presence of the *kami* just as one has to appreciate the beauty of nature even when it is not identified with a sign. There is a naturalness and freshness to a Shinto shrine that is hard to describe; it is expressed in the restraint of the decoration, and it creates an air of quiet peace. By contrast, the elaborate altar and statues of Buddhist temples can seem overwhelming. To sit in a dark temple with the flicker of candles casting light and shadow on gilded Buddhist statues is a memorable experience.

Ceremonies for Buddhas take place in large headquarters of Buddhist sects, in regional temples, in local parish temples, in small chapels, and in the home. Buddhism is more highly institutionalized than Shinto, and there is more ecclesiastical structure in Buddhism—for example, in the tie between a headquarters temple and its branch temples. The larger temples tend to combine some bureaucratic management with facilities for the study and practice of Buddhism. But most temples, large or small, enshrine Buddhist statues before which scriptures are recited and rituals performed. All these activities indirectly or directly are attempts to gain enlightenment and to request the help of Buddhas.

There are many Buddhas honored in Japan, and each has its own special benefits. **Kannon,** the goddess of mercy, is one of the most popular Buddhas, partly because Kannon grants requests for almost any kind of help. One specific form of Kannon, called Koyasu Kannon, or "Easy Childbirth Kannon," is popular with married women who want to conceive a child or who seek help in giving birth. Another form of Kannon, Bato Kannon ("Horseheaded Kannon"), once was popular with people who used horses and cows as beasts of burden, but even in highly mechanized contemporary Japan, Bato Kannon still has some followers.

Jizo is the patron saint of spirits of the dead, especially of dead children. Statues of Jizo, like other Buddhas, are found not only in large temples but also in wayside chapels (too small to enter), and such statues are seen even in the open air. Particularly for Jizo, a popular practice is to stack piles of stones near the statue (thought to help the spirits of dead children accumulate merit), and candies and crackers are often offered to Jizo.

Yakushi is the healing Buddha, and people who are sick or who are praying for a sick person will pay a visit to a Yakushi statue. The usual act of devotion before a Buddhist statue is to recite a brief passage from a Buddhist scripture; this helps enlighten the one reciting and also transfers the power of the scripture and the statue to this and other individuals.

Amida rivals Kannon and Jizo as one of the most important Buddhas. There are many physical representations of Amida that attract followers, but Amida is prayed to directly (even when no statue is present) by reciting the phrase *namu Amida Butsu* ("I take refuge in Amida Buddha"). Amida grants believers who practice this recitation assurance of rebirth in Amida's paradise after death. On medieval battlefields this cry was uttered by the wounded and dying who sought comfort from Amida, and it is still popular today.

These are but a few of the countless Buddhas honored within Japanese Buddhism. One interesting aspect of the veneration of these Buddhas is that most activities are carried out by laypersons with little or no priestly help and no national structure linking either the sites of worship for a Buddha or the followers of a Buddha. Often a group of laypeople in a local area form their own association or club for the worship of a particular Buddha, such as Kannon, and hold monthly meetings in homes, combining a social gathering with a simple service honoring Kannon. If members of such an association collect enough money, they might buy a small stone statue of Kannon and have it erected nearby. This is a good example of the presence of Buddhas in the life of the people.

Another aspect of the power of Buddhas is that the founders of Buddhist sects may also be considered as extremely powerful and able to grant benefits to believers. Nichiren, the founder of the Nichiren sect, declared himself to be the reincarnation of a previous Buddha. And Kobo Daishi (founder of the Shingon sect) is very popular in folktales—for example, one tale tells that because a kind girl walked a long distance to bring Kobo Daishi a drink of water, he used his staff to make a spring of water come forth so that she would not have to go so far for water. Such founders possess the power of Buddhas and are similar to "living *kami*."

People may travel to the headquarters of the parish Buddhist temple to which their family belongs or visit a regional temple that is famous for certain statues or for certain powers. Usually when a person enters such larger temples, a small amount of money is donated; also, incense is bought and lit from an altar candle and placed upright in a container filled with sand. Incense is a common offering to both Buddhas and spirits of the dead. A person may visit the family parish temple for special occasions, but the crucial link between the family and this temple is the family ancestors. Probably the most significant power of Buddhism, from a popular standpoint, is the use of Buddhist rituals to help transform the corpses of family dead into purified ancestors who grant blessings to the family. We will see in the next section that ancestors are one of the central features of Japanese religion. Funerals and memorials for family dead are conducted by Buddhist priests and temples, and this is the main source of income for such parish temples. In Tokugawa times (1600–1867), the government required each family to belong to a Buddhist temple, and even though this requirement was dropped after the opening of the Meiji era in 1868, most families have retained affiliation to a parish Buddhist temple.

In most homes it has been the custom to have a Buddhist altar (*butsudan*) in the main room of the house. Many traditional homes have had both Buddhist altar and Shinto altar (*kamidana*) in the same central room (one exception is families belonging to Pure Land denominations, which prohibit the use of *kamidana*). The Buddhist altar, an expensive lacquered or finished cabinet, contains not only pictures and statues of Buddhas and small containers for offerings of food, but more important, the wooden tablets representing the spirits of the family ancestors. It is interesting that a common word for ancestor, *hotoke,* can also mean "Buddha." Thus, an ancestor is considered a Buddha or has the power of a Buddha. Pious Japanese make daily offerings to the "Buddhas" (Buddhist divinities and family ancestors) and recite short sections of Buddhist scriptures in front of the Buddhist altar. In modern Japan more homes have Buddhist altars than Shinto altars, probably because of the great strength of the family bond (which is expressed through the Buddhist altar as respect for family ancestors).

The power of the Buddha and specific Buddhas is quite diverse, ranging from the lofty notion of enlightenment to very practical benefits. These two ideals—enlightenment and practical benefits—may seem contradictory, but actually they are only different aspects of the same principle. This principle is to live as close to the ideals of Buddhism as possible, eliminating personal defects and powerlessness and maximizing personal power. The way to a more powerful life may come either by following the example of the historical Buddha, overcoming uncontrolled emotions in order to become enlightened and living a life of tranquility and compassion for others, or by relying directly on the help of various Buddhist divinities to gain specific powers for solving problems in this life. (In the case of Amida, power is sought to assure peace in the next life.) In ancient times the powerful resources of Buddhas were monopolized by the state, but later, especially from Tokugawa times on, the power of Buddhas became an integral part of village and home life. Buddhist statues on village streets and Buddhist altars in homes brought the people in close daily contact with the presence and power of Buddhas. The world of Buddhas is both the power of enlightenment and the power to live.

The Blessings of Ancestors

A third object of worship and set of principles in Japanese religion is centered around ancestors, who are major sources of blessings. The role of ancestors is central to Japanese religion, but to understand this role, we must recognize the difference between the rather casual notion of ancestors in the West and the more significant concept of ancestors in Japan. In European and American usage, ancestors are all the dead people from whom a person is descended, both on the father's and the mother's side. Ancestry is considered part of a person's biological and social past, but it is of little importance for living one's life and is of no consequence religiously.

By contrast, in Japan ancestors refer especially to those from whom a person is descended in the father's line, as a continuation of family succession that directly affects personal fortune and religious behavior. Ancestors are much more than a biological and social fact, because family members do not automatically become ancestors when they die. Both a lapse of time and the transforming power of ritual are necessary to change the impure corpse into a purified ancestor. Religion is directly involved in the creation of ancestors: The major result of this ritual transformation is that the impure dead person becomes a benevolent source of blessings for descendants. Not only is a funeral performed for family dead, but memorial rites continue for many years, and a family prays to ancestors for protection and blessing.

Some features of ancestors have been seen in the earlier discussion of the power of Buddhas: Ancestors are enshrined in the home in Buddhist altars called *butsudan,* before which simple offerings and recitations are made by family members.

But exactly how does a person become an ancestor? The major procedures for handling the dead are Buddhist, especially since the time of the dominance of Buddhism during the Tokugawa period (1600–1867). In almost every culture, dead bodies and death generally are considered impure or defiling, and Japan is no exception. The ancient Japanese custom for disposing of the impure corpse was burial, but the Buddhist practice of cremation gradually became accepted and is standard today (encouraged partly for health reasons). The symbolism of cremation itself is clearly a means of driving out the impurity by destroying it with fire; in the smoke of cremation the "spirit" of the dead person ascends. Ashes of the person remaining after cremation are put in a small container and placed in the parish Buddhist temple to which the family belongs.

The key Buddhist ritual is the funeral mass and subsequent memorial masses. Details of such rituals vary considerably from denomination to denomination, but the gist of all these rituals is transformation. During the funeral mass, Buddhist scriptures are recited by priests to draw on their power as a means of transforming the dead person. As part of the transformation process, the Buddhist priest grants the dead person a special posthumous name, or "Buddhist name." This honorary name indicates, in Buddhist terms, that the material aspect of the dead person has been extinguished, and the person has gone on to enlightenment, or paradise. The Buddhist name is written on a memorial tablet for the individual; memorial tablets are used in the home for subsequent memorial rites. The time that it takes a dead person to be elevated to enlightenment or paradise varies with different denominations, but usually there are forty-nine days of mourning after death. This is considered the end of a period of impurity for both the dead person and his or her family. In formal Buddhist teaching, this indicates that the dead person has completed passage through stages of hell and is reborn; in popular understanding this means that the dead person's impurity has been eliminated and the person has been transformed into a benevolent ancestor.

To illustrate the significance of ancestors, it may help to explain the opposite situation—when a dead person does not become an ancestor. If the proper funeral and memorial rites are not performed for a dead person, there is always the possibility that the dead spirit will wander around the world and haunt people, causing misfortune and sickness not only for the dead person's family but for nearby people as well. There are special rituals to pacify such dead persons with "no relatives" so that they do not cause problems. This is a good example of the Japanese tendency to view human identity as an interrelationship of people, rather than as an individual existence. Both in life and in death, to be merely an individual (with no relation to other persons) is a dangerous condition, almost the same as being no one, having no identity. The dead individual who is not regularly memorialized is not transformed from impure corpse to pure ancestor, and therefore the person suffers and may also cause the living to suffer.

After memorial tablets are placed in the Buddhist altar in the home, they are regularly honored by the family with simple offerings and brief passages of scripture. The Buddhist priest of the family's parish temple is requested to perform memorial masses, especially on the annual anniversary of the person's death, and may come to the home for this purpose. Ritual observance of this "death day" is practiced for many years—usually thirty-three or fifty—after which the individual memorial tablet is no longer honored in the butsudan. According to Japanese custom, ancestors make special visits to family homes during the New Year celebrations and during the festival of the dead in late summer—these are two of the most important annual festivals.

The religious significance of the home is clear from the presence of ancestors in the home and the regular performance of rituals by the family in relationship to ancestors. In fact, the *butsudan,* whose literal translation is "Buddhist altar" might just as well be called a "family altar" or "ancestral altar," since the ancestral tablets are valued more highly than the Buddhist statues and pictures in the altar. If a house catches fire, the first thing to be saved is this altar, and if there is not time to save the entire altar, memorial tablets will be saved and Buddhist statues will be left behind.[3] This is perhaps an extreme example, but it shows that the blessing of ancestors is crucial to the values of the Japanese family.

Other aspects of ancestors highlight the significance of this family altar. Traditionally, ancestors were considered primarily through the father, and the first son of a family continued the family line, which meant keeping the ancestral tablets of the family. In some instances this continuation of the family line by the first son was called the main family, and other sons set up branch families. In traditional settings, it was customary for branch families to pay respects at the home of the main family, especially at the New Year, partly out of deference to their common ancestors. In the traditional setting, only the main family had a large *butsudan;* a branch family would buy a rather modest *butsudan* only when a member of this branch family died. In recent times customs have become much more flexible: There is less emphasis on main and branch families, and usually a family buys a *butsudan* after the first death in the immediate family.

The blessing that ancestors provide is life itself and protection within the ongoing unit of the family. Life is precious, and each person owes a debt to parents and ancestors for this gift of life. Members of a family pray to ancestors for offspring, health, and prosperity. In Japan, as in other countries, the family is the basic social unit for nurturing life and sharing experience. One of the distinctive features of the Japanese family, at least in contrast to the American family, is that the Japanese family extends from the dead ancestors through the living to the unborn in the future. The family is a religious institution in its own right, with family ancestors as its own objects of worship and the head of the family as its own leader of worship. The world of ancestors is defined by the mutual interaction of descendants providing sincere worship to ancestors and ancestors granting life and blessings to descendants.

Mediation by Holy Persons

A fourth object of worship and set of principles in Japanese religion is the mediation of sacredness and power by holy persons. There are holy persons or saints in most religions, but these figures have special significance in Japanese religion because they are not just holy in the sense of being more devout and set apart from others: In Japan holy persons mediate religious power and may become objects of worship themselves. Our treatment of *kami,* Buddhas, and ancestors has demonstrated that "deities" in Japanese religion are not far removed from human life; also, humans easily cross the boundary into sacredness and power. *Holy person* is a general term to indicate the kind of person who in his or her lifetime (and/or after death) is an object of worship or mediator of power for many people. Three major representatives of holy persons are (1) the founders of major Buddhist movements, some of whom are considered sources of Buddhist power; (2) the founders of New Religions during the past hundred and fifty years, some of whom are considered living *kami;* and (3) **shamans** within folk religion, who are mediums between this world and the next, between living and dead. We will look at the three kinds of holy persons separately, starting with founders.

Founders are important in any society or religion, because not only do they initiate an idea and incorporate the idea in a social group but they also as founders represent models to be followed. In Japanese society, founders of movements (for example, even artistic movements) are accorded special attention. Founders of Buddhist movements are singled out here because they are good examples of holy persons from earlier times who are still very important today. The power of Buddhist founders comes partly from the fact that they located the power of Buddhism for other people, making it available for a wider audience. In Japan this usually means that ordinary followers seek the power of Buddhism by believing in a founder, and practice devotions to a founder in order to obtain this power. The Buddhist founder is a model and also a means of obtaining power.

Two cases already mentioned of Buddhist founders as sources of power are Nichiren and Kobo Daishi. Nichiren was a very forceful personality who insisted on the absolute truth of the *Lotus Sutra* and absolute faith in this Buddhist scripture both for personal salvation and for national welfare. In fact he considered himself the reincarnation of an earlier Buddha for the purpose of spreading this message. In other words, Nichiren told his followers that he had been born in the form of a Buddhist divinity. This made him an absolute authority on the absolute truth; it is not surprising that followers have worshiped Nichiren down to the present day. Some believers even worship the title of the *Lotus Sutra* in Nichiren's handwriting, preserved in a major Nichiren temple.

Kobo Daishi was mentioned previously as the founder of the Shingon sect of esoteric Buddhism and a popular figure in folk legends. This founder is also worshiped, and there are many informal associations or clubs for this specific purpose. In the name Kobo Daishi, *daishi* is an honorary title that literally means "great teacher" or "saint." A number of Buddhist leaders were granted the title *daishi,* but the term *daishi-**ko,*** or "great teacher association," usually means a group of people who gather monthly for the purpose of worshiping Kobo Daishi. He is popularly believed to have been the one who devised the Japanese form of writing, so the power that he represents is both cultural and religious.

One scholar has called this tendency to focus on the power of individuals "the attitude of absolute devotion to a specific individual." This scholar quotes the devotion of Shinran (1173–1262) to his teacher Honen, the founder of Pure Land Buddhism, which centers around recitation of the ***nembutsu*** (taking refuge in Amida). Shinran wrote: "I do not know whether the *nembutsu* is actually the means to rebirth in the Pure Land, or whether perhaps it is the road to Hell.

Even though I were cajoled by Saint Honen that I should go to Hell through the *nembutsu,* I should do so and not regret it."[4] This shows the importance in Japanese religion of faith in an individual, rather than in the doctrine taught by the individual. This kind of "absolute devotion" is not limited to founders of Buddhist movements, but they are representative examples.

More recent examples of holy persons are the founders of New Religions during the past century and a half. Many of these have been women of extraordinary personal and religious experience who both founded New Religions and became objects of worship in their own New Religions. One is Miki Nakayama (1798–1887), the founder of the New Religion called Tenrikyo, who first became possessed during a healing ritual for her son. Such temporary possessions were not unusual. What was remarkable is that this deity refused to leave her body, insisting that Miki Nakayama should spread the message of rejecting materialism and selfishness for a true religious life. This founder is an example of *ikigami,* a "living *kami*," a human being who at the same time is filled with *kami* or is a *kami.*

For a person to be a *kami* can mean that everything associated with the person is also *kami* or sacred, and this has been true for Miki Nakayama. Her life and deeds became the sacred models for the religion she founded. Her writings became scriptures. Her songs became hymns. Her gestures became liturgy. To this day she is followed in the teaching and actual liturgy of Tenrikyo, as well as being worshiped herself. Another interesting aspect of Tenrikyo, shared with some other New Religions (and some Buddhist sects), is that the sacred character of the founding figure is inherited by descendants. After her death, Tenrikyo has been headed by a line of male descendants; each successor has the title *shimbashira,* usually translated as "patriarch," but the literal meaning is "sacred (*kami*) pillar." Even when it is a woman who founds a New Religion, the hereditary transmission is usually to male descendants.

This is only one of many interesting examples of holy persons, especially living *kami,* in New Religions. Miki Nakayama's career is but one instance in a rich and varied tradition of founders of New Religions. Many were female, but there have also been male founders. Some gained their *kami* character through possessions, like Miki Nakayama; others received a revelation from a deity, yet others underwent strict religious training as a means of acquiring power. Whatever the founder's approach to sacredness and power, followers usually have considered these founders as worthy of worship and as channels for obtaining power and blessings.

Holy persons are not limited to the founders of large movements. Another important category of holy person in Japanese religion is the shaman or medium who lives among people and serves individuals apart from organized movements. There are many local variations of such mediums, each given a particular Japanese name. The word *shaman* is a term used by ethnologists to refer to individuals with special religious powers, such as the ability to go into a trance and become a medium between this world and other worlds.

One important tradition of shamans in northern Japan is the blind female who undergoes special training and is able to talk with the dead. Such a shaman lives in an ordinary home (sometimes with other family members) and attracts people through word of mouth by those who have made use of her services. Usually people come to this shaman for specific requests about speaking to a dead relative, such as asking what offerings should be made for that person. A fee is paid, and the request is given to the shaman, who performs a ritual in order to get into contact with the dead spirit. The shaman makes offerings before a simple altar in the home and recites a simple liturgy she has learned as part of her training. The climax of the service is when she enters a trancelike state, at which time she becomes the mouthpiece for the dead relative and will answer simple questions put to her. After a brief exchange with the dead relative, the trancelike state ends and the person requesting the ritual leaves.

In this tradition of blind female shamans, there is a rather rigorous training period. The young woman may experience a "call" by a certain deity, indicating that she should become a shaman. She must find a senior shaman who will accept her for training and then undergo years of practice. She learns the rituals, recitations, and techniques of entering trance and speaking with the dead. Usually there is an intense initiation symbolizing marriage to the deity who called her. This initiation qualifies her to become a shaman and set up her own altar for communicating with the dead.

This brief description of the blind female shaman is but one example of the shamans within Japanese religion and does not include other kinds of holy persons who are able to draw on power and sacredness. This example was selected because it is a good illustration of a holy person as a mediator of power (rather than an object of worship). People who have specific problems and particular requests of the dead want to communicate with the other world, but ordinary people cannot do this. Only a person who has undergone special training and gained special power can become a medium between this world and the next, and traditionally the Japanese have perceived the blind female shaman to be able to do this. Today this kind of shaman is becoming rare, but there are a number of other kinds of holy persons who have similar powers.

The general principle applying to holy persons in Japanese religion is that sacredness and power are not completely outside the world but are often found within the world in living human beings (or human beings who once were alive). Some individuals, such as Nichiren, seem to have talent and persistence in pursuing religious power. Some people seem to become *kami* partly by accident, as in Miki Nakayama's accidental possession. Other founders of New Religions may undergo strict religious practice, and shamans may have to train for years before they are initiated. However this power is acquired, the understanding is that ordinary people, who do not have such powers, may make use of such power by following the model of holy persons: by imitating their practices (such as reciting the *nembutsu*), by worshiping the holy person, and/or by making requests to the holy person (through prayers or through direct request to a shaman).

The *kami*, Buddhas, ancestors, and holy persons interrelate to form a cluster of objects of worship and principles around which Japanese religion is organized. As a group of interrelated sources of sacredness, power, blessing, and mediation, they enable one to define what is "real," or at the heart of life and the universe. By conforming one's own life to this ideal picture of what is real and meaningful, one can experience a rich and rewarding career. Inevitably, as with any living system, there are tensions among these four objects of worship. However, most of the time they interact with each other in harmonious fashion to shape and support the Japanese religious worldview. [See Religions of Africa pp. 39–42, 64–69, Religions of Mesoamerica pp. 157–58, 186–89, Native Religions of North America pp. 274–75, 288–305, 330–32, Judaism pp. 414–15, Christianity pp. 537–38, Islam pp. 635–37, Hinduism pp. 739–41, 759–61, 780–84, Buddhism pp. 900–903, and Religions of China pp. 1024–26 for discussion of God, gods, and objects of worship.]

A person does not rely on just one object of worship but depends on all of them to lead a full religious life. *Kami* provide for the sacredness of local areas as local tutelary deities. Buddhas provide power as a philosophy of life and as solutions to particular problems. Ancestors nourish and sustain family life with blessings and protection. Holy persons mediate the richness of these traditions for ordinary people, making it possible for them to participate more fully in these sources of sacredness and power. The "world" of holy persons is a point of contact between powerless people and powerful figures, a bridge between this life and the next life.

These objects of worship are not separate from one another but constantly interact and overlap. Just as the Shinto altar (*kamidana*) and Buddhist altar (*butsudan*) are found in the same room, and just as Buddhas and ancestors are enshrined in the same Buddhist altar, these objects are organic parts of a living system. As a whole, these objects of worship define the "what" of the universe of Japanese religion.

The universe or cosmos of Japanese religion as one sacred way can be constructed (or reconstructed) in the accompanying diagram, which shows powers, rituals, and mediators in relationship to each other in a cosmic setting. Actually, the broken line of the large oval represents not only the cosmos, but also chaos or disorder in tension with the cosmos. At the top of the oval are the powers of the cosmos—holy persons, ancestors, *kami,* and Buddhas—above which are heaven and paradise. These powers are essentially benevolent but, like any power, can "backfire" and visit retribution or punishment upon humans. People come into contact with these powers especially through such rituals as divination, propitiation, devotions, memorials, offerings, purification, festivals, thanksgiving, and specific rites and prayers. These rituals are conducted particularly by shamans, popular practitioners, heads of families, Shinto priests, and Buddhist priests.

View the diagram from top to bottom; some mediation and rituals are directed *up* to powers, while rites of exorcism may be considered as directed *down* in the sense of suppressing or driving out essentially evil forces. Wandering spirits of the dead are the major evil forces to be driven away (or transformed into benevolent spirits as ancestors); impurity is the major condition to be avoided (or transformed through personal sincerity and ritual purification into purity). At the bottom of this diagram is the underworld, dominated by evil and purgatory. Mother earth, on the threshold between the world of the living

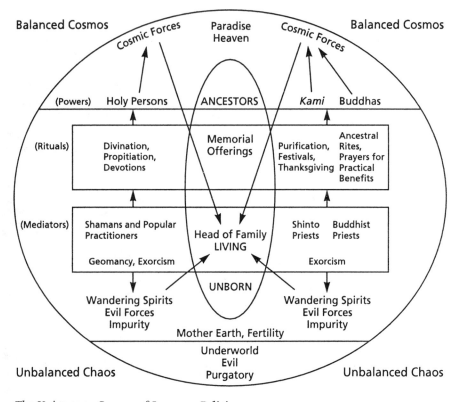

The Universe or Cosmos of Japanese Religions.

and the underworld, is in an ambiguous position of representing the fertility of earth and new life, but also being next to the underworld.

At the center of the oval is the religion of the family, which had its own pattern of ancestors for powers, memorial offerings for rituals, the head of the family for mediator, and the Unborn as the dimension of ambiguity and fertile possibilities. At the heart of families is the realm of the Living, which also is the center of the cosmos, seen from the human viewpoint. Religious action moves in two directions, up toward the powers, and down toward evil forces. The Living are related reciprocally to both the cosmic forces and evil forces, with the double intention of maximizing the harmonious relationship to the benevolent powers and receiving from them blessings and good fortune, and minimizing the evil forces by suppressing them and avoiding the sickness and misfortune they bring.

The levels of the powers and evil forces are not fixed, in fact the aim of religion is to maintain and enhance a balanced cosmos, and to avoid and diminish the unbalanced chaos. When individuals and the family are in harmony with the powers (through mediators and rituals, represented by the "up" arrows) the cosmos is balanced and blessings flow back from the cosmic forces (represented by the arrows from the cosmic forces to the Living). Individuals and the family attempt to drive out and suppress wandering spirits and evil forces (represented by the "down" arrows); when people neglect these rituals or the evil forces become dominant, the evil forces direct misfortune and sickness to the Living (represented by the arrows from evil forces to the Living).

This diagram provides a convenient graphic view of the world of worship and its prominence within the Japanese religious universe. However, we have more to see of this universe than the objects of worship. In the next chapter, we will examine other aspects of the worldview of Japanese religion, looking more closely at four smaller worlds of religious life: who (society), where (space), when (time), and how (life).

48

Japanese Religion's Worldview

OBJECTS OF WORSHIP provide the "what" around which the worldview of Japanese religion is centered. Four smaller worlds revolve around this center of worship: the organization of religious life in terms of who worships (society), where worship takes place (space), when worship takes place (time), and how worship directly affects people (human life). Each of these smaller religious worlds will be treated separately.

The Religious World of Society

The worldview of Japanese religion has been examined in terms of its objects of worship (such as *kami* and Buddhas); it can also be seen in terms of its subjects of worship (the people who carry out the worship). The present section focuses on the "who" of religion, the human rather than the divine. The way in which individuals and groups are involved in religion is an important factor in the practice of religious life. The religious world of society is the formation and use of social units (individuals and groups) for the purpose of preserving, celebrating, and transmitting religion. The role of individuals and groups varies from culture to culture. For example, in a modern country like the United States, the human organization of religion is usually considered as the relationship between an individual and a specially formed religious group such as a church or synagogue. In modern Japan, there is a similar pattern of relationship between an individual and a special religious group (for example, in a New Religion). But on the whole, Japanese religion presents a striking contrast with religion in modern America. During the past few centuries of Japanese religion, the individual has played less of a role than the family; also, special religious groups (such as churches) have been less important than such ordinary social groups as family, village, and nation. In fact, these "social" groups derive part of their identity and character from their involvement in religion. The major role of these social groups becomes apparent as we discuss units of human organization of religion in Japan: individual, family, village, nation, and specific religious groups.

The individual is less important in Japanese religion than in modern Western religion. In Japan people have participated in religion more as members of groups than as individuals; especially from Tokugawa times on, the family and village have been the major means of participating in religion. Not to be a member of such a group practically eliminates a person from participating in religion. A good example has already been seen in the ritual transformation of ancestors. One becomes an ancestor not through one's own achievements, virtue, or "salvation," but through the rituals that other family members perform (and have priests perform). If the funeral and memorial rites are not properly performed, then one is not transformed into a benevolent ancestor and is doomed to wander the earth and haunt people. The ideal, of course, is to have descendants perform the proper funeral and memorial rites so that the dead person can benefit the family line with protection and blessing. In death as in life, religious fulfillment is channeled more through groups than through individual existence.

Emphasis on group participation in religion does not mean that there is no individual experience in religion; rather, it means that religion is organized and experienced in the context of groups. This can be demonstrated in the Zen Buddhist ideal of being enlightened through meditation—which has often been misunderstood outside Japan as a highly individualistic experience. Enlightenment (or "awakening") does occur to individuals, but usually to individuals who are in the context of a Zen monastery—which is a tightly controlled community with rigid scheduling not only of meditation but of every detail of life from waking to sleeping. An individual who reaches the point of experiencing enlightenment does so by virtue of relationship to a Zen master and by means of the heightened concentration achieved within the structure of the monastic community.

The family may be considered the cornerstone of Japanese society as well as of Japanese religion. A Japanese person has a very strong sense of identity as a member of a family, much stronger than his or her identity as an individual. Ideally a person should always think and act with family interest ahead of personal interest. Participation in religion usually has been as a family, rather than by individual decision. Family residence determines participation in the Shinto shrine of the local tutelary *kami;* family birth determines participation in the hereditary Buddhist parish. These are the two most important centers of religious activity outside the home, and both are entered as a family rather than as an individual.

As we have seen, the family is a religious institution in its own right, with ancestors constituting the objects of worship, the male head acting as leader in worship, and the family as a unit serving as members of the religious institution. The particular anniversaries of death days observed by each family mean that a family even has its own calendar of religious events. The family home is the site of one or more altars. The family is practically a miniature religion itself, as is demonstrated in its inclusion of its own objects of worship (ancestors in the *butsudan*). As one scholar has phrased it, "Certain types of psychological security found in a relationship to a personal God in the West are found only in relation to the actual family in Japan."[5]

Social relationships are so important that ethical relationships are expressed more through social relationships than through universal principles; the family situation is the best example. The strong influence of Confucian thinking, developed especially during Tokugawa society, has shaped Japanese attitudes of filial piety and loyalty. Filial piety is the reverential obedience of children to parents: Because parents give life to children, children can never repay the debt they owe parents. Children should defer completely to parents (even when the "children" themselves are adults). Obedience to parents and reverence for ancestors are two of the basic virtues in Japanese society and religion. Parents are benevolent and protective of children. This model of social harmony in the family is the pattern for loyalty and benevolence outside the family in the local community, in work relationships, and in the nation as a whole.

Families participate in a local community, which for traditional Japan has been the village, and for modern urban Japan is more frequently a city or a district of a city. The traditional village pattern, although mostly replaced with city patterns, is important because it helped shape an understanding of life that is still influential today.

In the traditional countryside a number of farming families formed a small village community (or a smaller unit). The traditional village was the basic unit of economic and religious cooperation. In farming villages rice was a main crop for taxes and cash, and growing rice in irrigated fields required considerable cooperation. It was necessary for all the farmers in an area around a water source to agree on the time of planting and even the hours when water flowed from one field to another. Such practical decisions and many other matters affecting the common good of the community were decided in village councils. The people also cooperated in holding village celebrations. Such festivities varied greatly from village to village but usually included annual festivals such as the New Year (a ritual opening of the year and an asking of blessings for the villagers) and other seasonal rituals as well as special local traditions. In some areas there were elaborate rituals accompanying rice transplanting and festivals after the rice harvest; this defines a widespread spring and fall cycle of ritual in Japanese religion.

Most of these village celebrations were carried out by the villagers themselves, often without any professional religious leaders. Male heads of leading families often took turns being in charge of the rituals, and other leading families played key roles. In many villages it was the custom that a family had to live there for several generations before the male head of the family could participate in community decision-making councils and help perform annual festivals. Each village had its own customs and traditions about what celebrations would be held, when, and who could participate. Often young men were allowed to play a role in some public part of a festival, such as carrying a large wooden altar through the streets, as part of the recognition of their passing into manhood.

It is difficult to describe a general pattern for village religion, since there is so much local variation. But a universal feature is that one did not consciously "decide" to participate in a village festival—one did so almost automatically, by virtue of membership in the village and according to one's status in the village. Religion did not create villages, but it did help define the village as a community by mobilizing it for the performance of rituals. Even within cities, some communities performed annual rituals (especially the New Year, spring, and fall festivals) in a fashion similar to the village pattern. In modern Japan, especially after World War II, village festivals have been neglected, partly because of the rapid shift of the population from the countryside to the city. The weakening of involvement in traditional local celebrations is one factor that has encouraged participation in special religious groups like New Religions.

The nation is the largest social unit related to Japanese religion. Like the family and the village, the nation is considered primarily a social and political unit, but it has had a specific religious character in the past and continues to have a semireligious character today. As we have seen in previous chapters, traditional mythology describes the nation as a country founded by *kami,* led by an emperor who is descended from *kami,* and inhabited by a people united in worship of these *kami* and in loyalty to the emperor. In other words, from ancient times, "Japanese people" meant more than inhabitants of a certain area; it meant a group of people united by common practices of religious life.

One representative feature of this "national" religion is the Ise Shrine, where the Sun Goddess (from whom the imperial line is descended) is enshrined. This is considered the holiest of Shinto shrines, and since medieval times it has been popular practice to make pilgrimages there. Pilgrims take back special blessings to their homes, and many families buy a paper talisman from Ise annually to place in their *kamidana* (Shinto-style altar).

Another feature of the "national" religion is the round of rituals performed by the emperor for the sake of the Japanese people. Especially at harvest time, the emperor holds a special thanksgiving rite, and the enthronement ceremony for a new emperor is patterned after this rite. In traditional times the people had little contact with the emperor, but he carried out these religious activities behind the scenes; since World War II this has raised legal questions. It is well to remember that through the centuries there were various political forms, and the emperor never ruled Japan directly. In fact, the strong sense of patriotic and national identity as a country founded by *kami* and guided by the emperor is a more recent development, from the Meiji era (1868–1912) through World War II. The close association of religious support for nationalism, colonialism, and militarism leading up to World War II has caused widespread concern in Japan. Legally, the constitution written after World War II protects freedom of religion; it prohibits government support of any religion as well as discrimination against any religion. However, what the constitution means in practice is something still being debated today. One of the constitutional questions is whether national funds can and should be used to support the Ise Shrine and the rituals performed by the emperor. The relationship between religious commitment and national identity is a problem for Japan, just as it is for many other modern nations. In contemporary Japan the rather literal interpretation of the emperor as descended from *kami* and leading the Japanese people in the worship of *kami* is not widely held. But some scholars feel that, indirectly, much motivation for the enthusiasm, efficiency, and cooperation of the Japanese people in achieving economic success is a modern expression of the earlier notion of a "sacred" national entity.

Social units such as family, village, and nation have played major roles in Japanese religion, and special religious groups—those formed specifically for religious purposes—have been less important. There are institutional aspects of Japanese religion, especially Buddhism, however, that resemble some aspects of denominationalism in Protestant Christianity: There are numerous denominations of Buddhist sects, for example, subdivisions of Tendai and Shingon. But a family thinks of its affiliation to a local temple more as belonging to a parish Buddhist temple that helps memorialize family ancestors than to a particular Buddhist denomination. The consciousness of denominational ties is so weak that many people do not even know the exact denominational affiliation of their local parish temple.

One of the strongest traditional forms of the special religious group is the association or club (ko) formed locally for the purpose of honoring a particular deity, usually a Buddha such as Kannon. Sometimes a whole village belonged to this association; sometimes individuals joined freely. This informal group met at regular intervals (usually monthly) in homes to worship Kannon or another Buddha without any priestly supervision, and several members of the association used modest association funds to make a pilgrimage to a regional center honoring their object of worship. Such associations, because of their strong grassroots character, formed one of the most important special religious groups in traditional Japan. Some of these associations are still active today, but they have tended to decline along with other traditional village practices.

Since the nineteenth century, and especially in the twentieth century, New Religions have become the most important special religious groups. To become a member of a New Religion, it is necessary (at least for the first generation of members) to make a decision to join, in contrast to the traditional patterns of religious affiliation—the residential tie to the Shinto shrine of the local tutelary kami and the hereditary tie to the local parish Buddhist temple. The relationship between an individual and a New Religion is the closest parallel to the Western pattern of an individual joining a church. However, there are also some striking differences: For example, a member of a Christian church in a Western country usually does not form any other religious ties, whereas a Japanese member of a New Religion may continue to participate in several other religious groups.

Individuals join a New Religion when they are convinced, often through a relative or neighbor, of the truth of the teaching or the effectiveness of the ritual. Frequently an individual faces a personal problem, such as sickness or family tension, that prompts the quest for a religious answer. When the person is convinced of the New Religion's power to resolve this problem and meet the religious need, he or she joins the New Religion. Membership is in both a local branch and the nationwide religion, unifying all Japanese (and often foreign) members in the same forms of worship and principles of life. These nationwide and universal units of religious membership have increased in number and strength as village and local forms of religion have declined. But New Religions do not necessarily contradict or oppose traditional religious life; in fact, they often incorporate and renew traditional forms. The relation between the founder of a New Religion and an individual member is often seen as a "parent-child" relationship—the "child" (individual) should be grateful, obedient, and reverent to the "parent" (founder) who provides protection and blessing. In this fashion, traditional Confucian and family values are re-created in the framework of a New Religion.

The "who" of religious organization in Japan traditionally emphasized ordinary social units such as family and village, along with such special religious groups as the informal associations (*ko*) and the nation as a whole. In modern Japan, especially after World War II, New Religions are the most conspicuous and successful means of organizing people for religious purposes.

The Religious World of Space

Previous sections have approached the worldview of Japanese religion through what is worshiped and who does the worshiping; next we examine where the worship takes place, or the religious world of space. In the West, religious space is closely associated with churches and synagogues, since they are dedicated to the worship of God. In Japan there are similar examples of sacred space associated with deities enshrined in religious buildings (such as Shinto shrines and Buddhist temples), but in Japan sacred space is not so strictly limited to specific religious buildings. Space is considered as sacred wherever objects of worship are enshrined or wherever people can come into contact with them. Major locations of sacred space in Japanese religion are the home, village or local sacred sites, regional or special sacred sites, and national sacred sites. All these locations represent sacred space set aside for humans to contact objects of worship. Some of these places of sacred space correspond roughly to the units of society treated in the preceding section. For example, the family was discussed as the basic social and religious unit; correspondingly, the home is a basic location of sacred space.

The traditional home was sacred in the sense that it was built with the aid of religious rituals and continually honored with various rituals. There was a special ritual to consecrate the home site before the building was begun, as well as a special ritual for completion of the house frame, signified by the raising of the ridgepole. Various parts of the traditional house were considered sacred— the threshold, the central pillar, and the kitchen. *Kami* resided in these places, and some larger houses had a special family shrine on the land surrounding the house. Many of these traditional practices have fallen into disuse, but even some New Religions continue practices that honor the sacred character of the home.

Not only original construction, but also specifically religious contents of the home, make it sacred. It has been common for many homes to have both a

A kamidana *(Shinto-style altar) displayed for sale in a Tokyo department store: The price of 69,900 yen was then equivalent to about $300. When purchased, this type of small Shinto shrine is placed on a high shelf in the main room of a home, and* kami *are enshrined (often by means of papers bought at Shinto shrines and placed in the* kamidana*); small offering vessels will be placed on or before the* kamidana *to make offerings of food.*

kamidana (Shinto-style altar) and a *butsudan* (Buddhist-style altar). The *kamidana* helps make the home sacred by enshrining *kami* in the home—these may be the local tutelary *kami*, or the *kami* of more distant shrines, even the Ise Shrine. One means of enshrining *kami* is by making a visit to a shrine and paying a small fee for a special shrine paper with the seal of the shrine and its protective blessing; the paper is placed in the home (sometimes in the *kamidana*) but is usually removed and burned at the New Year, when it is replaced with another. The *butsudan* is doubly sacred because it enshrines Buddhas and ancestors, both of which are objects of worship and sources of blessing. Not only are offerings and rituals performed before the *butsudan*, but also special events in the life of the family are "announced" to the ancestors in front of the *butsudan*.

Traditionally, a number of other aspects of the home have made it sacred, including the seasonal events that center partly around the home. At the New Year, special decorations of evergreens are hung on the house gate; today these are just decorations, but they formerly signified the renewal of life. Twice a year, at the New Year and at the midsummer festival of the dead, spirits of family ancestors make a special visit to the home, and all family members try to be present at this time, which is a happy occasion of homecoming for both the living and the dead.

Thus, the home is built with the aid of rituals, is the location of enshrined objects of worship, and is the site of frequent festivities. More than modern Western homes, the Japanese home defines an important sacred space; it enables the family to come into contact with *kami,* Buddhas, and ancestors. As important as it has been, the home is not sacred in isolation from the rest of the world; rather, the home is reinforced and complemented by other sacred space.

In every area of Japan there are a number of sacred sites outside the home. In the traditional village, two of the key sacred sites are the Shinto shrine of the tutelary *kami* and the Buddhist parish temple. In a small community there may be only one tutelary shrine, whereas in a village there are usually several, each with its own area and its own families. Traditionally, families went to the

A rather ornate butsudan *(Buddhist-style altar) in the home of a man who also serves as a leader of Buddhist services in a rural area. Because this altar is also used for Buddhist worship services, the central figure is a statue of Amida, one of the most important Buddhist divinities. Memorial tables are often placed within the altar, but this family has a separate table for ancestral tablets to the left of the altar (not visible in the picture). The memorial tablet at the left (with four Chinese characters arranged vertically) is a general tablet for spirits of the war dead. A metal vessel for offering incense is in front of the statue; flowers and fruit are offered at the side of the altar. The gilded lotus flowers are an important part of Buddhism, because the lotus grows in mud but rises out of the mud to bloom as a pure white flower; similarly, humans can rise above the mud and filth of the world to bloom as enlightened beings. (Photo courtesy of Dr. Robert J. Smith, Department of Anthropology, Cornell University.)*

tutelary shrine during annual festivals to come into more direct contact with the local tutelary *kami;* often the custom was to bring home a printed shrine paper as the physical symbol of the *kami's* protective blessing. This practice makes clear that the shrine of the tutelary *kami* is a special sacred space in the village able to "charge" the homes of its territory with sacredness through contact with worshipers and distribution of its shrine papers. Families paid visits to the tutelary shrine at crucial junctures in life, as in the first time a child was taken out of the home—it was carried to the tutelary shrine and placed under the protective care of the tutelary *kami.*

The Buddhist parish temple has a double sacred character, somewhat like the *butsudan* in the home, because it enshrines both Buddhas and ancestors. Buddhist statues dominate the altar of a parish Buddhist temple; formal ceremonies are held before the Buddhas, and individuals may revere the Buddhas there from time to time. But from a popular point of view, the sacredness of the parish temple comes mainly from the family ancestors whose ashes are enshrined there. Usually a funeral mass is performed in the parish temple, and memorial observances are carried out both informally in the home and more formally in the parish temple. Since Tokugawa times, cemeteries have been located next to parish temples; these "cemeteries" are actually places for erecting memorial stones (rather than for burying bodies). Family members make annual or more frequent visits to the memorial stones of their ancestors and may offer flowers and incense. These parish temple cemeteries are crowded with people during the late summer festival of the dead; if at all possible, a person will visit the family memorial stone at this time, even if it means traveling hundreds of miles. The two busiest times of travel in Japan are at the New Year and during the late summer festival of the dead, when people leave cities and return to their home villages.

The parish Buddhist temple represents a sacred space somewhat different from that of the tutelary shrine. The parish temple is more closely related to the blessing of ancestors (through a social tie), providing blessings for families that have a hereditary relationship to this temple; the tutelary shrine is more directly related to *kami* of the local scene (through a residential tie), providing protection for homes located within this area. But there is a similarity in the relationship of both parish temple and tutelary shrine to the home: In both cases the space and character of the home are "charged" or reinforced by the power or sacredness of a sacred space outside it. The tutelary shrine makes it possible for a home to enshrine the tutelary *kami* annually. The parish temple helps sanctify the home memorial tablets in two ways: It ritually transforms the dead person into a benevolent ancestor through a funeral mass, and it maintains the blessings of ancestors through enshrining the ashes of the ancestors and performing memorials for them.

Just as the traditional home defined a sacred space of its own, the traditional village marked off a territory with its own sacred space. A village had boundary deities at the major entrance, in effect helping to sanctify and protect the village against any evil force attempting to enter; villagers going on pilgrimage were sent off and welcomed back at this sacred threshold of the village.

The traditional village also included other sacred sites, such as small chapels for specific Buddhas and small shrines for particular *kami*. Around the village there might have been a small waterfall, a hill, or a tree that according to local legend was the scene of some appearance of a *kami* or Buddha and was therefore considered a sacred site. Every village had its own pattern of sacred space made up of these different possibilities. As traditions and villages have changed, many of these practices have been discontinued, but there are still many small sacred spaces, even in contemporary Japanese cities. It is impossible to walk down the side streets of Tokyo without passing many small chapels and shrines. Most of the commuters and shoppers rush by these chapels and shrines, but the presence of fresh offerings indicates that some people continue to pay respects there. And the larger shrines and temples of major cities are thronged on such occasions as the New Year.

There are sacred sites outside both the home and the village (or city neighborhood), in regional or special sacred locations. Some of these are larger versions of the Shinto shrines and Buddhist temples in the local setting, providing special power and protection. For example, large Shinto shrines and Buddhist temples along the seacoast may "specialize" in praying for good fishing, protection on the sea, and repose of the souls of those who have drowned. A large shrine or temple may have a good reputation for providing a particular blessing, and individuals or groups may visit there to obtain that blessing. Several sacred mountains are famous as good places to memorialize ancestors (the spirits of the dead may be memorialized in any number of sacred places); families from several hundred square miles around such a sacred mountain travel there,

A Shinto shrine within the national headquarters of the New Religion Gedatsu-kai; this headquarters is called goreichi, *literally, "sacred land." The woman walking up the path toward the shrine has just purified her hands and mouth with water (at a site to the left of the path, not seen in the photograph) and is passing through the* torii *or sacred archway. She proceeds to the front of the shrine, where she will make an offering of money and bow her head in prayer. This setting is typical of many local Shinto shrines.*

This view from the front of a large Tokyo temple toward the entrance gate in the background shows the number of people who visit such temples. After entering the temple gate, each person follows his or her interest—admiring the old buildings, buying and burning incense (especially for spirits of the dead; note the smoke rising in the upper part of the picture), and entering the temple itself for offerings of money and brief prayers.

sometimes taking a portion of the ashes or an article belonging to the dead person to be part of the memorializing ritual.

Some sacred centers can be considered both regional and national. For example, the headquarters of Buddhist denominations often have a special quality, for a number of reasons: They are the places where founders of the denomination (holy persons) lived and worked, they are rich in history and local tradition, and they are favorite sites for families to memorialize their ancestors. Going to such a headquarters means coming into contact with the power of a holy person as well as the other traditions and the ancestors. Such headquarters are popular places for pilgrimage, especially for families whose parish temple belongs to that headquarters; families or groups of families travel to a headquarters and stay in temple buildings, attending special services honoring ancestors (and possibly participating in other devotional practices). In one respect, memorializing one's ancestor at a headquarters temple can be considered a level above services at the local parish temple and in the home. This makes the headquarters temple like a national center, but it can also be like a regional center if people of the surrounding area go there to come into contact with objects of worship associated with local legend. (The headquarters of New Religions represent another complex example of sacred space: They are sites of nationwide pilgrimage, making them a kind of "national" center, but only for the members of that New Religion.)

On the highest level, the religious organization of space in Japan makes the land itself a kind of sacred space. We have seen that Japan as a nation or political entity is a kind of sacred group of people; here we are looking at Japan as the land and physical space. From ancient times there has been the mythological tradition of the Japanese islands having been created by *kami*, and many local traditions of sacred space dedicated to *kami* are variations of this nationwide theme that Japan is the "land of the *kami*." The hundreds of sacred mountains in Japan, from the majestic Mount Fuji to the hill of the local village, are all examples of the land of Japan being filled with the presence of *kami*. The presence of many Buddhas in Japan is a reinforcement of this theme, for the popular notion is not of imported Buddhas but Buddhas who appeared in particular Japanese locations for the benefit of the local people.

Traditionally, one of the most sacred spots in Japan as a national center has been the Ise Shrine, because it enshrines the Sun Goddess, from whom the imperial line descended. Since medieval times people have made pilgrimages there to come into contact with the power that founded the nation. Several other shrines associated with emperors and traditional notions of the founding of Japan became important during the last hundred years, when Japan developed as a more centralized nation-state.

Another key shrine that has become part of the constitutional controversy over "national" shrines is the Yasukuni Shrine. During the past century, this shrine in Tokyo became the central site for enshrining the spirits of soldiers and sailors who died while on duty. One of the spiritual advantages of being enshrined at the Yasukuni Shrine is that, because these military men died while carrying out their loyalty to the emperor and nation, their spirits are directly associated with the spirits of past emperors. This direct contact with imperial ancestors is not possible for other people in Japanese society. Whatever one thinks about the constitutional issue (which revolves around national financing of a particular religion and the potential for encouragement of militarism), obviously the Yasukuni Shrine is a prime example of "national" sacred space.

The cities of Kyoto and Nara, both former capitals of Japan, also represent sacred space, because they are the places where so much of Japanese history was acted out. These two capitals are full of major shrines and temples and are extremely popular for both pilgrimage and tourism. Many of the shrines and temples are designated by the government as "national treasures" or "important cultural treasures" because of their historic significance, and some state funds are used to finance the restoration and maintenance of the buildings (but not rituals). When Japanese people visit these capitals—whether as individuals, families, or busloads of schoolchildren—even if they do not participate in specific religious ceremonies, they are coming into contact with the national heritage, and this makes the capitals part of the national tradition of sacred space. These two capitals are the best examples, but there are shrines and temples outside Kyoto and Nara designated "national treasures" that also qualify as part of the national organization of religious space.

The "where" of religious organization in Japan is extremely varied, with sacred space in the home and village as well as regional and national space. This is quite different from modern Western countries where sacred space is most often limited to religious buildings. Because sacred space is so widespread in

Japan, the question arises whether all space in Japan is sacred. It would be an exaggeration to say that the entire land space of Japan is sacred, but in contrast to modern Western countries, the religious organization of space in Japan is much more diffuse and expressed in a greater variety of forms. From the local scene of home and village to the larger scene of regional and national sacred centers, living in relation to these sacred spaces helps the Japanese people define their sense of place in the world—in other words, the religious world of space.

The Religious World of Time

The "when" of religious organization is the arrangement of religious events through time in a regular sequence, usually an annual pattern. Every religion has some kind of calendar that it follows to enact through time the religious ideals that it treasures. By acting out these ideals, not only is the message preserved and celebrated, but individuals and the community "realize" the message in their own lives. By participating in the rhythm of the annual celebrations, a person's life is regulated or organized into a meaningful rhythm. The religious world of time is this process of ordering religious events in a repeated annual sequence for all members of a community so that their participation in these events conforms to a set of religious ideals.

In a monotheistic religion like Christianity, the "church year" or "liturgical year" is oriented around the worship of God. In churches emphasizing liturgical worship, such as the Roman Catholic and Episcopal churches, the liturgy is printed in book form (the missal for the Roman Catholic Church and the Book of Common Prayer for the Protestant Episcopal Church) and followed closely in regular worship services. (American Christians also participate in popular festivals of a religious or semireligious nature, such as Memorial Day and Thanksgiving, but ordinarily they do not consider them as part of the church year.)

In Japanese religion, too, the religious organization of time is closely related to objects of worship, especially *kami* and ancestors. But the timing of annual events in Japanese religion presents two sharp contrasts with the liturgical year of Christianity: First, the Japanese religious year is not determined by just one religion but is regulated by several religious traditions; second, the Japanese religious year is more diffuse, corresponding more to the seasons, and depends more on custom and oral tradition than on a single liturgical book. In Japanese there is a general term, *nenju gyoji*, or "annual religious events," that refers to the ceremonies or events observed by all the people of an area on a certain day every year. In traditional Japan the day of an annual event was set apart from ordinary days by particular behavior, such as refraining from work (because in order to participate in the event one had to be "pure"). Every person or family in a traditional village was expected to participate in these annual events. Each village or region had some distinctive festivals or practices (for example, a seaside area would hold an annual harbor festival), but many annual events have been observed throughout Japan. Today some of these events are still held as religious festivals; others are seen more as days of recreation and times for the preparing of special foods.

Before treating the actual festivals, it is necessary to explain some of the general principles of time reckoning in Japan, for there are three kinds of calendars that help determine the dates for festivals. The calendar most Westerners use, the solar calendar of 365 days and twelve months (the Gregorian calendar, which also features a leap year), has been adopted in modern Japan and is used to determine many annual events; for example, by the solar calendar, New Year's Day is January 1. A second form of calendar used in Japan is the lunar calendar, following the twenty-eight-day cycle of the moon. Some festivals are held on the first day of the lunar calendar (the new moon), others, on the fifteenth day of the lunar calendar (the full moon). The lunar calendar begins with the first lunar month of twenty-eight days after the winter solstice. For example, one special New Year celebration was held traditionally on the first full moon following the winter solstice (just as the date of Easter in Christian countries varies each year according to the lunar patterns). The dates of the lunar festivals in Japan will not fall on the same day of the solar calendar every year.

A third form of calendar is the Chinese almanac, which was adopted by the Japanese so long ago that it has become part of Japanese tradition. The Chinese calendar is regulated by the rotation of two interlocking patterns: ten heavenly "stems" and twelve earthly "branches," which form a repeating cycle of sixty units. This is applied especially to days, and each day can be identified by the intersection of a stem and a branch within this sixty-day cycle. This calendar is used to designate some festivals and may also be consulted generally for lucky and unlucky days and for a personal horoscope. (New almanacs are printed every year and bought in large numbers by people who use them to follow festivals, lucky days, and personal fortunes.)

There are so many annual religious events in Japan that it is not possible to mention all of them. In fact, Japanese folklorists write whole books on the annual events of just one region, to record its particular practices. In this brief interpretation we will only highlight some of the major annual events observed throughout Japan, giving their names, dates of celebration, and general significance. We will start with a description of the New Year and then identify other major annual events through the course of a year.

The New Year is one of the most important and most widely celebrated annual events in Japan. As in other cultures, this time marks the end of one year and the beginning of another, but in Japan the celebration spans several weeks. Preparation begins in late December, when people clean their homes to purify them in readiness for the coming of the ancestors; also at the end of December, Shinto shrines perform a "great purification" rite to rid people of impurities and defilements from the previous half year. The New Year itself is very important both for homes and for shrines and temples. After the home is cleaned, a pine branch may be placed on the house gate and a rope made of rice straw hung over the entrance—both indicate renewal and sacred space. Inside the house a special altar (in addition to the *kamidana* and *butsudan*) is set up. In agricultural areas this may be seen as welcoming the rice *kami*; elsewhere it is seen as a welcoming of the ancestors.

People make their first visit of the year to shrines and temples late on New Year's Eve or on New Year's Day, as a lucky way of beginning the year. Huge crowds of people throng the shrines and temples, making small offerings of money and saying prayers for blessing in the coming year. For good measure, a fortune paper can be bought for a small sum, often from a vending machine; the fortune paper may predict good luck, or tell how to avoid bad luck. People also replace some shrine papers in the home at this time, bringing old papers with them to the shrine, throwing them away (often burning them), and buying new ones. The belief is that the old shrine papers have absorbed bad luck and illness during the year, protecting the family against this bad fortune; now they are used up and need to be replaced. There is another celebration called the Little New Year, falling on the first full moon of the new year (about January 15); although technically a separate festival, it is an extension of the New Year festivities. The highlight of this event is a bonfire at night; in some areas this is when old shrine papers and temple papers are burned. Generally this bonfire is a celebration greeting the *kami* of rice and seeking a plentiful and profitable new year.

The significance of this New Year celebration is almost as broad as Japanese religion itself. It is a replacement of impurity with purity. It is also a means by which humans establish a new beginning in harmony with the new beginning of nature. People purify their homes and give a special welcome to ancestors; they visit shrines and temples to come into contact with *kami* and Buddhas in order to start the year with sacredness and power. All these practices and beliefs demonstrate how crucial the New Year is, an excellent start for making human time conform to religious time.

The next annual event we look at is the "change of seasons" celebrated on February 3, considered the last day of winter and the opening of spring. This is another day that has been set aside for the driving out of evil and impurity. The festival has become associated with the throwing of soybeans. When it is celebrated at home, soybeans are thrown out of the house to expel evil and thrown into the house to bring in good luck. It is still a popular festival today, usually held at shrines and temples; children try to gather the soybeans thrown into a crowd as a sign of good luck for the year. This annual event is another means of marking the passage of the seasons, driving out impurities, and seeking good luck.

The doll festival, held March 3, is the second annual event that corresponds to a set of five Chinese festivals borrowed in ancient times and now completely adapted to Japanese customs. The Chinese way of reckoning these festivals is New Year's Day, the third day of the third month (the doll festival), the fifth day of the fifth month (boys' day), the seventh day of the seventh month (the star festival), and the ninth day of the ninth month (the chrysanthemum festival). The New Year celebration in Japan is so elaborate that it extends over a period of days and the Chinese precedent is largely forgotten. The doll festival today is especially for girls, who arrange an elaborate display of dolls in the home.

Nowadays the festival is mainly recreation for girls (and big business for department stores, which sell very expensive dolls), but in earlier times, paper dolls
were used and thrown into streams to carry away the impurities of the people.
The doll festival may once have signified purification, but today it is mainly a
day of relaxation and recreation.

The spring festival for the tutelary *kami* is celebrated according to the
Chinese-style almanac on a day close to the spring equinox in March. People
within the area of a tutelary *kami* pay visits to the tutelary shrine to make offerings and pray for the *kami's* blessing. This annual event signifies the asking of
protection from the tutelary *kami,* but at the same time it is celebrated according
to a seasonal rhythm that links humans and *kami* and home and shrine to the
rhythm of nature.

The spring equinox is associated with Buddhism and ancestors. The term
equinox in Japanese, *higan,* also means "the other shore," referring to both death
and the Buddhist goal of nirvana, or enlightenment. During this time, it is customary for people to return to their hometowns and honor family ancestors with
offerings and visits to memorial stones. This annual event is another in the
series of ceremonies centering on the blessing of ancestors.

The flower festival, falling on April 8, has been associated with various practices. It was widely regarded as the day when mountain *kami* descended, entered the rice fields, and became rice *kami* for the growing season, returning to
the mountains in the fall. People climbed mountains and brought flowers from
the mountain to their homes or rice fields, symbolizing the movement of *kami*
(which were also associated with ancestral spirits). People still celebrate this day
by having picnics on nearby mountains or hills and picking wild flowers. This
festival signifies the coming of spring and the bounty of nature, which in this
case is associated both with local *kami* and the blessings of ancestors. (April 8
is also the day the Japanese observe as the birthday of the historical Buddha,
and temples perform a special ritual pouring sweet tea over a small statue of the
infant Buddha.)

Boys' day, on May 5, is the third in the set of five Chinese festivals. The
earlier purpose of this summer festival may have been to drive away evil spirits
with dolls dressed as soldiers and placed outside the house gate. Later, the festival became more of a celebration of the growth and strength of boys, who
arranged a display of miniature warriors in the home. Like the doll festival on
March 3, boys' day has become mainly a form of recreation for children, and the
miniature warriors that boys display may be just as expensive as the dolls
bought by girls for the doll festival. A distinctive decoration of boys' day is a cloth
streamer fashioned in the shape of a carp and hung from a pole to wave in the
wind. Carp are symbolic of strength and vitality, and parents exhibit the streamers
to celebrate and encourage strength in young boys.

The "great purification" falls on June 30, in a month full of other observances
emphasizing avoidance of impurities. The "great purification" is performed at local
tutelary shrines, with the purpose of destroying all the impurities the people of
the shrine's area have accumulated since New Year's Day. Sometimes people
take to the shrine a simple paper doll that they have rubbed against their bodies,

thus symbolizing the transfer of impurities to the doll, which is left at the tutelary shrine and disposed of by Shinto priests. This "great purification" ceremony complements the similar ceremony at year's end (preparing for the New Year)—both are means of periodically purifying life and bringing it into harmony with the sacredness of *kami* generally, especially the tutelary *kami*.

The star festival is held July 7, another in the set of five Chinese festivals. It is called the star festival because, according to tradition, a weaver and her lover became stars and are able to meet only on this day. Traditionally, people celebrated this annual meeting of the stars representing the lovers by writing poems on colored papers and hanging them from bamboo poles. One of the benefits prayed for was greater facility in writing and crafts. In modern times some cities have made the star festival a major commercial undertaking, with entire city blocks elaborately decorated. Stores compete with one another to exhibit the largest and prettiest decorations in the streets in front of the stores. This festival, like others, has become more recreation and relaxation than religious ritual.

The festival of the dead, celebrated in mid-July (or later in the summer), is seen as a Buddhist event, but it is related completely to the ancestors. Spirits of the ancestors are welcomed in the home with special offerings. Families visit the memorial stones for ancestors and clean the area, often pouring water over the memorial stone. At this time of the year, the family may also pay a Buddhist priest to come to the home and recite a Buddhist scripture in front of the *butsudan*. Villages or city neighborhoods may arrange folk dances with a small musical group as a communal way of welcoming the presence of the ancestors. In traditional times there were colorful practices of greeting and sending off the ancestors, such as building small fires outside the gate to the house. The significance of the festival of the dead is greater than can be indicated in this brief description—in terms of the annual round of events, it is comparable in importance to the New Year, because it is the most important occasion for honoring the family ancestors.

The chrysanthemum festival falls on September 9. By Chinese reckoning this is the auspicious time of the ninth day of the ninth month; at present this "festival" is observed in Japan mainly as a viewing of specially grown chrysanthemums.

The fall festival for the tutelary *kami* is the counterpart of the spring festival for the tutelary *kami;* the fall festival is held according to the Chinese almanac on a day close to the fall equinox in September. The fall practices mirror those in spring; people of a given area visit the shrine of their tutelary *kami* with simple offerings and prayers. The fall festival again signifies asking protection from the tutelary *kami* and keeping in harmony people and nature, home and shrine. During the fall there are also many rituals marking the harvest of rice, usually a kind of thanksgiving ceremony. Harvest festivals are performed according to the lunar calendar but vary considerably due to the difference in climate from north to south and the ripening of rice from about August to November. Traditionally, this is the time when the *kami* of the rice fields return to the mountains, becoming the mountain *kami* once more; this balances the flower festival of April 8.

A child uses a dipper to splash water on a statue of Jizo, a Buddhist divinity. This statue is next to a cemetery; during the festival of the dead in late summer, families visit cemeteries to make offerings and burn incense at family memorial stones (note the smoke above the head of the small girl). Pouring water over memorial stones or splashing water on a Buddhist statue is a means of purifying the spirits of the dead or honoring a Buddhist divinity.

The fall *higan,* or "equinox," is celebrated for a week at the time of the fall equinox. During this counterpart of the spring equinox, people again visit family memorial stones and honor their ancestors. The significance of the fall *higan,* as of the spring, is to honor the ancestors and receive their blessings.

December ends the year with the preparation for the New Year, as has been indicated, with the celebration of the great purification that takes care of impurities accumulated from June 30 to the end of the year. This brings to a close the year's major annual religious events.[6]

The "when" of religious organization in Japan is a sequence of rituals and festivals that is repeated in the same fashion year after year. The strength of repetition in religion lies in its reinforcement of the power of the sacred model that it imitates. Just as the liturgical year of a Roman Catholic or Episcopal church repeats the same ritual pattern annually, drawing on the power of God, so the rhythm of annual events in Japan draws on the power of *kami,* Buddhas, and ancestors. The most important ritual events are emphasized by their being represented twice in the annual round. Major purification rituals come at year's end and mid-year. Ancestors are prominent in the home at the New Year and during the festival for the dead; formal respects are also paid to them during the spring and fall equinox celebrations. The tutelary *kami* is visited especially during spring and fall. Agricultural rhythms of spring and fall balance planting and harvesting with welcoming and sending off the mountain *kami* and rice field *kami.* Japanese religion organizes time in a regular schedule of events, so that human time can correspond to sacred time.

The religious ideals of living in close relation to *kami,* Buddhas, and ancestors are realized in the lives of people by acting out these ideals through the passage of time. This orderly pattern of annual events creates a religious world of time according to which people can regulate their lives with assurance of power and blessing. [See Religions of Mesoamerica pp. 159–60, 206–9, Native Religions of North America pp. 280–82, 351–54, Judaism pp. 431–33, Christianity pp. 551–53, Islam pp. 674, 707, Hinduism pp. 727, 793–94, Buddhism pp. 890–91, and Religions of China pp. 1021–24 for discussion of religious calendar and time.]

The Religious World of Human Life

The "how" of the religious world is the way in which religion is related to the course of human life. A person is born, matures, and dies, passing through a series of biological stages; but religion helps organize life into successive steps in the realization of a meaningful career. This career roughly follows biological states, but religious rituals have their own way of defining the stages and adding meaning to them. In the previous section, we viewed the religious organization of time as a series of annual events repeated in the span of a year for all or most people. Now we look at the religious organization of human activities as the cycle of life followed by an individual. One means of tracing the life cycle in any culture is to describe the religious rituals and observances that occur from birth to death—"from cradle to grave." After tracing the life cycle, other religious practices that an individual may use to enhance his or her spiritual experience will be mentioned. [See Religions of Africa pp. 42–51, 76–79, Religions of Mesoamerica pp. 201–6, Native Religions of North America pp. 278–79, 295–98, 306–8, Judaism pp. 445–50, Christianity pp. 542–43, 555–57, Islam pp. 677–78, 680–86, Hinduism pp. 747, 807–14, Buddhism pp. 915–17, 921, 931–37, and Religions of China pp. 1019–21 for description and discussion of rites of passage.]

In traditional Japan there were many rituals related to the life cycle, not all of which are practiced today. In modern Japan some religious and semireligious customs have come to be practiced in addition to, or replacing, the traditional rituals. In this brief overview we will cite some of the more important traditional rituals as well as some more recent customs, indicating the life stage, the practices associated with it, and its religious significance.

The first life stage is birth, which, in Japan, as in most cultures, is associated with various rituals. In traditional Japan there were many taboos or avoidances associated with birth, which was considered impure partly because of the blood involved. In former times a woman even gave birth and lived for a short while with her newborn child in a special isolation hut built for this purpose; it was important for the new mother to cook her food on a separate fire in order not to defile the rest of the family. Such practices have long since disappeared in Japan, but some traces remain (as seen below in the infant's first trip outside of the home).

When a child is born, it is given a soul or spirit by a birth *kami*, which once was considered separate from the tutelary *kami* but today is thought to be the same. A month after birth the taboos associated with birth end; in other words, the child is free from birth impurities and is taken by its parents to the shrine of the tutelary *kami*. Traditionally, the infant's first trip outside the home was when it was carried to the shrine of the tutelary *kami*. (This trip is comparable to christening in a Christian setting.) The traditional interpretation of the baby being presented to the tutelary *kami* is that the baby is (or becomes) the child of the tutelary *kami*. The individual has a special relationship to the tutelary *kami*: He or she should, for example, participate in the annual festivals at the tutelary shrine. This individual worships at the shrine of the tutelary *kami*, who protects him or her. Birth rituals usher the infant into life by affirming the source of life as the *kami* and by establishing a relationship between child and *kami*.

As medical facilities have advanced and birth takes place in modern hospitals, many of the traditions surrounding birth have disappeared. But some traditional practices survive even in a modern hospital. For example, there is a rich folklore related to the umbilical cord, which was preserved at birth and treasured. Later in life the cord was used to help a person recover from sickness. In some regions it was buried with the mother who bore the child, or it could be buried with the person to whom it belonged. Some modern hospitals still save the umbilical cord for parents; when my son was born in Japan in 1963, the hospital presented us with his umbilical cord in a camphor wood box. [See Religions of Africa pp. 45–46, 76, Native Religions of North America p. 307, Judaism pp. 385–86, 445–46, Christianity p. 556, Islam p. 682, Hinduism pp. 810–11, Buddhism p. 932, and Religions of China p. 1019–20 for description and discussion of birth rites.]

The family has special celebrations for the child associated both with the growth of the child and the child's entrance into annual events. On the first birthday, there is a special celebration. Also, there is a special celebration for the child's first participation in the doll festival (for girls) or in the boys' festival. A particular festival observed for children of both sexes occurs in the third, fifth, and seventh years: Girls participate at ages three and seven, boys only at age five. This annual festival is held November 15 and is named Shichigosan, literally, "seven-five-three," after the ages of children attending the festival. Children dress up in their finest clothes and visit their tutelary shrine. The purpose of these visits is to pray to the tutelary *kami* to protect them as they grow and mature. In other words, growth is not simply a biological matter but a process nurtured and protected by *kami* and other spiritual powers.

There are a number of rites that traditionally marked the passage of children into the status of young men and women or, later, adults. In some areas young men had their own associations, which they entered in their teens and left at marriage. Such associations have disappeared, but even today the point at which a young man first participates in a local festival, especially in the carrying of a portable altar around the shrine's territory, is a kind of "coming of age" event. In traditional Japan there was a collective ritual for teenage boys marking their adolescence with the granting of a loincloth. Adolescence for girls was celebrated individually after the first menstruation, marked by the granting of an underskirt. Such practices, which feature religious and social recognition of growth and sexual maturity, are no longer observed.

Today there is a national holiday on January 15, an official coming of age for all young men and women who will become twenty years old during that year. The present practice has a legal aspect, since these young people are now adults and can marry without parental consent. Another modern style of initiation is the ceremony admitting young people into the employment of a large company, or becoming the "child" of the company (comparable to becoming the child of the tutelary *kami*)—which includes formalities similar to adoption into a family.

A special religious aid for coping with life in modern Japan is the custom of praying at certain Shinto shrines famous for help in passing college entrance examinations. Before and at the time of examination, both mothers of students and the young people taking the examination may visit such shrines. Getting into a good university is crucial for securing a prestigious job, arranging a favorable marriage, and generally doing well in life, so the applicant can use all the help he or she can get. Of course the student must study hard, but this is an extra step to help one pass exams and be accepted into a university. This is a good illustration of how new rites arise even as old ones die out.

Marriages traditionally occurred in the home, and the crucial ceremony was the ritual exchange of *sake* (rice wine) between the bride and groom. Every locale had its own set of wedding customs. In many cases, the marriage was held in front of the *butsudan,* or at least the marriage was announced to the ancestors in the *butsudan.* No priest was needed for this traditional wedding, which was essentially an agreement between families. In recent times, weddings have become more formal and more expensive. During the past century there has arisen the custom of "marriage before the *kami,*" in other words, a marriage in a Shinto shrine. Some large shrines with beautiful grounds are popular as wedding sites and make considerable money from this business. Commercial wedding halls are also rented for this purpose. Very formal dress is required for weddings, either formal Japanese dress (kimono) or maybe a tuxedo for the groom and a Western-style wedding dress for the bride. "Christian"-style weddings have had considerable influence in Japan, even though very few Japanese are members of Christian churches. A marriage obviously is a ritual joining two lives, but in Japan this has meant even more—the joining of two families. Some traditional practices have largely passed away, taken over by the new customs developed at Shinto shrines and even commercial wedding halls. This is symptomatic of some of the secular tendencies in modern Japan. But tradition lives on, and the Chinese almanac is still a factor in determining a favorable day for a wedding. [See Religions of Africa pp. 48–51, 77–78, Judaism pp. 447–48, Christianity p. 556, Islam pp. 683–84, Hinduism pp. 809–10, Buddhism p. 935, and Religions of China p. 1020 for description and discussion of marriage rites.]

As a person grows older, there are specific years of danger and years of celebration. Every person can consult the almanac to watch for times of good luck and bad luck, but the most dangerous age for men is forty-two, for women, thirty-three. During this year of life a person should take pains to avoid any evil forces and, to counteract danger, should participate more actively in shrine festivals. Two years celebrated as auspicious are the sixty-first, since it begins the first year after a sixty-year cycle (according to the traditional almanac), and the seventieth, seen as a rare achievement. These notions reinforce the general understanding that life is not a simple biological continuity but has its bad times and good times. The almanac and related practices help the individual minimize or avoid bad times and maximize good times.

Rites for the dead are the last stage in this cradle-to-grave cycle, but in Japan the afterlife is more complicated than it is in Western countries. As we have seen in the treatment of ancestors, a person has a long "career" even after death, beginning with the funeral ceremony. In traditional times, there were many customs involved with the preparation of the body for the funeral; the general notion is that the soul leaves the body at death and must be prepared for the next world. For example, it was customary to place a bowl of rice by the body to help sustain the person in the next life and a sharp instrument to protect the person against evil spirits. In village settings members of the village cooperated to help prepare the body for the funeral, including washing the body, clothing it in white, and placing it in a coffin. The corpse is considered impure, and these preparatory acts, as well as the funeral and memorial rites, are intended to purify the body. The funeral service is conducted by Buddhist priests, who recite Buddhist scriptures, after which all accompany the body to the burial ground or crematorium. In modern times many of the preparations tend to be handled by an undertaker. As with weddings, the almanac is consulted for a favorable day for a funeral.

The general principles and practices for the transformation of the spirit of the dead person into an ancestor continue today, with some variations, depending on the Buddhist sect with which the person's family is affiliated. Usually the Buddhist posthumous name is granted by a Buddhist priest at the time of the funeral and written on a temporary memorial tablet, which is taken home from the funeral and set up in front of the *butsudan*. For forty-nine days, the family is in mourning, and it was formerly the custom for families not to visit or interact with other families during this time of mourning and taboo. (The forty-nine days also correspond to the time some Buddhist texts claim is required for a person to travel through purgatory.) The forty-ninth day signifies the completion of the purification of the dead person and his or her transformation into an ancestral spirit. At that time the temporary memorial tablet is removed, and a permanent memorial tablet is placed in the *butsudan*. Thereafter, memorial masses are held on the first anniversary of death and at regular intervals, especially on the annual anniversary of the death day, often ending with the thirty-third anniversary. The final memorial mass for the ancestor is significant, because it marks the end of the individual identity of the ancestral spirit; it then joins the "generations of ancestors."

The general belief is that as ancestral spirits lose their individual identity they merge with the ancestral *kami* of the family. In fact, it is felt that this vague group of ancestral family *kami* is responsible for birth, and an ancestral spirit may be reborn in the form of a baby born to the family. Japanese death rituals have much in common with death rituals throughout the world, which ease the transition from death and impurity to a new life. What is distinctive about the Japanese practice is the rather prolonged series of rituals after death and the strong association of spirits of the dead with the benefit of the ongoing family. It is interesting to note that death rituals actually circle back to birth, showing how the life cycle is complete and repeats itself in the career of individuals. [See Religions of Africa pp. 42–45, 78–79, Religions of Mesoamerica p. 144, Native Religions of North America pp. 300–301, 307–8, 335–37, Judaism pp. 448–50, Christianity p. 557, Islam pp. 684–85, Hinduism pp. 813–14, Buddhism pp. 935–37, and Religions of China pp. 1021, 1041–44 for description and discussion of death and funeral rites.]

Just as the series of annual events is repeated on a yearly basis in the lives of all people, so the cycle is repeated for each individual through the life span. A person learns this cycle of life not by formal teachings, but by observing other people pass through ritual events such as birth, marriage, and death; at the same time, a person is living out his or her career by passing through these life stages and rituals as they appear. In this fashion, the religious organization of life provides a spiritual blueprint by which people can plan and act out their lives in the attempt to fulfill the religious ideal: In Japan the ideal is to live a full and meaningful life in relation to *kami* and Buddhas, eventually becoming an ancestor and even a form of *kami*.

In addition to the rhythmic pattern of rituals from cradle to grave, there are many religious activities in which an individual can participate as an individual, rather than as part of a group. We have seen that usually the individual participates in religion through social groups such as the family, village, and nation. But as an individual a person has various other alternatives. One possibility already mentioned is the almanac, which includes predictions for individuals based on such personal variables as birth date. Also, anyone who experiences a personal problem may consult a fortune-teller or buy a fortune paper at a shrine or temple. As in Western countries, often horoscopes and fortune-telling are criticized as "superstitious" and joked about, but their popularity (and the abundance of printed material throughout the world) demonstrates the conscious and unconscious importance of such beliefs. Many traditional beliefs continue in modern Japan and influence individuals in their daily lives.

Some individual practices might be considered devotional, such as recitation of a devotional phrase (the *nembutsu*, for example, taking refuge in Amida). A family member may participate in simple offerings and prayers before the *butsudan*, but many also recite a part of a Buddhist scripture individually as a personal devotion before the *butsudan*. Most of the beliefs and practices of Japanese religion described in this chapter have to do with collective activity, but there is also room for individual conscience and action. Anyone who feels that he or she has done something wrong may go to a shrine, such as the tutelary shrine, to apologize to the tutelary *kami*, or pay a visit to a temple and recite a simple repentance. A typical case is when the individual feels "unfilial"—lacking in reverence to parents and ancestors—or thinks he or she is the cause of disharmony in the family. In this case a person may "apologize," or repent. A stronger form of this practice is the "hundredfold" repentance, called in Japanese *ohyakudo,* literally, "a hundred times." Some shrines and temples have a set of two stone markers for practicing this form of repentance within their precincts, and the conscience-stricken individual walks back and forth a hundred times between the two stones (usually barefoot) reciting a phrase of repentance.

More rigorous forms of practice depend on the individual's degree of religious commitment and the seriousness of the religious request. For example, a common means of intensifying religious commitment has been to make a pilgrimage to a sacred center, such as the Ise Shrine, or a regional sacred center. During World War II, one or both parents might have fulfilled a vow to visit a hundred shrines as a prayer of protection for a son in the war. Even today, people who wish to deepen their spiritual life may make a personal vow to visit a local shrine or temple a certain number of times, usually for early morning prayers. The individual gets up early (in traditional times the person might take a cold water shower as an ascetic practice to show strength of purpose), goes to the nearby shrine and says a simple prayer, and returns home or goes to work.

One of the common ways of advancing spiritually is to "study" religion, meaning to read popular books about Buddhism or Buddhist scriptures or to read explanations of doctrine distributed by denominations or New Religions. Popular books on religion sell very well in Japanese bookstores, and it is no accident that many New Religions got their start through publishing and still maintain sophisticated publishing facilities.

Another form of individual practice is meditation. Usually meditation is practiced in a group; it is rare for a person to leave home and become a Zen monk or nun meditating full-time. But even New Religions have simple techniques for meditation—sitting quietly in a formal posture and purifying the mind while thinking of one's own defects and concentrating on an object of worship. Usually these techniques are practiced in joint meetings, but they may be repeated at home individually, as part of daily devotions. [See Judaism pp. 422–27, Christianity pp. 500, 507, 519, Islam pp. 659–62, Hinduism pp. 752–53, Buddhism pp. 946–48, and Religions of China pp. 1032–34 for discussion of meditation and mysticism.]

These two means of organizing religious life—from cradle to grave, and by individual practice—show how Japanese religion is related to the flow of the human career and the meeting of personal problems. Life is more than mere biological development, it is the acting out of a drama of spiritual fulfillment with roles played by both human beings and objects of worship. A person is able to chart where he or she is in the life cycle by participating in the rituals for other people and by checking off his or her own ritual landmarks through life. If a particular problem arises, there are beliefs and practices to correct one's mistakes and deepen one's spirituality. All these practices—both the cycle from cradle to grave, and individual devotions—help an individual construct his or her own religious world of human life as a plan for spiritual fulfillment.

We have now viewed representative aspects and examples of the smaller "worlds" of Japanese religion, looking first at four kinds of objects of worship, and then surveying the religious significance of society, space, time, and human life. This selective treatment is intended to provide an interpretation of the nature of Japanese religion as a unified worldview. Each of these smaller worlds represents a unity of one aspect of religion and one dimension of religious practice. All these subworlds or smaller worlds of religion and dimensions of religious practice contribute to the total religious worldview in Japan, what we have called "one sacred way." This sacred way is not just a particular place or a specific building or an organized institution—it is the total understanding of the universe and how a human career can be lived meaningfully within it. Each "world" brings into order one aspect of this worldview or universe of meaning. These worlds are not separate entities but interlocking parts of this sacred way that is the implicit religious system at the heart of Japanese religious life.

49

The Dynamics of Japanese Religion

IN THIS CHAPTER Japanese religion will be presented more concretely and specifically. The previous chapters have provided overviews that help us better understand the Japanese religious heritage as a whole. Unfortunately, such generalizations may leave the false impression that Japanese religion is a dry historical framework or an abstract system. However, any religious tradition is much more than its recorded historical development or its implied systematic organization. When people actually participate in and experience religion, it is rich in detail and drama. Even as an "outsider" to Japanese religion, I have always been fascinated by and caught up in the human and spiritual drama of the festivals I have observed and the lives of people who have talked to me about their experiences. In previous chapters it has only been possible to give brief examples and illustrations that hint at the vitality of Japanese religion as it is acted out in actual lives and concrete events. The present chapter focuses on this concrete aspect—the "dynamics" of Japanese religion as it is acted out and experienced by Japanese people.

Two examples of religious dynamics that I have studied personally have been selected for description and discussion. From more than thirty years of studying Japanese religion, these examples stand out as interesting documents of important aspects of religious life today. The first is a village festival celebrating this rural community's religious welcoming of spring. The second is the life history of a Tokyo man who is a member of a New Religion. These examples cover much of the range of Japanese religion, from village to metropolis, from performance of a traditional festival to participation in a New Religion. Each example will be introduced briefly, described at greater length, and then interpreted in the context of Japanese religion as a whole.

The Spring Mountain Festival

Village festivals, in which all or most of the community participate, have been some of the most important annual events for the Japanese during the past few hundred years. These festivals are still held in some regions, even though their contemporary form is modified and shortened. One example of such a village festival is the *haruyama*, or "spring mountain," festival carried out by the people in the village of Toge in Yamagata Prefecture (in northeastern Honshu, facing the Sea of Japan). During the celebration of spring mountain, representatives of the village climb nearby mountains and symbolically welcome spring by bringing the mountain *kami* down to bless rice fields and homes.

Some knowledge about the village and local customs is necessary for understanding the festival. In the area around Toge are three sacred mountains—Haguro, Gassan,[7] and Yudono (see Gassan on map on p. 1081). Each mountain was believed to be the sacred abode of a mountain *kami* and a counterpart Buddhist divinity. (For Gassan the counterpart Buddha is Amida.) From Tokugawa times (1600–1867) these three mountains were considered a triad of sacred mountains for gaining power through Buddhist ascetic practices. Before and during the Tokugawa period, there were hundreds of sacred mountains throughout Japan where the priests of Shugendo groups gained their training and exercised their spiritual powers. Shugendo is the general name for the "mountain religion" emphasizing pilgrimage to mountains and ascetic retreats within mountains, treating the sacredness of the mountains from a combined perspective of Shinto notions of *kami* dwelling on mountains, Buddhist notions of Buddhist divinities manifested on mountains, and Daoist notions of mystical practice on mountains. Haguro, Gassan, and Yudono were known as the three sacred mountains of Shugendo in Dewa, the traditional name for this area of northern Honshu.

These mountains defined an important area of sacred space; there was a great deal of religious activity both on the mountains and between the mountains and the people of the surrounding area. Shugendo priests gained their powers while training at mountain headquarters and renewed these powers in ascetic practices on the mountains every year. Priests left the mountains during parts of the year to travel through specified territories to minister to the religious needs of the people, providing prayers and rituals of all kinds, especially healing rites. People from hundreds of square miles around made pilgrimages to these mountains, especially during the summer. [See Religions of Mesoamerica pp. 226–33, Judaism pp. 469–70, Christianity pp. 562–73, Islam pp. 645–47, Hinduism pp. 815–20, Buddhism p. 874, and Religions of China pp. 1041–44, for description and discussion of pilgrimage.]

Toge has been a very important village in the practice of Shugendo at these three sacred mountains, as seen in the fact that the village once was the location of many of the combination lodging houses and temples to which Shugendo priests guided pilgrims on their way to these sacred mountains. The geographical location and name of the village at the foot of Mount Haguro are also clues to its religious significance. The name Toge is a variation of the word for "mountain pass," and in Japanese folk belief a mountain pass was considered an opening from the ordinary world into the special area of the sacred mountains. The village of Toge still retains traditional practices related to Shugendo and these sacred mountains.

Toge is a relatively small village with several hundred families. It is a farming village large enough to have its own small shops, post office, and school system up through grade school. Growing rice and other agricultural products was traditionally the most important economic activity. In more recent times there has been some logging around the mountains, but there is still no major industry. In Toge, as in all areas of Japan, farming has become less important than industrial production and services. Increasingly, young people have been drawn to work outside the community. The major nearby city is Tsuruoka, which has its own high school and also railway connections; there is regular bus service between Toge and Tsuruoka.

Toge has experienced the general shift of young people from farms to industrialized cities, but its own traditions and customs have not been so severely undermined as those in the more urbanized and industrialized areas. Toge is true to its rural setting by being relatively more traditional and conservative than urban Japan. Neither Christianity nor the New Religions have won many members in Toge, which is an indication of the cohesiveness of the traditional practices in the village. The spring mountain festival is one of these traditional practices; it is described as I observed it in 1964.[8]

The spring mountain celebration is a spring festival performed by male representatives of Toge at the foot of Mount Haguro. The actual festival consists of two representatives (or proxies) from each of the eight *buraku,* or subdivisions, of Toge climbing Gassan (and perhaps making a round of the three sacred mountains) and bringing back to their respective *buraku* some mountain plants. The spring mountain ritual was performed on May 3, 4, and 5 in 1964: Preparations were made on the third, Gassan was climbed on the fourth, and the official return to the village was on the fifth. (The date is actually determined by the "eighty-eighth night"—or the day after the beginning of spring according to the lunar calendar.) Early on the morning of May 3, the two men from each of the eight *buraku* who were proxies for that year's festival climbed from Toge, via a stone staircase, several miles to the Dewa Shrine at the summit of Mount Haguro. While climbing to the mountaintop shrine, respect was paid at the various smaller shrines along the way, by a nod of the head and clap of hands. Wearing the Shinto-style white surplices around their necks, they entered Dewa Shrine and were led in a simple prayer by a Shinto priest, after which they all received a small drink of *sake* from another Shinto priest. Then they met in a separate room and discussed the practical plans for carrying out the spring mountain ritual. Since this was a village function, it was planned and carried out completely by the villagers and their *buraku* proxies.

On this morning, the villagers made some arrangements for lodging at the shrine's building, called Saikan ("Purification Hall"), the night of May 4 and decided to hire two trucks to take everyone as far as the "sixth station" of Gassan. In earlier times it was the custom to walk to Gassan, but with the coming of modern transportation, all forms of pilgrimage have changed drastically. The notion of "stations" requires further explanation. The route for climbing many Japanese mountains, including Fuji, came to be divided into ten "stations," each station usually marked by a shrine or holy site. Probably this symbolism came from the Buddhist scheme of ten stages between hell and heaven; climbing a sacred mountain is analogous to traveling from hell to heaven, from profane to sacred.

After all the arrangements were completed at Dewa Shrine, tiny cups of sacred *sake* were passed around for a toast before the meeting broke up. Then everyone descended the stone staircase to Toge. On the way to Toge, the *buraku* proxies left the stone pathway and picked leaves of the evergreen camellia for members of their *buraku*. Camellia, they say, is about the same as Shinto's sacred plant *sakaki*, also an evergreen plant. In this case, taking the camellia leaves to the village represents the symbolic descent of the mountain *kami* to the village or rice field. This is a change from the pre–World War II practice of picking plants during the actual climb of Gassan. After World War II, a large tract of land including most of the three mountains was made into a national park. The rules of the national park prohibit the removal of any plants or animals, thus making it impossible to bring back these plants from Gassan during the pilgrimage.

This morning trip took only several hours, and it was 9:30 A.M. when they returned to Toge. At this point the proxies went to their homes and awaited the truck ride to Gassan early the next morning. During the morning's activities, and throughout the spring mountain festival, these men obviously enjoyed themselves. They appreciated the break from their regular work, and as they climbed and descended the stone staircase, they chatted and joked with their friends. For special ceremonies, such as receiving *sake* from the Shinto shrine priest, they were quiet and attentive. But at no point were the participants solemn or long-faced.

A clue to the whole ceremony of spring mountain is found in the name that all the proxies share. They are called *gyonin,* a word similar to *gyoja,* or "ascetic," which means that they are carrying out a special religious duty. Formerly there were more severe restrictions for these "ascetics," but even today they should observe religious abstinence. This means at least abstaining from meat and not cohabiting with one's wife during the time of the festival, including the preparation period preceding the festival. The white clothes traditionally worn by each ascetic, as well as the small white surplice, indicate the purity of his religious task.

On the morning of May 4, everyone gathered at 4:30 for the truck ride to Gassan. Men other than the proxies could participate voluntarily. A number of voluntary participants, an official ranger of the national park (at the same time a member of the seventh *buraku*), and I increased the number of proxies from sixteen to just over thirty people. We crowded into the two small trucks headed for Gassan, passed the road leading to the summit of Mount Haguro, but did not stop at Dewa Shrine. The first stop was made about 5:00 at a small wayside shrine. This spot is called Daiman, technically the second station of Gassan. Everyone got out of the truck and gathered around the shrine to recite a simple prayer of purification. We then got back into the trucks, which began the rather steep ascent of Gassan. Already the remains of snowdrifts were visible in the valleys. Because we traveled by truck on the recently developed road, we did not visit the sites of the third, fourth, and fifth stations.

At 5:30 A.M. the trucks reached the end of the road, the sixth station. At this point we left the trucks for the climb on foot, amid deeper drifts of snow. About 6:15 the seventh station was reached after climbing up through brush and snow. The sixth station had seemed to be past the tree line, and by the seventh station, there were no trees at all. The seventh station was marked simply by piles of brush, with no sign of a shrine. After a well-deserved rest, we proceeded.

At about 6:45 we reached the eighth station. From the seventh to the eighth station a number of interesting sights appeared. The proxies passed some statues of Jizo and memorial stones in an area of the pilgrimage path called Sainokawara. Sainokawara is an important feature of the "otherworld" tradition at various sacred mountains, representing the boundary that dead spirits must cross to reach paradise. Jizo is well known as the Buddhist savior of the dead. People of the surrounding region often dedicate memorial stones here for family ancestors, and pilgrims usually place rocks on these piles when they pass, as an act of devotion and to help spirits of the dead accumulate merit in the next life. From this point on, there were memorial stones and many rock piles built up by generations of passing pilgrims. But the proxies passed this area without stopping, until we reached the eighth station, also known as Midagahara, the plain of **Mida** (the Buddhist divinity Amida). The prayer of purification was repeated at a small wooden shrine here, which is protected from wind and snow by eight-foot stone walls. Then breakfast was eaten, topped off with tea from a skier's hut.

Even from the seventh station, the scenery had been quite beautiful, with a view to the north of Mount Chokai, the highest mountain in northeastern Honshu. Other mountains, such as the famous skiing mountain Zao to the east, came into view near the summit of Gassan. From below the eighth station skiers were seen. Gassan is one of the mountains famous for late spring skiing, but of course skiing is a modern innovation that disregards the religious ceremony called "mountain opening." Traditionally, priests stayed on the mountain only during the summer pilgrimage season (because Gassan is uninhabitable in winter); these priests ceremonially "opened" the mountain to pilgrims when they entered the mountain in spring, and it was understood that people should not climb the mountain before the official opening.

From the seventh station on the climbing had become more difficult, and since the distance between the eighth and ninth stations is extraordinarily great, a rest was called in the snow at about 7:45. At 8:10 the ninth station was reached. Here there is a small shrine next to Bussho Pond, literally, "the pond where Buddhas live." The reference to Buddhas may mean *hotoke,* dead people who have become Buddhas, and surrounding the pond are various memorial stones. It is said that people bring cremation ashes here. Midway between the ninth station and the summit another rest was taken at 8:30, and at 9:00 we reached the summit of Gassan.

At the very summit is the tenth station, Gassan Shrine, entirely surrounded by an eight-foot wall of stone. Even though it was early May, heavy ice was on the nearby bushes. The proxies and others gathered inside the stone enclosure before the small shrine. As the prayer of purification was repeated, several

Some of the proxies worshiping at the shrine on the summit of Gassan, the tenth station. This photograph, taken from atop the eight-foot wall of stone, shows the corner of the shrine roof at the top.

bottles of *sake* brought along were offered and candles were lit. Later I was told that one feature of this ceremony was to divine the next year's crop or fortune by whether or not the candles stayed lit or went out during the recitation of the prayer.

If there is bad weather during the celebration of spring mountain, the proxies go directly from the tenth station of Gassan to Dewa Shrine on Mount Haguro. However, in 1964 the weather was remarkably clear, so the group of sixteen proxies, several voluntary participants, and I made a side trip from Gassan to Yudono. Because there was little time, we set out at once, making a very rapid descent down the steep slopes of snow—part of the time "skiing" down on our heels. One steep cliff was traversed by means of a steel ladder. Eventually the group reached its destination, a hot spring on the slopes of Mount Yudono.

The main object of worship here, a natural formation of outcropping rock, resembles the torso of a nude woman. It is stained red by the hot springs that gush forth even in winter. Again the participants gathered, facing the stone, to recite the simple prayer of purification. While resting and eating, various people drank the hot spring water, supposedly a healing cure, even though it had the characteristic "rotten egg" odor of hydrogen sulfide. Others dipped the tip of their white surplice in the water, or soaked their feet by standing in the running hot water. (Since they were wearing straw sandals, the water passed right through and warmed their feet.) Several bottles were filled with the spring water to take home. Some of the men paid respects to their ancestors' spirits in a spot still hidden in the snow, next to the object of worship.

The ascent from Yudono back to the summit of Gassan was quite arduous and slow. The height of Gassan is 1,980 meters (about 6,494 feet); the height of Yudono is 1,504 meters (about 4,933 feet). Since the shrine at Yudono is below the summit, this meant a rather sharp ascent of more than fifteen hundred feet up slippery snow. Finally the summit of Gassan was reached at about 1:30 P.M., and everyone was congratulated with sacred *sake*—sacred because it had been ceremoniously offered to the *kami* during the earlier prayer at Gassan Shrine. Before 2:00 the quick descent of Gassan started, following the same pilgrimage path as the ascent. Only one rest was taken, about 3:00, at the eighth station, and there was no religious activity during the descent.

The trucks, boarded at the sixth station about 4:00, went directly to Dewa Shrine on Mount Haguro, arriving at about 5:00. Everyone went immediately to the Saikan ("Purification Hall") in their white clothes. Individually, the participants paid their respects at the altar inside the Saikan. Until 1962, it was the custom to spend this final night of the spring mountain in a rough shelter, but in 1962 it was moved to the much nicer quarters in the Saikan. As the name *gyonin*, "ascetic," indicates, these people are considered to be performing *gyo*, or "asceticism," in their tour around the mountain. This is why they must observe abstinence. Thus, moving from the rough shelter to the Saikan marks another weakening or relaxing of asceticism. The Saikan is a fine, spacious shrine structure with kitchen and sleeping facilities for the shrine's pilgrims and general visitors. After everyone had a hot bath, a meal of celebration (with no meat or fish) was brought from homes in the village. Much *sake* was exchanged, a common village banquet the next night was discussed but not agreed on, and after more drinking and singing, everyone retired after 9:00. In previous times there was no bath, and the pilgrims went to sleep with their clothes on in the rough shelter. In 1964, apparently to retain the idea of asceticism, we were limited to two blankets for two people, sleeping on the straw mats found in all Japanese homes.

May 5, the final day of the spring mountain, began early. By 4:00 A.M., everyone was rising, exchanging cups of *sake*, and finishing the remainder of the previous night's meal. About 5:30 the children of these men came from the village via the stone staircase to pick up the lunch boxes and excess baggage. Then at 6:30, everyone walked to the Tenyu Shrine near the rough shelter. The Tenyu Shrine is the small shrine that honors Tenyu, the most illustrious leader in Haguro's history. After repeating the prayer of purification, they moved on to Dewa Shrine to listen to the Shinto priests recite a shrine prayer. Then the priests blessed the participants by swinging a pole with paper tassels over the heads of the participants and poured sacred *sake* for everyone. The participants then revered the shrine of Prince Hachiko, legendary founder of this sacred mountain. Next, we descended the stone staircase to the village, where we were greeted and congratulated by villagers. The last group recital of the prayer of purification was at the shrine office just above the entrance to the stone staircase. Leaving the shrine office, the pairs of proxies (or ascetics) gradually went their own way, paying their respects at their own *buraku's* shrine; this is their tutelary shrine, the first shrine each visited as a baby. Then the two proxies from each *buraku* attended the reception party in their own *buraku*.

I was able to witness the reception party of the seventh *buraku*, which retains the older traditional form. The "reception party" in Japanese is *sakamukae*. *Mukae* clearly means a "greeting" or "welcome," but many half-joking meanings have been attached to *saka*. A popular explanation is that it comes from the word *saka* for "slope," referring to the three steep sections in the stone staircase leading to Mount Haguro; another explanation is that *saka* is derived from the word *sake* (rice wine), since *sake* is a part of every welcome or party. But the original meaning surely goes back to *sakai*, or "boundary," that is, a welcome at the boundary of the village or *buraku*. Japanese scholars have analyzed this celebration of *saka-mukae*, or "boundary-welcome," which is widely observed to welcome pilgrims back from a visit to a distant shrine or temple. The most common practice is to go to the village boundary both to see off and to welcome back the pilgrims. The returning person was regarded either as sacred or as an actual *kami*; originally, the boundary-welcome was a religious rite in which villagers saw off and welcomed back the person who left the village and traveled to the world of the *kami*. In general the boundary-welcome represents a meeting between the sacred world, which the "ascetic" has just visited (or the sacred state he represents), and the profane world of the village.

Formerly, each of the eight *buraku* of Toge held the boundary-welcome on separate small hills or knolls outside the village. This hill or knoll was known as the *o-yama* ("mountain") of that *buraku*, or *saka-mukae-yama*, "boundary-welcome-mountain." At present only the seventh *buraku* retains the older custom; each other *buraku* gathers inside a house of that *buraku*. When the two proxies of the seventh *buraku* entered the village, not stopping at any house, they went to their "mountain" about ten-minutes' walk from the village. The "mountain" or knoll is not even fifty feet higher than the surrounding fields; it is covered with low brush and one taller tree at the top. About twenty men of the seventh *buraku* were waiting on top of the knoll, sitting on reed mats before a celebration meal. It was past 8:30 A.M. The shrine papers acquired from Dewa Shrine were placed beside a rock under the tree. This rock, called the "Gassan rock," had been brought from Gassan long ago to dedicate the seventh *buraku's* "mountain" to Gassan. After a short greeting, all faced the snowy form of Gassan on the horizon and chanted the familiar prayer that had been recited during the pilgrimage. This was followed by the formal feast of the spring mountain during which the shrine papers (in place of mountain plants) were distributed to the *buraku* members. The "red rice" (rice cooked with red beans) that is eaten on special occasions (such as weddings) was served, along with other special foods. The proxies excused themselves after eating a little and returned to the village. That night there were additional feasts, concluding the celebration of spring mountain.

Interpreting the Spring Mountain Festival

This description of spring mountain provides a good example of a village festival, illustrating the unity and dynamics of Japanese religion in a concrete case. To interpret this festival, we should recognize first that it has its own dramatic unity, with several climaxes. The festival begins with the proxies climbing Mount Haguro on May 3, practicing abstinence and indicating their pure state as pilgrims with their white clothing and surplices around their necks. The start of the pilgrimage is sealed with the ritual drinking of sacred *sake* given the proxies by the Shinto priests at Dewa Shrine. The festival moves toward its first climax on May 4, when the proxies recite their prayer of purification at each successive station of Gassan. Reaching the summit of Gassan is a climax in several senses. Gassan is a sacred mountain, and climbing it is to come into contact with sacred space and the *kami* of Gassan. At the same time, it is the attainment of the tenth station, which in Buddhist terms is to leave lower forms of earthly existence and enter a heavenly state. Another climax of the festival, especially from the viewpoint of the villagers, is the boundary-welcome, when the sacredness of the proxies rubs off on the others, and the shrine papers brought from the mountain are distributed to members of each home. This is a climax because it brings the power and blessing of the festival to each home.

By interpreting the major aspects of this festival in the context of Japanese religion, we can see how the worldview and dynamics of religion are expressed in a concrete example. The spring mountain festival includes all of the aspects or "worlds" of Japanese religion: objects of worship (*kami*, Buddhas, ancestors, and holy persons) as well as the religious ordering of social groups, space, time, and life.

The mountain *kami* of Gassan is the central object of worship for this festival, which symbolically brings the mountain *kami* to each village home in the form of shrine papers (which take the place of the traditional evergreens). Buddhas are also present on the mountain, especially in the statues of Jizo, savior of the dead, and in the area called the plain of Mida (Amida). Spirits of ancestors were venerated in several places, especially at the ninth station by the "pond where Buddhas live" and on Mount Yudono near the Yudono Shrine. In fact, some scholars think that the mountain *kami* and spirits of ancestors are similar if not identical. The proxies also honored a holy person when they paid respects at the Tenyu Shrine, honoring Tenyu, Mount Haguro's most illustrious leader. All these objects of worship played their roles in the drama of the spring mountain.

Religious ordering of social groups is expressed through families, *buraku*, and the village as a whole. Each of the eight *buraku* selected two male heads of families as proxies for the *buraku;* all proxies acted together to hold the festival for the village as a whole. Each home received a shrine paper as a symbol of the festival's blessing, and special rites were performed at each of the eight *buraku* shrines.

The religious ordering of space clearly specified certain locations around Toge as sacred space. Most important of all are the three sacred mountains, representing a kind of otherworld or heaven on earth. Also prominent are each of the ten stations leading to the summit of Gassan. On the village scene, in addition to the individual *buraku* shrines, there are the boundary-welcome-mountains, all of which are sacred space, too.

The religious ordering of time is demonstrated in the holding of the spring mountain on the eighty-eighth day of the year—the second day of spring—according to the lunar calendar. This is one of the major annual festivals for the village of Toge. In a larger sense, this festival is a collective action of the village to harmonize with the rhythm of the seasons and to open the agricultural year with a rite of spring.

The religious ordering of life is not prominent in this festival, which emphasizes collective action rather than cradle-to-grave rituals or individual practices. But because only male heads of families can participate as proxies, the festival is both a recognition of adult male status and a promise of future recognition to the young boys of the village. Even in small matters, such as the abstinence a man must observe while a proxy, it is obvious that this festival partially determines how these participants behave—what they can do and what they cannot do.

For the sake of analysis, this festival has been broken down into aspects or "worlds." But it is well to remember that the villagers of Toge do not experience religion through such analytical categories. Rather, they view the spring mountain as a precious tradition handed down to them, something they want to preserve and pass on to future generations. The participants told me this while they were celebrating on the night of May 4 in the Saikan, when they were drinking *sake*, dancing, singing, and having a good time. As the evening wore on they became more free in their conversation. Some of them had been in the Japanese military during World War II, and they assured me that Japan and the United States should not fight again but should be friends. They also told me that they were glad I had come on the festival with them, to see and record their tradition. They treasured this tradition and asked me to tell Americans not to send Christian missionaries—the people of Toge would preserve and respect their traditions, and Americans could follow their own traditions.

A proxy from the seventh *buraku* told me that having their young sons climb the stone staircase the next morning to take home some of the proxies' extra belongings was really not necessary, for these few belongings could be carried by the proxies themselves. Actually, he said, it was part of their sons' "education," to help them become a part of the spring mountain so that when they were heads of families they too would take their turns as proxies and keep alive the tradition. These comments helped me appreciate the importance of this festival for the people of Toge.

The spring mountain festival has changed through the years and will continue to change as long as it is practiced. The important thing is that these villagers treasure the festival and intend to hand down this tradition to their children. The same kinds of feelings and intentions are associated with village festivals in other areas of Japan, as well as with festivals held in cities. [See Religions of Africa pp. 74–75, Religions of Mesoamerica pp. 229–38, Native Religions of North America pp. 308–16, 351–57, Judaism pp. 439–45, Christianity pp. 551–55, Islam pp. 674, 677–79, Hinduism p. 829, Buddhism pp. 937–41, and Religions of China pp. 1021–24 for description and discussion of festivals and annual celebrations.]

The Life History of Mr. Negishi

The two examples of religious dynamics have been chosen partly because they represent quite different expressions of Japanese religious life. Spring mountain, the first example, is a traditional festival as it has been handed down by a village in an agricultural setting. The second example, the life history of a Tokyo member of a New Religion, presents a sharp contrast with the spring mountain: It is part of the recent wave of new religious movements, takes place within the largest metropolitan area in Japan, and is a personal statement (as contrasted with the collective action in spring mountain). But in spite of these differences between the two examples, there are also many similarities, as we will see.

During the past century and a half Japanese society has undergone considerable changes, especially a shift from a rural and agricultural way of life to an urban and industrial way of life. One aspect of this change has been a weakening of the village community and the decline of festivals like spring mountain. Another aspect of this change has been the emergence of many New Religions, such as Tenrikyo and Soka Gakkai mentioned in chapter 45. As traditional village structure weakened and collective participation in activities such as village festivals declined, New Religions became increasingly important. Many people moved from rural areas to cities, in the process disrupting the tie between the family home and a local tutelary *kami.* This is just one instance of the general weakening of participation in traditional forms of religion.

People who were separated from these traditional forms of religion often became involved in New Religions. Although New Religions incorporate many elements of traditional belief and practice, they are newly founded religious groups that individuals or families can join by their own choice. Previously, most religious life was not so much a matter of individual choice as a matter of residence and hereditary custom: The family participated in the local tutelary shrine where it lived, and the family participated in the Buddhist parish temple designated by family custom. What is most "new" about New Religions is that a person or family makes a decision to join a particular New Religion, not on the basis of residence or family custom, but on the basis of personal preference for that particular New Religion.

Although each New Religion has its own distinctive history and set of practices, some features are common to most of them. They are founded by powerful personalities who are able to attract others to the message each has discovered. This message usually consists of elements from Japanese religion that are reformulated and systematized through a decisive experience of the founder, such as a revelation. As the founder gathers together people who are attracted to this message (and personally devoted to the founder), an institutional arrangement of headquarters and branch groups emerges. People become members of these New Religions, replacing (or adding to) traditional practices with the rituals and festivals that form a daily and annual pattern for each New Religion. [See Religions of Africa pp. 25, 54–57, 79–82, Religions of Mesoamerica

p. 240, Native Religions of North America pp. 287, 320–22, 357–58, Judaism pp., 427–31, 456–75, Christianity pp. 529–33, Islam pp. 698–700, Hinduism pp. 770–74, 828–31, Buddhism pp. 952–56, and Religions of China pp. 998–1002, 1055–59 for discussion of new religious movements.]

The following example focuses on **Gedatsu-kai,** the New Religion joined by Mr. Negishi (a fictitious name used to protect his identity), whose life history provides us with an "inside" view of how a person joins and participates in a New Religion. Gedatsu-kai was officially founded in 1929 by Eizo Okano. Previous to his founding of Gedatsu-kai, Okano had a traditional upbringing and was familiar with the customs of Japanese religion, but he was more concerned with becoming a successful businessman than with religious life. Then, when he was forty-three, he became very ill and lost consciousness. In a dreamlike state, which he experienced as death and passage to the otherworld, he met the spirit of his dead father, and the power of *kami* and Buddhas was revealed to him. He considered his recovery from this illness a miracle of new life made possible by the *kami* and Buddhas. This experience forced him to rethink his life and stimulated him to practice religion more seriously. The name Gedatsu-kai comes from *gedatsu,* meaning "liberation," similar to the term nirvana (usually translated "enlightenment") and *kai,* meaning "society," and Okano felt he had experienced liberation or enlightenment (*gedatsu*), so he called his movement the "liberation society."

Gradually Okano left the business world and entered the world of religion full time, telling others about the message he had discovered. He felt that too often people disregard religion or mechanically go through the motions of religious practice but do not reflect deeply on the meaning of life and the nature of religion. He realized that people owe everything to *kami,* Buddhas, and ancestors and should pray sincerely to them. Okano taught that many of people's problems in daily life stem from neglect of such worship, especially disregard of ancestors.

He was skillful in counseling people with personal and spiritual problems and quickly gained a following. Eventually the following developed into an institutionalized religion with central headquarters and local branches. But Gedatsu-kai teaches that membership in Gedatsu-kai should not interfere with traditional religious practices; in fact, Gedatsu-kai members should intensify participation in the local tutelary shrine and parish Buddhist temple. Gedatsu-kai has its own distinctive rites, such as a daily rite for honoring family ancestors in individual homes; it also features regular worship services and occasional meditation sessions in local and regional meetings. Okano died in 1948, but the movement he founded continued to grow, expanding to more than three hundred local branches and several hundred thousand members in Japan. [See Religions of Africa pp. 29, 55–57, Religions of Mesoamerica pp. 152, 164–68, Native Religions of North America pp. 266–67, Christianity pp. 495–97, 531–32, 534–35, Islam pp. 622–28, 698–99, Hinduism pp. 769, 770–72, Buddhism pp. 860, 861–68, 892–99, and Religions of China pp. 993–95 for discussion of religious founders.]

Mr. Negishi is a member of Gedatsu-kai who told me about his experiences. We first met in 1969 when I began studying Gedatsu-kai, and we met again during 1979–1980 when I spent a half year studying Gedatsu-kai more thoroughly.[9] Part of this research was the recording of life histories of individual members, focusing on their religious experience. A life history is a personal story of how one remembers and interprets the course of one's own life. It was easy for Gedatsu-kai members to tell me their life histories, because a common practice in their meetings is for individuals to tell the other members present the story of their problems and how they resolved them. Mr. Negishi's life history is one of many I collected during 1979–1980. This kind of personal narration is about as close as non-Japanese can come to seeing how a Japanese person experiences and lives out religious life today.

Mr. Negishi was born in Tokyo, is a college graduate who lives in Tokyo, is financially independent, and donates much of his time to Gedatsu-kai. He has long been a member of this movement and now is an important member of the executive board of Gedatsu-kai. At the time of the interview, January 26, 1980, he was fifty-one years old. Mr. Negishi told his story in Japanese, which is translated into English here. The general import of his story is that religion is power, and the rationale for him to join Gedatsu-kai and participate in it is that Gedatsu-kai affords him the power to live. But it is best to let Mr. Negishi tell his own story. To retain the vividness of this personal document, it is quoted here in the first person singular—the "I" is Mr. Negishi speaking:

I entered Gedatsu-kai after I was ten years of age—between ten and twenty. There was a neighbor, an older person who was in a bank. And our family had leased land to him. This was an area formerly called Musashino—now a part of Tokyo. I am a real native of Tokyo. From ancient times my ancestors were here. They had land and rented it out. So I had a connection of **karma** with this person.[10]

I was still young at the time, and did not have much feeling for religion. But then there was our family situation at the time—our family was in poor health, and there was always someone sick. For example, my mother was sick for the longest period of time—she couldn't get out of bed for seven years. There were always two or three in the family sick, and it went on for ten years this way; I thought this was hard for my father.

But religion—well, in popular language, this is called newly arisen religions. As opposed to established religion, in the last hundred years or so these "newly arisen religions" had appeared as new forms of religion. And Gedatsu-kai seemed to be of a low level. This is how I felt about Gedatsu-kai. But I was told that the teaching was excellent in Gedatsu-kai. The bank person had encouraged my father to go to Gedatsu-kai, but my father didn't want to go, so I went instead.

I didn't like religion. Yet, at the same time, I was wondering about religion. In this world . . . in this world . . . is religion necessary? I thought, like most people, that what is most needed in the world are such things as politics, economics, and authority or power. In this light, in this world, religion is not really good, necessary.

But there were problems in this way of thinking. For example, if a law changes, then good and bad change overnight—what was good according to the law yesterday is bad according to the law today. This was just after Japan's defeat at the end of World War II, and we had no power.

At present young people, internationally—in Russia, everywhere, in all major countries—ask: What power does religion have? What purpose does religion serve? I thought this way, too—like all young people—at this time. Those who have power change their approval of religion, and the like, overnight.

Of course, people said that if you believed, it would be blessing—you would get well, and so on.

There are three main types of suffering: first, economic; second, feelings, that is, the family and human relations; and third, the body, that is, sickness. To resolve these problems of suffering, you should study religion, they said, but. . . . Throughout the world, there is religion. People always fight, even over religion, I thought. Most wars are religion-based. War is an argument among different peoples.

The bank person was a fine person, so my father told me to go study Gedatsu-kai. I was against this. I had a sibling, an older sister, and because my mother was always sick, my older sister was like a mother. So my father told my older sister, too, to go study; and because my older sister was more gentle than me, she went, and I went, too. This was just after World War II.

Even today the Japanese don't understand this. The Ise Shrine and Shrine Shinto were the cause of the war, so they say, but this is irrelevant. For example, the basis of religion, as we usually know it, is a teaching, ceremonies, propagation, rituals, and divinities—such as Buddhas. But this is irrelevant when we consider the practices of my family at the local tutelary *kami*. Where one lives—this is important.

Emperor Ojin is the deity worshiped.[11] Also, there are lots of small shrines, lots of spirits, but Emperor Ojin is the chief *kami*. My ancestors were venerating these spirits, opened up this faith. So I followed the flesh of my parents. I had this tradition. My religion I did not think of as an acquired "faith." My ancestors were born of this earth, they were part of the realm of nature. We must be in harmony with the realm of nature. In other words, the realm of nature is equal to a *kami*. It is nature that allows us to live. We must live in harmony with nature. This is the basic thinking of Japan.

Gedatsu's teaching is the same. It has the same view of nature. It emphasizes the local tutelary *kami*. And it stresses Buddhism. But Buddhism means our ancestors, as well as such divinities as the Buddha—this is how Japanese Buddhism is characteristically different from the Buddhism of other countries. So naturally Gedatsu-kai emphasizes the local Buddhist parish temple. So I was sympathetic to Gedatsu-kai.

I wondered about life, what a human being is. I was twenty-two years of age when my father died. While my father was alive—and then relatives, and even neighbors—they said about business dealings and work, you must not do bad things, you must be honest. And they helped me affirm this. My father died, but before he died he had taught me, and I remembered his words and sentences, about not lying, keeping promises, and so forth. But as I said before, I had been wondering about human beings, and how they can live. I thought that humans do not have power. But one must have power. To protect oneself, and one's family, one must have power. But what is one's own power? It does not just come from one's own circumstances. How do you get power? How can one maintain power?

In the teaching of the founder of Gedatsu-kai, and in Buddhism, there is the law of cause and effect. It is destiny. I studied genetics in the university. This is the scientific way of explaining it. The parents and children are the same—this is a genetic principle. "The actions of the parents are passed on to the children." The actions of the parents become the "result" of the children. Strong or weak, this is the karmic connection of the parent: the karma of cause and effect. This is the law of nature. This is the nature of the human race.

I learned this at school and thought it had no relation to religion—but then later I saw it in the founder's teaching! And was I surprised! The founder's disciples said that if I studied genetics, then I should understand the founder's teaching: "If you studied genetics, then you ought to understand Gedatsu-kai."

There were many people who didn't go on the first and fifteenth of the month to the local Shinto shrine of the tutelary *kami,* but my family was a shrine parish representative. And my family went not only on the first and fifteenth of the month, but every day. From my youth, I went every day. My family is still parish representative. I myself don't participate that much as parish representative, but my mother, who is seventy-eight and healthy now, goes to the shrine as parish representative. I go to the local shrine of the tutelary *kami* for "good morning" and "good night." My teachers in Gedatsu-kai said that if I did this, then I should understand Gedatsu-kai's teaching. In the morning, my "good morning" greeting is, "Again today your favor—blessing"; in the evening, my "good night" is, "Thank you for another safe day." I did this every day, as a custom, just as if I were greeting my parents.

Then there is another very important aspect of Gedatsu-kai's teaching, completely different, that I studied. As you know and as I have pointed out before, Japanese Buddhism is Mahayana Buddhism.[12] And this is fine, but in terms of human life, is the soul eternal? Worship is OK, but are there really *kami?* This is a doubtful matter. They say that even if the body is gone, people become *kami.* Is there a soul? Occasionally I practice the mediation ritual of **goho shugyo.**[13] I thought the teaching was wonderful but didn't believe in the practice of *goho shugyo.*

I was told to practice *goho shugyo.* The branch leader of Gedatsu-kai and others urged *goho shugyo.* Many times I was told this. At first when I practiced *goho shugyo,* there was no spiritual communication. Then suddenly I had a spiritual experience; this was after many practices of *goho shugyo.*

Members of a local branch of Gedatsu-kai meeting in a home perform the purification of spirit that begins the goho shugyo *ritual. Each member holds between joined palms a paper with a written Buddhist formula, as taught by the founder of Gedatsu-kai.*

In the plain around Tokyo there was one family named Toshima that had pioneered the area. This was one major family, like the Chiba, Itabashi, Akasaka families, who opened up the plain around Tokyo, and whose family names became place-names. There was also a man named Ota who built the Edo castle. There was a long battle between the Toshima and Ota families, and the Toshima family lost out. This was at the end of the Heian period [794–1185]. The fallen Toshima had a residence at Shakujii—located in Nerima ward of present-day Tokyo. I saw all this during the ritual of *goho shugyo*. It lasted for fifteen minutes. I saw the entire struggle, the landscape, and everything. This greatly surprised me.

There is only a little literature on this historical affair; Tokyo University has this literature. And there is some information in the Nerima local history. I saw all of this because I am a native of the area. It is only eight —or six—kilometers to this place Shakujii from my house, and to the site of the Toshima mansion, it is only one kilometer. My relatives all live in this area.

So the upshot is that the practice of *goho shugyo* and the study of literature are all the same—in my heart I didn't know this before. I didn't know it, I practiced the sacred *goho shugyo* and learned about history. Later I read literature and was surprised to find this experience confirmed. I heard their voices, the playing of the flute. I still remember it clearly today. So several hundred years pass, but souls still live—in our heart. They still express this through us. We are conscious of them. The soul is immortal.

And so I became quite interested in this. And the meaning may be a little different here, but I saw this in other families: "Ah, because the father did such and such, the child becomes so and so." And because I am a native of the area, and mine is an old family, I know five or six generations of neighboring people—I can even recite the names of the heads of neighboring families going back that many generations. And I see the influence of older generations in the present. The suffering older generation affects the present generation, too. This is genetics.

And when we rejoice, the ancestors do, too; this is because the ancestors are the same as *kami*. The soul is immortal. This is the essence of how things should be. Do good today, and it becomes tomorrow's blessing. Today's evil, tomorrow's sorrow. And it is not just oneself, but one's child, and grandchild. It is the divine providence of nature. A mistake goes back to the *kami*. A white flower should be the same for three generations, and so on—it all goes back to the same source. And a human, even if he makes mistakes—it all returns to the *kami!*

The realm of nature is the "way" the *kami* have created.[14] And we must live according to the principles of nature. For example, there are the sacred teachings of the founder—how man can live—there is destiny. But what is humanity? It is as a human being that the *kami* have created man. And it is according to this destiny that one matures and lives. And because we have this human quality, we must live as humans. And human nature—human quality, this quality—knowing this is a level of maturing, a level of learning, therefore we must practice this "way." We must study, practice, this "way." We must study, practice, learn. Thus we make happiness for others. The *kami* make everything: objects, persons, principles. We should give thanks for food—help create happiness for others. We have karmic connection with all things. We give thanks to the *kami* for this day, for everything.

In our own hearts we grow and can understand this. Questions of what denomination we belong to, what sect—these are not important.

For example, even if I take but one grain of rice and eat it, then it will never enter anyone else's mouth—this life was given just for my existence. For this we are very grateful! We must see that every day we live is given by the *kami*. To take good care of parents is the same thing. This is gratitude. And by this we know that it is due to the *kami's* heart that man lives.

In our own hearts, we grow, and can understand this. Questions of what denomination, what sect—it is not just what is "correct" according to the *kami*, or what the Buddha does not allow—rather, everything depends on the people, and the locale, and living in terms of this. Because this is what enables us to live. For example, take a teacup. We can use it to drink tea, or we can throw it at an enemy. So it is not the orthodox teaching, but the social, local relevance. We are enabled to live.

So our power comes from the generations of ancestors. This is genetics. So for the descendants this is extremely important for their fortune. It is what the ancestors have done for us.

Interpreting the Life History of Mr. Negishi

As we attempt to interpret this human document, it is interesting to note that, like the spring mountain festival, this life history has its own dramatic unity. In this case, the drama centers around Mr. Negishi's personal quest for meaning.

In childhood Mr. Negishi participated naturally in traditional religious practices, visiting the local tutelary shrine for a "good morning" and "good night" just as if he were greeting his parents. But in his teenage years after World War II, there was a great deal of uncertainty, and he was unsure about the power that would help him live his life meaningfully. The answer came in the teaching and practices of Gedatsu-kai, which did not contradict traditional beliefs but expanded them into a total philosophy of life. Mr. Negishi considered the founder Okano's teaching about gratitude to nature, parents, and ancestors a significant reformulation of traditional notions. After he had accepted Gedatsu-kai teachings in principle, Mr. Negishi had a transforming spiritual experience in which he communicated directly with the other world. On the basis of reasoning out traditional practices, as well as on the basis of personal experience, Mr. Negishi found in Gedatsu-kai a way of life that provides him with power to live meaningfully.

This single life history cannot speak for all Japanese today, but it provides a valuable inside view of how one person became a member of a New Religion and continues to participate in it. If we interpret this life history in terms of the worldview of Japanese religion, it is remarkable how closely it follows this pattern of objects of worship (kami, Buddhas, ancestors, and holy persons), as well as the religious ordering of society, space, time, and life.

Mr. Negishi honors the whole range of objects of worship. He greets the local tutelary kami morning and night, like his own parents. He senses a deep gratitude toward nature, which provides human beings with life. He regularly visits the local Buddhist parish temple, expressing his concern for both ancestors and Buddhas. Not mentioned explicitly, but practiced by Mr. Negishi, are Gedatsu-kai's morning and evening devotions in the home, which include veneration of the Gedatsu-kai triad of the kami of nature, a Buddhist divinity, and the founder, Okano. Ancestors are very important and should be ritually revered morning and night.

As Mr. Negishi reminds us, we are totally indebted to our ancestors, and we are equally responsible to future generations. In Mr. Negishi's eyes, there is little difference between ancestors and kami, and nature is equivalent to kami. He also reveres the founder of Gedatsu-kai, Eizo Okano, a kind of holy person. All these objects of worship form the resources of power Mr. Negishi draws on to live his life more fully.

The ordering of social groups is somewhat different from what was seen in the village festival of spring mountain. In that case the village automatically functioned as a unit to perform the festival. In the case of Mr. Negishi, it took some time and persuasion before he finally agreed to participate in the new movement of Gedatsu-kai. But his participation was based on a conscious decision to join, a kind of decision not usually made in village festivals like spring mountain. In joining Gedatsu-kai, Mr. Negishi chose to share religious practice with others both in local branch meetings and in national meetings of Gedatsu-kai members. In this fashion, Gedatsu-kai (like New Religions generally) represents a significant reordering of social and religious units. However, membership in Gedatsu-kai does not cause Mr. Negishi to stop traditional practices;

in fact, it reinforces active involvement in both the local tutelary shrine and the parish temple. Gedatsu-kai is not only a form of reordering social units but also a means of reinterpreting the significance of society. Like other members of Gedatsu-kai, Mr. Negishi could see, as the founder had taught, that both personal and social problems often are caused by disregard for proper social relations and proper rituals for ancestors.

The religious ordering of space according to Gedatsu-kai both reinforces traditional notions and develops some new features. Mr. Negishi does not mention this directly, but it is implied in his story. Gedatsu-kai presents a total philosophy that explains the significance of the local tutelary shrine and Buddhist parish temple. In this sense, traditional notions of sacred space, which had tended to decline, are given new support. In a similar sense, the home is reinforced as a sacred site, not merely because of the presence of *kamidana* and *butsudan*, but also because Gedatsu-kai practices daily veneration of ancestors in the home with a distinctive ritual. One of the new aspects of sacred space in Gedatsu-kai is that the native village of the founder has become a sacred headquarters and holy site of pilgrimage. In this way, the traditional village religion of the founder has become a "national" village tradition for all members of Gedatsu-kai.

The religious ordering of time within Gedatsu-kai, as with its other key features, combines old and new. The traditional daily pattern of ritual is reinforced with specific Gedatsu-kai rituals in the home, especially the honoring of family ancestors. A new pattern that Gedatsu-kai has laid down is regular monthly meetings on both the local branch level and the regional level. This is more like an institutional "church." Gedatsu-kai has its own annual religious calendar, combining traditional festivals such as the New Year, spring festival, and fall festival with its own distinctive celebrations (for example, the anniversaries of the birth and death of the founder).

The religious ordering of life in Gedatsu-kai has some aspects of "cradle-to-grave" not mentioned by Mr. Negishi—such as special youth groups. But the major organization of life in Gedatsu-kai is a reformulation of traditional notions into a complete philosophy of life. Gedatsu-kai incorporates traditional practices at both the tutelary shrine and the parish temple with a renewed sincerity. Also, Gedatsu-kai helps people understand the karmic connection they have with all others as well as how they should properly behave toward other people. A person's life is not merely a biological fact but is granted by *kami* and nourished by ancestors.

Mr. Negishi's story has its own dramatic unity. The story has been broken down into components to help us better understand various aspects of the worldview of Japanese religion. But Mr. Negishi experiences the dynamics of Gedatsu-kai as it helps him resolve the problem of meaning, providing him with a total philosophy of life. This same theme is found in all the life histories of Gedatsu-kai members I collected during 1979 and 1980.[15] Such a life history is a good illustration of the dynamics of religious experience in contemporary Japan, especially within the highly successful New Religions. [See Religions of

Africa pp. 45–51, 75–79, Native Religions of North America pp. 318–20, Judaism pp. 457–69, Christianity pp. 573–86, Hinduism pp. 820–26, and Religions of China pp. 1040–54 for discussion of life histories and personal accounts.]

The Japanese Religious Way

We have now seen Japanese religion from three views: its historical origins and development, its overall systematic unity, and two examples of its dynamics. The richness of Japanese religious life can only be suggested by brief glimpses through these three approaches; any tradition is too complex to be captured by a short treatment. Nevertheless, we must attempt to provide a general overview of the Japanese religious situation. How can we draw together the insights of our study? The following chart draws on the materials included in the three approaches, presenting them in a concise pattern of interrelated principles, institutions, beliefs, practices, and objects.

This chart is read from the upper left to the bottom and from the upper right to the bottom. The first box of the chart is the basic principle or predicament of Japanese religion—the notion that people are born into the world thanks to the *kami,* Buddhas, and ancestors, with the obligation to maintain purity and harmony. According to the Japanese tradition, this is how people find themselves in the world—this is what defines the basic human condition.

The next box contains the solution to this predicament or situation—to maximize purity and harmony while minimizing impurity and disharmony by following the religious way of sincerity and ritual propriety in the Japanese community.

The lower box titled "The Japanese Community" indicates the institutions that enable people to realize the religious solution: These institutions are the home, Shinto shrines and Buddhist temples, and the whole range of human groups from family and village to nation. The left side of the chart as a whole represents the ethos of Japanese religion.

The right side of the chart is the implementation of the ethos through comprehensive patterns of religious life, rituals and practices, and contact with holy things. The first row of "patterns" includes the major resources on which people can base their religious career. The row of "rituals and practices" singles out the basic activities by which a person acts out his or her religious life. The row of "holy things" lists some of the objects of sacred power a person comes into contact with in the acting out of religion. This chart provides a convenient overview of the Japanese religious way.

People are born into the world thanks to the *kami*, Buddhas, and ancestors, with the obligation to maintain purity and harmony.

Purity/harmony can be maximized, and impurity/disharmony can be minimized, by following the religious way of sincerity and ritual propriety in the Japanese community.

THE JAPANESE COMMUNITY

is centered around the home with its Shinto and Buddhist altars as a grass roots religious institution;

draws on Shinto shrines and Buddhist temples as powerful resources for maintaining purity and harmony;

and attempts to lead family, village, and nation into natural and social harmony.

The ethos of Japanese religion

THE RELIGIOUS LIFE OF THE JAPANESE COMMUNITY

to bring about purity and harmony on the personal, social, and national levels

Patterns for the religious life:

| CONFUCIAN ETHICS | BUDDHIST DEVOTION | SHINTO PURITY/SINCERITY | ANCESTRAL POWER |

Rituals and practices:

| ANNUAL/ SEASONAL | HOME DAILY/SEASONAL | | INDIVIDUAL DEVOTIONS |

(New Year, Spring, Summer, Bon, Fall)
rites of passage (birth, marriage, death)

repentance
meditation
fortunes/divination
purification
pilgrimage
filial piety
prayer

Contact with holy things:

| HOME ALTARS | SHINTO SHRINES | BUDDHIST TEMPLES (STATUES) | WAYSIDE STATUES AND STONES | NATURAL FORCES |

The ongoing practices that enable individuals and groups to experience and celebrate this ethos

The Japanese Religious Way.

50

Conclusion: The Contemporary Religious Situation

THE JAPANESE RELIGIOUS tradition is so rich and varied that many aspects cannot be mentioned in such a brief treatment. Previous chapters have surveyed some key aspects of this tradition: the outlines of Japanese culture and Japanese religion, the historical development of Japanese religion, the world of worship, Japanese religion's worldview, and two examples of religious dynamics. There is much more to Japanese religion that is not included in these few chapters, but before we leave the subject, it is well to ask what the religious situation is in Japan today.

The Sacred Way in Modern Japan

The general picture of Japanese religion is that it features many separate traditions, such as Shinto and Buddhism, within one sacred way. In the celebration of a village festival or in the personal story of a member of a New Religion, there is not just a single tradition or a combination of traditions but a total way of life that draws on all these resources. The spring mountain festival has its own dramatic unity that is re-created every time it is celebrated. And the personal drama of Japanese religion is reenacted every time a person enters a New Religion—simultaneously resolving an individual quest for religious meaning and reformulating traditional practices. This is part of the total religious heritage in Japan—in other words, the "sacred way of Japanese religion."

This is the general picture of Japanese religion, but what are the problems and possibilities facing religious life in Japan today? Is the "sacred way" a remnant of the past, likely to fade away in the near future? What are the pressures that modern Japan places on religious commitment, and what changes are likely to take place within this sacred way? There is no one, either in Japan or outside Japan, who can answer such questions completely, because this is a matter of speculation about the future rather than a description of present or past. However, we may prepare for the future by reflecting on the possibilities

1174

that are suggested in the past and present of Japanese religion. There seem to be three major possibilities for the unfolding of religion in Japan from the present moment. One possibility is the continued practice of traditional religion. A second possibility is the further success of recent movements such as the New Religions, which develop somewhat different patterns than traditional religion. A third possibility that should be mentioned is choosing not to be religious—practicing no religion at all.

The first possibility, continued practice of traditional religion, is the extension of practices that have been very important during the past few centuries, such as maintaining a *kamidana* or *butsudan* within the home and venerating *kami* and ancestors. This "traditional" possibility includes religious activities carried on within a family, a village, or a section of a city as part of the collective social and religious life, much as was seen in the spring mountain festival. Obviously there are factors in modern Japan that make it difficult to continue these traditional practices as they were carried out in the past.

A key component of the sacred way throughout Japanese history has been the sacredness of *kami*. One modern factor that interrupts the traditional worship of *kami* is the changing lifestyle, especially the shift from a rural-agricultural way of life to an urban-industrial one. Many of the beliefs and practices associated with *kami* were directly related to agricultural activities. The spring mountain festival was considered the beginning of the rice growing season, ushering the mountain *kami* into the rice fields. However, many young people have left agriculture and taken jobs in the cities. For these young people, who may work a forty-hour (or more) week in a factory, it is difficult to recapture the traditional sense of the seasonal rhythm of spring and fall, with their appropriate spring and fall festivals. Factory workers are more likely to be concerned with leisure time on weekends and vacations than with the periodic "break" provided by festivals. It is not surprising that fewer Japanese homes today have *kamidana,* and that those that do, observe fewer ceremonies at the *kamidana*. It is obvious that for many contemporary Japanese people, the sense of the sacredness of *kami* is not the same as it was for farmers living in a traditional village some time ago.

This is one illustration of how "traditional religion" is changing. The earlier notion of *kami* and practices associated with *kami* may be continued, but not exactly as they were in the past. Some changes may be minor, as with some of the changes in the spring mountain festival: Village representatives still venerate the mountain *kami* of Gassan, but they make the trip by truck, rather than on foot. Other changes, such as the dying out of some customs and festivals, are more significant. Changes may occur in how *kami* are perceived, and, in fact, changes have taken place through the centuries. As cities grew, some *kami* formerly associated with fertility and agricultural festivals came to be associated with good luck in business. In a case like this, the veneration of a particular *kami* is continued, but its significance is reinterpreted.

Undoubtedly some practices will survive and flourish: Although many homes do not have *kamidana,* it is still a widespread custom to have *butsudan.* Some family and village ceremonies will continue, in spite of the difficulties.

Some practices die, some flourish, and others continue in changed form. It is well to remember that *tradition* means something that is handed down from one generation to another. And whatever religion Japanese people hand down to their children is in this sense traditional. One reason for the usual distinction between traditional and modern is that in times of rapid social change there is a greater degree of discontinuity and change in the culture that is handed down. This is the ambiguity of traditional religion in modern Japan: Something will be handed down, but it will have a greater degree of change than that handed down several hundred years ago.

The second possibility is the further success of movements such as the New Religions, which represent considerable discontinuity from earlier religious tradition, such as village practices. The New Religions were founded outside the major religions and are alternatives to the almost automatic participation in tutelary shrine and parish temple. Joining a New Religion involves a conscious decision to enter a specific institution. The same conditions that contributed to the disappearance or change in traditional religious practices have tended to help movements such as the New Religions continue and expand.

When people move from villages to cities and become rather separated from the agricultural way of life, they are more likely to join a New Religion. To put it the other way around, people who are caught up in village festivals and are participating as members of villages and families do not tend to join New Religions. It is especially people who see themselves more as individuals, or at least as individual families, who tend to make a conscious decision to join New Religions. This trend is likely to continue, because once the fabric of village life is torn, it is not a simple matter to reconstitute the earlier uniformity and cooperation of the village. One trend in modern Japan that is likely to continue is the movement of people both geographically (from area to area) and socially (from farm life to factory life and from one industry to another).

What are some of the implications of the success of the New Religions? It does not mean the end of Japanese religion but its transformation into new forms. While some *kami* may be neglected, other *kami* are reinterpreted and incorporated into the worship of a New Religion. A significant change brought about by these New Religions is the emphasis on the powerful personalities of founders, who are viewed as living *kami*. In the earlier centuries of Japanese religion there were holy persons, but the living *kami* of New Religions are more numerous and more prominent than the holy persons of medieval times.

The founder of Gedatsu-kai is revered by Mr. Negishi as the one who reformulated the many traditional practices into a more meaningful philosophy of life, setting up effective social groups (branches of Gedatsu-kai) and practical rituals for carrying out this philosophy. This newer style of social organization, with its emphasis on providing a total way of life in an explicit teaching, is one of the major contributions of the New Religions. However, as many scholars have pointed out, the New Religions are not completely "new"; in fact, they are mainly the reworking of old elements, such as veneration of ancestors, for example. This is another way of saying that as the New Religions come to be handed down to future generations (and not primarily joined by individuals through conscious decision), they in turn become "traditions," and all the New Religions as a whole may eventually be viewed as "traditional religion" as they become a major channel for transmitting such earlier beliefs as veneration of *kami* and ancestors.

The third possibility is that the Japanese may choose not to be religious, participating neither in the more traditional family and village religious activities nor in the newer forms found in New Religions. This is not only a possibility, but for a large number of Japanese people today, an actuality: They do not participate in religion and are much more concerned with matters such as economic activities than spiritual advancement. Most Japanese share with other "modern" people—those who live in highly urbanized, industrialized, and commercial settings—a preoccupation with getting ahead in the world. In fact, the special term *economic animal* was coined by the Japanese to deplore the dominant drive for money and consumption in Japanese life today.

Religious leaders in Japan, especially within Buddhism and the New Religions, have joined the criticism of the economic animal, either directly or indirectly. These leaders view with alarm the trend toward international dilemmas of pollution and warfare: They say that it is uncontrolled materialism that leads to pollution and nationalistic greed and ambition for power that leads to war. In this light, modern people may enjoy a higher standard of living without finding true satisfaction and enjoyment of life. It is interesting that many surveys of Japanese people show a relatively low percentage of people who are active in religion but a majority of people who say that religion is necessary for living a meaningful life. Therefore, a large number of Japanese people who are not involved in religion are either looking for religious solutions or are potential participants in religious activities. One of the ironies of modern life—with all its technology and conveniences—is that it does not free people from religion; in fact, it may help turn people to religion.

A common misperception of Japan is that as it becomes more modern, it becomes more Westernized and less traditional. It is true that Japan has borrowed considerably from other countries—and will borrow more in the future. But whatever Japan has borrowed from the West it has modified and adapted to Japanese culture, and it will keep on doing so in the future. The important thing to remember is that two processes are occurring simultaneously: Japan is borrowing and adapting foreign technology and culture, and Japan is continuing and modifying Japanese culture. Japan has refined Western technology (cameras and electronics, for example) but has utilized aspects of Japanese culture to organize and manage industry.

The present tradition of beliefs, practices, and customs constitutes the distinctive Japanese heritage of religion—an ideal against which human life can be measured. In Japan, as in other modern countries, there will be a large number of people uncommitted to a specific religion or not active in religious life. But the ideal remains in the background and is handed down by people committed to and active in religious life and is made available for others. Often people who had no idea of becoming involved in religion face a crisis and realize personal significance in the ideal that has been kept alive. Just as Japanese religion is constantly changing, so is the life of every individual Japanese: No one can predict when any individual will turn to religion, but many Japanese admit the necessity of religion and may become active when the time is ripe for them.

The modern scene in Japan is so complex that probably all three possibilities for religion will continue to coexist in the future. In some places the older forms of traditional religion will continue, although changes inevitably will occur in the process of handing down older forms. At the same time, new forms such as New Religions will probably expand, and their style of organizing religious life may spread to other areas. It is likely that Shinto shrines and Buddhist temples will come to depend more on the conscious decision of individuals and individual families to participate in their observances. And it is probable that the dominance of the urban-industrial way of life will help keep most people preoccupied with economic matters rather than religious matters. However, this concern for the physical and material may wear thin and give way to interest in the spiritual and religious.

Although no one can predict the exact religious career for specific individuals, it can be safely assumed that Japanese religion will continue into the future. It will not be the same as it has been, but it will be distinctively Japanese. *Kami,* Buddhas, ancestors, and holy persons will probably remain at the core of Japanese religion and continue to form a distinctive pattern or "sacred way" that has been characteristic of the Japanese religious heritage.

Study Questions

Before you begin to read this part, take a mental inventory of what you know and think about Japan. What images do you have of Japan and Japanese people? Make a list of Japanese things that you recognize, from technology to culture. What would you imagine religion in Japan to be like? Keep these images and things in mind as you read this part and develop new notions about Japan.

CHAPTER 45

Introduction: Japan and Japanese Religion

1. Identify Japan in terms of its geographical location and various aspects: social, national, economic, and political patterns as well as cultural heritage.
2. Identify the chief characteristics of the religious traditions found in Japan: Shinto, Buddhism, Daoism, Confucianism, Christianity, folk religion, and New Religions.
3. What does it mean to interpret Japanese religion as "many traditions within one sacred way"?

CHAPTER 46

The Historical Development of Japanese Religion

1. How are fertility, rice, and family related to early religious customs?
2. What are *kami?*
3. Interpret the mythological account of the creation of Japan.
4. How did Buddhism, Daoism, and Confucianism enter Japan and what influences did they have on the Japanese tradition? How did the Japanese tradition influence them?
5. How did Japanese Buddhism "flower" in the development of the Shingon, Tendai, Pure Land, and Zen sects?
6. During the medieval period (fourteenth through eighteenth centuries), what were the major trends in Shinto and Buddhism?
7. How did Christianity enter Japan and how did it fare during the "Christian century"?
8. How did Confucian teachings help support the social and political order?
9. Why are 1867 and 1945 the "two major turning points" in recent Japanese religious history?
10. Trace the relationship between state and religion for Shinto, Buddhism, and Christianity from 1867 to the present.

CHAPTER 47

The World of Worship

1. How does studying religion as a worldview (or unified system) differ from studying religion as historical development? (Note the subworlds of Japanese religion—the what, who, where, when, and how.)
2. Define *kami* as objects of worship.
3. How does the notion of *kami* differ from the doctrine of God in Judaism and Christianity?
4. How is the notion of *kami* central to Shinto?
5. Where and how are *kami* worshiped?
6. What is the ideal of the close harmony among humans, *kami,* and nature?
7. Define Buddhas as objects of worship.
8. What is the relationship between the sacredness of *kami* and the power of Buddhas?
9. Distinguish between the historical Buddha and Buddhist divinities.
10. Where and how are Buddhas worshiped?
11. How is the power of Buddhas expressed in the two ideals of enlightenment and practical benefits?
12. Define ancestors as objects of worship.
13. Where and how are ancestors worshiped?
14. How does a dead person become ritually transformed into an ancestor, and what is the blessing of ancestors?
15. Define holy persons as objects of worship.
16. How does someone become a holy person?
17. Interpret as holy persons: founders of Buddhist movements, founders of New Religions, and shamans.
18. Where and how are holy persons worshiped?
19. How do holy persons provide mediation?
20. Interpret *kami,* Buddhas, ancestors, and holy persons as the world of worship (the "what") for Japanese religion.

CHAPTER 48

Japanese Religion's Worldview

1. What constitutes the religious world of society in Japan?
2. Identify who worships—the individual and various groups in Japanese religion.
3. What constitutes the religious world of space in Japan?
4. Identify the major examples of where worship takes place in Japanese religion.
5. What constitutes the religious world of time in Japan?
6. Identify the major examples of when worship takes place in Japanese religion.

7. What constitutes the religious world of human life in Japan?
8. Identify the major examples of how worship is related to the course of human life.
9. Interpret the four objects of worship (*kami,* Buddhas, ancestors, and holy persons) and the four subworlds (who, where, when, and how) as the total religious worldview or "one sacred way."

CHAPTER 49

The Dynamics of Japanese Religion

1. What are the major events of the pilgrimage of the spring mountain festival and how are they part of the religious experience of the participants?
2. How can the spring mountain festival be seen as including all the worlds of Japanese religion (the objects of worship and religious groups, space, time, and life)?
3. What are the major religious events of Mr. Negishi's life and how do they provide him with the "power" to live?
4. How can Mr. Negishi's life history be seen as including all the worlds of Japanese religion (the objects of worship and religious groups, space, time, and life)?

CHAPTER 50

Conclusion: The Contemporary Religious Situation

1. What are the problems and possibilities facing the sacred way in modern Japan?

Recall the mental inventory of Japanese images that you made before reading this part. What is there in Japanese religion that is most like your own religious tradition? What in Japanese religion is most different from your own tradition? What is most interesting? How has your understanding of Japan changed as a result of reading this part? Can you now imagine yourself participating in Japanese religion?

Notes

This work is dedicated to Mircea Eliade and Joseph M. Kitagawa, who were my dissertation advisors at the University of Chicago; their teaching and help, both during graduate school and subsequently, have been invaluable for all my research and teaching, including this study.

Special thanks go to my son David, who carefully read the first draft of this work, making valuable suggestions for improving it.

Western Michigan University, through its Faculty Research Fund, has from time to time supported my research in Japanese religion; although no direct support was provided for this work, acknowledgment is gratefully noted for helping make possible the previous research on which it is based.

The editorial and production staff of Harper San Francisco transformed the manuscript into published form.

1. Donald Keene, *Japanese Literature: An Introduction for Western Readers* (New York: Grove Press, 1955), 22.
2. This mode of interpreting religious material is demonstrated in the work of Mircea Eliade, as in *The Sacred and the Profane: The Nature of Religion,* trans. Willard R. Trask (New York: Harcourt, Brace, 1959); and *From Primitives to Zen: A Thematic Sourcebook of the History of Religions* (New York: Harper & Row, 1967).
3. For more information on ancestors, see Robert J. Smith, *Ancestor Worship in Contemporary Japan* (Stanford, CA: Stanford University Press, 1974), esp. 84–85, for the example of saving memorial tablets from fire.
4. Hajime Nakamura, *Ways of Thinking of Eastern Peoples: India-China-Tibet-Japan* (Honolulu: East-West Center Press, 1964), 450.
5. George DeVos, quoted in David W. Plath, "Where the Family of God is the Family: The Role of the Dead in Japanese Households," *American Anthropologist,* 66, no. 2 (April 1964): 300–17.
6. For a more complete account of annual events, see Hitoshi Miyake, "Folk Religion," in *Japanese Religion,* ed. Ichiro Hori (Tokyo: Kodansha International, 1972), 126–32.
7. The Japanese word for mountain is *san,* and Gassan is literally "moon mountain." Because Gassan includes *san* or "mountain" within its name as a proper noun, it will be referred to simply as Gassan.
8. This festival is treated at greater length in my article "The Celebration of Haru-Yama (Spring Mountain): An Example of Folk Religious Practices in Contemporary Japan," *Asian Folklore Studies* 27, no. 1 (1968): 1–18.
9. This research, including other life histories, is presented in *Gedatsu-Kai and Religion in Contemporary Japan* (Bloomington: Indiana University Press, 1989).
10. This popular notion of "connection of karma" means a close social relationship that has its own destiny; Mr. Negishi uses this term several times during his story, especially to refer to the karma of family ancestors.
11. According to tradition, Emperor Ojin was the fifteenth emperor and reigned 270–310 C.E. Emperor Ojin is identified with Hachiman, a composite object of worship with both Shinto and Buddhist features.

12. Buddhism is usually divided into two major groups: the Theravada, or more strict monastic tradition, of south Asian countries (such as Sri Lanka), and the Mahayana, or more liberal tradition, now dominant in east Asian countries.

13. *Goho shugyo* is a ritual technique combining meditation and mediation with spirits of the other world, especially spirits of ancestors.

14. In this case, the "way" means a way of life, as in a philosophy of life.

15. Another life history from this research is "Gedatsu-kai: One Life History and Its Significance for Interpreting Japanese Religion," *Japanese Journal of Religious Studies* 7, nos. 23 (June–September 1980): 227–57; this and other life histories are included in my *Gedatsu-kai and Religion in Contemporary Japan.*

Glossary

Amaterasu See Sun Goddess.

Amida One of the most popular Buddhist divinities, especially in Pure Land Buddhism; people who take refuge in Amida are enabled to be reborn in the paradise of Amida (abbreviated as Mida).

ancestors In Japanese practice, the spirits of the dead, especially in the male line of the family, who have been transformed by funeral and memorial rituals into benevolent sources of blessing for descendants.

Buddha The historical person named Siddhartha Gautama, who lived in India during the sixth and fifth centuries B.C.E. and founded Buddhism. Also refers to Buddhist divinities, which are worshiped in the form of statues (and pictures) especially in Buddhist temples and also in *butsudan* in homes.

Buddhism A religion emphasizing enlightenment, founded in India by the historical Buddha (Siddhartha Gautama) about the sixth century B.C.E. Brought to Japan about a thousand years later, it was adapted to Japanese culture.

buraku Subdivision of a village (as in the village of Toge); can also mean a small community or hamlet.

butsudan A Buddhist-style altar in the home, a lacquered or finished cabinet in the main room of the home in which Buddhist divinities and family ancestors are enshrined.

Christianity A religion introduced to Japan by the Jesuit missionary Saint Francis Xavier in 1549 but banned in the next century; Protestant and Catholic missionaries reintroduced Christianity in the mid-nineteenth century.

Confucianism A Chinese teaching emphasizing social harmony set forth by Confucius about the fifth century B.C.E.; it became an important guide for ethics and social relations in Japan.

Confucius The Chinese philosopher (551–479 B.C.E.) who set forth a teaching emphasizing social harmony by a return to virtue; this teaching was the basis for the social and ethical systems known as Confucianism.

Daoism (Taoism) A Chinese teaching, which became influential within Japanese culture, that emphasizes return to nature or harmony with nature; generally associated with Chinese folk traditions of the almanac and cosmology.

enlightenment A Buddhist goal, achieved by overcoming human suffering and "awakening" to a higher peace.

folk religion The beliefs and practices held and transmitted by the people apart from formal religions.

Gedatsu-kai A New Religion founded in 1929 by Eizo Okano, emphasizing self-reflection and a return to traditional values, especially veneration of *kami* and ancestors; it has several hundred thousand members.

goho shugyo A ritual technique in the New Religion Gedatsu-kai combining meditation and mediation with spirits of the other world, especially spirits of ancestors.

holy person In Japanese religion, a person, such as a founder of a sect or New Religion, who in his or her lifetime and/or after death is an object of worship or mediator of power for many people.

Jizo One of the most popular Buddhist divinities, known as the savior of the dead, especially the patron saint of dead children.

kami The Japanese term for spirits or divinities, which may include mythological figures, the power within natural objects, the emperor, or powerful religious figures; the term *kami* can be singular or plural. Generally *kami* signifies anything sacred. *Kami* are worshiped especially at Shinto shrines and also before *kamidana* in homes.

kamidana A Shinto-style altar, in the form of a miniature Shinto shrine, in the main room of the home, on which offerings are placed.

Kannon One of the most popular Buddhist divinities, sometimes known as the goddess of mercy; there are a number of forms of Kannon that grant various requests to people.

karma A Buddhist term (in Sanskrit) whose formal meaning is the actions and the results of prior actions; in popular Japanese usage, it also means the destiny of social relationships, especially the destiny passed down by family ancestors.

ko Associations or clubs formed locally for the purpose of honoring a particular deity and making pilgrimages.

Kojiki A Japanese mythological writing from the eighth century that records the ancient traditions of *kami.*

Lotus Sutra One of the most popular Buddhist scriptures in east Asia, it teaches the possibility of enlightenment for all people through simple acts of devotion.

Mida See Amida.

nembutsu Recitation of faith or refuge in Amida (*namu Amida Butsu*) as an act of devotion, especially in Pure Land Buddhism.

New Religions The many new religious movements founded by powerful personalities during the last century and a half, such as Tenrikyo, Soka Gakkai, and Gedatsu-kai.

Nichiren A form of Buddhism—named after the man Nichiren—emphasizing absolute faith or refuge in the *Lotus Sutra* and Japanese nationalism.

Nihongi A Japanese mythological writing from the eighth century that records the ancient traditions of *kami;* it contains more explicit Chinese influence than the *kojiki.*

nirvana The Buddhist term (in Sanskrit) for enlightenment. See also enlightenment.

norito Ancient Shinto prayers, still used in Shinto ceremonies.

Pure Land A form of Buddhism emphasizing faith or refuge in Amida and rebirth in the paradise of Amida; developed in China and stressed by Japanese Buddhists such as Honen.

shaman A person (in Japan, usually a woman) who has undergone special training and is able to go into a trance and be a medium between this world and other worlds.

Shingon A form of esoteric Buddhism brought from China to Japan by Kukai (Kobo Daishi).

Shinto The Japanese religion that developed out of prehistoric practices, especially worship of *kami,* and became a national tradition.

shogun A military dictator; *Shoguns* ruled Japan from late medieval times until 1867.

shrine A Shinto building where *kami* are enshrined and prayers and offerings are made to *kami.*

Soka Gakkai A New Religion founded before World War II and refounded in 1950; emphasizing faith in the *Lotus Sutra,* it has attracted millions of followers since the 1950s and is the largest New Religion in Japan.

Sun Goddess (Amaterasu) One of the most important Shinto *kami,* from whom the imperial line descended; now enshrined at the Ise Shrine.

Taoism See Daoism.

temple A Buddhist building where Buddhist divinities are enshrined; scriptures are recited and rituals performed before the Buddhist divinities.

Tendai A form of Buddhism emphasizing the *Lotus Sutra* and comprehensive philosophy brought from China to Japan by Saicho (Dengyo Daishi).

Tenrikyo A New Religion founded by Miki Nakayama in 1838, emphasizing purification of personal life in order to lead a joyous life; the first New Religion to develop a large membership and effective organization.

tutelary *kami* The guardian *kami* of local Shinto shrines, which protect the people living in the area around these shrines.

Yakushi A popular Buddhist divinity, known as the healing Buddha.

Zen A form of Buddhism emphasizing enlightenment through meditation. It developed in China and was stressed by Japanese Buddhists such as Eisai and Dogen.

Selected Reading List

(For a comprehensive annotated bibliography on Japanese religion, see below: Earhart. *Japanese Religion: Unity and Diversity,* 213–54.)

Anesaki, Masaharu. *History of Japanese Religion.* London: Kegan Paul, Trench, Trubner, 1930. Reprint. Rutland, VT: Charles E. Tuttle, 1963.

Drummond, Richard H. *A History of Christianity in Japan.* Grand Rapids, MI: Eerdmans, 1971.

Earhart, H. Byron. *Gedatsu-kai and Religion in Contemporary Japan: Returning to the Center.* Bloomington: Indiana University Press, 1989.

———, ed. *Japanese Religion: Unity and Diversity.* 3d ed. Belmont, CA: Wadsworth, 1982.

———. *Religion in the Japanese Experience: Sources and Interpretations.* Belmont, CA: Wadsworth, 1974.

Eliot, Sir Charles. *Japanese Buddhism.* London: Edward Arnold, 1935. Reprint. London: Routledge & Kegan Paul, 1959.

Hardacre, Helen. *Kurozumikyo and the New Religions of Japan.* Princeton: Princeton University Press, 1986.

Holtom, Daniel C. *The National Faith of Japan: A Study in Modern Shinto.* New York: Dutton, 1938. Reprint. New York: Paragon Book Reprints, 1965.

Hori, Ichiro. *Folk Religion in Japan: Continuity and Change.* Edited by Joseph M. Kitagawa and Alan L. Miller. Chicago: University of Chicago Press, 1968.

———, ed. *Japanese Religion.* Translated by Yoshiya Abe and David Reid. Tokyo: Kodansha International, 1972.

Itasaka, Gen, ed. *Kodansha Encyclopedia of Japan.* 9 vols. Tokyo: Kodansha, 1983.

Kishimoto, Hideo, ed. *Japanese Religion in the Meiji Era.* Translated by John F. Howes. Tokyo: Obunsha, 1956.

Kitagawa, Joseph M. *On Understanding Japanese Religion.* Princeton: Princeton University Press, 1987.

———. *Religion in Japanese History.* New York: Columbia University Press, 1966.

Matsunaga, Daigan, and Alicia Matsunaga. *Foundations of Japanese Buddhism.* 2 vols. Los Angeles: Buddhist Books International, 1974.

Miyake, Hitoshi. "Folk Religion." In *Japanese Religion.* Edited by Ichiro Hori and translated by Yoshiya Abe and David Reid. Tokyo: Kodansha International, 1972. 121–43.

Murakami, Shigeyoshi. *Japanese Religion in the Modern Century.* Translated by H. Byron Earhart. Tokyo: University of Tokyo Press, 1980.

Nakamura, Hajime. *A History of the Development of Japanese Thought from 592 to 1868.* 2 vols. Tokyo: Kokusai Bunka Sinkokai, 1967.

Ono, Sokyo. *Shinto: The Kami Way.* Tokyo: Bridgeway Press, 1962.

Reader, Ian. *Religion in Contemporary Japan.* Honolulu: University of Hawaii Press, 1991.

Saunders, B. Dale. "Koshin: An Example of Taoist Ideas in Japan." In *Proceedings of the IXth International Congress for the History of Religions.* Tokyo: Maruzen, 1960. 423–32.

Smith, Robert J. *Ancestor Worship in Contemporary Japan.* Stanford: Stanford University Press, 1974.

Tomikura, Mitsuo. "Confucianism." In *Japanese Religion.* Edited by Ichiro Hori and translated by Yoshiya Abe and David Reid. Tokyo: Kodansha International, 1972. 105–22.

Index

Note: Items that are boldfaced in the index can be found in the glossaries; boldfaced page numbers indicate where.